W9-CAI-945

Sweden

written and researched by

James Proctor and Neil Roland

ROUGH
GUIDES

www.roughguides.com

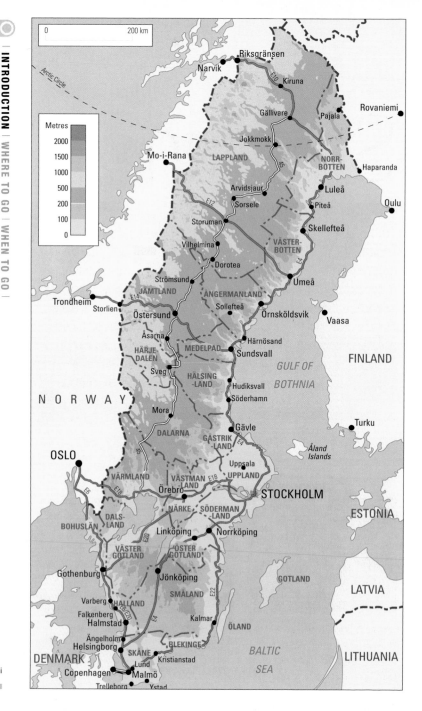

0   200 km

Metres
2000
1500
1000
500
200
100
0

Arctic Circle

Riksgränsen
Narvik
Kiruna
Gällivare
Pajala
Rovaniemi
Jokkmokk
Mo-i-Rana   LAPPLAND   NORR-
BOTTEN   Haparanda
Arvidsjaur   Luleå
Sorsele   Piteå   Oulu
Storuman   Skellefteå
Vilhelmina   VÄSTER-
BOTTEN
Dorotea
Strömsund   Umeå
JÄMTLAND   ÅNGERMANLAND
Trondheim   Sollefteå   Örnsköldsvik   Vaasa
Storlien
Östersund
Åsarna   Härnösand   FINLAND
HÄRJE-   MEDELPAD   Sundsvall
DALEN
Sveg   HÄLSING   GULF OF
-LAND   BOTHNIA
Hudiksvall
N O R W A Y   Söderhamn
Mora   Turku
DALARNA   Gävle
GÄSTRIK
-LAND
OSLO   Uppsala
VÄRMLAND   VÄSTMAN   UPPLAND
-LAND
Örebro   STOCKHOLM
NÄRKE   SÖDERMAN
DALS-   LAND   ESTONIA
BOHUSLÄN   LAND   Linköping   Norrköping
VÄSTER   ÖSTER
GÖTLAND   GÖTLAND   Åland
Gothenburg   Islands
Jönköping   GOTLAND
Varberg   HALLAND   SMÅLAND   LATVIA
Falkenberg
Halmstad   Kalmar
Ängelholm   ÖLAND
Helsingborg   BLEKINGE   BALTIC
SKÅNE   LITHUANIA
DENMARK   Lund   Kristianstad   SEA
Copenhagen   Malmö
Trelleborg   Ystad

Introduction to

Sweden

The mere mention of Sweden conjures up resonant images: snow-capped peaks, reindeer wandering in deep green forests and the 24-hour daylight of the midnight sun. But beyond the household names of ABBA, IKEA and Volvo, Sweden is relatively unknown. The largest of the Scandinavian countries, with an area twice that of Britain (and roughly that of California), but a population of barely nine million, Sweden is still one of Europe's best-kept secrets. Its cities are safe, carefree places where the cheap public transport runs on time and life is relaxed. Sweden's countryside boasts pine and birch forest as far as the eye can see, crystal-clear lakes perfect for a summer afternoon dip, not to mention possibly the purest air you'll ever breathe, and the country's south and west coasts feature some of the most exquisite beaches in Europe.

Forget anything you've heard about Sweden's reputedly high **prices** — over recent years, the Swedish *krona* has depreciated significantly against most other Western currencies, putting Sweden within the scope of many visitors' budgets. For accommodation, there's a range of decent hotels, guesthouses and hostels to suit every pocket, and many hotels drop their prices in summer (and at weekends all year round). What's more, Sweden is now one of the least expensive countries to reach from within Europe: "no-frills" air fares have opened up the country as never before.

Many tourists come to Sweden looking forward to wild sex and easy pick-ups. Most return home disappointed. Somehow over the years the open Swedish attitude to nudity and sexuality has become confused with sex. Contrary to popular belief though, Sweden isn't populated solely with people waiting for any opportunity to tear their clothes off and make passionate love under the midnight sun. People may talk about sex openly, but when it comes down to it the Swedes can be rather puritanical. **Nudity**, though common, is quite unrelated to sex: go to a beach in Sweden on a hot summer's day and you'll doubtless see people sunbathing naked, but this state of affairs is certainly not an invitation for a love-in. However, the Swedes' **liberal** and open attitude to virtually every aspect of life is certainly one of their most enviable qualities; people are generally left to do their own thing providing it doesn't impinge on the rights and freedoms of others. In Sweden, rights go hand in hand with duties, and there's a strong sense of civic obligation (count how few times you see people dropping litter, for example), which in turn makes for a well-rounded and stable society.

Where to go

Sweden is principally a land of **forests** and **lakes**. Its towns and cities are small by European standards and mostly

This is the land of reindeer and elk, of swiftly flowing rivers and coniferous forest

Fact file

● Sweden is the **third largest country** in western Europe – behind only France and Spain – stretching 1600km from north to south. If the country were pivoted around on its southernmost point, the top of the country would reach as far south as Naples in Italy.

● More than half Sweden's land surface is **forest** – mostly coniferous – amongst which there are an astonishing **100,000 lakes**.

● The **Swedish parliament** has one chamber and the 349 members are elected by **proportional representation** in elections held every four years on the third Sunday in September. At 43 percent the country has the highest proportion of female members of parliament in the world.

● Although the **Sámi**, the indigenous population of Swedish Lapland, constituted the only distinct minority of any size before World War II, today twenty percent of Sweden's inhabitants are of foreign extraction.

● There is no translation for the Swedish word **lagom**, one of the most commonly used terms in the language. Roughly speaking it means "just the right amount, not too much but not too little", a concept that is the very essence of Swedishness.

to be found in the southern third of the country, where most Swedes live. Of the **cities**, serenely beautiful **Stockholm** is supreme. Sitting elegantly on fourteen different islands, where the waters of Lake Mälaren meet the Baltic Sea, the city boasts some fantastic architecture, fine museums and by far the best culture and nightlife in the country. Its wide tree-lined boulevards, the narrow medieval streets of the Old Town and some modern, state-of-the-art buildings make Stockholm one of the most beautiful cities in Europe. The 24,000 islands which comprise the Stockholm **archipelago** begin just outside the city limits and are a perfect antidote to the bustle of the capital, offering endless opportunities to

explore unspoilt island villages – and, of course, to go swimming. On the west coast, **Gothenburg**, the country's second city, is also one of Sweden's most appealing destinations. Gothenburgers have a reputation for being among the friendliest people in Sweden, and the city's network of canals, and spacious avenues is reminiscent of Amsterdam, whose architects designed it.

The **south** is the most cosmopolitan part of the country, owing to the proximity of Denmark and the rest of the European continent. Its surprisingly varied western coast has bustling towns all the way along its length. **Helsingborg**, near where the Danish island of Zeeland and Hamlet's Elsinore is situated, is small yet breezily continental. To the north lies the Bjäre peninsula, offering some of the country's best cycling and hiking, with the home of

> **Sweden is still one of Europe's best-kept secrets**

Swedish tennis, **Båstad**, nestling at the peninsula's base. Just over 50km south of Helsingborg is the glorious ancient university seat of **Lund**, while nearby **Malmö**, Sweden's third city, heaves with youthful nightlife around its medieval core. The south coast is brimming with chocolate-box villages and a few cultural surprises; inland, southern Sweden boasts some handsome lakes, the two largest of which, Vänern and Vättern, provide exceptional fishing and splendid backdrops to some beautiful towns, not least the evocative former royal seat and monastic centre of **Vadstena**. To the east of

the mainland lie the islands of **Öland** – featuring some stunning scenery – and **Gotland**, justifiably raved about as a haven for summer revelry within the medieval walls of its unspoilt Hanseatic city, **Visby**.

Central Sweden and **Swedish Lapland** are what most outsiders imagine Sweden to look like. In the country's centre is **Dalarna** (literally, "The Dales"), an area of rolling hills and villages of red-and-white wooden houses that is, for Swedes, the most quintessentially Swedish part of the country; it's also home to **Lake Siljan**, one of Sweden's most beautiful lakes. From Dalarna, the private Inlandsbanan train line strikes north through some of the country's most beautiful scenery, with reindeer – and occasionally bears – having to be cleared off the track as the trains make their way from village to village. To the east, the other train line linking the north with the south runs close to the **Bothnian coast**. Most towns and cities in the north are located along here: **Sundsvall**, **Umeå** and **Luleå** are all enjoyable, lively places to break your journey on the long trek north. Equally, the **High Coast** north of Sundsvall is an excellent introduction to northern Sweden, with its array of pine-clad islands and craggy inlets, which extend deep inland around a patchwork of flower meadows and rolling hillsides.

Both train lines eventually meet in the far north of Sweden, within the **Arctic Circle**, in the home of the Lapps or **Sámi** – Sweden's (and Scandinavia's) oldest indigenous people. The further north you travel into **Swedish Lapland**, the more isolated the towns become – you'll often be covering vast distances in these regions just to get to the next village, and you shouldn't be surprised if you drive for hours without seeing a soul. This is the land of reindeer and elk, of swiftly flowing rivers and coniferous forest, all traversed by endless hiking routes. The **Kungsleden**, a trail that stretches for 500km from Hemavan to Abisko,

Midsummer mayhem

Midsummer Solstice, which falls annually on the weekend closest to June 24, dates back to prehistoric times. Maypoles are erected as giant fertility symbols in gardens across the country, and an atmosphere akin to Mediterranean *joie de vivre* takes over. From the winter months people discuss where and with whom they'll celebrate the festival. This is not a time for staying in towns – everyone heads to the countryside and coasts – Dalarna, the island of Öland and the Bohuslän Coast are just a few of the most popular spots. Aided in no small part by copious quantities of alcohol, for this weekend the population's national characteristics of reserve and restraint dissolve. Long trestle tables draped in white cloths sagging under the weight of multiple varieties of herring, potatoes with dill and gallons of schnapps are set up outside. Parties go on through the light night with dancing to the strains of accordions.

Jugendstil – Swedish style

When thinking of Sweden's design awareness, it may be blond-wood simplicity and flatpacks that first spring to mind, but one of the country's most splendid periods for architecture and design was the end of the nineteenth century and the first decade of the twentieth – the era of Art Nouveau or Jugendstil.

This free-flowing style was employed to decorate the facades of urban landscapes across Europe but the luxuriant curves and organic shapes were never so resonant as in nature-loving Sweden. Towns across the country still boast a wealth of beautiful examples from this elegant era. Stockholm's Östermalm area is rich in the style, while in Gothenburg, the curves and curls are most apparent in Vasastan. In Malmö, Helsingborg and Lund the best houses – often cream-stuccoed with green paintwork – are peppered with images of quirky faces, rising suns and stylized flowers.

passes through some of Sweden's wildest and most beautiful terrain, offering the chance to experience nature in the raw. Two of Sweden's northernmost towns, **Kiruna** and **Gällivare**, make excellent bases for exploring Lapland's **national parks**, which can all be reached easily from there by train or bus, and for visiting the world-famous **Icehotel** located in nearby **Jukkasjärvi**. Lapland is also where you will experience the **midnight sun**: in high summer the sun never sets, allowing you to read the newspaper outdoors or play golf at midnight. In midwinter the opposite is true, and the complete darkness (not to mention temperatures as low as –30°C) can make this one of the most magical parts of the country to travel through, as the sky is lit up by the multi-coloured patterns of the **northern lights**, or Aurora Borealis (see p.xiii).

When to go

I n general, **May to September** is a good time to visit Sweden – north or south. **Summer** in Sweden, though short, can be hot; the summer of 2002 was the hottest since records began with around six weeks of temperatures in Stockholm constantly above 25C. Most Swedes take their summer holiday between mid-June and mid-August, which is when the weather is at its best and festivals are thick on the ground. Generally, if southern Sweden is having a hot summer, it'll be miserably cold and rainy in the north – and vice versa.

By the end of August, in northern Sweden the leaves are starting to turn colour and night frosts are not uncommon; the first snows fall in September. In Stockholm, snow starts to fall in October but doesn't generally settle; by November, though, the ground is usually covered in a blanket of snow, which will last until the following March or even April, when there can still be snow showers. **Winters** in the south of Sweden are often mild, and the southern province of Skåne often escapes snow completely. Swedes go to great lengths, however, to point out that a cold, snowy winter is far better than a milder, greyer one: a cover of snow on the ground acts as a reflector for the little light there is in the winter months and goes a long way to brightening things up. In the south of the country, the winter snow has generally gone by the end of March or beginning of April, when temperatures are slowly starting to rise. Bear in mind, though, that if you're heading north in late spring you're likely to encounter snow until well into May.

Daylight is in short supply in winter. In December, it doesn't get light in Stockholm until around 9.30am, and it's normally dark again by 3pm. North of the Arctic Circle – in Kiruna, for example – there's 24-hour darkness from mid-December to mid-January, and the merest glow of

Northern lights

Also known by the Latin name, *aurora borealis*, the northern lights are visible all across northern Sweden during the dark months of winter. These spectacular displays of green-blue shimmering arcs and waves of light are caused by solar wind, or streams of particles charged by the sun, hitting the atmosphere. The colours are the characteristic hues of different elements when they hit the plasma shield that protects the Earth: blue is nitrogen and yellow-green oxygen. Although the mechanisms which produce the aurora are not completely understood, the displays are generally more impressive the closer you get to the poles – low temperatures are also rumoured to produce some of the most dramatic performances. Gällivare and Kiruna, both well inside the Arctic Circle, are arguably the best places in Sweden to catch a glimpse of the aurora, particularly during the coldest winter months from December to February. Although displays can range from just a few minutes to several hours, the night sky must be clear of cloud to see the northern lights from Earth.

Average daily temperatures (°C) and precipitation (mm)

	Jan	Mar	May	June	July	Aug	Oct	Dec
Jokkmokk								
°C	-17	-8	6	12	14	12	1	-14
mm	30	24	35	48	78	74	41	32
Umeå								
°C	-9	-4	7	13	15	14	4	-7
mm	49	41	41	44	53	78	65	56
Östersund								
°C	-7	-4	7	12	13	12	4	-6
mm	27	23	35	57	76	60	37	31
Stockholm								
°C	-3	0	11	16	17	16	8	-1
mm	39	26	30	45	72	66	50	46
Gothenburg								
°C	-2	1	11	15	16	16	9	0
mm	62	50	51	61	68	77	84	75
Visby								
°C	-1	0	10	14	16	16	8	1
mm	48	32	29	31	50	50	50	51
Lund								
°C	-1	2	11	15	17	17	9	1
mm	54	44	43	54	66	63	60	65

light at noon during the months immediately either side.

Conversely, at the height of summer there's no part of Sweden which is dark for any length of time. Even the south of the country only experiences a few hours of darkness; in Stockholm it doesn't get properly dark at all in June. From 11pm or midnight there's a sort of half-light, with the sun only just below the horizon, which lasts just a few hours; at 3am it's bright daylight again. In the far north there's 24-hour daylight from the end of May to the end of June, and April and July are very light months.

31

things not to miss

It's not possible to see everything that Sweden has to offer in one trip – and we don't suggest you try. What follows is a selective and subjective taste of the country's highlights, from snowmobiling to smörgåsbord. They're arranged in five colour-coded categories to help you find the very best things to see, do and experience. All entries have a page reference to take you straight into the guide, where you can find out more.

02 Nimis, Kullen Peninsula Page **223** • Clamber over this sprawling sculpture of driftwood towers and corridors on Sweden's west coast.

01 Herring Page **40** • The quintessentially Swedish culinary experience: herring washed down with a shot of vodka.

04 **Midnight sun** Page **54** • The Midnight Sun: from late May to mid-July the sun never sets in northern Sweden.

03 **Vasa ship, Stockholm** Page **87** • After lying in mud for cen-turies at the bottom of Stockholm harbour, the mighty Vasa warship has now been restored to her former glory.

05 **Gamla Stan, Stockholm** Page **72** • Gamla Stan, Stockholm one of Europe's best preserved medieval cities.

06 **Swimming in a lake** Page **88** • One of Sweden's 100,000 lakes – perfect for a refreshing dip.

07 **Sámi culture, Arvidsjaur** Page **472** • Still used by the Sámi today, Lappstaden in Arvidsjaur is a monument to the thriving culture of Sweden's indigenous population.

08 **Icehotel** Page **492** • A night spent in the Icehotel is a must for anyone travelling in Swedish Lapland in winter.

09 **Having a sauna** Page **54** • A Swedish sauna is the perfect end to a long day.

10 **St. Karins ruin, Visby** Page **345** • One of fifteen medieval churches soaring above the cobbled lanes of Gotland's capital city.

11 **Snowmobiling in winter** Page **47** • Snowmobiling across Lapland is an exhilarating way to see winter Sweden.

12 Fiskebaäckskil, Bohuslån Coast Page 170

• The picture-perfect fishing village on this craggy western coast is home to painter Carl Wilhelmson.

13 Crossing the Arctic Circle Page 478

• Don't leave Sweden without crossing the Arctic Circle: 66° 33' north.

14 Högbonden, High Coast Page 379

• A visit to this idyllic island in the Gulf of Bothnia, with its converted lighthouse, is an essential trip in northern Sweden.

15 **Glass Kingdom, Småland** Page **303** • Scattered within the forest in southeast Sweden, fifteen glass factories produce some of the world's finest glass.

16 **Vadstena** Page **315** • This attractive lakeside town is a fusion of royal and ecclesiastical history with its great palace and abbey founded by Sweden's first female saint, Birgitta.

17 **Jokkmokk Winter Market** Page **481** • The Jokkmokk winter market has everything from bearskins to candlesticks.

18 **South Coast beaches** Page **281** • Stretches of white sandy beaches and clear, warm waters are perfect places to relax in the summer sun.

19 **Gothenburg's Konst Museet** Page **147** • The Furstenburg Galleries boast some of Sweden's finest late nineteenth century-paintings.

20 **Gammelstad, Luleå** Page **403** • Proudly listed on the UNESCO World Heritage list, Gammelstad is Sweden's largest parish village.

21 **Walking the Kungsleden trail** Page **48** • Hiking the Kungsleden trail in northern Sweden is the best way to experience nature in the raw.

23 Marstrand Page **165** • Just a ferry ride from Gothenburg this historic fortress island buzzes in summer with people who head here for the sailing and bathing.

22 Foteviken Viking Museum, Southwest Skåne Page **248** • Spend a night in a Viking tent in this working village.

24 Lund Cathedral Page **233** • This twelfth-century cathedral in Sweden's principal university town is the finest Romanesque building in northern Europe.

25 **Norrköping's industrial landscape** Page **329** • An appealing textile town with some sensational industrial buildings set around the crashing Motala Ström.

27 **Henry Dunker Museum, Helsingborg** Page **227** • A sensational new museum that brings to life the history of this bustling little city.

26 **Kirke Möss Car Cemetery** Page **305** • The bizarre sight of nearly one hundred veteran cars abandoned in a forest south of Växjö.

28 **Stockholm archipelago** Page **104–112** • No visit to Stockholm is complete without a trip to one of the 24,000 islands that make up the archipelago right on the capital's doorstep.

29 **Ystad** Page **254** • A perfect medieval town where a bugler plays a haunting note from the ancient church's tower through every night.

30 **Smörgåsbord** Page **42** • Eat until you drop: the smörgåsbord is an excellent way to sample Sweden's excellent cuisine.

31 **Inlandsbanan** Page **32** • A trip on the Inlandsbanan through northern Sweden is one of Europe's great railway journeys.

Contents

Using this Rough Guide

We've tried to make this Rough Guide a good read and easy to use. The book is divided into six main sections, and you should be able to find whatever you want in one of them.

Colour section

The front colour section offers a quick tour of Sweden. The **introduction** aims to give you a feel for the place, with suggestions on where to go. We also tell you what the weather is like and include a basic country fact file. Next, our authors round up their favourite aspects of Sweden in the **things not to miss** section – whether it's great food, amazing sights or a special hotel. Right after this comes a full **contents** list.

Basics

The Basics section covers all the **pre-departure** nitty-gritty to help you plan your trip. This is where to find out which airlines fly to your destination, what paperwork you'll need, what to do about money and insurance, about Internet access, food, security, public transport, car rental – in fact just about every piece of **general practical information** you might need.

Guide

This is the heart of the Rough Guide, divided into user-friendly chapters, each of which covers a specific region. Every chapter starts with a list of **highlights** and an **introduction** that helps you to decide where to go, depending on your time and budget. Likewise, introductions to the various towns and smaller regions within each chapter should help you plan your itinerary. We start most town accounts with information on arrival and accommodation, followed by a tour of the sights, and finally reviews of places to eat and drink, and details of nightlife. Longer accounts also have a directory of practical listings. Each chapter concludes with **public transport** details for that region.

Contexts

Read Contexts to get a deeper understanding of what makes Sweden tick. We include a brief history, articles about architecture and wildlife, and a detailed further reading section that reviews dozens of **books** relating to the country.

Language

The **language** section gives useful guidance for speaking Swedish and pulls together all the vocabulary you might need on your trip, including a comprehensive menu reader. Here you'll also find a glossary of words and terms peculiar to the country.

Index + small print

Apart from a **full index**, which includes maps as well as places, this section covers publishing information, credits and acknowledgements, and also has our contact details in case you want to send in updates and corrections to the book – or suggestions as to how we might improve it.

Chapter list and map

Contents

Contexts

507–539

Language

541–552

Index + small print

553–563

Map symbols

maps are listed in the full index using coloured text

‑‑‑‑‑‑	International boundary	▲	Mountain peak
‑‑‑ ‑‑ ‑	County boundary	⛷	Viewpoint
‑ ‑ ‑ ‑ ‑	Chapter division boundary	🕯	Lighthouse
▬▬▬	Motorway	✈	Airport
═══	Major road	Ⓣ	T-bana station
───	Minor road	★	Bus stop
▬▬▬	Pedestrianised street	🅿	Parking
⫿⫿⫿⫿	Steps	⛽	Petrol station
‑ ‑ ‑ ‑	Path	◉	Accommodation
▬●▬●▬	Railway	△	Youth hostel
‑ ‑ ‑	Ferry route	⚊	Campsite
────	Waterway	⊞	Hospital
┴┴┴┴	Canal	ⓘ	Tourist office
▬■▬■▬	Wall	⊠	Post office
◆	General point of interest	ⓒ	Telephone
🏛	Archeological site	@	Internet access
∴	Ruin	🏊	Swimming pool
♔	Castle	🎿	Ski trail
🏛	Stately home	▬	Building
⛲	Gardens	✛	Church (town maps)
⊙	Statue	⁺₊⁺	Cemetery
♟	Museum	▒	Park
ⵜ	Church (regional maps)	⌁	Forest
⛪	Monastery	⋰	Beach
✡	Synagogue		

Basics

Basics

Getting there

Given the long distances involved in reaching Sweden, especially the northern stretches of the country, flying is by far the quickest and cheapest option. The main gateways are Stockholm and Gothenburg, both with two international airports to choose between, and Copenhagen, in neighbouring Denmark, now just a twenty-minute train ride away from Malmö. However, if you're making Sweden part of a longer European trip, visiting other countries along the route, it may be a better idea to travel by train, using one of the handful of rail passes available.

Air fares always depend on the **season**, with the highest being around June to mid-August, when the weather is best; fares drop during the "shoulder" seasons – April, May and mid-August to October – and you'll get the best prices during the low season, November to March (excluding Christmas and New Year when prices are hiked up and seats are at a premium).

The proliferation of **no-frills airlines** has dramatically cut the price of tickets to Sweden from Europe, leading to thoroughly affordable flights. Another way to cut costs is to contact a **specialist flight agent** – either a consolidator, who buys up blocks of tickets from the airlines and sells them at a discount, or a **discount agent**, who in addition to dealing with discounted flights may also offer special student and youth fares and a range of other travel-related services such as travel insurance, rail passes, car rentals, tours and the like.

Booking flights online

Many airlines and discount travel websites offer you the opportunity to book your tickets online, cutting out the costs of agents and middlemen. Good deals can often be found through discount or auction sites, as well as through the airlines' own websites.

ⓦ **travel.yahoo.com** Incorporates a lot of Rough Guide material in its coverage of destination countries and cities across the world, with information about places to eat, sleep and see.
ⓦ **www.cheapflights.com** Bookings from the UK and Ireland only. Flight deals, travel agents, plus links to other travel sites.
ⓦ **www.cheaptickets.com** Discount flight specialists.

ⓦ **www.etn.nl/discount.htm** A hub of consolidator and discount agent Web links, maintained by the non-profit European Travel Network.
ⓦ **www.expedia.com** Discount air fares, all–airline search engine and daily deals.
ⓦ **www.flyaow.com** Online air travel info and reservations site.
ⓦ **www.hotwire.com** Bookings from the US only. Last-minute savings of up to forty percent on regular published fares. Travellers must be at least 18 and there are no refunds, transfers or changes allowed. Log-in required.
ⓦ **www.lastminute.com** Offers good last-minute holiday package and flight-only deals.
ⓦ **www.priceline.com** Name-your-own-price website that has deals at around forty percent off standard fares. You cannot specify flight times (although you do specify dates) and the tickets are non-refundable, non-transferable and non-changeable.
ⓦ **www.travelocity.com** Destination guides, hot fares and best deals for car hire, accommodation and lodging. Provides access to the travel agent system SABRE, the most comprehensive central reservations system in the US.
ⓦ **www.travelshop.com.au** Australian website offering discounted flights, packages, insurance, online bookings.

From Britain

The most convenient and economical way to get to Sweden from Britain is to **fly**. There are direct flights to Stockholm, Gothenburg and Copenhagen from most major British airports, though the cheaper deals with the no-frills airlines are still restricted to London. From smaller regional airports where no direct flights exist, connections can be made in either London or Amsterdam. Although it is possible to travel to Sweden by both **train** and **ferry**, either way will involve a journey of at least 24 hours, flying will always be cheaper – and a good deal quicker; flight time to Sweden from Britain is just two hours. Travelling by train involves changing three or four times, whilst direct ferries only leave from one UK port, Newcastle.

Flights

The decision in recent years by the budget airline, **Ryanair**, to target the Swedish market and introduce several daily flights to Sweden's three main cities has seen prices plummet. As a result, Sweden is now one of the cheapest European countries to reach from the UK. From London Stansted, Ryanair flies to four airports in Sweden, whose three-letter codes are given here in brackets: Stockholm (Skavsta NYO; Västerås VST), Gothenburg City (GSE) and Malmö (MMX). Neither of Ryanair's Stockholm airports is particularly close to the capital; near the town of Nyköping, Skavsta is about an hour's drive southwest from Stockholm, whilst Västerås is a similar distance to the west. Conversely, Gothenburg City is considerably closer to the city centre than Landvetter airport used by British Airways and SAS. Malmö airport, on the outskirts of the city, has a direct bus link with the centre, while neighbouring Copenhagen airport, just over the Öresund strait in Denmark, has a direct rail link (from the train station immediately beneath Copenhagen airport) with Malmö, Gothenburg and Stockholm. Ryanair's return fares to all four Swedish destinations generally hover around the £50–80 mark (Mon–Thurs), rising by around £30–50 for departures involving travel on a Friday, Saturday or Sunday. Special promotions are often run when business is slow; for information on these contact Ryanair (see p.13 for details).

It's worth trying other **airlines** who operate to Sweden, not just for the option of flying from an airport closer to home, but also because these companies now try to match the higher fares offered by Ryanair. Of all the airlines, SAS has the most direct flights to Sweden from the largest number of British cities, whilst BA also operates various daily flights for around the same prices. City Airline, Finnair and the Danish airline, Maersk, all offer regular services from a number of regional airports; see below for a full list of possibilities.

The cheapest non-discounted deals no longer require your stay to include a minimum of one Saturday night. Flights in June, July and August (particularly at weekends) are often sold out months before at these lower fares. Scheduled flights generally start at around £100–£180 return. If you're under 25, ask about the availability of **youth fares**, although generally they're nothing to write home about. **SAS Airpasses** are sold in connection with the company's return flights and can be useful for travelling around Sweden by air (see "Getting around", p.29).

Via Copenhagen

Flights to **Copenhagen** are competitively priced and can be useful for **southern Sweden**, particularly Malmö. The new Öresund bridge has transformed travel between Copenhagen and Malmö and regular direct train services now link Copenhagen airport (Kastrup, CPH) with Malmö (also less frequently with Gothenburg and Stockholm); the journey time, for example, from Copenhagen airport to Malmö central station is just 20min. Airlines flying from **London to Copenhagen** include SAS, BA, Maersk, Varig and easyJet, while SAS, BA and bmi serve several British regional cities; see below for details.

Airlines and routes

bmi ☎0870/607 0555, ⊛www.flybmi.com. Edinburgh–Copenhagen (1 daily); Glasgow–Copenhagen (Mon–Fri 2 daily, Sat & Sun 1 daily); Leeds Bradford–Copenhagen (1 daily). **British Airways** ☎0845/77 333 77, ⊛www.ba.com. Heathrow–Stockholm (Mon–Fri & Sun 6 daily, Sat 4 daily); Heathrow–Copenhagen (Mon–Fri & Sun 5 daily, Sat 4 daily); Birmingham–Stockholm (Mon–Fri 2 daily, Sat & Sun 1 daily, operated by Maersk); Birmingham–Gothenburg (Mon–Fri 2 daily, Sun 1 daily, operated by Maersk); Birmingham–Copenhagen (Mon–Fri 3 daily; Sat & Sun 1 daily); Manchester–Gothenburg (Mon–Fri & Sun 1 daily). **City Airline** ☎0870/330 8800, ⊛www.cityairline.com. Gatwick & Manchester to Gothenburg (both 3 daily). **easyJet** ☎0870/600 0000, ⊛www.easyjet.com. Stansted–Copenhagen (3 daily).

Finnair ☎020/7408 1222, ⊛www.finnair.co.uk. Manchester–Stockholm (Mon–Fri 2 daily, Sat & Sun 1 daily).
KLM ☎0870/507 4074, ⊛www.klmuk.com. Flights from Aberdeen, Glasgow, Edinburgh, Newcastle, Teesside, Leeds Bradford, Humberside, Manchester, Birmingham, Cardiff, Bristol, Norwich and London Heathrow to Copenhagen, Gothenburg and Stockholm via Amsterdam.
Ryanair ☎0871/246 0000, ⊛www.ryanair.com. Stansted–Stockholm Skavsta (2 daily); Stansted–Västerås (1 daily); Stansted–Gothenburg City (2 daily); Stansted–Malmö (2 daily).
SAS Scandinavian Airlines ☎0845/607 2772, ⊛www.scandinavian.net. Heathrow–Stockholm (Mon–Fri 8 daily, Sat 5 daily, Sun 9 daily); Heathrow–Gothenburg (2 daily); Heathrow–Copenhagen (Mon–Fri & Sun 7 daily, Sat 6 daily); Gatwick–Copenhagen (Mon–Sat 3 daily, Sun 2 daily, operated by Maersk); Birmingham–Copenhagen (Mon–Fri 2 daily; Sun 1 daily); Manchester–Stockholm (Mon–Fri 2 daily, Sun 1 daily, operated by Skyways); Manchester– Copenhagen (Mon–Fri 3 daily, Sat & Sun 2 daily).
Varig ☎020/8321 7170, ⊛www.varig.com. Heathrow–Copenhagen (Mon–Fri & Sun 1 daily).

Flight and travel agents

Bridge the World ☎0870/444 7474, ⊛www.bridgetheworld.com. Specializing in good deals aimed at the backpacker market.
Flightbookers ☎0870/010 7000, ⊛www.ebookers.com. Low fares on an extensive selection of scheduled flights.
North South Travel ☎ & ℗01245/608 291, ⊛www.northsouthtravel.co.uk. Friendly, competitive travel agency, offering discounted fares – profits are used to support projects in the developing world, especially the promotion of sustainable tourism.
Norvista Travel ☎0870/744 7315, ⊛www.norvista.co.uk. Discounted flights to Sweden using Finnair and other carriers.
STA Travel ☎0870/1600 599, ⊛www.statravel.co.uk. Worldwide specialists in low-cost flights and tours for students and under-26s, though other customers welcome.
Top Deck ☎020/7244 8000, ⊛www.topdecktravel.co.uk. Long-established agent dealing in discount flights.
Trailfinders ☎020/7628 7628, ⊛www.trailfinders.com. Very well-informed agents for independent travellers.

Package holidays

Don't be put off by the idea of an inclusive **package**, as it can sometimes work out the cheapest way of doing things, and may be a much easier way of reaching remote areas of northern Sweden in winter. **City breaks** invariably work out less costly than arranging the same trip independently: prices include return travel, usually by plane, and accommodation ranging from hostels to luxury-class hotels. As a broad guide, on a package, four-night stays in Stockholm and Gothenburg go for around £300–350 a head; go for a week, and rates per night fall considerably.

There are also an increasing number of operators (see below) offering **special-interest holidays** to Sweden, from camping tours to Arctic expeditions. Many also offer good-value **skiing** and **winter sports holidays**: in January with Ski Scandinavia, a week in one of the major resorts – Storlien – costs around £350 (including flight and half board). General information on skiing holidays in Sweden can be obtained from the Swedish Travel and Tourism Council. For more on skiing and winter sports in Sweden, see "Sports and outdoor pursuits", p.47.

Specialist operators

Anglers World Holidays 46 Knifesmith Gate, Chesterfield, S40 1QR ☎01246/221717, ⊛www.anglers-world.co.uk. Angling holidays plus cottage and hotel stays.
Arctic Experience 29 Nork Way, Banstead, SM7 1PB ☎01229/467000, ⊛www.arctic-discover.co.uk. Specializes in trips to Lapland.
Crystal Cities, Crystal House, The Courtyard, Arlington Rd, Surbiton, Surrey KT6 6BW ☎0870/166 4951, ⊛www.crystalholidays.co.uk. The biggest ski operator on the market, with packages to Åre and Storlien at reasonable prices.
DFDS Seaways Scandinavia House, Parkeston Quay, Harwich, CO12 4QG ☎0870/5333 000, ⊛www.dfdsseaways.co.uk. Extensive range of motoring and cabin holidays as well as city breaks – good out-of-season deals.
Mountain & Wildlife Ventures Compston Road, Ambleside, Cumbria LA22 9DJ ☎015394/433285. Hugely experienced company dealing in Nordic ski touring, skiing courses, mountain skiing and expeditions.
Norvista 227 Regent St, London W1R 8PD ☎0870/744 7315, ⊛www.norvista.co.uk. Hiking

holidays around Arvidsjaur, and a four-day Arctic safari – expensive but well worth it.

Scantours 21–24 Cockspur St, London, SW1Y 5BN ☏020/7839 2927, ⊛www.scantoursuk.com. City breaks, cruises on the Göta canal, and trips out to lakes and mountains.

Tracks Travel Evegate Park Barn, Smeeth, Ashford, Kent TN25 6SX ☏020/7937 3028, ⊛www.tracks-travel.com. Group camping tours for 18- to 38-year-olds.

Travellers Waterside, Kendal, Cumbria LA9 4HE ☏015396/20196. Dog-sledging holidays in Jämtland and Arctic Sweden, with accommodation in mountain cabins in the national parks.

By train

Getting to Sweden by **train** is much more expensive than flying, and is only worth considering if you're travelling on a rail pass. A number of discounted tickets and passes make it possible to cut costs.

From London, trains to Sweden go via Brussels, Cologne, Hamburg and Copenhagen: a typical journey will involve changing trains three or four times. The fastest and easiest connection in summer is to take the Eurostar, leaving Waterloo mid-evening for Brussels Midi. From there, you can connect onto the sleeper to Hamburg, where you change again for a morning train to Copenhagen, changing again in Copenhagen for a lunchtime train to Stockholm. The times of trains can change, particularly if you're travelling outside the summer season, but the above pattern generally holds. With the optimal choice of connections, the total journey takes around 21 hours, otherwise it could take up to 26 hours. The standard London–Stockholm return fare is around £450.

Travelling **from the north of England or Scotland**, you may well prefer to take the overnight P&O Ferries service from Hull to Rotterdam (passenger fare from £48 return with cabin; discounts for students, under-26s and over-60s), and then a train from Rotterdam via Amersfoort, Osnabrück, Hamburg and Copenhagen. There is no through ticket for this journey; the cheapest way to do it is with an InterRail pass. Despite all the connections on this route, it's a decent way to get from northern England and Scotland cutting out the hassle of crossing London.

Discount train tickets and passes

An **InterRail pass**, available to anyone resident for six months in the participating European countries, is an excellent way of getting to Sweden and seeing a good chunk of northern Europe on the way. A zoning system applies to all of the countries covered by the scheme; to reach Sweden you'll need a pass covering zone E (France, Belgium, Netherlands, Luxembourg), zone C (Germany, Switzerland, Austria and Denmark), and zone B (Sweden itself; also covers Norway and Finland) if you intend to see the country by train. A one-month pass for three zones currently costs £225. The equivalent **InterRail "26-Plus" pass** for those over 26 costs £320. The passes are available from Rail Europe and youth/student travel agencies.

A serious rival to InterRail, and invaluable if you're planning to visit the rest of Scandinavia as well, is the **ScanRail pass** (⊛www.scanrail.com). Valid on the rail networks of all four countries, the pass comes in two forms, ScanRail and ScanRail Flexi. A full 21-day ScanRail pass in standard class costs £216/$332; 12- to 25-year-olds pay £162/$249; over-60s £192/$295. ScanRail Flexi is available for travel on any five days in a two month period (adult £139/$214; youth £105/$161; over-60s £123/$190) or any ten days in two-months (adult £187/$288; youth £140/$216; over-60s £166/$256). More expensive passes for first-class travel are also available. ScanRail passes are valid on the Inlandsbanan (see p.32) as well as on buses connecting Boden, Haparanda and Kemi in Finland. They also give discounts on a number of ferry routes, including Stockholm–Helsinki, Stockholm–Turku and Gothenburg–Fredrikshavn.

Another alternative for travelling in Sweden (and through Scandinavia) is the **Eurodomino pass**, which offers unlimited train travel (including supplements for high-speed trains) within any one of 25 European countries including Sweden, Denmark, Finland and Norway and can be bought through RailEurope. For each country you have to buy a separate pass, which is good for a certain number of travel days (3, 4, 5, 6 & 7) within a one-month period, and comes in under-26 and standard-class versions. The prices for Sweden, for example, are:

three days for £105 (under-26 £85); five days for £132 (£105); and seven days for £159 (£125).

Information on **Swedish rail passes** is given in "Getting around" on p.29.

Train information

Eurostar UK ☎0870/160 6600, ⓦwww.eurostar.com. Although they don't sell tickets to Sweden, you're likely to use their services to cross the Channel for connections in Brussels.

Eurotunnel UK ☎0870/535 3535, ⓦwww.eurotunnel.com.

European Rail ☎020/7387 0444, ⓦwww.europeanrail.co.uk The place to buy train tickets for Sweden.

By car, ferry and Le Shuttle

Only one ferry company, **DFDS Seaways**, provides a direct link between Britain and Sweden sailing between Newcastle and Gothenburg – it's direct, though not particularly cheap. Although direct crossings to Sweden are long, they do save a lot in petrol and frayed tempers – if you do choose a Channel crossing instead don't underestimate the length of the drive up from France or Belgium through the Netherlands, Germany and Denmark before southern Sweden finally comes into sight. The drive from Copenhagen to Stockholm itself will take around eight to ten hours depending on the weather, and much longer in winter. This long haul north makes taking your car across to France on Le Shuttle services not worth the bother. DFDS Seaways' **fares** are expensive; the cheapest ticket from Newcastle to Gothenburg for a car and five passengers, with couchette accommodation, costs from £374 though this must be booked at least 42 days before departure. For foot passengers, the cheapest tickets start at £84, when booked at least 90 days in advance. Students get a twenty-five percent discount on economy accommodation for departures on Sunday to Thursday. Facilities on board are extremely good, with saunas, cinemas and discos helping to while away the long hours. Bear in mind, though, that a 24-hour crossing of the North Sea can be a stomach-wrenching experience, especially in winter.

The only other ferry routes that make any sense are those to the Netherlands, giving you a head start on the drive to Sweden.

Ferry companies and Le Shuttle

DFDS Seaways ☎08705/33 30 00, ⓦwww.dfdsseaways.co.uk. Newcastle–Gothenburg, 2 weekly, 25–27hr; Harwich–Esbjerg (Denmark), 3–4 weekly, 17hr.

Eurotunnel (Le Shuttle) UK ☎0870/535 3535, ⓦwww.eurotunnel.com.

P&O Ferries ☎08701/29 60 02, ⓦwww.mycruiseferries.co.uk. Hull–Rotterdam, 1 daily, 10hr.

Stena Line UK ☎08705/70 70 70, ⓦwww.stenaline.co.uk. Harwich–Hook of Holland, 2 daily, 4hr.

By bus

Travel by **long-distance bus** is the stuff horror movies are made of, and isn't recommended – it will nearly always be cheaper to fly. From London, Eurolines operate a service up to three times a week from Victoria Bus Station to Stockholm (31hr; from £154 return) with stops at around sixteen destinations in Sweden.

Alternatively, direct daily buses run from various points across the north of England and Scotland to the Hull ferry terminal for the P&O nightly sailing to Rotterdam. Principal pick-up points are Bradford, Edinburgh, Glasgow, Leeds, Manchester, Middlesborough, Newcastle, Sunderland, Thirsk, York and Liverpool; details from National Express (see below). Once in Rotterdam though, you're best returning to the train service to get you to Sweden.

Bus information

National Express ☎08705/80 80 80, ⓦwww.gobycoach.com. Details of bus services from across Britain to London to connect with Eurolines departures to Sweden. Also information on the bus to the P&O Ferries terminal in Hull for the overnight ferry to Rotterdam.

Eurolines UK ☎08705/14 32 19, Republic of Ireland ☎01/836 6111; ⓦwww.eurolines.co.uk. Information on bus services from London Victoria Coach Station to Sweden.

From Ireland

With no ferry services from Ireland to any Scandinavian port, the most straightforward way to travel to Sweden is to fly. If you are planning a wider European tour, travelling by train on an InterRail pass is an option worth considering. Alternatively, you might find it more economical to make your way to Britain and pick up a flight, ferry, bus or package deal from there – all of which are detailed on p.12–15.

The cheapest way of getting to Stockholm or Gothenburg **from Belfast** is to buy two individual tickets. Firstly, take one of the budget airlines to London and then, with a second ticket, take a flight to Stockholm or Gothenburg with either Ryanair, British Airways or SAS. **From Derry** the best bet is usually to fly with Ryanair into London Stansted and then pick up another flight to Sweden.

From the Republic of Ireland, SAS, and their partners, Skyways, are the only airlines offering direct flights to Scandinavia. SAS operate daily services (Mon–Sat 3 daily, Sun 2 daily) **from Dublin** to **Copenhagen** (€210; 2hr) from where you can take the train to Sweden from Copenhagen airport. Skyways operate direct flights (2 daily) **from Dublin to Stockholm** (€300; 2hr 45min). However, it's likely to be cheaper to fly with Ryanair from Dublin to **Stansted**, and then pick up a flight on to Sweden. This is also the case for departures **from other Irish cities** served by Ryanair, currently Knock, Shannon, Cork and Kerry.

Airlines and routes

Aer Lingus Northern Ireland ☎0845/084 4444, Republic of Ireland ☎0818/365 000; ⊛www.aerlingus.ie. Daily flights from Dublin to London Heathrow.
bmi Northern Ireland ☎0870/607 0555, Republic of Ireland ☎01/407 3036; ⊛www.flybmi.com. Flights from Belfast to London Heathrow.
British Airways Northern Ireland ☎0845/77 333 77, Republic of Ireland ☎1800/626 747; ⊛www.ba.com. Daily direct flights from Dublin to London Heathrow, Manchester and Birmingham.
easyJet UK ☎0870/600 0000, ⊛www.easyjet.com. Daily flights from Belfast to Stansted and Luton.
KLM ☎0870/507 4074, ⊛www.klm.com. Flights from Dublin and Cork to Copenhagen, Gothenburg and Stockholm via Amsterdam.
Ryanair Northern Ireland ☎0871/246 0000, Republic of Ireland ☎01/609 7800; ⊛www.ryanair.com. Flights from Derry, Knock, Dublin, Shannon, Cork and Kerry to London Stansted.

SAS Scandinavian Airlines Northern Ireland ☎0845/607 2772, Republic of Ireland ☎01/844 5440; ⊛www.scandinavian.net. Dublin to Copenhagen (Mon–Sat 3 daily, Sun 2 daily).

Ferry operators

Irish Ferries Northern Ireland ☎0800/0182 211, Republic of Ireland ☎1890/313 131; ⊛www.irishferries.com. Dublin to Holyhead and Rosslare to Pembroke.
P&O Northern Ireland☎0870/242 4777, Republic of Ireland ☎1800/409 049; ⊛www.poirishsea.com. Larne to Cairnryan and to Fleetwood; Dublin to Liverpool.

Specialist agents and tour operators

Co-op Travel Care Belfast ☎0870/902 0033, ⊛www.travelcareonline.com. Flights and holidays around the world.
Joe Walsh Tours Dublin ☎01/676 0991, ⊛www.joewalshtours.ie. General budget fares agent.
Lee Travel Cork ☎021/277 111, ⊛www.leetravel.ie. Flights and holidays worldwide.
McCarthy's Travel Cork ☎021/427 0127, ⊛www.mccarthystravel.ie. General flight agent.
Neenan Travel Dublin ☎01/607 9900, ⊛www.neenantrav.ie. Specialists in European city breaks.
Rosetta Travel Belfast ☎028/9064 4996, ⊛www.rosettatravel.com. Flight and holiday agent.
Student & Group Travel Dublin ☎01/677 7834. Student and group specialists, mostly to Europe.
Trailfinders Dublin ☎01/677 7888, ⊛www.trailfinders.ie. One of the best-informed and most efficient agents for independent travellers.
usit NOW Dublin ☎01/602 1600, ⊛www.usitnow.ie. Student and youth specialists for flights and trains.

From North America

With only one airline (Scandinavian Airlines from New York and Chicago) operating direct flights from the USA to Sweden, and with no direct flights from Canada, you will more than likely have to transit via another European city. You may actually find it cheaper to fly on a European airline via its home hub, such as British Airways which flies from various US cities via London, Lufthansa via Frankfurt, KLM via

Amsterdam, Air France via Paris or Icelandair via Reykjavík, the latter being very often a source of reasonable fares to Sweden, rather than to take one of the few direct flights to Stockholm.

From the US

From **New York**, a round-trip midweek **fare** to Stockholm (8hr on a nonstop flight; otherwise around 10hr) will cost US$700–1000 in high season, US$650–800 during the shoulder seasons, and anywhere between US$500 and 650 in the low season. British Airways are currently offering some of the best deals, at the lower end of the price range in summer or winter. From **Chicago** (9hr on a nonstop flight; at least 11hr otherwise), prices are much the same, although some airlines charge US$70 more than the top fares from New York. Travelling from the **West Coast** (journey time at least 12hr), you'll pay around US$1300 in high season, US$1100 in the shoulder and low seasons for a direct flight – roughly around US$400 less for an indirect one, for example via London with British Airways, who are currently offering Seattle to Stockholm for US$885.

From Canada

Travellers in **Canada** can fly to Stockholm from **Toronto** via Helsinki with Finnair (summer only). Several other airlines also operate flights from Toronto and Vancouver to European cities, with connections on to Stockholm. **Fares** from Toronto (journey time 9–13hr depending on connections) are CAN$1100–1400 in high season, CAN$900–1050 in shoulder season, and CAN$850–1150 in low season. In comparison, fares from Vancouver (13–18hr) are around CAN$500 higher in all seasons. The cheapest fares are once again with British Airways. It might well also be worth investigating cheap flights to New York, Chicago or Seattle and linking up with one of SAS's nonstop flights from there.

Airlines and routes

Air Canada ☎1-888/247-2262, ⊛www.aircanada.ca. Toronto to Copenhagen, Frankfurt, or London, with connections to Stockholm on SAS and Lufthansa.

Air France US ☎1-800/237-2747, ⊛www.airfrance.com, Canada ☎1-800/667-2747, ⊛www.airfrance.ca. Flies daily from many major US and Canadian cities to Paris with connections to Stockholm.
American Airlines ☎1-800/433-7300, ⊛www.aa.com. Direct flights to London from a number of US cities, from where BA connections are available to Stockholm.
British Airways ☎1-800/247-9297, ⊛www.british-airways.com. Flies in connection with American from a number of different US and Canadian cities to London, with connecting flights to Stockholm.
bmi (British Midland) ☎1-800/788-0555, ⊛www.flybmi.com. Flights from Washington and Chicago to Manchester, from where there are SAS partner connections to Sweden.
Continental Airlines domestic ☎1-800/523-3273, international ☎1-800/231-0856, ⊛www.continental.com. New York to Paris and Frankfurt with connecting flights to Stockholm on Air France or SAS.
Delta Air Lines domestic ☎1-800/221-1212, international ☎1-800/241-4141, ⊛www.delta.com. Direct flights from New York to Paris with onward connections to Stockholm with a number of different European carriers.
Finnair ☎1-800/950-5000, ⊛www.finnair.com. Flights from New York to Stockholm via Helsinki; also from San Francisco (summer only; 3 weekly) and Toronto (summer only; 2 weekly).
Icelandair ☎1-800/223-5500, ⊛www.icelandair.com. Flies to Stockholm and Copenhagen via Reykjavík from New York, Minneapolis, Baltimore, Boston and Orlando – you'll have the option to break your journey with 1–3 nights' stay in Reykjavík.
Lufthansa US ☎1-800/645-3880, Canada ☎1-800/563-5954, ⊛www.lufthansa-usa.com. Flights from Atlanta, Boston, Chicago, Dallas, Miami, New York, San Francisco, Washington, Toronto and Vancouver to major cities in Germany, from where there are onward Lufthansa and SAS connections to Sweden.
SAS (Scandinavian Airlines) ☎1-800/221-2350, ⊛www.scandinavian.net. Direct daily flights from New York and Chicago to Stockholm; also operates daily flights from Seattle to Copenhagen, where there are connections to Stockholm. You can connect up on United with all their flights from other North American cities.
United Airlines domestic ☎1-800/241-6522, international ☎1-800/538-2929, ⊛www.ual.com. Connects most major North American cities with SAS direct flights from New York or Chicago to Stockholm.

Virgin Atlantic Airways ☎1-800/862-8621, ⊛www.virgin-atlantic.com. Daily flights from the major US and Canadian cities to London, with connections to Stockholm.

Discount agents, consolidators and travel clubs

Air Brokers International ☎1-800/883-3273, ⊛www.airbrokers.com. Consolidator and specialist in round-the-world and Circle Pacific tickets.
Airtech ☎212/219-7000, ⊛www.airtech.com. Standby seat broker; also deals in consolidator fares and courier flights.
Airtreks.com ☎1-877-AIRTREKS or 415/912-5600, ⊛www.airtreks.com. Round-the-world and Circle Pacific tickets. The website features an interactive database that lets you build and price your own round-the-world itinerary.
Council Travel ☎1-800/2COUNCIL, ⊛www.counciltravel.com. Nationwide organization that mostly specializes in student/budget travel. Flights from the US only. Owned by STA Travel.
Educational Travel Center ☎1-800/747-5551 or 608/256-5551, ⊛www.edtrav.com. Student/youth discount agent.
New Frontiers ☎1-800/677-0720 or 310/670-7318, ⊛www.newfrontiers.com. French discount-travel firm based in New York City. Other branches in LA, San Francisco and Quebec City.
Skylink US ☎1-800/247-6659 or 212/573-8980, Canada ☎1-800/759-5465, ⊛www.skylinkus.com. Consolidator.
STA Travel ☎1-800/781-4040, ⊛www.sta-travel.com. Worldwide specialists in independent travel; also student IDs, travel insurance, car rental, rail passes, etc.
Student Flights ☎1-800/255-8000 or 480/951-1177, ⊛www.isecard.com. Student/youth fares, student IDs.
TFI Tours ☎1-800/745-8000 or 212/736-1140, ⊛www.lowestairprice.com. Consolidator.
Travac ☎1-800/TRAV-800, ⊛www.thetravelsite.com. Consolidator and charter broker with offices in New York City and Orlando.
Travel Avenue ☎1-800/333-3335, ⊛www.travelavenue.com. Full-service travel agent that offers discounts in the form of rebates.
Travel Cuts Canada ☎1-800/667-2887, US ☎1-866/246-9762, ⊛www.travelcuts.com. Canadian student-travel organization.
Travelers Advantage ☎1-877/259-2691, ⊛www.travelersadvantage.com. Discount travel club; annual membership fee required (currently $1 for 3 months' trial).
Worldtek Travel ☎1-800/243-1723,

⊛www.worldtek.com. Discount travel agency for worldwide travel.

Specialist tour operators

Abercrombie & Kent ☎1-800/323-7308 or 630/954-2944, ⊛www.abercrombiekent.com. Tours of Scandinavia by land and sea.
American Express Vacations ☎1-800/446-6234, ⊛www.americanexpress.com/travel Flight-plus-hotel packages to Stockholm.
Bennett Tours ☎1-800-221-2420, ⊛www.bennett-tours.com. Scandinavia specialists offering cheap weekend breaks (in winter) or fully escorted bus tours (in summer) throughout Scandinavia.
Contiki Tours ☎1-888/CONTIKI, ⊛www.contiki.com. Tours of Scandinavia and Russia for 18- to 35-year-olds.
Euro-Bike & Walking Tours ☎1-800/321-6060, ⊛www.eurobike.com. Offers a summer bicycling tour of Sweden and Denmark.
EuroCruises ☎1-800/688-3876 or 212/691-2099, ⊛www.eurocruises.com. For cruises of the Baltic Sea and the canals of Sweden.
Euroseven ☎1-800/890-3876, ⊛www.euroseven.com. Independent hotel-plus-flight packages from New York, Baltimore or Boston to Scandinavia.
Passage Tours ☎1-800-548-5960, ⊛www.passagetours.com. Specializes in Scandinavia. Offers escorted and unescorted tours and cheap weekend breaks.
REI Adventures ☎1-800/622-2236, ⊛www.rei.com/travel. Climbing, cycling, hiking, cruising, paddling and multisport tours to Sweden.
Scanam World Tours ☎1-800/545-2204 or 201/835-7070, ⊛www.scanamtours.com. Specializes in Scandinavian tours and cruises for groups and individuals. Also cheap weekend breaks.
SAS (Scandinavian Airlines) ☎1-800/221-2350, ⊛www.scandinavian.net. Offers tours and fly-drive deals.
Scantours ☎1-800/223-7226, ⊛www.scantours.com. Major Scandinavian holiday specialists offering vacation packages and customized itineraries, including cruises and city sightseeing tours.

European rail passes

There are a number of **European rail passes** that can only be purchased before leaving home, though consider carefully how much travelling you are going to be doing:

these all-encompassing passes only really begin to pay for themselves if you intend to see a fair bit of Sweden and the rest of Europe by train.

The best known and most flexible is the **Eurail Youthpass** (for under-26s), which costs US$401 for fifteen days; there are also one-month and two-month versions. If you're 26 or over, you'll have to buy a first-class **Eurail** pass, which costs US$572 for the fifteen-day option. You stand a better chance of getting your money's worth out of a **Eurail Flexipass**, which is good for a certain number of travel days in a two-month period. This, too, comes in under-26/first-class versions: ten days for under-26s costs US$473, for over-26s US$674; and fifteen days costs US$622 and US$888.

North Americans are also eligible to purchase a pass specifically for travel in Scandinavia only (Sweden, Denmark, Finland and Norway) called the **ScanRail pass**. These also come in under-26/over-26 versions and are valid for five days of travel within two months (under-26s US$161; over-26s US$214), ten days within two months (US$216; US$288) and twenty-one consecutive days (under 26s US$249; over 26s US$332). These fares are for the well-regarded second-class ticket; there are also first-class versions for both youth and adult passengers that are slightly more expensive but not worth the extra money because many Swedish trains don't offer first-class carriages. For information on passes that you can buy at home for travel in Sweden only, see "Getting Around", p.29.

Rail agents in North America

DER Tours/German Rail ☏1-800/421-2929 or in Canada ☏416/695-1209; ⊛www.der.com. Eurail and ScanRail passes.
Rail Europe US ☏1-877/257-2887, Canada ☏1-800/361-RAIL; ⊛www.raileurope.com. Official Eurail pass agent in North America; also sells the ScanRail pass.
ScanTours ☏1-800/223-7226, ⊛www.scantours.com. Eurail and ScanRail passes.

From Australia and New Zealand

There are **no direct flights** from Australia or New Zealand to Sweden; instead you have to fly to a gateway city in either Europe or Asia, from where you can get a connecting flight or alternative transport. Fares are pretty steep, so it's worth heading to London (see "Getting there from Britain"), Amsterdam or Frankfurt first, as it's easier to get a cheap onward flight from there. Air fares vary significantly with the season. For most major airlines, low season is mid-January to the end of February, and October and November; high season is from mid-May to the end of August and from December to mid-January; shoulder seasons cover the rest of the year. The fares we list for Australia are for flights from any of the major eastern Australian cities; in comparison, flying from Perth and Darwin via Asia costs A$100–200 less, or A$300–400 more via North America. The New Zealand fares we give are for flights out of Auckland; fares from Christchurch and Wellington cost NZ$200–300 more. Tickets purchased direct from the airlines tend to be expensive, with published fares listed at A$2550/NZ$2869 (low season); A$2959–3249/NZ$3239–3450 (shoulder season); and A$3499/NZ$4099 (high season). Travel agents offer better deals on fares and have the latest information on limited special deals, such as free stopovers en route and fly-drive/accommodation packages. Flight Centre and STA (which has fare reductions for ISIC-card-holders and under-26s) generally offer the best discounts – see overleaf for contact details. All the prices quoted below are for discounted fares.

Lauda Air, KLM and Thai, in conjunction with airlines operating out of Australia and New Zealand, offer the best fares for Sweden, with daily flights to **Stockholm** and **Gothenburg**, via Vienna, Amsterdam and Bangkok, for around AUS$1600/2030/2199/NZ$2300/2700/3100 (low/medium/high season). Generally you can expect to pay AUS$1600–AUS$1800/NZ$2200–NZ$2500 on Garuda, Gulf, Korean or Japan Airlines; AUS$1849–AUS$2229/NZ$2459–NZ$2810 on Malaysia Airlines and Lufthansa; and AUS$2000–AUS$2800/NZ$2500–NZ$3300 on British Airways, Qantas, Singapore Airlines, Air New Zealand and Canadian Airways.

Airlines and routes

Air New Zealand Australia ☏13 24 76, New Zealand ☏0800/737 000; ⊛www.airnz.com. Several flights weekly to London from Australia, via

Auckland and LA; also daily flights to Bangkok (to connect with SAS) from major cities in Australia and New Zealand.

British Airways Australia ☎02/8904 8800, New Zealand ☎0800/274 847 or 09/357 8950; ⓦwww.ba.com. Daily flights to London from major Australian cities via Asia, and from New Zealand cities via Los Angeles, in conjunction with Qantas. Free side-trips to Europe, including to Stockholm, and fly-drive deals.

Finnair Australia ☎02/9244 2299, ⓦwww.finnair.com. Daily flights from Sydney and Auckland to Helsinki via Singapore (code-share with Qantas) and then on to Stockholm and Gothenburg.

Garuda Indonesia Australia ☎02/9334 9970, New Zealand ☎09/366 1862; ⓦwww.garuda -indonesia.com. Flies several times weekly to London and Amsterdam from major Australian cities, via Jakarta or Denpasar, and from Auckland twice weekly.

Japan Airlines Australia ☎02/9272 1111, New Zealand ☎09/379 9906; ⓦwww.japanair.com. Daily flights to London from Brisbane and Sydney, via Tokyo or Osaka, plus several flights weekly from Cairns and Auckland.

Korean Air Australia ☎02/9262 6000, New Zealand ☎09/914 2000; ⓦwww.koreanair.com.au. Several flights a week to London from Sydney, Brisbane, Auckland and Christchurch, via Seoul.

Lauda Air Australia ☎1800/642 438 or 02/9251 6155, New Zealand ☎09/522 5948; ⓦwww.aua.com/default_e.asp. Bookings through Austrian Airlines. Several flights weekly to Stockholm from Sydney and Melbourne via Vienna and Kuala Lumpur, in conjunction with Austrian Airlines.

Lufthansa Australia ☎1300/655 727, ⓦwww.lufthansa-australia.com, New Zealand ☎09/303 1529, ⓦwww.lufthansa.com/index_en.html. Daily flights to Frankfurt from major Australian cities and Auckland, through arrangements with Singapore Airlines and Thai Airways, connecting with Lufthansa flights in either Singapore or Bangkok.

Malaysia Airlines Australia ☎13 26 27, New Zealand ☎0800/777 747; ⓦwww.mas.com.my. Several flights weekly to London, Amsterdam, Paris and Zürich from major Australian and New Zealand cities, via Kuala Lumpur.

Qantas Australia ☎13 13 13, ⓦwww.qantas.com.au, New Zealand ☎09/357 8900, ⓦwww.qantas.co.nz. Daily to London, Singapore and Bangkok from major cities in Australia and New Zealand, connecting with SAS

and Finnair to Stockholm and Gothenburg.

Scandinavian Airlines (SAS) Australia ☎1300/727 707, New Zealand agent: Air New Zealand ☎09/357 3000; ⓦwww.scandinavian.net. SAS, through a partnership with Qantas and Air New Zealand, have several flights weekly to Stockholm and other destinations in Scandinavia from major cities in Australia and New Zealand, via Bangkok, Singapore or Tokyo and Copenhagen.

Singapore Airlines Australia ☎13 10 11, New Zealand ☎09/303 2129; ⓦwww.singaporeair.com. Several flights weekly to London from major Australian cities, via Singapore, and twice weekly from Auckland.

Thai Airways Australia ☎1300/651 960, New Zealand ☎09/377 0268; ⓦwww.thaiair.com. Several flights weekly to Stockholm from major Australian cities and from Auckland (connects with Lufthansa).

Discount agents

Budget Travel New Zealand ☎0800/808 480, ⓦwww.budgettravel.co.nz
Destinations Unlimited New Zealand ☎09/373 4033
Flight Centre Australia ☎13 31 33 or 02/9235 3522, ⓦwww.flightcentre.com.au, New Zealand ☎0800 243 544 or 09/358 4310, ⓦwww.flightcentre.co.nz
STA Travel Australia ☎1300/733 035, ⓦwww.statravel.com.au, New Zealand ☎0508/782 872, ⓦwww.statravel.co.nz
Student Uni Travel Australia ☎02/9232 8444, New Zealand ☎09/300 8266; ⓦwww.sut.com.au
Trailfinders Australia ☎02/9247 7666, ⓦwww.trailfinders.com.au

Specialist tour operators

Bentours Australia ☎02/9241 1353, ⓦwww.bentours.com.au. Ferry, rail, bus and hotel passes, and a host of scenic tours throughout Scandinavia, including a four-day ferry journey down the Göta Canal between Stockholm and Gothenburg (from AUS$1410/NZ$1700, including meals).

Explore Holidays Australia ☎02/9857 6200 or 1300/731 000, ⓦwww.exploreholidays.com.au. Wholesaler of Stockholm mini-stays, from AUS$730/NZ$880 twin sharing for three nights' accommodation with city sightseeing tour and evening meals.

Wiltrans Australia ☎02/9255 0899 or 1800/251 174. Luxury, all-inclusive thirteen-day tours of Scandinavia and the Baltic, departing by boat from the UK, from around US$7000 (when you buy, prices are converted to AUS$ at the prevailing exchange rate).

Travel Plan Australia ☎ 02/9958 1888 or 1300/130 754, ⊛ www.travelplan.com.au. Skiing in Europe, Scandinavia and Canada.

Red tape and visas

American, Canadian, Australian and New Zealand citizens need only a valid passport to enter Sweden, and can stay for up to three months. If you want to stay longer, you can often get a short extension via the local police. Once this extension has expired, you won't be allowed back into Sweden, or any of the other Nordic countries, for a further six months. European Union and European Economic Area nationals can stay in Sweden for an unrestricted period but require a **resident's permit** (*uppehållstillstånd*) for visits longer than three months. For further information on where to obtain the permits, contact the Swedish embassy in your home country (see below).

In spite of the relative lack of restrictions on entering Sweden, checks are sometimes made on travellers at the ports in Malmö, Helsingborg, Gothenburg and Stockholm. Especially if you are young and have a rucksack, be prepared to prove that you have enough money to support yourself during your stay. You may also be asked how long you intend to stay and what you are there for; be polite in your responses, and you'll avoid unnecessary trouble.

Swedish embassies abroad

Australia 5 Turrana St, Yarralumla, ACT 2600 Canberra, ☎ 06/270 2700, ⊛ www.embassyofsweden.org.au
Canada 377 Dalhousie St, Ottawa, Ontario K1N 9NB, ☎ 613/241-8553, ⊛ www.swedishembassy.ca
New Zealand Consulate General, 13th Floor, Aitken St, Wellington, ☎ 04/499 9895
Republic of Ireland 13–17 Dawson St, Dublin 2, ☎ 01/671 5822, ⊛ www.swedishembassy.ie

UK 11 Montagu Place, London W1H 2AL, ☎ 020/7917 6400, ⊛ www.swedish-embassy.org.uk
USA 1501 M Street NW, Suite 900, Washington, DC 20005-1702, ☎ 202/467-2600, ⊛ www.swedish-embassy.org

Customs allowances

The **duty-free allowance** for visitors aged 20 and over arriving from the EU is five litres of spirits (more than 22° of alcohol by volume) or 6 litres of fortified or sparkling wine (15 percent to 22 percent alcohol by volume), plus 52 litres of wine (up to 15 percent by volume), and 64 litres of strong beer (more than 3.5 percent alcohol by volume) provided the tax on all these has already been paid in another EU country. Visitors aged 18 and over can also take in 400 cigarettes, or 200 cigarillos, or 100 cigars, or 500g of pipe tobacco. Allowances for people arriving directly from North America, Australia and New Zealand are lower – but are still duty-free.

Insurance

Even though EU health-care rights apply in Sweden, you'd do well to take out an **insurance** policy before travelling to cover against theft, loss and illness or injury. Before paying for a new policy, however, it's worth checking whether you are already covered: some all-risks home insurance policies may cover your possessions when overseas, and many private medical schemes include cover when abroad. In Canada, provincial health plans usually provide partial cover for medical mishaps overseas, while holders of official student/teacher/youth cards in Canada and the US are entitled to meagre accident coverage and hospital inpatient benefits. Students will often find that their student health coverage extends during the vacations and for one term beyond the date of last enrolment.

After exhausting the possibilities above, you might want to contact a specialist **travel insurance** company, or consider the travel insurance deal we offer (see box). A typical policy usually provides cover for the loss of baggage, tickets and – up to a certain limit – cash or cheques, as well as cancellation or curtailment of your journey. Most of them exclude so-called **dangerous sports** unless an extra premium is paid: in Sweden this can mean skiing, white-water rafting, windsurfing and trekking, though probably not kayaking or hiking.

Many policies can be chopped and changed to exclude coverage you don't need – for example, sickness and accident benefits can often be excluded or included at will. If you do take **medical coverage**, ascertain whether benefits will be paid as treatment proceeds or only after return home, and whether there is a 24-hour medical emergency number. When securing **baggage cover**, make sure that the per-article limit – typically under £500 – will cover your most valuable possession. If you need to make a claim, you should keep receipts for medicines and medical treatment, and in the event you have anything stolen, you must obtain an official statement from the police.

Rough Guides travel insurance

Rough Guides offers its own travel insurance, customized for our readers by a leading UK broker and backed by a Lloyd's underwriter. It's available for anyone, of any nationality and any age, travelling anywhere in the world.

There are two main Rough Guide insurance plans: **Essential**, for basic, no-frills cover; and **Premier** – with more generous and extensive benefits. Alternatively, you can take out **annual multi-trip insurance**, which covers you for any number of trips throughout the year (with a maximum of 60 days for any one trip). Unlike many policies, the Rough Guides schemes are calculated by the day, so if you're travelling for 27 days rather than a month, that's all you pay for. If you intend to be away for the whole year, the Adventurer policy will cover you for 365 days. Each plan can be supplemented with a "Hazardous Activities Premium" if you plan to indulge in sports considered dangerous, such as skiing, scuba-diving or trekking.

For a policy quote, call the Rough Guides Insurance Line on UK freefone ☏0800/015 0906, or, if you're calling from elsewhere ☏+44 1243/621 046. Alternatively, get an online quote or buy online at ⊛www.roughguidesinsurance.com.

Information, websites and maps

Before you leave, it's worth contacting the Swedish Travel and Tourism Council (the national tourist board) in your own country (see below) for free maps and brochures – though you don't need to go overboard, as the same can easily be obtained once you're in Sweden.

Swedish Travel and Tourism Council

Australia No office but the Swedish Embassy handles tourist information (see p.21).
Britain 11 Montagu Place, London, W1H 2AL ☎020/7870 5600, ⊛ www.visit-sweden.com.
Canada Contact the Swedish Embassy for tourist information (see p.21).
Ireland No office but the Swedish Embassy handles tourist information (see p.21).
New Zealand No office but the Swedish Consulate supplies tourist information (see p.21).
USA PO Box 4649, Grand Central Station, New York, NY 10163–4649, ☎212/885-9700, ⊛ www.gosweden.org & ⊛ www.visit-sweden.com.

Tourist offices in Sweden

All towns – and some villages – have a **tourist office** from where you can pick up free town plans and information, brochures and other literature. Many tourist offices can book private rooms (and sometimes youth hostel beds), rent bikes, sell local discount cards and change money. During the summer they're open until late evening; out of season it's more usual for them to keep shop hours, and in the winter they're normally closed at weekends. You'll find full details of individual offices throughout the text.

Maps

The **maps** and plans printed in this guide are intended for general reference, but drivers, cyclists and hikers will probably require something more detailed.

The most useful map of **Stockholm** can only be bought in the city itself: the Stockholmskartan (50kr) is available from the

local transport authority, Storstockholms Lokaltrafik, at their offices underneath the central train station, and also at the entrance to Sergels Torg metro station and at Slussen metro. This map has the particular advantage of showing all bus and metro routes in the capital, and includes a street index. For maps of the whole country, go for the Terrac (1:1,000,000) or Hallwag maps. There are also regional maps produced by Kartförlaget (1:400,000), which are excellent.

If you're staying in one area for a long time, or are **hiking** or walking, you'll probably need something more detailed still, with a minimum scale of 1:400,000 – though preferably much larger for serious trekking. The 1:300,000 Esselte Kartor are excellent, but the ones to beat them are the Fjällkartan series, covering the northwestern mountains; these maps, produced by Lantmäteriverket, at a scale of 1:100,000, are unfortunately rather expensive, both in Sweden and abroad. You'll find that the larger tourist offices usually have decent hiking maps or leaflets giving descriptions of local hiking routes.

Map Outlets

Australia and New Zealand

The Map Shop 6–10 Peel St, Adelaide, SA 5000 ☎08/8231 2033, ⊛ www.mapshop.net.au
Specialty Maps 46 Albert St, Auckland 1001 ☎09/307 2217, ⊛ www.ubdonline.co.nz/maps
MapWorld 173 Gloucester St, Christchurch ☎0800/627 967 or 03/374 5399, ⊛ www.mapworld.co.nz
Mapland 372 Little Bourke St, Melbourne, Victoria 3000 ☎03/9670 4383, ⊛ www.mapland.com.au
Perth Map Centre 1/884 Hay St, Perth, WA 6000 ☎08/9322 5733, ⊛ www.perthmap.com.au

Britain and Ireland

Blackwell's Map and Travel Shop 50 Broad St, Oxford OX1 3BQ ☎01865/793 550, ⊛maps.blackwell.co.uk

Easons Bookshop 40 O'Connell St, Dublin 1 ☎01/858 3881, ⊛www.eason.ie

Heffers Map and Travel 20 Trinity St, Cambridge CB2 1TJ ☎01865/333 536, ⊛www.heffers.co.uk

Hodges Figgis Bookshop 56–58 Dawson St, Dublin 2 ☎01/677 4754, ⊛www.hodgesfiggis.com

The Map Shop 30a Belvoir St, Leicester LE1 6QH ☎0116/247 1400, ⊛www.mapshopleicester.co.uk

National Map Centre 22–24 Caxton St, London SW1H 0QU ☎020/7222 2466, ⊛www.mapsnmc.co.uk

Newcastle Map Centre 55 Grey St, Newcastle-upon-Tyne, NE1 6EF ☎0191/261 5622

Ordnance Survey Ireland Phoenix Park, Dublin 8 ☎01/802 5300, ⊛www.osi.ie

Ordnance Survey of Northern Ireland Colby House, Stranmillis Ct, Belfast BT9 5BJ ☎028/9025 5755, ⊛www.osni.gov.uk

Stanfords 12–14 Long Acre, WC2E 9LP ☎020/7836 1321, ⊛www.stanfords.co.uk

The Travel Bookshop 13–15 Blenheim Crescent, W11 2EE ☎020/7229 5260, ⊛www.thetravelbookshop.co.uk

US and Canada

Adventurous Traveler.com US ☎1-800/282-3963, ⊛adventuroustraveler.com

Book Passage 51 Tamal Vista Blvd, Corte Madera, CA 94925 ☎1-800/999-7909, ⊛www.bookpassage.com

Distant Lands 56 S Raymond Ave, Pasadena, CA 91105 ☎1-800/310-3220, ⊛www.distantlands.com

Elliot Bay Book Company 101 S Main St, Seattle, WA 98104 ☎1-800/962-5311, ⊛www.elliotbaybook.com

Globe Corner Bookstore 28 Church St, Cambridge, MA 02138 ☎1-800/358-6013, ⊛www.globercorner.com

Map Link 30 S La Patera Lane, Unit 5, Santa Barbara, CA 93117 ☎1-800/962-1394, ⊛www.maplink.com

Rand McNally US ☎1-800/333-0136, ⊛www.randmcnally.com. Around thirty stores across the US; dial ext 2111 or check the website for the nearest location

The Travel Bug Bookstore 2667 W Broadway, Vancouver V6K 2G2 ☎604/737-1122, ⊛www.swifty.com/tbug

World of Maps 1235 Wellington St, Ottawa, Ontario K1Y 3A3 ☎1-800/214-8524, ⊛www.worldofmaps.com

Costs, money and banks

Although often considered the most expensive country in Europe, Sweden is in fact cheaper than all the other Nordic countries and no more expensive than, say, France or Germany. If you don't mind having your main meal of the day at lunchtime – like the Swedes – or having picnics under the midnight sun with goodies bought from the supermarket, travelling by the efficient public transport system and going easy on the nightlife, you'll find Sweden isn't the financial drain you thought it was going to be.

Cash and credit cards

The Swedish **currency** is the *krona* (kr; plural *kronor*), made up of 100 *öre*. It comes in coins of 50 *öre*, 1kr, 5kr and 10kr; and notes of 20kr, 50kr, 100kr, 500kr, 1000kr and 10,000kr. There's no limit on the amount of Swedish and foreign currency you can take into Sweden. At the time of going to print, the exchange rate was around 14–15kr to £1, or 8kr to US$1.

The cheapest and easiest way of accessing money whilst you're in Sweden is from ATMs with your **debit card**. Check with your bank that your card is suitable and make sure you have a personal identification number (PIN) that's designed to work overseas.

There will be a flat transaction fee, which is usually quite small, but no interest payments.

Credit cards are a very handy backup source of funds, and can be used either in ATMs or over the counter. Mastercard, Visa, American Express and Diners Card are accepted just about everywhere for goods or cash; Visa and, to a lesser extent, Mastercard can also be used in Swedish ATMs. Remember that all cash advances are treated as loans, with interest accruing daily from the date of withdrawal; there may be a transaction fee on top of this.

Traveller's cheques are a safe and simple way of carrying your money, although there can be some hefty commission when you come to change them. Some places charge per cheque, others per transaction, so it's common sense to take large denominations with you, or to try to change in one go as much as you feel you can handle.

Banks and exchange

Banks (Mon–Wed & Fri 9.30am–3pm, Thurs 9.30am–5.30pm; in some cities, banks may stay open to 5.30pm every weekday) have standard exchange rates but commissions can vary enormously, so it's always worth shopping around. Banks at airports, ports and main train stations generally have longer opening hours – but often inferior rates of exchange. All banks are closed at weekends and on public holidays.

The best place to change money is at the yellow **Forex** offices (ⓦwww.forex.se), which offer 3–18 percent more *kronor* for your currency than the banks. You'll find Forex branches in city centres – Gothenburg, Helsingborg, Linköping, Luleå, Lund, Malmö, Norrköping, Nyköping, Örebro, Stockholm, Trelleborg, Umeå, Uppsala, Västerås and Ystad. Branches are also available at major airports, including Stockholm (Arlanda Terminal 2), Stockholm (Skavsta), Gothenburg (Landvetter) and Malmö (Sturup), plus the ferry terminals in Helsingborg and Ystad and major railway stations. In the more remote areas, you'll often find that hostels, hotels and campsites will change money, but the rates at hotels are usually abysmal.

Costs

Accommodation in Sweden is good value: youth hostels are of a very high standard and

charge around 130kr (£9/$14) a night for members; hotels offer special low prices to tourists in summer; and campsites are plentiful and cheap. **Admission prices** to museums and galleries are also low or nonexistent; and if you flash an ISIC card (see below), it's likely to bring a reduction. At most places, there are also reductions of around thirty to fifty percent for children and senior citizens, and younger children often get in for free.

If you're **self-catering** and shopping for **food**, look for produce marked "*extrapris*", which denotes a special offer, or "*fynd*", which is supposed to be literally that – a bit of a find. It's best to avoid anything frozen or in tins, as fresh food is reasonably priced in comparison. There are **supermarkets** in even the smallest town and village, though it is rare to find the big "hypermarket" style supermarkets common in Britain and the US; a common chain to look for across Sweden is ICA.

Restaurant eating can work out a good deal if you stick to the *Dagens Rätt* (dish of the day), served at lunchtime in most restaurants and cafés, and generally consisting of salad, a main meal (often a choice between two or three dishes), bread, a drink and a coffee – for 60–75kr all-in (£5/$8). What will cost you serious money in Sweden is **alcohol**: a strong beer in a bar outside Stockholm costs a dizzy 45–55kr (£3–4/$5–8), in Stockholm you'll pay around 30–45kr (£2–3/$3–5) making a beer roughly the same price as in London; however, a bottle of wine in a restaurant will set you back around 250kr (£17/$23); and the cost of a whisky or cognac is likely to bring on heart trouble.

Put all this together and you'll find you can exist – camping, self-catering, hitching, no drinking – on a fairly low budget (around £15/$22 a day), though it will be a pretty miserable experience and only sustainable for a limited period of time. Stay in hostels, eat the *Dagens Rätt* at lunchtime, get out and see the sights and drink the odd beer or two and you'll be looking at doubling your expenditure. Once you start having restaurant meals with wine, taking a few taxis, enjoying coffees and cakes and staying in hotel accommodation, you'll probably spend considerably more (£60–75/US$90–115).

Youth/student discounts

Once obtained, various official and quasi-official **youth/student ID cards** soon pay for themselves in savings. Full-time students are eligible for the International Student ID Card (ISIC; ⓦwww.isiccard.com), which entitles the bearer to special air, rail and bus fares and discounts at museums, theatres and other attractions. For Americans there's also a health benefit, providing up to $3000 in emergency medical coverage and $100 a day for 60 days in the hospital, plus a 24-hour hotline to call in the event of a medical, legal or financial emergency. The card costs $22 for Americans; Can$16 for Canadians; AUS$16.50 for Australians; NZ$21 for New Zealanders; and £6 in the UK.

You have to be 26 or younger to qualify for the **International Youth Travel Card**, which costs US$22/£7 and carries the

same benefits. Teachers qualify for the **International Teacher Card**, offering similar discounts and costing US$22, Can$16, AUS$16.50 and NZ$21. All these cards are available in the US from Council Travel, STA, Travel CUTS and, in Canada, Hostelling International (see p.37 for addresses); in Australia and New Zealand from STA or Campus Travel; and in the UK from STA.

Several other travel organizations and accommodation groups also sell their own cards, good for various discounts. A university photo ID or an ISIC card might open some doors, but they are often not accepted as valid proof of age, for example in bars or Sweden's liquor stores, the Systembolaget.

Post, phones and email

Communications within Sweden and abroad are good; in general it is easy to phone anywhere in the world, even from smaller towns. Most Swedes speak some English, and the operators are usually fluent. International mail deliveries work very efficiently and postal services are easy to use if you don't know Swedish, though in remoter places collections and deliveries can take a bit longer. Surprisingly for such an IT-savvy country, Sweden has few Internet cafes; instead, you'll find access at every library.

Postal services

The Swedish **post office** is a thing of the past. True, a couple still exist in the bigger towns and cities but, more and more, postal services are to be found in local supermarkets or at filling stations keeping the same (longer) hours as their new hosts. It's a recent change which the Swedes themselves are having trouble coming to terms with, despite a vigorous advertising campaign to persuade them to the contrary; the idea is that providing postal services in shops and at filling stations will encourage more people to use them, not least because they will also be open longer hours. Where post offices do still exist they are open Monday to Friday (9am–6pm) and Saturday

(10am–1pm) but closed Sunday. You can buy **stamps** (*frimärken*) at post offices, most newspaper kiosks, tobacconists, hotels, bookshops and stationers' shops – as well as at supermarkets and filling stations. Letters and postcards to Europe, North America, Australia and New Zealand cost 10kr for up to 20g. Within Sweden, letters cost 5.50kr for first class or 5kr for "Ekonomipost" (second class).

You can have letters sent **poste restante** to any post office in Sweden by addressing them "Poste Restante" followed by the name of the town and country. When picking up mail you'll need to take your passport, and make sure they check under middle names and initials as letters can get misfiled.

Telephone

All public payphones in Sweden are **cardphones** and you'll generally find one in even the smallest village. You call anywhere in the world from a public cardphone using **phonecards**, which are sold at newsagents (Pressbyrån). It's better value to buy a larger card for 120 units (100kr) since the larger the denomination of units, the cheaper the cost per unit. English instructions on how to use a cardphone are generally displayed inside each booth. Alternatively, a last resort, whip out your **credit card** and dial from a credit-card phone marked "CCC"; these are widely found though more expensive to use than regular cardphones.

Paying for international calls made from hotel rooms will give you nightmares for months after, and is only worth it in emergencies. For **collect calls**, use the overseas operator on ☏ 118 119; for domestic directory enquiries call ☏118.

Major towns and their surrounding areas each have an **area code**, which must be used when phoning from outside that zone. Area codes are included in telephone and fax numbers throughout the guide – omit them if dialling from within the area.

It's worth knowing that general **information lines** (SAS and the like) are often ☏020 numbers, which are toll-free. These numbers cannot be dialled from outside Sweden. In **emergencies**, call ☏112 for the police, fire brigade or ambulance.

Making international calls to and from Sweden

To **call Sweden from abroad**, dial your country's international access code followed by 46 for Sweden, then dial the area code (without its first 0) and the number. To **call abroad from Sweden**, dial 00 followed by the required country code (see below), then the area code (without its first 0) and the number. Within Sweden, international directory enquiries is on ☏118 119.

Useful country codes

Sweden ☏46	Australia ☏61
Britain ☏44	Canada ☏1
Ireland ☏353	New Zealand ☏64
USA ☏1	

Mobile phones

In the land of *Ericsson*, mobile phones work virtually everywhere and almost every Swede has at least one. Even in the most remote village in Norrland there's some kind of network coverage; with international roaming this means you can use your phone virtually wherever you happen to be. However, once outside the towns and villages, particularly in the north, coverage can be limited to major roads and junctions. Buying phone cards is easily done as they are available at all Pressbyrå newsagents.

Internet access

Internet cafés are surprisingly thin on the ground in Sweden; they only really exist in the larger cities. As an alternative, try the local **library** where it can be a good idea to book a time slot to save hanging around. Access at libraries is free, and in cafés it usually costs 40–60kr per hour.

Opening hours, holidays and festivals

Shop opening hours are generally from 9am to 6pm on weekdays and 10am to 4pm on Saturdays. In larger towns, department stores remain open until 8pm or 10pm on weekdays, and some are also open on Sundays between noon and 4pm. In country areas, shops and petrol stations generally close for the day between 5pm and 6pm. Museums and galleries operate various opening hours, but are generally closed on Mondays. Banks, offices and shops are closed on public holidays (see below). They may also close or have reduced opening hours on the eve of the holiday. For banking hours, see p.25; for post office hours, see p.26.

Swedish **festivals** are for the most part organized around the seasons. Most celebrations are lively events, as Swedes are great party people – especially when the beer begins to flow. The highlight of the year is the Midsummer festival when the whole country gets involved, and wild parties last well into the early hours. The date of Midsummer's Day varies from year to year but is the Saturday closest to the actual summer solstice.

Public holidays in Sweden

New Year's Day	Jan 1
Epiphany	Jan 6
Good Friday	
Easter Sunday	
Easter Monday	
Labour Day	May 1
Ascension Day	Fortieth day after Easter Sunday
Whit Sunday	Seventh Sunday after Easter
Whit Monday	Monday after Whit Sunday
Midsummer's Eve	Always on a Friday
Midsummer's Day	Saturday closest to the summer solstice
All Saints' Day	Closest Sat to Nov 1
Christmas Eve	Dec 24
Christmas Day	Dec 25
Boxing Day	Dec 26
New Year's Eve	Dec 31

Major festivals and events

Valborgsmässoafton (April 30): Walpurgis Night; bonfires and songs welcome the arrival of spring nationwide.

Labour Day (May 1): a marching day for the workers' parties.

Stockholm Marathon (June 1): one of the biggest events of its kind.

Swedish National Day (June 6): in existence since 1983, a bit of a damp squib and not a public holiday; worthy speeches are delivered in the evening.

Midsummer (June 21–23): the celebration to beat them all, during which the Swedish maypole, an old fertility symbol, is erected at popular gatherings across Sweden. The maypole is raised in June because it's often still snowing in northern Sweden in May.

Crayfish parties (throughout Aug): held in the August moonlight across the country to say a wistful farewell to the short Swedish summer.

Surströmming (late Aug): in northern Sweden, parties are held at which people eat foul-smelling fermented Baltic herring (see p.380).

Eel parties (Sept): held in the southern province of Skåne, a region known for its smokehouses and the smoked eel they produce.

St Martin's Eve (Nov 10): people from Skåne get together to eat goose – the traditional symbol of the province.

Nobel Prize Day (Dec 10): ceremonies are held in Stockholm.

St Lucia's Day (Dec 13): a procession of children, led by a girl with a crown of candles, sings songs as they bring light into the darkest month.

Getting around

The public transport system in Sweden is one of Europe's most efficient; it operates on time in all weathers. There's a comprehensive train network in the south of the country; in the north travelling by train isn't quite so easy – many branch lines have been closed as Swedish State Railways (SJ) tries to save money on loss-making routes. However, it's still possible to reach the main towns in the north by train, and where train services no longer exist, buses generally cover the same routes (rail passes are valid for some of these journeys).

Look out for city and regional **discount cards**, which often give free use of local transport, free museum entry and other discounts. Often these cards are only on sale during the summer (notable exceptions are those in Stockholm, Gothenburg and Malmö); the most useful ones have been detailed in the text. Elsewhere, it's worth asking at local tourist offices as discount schemes frequently change.

Timetables

The most important train, bus and ferry schedules are contained in the handy booklet **Tågtider**, which is currently available free of charge from main train stations. Inside you'll find a map of Sweden's rail routes and times of all trains. Although it's in Swedish, the tables are easy to figure out.

In winter, train and bus services are reduced, especially in the north (where they may even stop altogether). At holiday times (see "Opening hours, holidays and festivals", opposite) and between mid-June and mid-August, services are often heavily booked; it's worth making reservations (often compulsory) as far in advance as you can. This is also possible from abroad: contact Sweden Booking on ☎0046/498 20 33 80 or ⓔinfo@swedenbooking.com.

If you're planning on jetting round the country by plane using the airpass system operated by SAS, you'll find it handy to have a copy of the **Inrikes tidtabell** (*Domestic Timetable*), which lists every route within Sweden operated by SAS and its partner airline, Skyways; the booklet is available free from airports, tourist offices, travel agents and airline offices.

Trains

Other than flying, **train** travel is the quickest and easiest way of covering Sweden's vast expanses. The service is generally excellent and prices are not that expensive, irrespective of whether you travel on Swedish State Railways (usually abbreviated to SJ), or one of the regional services (Länstrafiken) operated by Sweden's county councils, or on the increasing number of private services. Examples of these independent are those to Swedish Lapland operated by Connex or on the trans-Scandinavia routes Oslo-Gothenburg-Copenhagen and Oslo-Karlstad-Stockholm, operated by Linx, a joint venture between Swedish and Norwegian Railways. Many station names in Sweden carry the letter C after the name of the city, for example, Stockholm C; this is a railspeak abbreviation of Central.

SJ (*Statens Järnvägar*; from abroad ☎00 46 771 75 75 75, in Sweden ☎0771/75 75 75, ⓦwww.sj.se) runs an extensive network of train services stretching from the far south of the country up to Östersund and Sundsvall in central Sweden.

For trains from Gothenburg and Stockholm to Swedish Lapland and across the border to Narvik into Norway, services are operated by the private company, Connex (☎0771/260000, ⓦwww.connex.se), although rail passes (see p.14) are valid on these services too.

For train (SJ and other companies) and connecting bus information visit ⓦwww.tagplus.se.

High-speed trains (X2000)

The pride and joy of Swedish Railways is its network of **high-speed trains**, the X2000,

which operates on most main routes, including from Stockholm to Copenhagen via the Öresund bridge. Using these services can save you a couple of hours, particularly on the Stockholm–Gothenburg and Stockholm–Malmö runs. The trains have overhead sockets for listening to the radio (bring your own headphones), telephones, a bistro car and, in first-class only, fax machines and photocopying services. Fares are, not surprisingly, higher: for example, the non-discounted X2000 Stockholm–Gothenburg one-way fare in standard class is 1041kr – 600kr more than on a normal service. When you buy an X2000 ticket, the price includes a mandatory seat reservation; if you have a rail pass, you'll pay 60kr for the seat reservation.

Tickets and discounts

Individual train tickets are rarely cost-effective and visitors doing a lot of touring by train are much better off buying a **train pass** (see p.14). If you do need to buy an individual ticket, it's worth being aware of the main discount system for SJ train tickets, the **förköpsbiljett** (advance purchase ticket) which is available every day (higher prices apply, however, on Fri and Sun) for most trains in second class. This ticket can be bought between seven and ninety days before departure and includes all seat reservations. Under-26s are entitled to a thirty percent discount on most fares, but must be able to prove their age (show your passport). **Reserved seats** on Swedish trains are not marked, so although it may appear that a seat is free it may not be so – always ask *"är det ledigt här?"* – "is anyone sitting here" – before you sit down. Incidentally, *"några nya påstigare"* is what you're likely to hear the conductor saying as he/she comes through the train after each station, which literally means "any new boarders": only show your ticket if you've just got on. *"Biljetterna, tack"*, on the other hand, is "all tickets please".

In the end most people are best off avoiding the headache of choosing discount tickets by getting a pass instead, such as InterRail, Eurail or ScanRail (see the relevant "Getting there" section for details) or, if you are touring Sweden only, a **Sweden Rail Pass**. This gives unlimited travel throughout the country on all SJ trains. A seven-day pass costs £130 in standard class and £171 in first class; a fourteen-day version costs £174 and £226 respectively. Supplements are payable on InterCity and express services. You have to buy the pass before you leave home; it is not available in Sweden. In countries where there is no agent, for example, Australia or New Zealand, you can email ℮info@swedenbooking.com to buy the pass before you leave home.

Bicycles cannot simply be taken on board the train. As in most European countries, you'll need to register the bike as luggage and send it ahead; in Swedish this service is called *pollettera*, and generally costs around 375kr. This facility is provided by *Day and Night Expressgods* (℡0771/71 71 71), who guarantee that your bike will arrive in three days, although the time needed can often be much less, especially between Stockholm and Gothenburg.

Overnight train journeys

In recent years the number of overnight services operating in Sweden has been reduced. At present **sleeper trains** only operate on the following routes: Stockholm-Malmö (SJ), Gothenburg/Stockholm-Östersund and Storlien (SJ), Stockholm-Luleå-Kiruna-Narvik (Connex) and Gothenburg-Luleå (Connex). Overnight services between Stockholm and Oslo, Stockholm and Copenhagen and between Malmö and Oslo have been withdrawn. Nonetheless, if you plan to travel overnight in Sweden, it's worth paying for a couchette or a sleeping car – Swedish train seats don't pull out to form a bed, unlike their equivalents in many other European trains. If you want to travel by couchette or sleeper without a rail pass, you have to buy an all-in-one ticket which includes your train fare, sleeping accommodation and supplement. **Prices** vary according to distance and train company: for example, a couchette on the Stockholm–Kiruna journey with Connex costs 600kr one-way (750kr in a three-berth sleeper), whereas a couchette on the Stockholm–Malmö run with SJ costs 750kr one-way (950kr in a three-berth sleeper). All these fares also include the cost of the train ticket itself. With a **rail pass**, prices are low: a couchette costs 90kr (less than a night in a youth hostel) whereas a three-berth standard-class sleeping car is a little more at 165kr; a two-berth costs 280kr per person – altogether excellent value.

Couchettes in **women-only compart-ments**, unique to Sweden, are available. Sleepers are single-sex only though couples travelling together can share a two-berth compartment. There's a toilet, hot shower and a hair dryer in the sleeper compartment itself as well as a socket for the radio (bring your own headphones). The night trains from Stockholm to Kiruna and Luleå and from Gothenburg to Luleå are an experience in themselves. There's even a cinema on board where you can catch up on the latest releases before heading off to the bistro for a bite or a quick jive to your favourite tunes from the jukebox – all as you slip painlessly through the Swedish night.

The Inlandsbanan

If you're in Sweden for any length of time, travelling at least a section of the **Inlandsbanan** (Inland Railway; ☎020/53 53 53, outside Sweden ☎00 46 63 19 44 09, ⌨www.inlandsbanan.se), which runs through northern Sweden, is a must. The route takes in some of the country's most unspoilt terrain – kilometre after kilometre of forests, and several lakes (the train stops at one of them, Varjisträsk, for passengers to take a quick dip), and offers a chance to see real off-the-beaten-track Sweden. For more information, see p.424.

The Pågatågen

In Sweden's southernmost province, Skåne, a local private company, **Pågatågen** (⌨www.skanetrafiken.se), operates trains between Ängelholm, Helsingborg, Lund and Malmö, and between Malmö and Ystad. Prices on the short hops are low; ticketing is fully automated – you buy your tickets from a machine on the platform. InterRail and ScanRail cards are valid for travel on these routes.

Buses

Although bus travel is about half as expensive as going by train, **long-distance buses** are generally less frequent, and so much slower that they aren't a good choice for long journeys (for example, Stockholm to Malmö takes 4hr 15min on the X2000, but 9hr 20min by bus). Most long-distance buses are operated by two companies,

Swebus (☎0200/218 218, ⌨www.swebus-express.se) and Svenska Buss (☎0771/67 67 67, ⌨www.svenskabuss.se). Swebus have the most extensive network in Sweden, with departures to around three hundred destinations ranging from Malmö in the south to as far north as Dalarna. Svenska Buss also operate in the south of the country, going no further north than Falun and Borlänge. On Swebus, fares depend on the length of the journey, with under-17s going for half price and children under 6 for free. Anyone aged 17–24 and senior citizens get a twenty percent discount on the day of travel (Fri, Sat & Sun departures are always more); a single ticket from Malmö to Stockholm, for example, is 305kr for travel Mon–Thu, 435kr for Fri–Sun. Fares on Svenska Buss are similar.

Between Stockholm and the north of Sweden, there are a number of smaller companies running only one or two routes, including Y-Bussen (☎08/440 85 70 in Stockholm, ☎060/17 19 60 in Sundsvall, ⌨www.ybuss.se), the only company operating services from Stockholm to Sundsvall (200kr), the High Coast (270kr), Örnsköldsvik (280kr) and Umeå (320kr), as well as across to Östersund (255kr); and Lapplandspilen (☎0951/779 50, ⌨www.lapplandspilen.se), which operates buses between Stockholm and Vilhelmina (510kr), Storuman (525kr), Tärnaby (545kr) and Hemavan (545kr).

Regional buses are particularly important in the north, where they carry mail to isolated areas. Several companies operate daily services, and their fares are broadly similar to one another's (usually 200–300kr for a 1hr to 2hr journey). Major routes are listed in the "Travel Details" at the end of each chapter, and you can pick up a comprehensive timetable at any bus terminal.

Planes

The **domestic plane network** is currently undergoing a major shake-up. The decision by Malmö Aviation to launch its curiously named *snålskjutsen* service (literally "tight-fisted lift"; ⌨www.snalskjutsen.com) on the Stockholm–Gothenburg and Stockholm–Malmö routes with single fares from just 290kr has sent a shiver down the spine of the two existing companies who had neatly carved up the domestic market between them: SAS (☏020/727 727, ✆www.sas.se) and Skyways (☏020/95 95 00, w✆www.skyways.se). SAS fares on the corresponding routes are still a little higher – though this is likely to change.

Away from the core Stockholm-Gothenburg-Malmö triangle, various deals can make flying a real steal, especially considering the time saved (see below). Individual so-called *privatpris inrikes* tickets, though, which must be booked at least one week before departure, aren't particularly cheap (around 1000–3000kr return depending on destination, generally 2000–3000kr for Thurs–Sun departures). Flying to or from Stockholm, anyone travelling with you goes for just 650kr or 850kr depending on the length of the flight – ask for a *medföljandepris*. This fare is supposed to be only for accompanying partners (male or female, gay or straight) – it's worth pretending even if you're not quite so familiar with your travelling companion.

SAS operates between Stockholm and the following destinations: Gothenburg, Karlstad, Kiruna, Luleå, Malmö, Ronneby/Karlskrona, Sundsvall, Umeå, Växjö, Ängelholm/Helsingborg, Östersund, Örnsköldsvik. Skyways flies between Stockholm and Arvidsjaur, Borlänge/Falun, Gällivare, Halmstad, Hemavan, Hultsfred, Jönköping, Kalmar, Kramfors/ Sollefteå, Kristianstad, Linköping, Lycksele, Mora, Oskarshamn, Skellefteå, Skövde, Storuman, Söderhamn, Vilhelmina, Sveg, Söderhamn, Trollhättan/Vänersborg, Visby and Örebro; between Gothenburg and Borlänge/ Falun, Sundsvall/Härnösand and Västerås; between Luleå and Sundsvall/ Härnösand; and between Malmö and Västerås and Örebro.

Air passes and stand-by tickets

SAS and Skyways offer a joint **Visit Scandinavia Airpass**, which can make flying a serious alternative to InterRail or ScanRail. The airpass has to be bought in conjunction with an SAS or Skyways return ticket to Sweden. With each international ticket, you can buy up to eight coupons, each valid on one flight; so two coupons are needed on journeys involving one change of plane (for example Malmö to Östersund via Stockholm). The coupons cost €69 (£45/US$75) on all flights within Sweden

except on the Stockholm–Kiruna route, for which a coupon costs €122 (£80/US$132). The passes are also valid on flights between Sweden and the other Scandinavian countries, though coupons for these routes cost €80 each (£52/US$86).

People under 26 can save substantially by flying **stand-by**. Buy tickets at any domestic airport when you arrive, and on the day you want to catch an internal flight, go to the airport and get in the appropriate queue. A single **stand-by ticket** (for example Stockholm–Luleå) currently costs a ridiculously cheap 340kr; for 470kr you can get priority on a particular flight. If you buy eight one-way stand-by tickets you get two single tickets within Sweden free. Buy sixteen single tickets and you're entitled to a free return ticket from Sweden to any SAS European destination north of the Alps. You can avoid lengthy waits at airports by checking seat availability first (in Swedish only, ☏020/72 78 88 or visit ✆www.sas.se/ungdom). If you don't speak Swedish, call SAS on ☏020/727 727 and ask them whether you're likely to get a seat.

Ferries and boats

In a country with such an extensive coastline and many lakes, it is only natural that domestic ferry services in Sweden are many and varied. The main route is between Visby, on the Baltic island of Gotland, and Nynäshamn, on the mainland near Stockholm and Oskarshamn. High-speed catamarans as well as regular ferries operate on both routes. Departures are very popular in summer and you should try to book ahead. The ScanRail pass gives a fifty percent discount on the Gotland crossings (for more details see p.14).

Each of the various archipelagos off the coast – particularly the Stockholm archipelago with its 24,000 islands – has ferry services which link up the main islands in the group. If you're in Stockholm, make sure you venture out into the archipelago – the peace and quiet, and the vistas of water, rocks and islets, are something special. A boat pass, which covers travel within the archipelago, is available in Stockholm; see p.106 for more details. There's also an extensive archipelago off Luleå which is worth visiting; details of boat services there are given on p.404.

It's possible to cross between Stockholm and Gothenburg on the **Göta Canal**, either on your own boat or by taking one of the rather pricey cruises along the route on an atmospheric old steamboat; ticket and journey details are given on p.179. Cheaper day cruises are possible along stretches of the Göta Canal and the Trollhättan Canal; more details are given in Chapter 2.

Driving and hitching

As far as road conditions go, **driving** in Sweden is a dream. Traffic jams are rare (in fact in the north of the country yours will often be the only car on the road), roads are well maintained and motorways, where they exist, are toll-free. The only real **hazards** are reindeer (in the north) and elk (everywhere), which wander onto the road without warning. It's difficult enough to see them at dusk, and when it's properly dark all you'll see is two red eyes as the animal leaps out in front of your car. The Swedes have now taken to spraying pungent-smelling artificial wolf urine on the edges of roads where accidents involving elk are common – elk and wolves don't get on at all well. If you hit an elk or deer, not only will you know about it (they're as big as a horse), you're bound by law to report it to the police.

To drive in Sweden you'll need a full licence; an international driving licence isn't required, though a green card or other insurance documents are essential. **Speed limits** are 110kph on motorways, 90kph on dual carriageways and many other roads, 50kph in built-up areas, and 70kph elsewhere if unsigned; for cars towing caravans, the limit is 80kph. Fines for speeding are levied on the spot. You must drive with your headlights on 24hr a day (don't forget to turn them off when you leave the car!), and it's useful to fit a headlamp adaptor if you're bringing over a right-hand drive car to avoid dazzling oncoming traffic with your lights. Warning triangles are compulsory, as is the wearing of seat belts both in the back and in the front; children can use any seat but must use a seat belt or a special child safety seat. Studded tyres for driving on snow and ice are allowed between October 1 and April 30, longer if there's still snow on the ground; when in use they must be fitted to all wheels. In northern Sweden, it's worth fitting mud-flaps to your wheels and stone-guards to the fronts of caravans.

Swedish **drink-driving laws** are among the strictest in Europe, and random breath tests are commonplace. Basically, you can't have even one beer and still be under the limit; the blood alcohol level is 0.2 percent. If you're found to be over the limit you'll lose the right to drive in Sweden, face a fine (often) and a prison sentence (not infrequently).

The cost of **petrol** (*bensin*) is in line with the European average (about £0.70/US$1 a litre). Types of petrol normally available are 98 octane (equivalent to four-star), unleaded (*blyfri*) and diesel. Most filling stations are self-service (*Tanka själv*), where you either pay a machine at the pump that accepts 20kr, 50kr or 100kr notes (though not for diesel), or head for the pumps marked "*Kassa*", which allow you to pay inside at the till.

If you **break down**, call either the police or the Larmtjänst on freephone ☏020/91 00 40, a 24-hour rescue organization run by Swedish insurance companies. You should only use the emergency telephone number (☏112) in the event of an accident and injuries. It's not mandatory to call the police in the event of an accident, but drivers must give their name and address to the other parties involved and shouldn't leave the scene until that's done. Drivers who don't stop after an accident may be liable to a fine or even imprisonment.

Car rental

Roads in Sweden may be a dream, but forking out for **car rental** is more the stuff of nightmares. Car rental is uniformly expensive; the only way to bring down the ludicrous prices is to hunt for special weekend rates (tourist offices are a good source of information on these, or try the national chain of filling stations, Statoil (☏www .statoil.se), which often rents out vehicles at near-bargain prices (1000kr) over weekends (generally Friday afternoon to Monday morning). If you fail to find a special deal, in the summer months reckon on paying 3500kr and upwards a week for a VW Golf or similar-sized car, with unlimited mileage. Be warned, though, that deals in the remoter parts can be even more expensive than this. The major international companies are represented in all the main towns and cities (in out-of-the-way places, airports are often the only source of car rental). To rent a car in Sweden you must be over 21 and have held a driving licence for at least one year.

You may well find it cheaper, especially if you are travelling from North America, to arrange things before you go; airlines sometimes have special deals with car rental companies if you book your flight and car through them. Alternatively, if you don't want to be tied down, try an agency such as Holiday Autos, who will arrange advance booking through a local agent and can usually undercut the big companies considerably; see below for details of car rental companies.

Car rental outlets

AUSTRALIA
Avis ☎13 63 33, ⓦwww.avis.com
Budget ☎1300/362 848, ⓦwww.budget.com
Hertz ☎13 30 39, ⓦwww.hertz.com

BRITAIN
Avis ☎0870/606 0100, ⓦwww.avisworld.com
Budget ☎0800/181 181,
ⓦwww.budget.co.uk
Europcar ☎0845/722 2525,
ⓦwww.europcar.co.uk.
Hertz ☎0870/844 8844, ⓦwww.hertz.co.uk
Holiday Autos ☎0870/400 00 99,
ⓦwww.holidayautos.co.uk

IRELAND
Avis Northern Ireland ☎028/9024 0404, Republic of Ireland ☎01/605 7500; ⓦwww.avis.co.uk
Budget ☎01/9032 7711,
ⓦwww.budgetcarrental.ie
Europcar Northern Ireland ☎028/9442 3444, Republic of Ireland ☎01/614 2800;
ⓦwww.europcar.ie
Hertz ☎01/660 2255, ⓦwww.hertz.ie
Holiday Autos ☎01/872 9366,
ⓦwww.holidayautos.ie

NEW ZEALAND
Avis ☎09/526 2847, ⓦwww.avis.co.nz
Budget ☎09/976 2222, ⓦwww.budget.co.nz
Hertz ☎0800/654 321, ⓦwww.hertz.co.nz

NORTH AMERICA
Avis US ☎1-800/331-1084, Canada ☎1-800/272-5871; ⓦwww.avis.com
Budget ☎1-800/527-0700,
ⓦwww.budgetrentacar.com
Hertz US ☎1-800/654-3001, Canada ☎1-800/263-0600; ⓦwww.hertz.com

Hitching

Despite the amount of holiday traffic and the number of young Swedes with cars, **hitching** is rarely worth the effort, as long-distance lifts are few and far between. Shorter hops are easier to find, especially when travelling along the coasts and in the north, but don't rely on hitching as your main means of transport. If you do try it, always use a sign; be prepared for long, long waits and to be scoffed at by passing drivers.

City transport

Since most Swedish towns and cities are small by European standards they're usually easy to explore comfortably on foot. If, however, you want to use public transport to get across town quickly or head for a distant hotel or campsite, you'll find **buses** can be very useful. Flat fares are around 15kr to 25kr, the ticket usually being valid for an hour. Most large towns operate some sort of discount system allowing you to buy a book of tickets, which is better value than buying them individually – details of such schemes are in the text or can be obtained from the local tourist offices.

Taxis should only be used as a last resort since fares are quite simply horrific. Before you get in the taxi the meter will be showing at least 35kr; it will continue to tick over as you wait at traffic lights. A three-kilometre ride can easily set you back around 150kr. Given the phenomenal fares they charge, taxi drivers don't expect a tip. In some areas there are also surcharges for booking a taxi by phone.

Cycling

Some parts of the country are made for **cycling**: Stockholm, the southern provinces and Gotland, in particular, are ideal for a leisurely bike ride. Many towns are best explored by bike, and tourist offices, campsites and youth hostels often rent them out from around 100kr a day, 400kr a week. Taking a bike on the train involves a bit of forward planning, however; see p.31.

Although not as cycle-friendly as Holland, for example, there are still a lot of cycle paths in towns, which are often shared with pedestrians. You should make sure you cycle on the correct section of the path, indicated by a cycle sign painted on the ground. Sweden has a large number of signposted **cycle trails**; one of the most popular is the Sweden Trail (Sverigeleden), which stretches all the way from Helsingborg in the southwest to Karesuando near the Finnish border, taking in many of the country's main sights.

Svenska Cyckelsällskapet (Swedish Cycling Association), Box 6006, S-164 06 Kista, Stockholm (☎08/751 62 04, ⓦwww.svenska-cyckelsallskapet.se) has more information. The STF (see opposite) has details of Swedish cycling holidays that include hostel accommodation, meals and cycle rental.

Accommodation

Finding somewhere cheap to stay in Sweden isn't difficult. There's an extensive network of youth hostels (of an exceptionally high standard) and campsites, while private rooms and bed-and-breakfast places are common in the towns and cities. Self-catering accommodation is generally restricted to youth hostels and campsites, where cabins are often equipped with kitchens.

Accommodation prices in Sweden tend to vary according to the day of the week or the season. The highest prices are frequently charged from Sunday to Thursday during non-summer months; cheaper rates are usually available at weekends throughout the year and daily in summer. The definition of when summer begins and ends can vary a little from establishment to establishment but it is generally accepted as mid-June to mid-August. In some places in the north summer may not be deemed to start until the beginning of July. Remember though that this rule does not apply across the board and there are some places that actually charge higher prices in summer in line with most other countries. When we give two price codes in the guide, the higher price is the non-summer weekday price, the lower one the summer and weekend price. Single rooms, where

available, usually cost between 60 and 80 percent of a double. Special accommodation deals, which form part of the discount-card schemes available in many of the larger towns, can also help to bring down the cost.

Youth Hostels

Youth hostels in Sweden (*vandrarhem*: literally "wanderers' home") turn up in the unlikeliest of places. There are over three hundred of them dotted across the country, in converted lighthouses, old castles and prisons, historic country manors, schoolrooms and even on boats. Quite simply, they offer some of the best accommodation in the country. Forget any preconceptions about youth hostelling: in Sweden, dormitories are few, and rooms are family-oriented (usually sleeping four people), modern, clean and hotel-like.

Accommodation prices

The hotels listed in the guide have been graded according to the following price codes, based on the cost of the least expensive double room available. When two codes are given the first one is for double rooms during high season and the second one applies for the rest of the year. For more details and information on hostel prices, see opposite.

❶ under 500kr	❸ 701–900kr	❺ 1201–1500kr
❷ 501–700kr	❹ 901–1200kr	❻ over 1500kr

The majority of hostels are run by STF – short for **Svenska Turistföreningen**, Box 25, S-101 20 Stockholm, ☎08/463 22 70, ✆www.meravsverige.nu. To get members' rates at Swedish hostels you can either join the youth hostel association in your home country (see below for details) or get a Hostelling International (HI) card at any Swedish hostel (275kr per calendar year). The **cost** of hostel accommodation varies from 80–200kr but is generally around 120–200kr per person per night for members; the surcharge for non-members is 45kr a night. Children pay 30–100kr per bed per night. Throughout the guide, we have quoted prices if they are outside the 80–200kr range and when the hostel offers double rooms, we have given a price code.

Beds are either in a small room (usually shared with one to three others), or in a larger **dorm**. Out of season it's generally possible to have a double room (for one or two people) and still pay the per person price; the remaining bunks will remain empty. During the busier summer months, you're likely to have to share any room that the hostel has available. Most hostels also have some **family rooms** which are available for sole-occupancy by families, and some of the places in the south of the country offer double rooms all year round; details are given in the text.

Nearly all hostels have well-equipped **self-catering** kitchens and serve a buffet breakfast. If you're planning to cook for yourself using youth hostel kitchens, bear in mind that a few don't provide kitchenware and utensils – take at least basic equipment with you. To stay at an STF hostel it's best to have your own sheets, although they can be rented at the hostels for around 50kr. You are allowed to use a sleeping bag provided you put a sheet between it and the mattress to keep the latter clean.

Hostels are popular with Swedish families as cheap hotel-standard accommodation and can fill quickly, so always ring ahead, particularly in the summer. They usually close between 10am and 5pm, with curfews commencing at around 11pm or midnight; some are closed out of season, particularly those in the north.

It would be impossible to list all youth hostels in Sweden in this guide; for details, see *Hostelling International: Europe and the Mediterranean*, available from your local

youth hostel association. Apart from the STF hostels there are a number of independently run hostels, usually charging similar prices; we've mentioned the most useful in the text, and tourist offices will have details of any other local independent hostels.

Youth hostel associations

AUSTRALIA
Australia Youth Hostels Association ☎02/9261 1111, ✆www.yha.com.au. Adult membership rate AUS$52 (under-18s, AUS$16) for the first twelve months and then AUS$32 each year after.

CANADA
Hostelling International Canada ☎1-800/663 5777 or 613/237 7884, ✆www.hostellingintl.ca. Rather than sell the traditional 1- or 2-year memberships, the association now sells one individual adult membership with a 28- to 16-month term. The length of the term depends on when the membership is sold, but a member can receive up to 28 months of membership for just $35. Membership is free for under-18s and you can become a lifetime member for $175.

ENGLAND AND WALES
Youth Hostel Association (YHA) ☎0870/770 8868, ✆www.yha.org.uk and www.iyhf.org. Annual membership £13; under-18s £6.50; lifetime £190 (or five annual payments of £40).

IRELAND
Irish Youth Hostel Association ☎01/830 4555, ✆www.irelandyha.org. Annual membership €15; under-18s €7.50; family €31.50; lifetime €75.
Hostelling International Northern Ireland ☎028/9032 4733, ✆www.hini.org.uk. Adult membership £10; under-18s £6; family £20; lifetime £75.

NEW ZEALAND
Youth Hostelling Association New Zealand ☎0800/278 299 or 03/379 9970, ✆www.yha.co.nz. Adult membership NZ$40 for one year, NZ$60 for two and NZ$80 for three; under-18s free; lifetime NZ$300.

SCOTLAND
Scottish Youth Hostel Association ☎0870/155 3255, ✆www.syha.org.uk. Annual membership £6, for under-18s £2.50.

US
Hostelling International-American Youth Hostels ☎202/783-6161, ✆www.hiayh.org. Annual membership for adults (18–55) is $25, for seniors (55 or over) is $15, and for under-18s and groups of ten or more is free. Lifetime memberships are $250.

Fell stations and mountain cabins

Fell stations (*fjällstationer*) provide top quality hostel-like accommodation along mountain hiking routes; charging 150–400kr per person, depending on their standard and the time of year. They're usually better equipped than the average youth hostel: rooms are private rather than dorms and each fell station has a sauna, a shop, a kitchen and – Sylarna fell station, south of Storlien, apart – a restaurant. There are eight fell stations in all, found in or near the chain of mountains which form the border between Sweden and Norway, and always located on walking paths. During the ski season it is wise to book ahead.

Mountain cabins (*fjällstugor*), of which there are around ninety, are often no more than simple huts out in the wilds and are wonderful for getting away from it all. Run by the STF, they generally cost between 160–220kr depending on season and are often located at convenient intervals along popular walking routes. Some of them have a warden who can sell you food supplies and, more often than not, there'll also be a kitchen where you can prepare your own food. The odd one or two also have saunas (40kr per person), making for a perfect end to a day's hiking. Both fell stations and mountain cabins allow you to use a sleeping bag without a sheet underneath.

Hotels, pensions and private rooms

Hotels and **pensions** (usually family-run bed and breakfast establishments) needn't be expensive, and although there's little chance of finding any kind of room under 450kr a night, you can often find good-value hotel rooms in summer, especially in July, when business people who would otherwise fill the hotels during the week are on holiday (many Swedes also head south, out of the country, at this time of year). If you turn up at some of the larger hotels after 6pm in summer without a booking, you may find they drop their prices even lower than their usual discount rate. This is obviously a risky strategy (and breakfast often isn't included in these late deals), but it can land you some very cheap rooms. The only parts of the country where summer discounts don't apply are in some of the popular holiday destinations in southern Sweden, where prices can actually go up in summer.

Out of summer, rooms are much cheaper on Friday and Saturday (when the business people are at home) than Sunday to Thursday; for example, a room with TV and bathroom will on average cost from 450kr for a single, and from 600kr for a double at weekends outside summer, but around 700kr for a single and 1000kr for a double Sunday to Thursday outside summer. Nearly all hotels include a huge self-service buffet **breakfast** in the price, which will keep you going for much of the day.

The best **package deals** are those operated in Malmö, Stockholm and Gothenburg, where 400–500kr gets you a double room for one night, with breakfast and the relevant city discount card thrown in. These schemes are often valid from mid-June to mid-August and at weekends throughout the year, but see the accommodation details under the city accounts for specific information.

The other option is to buy into a **hotel pass scheme**, where you buy in advance a series of vouchers that pay for a room or give you a discounted rate in various chain hotels throughout the country. These vouchers can be bought before you leave for Sweden; for the latest details, it's best to consult the Swedish Tourism and Travel Council (see p.23 for their addresses outside Sweden), whose publication *Hotels in Sweden* contains a comprehensive listing of hotels with information on the various discount schemes. The drawback of having a hotel pass is that you may feel bound to stay in hotels all the time and will be limited to particular chains.

Another accommodation option is renting **private rooms** in people's houses. Most tourist offices can book these for you in any reasonably sized town, and at around 100–200kr a head (plus a 30–50kr booking fee), they're an affordable and pleasant option. In the countryside, these rooms are advertised with roadside signs saying "*Rum*" or "*Logi*". All rooms have access to showers and/or baths and sometimes a kitchen, and hosts are rarely intrusive.

Self-catering and B&B

Self-catering is a good way to keep costs down. **Self-catering** apartments (*stugor* in

Swedish) can be found across the country, from mountain-tops to city campsites. Most include a bathroom and a kitchen, although in the simpler cabins the bathroom may be in a communal service building close by. **Bed and breakfast** accommodation on a farm is only found in the south of Sweden, since farming is concentrated in these climatically warmer districts and can offer an insight into the difficulties of farming so far north.

Self-catering apartments

If you fancy renting a **self-catering cottage**, private apartment or a couple of rooms for a week or so, contact local tourist offices (details given in the text), where staff will book them for you. Alternatively, in towns, approach one of the companies listed in the box above. Apartments for four people cost between 2500kr and 3000kr a week.

Farms throughout Sweden offer **bed and breakfast accommodation** as well as self-catering facilities. For more information, contact local tourist offices or an organization called Bo på Lantgård (Living on a farm), Box 8, S-668 21 Ed, Sweden (☎0534/120 75, ☻www.bopalantgard.org). Accommodation on a farm costs roughly 250–300kr a night per person, with discounts for children. The Swedish Travel and Tourism Council (see p.23) have the latest details on farm B&Bs and farm holidays, and should be able to help you book your accommodation before you leave for Sweden.

City apartment agencies

Stockholm
Hotelltjänst/Caretaker ☎08/10 44 37, ☏ 21 37 16.
Gothenburg
Foretagsbostäder ☎031/17 00 25, ☻www.foretagsbostader.se.
SGS ☎031/708 13 30, ☻www.vb.sgsbostader.com
Svenska Turistlägenheter ☎031/340 03 50, ☻www.svturist.se.
Malmö
City Room ☎040/795 94.

Campsites and cabins

Practically every town or village has at least one **campsite**, and they are generally of a high standard. To pitch a tent at any campsite you'll need the Camping Card Scandinavia, which costs 90kr and includes accident insurance while staying at the site. Cards can be issued at the first site you visit or before you leave; contact the Swedish Camping Site Owners' Association (Box 255, S-451 17 Uddevalla; ☻www.camping .se). It costs around 80–160kr for two people to pitch a tent at an official campsite. Most sites are open from June to September, some – including around two hundred in winter sport areas – throughout the year. A camping brochure with details of all sites, plus a detailed motoring and camping map, is available from offices of the Swedish Travel and Tourism Council (see p.23 for details).

Thanks to a tradition known as *Allemansrätten* (Everyman's Right; see p.47), it's perfectly possible to **camp rough** in Sweden. This gives you the right to camp anywhere for one night without asking permission, provided you stay a reasonable distance (100m) away from other dwellings. In practice (and especially if you're in the north), there'll be nobody around to mind if you camp in one spot for longer, although it's as well – and polite – to ask first should you come across someone. The wide-open spaces within most town and city borders make free camping a distinct possibility in built-up areas too.

Many campsites also boast **cabins**, each of which is usually equipped with bunk beds, a kitchen and utensils, but not sheets. For a group or a couple, the cabins are an excellent alternative to camping; cabins go for around 350–450kr for a four-bed number. As usual, it's wise to ring ahead to secure one. Sweden also has a whole series of cabins for rent in spots other than campsites, often in picturesque locations, such as in the middle of the forest, by a lakeshore or on the coast. On the whole, these cabins offer high-standard accommodation at prices to match. For information and to make a booking, contact the local tourist office or the Swedish Travel and Tourism Council.

Note also that only **propane** gas – for example, Primus – is normally available in Sweden. It's illegal and also highly dangerous to burn propane in equipment designed for butane. Propane and the associated cooking, heating or lighting equipment are inexpensive, and widely available throughout Sweden.

Eating and drinking

There's no escaping the fact that eating and drinking is going to take up a large slice of your budget in Sweden – though no more so than in any other northern European country. Swedish food – based largely on fish, meat and potato, and very varied in preparation – is always tasty and well presented, and, at its best, delicious. Unusual specialities generally come from the north of the country and include reindeer, elk meat and wild berries; while herring and salmon come in so many different guises that fish fiends will always be content. Vegetarians, too, should have no problems, with plenty of non-meat options available especially in the bigger towns; elsewhere their choice may be limited to pizzas and salads. Alcoholic drinks are available in most establishments, with lager-type beers and imported wines providing no surprises; the local spirit *akvavit*, however, is worth trying at least once. It comes in dozens of weird and wonderful flavours, from lemon to cumin-and-dill.

Eating well and eating cheaply needn't be mutually exclusive aims in Sweden. The best strategy is to fuel up on breakfast and lunch, both of which offer good-value options. **Breakfast** is often included in the cost of a night's accommodation, and most restaurants have **lunchtime specials** (*Dagens Rätt*) that time and again are the best-value meals you'll find.

Food

Sweden's various **salmon** dishes are among the very best the cuisine has to offer – they're divine either warm or cold, and a mainstay of any Swedish *smörgåsbord* worth its salt. **Herring** is mostly served raw, but don't let that put you off as it tastes surprisingly good. Of the dishes from the north, **reindeer** is the most obvious one to try; it has a delicious flavour when smoked and is akin to beef in taste and texture, but with virtually no fat; elk meat is decidedly less appetizing, but is good for burning up calories – you'll expend as many chewing the stuff as you'll get from it. **Sauces** feature prominently in Swedish cooking, often flavoured with dill or parsley; alternatively there are many delicious creamy concoctions too.

Wild berries appear in many dishes, especially the lingonberry, which is something like cranberry, and makes a good accompaniment to Swedish meatballs, a combination praised by many a Swede as a delicacy of the country. You'll also be able to taste orange-coloured sweet cloudberries, which grow in the marshes of Lapland and are delicious with ice cream.

Vegetarian food

It's not too tough being **vegetarian** in Sweden: buffet-type meals are commonplace, and most are heavy with salads, cheeses, eggs and soups. For those who eat fish, there'll be no problem at all. The cities, too, have salad bars and sandwich shops where you'll have no trouble feeding yourself; and if all else fails the local pizzeria will always deliver the non-meaty goods. At lunchtime you'll find that the *Dagens Rätt* in many restaurants has a vegetarian option; it's always worth asking about if one isn't mentioned.

Breakfast

Breakfast (*frukost*) is almost invariably a help-yourself buffet in the best Swedish tradition; you can go up to the serving table as many times as you like and eat until you're fit to explode. There's generally an endless supply of breakfast cereals, muesli, cheeses, ham, salad, caviar (generally not the genuine article, but roe from fish other than sturgeon), pâté, boiled eggs, Danish pastries, coffee, tea and juice. Swankier venues will usually also offer porridge, herring, yoghurt and fruit, as well as hot food, often bacon, scrambled egg and sausages. Youth hostels charge around 50kr for breakfast; if you stay in a hotel, it'll be included in the price of your accommodation.

Something to watch out for is the jug of *filmjölk* (sometimes just called *fil*) or soured milk that you'll find next to the ordinary milk on the breakfast table. Swedes rave about the stuff and pour lashings of it on their cereals. It's thicker than normal milk, and you might find it tastes better if you mix it with some of the regular stuff. It's also eaten by itself, sometimes with a dollop or two of jam and a pinch of cinnamon.

Coffee is something the Swedes excel at: always freshly brewed, strong and delicious. Coffee breaks are a national institution, encapsulated in the verb *fika*, which is rendered rather long-windedly in English as "to put your feet up and enjoy a good cup of coffee". A coffee costs 15–25kr, but the price usually buys you more than one cup; the word *påtår* indicates that all cups after the first are either free or cost just a few *kronor*. **Tea** isn't up to scratch – weak Liptons as a rule – and costs just one or two *kronor* less than coffee. There are, however, some excellent speciality teas available in Sweden – look around for some when you're in a café, and if they have Södermalmsblandning (a variety that tastes of flowers and spices, and is named after Stockholm's south island), give it a try.

Snacks and light meals

For **snacks** and **light meals** you're really looking at the delights dished up by the Gatukök (street kitchen) or Korvstånd (sausage stall). A **Gatukök** is often no more than a hole in the wall – generally conspicuous by the snaking queue and gaggle of teenagers it attracts – serving sausages, burgers, chips, soft drinks and sometimes pizza slices or chicken pieces. Chips with a sausage or burger generally comes to around 50kr. The **Korvstånds** usually limit themselves to sausages (hotdogs are usually around 20kr), though some have chips and burgers as well. These outlets are to be found on every street, and until quite recently were often the only source of nourishment open after 5pm in the smaller towns and villages.

Thankfully things have changed now. If you feel like really pushing the boat out, you could hit one of the country's burger bars: *Clockburger* is Sweden's own chain and usually a couple of *kronor* cheaper than *McDonald's* or *Burger King*. At the very best, these places offer the cheapest source of coffee – if you can stomach the surroundings.

For coffee, it's far better to hit the **konditori**, a coffee and cake shop of the first order. You should try at least one *konditori* while you're in Sweden: coffee and cake will typically set you back 60–70kr (remember, though, that coffee refills are generally free). The *konditori* is as good a place as any to try a Swedish **open sandwich** (45–55kr), generally using white or rye bread, piled high with an elaborate variety of toppings. Favourites include prawns in mayo (with or without caviar), smoked salmon, egg slices and anchovy, cheese (often with green peppers or cucumber), pâté, meatballs and, in the north, sometimes reindeer.

Self-catering

For the cheapest eating it's hard to beat the supermarkets and market stalls. Of the supermarket chains, ICA and Konsum have the biggest range of produce but most of the supermarkets in Sweden are small local affairs selling just the basics and a few other bits and pieces. If it's choice you're after, and you're in one of the bigger towns and cities, you should try the food halls in the department stores, Åhléns and Domus, which have a much wider selection than the average supermarket. Alternatively head for the indoor or outdoor markets, which often have fresher produce than the supermarkets, and at lower prices.

Fish is always excellent value, especially salmon. Pork and beef aren't too bad either; chicken is slightly more expensive. As for **bread**, it's best to avoid the fluffy white loaves that you'll hardly notice you've eaten; go instead for those made from rye, which are darker and more filling. Sweden is a country rich in **cheeses**, all of which are reasonably good value and make great sandwich fillers; the range runs from stronger ripened cheeses such as Västerbotten and Lagrad Svecia to milder types like Grevé and Herrgårdsost; Prästost (literally "priest's cheese"), a medium-strong cheese akin to a crumbly Cheddar, is also a particular favourite here. Also handy for sandwiches is Kalles Kaviar, packaged in blue tubes with a smiling little boy on the label – he's Kalle (Charlie) and something of a folk hero. The contents, which are orange in colour, aren't real caviar but made from cod roe; the stuff is especially good on crispbread (*knäckebröd*) – which is another area where the Swedes excel: it's easy to be overwhelmed by the different crispbread varieties available, but you can try a good few as prices are low.

There are also loads of different yoghurts and varieties of *filmjölk* (see p.41) to choose from – all very healthy and inexpensive – as is milk, which comes in three varieties: *lättmjölk* (skimmed), *mellanmjölk* (semi-skimmed) and *mjölk* (full-fat). Fruit and vegetables are expensive but not exorbitantly so, with bananas and mushrooms generally the priciest items. A pack or jar of coffee constitutes a serious financial investment; tea less so, but it is still not especially cheap. Pasta, rice, potatoes, eggs, onions and bacon are relatively inexpensive. The only goods to steer well clear of are those in tins (except mussels, mackerel and tomatoes), which are invariably extremely costly for what they are.

Restaurants

Don't treat **restaurants** (*restaurang*) as no-go areas: they can be perfectly affordable, and offer some delicious high-quality food. Swedes eat their main meal of the day at lunchtime; do likewise and you'll save lots of cash. But you don't have to restrict yourself to eating out at lunchtime; many restaurants also offer special deals in the evening, and even if they don't you're bound to find something on their menu that will fit your pocket. Remember that Swedish portions are generous and you'll often find that a starter is unnecessary and that cutting it out is a good way to save money. **Prices** given in the guide are for a main course dish in the evening, unless otherwise stated. A not-too-upmarket evening meal in a restaurant will cost you 90–120kr without alcohol. A three-course meal will naturally cost more; expect to pay something in the region of 250–400kr. Add around 40kr for a strong beer, or 250kr for an average bottle of wine. Dishes usually have some sort of salad accompaniment and come with bread. Bear in mind that Swedes eat early; lunch will be served from 11am, dinner from 6pm.

At lunchtime, go for the **Dagens Rätt** or dish of the day, which costs between 60kr and 75kr and is one way to sample Swedish *Husmanskost* (home cooking). Served from 11am to 2pm, *Dagens Rätt* offers the choice of a main meal, along with salad and bread/crispbread, a soft drink or light beer, and coffee. Some Swedish dishes like *pytt i panna* (a fry-up of potatoes and meat with beetroot and a fried egg) and *köttbullar* (meatballs) are standards. You'll also find various pizza and pasta dishes on offer in Italian restaurants, basic meals in Chinese restaurants (sometimes a buffet-type spread). Most cafés also offer some sort of *Dagens Rätt* but their standard of cooking is often not as good as in restaurants; cafés in train stations and department stores, however, are worth trying. If you're travelling with children, look out for the **childrens' menu** (*Barnmatsedel*).

While you're in Sweden you should try a **smörgåsbord**, available in the larger restaurants and in hotels for around 250kr – expensive, but good for a blowout. A good table will be groaning under the weight of dishes: salmon (both boiled and smoked), *gravad lax*, shrimps, herring, eel, *Janssons frestelse*, scrambled eggs, oven-baked omelettes, fried sausages, smoked reindeer, liver paté, beef, hot and cold meats, eggs, fried and boiled potatoes, vegetables, salad, pastries, desserts, fruit, cheese – the list is endless. It's important to pace yourself: don't feel compelled to fill up your plate the first time you go to the table, as you can return as many times as you like. If you're a traditionalist you should start with *akvavit*, drink beer throughout and finish with coffee. Coffee will be included in the price – alcohol won't be, except on Sundays when fancier and dearer spreads generally include it.

A variation on the theme is the **sillbricka** or herring table, made up of a dozen or so dishes based on Sweden's favourite food, cured and marinated herring. Once again this is excellent – if you like raw fish – and runs to about the same price as the *smörgåsbord*.

Many of the **traditional Swedish dishes** on offer in most restaurants are listed in the box on pp.548–551 and an indication of prices is given opposite.

Foreign restaurants

For years the only ethnic choice in Sweden was between pizzerias and the odd Chinese restaurant; in provincial towns this is often still the case, but even here the number of ethnic restaurants has increased dramatically. Pizzerias offer the best value; you'll get a large, if not strictly authentic, pizza for 50–60kr, usually with free coleslaw and bread. Chinese restaurants nearly always offer a cheapish set lunch, but in the evenings prices shoot up. They aren't particularly good value for money and the food is often bland and inauthentic. If there's a group of you, however, putting dishes together can work out reasonably in terms of price. Middle Eastern kebab takeaways and cafés have also sprung up over recent years; here you can find something substantial in pitta bread for around 35–45kr. Japanese is popular and not too pricey, but other options are not such good deals: Indian food is hard to find and quite expensive; while anything French is expense-account stuff and only worth considering if you want a splurge.

Drinks

Drinking in Sweden can be expensive, but there are ways of softening the blow. Either you forgo bars and buy your booze in the state-run liquor shops, the **Systembolaget** (see below), or you seek out the happy hours (same term in Swedish) offered at many pubs and bars. The timing of happy hours has no rhyme or reason to it, so keep your eyes peeled for signs either in bar windows or on the pavement outside. During happy hours, the price of a strong beer can come down to under 25kr. If you miss happy hour, content yourself with the fact that Swedes, too, think booze is overpriced, and you won't be expected to participate in buying expensive rounds of drinks. It's also perfectly acceptable to nurse one drink through the entire evening, if that's all you can afford. Drinking in public is frowned upon in Sweden and you're not allowed to take alcohol onto a train or the street for your own consumption (drinking alcohol purchased on trains or pavement cafés is permitted).

The Systembolaget

In any Swedish town or city, the **Systembolaget** is the only shop that sells wine, strong beer and spirits. It's run by the state, is only open office hours from Monday to Friday and on Saturday mornings, and until quite recently kept all its alcohol on display in locked glass cabinets. Quite unthinkable just a couple of years ago in alcohol-obsessed Sweden, a number of stores have now gone self-service, giving buyers the chance to actually fondle the hard stuff before purchasing. Walking into any Systembolaget – be it counter or self-service – really is a trip into the twilight zone, if you can find one at all: stores are often tucked away in obscure places, and they're forbidden to advertise by law, but we have listed them in the text for largish towns.

Buying alcohol is made as unattractive as possible: first you take a queue number from the machine by the door. This will give you your place in the queue and may even state the likely waiting time: a quarter of an hour is about average, though on Friday afternoons it can be up to an hour and over. You select your bottles by number (each bottle in the cabinets has its number displayed alongside); when your turn comes you then quote your number to the cashier, who scuttles off to retrieve your booty. Hand over your cash and the dirty business is over. You need to be at least 20 to buy alcohol, and may have to show ID.

The system is designed to make Swedes think about how much they drink, and prices are accordingly very high – 70cl of whisky costs 300kr. But it's estimated that for every four bottles of booze consumed in Sweden only two are bought from the Systembolaget; one is smuggled into the country while the last is moonshine, distilled illegally at home.

What to drink

Beer is the most common alcoholic drink in Sweden, and even though it's expensive the local brands are very good. Competition among bars within Stockholm, Gothenburg and Malmö has brought down the price considerably; be prepared to pay a third more in the provinces for the same thing. Whether you buy beer in a café, restaurant or a bar, it'll cost roughly the same: on average 35–45kr for half a litre of lager-type brew; in nightclubs, it'll be more like 55–65kr.

Unless you specify a type, the beer you get in a bar will be *starköl* (also referred to as *storstark*), the strongest Class IV beer with an alcohol content of 5.6 percent by volume. Outside bars and restaurants, Class IV is only available in the Systembolaget, where it's around a third of the price you'll pay in a bar. *Mellanöl*, a Class III brew, costs slightly less than a *starköl* because it contains less alcohol; a good brand is Three Towns (green-labelled bottle) – once again, it's not available in the shops, only at the Systembolaget and in bars and restaurants. Class II or *folköl* is very similar in strength to *mellanöl* though contains slightly less alcohol. Cheapest of all is the Class I *lättöl*, the beer served with *Dagens Rätt* at lunchtime. It's palatable with food, though it contains virtually no alcohol; Pripps and Spendrups are the two main brands. Both *folköl* and *lättöl* are the only beers available in supermarkets.

Wine in restaurants is pricey; a bottle will set you back something like 250kr, and a glass around 45kr. You can buy a good bottle of red or white in the Systembolaget for just 50–60kr.

It's also worth trying the **akvavit** or schnapps, which is made from potatoes, served ice-cold in tiny shots and washed down with beer. There are numerous different flavours of *akvavit*: spices, herbs or citrus fruits, to name a few, are added to the finished concoction, giving rise to some memorable headaches. If you're in Sweden at Christmas, don't go home without having sampled **glögg**: mulled red wine with cloves, cinnamon, sugar and more than a shot of *akvavit*.

Where to drink

With the fall in the price of alcohol over recent years, more and more people are now going out to **bars** of an evening. On Friday and Saturday nights in particular, they're the place to be seen. You'll find bars in all towns and villages. In Stockholm and the larger cities the trend is towards brasserie-type places – smart and flash. The British pub – and, more recently, the Irish pub – is also popular in Sweden, although the atmosphere inside never quite lives up to the original. Elsewhere – particularly in the north of the country – you'll come across more down-to-earth drinking dens, occasionally sponsored by the local trades union. Drink is no cheaper here, and the clientele is heavily male and usually drunk: they can be intimidating places for outsiders, especially in small provincial villages, where drinking seems to be the main way of coping with eight months of winter.

In the summer, **café-bars** spill out onto the pavement, which is a more suitable environment for children and handy if all you want is a coffee. When you can't find a bar in an out-of-the-way place, head for the local hotel – but be prepared to pay for the privilege. Bar **opening hours** are elastic and drinking-up time is generally some time after midnight; in the big three cities – Stockholm, Gothenburg and Malmö – you can go on drinking all night, if your wallet can take the pace.

Health

EU nationals can take advantage of Sweden's health services under the same terms as residents of the country. For this you'll need form E111, available in the UK through post offices and Department for Work and Pensions offices. You'll have to show your E111 if you need medical treatment. Citizens of non-EU countries will be charged for all medical services; US visitors will find that medical treatment is far less expensive than they are accustomed to at home. Even so it is advisable to take out travel insurance (see p.22).

There's no **local doctor** system in Sweden: go to the nearest hospital with your passport (and E111, if applicable) and they'll treat you; the casualty department is called *Akutmottagning* or *Vårdcentral*. For a clinic visit, the charge is up to 240kr; overnight stays in hospital cost 80kr per 24 hours (free for children under 16).

For **dental treatment**, EU citizens have to pay in full any bill up to 800kr, then 65 percent of the next 700kr of the cost, and 30 percent of any remaining charge. You can spot a dental surgery by looking out for the sign "Tandläkare" or "Folktandvården". An emergency dental service is available in most major towns and cities out of hours – look in the windows of the local pharmacy for contact telephone numbers.

Medicines may be taken into Sweden if intended for your own use; you must have a medical certificate proving that you need them. Prescriptions can be taken to the nearest **pharmacy** (*apotek*); those from Scandinavian doctors will be filled routinely, but if your prescription is from another EU country you'll also need to show your E111 form to get your medicine. Minor painkillers, such as aspirin, are not available over the counter in Sweden, so bring some with you – otherwise you'll need a prescription to get them.

Coping with mosquitoes

The **mosquito** goes by the rather fetching name of *mygg* in Swedish – it's a word you'll become uncomfortably familiar with during your stay. If you're planning to spend any time at all outside the confines of towns and cities (and even in built-up areas the little critters can be merciless), it's imperative that you protect yourself against bites. Swedish mosquitoes don't carry diseases, but they can torment your every waking moment from the end of June, when the warmer weather causes them to hatch, until around mid-August. They are found in their densest concentrations in the north of the country, where there's swampy ground; there the sky has been known to darken when swarms of the things appear from nowhere.

Mosquitoes are most active early in the morning and in the late afternoon/early evening; the best way to protect yourself is to wear thick clothing (though not dark colours, which attract them) and apply mosquito **repellent** to any exposed skin. When camping, make a smoky fire of (damp) peat if feasible, as mosquitoes don't like smoke. And, easier said than done, don't scratch mosquito bites (*myggbett*); treat them instead with Salubrin or Alsolsprit creams, or something similar, available from local chemists.

Keeping warm and safe in winter

There's no two ways about it: seven to eight months of snow can make **winter in Sweden** pretty grim. But visiting in the depths of winter can be quite fun if you protect yourself against the **extreme cold** – temperatures are often below -30°C in the north of the country. Swedes cope by wearing several layers of clothes, preferably cotton, which is good at keeping out the cold. A warm winter coat alone won't suffice. You'll need a good woolly hat, snug-fitting gloves or mittens, and thick socks as well – between thirty to fifty percent of body heat is lost from the feet and head. Be prepared, though, to shed layers when you go into shops and other buildings, which are often heated to seemingly oven-like temperatures.

Bring **boots** or stout shoes with good grips which will hold onto the finely polished compacted snow that covers streets and pavements in winter. Venturing onto the ice isn't advisable, but if you feel you must do so, first ask the advice of local people as to whether it'll hold your weight. **Drivers** often take shortcuts in their cars across frozen lakes in winter – if you're going to do this, too, make sure you stick to the route that has either been marked out or the existing well-worn tracks in the ice. In towns and cities, keep your eyes peeled for **icicles** hanging from roofs and gutters; sooner or later they'll come crashing to the ground and you don't want to be underneath when that happens.

Crime and personal safety

Sweden is in general a safe country to visit, and this extends to women travelling alone. However, it would be foolish to assume that the innocent, trouble-free country of just a few years ago still exists. It doesn't, but although people no longer leave their doors unlocked when they go out shopping, Sweden is still a far cry from crime-ridden London or New York. As long as you take care, in particular at night in the bigger towns and cities, you should have no problems. If you do meet any trouble, dial ☏112 for emergency assistance from the police, fire brigade or ambulance; emergency calls from cardphones are free of charge.

Stockholm and the bigger cities have their fair share of petty crime, fuelled as elsewhere by a growing number of drug addicts and alcoholics after easy money. But keep tabs on your cash and passport (and don't leave anything valuable in your car when you park it) and you should have little reason to visit the police. If you do, you'll find them courteous, concerned and, perhaps most importantly, usually able to speak English. If you have something stolen, make sure you get a **police report** – it's essential if you want to make a claim against your insurance.

Petty crime and minor offences

As for offences *you* might commit, the big no-nos are drinking alcohol in public places (which includes on trains), and being drunk in the streets can get you arrested – drink-driving is treated especially rigorously (see p.34). Drugs offences, too, meet with the same harsh attitude that prevails throughout the rest of Europe.

Otherwise, Sweden is a pretty liberal place. Camping rough creates no problem and is a right enshrined in law (see box opposite). Topless sunbathing is universally accepted in all the major resorts (elsewhere there'll be no one around to care). Nude bathing is best kept for quieter spots but is very common and perfectly accepted – you'll have no problems finding a beach or a shady glade in a forest where you can work on your all-over tan; should anyone stumble on you they'll either ignore you or apologize for cramping your style.

Racism

Although **racism** is not a major problem in Sweden, it would be wrong to say it doesn't exist. It stems mainly from a small but vocal neo-Nazi movement, VAM (their full name translates as "White Aryan Resistance") who occasionally daub slogans like "*Behålla Sverige Svenskt*" (Keep Sweden Swedish) on walls in towns and cities and on the Stockholm metro. In recent years, the unemployment rate has shot up from the steady 1–2 percent during the heyday of Social Democratic governments and these days Sweden's skinheads blame the country's one million immigrants for stealing jobs from Swedes. Although there have been several racist murders and many attacks on dark-skinned foreigners over the past couple of years, it's still the exception rather than the rule. Keep your eyes and ears open and avoid trouble, especially on Friday and Saturday nights when drink can fuel these prejudices.

Sports and outdoor pursuits

Sweden is a wonderful place if you love the great outdoors, with fantastic hiking, fishing and, of course, winter sports opportunities. Best of all you won't find the countryside overcrowded – there's plenty of space to get away from it all, especially in the north. You'll also find Swedish beaches refreshingly relaxed and always clean.

Skiing and Winter Pursuits

During the winter months, **skiing** – a sport which began in Scandinavia – is incredibly popular; in the north of Sweden people even ski to work. Some of the most popular ski resorts include Åre, Sälen, Storlien and Riksgränsen; these and many others are packed out during the snow season when prices hit the roof. If you do intend to come to ski, it is essential to book accommodation well in advance or take a package holiday – see the relevant "Getting there" sections.

In northern Sweden you can ski from the end of October well into April, and at Riksgränsen in Lapland you can ski under the midnight sun from late May to the end of June when the snow finally melts; the ski lifts are open from 10pm to 1am. Riksgränsen is also the place to head for if you're into **snowboarding**. Kiruna is a good bet as a base for other winter pursuits, whether you fancy **dog sledging**, snowmobile riding, a night in the world's biggest igloo (the Ice Hotel at Jukkasjärvi, see p.493), **ice fishing** or even a helicopter tour out into the snowy wilderness. Bear in mind, though, that the area around Kiruna is one of the coldest in the country, and temperatures in the surrounding mountains can sink to -50°C during a really cold snap (also see "Keeping warm and safe in winter" on p.45). If the mere thought of such temperatures chills you to the bone, it's worth noting that milder Stockholm also has a ski slope within the city boundary.

The countryside – some ground rules

In Sweden you're entitled by law to walk, jog, cycle, ride or ski across other people's land, provided you don't cause damage to crops, forest plantations or fences; this is the centuries-old **Allemansrätten** or Everyman's Right. It also allows you to pick wild berries, mushrooms and wild flowers (except protected species), fish with a rod or other hand-tackle, swim in lakes, and moor your boat and then go ashore where there are no nearby houses. But this right brings with it certain obligations: you shouldn't get close to houses or walk across gardens or on land under seed or crops; pitch a tent on land used for farming; camp close to houses without asking permission; cut down trees or bushes; or break branches or strip the bark off trees. Nor are you allowed to drive off-road (look out for signs saying "*Ej motorfordon*", no motor vehicles; or "*Enskild väg*", private road); light a fire if there's a risk of it spreading; or disturb wildlife.

It's common sense to be wary of frightening reindeer herds in the north of Sweden; if they scatter it can mean several extra days' hard work for the herders; also avoid tramping over the lichen – the staple diet of reindeer – covering stretches of moorland. If you'd like to pick flowers, berries or mushrooms it's worth checking the latest advice from the authorities as to any health risks this may pose – post-Chernobyl. As you might expect, any kind of hunting is forbidden without a permit. National parks have special regulations which are posted on huts and at entrances, and these are worth reading and remembering.

Hiking

Sweden's Right of Public Access, *Allemansrätten*, means you can **walk** freely right across the entire country (see box on p.47 for more details). A network of more than forty long-distance footpaths covers the whole of Sweden, with overnight accommodation available in mountain stations and huts. The most popular route is the northern **Kungsleden**, the King's Route, which can get rather busy in July at times, but is still enjoyable. The path stretches for 460km between Abisko (on the train line between Kiruna and Narvik in Norway) and Hemavan, passing through some spectacular landscape in the wild and isolated northwest of the country; the trail also takes in Sweden's highest mountain, Kebnekaise (2078m). For more information, see p.495–500.

To find out more about walking in Sweden, contact the very helpful Svenska Turistföreningen (Swedish Touring Club; Drottninggatan 31–33 in Stockholm; Drottningtorget 6 in Gothenburg, ⊛www.meravsverige.nu. For a guide to the dos and don'ts of hiking in Sweden, see p.487.

Canoeing and whitewater rafting

There are almost one hundred thousand lakes and thousands of kilometres of rivers and canals in Sweden. Needless to say, on summer afternoons taking to a **canoe** is a popular pastime; an excellent area for this is Strömsund (see p.462). For more fast-flowing action, the northern rivers are ideal for **whitewater rafting**, with particularly good spots including the Pite river near Moskosel, north of Arvidsjaur (handy for the Inland Railway); the Kukkola rapids (see p.408) in the Torne Valley, north of Haparanda (and the Torne river in general between Haparanda and Pajala in the far northeast, where there are various lengths and grades of difficulty); and the Indalälven river, in Jämtland on the border with Norway, which offers moderately difficult to difficult rafting. The Strängforsen rapids in Värmland are somewhat tamer, with easy whitewater trips in paddle boats.

Golf and fishing

Golf has become incredibly popular in Sweden in recent years. There are now over three hundred courses in the country; most are concentrated in the south and are playable year-round, but it's also possible to play north of the Arctic Circle in the light of the midnight sun. For more information, contact the Swedish Golf Federation (PO Box 84, S-182 11, Danderyd, Stockholm; ☎08/622 15 00, ℻753 05 22, ⊛www.golf.se).

Sweden is an ideal country for **anglers**; in fact salmon are regularly caught from opposite the Parliament building right in the centre of Stockholm, because the water is so clean and fishing there is free. Fishing is also free along the coastline and in the larger lakes, including Vänern, Vättern (particularly good for salmon and char) and Mälaren. In the north of the country, Hemavan (see p.468) is known for top-class mountain fishing for trout and char, whereas nearby Sorsele (see p.469) is good for fly-fishing for trout, char and grayling. For salmon fishing, the river running up through the Torne Valley (see p.500) is among the very best places. Char are said to be most easily caught in summer on flies and small spinners; for grayling, fly-fishing on late summer evenings using flies resembling mayflies, stoneflies or nymphs is likely to give the best results.

In most areas you need a permit for freshwater fishing; ask at local tourist offices. For more information, contact Top 10 Fishing ☎031/338 4485, ⊛www.top10fishing.se.

The media

Stockholm is the centre of the Swedish media world; all national radio and television stations are broadcast from the capital, and the country's four main daily newspapers are also based here. As in most other countries, the media are justifiably accused of being obsessed with events in the capital and rarely venturing beyond the city's boundaries in their coverage. However, as you travel around the country, you'll doubtless come across the wide array of regional newspapers, as well as local TV and radio stations, that help to fill this gap. Every region or city has its own newspaper, for example *Göteborgsposten* in Gothenburg or *Norrbottens tidning* in Lapland. In remote parts of the country, particularly in the north, these local media really come into their own; in winter, people depend on them for accurate and up-to-date information on everything from local political machinations to snow depths in the vicinity.

Throughout the country the quality of the Swedish media is generally high. It's worth pointing out one cultural difference though: some interviews in Swedish news broadcasts can come across as rather plodding to outsiders, but will sound normal to Swedes. In Sweden, having long pauses between words shows that the speaker is talking in a considered way (to outsiders, it'll sound as if the interviewee is about to fall asleep).

Newspapers

Assuming you don't read Swedish, you can keep in touch with world events by buying **English-language newspapers** in the major towns and cities, sometimes on the day of issue, more usually the day after. Municipal libraries across the country often have good selections of British broadsheets but they can sometimes be a little out of date. The main Swedish papers are *Dagens Nyheter* and *Svenska Dagbladet* (their Friday supplements, often available free in the entrances to bookshops, may be useful for Stockholm listings) and the tabloids, *Expressen* and *Aftonbladet*. If you're in Stockholm you can pick up a copy of *Metro*, a free newspaper available at tube stations, which has lots of information about what's on in the capital; its listings are in Swedish only, but will be comprehensible enough even if you don't speak the language.

TV and radio

Swedish TV won't take up much space on your postcards home. There are two state channels, SVT 1 and SVT2, operated by Sveriges Television (SVT), worth watching if only for the wooden in-vision continuity announcers. TV3 is a pretty dire cable station shared with Norway and Denmark, although there's a good chance of catching an old episode of *Kojak* – if you like that sort of thing. Sweden's only terrestrial commercial station is TV4, whose evening news programme, *Nyheterna*, is an attempt to portray news as entertainment; unfortunately, though, the end result is pretty tasteless. TV5 is a cheesy cable channel available in most hotels that seems to show nothing but a string of American sitcoms – news, on this channel, is virtually nonexistant. On all the channels, foreign programmes are in their original language, which makes for easy viewing; SVT 1 and SVT2 show a lot of excellent BBC documentaries and comedy programmes.

On the **radio**, you'll find pop and rock music on P3, classical music on P2, and Swedish speech on P1 (frequencies differ throughout the country) – all operated by Swedish Radio (ⓦwww.sr.se), the state broadcaster. Commercial stations have now sprung up in towns and cities across Sweden, and in Stockholm the ones worthy of your interest if you like pop music are Radio City 105.9 FM, Mix Megapol 104.3 FM and Rix 105.5 FM.

You'll find **news in English** courtesy of Radio Sweden (Swedish Radio's international arm; ☎08/784 7287, ⓦwww.sr.se/rs). Their English news programme, *60 Degrees North*, can be heard weekdays in Stockholm on 89.6MHz FM at 3.30pm, 7.30pm, 9.30pm and at 2.30am. The evening broadcasts should be audible on 1179kHz medium wave throughout Sweden, although reception can vary considerably. These Stockholm FM broadcasts comprise a service called "Stockholm International" (ⓦwww.sr.se/p6), which additionally carries material from foreign broadcasters, including BBC World Service (Mon–Fri 6–7.30am; Sat 6–6.30am & 7–7.30am; Sun 5–5.30 and 6–6.30am; also on 6195, 9410, 12095 and 15070 kHz short wave; ⓦwww.bbc.co.uk/worldservice) and America's National Public Radio (ⓦwww.npr.org).

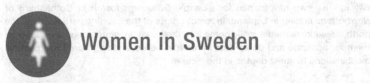

Women in Sweden

In general the social and economic position of women in Sweden is one of the most advanced in Europe – something that becomes obvious after just a short time here. Women travellers will rarely feel uncomfortable in the large cities and even in the depths of the countryside, where a lumberjack attitude holds sway, people are usually reserved and courteous.

Sweden has one of the highest percentages in the world of women in the workplace, and international surveys continually put Sweden at the top of the list when it comes to equality: around half of Sweden's government ministers are women. Many women are in traditionally male occupations which means that Swedish men have been forced to become more aware of the rights of women. The women's movement is strongly developed, riding on the back of welfare reforms introduced by the Social Democratic governments since World War II.

Women can walk around almost everywhere in comparative comfort and safety, although in Stockholm and Gothenburg you can occasionally expect to receive unwelcome attention. Sexual harassment in Sweden is rare. If you do have any problems, the fact that almost everyone understands English makes it easy to get across an unambiguous response.

Gay and lesbian Sweden

Swedish attitudes to **gay men** and **lesbians** are remarkably liberal – on a legal level at least – when compared to most other Western countries, with both the government and the law proudly geared towards the promotion of gay rights and equality (the official age of sexual consent is 15 whether you are gay or straight).

In 1995, Sweden introduced its registered-partnership law, despite unanimous opposition in parliament from the right-wing Moderates and Christian Democrats (needless to say, the Swedish Church wasn't best pleased either). Under the law, gay couples can, in effect, marry, by registering their relationships with the state. They are then guaranteed the same legal rights enjoyed by married straight couples; the law even permits the exchange of rings.

That said, the acceptance of gays and lesbians in society as a whole can at best be described as paradoxical, and in fact homosexuality was regarded as a psychological disease in Sweden until 1979. Outside the cities, and particularly in the north of the country where the lumberjack mentality rules supreme, there can still be widespread embarrassment and unease whenever the subject is mentioned in public. On the other hand, some of Sweden's best-loved entertainers are gay – and accepted as such.

Sweden's **gay scene** is less visible than in countries with more regressive official policies towards minority sexuality; even in Stockholm and Gothenburg, you're unlikely to see gay or lesbian couples holding hands or kissing in public. Gay community life in general is supported by the state-sponsored Riksförbundet för Sexuellt Likaberättigande, or RFSL (National Association for Sexual Equality; Sveavägen 57–59, PO Box 350, 10126 Stockholm; ☎08/736 02 11, ⊛www.rfsl.se). Founded in 1950 as one of the first gay rights organizations in the world, RFSL today operates a switchboard and helpline in most of the larger towns, though it's usually necessary that callers leave messages for someone to ring them back. It runs discos and pub nights in local venues either once a week or, more likely, once a month. RFSL also organizes a midsummer party in Stockholm to which foreign visitors are very welcome. Tourist offices invariably have no details of gay venues or events, so it's worth contacting the main RFSL offices in Stockholm or Gothenburg for information, or checking out their regular publication *Kom Ut* or the excellent *QX* paper, both available from gay venues. The international gay guide, *Spartacus*, has lots of useful information about gay and lesbian happenings in Sweden, and listings of bars, discos, cafés and restaurants; it's best to stick to places described as "mainly gay", as many of the "mixed gay" venues are not particularly gay-oriented compared to those at home.

Travellers with disabilities

There are numerous organized tours and holidays specifically for people with disabilities – the contacts below will be able to put you in touch with any specialists in Sweden. Once you're there, you'll find Sweden in many ways a model of awareness in terms of disabled travel, with assistance forthcoming from virtually all Swedes, if needed. A useful holiday guide for people with disabilities is available from Swedish tourist offices (see p.23 for their addresses outside Sweden).

Contacts for travellers with disabilities

BRITAIN AND IRELAND

Holiday Care 2nd floor, Imperial Building, Victoria Rd, Horley, Surrey RH6 7PZ ☎01293/774 535, Minicom ☎01293/776 943, ⊛www.holidaycare.org.uk. Provides free lists of accessible accommodation. Information on financial help for holidays available.

Irish Wheelchair Association, Blackheath Drive, Clontarf, Dublin 3 ☎01/818 6400, ⊛www.iwa.ie. Useful information provided about travelling abroad with a wheelchair.

RADAR (Royal Association for Disability and Rehabilitation) 12 City Forum, 250 City Rd, London EC1V 8AF ☎020/7250 3222, Minicom ☎020/7250 4119, ⊛www.radar.org.uk. A good source of advice on holidays and travel; their website is useful and well organized.

SWEDEN

De Handikappades Riksförbund, Katrinebergsvägen 6, S-117 43, Stockholm (DHR; Swedish Federation of Disabled Persons; ☎08/18 91 00, ⊜645 65 41. A good general source of information on disabled people's rights in Sweden and on facilities available from hotels to train travel.

Svenska Handikappidrottsförbundet Idrottenshus, S-123 87, Farsta, Sweden ☎08/605 60 00, ⊜724 85 40. Information on all manner of sports facilities for people with disabilities with a list of local organizations.

US AND CANADA

Access-Able ⊛www.access-able.com. Online resource for travellers with disabilities.

Directions Unlimited 123 Green Lane, Bedford Hills, NY 10507 ☎1-800/533-5343 or 914/241-1700. Travel agency specializing in bookings for people with disabilities.

Mobility International USA 451 Broadway, Eugene, OR 97401 ☎541/343-1284, ⊛www.miusa.org. Information and referral services, access guides, tours and exchange programmes. Annual membership $35 (includes quarterly newsletter).

Society for the Advancement of Travelers with Handicaps (SATH) 347 5th Ave, New York, NY 10016 ☎212/447-7284, ⊛www.sath.org. Non-profit educational organization that has actively represented travellers with disabilities since 1976.

Wheels Up! ☎1-888/389-4335, ⊛www.wheelsup.com. Provides discounted air fare, tour and cruise prices for disabled travellers, also publishes a free monthly newsletter and has a comprehensive website.

Planning a holiday

If there's an association representing people with your specific disability, it's worth contacting them early in the planning process. The more independent you want to be when travelling, the more important it is to become an authority on where you must be self-reliant and where you may expect help, especially regarding transport and accommodation. Assess your limitations and make sure other people – travel agencies, insurance companies and travelling companions – know about them, too.

People with a pre-existing medical condition are sometimes excluded from travel **insurance policies**, so read the small print carefully. To make your journey simpler, ask your travel agent to notify airlines or bus companies of your arrival, as they may be able to arrange assistance, for example, providing a wheelchair at airports and staff primed to help. A medical certificate of your fitness to travel, provided by your doctor, is also extremely useful; some airlines or insurance companies may insist on it. Make sure that you have extra supplies of drugs – carried with you if you fly – and, in case of emergency, a prescription that includes the generic name of any medicine you need. Carry spares of any clothing or equipment that might be hard to find. If you use a wheelchair, it's always wise to have it serviced before you go, and carry a repair kit. If you don't use the wheelchair all the time, but your walking capabilities are limited, remember that you are likely to need to cover greater distances while travelling than at home (sometimes over rougher terrain and in colder temperatures than you are used to), and plan your route with this in mind.

Disabled travel in Sweden

Getting to Sweden is becoming easier for disabled visitors: DFDS Seaways ferries now have specially adapted cabins, and Silja Line offers discounts for travellers with disabilities on its routes between Sweden and Finland. **Public transport** throughout the country is also geared up for people with disabilities. Wheelchair access is usually available on trains (InterCity trains have wide aisles and large toilets, and often have special carriages with hydraulic lifts), and there are lifts down to the platforms at almost every Stockholm metro station. In every part of the country there'll be some taxis in the form of minivans specially converted for disabled use.

Accommodation suitable for the disabled is often available: most hotels have specially adapted rooms, while some chalet villages have cabins with wheelchair access. Any building with three or more storeys must, by law, have a lift installed, while all public buildings are required by law to be accessible to people with disabilities and have automatic doors. Generally, hotels, hostels, museums and other public places are very willing to cater to those with disabilities.

Directory

Addresses In Sweden addresses are always written with the number after the street name. In multi-floor buildings the ground floor is always counted as the first floor, the first the second, etc.

Alphabet The letters å, ä and ö come at the end of the alphabet after z.

Arctic circle An imaginary line drawn at approximately 66° 33' latitude that stretches across northern Sweden and denotes the limit beyond which there is at least one day in the year when the sun never sets and one on which it never rises.

Beaches The southern province of Skåne has the sandiest beaches in the country. The further north you travel the rockier the beaches become. The Bohuslän coast north of Gothenburg has some gently sloping rocks which are ideal for sunbathing, and so do the islands in the Stockholm archipelago. Many of Sweden's thousands of lakes also have sandy stretches of shoreline.

Books You'll find English-language books in almost every bookshop and in the bigger department stores, though at roughly twice the price you're used to paying. Libraries, too, stock foreign-language books.

Children Sweden is a model country when it comes to travelling with children. Most hotels and youth hostels have family rooms and both men's and women's toilets – including those on trains – usually offer baby-changing areas. Always ask for children's discounts as many activities, particularly during the summer months, are geared towards families.

Crossing borders The land borders with Norway and Finland are relaxed affairs, and in fact on minor roads you'll hardly notice you've passed from one country to the other. It's wise to have your passport with you, though it's unlikely you'll be asked to show it.

Electricity The supply is 220V, although appliances requiring 240V will work perfectly well. Plugs have two round pins. Remember that if you're staying in a cottage out in the wilds, electricity may not be available, so take candles in case.

Emergencies Dial ☎112 (free) for the police, ambulance and fire brigade.

Luggage In most train stations, ferry terminals and long-distance bus stations there are lockers where you can leave your bags for a small fee. At some train stations you hand in your baggage for storage. Tourist offices may also watch your stuff bags, but generally make a charge.

Medication You need a doctor's prescription even to get minor painkillers in Sweden, so bring your own supplies.

Midnight sun The midnight sun can be experienced in the far north of Sweden for about two months during the summer. At Abisko and Riksgränsen it is visible from about May 27 to July 15; in Kiruna from 31 May to July 11; in Gällivare from June 4 until July 12; and at Jokkmokk between June 8 and July 3; all dates are approximate.

Northern lights (*Aurora Borealis*) A shifting coloured glow visible during winter in northern Sweden, thought to be of electrical origin – though you'll need to be in luck to see a really good display. The sky often turns peculiar colours on winter nights in the far north.

Nude bathing Although there are few official nudist beaches in Sweden, the country does boast around 100,000 lakes and one of the lowest population densities in Europe which means that sooner or later you'll find your very own lake where you can swim and sunbathe naked undisturbed. If other people are around, show them consideration, but you're unlikely to meet opposition.

Photography Film is available in most supermarkets, generally at 35–100kr per roll; developing is also very expensive and slow. It's best to bring more rolls than you think you'll need.

Saunas Most public swimming pools and hotels, even in the smallest towns, will have a sauna. They're generally electric and extra steam is created by gently tossing water onto the hot elements. The temperature inside will range from 70–120°C. Traditional wood burning saunas are often found in the countryside and give off a wonderful smell. Public saunas are always single-sex and nude; you'll often see signs forbidding the wearing of swimming costumes, as these would collect your sweat and allow it to soak into the wooden benches inside. Take a small paper towel to sit on; these are often available in the changing rooms. It is common practice to take a cold shower afterwards or, if you're in the countryside, to take a dip in a nearby lake. In the winter people will even roll in the snow to cool off.

Smoking Smoking is frowned upon in Sweden and is outlawed on most public transport and in many public buildings such as libraries. Smoking in restaurants is permitted (although some are completely no-smoking) but be aware of your fellow diners. A pack of twenty cigarettes costs 35–40kr, and the minimum age is 18.

Time Sweden conforms to Central European Time (CET) which is always one hour ahead of Britain and Ireland. For most of the year Sweden is six hours ahead of New York; nine hours behind Sydney and eleven hours behind Auckland. Clocks go forward by one hour in late March and back one hour in late October (on the same days as in Britain and Ireland).

Tipping In restaurants, the service charge is normally included in the price of your food so there's no need to tip. However it is customary to round the bill up to the nearest 10kr. Do not tip taxi drivers, though you should tip cloakroom attendants in bars and discos around 10kr a time.

Guide

Guide

Stockholm and around

CHAPTER 1 # Highlights

---

* **Gamla Stan, Stockholm**
Wander through the narrow
streets and alleyways of the
Old Town for a taste of
medieval Stockholm. See
p.72.

* **Vasa museum, Stockholm**
Fascinating seventeenth-
century warship raised from
Stockholm harbour and
painstakingly restored to her
former glory. See p.87.

* **Drottningholm, Stockholm**
Take a boat trip to the
Rococo-inspired home of
the Swedish royal family,
beautifully set on the shores
of Lake Mälaren. See p.102.

* **Af Chapman youth hostel,
Stockholm** A bunk on board
this elegant square-rigged
ship-cum-hostel, moored
right in the heart of the capi-

tal, is one of Sweden's best
bargains. See p.70.

* **Birka, Lake Mälaren** Get to
grips with Viking history on
the site of Sweden's oldest
town. See p.103

* **Gällnö island, Stockholm
archipelago** Walk through
deep green forest and swim
from the shores of this island
edged by purple reeds and
carpets of wildflowers. See
p.108.

* **Gamla Uppsala** Royal burial
mounds and a beautiful
medieval church add mys-
tery to this ancient pagan
settlement. See p.127.

* **Boat trips from Västerås**
Take a trip on the crystal
clear waters of Mälaren for
the best lakeside vistas in
Sweden. See p.118.

Stockholm and around

S tockholm is without a shadow of a doubt one of the most beautiful cities in Europe. Built on no fewer than fourteen **islands**, where the fresh water of Lake Mälaren meets the brackish Baltic Sea, clean air and open space are in plentiful supply here. One-third of the area within the city limits is made up of water, while another third comprises parks and woodlands, including the world's first urban national park, where you can swim and fish just minutes from the city centre. Broad boulevards lined with elegant buildings are reflected in the deep blue water, and alongside the cobbled waterfront, rows of painted wooden houseboats bob gently. Yet Stockholm is also a hi-tech metropolis, with futuristic skyscrapers and a bustling commercial hub. The modern centre is a consumer's heaven, full of stylish shops and a myriad of bars and restaurants – of which Stockholm has more per capita than most other European capitals. Quality of life is important to Stockholmers – a seat on the metro and elbow room on even the most crowded shopping street are regarded as virtual birthrights. As a result, the capital is one of Europe's saner cities and a delightful place in which to spend time.

Move away from Stockholm, and it's not difficult to appreciate its unique geographical location. Water surrounds the city and, although you can travel by train and bus, it's worth making the effort to ply the serene waters of Lake Mälaren or the Stockholm archipelago by boat. The **archipelago** is made up of a staggering 24,000 islands, islets and rocks as the Swedish mainland slowly splinters into the Baltic Sea. A summer paradise for holidaying city dwellers, the islands are easily accessible from the centre. Another must is a boat trip inland along Lake Mälaren, either to the Viking island of **Birka**, where you can see the remains of Sweden's most important medieval trading centre and a dizzying array of ancient finds, or to **Drottningholm**, the seventeenth-century royal residence right on the lakeside. Another easy trip on Lake Mälaren leads to the impressive castle of **Gripsholm** at Mariefred. Also within reach on a day-trip are the ancient Swedish capital and medieval university town of **Uppsala** and the country's oldest village, **Sigtuna**, complete with its rune stones and ruined churches; both these places are accessible by frequent train services from Stockholm's Central Station or by the occasional boat. Lakeside **Västerås**, a fascinating mix of the new and old – including a sixth-century royal burial mound – is also worth exploration and is easily reached by regular trains from Stockholm.

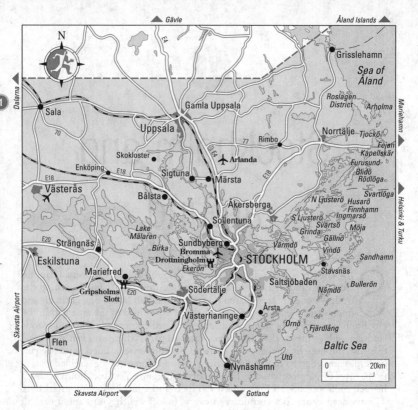

Stockholm

"It is not a city at all," he said with intensity. "It is ridiculous to think of itself as a city. It is simply a rather large village, set in the middle of some forest and some lakes. You wonder what it thinks it is doing there, looking so important."
Ingmar Bergman, interviewed by James Baldwin

At times, **STOCKHOLM**'s status as Sweden's most contemporary, forward-looking city seems at odds with the almost pastoral feel of its wide open spaces and ageing monumental buildings. First impressions of the city can be of a distant and unwelcoming place, and it comes as no surprise that in the provinces self-important Stockholm is sometimes known as the *"isdrottning"* (Ice Queen). But don't be put off; on a Friday or Saturday night you'll see its other side – when Stockholmers let their hair down, and the night air is abuzz with conversation.

Gamla Stan (Swedish for "Old Town") was the site of the original settlement of Stockholm, first mentioned as a town in 1252. Today the area is an atmospheric mixture of ornate historical buildings surrounded on all sides by a latticework of medieval lanes and alleyways. Close by and easily reached by ferry is the tiny island of **Skeppsholm**; conveniently, the island is also the site of the two most central youth hostels (see p.70). To the north of the Old Town, the district of **Norrmalm** swaps tradition for a thoroughly contemporary feel – shopping malls, huge department stores and a conspicuous, showy wealth; the lively **central park**, Kungsträdgården, and Central Station are here, too. Most of Stockholm's eighty or so **museums and galleries** are spread across this area and two others: to the east, the more residential **Östermalm**, with its mix of grand avenues and smart houses; and to the southeast, the green park island of **Djurgården**. Here the extraordinary seventeenth-century warship, **Vasa**, rescued and preserved after sinking in Stockholm harbour, and **Skansen**, oldest and best of Europe's open-air museums, both receive loud and deserved acclaim. The island of **Södermalm**, to the south of the Old Town, is sometimes known as "the Southside" (when Swedes talk about it in English) or as plain "Söder" (as its right-on inhabitants call it). This was traditionally the working-class area of Stockholm, but today is known for its cool bars and restaurants and lively street life. Indeed, any visit to Stockholm is not complete without sampling one of the growing number of eateries in this neighbourhood – an ideal place to watch, and join, the city's population at play. To the west of the centre, the island of Kungsholmen is fast becoming a rival to its southern neighbour for trendy restaurants and drinking establishments.

Arrival and information

Most international and domestic flights arrive at **Arlanda airport** (T08/797 61 00, W www.arlanda.se), an inconvenient 45km north of Stockholm. High-speed trains leave every fifteen minutes from the two dedicated **Arlanda Express** stations beneath the airport (Arlanda North for Terminal 5, Arlanda South for the other terminals) for the Central Station in Stockholm (daily 5.05am–12.35am; 20min; 140kr). SJ and Tågkompaniet trains use a separate station, Arlanda C, also beneath the airport and accessed from Sky City (the central shopping and restaurant area between Terminals 5 and 4), for most northbound destinations. **Airport buses**, Flygbussarna, call at all terminals and run from Arlanda to Stockholm's long-distance bus station, Cityterminalen (daily 6.30am–11.45pm; every 5–10min; 40min; 80kr); you buy your ticket on the bus. After 11pm bus departures are timed to coincide with incoming flights. **Taxis** from the airport into town should cost around 350kr and are an affordable alternative for a group; choose those vehicles that have prices displayed in their back windows.

Some domestic flights operated by Malmö Aviation arrive at the more central **Bromma airport** midway between Brommaplan and Sundbybergs Centrum T-bana stations, which is also connected to the bus station, Cityterminalen, by Flygbussarna – buses run in connection with flight arrivals and departures (20 min; 60kr). Ryanair's Stockholm flights arrive at **Skavsta airport**, 100km to the south of the capital close to the town of Nyköping, and at **Västerås**, 100km to the west of Stockholm; Skavsta and Västerås buses operate in connection with flight arrival and departure times (both routes 80min; 100kr single).

By **train**, you'll arrive at **Stockholm C** (C is an abbreviation of Central in railspeak throughout Sweden), a cavernous structure on Vasagatan in the cen-

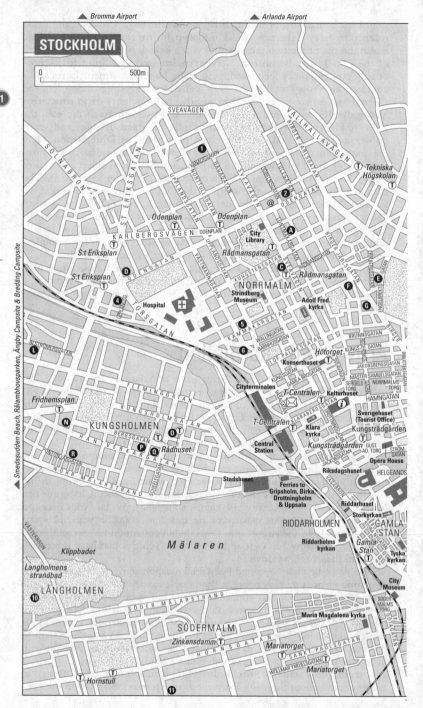

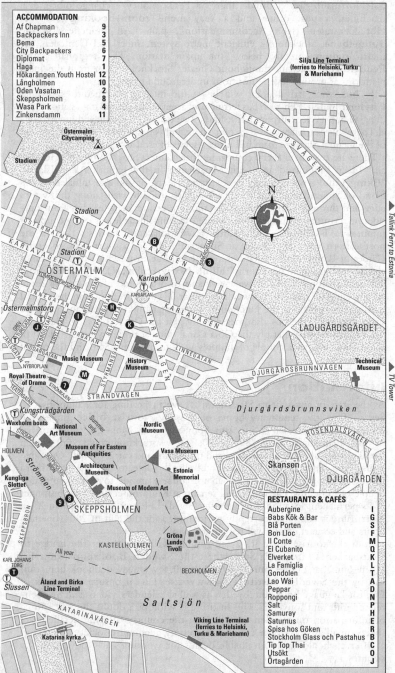

ACCOMMODATION

Af Chapman	9
Backpackers Inn	3
Bema	5
City Backpackers	6
Diplomat	7
Haga	1
Hökarängen Youth Hostel	12
Långholmen	10
Oden Vasatan	2
Skeppsholmen	8
Wasa Park	4
Zinkensdamm	11

▲ *Ropsten*

Silja Line Terminal
(ferries to Helsinki, Turku
& Mariehamn)

▲ *Tallink Ferry to Estonia*

Östermalm
Citycamping

Stadium

ÖSTERMALM

Stadion

Stadion

Karlaplan

Östermalmstorg

Music Museum

History
Museum

Royal Theatre
of Drama

LADUGÅRDSGÄRDET

Technical
Museum

▲ *TV Tower*

Kungsträdgården

Waxholm boats

National
Art Museum

Museum of Far Eastern
Antiquities

Architecture
Museum

Museum of Modern Art

HOLMEN

Kungliga
Slottet

SKEPPSHOLMEN

KASTELLHOLMEN

All year

KARL JOHANS
TORG

Slussen

Åland and Birka
Line Terminal

Katarina kyrka

Nordic
Museum

Vasa Museum

Estonia
Memorial

Djurgårdsbrunnsviken

ROSENDALSVÄGEN

Skansen

DJURGÅRDEN

Gröna
Lunds
Tivoli

BECKHOLMEN

Saltsjön

Viking Line Terminal
(ferries to Helsinki,
Turku & Mariehamn)

RESTAURANTS & CAFÉS

Aubergine	I
Babs Kök & Bar	G
Blå Porten	S
Bon Lloc	F
Il Conte	M
El Cubanito	Q
Elverket	K
La Famiglia	L
Gondolen	T
Lao Wai	A
Peppar	D
Roppongi	N
Salt	P
Samuray	H
Saturnus	E
Spisa hos Göken	R
Stockholm Glass och Pastahus	B
Tip Top Thai	C
Utsökt	O
Örtagården	J

63

▼ 12

tral Norrmalm district. Inside, there's a Forex money exchange office, cash machines, a post office and a very useful **room-booking service**, Hotellcentralen (see "Accommodation", p.68). All branches of the **Tunnelbana**, Stockholm's efficient metro system, meet at T-Centralen, the metro station directly below the main station. The regional trains, **Pendeltågen**, that run throughout Greater Stockholm leave from the main platforms at ground level – not from underground platforms.

By **bus**, your arrival point will be at the huge glass structure known as **Cityterminalen**, a Hi-tech bus terminal adjacent to the central train station, handling all bus services: airport, ferry shuttle (see below), domestic and international. There's also a money exchange office here, and you can get to the northern end of the Central Station's main hall using a series of escalators and walkways.

There are two main **ferry** companies that connect Stockholm with Helsinki and Turku in Finland and with Mariehamn in the Finnish Åland Islands. **Viking Line** (ⓦwww.vikingline.se) services arrive at Vikingterminalen on the island of Södermalm, from where it's a thirty-minute walk along the water's edge and through Gamla Stan to the modern centre; or take a bus from outside the terminal to Slussen, from where the Tunnelbana leaves every couple of minutes to T-Centralen. **Silja Line** (ⓦwww.silja.com) ferries arrive on the northeastern edge of the city at Siljaterminalen; it's a short walk to either Gärdet or Ropsten metro stations, on the red line, from where trains run into town. The third main operator is **Tallink** (ⓦwww.tallink.se), with sailings from Tallinn in Estonia. These arrive at Frihamnen, at the end of the #1 bus route which will take you all the way into town. If you're heading for the central train station, get off at the junction of Kungsgatan and Vasagatan and walk the short distance – the bus also goes directly past the Cityterminalen. The boats from **Gothenburg** that ply the Göta Canal dock at the quay on the island of Riddarholmen, just a couple of minutes' walk from Gamla Stan and the rest of the centre.

Information

At the start of any visit to Stockholm it's worth heading for Kulturhuset in Sergels Torg, the temporary home of the city's **tourist office** (June–Aug Mon–Fri 8am–7pm, Sat & Sun 9am–5pm; Sept–May Mon–Fri 9am–6pm, Sat & Sun 10am–3pm; ☎08/789 24 90, ⓦwww.stockholmtown.com) which hands out fistfuls of free brochures and timetables, and carries *What's On*, a free listings and entertainments guide. You'll also be able to buy the Stockholm Card (see p.66) which can be valuable if you're planning to visit more than a couple of museums. The office will remain at Kulturhuset until refurbishment of its permanent location, Sverigehuset (Sweden House), at Hamngatan 27 in Norrmalm, is complete, currently programmed for the end of 2004; opening hours and contact details will remain as above.

From the tourist office it's a ten-minute walk south over the bridge to Slottsbacken 10 in Gamla Stan, where the **Sweden Bookshop** (Mon–Fri 10am–6pm, Sat 11am–3pm; ☎08/453 78 00, ⓦwww.swedenbookshop.com) run by the **Swedish Institute** (ⓦwww.si.se) has an unsurpassed stock of English-language books on Sweden as well as calendars, videos and Sweden-related gifts and souvenirs. The Institute is without a doubt the best source of information on Sweden anywhere in the country offering detailed fact sheets on all aspects of the country (economy, geography, society and so on) at 10kr each, alongside invaluable details for working and studying in the country.

City transport

At first, Stockholm can be a confusing place, winding and twisting its way across islands, over water and through parkland. To find your way around, the best bet is to **walk**: it takes about half an hour to cross central Stockholm on foot, from west to east or north to south. Sooner or later, though, you'll probably want to use some form of **transport** and, while routes are easy enough to master, one thing to avoid is paying per trip on the city's transport system – a very expensive business. The city is zoned, a trip within one zone costing 20kr, with single tickets valid within that zone for one hour. So you can make several short journeys within one hour without buying another ticket providing you stay in the same zone; cross a zone and it's another 10kr. Most journeys you will want to make will generally cost 30kr. It's better to make use of the bewildering array of **passes** and **discount cards** available, described on p.66.

Storstockholms Lokaltrafik (**SL**; Ⓦ www.sl.se) operates a comprehensive system of buses and trains (metro and regional), which extends well out of the city centre. Their main information office is the **SL-Center** at Sergels Torg (Mon–Fri 7am–6.30pm, Sat & Sun 10am–5pm), just by the entrance to T-

STOCKHOLM TUNNELBANA

Centralen. It stocks timetables for the city's buses and metro system, regional trains and archipelago boats. For details of other SL offices, see "Listings", p.99. Up-to-date information on the public transport system can also be obtained by phoning ℡08/600 10 00.

The quickest and most useful form of transport is the **Tunnelbana** (T-bana; ⓦwww.tunnelbana.com), Stockholm's metro system, which comprises three main lines (red, green and blue) and a smattering of branches. It's the swiftest way to travel between Norrmalm and Södermalm, via Gamla Stan, and it's also handy for trips out into the suburbs – to ferry docks and to distant youth hostels, campsites and museums. Station entrances are marked with a blue letter "T" on a white background, and displays above each platform give the final destination of each train. Trains usually run from early morning until around midnight, but on Fridays and Saturdays there are services all through the night. The Tunnelbana is something of an artistic experience, too, many of the stations looking like Functionalist sculptures: T-Centralen is like a huge papier-mâché cave, and Kungsträdgården is littered with statues, spotlights and fountains. Other stations to look out for are Akalla (ceramic images of daily life), Rissne (maps of the world, each region labelled with key historical events and their dates) and Midsommarkransen (massive wooden sculptures of garlands of flowers).

Travel passes and tickets

There are a number of **travel passes** that represent good value for money if you're travelling around the city. The **one-day card** is valid for 24 hours (80kr) and the **3-day card** for 72 hours (150kr); these cover unlimited travel by bus, T-bana and regional train, plus travel on ferries to Djurgården. These cards were formerly known as tourist cards and you may still find some confusion surrounding the new names. Discounts for under-18s or over-65s bring the cost down to 45kr (1 day) and 90kr (3 days). These cards can be bought from Pressbyrå newsagents or SL travel centres and really are excellent value, when compared to the price of a single journey in the city.

Otherwise you can buy a strip of twenty reduced-price SL **ticket coupons** known as *rabattkuponger* (110kr) – valid on the metro and the buses – from bus drivers or at any metro station; you'll have to stamp at least two for each journey.

If you're staying in Stockholm for a week or two, it's worth considering a Månadskort or **Monthly Card**, which brings fares tumbling down: for a mere 500kr, the card offers unlimited travel for 31 days on virtually everything that moves throughout the whole of Greater Stockholm. The card isn't specific to an individual, so any number of different people can use it – though not at the same time. If you're spending several months in the city, there are some great-value Säsongskort (**season cards**) available. Monthly and season cards can be bought from any SL-Center and, once again, reduced fares are available on all cards for under-18s and senior citizens.

The Stockholm Card

If you're planning to visit several museums, the best pass to have is the **Stockholm Card (Stockholmskortet)**, which gives unlimited travel on the metro, city buses, the Djurgården ferry and regional trains as well as free entry to around seventy museums plus free parking and sightseeing boat trips. Cards are sold undated and are stamped on first use, after which they're valid for 24, 48 or 72 hours (220/380/540kr respectively); each card covers one adult and two children under seven. The sightseeing boat tours included on the card leave from in front of the *Grand Hotel* on Strömkajen (mid-May to end Aug; 1hr). The card is available from the tourist office, Hotellcentralen in Central Station or any SL Center.

Buses and ferries

Buses are often less direct than the metro because of the city's layout – the route maps on the back of the *Stockholms innerstad* bus timetable will give an idea as to how convoluted your journey might be. Tickets are bought from the driver; board buses at the front and get off at the back or in the middle. **Night buses** replace the metro after midnight, except on Friday and Saturday, when it runs all night. In an effort to cut pollution, many city buses now run on ethanol, partly produced from Spanish red wine, which is supposedly better for the environment than diesel; you'll notice a strange smell when one of these vehicles goes by. Stockholm's buses are also pushchair- and pram-friendly; a special area halfway down the bus has been set aside for these. If you're travelling with a dog, sit as far back as you can, as the seats at the front of the buses are intended for people with allergies.

Ferries provide access to the sprawling archipelago, sailing from outside the *Grand Hotel* on Strömkajen (see p.106 for more details); they also link some of the central islands: Djurgården is connected with Nybroplan in Norrmalm (a small square behind the *Grand*) via the Vasa museum and Skeppsholmen (early May to late Aug only), and with Skeppsbron in Gamla Stan (year-round). **Cruises** on Lake Mälaren leave from outside Stadshuset on Kungsholmen, and **city boat tours** leave from outside the *Grand Hotel*, as well as from round the corner on Nybroplan. **Tickets** for ferries linking the central islands cost 20kr one-way, and longer trips out into the archipelago up to 100kr, depending on how far you are going. They can be bought from the offices of the ferry company that operates the majority of sailings into the archipelago, Waxholmsbolaget (ⓦ www.waxholmsbolaget.se), on Strömkajen in front of the *Grand Hotel*, or on the boats themselves. If you are intending to spend a week or so exploring different islands in the archipelago, there are a couple of cards available that will help cut costs; see opposite.

Bikes, taxis and cars

Bike rental is centrally available from Skepp O'Hoj at Galärvarvsvägen 2 (ⓣ08/660 57 57), just over the bridge that leads to Djurgården, or from Cykelstället Servicedepån at Scheelegatan 30 (ⓣ08/651 00 66); reckon on paying 200kr per day or 800kr per week for the latest mountain bike, less for a boneshaker. There is also an outlet of Cykelstället Servicedepån at Kungsholmsgatan 34 on Kungsholmen.

Taxis can be hailed in the street, from a taxi rank (there's one outside Central Station) or ring one of the four main operators: Taxi Stockholm (ⓣ08/15 00 00), Taxi Kurir (ⓣ08/30 00 00), Top Cab (ⓣ08/33 33 33) or Taxi 020 (ⓣ020/93 93 93). The meter will show around 35kr when you get in and will then race upwards at an alarming speed: 100kr or thereabouts for every 10km during the day (more between 7pm & 6am and at weekends). A trip across the city centre will cost 150–200kr, more in the evenings and at weekends.

When **driving**, be extremely careful when **parking**: you aren't allowed to park within 10m of a road junction, whether it be a tiny residential cul-de-sac or a major intersection, and you'll often see people goose-stepping in an attempt to measure out the exact distance. Parking is also prohibited within 10m of a pedestrian crossing, and in bus lanes and loading zones. Disabled parking spaces are solely for the use of disabled drivers, a rule which is rigorously enforced – it can cost you over 1000kr if you disobey. In the centre, parking isn't permitted one particular night a week to allow for cleaning (see the rectangular yellow street signs with days and times in Swedish, below the "no stopping" sign on every street. In winter the same applies to allow for snow clearance. In short, if in doubt, don't park there – also remember that the closer you drive to a city centre the more it will cost to park your car. For **car rental**, see "Listings", p.99.

Canoes and kayaks

The dozens of **canoes** and **kayaks** you see being paddled around Stockholm are a testimony to the fact that one of the best ways to see the city is from the water. Skepp O'Hoj, at Galärvarvsvägen 2 (℡08/660 57 57), and Tvillingarnas Båtuthyrning, just by Djurgårdsbron (℡08/663 37 39), are two of the best places in town to rent boats. Special weekend deals are often available from Friday evening to Monday morning, when a canoe can be rented for 300kr; otherwise they cost about 120kr per day. For canoes in the archipelago, try Skärgårdens Kanotcenter at Vegabacken 22 on Vaxholm (℡08/541 377 90), or ask locally on the other islands – corner shops often have a couple of canoes or boats for rent.

Accommodation

Stockholm has plenty of **accommodation** to suit every taste and pocket, from elegant up-market hotels with waterfront views to youth hostels in unusual places – two on boats and another in a former prison. If you are looking for one of the cheaper hotel rooms or a hostel bed in the centre of town, don't turn up late in summer. In fact, from mid-June to mid-August it is always a good idea to book your accommodation in advance either directly with the hotel or hostel or, alternatively use the excellent room-booking service, **Hotellcentralen**, in the main hall of the Central Station (daily: June–Aug 8am–8pm; Sept–May 9am–6pm; ℡08/789 24 90, ✉hotels@stoinfo.se), which holds comprehensive listings of hotels and hostels. They score over ringing for yourself in that they have the latest special offers direct from the hotels; if you book accommodation through them you'll be charged a booking fee of 50kr for a hotel room, or 20kr for a hostel room. It's best to call at their office in person rather than phone, as they're often too busy to answer many calls. Hotellcentralen can also make bookings under the Stockholm Package scheme (see below).

Hotels and pensions

Summer in Stockholm means a buyer's market for **hotel** rooms as business travel declines, with double rooms costing as little as 580kr. The cheapest choices on the whole are found to the north of Cityterminalen in the streets to the west of Adolf Fredriks kyrka. But don't rule out the more expensive places either: there are some attractive weekend and summer prices that make a spot of luxury nearer the waterfront a little more affordable. Most of the hotels and pensions also offer the **Stockholm Package**, an arrangement whereby accommodation booked at participating establishments is charged at a much reduced room rate. At the bottom end of the scale it can work out cheaply: 450kr per person in a twin room with breakfast, rising to around 870kr in quite a posh hotel. This package can be booked through Hotellcentralen (see above); if you ring ahead you can specify which hotel you'd like, while if you book on the day you'll be given what's available. At the time of writing, most of the hotels and pensions given below were part of the scheme, but the list of participants is prone to change. All of the following establishments include breakfast in the price, unless otherwise stated.

Norrmalm

The following hotels are marked on the maps on p.63 & p.73.

Bema Upplandsgatan 13 ☎08/23 26 75, ☏20 53 58. Bus #47 or #69 from Central Station. Ten minutes' walk from the station, this small pension-style hotel has twelve en-suite rooms with beech-wood furniture and modern Swedish decor. Summer and weekend deals bring the cost down. ❸/❷

Central Vasagatan 38 ☎08/566 208 00, ☗www.centralhotel.se. T-Centralen T-bana. A modern, comfortable place, handy for the station. ❻/❹

Diplomat Strandvägen 7C ☎08/459 68 00, ☗www.diplomathotel.com. Östermalmstorg T-bana or buses #47 or #69. One of the city's top hotels offering rooms with wonderful views over Stockholm's inner harbour and grandest boulevard. Although the suites in this turn-of-the-twentieth-century town house are at the top end of the price range, they represent much better value than the cheaper double rooms at the *Grand*. Non-discounted double rooms start at 2195kr; there are summer and weekend discounts from 1295kr. ❻/❺

Grand Södra Blasieholmshamn 8, Norrmalm ☎08/679 35 00, ☗www.grandhotel.se. Kungsträdgården T-bana. A late nineteenth-century harbourside building overlooking Gamla Stan, Stockholm's most refined hotel provides the last word in luxury – with prices to match. Only worth it if you're staying in the best rooms; otherwise, the *Diplomat* has suites with a view for the same price as a double here. Summer and weekend reductions with doubles from 1890kr. ❻

Haga Hagagatan 29, Norrmalm ☎08/545 473 00, ☗www.hagahotel.se. Odenplan T-bana. Thirty-eight good-value, modern rooms in a quiet road a little out of the centre, within easy striking distance of the top of Sveavägen. ❹/❸

Mälardrottningen Riddarholmen ☎08/545 187 80, ☗www.malardrottningen.se. Gamla Stan T-bana. Moored by the side of the island of Riddarholmen, this elegant white ship was formerly the gin palace of American millionairess Barbara Hutton. Its cabin-style rooms are a little cramped and in need of a lick of paint and bit of a polish, but offer good value for such a central location. ❺/❹

Nordic Light Vasaplan 7, Norrmalm ☎08/505 630 00, ☗www.nordichotels.se. The last word in Nordic design – each room is individually decorated in shades of white and steely grey – but, sadly, the emphasis is too much on looks rather than comfort. Painfully contemporary. ❻/❺

Nordic Sea Vasaplan 2–4, Norrmalm ☎08/505 630 00, ☗www.nordichotels.se. As with its more expensive sister hotel opposite, focus here is on bold designs and colours – maritime blues and greens predominate throughout. Some of the rooms are tiny and only have views of the train station, although the superb buffet breakfast is certainly a bonus. ❻/❺

Pensionat Oden Odengatan 38, Norrmalm ☎08/612 43 49, ☗www.pensionat.nu. Rådmansgatan T-bana. Second-floor hotel offering elegant modern rooms with shared bathrooms which represent excellent value for money. Good central location. Non-discounted rooms here are a little cheaper than at its sister establishment (see below). ❸/❷

Queen's Drottninggatan 71A, Norrmalm ☎08/24 94 60, ☗www.queenshotel.se. Hötorget T-bana. Shabby mid-range pension-style hotel, with en-suite rooms and breakfast buffet. Summer and weekend deals. ❸

Wallin Wallingatan 15, Norrmalm ☎08/506 161 00, ☗www.wallinhotel.com. Buses #47 or #69 from Central Station. Decent central hotel with en-suite rooms; a 10min walk from the station. ❻/❹

Wasa Park St Eriksplan 1, Norrmalm ☎08/545 453 00, ☏545 453 01. Sankt Eriksplan T-bana. A clean, simple hotel; a bit out of the centre but cheap, although there are no en-suite rooms. Summer and weekend deals. ❷

Gamla Stan

The following hotels are marked on the maps on p.73.

First Hotel Reisen Skeppsbron 12 ☎08/22 32 60, ☗www.firsthotels.com. Gamla Stan or Slussen T-bana. Traditional hotel with heavy wood-panelled interior. All rooms have bathtubs (not the norm in Sweden), plus wonderful views over the Stockholm waterfront. ❻/❺

Lady Hamilton Storkyrkobrinken 5 ☎08/506 401 00, ☗www.lady-hamilton.se. Gamla Stan T-bana. Traditional hotel in a building dating from the 1470s with rooms tastefully decorated in old-fashioned Swedish style – lots of antique furniture and folk artefacts. ❻

Lord Nelson Västerlånggatan 22 ☎08/506 401

20, @www.lord-nelson.se. Gamla Stan T-bana.
This cosy hotel – the narrowest in Sweden at just
5m wide – is stuffed full of naval antiques and
curiosities including an original letter from Nelson
to Lady Hamilton. Rooms are small but have ship's
teak floorboards and lots of mahogany and brass.
Better value than the *Lady Hamilton*. ⑥/⑤
Rica City Gamla Stan Lilla Nygatan 25 ℡08/723
72 50, @www.rica.se. Gamla Stan T-bana. Like
other hotels in the Old Town this one doesn't come
cheap though it is wonderfully situated in an elegant medieval building with stylish yet old-fashioned rooms to match; all 51 are individually decorated. ⑥/⑤

Södermalm

The following hotels are marked on the map on
p.89.
Alexandra Magnus Ladulåsgatan 42 ℡08/84 03
20, @www.alexandrahotel.se. Medborgarplatsen
T-bana. This small, modern hotel is in a peaceful
Södermalm location. The summer and weekend
reductions make it a pleasant and affordable
option. ④/③
Anno 1647 Mariagränd 3, near Slussen,
Södermalm ℡08/442 16 80, @www
.swedenhotels.se. Near Slussen in Södermalm;
Slussen T-bana. Located in a seventeenth-century
building handy for the Old Town, with pine floors
and period furniture, though not recommended for
people with mobility difficulties. ⑥/⑤

Columbus Tjärhovsgatan 11, Södermalm
℡08/503 112 00, @www.columbus.se.
Medborgarplatsen T-bana. Simple rooms with
shared bathrooms in a plain, almost school-like
building. ④/③
Oden Söder Hornsgatan 66B, Södermalm
℡08/612 43 49, @www.pensionat.nu. Mariatorget
T-bana. This is a good-value choice in the heart of
Söder, with tastefully decorated rooms – some en
suite – at excellent prices. ③/②
Scandic Hotel Slussen Guldgränd 8, Södermalm
℡08/517 353 00, @www.scandic-hotels.com.
Slussen T-bana. Luxurious chain hotel with wood-
en floors throughout. It's really only worth considering if you can get one of the rooms at the front
with fantastic views out over Gamla Stan. Non-discounted double rooms start at a totally outrageous
3033kr. ⑥
Tre Små Rum Högbergsgatan 81, Södermalm
℡08/641 23 71, @www.tresmarum.se.
Mariatorget T-bana. A clean, modern option in the
heart of Södermalm. The seven, simple basement
rooms with shared bathrooms are very popular, so
book in advance. Help-yourself breakfast from the
kitchen fridge. ②
Zinkensdamm Zinkens Väg 20, Södermalm
℡08/616 81 10, @www.zinkensdamm.com.
Hornstull or Zinkensdamm T-bana. Comfortable
and well-appointed hotel rooms, all en suite, in a
separate wing of the youth hostel (see opposite).
⑤/④

Youth hostels and private rooms

Stockholm has a wide range of good, well-run **hostels**, nearly all in the city centre or within easy access of it, and costing 120–200kr a night per person. There
are no fewer than six official STF youth hostels in the city, two of which – *Af
Chapman* and *Långholmen* – are among the best in Sweden. There are also a number of independently run places, which tend to be slightly more expensive.

Another good low-cost option is a **private room**, generally in a family
house; to book one, contact an agency called Hotelltjänst, Vasagatan 15–17
(℡08/10 44 67), just a few minutes' walk from Central Station. Tell them how
much you want to pay, and where in the city you want to stay (some rooms
are out of the centre), and they should land you somewhere with fridge and
cooking facilities for around 250kr per person per night; you can often arrange
better-value deals for longer stays.

STF hostels

The following hostels are marked on the map on
p.62.
Af Chapman Flaggmansvägen 8, Skeppsholmen
℡08/463 2266, @www.stfchapman.com.
Kungsträdgården T-bana or bus #65 direct from
Central Station. This square-rigged 1888 ship – a
landmark in its own right – has views over Gamla
Stan that are unsurpassed at the price. Without an

advance reservation (try to book a fortnight before
you arrive), the chances of a space in summer are
slim. The drawbacks to nautical accommodation
are a lockout (11am–3pm) and the lack of a
kitchen. Reception 7am–noon & 3–10pm, curfew
at 2am. Closed first week of Jan.
Backpackers Inn Banérgatan 56, Östermalm
℡08/660 75 15, ℉665 40 39. Karlaplan T-bana,
exit Valhallavägen, or bus #4. Quite central former

school residence, with washing machines available. Three hundred beds in large dorms. Late June to early Aug only.

Hökarängen Munstycksvägen 18 ☏ & ☏08/94 17 65. Nice old place with 46 beds 20 minutes out of the city on the green metro line in the direction of Farsta Strand; get off at Hökarängen and walk 10min from the station south along Pepparvägen. Swimming is possible in the bay 2km from the hostel. Late June to early Aug only.

Långholmen Kronohäktet, Långholmen ☏08/668 05 10, ☻www.langholmen.com. Hornstull T-bana and follow the signs. On the island of Långholmen, Stockholm's grandest STF hostel is inside the former prison building dating from 1724. The cells are converted into smart private and dormitory rooms, still with their original, extremely small windows. This is a great location, with beaches nearby, buses to Kungsholmen, and the whole of Södermalm on the doorstep. Fantastic views of Stockholm and of Lake Mälaren.

Skeppsholmen Flaggmansvägen 8, Skeppsholmen ☏08/463 22 66, ☻www.stfchapman.com. Kungsträdgården T-bana or bus #65 direct. Right in the centre and immensely popular, this former craftsman's workshop is of a similar standard to *Af Chapman*, at the foot of whose gangplank it lies; there are no kitchen or laundry facilities.

Zinkensdamm Zinkens Väg 20, Södermalm ☏08/616 81 00, ☻www.zinkensdamm.com. Hornstull T-bana or Zinkensdamm. Huge hostel with 490 beds in an excellent location for exploring Södermalm though a 30min walk from the city centre. Kitchen and laundry facilities (also see "Hotels and pensions").

Independent hostels

The following hostels are marked on the maps on p.62 & p.89.

City Backpackers Upplandsgatan 2A ☏08/20 69 20, ☻www.citybackpackers.se. T-Centralen T-bana. Friendly, non-HI hostel with 65 beds, only 5min from the Central Station. The owners and staff have travelled widely and specialize in catering for backpackers; facilities include all-day Internet access, cable TV and a sauna. A twin-bed room is 470kr. Otherwise 160–190kr per bed.

Gustav af Klint Stadsgårdskajen 153, Södermalm ☏08/640 40 77, ☻www.hem.fyristorg.com/gustafafklint. Slussen T-bana. Housed in an old fishing boat, this rather down-at-heel hostel has rather cramped rooms; if they're full, don't be tempted to take one of its private rooms – they're not worth the money. The place has a good central location, just a few minutes' walk from the Old Town.

Campsites

With the nearest year-round campsites a good half an hour out of the city centre, **camping** out of season in Stockholm can prove rather inconvenient. However, a summer-only city campsite does exist in Östermalm (see below). The tourist offices have free camping booklets available, detailing facilities at all Stockholm's campsites. Pitching a tent costs around 100kr for two people in July and August, or 50kr at other times of year. This being Sweden, all sites listed below are well equipped with modern service buildings providing showers and laundry facilities.

Ängby ☏08/37 04 20, ☻www.angbycamping.se. T-bana Ängbyplan on the green line towards Hässelby and turn left when leaving the station. West of the city on the lakeshore. Open all year, but phone ahead to book Sept–April.

Bredäng ☏08/97 70 71, ☻www.camping.se/plats/A04. T-bana Bredäng on the red line towards Norsborg. Southwest of the

city with views over Lake Mälaren. Open all year, but phone ahead to book Nov–April.

Östermalm Citycamping ☏08/10 29 03. T-bana Stadion. The most centrally located of all Stockholm's campsites but only open from late June to mid-Aug. Adjacent to the Östermalm sportsground and walkable from the city centre in around 30min.

The City

Visitors have been enchanted by Stockholm for the past 150 years, though the sights and museums have changed radically during that time. Once, in the centre, there were country lanes, great orchards, grazing cows, and even windmills.

The downside then was the lack of pavements (until the 1840s) or piped water supply (until 1858), and the presence of open sewers, squalid streets and crowded slums. In the twentieth century, a huge **modernization** programme was undertaken as part of the Social Democratic out-with-the-old-and-in-with-the-new policy: Sweden was to become a place fit for working people to live. Old areas were torn down as "a thousand homes for a thousand Swedes" – as the project was known – were constructed. The result, unfortunately, can be seen only too clearly around Sergels Torg: five high-rise monstrosities and an ugly rash of soulless concrete buildings that blot the city-centre landscape. There was even a plan to tear down the whole of the Old Town and build a modern city in its stead; thankfully the scheme was quickly rescinded.

Stockholm is now, for the most part, a bright and elegant place, and, with its great expanses of open water right in the centre, it offers a city panorama unparalleled anywhere in Europe. Seeing the sights is a straightforward business: everything is easy to get to, opening hours are long, and the pace is relaxed. For most visitors the first stop is the Old Town, **Gamla Stan**, a medieval jumble of cobbled streets and narrow alleyways huddled together on a triangular-shaped island sandwiched between Stockholm's modern centre, **Norrmalm**, home to the capital's main area of shops as well as the train and bus stations, and the fashionable southern island of **Södermalm**, whose grids of streets lined with lofty stone buildings create an altogether more homely ambience than the grand and formal buildings of the city centre. It's here, south of the main city, that you'll find some of the city's most enjoyable bars and restaurants, as well as a couple of popular beaches on the neighbouring island of Långholmen. In this city of islands, you'll find more waterside greenery and relaxation opportunities on **Djurgården**, a vast area of parkland right on the edge of the modern city. Stockholm boasts an amazing range and number of **museums**, found in most districts of the city; we've described the most interesting ones in detail. Stockholm's many **churches** are also worthy of your attention as you amble round the city.

Old Stockholm: Gamla Stan and Riddarholmen

Three islands – Riddarholmen, Staden and Helgeandsholmen – make up the **oldest part of Stockholm**, a history-riddled cluster of seventeenth- and eighteenth-century buildings backed by hairline medieval alleys. It was on these three adjoining polyps of land that Birger Jarl erected a fortification in 1255, an event that was to herald the beginnings of the present city. Rumours abound about the derivation of the name "Stockholm", though it's now widely believed to mean "island cleared of trees", since the trees on the island that is now home to Gamla Stan were probably felled to make way for settlement. Incidentally, today the words *holm*, island, and *stock* meaning log are still in common use.

A taste of Stockholm's medieval past can be had at the excellent **Medeltidsmuseum**, at the northern end of the two bridges, Norrbron and Riksbron, which lead across to Gamla Stan. Although, strictly speaking, only the largest island, Staden, contains **Gamla Stan** (the Old Town), this name is usually attached to the buildings and streets of all three islands. Once Stockholm's working centre, nowadays Gamla Stan is primarily a tourist city, an eminently strollable area around the **Kungliga Slottet** (royal palace), **Riksdagshuset** (parliament building) and **Storkyrkan** (cathedral). The central spider's web of streets – best approached over the bridges Norrbron or Riksbron – is a sprawl of monumental buildings and high airy churches that

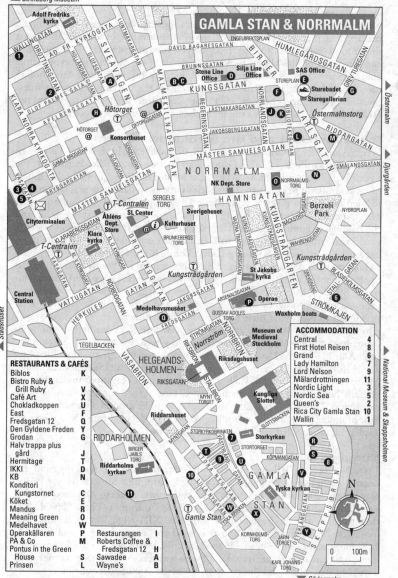

GAMLA STAN & NORRMALM

RESTAURANTS & CAFÉS

Biblos	K
Bistro Ruby & Grill Ruby	V
Café Art	X
Chokladkoppen	U
East	F
Fredsgatan 12	Q
Den Gyldene Freden	Y
Grodan	G
Halv trappa plus gård	J
Hermitage	T
IKKI	D
KB	N
Konditori Kungstornet	C
Köket	E
Mandus	R
Meaning Green	O
Medelhavet	W
Operakällaren	P
PA & Co	M
Pontus in the Green House	S
Prinsen	L
Restaurangen	I
Roberts Coffee & Fredsgatan 12	H
Sawadee	A
Wayne's	B

ACCOMMODATION

Central	4
First Hotel Reisen	8
Grand	6
Lady Hamilton	7
Lord Nelson	9
Mälardrottningen	11
Nordic Light	3
Nordic Sea	5
Queen's	2
Rica City Gamla Stan	10
Wallin	1

0   100m

form a protective girdle around the narrow lanes. Some of the impossibly slender alleys lead to steep steps ascending between battered walls, others are covered passageways linking leaning buildings. The tall dark houses in the centre were mostly owned by wealthy merchants, and are still distinguished by intricate doorways and portals bearing coats of arms. The main square of the Old Town is **Stortorget**, an impressive collection of tall pastel-coloured stone buildings with curling gables which saw one of the medieval city's most ferocious battles, the Stockholm Bloodbath (see p.513). It's easy to spend hours wandering around here, although the atmosphere these days is not so much medieval as mercenary: there's a dense concentration of antique shops, art showrooms and chi-chi cellar restaurants. Not surprisingly, this is the most exclusive part of Stockholm in which to live. Off the western shore of Gamla Stan, the tiny islet of **Riddarholmen** not only houses one of Stockholm's most beautiful churches, **Riddarholmskyrkan**, the burial place for countless Swedish kings and queens over the centuries, but also the Baroque **Riddarhuset** a reminder of the glory days of the Swedish aristocracy.

Riksdagshuset and the Medeltidsmuseum

Perched on Helgeandsholmen, a small oval-shaped island wedged between Norrmalm to the north and Gamla Stan to the south, **Riksdagshuset**, the Swedish parliament building (May–Aug Mon–Fri guided tours in English at noon & 1.30pm; free) is where Sweden's famous welfare state was shaped and formed during the postwar years of the 1940s and 50s. The building was completely restored, though, in the 1970s, just seventy years after it was built, and the original, columned facade (viewed to best effect from Norrbron) is rarely used as an entrance today; the main entrance is on Riksgatan, the short street between the bridges of Riksbron and Stallbron. It is the glassy bulge at the back (which you see when coming into Stockholm from the south by train) that is the hub of most activity, and where you're shown round on **guided tours**. This being Sweden, the seating for members is in healthy, non-adversarial rows, grouped by constituency and not by party, and it is not unknown for some politicians to breastfeed their offspring in the chamber.

In front of the Riksdag, accessed by a set of steps leading down from Norrbron, is the **Medeltidsmuseum** (Museum of Medieval Stockholm; July–Aug Fri–Mon 11am–4pm, Tues–Thurs 11am–6pm; Sept–June Tues–Sun 11am–4pm, Wed 11am–6pm; 40kr; ⓦwww.medeltidsmuseet.stockholm.se). Medieval ruins, tunnels and walls discovered during excavations under the parliament building have been incorporated into a walk-through underground exhibition. There are reconstructed houses to poke around alongside a selection of models, pictures, boats and skeletons. With detailed English labelling, it's a splendid display that's great fun for children too.

Kungliga Slottet

Cross Norrbron or Riksbron from the Riksdagshuset and up rears the most distinctive monumental building in Stockholm, **Kungliga Slottet** (Royal Palace, ⓦwww.royalcourt.se) – a low, square, yellowy-brown building, with two arms that stretch down towards the water. Stockholm's old Tre Kronor (Three Crowns) castle burnt down at the beginning of King Karl XII's reign, leaving his architect, Tessin the Younger (see p.102), a free hand to design a simple and beautiful Baroque structure in its stead. Finished in 1754, the palace is a striking achievement: uniform and sombre outside, but with a magnificent Rococo interior that's a swirl of staterooms and museums. Its sheer size is quite overwhelming and it's worth focusing your explorations on one or two sections of the palace.

The palace's **Apartments** (mid-May to Aug daily 10am–4pm; Sept–April Tues–Sun noon–3pm; 70kr) hold a relentlessly linear collection of furniture and tapestries, all too sumptuous to take in and inspirational only in terms of colossal size. The **Treasury** (same times; 70kr), on the other hand, is certainly worth a visit for its ranks of jewel-studded crowns. The oldest one was made in 1650 for Karl X, while the two most charming belonged to princesses Sofia (1771) and Eugène (1860).

Also worth catching is the **Armoury** (June–Aug daily 10am–5pm; Sept–May Tues, Wed & Fri–Sun 11am–5pm, Thurs 11am–8pm; 65kr; Ⓦwww.livrustkammaren.nu), which is not so much about weapons as ceremony – with suits of armour, costumes and horse-drawn carriages from the sixteenth century onwards. Also on display is the stuffed horse of King Gustav II Adolf, who died in the Battle of Lützen in 1632, and his blood- and mud-spattered garments, retrieved after the enemy had stripped him down to his boxer shorts on the battlefield.

Nearby, two other museums are worth a quick look if you're a real palace junkie: the **Museum Tre Kronor** (same times as Apartments; 70kr; Ⓦwww.royalcourt.se) contains part of the older Tre Kronor castle, its ruins underneath the present building, while the **Royal Coin Cabinet**, Slottsbacken 6 (Tues–Sun 10am–4pm; 45kr), is home to a stash of coins, banknotes and medals from across the centuries, as well as a number of silver hoards from Viking days.

Into Gamla Stan: Stortorget and around

South of the Royal Palace, the streets are suddenly narrower and darker and you're into Gamla Stan proper. The highest point of the old part of Stockholm is crowned by **Storkyrkan** (daily: mid-May to mid-Sept daily 9am–6pm; 10kr; rest of year 9am–4pm; free), consecrated in 1306, and almost the first building you'll stumble upon. Pedantically speaking, Stockholm has no cathedral, but this rectangular brick church is now accepted as such, and the monarchs of Sweden married and were crowned here. Storkyrkan gained its present shape at the end of the fifteenth century, and then was given a Baroque remodelling in the 1730s. The interior is marvellous: twentieth-century restoration has removed the white plaster from the red-brick columns, and the effect has given a warm colouring to the rest of the building. Much is made of the fifteenth-century Gothic sculpture of St George and the Dragon (see p.513), certainly an animated piece but easily overshadowed by the royal pews – more like golden billowing thrones – and the monumental black-and-silver altarpiece. Fans of organ music might like to visit the frequent recitals that often take place on Saturdays around 1pm.

Stortorget, Gamla Stan's main square, one block south of Storkyrkan along either Trångsund or Källargränd, is a handsome and elegantly proportioned space crowded by eighteenth-century buildings. In 1520, Christian II used the square as an execution site during the "Stockholm Blood Bath" (see p.513), dispatching his opposition en masse with bloody finality. Now, as then, the streets **Västerlånggatan**, **Österlånggatan**, **Stora Nygatan** and **Lilla Nygatan** run the length of the Old Town, although today their time-worn buildings harbour a succession of art-and-craft shops and restaurants. Happily the consumerism here is largely unobtrusive, and, in summer, buskers and evening strollers clog the narrow alleyways, making it an entertaining place to wander or to stop for a bite to eat. There are few real targets, though at some stage you'll probably pass **Köpmantorget** square (off Österlånggatan), where there's a replica of the George-and-Dragon statue from inside the Storkyrkan. Take every opportunity, too, to wander up side streets, where you'll find fading coats of arms, covered alleys and worn cobbles at every turn.

On Tyska Brinken, just off Västerlånggatan, is the **Tyska kyrkan** (German Church; early May to late Sept daily noon–4pm; rest of year Sat & Sun noon–4pm; free). Once belonging to Stockholm's medieval German merchants, the church served as the meeting place of the Guild of St Gertrude. A copper-roofed red-brick building atop a rise, it was enlarged in the seventeenth

△ Caption

century when Baroque decorators got hold of it: the result, a richly fashioned interior with the pulpit dominating the nave, is outstanding; the royal gallery in one corner – designed by Tessin the Elder – can only add to the overall elegance of this church, one of Stockholm's most impressive.

Riddarhuset and Riddarholmen

From Storkyrkan, it's a five-minute stroll west along Storkyrkobrinken to the handsome, seventeenth-century Baroque **Riddarhuset** (daily Mon–Fri 11.30am–12.30pm; 40kr; ⓦwww.riddarhuset.se), or House of Nobles. Its Great Hall was where the Swedish aristocracy met during the Parliament of the Four Estates (1668–1865); their coats of arms – around two and a half thousand of them – are splattered across the walls. Take a peek downstairs, at the Chancery, which stores heraldic bone china by the shelf-load and has racks full of fancy signet rings – essential accessories for the eighteenth-century noble-about-town.

Riddarhuset shouldn't really be seen in isolation. It's only a matter of seconds to cross the bridge onto **Riddarholmen** island, and to **Riddarholmskyrkan** (May–Aug daily 10am–4pm; Sept Sat & Sun noon–3pm; 30kr). Originally a Franciscan monastery, the church has been the burial place of Swedish royalty for over six centuries. Since Magnus Ladulås was sealed up here in 1290, his successors have rallied round to create a Swedish royal pantheon. Among others, you'll find the tombs of Gustav II Adolf (in the green marble sarcophagus), Karl XII, Gustav III and Karl Johan XIV, plus other innumerable and unmemorable descendants. Walk around the back of the church for stunning views of Stadshuset, the City Hall, and Lake Mälaren. In winter, the lake often freezes from here right up to the Västerbron bridge, 1km away, and people skate and take their dogs for walks along the ice.

Skeppsholmen, Kastellholmen and the Nationalmuseum

Off Gamla Stan's eastern reaches lies the island of **Skeppsholmen** (a 10min walk from Stortorget: cross Strömbron, turn right and cross Skeppsholmbron; you can also take a ferry from Nybroplan, see p.67, or bus #65 from Central Station), home to two of Stockholm's best youth hostels. However, it's the eclectic clutch of **museums**, the first of which, the National Art Museum, is actually just before the bridge, Skeppsholmsbron, that draws most people here. There's little else to detain you on Skeppsholmen or on the tiny, adjacent **Kastellholmen**, connected by a bridge to the south. The fact that both islands are in the Baltic proved attractive enough for the Swedish Navy to build camps here in the nineteenth century; some of the abandoned old barracks are still visible.

Nationalmuseum

As you approach Skeppsholmsbron, on the way to Skeppsholmen, you'll pass the striking waterfront **Nationalmuseum** (National Art Museum; Tues & Thurs 11am–8pm, Wed, Fri–Sun 11am–5pm; 75kr; ⓦwww.nationalmuseum .se), overlooking the Royal Palace. This impressive collection of Swedish and European fine and applied arts from the late medieval period to the present day is contained on three floors.

Changing exhibitions of prints and drawings take up the **ground floor** as well as *Design 19002000*, a permanent exhibition of twentieth-century Swedish design with extensive displays of furniture and glassware, which, partly thanks to IKEA, Sweden is now justifiably famous for abroad. There is also a museum shop and café, plus lockers to leave your bags in on the ground floor.

The **first floor** is devoted to applied art, and those with a penchant for royal curiosities will be pleased to find that this museum has the lot – beds slept in by kings, cabinets leaned on by queens, plates eaten off by nobles – mainly from the centuries when Sweden was a great power. There's modern work alongside the ageing tapestries and furniture, including Art Nouveau coffeepots and vases, and a collection of simply and elegantly designed Swedish wooden chairs.

It's the **second floor**, though, that's most engaging. There's a plethora of European and Mediterranean sculpture along with some mesmerizing six-teenth- and seventeenth-century Russian icons. The paintings on this floor include works by El Greco, Canaletto, Gainsborough, Gauguin and Renoir. Something of a coup for the museum is Rembrandt's *Conspiracy of Claudius Civilis*, one of his largest monumental paintings. Depicting a scene from Tacitus's *History*, the bold work shows a gathering of well-armed chieftains. There are also some fine works by **Swedish artists** from the sixteenth to early twentieth centuries – most notably paintings by the nineteenth-century mas-ters Anders Zorn and Carl Larsson, and one, by Carl Gustav Pilo, a late eigh-teenth-century painter, depicting the coronation of Gustav III in Gamla Stan's Storkyrkan. Note the white plaster columns of the church rather than the red brick of today.

Skeppsholmen's museums

On Skeppsholmen itself, Stockholm's **Moderna Muséet** (Modern Museum; Tues–Thurs 11am–8pm, Fri–Sun 11am–6pm; 70kr; ⓦ www.modernamuseet .se), due to reopen during 2003, is one of the better modern art collections in Europe, with a comprehensive selection of work by some of the twentieth century's leading artists. Take a look at Dali's monumental *Enigma of William Tell*, showing the artist at his most conventionally unconventional, and Matisse's striking *Apollo*. Look out for Picasso's *Guitar Player* and a whole host of Warhol, Lichtenstein, Kandinsky, Miró and Magritte. Next door is the **Arkitekturmuséet** (Architecture Museum; same times; 55kr; ⓦ www .arkitekturmuseet.se), once again due to reopen late-2003 after refurbishment, serving up a taste of Swedish architecture through the ages in one of the most inspired buildings in the city – all glass and airy.

Perhaps one for a rainy day, unless you're particularly interested in the disci-pline, the museum also stages temporary exhibitions on various aspects of architecture and urban planning within the country.

Due to ongoing renovation work caused by damp and mould damage in the building which contains both the Moderna Muséet and the Arkitekturmuséet, both museums will be housed in **temporary accommodation** until at least the end of 2003. Exhibits from the Arkitekturmuséet can be seen in the adja-cent Skeppholmskyrka church (Tues–Sun 1pm–5pm) as well as at the Konstakademien at Fredsgatan 12 (Tues–Thurs 11am–8pm, Fri–Sun 1pm–5pm), close to the Riksdagshuset. The Moderna Muséet has temporarily moved to Klarabergsviadukten 61, near the main station (Tues–Thurs 10am–8pm, Fri–Sun 10am–6pm).

A steep climb up the northern tip of the island brings you to **Östasiatiska Muséet** (Museum of Far Eastern Antiquities; Tues noon–8pm, Wed–Sun noon–5pm; 50kr; ⓦ www.ostasiatiska.se). A visit here is half a day well spent: you'll be rewarded by an array of objects displaying incredible craftsmanship, including many exhibits from China – the favourite hunting ground of Swedish archeologists. There are fifth-century Chinese tomb figurines, intricate ceramics from the seventh century onwards and fine Chinese paintings on paper and silk. Alongside these, take a look at the astounding assembly of sixth-century Buddhas, Indian watercolours and gleaming bronze Krishna figures, and a magnificent set of Samurai armour, a gift from the Japanese crown prince in the 1920s.

Norrmalm and Kungsholmen

Immediately to the north and west of Gamla Stan, modern Stockholm is split into two distinct sections. **Norrmalm**, to the north, is the commercial heart of the city, a compact area full of shops and offices, restaurants, bars and cinemas, always bustling with people and street life – unfortunately, it also has a high count of ugly modern buildings. To the west, **Kungsholmen** has a very different feel, with wider, residential streets, larger parks, select shops and Stockholm's town hall. Norrmalm is easy to get round on foot, and from there it's only a short walk across Stadshusbron to Kungsholmen.

Gustav Adolfs Torg and around

Down on the waterfront, at the foot of Norrbron, is **Gustav Adolfs Torg**, more a traffic island than a square these days, with the nineteenth-century **Operan** (Opera House; ⊛www.operan.se) its proudest, most notable – and ugliest – building. It was here, in an earlier opera house on the same site, that King Gustav III was shot at a masked ball in 1792 by one Captain Ankarström, an admirer of Rousseau and member of the aristocratic opposition. The story is recorded in Verdi's opera *Un ballo in maschera*, and you'll find Gustav's ball costume, as well as the assassin's pistols and mask, displayed in the Palace Armoury in Gamla Stan (see p.75). The opera's famous restaurant, *Operakällaren* (see p.93), which faces the water, is hellishly expensive, the trendy café less so.

A statue of King Gustav II Adolf marks the centre of the square, between the Opera and the Foreign Ministry opposite. Look out, too, for fishermen pulling salmon out of **Strömmen**, the fast-flowing stretch of water that winds its way through the centre of the city. Since the seventeenth century, Stockholmers have had the right to fish this outlet from Lake Mälaren to the Baltic; landing a catch here isn't as difficult as it sounds, and there's usually a group of hopefuls on one of the bridges around the square.

Just off the square, at Fredsgatan 2, in the heart of government (several ministries are located in the surrounding streets), is **Medelhavmuséet**, a sparkling museum devoted to Mediterranean and Near Eastern Antiquities (Tues 11am–8pm, Wed–Fri 11am–4pm, Sat & Sun noon–5pm; 50kr; ⊛www.medelhavsmuseet.se). Its enormous display on Egypt includes several whopping great mummies; the most attractive pieces are the bronze weapons, tools and domestic objects from the time before the Pharaohs. The Cyprus collections are also huge, the largest such assemblage outside the island itself, depicting the island civilization over a period of six thousand years. The museum also contains strong Greek displays and comprehensive collections of Etruscan and Roman art. A couple of rooms examine Islamic culture through pottery, glass and metalwork, as well as decorative elements from architecture, Arabic calligraphy and Persian miniature painting.

Walking back towards the Opera House and continuing across the main junction onto Arsenalsgatan, you'll soon come to **St Jakobs kyrka** (daily 11am–3pm). Although the church is located in a prime location it is often curiously overlooked by visitors to the city. It stands on the site of an earlier chapel of St James (Jakob in Swedish) and was completed some 52 years after the death of its founder, Johan III. Although the church's doors are impressive – check out the south door with its statues of Moses and St James on either side – it's the great, golden pulpit that draws most attention. The date of the church's completion (1642) is stamped high up on the ceiling in gold relief. Organ and choir recitals are held here, generally on Saturday at 3pm.

Kungsträdgården

One block east of Saint Jakobs kyrka and the Opera House, Norrmalm's eastern boundary is marked by **Kungsträdgården**, the most fashionable and central of the city's numerous parks, reaching northwards from the water as far as Hamngatan. The mouthful of a name literally means "the king's gardens", though if you're expecting perfectly designed flowerbeds and rose gardens you'll be sadly disappointed – it's a great expanse of concrete with a couple of lines of trees, its days as a royal kitchen garden long gone. Today the area is Stockholm's main meeting place, especially in summer, when there's almost always something going on: free music, live theatre and other performances take place on the central open-air stage. There are also several popular **cafés** – the open-air one off Strömgatan at the square's southern edge is popular in spring as a place for winter-weary Stockholmers to lap up the sunshine. In winter, the park is as busy as in summer: the **Isbanan**, an open-air ice rink at the Hamngatan end of the park, rents out skates (mid-Nov–March daily 9am–6pm; skate rental 35kr). There is a tourist office here, too, at the corner of Hamngatan and Kungsträdgårdsgatan in Sverigehuset (see p.64 for details).

North of the park, Hamngatan runs east to **Birger Jarlsgatan**, the main thoroughfare that divides Norrmalm from Östermalm, which has become a Mecca for increasingly trendy eating and drinking in recent years. Look out for the stone pillars near the water, with panels that illuminate to give an electronic display indicating the current levels of pollution (low compared to other capitals) in the city's air and water.

Sergels Torg to Hötorget

At the western end of Hamngatan, past the enormous NK department store, lies **Sergels Torg**, the ugliest square in modern Stockholm. It's an open-air meeting area and venue for impromptu music performances or demonstrations, centred around the five seething floors of **Kulturhuset** (Tues–Fri 11am–7pm, Sat & Sun 11am–5pm; free, though entrance fees are charged for exhibitions), whose windows overlook the milling concrete square. Inside this building, devoted to contemporary Swedish culture, are temporary art-and-craft exhibitions, together with workshops open to anyone willing to get their hands dirty. The reading room (Läsesalongen) on the ground level is stuffed with foreign newspapers, books, records and magazines – especially handy when it's wet and windy outside. As you come in, check with the information desk for details of poetry readings, concerts and theatre performances. At the **café** on the top floor, you can indulge in delicious apple pie and custard – and take in the best **views** of central Stockholm. One thing you'll have a bird's-eye view of is the eyesore tall, wire-like column, surrounded by a spewing fountain (sometimes clouded by soap suds – the local youth think it's a real wheeze to pour packets of washing powder into it), that dominates the massive square outside.

Down the steps, below Sergels Torg, is **Sergels Arkaden**, a set of shabby underground walkways that are home to buskers, brass bands and demented lottery ticket vendors. There are sometimes political rallies and demonstrations, too, or oddball games including one known as *klädsträcket*, where students run around shivering in their underwear or less, having tied their clothes together in a line to see whose line is longest – somehow a very Swedish pastime. There's also an entrance to **T-Centralen**, the central T-bana station, as well as a gateway to Stockholm's other main department store, Åhléns, not quite as posh as NK, and an easier place to find your way around.

A short walk along Klarabergsgatan, west of Kulturhuset, brings you to the **Central Station** and **Cityterminalen**, hub of virtually all Stockholm's transport. The area around here is given over to unabashed consumerism, but there's little to get excited about in the streets around the main drag, **Drottninggatan**, just run-of-the-mill shops selling clothing and twee gifts punctuated by a *McDonald's* and the odd sausage stand. There is one highlight, however, in the **Klara kyrka** (Mon–Fri 10am–6pm, Sat 10am–7pm, Sun 8.30am–6pm), just to the south of Klarabergsgatan. Hemmed in on all sides, with only the spires visible from the streets around, the church is particularly delicate, with a light and flowery eighteenth-century painted interior and an impressive golden pulpit. Out in the churchyard, a memorial stone commemorates the eighteenth-century Swedish poet Carl Michael Bellman, whose popular, lengthy ballads are said to have been composed extempore; his unmarked grave is somewhere in the churchyard.

Three blocks further up Drottninggatan in the cobbled square, **Hötorget**, you'll find an open-air fruit, vegetable and flower market, as well as the wonderful **Hötorgshallen**, an indoor market boasting a tantalizing array of Middle Eastern sights and smells. Grab an ethnic snack here and sit yourself on the steps of the **Konserthuset** in the square; if you're lucky you might catch one of the summer classical music recitals (usually Sunday afternoons). The tall building across the square, PUB, is a former department store where **Greta Garbo** began her working life as a sales assistant in the hat section. In its basement, the small commemorative Garbo Room contains a table, sofa, bureaux, lamps, carpets and paintings from her apartment at 450 East 52nd St in New York. Beside the room are several pictures capturing the star at her best. Although she died in New York in 1990, it wasn't until 1999 that her ashes were returned to Stockholm and buried in the Skogkyrkogården cemetery. Fittingly, Hötorget, is also home to Stockholm's biggest cinema complex, Filmstaden Sergel; to the east, **Kungsgatan**, running down to Stureplan and Birger Jarlsgatan, has most of the rest of the city's cinemas (see p.98), interspersed with agreeable little cafés and bars.

North of Hötorget

From Hötorget, the city's two main streets, **Drottninggatan** and **Sveavägen** – the latter with some excellent restaurants and bars – run parallel uphill and north as far as Odengatan and the Stadsbiblioteket, or City Library, set in a little park. In secluded gardens on Sveavägen, not far north of Hötorget, sits eighteenth-century **Adolf Fredriks kyrka**, its churchyard popular with lunching office workers. Although the church has a noteworthy past – the French philosopher Descartes was buried in the church's cemetery for eleven years before his body was taken back to France in 1661 – it would have remained unremarkable, were it not for one of the most tragic – and still unexplained – events in modern Swedish history: the murder of the former prime minister **Olof Palme** in 1986 (see box overleaf).

Continuing north along Drottninggatan, you'll soon come to the intriguing **Strindbergsmuséet** at no. 85 (Strindberg Museum; Tues–Sun noon–4pm; 40kr; Ⓦ www.strindbergsmuseet.se), housed in the "Blue Tower", the last building in which the writer August Strindberg lived in Stockholm, which provides an illuminating insight into the author's curious life. The house, which was the writer's home between 1908 and 1912, is so carefully preserved that you must put plastic bags over your shoes on entering to protect the floors and furnishings. The study is a dark and gloomy place just as he left it on his death; he always wrote with the Venetian blinds and heavy curtains closed against the sunlight. Upstairs his library is a musty room with all the books firmly behind glass, which is a great shame as Strindberg was far from a passive reader. He underlined heavily and criticized in the margins as he read, though rather less eruditely than you'd expect – "Lies!", "Crap!", "Idiot!" and "Bloody hell!" tended to be his favourite comments. Good English notes are supplied free, and the nearest T-bana stop is Rådmansgatan, on the green line (direction Fridhemsplan).

Heading further north, the city gradually peters out into a number of parks and gardens (for more on which see p.85). The closest to town – officially in the area north of the centre called **Vasastaden**, and only a twenty-minute walk along Sveavägen from Adolf Fredriks kyrka – is **Vanadislunden**. Inside the park is a watersports and activities centre – **Vilda Vanadis** (June–Aug daily 10am–6pm; 50kr) – containing an outdoor pool and water slides. To get there from the centre, you can either walk from the T-bana at Odenplan, or take bus #52 from Central Station or Sergels Torg towards Karolinska Sjukhuset.

The assassination of Olof Palme

Adolf Fredriks kyrka is of immense significance to modern Swedes as the final resting place of **Olof Palme**; a simple headstone and flowers mark his grave. The then prime minster of Sweden was gunned down in front of his wife on February 28 1986, while they were on the way home from the Riviera cinema on Sveavägen. Like most Nordic leaders, Palme's fame was his security, and he had no protection staff with him when he died. A simple **plaque** on the pavement, often respectfully bedecked with flowers, now marks the spot, near the junction with Olof Palmes Gatan, where the prime minister was gunned down; the assassin escaped up the nearby flight of steps.

Sweden's biggest-ever murder inquiry was launched, and as the years went by, so the allegations of police cover-ups and bungling grew. When Christer Pettersson, a smalltime criminal, was convicted for the murder in July 1989, most Swedes thought that was the end of the story, but his release just five months later for lack of evidence only served to reopen the bitter debate, with consequent recriminations and resignations within a much-derided police force. Although it used to be that the finger of suspicion was most often pointed at immigrant Kurdish extremists, right-wing terror groups or even a hitman from within the police itself, recent theories have suggested that the corrupt regime in South Africa was behind the killing; Palme was an outspoken critic of apartheid, leading calls for an economic blockade against Pretoria.

Palme's death sent shockwaves through a society unused to political extremism of any kind, and has sadly led to a radical rethink of the open-government policy Sweden had pursued for decades. Government ministers now rarely go unescorted; security guards and self-locking doors are now commonplace in all public buildings.

The island of **Kungsholmen** and Stockholm's City Hall is only a matter of minutes from the Central Station, across Stadshusbron. Finished in 1923, **Stadshuset** (mid-May to Sept daily guided tours 10am, noon & 2pm; rest of year daily 10am & noon; 50kr; ⓦwww2.stockholm.se/stadshuset) is one of the landmarks of modern Stockholm and one of the first buildings you'll see when approaching the city from the south by train. Its simple, if somewhat drab, exterior brickwork is no preparation for the intriguing detail inside. If you're a visiting head of state you'll be escorted from your boat up the elegant waterside steps; for lesser mortals, the only way to view the innards is on one of the guided tours, which reveal the kitschy Viking-style legislative chamber and impressively echoing Golden Hall. The Stadshuset is also the departure point for **ferries** to Drottningholm, Birka, Mariefred and Gripsholm, Sigtuna and Uppsala (see "Around Stockhom", p.101).

But don't stop just at the Stadshuset; venture further into Kungsholmen and you'll discover a rash of great new bars and restaurants (see p.91), and an excellent **beach** at Smedsudden (buses #1, #4 and #62 to Västerbroplan, then a 5min walk). There's also the popular park, **Rålambshovsparken**; head through it to get to Smeduddsbadet, where you can swim in Lake Mälaren and enjoy fantastic views of the City Hall and the Old Town.

Östermalm

East of Birger Jarlsgatan, the streets become noticeably broader and grander, forming a uniform grid as far as Karlaplan. **Östermalm** was one of the last areas of central Stockholm to be developed and, with the greenery of Djurgården (see p.85) beginning to make itself felt, the impressive residences here are as likely to be consulates and embassies as fashionable homes. The first place to head for is **Nybroplan**, a square at the water's edge, a ten-minute walk just east along Hamngatan from Sergels Torg (from Gamla Stan, it's a 15min stroll from Strömbron, or take the T-bana to Östermalmstorg or bus #55) and marked by the white-stone **Kungliga Dramatiska Teatern**, Stockholm's showpiece theatre, more commonly known as Dramaten. The curved harbour in front is the departure point for all kinds of archipelago **ferries** and tours (see p.106), including a summertime ferry that makes the short journey to Djurgården via Skeppsholmen (early May to late Aug daily every 15min; 20kr).

At the back of the theatre, at Sibyllegatan 2, is the innovative **Musikmuséet** (Tues–Sun 11am–4pm; 30kr; ⓦwww.musikmuseet.se), charting the history of music in Sweden using photographs, instruments and sound recordings, and containing a range of instruments that visitors can play ("carefully", pleads the notice). Best are the sections that deal with the late nineteenth century – a time when *folkmusik* had been given fresh impetus by the growing labour movement – and inevitably, Sweden's most famous pop export **ABBA**. You can pray at the shrine of Benny's piano, stare in awe at some of the group's gold discs and jive to *Dancing Queen*, or indeed any other song ABBA recorded, all available for your listening pleasure on a computer jukebox; see the box overleaf for more.

The chief feature of this end of the city was once the barracks, part of which houses today the **Armémuséet** (Army Museum; Tues 11am–8pm, Wed–Sun 11am–4pm; ⓦwww.armemuseum.org; 60kr), opposite the Musikmuséet at Riddargatan 13. Inside are exhaustive and exhausting exhibitions covering a thousand years of war and military life – everything from precision killing machines to uniforms, swords and medals. This really is a last resort museum

Sweden's fab four: ABBA

Overturning odds of 20–1, Anni-Frid Lyngstad, Benny Andersson, Björn Ulvæus and Agnetha Fältskog first came to the world's attention as they stormed to victory in April 1974 at the Eurovision Song Contest with *Waterloo*. They went on to become the biggest-selling group in the world, topping the charts for a decade with hits like *Dancing Queen* (performed to celebrate the marriage of Swedish King Carl Gustaf to German commoner, Silvia Sommerlath in 1976), *Mamma Mia* and *Money Money Money*, and became second only to Volvo as Sweden's biggest export earner. The winning combination led to a string of Number One hits and even a film, *ABBA – The Movie*, released to popular acclaim in 1978.

However, the relentless workload of recording and touring took its toll; frictions within the group surfaced and the two couples, Agnetha and Björn and Anni-Frid and Benny, divorced and **ABBA** called it a day in 1983. News of the split was broken by the Swedish newspaper, *Dagens Nyheter* – Agnetha had casually dropped the bombshell into a conversation and to this day carries the blame for the break-up. Having withdrawn completely from public life, she now lives as a recluse on the island of Ekerö in Lake Mälaren. Anni-Frid, on the other hand, married to a German prince, lives in Switzerland and spends her time championing environmental causes. After a spell in Henley-on-Thames, near London, during the 80s, Björn is now back in Stockholm where he writes and produces music with Benny. Together they've worked on a string of musicals including *Chess* and *Mamma Mia,* which uses 27 ABBA songs to tell the tale of the relationship between a mother and her daughter.

ABBA may be no more but their memory and their music lives on: having spearheaded a worldwide revival in Seventies music, ABBA songs have provided the Australian tribute group *Björn Again* with rich pickings. Even more remarkable, though, is the number of new Swedish groups who've made the big time thanks to ABBA opening the world's eyes to Swedish music: Roxette, The Cardigans, The Wannadies, Ace of Base, Whale and Army of Lovers to name but a few. In 1999 events came full circle when Swedish singer, Charlotte Nilsson, won the Eurovision Song Contest with her ABBA-style song, *Take me to your heaven*, 25 years after the super-group's success in Brighton.

unless you have a particular interest in military history, so spare yourself the torture and stroll instead up the hill of Sibyllegatan, just west of the museums, to **Östermalmstorg** – an elegant square that's home to the quite ritzy **Östermalmshallen**, a wonderful indoor food-market. Although it looks very similar to Norrmalm's Hötorgshallen, the items here are more akin to what you might find in a smart delicatessen, along with various oddities including reindeer hearts and the wicked-smelling *surströmming* (see p.380). Wander round at lunchtime and you'll spot well-heeled ladies and gents sipping Chardonnay and munching on shrimp sandwiches.

Historiska Muséet

As you wend your way around Östermalm's well-to-do streets, sooner or later you're bound to end up at the circular **Karlaplan**, a handy T-bana and bus interchange, full of media types coming off shift from the Swedish Radio and Television buildings at the eastern end of Karlavägen. From here, it's a short walk down Narvavägen – or you can jump on a #44 bus – to the **Historiska Muséet** at nos. 13–17 (History Museum; Tues–Sun 11am–5pm; 70kr; ⓦ www.historiska.se); from Norrmalm, hop on bus #56, which runs there via Stureplan and Linnégatan. The most wide-ranging historical display in

Stockholm, it's really two large collections – a Museum of National Antiquity and the new Gold Room, with its magnificent fifth-century gold collars and other fine pieces of jewellery housed in an underground vault. On the ground floor, the prehistory section has labelling in English, and highlights include the idealized Stone Age household: flaxen-haired youth amid stripped-pine benches and rows of neatly labelled herbs and a mass of Viking weapons, coins and boats, including jewellery and bones from Birka (see p.103). Upstairs, there's a worthy collection of medieval church art and architecture, with odds and ends gathered from all over the country, evocatively housed in massive vaulted rooms. If you're moving on from Stockholm to Gotland (see p.336), be sure to take in the reassembled bits of stave churches uncovered on the Baltic island – some of the few examples that survive in Sweden.

Lidingö and Millesgården

Northeast of the city centre, **Lidingö**, is a commuter island which you'll already have glimpsed if you arrived from Finland or Estonia by ferry, as the terminal is immediately opposite on the mainland. The residential district of Stockholm's well-to-do, the island is also home to the startling **Millesgården** at Carl Milles Väg 2 (May–Sept daily 10am–5pm; Oct–April Tues–Thurs noon–4pm, Sat & Sun 11am–5pm; 75kr; ⓦwww.millesgarden.se), the outdoor sculpture collection of **Carl Milles** (1875–1955), one of Sweden's greatest sculptors and art collectors. To get to Millesgården, take the T-bana to Ropsten, then the rickety Lidingöbanan train over the bridge to Torsvikstorg, and walk down Herserudsvägen.

Phalanxes of gods, angels and beasts sit on terraces carved into the island's steep cliffs, many of the animated, classical figures also perching precariously on soaring pillars, overlooking the distant harbour. A huge *Poseidon* rears over the army of sculptures, the most remarkable of which, *God's Hand*, has a small boy delicately balancing on the outstretched finger of a monumental hand. Those who've been elsewhere in Sweden may find much of the collection familiar, as it includes copies and casts of originals adorning countless provincial towns. If this collection inspires, it's worth tracking down three other pieces by Milles in the capital – his statue of *Gustav Vasa* in the Nordic Museum on Djurgården; the *Orpheus Fountain* in Norrmalm's Hötorget; and, out at Nacka Strand (bus #404 from Slussen or Waxholm boat from Strömkajen), the magnificent *Gud på Himmelsbågen*, a claw-shaped vertical piece of steel topped with the figure of a boy, forming a stunning entrance marker to Stockholm harbour.

Lidingö is also the venue for the world's biggest cross-country race, the **Lidingöloppet**, held on the first Sunday in October. It's been staged since 1965, the thirty-kilometre course attracting an international field of around thirty thousand runners – quite a sight as they skip or crawl up and down the island's hills. For more information, or if you want to take part, ask the tourist offices in Stockholm.

Djurgården and around

East of Gamla Stan and south of Östermalm, occupying a forested island in Stockholm harbour, **Djurgården** (pronounced "Yoor-gorden") is Stockholm's most enjoyable city park. This finger-shaped island stretches over three kilometres in length from Djurgårdsbron bridge in the west (linking it to Strandvägen in Östermalm) to Blockhusudden point in the east. Royal hunting grounds throughout the sixteenth to eighteenth centuries, these days

Djurgården is in fact just one half of the *nationalstadsparken* (national city park) which helps to make Stockholm one of Europe's greenest capitals. Composed of two distinct areas of parkland, Djurgården and **Ladugårdsgärdet** (or more commonly plain Gärdet), separated by a small bay, **Djurgårdsbrunnsviken**, which is a popular area for **swimming** in summer and **skating** in winter, when it freezes over, the city park is a perfect place to escape the bustle of the capital amongst the clumps of pines. Besides taking time out from the city, you can also sample some of Stockholm's finest **museums** here.

Top of the list are the massive open-air **Skansen**, an amazing conglomeration of architecture and folk culture from around the country, and **Vasamuséet**, which houses a wonderfully preserved seventeenth-century warship. In addition, Djurgården is also home to **Nordiska Muséet**, at the foot of the Djurgårdsbron bridge, Stockholm's premier museum of exhibitions on all things Swedish, both contemporary and historical, and **Thielska Galleriet**, at Blockhusudden, a superb collection of work by Swedish artists. A full day is just about enough to see everything on Djurgården.

You can walk here through the centre out along Strandvägen, but it's quite a hike – around half an hour on foot from Sergels Torg to the Djurgårdsbron bridge across to the island. Using public **transport**, take bus #44 from Karlaplan; or from Norrmalm, buses #47 and #69 (only as far as the bridge, Djurgårdsbron); or from Gamla Stan, the ferries from Skeppsbron (all year; see p.67) or Nybroplan (early May to late Aug; see p.67).

The Nordic Museum, Skansen and Gröna Lunds Tivoli

Starting with the palatial **Nordiska Muséet** (Nordic Museum; Tues–Sun 10am–5pm, plus Mon same times late June to Aug; 60kr; ⓦwww.nordm.se), just over Djurgårdsbron from Strandvägen, is the best idea, if only because it provides a good grounding to what makes, and indeed has made, the Swedish nation tick over generations – the same cultural themes pop up repeatedly in museums not only across the capital, but across the country. The displays are a recent attempt to represent the last five hundred years of Swedish cultural history in an accessible fashion, and the *Sámi* section is particularly good. On the ground floor of the cathedral-like interior, you can't fail to spot Carl Milles's phenomenal statue of Gustav Vasa, the sixteenth-century king who drove out the Danes, and an inspirational figure who wrought the best from the sculptor (for more on whom, see p.85).

It's for **Skansen**, though, a ten-minute walk south along Djurgårdsvägen from the Nordiska Muséet, that most people come: a vast open-air museum with 150 reconstructed buildings, from a whole town to windmills and farms, laid out on a region-by-region basis (daily: May 10am–8pm; June–Aug 10am–10pm; Sept 10am–5pm; Oct–April 10am–4pm; June–Aug 60kr, otherwise 30kr; ⓦwww.skansen.se). Each section boasts its own daily activities – traditional handicrafts, games and displays – that anyone can join in. Best of the buildings are the warm and functional *Sámi* dwellings, and the craftsmen's workshops in the old-town quarter. You can also potter around a small **zoo** and a bizarre **aquarium**, fish cheek-by-jowl with crocodiles, monkeys and snakes. Partly because of the attention paid to accuracy, partly due to the admirable lack of commercialization, Skansen manages to avoid the tackiness associated with similar ventures in other countries. Even the snack bars dole out traditional foods and in winter serve up great bowls of warming soup.

Immediately opposite Skansen's main gates and at the end of the #44 bus route (bus #47 also goes by), **Gröna Lunds Tivoli** (daily: May–Sept noon–midnight; Oct–April shorter hours – check at the tourist office; admission 50kr, or 220kr for unlimited rides; ⓦ www.gronalund.com) is not a patch on its more famous namesake in Copenhagen, though decidedly cleaner and less seedy. It's definitely more of a place to stroll through rather than indulge in the rides, most of which are fairly tame, a notable exception being the Fritt Fall, a hair-raising vertical drop of 80m in just six seconds – do lunch later. At night the emphasis shifts as the park becomes the stomping ground for hundreds of Stockholm's teenagers.

Vasamuséet

Housed in an oddly shaped building, close to Nordiska Museet, **Vasamuséet** (Vasa Museum; daily: mid-June to mid-Aug 9.30am–7pm; mid-Aug to mid-June 10am–5pm, Wed until 8pm; 70kr; ⓦ www.vasamuseet.se) is without question head and shoulders above anything else that Stockholm has to offer in the way of museums. The *Vasa* warship, the pride of the Swedish fleet built on the orders of King Gustav II Adolf, sank in Stockholm harbour on her maiden voyage in 1628. A victim of engineering miscalculation and insufficient maritime knowledge, the *Vasa's* hull was simply too narrow to withstand even the slightest swell which, when coupled with top-heavy rigging, made her a maritime disaster waiting to happen. On August 10 she went down with all hands barely a few hundred metres from her moorings.

Preserved in mud for over three hundred years, the ship was raised along with twelve thousand objects in 1961, and now forms the centrepiece of a startling, purpose-built hall on the water's edge. The museum itself is built over part of the old naval dockyard. Impressive though the building is, nothing prepares you for the sheer size of the **ship**: 62m long, the main mast originally 50m above the keel, it sits virtually complete in a cradle of supporting mechanical tackle. Surrounding walkways bring you nose-to-nose with cannon hatches and restored decorative relief, the gilded wooden sculptures on the soaring prow designed to intimidate the enemy and proclaim Swedish might. Carved into the ship's stern, the resplendent figures of two naked cherubs complete with podgy stomachs and rosy cheeks, proudly bearing the Swedish crown between them, are truly remarkable for their fine detail and garish colours. Adjacent **exhibition halls** and presentations on several levels take care of all the retrieved items which give an invaluable insight into life on board – everything from combs to wooden barrels for preserving food supplies. There are reconstructions of life on board, detailed models of the *Vasa*, displays relating to contemporary social and political life, films and videos of the rescue operation, excellent English notes and regular English-language **guided tours** – in short, a must.

The Estonia Memorial

Adjacent to the museum, a more recent reminder of the power of the sea deserves your attention. Located on the Stockholm waterfront, the three 2.5-metre-high granite walls of the **Estonia Memorial**, arranged in a triangle, bear the engraved names of the 852 people who died on board the *Estonia* ferry which sank in the Baltic Sea in September 1994, while crossing from the Estonian capital, Tallinn, to Stockholm. The inscription reads simply "their names and their fate, we shall never forget".

Following the disaster, an official three-nation investigation involving Sweden, Finland and Estonia was launched to try to determine the cause of the tragedy. After much deliberation, and to great derision from the relatives of those who died on the ferry, the investigators declared that poor design by the original German shipbuilders of the huge hinges which held the bow door in place was to blame for the accident. The shipyard immediately refuted the claim and said the fault lay squarely with the ferry operator, Estline, for shoddy maintenance of the vessel. Following the publication of the official accident report, a number of conspiracy theories have surfaced, most alarmingly suggesting that the Russian mafia had weapons onboard, exploding a bomb on the car deck once it became clear that Swedish customs had been tipped off about their illicit cargo and imminent arrival in Stockholm. The wreck of the Estonia now lies on the sea bed southwest of the Finnish Åland islands covered in a protective layer of concrete to prevent plundering.

Thielska Galleriet

At the far eastern end of Djurgården (bus #69 from Norrmalm), **Thielska Galleriet** (Thiel Gallery; Mon–Sat noon–4pm, Sun 1–4pm; 50kr; Ⓦwww.thielska-galleriet.a.se) is one of Stockholm's major treasures, a fine example of both Swedish architecture and art. The house was built by Ferdinand Boberg at the turn of the twentieth century for banker Ernest Thiel, and turned it into an art gallery after he sold it to the state in 1924. Thiel knew many contemporary Nordic artists personally and gathered an impressive collection of paintings over the years, many of which are on display today. There are works by Carl Larsson, Anders Zorn – most notably his portraits and female nudes – Edvard Munch, Bruno Liljefors and even August Strindberg, whose wild Swedish landscape pictures are on display. The museum enjoys a dramatic setting at Blockhusudden, the very tip of Djurgården, and the views out over Stockholm harbour and across to the district of Nacka on the southern shore are attractive enough to warrant a trip out here.

The Kaknäs TV tower and around

It's possible to walk from Djurgården to Stockholm's famous **Kaknästornet** (Kaknäs TV tower; daily: May–Aug 9am–10pm; Sept–April 10am–9pm; 25kr), in the northern stretch of parkland known as **Ladugårdsgärdet** – head eastwards across the island on Manillavägen, over Djurgårdsbrunnsviken. At 160m, the tower is one of the tallest buildings in Scandinavia, providing excellent views over the city and archipelago, and there's a restaurant about 120m up for an elevated cup of coffee. Bus #69 from Norrmalm will also take you directly here. Beyond Ladusgårdsgärdet, north of the tower, where windmills used to pierce the skyline, lies first Frihamnen, where the Tallink ferries from Estonia dock, and just beyond that is Värtahamnen harbour and the Silja Line ferry terminal for Finland.

Ekoparken

The royal park of Djurgården, together with its northern neighbours, Haga and Ulriksdal, make up Stockholm's National City Park, **Ekoparken** (Ⓦwww.ekoparken.com). This vast stretch of urban parkland reaches all the way to the shimmering chrome-and-glass headquarters of Scandinavian Airlines, which you may have glimpsed if you came into Stockholm by bus from Arlanda airport. Once you tire of the city streets, this is the place to come, not least for the excellent **swimming** opportunities at Brunnsviken lake which runs through the northern section of the park. If you don't fancy walking all the way here – and it's a good one-hour walk from the city centre – take the T-bana to Universitetet, from where you can walk through the woods to the lake.

Södermalm and Långholmen

Whatever you do in Stockholm, don't miss the delights of the city's southern island, **Södermalm**, more often known simply as "Söder", whose craggy cliffs,

SÖDERMALM

RESTAURANTS & CAFÉS

Blå Dörren	A
Blå Lotus	R
Bonden	P
Bröderna Olssons	F
Creperie Fyra Knop	L
Dionysos	M
Folkhemmet	T
Hosteria Tre Santi	C
Indigo	N
Kvarnen	H
Lasse i Parken	B
Mellis	O
Mosebacke	D
Pelikan	S
Sjögräs	E
Snaps/Rangus Tangus	G
Soldaten Svejk	J
String	K
Tre Indier	Q

ACCOMMODATION

Alexandra	8
Anno 1647	4
Columbus	7
Gustav af Klint	3
Hökasängen	9
Youth Hostel	
Oden Söder	2
Scandic Hotel Slussen	1
Tre Små Rum	5
Zinkensdamm	6

▼ Main Line South, also Pendeltåg to Nynäshamn for Ferry to Gotland

turrets and towers rise high above the clogged traffic interchange at Slussen. The perched buildings are vaguely forbidding, but venture beyond the main roads skirting the island and a lively and surprisingly green area unfolds, one that is at heart emphatically working class. On foot from Gamla Stan, head south along any of the parallel streets that head towards Kornhamnstorg or Järntorget squares, continue past the Slussen metro station where Götgatan, Södermalm's main north-south thoroughfare, begins. To get here by public **transport**, you can either take bus #46 from Norrmalm and get off at Bondegatan, or jump on the #53 to Folkungagatan; alternatively ride the T-bana to either Slussen or, to save an uphill trek, Medborgarplatsen or Mariatorget.

Just south of Södermalmstorg is the rewarding **Stadsmuséet** (Stockholm City Museum; June–Aug daily 11am–7pm; Sept–May Tues–Sun 11am–5pm, Thurs 11am–9pm; 50kr; ⓦwww.stadsmuseum.stockholm.se), hidden in a base-ment courtyard. The Baroque building, designed by Tessin the Elder and fin-ished by his son in 1685, was once the town hall for this part of Stockholm; now it houses collections relating to the city's history as a seaport and indus-trial centre.

Fifteen minutes' walk to the southeast, the Renaissance-style **Katarina kyrka**, on Högbergsgatan, stands on the site where the remains of the victims of the so-called "Stockholm Blood Bath" (see p.513) – the betrayed nobility of Sweden who had opposed King Christian II's Danish invasion – were buried in 1520. They were burned as heretics outside the city walls, and it proved a vicious and effective coup, Christian disposing of the opposition in one fell swoop.

It's worth wandering westwards to **Mariatorget**, a spacious square where the influence of Art Nouveau on the buildings is still evident. This is one of the most desirable places for Stockholmers to live, close to the stylish bars and restaurants that are the favourite haunts of Stockholm's young and terminally hip. On bad-hair days, you can escape the latest fashions and regress to your childhood at the **Leksaksmuseum**, Mariatorget 1C (Toy Museum; Tues–Fri 10am–4pm, Sat & Sun noon–4pm; 45kr, children 25kr; ⓦwww.hotel.telemu-seum.se/leksaksmuseet), which contains everything from tin soldiers to space guns, although there's more to interest big kids than little ones, as you can't actually play with most of the toys.

Södermalm is also home to one of Stockholm's most popular parks, **Tantolunden**, located close to the Hornstull T-bana at the end of Lignagatan, and complete with an open-air theatre where performances are held in sum-mer. The island is also the place to come for **swimming pools**, as there are three in fairly close proximity: Forsgrénskabadet (Mon noon–9pm, Tues & Thurs 6.30–9pm, Wed 6.30am–6pm, Fri 6.30–7pm, Sat 9am–4pm, Sun 10am–5pm; Medborgarplatsen T-bana), Erikdalsbadet (Mon–Thu 6.30am–9pm, Fri 6.30am–8pm, Sat 9am–5pm, Sun 9am–6pm; Skanstull T-bana) with an open-air pool; and the wonderful little Liljeholmsbadet (Mon 7am–7pm women only (nude swimming), Tues & Wed 7am–4pm, Thurs 7am–5pm, Fri 7am–7pm men only (nude swimming), Sat 8am–2pm; Hornstull T-bana), a pool in a boat-like pontoon contraption that floats in Lake Mälaren. The water at Liljeholmsbadet is never cooler than 30°C, and there's an excel-lent sauna and terrace from where you can look out over the waters of the lake.

Although you'll probably end up in one of Söder's bars or restaurants (see p.94 and p.96) when night falls, it's best to get your bearings during the day, as the grids of streets become confusing in the dark. The main streets to aim for are **Götgatan**, **Folkungagatan**, **Bondegatan** and **Skånegatan** (see p.94 and p.96 for listings).

Långholmen

True to its name, which means "long island", **Långholmen** is a skinny sliver of land that lies off the northwestern tip of Södermalm, crossed by the mighty Västerbron bridge linking Södermalm with Kungsholmen. There are a couple of popular **beaches** here: **Långholmens strandbad** to the west of the bridge, rocky **Klippbadet** to the east, and – over the bridge from here – at **Smeddsudden**, on Kungsholmen. Leafy and peaceful, Långholmen is a delightful place to take a walk; on the way you'll also get some stunning views of the city, towards Stadhuset and Gamla Stan. Get to Långholmen by taking the T-bana to Hornstull and following the signs to the youth hostel, or on bus #4, which crosses Västerbron on its way from Södermalm, Kungsholmen, Norrmalm and Östermalm – incidentally, this bus ride is an excellent way of seeing a lot of the city for very little cost.

One of the better places to stay in the city is the **youth hostel** (see p.71), sited in what used to be Långholmen's large prison building. There's a **café** here in the summer, where you can sit outside in the former exercise yard – full of narrow, bricked-up runs with iron gates at one end. Alternatively, you could nip back over onto Södermalm and sample the excellent *Lasse i Parken* café (see p.95).

Eating

Eating out in Stockholm needn't be expensive – observe a few rules and you'll manage quite well. If money is tight, switch your main meal of the day to lunchtime, when on weekdays almost every café and restaurant offers an excellent-value set menu, known as *Dagens Rätt*, for 60–70kr. For evening meals, don't assume that Italian and Chinese places will be the least expensive; more often than not they're overpriced and serve food that's pretty tasteless. You're much better off seeking out one of Stockholm's many Swedish restaurants, where you're likely to find an extensive menu of traditional fare as well as some good international dishes. In fact the culinary craze in Stockholm for "fusion" dishes, a blend of Swedish cooking with other world cuisines that can lead to some surprising and delicious combinations, is still going strong.

The scourge of Swedish nightlife – high alcohol prices – is gradually being neutralized due to increased competition. In fact, drinking in Stockholm now costs roughly the same – and often less – than in London; the tired old stories about beer in Stockholm requiring a second mortgage are quite simply no longer true. Over recent years, there's been a veritable explosion in the number of **bars and pubs** in the capital, in particular British and Irish-style ones. **Beer prices** have dropped considerably and, on Södermalm especially, there are some very good deals. **Happy hours** at various places also throw up some bargains – watch out for signs outside bars and pubs advertising their particular times.

Breakfasts and snacks

Breakfasts are a Swedish speciality. If you're staying in a hotel, you're likely to be faced with a bewildering array of cereals, cheeses, cold meats and yoghurts for breakfast, to which you simply help yourself. You can return to the buffet table as many times as you want – needless to say coffee and other beverages, such as orange juice, are also included in the eat-and-drink-as-much-as-you-want spreads. Hotels are the only places that offer such extensive breakfasts, although you'll find a smaller selection in most youth hostels and plenty of good coffee, cakes and sandwiches at Stockholm's many cafés. When the hunger pangs strike, the locals pick up a *korv*, a large grilled or fried sausage in bread for 10–15kr from one of the many street vendors.

Markets and supermarkets

Of the indoor **markets**, Hötorgshallen (Mon–Thurs 10am–6pm, Fri till 6.30pm, Sat 10am–4pm) in Hötorget (see p.81) is cheaper and more varied than the posher and downright expensive Östermalmshallen (Mon 10am–6pm, Tue–Fri 9am–6pm, Sat 9am–3pm) in Östermalmstorg (see p.84). **Hötorgshallen** is awash with small cafés and ethnic snacks, but for **fruit and vegetables**, buy either from the cheaper open-air market outside, or from the summer stalls outside most T-bana stations, especially in the suburbs (conveniently, the ones outside Slussen and Brommaplan T-bana stations are open all year). Pleasant for a wander, **Östermalmshallen** has all kinds of unusual eats; however, most of what's on sale here can be bought at lower prices from the city's biggest **supermarket**, in the basement of Åhléns department store at Sergels Torg. There are also several other central supermarkets: try Konsum in Järntorget in Gamla Stan and Tempo at the Gamla Stan T-bana station.

Cafés and restaurants

Day or night, the main areas for decent eating are, in the city centre, the triangle marked out by Norrmalmstorg, Birger Jarlsgatan and Stureplan; in Östermalm, Grev Turegatan; and in Södermalm, around Folkungagatan, Skånegatan and Bondegatan. In Kungsholmen, restaurants are more spread out, so it helps to know your destination before you set off. Several restaurants in Gamla Stan are also worth checking out, though they tend to be a little expensive. For the best choice in terms of price and variety, head south for Södermalm, where you'll find the more trendy and chic **cafés** and **restaurants**, and a broader range of cuisines. A good way to keep costs down when eating out is to resist the temptation to order a starter – throughout Sweden portions are generous and most main dishes are large enough to fill even the emptiest stomach.

In recent years, a rash of good daytime **cafés** has appeared, where you can sit over coffee and cake and just watch the world go by. It's worth noting the best ones: *Wayne's* and *Robert's Coffee* in the city centre; *Chokladkoppen* in Gamla Stan; *Saturnus* in Östermalm; and in Södermalm, *Indigo* and the studenty *String* and *Lasse i Parken* (see pp.93–95).

Some of the places listed below also appear in the "Nightlife and culture" section (p.95), as there's a fairly fine line between restaurants and bars in Sweden, with many places offering music and entertainment in the evening as well as food throughout the day.

Norrmalm

The following cafés and restaurants are marked on the maps on p.62 & p.73.

Babs Kök & Bar Birger Jarlsgatan 37. Young, trendy, atmosphere at this quirky restaurant/bar serving mostly meat dishes including a tasty duck terrine with pear and raisin. Mains around 120kr.

Biblos Biblioteksgatan 9. A wonderfully trendy café and restaurant right in the centre of town – a good place to people-watch whilst sampling a dish from the eclectic menu at 120–150kr each.

Bon Lloc Regeringsgatan 111 ☎08/660 60 60. One of the capital's best restaurants. The award-winning Euro-Latino dishes with a hint of Swedish home-cooking are accompanied by an impressive array of top Spanish wines. Starters from 165kr, mains from 275kr. Reservations necessary.

East Stureplan 13. One of the city's finest restaurants. Trendy to a T, with excellent food – lots of fish and Asian-style dishes: lunch around 75kr; dinner from 150kr.

Fredsgatan 12 Fredsgatan 12. A delicious mix of

Swedish and international cuisine, though on the expensive side. Check out the outside bar in summer.

Halv trappa plus gård Lästmakargatan 3, at Stureplan. This is one of Stockholm's most popular eateries, serving modern European dishes – particularly fish. It's a good place to people-watch especially outside in summer in the rear garden. Main courses for 150kr.

IKKI Kungsgatan 44, upstairs in the *Kungshallen*. A Japanese sushi bar that's very popular, especially at lunchtime. Lots of fish and grilled things on skewers. Main dishes from 150kr.

KB Smålandsgatan 7. Excellent Swedish food in posh surroundings and a favourite haunt of authors and artists – quite simply, a Stockholm institution. Reckon on at least 250kr for a main course.

Konditori Kungstornet Kungsgatan 28. Popular 1950s-style Swedish coffee house with excellent cakes and sandwiches around 60kr.

Köket Sturegallerian 30. Very popular (though rather pricey) place for snacks (from 100kr) when the nightclubs have closed. Thurs–Sun open until 3am.

Lao Wai Luntmakargatan 74. This was Sweden's first East Asian restaurant and is decidedly good, though not especially cheap. Chinese and Vietnamese main courses around 200kr.

Operakällaren Operahuset, Gustav Adolfs Torg. A bill at the famous Opera House restaurant will make a serious dent in your wallet (starters from 175kr) but the daily smorgasbord (Mon–Sat 11.30am–3pm, Sun noon–6pm) is fabulous, although it's still around 495kr per person. A better bet is the *Bakfickan* around the back where simpler (and much cheaper) dishes are served from the same kitchen – main courses range from 85kr–192kr.

Peppar Torsgatan 34. Attractive, moderately priced Cajun restaurant with decent-sized portions. Unfortunately, dishes are geared towards a none-too-adventurous Swedish palate and can sometimes be disappointingly bland.

Prinsen Mäster Samuelsgatan 4. Traditional old place frequented by artists, musicians and writers. Very expensive, though delicious, Swedish food.

Restaurangen Oxtorgsgatan 14. No starters or main courses here – you simply put together a Swedish meal consisting of three or five small dishes. Run by one of Stockholm's top chefs and accordingly expensive.

Roberts Coffee Kungsgatan 44. Just inside the door of the *Kungshallen* food hall, and a popular place to meet friends for a good cup of coffee.

Rolfs Kök Tegnergatan 41. Popular central restaurant close to Hötorget with a special line in Asian and Cajun stir-fried food; fairly expensive prices – count on at least 150kr per dish.

Sawadee Olofsgatan 6. Next to Hötorget T-bana. Attractive Thai restaurant with a wonderful 165kr special dinner and reasonably priced drinks.

Tip Top Thai Sveavägen 57. A style-conscious place serving a range of Thai food – everything from *tom kha gai* chicken soup to coconut ice cream – plus some Swedish home-cooking, although it's all a bit pricey. Very popular gay venue.

Wayne's Kungsgatan 14. A popular café for smart city types and trendy young things, who sip cappuccinos while pretending to read foreign newspapers.

Östermalm

The following cafés and restaurants are marked on the maps on p.62 & p.73.

Aubergine Linnégatan 38. An up-market and expensive place on one of Östermalm's busiest streets. Lots of wood and glass. The separate bar menu brings prices within reach – chicken on a skewer is good at 90kr – though otherwise it's fusion fare costing around 170kr.

Blå Porten Djurgårdsvägen 64. The best café in all of Stockholm is actually on Djurgården in a glass-walled building overlooking a courtyard where outdoor seating is arranged around an old fountain. The open sandwiches and lunches here are inspired by French Provençal cuisine – the carrot salad with flatleaf parsley and vegetarian bean soup are excellent. Mains from 65–98kr, cakes 10–30kr.

Elverket Linnégatan 69. Tasty international food served up in a restaurant attached to a theatre. Spacious lounge for drinks before dinner or relaxation afterwards.

Grodan Grev Turegatan 16. Swedish for "the frog", hence the name *La Grenouille* on the outside, and a favourite haunt for many Stockholmers. French cuisine at moderate prices –150–200kr.

Il Conte Grevgatan 9. This restaurant is rumoured to be the best Italian in town; the pasta is excellent and very good value at around 130kr per dish.

Meaning Green Norrlandsgatan 2. Decent veggie food served at one of the city's better vegetarian restaurants at quite reasonable prices.

PA & Co Riddargatan 8. Fashionable restaurant with international dishes, some good old Swedish favourites and a few inventive "crossovers" dishes – count on around 150–200kr per dish.

Samuraj Kommendörsgatan 40. A good Japanese place known for its fine food and friendly staff but it's generally over 200kr per dish.

Saturnus Erikbergsgatan 6. Good, moderately priced pasta, huge cakes and massive sandwiches – a café by day, with a formal restaurant service in the evening.

Stockholms Glass och Pastahus Valhallavägen 155. Excellent fresh pasta and home-made ice cream at this inexpensive place. Closed evenings.

Wedholms Fisk Nybrokajen 17. Classy fish restaurant with an extensive menu but rather steep prices – mains start at around 170kr.

Örtagården Nybrogatan 31. Top-notch, though still affordable, vegetarian fare dished up under a huge chandelier in turn-of-the-twentieth-century surroundings. Dozens of different salads, hot main courses and soups.

Gamla Stan

The following cafés and restaurants are marked on the maps on p.62 & p.73.

Bistro Ruby and **Grill Ruby** Österlånggatan 14. *Bistro Ruby* is a pricey French bistro in the heart of the Old Town, tastefully done up in Parisian style but expensive. Next door, though in the same building, is *Grill Ruby*, a favourite among hungry journalists and writers, serving up American-style grills of meat and fish (85–192kr) and weekend brunches.

Café Art Västerlånggatan 60–62, Gamla Stan. A fifteenth-century cellar-café with sandwiches plus good coffee and cakes. The works of art on the walls are for sale.

Chokladkoppen Stortorget 18, Gamla Stan. A fabulous café specializing in rich chocolate tart and overlooking the grand old square. Coffee served in badly designed handless cups. Popular with the city's gay coffee drinkers.

Den Gyldene Freden Österlånggatan 51. Stockholm's oldest restaurant, housed in vaulted cellars and adorned with elegant wall paintings, was opened in 1772. Prices are a bit steep at around 450kr for two traditional Swedish courses without drinks, but the atmosphere, food and style are unparalleled.

Gondolen Stadsgården 6. At the top of the Katarina lift. Breathtaking views over Stockholm from this high-level restaurant right on the seafront. The place is divided into two restaurants, one of which is dramatically cheaper (where main dishes from the eclectic menu go for about 150kr).

Hermitage Stora Nygatan 11. Vegetarian restaurant that's well worth checking out for its hearty dishes; lunches for 50kr, main courses cost 60–120kr. Mon–Sat till 8pm, Sun to 7pm.

Medelhavet Lilla Nygatan 21. Good central Mediterranean restaurant with an intimate bar,

Bläckfisken, next door.

Pontus in the Green House Österlånggatan 17. With main courses at 300–450kr, this is the place to come if you want to splash out. Luxury Swedish-style food served by one of the city's top chefs, though the atmosphere can be a little stuffy.

Södermalm

The following cafés and restaurants are marked on the map on p.89.

Blå Dörren Södermalmstorg 6. Beer hall and restaurant with excellent, but expensive (around 175kr per dish), Swedish food.

Blå Lotus Katrina Bangata 21. Oriental decor covers the basement walls of this hangout for a young alternative crowd. There's outdoor seating in summer. Breakfast available.

Bonden Bondegatan 1C. Small, cosy restaurant with rough brick walls. Main courses here go for around 130kr: try the delicious fillet of chicken with morel mushrooms in red wine sauce and potato gratin.

Bröderna Olssons Folkungagatan 84. If you like garlic this is definitely the place for you, with every conceivable dish laced with the stuff. Main courses from 200kr, washed down by an extensive choice of different vodkas and akvavit.

Creperie Fyra Knop Svartensgatan 4. A rare treat in Stockholm – excellent, affordable crepes at around 50kr each served in this dark, evocative restaurant which is fashionably tatty and plays the likes of Leonard Cohen.

Dionysos Bondegatan 56. Tasteful Greek decor gives this place a homely feel, and the food is excellent: grilled *halloumi* for 68kr, *souvlakia* for 140kr.

Folkhemmet Renstiernas Gata 30. Very popular place serving Swedish home-cooking and international dishes (150kr for a main course) to young trendies and media types. Packed at weekends.

Hannas Krog Skånegatan 80. A firm favourite and popular haunt of Söder trendies. It's crowded and noisy with lunch deals for around 60kr, evening dishes for around 100–150kr. Also a popular evening drinking haunt.

Hosteria Tre Santi Blekingegatan 32. One of Södermalm's better Italian restaurants and excellent value for money – always busy.

Indigo Götgatan 19. Near Götgatan exit from Slussen T-bana. The ideal place to stop off for an afternoon cappuccino. Good pastries and cakes, too – the carrot cake is a house speciality.

Indira Bondegatan 3B. The area's biggest Indian restaurant, with a good tandoori-based menu. Takeaway food also. Main dishes cost 80–110kr.

Kvarnen Tjärhovsgatan 4. Small beer hall with simple Swedish food – lunch for around 50kr. Evening dishes, fish and meat, for 150kr. Open till 3am.

Lasse i Parken Högalidsgatan 56. Daytime café housed in an eighteenth-century house, with a pleasant garden that's very popular in summer. Also handy for the beaches at Långholmen. June–Aug only daily 11am–5pm.

Mellis Skånegatan 83–85. Another popular restaurant on this busy restaurant street. Greek, French and Swedish dishes served at reasonable prices. A nice place for coffee and cakes, too.

Mosebacke Mosebacke Torg 3. The place to come on a sunny lunchtime: sit outside and enjoy views over the harbour and the old town. The salmon is particularly good.

Pelikan Blekingegatan 40. Atmospheric, working-class Swedish beer hall (from the entrance hall turn right) with excellent traditional food, such as *pytt i panna* for 89kr. Left of the entrance hall is a smarter restaurant with a more up-market menu, though still based on Swedish home-cooking – mains around 120kr.

Sjögräs Timmermansgatan 24. A modern approach to Swedish cooking, influenced by world cuisines; with mains for around 180kr. Stylish interior with plain walls and cosy sofas that are always packed.

Snaps/Rangus Tangus Medborgarplatsen. Good old-fashioned but reasonably priced Swedish food in a 300-year-old building. Very popular – especially in summer, when there's outdoor seating in the square.

Soldaten Svejk Östgötagatan 35. Lively Czech-run joint that draws in a lot of students. Simple menu with dishes around the 120kr mark. Large selection of Czech beers; Staropramen for 44kr.

String Nytorgsgatan 38. If you fancy yourself as a writer, or if you just fancy yourself, you'll fit in well at this retro studenty café. Good for cheapish coffee with muffins or brownies for 15–30kr.

Tre Indier Möregatan 2. Slightly tucked away in a tiny street off Åsögatan (take bus #55 in the direction of Södra Hammarbyhamnen to the junction of Västgötagatan and Åsögatan), but well worth seeking out. A lively evening Indian restaurant. 150kr.

Kungsholmen

The following cafés and restaurants are marked on the map on p.62.

El Cubanito Scheelegatan 3. Delicious, reasonably priced Cuban food that deservedly attracts people from across town – be sure to try the delicious marinated squid – starters from 69kr, mains 89–198kr. Impressive choice of Caribbean rums and cocktails also available. Always packed.

La Famiglia Alströmergatan 45. One of Kungsholmen's better Italian places and a good one for a first date; even Frank Sinatra once ate here. Expensive.

Roppongi Hantverkargatan 76. The best place on the island for sushi and other Japanese delights – though none of it comes cheap.

Salt Hantverkaregatan 34. On the island's main road, it serves stodgy traditional Swedish fare (around 150kr per dish), including elk burgers, though ask for plenty to drink if you're eating the salty slabs of pork. The restaurant is as Swedish as they come – red painted walls, elk antlers and assorted souvenirs from past caravanning holidays.

Spisa hos Göken Pontonjärgatan 28. This small gay-run neighbourhood restaurant is an excellent choice for modern Swedish food, as well as Thai-inspired dishes, all served up in a restaurant with outdoor seating in summer and great views out towards Långholmen and Södermalm. Sat & Sun brunch (noon–4pm) are inordinately popular.

Utsökt Scheelegatan 12. A good choice for Swedish specialities such as salmon, venison and flounder – all around 175kr. This is a place to experience fine dining in formal surroundings while admiring the well-manicured garden at the rear.

Nightlife and culture

There's plenty to keep you occupied in Stockholm, from pubs and clubs to the **cinema** and **theatre**. Many establishments have an unwritten dress-code so it's best to leave your jeans and trainers at home if you want to get past the bouncers. Be prepared, too, to cough up around 15–20kr to leave your coat at the cloakroom, a requirement at many bars and pubs as well as at discos, particularly in winter. As well as Friday and Saturday night, Wednesday night is an active time in Stockholm, with lots going on and queues outside the more popular places. Swedes, and especially Stockholmers, are fairly reserved, so don't expect to immediately get chatting to people – in fact it is positively fashionable to be cool and aloof. However, after a few drinks, it's usually easy enough to strike up conversation. Most places will open around 10pm although they don't fill up for an hour or so and close around 3-4am.

For **information** on what's happening in Stockholm, the aptly–named *What's On*, free from the tourist office, is particularly good for all kinds of listings. It contains day-by-day information about a whole range of events – gigs, theatre, festivals, dance – sponsored by the city, many of which are free and based around Stockholm's many parks. The publication is year round though the open-air events only take place in summer. There's also a free Saturday supplement to the *DN* newspaper, *på stan* — get someone to translate if your Swedish isn't up to it – that details all manner of entertainments, from the latest films to club listings; it's available in bars and restaurants.

Popular venues in summer are Kungsträdgården and Skansen, where there's always something going on. **Kulturhuset** in Sergels Torg has a full range of artistic and cultural events – mostly free – and the information desk on the ground floor has programmes to give away.

Bars, brasseries and pubs

The majority of Stockholmers do their drinking and eating together, and several of the places listed below also serve food. If you just want to do some serious **drinking**, the capital certainly has enough establishments to choose from, nearly all open seven days a week.

Norrmalm and Östermalm

Berns Berzelii Park, Nybroplan. One of the chicest brasseries in town, with the current interior design by London's Sir Terence Conran. Originally made famous by writer August Strindberg, who picked up character ideas here for his novel, *The Red Room*.

Café Opera Opera House, Gustav Adolfs Torg. If you don't mind your Gucci gear getting crumpled, and you can stand just one more Martini, join the queue outside. Daily till 3am.

Dubliner Smålandsgatan 8. One of the busiest Irish pubs in town, with live music most evenings.

East Bar Stureplan. Loud tunes, loud dress and loud mouths. Great fun.

Lydmar Sturegatan 10. Definitely one of the most popular bars in Stockholm. The clientele are very elegant so dress up to get past the bouncers.

Storstad Odengatan 41. A popular hangout with Stockholm's media crowd and local celebrities. Packed at weekends with a card-flashing crowd.

Sturecompagniet Sturegatan 4. One of Stockholm's leading nightspots with three floors of bars; something for everybody and worth a look, although it can get packed. Expensive beer.

Tranan Karlbergsvägen 14. An atmospheric old workers' beer hall, in the basement, which is one of Stockholm's best and most popular drinking holes.

Gamla Stan

Gråmunken Västerlånggatan 18. Cosy café-bar that's usually very busy. Sometimes has live music to jolly things along.

Kaos Stora Nygatan 21. An unpretentious young

fashion-conscious crowd gathers here for a good time. DJs at weekends.

Kleins Kornhamnstorg 51. One of the bigger bars in Gamla Stan and definitely worth a look.

Södermalm

Akkurat Hornsgatan 18. This famous spot is known for its 200 different types of whisky and extensive beer selection, including an impressive array of Belgian varieties.

Bonden Bar Bondegatan 1B. Just along from the *Bonden* restaurant and down a series of steps. A good choice for an evening beer before strutting

your stuff on the adjoining dance floor.

Fenix Götgatan 40. A loud and brash American-style bar that's always busy with clientele who are here for the sole purpose of drinking large quantities of beer.

Folkhemmet Renstiernas Gata 30. Trendy hangout for 20- to 30-somethings. Inordinately popular at weekends.

Gröne Jägaren Götgatan 64. Some of the cheapest beer in Stockholm; *storstark* is 24kr until 9pm – perhaps inevitably, its clientele tend to get raucously drunk.

H₂O/Eld Tjärhovsgatan 4. In the basement underneath the *Kvarnen* beer hall, these two trendy new bars are always popular. Open till 3am. *H₂O*, decorated entirely in blue and white ceramic tiles and resembling a public toilet, is the better of the two, where hanging out at the bar is the in-thing to do. *Eld* has a resident DJ most nights of the week.

Both places attract Stockholm's well-dressed, well-heeled and well-tipsy.

Kvarnen Tjärhovsgatan 4. Another busy beer hall; this one is a favourite haunt of southside football fans.

O'Learys Götgatan 11–13. Södermalm's most popular Irish pub is good for watching sport on the widescreen TV and then for stumbling back to the nearby Slussen T-bana.

Pelikan Blekingegatan 40. A fantastic old beer hall full of character – and characters.

Clubs

The **club scene** in Stockholm is limited, and several clubs also function as restaurants and bars. Cover charges aren't too high at around 100kr, but beer gets more expensive as the night goes on, reaching as much as 55kr, a glass and in the places that function as restaurants you'll have to order food, too. In Stockholm, as in the rest of Sweden, there is very little real crossover with the gay scene; for more on gay Stockholm, see p.98.

Aladdin Barnhusgatan 12–14, Norrmalm ☎08/10 09 32. One of the city's most popular dance-restaurants, close to the Central Station, often with live bands. Expensive.

Blacknuss & Jazzjoint Mosebacke torg 3, Södermalm. One of the longest-established clubs in town; every second Fri (odd weeks) groove to an eclectic mix of soul, funk, R'n'B and live bands

Dailys Kungsträdgården The *G-Klubben* section inside this nightclub complex, complete with strip-lights on the stairs, is where you'll find Stockholm's movers and shakers. Be young, beautiful and trendy.

Fasching Kungsgatan 63, Norrmalm ☎08/21 62 67, ⊛www.fasching.se. Stockholm's premier jazz venue, with local acts and big international names.

Patricia Stadsgårdskajen, Slussen, Södermalm ☎743 05 70, ⊛www.patricia.st. Formerly the royal yacht of Britain's Queen Mother, today a restaurant-disco-bar with fantastic views of the city across the harbour. The menu, with a huge variety of imaginative main courses (from Thai stir-fries to fresh lobster or chicken *fajitas*) is quite simply terrific. Wed–Sun; gay on Sun (see p.99).

Club Nocturna Mosebacke torg 3, Södermalm. *The* place for latin, salsa, mambo and rumba. Sat only.

Sturecompagniet Sturegatan 4, Norrmalm. Strut to house and techno and a fantastic light show, or work your way through three floors of bars. Very popular.

Live music: rock and jazz

When there's live **rock** and **jazz** music at bars and cafés, it will mostly be provided by local bands, for which you'll pay around 100kr entrance. Most international big names make it to Stockholm, playing at a variety of seated halls and stadiums – tickets for these are, of course, much more expensive. The main **large venue** is the Stockholm Globe Arena (the largest spherical building in the world), Johanneshov (T-bana Gullmarsplan; ☎08/600 34 00, ⊛www.globen.se).

Cirkus Djurgårdsslätten 43 ☎08/587 987 00, ⊛www.cirkus.se. Occasional rock and R&B performances.

Daily News Kungsträdgården, Norrmalm ☎08/21 56 55, ⊛www.dailys.nu. This central rock venue hosts the most consistent range of live music in town – everything from grunge to techno.

Engelen Kornhamnstorg 59, Gamla Stan ☎08/20

10 92, ⊛www.wallmans.com. Live jazz, rock or blues nightly until 3am, but arrive early to get in; the music starts at 8.30pm (Sun 9pm).

Fasching Kungsgatan 63, Norrmalm ☎08/21 62 67, ⊛www.fasching.se. Local and foreign contemporary jazz; a good place to go dancing too. Closed Sun.

Nalen Regeringsgatan 74 ☎08/566 398 00,

ⓦwww.landh-taube.se/gn. Once *the* place to hear music in the city (even the Beatles were booked to play here), now offering jazz, swing and big band. **Södra Teatern** Mosebacke torg 3, Södermalm ⓣ08/556 972 30. This is one of the best places in the capital for world music, hip hop, rock and pop – if it's happening anywhere, it's happening here. Weekends only.

Stampen Stora Nygatan 5, Gamla Stan ⓣ08/20 57 93. Long-established and rowdy jazz club, both trad and mainstream; occasional foreign names, too.

Tre Backar Tegnérgatan 12–14, Norrmalm ⓣ08/673 44 00; T-bana Rådmansgatan. Good, cheap pub with a cellar for live music performances. Rock and blues nightly Mon–Sat until midnight.

Classical music, theatre and cinema

Classical music is always easy to find in Stockholm; many museums – particularly the History Museum and Music Museum – have regular programmes, and there's generally something on at one of the following venues: Konserthuset in Hötorget, Norrmalm (ⓣ08/10 21 10); Berwaldhallen, Strandvägen 69, Östermalm (ⓣ08/784 18 00, ⓦwww.sr.se/berwaldhallen); and Musikaliska Akademien, Blasieholmstorg 8, near the National Art Museum (ⓣ08/20 68 18). **Organ and choral music** can be heard at Adolf Fredriks kyrka, Holländargatan 16 in Norrmalm and St Jakobs kyrka in Kungsträdgården Norrmalm, Gustav Wasa kyrka in Odenplan, and Storkyrkan in Gamla Stan; for more details consult *What's On*. Operan, on Gustav Adolfs Torg, is Stockholm's main **opera** house (ⓣ08/24 82 40, ⓦwww.operan.se); for less rarefied presentations of the classics, check out the programme at Dramaten, Nybroplan in Östermalm (ⓣ08/667 06 80, ⓦwww.dramaten.se).

Theatre and cinema

There are dozens of **theatres**, but only one has regular performances of **English-language productions**: Vasa Teatern, Vasagatan 19 (ⓣ08/24 82 40). If you want tickets for anything else theatrical, it's often worth waiting for reduced-price standby tickets, available from the kiosk in Norrmalmstorg.

Cinema-going is an incredibly popular pastime in Stockholm, with screenings of new releases nearly always full. The largest venue in the city centre is Filmstaden Sergel in Hötorget (ⓣ08/562 600 00, ⓦwww.sf.se), but there are also a good number of cinemas the entire length of Kungsgatan between Sveavägen and Birger Jarlsgatan, always very lively on Saturday night. Tickets cost around 80kr and films are never dubbed into Swedish.

Finally, **Kulturhuset**(ⓦwww.kulturhuset.stockholm.se) in Sergels Torg has a full range of artistic and cultural events, most of them free; the information desk on the ground floor has free programmes.

Gay Stockholm

Given that Stockholm is a capital city, the **gay scene** (ⓦwww.stockholmtown .com/gay) is disappointingly small and closeted. Attitudes in general are tolerant, but expectations of gay couples walking hand-in-hand or kissing in the street are just another false assumption about Sweden. Until just a few years ago, there was only one gay place in the whole of the city. Thankfully, the country has now freed itself from the tax rules that made it hard for the smaller bars to stay afloat, and gay bars are springing up all over the place. The main **bars** and **clubs** to be seen at – and definitely to do the seeing – are listed below. However, they are all mostly male hangouts; lesbians in Stockholm have an even lower profile, and even the beaches listed below are male only.

The city's main **gay centre** is at Sveavägen 57; the upstairs offices house the headquarters of Sweden's **gay rights group**, Riksförbundet för sexuellt lik-aberättigande (National Association for Sexual Equality), which is a great source of information (☎08/736 02 12, ⓦwww.rfsl.se). Besides offering HIV advice (☎08/736 02 11), they run a free newspaper, *Kom Ut*; a bookshop, Rosa Rummet; a restaurant, café, bar and club (see below) and a radio station. A second newspaper, *QX* (ⓦwww.qx.se) is also available at gay bars and clubs and is handy for listings. **Gay Pride Week** (☎08/33 59 55, ⓦwww.stockholm-pride.org) is the second week of August and features special events ranging from live bands to discussion forums.

Bars, restaurants and clubs

Bitch Girl Club Kolingsborg, Slussen ☎070/748 14 24. Scandinavia's biggest lesbian club, held every other Friday in summer. Saturday rest of year. Close to the main exit of the Slussen T-bana (9pm–3am).

Häktet Hornsgatan 82 ☎08/84 59 10; T-bana Zinkensdamm. A wonderful place with two bars, front and back, as well as a quiet sitting room and a beautiful outdoor courtyard – a real haven in summer. Open Wed & Fri nights only. Mostly women on Wed.

Mandus Österlånggatan 7 ☎08/20 60 55. Kitsch and unpretentious gay restaurant where the service is as fun as the food – a tasty mix of Swedish, Thai and Mediterranean cuisines. Evenings are often busy (no bookings taken) so it pays to arrive early to secure a table or enjoy a beer – and a lot of attention from the bar staff – before dining.

Patricia Stadsgårdskajen ☎08/743 05 70, ⓦwww.patricia.st. The Queen Mother's former yacht attracts queens from across Stockholm for fun on Sunday nights (no entrance fee if you eat in the restaurant), often with drag acts or stand-up comedy. A great place for romantic evenings with views across the harbour. The food is top-quality crossover style with some Swedish home-cooking too. Reckon on 170kr per dish.

Regnbågsrummet Sturecompagniet, Stureplan (Fri & Sat 10pm–5am). Currently the hippest club hence long queues.

Sidetrack Wollmar Yxkullsgatan 7 ☎08/641 16 88, ⓦwww.sidetrack.nu. Dark and smoky British-style pub popular with leather and denim boys. Men only.

TipTop Sveavägen 57 ☎08/32 98 00. Stockholm's main gay men's venue – a club, restaurant and bar all rolled into one – and very popular, especially on Friday and Saturday nights. Open daily.

Torget Mälartorget 13, Gamla Stan ☎08/20 55 60, ⓦwww.torgetbaren.nu. Opposite Gamla Stan tube station and an elegant place for a drink at any time of the evening. Always busy and full of beauties. Open daily.

Gay beaches

Freskati Universitetet T-bana. Turn left out of the underground station, past the Pressbyrån kiosk, walk under the bridge and towards the trees. A popular sunbathing spot.

Kärsön Brommaplan T-bana, then buses #177, #301–323, #336 or #338 towards Drottningholm palace. Get off at the stop over the bridge and take the path to the right along the water's edge. If you want to sunbathe nude and swim in Lake Mälaren, this island is where to come: woodpeckers in the trees, deer in the forest and men dozing in the sunshine; a truly wonderful place.

Listings

Airlines American Airlines ☎08/78 03 55; British Airways ☎020/78 11 44; Delta Air Lines ☎08/587 691 01; Finnair ☎020/78 11 00; Icelandair ☎08/690 98 00; KLM and Northwest ☎08/593 624 30; Malmö Aviation, Bromma airport ☎08/597 915 62; Ryanair ☎0911/23 36 88; SAS Stureplan 8 ☎020/72 77 27; United Airlines ☎020/79 54 02.

Airport enquiries Arlanda ☎08/797 61 00; Arlanda SAS domestic flights ☎08/797 50 50; Bromma ☎08/797 68 00; Skavsta ☎0155/28 04 00; Västerås ☎021/80 56 00.

Banks and exchange Banks generally stay open later in central Stockholm than in the rest of the country – usually Mon–Fri 9.30am–3pm, though some stay open until 5.30pm; the bank at Arlanda is open even longer hours. Forex exchange offices offer better value than the banks for changing money; branches can be found in the main hall at Central Station (daily 7am–9pm); at Cityterminalen (Mon–Fri 7am–8pm, Sat & Sun 8am–5pm); Vasagatan 14 (Mon–Fri 9am–7pm, Sat 9am–4pm); in the Sverigehuset (Mon–Fri 8am–7pm, Sat & Sun 9am–5pm); and at Arlanda airport Terminal 2 (daily 6am–9pm).

Beaches City beaches are Långholmens Strandbad and Klippbad on Långholmen – T-bana Hornstull; Smedsudden on Kungsholmen – buses #1, #4 and #62 from Central Station towards Fredhäll, get off at Västerbroplan; Hellasgården lake in Nacka (an eastern suburb of Stockholm) – bus #401 from Slussen; Saltsjöbaden – take the Saltsjöbanan train from Slussen. There are also good, if small, sandy beaches in the archipelago on the island of Grinda (see p.107) – boats from Strömkajen.

Bookshops English-language books are available at Akademibokhandeln, corner of Regeringsgatan & Mäster Samuelsgatan; Aspingtons second-hand bookshop, Västerlånggatan 54; Hedengrens Bokhandel, Sturegallerian, Stureplan 4; Sweden Bookshop, Sverigehuset, Hamngatan 27.

Bus enquiries For SL bus information see "SL travel information" below; for long-distance bus information call Swebus Express on ☎0200/218 218 or visit ⓦwww.swebusexpress.se; for Svenska Buss call ☎0771/67 67 67.

Car breakdown recovery Larmtjänst ☎020/22 00 00).

Car rental Avis, Vasagatan 10B, and Arlanda and Bromma airports ☎020/78 82 00, ⓦwww.avis-se.com; Budget, Klarabergsviadukten 92 ☎08/411 15 00, ⓦwww.budget-sweden.com; Europcar, Tegelbacken 6 ☎08/611 45 60, ⓦwww.europcar.se; Hertz, Vasagatan 26 ☎020/211 211, ⓦwww.hertz.se.

Dental problems Emergency dental care at St Eriks Hospital, Fleminggatan 22; daily 8am–8.30pm. Out of hours ring Stockholm Care on ☎08/672 24 00.

Doctor Tourists can get emergency outpatient care at the hospital for the district they are staying in; check with Stockholm Care ☎08/672 24 00.

Embassies and consulates Australia, Sergels Torg 12 ☎08/613 29 00; Canada, Tegelbacken 4 ☎08/453 30 00; Ireland, Östermalmsgatan 97 ☎08/661 80 05; New Zealand – use the Australian Embassy; UK, Skarpögatan 6–8 ☎08/671 30 00; US, Dag Hammarskjöldsväg 31 ☎08/783 53 00.

Emergencies Ring ☎112 for police, ambulance or fire services.

Ferries Tickets for Finland from Silja Line at Stureplan or Värtahamnen (☎08/22 21 40, ⓦwww.silja.com), and from Viking Line at Stadsgårdsterminalen (☎08/452 40 00, ⓦwww.vikingline.se); tickets for Estonia from Tallink, Frihamnen (☎08/667 00 01, ⓦwww.tallink.se); for the archipelago from Waxholms Ångfartygs AB, Strömkajen (☎08/679 58 30, ⓦwww.waxholmsbolaget.se).

Internet access *Internet Café*, 3rd floor, Pub department store, 63 Drottningatan; *Café Access*, Kulturhuset, Sergels torg ; *Nine*, Odengatan 44; *Cafe Zenit*, Sveavägen 20; reckon on 40–60kr per hour.

Laundry Self-service laundry at Västmannagatan 61; or try the youth hostels.

Left luggage There are lockers at Central Station (from 30kr per day), the Cityterminalen bus station and the Silja and Viking ferry terminals.

Lost property Östra Kyrkogatan 4 at the Central Station ☎08/412 69 60.

Newspapers Buy them at kiosks in the central train station, Cityterminalen or at the Press Stop which has branches in the Gallerian shopping centre on Hamngatan and also at Sveavägen 52. Read them for free at Stadsbiblioteket (City Library), Sveavägen 73, or at Kulturhuset, Sergels Torg.

Pharmacy 24-hour service at C. W. Scheele, Klarabergsgatan 64 (☎08/454 81 30).

Police Headquarters at Agnegatan 33–37, Kungsholmen (☎08/401 00 00), but the city-centre station is at Tulegatan 4 ☎08/401 12 00.

Post office Most useful office is in the Central Station (Mon–Fri 7am–10pm, Sat & Sun 10am–7pm). Poste restante mail can be addressed to any post office; you'll need to show your passport when collecting your letters.

Radio BBC, NPR, Radio Australia, Radio New Zealand, RTE and CBC programming can be heard on Stockholm International 89.6 FM. Radio Sweden also provide news in English – about Sweden only – on the same frequency several times during the day – for schedules call ☎08/784 72 88, visit ⓦwww.sr.se/p6, or look in the *Dagens Nyheter* newspaper.

Swimming pools Outdoors at Vilda Vanadis, in Vanadislunden park, Sveavägen, and at Eriksdalsbadet, Eriksdalslunden, Södermalm (see p.90). Indoors at Forsgrénskabadet, Medborgarplatsen 2–4; Centralbadet, Drottninggatan 88; Storkyrkobadet, at Svartmangatan 20–22 in Gamla Stan; Sturebadet, inside Sturegallerian shopping centre, Stureplan; and at Liljeholmsbadet, Bergsunds Strand, Liljeholmen (see p.90).

Systembolaget Norrmalm: Klarabergsgatan 62;

Regeringsgatan 55; Sveavägen 66; Vasgatan 25; Odengatan 58 and 92. Gamla Stan: Lilla Nygatan 18. Södermalm: Folkungagatan 56 & 101; Götgatan 132; and inside the Söderhallarna shopping centre in Medborgarplatsen. Stores are generally open Mon–Wed 10am–6pm, Thu & Fri 10am–7pm, Sat 10am–2pm.

Train information For tickets and information for domestic and international routes with SJ (Swedish State Railways), call ☏0771/75 75 75; from abroad ring ☏00 46 771/ 75 75 75; for Tågkompaniet call ☏020/44 41 11.

Travel agents Kilroy, Kungsgatan 4 (☏0771/54 57 69), for discounted rail and air tickets and ISIC cards; Ticket: branches at Kungsgatan 60 (☏08/24 00 90), Sturegatan 8 (☏08/611 50 20) and Sveavägen 42 (☏08/24 92 20); for cheap international flights check the travel section of the main *Dagens Nyheter* newspaper.

Travel information (SL) Bus, T-bana and regional train (*pendeltåg*) information on ☏08/600 10 00. There are SL-Centers at Sergels Torg (Mon–Fri 7am–6.30pm, Sat & Sun 10am–5pm); Slussen (Mon–Fri 7am–6pm, Sat 10am–1pm); Gullmarsplan, Södermalm (Mon–Thurs 7am–6.30pm, Fri 7am–6pm, Sat 10am–5pm); and Fridhemsplan, Kungsholmen (Mon–Fri 7am–6.30pm, Sat 10am–5pm).

Moving on from Stockholm

Mainline **trains** from Stockholm, as well as Arlanda Express services (5.05am–11.35pm; every 15min; 20min; 140kr) to Arlanda airport, leave from the Central Station. Long distance **buses** depart upstairs from the adjoining Cityterminalen. **Airport buses** to Stockholm's four airports, Arlanda, Bromma, Skavsta and Västerås, also leave from here; those for Bromma and Västerås always go from Gate 23, and those for Skavsta from Gate 24. Buses for Arlanda call first at Terminal 5 then continue onto Terminals 4, 3 and 2. Waxholmsbolaget **boats** for the archipelago leave from in front of the *Grand Hotel* on Strömkajen, whereas services to Drottningholm, Mariefred and Gripsholm, as well as to Uppsala via Sigtuna, leave from Stadshuset on Kungsholmen. Silja Line **ferries** to Helsinki, Mariehamn and Turku in Finland sail from Värtahamnen in Östermalm; Viking Line, which sails to the same Finnish destinations, uses Stadsgårdsterminalen on Södermalm. Note the Swedish names for two of these places: Helsinki is *Helsingfors* and Turku confusingly is *Åbo*.

Around Stockholm

Such are Stockholm's attractions that it's easy to overlook the city's surroundings, yet if you did so you'd be missing some of Sweden's most fascinating sights – all of which make ideal day-trips as they're within easy striking distance of the capital – most enjoyably by boat. One hour from the city centre stands **Drottningholm**, Sweden's greatest royal palace, while a little further out in the lake is the World Heritage island of **Birka**, with its magnificent archeological remains of Viking dwellings. Stockholm's stunning **archipelago** makes another excellent waterborne day-trip with dozens of pine-clad islands, all served by regular ferries; we've listed the best destinations in the guide. Alternatively, west of the capital, the little lakeside village of **Mariefred**, containing Sweden's other great castle, **Gripsholm**, is not only accessible by a fine boat ride on the waters of Lake Mälaren but also by train. On the opposite shore lively **Västerås**, one of Sweden's most likeable cities, is most readily reached by train from Stockholm, though also by changing boats at Birka (see p.104). North of Stockholm, **Sigtuna** is Sweden's oldest town and even today is full of ruined medieval churches and runestones. Nearby **Skokloster** castle is equally worthy of a trip and is an absolute must for fans of over-the-top Baroque. Beyond both, the charming university town of **Uppsala** is readily reached from both Stockholm and Arlanda airport, and can, in principle, be visited on a day-trip from the former, or as a first destination in any Swedish tour from the latter, though to do Uppsala justice it really merits a longer stay.

Stockholm Cards and 1- and 3-day travel cards are not valid on the boat services to Drottningholm or in the archipelago, but they can be used on the bus, T-bana and regional train services within Greater Stockholm, which helps cut travel costs for at least part of some journeys.

Drottningholm and Birka

Just to the west of the capital on the banks of Lake Mälaren stands the stately royal residence of **Drottningholm** with sweeping views across the water. Less than an hour away from Stockholm the palace makes a relaxing day-trip and can be coupled with a visit to the dizzying array of ancient finds at the Viking town of **Birka**, on the nearby island of Björkö.

Drottningholm

Even if your time in Stockholm is limited, try to see the harmonious royal palace of **Drottningholm** (May–Aug daily 10am–4.30pm; Sept daily noon–3.30pm; Oct–April Sat & Sun noon–3.30pm; 60kr; ⓦwww.royalcourt .se). The finest way to reach the palace is by **ferry** (May to early Sept daily 9.30am–6pm; 70kr one-way, 100kr return), which leaves every hour from Stadshusbron on Kungsholmen and takes just under an hour each way. Otherwise take the T-bana to Brommaplan and then buses #177, #301–323, #336 or #338 from there – a less thrilling ride, but covered by the Stockholm Card as well as the one- and three-day travel cards.

Beautifully located on the shores of leafy **Lovön**, an island 11km west of the centre, Drottningholm is perhaps the greatest achievement of the two architects **Tessin**, father and son. Work began in 1662 on the orders of King Karl X's widow, Eleonora, with Tessin the Elder modelling the new palace in a thoroughly French style – giving rise to the stock comparisons with Versailles. Apart from anything else, it's considerably smaller than its French contemporary, utilizing false perspective and trompe l'oeil to bolster the elegant, though rather narrow, interior. On Tessin the Elder's death in 1681, the palace was completed by his son, then already at work on Stockholm's Royal Palace.

Inside, good English notes are available to help you sort out the riot of Rococo decoration in the rooms which largely date from the time when Drottningholm was bestowed as a wedding gift on Princess Louisa Ulrika (a sister of Frederick the Great of Prussia). No hints, however, are needed to spot the influences in the Baroque "French", and the later "English", **gardens** that back onto the palace. Since 1981, the Swedish royal family has slummed it out at Drottningholm, using it as a permanent home. This move has accelerated efforts to restore parts of the palace to their original appearance, and the monumental **grand staircase** is now once again exactly as envisaged by Tessin the Elder. Another sight worth visiting is the **Court Theatre** (Slottsteater), nearby in the palace grounds (May–Sept only guided tours every 30min; 60kr; Ⓦ www.drottningholmsteatern.dtm.se). It dates from 1766, but its heyday was a decade later, when Gustav III imported French plays and theatrical companies, making Drottningholm the centre of Swedish artistic life. Take the guided tour and you'll get a florid but accurate account of the theatre's decoration: money to complete the building ran out in the eighteenth century, meaning that things are not what they seem – painted papier-mâché frontages are *krona*-pinching substitutes for the real thing. The original backdrops and stage machinery are still in place, though, and the tour comes complete with a display of eighteenth-century special effects including wind and thunder machines, trapdoors and simulated lighting. Also within the extensive palace grounds is a **Chinese Pavilion** (May–Aug daily 11am–4.30pm; 60kr), a sort of eighteenth-century royal summerhouse.

You might be lucky enough to catch a **performance** of drama, ballet or opera here (usually June–Aug). The cheapest **tickets** cost around 170kr, though decent seats are more in the region of 300–600kr – check the schedule at Drottningholm or ask at the tourist offices in the city.

Birka

Björkö (the name means "island of birches"), in Lake Mälaren, is known for its rich flora, good beaches, ample swimming opportunities, but most of all for the Viking town of **BIRKA** (Ⓦ www.raa.se/birka), which is a UNESCO World Heritage site. Sweden's oldest town, founded around 750AD, Birka was once the most important Viking trading centre in the northern countries, benefiting from its strategic location near the mouth of Lake Mälaren on the portage route to Russia and the Byzantine Empire. Tradesmen and merchants were drawn to the prosperous and rapidly expanding village and the population soon grew to around one thousand. The future patron saint of Scandinavia, **Ansgar**, came here in 830 as a missionary at the instruction of the Holy Roman Emperor, Louis I, and established a church in an attempt to Christianize the heathen Swedes. They showed little interest and the Frankish monk preached on the island for just over a year before being recalled. Birka reached its height during the tenth century before sliding into decline; falling water levels in Lake Mälaren, the superior location of the Baltic island of Gotland for handling Russian-Byzantine trade and the emergence of nearby rival, Sigtuna, all led to its gradual disappearance after 975. Today a few obvious remains lie scattered about, including the remnants of houses and most notably a vast cemetery, the largest Viking-age burial ground in Scandinavia, which totally surrounds the site of the former village. Major excavations began here in 1990 and the **Birka museum** (May to mid-Sept daily 10am–5pm; 50kr) now displays historical artefacts as well as scale models of the harbour and craftsmen's quarters.

In Viking times, Björkö was actually two separate islands, with the main settlement located in the northwest corner of the one further north. As the land rose after the last Ice Age, the narrow channel between the two islands vanished, resulting in today's single kidney-shaped island; remains of jetties have been found where the channel would have been, as well as a rampart which acted as an outer wall for the settlement. It's reckoned that, from the eighth to the late tenth century, the relatively prosperous population here was around a thousand. The developed nature of their society is evident from modern finds: scissors, pottery and even keys have all been excavated. Among the remains of Viking-age life, the most striking is Birka's graveyard, which can be found outside the rampart; turn right from where the boat arrives and you'll come across around four hundred burial mounds, some with standing stones. A fort complete with earth ramparts was located at the island's highest point; today the rampart is still visible.

Getting there

From **Stockholm** there are two main routes to Birka: the most enjoyable is the Strömma Kanalbolaget (May to late Sept daily 10am, return trip from Birka at 3.30pm; ⓦ www.strommakanalbolaget.com) boat (1hr 45min) from Stadshusbron outside the Stadshuset on Kungsholmen; tickets can be bought on board and cost 113kr single, 225kr return, which includes entry to the museum. The second option involves taking bus #312 from **Brommaplan** via Drottningholm to Rastaholm on Ekerö, from where there are three boats daily in July & August (10.30am, noon & 1.30pm; 30min; 140kr; ☏08/711 14 57, ⓦ www.malaroskargardstrafik.a.se) to Birka.

It's also possible to get to Birka from **Västerås** (see p.114): Strömma Kanalbolaget boats depart from Östra Hamnen in Västerås (early June to mid-Aug daily; early May to early June & mid-Aug to early Sept, Sat & Sun only) at 10am with single tickets costing 103kr, returns 205kr; the boat arrives in Birka at 1pm. It is therefore possible to travel between Stockholm and Västerås, in both directions, entirely by boat by changing in Birka – the boat from Birka to Västerås leaves at 3.30pm (same dates as above) arriving at 6.30pm.

The archipelago

If you arrived in Stockholm by ferry from Finland or Estonia, you'll already have had a tantalizing glimpse of the **Stockholm archipelago**. In Swedish the word for archipelago is *skärgården* – literally "garden of skerries" and a pretty accurate description: the array of hundreds upon hundreds of pine-clad islands and islets is the only one of its kind in the world. Most of the islands are flat and make wonderful places for **walking**; we've suggested a few routes which aren't meant to take you to any particular destination, but are the best way to take in the sweeping sea vistas and unspoilt nature here. Of the vast number of islands in the archipelago, several are firm favourites with Stockholmers; others offer more secluded beaches and plenty of opportunity for walking amid undiscovered beautiful surroundings. The archipelago, though, holds another secret, little known even to most Swedes – many of **ABBA**'s most famous hits were written out here, on the island of Viggsö where the famous foursome owned a couple of summer cottages (see p.108).

From November to April, life in the archipelago can be tough, with the winter ice stretching far out into the Baltic, throwing the boat timetables into confusion. But in summer the archipelago is at its best: the air is heavy with the scent of fresh pine, and seemingly endless forests are reflected in the deep blue of the sea. It's worth bearing in mind that when it's cloudy in Stockholm, chances are the sun is shining somewhere out in the islands.

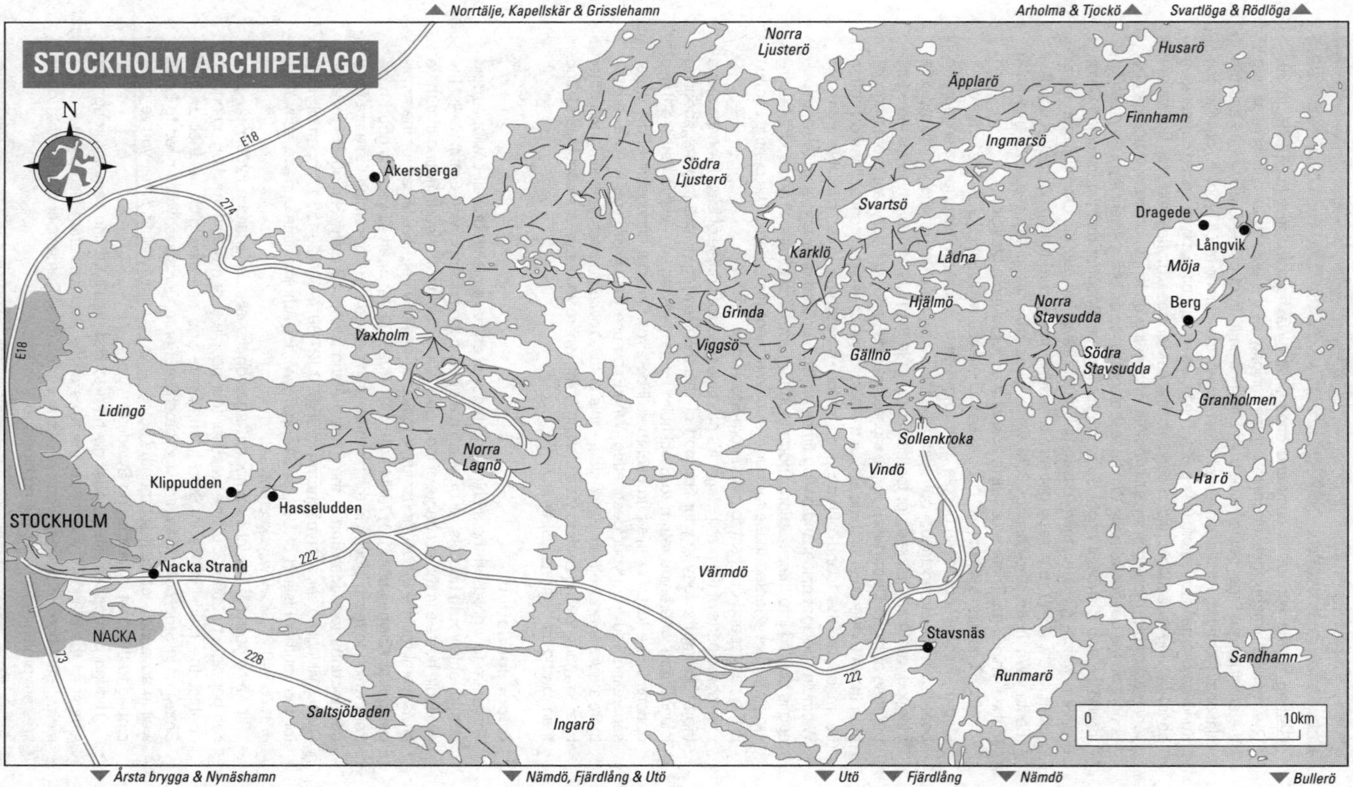

STOCKHOLM ARCHIPELAGO

N

◄ Norrtälje, Kapellskär & Grisslehamn   ◄ Arholma & Tjockö   ◄ Svartlöga & Rödlöga

Husarö
Finnhamn
Äpplarö
Ingmarsö
Norra
Ljusterö
Svartsö
Ladna
Hjälmö
Karklö
Södra
Ljusterö
Grinda
Viggsö
Gällnö
Sollenkroka
Vindö
Åkersberga
Norra
Lagnö
Vaxholm
Hasseludden
Klippudden
Lidingö
Nacka Strand
STOCKHOLM
NACKA
Saltsjöbaden
Ingarö
Värmdö
Stavsnäs
Runmarö
Långvik
Dragede
Möja
Berg
Granholmen
Norra
Stavsudda
Södra
Stavsudda
Harö
Sandhamn

E18
274
272
272
228
73

10km
0

1

105

◄ Årsta brygga & Nynäshamn   ◄ Nämdö, Fjärdlång & Utö   ▼ Utö   ▼ Fjärdlång   ▼ Nämdö   ▼ Bullerö

Island practicalities

Getting to the islands is easy and cheap, with Waxholmsbolaget (℡08/679 58 30, ⓦwww.waxholmsbolaget.se) operating the majority of the passenger-only sailings into the archipelago. Most boats leave from Strömkajen in front of the *Grand Hotel* and the National Museum; others leave from just round the corner at Nybroplan, next to the Kungliga Dramatiska Teatern (see p.83). The boats usually have a well-priced cafeteria on board serving reasonably priced sandwiches, cakes, beers, coffee and tea. Tickets are very reasonable, ranging from 30kr to 95kr depending on length of journey, and can be bought on the boat or from the Waxholmsbolaget office on Strömkajen. If you're planning to visit several islands, it might be worth buying the **Båtluffarkort** (Interskerries Card; 385kr), which gives sixteen days' unlimited travel on all Waxholmbolaget lines. Alternatively, if you've already got an SL monthly travel card (see p.66), buy a supplementary **Waxholm card** costing 385kr, which gives you one month's free travel anywhere in the archipelago. There is usually a 25kr charge for taking a **bicycle**.

When boarding the boat, you'll be asked where you're heading for, as the boats don't stop at every island unless people want to get on or off there. If you're waiting for the boat out in the archipelago, you must raise the semaphore flag on the jetty to indicate that you want to be picked up; torches are kept in the huts on the jetties for the same purpose at night. **Departures** to the closest islands (around 4 daily) are more frequent than those to the outer archipelago; if there's no direct service, connections can often be made on the island of Vaxholm. In the **timetables** (free; available from the Waxholmsbolaget office, and sailing times are also posted on every jetty), the archipelago is divided into three sections: *norra* (northern), *mellersta* (central) and *södra* (southern); we have adopted these for our own coverage of the islands. The central section is the easiest and quickest to reach from Stockholm.

In some parts of the archipelago, it's possible to visit a couple of islands on the same trip by taking the ferry to your first port of call, then **rowing** across to a neighbouring island, from where you return to Stockholm by the ferry again – we've detailed these options in the text. For this purpose, there'll be a rowing boat either side of the water separating you from your destination. When you use the boats, you have to ensure there's always one left on either side – this entails rowing across, attaching the other boat to yours, rowing back to your starting point, where you leave one boat behind, and then rowing across one last time.

Accommodation

There are few hotels in the archipelago but it does have plenty of well-equipped and comfortable **youth hostels**, all of which are open in the summer (May–Sept); we list the available hostels in the accounts of individual islands below. It's worth noting that there are several mainland hostels usefully located at points where boats sail for the archipelago: at **Kappelskär** (℡0176/441 69, ℻0176/23 90 46; open all year), a good base from which to reach Tjockö in the northern archipelago and from which there are **ferry connections** to Mariehamn in the Finnish Åland islands (3 daily; 3hr, 50–80kr single; ⓦwww.vikingline.se); at **Nynäshamn** (℡08/520 127 80, ℻08/520 153 17; open all year), for the southern island of Utö; at **Skeppsmyra**, for Arholma (late June to early Aug; ℡0176/940 27, ⓦwww.lyckhemhb.se).

It's also possible to rent summer **cottages** on the islands for around 200kr per person per night or 2000–2500kr a week for four people – for more information on prices, contact the tourist office in Stockholm, where you can also pick up their *Bed & Breakfast in Stockholm's Archipelago* brochure. For longer stays, you'll need to book well in advance – at least six months before – or you may well find that you've been pipped to the post by holidaying Swedes.

Though **campsites** are surprisingly hard to find, you'll be fine camping rough on almost all the islands if you follow the rules of the *Allemansrätten* (see p.47) – a few nights' stay here and there won't cause any problems. Remember though that open fires are prohibited all over the archipelago.

The central archipelago

The easiest section of the archipelago to reach, and consequently the most popular with day-tripping Stockholmers, the **central archipelago** is the islands at their most stunning. Here hundreds of rocks, skerries, islets and islands jostle for space in the pristine waters of the Baltic, giving the impression of giant stepping-stones leading back to the mainland. Navigating this maze of islands certainly takes experience and at times boats here are forced to cut their speed to chug through narrow sounds and passageways. This is especially true on the narrow approach to **Vaxholm**, the first and most popular island in the central archipelago, whose charms lie in strolling the town's couple of main streets and browsing in the handful of small shops. Nearby, **Grinda**, can also be busy though it does boast a number of sandy and rocky beaches to help disperse the summer crowds. For a more back-to-nature experience **Gällnö** and, more so, neighbour **Karklö**, are better destinations to head for. They are tranquil, unspoilt havens of peace and solitude where the simple pleasures of walking through the forest, **nude sunbathing** (very popular in the archipelago) or swimming in the sea are the main attractions. **Svartsö**, on the other hand, is a little more developed than its southerly neighbours with a number of small settlements and a shop selling provisions in addition to large expanses of forest and coastline to enjoy. One of the best **walks** can be found on **Ingmarsö**, in terms of appearance very similar to neighbouring Svartsö, leading through untouched forest to a narrow sound where rowing boats will take you over to tiny **Finnhamn**, a small hilly island, with fine sea views – in terms of distance from Stockholm, this is one of the last inhabited islands of the archipelago. Larger **Möja** gives the impression of a small Swedish village rather than an island and its main attraction is the enjoyable walk, along the island's quiet main road, from hamlet to hamlet.

Vaxholm

The island of **Vaxholm** lies only an hour from the capital by boat, and is a popular weekend destination for Stockholmers. Its eponymous town has an atmospheric wooden harbour, whose imposing fortress once guarded the waterways into the city, superseding the fortifications at Riddarholmen. Having successfully staved off attacks from Danes and Russians in the seventeenth and eighteenth centuries, nowadays the fortress is an unremarkable museum of military bits and pieces (June–Aug daily noon–4pm; 30kr). However, since all boats to and from Stockholm dock here, it's often swarming with visitors – do yourself a favour, stay on the boat and seek out one of the archipelago's quieter islands, which are quite frankly, more worthy of your attention.

Grinda and Viggsö

Another firm favourite, though a much-overrated destination, is **Grinda** (1hr 20min from Stockholm by boat), a thickly wooded island typical of the central archipelago, with some sandy beaches. It's particularly popular with families and so can be busy, particularly at weekends. In its favour, Grinda has frequent boat connections, a **youth hostel** (℡08/542 490 72, ℻08/542 493 45; May to late Oct) on the south coast east of the southern jetty, several ad-hoc **campsites**, a **restaurant** and a **café** in the centre of the island. To enjoy the sunshine on summer afternoons, head for beaches on the southern side of the island, as the tall trees on the northern side block out the sun. Boats dock at two jetties on the island, at its southern (Södra Grinda) and northern ends (Norra Grinda); a walk between the two takes thirty to forty minutes.

It is, however, on the approach to Södra Grinda that you'll pass a tear-shaped island tightly sandwiched in the narrow channel between Grinda and much larger Värmdö to the south: this unassuming rocky outcrop topped by dense pine forest is **Viggsö**, the place where **ABBA** composed *Dancing Queen*, *Fernando* and several other chart-topping hits; shots of the island were also used in *ABBA The Movie*. Agnetha and Björn bought a summer cottage on Viggsö in 1971, closely followed in 1974 by Benny and Frida, who became neighbours on the other side of the island – the sound of piano music drifting across the treetops a sure sign that one or other couple had sailed their boat out from Stockholm to spend a few days away from the city. In fact, the members of the group often retreated to the island throughout their career and the two men would spend entire days in Björn's yellow wooden outhouse hammering away at a battered upright piano and strumming an old guitar to produce perhaps some of the greatest pop hits the world has ever known – the restorative calm of Viggsö was at the very heart of much of ABBA's music-making.

Gällno and Karklö

A beautiful low-lying island covered with thick pine forest, **Gällnö** (1hr 30min–2hr from Stockholm by boat)is the archipelago at its best. Home to just thirty people, a couple of whom farm the land near the jetty, the island has been designated a nature reserve: you can spot deer in the forest or watch eider ducks diving for fish. It takes around two hours to get here from Stockholm. The idyllic **youth hostel** (T08/571 661 17, F08/571 662 88; May–Sept), sur-rounded by low-hanging trees, is easy enough to find; the track leading to it is well signposted from the tiny main village, where there's also a small **shop** sell-ing provisions. From here, there's the choice of two **walks**: either head east through the forest for Gällnönäs, from where you can pick up boats either back to Stockholm or further out into the islands, or alternatively, continue past the youth hostel, following signs for Brännholmen, till you arrive at a small bay popular with yachties. Now look for the hut where the toilet is, as one of its walls bears a map and sign on the outside showing the path leading from here to the rowing boats – these enable you to cross the narrow sound separating Gällnö from its neighbour, Karklö. When you head across, remember to leave one boat on either side of the sound (see p.106).

Karklö (2hr from Stockholm by boat) is one of the most unspoilt islands in the archipelago and, combined with Gällnö, makes for an excellent day-trip from Stockholm. There are no shops or roads here, only tracks which meander across the island and around farmers' fields, connecting the spot where the rowing boats are moored with the main jetty on the other side, where the boats from Stockholm dock. The paths can be difficult to find at times, so it's best to ask directions in the main village, which is close to the rowing-boat moorings.

Svartsö

North of Gällno (2hr–3hr from Stockholm), **Svartsö** is a busier island than its neighbour, though it's never overrun with visitors and there's plenty of space here to unwind and sunbathe on the rocky shores – particularly on the west-ern edge of the island (see below). With its fields of grazing sheep, thick virgin forest and crystal-clear lakes, Svartsö has a more pastoral feel than some of the other surrounding islands where forest predominates. There are also good roads that make the island ideal for cycling or walking. From the northern jetty, where most boats from Stockholm arrive, there's a pleasant walk – lasting about ninety minutes – which first takes you along the road towards the two lakes in the centre of the island. Just before you arrive at the lakes, turn right into the path that follows the lakeside, passing a few houses on the way. The road then becomes a track which heads into the forest. Continue past a couple of hay-fields in a forest clearing, and eventually you'll glimpse the sea through the trees at the forest edge; this is an ideal place to sunbathe nude or stop for a picnic. Past a farmhouse and a couple of barns, the track eventually turns into a road again; from here it's another twenty- to thirty-minute walk to the village of **Alsvik**, with its **shop** where you can buy snacks and refreshments, post office and ferry connections back to the capital (2hr).

Ingmarsö and Finnhamn

Ingmarsö is an excellent island for walkers. Between 2hr 30min and 3hr by boat from Stockholm, the northern jetty (Norra Ingmarsö) is where most boats dock. From here you can do an enjoyable roundabout **walk** that takes you across the island and on to neighbouring Finnhamn, from where you can catch a boat back. Follow the main road away from the northern jetty; after about fifteen minutes, turn left at the signpost marked "Båtdraget" and "Femsund". Before making this turn you may want to continue straight ahead for five minutes to the island's **supermarket** to stock up on provisions before retracing your steps to the signpost. The road to Femsund eventually turns into a track – marked by blue dots on tree trunks – which strikes out through the forest heading for Kålmårsön. After about an hour, the path skirts a wonderfully isolated lake, where you can swim and sunbathe, before passing through more unspoilt forest and emerging at a small bay filled with yachts. Look carefully here for the continuation of the path – still marked with blue dots – which will take you to rowing-boat moorings at the narrow sound between here and neighbouring Finnhamn. If you fail to locate the path, follow the coast round to the right for roughly ten to fifteen minutes while facing the yachts in the bay. It takes about two and a half hours to get to the sound from the northern jetty. Row over to Finnhamn, remembering to leave one rowing boat on either side of the sound (see p.106).

Although only a tiny island, **Finnhamn** is often busy because of its popular **youth hostel** (☎08/542 462 12, ⓦwww.finnhamn.nu) – complete with waterfront sauna – which is a dramatically located yellow building perched on rocks looking out to sea. To walk from the rowing-boat moorings to the main jetty and the youth hostel takes around forty minutes; the journey time back to Stockholm is around two hours. During summer, the *Finnhamn café* by the jetty serves up simple snacks and refreshments. If the crowds are too much here, head southeast from Finnhamn's tiny main village for the islet of Lilla Jolpan, where there are some good bathing opportunities.

Möja

One of the most popular, though still uncrowded, islands to visit, **Möja** (3hr from Stockholm by boat) is home to around three hundred people, who make their living from fishing and farming. There's a small craft museum in the main town, **Berg**, and even a cinema, *Konsum* supermarket, post office and **restaurant**. There's a pleasant afternoon to be had here doing an easy six-kilometre walk from the main ferry jetty, named Berg, where you should disembark when arriving from Stockholm. The walk takes you along the well-made road to the tiny settlement of **Långvik** in the north of the island, and gives you a chance to have a peep at some of the wooden cottages and well-tended gardens on the way. Just before Långvik, itself nothing more than a few houses grouped around a tiny harbour and another small *Konsum* supermarket, a well-trodden path heads left into the forest, past a small store that sells bread, and on to **Dragede**, a cluster of wooden cottages romantically situated deep in the forest. It should take you about twenty minutes to arrive here from Långvik; once at Dragede you can catch a boat for Stockholm via Berg (journey time 2hr 30min–3hr 30min).

The northern archipelago, Norrtälje and Grisslehamn

Though similar in nature to their counterparts in the central archipelago, the islands in the northern stretches of the *skärgård* are far fewer in number. As a result, the appearance of the **northern archipelago** is very different; characterized by open vistas and sea swells rather than narrow sounds and passageways, the islands here are very much at the mercy of the sea and weather. Surprisingly for such an exposed location, a couple of the islands, notably **Arholma** and **Tjockö** depend on agriculture for their survival. Meanwhile it's untouched nature not farming that proliferates on **Svartlöga** and **Rödlöga**, which are recommended for those seeking to get away from it all – if you're looking for your very own clearing in the forest or rocky beach you won't go far wrong here. Although Stockholm is, on average a three-hour boat ride away, the islands can also be reached by changing buses in **Norrtälje,** an uneventful little place whose best feature is its proliferation of onward bus connections, (reached by bus from Stockholm) and then a shorter ferry ride from one of the northern jetties: Simpnäs for Arholma; Räfsnäs or Kapellskär for Tjockö; Furusund for Svartlöga and Rödlöga. Mainland **Grisslehamn**, north of the island of Arholma, is notable for its frequent ferry connections to Eckerö on the Finnish Åland islands – an easy day-trip destination.

Arholma

One of the most northerly islands in the Stockholm archipelago (4hr by boat from Stockholm), **Arholma** was the scene of a dramatic confrontation with Russia in July 1719, when thirty Russian warships carrying five thousand men appeared on the horizon. Their arrival was part of a strategic campaign mounted by the tsar, Peter the Great, to force Sweden to accept Russian dominance of the Baltic. As the terrified islanders fled to the mainland, their farms were set ablaze and animals slaughtered by the invading Russian forces.

Today, Arholma is a working agricultural island, the countryside characterized not by forest, as with many other islands hereabouts, but by agricultural fields, the result of centuries of farming tradition. Other than the eighteenth-century lighthouse to the east of the jetty served by boats to and from Stockholm, there's little else to see on the island; the main attraction is simply wandering around the country lanes and enjoying the tranquil setting – it's possible to get down to the water's edge at several points around the island though there are no real beaches.

A couple of minutes' stroll from the jetty is the **youth hostel** (℡0176/560 18; advance booking required), located where the track from the jetty meets Arholma's main road. There's also a simple **campsite** in the tiny bay to the north of the jetty. During the short summer months there's a small unsophisticated **café** down at the harbour, where you'll also find a year-round **shop** selling basic provisions. The best **swimming** can be had south of the youth hostel in another tiny unnamed bay reached by following the main road south to the narrow inlet which marks the beginning of the Granö peninsula; from here, take the small road to the right which then becomes a track as it heads west to the sea – roughly a fifteen-minute walk. In addition to the direct boat from Stockholm to Arholma, it's also possible to get here by taking a bus from Norrtälje to Simpnäs (#636; 1hr; see the *Norra Skärgården* timetable for times) and then a ferry over to Arholma (20min).

Tjockö, Svartlöga and Rödlöga

Close to the mainland (10min from Räfsnäs; 3hr 20min from Stockholm by boat) is **Tjockö**, an island where life is much as it was decades ago. A wonderful little place with forests, meadows and open fields, Tjockö also has a good sandy beach with smooth rocks that make an ideal spot for soaking up the sun. To get here, take bus #640 from Tekniska Högskolan T-bana (on the red line towards Mörby centrum) to Norrtälje, then bus #631 to Räfsnäs, from where it's a ten-minute boat trip.

To the south, and much further out towards Finland, are Svartlöga and Rödlöga. **Svartlöga** is the only island in the archipelago whose forest is totally deciduous, and was one of the few to escape Russian incursions in 1719, during the Great Northern War. There are several good rocky beaches on which to relax after your long journey here. Neighbouring **Rödlöga** is a much tinier red-granite affair, with no roads, just leafy paths; overgrown hedgerows, thick with wild roses; and wonderful secluded beaches. The boat journey time from Stockholm to both islands is roughly four hours (they are only 10min apart and the same boat calls at both islands), or ninety minutes from Furusund, a coastal town which is reached on bus #640 from Tekniska Högskolan T-bana to Norrtälje, where you change to the #632 or #634 to Furusund.

Norrtälje and Grisslehamn

Heading for the northern islands, there's a fair chance you'll end up changing buses in the mainland town of **NORRTÄLJE**, where there's a **tourist office** at Danskes gränd 6 (June to mid-Aug Mon–Fri 9.30am–7pm, Sat 9.30am–5pm, Sun 11am–5pm; mid-Aug to May Mon–Fri 9.30am–5pm; ☏0176/719 90, ⓦwww.norrtalje.se) and a comfortable **youth hostel** (☏50176/715 69, ⓕ0176/715 89; early June to mid-Aug), at Bältartorpsgatan 6, in an old timber building dating from the turn of the last century. Though the town is pleasant enough, it's only worth a quick look round between buses rather than an overnight stay. This is an old spa town and capital of the Roslagen district, with a regional museum, Roslagsmuséet (Mon–Fri 11am–4pm; June–Aug Mon–Sat 11am–2pm; 30kr), at Hantverkaregatan 23, housed in an old gun factory in the centre of town, recounting the district's strong maritime links.

Norrtälje is also a handy jumping-off point for trips to **GRISSLEHAMN** in the north, a small fishing village where you'll find the pretty home of the early twentieth-century writer and artist Albert Engström, with paintings and knick-knacks displayed inside. Note that there are **ferry connections** from Grisslehamn to Eckerö on the Finnish Åland islands with Eckerölinjen (2–5 daily; 2hr; 80kr one-way late June to early Aug, otherwise 50kr; ⓦwww.eckerolinjen.fi).

The southern archipelago

Although sharing more in appearance with the denser central archipelago than its more barren northern counterpart, the **southern archipelago**, is much quieter in terms of visitor numbers because it is harder to reach from central

Stockholm. The one notable exception, however, is **Sandhamn**, a yachting Mecca which draws sailors from all across Sweden and surrounding Baltic Sea countries. Though enjoyable, the island is often overrun with visitors and prices are inflated as a result. At the other extreme, **Bullerö**, a tiny dot on the map off the nearby island of Nämdö, is a naturalist's paradise – and a nature reserve. However, it's **Fjärdlång** and much larger **Utö**, both further to the south, that remain the southern's archipelago's most likeable destinations – the former, although not suitable for bathing, is an ideal place to get away from it all, whereas the latter has good opportunities for swimming and cycling.

Sandhamn and Bullerö

With its fine harbour, the island of **Sandhamn** (2hr from Stockholm by boat) has been a destination for seafarers since the eighteenth century and remains so today, attracting large numbers of yachts of all shapes and sizes. The main village is a haven of narrow alleyways, winding streets and overgrown verandahs. If you fancy staying overnight on the island there are a couple of options: an exclusive and rather swanky **hotel**, *Sandhamn Hotell & Konferens* (℡08/574 504 00, Ⓦwww.sandhamn.com; ❻), catering for wealthy yachties, and *Sandhamns Värdshus* (℡08/571 530 51, Ⓦwww.sandhamns-vardshus.se; ❸), a much smaller and altogether more agreeable bed-and-breakfast establishment – both places serve excellent seafood.

In the southern stretch of the archipelago, **Bullerö** (3hr from Stockholm) is about as far out as you can go in the archipelago. This beautiful island is a nature reserve, with attractive walking trails. To get here, take the Saltsjöbanan train from Slussen station to Saltsjöbaden, from where boats leave for the island of Nämdö; change at the Idöborg jetty on Nämdö for a shuttle service to Bullerö. Although far out in the archipelago, the boat journey time to Nämdö is now just two hours from Stockholm after recent timetabling improvements.

Fjärdlång and Utö

Fjärdlång (3hr 15min from Stockholm) was closely linked for a time with businessman Ernest Thiel, who established the Thiel Gallery on Djurgården in Stockholm. Inspired by his friend, Bruno Liljefors, who once bought nearby Bullerö, Thiel purchased Fjärdlång (or Fjällång as the islanders call it) in 1909 and built a large and well-appointed villa on the island as his new residence. Today the building has been converted into a top-notch **youth hostel** (℡08/510 560 92, ℻08/501 566 34; early June to mid-Sept), which is next to the jetty where boats from Stockholm put in. Although the island is not suitable for bathing, as the trees stretch down to the water's edge, Fjärdlång is an ideal place to relax and enjoy nature. Lying on the very eastern edge of the archipelago, it offers superb views of the surrounding skerries of the Baltic. To get here, either take the boat from Stockholm or pick up the train from Slussen to Saltsjöbaden and catch a boat there (journey times 3hr 15min and 2hr respectively).

Far out in the southern reaches of the archipelago, **Utö** (3hr 30min from Stockholm) is flat and thus ideal for cycling around; it's not bad for bathing and picnics either. There are excellent views from the island's windmill, on a hill, Kvarnbacken, a ten-minute walk southwest of the jetty. It takes three and a half hours to get here by boat from Stockholm; alternatively you can get the Pendeltåg to Västerhaninge from where bus #846 goes to Årsta brygga for the ferry to the island (50min). The comfortable **youth hostel** (℡08/504 203 15, Ⓦwww.uto-vardshus.se) is near where the ferry docks and has three elegant wooden verandahs overlooking the sea.

Around Lake Mälaren

Freshwater **Lake Mälaren** dominates the countryside west of Stockholm and provides the backdrop to some of the capital region's most appealing destinations – all suitable for day-trips. Frequent **train services** run to **Västerås**, a modern and thoroughly enjoyable city on the northern shore of the lake, which is about an hour from Stockholm, and also boasts some excellent sandy **beaches** on a couple of islands just beyond the harbour. Closer to the capital, however, it's the enchanting lakeside village of **Mariefred** that really steals the show with its magnificent castle, **Gripsholm**. Trains link both places, making it possible to complete a circuit around the lake without having to return to Stockholm – total travel time for this circuit is around five hours.

Mariefred

If you've only got time for one boat trip outside Stockholm, make it to **MARIEFRED**, a tiny quintessentially Swedish village about an hour west of the city, whose peaceful attractions are bolstered by one of Sweden's most enjoyable castles. Its Swedish name is derived from that of an old monastery, Pax Mariae ("Mary's Peace"). A couple of minutes up from the quayside and you're strolling through narrow streets where well-kept wooden houses and little squares haven't changed much in decades.

Steam-train fans will love the **Railway Museum** at the railway station in Läggesta – you'll probably have noticed the narrow-gauge tracks running all the way to the quayside. There's an exhibition of old rolling stock and workshops, given added interest by the fact that narrow-gauge **steam trains** still run between Mariefred and **Läggesta**, a twenty-minute ride away, on the Östra Sörmlands Järnväg railway (ⓦwww.oslj.nu). These trains leave Mariefred roughly hourly between 11am and 5pm (mid-June to late June & early Aug to Sept Sat & Sun; late June to early Aug daily; ☎0159/210 00; 48kr second class return; half-price for children and rail-pass holders). From Läggesta, it's possible to pick up the regular SJ train back to Stockholm; check for connections at the Mariefred tourist office. Of course, you could always come to Mariefred from Stockholm by this route too (see p.114).

Gripsholms slott

Lovely though the village is, touring around it is really only a preface to seeing **Gripsholms slott**, the imposing red-brick castle built on a round island just to the south (mid-May to mid-Sept daily 10am–4pm; rest of year Sat & Sun noon–3pm; 60kr; ⓦwww.royalcourt.se). Walk up the quayside, and you'll see the path to the castle running across the grass by the water's edge.

In the late fourteenth century, Bo Johnsson Grip, the Swedish high chancellor, began to build a fortified castle at Mariefred, although the present building owes more to two Gustavs – Gustav Vasa, who started rebuilding in the sixteenth century, and Gustav III, who was responsible for major restructuring a couple of centuries later. Rather than the hybrid that might be expected, the result is rather pleasing – an engaging textbook castle with turrets, great halls, corridors and battlements. There are optional English-language **guided tours** (mid-May to mid-Sept 1pm; 10kr extra), on which the key elements of the castle's construction and history are pointed out: there's a vast portrait collection that includes recently commissioned works depicting political and cultural figures as well as assorted royalty and nobility; some fine decorative and architectural work; and, as at Drottningholm (see p.102), a private theatre, built for Gustav III. It's too delicate to be used for performances these days, but in summer, plays and other events are staged out in the castle grounds; more information can be obtained from Mariefred's tourist office (see opposite). Even **ABBA** have put in an appearance here – in February 1974 Gripsholm was used as the cover shot for their *Waterloo* album.

Practicalities

To get here by public transport, take the **train** from Stockholm to Läggesta, from where connecting buses and, at certain times of year, steam trains (see p.113) shuttle passengers into Mariefred. In summer, you can even get here on a **steamboat** from Stockholm, the *S/S Mariefred*, which leaves from Klara Mälarstrand, near Stadshuset on Kungsholmen (mid-May to mid-June Sat & Sun 10am; mid-June to mid-Aug Tues–Sun 10am; mid-Aug to mid-Sept Sat & Sun 10am; 3hr 30min each way; 120kr one way, 180kr return); buy your ticket on board. The **tourist office** is in the fine eighteenth-century timber Rådhuset, the building with the large spire on top that's easily visible from the quay (June–Aug Mon–Sat 10am–6pm, Sun 10am–4pm; Sept–May Mon–Thurs 9am–4pm, Fri 9am–3pm; ☏0159/297 90; ⓦwww.mariefred.se). You can ask here about free maps and **bike rental** (85kr per day; 400kr per week).

Mariefred warrants a night's stay, if not for the sights – which you can exhaust in half a day – then for the pretty, peaceful surroundings. There's only one **hotel**, *Gripsholms Värdhus*, Kyrkogatan 1 (☏0159/347 50, ⓦwww.gripsholms -vardshus.se; ⓖ), a beautifully restored inn (the oldest in Sweden) that's a wonderfully luxurious option, overlooking the castle and the water. The **youth hostel** is beyond the castle, in the Red Cross education centre (☏0159/367 00; ⓦwww.redcross.se/gripsholm; mid-June to mid-Aug). Otherwise, ask in the tourist office about **rooms** in the village, which range from 200 to 400kr per person per night. There are also six-person **cabins** (550kr), which you can rent at the tourist office.

As for **eating**, treat yourself to lunch in *Gripsholms Värdhus*, at Kyrkogatan 1. The food is excellent, and around 200kr will get you a turn at the herring table, a main course, a drink and coffee – all enhanced by the terrific views over to Gripsholm. Alternatively, try the much simpler *Skänken* at the back of the *Värdhus*, where lunch goes for around 75kr – although the price is lower, the quality is just as high, as it all comes from the same kitchen. Another good spot is the classy *Strandrestaurangen* on the lakeside near the church, which serves up delicious lunches for 65kr and seafood mains in the evening – try the fish in saffron with shellfish and aioli at 135kr. For friendly service but less inspiring fare, there's *Mariefreds Bistro*, opposite the castle at Storgatan 16, and *Gripsholms Grill & Pizzeria*, at Gripsholmsvägen 1. For **coffee** and cakes, head for *Konditori Fredman* in the main square, opposite the town hall, at Kyrkogatan 11.

Västerås and around

Capital of the county of Västmanland and Sweden's sixth biggest city, **VÄSTERÅS** is an immediately likeable mix of old and new. Today the lakeside city carefully balances its dependence on ABB, the industrial technology giant, with a rich history dating back to Viking times. If you're looking for a place that's lively and cosmopolitan, yet retains cobbled squares, picturesque wooden houses and even a sixth-century royal burial mound, you won't go far wrong here. Västerås also boasts some of Lake Mälaren's best **beaches**, a short ferry ride away from the city centre.

Arrival, information and accommodation

As the train pulls into Västerås, the first thing you'll notice is a sea of bicycles neatly standing in racks right outside the **train station** on Södra Ringvägen; arriving by **bus** you'll be dropped at the adjacent terminal. The **airport**, served by Ryanair flights from London Stansted as well as services from Copenhagen, Gothenburg and Malmö with Skyways, is just 6km east of the city, from where **bus #L41** runs to the centre (Mon–Fri hourly 9.35am–11.45pm, Sat & Sun 1 only; 16kr). However, undoutbedly the best way to arrive in Västerås is by **boat** (leaves from outside the city hall on Stadshusbron, change at Birka), the shimmering waterfront slowly unfolding as you pull into the harbour, highlighted to the rear by the towering skyscraper that houses the *Radisson SAS* hotel.

From the train station, the **tourist office** at Stora Gatan 40 is a ten-minute walk away (mid-June to mid-Aug Mon–Fri 9am–7pm, Sat 9am–3pm, Sun 10am–2pm; mid-Aug to mid-June Mon–Fri 9.30am–6pm, Sat 10am–3pm; ☎021/10 38 30, ⊛www.vastmanland.se), through Vasaparken towards the centre of town. From the harbour, it's a five-minute walk north along Hamngatan, across Södra Ringvägen into Vasaparken and onto the tourist office.

The **youth hostel** (☎021/18 52 30; ⊛www.lovudden.nu), complete with sauna, is located at Lövudden, 5km west of the city on Lake Mälaren; take bus #25 (Mon–Sat roughly hourly, Sun restricted service) from the bus terminal. The following are some of the city's better **hotels**.

Aaros Metro Vasagatan 22 ☎021/18 03 30, ⊛www.aarosmetro.se. The cheapest hotel in town and located right in the centre of the city with basic, though modern and adequate rooms. ❸/❷

Arkad Östermalmsgatan 25 ☎021/12 04 80, ⊛www.arkad-hotell.se. A new building, decorated in old-fashioned style, that is good value for money, especially in summer. ❺/❷

Elite Stadshotellet Stora Torget ☎021/10 28 00, ⊛www.vasteras.elite.se. This hotel has been here as long as anyone can remember and the good-quality modern rooms, right in the heart of the city, have become a fixture of Västerås. However, although they cost the same as the *Radisson SAS* they don't enjoy the same views. ❺/❸

Klipper Kungsgatan 4 ☎021/41 00 00, ℗14 26 70. This centrally located option, close to the lazy Svartån river in the old town, offers charming rooms and good service. ❹/❷

Radisson SAS Plaza Karlsgatan 9A ☎021/10 10 10, ⊛www.radisson.com. Known locally as the "Skyscraper", this 25-storey glass-and-chrome structure is the last word in Scandinavian chic and particularly good value in summer. ❺/❸

The City

From the tourist office, it's a short stroll up Köpmangatan to the twin cobbled squares of Bondtorget and Stora Torget. The slender lane from the southwestern corner of Bondtorget leads to the narrow **Svartån river**, which runs right through the centre of the city; the bridge over the river here (known as Apotekarbron) has great views of the old wooden cottages which nestle eave-to-eave along the riverside. Although it may not appear significant (the Svartån is actually much wider further upstream), the river was a decisive factor in making Västerås the headquarters of one of the world's largest engineering companies, Asea-Brown-Boveri (ABB), which needed a ready source of water for production; if you arrived by train from Stockholm you'll have passed their metallurgy and distribution centres on approaching the station. Back in the square, look out for the striking sculpture of a string of cyclists, the *Asea Stream*, which is supposed to portray the original workers of ABB as they made their way to work; today the sculpture is also a reminder of the impressive fact that Västerås has over 300km of cycle tracks and is a veritable haven for cyclists.

North of the two main squares, the brick **Domkyrkan** (Mon–Fri 8am–5pm, Sat & Sun 9.30am–5pm) dates from the thirteenth century, although its two outer aisles are formed from a number of chapels built around the existing church during the following two centuries. The original tower was destroyed by fire, leaving Nicodemus Tessin the Younger (who also built the Royal Palace in Stockholm, see p.74) to design the current structure in 1693. The highly ornate gilded oak triptych, above the altar, was made in Antwerp and depicts the suffering and resurrection of Christ. To the right of the altar lies the tomb of Erik XIV, who died an unceremonious death imprisoned in Örbyhus castle in 1577 after eating his favourite pea soup – little did he realize it was laced with arsenic.

Local rumour has it that the king's feet had to be cut off in order for his body to fit the coffin, which was built too small. Today though, his elegant, black-marble sarcophagus rests on a plinth of reddish sandstone from Öland.

Beyond the cathedral is the most charming district of Västerås, **Kyrkbacken**, a hilly area that stretches just a few hundred metres. Here, steep cobblestone alleys wind between preserved old wooden houses where artisans and the petit bourgeoisie lived in the eighteenth century. Thankfully the area was saved from the great fire of 1714 — which destroyed much of the rest of the city – and the wholesale restructuring of the 1960s. The area's sleepy appearance today belies the fact that this was once the very centre of activity in the city, not least because it was here that the local students had their rooms. At the top end of Djäknegatan, the main street of the district, look for a narrow alley called Brunnsgränd, along which is a house bearing the sign "Mästermansgården": it was once the abode of the most hated and ostracized man in the district – the town executioner.

A quick walk past the restaurants and shops of Vasagatan will bring you to Stora Gatan and eventually to the eye-catching modern **Stadshuset** in Fiskatorget – the building is a far cry from the Dominican monastery which once stood on this spot. Although home to the city's administration, the Stadshuset is best known for its 47 bells, the largest of which is known as The Monk and can be heard over the city at lunchtimes.

Across the square, once home to a fish market, the old town hall has now been transformed into an **art museum** (mid-May to mid-Aug Tues–Fri 11am–4pm, Sat & Sun noon–4pm; rest of year Tues–Fri 10am–5pm, Sat & Sun 11am–5pm; free). It's worth a quick look for its contemporary collections of Swedish and other Nordic art – don't expect too much though. Continue across Slottsbron to the **castle**, today home to a dull collection of local para-phernalia inside the **county museum** (Tues–Sun noon–4pm; free). The best exhibit lies just inside the entrance: the most lavish female burial in Sweden, in the form of a Viking boat grave from nearby Tuna, Badelunda. The boat sat in clay for hundreds of years, which accounts for its remarkable state of preser-vation. The gold jewellery worn by the woman found in the boat dates from the Roman Iron Age, and is also on display.

Eating and drinking

Västerås easily has the best **restaurants** of any town around Lake Mälaren. You'll find all kinds of cuisine, from Thai to Greek, traditional Swedish to British-style pub food. The city also has a lively **drinking scene** – including one cocktail bar 24 floors up, from where there are unsurpassed views of the lake.

Atrium Corner of Smedjegatan and Sturegatan. Greek favourites from 89kr, starters from 20kr.
Bellman Stora Torget 6. Very elegant restaurant done out with eighteenth-century furniture and decor. Count on at least 150kr per dish although lunch, at 63kr, is excellent value.
Bill o Bob Stora Torget 5. Handily located in the main square, with outdoor seating in summer. Usual meat and fish dishes for around 100kr, plus a selection of salads.

Bishops Arms Östra Kyrkogatan. British-style pub with a large selection of beer and single malt whiskies. Pub food also available. Over-23s only
Brogården Stora Gatan 42 adjacent to the tourist office. Riverside café with good views of the water and old wooden houses.
Kalle på Spången Kungsgatan 2. Great old-fashioned café with outdoor seating, close to the river. *The* place for coffee, cakes, grilled baguettes and fresh orange juice.
Karlsson på taket Karlsgatan 9A. Chi-chi café-restaurant on the 23rd floor of the *Radisson SAS Plaza*. Expensive, but the views are fantastic. Reckon on around 170–200kr per main dish.
Kina Thai Gallerian 36. Next to the Filmstaden cinema. Usual Chinese and Thai dishes for around 138kr. Lunch for 63kr.
Limone Stora Gatan 4. Stylish modern Italian restaurant serving top-notch pasta-only dishes (80kr); also pasta with lamb (178kr) or fish

(140kr).
Möller Mat o Musik Kungsgatan 4. Lunch for 75kr, meat and fish mains 75–195kr. The restaurant turns into a nightclub in the evening.
Piazza di Spagna Vasagatan 26. The best pizzeria in town and a very popular place for lunch at 65kr. Pizzas from 63kr; pasta from 76kr; meat dishes start at 162kr.
Sky Bar Karlsgatan 9A. On the 24th floor of the *Radisson SAS Plaza* hotel. Great cocktails and an unsurpassed view of the city. Light snacks also available.
Stadskällaren Stora Torget. Smart restaurant with rough brick interior and windows overlooking the main square. Meat and fish dishes start at 150kr.
Tabazco Sturegatan 20A. One of the city's most popular eateries with a menu that's heavily influenced by Mediterranean and Oriental cooking: try the chicken or pork kebab at 140kr, or grilled beef 154kr. Lunch here is 59kr.

Around Västerås: the Anundshög burial mound

Whilst in Västerås, try not to miss nearby **Anundshög**, the largest royal burial mound in Sweden, just 6km northeast of the city. Dating from the sixth century, the mound is thought to be the resting place of King Bröt-Anund and his stash of gold. Anundshög was also used for sessions of the local *ting*, or Viking parliament and several other smaller burial mounds nearby, suggest that the site was an important Viking meeting place over several centuries. Beside the main mound lie a large number of **standing stones** arranged end-to-end in the shape of two ships. The nearby **rune stone** dates from around 1000, its inscription reading "Folkvid erected all these stones for his son, Hedin, brother of Anund. Vred carved the runes." To get here, take **bus** #12 from the centre of town to its final stop, Bjurhovda, from where it's a short walk of around 20min – it's a good idea to ask for precise details at the tourist office in Västerås before setting out because Anundshög is not signposted from the bus stop.

Listings

Airport 6km southwest of the city. Information on ☎021/80 56 00.
Banks FöreningsSparbanken, Hantverkargatan 5; Handelsbanken, Vasagatan 20A; Nordea, Stora Gatan 23.
Bike rental Prylhuset, Kopparbergsvägen 29 ☎021/121210.
Buses Operated by Västmanlands Lokaltrafik. Information on ☎0200/25 50 75 or ⊛www.vl.se.
Car rental Avis, Södra Ringvägen 3, ☎021/80 01 88; Budget, Sjöhagsvägen 1, ☎021/14 39 27; Europcar, Kopparbergsvägen 47, ☎021/12 41 43; Hertz, Strömledningsgatan 11, ☎021/17 88 47
Cinemas Filmstaden, Gallerian 34, opposite the *Radisson SAS Plaza*; Royal, Torggatan, close to Stora Torget.
Doctor Emergency service available by calling ☎021/17 30 00.

Left luggage Lockers available at the train station on Södra Ringvägen.
Pharmacy Stora Gatan 34 (Mon–Sat 9am–9pm, Sun 10am–9pm)
Police Västgötegatan 7 (☎021/15 20 00)
Swimming Östra Holmen and Ridön islands (see above); Lövudden campsite (see above), where there's a sandy beach plus pedal boats, windsurfing equipment and canoes for rent.
Systembolaget Stora Gatan 48; Mon–Wed 10am–6pm, Thurs & Fri 10am–7pm, Sat 10am–2pm.
Taxi Taxi Västerås (☎021/18 50 00); Taxi Kurir (☎021/12 22 22).
Trains Information on ☎0771/75 75 75.
Travel agent Ticket, in Köpmangatan, next to the tourist office (Mon–Fri 9am–6pm, Sat 10am–2pm).

Beaches and boat trips on Lake Mälaren

It's easy to forget that Västerås is situated on Lake Mälaren, as the centre of town is removed from the waterfront. Yet it is very easy to get out onto the lake, with **boat trips** operating to Västeråsfjärden and Ridöfjärden, the sections of the lake south of the city, where there is a string of small islands blessed with great **beaches**.

The closest island to Västerås is **Östra Holmen**, which is the easternmost of three islets located immediately off the coast. Noted for its three excellent **nudist beaches** on the southern shore, the island is popular with locals who come here to enjoy the wide open views of Lake Mälaren and to explore its undisturbed shoreline – an easy circular walk of around 2km. *M/F Elba* sails here hourly (10–15mins June to mid-August daily 10.15am–6.15pm; 40kr return; ⓦwww.vasteras.se/tif) from Färjkajen quay in the harbour, southwest of the train station.

Further south, sitting roughly halfway between the northern and southern shores of the lake, the much larger island of **Ridön** traces its history back to Viking times when it was home to a small fishing community. Today though, Ridön is a peaceful haven of forest, sheltered coves ideal for **swimming** and paths which lead around the entire coast, whilst a country lane winds its way across the centre of the island from west to east; there's a small **café** and wooden belltower at the point where this lane meets the path leading up from the ferry jetty. *M/F Silvertärnan* sails roughly every two hours (daily: June–Aug 7am–7pm; May, Sept & Oct Mon–Fri 3 daily, Sat & Sun 7am–7pm; 20 min; 40kr single; ⓦwww.vasteras.se/tif) daily to Ridön from Färjkajen quay in the harbour.

En route the ferry calls in at two smaller islands, **Almö-Lindö** and tiny **Skåpholmen**, both perfect for seekers of total solitude. Of these two uninhabited islands, cashew nut-shaped Almö-Lindö, which the boat reaches first, is the better bet since it is larger, has more varied terrain and some good bathing beaches – though no facilities. **Skåpholmen** is a skinny sliver of an island just off the southern shore of its larger neighbour, whose main attraction is total seclusion – if you're keen to spend a people-free day and are looking for your very own island where you can cast off your clothes and amble at will around the shoreline or through the forest – a quintessentially Swedish experience – this is the place to make for as you're likely to be the only person here: once again, there are no facilities. Although all ferries will stop here, both islands are request stops and on the return journey to Västerås you must make sure to raise the metal semaphore on the jetty to alert the boat that you wish to be picked up – forget and you'll be left waiting for the next boat.

However, if you're looking for a longer **cruise** on the lake, *M/S Nya Hjelmare Kanal* sails from Östra Hamnen harbour to Birka (10am daily early June to mid-Aug; 10am Sat & Sun early May to early June & mid-Aug to early Sept Sat and Sun only; 103kr single), a journey of three hours taking in some spectacular lakeside vistas. For more information contact the boat operator (☎08/587 140 00, ⓦwww.strommakanalbolaget.com) or the tourist office.

Sigtuna and Skokloster

SIGTUNA is a compact little town that has an impressive history dating all the way back to Viking times, with extensive ruined churches and rune stones right in the town centre. Just 40km north of Stockholm, this place is quietly

△ Caption

understated – it doesn't shout medieval history at you – in fact, apart from its ruins, it looks like any other old Swedish town with cobbled streets and squares – but scratch the surface and you'll soon understand what made Sigtuna so important. Founded in 980 by King Erik Segersäll, Sigtuna grew from a village to become Sweden's first town. Fittingly, it contains Sweden's oldest street, Storagatan – the original – laid out during the king's reign, still lies under its modern-day counterpart, beneath three metres of historical and cultural debris. Sigtuna also boasts three **ruined churches**, dating from the twelfth century, which give a good idea of the important role the town played in the Middle Ages when, in fact, Sigtuna supported no less than seven churches. Impressively, two of the three are very much still standing.

Two of the most impressive ruins, the churches of **St Per** and **St Olof**, lie along Stora gatan itself. Much of the west and central towers of St Per's still remain from the early 1100s; experts believe it likely that the church functioned as a cathedral until the diocese was moved to nearby Uppsala (see opposite). The unusual formation of the vault in the central tower was influenced by church design then current in England and Normandy. Further east along Stora gatan, St Olof's, dating from the mid-twelfth century has impressively thick walls and a short nave, the latter suggesting that the church was never completed. Sadly, the third ruined church, **St Lars**, is little more than a pile a stones nearby on Prästgata; only the remains of the tower are still standing.

Close by, on Olofsgatan (daily 9am–4pm; free), is the very much functioning **Mariakyrkan**, constructed of red brick during the mid-thirteenth century to serve the local Dominican monastery. Inside, the walls and ceiling are richly adorned with restored paintings from the fourteenth and fifteenth centuries. The Sigtuna district contains more rune stones than any other area in Sweden – around 150 of them have been found to date – and several can be seen close to the ruins of the church of St Lars along Prästgatan.

Further along the main road the **Sigtuna museum**, at no. 55 (June–Aug daily noon–4pm; Sept–May Tues–Sun noon–4pm; 20kr; ⓦwww.sigtuna.se/museer), exhibits archeological remnants, including material on Sigtuna's past role as Sweden's foremost trading centre. There are coins bearing witness to the town's status in 995 as the first town in the land to mint coins; alongside the head of the king are imprinted the words "Olof king in Sigtuna". However, the museum's prize exhibits are the booty the local pillaging populace brought home after various raids abroad: more coins, gold rings even an intricately decorated clay egg, dating from the eleventh century and originating in Kiev.

Practicalities

To reach Sigtuna from Stockholm, take either the SJ train or the Pendeltåg to Märsta, from where **buses** #570 and #575 run the short distance to the town – total journey time is around an hour. In summer it's also possible to reach Sigtuna by **boat** from Stockholm (late June to mid-Aug Wed & Sat only; 3hr; single 550kr including on-board lunch): the *M/S Östanå I* leaves Stadshusbron at 9.30am and returns to Stockholm on Thurs & Sun (also late June to mid-Aug) at 4.15pm.

Sigtuna's **tourist office** is at Stora gatan 33 (June–Aug Mon–Fri 10am–6pm, Sat 10am–5pm, Sun 11am–5pm; Sept Mon–Fri 10am–5pm, Sat & Sun 11am–4pm; rest of year Mon–Fri 9am–4pm; ⓣ08/592 500 20, ⓦwww.sigtuna.se/turism). Should you decide to stay, the good-value **youth hostel** is at Manfred Björkquists allé 12 (ⓣ08/592 582 00; ⓦwww.amica.se/ansgarsliden; late June to early Aug), at the bottom of the hill right by Lake Mälaren. However, total

luxury is also available at *Sigtuna Stadshotell* (☎08/592 501 00, ✇www
.sigtunastadshotell.se; ❻), Stora Nygatan 3, where discounted doubles go for
1550kr in a recently renovated building stuffed full of period fittings from the
early 1900s.

There are a couple of places to **eat** located off the main street: the atmospheric *Tant Brun*, at Lauräntii gränd 3, a café in a seventeenth-century building with outdoor seating in summer, specializes in home-made bread; *Amandas
Krog*, Långgränd 7, serves excellent Swedish home cooking. Also worth a look
is the floating *Båthuset* on Strandpromenaden, a pontoon supporting a little
wooden restaurant dishing up delicious fish and beef mains for around 120kr.
The best place to **drink** is *The Corner Pub*, Stationsgatan 3, which also has bar
meals and an impressive range of beers and whiskies.

Skokloster

Fans of exuberant Baroque shouldn't miss the seventeenth-century castle at
Skokloster (April–Oct mandatory English-language guided tours,
12.10pm–4.10pm; hourly at 10min past the hour; 65kr; ☎018/38 60 77,
✇www.lsh.se/skokloster), one hour north. Commissioned in 1654 by the
Estonian, Carl Gustav Wrangel, on the orders of King Karl IX, the white brick,
stone and marble exterior of this supreme example of high camp took fourteen years to complete, yet when the king died 22 years later, the interior
remained incomplete, as parts still do to this day. However, what remains is a
flamboyant mélange of stucco ceilings, carved fireplaces, gilt wall coverings,
elegant tapestries and quite simply some of the most over-the-top furniture
ever graced by aristocratic Swedish bottoms. Don't miss the count's extravagant
bedroom on the first floor, accessed from the top of a sweeping staircase of
Öland limestone, where visitors were received from the double bed in the centre of the room draped in red silk dotted with sequins; Dutch tapestries dating
from the seventeenth century crowd the walls and there is a small cabinet inlaid
with tortoiseshell.

From Skokloster hourly daily **buses** run via Bålsta to Uppsala (journey time
1hr 40min). However, it's also possible to travel in greater style by direct **boat**
from Skokloster to Uppsala (Wed & Sat at 4.45pm) and Stockholm (Thurs &
Sun at 1.45pm) from late June to mid-Aug). **Skokloster** is easily reached by
hourly daily bus from Sigtuna (change at Bålsta; 1hr) or by the Strömma
Kanalbolaget boat to Uppsala (see above for days of operation). If the palace
has left you longing for opulence, the *Skokloster Wärdshus* (☎018/38 61 00,
✇www.skokloster.se; ❺/❸) has tastefully old-fashioned **rooms** and a **restaurant** located in the castle's former stables.

Uppsala and around

First impressions as the train pulls into **UPPSALA**, only an hour northeast of
Stockholm, are encouraging, as the red-washed castle looms up behind the railway sidings with the cathedral dominant in the foreground. A medieval seat of
religion and learning, Uppsala clings to the past through its cathedral and university, and a striking succession of related buildings in their vicinity. The city
is primarily regarded as the historical and religious centre of the country, and
it's as a tranquil daytime alternative to Stockholm (and as a place with an active
student-geared nightlife) that Uppsala draws the traveller.

ACCOMMODATION

Årsta Gård	1
Basic	3
First Hotel Linné	2
Grand Hotell Hörnan	7
Radisson SAS Gillet	5
Scandic Hotel Uplandia	4
Svava	6
Youth Hostel	8

RESTAURANTS & CAFÉS

Alexander	L	Kung Krål	E
Amazing Thai	F	Landings	D
Domtrappkälaren	G	Ofvandahls	C
Elaka Måns	H	Sten Sture & Co.	N
Fågelsången	M	Svenssons krog/	
Guntherska		bakficka	A
hovkonditori	K	Svenssons taverna	B
Hambergs		Wayne's Coffee	J
fisk o kräft	I		

UPPSALA

Bror Hjorth Museum ▼   ▼ Campsite & ⑧

Arrival and information

The quickest way to get from Stockholm to Uppsala is by SJ train from the central station, although from July to mid-August there's also a boat service to Uppsala (Wed & Sat only; ☎08/587 140 00, ⓦwww.strommakanalbolaget .com), which leaves Stadshusbron (next to City Hall on Kungsholmen) at 9.30am, calling at Sigtuna and Skokloster on the way, arriving in Uppsala at 6.30pm. From the terminus at Islandsbron walk north along Västra Ågatan for ten minutes to reach the tourist office. Uppsala's **train** and **bus stations** are adjacent to each other off Kungsgatan, separated only by an erotic statue of a man with an oversized penis by local sculptor and painter, Bror Hjorth (see p.125). It's a fifteen-minute walk west to the **tourist office** at Fyris Torg 8 (Mon–Fri 10am–6pm, Sat 10am–3pm, plus end June to mid-Aug Sun noon–4pm; ☎018/27 48 00, ⓦwww.res.till.uppland.nu), where you can pick up bundles of leaflets about the city. Arlanda is Sweden's main **airport** serving the major scheduled airlines; bus #801 runs between the airport and Uppsala bus station (daily 4am–midnight every 15–30min; 40min; 75kr).

Accommodation

Though it's so close to Stockholm, staying over in Uppsala can be an attractive idea. The **youth hostel** is at Sunnerstavägen 24 (☎018/32 42 20, ☎018/32 40 68), 6km south of the centre at STF's beautifully sited *Sunnersta Herrgård* – take bus #20, #25 or #50 from Nybron, by Stora Torget. For a night's **camping**, head the few kilometres north to the open spaces of Gamla Uppsala (see p.127), or use the official campsite, *Sunnersta Camping* (☎018/27 60 84), at Graneberg, 7km out near the youth hostel (bus #20 from Nybron), where there are also two-person cabins by Lake Mälaren (❶). Uppsala has a fair range of central **hotels** (see below), but the cheapest, *Hotell Årsta Gård*, is a bus-ride away in suburbia.

Årsta Gård Jordgubbsgatan 14 ☎018/25 35 00. This large cottage-style building on the outskirts is the cheapest hotel in town; take bus #7 daytime or #56 evenings to Södra Årsta (15min). ❷

Basic Kungsgatan 27 ☎018/480 50 00, ⓦwww.basichotel.com. Simple, bright and clean rooms with en-suite bathrooms and a tiny shared kitchen. Same price all year. ❸/❷

First Hotel Linné Skolgatan 45 ☎018/10 20 00, ⓦwww.firsthotels.com. Completely overpriced tiny rooms – a last resort when everything else is full. ❺/❸

Grand Hotell Hörnan Bangårdsgatan 1 ☎018/13 93 80, ⓦwww.eklundshof.se. A wonderfully elegant place with large old-fashioned rooms and a restaurant. Try for a room overlooking the Fyrisån

river at the front. ❺/❹

Radisson SAS Gillet Dragarbrunnsgatan 23 ☎018/68 18 00, ⓦwww.radisson.com. A stone's throw from the cathedral but with run-of-the-mill, overpriced, rooms. Fans of kitsch should head for the restaurant. ❺/❸

Scandic Hotel Uplandia Dragarbrunnsgatan 32 ☎018/495 26 00, ⓦwww.scandic-hotels.com. A modern chain hotel that's opted for small rooms with wood fittings. ❻/❸

Svava Bangårdsgatan 24 ☎018/13 00 30, ⓦwww.hotelsvava.com. Modern hotel with all creature comforts, including specially designed rooms for people with disabilities and those with allergies. ❻/❹

The City

A fifteen-minute walk west from the train station, the great **Domkyrkan** is Scandinavia's largest cathedral (ⓦwww.uppsaladomkyrka.nu; daily 8am–6pm; free), and the centre of the medieval town. Built as a Gothic boast to the people of Trondheim in Norway that even their mighty church, the Nidarosdom, could be overshadowed, it loses out to its rival only on building materials – local brick rather than imported stone. The echoing interior remains impressive, particularly the French Gothic ambulatory, flanked by tiny chapels and bathed in a golden, decorative glow. One chapel contains a lively set of restored fourteenth-century wall paintings that recount the legend of St Erik, Sweden's patron saint: his coronation, subsequent crusade to Finland, eventual defeat and execution at the hands of the Danes. The Relics of Erik are zealously guarded in a chapel off the nave: poke around and you'll also find the tombs of the Reformation rebel Gustav Vasa and his son Johan III, and that of the botanist Linnaeus (see overleaf), who lived in Uppsala. Time and fire have led to the rest of the cathedral being rebuilt, scrubbed and painted to the extent that it resembles a museum more than a thirteenth-century place of worship; even the characteristic twin spires are late nineteenth-century additions.

The other buildings grouped around the Domkyrkan can all claim a purer historical pedigree. Opposite the west end of the cathedral, the onion-domed **Gustavianum** was built in 1625 as part of the university (May–Sept daily 11am–5pm; Sept–April Tues–Sun 11am–4pm; 40kr), and is much touted by the tourist office for its **Augsburg Art Cabinet** – an ebony treasure chest presented to Gustav II Adolf by the Lutheran councillors of Augsburg in 1632 – and its tidily preserved anatomical theatre. The same building houses a couple of small collections of Egyptian, Classical and Nordic antiquities with a small extra charge for each section.

The current **University** building (Mon–Fri 8am–4pm) is the imposing nineteenth-century Renaissance-style edifice opposite Gustavianum. Originally a seminary, today it's used for lectures and seminars and hosts the graduation ceremonies each May. Among the more famous alumni are Carl von Linné (Linnaeus; see overleaf) and Anders Celsius, inventor of the temperature scale. No one will mind you strolling in for a quick look, but the rest of the building is not open to the public.

From the university, Övre Slottsgatan leads south to the **Carolina Rediviva** (mid-June to mid-Aug Mon–Fri 9am–5pm, Sat 10am–5pm, Sun 11am–4pm; 20kr; rest of year Mon–Fri 9am–8pm, Sat 10am–4pm; free), the university library and one of Scandinavia's largest, with around five million books. On April 30 (Valborgsmässoafton) each year the students meet here to celebrate the official first day of spring (usually in the snow), all wearing the traditional student cap that gives them the appearance of disaffected sailors. Adopt a studenty pose and you can slip in for a wander round and a coffee in the common room. More officially, take a look in the **manuscript room**, where there's a collection of rare letters and other paraphernalia. The beautiful sixth-century Silver Bible is on permanent display, as is Mozart's original manuscript for *The Magic Flute*.

After this, the **castle** (guided tours June–Aug 1pm & 3pm; 60kr) up on the hill, built by Gustav Vasa in the mid-sixteenth century, is a disappointment. Certainly over the centuries significant chapters of Sweden's history were played out here: the Uppsala Assembly of 1593, which established the supremacy of the Lutheran Church, took place in the Hall of State, where also, in 1630, the Parliament resolved to enter the Thirty Years' War. Sadly though, much of the castle was destroyed in the 1702 fire that also did away with three-quarters of the city, and only one side and two towers – the L-shape of today – remain of what was once an opulent rectangular palace. Inside, admission also includes access to the castle's art museum but, quite frankly, it won't make your postcards home.

The Linnaeus Garden

Seeing Uppsala – at least its compact older parts – will take up a good half-day; afterwards, take a stroll along the Fyrisån river that runs right through the centre of town. In summer, there are several resting places here that are good for an hour or two's sunbathing, and there's enough greenery to make for a pleasant wander. One beautiful spot is the **Linnaeus Garden** (daily: May–Sept 7am–8.30pm; rest of year 7am–7pm; access to greenhouses 20kr; ⓦwww .linnaeus.uu.se), over the river on Svartbäcksgatan, containing around 1300

Carl Von Linné

Born in Småland in 1707, **Carl von Linné**, who styled himself Carolus Linnaeus, is undoubtedly Sweden's most revered scientist: any Swedish town of a decent size has a street named Linnégatan, one of Gothenburg's most appealing districts (see p.152 is named after him – and his face appears on all 100kr notes. His international-al reputation was secured by the introduction of his **binomial classification**, a two-part nomenclature that enabled plants to be consistently named and categorized into families. Only very recently has the basis of his classifications been undermined by genetic methods, resulting in the complete realignment of certain plant families. In 1732, while still a university student, he secured funds from the bishop of Växjö to undertake a botanical expedition to Lapland. His later expeditions to the Baltic islands of Öland and Gotland, and the mainland provinces of Västergotland and Skåne, were to provide the cornerstones for the creation of his ground-breaking system of plant classification. In 1754 he acquired an estate at **Hammarby**, 13km southeast of the town, and built a house there. Today, the beautiful homestead, with lush gardens including a collection of Siberian plants and a gene bank for the fruit species of the Lake Mälaren region, is managed by the university (May–Sept daily 8am–8pm; bus #808 runs here from town). The house contains some of Linné's own hand-coloured drawings of plants; also here is his private natural history museum, now the property of the Linnéan Society in London, in a stone pavilion on a hill nearby (Tues–Sun noon–4pm; 10kr).

varieties of plants. These are Sweden's oldest botanical gardens, established in 1655 by Olof Rudbeck the Elder, and relaid by Linnaeus (see box, opposite) in 1741; some of the species he introduced and classified still survive here. The adjoining **museum** (same times; 20kr) was once home to Linnaeus and his family, and attempts to evoke his life through a partially restored library, writing room and a collection of natural history specimens. While you're in Uppsala, you may also wish to visit the great man's former house at Hammarby, south of town (see box).

The Bror Hjorth museum

Travelling around Sweden, you can't help but spot the work of Uppsala-born sculptor and painter, Bror Hjorth (1894–1968). Once professor of drawing at the Swedish Royal Academy of Fine Arts, today he's considered one of Sweden's greatest artists. A modernist with roots in folk art, his numerous public art commissions can be seen right across the country – perhaps most strikingly in the church in Jukkasjärvi in Lapland (see p.492). Arriving in Uppsala by train or bus, you'll have come face-to-face with one of his statues right outside the main stations, and will understand why his work so much contraversy. The central theme in his sculptures and paintings, which concentrate mostly on love, life and music, was to seek out the intensity which art can evoke. His former home and studio in Uppsala have now been turned into a **museum** (early June to Aug Tues–Sun noon–4pm; mid-Aug to May Thurs, Sat & Sun noon–4pm; 30kr), containing the largest and most representative collection of his work in the country. Buses #6 and #7 run from Stora Torget to the museum, located a ten-minute ride west of the centre at Norbyvägen 26.

Eating, drinking and nightlife

In keeping with its status as one of Sweden's largest cities and major university centres, Uppsala boasts an impressive range of sophisticated **restaurants** and **bars**. Almost all of them are located in the grid of streets bordered by the Fyrisån river, St Olofsgatan and Bangårdsgatan, and, although in summer it can be busy in Uppsala, it's not necessary to book a table. If you're travelling north from here into the Swedish provinces, it's a good idea to splurge and make the most of the city's eateries, which offer everything from mouthwatering cakes to moussaka.

Cafés

Güntherska hovkonditori Östra Ågatan 31. Old-fashioned café with simple lunch dishes for around 65kr.

Fågelsången Munkgatan 3. Café and lunch place that's full of posey students. Coffee and cake here is around 50–60kr.

Landings Kungsängsgatan 5. Busy café in the main pedestrian area where good open sandwiches go for around 50–70kr.

Ofvandahls Sysslomangatan 3–5. Near the old part of town, this lively café, with old wooden tables and sofas, originally opened in 1878. Don't leave town without trying the home-made cakes; around 40–50kr a slice.

Wayne's Coffee Smedgränd 4. The best café in Uppsala – modern and airy with large windows which open right out onto the street.

Restaurants and bars

Alexander Östra Ågatan 59. Completely over-the-top Greek place with busts of famous Ancient Greeks at every turn. Main dishes 95–165kr

Amazing Thai Bredgränd 14. Small and friendly place serving up all your favourite Thai main dishes for around 100kr; lunch is 60kr. Also does takeaways.

Domtrappkälaren St Eriks Gränd 15. One of the most chi-chi places in town with an old vaulted roof and a great atmosphere. Dishes around 200kr; excellent lunch upstairs for 110kr.

Elaka Måns Smedsgränd 9. A modern bistro-style restaurant with the usual run of fish and meat dishes. Very popular and not too pricey.

Hambergs fisk o kräft Fyris Torg 8. Located next to the tourist office and serving very good fish and seafood. Particularly popular at lunchtime. Reckon on 150kr per dish.

Kung Krål St Persgatan 4. Across the river from the tourist office, housed in a fantastic old stone building with outdoor seating in summer. Swedish home-cooking and international dishes for around 120kr.

Sten Sture & Co Nedre Slottsgatan 3. This large ramshackle wooden house immediately below the castle serving trendy and inspired cooking is one of the best spots in town. There's often live jazz while you eat and outdoor tables in summer.

Svenssons krog/bakficka Sysslomangatan 15. A wonderful restaurant decked out in wood and glass, with everything from Swedish home-cooking to elaborate salmon dishes. The cheaper *bakficka* section serves good pasta at around 100kr.

Svenssons taverna Sysslomangatan 14. Across the road from its sister-restaurant, one of Uppsala's best eateries offers an international menu for around 120kr per dish. There's a large outdoor seating area in the shade of huge beech and oak trees.

Bars, clubs and live music

At night, most of the action is generated by the **students** in houses called "Nations", contained within the grid of streets behind the university, backing onto St Olofsgatan. Each a sort of college student club or association, they run dances, gigs and parties of all hues, and most importantly boast very cheap bars. The official line is that if you're not a Swedish student you won't get into most of the events advertised around the town; in practice being foreign and nice to the people on the door generally yields entrance, and with an ISIC card it's even easier. As many students stay around during the summer, functions are not strictly limited to term time. A good choice to begin with is *Uplands Nation*, off St Olofsgatan and Sysslomangatan near the river, with a summer outdoor café open until 3am.

Among the **non-student bars** is *Svenssons Taverna*, Sysslomangatan 14, which is a great place for a beer and nibbles; but it's *O'Connors*, a first-floor Irish pub with food, tucked away at Stora Torget 1 above the fast-food place *Saffet's*, which is *the* place to do your drinking – it's quite astounding just how many people can crowd into this pub. Also inordinately popular is the new *Escobar*, Smedsgränd 9, a glass and chrome place that's both bar and restaurant serving up different types of lasagne as well as large amounts of attitude. *Sten Sture & Co* puts on **live bands** in the evenings, while *Katalin and all that jazz* is open late and puts on **jazz** nights in the long, low goods shed behind the train station.

Listings

Banks and exchange Handelsbanken, Vaksalagatan 8; Nordea, Stora Torget; SEB, Kungsängsgatan 7–9; Upplandsbanken at the corner of Östra Ågatan and Drottninggatan. There's a Forex exchange at Fyris Torg 8, left of the tourist office. Mon–Fri 9am–7pm, Sat 9am–3pm; ☏018/10 30 00.

Buses City buses leave from Stora Torget; they're operated by Uppsalabuss ☏018/27 37 00; long-distance buses from the bus station adjacent to the train station (see Stockholm "Listings" for phone numbers).

Car rental Avis, Stålgatan 8 ☏018/15 16 80; Europcar, Kungsgatan 103 ☏018/17 17 30; Hertz, Kungsgatan 97 ☏018/16 02 00.

Cinemas Filmstaden, Västra Ågatan 12 & 16.

Pharmacy At Bredgränd ☏020/66 77 66; Mon–Fri 9am–6.30pm, Sat 10am–3pm.

Police Salagatan 18 ☏018/16 85 00.

Swimming pool Centralbadet, Gamla Torget to the right of the Kung Krål restaurant.

Systembolaget Svavagallerian, Mon–Wed 10am–6pm, Thu & Fri 10am–7pm, Sat 10am–2pm.

Taxis Taxi Kurir ☏018/12 34 56; Uppsala Taxi ☏018/10 10 10.

Train station Information on ☏018/65 22 10.

Travel agent Kilroy, Bredgränd (Mon–Fri 10am–6pm); Ticket, Östra Ågatan 33 & Bångårdsgatan 13 (Mon–Fri 9am–6pm, Sat 10am–2pm).

Gamla Uppsala

Five kilometres to the north of Uppsala, three huge royal **burial mounds**, dating back to the sixth century mark the original site of the town – **Gamla Uppsala** (ⓦ www.raa.se/gamlauppsala). According to legend, they are the final resting places of three ancient kings Aun, Egil and Adlis. Though the site developed into an important trading and administrative centre, it was originally established as a pagan settlement and a place of ancient sacrificial rites by the Svear tribe. In the eleventh century, the German chronicler, Adam of Bremen, described the cult of the *æsir* (the Norse gods Odin, Thor and Freyr) practised in Uppsala: every ninth year, the deaths of nine people would be demanded at the festival of Fröblot, the victims left hanging from a nearby tree until their corpses rotted. Two centuries later, the great medieval storyteller, Snorri Sturluson of Iceland, depicted Uppsala as the true home of the Ynglinga dynasty (the original royal family in Scandinavia who also worshipped Freyr), a place where grand sacrificial festivals were held in honour of their god.

The pagan temple where these bloody sacrifices took place is now marked by the Christian **Gamla Uppsala kyrka** (daily: April–Sept 9am–6pm; rest of year 9am–4pm), which was built over pagan remains when the Swedish kings first took baptism in the new faith. Built predominantly of stone yet characterized by its rear nave wall of stepped red-brick gabling, this is one of the most breathtakingly beautiful churches in Sweden with an understated simplicity at the very heart of its appeal. Although what survives of the church today is only a remnant of the original cathedral, the relics inside more than compensate for the downscaling. In the porch are two impressive collecting chests, one made from an oak log and fitted with iron locks, which dates from the earliest days of the church. Entering the nave, look out for the cabinet on the left containing a superb collection of church silver, including a fourteenth-century chalice and a censer from the 1200s. Nearby, in the nave wall, a stone memorial to Anders Celsius, inventor of the temperature scale that bears his name, is a worthy tribute. The overpowering feeling of early ecclesiastical design is enhanced by the fifteenth-century faded wall and ceiling paintings, all round the nave, which boldly portray the horns of an ox, the arms of the Oxenstierna family. Outside, if you haven't yet set eyes on a genuine rune stone in Sweden, look carefully in the church walls at the back to find a perfectly preserved example from the eleventh century.

The burial mounds and the Historical Centre

Southeast of the church, the **tinghög** or parliament hill, the only mound not fenced in, was once the site of the local *ting,* where, until the sixteenth century, a Viking parliament was held to deliberate on all matters affecting Uppsala. Immediately west of here, a path leads around the three main mounds, the first of which, **östhögen**, the east mound, dates from around 550. Following the 1846–7 excavations of Gamla Uppsala, this hill yielded the site's most astonishing artefacts: the cremated remains of a woman – possibly a priestess for the god Freyr – buried in magnificent wool, linen and silk clothing, as well as a necklace bearing a powerful image of a Valkyrie. The adjacent central mound, **mitthögen**, is thought to be around fifty years older than its neighbour but has still to be excavated. Finally, the western **västhögen** has been dated from the late sixth century and following excavations in 1874 revealed male bone fragments and jewellery commensurate with high status.

The finds are proudly displayed in the new and enjoyable **Historical Centre** (mid-May to mid-Aug daily 10am–5pm; mid-April to mid-May & mid-Aug to Sept Tues–Sun 10am–4pm; Oct–Dec Sat & Sun noon–3pm; 50kr), at the entrance to the site. It's a brave and successful attempt to portray early Swedish history in a wider non-Viking context. Here you can gawp at an archeologist's dream – gold fragments, ancient pieces of glass and precious ivory game pieces – as well as ambling through exhibitions illustrating the origin of local myths and a full account of Uppsala's golden period which ended in the thirteenth century.

Practicalities

Buses #2, #24 or #54 from Stora Torget in Uppsala drop you at the Gamla Uppsala terminus, in reality nothing more than a bus stop next to a level crossing opposite the Historical Centre. From the bus stop cross the busy Stockholm-Uppsala mainline at the level crossing to reach the site; from the Centre paths lead to the church and burial mounds. If the nibbles strike after an afternoon of pillaging and plundering, there's a simple **restaurant** nearby: *Odinsborg*, halfway between the Historical Centre and the church, was built in the Swedish national romantic style and serves lunches and light snacks for around 70kr, though nothing else – it is precisely this absence of touristy adornments, something the Swedes have understood, that has helped Gamla Uppsala remain so mysterious and atmospheric.

Travel details

Trains

Stockholm to: Boden (2 daily; 14hr); Gällivare (2 daily; 16hr); Gävle (hourly; 1hr 20min); Gothenburg (hourly; 3hr 10min by X2000, 5hr by Inter-City); Helsingborg (hourly; 5hr); Kiruna (2 daily; 17hr); Läggesta (for Mariefred; 8 daily; 40min); Luleå (2 daily; 14hr); Malmö (hourly; 4hr 30min); Mora (4 daily; 4hr); Östersund (3 daily; 6hr); Sundsvall (7 daily; 3hr 30min); Umeå (1 daily; 10hr); Uppsala (hourly; 40min)

Läggesta to: Stockholm (hourly; 40min); Västerås (hourly; 1hr 30min).

Uppsala to: Gällivare (2 daily; 15hr); Gävle (hourly; 40min); Kiruna (2 daily; 16hr); Luleå (2 daily; 13hr); Mora (4 daily; 3hr); Östersund (3 daily; 4hr 30 min); Stockholm (hourly; 40min); Sundsvall (7 daily; 2hr 45 min); Umeå (1 daily; 9hr 30min).

Västerås to: Stockholm (every 30min; 50min); Läggesta (hourly; 1hr 30min); Gothenburg (7 daily; 4hr)

Buses

Bålsta to: Skokloster (hourly; 25min)
Märsta to: Sigtuna (4 hourly; 20min)
Sigtuna to: Bålsta (hourly; 40min)
Stockholm to: Gothenburg (Mon–Wed 2 daily, Thurs 3 daily, Fri & Sun 5 daily, Sat 1 daily; 4hr 30min, or 7hr 20min via Kristinehamn or Jönköping); Gävle (daily; 2hr 20min); Halmstad (Fri & Sun 1 daily; 7hr 30min); Helsingborg

(Mon–Thurs 1 daily, Fri & Sun 2 daily; 8hr); Jönköping (Mon–Thurs 1 daily, Fri & Sun 2 daily; 4hr 50min); Kalmar (5 daily; 6hr 30min); Kristianstad (Mon, Thurs, Fri & Sun 1 daily; 9hr 30min); Kristinehamn (Mon–Thurs & Sat 2 daily, Fri & Sun 3 daily; 3hr); Malmö (Fri 1 daily, Sun 2 daily; 10hr 20min); Norrköping (Mon–Wed 2 daily, Thurs 3 daily, Fri & Sun daily, Sat daily; 2hr); Sollefteå (1 daily; 8hr 15min); Umeå (1 daily; 9hr 20min); Östersund (1 daily; 8hr 30min).

Ferries

For details of Stockholm city ferries, see p.67; for the services to the archipelago, see p.106; for Birka see p.104.

International trains

Stockholm to: Copenhagen (5 daily; 5hr); Narvik (1 daily; 20hr); Oslo (3 daily; 5hr).
Uppsala to: Narvik (1 daily; 18hr 30min).

International ferries

Grisslehamn to: Eckerö on the Åland Islands (2–5 daily; 2hr); a bus leaves Tekniska Högskolan T-bana 2hr before the ferry's departure from Grisslehamn
Stockholm to: Helsinki (1 Viking Line and 1 Silja Line daily; 17hr); Mariehamn (6 daily; 4hr); Tallinn (1 daily; 13hr); Turku (4 daily; 12–14hr).

Gothenburg and around

RUSSIA

Arctic Circle

NORWEGIAN SEA

⑦

⑤

Gulf of Bothnia

FINLAND

NORWAY

⑥

Gulf of Finland

①

ESTONIA

RUSSIA

❷

④

Gotland

LATVIA

③

Öland

DENMARK

BALTIC SEA

LITHUANIA

BELARUS

CHAPTER 2

Highlights

✷ **Fürstenburg galleries** The highlight of the city's grand Art Museum are the paintings by Sweden's finest nineteenth- and early twentieth century artists. See p.147

✷ **Café life in Haga** Sip a coffee at the laid-back pavement cafés in Gothenburg's old working-class neighbourhood. See p.151

✷ **Marstrand** This glorious fortress island on the Bohuslän Coast buzzes with summer activity when the yachting set joins the sea bathers. See p.165

✷ **Smedje Volund** The home-cum-studio of Sweden's celebrated blacksmith Berthe Johansson is carved from pink granite and filled with the shipwrecks he reworks into furniture. See p.169

✷ **Fiskebäckskil** A picture-perfect Bohuslän coast fishing village is the location of the studio of painter Carl Wilhelmson. See p.170

✷ **Fallensdagar, Trollhättan** Each July, this three-day festival of music and dancing centres round the town's dramatically lit crashing waterfalls. See p.180

✷ **Kinekulle** "Flowering Mountain" on the southern shores of Lake Vänern is pure pastural beauty, dotted with historical sites from runic stones to medieval churches. See p.187

Gothenburg and around

Of all the cities in southern Sweden, the grandest and most varied is the western port of **Gothenburg**. Designed by the Dutch in 1621, the city boasts splendid Neoclassical architecture, masses of sculpture-strewn parkland and a welcoming and relaxed spirit.

Gothenburg is Sweden's second largest city and Scandinavia's largest seaport; these facts, allied with its industrial heritage as a shipbuilding centre, have been enough to persuade many travellers arriving in the country by ferry to move quickly on into the surrounding countryside. The cityscape of broad avenues, elegant squares, trams and canals, however, is not only one of the prettiest in Sweden, but also the backdrop to a well-established arts and youth scene, and a well-developed café society. There is a certain resentment on the west coast that Stockholm wins out in the national glory stakes, but Gothenburg's easier-going atmosphere – and its closer proximity to western Europe – makes it first choice as a place to live, ahead of the capital, for many Swedes. Talk to any Gothenburger and he or she will soon disparage the more frenetic lives of the "08-ers" – 08 being the telephone code for Stockholm. Gothenburg has a buoyancy of its own though – thanks to its highly visible student population – that inspires exploration; those who try soon discover that the place is worth a lot more time than most ferry arrivals give it.

The counties to the north and east of the city are prime targets for domestic tourists. To the north, the craggy **Bohuslän coastline**, with its uninhabited islands, tiny fishing villages and clean beaches, attracts thousands of holiday-makers all the way to the Norwegian border. The coast is popular with the sail-ing set, and there are many guest harbours along the way. One highlight is the glorious fortress island of **Marstrand**, which makes for an easy and enjoyable day-trip from Gothenburg, while further north, islands such as the **Kosters** offer splendid isolation and unexpectedly exuberant wildlife.

To the northeast of the city, the vast and beautiful lakes of **Vänern** and **Vättern** provide the setting for a number of historic towns, fairy-tale castles and some splendid inland scenery, all of which are within an hour's train jour-ney of Gothenburg. The lakes are connected to each other (and to the east and west coasts) by the cross-country **Göta Canal**, allowing you to travel all the way from Gothenburg to Stockholm by boat: a lovely trip. The first leg of this journey is up the Trollhättan Canal to **Trollhättan**, a low-key, winning little

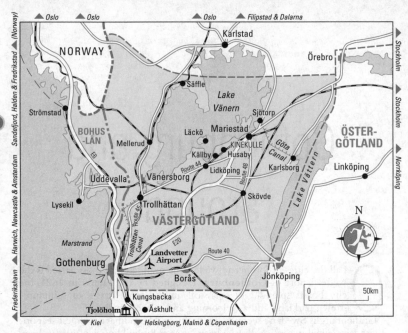

town built around the canal, and a good place to aim for if you only have time for a short trip out from the city. Beyond here, though, other agreeable lakeside towns vie for your attention, with attractions including the elk safaris on the ancient plateaux of Halleberg and Hunneberg, near **Vänersborg** on the tip of Lake Vänern; the historically fascinating natural haven of **Kinnekulle**, a hill rising to the east of Lake Vänern; the picturesque medieval kernel of **Mariestad**, further up the lake's eastern shore; and the huge military fortress at **Karlsborg**, on the western shore of Lake Vättern. Just beyond the southernmost suburbs of Gothenburg, a couple of charming excursions within easy reach of the city include the elaborate manor house **Tjolöholm** and **Äskhult**, a rare example of a perfectly preserved early nineteenth-century farmstead.

Trains and **buses** provide most of the region with a regular, efficient service; the only area you may find difficult to explore without a car is the Bohuslän coast. **Accommodation** is never a problem, with plenty of hotels, hostels and campsites in each town.

Gothenburg

With its long history as a trading centre, **GOTHENBURG** (Göteborg in Swedish; pronounced "Yur-te-boy") is a truly cosmopolitan city. Founded on its present site in the seventeenth century by Gustav II Adolf, Gothenburg was the fifth attempt to create a centre not reliant on Denmark – the Danes had enjoyed control of Sweden's west coast since the Middle Ages, and had extracted extortionate tolls from all water traffic into Sweden. The medieval centre of trade had been 40km up the Göta River, but to avoid the tolls it was moved to a site north of the present city. It wasn't until Karl XI chose the island of Hisingen, today the site of the city's northern suburbs, as the location for Sweden's trading nucleus that the settlement was first called Gothenburg. This, however, fell to the Danes during the battle of Kalmar and it was left to Gustav II Adolf to find the vast ransom demanded for its return. Six years later, when it had finally been paid off, he founded the city where the main square is today.

Although Gothenburg's reputation as an industrial and trading centre has been severely eroded in recent years – clearly evidenced by the stillness of its shipyard cranes – the British, Dutch and German traders who settled here during the eighteenth and nineteenth centuries left a rich architectural and cultural legacy. The city is graced with terraces of grand **merchant houses**, all carved stone, stucco and painted tiles. The influence of the Orient was also strong, reflecting the all-important trade links between Sweden and the Far East, and is still visible in the chinoiserie detail on many buildings. This trade was monopolized for over eighty years during the nineteenth century by the hugely successful **Swedish East India Company**, whose Gothenburg auction house, selling exotic spices, teas and fine cloths, attracted merchants from all over the world.

Today the city remains a business centre, but the flashy hotels in the centre are much less striking for the visitor than the restrained opulence of the older buildings, which echoes not only its bygone prosperity but also the understated tastes of its citizens. In the 1960s, parts of the city lost their grandest old buildings, and the new apartment blocks that replaced them, while lacking the beauty of their predecessors, are far less hideous than their equivalents in other European cities. Gothenburgers may tell you that they think their surroundings are nothing special, but these assertions are simply an expression of Swedish reserve and Gothenburg modesty. They also have a justified reputation for friendliness, and though a one night stopover may not reveal it, there is a relaxed geniality among many of the city's folk, making this one of the few places in Sweden where the locals may strike up a conversation with you, rather than vice versa.

Arrival and information

All **trains** arrive at **Central Station**, which forms one side of Drottningtorget. **Buses** from towns north of Gothenburg use **Nils Ericsonsplatsen**, just behind the train station; arriving from places south of Gothenburg, you'll disembark at **Heden** terminal at the junction of Parkgatan and Södra Vägen, with easy tram connections to all areas of the city. From **Landvetter airport**, 25km east of the city, Flygbuss (airport buses; daily 5am–11.15pm; 30min; 60kr) run every fifteen minutes into the centre, stopping at Liseberg, Korsvagen, Avenyn and Parkgatan before arriving in front of the train station.

DFDS Seaways **ferries** (☎031/65 06 50, ⓦwww.dfdsseaways.se) from Newcastle in England (see p.15) arrive at **Frihamnspiren** on Hisingen, north of the river, from where buses run to Nils Ericsonsplatsen, behind the train station (20mins; 40kr). **Stena Line** (ⓦwww.stenaline.com) also operates ferries from Fredrikshavn in Denmark, which dock just twenty minutes' walk from the city centre, close to the Masthuggstorget tram stop on lines #3, #4 and #9; their services from Kiel in Germany put in 3km away from the city, from where bus #491 or trams #3 or #9 will bring you into the centre.

The Gothenburg Pass

A boon if you want to pack in a good bit of sightseeing, the **Gothenburg Pass** provides unlimited bus and tram travel within the city; free entry to all the city museums except for the Liseberg Amusement Park (see p.149); free boat trips to Nya Elfsborg (see p.144); and two-for-one reductions at several other sights. It includes a bus tour and paddan boat trips and one free trip on a vintage tram. The only transport not covered by the card are the special buses to and from the airport and port (see p.133). The Gothenburg Pass comes with a second card entitling the holder to free parking in roadside spaces (but not at privately run or multistorey car parks). You can buy the card, which is valid on the day of purchase, from either of the tourist offices, and from hotels and Pressbyrån kiosks or at ⓦwww.goteborg.com (75kr for a 24-hour pass, 295kr for a 48-hour pass). An accompanying booklet explains in detail where and how it can save you money.

Gothenburg has two **tourist offices**; the one handiest for those arriving by train or bus is at the kiosk in Nordstan, the indoor shopping centre near Central Station (Mon–Fri 9.30am–6pm, Sat 10am–4pm, Sun noon–3pm). The main office is, however, on the canal front at Kungsportsplatsen 2 (May Mon–Fri 9am–6pm, Sat & Sun 10am–2pm; June & mid–Aug to late Aug daily 9am–6pm; July to mid–Aug daily 9am–8pm; Sept–April Mon–Fri 9am–5pm, Sat 10am–2pm; ☎031/61 25 00, ⓦwww.goteborg.com), just five minutes' walk from the train station, across Drottningtorget and down Stora Nygatan; the tourist office is opposite the "Copper Mare" statue (see p.146). Both offices provide information, a room-booking service, and a restaurant; the bilingual, annually renewed *Guide Göteborg* detailing events, music and night spots in town, is available from either. The tourist offices also sell the Gothenburg Pass (see above), obtainable on its own or with hotel accommodation as part of the Gothenburg Package (see p.137).

City transport

Apart from sights north of the river or out in the islands, it's easy to **walk** to almost anywhere of interest in Gothenburg. The streets are wide and pedestrian-friendly, and the canals and the grid system of avenues make orientation simple. The city is one of the best in Europe for **cycling**: most main roads have cycle lanes, and motorists really do seem to give way to those on two wheels. The tourist office can provide you with the excellent *cykelcarte* which shows clearly all the cycle routes throughout the city, and out to the archipelago.

That said, access to some form of **public transport** is always handy, particularly if you've just arrived at one of the central transport terminals or end up staying further out from the centre. The **tram** system is efficient and frequent and more easily negotiated than buses for travel within the city. A free **transport map** (*linje kartan*) is available at both tourist offices.

Trams and buses

The most convenient form of public transport is the **tram** system. A colour-coded system of eleven tram lines serves the city and its outskirts, and a tram will pass through all central areas every few minutes – you can tell at a glance which line a tram is on, as the route colour will appear on the front. Trams run

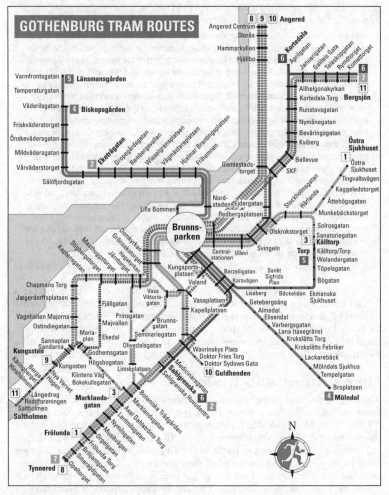

GOTHENBURG TRAM ROUTES

from 5am to midnight, after which there is a less frequent night service. The main pick-up points are outside Central Station and in Kungsportsplatsen. During summer, there are even vintage trams on the network, plying the Liseberg route (see box overleaf). Gothenburg also has a fairly extensive **bus** network, using much the same routes, but central pedestrianization can lead to some odd and lengthy detours. You shouldn't need to use buses in the city centre; routes are detailed in the text where necessary.

Tickets are available from tram and bus drivers. There are no zones, and fares cost a standard 16kr for adults, while 7- to 16-year-olds go for half price; tickets for the night service on the trams cost double the usual price. Ticket inspectors, in yellow jackets, are on the increase, and there's an instant fine of 600kr if you're caught travelling without a valid ticket – since all the ticket information is in English and posted on boards at bus and tram stops, ignorance is no defence.

If you are staying for a couple of days and travelling around the city quite a bit, it's better value to buy **carnets** from the Tidpunkten offices – travel information centres – at Brunnsparken, Drottningtorget and Nils Ericsonsplatsen, or from Pressbyrån kiosks. A ten-trip carnet costs 100kr. Stick these in the machines on a tram or bus, press twice for an adult, once for a child. With a **Gothenburg Pass** (see p.134), most public transport within the city is free.

Bikes, cars and taxis

Cycling in the city is easy and popular; there's a comprehensive series of cycle lanes and bike racks. You can rent a bike at Millennium Cykel at Chalmersgatan 19 (ⓣ031/18 43 00; 60kr/day), a street to the south of and parallel to Avenyn; the *Slottskogens* and *Stigbergssliden* hostels (see p.140) also rent bikes for 50kr a day.

There is no shortage of **car parks** in the city, with a basic charge of 20kr per hour in the centre. The most useful of these are the new Ullevigarage at Heden, near the bus terminal; the Lorensbergs car park near Avenyn; Gamla Ullevi on Allen, south of Kungsportsplatsen; and two multistorey car parks: at Nordstan near Central Station, and at Garda-Focus, close to Liseberg. Guests at some of the larger hotels can claim a discount at the multistorey car parks. Roadside parking areas marked with blue signs, where you pay at machines, are cheaper than metered spaces. The Gothenburg Pass comes with a second card entitling the holder to free parking in certain areas (see p.134). For information on **car rental**, see p.162.

Taxis can be summoned by calling ⓣ031/65 00 00; you can also pick one up at the rank at Central Station. There is a twenty percent reduction for women travelling at night – check with the driver first.

Accommodation

Gothenburg has plenty of good accommodation to choose from, with no shortage of comfortable **youth hostels** (a couple of which are very central) and **private rooms**. Most of the central **hotels** are clustered around the train station; they offer a high standard of service, though they're designed with business people in mind, so tend to be flashy but characterless. You should have little trouble finding accommodation whenever you turn up, though in summer it's a good idea to book ahead if you are on a tighter budget, or if you want to stay in the most popular youth hostels. There are several **campsites**, though none of them very central, the closest being just beyond Liseberg Amusement Park.

Hotels and pensions

Summer reductions mean that even the better hotels can prove surprisingly affordable, and most places also take part in the **Gothenburg Package**, a scheme coordinated by the tourist office. This is a real bargain as it offers accommodation in a twin bedroom, breakfast and a Gothenburg Pass, all from 450kr per person per night, daily, all year round. There is a fifty percent discount for **children** sharing with one parent at some hotels, while others allow extra beds in single rooms – the tourist office can advise. To take advantage of the Gothenburg Package, contact the tourist office (see p.134). Breakfast is included in our prices, unless otherwise stated.

Old town and harbour

Barken Viking Gullbergskajen ☎031 63 58 00, ℮barken.viking@liseberg.se. Moored by the Opera House, this hotel on a 1906, Danish-built training ship is a charismatic and comfortable choice with dark, cosy rooms and good service. ❷

Eggers Drottningtorget ☎031/80 60 70, ℗www.bestwestern.se. The original station hotel, this characterful establishment has individually furnished bedrooms and a wealth of grand original features; the place is believed to have been used during World War II for secret discussions between British and Nazi military negotiators. With a low Gothenburg Package price, this is one of the best-value central hotels. ❻/❹

Elite Plaza Västra Hamngatan 3 ☎031/720 40 40, ℗www.euro-hotel-discounts.com. The magnificent facade of this opulent hotel hides a stunning blend of contemporary and classic decor. Grand vaulted ceilings and mosaic floors are complemented by striking modern paintings. Worth pushing the boat out for. ❻/❺

Europa Köpmansgatan 38 ☎031/751 65 00, ℮europa@scandic-hotels.com. With 460 rooms behind an amorphous facade adjoining the Nordstan shopping centre, this is one of the largest hotels in the country. The interior is very plush, with lots of marble and a – unusually for Sweden – the bathrooms have bathtubs. A huge buffet is served for breakfast. ❻/❸

Hotel 11 Maskingatan 11 ☎031/779 11 11, ℗www.hotel11.se. With contemporary rooms boasting views across to Hisingen and dramatic summer reductions, this is one of the city's most stylish places to stay, built on the site of a former shipyard. Take tram #5 to Lilla Bommen, then the boat, *Älv Snabben* (Mon–Fri 6am–11.30pm, shorter hours at weekend; every 30min; 16kr, free with Gothenburg Pass), in the direction of Klippan – get off at Eriksberg. ❺/❸

Opera Hotel Norra Hamngatan 38 ☎031/80 50 80, ℗www.hotelopera.se. A merger of two hotels has resulted in this big, central establishment, which has good facilities, including a sauna and Jacuzzi, but is rather soulless. ❹/❸

Rica City Hotel Burggrevegatan 25 ☎031/771 00 80, ℗www.rica.se. Close to Central Station and the airport bus stop. All rooms in this comfortable hotel are en suite and have cable TV. Residents can take advantage of the free sauna and the solarium (30kr). ❸

Robinson Södra Hamngatan 2 ☎031/80 25 21, ℗www.hotelrobinson.com. Facing Brunnspark, this mediocre but economical hotel is housed in part of the old Fürstenburg Palace, complete with the original facade. A few other original features, like the lift's etched windows depicting Skansen Leijonet, have survived decades of architectural tampering. En-suites are 160kr extra and there are also some family rooms. Not in Gothenburg Package. ❸/❹

SAS Radisson Scandinavia Södra Hamngatan 59–65 ☎031/80 60 00, ℮info.scandinavia.gothenburg@radissonsas.com. Opposite the train station with a facade of hideous pink panels and glass lifts and fountains, the atrium foyer of this business-oriented option resembles a shopping mall; the bedrooms are all pastel shades and birch wood. Also within the complex is an elegant restaurant. ❻/❹

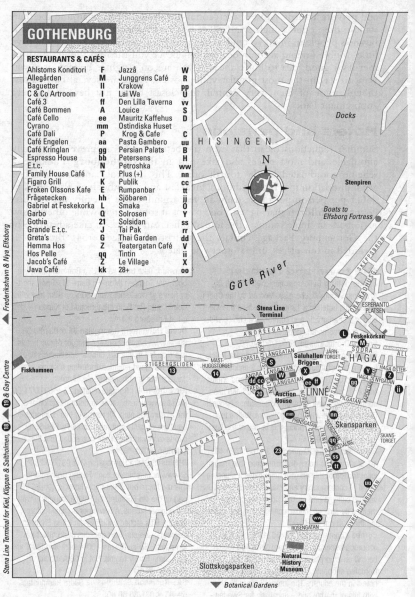

GOTHENBURG

RESTAURANTS & CAFÉS

Ahlstoms Konditori	F	Jazzå	W	
Allegården	M	Junggrens Café	R	
Baguetter	ll	Krakow	pp	
C & Co Artroom	I	Lai Wa	U	
Café 3	ff	Den Lilla Taverna	vv	
Café Bommen	A	Louice	S	
Café Cello	ee	Mauritz Kaffehus	D	
Cyrano	mm	Ostindiska Huset		
Café Dali	P	Krog & Cafe	C	
Café Engelen	aa	Pasta Gambero	uu	
Café Kringlan	gg	Persian Palats	B	
Espresso House	bb	Petersens	H	
E.t.c.	N	Petroshka	ww	
Family House Café	T	Plus (+)	nn	
Figaro Grill	K	Publik	cc	
Froken Olssons Kafe	E	Rumpanbar	tt	
Frågetecken	hh	Sjöbaren	jj	
Gabriel at Feskekorka	L	Smaka	O	
Garbo	Q	Solrosen	Y	
Gothia	21	Solsidan	ss	
Grande E.t.c.	J	Tai Pak	rr	
Greta's	G	Thai Garden	dd	
Hemma Hos	Z	Teatergatan Café	V	
Hos Pelle	qq	Tintin	ii	
Jacob's Café	Ž	Le Village	X	
Java Café	kk	28+	oo	

HISINGEN

Docks

Stenpiren

Boats to
Elfsborg Fortress

Göta River

Stena Line
Terminal

Feskekörkan

SÖDRA

HAGA

Fiskhamnen

LINNÉ

Auction
House

Skansparken

SKANS-
TORGET

Slottskogsparken

Natural
History
Museum

▼ Botanical Gardens

◀ Frederikshavn & Nya Elfsborg

Stena Line Terminal for Kiel, Klippan & Saltholmen, ⑱ ◀⑲ & Gay Centre

Avenyn and around

Allen Parkgatan 10 ☎031/10 14 50, ⓔhotel.allen@telia.com. Very central, sensibly priced hotel close to Avenyn and the old town. Prices include parking. ③/②

City Lorensbergsgatan 6 ☎031/708 40 00, ⓦwww.cityhotelgbg.se. Not to be confused with

Rica City Hotel (above) this is a cheapish and popular place, excellently positioned close to Avenyn. En-suite rooms cost an extra 300kr. ①

Gothia Towers Mässansgata 24, ☎031/750 8800, ⓔinfo@gothiatowers.com. Inside the mirrored towers, just opposite Liseberg is a subtle, well-designed, contemporary hotel. The upper

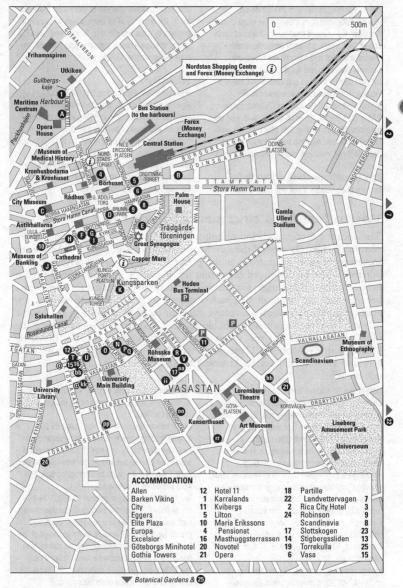

| 0 | | 500m |

Map labels:

Frihamnspiren
Utkiken
Gullbergs-kaje
Maritima Centrum — Harbour
Opera House
Museum of Medical History
Kronhusbodarna & Kronhuset
Rådhus — Börshuset
City Museum
Antikhallarna
Museum of Banking — Cathedral
Saluhallen
Rosenlunds Canal
Stora Hamn Canal
Palm House
Trädgårds-föreningen
Great Synagogue
Copper Mare
Kungsparken
Heden Bus Terminal
Röhsska Museum
University Main Building
University Library
Konserthuset
Art Museum
VASASTAN
Lorensberg Theatre
Götaplatsen
Liseberg Amusement Park
Universeum
Museum of Ethnography
Scandinavium
Gamla Ullevi Stadium

Nordstan Shopping Centre and Forex (Money Exchange)
Bus Station (to the harbours)
Forex (Money Exchange)
Central Station
Odinsplatsen

ACCOMMODATION

Allen	12	Hotel 11	18	Partille		
Barken Viking	1	Karralands	22	Landvettervagen	7	
City	11	Kvibergs	2	Rica City Hotel	3	
Eggers	5	Lilton	24	Robinson	9	
Elite Plaza	10	Maria Erikssons		Scandinavia	8	
Europa	4	Pensionat	17	Slottskogen	23	
Excelsior	16	Masthuggsterrassen	14	Stigbergssliden	13	
Göteborgs Minihotel	20	Novotel	19	Torrekulla	25	
Gothia Towers	21	Opera	6	Vasa	15	

▼ Botanical Gardens & 25

floors have wonderful uninterrupted views over the city. Substantial summer and weekend reductions make this an affordable option. 6 / 4

Vasastan

Excelsior Karl Gustavsgatan 7 ⊕031/17 54 35, ⊛www.hotelexcelsior.nu. A stylish yet homely 1880 building in a road of classic Gothenburg houses, between Avenyn and Haga, this is one of the best places in town for character. Greta Garbo and Ingrid Bergman both stayed here. Classic suites – Garbo's was no. 535 – with splendid nineteenth-century features cost no more than ordinary rooms. 4 / 2

Lilton Föreningsgatan 9 ☏ 031/82 88 08, ⓦ www.hotellilton.com. Close to the Haga district, this cosy, ivy-covered fourteen-bedroom place is one of Gothenburg's hidden gems. Australian-owned, it's quiet and friendly, with splendid National Romantic and Art Nouveau buildings close by, plus there's free tea and coffee and use of a kitchen. 100kr reduction at weekends. ❸

Maria Erikssons Pensionat Chalmersgatan 27A ☏ 031/20 70 30, ⓕ 16 64 63. With just ten, pleasant enough rooms, this place is well positioned on a road running parallel with Avenyn. Breakfast not included; not in Gothenburg package. ❸/❷

Vasa Hotel Viktoriagatan 6 ☏ 031/1736 30, ⓦ www.hotelvasa.se. What this plain but comfort-able hotel lacks in glamour is more than made up for by the geniality of its owners and its excellent position in Vasastan, close to Avenyn and even closer to Haga. There's a sauna, solarium and 24-hour reception too. ❹/❸

Klippan

Novotel Hotel Klippan 1 ☏ 031/14 90 00, ⓦ www.novotel.se. An attractive pile converted from the old Carnegie Porter Brewery in delightful Klippan, just west of the city (see p.154). It's a mishmash of architectural styles on the inside, but has great views from the upper storeys. There's also a huge central atrium dripping with fake foliage, and an expensive, traditional restaurant, *Carnegie Kay*, is attached. ❺/❸

Youth hostels and private rooms

The cheapest accommodation option is staying in one of the numerous STF-run **youth hostels** around the city. Most hostels have a range of rooms, from singles through to dormitories with up to ten beds. Prices for private rooms, whether single or double, all fall within the ❶ price range and dorm beds are between 100–150kr a night for members, 40kr more per person for non-members. Hostels are open all year unless otherwise stated. **Private rooms** are another good economical alternative that can be booked through the tourist office (175kr per person in a double room, 225kr for a single; booking fee 60kr). For stays of a week or more, it's worth contacting SGS Bostader, Utlandgatan 24 (Mon–Fri 11am–3pm), who rent out **furnished rooms**, with access to kitchen facilities, for around 1200kr a week; sheets are provided, but not utensils.

Göteborgs Minihotel Tredje Långgatan 31 ☏ 031/24 10 23, ⓦ www.minihotell.se. This uninspiring building is nevertheless well placed for the alternative scene around the Linné area.

Karralunds Vandrarhem Olbergsgatan 1 ☏ 031/84 02 00, ⓦ www.liseberg.se. Four kilometres from the centre, close to Liseberg Amusement Park – take tram #5 to Welandergatan, direction Torp. Non-smoking rooms available, plus cabins and a campsite. Breakfast can only be ordered by groups; book ahead in summer.

Kvibergs Vandrarhem Kvibergsvägen 5 ☏ 031/43 50 55, ⓦ www.vandrarhem.com. In Gamlestad, 10min by tram #6 or #7 from Central Station.

Masthuggsterrassen Masthuggsterrassen 8 ☏ 031/42 48 20, ⓔ masthuggsterrassen.van-drarhem@telia.com. Up the steps from Masthuggstorget (tram #3 or #4) and a couple of minutes' walk from the terminal for the Stena Line ferry from Denmark.

Partille Landvettervagen, Partille ☏ 031/44 65 01, ⓦ www.partillevandrarhem.com. Fifteen kilometres east of the city (bus #513 from Heden bus terminal to Astebo; 30min) right by Lake Kåsjöns, this family-run hostel has a solarium and TV lounge plus laundry facilities.

Slottskogen Vegagatan 21 ☏ 031/42 65 20, ⓔ mail@slottskogenvh.se. Superbly appointed and well-designed family-run hostel, just two minutes' walk from Linnégatan and not far from Slottskogen Park. Take tram #1 or #2 to Olivedahlsgatan. The 40kr breakfast is wonderful.

Stigbergssliden Stigbergssliden 10 ☏ 031/24 16 20, ⓦ www.hostel-gothenburg.com. Excellent hostel that was built in 1830 as a seamen's house, well placed for ferries to Denmark as it's just west of the Linné area down Första Långgatan. All rooms have basins, and there's disabled access, laundry facilities (20kr) and a pleasant back courtyard. Breakfast is 40kr, and bike rental costs 50kr per day.

Torrekulla Kallered ☏ 031/795 14 95, ⓦ www.stf-turist.se. Fifteen kilometres south of the city, this is a pleasantly situated hostel with a free sauna and a nearby lake where you can take a dip. Bus #705 from Heden, or a ten-minute train journey from Central Station (direction Kungsbacka) to Mölndal, then a fifteen-minute walk.

Cabins and campsites

Two of the following campsites also provide **cabins**, which are worth considering, especially if there are more than two of you. Facilities are invariably squeaky clean and in good working order – there's usually a well-equipped kitchen too – but you'll have to pay extra for bedding. Prices for cabins are given below; if you want to **camp**, you'll pay around 100kr for two people in July or August, 50kr the rest of the year.

Askims ☎031/28 62 61, ⊛www.liseberg.se. Set beside sandy beaches, 12km from the centre (tram #1 or #2 to Linnéplatsen, then bus #83, or the Blå Express, direction Saro, from outside Central Station on Drottningtorget), this campsite also has four-bed cabins (615kr high season, 495kr low). Open early May to late Aug (office daily 9am–noon & 3–6pm, slightly later Thurs–Sat).

Karralunds Vandrarhem Olbergsgatan 1 ☎031/84 02 00, ⊛www.liseberg.se. Four kilometres from the centre, close to Liseberg Amusement Park (tram #5 to Welandergatan, direction Torp) and set among forest and lakes, the site offers four-bed cabins costing 615kr; 695kr with your own toilet; 50kr discount outside June–Aug. Open all year.

Lilleby Havsbad ☎031/56 50 66, ℗56 16 05. About an hour from the city centre (bus #21 from Nils Ericsonsplatsen and change to #23 at Kongshallavagen), this splendid seaside location is some compensation for the trek. May–Aug.

The City

Nearly everything of interest in Gothenburg is south of the **Göta River** and, unless you fancy a trip to the **Volvo factory** on the northern island of **Hisingen**, there's no real need to cross the water. At the heart of the city is the historic **old town**, about the best place to start, although Gothenburg's attractions are by no means restricted to this area. Tucked between the Göta River to the north and the zigzagging canal to the south, the old town's tightly gridded streets are lined with impressive facades, interesting food markets and a couple of worthwhile museums, most notably the **Stadsmuseum** and, up by the harbour, the **Museum of Maritime History**. Just across the canal that skirts the southern edges of the old town is **Trädgårdsforeningen** park, in summer full of floral colour and picnicking city dwellers.

Heading further south into the modern centre, **Avenyn** is Gothenburg's showcase boulevard, alive with showy restaurants and bars. However, it's the roads off Avenyn that hold the area's real interest, with more alternative 24-hour café-bars and some of Gothenburg's best museums, including the city's **Konstmuseum** further south in **Götaplatsen**. For family entertainment day or night, the classic **Liseberg Amusement Park**, just to the southeast of the Avenyn district, has been a focal point for Gothenburgers since the 1920s.

In Vasastan, a small district to the west of Avenyn, crammed with intricately decorated late nineteenth-century apartment buildings and peppered with appealing little cafés, you'll find the **Röhsska Museum** of applied arts. Vasastan stretches west to **Haga**, the old working-class district, now a haven for the trendy and moneyed. Haga Nygatan, the main thoroughfare, leads on to Linnégatan, the arterial road through **Linné**. Fast establishing itself as the most vibrant part of the city, it's home to the most interesting evening haunts, with new cafés, bars and restaurants opening up alongside long-established antique emporiums and sex shops. Further out, the rolling **Slottskogen** park holds the **Natural History Museum**, but is more alluring as a pretty place to sunbathe.

Gothenburg is a fairly compact and easy city to get around, so you can cover most of the sights even if you only have a day or two here. But to get the most from your stay, give the city at least four days and slow your pace down to a stroll – which will put you in step with the locals.

The old town and the harbour

The **old town** is divided in two by the **Stora Hamn Canal**, to the north of which is the harbour, where the decaying, but still impressive, shipyards make for a dramatic backdrop. The streets south of the Stora Hamn stretching down to the southern canal are perfect for an afternoon's leisurely stroll, with some quirky cafés, food markets and antique/junk shops, along with the excellent Stadsmuseum as well as mainland Sweden's oldest synagogue at the water's edge. Straddling the Stora Hamn is the stately main square, **Gustav Adolfs Torg**; an early start here will mean you can see the whole area the same day, without rushing.

Gustav Adolfs Torg

At the centre of **Gustav Adolfs Torg**, a copper statue of Gustav II Adolf points ostentatiously to the spot where he reputedly declared: "Here I will build my city." This, however, isn't the original German-made statue of the city founder: that one was kidnapped on its way to Sweden, and rather than pay the ransom demanded, the Gothenburgers commissioned a new one.

Although there is little attempt to encourage visitors to enter the buildings surrounding the square, a little persistence will allow you to discover some exceptional interiors. To the east of the square, with the canal behind you, stands the **Rådhus**, which isn't a town hall as the name suggests, but has housed the criminal law courts since 1672. The dull Neoclassical facade is dramatically improved by the extension designed by the ground-breaking Functionalist architect E.G. Asplund in 1936. Inside, it retains its original glass lifts and features mussel-shaped drinking fountains and huge panels of laminated aspen – the latter creating the impression of standing inside a giant 1930s cocktail cabinet.

Also tucked away in the old building are some rather fine rooms with grand chandeliers and trompe l'oeil ceilings; to see them you'll have to attract the attention of a court assistant and wait for the rooms to be opened. Your time is better spent trying to convince attendants at the white, double-columned 1842 **Börshuset** to let you in. Facing the canal, this former Exchange has magnificent banqueting and concert halls of great opulence, while the smaller rooms are a riot of red and blue stucco, inspired by the eighteenth-century excavations at Pompeii. Visitors are not encouraged in any numbers as the fabric of the building is under strain, but once you're inside, the staff will usually give an enthusiastic and informed commentary.

North to the harbour

Heading north from the square along Östra Hamngatan, you'll pass Sweden's biggest shopping centre, the amorphous **Nordstan**. Despite valiant attempts at face-lifts, it's still a dark and dreary complex, its few saving graces including a late-opening pharmacy (daily 8am–10pm), a tourist office and ticket offices for all the ferry companies (see p.134). If you have time to spare and haven't yet seen the city's impressive **Central Station**, take a short detour along Burggrevegatan to Drottningtorget. Dating from 1856, this is the oldest train station in the country and its period facade fronts a grand and marvellously preserved interior – take a look at the wood beam-ends in the ticket hall, every one carved in the likeness of the city-council members of the day. Although it's usually behind closed doors, you might be able to persuade a guard to let you see the staff room, once the royal waiting room and still resplendent with its hand-painted ceilings and gilt-topped pillars.

New transport links to the harbour

A far-reaching programme designed to eradicate the one non-user-friendly aspect of Gothenburg was launched in 1999 – and has been warmly received by Gothenburgers despite a certain degree of chaos during the work. For years now, the harbourside has been effectively severed from the city by the huge amount of traffic along Marten Krakowsgatan and Skeppsbron, which makes crossing to the water from Lilla Bommen a treacherous task, and a tedious one from Nordstan. Now that the harbour area is becoming upmarket, a huge **traffic relief tunnel** is being built from the Järntorget area just south of the Feskekorka, right up to the Opera House. Apartments are to be built all along the waterfront, with car access for residents only. New tram lines will be added to the existing system to bring people to and from the area (the overall transport plan even extends to having a ring of tram lines right around the city), and getting around on foot in the centre will become even easier. The previous layout of tram lines around Järntorget has already been rejigged, and the square has been transformed with cafés and fountains. New stops have been built for trams #2, #3, #9 and #11. This project, the biggest the city has seen in decades, is expected to be completed around 2005.

Back on Östra Hamngatan at no. 11 is the **Museum of Medical History** (Medicinhistoriska Museet; Tues, Wed & Fri 11am–4pm, Thurs 11am–8pm; 30kr), owned by the Sahlgren Hospital and charmingly set in the 200-year-old house which was home to the hospital during the mid-nineteenth century. The rooms exploring disease through the ages are unlikely to inspire those without a ready interest in pathology. More diverting are an 1870s ambulance, like a vast wicker pram, and an old dental surgery, complete with a hand-decorated dentist's chair.

At the northern end of Östra Hamngatan, on Lilla Bommen, Gothenburg's industrial decline is juxtaposed with its artistic regeneration to dramatic visual effect. To the west, beyond the harbour, redundant shipyard cranes loom across the sky, making a sombre background to the industrially themed bronze and pink-granite sculptures dotted along the waterfront. A couple of minutes' walk to the west is the striking, modern **Opera House** (daily noon–6pm; guided tours July Tues & Wed noon–3pm; T031/10 82 03 for programme and tour details, Wwww.opera.se), which is worth a quick wander inside, whether you're an opera buff or not.

North along the riverbank from the Opera House is the **Utkiken** (Lookout Point; Jan to mid-May & early Sept to mid-Dec Sat & Sun 11am–4pm; mid-May to early Sept daily 11am–7pm; 30kr); designed by the Scottish architect Ralph Erskine (author of the Sydney Opera House) in the late 1980s, this 86-metre-high office building resembles a half-used red lipstick. Its top storey (the lift takes you to the 22nd floor) offers panoramic views of the city and harbour and there's a café too.

Walking west along the quay, it's just a couple of minutes to the **Maritima Centrum** (May–June daily 10am–6pm, July & Aug till 8pm; 45kr, free with a Gothenburg Pass; Wwww.gmtc.se), which describes itself as "the largest ship museum in the world". An interesting experience, even for non-enthusiasts, it comprises a dozen boats including a 1915 lightship, a submarine and a firefloat (a sort of nautical fire engine), each giving a glimpse of how seamen lived and worked on board. The most impressive ship is a monstrous naval destroyer, complete with a medical office, where the display showing the amputation of a leg and hand is more amusing than informative – far-fetched clothes-shop dummies do the honours. There is a rather good café-restaurant on the ship. Disabled access to the ship is good; anyone wanting to avoid its steep stairs can use a special route indicated by blue arrows.

Nya Elfsborg

Boats leave from Lilla Bommen, near the Opera House, for the popular excursion to the island **fortress** of **Nya Elfsborg** (early May to Aug hourly 9.30am–5pm; 30min; 85kr, free with a Gothenburg Pass), built in the seventeenth century to defend the harbour and the city. The surviving buildings have been turned into a **museum** and café. On the half-hour-long guided tours of the square tower, chapel and prison cells (included in the price of the boat trip), you'll hear about violent confrontations with the Danes and some of the methods used to keep prisoners from swimming away – check out the set of iron shackles weighing over 36kg.

The Kronhuset and the Stadsmuseum

From the maritime museum, it's a short walk southwest to Gothenburg's oldest secular building, **Kronhuset**, on Kronhusgatan (Tues–Fri 11am–4pm, Sat & Sun 11am–5pm). Built by the Dutch in 1642 as an artillery depot for the city's garrison, it was where 5-year-old Karl XI was proclaimed king in 1660. Set picturesquely in the eighteenth-century wings that flank the original building is **Kronhusbodarna** (Mon–Fri 10am–5pm, Sat 10am–2pm), a cluster of small, pricey shops specializing in making gold, silver and glass ornaments and jewellery. The silversmith here can sell you a replica of the city's oldest key, but your money would be better spent at the atmospheric vaulted café, which serves heaps of meringues as well as sandwich lunches.

A couple of blocks further south, the **Stadsmuseum**, Norra Hamngatan 12 (City Museum; May–Aug daily 11am–4pm; Sept–April Tues & Thurs–Sun 11am–4pm, Wed 11am–8pm; 40kr; ⓦwww.stadsmuseum.goteborg.se) has emerged, after an extensive reshuffle of the city's museums, as the mother of them all, incorporating several in one building. It is located in the Ostindiska Huset, built in 1750, which housed the offices, goods store and auction house of the enormously influential **Swedish East India Company**. Envious of the major maritime nations, two Gothenburg-based industrialists, Colin Campbell and Niklas Sahlgren, set up the firm in the early eighteenth century. Granted the sole Swedish rights to trade with China in 1731, the company monopolized all Swedish trade with the Far East for over eighty years, the only condition being that the bounty – tea, silk, porcelain, spices and arrack (an East Indian schnapps used to make Swedish punch) – had to be sold and auctioned in Gothenburg. The Chinese influence acquired on these great sea voyages pervaded Gothenburg society, and wealthy financiers adorned their homes and gardens with Chinese motifs. By 1813, the unrest of the French Revolution and competition from British and Dutch tea traders meant profits slid, and it was decreed in Sweden that "East India trade could be pursued by anyone so inclined". The headquarters, however, remains an imposing reminder of the power and prestige the company – and Gothenburg – once had. Very informative **guided walks** of the seventeenth-century streets, canals and buildings of old *Giöteborgh*, emphasizing the legacy of the East India Company, are organized by the museum (in English; cost included in the museum admission fee, otherwise 40kr or free with Gothenburg Card).

The museum itself is well worth a browse, not least for its rich interior, a mix of squat, carved stone pillars, stained glass and frescoes. Your first port of call should be the third floor, where there are exhibitions on the Company itself. There is very little English labelling, but the numerous display cabinets, full of Chinese goods and treasures, give a wonderful insight into the company's history. The renovated hall where the city's grandest auctions took place is, however, surprisingly modest. From here you move on to the rather incongruously located exhibition of **1950s life**, based around fashions and film stars; among the displays are showcases of pointy bras and Vespa bikes.

The museum's most impressive section is the **industrial history** exhibition. Using sound effects, clever design and plenty of English commentary, the exhibition focuses on twentieth-century commerce, starting with the textile and timber trades, which were central to Gothenburg's wealth. At the beginning of the century, working conditions in the city's factories were extremely poor, and at some textile factories up to a third of the workforce were children. The main working-class neighbourhood was Haga (see p.151), and the exhibition highlights the importance of Järntorget (Iron Square), just northwest of Haga Nygatan, which was a hotbed of unrest during the great strike of 1909. The exhibition then moves on to the middle decades of the century, when massive industrial growth saw the building of the shipyards, and the rise of the ball-bearings and motor-vehicle industries. By the 1950s and 1960s, the first foreign labour had to be recruited to deal with demand, and the present situation is summed up by a plaque at the end: "Once, the city had one engineer and one hundred workers to make a ship engine. Now, a large group of engineers design part of an engine to be built by factories abroad."

South of Stora Hamn – Lilla Torget to Brunnsparken

Most of the city's smaller and none-too-thrilling museums have been incorporated within the Stadsmuseum, with the exception of one, the **Banking Museum** (Bankmuseet), Södra Hamngatan 11, on the south side of Stora Hamn canal (Sun noon–3pm, guided tours in English at 2pm; ☎031/40 11 05). The building's facade is really the best bit although you can also visit the vaults inside. Also on this side of the canal, and just to the west of the Stadsmuseum, is **Lilla Torget**. In itself, the square is nothing to get excited about, but, having nodded at the statue of Jonas Alstromer – the man who introduced the potato to Sweden in the eighteenth century – it's worth taking the tiny opening on the western side of the square and making the steep but short climb to **Drottning Kristinas Jaktslott** (Queen Kristina's Hunting Lodge) at Otterhallegatan 16. Never a hunting lodge, and absolutely nothing to do with Queen Kristina, who died before it was built, it is now a quaint **café** that serves particularly good waffles (daily 11am–4pm).

A couple of minutes' walk west from the square brings you to the quayside where, at **Stenpiren** (Stone Pier), hundreds of emigrants said their last goodbyes before sailing off in 1638 to "New Sweden" in the United States. The granite **Delaware Monument** was carted off to America from Gothenburg in the early part of the last century, and it wasn't until 1938 that celebrated sculptor Carl Milles cast a replacement in bronze, which stands here looking out to sea.

Back in Lilla Torget, it's only a short walk down Västra Hamngatan, which leads off from the southern side of the square, to the city's cathedral; on the way you'll pass **Antik Hallarna** (Mon–Fri 10am–6pm, Sat 10am–2pm), a clutch of pricey antique shops. The most affordable stuff here is towards the back, along with the tat. It's the grand mid-nineteenth century building, however, that warrants your attention, with its fantastic gilded ceiling and regal marble stairs leading up to the second floor, where there's a decent enough café.

A few blocks south of Antik Hallarna and left off Västra Hamngatan is the Neoclassical cathedral, **Domkyrkan** (daily Mon–Fri 8am–8pm, Sat 9am–6pm, Sun 10am–3pm), built in 1827 – the two previous cathedrals were destroyed by fires at a rate of one a century. Four giant sandstone columns stand at the portico, and inside there's an altarpiece that's a picture of gilded opulence. The plain white walls concentrate the eye on the unusual post-Resurrection cross

– devoid of a Jesus, his gilded grave clothes strewn around, summoning images of an adolescent's bedroom floor. Another quirky feature is the twin glassed-in verandas that run down either side; looking like glamorous trams with net curtains, they were actually designed for the bishop's private conversations.

Continuing east past the cathedral and north towards Stora Hamn, the leafy square known as **Brunnspark** soon comes into view, with Gustav Adolfs Torg just across the canal. The sedate house facing the square is now a snazzy restaurant and nightclub called *The Palace* (see p.159), but in the late nineteenth century the house was home to Pontus and Gothilda Fürstenburg, the city's leading arts patrons. They opened up the top floor as an art gallery, the first in Gothenburg to make use of electric as well as natural light, and later donated their entire collection – the biggest batch of Nordic paintings in the country – to the city's Art Museum. As a tribute to the Fürstenburgs, the museum made over the top floor into an exact replica of the original gallery (see p.149). Staff at *The Palace* seem to know little of its history, but won't prevent you wandering upstairs to see the richly ornate plasterwork and gilding, much as it was.

West from Stora Nygatan along the canal

Following the zigzagging canal that marks the southern perimeter of old Gothenburg – a moat during the days when the city was fortified – makes for a fine twenty-minute stroll, past pretty waterside views and a number of interesting diversions. Just east of Brunnspark, **Stora Nygatan** wends its way south along the canal's most scenic stretch; to one side are Neoclassical buildings all stuccoed in cinnamon and cream, and to the other is the green expanse of Trädgårdsföreningen park (see opposite). Amid all the architectural finery sits the **Great Synagogue** (☎031/17 72 45 to arrange a visit), inaugurated in 1855, making it mainland Sweden's oldest. Its simple domed exterior belies the existence of one of the most exquisite interiors of any European synagogue: the ceiling and walls are covered in rich blues, reds and gold, and Moorish patterns are interwoven with Viking leaf designs. A restoration programme is re-creating the original brilliance of colour. There are also some unusual features: the lofty interior contains two upper levels of women's galleries and at the back, a splendid organ – extremely rare in synagogues – first played at the inauguration ceremony. The original congregation were Orthodox German Jews, who were encouraged to settle here as they promoted and encouraged trading links with the rest of Europe, though it now serves as a Conservative synagogue for all the community.

South from the synagogue, you'll pass **Kungsportsplatsen**, in the centre of which stands a useful landmark, a sculpture known as the "Copper Mare" – though it's immediately obvious if you look from beneath that this is no mare. A few minutes further on, and one block in from the canal at Kungstorget, stands **Saluhallen** (Mon–Fri 9am–6pm, Sat 9am–2pm), a pretty barrel-roofed indoor market built in the 1880s. Busy and full of atmosphere, it's a great place to wander through (for more on food markets in Gothenburg see p.155); outside there's also a flower market.

Five minutes' walk west from here is Gothenburg's oldest food market, the Neo-Gothic **Feskekorka**, or "Fish-church" (Tues–Thurs 9am–5pm, Fri 9am–6pm, Sat 9am–1.30pm), whose strong aromas may well hit you long before you reach the door. Despite its undeniably ecclesiastical appearance, the nearest this 1874 building comes to religion is the devotion shown by the fish lovers who come to buy here. Inside, every kind of fish, from smoked to shellfish, lies in gleaming pungent silver, pink and black mounds, while in a gallery upstairs, there's a very small, very good restaurant (see p.157).

Trädgårdsföreningen

From Kungsportsplatsen, cross the bridge over the southern canal, and the main entrance to the well-groomed **Trädgårdsföreningen** (Garden Society Park; May–Aug 7am–9pm; Sept–April 7am–6pm; May–Aug 10kr, rest of year free) is just to the east. There are a number of attractions to visit, the most impressive of which is the 1878 **Palm House** (daily: June–Aug 10am–6pm; Sept–May 10am–4pm; 20kr fee also gives entry to the Botanical Gardens; see p.153). Designed as a copy of London's Crystal Palace, and looking like a huge English conservatory, it contains a wealth of very un-Swedish plant life: tropical, Mediterranean and Asian flowers. Close by is the **Butterfly House** (April, May & Sept Tues–Sun 10am–4pm; June–Aug daily 10am–5pm; Oct–March Tues–Fri 10am–3pm, Sat & Sun 11am–3pm; 35kr), where you can walk among free-flying butterflies from Asia and the Americas that flit about here in eighty percent humidity. Further on is the **Rosarium**, with nearly three thousand varieties of rose, providing a myriad of colours throughout the year. During summer the place goes into overdrive, with lunchtime concerts and a special children's theatre.

Avenyn and around

Running all the way from the canal southeast to Götaplatsen is the wide, cobbled length of Kungsportsavenyn. Known more simply as **Avenyn**, this "avenue" teeming with life is Gothenburg's showiest thoroughfare. The ground floor of almost every grand old nineteenth-century home has been converted into a café, bar or restaurant; the young and beautiful inhabit this place sipping overpriced drinks while posing at the tables that, from mid-spring to September, spill out onto the street. It's enjoyable enough to sit and watch people go by, but for all its glamour, the tourist-oriented shops and brasseries are mostly bright and samey, and the grandeur of the city's industrial past is easier to imagine in the less spoiled mansions along Parkgatan – running at right angles to Avenyn and parallel to the canal – and other roads to the southwest off the main drag. At the southern end of the avenue on **Götaplatsen**, is the fascinating **Konstmuseum**, which contains a fine collection of international art from various periods.

Götaplatsen

At the top of Avenyn, **Götaplatsen** is modern Gothenburg's main square, in the centre of which stands Carl Milles's **Poseidon** – a giant, nude, bronze body-builder with a staggeringly ugly face. The size of the figure's penis caused moral outrage when the sculpture first appeared in 1930, and was subsequently dramatically reduced. Today, although from the front Poseidon appears to be squeezing the living daylights out of what looks like a large-fanged fish, if you climb the steps of the **Concert Hall** to the right, it becomes clear that Milles won the battle over Poseidon's manhood to stupendous effect. To the left of the statue and standing back from the City Library is the columned **Lorensberg theatre**, one of Gothenburg's few private theatres, and originally designed as the first people's theatre in the country – with no expensive boxes, just standard-price stalls. The Lorensberg (like many other theatres in Sweden) is closed during the summer and only puts on shows in Swedish (for more on theatre in Gothenburg, see p.162).

Konstmuseum

Behind *Poseidon* stands the Götaplatsen's most impressive attraction, the superb **Konstmuseum** (Art Museum; May–Aug Mon–Fri 11am–4pm; Sept–April

△ Poseidon sculpture, Gothenburg

Tues, Thurs & Fri 11am–4pm, Wed 11am–9pm, Sat & Sun 11am–5pm; 35kr; ⓦ www.konstmuseum.goteborg.se). Though its massive, symmetrical facade is reminiscent of fascist architecture of 1930s Germany, this is one of the city's finest museums, and it's easy to spend half a day absorbing the diverse and extensive collections. The following is only a brief guide to some of the highlights.

On the ground floor, the **Hasselblad Centre** (ⓦ www.hasselbladcenter.se), shows excellent photographic exhibitions, while on the floor above, a display of post-1945 Nordic art gives space to changing displays of the work of contemporary Scandinavian painters and sculptors. Another room on this floor has some works by the celebrated masters of French Impressionism; the next couple of floors hold a range of minor works by Van Gogh, Gauguin and Pissarro, a powerful and surprisingly colourful Munch and a couple of Rodin sculptures. Moving on to floor five, you'll find Italian paintings from 1500 to 1750, including works by Canaletto and Francesco Guardi, as well as Rembrandt's *Knight with Falcon* and Rubens' *Adoration of the Magi*.

Best of all, however, and the main reason to visit, are the **Fürstenburg Galleries** on the sixth floor. These celebrate the work of some of Scandinavia's most prolific and revered turn-of-the-twentieth-century artists; well-known works by Carl Larsson, Anders Zorn and Carl Wilhelmson reflect the seasons and landscapes of the Nordic countries and evoke a vivid picture of Scandinavian life at that time. Paintings to look out for include Larsson's *Lilla Suzanne*, which touchingly depicts the elated face of a baby and is one of his most realistic works; Anders Zorn's *Bathers*, flushed with a pale pink summer glow and exemplifying the painter's feeling for light and the human form; and the sensitive portraits by Ernst Josephson, most notably his full-length portrait of Carl Skånberg – easily mistaken for the young Winston Churchill. The Danish artist Peter Kroyer's marvellous *Hip Hip Hooray* again plays with light, and a couple of works by Hugo Birger also deserve your attention. One depicts the interior of the original Fürstenburg Gallery (see p.146), complete with electric lights, while his massive *Scandinavian Artists' Breakfast in Paris,* dominating an entire wall, puts some faces to the artists' names – a brief pamphlet in the room will help identify them. Also worth a look is an entire room of Larsson's bright, fantastical wall-sized paintings.

A delightful little park, **Nackros Dammen** ("Waterlily Park"), lies just behind the museum; with its late-spring rhododendrons and big pond full of ducks, it's a lovely place for a stroll.

Liseberg and around

Just a few minutes' stroll southeast from Avenyn – left up Berzeliigatan and right into Södravägen is the most direct way – leads to the **amusement park** Liseberg, alive both during the day and at night throughout the summer. In its shadow to the south, Gothenburg's newest museum, **Universeum** is fascinating, particularly for children, while the absorbing **Museum of World Culture** is just two blocks north.

Liseberg Amusement Park

Just a few minutes' walk southeast from Götaplatsen (or take tram #5 from the old centre), **Liseberg Amusement Park** (late April to June & late Aug daily 3–11pm; July to mid-Aug daily noon–11pm; Sept Sat 1–11pm, Sun noon–8pm; 45kr, under-7s free; all-day ride pass 215kr, tickets for a fixed number of rides 90kr or 150kr; ⓦ www.liseberg.se) is a riot of party lights and gum-pink paintwork. Opened in 1923, Scandinavia's largest amusement park, with its flowers, trees, fountains and clusters of lights, is great fun for adults as well as children, a league away from the hyped neon and plastic mini-cities that constitute so many theme parks around the world. Old and young dance to live bands most evenings, and although louder and more youth-dominated at night (especially on Saturdays), it's all good humoured. One of the most popular attractions is an ambitious roller coaster called "Hangover", best avoided if you've got one, while the new "Balder" roller coaster, due to open in 2003, will be built entirely of wood in the traditional manner.

Universeum and Museum of World Culture

Within just a few steps of the theme park the city's newest museum, designed by Gothenburg architect Gert Wingårdh, **Universeum** (early June to mid-Aug daily 10am–8pm; rest of year Tues–Sun 10am–6pm; 110kr; ⓦwww.universeum.se), is well worth an hour or so of your time. Contained within a splendidly organic building with soaring glass, wood and concrete walls, it couldn't be more in contrast to the fairy lights and pink of the amusement park reflected in its vast windows. This museum of the environment has plenty of information in English and is definitely a must for children. Water is a major theme (the complex holds the world's largest recirculating water system, processing three million litres a day), and once inside, you can walk some 3km through various different environments – Swedish mountain streams, rainforest, open ocean – all of which feel extremely authentic; expect to emerge dripping. There's also an interactive "inventors' corner" for kids and a vast circular pool containing tame plaice-like rays that children are encouraged to stroke. The **café** is good value too, with full meals for no more than 90kr.

Just a couple of blocks north of Liseberg (head up Skånegatan and right into Levgrensvägen), is the unusually interesting **Museum of World Culture**, at Avagen 24, a ten-minute walk north of the park (May–Aug Mon–Fri 11am–4pm, Sat & Sun 11am–5pm; 50kr; ⓦwww.etnografiska.se), just over the highway. The best exhibits are those on Native American culture, with brilliantly lit textiles that are almost 2000 years old and some other more grisly finds, including skulls deliberately trephined (small circular sections of bone were removed) to ward off bad spirits.

Vasastan

Back at Avenyn, you can take one of the roads off to the west and wander into the **Vasastan** district, where the streets are lined with fine nineteenth-century and National Romantic architecture, and the cafés are cheaper, more laid-back and much more charismatic. The area also boasts Gothenburg's collection of applied arts, the **Röhsska Museum**, as well as several fine University buildings.

Vasagatan and the Röhsska Museum

Along Vasagatan, the main street through the district, and parallel **Engelbrektsgatan**, you'll come across solid, stately and rangy buildings that epitomize Gothenburg's nineteenth-century commercial wealth and civic pride. White-stuccoed or red-and-cream brick facades are decorated with elaborate ceramic tiles, intricate stone-and-brick animal carvings, shiny metal cupolas and classical windows. With the detail spread gracefully across these six-storey terraces, the overall effect is of restrained grandeur. Many of the houses also have Continental-style wrought-iron balconies; it's easy to imagine high-society gatherings spilling out into the night on warm summer evenings. In contrast, interspersed among all this nineteenth-century swagger are some perfect examples of early twentieth-century National Romantic architecture, with rough-hewn stone and Art Nouveau swirls in plaster and brickwork; look particularly at the low-numbered buildings along Engelbrektsgatan, south from the main drag.

At Vasagatan 37–39, is the excellent **Röhsska Museum**, Sweden's main museum of applied arts (May–Aug Mon–Fri noon–4pm, Sat & Sun noon–5pm; Sept–April Tues noon–9pm, Wed–Fri noon–4pm, Sat & Sun noon–5pm; 40kr; ⓦwww.designmuseum.se). This 1916 museum is an aesthetic Aladdin's cave, with each floor concentrating on different areas of decorative and functional art, from early-dynasty Chinese ceramics to European arts and crafts from the sixteenth and seventeenth centuries. Most arresting is the first floor, devoted to twentieth-century decor and featuring all manner of recognizable designs for domestic furniture and appliances from the 1910s to the 1990s – enough to send anyone over the age of 10 on a giddy nostalgia trip. Attached to the contemporary design shop is a pleasant **café**, serving light lunches (55–60kr).

The University buildings

A couple of blocks down from the museum, the glorious main **University building** stands in a small park; it's worth trying the doors of this 1907 classic to peek at the stunningly renovated interior – all pale marble coolness, an enormous Art Nouveau light fitting and a main hall with impressive wall paintings.

Further down still, towards the west end of the street where the Haga district begins, and on the right, overlooking Haga Park, is the original **University Library**, now housing newspaper archives (☏031/773 27 20). Here you can read the British, American and French national papers – but the real draw is that the whole place has been restored, with spectacular reading areas beneath vaulted, hand-painted arches. In the main reading area, one wall is filled with a vast Impressionist **painting**, *The Giving of Wisdom*, which Pontus Fürstenburg (see p.146) commissioned for the library from Carl Wilhelmson, one of Sweden's most celebrated late nineteenth-century artists (see p.170).

Haga

A ten-minute stroll west up Vasagatan (alternatively take tram #1 or #2 to Olivedalsgatan) is the city's oldest working-class suburb, **Haga**, once so run-down that its demolition was on the cards, but today one of Gothenburg's most picturesque quarters. The transformation took place in the early 1980s, after someone saw potential in the web of artisans' homes known as "governor's houses". These distinctive early nineteenth-century buildings are constructed with a stone ground floor and two wooden upper storeys. There had been a recent declaration that no building should have more than two floors of wood to minimize the devastation caused by city fires, but stone was expensive at the time and was heavy for the clay ground to support so a combination of materials was employed to maximize the space available.

Haga is now Gothenburg's miniature version of Greenwich Village, with well-off and socially aware 20- and 30-somethings hanging out in the style-conscious cafés and shops along its cobbled streets. Although there are a couple of good restaurants (see p.158) along the main thoroughfare, **Haga Nygatan**, this is really somewhere to come during the day, when there are tables out on the street and the atmosphere is friendly and villagey – if a little self-consciously fashionable. Apart from the boutiques, which sell things like Art Deco light fittings, calmative crystals and nineteenth-century Swedish kitchenware, it's worth noting the intervening apartment buildings. These red-brick edifices were originally almshouses funded by the Dickson family, the city's British industrialist forefathers who played a big part in the success of the East India Company – the name of Robert Dickson is still emblazoned on the facades.

Next door to the beautiful F.D. Dickson People's Library on Allegatan, is **Haga Badet** (July & Aug Mon–Fri 7am–8pm, Sat 9am–5pm, Sun 10am–5pm, rest of year Mon–Fri 7am–9.30pm, Sat 9am–6pm, Sun 10am–6pm; one-day card allowing use of the sauna, gym & pool June–Aug 95kr; rest of year 320kr), a superbly renovated bathhouse constructed with funds donated by Sven Renström, one of Gothenburg's non-British philanthropists at the end of the nineteenth century. These days it has a very different sort of clientele: it's a rather fine health spa, with pretty Art Nouveau-style pools, a Roman bath and a massage area. There's also a very pleasant **café** with a buffet (Mon 11.30am–2.30pm, Tues–Fri 11.30am–10pm, Sat 11.30am–7pm, Sun 1–4pm; closed in summer).

Adjoining Haga to the south, **Skansparken** is hardly a park at all, more just a raised mound of land on which stands the **Military Museum** (Tues & Wed noon–2pm, Sat & Sun noon–3pm; 30kr; guided tour in English, included with admission, first Sun of each month at 1pm; ☎031/14 50 00), housed in the newly gilded Skansen Kronan, one of Gothenburg's two surviving seven-teenth-century fortress towers. The steep climb is worth it for the views north across the city to the harbour, rather than for the feeble collection of wax models dressed in military uniforms from throughout the ages.

Linné

To the west of Haga, the cosmopolitan district of **Linné** is named after the botanist Carl Von Linné, who originated the system for classifying plants used the world over (see p.124). To get there turn south off Haga Nygatan into Landsvagsgatan, which joins up with Linnégatan – the main thoroughfare. In recent years, so many stylish cafés and restaurants have sprung up along the main drag that Linné is now considered Gothenburg's "second Avenyn" – but without the attitude. The street is lined with Dutch-inspired nineteenth-cen-tury architecture, tall and elegant buildings interspersed with steep little side roads.

However, it's the main roads leading off Linnégatan, prosaically named Long Street First (Långgatan Första), Long Street Second (Andra) and so on up to Fourth, that give the area its real character. The not-very-long Second and Third streets contain a mix of dark antique stores, basement cafés and upfront sex shops. If you're interested, check out the popular **Auction House**, Trådje Långgatan 9 (the third 'Long Street') (closed July; ☎031/12 44 30), where a large amount of silver, porcelain and jewellery is mixed in with total tat; view-ings (Mon 4–7.30pm, Tues 9am–noon) precede the weekly auctions (Wed & Thurs 9am–3pm).

On the right as you head up Linnégatan towards Järntorget is one modern apartment block that's worth a second glance, as is the forbidding building directly opposite, where King Oskar II had his private apartment – and his women. The block on the right replaced a property whose republican owner so hated both the monarchy and the morals of the king that he had a run of colourful ceramic panels, depicting the devil, set facing the royal apartment. Sadly, the Gothenburg propensity for doing away with its own past meant the "devil building", as it was known, was recently demolished, but two of the grotesque panels have been incorporated into the new apartment block.

Slottskogen

Slottskogen, a five-minute walk south from Linnégatan (tram #1 or #2 to Linnéplatsen), is a huge, tranquil expanse of parkland, with farm animals and birdlife, including pink flamingos in summer. The rather dreary **Natural History Museum** (Naturhistoriska Museet; daily 11am–5pm; 40kr; Ⓦwww.gnm.se), within the grounds of the park, prides itself on being the city's oldest museum, dating from 1833. Its endless displays of stuffed birds appear particularly depressing after seeing the living ones outside, and although the museum supposedly contains ten million animals, most of these are minute insects, which sit unnoticed in drawers that fill several rooms. The most worthwhile item is the world's only stuffed blue whale, which was killed in 1865 and contains a Victorian café complete with original red velvet sofas – unfortunately, it's only opened in election years (the Swedish word for whale also means election).

On the south side of Slottskogen are the impressive **Botanical Gardens** (Botaniska Trädgården; daily 9am–dusk; glasshouses May–Aug daily 9am–6pm; Sept–April Mon–Fri 10am–3pm, Sat & Sun noon–4pm; 20kr or included in the entrance to the Palm House), which hold some 12,000 species of plants; highlights are the Japanese valley and the rock gardens.

North of the river

The main reasons to venture north across the Göta river onto Hisingen, Sweden's fourth largest island, are to visit the **Volvo Factory** and, nearby, the **Volvo Museum**. To reach the factory from the centre of town, bus #29 runs in summer from Drottningtorget platform M, outside the main post office, right up to the gates (40min.). To get to the museum from the factory, take bus #28 to Eketrägatan and then change onto bus #29; or from the centre of town, take tram #2 or #5 to Eketrägatan, then bus #28 to Götaverken Arendal.

The factory (Ⓣ031 325 1093; free) runs daily tours in English and is an illuminating experience. From its humble beginnings in 1927, when the company was founded by two engineers from a Gothenburg ball-bearings factory, the **Volvo factory** has developed into a vast, city-like complex, with buses wending their way across leafy hills and stopping at places called Volvo Hall and Volvo Park. Geared towards people who are contemplating buying a car, the (compulsory) tour here includes film shows and commentaries in English that are one long advertisement. To see just how advanced technology is used at each stage in a car's creation, take the more interesting **Blue Train tour** (free), on a tram-like series of carriages that transports visitors through the vast site and the two-kilometre-long factory building, where you can watch robots (and even a few humans) build the cars from start to finish. There's a full commentary in English, which steers clear of technical jargon.

The **Volvo Museum** (June–Aug Tues–Fri 10am–5pm, Sat & Sun 11am–4pm; Sept–May Tues–Fri noon–5pm, Sat 11am–4pm; 30kr; Ⓦwww.volvo.se/history/museum) is also worth a look, especially for aficionados. There is little effort made at the museum to create a special ambience for the many pristine exhibits, but fans of classic cars will enjoy seeing rare examples of many models. There is the unique prototype of "Phillip", an unusual American-style Volvo with fins that never went into production, and plenty of other gleaming specimens, such as Volvo Amazons and the sporty P1800s, along with some pretty uninteresting commercial vehicles – lorries and the like.

West to Klippan and the Gothenburg Archipelago

On a fine day, Gothenburgers make for the nearest **coastal islands**, where bathing in the sea and sun are a real pleasure and it's hard to imagine you're so close to a city at all. One of the best ways of exploring the area is by bike, taking in the industrial heritage of the city on your way out to the beaches.

Along the waterfront to Klippan

Starting from the Opera House (see p.143), follow the route past the ferry terminals used by Stena Line's Denmark services and the **Amerika House**, the building that once housed the shipping line operating services to the USA. This was where countless Swedes left their native shores for the last time – and also the spot from where Sweden's small clutch of film stars (most notably Garbo and Bergman) sailed. Around 1km on, the gold-topped spire of the Karl Johan Church appears in foliage to the left, and a small lane, also on your left, leads to the city's gay centre (see p.160); just on the right Fiskhamnen (see opposite) holds Gothenburg's famed **fish auctions** which make a dramatic sight at six in the morning.

A few hundred metres straight on is **Klippan**, a charming old enclave of red houses once used in both the sugar and brewing industries; the area was at one time also the home port of the East India Company. Today, the buildings are largely converted for tourist purposes, the sugar mill having closed in the late 1950s and the brewery shut down in 1975. The first building you see is the red-painted East India Company warehouse, now a chic restaurant, *Sjömagasinet* (see p.158.)

A number of preserved houses are dotted about, including the low cottages of the workers, and the old sugar mill. Taken over by Sir David Carnegie in 1836, the mill now houses artists' studios which are not really open to the public, but from the outside you'll be able to see work in progress. The most imposing building, the **Carnegie Porter Brewery** itself, is now a *Novotel* hotel (see p.140). To rest a while, the best spot is the **café**/art gallery (Mon–Fri 11am–8pm, Sat & Sun noon–8pm) in an old factory office, beyond the turquoise-painted Älfsborgs bridge, with views over the water to the Öresund. You'll also find the ruins of Älvsborg Castle hereabouts, but it's only a few paltry mounds of stones, and not to be confused with the similar sounding Nya Elfsborg fortress (see p.144), at the mouth of the river, to which there are regular **boat trips**.

Just a few steps further west, the newest and most exciting development at Klippan for anyone interested in contemporary art is **Röda Sten** (daily noon–4pm; free), an old graffiti-covered warehouse which lacks charm in itself, but has been turned into a huge gallery space for temporary exhibitions. The only permanent exhibits are outside, a smattering of large and powerful granite sculptures by Claes Hake, reflecting the once industrial character of the area.

A few metres beyond Röda Sten is a small inlet in which children like to splash about. It's said locally that in a seventeenth-century river battle between Swedes and Danes, one surviving Swede climbed up on the largest stone in the water and, while his own blood dripped onto it, declared victory; today the biggest stone in the water is painted blood red. A cycle track leads from the inlet through to **Nya Varvet** (New Wharf), a pleasant harbour area filled with small pleasure boats. There's not much to do here except fill up at the restaurant, *Reveljen* (see p.158).

Saltholmen and the offshore islands

Around 3km west of Klippan is **Saltholmen**, at the tip of Gothenburg's most westerly peninsula. Outcrops of smooth rocks provide a multitude of hidden sunbathing areas where nude bathing is quite the norm. The zone around to your left, on the south side of the peninsula, has become a recognized gay bathing area. Climbing to Saltholmen's highest point the views are quite idyllic, with boats flecking the water and the offshore islands stretching out into the distance.

From Saltholmen, regular ferries make the short trips to the most popular islands, stopping first at **Brännö**, an island mainly given over to summer houses converted from fishermen's shacks, and crowded with Gothenburgers through high season. **Styrsö** is the next island, with three hamlets where most of its residents live all year. The furthest of the main islands is **Vrångö**, which has one small village and a perfect lagoon with a great beach: on leaving the boat, turn left, follow the short path and you'll find a spit of flat stone forming one side of the lagoon.

Tram #4 runs all the way to Saltholmen, and the ferries cost 10kr (free with tram ticket). There's a delightful little outdoor **café** at Saltholmen run by a Thai family, selling coffee, cake and ice cream.

Eating

Gothenburg has a multitude of eating places, catering for every budget and for most tastes. Despite the historical association of the town with foreign nations, the upsurge in foreign **restaurants** that characterized the 1990s has been overtaken by simpler, pan-European eateries which draw on Swedish staples such as good breads, exceptional herring and salmon dishes and, in summer, glorious soft fruits. The emphasis these days is much more on casual eating than it was ten years ago. When eating out, Gothenburgers are as likely to munch on filled ciabattas served with salad as sit down to three-course meals. When formal fare is called for, the city excels in fish restaurants. There's also a growing trend towards low-priced pasta places providing healthier alternatives to the pizza parlours and burger bars.

Markets and snacks

The bustling, historic **Saluhallen** at Kungstorget is a delightful sensory experience, with a great choice of meats, fish, fruits, vegetables and a huge range of delectable breads; there are also a couple of cheap coffee and snack bars here. A more recent arrival on the market scene is **Saluhall Briggen**, on the corner of Tredje Långgatan and Nordhamsgatan in the Linné area. Housed in an old fire station, it specializes in good-quality meats, fish and cheese and mouthwatering deli delights. For excellent fresh fish, **Feskekorka** (see p.146) is an absolute must; while for the serious fish aficionado, there's the auction at **Fiskhamnen** (Fish Harbour; Tues–Fri 7am), a couple of kilometres west of the centre – take tram #3 or #4 to Stigbergstorget. For a superb **delicatessen**, head for Delitalia, Övre Husargatan 12, a terrific Italian place in the Linné area, selling anything you could want for a picnic. The conveniently located **Konsum** supermarket on Avenyn (daily till 11pm) sells a wide range of fruits, fish and meats, and also has a good deli counter. For excellent takeaway baguette and coffee deals, head for the Liseberg end of Södravagen, where a clutch of café-shops sell full-to-bursting sandwiches and coffee for just 20kr – and all just a couple of minutes' walk from the much pricier Avenyn.

Cafés and Konditori

During the past few years, **café life** has really come into its own in Gothenburg, the profusion of new places throughout the city adding to the more traditional **konditori** (bakery with tea-room attached). Nowadays, it's easy to stroll from one café to another at any time of day or night, and tuck into humungous sandwiches and gorgeous cakes. Cafés also offer a wide range of light meals and are fast becoming about the best places to go for good food at reasonable prices. The most interesting cafés are concentrated in the fashionable Haga and Linné districts.

The old town

Ahlstroms Konditori Korsgatan 2. Dating from 1901, this traditional café/bakery is very much of the old school, much like many of its patrons. The original features have been watered down by modernization, but it's still worth a visit for its good selection of cakes, plus *Dagens Rätt* at 52kr.

C & Co Artroom Kyrkogatan 31. A perfect example of Gothenburg's foray into cool little cafés and bagel bars, attracting the kind of people who just have to have excellent filled bagels at 35–40kr, and really good coffee. Mon–Fri 10am–5pm, Sat 9am–2pm.

Café Bommen at the harbour. Standard café food, but a lovely spot to have a coffee by the water's edge, facing the Opera House. Daily 11am–6pm.

Froken Olssons Kafe Östra Larmgatan 14. Heaps of sandwiches, salads and sumptuous desserts served up in a rural-style atmosphere. Look out for the mountains of giant meringues on tiered, silver cake trays. Sandwiches for 30–50kr, and a good-value lunchtime vegetarian salad buffet for 50kr.

Mauritz Kaffehus Fredgatan. Very small and unassuming, this place is run by the founder's great grandson; the family have been importing coffee into Gothenburg since 1888. Come here for espresso and cappuccinos standing at the bar; drinks served with apple buns or rye rolls with cheese.

Petersens Korsgatan 15. A *konditori* with good cakes and the best bread in town. Mon–Fri 9am–7pm, Sat 8.30am–5pm.

Avenyn, Vasastan and around

Baguetter Södra Vägen 59. Big, freshly made sandwiches in a very small, basic café, well worth the five-minute walk here from Avenyn or Liseberg. Prices around 20kr.

Café Dali Vasagatan 42. A friendly, stylish place for sandwiches and cakes in an orange-painted basement. Popular with students.

Café Engelen Engelbrektsgatan 26. Friendly, studenty 24-hour café serving home-made, excellent-value food such as baked potatoes, lasagne and big sandwiches for 45kr, plus glorious ice cream and a massive range of fruit teas. There's always a vegetarian selection and a good 36kr breakfast.

Espresso House Vasagatan 22. This excellent, ubiquitous chain of Swedish coffee houses has at last made it north to Gothenburg. This branch is full of hip students in relaxed mode. Delicious salads (50kr), cakes (30kr) and a great variety of good coffees.

Family House Café Storgatan 10. With a wacky, cosily designed setting within an old house, this place is an absolute gem and a must for its superbly relaxed atmosphere. Terrific breakfasts, sumptuous and healthy lunches including three home-made pies each day, and wonderful soups and desserts. You name the price for your breakfast, based on what you think it's worth, and on the 18th, 19th and 20th of each month, breakfasts are free.

Java Café Vasagatan 23, There's a Parisian feel to this studenty coffee house that's stood the test of time serving breakfasts at 30kr and a wide range of coffees. Decor includes a collection of thermos flasks dotted among shelves of books. A good Sunday-morning hang-out. Mon–Fri 8am–11pm, Sat & Sun 10am–11pm.

Junggrens Café Avenyn 37. One of only a couple of reasonably priced Avenyn cafés, with good snacks and sandwiches. Atmospheric and convivial, it's been run for decades by a charismatic old Polish woman and her sulky staff. Coffee for only 13kr, sandwiches 15–40kr.

Muffinsmm Avenyn 39. A more recent arrival, near Göteplatsen, serving delicious, light muffins, a range of salads, pannini and wraps. There's no seating but there are benches outside and the prices are very low.

Garbo Vasagatan 40. With homage to the silver screen ice queen on the walls, this sociable, relaxed café serves good, light food. Same owners as *Greta's* opposite.

Teatergatan Café Teatergatan 36. Somewhat posey place where you can sit at one of the black-and-white swivel chairs and try sandwiches at 50kr and salads at 60kr.

Tintin Café Engelbrektsgatan 22. Very busy 24hr café with mounds of food and coffee at low prices (try a big plate of chicken salad for 45kr) and a laid-back, student atmosphere.

Haga

Allegården Södra Allegatan 4, looking onto Feskekorka. Originally built by F.D. Dickson as a people's library in 1897, this fairy-tale concoction of engraved stone and pink brick is a friendly place for a coffee. Mon–Fri 8.30am–4pm.

Jacob's Café Haga Nygatan 10. *The* place to sit outside and people-watch; inside, the decor is fabulous, with some fine Jugend (Swedish Art Nouveau) lamps.

Café Kringlan Haga Nygatan 13. The best spot in town for wonderful chocolate pies, bagels, strudels and generous open sandwiches. A prime place to people-watch in the summer.

Linné

Café 3 Linnégatan 3, at the corner of Tredje

Långgatan. A cosy, all-day café serving filled-baguettes (25kr take away or 30kr eat in), and lovely fruit crumbles.

Café Cello Andre Långgatan 6. A pleasant, Greek-owned café, where you can buy the antique ornaments and furniture around you. Food is home-baked and lunches cheap. Sandwiches from 22kr.

Publik Andra Långgatan 20. Young, funky and unashamedly retro place where people come to smoke, drink and lounge, with old velvet sofas and scores of LPs to leaf through on a nostalgia trip. Coffee and muffins, or nachos and ciabattas cost 35–45kr.

Saluhallen Briggan (see markets above). Amid the delicatessen, fish and cheese counters, this market-café serves baked potatoes, pies, and pizzas for 55kr each plus pasta dishes and sizeable grills at 60kr.

Solsidan Café Linnégatan 42. Lovely café with outdoor seating that's very popular with Linné locals, serving delicious cakes and lunches. Pasta salad and coffee 49kr. Daily 10am–11pm.

Restaurants

If you want to avoid paying over the odds, it's generally a good idea to steer clear of Avenyn itself (where prices are almost double what you'll pay in Haga or Linné) and to eat your main meal at **lunchtime**, when you can fill up on *Dagens Rätt* deals for 50–70kr. Otherwise, expect to pay 80–120kr for a main dish in most restaurants, a lot higher in the more exclusive places.

It's not usually necessary to **book** tables, but we've given numbers for places where you might need to; things get especially busy between the peak hours of 7pm to 9pm. Restaurants usually open for lunch from 11.30am to 2.30pm, and for dinner from 6pm until 11pm. Again, we have listed opening times which differ from this.

The old town

Gabriel at Feskekorka Feskekorkan fish market ☎031/13 90 51. Excellent fish restaurant, though prices seem particularly high when you can see the real cost of the ingredients below. It's much cheaper to fill up at the tiny eight-seat *Café Feskekorke* at the opposite end of the market. Closed Sun.

Grande E.t.c. Kungsgatan 12 ☎031/701 77 84. Big brother to *E.t.c.* at Vasaplatsen, serving similar, very fresh pasta dishes from 85kr.

Greta's Drottninggattan 35. Stylish and popular bar-restaurant drawing a mixed gay and straight clientele. These days the pan-European food is given less priority than it used to be before it also became a nightclub.

Ostindiska Huset Krog & Café Norra Hamngatan 12, next door to the Stadsmuseum. Delightful eatery serving regular Swedish fayre in the vaulted white Ostindiska House. Lunch menu for around 60kr and

more costly evening menu in a romantic setting.

Persian Palats Stampgatan 4, close to the train station ☎031/15 61 22. Excellent and reasonably priced Persian cooking with an amazing selection of own-baked cakes. Very good daily lunch with vegetarian options.

Avenyn, Vasastan & Around

E.t.c. Vasaplatsen 4, Vasastan. This cool, elegant grey-painted basement is the best place in town for superb home-made pasta. Lunch 55kr; dinner menu also offers meat and fish dishes. Very busy in the evenings.

Figaro Grill & Café Bar Stora Teatern, at the foot of Avenyn. Excellent-value grilled meats and burgers plus good desserts; lunch specials at 65kr. Serve yourself at the bar and sit in the dappled light of ancient beech trees overlooking the canal and Old Town.

Restaurant Frågetecken Södra Vägen 20. Very popular spot just a minute's walk from Götaplatsen, with a name that translates as "restaurant question mark". Eat out in the conservatory, or inside to watch the chefs at work, carefully preparing Balkan-influenced food. They boast of being "famous for breasts": duck at 230kr is the most expensive thing on the menu, but there's also pasta for under 100kr.

Gothia Hotel Restaurant Massangsgatan 24 ☎031/40 93 00. This glass-walled top-floor piano-bar restaurant offers panoramic views across the city. Meals, geared around fish and meat with subtle sauces are fabulously expensive, but they also serve cheaper snacks including superb king-prawn sandwiches, though still at a whopping 110kr.

Lai Wa Storgatan 11, Vasaplan. One of Gothenburg's better Chinese restaurants with a wide variety of dishes at reasonable prices – try the Peking soup. Good lunches.

Reveljen Nya Varvet west of Klippan (Mon–Fri 11am–2pm), a vast self-service eatery with scores of large bowls containing salads, fish or meat – excellent budget lunches at 60kr for as much as you can gorge.

Sjömagasinet, Klippan. Serving piles of turbot and lobster at prices to test any expense account, this stylish place is housed in a former East India Company warehouse (Mon–Fri 11.30am–2.30pm & 5–11pm, Sat 5–11pm, Sun 2–9pm).

Smaka Vasaplatsen 3, Vasastan ☎031/13 22 47. Moderately priced traditional Swedish dishes enjoyed by a lively, young crowd in a striking, modern interior.

Tai Pak Arkivsgatan, 4 just off Avenyn near Götaplatsen. Decent Chinese traditional-style restaurant serving a two-course special for 69kr, and individual courses for 65–75kr.

28+ Götabergsgatan 28, ☎031/20 21 61. Very fine French-style gourmet restaurant, whose name refers to the fat percentage of its renowned cheese, also sold in the shop (9am–11pm) near the entrance. Specialities include goose-liver terrine. Service is excellent though prices are high with main dishes at close to 200kr. Closed Sun.

Haga

Hemma Hos Haga Nygatan 12 ☎031/13 40 90. Popular restaurant full of quaint old furniture, serving upmarket and expensive Swedish food including reindeer and fish dishes. Mon–Fri 5pm–midnight, Sat 1pm–midnight.

Sjöbaren Haga Nygatan 27. Small fish and shellfish restaurant on the ground floor of a traditional governor's house building. Moderate prices.

Solrosen Kaponjargatan 4a ☎031/711 66 97. The oldest vegetarian restaurant in Gothenburg, this is the place to come for well-prepared veggie and vegan delights: starters such as falafel, Greek salad and fried cheese are 40kr upwards, while mains such as artichoke au gratin and fried aubergine are 90–180kr. The daily special – soups, hot food such as lasagne and salads –is good value at 65kr. There are six beers on tap and smoking is allowed.

Linné

Cyrano Prinsgatan 7 ☎031/14 31 10. A superb Provençal-style bistro with a laid-back atmosphere and great service. They also do fantastic wood-fired pizzas. Very popular, so book ahead.

Den Lilla Taverna Oliver Dahlsgatan 17 ☎031/12 88 05. A very good and very popular Greek restaurant, with paper tablecloths and Greek scenes painted on false windows. Most dishes cost 65–90kr. Live bazouki music Wed & Sat. Mon–Thurs 5–11pm, Fri 5pm–midnight, Sat 1pm–1am, Sun 1pm–10pm.

Hos Pelle Djupedalsgatan 2 ☎031/12 10 31. Sophisticated wine bar off Linnégatan, not cheap, but serving snacks as well as full meals, and decorated with intriguing abstract artwork.

Jazzå Andre Långgatan 4. Pleasantly dark bar and restaurant serving European dishes at standard prices with jazz and blues nights and interesting modern art on the yellowing walls.

Krakow Karl Gustavsgatan 28 ☎031/20 33 74. Burly staff serving big, basic and very filling Polish food in a large, dark restaurant. Moderate prices.

Le Village Tredje Långgatan 13 ☎031/24 20 03. Lovely candle-lit restaurant connected to a big antique shop, serving very well-presented if smallish dishes. The main dining area is expensive – sit in the cheaper bar area where meals start at 65kr.

Louice Värmlandsgatan 18, off Andra Långgatan ☎031/12 55 49. Justifiably popular and unpretentious neighbourhood restaurant, with occasional live music. Standard main courses are expensive, but look out for the excellent-value daily specials at 79kr. There's a full children's menu, with an English translation available, at 35kr.

Pasta Gambero Övre Husargatan 5 ☎031/13 78 38. The best of a number of good, reasonably priced Italian eateries on this long street at the end of Linnégatan. The servings are generous and the service very obliging. Next door is an excellent pizzeria, run by the same family.

Petroshka Oliver Dahlgatan 10 ☎031/24 38 80. Bizarre Russian restaurant – the tables are decked out with cut-glass crystal and candelabras, but the atmosphere is that of a St Petersburg living room. Plentiful, traditional Russian food from borsch to caviar and blinis. This place manages to glitter grandly yet cheaply.

Plus (+) Corner of Linnégatan and Landsvägsgatan ☎031/24 08 90. Sit at polished tables beneath chandeliers in this beautifully restored wooden house nestling in rough-hewn rock. Fish and meat dishes go for 160–180kr, and there's a wide drinks list and terrace seating.

Rumpanbar Linnégatan 38. A popular, stylish place with a great corner location and huge windows. Excellent pizzas and good meat and fish dishes too. Open till 1am.

Nightlife and entertainment

There's an excellent choice of places to **drink**, and even the hippest bars often serve food and so have a bit of a restaurant atmosphere, the exceptions being a small number of British- and Irish-style pubs. Although it's not uncommon for Gothenburgers to drink themselves to oblivion, the atmosphere around the bars is generally non-aggressive.

The city also has a brisk **live music scene** – jazz, rock and classical – as well as the usual cinema and theatre opportunities. The details below should give you some ideas, but it's worth picking up the Friday edition of the *Göteborgs Posten*, which has a weekly supplement, *Aveny*, full of listings for bars, concerts, clubs and almost anything else you might want to know about – it's in Swedish but not very difficult to decipher. The notice boards in the main hall at the entrance to *Studs*, the student bar in Haga, are also good for information on gigs and what's going on generally in the city.

Bars and pubs

We've listed some of the city's most popular **pubs** and **bar-restaurants** below; however, it's worth noting that many of the cafés and restaurants listed on pp.156–159 are also good places to have a beer, especially in the busier night-time areas of Avenyn and Linné. In Vasaplan, just west of Avenyn, and in Haga, further west, the 24-hour studenty cafés listed earlier are great places to drink into the early hours, and on Avenyn itself, it's less a matter of choosing the best place than spotting a table. Although there are a number of long-established bars in the old town, the atmosphere is generally a bit low-key at night.

The old town

Beefeater Inn Plantagegatan 1. One of a bevy of British-oriented neighbourhood pubs that's very much in vogue with Gothenburgers. This one really goes overboard, with a stylistic mishmash of red-telephone-box doors, tartan walls and staff in kilts.

Bishops Arms Västra Larmgatan 1. Attached to the glamorous *Elite Plaza* hotel (see p.137), this pub boasts a wide range of beers. It's all faux "olde Englishe" inside, but nicely done and a cut above similarly styled places around the country.

Dubliners Östra Hamngatan 50b. For a while, Swedes have been overtaken with a nostalgia for all things old and Irish – or at least a Swedish interpretation of what's old and Irish. This is the most popular exponent.

Gamle Port Östra Larmgatan 18. The city's oldest watering hole, with British beer in the downstairs pub and an awful disco upstairs (see overleaf).

Palace Brunnsparken. The rather splendid former home of the Furstenburgs and their art galleries (see p.146) is very popular spot, with live bands on Thursdays.

Pelican Kungstorget, behind Saluhall. Elegant yet relaxed place with contemporary, minimalist decor, serving good steaks along with a long list of drinks.

Avenyn and around

Avenyn 10 Avenyn 10. Very loud young crowd. Not a place for a drink and a chat, unless you want to stand out on the street.

Brasserie Lipp Avenyn 8. Although no longer the hippest place on Avenyn, *Lipp* is expensive and so attracts a slightly older crowd – but a crowd it is, especially during summer.

Napoleon Vasagatan 11. It's the fabulous decor of this old house that makes a drink here fun:

even the exterior walls are covered in delicate old paintings. Though really a bar, this lovely, dark, mellow place also serves light meals. Mon–Thurs & Sun 10am–midnight, Fri & Sat 10am–3am.

Nivå Avenyn 9. Stylish, popular bar with a modern interior heavy on mosaic decor, and a bar and restaurant on different levels.

Scandic Rubinen Bar Avenyn 24. Glitzy hotel-foyer type of bar. Always packed with tourists and right at the heart of Avenyn.

Haga

Stars & Stripes Järntorget 4J Though rather unappealing on the outside and slightly rough within, *Stars & Stripes* boasts some remarkable painted ceilings and a very down-to-earth atmosphere.

Studs Götabergsgatan 17, off Engelbrektsgatan, behind Vasa Church. This is the hub of Gothenburg student life, with a pub, bar and restaurant. The main advantage of the student bar is its prices, with two-for-one beers before 9pm in summer. If

you haven't got student ID, friendly bluffing should get you in.

Linné

Cigarren Järntorget 6, opposite the Folketshus. Looks as if it's been here forever, but has actually only existed since the revamping of this classic old workers' square. Huge range of cigars and lots of coffees and teas alongside the beers and wines.

Gillestugan Järntorget 6. Cosy and panelled without being over the top, this bar has plenty of outdoor seating and offers full meals such as beef fillet at 98kr or seafood burgers at 125kr.

The Rover Andra Långgatan 12. Run-of-the-mill Anglo-Irish pub selling Boddingtons, with other lagers, ales and cider on tap, plus a wide range of bottled beers. Lamb, steaks and trout dishes for 59–105kr.

1252 Linnégatan 52. The first of the bars in this area to become trendy, this long-term survivor put the Linné area on the nightlife map. Reasonably priced food considering the location, with outdoor tables in summer.

Clubs

During the past few years, the city's old, mediocre **clubs** have been usurped by a cluster of smaller, laid-back joints around the junction of Victoriagatan and Storgatan in Vasastan. There are, however, a few big, classic nightclubs around the city which consistently pull the biggest crowds.

Ici Viktoriagatan 3 ☎031/711 02 00. Around the corner from Vasastan, this place fills to the gills with revellers, mostly in their early 20s; the queues reach out of the door.

Klara Viktoriagatan 1 ☎031/ 13 38 54. The best of all the more alternative night spots, next door to *La Bas* (see below). A long-established and eminently likeable bar with live music and a more catholic mix of people and conversation when the latter can be heard at all. Monday nights are dedicated to the 80s, Tuesday has reggae and Wednesday has jamming sessions with local DJs.

La Bas Viktoriagatan ☎031/711 02 05. Next door to *Ici*, this club attracts a slightly older crowd (but still not hitting 30), with a more preppy, sophisticated scene and more elbowroom.

Park Lane Avenyn 36 ☎031/20 60 58. A hot, crowded club with three bars, a casino and live entertainment.

Rondo Liseberg. People of all ages dancing in a friendly atmosphere, often to live bands, on Sweden's biggest dance floor (if that's a boast).

Träga@rn Nya Alleyn, near Heden ☎031/10 20 90. One of the city's liveliest haunts. this hip club offers five bars, a casino, a disco and show bands. Open daily 9pm–3am, with a minimum age of 25; free before 10pm, otherwise, admission is 80kr (60kr on Friday nights, when the age limit drops to 22).

Valand Vasagatan 3, just off Avenyn. The oldest of the traditional nightclubs in town, and still always crowded. It boasts two dance floors and four bars.

Vasastan Viktoriagatan 2A. A suave spot where confident twenty- and thirty-somethings enjoy a mellow atmosphere.

Yaki Da Östra Larmgatan 18 (upstairs from *Gamle Port*, see p.159). Despite having three bars, a stage and a casino, there's often a pretty depressing atmosphere.

Gay Gothenburg

Gothenburg's **gay scene** appears surprisingly half-hearted to visitors. The burgeoning reliance on personals sites on the Internet has hit traditional gay café life profoundly. Despite this, there is now something approaching choice for gay Gothenburgers, though it's still very limited compared to cities of this size in other countries. **RFSL**, the official organization for gay rights is based at

Karl Johansgatan 31, in a charming old wooden vicarage inconveniently far from the town centre (☎031/775 40 10, ✉goteborg@rfsl.se). By bike or on foot, head out west towards Klippan, and when you see the gold-topped spire of Karl Johan Church, follow the sign, under the freeway, pointing to Majorna. While there are occasional café and party nights here, they are ignored by most gay Gothenburgers. Gay clubs emerge and disappear at an alarming rate here, below are the more established and popular.

Gay bars & clubs

Cosmopolitan at *Restaurang Enter Lounge*, Vasaplatsen. This is one of the newest venues on the scene, with guest DJs each week, two bars and two dance floors. Try Saturdays 10pm–3am.
Eros at *Restaurang Haket*, Första Långgatan 32 ☎031/701 49 47. One of the longest-standing clubs with a mixed age range in something of an uninspired down-at-heel setting.

Greta's Drottninggatan 35. The city's first gay restaurant/bar/café to be open every day. Though its popularity has waned among the gay fraternity recently, it's still worth checking out for a drink or its more popular themed club nights.
Shame at *Restaurant Räkan*, behind *McDonald's* on Avenyn. There's a 60kr entry fee and the time to go is Fridays 8pm–3am.

Live music

Gothenburg's large student community means there are plenty of **local live bands**. The best venue, with an emphasis on alternative and dance music, is *Kompaniet*, at Kungsgatan 19 (☎031/711 99 46). The top floor is a bar, while downstairs there's dancing to Eurotechno and drinks are half-price between 8pm and 10pm. The place stays open until 3am daily in summer (winter Wed–Sat only). Other bars worth checking out are *Klara*, Vallgatan 8, which has wannabe poets by day and, on Monday nights, a diverse range of indie and rock bands; and *Dojan*, Vallgatan 3, a small, smoky and crowded rock pub, with a mixed-age clientele, and live bands every night. Just round the corner in Kaserntorget is *Sticky Fingers*, a rock club with live bands several nights a week. For **international groups**, there are some sizeable stadia in the city, notably Scandinavium (☎031/81 10 20), which hosts big-time acts, as does the colossal arena, Ullevi Stadium, not to be confused with Gamle Ullevi close by, where football matches are held. Both are off Skånegatan to the east of Avenyn; take tram #1, #3 or #6.

Jazz enthusiasts should head for the trendy *Neffertiti* jazz club at Hvitfeldtsplatsen 6 (☎031/711 15 33; Mon–Sat from 9pm). There's modern jazz, big band and folk music here as well as reggae, blues and soul. You may have to queue. *Jazzhuset*, Eric Dahlbergsgatan 3 (☎031/13 35 44; Wed–Sat 8pm–2am), puts on trad and Dixieland jazz, and swing, and is something of a pick-up joint for executives. **Classical music** concerts are held regularly in the Konserthuset, Götaplatsen (☎031/726 53 10, ⊛www.gso.se), and at the Stora Theatre, Avenyn; programme details can be obtained from the tourist office. For opera, head to Gothenburg's renowned Opera House at Christina Nilssons Gata at the harbour (☎031/13 13 00, ⊛www.opera.se).

Cinema and theatre

There are plenty of **cinemas** around the city, and English-language films (which make up the majority of what's shown) are always subtitled in Swedish, never dubbed. The most unusual of the cinemas is Bio Palatset, on Kungstorget. In a building that was originally a meat market and then a failed shopping mall, this ten-screen picture house has an interior painted in clashing fruity colours; the foyer has been scooped out to reveal rocks, now floodlit, studded with Viking spears. Another multi-screen complex is Filmstaden, at

Kungsgatan 35, behind the cathedral. For a great **art-house cinema**, check out Hagabion on Linnégatan (Mon–Fri 6–9.15pm, Sat & Sun 2.30–9.15pm; ☏031/42 88 10). Converted from an old creeper-strewn school, it has a pleasant café for cake, soup and sandwiches. A remarkable range of films is offered at the **Gothenburg Film Festival** (ⓦ www.filmfestival.org; Jan & Feb), at the Draken cinema on Järntorget, but the place is closed during summer.

Theatre in Gothenburg is unlikely to appeal to many visitors: the city's council-run theatres put on plays that would make Strindberg look like farce, what's more, they are all in Swedish. The Lorensberg, a privately run theatre on Lorensbergsgatan off Götaplatsen, goes for light comedy shows in Swedish only and is closed during the summer months.

Listings

Airlines British Airways, at the airport ☏020/78 11 44; Finnair, Fredsgatan 6 ☏020/78 11 00; KLM, at the airport ☏031/94 16 40; Lufthansa, Fredsgatan 1 ☏031/80 56 40; SAS, at the airport ☏020/91 01 10.

Airport General information on ☏031/94 10 00.

Banks and exchange Most banks are found on Östra Hamngatan, Södra Hamngatan and Västra Hamngatan. There are four Forex exchange offices, which accept American Express, Diners Club, and travellers' cheques: Central Station ☏031/15 65 16 (daily 8am–9pm); Avenyn 22 ☏031/18 57 60 (daily 8am–9pm); Nordstan shopping centre ☏031/15 75 30 (daily 9am–7pm); and Kungsportsplatsen ☏031/13 60 74 (daily 9am–7pm).

Buses Reservations are obligatory for buses to Stockholm, Helsingborg and Malmö; book at Bussresebyra, Drottninggatan 50 (☏031/80 55 30).

Car rental Avis, Central Station (☏031/80 57 80) and at the airport (☏031/94 60 30); Budget, Kristinelundsgatan 13 (☏031/20 09 30), at the airport (☏031/94 60 55); Europcar, Stampgatan 22D (☏031/80 53 90), at the airport (☏031/94 71 00); Hertz, Stampgatan 16A (☏031/80 37 30), at the airport (☏031/94 60 20). Also many of the larger petrol stations such as Q8, Statoil & Shell.

Dentist Akuttandvården, Stampgatan 2 close to the train station ☏031 80 78 00.

Doctor Medical Counselling Service and Information (☏031/41 55 00); Sahlgrenska Hospital at Per Dubbsgatan (☏60 10 00). City Akuten, a private clinic, has doctors on duty 8am–6pm at Drottninggatan 45 (☏031/10 10 10).

Emergency services Ambulance, police, fire brigade on ☏112.

Hospital Sahlgrenska University Hospital ☏031 342 10 00

Internet access Gameonline, Magasinsgatan 26 ☏031/13 51 71; IT-Grottan, Chalmersgatan 27 ☏031/778 73 77; IT-Palatset Jaremans, Viktoriagatan 14 ☏031/13 31 13 (daily 11am–midnight; 48kr/hour);

Laundry At Nordstan Service Centre, the shopping centre near Central Station.

Left luggage Lockers at Nordstan Service Centre and Central Station. 20–40kr.

Petrol stations Preem, Skånegatan, facing Ullevi Stadium; Statoil, Frabriksgatan on opposite side of Ullevi Stadium.

Pharmacy Apoteket Vasen, Götagatan 10, in Nordstan shopping centre, daily 8am–10pm; ☏031/80 44 10.

Police Headquarters at Ernst Fontells Plats ☏031/739 20 00 (Mon–Fri 9am–2pm).

Post office Main post office for poste restante is in Nordstan shopping centre (☏031/62 39 76; daily 10am–6pm)

Public telephones Phone cards can be bought at Pressbyrån and the tourist offices.

Swimming The biggest and best pool is the 1950s Valhallabadet, on Skånegatan, next to the Scandinavium sports complex.

Systembolaget Nordstan shopping centre or Kungsportsavenyn (Avenyn) 18.

Train information Domestic trains on ☏020/75 75 75; international train information on ☏031/80 77 10.

Travel agents KILROY travels, Berzeliigatan 5, not far from Götaplatsen (Mon–Fri 9.30am–5pm; ☏031/20 08 60).

Around Gothenburg

North of Gothenburg, the rugged and picturesque **Bohuslän coast**, which runs all the way to the Norwegian border, attracts countless Scandinavian and German tourists each summer. The crowds don't detract, though, from the wealth of natural beauty – pink-and-black-striped granite rocks, coves, islands and hairline fjords – nor from the many fishing villages that make this stretch of country well worth a few days' exploration. The most popular destination is the island town of **Marstrand**, with its impressive fortress and richly ornamental ancient buildings, but there are several other attractions further up the coast that are also worth visiting, not least the Bronze Age **rock carvings** at **Tanumshede**, near Strömstad.

Northeast of the city, the county of **Västergötland** encompasses the southern sections of Sweden's two largest lakes, **Vänern** and **Vättern**. Here the scenery is gentler, and a number of attractive lakeside towns and villages make good bases from which to venture out into the forested countryside and onto the **Göta Canal** proper. This connects the lakes with each other, and is part of a larger waterway, also referred to as the Göta Canal, running from the North Sea to the Baltic. There are a number of ways to experience the canal, from cross-country cruises to short, evening hops on rented boats or organized ferry rides. The use of **bikes** is a great alternative for exploration of Västergötland, by means of countless cycling trails, empty roads and the canal towpaths. Nearly all tourist offices, youth hostels and campsites in the region rent out bikes, for around 80kr a day or 400kr a week.

While the south of Gothenburg is mostly unspectacular suburbs and countryside, there are a couple of specific sites which would make an appealing daytrip. The spectacular manor house at **Tjoloöholm** brings English Elizabethan and Swedish Romanticism together, while nearby **Åskhult** is one of the very few early nineteenth-century villages to survive land reforms.

The Bohuslän coast

A chain of **islands** linked by a thread of bridges and short ferry crossings make up the county of **Bohuslän** where, despite the summer crowds, it is still easy enough to find a private spot to swim. Sailing is also a popular pastime among Swedes, many of whom have summer cottages here, and all the way along the coast you'll see yachts gliding through the water. Another feature of the Bohuslän landscape you can't fail to miss is the large number of **churches** throughout the county. Although church crawls may not be everyone's idea of a holiday, for long stretches these are the only buildings of note. The county has a long tradition of religious observance, fuelled in the early nineteenth century by the dogmatic Calvinist clergyman Henric Schartau, who believed that closed curtains were a sign of sin within – even today, many island homes still have curtainless windows. The churches, dating from the 1840s up until the 1910s, are mostly white, simple affairs, looking like windmills without sails. They are almost all built 1300m from their villages, and all are surrounded by graveyards. Once you've seen the inside of one of these churches, you've seen most, but those few that are exquisite or unusual have been highlighted in the

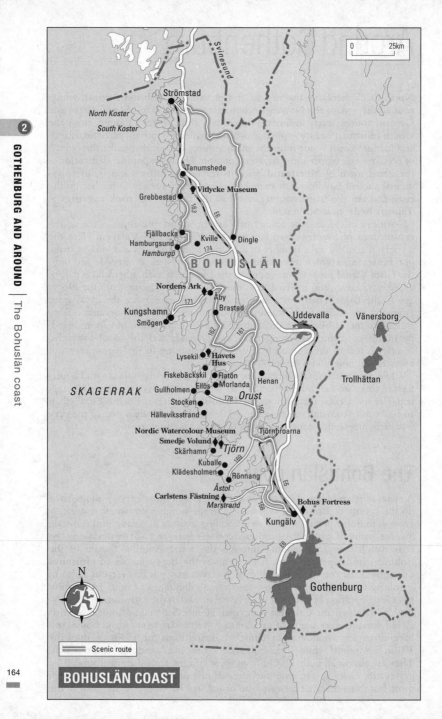

BOHUSLÄN COAST

text. Each church is usually open between 10am and 3pm, but the clergyman invariably lives next door and will be happy to unlock the building.

Train lines travel up the coast from Gothenburg through industrial Uddevalla and on to **Strömstad** (the northernmost town of any size before you enter Norway), but you will be limited to visiting the main towns. Although **bus services** do run, these are patchy and infrequent (on some routes, there is only one bus a week). If you really want to explore Bohuslän's most dramatic scenery and reach its prettier villages, you'll need a car. From Gothenburg, the **E6** motorway is the quickest road north, with designated scenic routes leading off it every few kilometres. For Marstrand alone, one of the most pleasant, if not the quickest ways, is to take a **ferry** from Gothenburg to the island.

Kungälv and the Bohus Fortress

Just under 20km north of Gothenburg on the E6, the quaint old town of **KUNGÄLV**, overshadowed by the fourteenth-century ruins of Bohus Fortress, is a gem of a place to stop for a few hours. Rebuilt after the Swedes razed it in 1676 to prevent the Danes finding shelter during one of their many skirmishes, the town now consists of sprawling cobbled streets and pastel-painted wooden houses, all leaning as if on the verge of collapse. The **tourist office** (℡0303/992 00, ⓦwww.kungalv.se), in the square below the fortress, will provide you with a useful walking-tour map detailing the history of almost every seventeenth-century property here.

The main reason most people visit the town, though, is to see the remains of **Bohus Fortress** (May–Aug daily, Sept Sat & Sun only; guided tours, concerts and opera performances in July & Aug – for details ℡0303 156 62). The first defensive fort here, a wooden affair, was built by the Norwegian king in the fourteenth century, on what was then Norway's southern border. This was replaced by a solid stone building, surrounded by deep natural moats, a complex which came to be known in Sweden for its impregnability. After withstanding six Swedish attacks in the 1560s, the colossal stronghold was rebuilt, this time enclosing a Renaissance palace. When the area finally became Swedish in 1658, Bohus didn't enjoy much of a respite: during the next twenty years, a further fourteen sieges here saw some spectacular bombardment by the Danes: records show that 15,000 men fired 30,000 red-hot cannonballs at the unfortunate fortress, which somehow managed not to fall. Where attack failed, Swedish weather has succeeded, however, and today the building is very much a ruin – albeit a well-kept, grassy one.

Once you've seen the fortress and wandered round the village, there is little else to do here. For accommodation, there's an STF **youth hostel** a stone's throw from the fortress at Farjevagen 2 (℡0303/189 00, ⓕ192 95; 110kr).

Marstrand

About 25km to the west of Kungälv, the island of **Marstrand** buzzes with summer activity, as holiday-makers come to sail, bathe and take one of the highly entertaining historical tours around its impressive **castle**, Carlstens Fästning. With ornate wooden buildings lining the bustling **harbour**, Marstrand is a delightful place to visit and as an easy day-trip from Gothenburg, it shouldn't be missed.

The town's colourful **history** – as so often in Sweden – mainly revolves around fish. Founded under Norwegian rule in the thirteenth century, it achieved remarkable prosperity through herring fishing in the following century, when the ruling king, Håkon of Norway, obtained permission from the pope to allow fishing in the town even on holy days. Rich herring pickings, however, eventually led to greed and corruption, and Marstrand became known as the most immoral town in Scandinavia. The murder of a cleric in 1586 was seen as an omen, and soon after, the whole town burned to the ground and the herring mysteriously disappeared from its waters. The fish – and Marstrand's prosperity – eventually returned in the 1770s. Around this time, the king announced an open-door policy, or *Porto Franco*, for Marstrand, which for the first time allowed foreigners to settle in Sweden, resulting in an influx of Jewish people onto the island. Unfortunately, in 1808 the fish disappeared again, and never came back. In his anger, the king abolished *Porto Franco*, forcing the Jewish community to move to Gothenburg (where pressure from the East India Company had also brought a change in the law, allowing Jews to settle). Meanwhile, the town, without its main source of income, fell behind Gothenburg and Kungälv in importance. By the 1820s, the old herring salting-houses had been converted into bathhouses as Marstrand reinvented itself as a fashionable bathing resort.

Arrival, information and accommodation

Boats leave from Gothenburg from Lilla Bommen at 9.30am, arriving in Marstrand at 12.30pm, with a return trip at 2.30pm arriving back at Lilla Bommen at 5.20pm (May & June selected dates; July & Aug daily). If you have a Gothenburg Pass, you can get two day-trip tickets for the price of one (160kr). To save time, take **bus** #312 from Nils Ericsonsplatsen in Gothenburg to its terminus, where you can catch the ferry. Buy a 100kr carnet at Tidpunkten, next to the bus terminal (once on the bus, insert the carnet into the machine and press "5"); it's half the cost of buying a ticket on the bus and also covers the two-minute ferry journey from the mainland. By **car**, take the E6 north out of Gothenburg, and then Route 168 west, leading right to the ferry stop. Cars are not permitted on the island; you must park on the mainland (25kr a day at car park close to terminal; 15kr a day if you use one of the car parks slightly further away). Leaving the island between midnight and 5am, you press a button at the **ferry** stop and they'll send a boat to pick you up (15min; 13kr return).

The **tourist office** (June Mon–Fri 9.30am–4.30pm, Sat & Sun noon–4pm; late June to early Aug Mon–Fri 9.30am–6pm, Sat & Sun 11am–5pm; mid-Aug to May Mon–Fri 10am–4pm; ☎0303/600 87, ⓦwww.marstrandshamn.nu) currently moves home each year, but is always somewhere close to the harbour where the ferries arrive. Outside summer, it's best to check at Kungälv tourist office (see p.165) which deals with out-of-season enquiries for Marstrand. The staff can book **private rooms** in an old barracks with a small kitchen; bookings must be for a minimum of two people (prices start from 370kr). They will also book **apartments** (a minimum of two people, but fitting up to four; 600kr) and more pleasant en-suite rooms with their own kitchens in private homes or cottages (450kr for two people). The island's STF *Båtellet* **youth hostel** (☎0303/600 10, ⓕ606 07; 235kr) is wonderfully set in an old bathhouse and looks out onto idyllic islands but the rooms are nothing special although the facilities are good: it boasts a sauna, laundry, a swimming pool and a restaurant (see p.168). Of the several very pleasant **hotels** on the island, the *Grand Hotel*, at Paradis Parken (☎0303/603 22, ⓦwww.grandmarstrand.se; ❺), just 50m from the tourist office and left through the park, dating from 1892, is a real classic. Expertly refurbished, this very fine hotel lives up to its name, but ask for a room away from the street – loud late-night revellers can otherwise keep you awake. The more standard but still very pleasant *Hotel Nautic*, at Långgatan 6 (T0303/610 30, Wwww.hotellnautic; ④), has a lovely setting, surrounded by water and sailing boats.

The Town

Turning left when you leave the boat, head up cobbled Kungsgatan and past the *Grand Hotel* (see above). After about a minute, you'll arrive at a small square, surrounded by beautiful wooden houses painted in pastel hues; the locals play *boules* here beneath the shade of a huge, ancient beech tree. Across the square is the squat, white **St Maria kyrka**, named after a girl who was shipwrecked here in the twelfth century. The church, whose interior is simple and unremarkable, was originally called Maria Strand (Maria's Beach), hence the name of the island. From here, all the streets, lined with wooden villas, climb steeply to the castle.

Carlstens Fästning is an imposing sweep of stone walls solidly wedged into the rough rock above (mid-June to mid-Aug daily 11am–6pm: early June & late Aug till 5pm; rest of year Sat & Sun noon–4pm; 60kr including guided tour; for English, book ahead on T0303/602 65). You could easily spend half a day clambering around the castle walls and down the weather-smoothed rocks to the sea, where there are always plenty of places to bathe in private. The informal **tours** take an hour and, though not officially in English, guides are happy to oblige. The most interesting tales they'll tell are down in the prison cells: Carlstens' most noted prisoner-resident was **Lasse Maja**, a thief who got rich by dressing as a woman to seduce and rob wealthy farmers. A sort of Swedish Robin Hood, Maja was known for giving his spoils to the poor. Incarcerated here for 26 years, Maja ingratiated himself with the officers by deploying his cooking skills in a kitchen not renowned for its cuisine. His culinary expertise eventually won him a pardon: when the new king, who was reputed to hate Swedish cooking, visited, Maja had the foresight to serve him French food.

In Maja's cell you can view the neck, waist and ankle shackles that prisoners wore for years on end. More unnerving, though, are the cell designs with a floor area of just two metres by three metres, and pitch dark. In 1845, one prisoner was chosen for one of these cells on the grounds that he was the least observant Christian in town; records show that the only person he was allowed to speak to was a pastor, just once a year, on Christmas Eve. His drawings in his own blood are still visible, as is the dip in the barred windowsill where his hand tapped constantly until his death.

Some tours include climbing the 100-metre-high towers, built in 1658. The views from the top are stunning, but you have to be fit to get up there: the steep, spiral climb is quite exhausting. Once a year, around July 20, the fortress hosts a huge, colourful **festival**, with an eighteenth-century-style procession and live theatre that's well worth catching.

On your way back down from the castle, you can take a detour and visit the remains of **Fredriksborg**, one of the original twelve fortresses on the island, reduced now to a neat wall around the shore. Walking down Villagatan, before you get to the shore, there's a small gateway on the right that leads to a house covered with black, wooden tiles. Its friendly owner will allow you (if you ask first) to walk along his garden path to a vault, originally used to fire cannons at enemy boats, in the old fortress wall; inside are the dusty remains of Scandinavia's first synagogue, soon to be restored. To get back to the town centre, carry on down Villagatan to the shore and walk along the path till you reach Långgatan, which leads back to the main square.

Eating, drinking and nightlife

For a daytime **coffee**, the most atmospheric place is the café in the old officers' mess at the fortress. At night, the relaxed *American Bar* and neighbouring
Oscars, close to the harbour, are good **drinking** haunts. *Oscars* became
Sweden's first discotheque in 1964, and today part of it is still a **nightclub**
playing disco and popular rock music principally to an older crowd. The
Societetshuset (see below) has a disco throughout the summer (Thurs–Sat;
entrance 80kr after 10pm).

Marstrand is nowadays known as something of an **eating** Mecca, though the
fare mostly comes at considerable cost, with main dishes at 180–250kr, though
there are one or two cheap eats too.

American Bar close to the harbour where the ferries arrive. One of Sweden's first bars when it
opened in 1919, today it has a worn 1940s
America feel with posters of cruise ships sailing
between Sweden and the US. The food – mostly
chicken, fish and meat – is good but pricey with
mains all between 125kr and 225kr. It's best to
just have a drink.

Arvidsons at the harbour. Those in the market for
cheap eats will be restricted to this very good
smoked fish stall. Bread and other provisions to go
with the fish can be found at Skepps Handel, also
on the harbourfront, at the corner of
Drottninggatan (daily 7.30am–9pm).

Lasse Majas Krog at the harbour. Located in a
cheerful old house with yellow walls this spot is
very popular with locals and tourists alike. A wide-
ranging meat and fish menu has main courses from
110kr to 220kr, as well as pizzas at around 100kr.

Marstrands Värdshus at the harbour. Very popular for eating at basic wooden tables outside.
Chicken salad costs 125kr, or try the smoked
salmon with dill and potatoes at 135kr.

Oscar's at the harbour, next to the *American Bar*.
First opened originally as a hotel in 1898, this
restaurant has been restored to its former glory
and is now a stylish place for a meal.

Restaurant Drott at the youth hostel ☎0303/618
70. Attractive spot serving very pleasant lunches
and dinners in an 1858 bathhouse with delightful
views. Daily pasta dishes for 49kr, and meat or
seafood meals for 100–200kr. To get there, turn
right from the ferry pier and follow the water's
edge from the harbour as far as you can go.

Restaurant Tenan in the *Grand Hotel*. A charming
option overlooking the bandstand at the front of
the hotel. Dishes include a mixture of local specialities and more international fare.

Societetshuset by the youth hostel ☎0303/606
00. Three restaurants within one classic old house,
all serving a good range of meat and fish dishes in
an old-fashioned atmosphere, though prices are
high.

Villa Maritime on the harbour front. The newest
place in town is hugely overpriced for its relatively
standard dishes.

Tjörn and Orust

Back on the mainland, Route 160, the first coastal scenic route north of
Kungälv, begins 23km from the town; if you're driving from Gothenburg, you
can get to Route 160 off the E6. From Marstrand, though, it's far more appealing to cut east on Route 168, then north on the tiny road signed
"Stenungsund", turning onto Tjörn island on Route 160. Once off the main
road, you'll soon reach **Tjörnbroarna**, a five-kilometre sequence of three
graceful bridges connecting the islands of Tjörn and Orust, and affording spectacular views over the fjords.

While the rugged pink granite outcrops, natural pools of water and jagged
coastline are pleasure enough, the islands offer some cultural diversions too,
particularly the artistic community on Tjörn with its smithy and the **Nordic
Watercolour Museum**, while the beautiful, tiny island of **Klädesholmen**
which retains the atmosphere of the old fishing communities of this area.

Tjörn and surrounding islands

Buses go from Nils Ericsonsplatsen in Gothenburg directly to the village of
Kuballe (bus times from the Tidpunkten on ☎031/80 12 35), on the island of
TJÖRN, 2km from its southernmost tip.

Skärhamn, 4km north of Kuballe, is a charming village centred around a tranquil and picturesque harbour. The most celebrated attraction here is the **Nordiska Akvarellmuseet** (Nordic Water colour Museum; May–Aug daily 11am–6pm; rest of year Tues–Sun noon–5pm; 60kr; ⓦwww.akvarellmuseet.org) in a striking new wood and glass building reflected in the surrounding pools of water. The main criteria for inclusion in the collection – apart from being a Nordic watercolour artist – is to be living. While there's a very charming **café** overlooking the water, the temporary exhibitions can lean on the edge of pretension.

For a real treat, though, follow the sign for **Smedje Volund** (Mon–Fri 10am–4pm, or call to arrange a visit ⓣ0304/67 17 55, ⓦwww.volund.se; free), a few steps beyond. In a stunning house hewn from the pink granite surroundings and floored with ancient kiln bricks is the home and studio of Sweden's most celebrated blacksmith artist **Berth Johansson**, who designed the striking gates at Gothenburg Art Museum. You can watch this charismatic craftsman creating stunning furniture from wrecked ships and the ruins of old factories, while upstairs glass-blowers create wonderful designs and then sell their work at a fraction of the cost of shops elsewhere. There's also a cosy **café** serving tasty cake.

The small **tourist office** at Skärhamn (June–Aug Mon–Sat 9.30am–6pm, Sun 11am–3pm; rest of year Mon–Fri noon–5pm, Sat 11am–3pm; ⓔskarhamn@bastkusten.se) also offers **Internet** connection (10kr for 15min). If you're looking for a **restaurant**, try the harbourside *Haddock's Restaurant* for main meals, though a delicious alternative is to picnic from Kenneth & Lars' fish shop next door, which is brimming with wonderful smoked fish and freshly baked baguettes.

From Kuballe, a bridge makes for an easy journey to **Klädesholmen**, an island of lovely wooden cottages on steep inclines. The landscape around here is all pink granite islets, smoothed down but still somehow raw. There are no trees, just little lakes with ducks and swans. Past the duller outskirts of this herring-canning island, a sign shows the way to a small museum, **Silleboa** (early June Sat & Sun 3–7pm; June to mid-Aug daily 3–7pm; late Aug Sat & Sun 3–7pm), which uses artefects and photographs to depict life in this tucked-away place.

Just 3km south of Kuballe is the blandly built-up village of **Rönnäng**, from where ferries head out to **Åstol** (48kr return), a tiny island so crammed with pretty houses it's known locally as having "no industry, no fishing and no soil". Rönnang has a charming **youth hostel**, clearly signposted, in an appealing yellow-painted wooden house at Nyponvägen 5 (ⓣ0304/67 71 98, ⓕ67 76 74; 115kr, ❶). There's a decent little **pizza place** at Dalenvägen 12, also in Rönnang.

Orust and Gullholmen

A centre for boat-building since Viking times, the island of **Orust** is bare on its windward coasts, yet has forest right up to its eastern shores. Henan, the largest village, is unremarkable; you are much better off avoiding it altogether and heading west off Route 160 onto Route 178, for the town of **Ellös**, where there are places to stay and eat. The most economical **accommodation** option is the *Ellös Brygga* apartments, signposted from the centre (ⓣ0304/509 93; closed in winter). A two-room place with cooking facilities and a balcony overlooking the water costs 550kr in summer, 390kr spring and autumn. In summer the building is also home to a reasonable **restaurant**, offering everything from baked potatoes with prawns to fillet steaks – all at fair prices. In the centre of the village is a bright, elegant restaurant, *Kök & Fisk*, at Skandiavägen 10 (℡0304/500 04), with a bar made out of an old boat. Mains of duck, lamb, turbot and veal are not cheap (around 180kr), but the daily special at 75kr is always a good choice. Just outside the nearby village of **Stocken**, to the south of Ellös, is the splendidly situated STF **youth hostel** at Tofta (℡0304/503 80, ⓦwww.toftagard.se/toftauk/; 140kr; May to mid-Sept), a wooden manor built in 1770, and set in huge grounds, making a wonderful base from which to explore the locality.

Due west of Ellös is the island of **Gullholmen**, where there's a fine example of an unspoilt fishing village, reached by a frequent ferry crossing. Founded in the thirteenth century, the village has a substantial church surrounded by a huddle of red-and-white wooden homes. The rest of the island is a nature reserve where birds nest undisturbed beneath smooth, granite rocks.

A couple of kilometres northeast of Ellös, the little village of **Morlanda** contains a nineteeth-century **cholera cemetery**, where the locals who died of the disease are buried. It's a quiet spot that comes as a poignant reminder of how insular and remote the communities here used to be. To get there, take the narrow road just before the church (which, incidentally, contains Sweden's oldest organ, dating from the seventeenth century), follow it for about 700m and you'll see a path which takes you into some gardens, where the path peters out. From here, wander through the meadow and some lovely woodland until you see a sign, marked "Kolerakyrkogård". A crude stone wall surrounds the site and a bronze cross at the centre commemorates the 1834 epidemic.

Fiskebäckskil

Just north of Morlanda, a free car ferry carries you over to the next island north, where, having stopped at Malö, you reach Flatön. There are superb views over the islands from just after the point where the tiny ferry drops you. Nearby is the lovely and inexpensive restaurant *Flinks*, which serves simple, filling dishes. It's worth peeking in the attached shop too; behind the twee tourist souvenirs, the shelves are full of authentic 1940s paraphernalia, such as magazines and confectionary tins, kept as they were when Sweden's most famous folk singer **Evert Taube** used to stay here and write some of his best loved songs.

From here, the road leads on for a couple of kilometres, past undulating meadows and cottages, to another ferry ride (free), lasting just thirty seconds, to **FISKEBÄCKSKIL**. The locals here once eked out a living making herring-oil lamps, until the advent of electric light put paid to that trade.

The village is peppered with imposing old wooden houses, many with fancily carved porchways and intricate glazed verandahs, perched high up on rocky rises, and boasts several attractions that are well worth exploring.

Arriving by road from the south, you'll find the remarkably stylish **art café**, *Salt Arvet* (℡0523/229 00; July Wed–Sun noon–6pm; May, June & Aug Sat & Sun only, noon–6pm), just on the right where the road enters the village. The galleries (40kr) display constantly changing exhibitions of international standard, such as works by Lichtenstein and Picasso. The café is also a lovely spot for a bite – moussaka (60kr), filled baguettes (45kr) or home-made apple cake (60kr) can be enjoyed while you look out through the glass walls onto the picturesque natural harbour.

Fiskebäckskil's most famous son is the artist **Carl Wilhelmson**, who was born in a cottage near the marina. He made his name nationally with his powerful, evocative portraits and landscapes, which beautifully reflect west-coast Swedish life at the end of the nineteenth century. In 1912, he had a strikingly elegant cottage built close to his birthplace, with splendid views over the waters towards Lysekil. Today, Wilhelmson's grandson, a retired sea captain, still spends his summers in the airy, elevated wooden house, and is happy to show interested visitors around (℡0523/221 28). The cottage's sitting room is Wilhelmson's former studio, its double-height windows letting the famous Nordic light flood in. Reproductions of his work line the walls (the originals are mostly in the Gothenburg Art Museum, see p.147; or the National Art Museum in Stockholm, see p.77), the subjects often being the scenery just outside these windows. The most poignant of the prints, *On The Hill* (original in Gothenburg), shows a scene from Wilhelmson's childhood. Aged 9, he had stood unnoticed behind a group of old men sitting on a rock in Fiskebäckskil, while they discussed a hurricane which had wrecked twenty ships the day before, killing his father, a sea captain. When they became aware of the boy's presence, they asked him not to say anything, and he kept the secret from his mother, who only learnt of her husband's death from the post-boat captain a month later.

Not far away, close to the marina, the 1772 **church** (daily 10am–9pm) has an opulent yet almost domestic feel about its interior. There are chandeliers, gold-plated sconces, etched glass mirrors with hand-carved wood frames, and fresh flowers at the ends of each pew. The luxuriance of the decor is thanks to donations from Bohuslån's richest eighteenth-century landowner, Margareta Huidtfeldt, who also paid for the wrought-iron-and-sheet-metal spire, crowned with a gold-plated weathercock. The wooden, barrel-vaulted ceiling is worth a glance, too: it's covered in eighteenth-century murals, the oddest aspect of which is the scattering of angels' heads. Outside in the graveyard close to the main door is Wilhelmson's rather plain grave, his likeness carved into the granite tombstone. More unusual is the grave in the far corner, where an English officer and a German soldier who died together in the Great North Sea Battle of 1916 were buried together.

Practicalities

Though Fiskebäckskil is a quiet, hidden-away sort of place, it does have a fine **hotel** and a couple of excellent eating opportunities. The stylish *Gullmarsstrand Hotel* (℡0523/222 60, ℻228 05; ❹) is right on the water, next to the Lysekil ferry pier but it's only open during the summer. The hotel also boasts a decent **restaurant**, which is open in July only for lunch and dinner (other times by arrangement). For a really exceptional meal, though, head to *Kapten Sture's Restaurant* (summer daily 2–11pm; rest of year shorter hours; ℡0523/221 25), up Kaptensgatan from the church. The interior is decorated like an old ship and the best dishes use the locally caught fish, fresh from the boats. Another possibility is the pleasant *Brygghuset* on the marina waterfront, which does good meat dishes as well as local fish plates. (Mon–Fri 6pm–1am, Sat & Sun noon–1am). All three restaurants have main dishes at 100–160kr.

Lysekil and around

The largest coastal town in this area is **LYSEKIL**, at the tip of a peninsula with the Gullmar fjord twisting to the east and the Skagerrak to the west. While the journey by Route 162 into town does not reveal it as immediately attractive, Lysekil does still have plenty to recommend it. From the tourist office (see overleaf), it's just five minutes' walk through the village to **Havets Hus** (July to mid-Aug daily 10am–6pm; rest of year 10am–4pm; 60kr; ℡0523/165 30), an amazing museum of marine life. The chief attraction here is an eight-metre-long underwater tunnel with enormous fish swimming over and around you, although the view is a little distorted as you're looking through curved glass. Fish with such delightful names as Father Lasher, Picked Dogfish and Five Bearded Rockling feature, along with varieties usually associated with lemon-wedges in restaurants; children can enjoy feeling the slimy algae or starfish in the touch pool.

The villas en route to Havets Hus, with their intricately carved eaves, porticoes and windows, are worth a look, too. Lysekil was a popular bathing resort in the nineteenth century, and these ornate houses are a reminder of the time when the rich and neurotic came to take the waters. The bizarre, castellated rough granite house on the inland side of the main road was built as home for a Mr Laurin, then Lysekil's wealthiest man; it now plays host to the offices of the local newspaper. A better-known local figure of the past is Carl Curman, a self-styled health guru. Of the town's ornate Hansel-and-Gretel houses on the waterside of the main road – painted mustard and chocolate brown – his was the most fancy (a bronze bust of him stands behind it, at the water's edge). In his day, Curman managed to convince his patients that sunbathing on the exposed rock was dangerous "as the amount of air must be regulated" and persuaded them that it was in the interest of their health to pay to use the bathhouses, which he conveniently owned. Today, the classic old bathhouses, along the waterfront, are a popular place for (segregated) nude bathing (free).

Walk up any set of steps from the waterfront and you'll reach the **church** (daily 11am–7pm; shorter hours in winter), the town's most imposing landmark, visible for miles around. It's hewn from the surrounding pink granite, with beaten copper doors and windows painted by turn-of-the-twentieth-century artist Albert Eldh.

Much of the shoreline has been turned into a **nature reserve** with over 250 varieties of plant life – all due to Carl Curman's wife Carla, who bought the whole coast here to prevent the stone-cutting industry, which became big business locally in the nineteenth century, from destroying it. For guided botanical and marine walks (late June to Aug Wed; 30kr), ask at the tourist office.

Practicalities

From Fiskebäckskil, an hourly passenger ferry (15 minutes; 18kr) goes to Lysekil from the end of Kaptensgatan. To get here by car, head back out of Fiskebäckskil in an eastward direction (towards Uddevalla) for 10km, then take the free ferry over. Express **bus** #840 comes here from Gothenburg, via Uddevala (2 hourly; 2 hours 30 minutes), or bus #841 is direct from Gothenburg and takes just two. By **car**, take Road 162, which leads off the E6 at Uddevalla.

Lysekil's **tourist office** is located at Södra Hamngatan 6 (mid-June to mid-Aug Mon–Sat 9am–7pm, Sun 11am–3pm; mid-Aug to mid-June Mon–Fri 9am–5pm; ☎0523/130 50, ⊛http://cityguide.se/lysekil), the main road along the waterfront. If you want to **stay**, there's a hostel (contrary to its name), *Kust Hotel Strand*, Strandvägen 1 (☎0523/79751, ℗122 02; 195kr, ❶), pleasingly placed on the waterfront next to Havets Hus. Another attractive place is the grand old *Stadshotel Lysekil*, on Kungstorget (☎0523 14030, ⊛www.stadshotellet -lysekil.se; ❸), which faces the appealing town park. The best and most characterful option, *Lysekil Havshotell*, Turistgatan 13 (☎0523/797 50, ⓔinfo@strandflikorna.se; ❹), is in an archetypal red and white house built in 1904, with a bright, cosy interior. Its sea views are all but obliterated by a huge granite boulder – though you can climb up for a windy panoramic view of miles around.

Lysekil has plenty of mid-range family **restaurants** serving big portions with a choice of fish and meat dishes. One good option is *Rosvik*, on Rosviksvagen just back from the waterfront, where daily specials are very good value at 98kr. For a meal of fish and a beer, *Pråmen*, a **restaurant-bar** jutting out over the water, makes for a pleasant spot, with views back over Fiskebäcksil and dishes from 90kr. Nestling beneath the church, *Konditori Jönssons Katt* is best for light meals, salads and sandwiches (Mon–Fri 7am–8pm, Sat 8am–8pm, Sun 10am–8pm).

North to Nordens Ark and Smögen

From Lysekil, head back along Route 162 and turn left (west) for **Nordens Ark**, a wildlife sanctuary, near Åby. It's a twenty-minute drive north from Lysekil, and on the way you'll pass a couple of notable churches, in particular the one at **Brastad**, an 1870s Gothic building with an oddly haphazard appearance: every farm in the neighbourhood donated a lump of its own granite towards the construction, but none of the bits matched.

Don't be put off by the yeti-sized inflatable puffin at the entrance to **Nordens Ark**, on the Åby fjord (daily: June–Aug 10am–7pm; Sept–May 10am–4pm; 105kr; ⓦwww.nordensark.se). This non-profit-making place is a wildlife sanctuary for endangered animals, where animal welfare takes priority over human voyeurism. Red pandas, lynxes, snow leopards and arctic foxes are among the rare creatures being bred and reared. The mountainous landscape of dense forest and grassy clearings is kept as close as possible to the animals' natural habitat. The enclosures are so large, and the paths and bridges across the site so discreet, that you may not see any animals at all. Your best bet for a glimpse is to follow behind the little truck that trundles around at feeding times. Tickets and a full English-language guide are available in the fine eighteenth-century Åby manor house on the grounds.

Smögen

From Lysekil, to reach the old fishing village of **SMÖGEN**, 15km west of Nordens Ark along the coast (there's no public transport between the two), you'll have to return on Road 162, then take road 171, as there is no crossing over the Åby fjord. It's well worth the trouble, though – the attractive village is all ice-cream parlours, and boutiques in old seafront wooden houses, and has a quay that runs for several hundred metres. In July and August, however, Bohuslän's entire teenage population besieges the village for an orgy of drinking – fascinating to watch, and impossible to sleep through.

Smögen has its own summer-only **tourist office** at Brunnsgatan (end June to early August daily 4–8pm, ☏0523/375 44); for the rest of the year try the tourist office in the adjoining village of Kungshamn, at Hamngatan 6 (daily 9am–6pm; ☏0523/66 55 50, ⓔinfo@sotenasturism.se.) The Smögen office organizes enjoyable **guided tours** (summer daily 5pm lasts 90mins; 40kr) leading through the alleys and lanes, explaining how people lived here over the centuries, and where the singer Evert Taube (see p.170) lived and performed. For **accommodation**, there is a **youth hostel**, *Makrillvikens*, Makrillgatan (☏0523/315 65, ⓦwww.makrillviken.se; 170kr, ❶) in a simple, cream wooden house set well back from the crowds amid rocky outcrops of granite, with open sea views and a sauna (25kr). Breakfast is 50kr extra but you'd do better to head to *Coffeeroom* (see overleaf). Alternatively, *Smögens Havsbad*, Hotellgatan 26 (☏0523/66 84 50, ⓦwww.smogenshavsbad.se; ❺/❹) is a stylish place, five minutes' walk from the quay, away from the summertime hubbub. In an attractive fin-de-siècle house bordered by granite boulders, the rooms are more modern than you might expect and there's a fine sauna and lounge; it also has a good **restaurant** and bar. The cheapest option is to go for one of the **private rooms** in the red wooden houses clustered at the harbourside (300kr for a double). Otherwise, contact one of the tourist offices above as they can find private rooms for around 400kr for a double.

There are plenty of places for a cheap bite, though the real culinary draw is the terrace of open-fronted **fishmongers' shops** selling mounds of shrimp, langoustine, crab and all manner of smoked seafood. The most popular **restaurant** and bar in the village is *Brasserie Brygget* by the water, though drinking hordes raise the decibel levels alarmingly in the evening. *Lagergrens* close by is far more pleasant for a laid-back, quiet drink and a wide range of à la carte meals, or pizzas at 84kr. By far the best **café** in the villages is *Coffeeroom* at Sillgatan 10 (mid-June to mid-Aug daily 9am–8pm), just 50m from the foot of Storgatan. They serve a breakfast buffet, excellent home-baked bread, cakes, warm baguettes and pies, though their speciality is giant warm, cinnamon buns. Next door is the best of the old-fashioned sweet shops, *Sommar Godd*, selling boxes of candy.

Fjällbacka

Thirty-five kilometres north along the coast from Smögen, **FJÄLLBACKA** was long regarded as a picture-perfect village: nestling at the base of a huge granite rock formation, its houses are painted in fondant shades, with a wealth of intricate gingerbreading known in Swedish as *snickargladje* ("carpenter's joy"). Today, though, that image is spoiled by the rooftop television antennae and satellite dishes, while the rocks are mostly under safety netting. To get here from Smögen, drive north along Route 174, then either take the tiny, unnamed coastal route here, or head on up to Dingle from where you get Route 163.

When you arrive in Fjällbacka, it will immediately be apparent that a certain celebrated actress holds sway in the little town. Her statue, in the eponymous **Ingrid Bergmans** Torg, looks out to the islands where she had her summer house, and to the sea, over which her ashes were scattered. Steps behind Bergman's statue lead to a dramatic ravine between some cliffs, known as Kungskliftan (King's Cliff); in 1887, Oscar II etched his name into the rock here, and so started a trend.

The **tourist office** (June–Aug daily 10.30am–12.30pm & 2–7.30pm; ☎0525/321 20, ⊛www.fjallbacka.com) is in a tiny red hut on Ingrid Bergmans Torg. For a really glamorous **hotel**, there's the costly *Stora Hotellet,* Galärbacken (☎0525/310 03, ⊛www.storahotellet-fjallbacka.se; ❺), with individually decorated rooms and a host of interesting design features. There are also plenty of **camping** opportunities in Fjällbacka, and a **youth hostel** a couple of minutes away on an unnamed island (☎0525/312 34; May–Aug) – though its setting is more frustrating than romantic when the ferryman is too busy to carry visitors to the mainland. A more convenient hostel is *Badholmen*, just on the pier, two minutes' walk from the tourist office in a cream-coloured house with a black roof (☎0525/321 50; 150kr, 200kr in July). It has just four rooms, and breakfast can be provided. A good non-STF hostel alternative is *Åsleröd Vandrarhem* (☎0525/312 77, ☎325 33; ❶), 2km north of town. There are a couple of pleasant places to **eat** including *Restaurant Mässen*, on the waterfront just off Ingrid Bergmans Torg, which has a 65kr lunch, pizzas and à la carte items such as catfish with shrimp sauce for 120kr. Better for a relaxed beer and baguette is *Café Bryggan*, nestling beneath the rock formation, right on the square and with outside seating.

Tanumshede and Grebbestad

The town of **TANUMSHEDE**, around 15km north of Fjällbacka on the E6, has the greatest concentration of **Bronze Age rock carvings** in Scandinavia, with four major sites not far away in the surrounding countryside. The E6 express **bus** runs from Gothenburg to Tanumshede (5 daily; 2 hr); bus #875 runs here from Fjällbacka (Mon–Fri 6 daily; Sat & Sun 2 daily). Tanumshede was coastal during the Bronze Age, when the sea level was 15m higher than today. Between 1500 and 500 BC, Bronze Age artists scratched images into the ice-smoothed rock, and at Tanumshede you'll see some fine examples of the most frequent motifs: the simple cup mark is the most common, and there are also boats, humans and animals. In 1994, the Tanumshede carvings were added to the UNESCO World Heritage List.

The carvings are mostly to be found on sloping, smooth rock surfaces (these are very slippery when wet) and it's well worth heading straight for the **tourist office** (July to mid-Aug Mon–Sat 10am–6pm; mid-Aug to June Mon–Thurs 9am–4.30pm, Fri 9am–3pm; ☎0525/204 00, ℮tanum.turist@swipnet.se), oddly sited in a Texaco filling station on the main road, where the staff will provide you with English booklets (10kr) detailing the types of images at the four sites. A good way to visit the carvings is on a **bike**, which you can rent from Westmans Tanumshede at Riksvägen 67,500m south of the church in the town centre (☎0525/201 00; 80kr a day).

The **Vitlycke Museum** (April–Sept daily 10am–6pm; Oct–Dec Thurs–Sun 11am–5pm; rest of year phone ahead for times ☎0525/209 50; ⓦwww.vitlycke.bohusmus.se), which opened in Tanumshede in 1998, explores the meaning of the images in the carvings. The interpretations it presents are wildly liberal and often contradictory: take, for example, the celebrated Fossum Woman, who is variously described as "giving birth to the egg of life", "a male trophy" or "displaying nether-region jewellery". One of the best-known is the so-called "Bridal Couple", who appear to be fornicating standing up. There's a good **restaurant** at the Vitlycke Museum, delighting in using what it calls "Bronze Age raw materials" – which actually means eschewing food processors. They serve venison, fish and shellfish, with sauces flavoured with parsley root, sorrel and chickweed.

Grebbestad

There is a smattering of restaurants and nightlife opportunities at **GREBBESTAD**, just a couple of kilometres southwest of Tanumshede. Staff at the **tourist office** here (July Mon–Fri 9am–8pm, Sat & Sun 10am–8pm; rest of year Mon–Thurs 11am–2pm, Fri & Sat 11am–5pm; ☎0525/100 80, ℮grabbestadturist@telia.com) will book **private rooms** from 180kr per person with no booking fee. Among the best **cafés** are the very relaxed *Greby's*, where you can eat well in a 1901 former factory at Grebbestadsbryggan; or try the waterfront Skafferiet, at Nedre Långgatan 40, which serves good-value savoury pies and filling salads, as well as cakes and a wide selection of unusual ice creams. The best **accommodation** option here is *Grebbestads Vandrarhem & Mini Hotel*, at Nedre Långgatan 15 (☎ & ℗0525/614 14; ❷), right on the waterfront in a pleasant, wooden house.

Strömstad

Around 25 kilometres north of Tanumshede, the once fashionable eighteenth-century spa resort, **STRÖMSTAD**, has an air of faded grandeur, though these days it's pretty lifeless outside midsummer. Everywhere of interest is easily accessible from its train station, and with ferry connections to the Norwegian towns of Sandefjord, Fredrikstad and Halden, the town is a good spot for a breather before you head north. Aside from its close proximity to the Koster Islands (see opposite), the town boasts a couple of quite remarkable public buildings that are well worth a look.

Although you wouldn't guess it from its run-of-the-mill exterior, inside Strömstad's **church**, a few minutes' walk from the train and bus stations, there's an eclectic mix of unusual decorative features, including busy frescoes, model ships hanging from the roof, gilt chandeliers and 1970s brass lamps. During the summer numerous concerts are held here, from jazz to gospel; they're free and usually begin at 8pm. The town's newest arts venue is **Lokstallet Konsthall**, at Uddevallavägen 1 (end June to early Aug daily 11am–5pm, Wed till 7pm; early Aug to late Sept closed Mon; 20kr; ☎0526/146 95). Right opposite the ferry terminals at Södra Hamn, there are some striking contemporary art exhibitions in a former steam-engine warehouse.

The town's most bizarre building, which overlooks the whole town, is the massive, copper-roofed **Stadshus**, the product of a millionaire recluse. Born to a Strömstad jeweller in 1851, Adolf Fritiof Cavalli-Holmgren became a financial whizz-kid, moved to Stockholm and was soon one of Sweden's richest men. When he heard that his impoverished home town needed a town hall, he offered to finance the project, but only on certain conditions: the building had to be situated on the spot where his late parents had lived, and he insisted on complete control over the design. By the time the mammoth structure was completed in 1917, he was no longer on speaking terms with the city's politicians, and he never returned to see the building he had battled to create, which had been topped with a panoramic apartment for his private use. Much later, in 1951, it was discovered that his obsessive devotion to his parents had led him to design the entire building around the dates of their birthdays – January 27 and May 14 – and their wedding day – March 7. The dimensions of the over one hundred rooms were calculated using combinations of the numbers in the dates, as were the sizes of every window, every flight of stairs and every cluster of lamps. Furthermore, in all the years of dealing with city officials, he only ever responded or held meetings on these dates. Built entirely from rare local apple-granite (so named because it contains circular markings), the town hall is open to the public, but to view the most interesting areas you have to arrange a private tour (July Tues; 20kr or ask at the town hall). Adolf's portrait, which bears a false date (unsurprisingly, one of his three favourites), can be seen in the main council chamber. Despite his animosity towards the city administration, Adolf still chose to be buried in the graveyard at Strömstad's church – his rough-hewn granite tombstone is by far the grandest here, its inscription translating as "From Strömstad town, with grateful thanks to this most memorable son".

Practicalities

Strömstad can be reached by **train** from Gothenburg or by the E6 express **bus** between Gothenburg and Oslo; by car, take Route 176 off the E6. There's also a local bus from Tanumshede. Both the **train and bus stations** are on Södra Hammen, opposite the **ferry** terminal for services to Sandefjord in Norway (ColorLine; ☎0526/620 00). Ferries to Halden use Norra Hamnen, 100m to the north on the other side of the rocky promontory, Laholmen, as do the ferries to the Koster Islands (see opposite).

The **tourist office**, on the quay (May to mid-June & mid-Aug to end Aug Mon–Fri 9am–6pm, Sat & Sun 10am–4pm; mid-June to mid-Aug Mon–Sat 9am–8pm, Sun 10am–8pm; Sept–April Mon–Fri 9am–5pm; ☎0526/623 30,

@www.stromstadtourist.se), has full details of ferry times. **Private rooms** can be booked at *Västkustbokningen*, just a few metres away on Västra Klevgatan (☎0526/109 49). The STF **youth hostel**, *Crusellska House*, is at Norra Kyrkogatan 12 (☎0526/101 93; 160kr, ❶; closed mid-Dec to mid-Jan), close to the church. There's also an independent hostel, *Gästis Roddaren Hostel*, at Fredrikshaldsvägen 24 (☎0526/602 01; 150kr), ten minutes' walk along the road fronting the Stadshus. For a central **hotel**, try *Krabban*, on Södra Bergsgatan 15 (☎0526/142 00, @www.hotellkrabban.se; ❸) which has clean, unexceptional rooms, or the modern *Hotel Laholmen* (☎0526/19700, ✉laholmen@top-stromstad.se; ❺/❸), with a prime waterfront position enjoying wonderful views, and serving good **breakfasts** (Mon–Fri 7–9am, Sat & Sun 8–10am; only 30kr for nonresidents, but not available during July). There is a **campsite** (☎0526/611 21; May–Sept) with cabins, a kilometre from the train station, along Uddevallavägen, or a larger one at Daftö, 4km south, (☎0526/260 40, @www.dafto.nu) with tiny triangular-shaped cottages (a bus runs here from the centre).

Strömstad has a good number of places to eat and drink, most of which are easily found by just wandering around near the harbour area. Among the **restaurants** worth trying are *The Cod*, a few metres towards the centre from the Color Scandi Line terminal (☎0526/615 00), and opposite, the *Prämen*, jutting into the water. Both specialize, like most of the places in these parts, in fresh fish dishes. The best of the **cafés** are *Backlund's* (Mon–Fri 8am–7pm, Sat 8am–3pm), a locals' haunt in the old bathhouse building just behind the tourist office, with sandwiches at about 18kr; *Kaffe Kompaniet*, on Södra Hamngatan, on the site of Strömstad's first coffee house, opened in 1882, where they offer an excellent smörgasbord and a wide range of unusual coffees; or try *Kaff Doppet*, a more characterful *konditori* by the station. There are also a number of fish shops doubling as **fish-snack cafés**. Excellent value is *Skaldjurs Café*, hidden away behind the Sandefjord ferry terminal in a row of red wooden sheds. For 20kr, you get smoked mackerel and bread, and for not much more they'll serve a plateful of fish, bread and potato salad.

Nightlife in Strömstad is, unsurprisingly, not really kicking. The only place that really comes alive on a summer evening is *Skagerack*, in a tired-looking wedding cake of a building where the Stockholm elite once partied; it's in the centre, opposite the church. At night in summer it is very loud, very young and the place for big-name bands to play, if they hit the Bohuslän coast at all. An older crowd fills the more sedate (and expensive) terraces of *Hotel Laholmen* (see above). Some awful troubadours can be heard at *Beer Palace*, next door to the tourist office, where there's also reasonable, if simple, food. A better bet might be the more popular nightclub at *The Cod* (see above).

The Koster Islands

Sweden's two most westerly inhabited islands (population 300), the **Kosters** enjoy more sunshine hours than almost anywhere else in the country. To get here, pick up the **ferry** at Norra Hamn, outside Strömstad's tourist office (90kr return; 15mins). Outside high season, you'll have to take an early-morning ferry to North Koster (80kr) to see both islands; if you leave later, the only way of making it across onto the south island is to hitch a lift on a local's boat. The boat stops first at **North Koster** (35min), the more rugged of the pair; the island is a grand **nature reserve**, which takes a couple of hours to walk around. It's just another five minutes on the ferry to Långegärde, the first stop on **South Koster**, an island three times the size of its neighbour. You could stay on another fifteen minutes to reach **Ekenäs**, the only settlement of any size, but it doesn't make much difference where you disembark as one spot is much like any other here. These ferries apart, you can also get **taxi boats** (℡0526/202 85) to the islands from outside Strömstad's tourist office (500kr); they are the only choice if you miss the last ferry back at 9.30pm.

No vehicles are allowed on either island except for curious, motorized buggy bikes with wooden trays in front for carrying provisions. There are no dramatic sights – the pleasure of being here is in losing yourself in an atmosphere of complete calm, the silence broken only by the screeching of birds. Mostly, the place is made for cycling in the sun, along the easy paths through wild-flower meadows; once in a while you can have refreshments at the smattering of small cafés and ice-cream parlours. During the summer, there are also **bird- and seal-watching expeditions** (170k); more information from Strömstad's tourist office).

Practicalities

Wherever you disembark from the ferry, you'll be met by a sea of **bikes** to rent, all for 70kr a day; they're the best way to explore the gently undulating landscape of the south island. You can also take a **map** of the island free from Strömstad tourist office, but you don't really need one: all the tiny tracks lead to coves and also interconnect, so finding your way around should be simple.

Camping on the islands is restricted to just one site on North Koster, *Vettnet* (℡0526/204 66), and there's a **youth hostel** (℡0526/201 23; 150kr; May to mid-Sept), 800m from the ferry stop at Kilesand on the south island, which has cabins and self-catering accommodation. Before you reach either of these options, however, expect to be inundated by people prepared to rent out their **apartments** for 250–300kr a night, excellent value if there are three or more of you. There's also one **hotel** on South Koster, and surprisingly stylish it is too: the *Skärgårdshotell* at Ekenäs, just 100m from the harbour (℡0526/202 50, ✪http://home.swipnet.se/ ~w-84681; ❹), with a warm apricot interior. There's a good **restaurant** here too, (main course at 100–150kr) but outside high season you must ring to find out if they're open. Alternatively, there's a good **café**, *Skaldjurscafé*, by where the boat comes in at Långegärde. Located in a big red wooden house, and serving meat and fish dishes, as well as light bites like *pytt i panna*, home-baked bread and shrimp (known locally as "Toast Koster") and mussel soup.

The Göta Canal: Trollhättan, Vänersborg and around

The giant waterway that is the **Göta Canal** leads from the mouth of the River Göta on the western seaboard to Sweden's largest lake, **Vänern**, via the **Trollhättan Canal**, then links up with another formidable lake, **Vättern**, and

runs right through southeastern Sweden to the Baltic Sea. Centuries ago, it was realized that Vänern and Vättern could be linked as part of a grand scheme to create a continuous waterway across the country, from Gothenburg to the Baltic. This would not only make inland transport easier, but also provide a vital trade route, a means of both shipping iron and timber out of central Sweden, and of avoiding Danish customs charges levied on traffic through the Öresund. It was not until 1810 that Baron Baltzar Von Platen's hugely ambitious plans to carve out a route from Gothenburg to Stockholm were put into practice by the Göta Canal Company. Sixty thousand soldiers took 22 years to complete the mammoth task, and the canal opened in 1832, shortly after Von Platen's death.

Without your own transport, some of the easier places to see from Gothenburg are the few small towns that lie along the first stretch of the river/canal to Lake Vänern, in particular **Trollhättan**, where the canal's lock system tames the force of the river to dramatic effect. A few kilometres north of Trollhättan, **Vänersborg**, at the southernmost tip of Lake Vänern, provides a useful base for exploring the natural beauty of the nearby hills, home to Sweden's largest population of elks. From Gothenburg, there are regular **trains** stopping at Trollhättan, or by car, take Route 45; the area is even closer at hand from Uddevalla in Bohuslän, via Route 44.

The Göta canal by boat

Although the Trollhättan Canal is still used to transport fuel and timber, the Trollhättan segment and the Göta Canal proper, between Vänern and Vättern, are extremely popular tourist destinations, with a wide range of canal trip deals on offer. There's a seemingly endless range of options for boat trips along the canal through the Göta Canal Company in Gothenburg (☏031/80 63 15, ⊛www.gotakanal.se), many of which involve a mixture of cycling and relaxing on the boats, though others include canoeing, Icelandic pony riding and even ice-skating trips in winter. Prices vary dramatically, depending on the length of trip and what is included, such as accommodation, bus transfers, museum entry and guided tours. For example, a trip through sixteen locks in one day on *M/S Bellevue* between Sjötorp, Lyrestad and Töreboda costs a good-value 250kr. It runs from mid-May to early Sept and includes a bus back to where you started. There's a restaurant and café on board and children under-7 travel free. More glamorously, and correspondingly more expensive is a two-day round trip to and from Motala on *M/S Diana*. It costs 2395kr per person including full board and one night on the boat, with a stop at Berg with its impressive flight of locks.

To cut down on expenses and time, you can take in a selection of locks on a **day-trip** from towns along the canal route; alternatively you can **rent a boat** or use your own; the tourist office (see p.180) can advise on prices and mooring places. The cheapest way to explore the picturesque towpaths is by **renting a bike**.

Trollhättan

Seventy kilometres northeast of Gothenburg, **TROLLHÄTTAN** is the kind of place you might end up staying in for a couple of days without really meaning to. A small town, it nevertheless manages to pack in plenty of offbeat entertainment along with some peaceful river surroundings. Built around the fast river that for a couple of hundred years powered its flour- and saw-mills, Trollhättan remained fairly isolated until 1800, when the Göta Canal Company successfully installed the first set of locks to bypass the town's furious waterfalls. River traffic took off and better and bigger locks were installed over the years. The best time to visit is during the **Fallensdagar** (⊛ fallensdagar.trollhattan .nu) on the third Friday in July, a three-day festival of dancing and music based around the waterfalls. Summer is the best time to come, when the sluices are open and you can see the **falls** in all their crashing splendour (May & June Sat & Sun 3pm; July Fri 11pm; Aug Wed, Sat & Sun 3pm). There is a good system of paths with orientation maps along the canal system to help you enjoy the locks and the falls.

Arrival and information

The **train station** is just north of the town centre on Järnvägsgatan. Trollhättan's **tourist office** (mid-June to mid-Aug daily 10am–6pm; mid-Aug to mid-June Mon–Fri 10am–noon & 1.30–4pm; ☎0520/48 84 72, ⊛www.visittrollhattan.se), is south of the centre, next door to the Saab museum at Åkerssjövägen 10. You can buy the **Sommar Card** here (valid mid-June to mid-Aug; 100kr), which gives free entrance to Innovatum, the Saab and Canal museums, plus free cable-car trips (see opposite). This is also the spot to **rent bikes** (75kr/day). From late June to mid-August, there are **boats** (☎0520/321 00) up the canal to Vänersborg; the four-hour round trip costs 100kr, and there are also evening trips including dinner (265kr). There are boat trips on *M/S Strömkarlen* (late June to mid-Aug; ☎0520/321 00; 100kr or evening trips including food, 265kr), heading to the locks and Canal Museum at 11am, and 6.30pm; the boats leave from outside *Strandgatan Café* (see below). Otherwise, buses #600 and #605 ply the route regularly.

The tourist office can also book **private rooms** from 100kr per person (booking fee 26kr), or for only a little more money, there is an STF **youth hostel** a couple of blocks from the train station at Tingvallavägen 12 (☎ & ⓕ0520/129 60, ⊛www.meravsverige.nu; 120kr, ❶); it has double and family rooms, serves breakfast and also rents bikes. For a central, comfortable **hotel**, try *Hotel Swania*, Storgatan 49 (☎0520/890 00, ⊛www.scandic-hotels.com; ❻/❸). As well as having an attached brasserie and nightclub (see p.182), it serves an exceptionally varied breakfast buffet, also available to nonresidents at 65kr. *Hotel Turisten*, Garvaregatan 18 (☎0520/41 11 39, ⊛www.turisten.com/ index.htm; ❶), also has cheap, functional rooms with shared bathrooms. Overlooking the river, the *Hotel Albert* (☎0520/129 90, ⊛www.alberthotell .com; ❹/❸) is set in a historic house, but is across the bridge on the other side of the water from the rest of town. Although the annexe rooms are not in keeping with the original building, breakfast served in the old house is unusually good (75kr for nonresidents). There's a **campsite** ten minutes' walk south from the train station by the river (☎0520/306 13, ⊛www.camping.se/ plats/p06; June–Aug). Four two-berth cabins, that will easily sleep four, cost 350kr with shower included and there's a heated swimming pool close by, plus tennis and golf facilities.

The town and the canal

Downtown Trollhättan is fairly mundane, but one worthwhile foray if you like contemporary art is a visit to the **Folketshus** on the pedestrianized main shopping street, at Kungsgatan 25 (June–Aug Tues–Sun noon–4pm, rest of year Sun–Thurs to 7pm, Sat 11am–2pm). On the first floor an impressive hall is given over to dramatic, constantly changing exhibitions and installations of modern art.

From Strandgatan, three streets to the west of Kungsgatan, you can follow the river south, towards the **locks**. Strolling south along the riverside path with the network of canal locks to your left and the beautiful winding river to your right, you pass a grand, red-brick nineteenth-century church perched on rocks between the waterways. A little further down you come to the **Olidan hydroelectric power station** (June–Aug daily guided tours noon–4pm), a fine 1910 castle-like building with thirteen massive generators. Climbing beyond the power station, a road twists up to the striking **Elvius Lock**, the lowest in the system, built in 1717 and known as "Polhem's lock" after its designer (you can see Polhem's irate-looking face peering out from all 500kr bank notes); it was never used as the design was regarded as flawed. From here, a **forest walk** along the top of a steep, raised bank above the river offers a lovely twenty-minute saunter to the **Lower Locks**, built during the first forty years of the nineteenth century. These locks were rather more successful, being built away from the falls instead of directly in their course. If you carry on up Nedre Slussvägen, the road by the side of the locks where the forest gives way to meadows, you'll reach the 1893 **Canal Museum** (mid-June to mid-Aug daily 11am–7pm; first weekend in April & Sept Sat & Sun noon–5pm; 10kr; ☎0520/47 22 51) at Slussledsvägen 2–8, which puts the whole thing in perspective, with a history of the canal and locks, as well as model ships, old tools and fishing gear.

Crossing the canal via the bridge adjacent to the museum and heading into the town's industrial hinterland, you'll soon reach the **Saab Museum** (June–Aug daily 10am–6pm; Sept–May Tues–Fri 11am–4pm; 30kr; call to arrange a tour on ☎0520/843 44). Every model of Volvo's arch rival is lined up, including the first bullet-shaped coupé (1946) and the Monte-Carlo-winning sports model of the 1960s. Year-long temporary exhibitions focus on different aspects of the car's design, such as rally driving or convertibles.

Cinema enthusiasts may be interested to know that just a few steps away in the old brick foundry, just behind the tourist office, are the largest **film studios** in Scandinavia. Film i Väst has taken over thirty film awards from international film festivals during the past few years and what is now dubbed "Trollywood" is churning out an increasing number of movies on international release. Nicole Kidman, Lauren Bacall and Björk are a few of the names to find themselves starring in Trollywood films. While there is not yet an official tour available, you can check out ⓦwww.filmivast.se and arrange to see inside the studios.

The newest attraction in town, just outside the tourist office and close to the Saab Museum, is the Innovatum **cableway** (☎0520/48 84 80), which makes the odd boast of being Sweden's most southerly cable-car ride. The futuristic cable cars make a six-minute journey 30m above the water, offering superb views over the river (early April, May & Sept Sat & Sun only 11am–4pm; early June noon–6pm; mid-June to mid-Aug daily 10am–6pm; mid-Aug to end Aug daily noon–4pm; 40kr). The trip starts at **Innovatum**, a centre dedicated to exhibitions on Swedish inventions, next door to the tourist office (mid-June to mid-Aug daily 10am–6pm; rest of year Tues–Sun 11am–4pm; ℡0520/48 84 80; free).

Eating and drinking

Trollhättan's best **cafés** are mostly along Strandgatan by the canal; particularly popular is *Strandgatan*, at no. 34, where drinks or filled bagels and good-value cooked meals are served to a young crowd, on a terrace in summer. The nearby *Sluss Caféet* (daily: May & Aug 10.30am–9pm; June & July 10.30am–10pm), is a classic outdoor summer place overlooking the locks. The most delightful of them all is *Café Smulan*, at Föreningsgatan 6 (Tues–Sat 11am–3pm), which serves delicious cakes as well as terrific, good-value vegetarian meals. If you're striking out further along the Göta Canal, then a superb stop is the canal-side *Slusscafeet* (summer 11am–10pm; winter shorter hours), at Brinkebergskulle, between Trollhättan and Vänersberg. The most delectable chocolate fudge brownies, pear tart and massive sandwiches (around 40kr) plus a wide range of freshly prepared lunches are served in an idyllic setting.

For fine dining, the **restaurant** at *Hotel Albert* (Mon–Fri 11.30am–2pm & 6–9pm, Sat 6–9pm, Sun 2–5pm) is well worth a visit. This charming old house was home to Edward Albert, a German who came to Trollhättan in 1880 and presided over some of the first urban-planning for working-class housing in Sweden. After his wife Maria died in childbirth, he founded a hospital; the hotel/restaurant is lined with pictures of how his family lived.

The best **bar/restaurant** for lively nights out is *M/S Nitlotten*, positioned beneath a spread of huge trees at the water's edge in the centre of town. It's always heaving, with classic and mainstream hits generating a lively atmosphere, and filling meat and fish dishes. *The Grand Bar*, at *Hotel Swania* directly opposite, is a fair rival (Mon–Sat). The most popular **pubs**, which are also good for evening meals, are *Oscar's* at Storgatan 44 (Mon & Tues 5–11pm, Wed–Sat 5pm–1am), and *Butler's*, at Spanmålsgatan 19, a late-opening Irish-style pub.

Later in the evening entertainment revolves around the **nightclubs** at *Hotel Swania*, entrance in Strandgatan (till 2am), and *KK's Bar & Nightclub*, at Torggatan 3, which has a young crowd, except on Thursdays, when 25- to 30-year-olds hit the dance floor. Trollhättan's **gay** community is served by the organization RFSL Trestad (covering Trollhättan, Vänersborg and Uddevalla; ℡0520/41 17 66), who run the friendly *Rainbow Café* (Wed 6–9pm & extra hours during the Fallensdagen), serving cheap coffee and cakes at Strindsbergsgatan 8 – continue down Garvaregatan heading away from the town centre.

Vänersborg and around

On the westerly tip of Lake Vänern, 14km north of Trollhättan, **VÄNERSBORG** was dubbed "Little Paris" in the nineteenth century by the celebrated local poet Birger Sjoberg. The similarities would be lost on anyone who has visited the French capital, though Vänersborg is a pleasant enough little resort town. Its main attractions are the nearby twin plateaux of **Hunneberg** and **Halleberg** (see opposite), both of which are not only of archeological interest but also support a wide variety of wildlife.

Vänersborg's old town is compact, if a bit lacklustre, pivoting around a central market square; it's pleasant to stroll past the numerous grand buildings – though all are overlooked by the bleak old prison at the end of Residensgatan. **Skräcklan Park**, just a few minutes from the centre, is a pretty place to relax, with its 1930s coffee house and promenade. There's a bronze statue of Sjoberg's muse, Frida, who always has fresh flowers in her hand – even in winter, when the lake is solid ice, locals brave the subzero winds to thrust rhododendrons through her fingers.

Vänersborg's **museum**, behind the main square (Tues–Thurs, Sat & Sun noon–4pm; 20kr), is worth viewing not so much for its contents per se (stuffed birds obscured by century-old dust) but rather for the sheer antiquity of the presentation: you can't touch anything and the pervading darkness means you can't see much either. It's the oldest such museum in the country, and the gloomy interior and the collections have hardly altered since the doors first opened to the public in 1891. The biggest collections are of African birds, perched in massive glass cases in a room with a hand-painted ceiling. Also worth a glance is the caretaker's apartment, preserved in all its 1950s gloom, and a reconstruction of Sjoberg's home, which is darker still.

Practicalities

The **tourist office** is at the train station (June–Aug Mon–Fri 8am–7pm, Sat & Sun 10am–4pm; Sept–May Mon–Fri 10am–4pm; ☎0521/27 14 00, Ⓦwww.vanersborg.se/turist). The cheapest **B&B** is the friendly and central *Hotel 46*, at Kyrkogatan 46 (☎0521/71 15 61; ❷); there's no reception, so calling first is essential. If you would prefer a **hotel**, the *Strand*, at Hamngatan 7, is a decent enough place (☎0521/138 50, Ⓕ159 00; ❹/❷). Otherwise there's an attractive lakeside **campsite** at *Ursands Camping* (☎0521/186 66, Ⓦwww .softwarehotels.se/ronnum), which needs to be booked at least two hours ahead on ☎020/91 90 90; get there on **bus** #661 (6 daily). A good place to **eat** is *Konditori Princess*, at Sundsgatan, a pleasant bakery with a café that's popular with locals. You can also find decent and remarkably cheap food at the train station's own café (Mon–Fri 11.30am–3pm), which serves dishes like meat balls with salad, bread and coffee for 40kr. **Nightlife** is pretty limited, the only options being the bars *Club Roccad* on Kungsgatan 23 and *Oslagbar* at Edsgatan 8.

The tiny town of **Värgon**, just a kilometre from Vänersborg and reached along Östravägen (or take bus #62) is home to a renowned restaurant and **hotel**, *Ronnums Herrgård* (☎0521/26 00 00, Ⓕ26 00 09; ❹). If you stay, insist on a room in the main building (the ones further away are less chic). The **restaurant** offers Swedish and international cuisine (☎0521/26 00 30; lunches 200kr for two courses; evening meals in summer only 350kr for three courses). Alternatively, you can save your *kronor* and get a good pizza and salad for 40kr at *Pizzeria Roma*, Nordkroksvagen 1 (☎0521/22 10 70; Mon–Fri 11am–10.30pm, Sat & Sun noon–10.30pm), on the opposite side of the main road.

East of Vänersborg: Halleberg and Hunneberg

East of Värgon, the road runs between the twin plateaux of **Halleberg** and **Hunneberg**, difficult to get to without your own transport, but well worth the trouble. There are regular **buses** to Hunneberg from Vänersborg, which are replaced in summer by a **taxi** service for the same price; there are just three a day and you need to ring an hour ahead (☎020/91 90 90). From Trollhättan, bus #619 runs straight to Hunneberg in about ten minutes.

Thought to be five hundred million years old, the hills are remarkable products of erosion, the result of water and sun cracking and grinding down the rock until the original peaks were reduced to their present flat-topped form. They're covered in a forest of blueberry and spruce where ospreys feed, which in turn is surrounded by dense clumps of oaks and pine. At the foot of the mountains are deciduous trees like linden, ash and maple; it's not uncommon to see hawfinches, herons and greenfinches here.

Early human remains have been found in the vicinity, as well as the traces of an old Viking fort, but this ancient landscape is best known as the home of Sweden's biggest herd of elks. **Elk safaris** run from late June to mid-August (240kr booked through the tourist office). The three-hour bus tours start at 7pm from the station, touring the town itself first before heading to Hunneberg and stopping at the small Royal Hunting Museum. The old practice of offering money back if no sightings are made has been dropped, since a disease has reduced the stock to just 100.

Oscar II began shooting elk here in 1872, and the Royal Hunt continues to claim elk lives: the present king shoots a maximum of fifty during two days at the beginning of October (new animals are then brought in to keep the number steady). Without going on a safari, the easiest way of spotting the elks is to be on the five-kilometre track around Halleberg at dawn or dusk; you can drive, cycle or walk up. The elks are well worth the trouble: leggy and long-faced, these massive creatures are so inquisitive they have no qualms about eating apples from your hand.

The excellent **youth hostel**, at Bergagårdsvägen 9, at the foot of Hunneberg, is housed in a building dating from 1550 (reception daily 9–11am & 5–8pm; ℡0521/22 03 40 or 070/634 11 23, ⊛www.svif.se/067.htm; 140kr; closed mid-Dec to mid-Jan); in the seventeenth century the place was used by Danish soldiers as a base from which to drive the Swedes into the hills. You can walk or cycle (**bike rental** at youth hostel; 60kr) along the Swedes' line of retreat up Hunneberg, a route that brings you to the **Naturskola Nature Centre** (daily: mid-May to late June & early-Aug 11am–8pm; mid-Aug to mid-May 11am–4pm, late June & July closed; ℡0521/22 37 70; free). A web of nature trails begins outside the centre, including special trails for wheelchair users; there's also a great **café**, which serves home-made cakes and endless refills of coffee for 12kr, and has lots of information about the wildlife in the hills.

Between the lakes: Västergötland

The county of **Västergötland** makes up much of the region between lakes Vänern and Vättern – a wooded, lakeland landscape that takes up a large part of the Gothenburg-to-Stockholm train ride. The most interesting places lie on the southeastern shore of Lake Vänern, notably the fascinating countryside around **Kinnekulle**, and the pretty town of **Mariestad**, easily reached from Gothenburg. With more time, you can cut south to the western shore of Lake Vättern, and in particular to the colossal fortress at **Karlsborg**. In between the lakes runs the **Göta Canal** which, along with the **Tiveden National Park**, is the main regional target for Swedes taking their holidays in July and August.

Lidköping

Flanking a grassy-banked reach where the River Lidan meets Lake Vänern, **LIDKÖPING**, around 140km northeast of Gothenburg, won't detain you long, though its layout is pleasant enough, due to an age-old decree that the height of a house may not exceed the width of the street on which it stands. On the east bank, the old town square, dating from 1446, faces the new town square, Nya Stadens Torg, created on the west bank by Chancellor Magnus de la Gardie in 1671, and graced by a wooden hunting lodge brought from his estate. Both squares enjoyed a perfect panorama of Vänern until an unsightly concrete screen of coal-storage cylinders and grain silos was plonked just at the

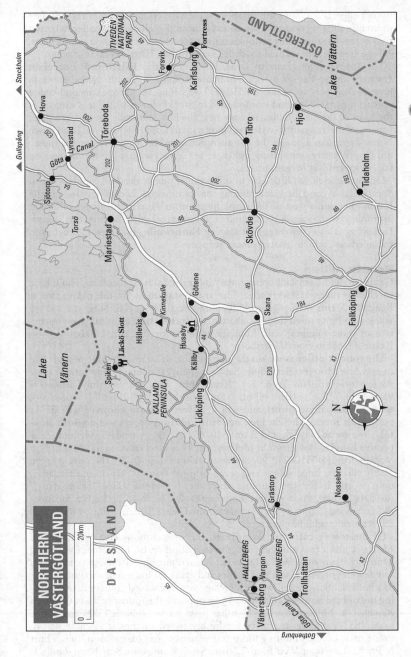

NORTHERN VÄSTERGÖTLAND

20km

OSTERGÖTLAND

TIVEDEN NATIONAL PARK

Fortress

Forsvik

Karlsborg

Stockholm

Hova

Göta Canal

Lyrestad

Töreboda

Gullspång

Sjötorp

Torsö

Mariestad

Lake Vänern

Hällekis

Läckö Slott

Spiken

KALLAND PENINSULA

Kinnekulle

Husaby

Källby

Lidköping

DALSLAND

Götene

Skara

Skövde

Tibro

Hjo

Lake Vättern

Tidaholm

Falköping

Grästorp

Nossebro

HALLEBERG

Vänersborg

Vargön

HUNNEBERG

Trollhättan

Göta Canal

Gothenburg

water's edge; the squares still make for a pleasant-enough wander though. The most appealing section of town to stroll around is along Esplanaden where it runs across Mellbygatan overlooking the park, ablaze with flowers in summer. All the houses here seemed modelled on Norman Bates' home in *Psycho*.

The town's chief claim to fame, however, is the **Rörstrand Porcelain Factory** (Mon–Fri 10am–6pm, Sun noon–4pm; free, with guided tours in June & Aug only for 15kr; ℡0510/823 48). Run by Europe's second-oldest porcelain firm (Rörstrand was founded in Stockholm in 1726), it is situated at the heart of the bleak industrial zone near the lake, and easily spotted, as a giant version of their signature-style logo looms up in front of you as you head down Norra Torngatan. Though the company is revered by many Swedes, the museum here is pretty uninspiring but there are some pleasing classical designs on sale, supposedly at bargain prices.

Lidköping itself has little else to offer, and is utterly dead on Sundays, but it does make a good base for visiting the picturesque **Läckö castle**, on the Kalland peninsula west of the town. Jutting into Vänern, this finger of land is brimming with scenic routes and a number of other architectural gems. Lidköping is also convenient for visiting **Kinnekulle**, just a few kilometres to the northeast, which has even more surprises.

Practicalities

Getting to and from Lidköping is easy by **train**; from Gothenburg, you'll have to change trains at Herrljunga. The **train station** is by the old square at Bangatan 3. **Bus** #1 comes to Lidköping directly from Karlsborg, and bus #5 will get you into town from Trollhättan; the **bus station** is on the main square, two or three minutes' walk from the train station. By **car**, Lidköping is on Route 44, 53km from Vänersborg.

The **tourist office** is within the train station (May to early June & mid-Aug to end Aug Mon–Fri 9am–5pm, Sat 9am–1am; early June to end June & early Aug Mon–Fri 9am–7pm, Sat 10am–7pm, Sun 2–7pm; July Mon–Fri 9am–8pm, Sat 10am–8pm, Sun 2–8pm; ℡0510/77 05 00, ☺www.lidkoping.se/turist), and will help with **private rooms** (from 350kr per double room). The cheapest **accommodation** option is the **youth hostel**, close by at Nicolaigatan 2 (℡0510/664 30; ❶). A really lovely and inexpensive **hotel** is *Park Hotell*, at Mellbygatan 24, a street running south from Nya Stadens Torg (℡0510/243 90, ☺www.parkhotell.org; ❸/❷); the pink-painted 1920s villa has huge rooms and some original features. A pricier alternative, only worth it for the summer discount, is *Edward Hotell*, Skaragatan 7 (℡0510/790 00, ☺www.edwardhotel.se; ❻/❸). An even better bet for more old-fashioned luxury, is the *Stadtshotel*, on Gamla Stadens Torg (℡0510/220 85, ✉hotel@stadtlidkoping.se; ❺/❸).

Of the town's **cafés** and **konditori**, the most atmospheric by far is *Café Limtorget*, just a few minutes from the tourist office, on Limtorget (May–Aug Mon–Fri 10am–8pm, Wed till 9pm Sat 10am–2pm, Sun 10am–5pm). Here you can devour gorgeous cakes and waffles and drink tea from delicate antique cups in a butterscotch-painted wooden cottage with a cobbled courtyard, overlooking the old red houses in Gamlastad. Just opposite the tourist office is *Garstroms Konditori*, at Mellbygatan 2, which has been serving reliable cakes and coffee since 1857. An appealing place for freshly baked muffins is *Rådhuskonditori*, inside de la Gardie's hunting lodge in the new square (daily: Mon, Tues, Thurs & Fri 8.30am–6pm, Wed from 7.30am, Sat 7.30am–4pm, Sun 10am–6pm). It also serves filled baguettes for 28kr, and the warm apple cake with ice cream is well-worth trying at 22kr. For true **restaurant** fare, try *Källaregatan 3*, at that address for Swedish classics plus a few pan-European dishes and a good selection of wines, served up at reasonable cost in bright, pleasant surroundings.

North from Lidköping: to Läckö castle

If you have your own transport, it's worth taking in some of the little-visited sights along the 25km route north to Läckö Castle, notably **Riddargardskvarnen**, a pristine, mid-nineteenth-century windmill around 11km north of town. A remarkable structure, it was run as a flour mill until its owner died in 1978, and is now maintained by local people – the public are allowed to wander around inside. Opposite, the sign "*Gravfalt*" marks a huge **Viking burial site** – though there are rather fewer graves to pick out than sheep droppings; it's a beautiful setting all the same. For a real trip into the past, though, follow the small lane marked "*Froslunda*" to a potato farm, then carry on along this route for a couple of kilometres to the avenue that leads to the secluded **Stola Herregård**, one of Sweden's finest Carolean estates (May–Sept tours by appointment; mid-June to mid-Aug Tues, Thurs & Sun 2pm & 4pm; 50kr; ☎0510/180 30, ⓦwww.lidkoping.se/stola), in private hands since the Middle Ages. The present manor was built in 1713, the faded grandeur of its interior a wonderfully authentic example of Rococo ornamentation. The whole estate has changed very little in several hundred years.

Officially billed as being on its own island, but surrounded by water on just three sides, **LÄCKÖ CASTLE** (May–Sept 10am–6pm; 70kr, end Aug & Sept 50kr; ☎0510/103 20) is everyone's idea of a fairy-tale castle: its turrets and towers all creamy white as if it had been dipped in yoghurt. The castle dates from 1290, but was last modified and restructured by Lidköping's chancellor, de la Gardie, when he took it over in 1652. Inside, there is a wealth of exquisite decoration, particularly in the apartment that belonged to de la Gardie's wife, Princess Marie Euphrosyne. There are celebrated annual art exhibitions here in summer (ask at Lidköping tourist office for details) and frequent guided tours (May–Aug daily 10am–4pm, Sept daily 11am–1pm; 30kr). Läckö's charms are no secret, so if you visit during summer, be prepared for the crowds. **Bus** #132 from Lidköping travels out here every hour during summer (20kr including entrance), via the tiny village of **Spiken**, 3km south of Läckö, which is a haven for lovers of smoked fish, sold at little stalls here.

East from Lidköping: Kinnekulle

Unlike many other areas of southern Sweden known primarily for their natural beauty, the delightful **Kinnekulle** region, stretching east from Lidköping along the southeastern edge of Vänern, is peppered with points of historical and social interest and makes for a splendid day amid a picturesque wilderness. Although the area is very much of the mainland, it has an insular feel, with the locals seeing themselves as living autonomously. The region has always been considerably wealthy, with some magnificent manor houses, some of which continue to be run privately (one or two have become hotels, see p.189); each has its own immaculate railway station, where minature trains stop regularly. The whole area is easily covered by bike, and makes for a delightful day's cycling as the land undulates gently offering a wide range of attractive vistas.

Källby and Husaby

Twelve kilometres east and the first stop on the Kinnekullebanan regional train from Lidköping, **KÄLLBY** has an Iron Age burial site (turn left at the main road junction), where two impressive stones face each other, one carved with a comical, goblin-like figure, supposedly the god Thor. Not far beyond, **HUS-ABY** village makes for a tranquil diversion, but one of great religious and cultural significance. It was at the church here that, in 1008, the English missionary St Sigfrid baptized Olof Skotkonung, the first Swedish king to turn his back on Viking gods and embrace Christianity. The present, three-towered church was built in the twelfth century, and just to the east is the well where the baptism is said to have taken place. King Oscar had his name carved in the rock above the well in 1900 and it's become a magnet for royal graffiti ever since. Most recently Crown Princess Victoria added her name on the ancient site in 2001. Close by, if you take a path just a few metres west of the church and follow a sign to **Lasse i Bergets Grotta** (Lasse's Grotto), 200m off the main road is a remarkable sight. Sunk into the rock and entirely camouflaged by trees, there's a grotto where a local man, Lars Eriksson, and his wife made their home in 1881; they remained in this two-chambered cave until his death in 1910. Born in 1828 and known as Lasse, this illiterate man made his own guns, hunted and picked all his own food, and was said to practise witchcraft; more mundanely, his wife made clothes to sell locally. Today, you can walk into the dark rock "rooms" which are made additionally fascinating by the photographs, on the display board outside, taken in 1907 of Lasse and his cosy, cluttered interior. From outside, there's no sign that anyone ever lived here.

From Husaby to Hällekis

A couple of kilometres onward from Husaby lies the "flowering mountain", **Kinnekulle** (all trains from Källby will take you there), an area of woods and lakes interwoven with paths and boasting hundreds of varieties of flowers, trees, birds and other animals. The strange, flat-topped shape of the hill is due to its top layer of hard volcanic rock, which even four hundred million years of Swedish weather has not managed to wear down, making for something of a botanical and geological treasure trove. For views of the surrounding landscape and the water beyond, pop in to **Högkullen**, a wooden look-out tower on the hill, built in the National Romantic style in 1892.

At the northernmost point of the region, the only town as such is **HÄLLEKIS**, an unglamorous little place where concrete-making was the local industry until the 1970s, but which now concentrates on the insulation trade. The unlovely buildings connected with this business are thankfully restricted to the periphery of the town. An unexpected diversion here is **Falkängen,** a street of former workers' cottages renovated and prettified into a sort of Swedish *Stepford Wives* village where appallingly twee hand-crafted knick-knacks are sold from the pastel houses. The village is a must-see, though, for the unlikely combination of permanently smiling women (no men seem to be involved) making clothes and ornaments, and the charming coffee houses serving home-made cakes. The **youth hostel** is right in the middle of all this (see opposite), and sheep and ducks have been encouraged to live among the houses, creating the appearance of a toy farm.

Practicalities

Husaby has a summer **tourist office** by the ancient church (June–Aug daily noon–6pm; ☎ & ☎0511 34 32 60, ✆husabyturist@telia.com). There's a fine, beautifully sited **restaurant** at Högkullen, just south of Hällekis, *Vin Och Pimpinella* (☎0510/544 256; ☻www.vinopim.com) which serves splendid Swedish dishes from a very short but stylish daily menu that always includes a vegetarian option. The views from the restaurant's vast windows are superb. Another good place is *Blombergs* (☎0510 54 23 06), in between Källby and

Hällekis, which has its own immaculate little station close by. This large, barn-like place offers lunch specials and à la carte dishes (Mon–Fri noon–3pm, Sat noon–8pm, Sun till 5pm); there's a pleasant delicatessen here too. The beauti-fully renovated STF **youth hostel**, *Falkängen* (⌕0510/54 06 53, ⌕info@ falkangen.nu; 145kr, ❶), set amid the former workers' cottages close to Hällekis, has a real community atmosphere; **bikes** are available for rent (50kr a day or 200kr a week). A charming **bed & breakfast** prettily situated at Gössätter, just south of Hällekis and close to the Medel, Väster and Österplana churches, is *Blå Pensionatet* (⌕ & ⌕0510 54 00 07), an appropriately bright-blue-painted wooden house with old country furniture. It has superb beds and a big buffet breakfast.

Around Hällekis

Heading back south from Hällekis, the grand Naples yellow facade of **Hönsäter Slott**, just half a kilometre away, comes as quite a surprise. Now a fine restaurant and a lovely **hotel**, this castle dates from the fourteenth centu-ry, though most of the present building was constructed in the 1660s. Even if you're not staying, staff are relaxed about visitors peeking into the beautiful rooms. Note the ancient square piano and the run of glorious first-floor rooms, each one opening onto the next, as though an image infinitely reflected in two facing mirrors.

Three kilometres south of Hönsäter, **Hällekis castle** is a very grand mansion at the end of an avenue cut through the forest and lined with horse-chestnut trees. A dreary clothes shop specializing in tartans and V-neck sweaters is housed within the building nearest the entrance, but otherwise the grounds of this private estate contain a range of design workshops, all worth a look (June–Aug Tues–Sun noon–4pm, July daily; Sept–May Sat & Sun noon–4pm); their products range from ceramics to ironware and glassware. It is the **gardens** (10kr), however, that are the real draw. The headily scented perennial borders were devised by the British garden designer Simon Irvine, who also created the gardens at Läckö Castle (see p.187). There's an appealing, vine-covered **café** that's open in summer. At the start of the avenue into the grounds, a long flight of half-hidden, mossy stone steps leads to a path through some of the prettiest forest. The stairs were built for King Oscar II to enable him to climb Kinnekulle without having to hike, and an inscription commemorating his first visit is engraved on gravestone-like tablets at the foot of the stairs. Once at the top, follow the path to the right, opening onto a clearing blushing with wild roses. From here, there's a striking vista down into the huge canyon-like quar-ry below.

Just a little further on from Hällekis Castle is an extraordinarily fine mansion named **Råbäcks**, fronted by yellow-striped awnings and framed by climbing roses and honeysuckle. A few strides away, Råbäck station is doll's-house per-fect. Wild poppies grow on the track undisturbed by the six trains that run through each day. Just a few metres on, Munkängarna is a meadowland **nature reserve** owned by the monastery at Vadstena (see p.317) until the fifteenth century. In spring, the area is fragrant with wild flowers, but sadly the only English text amid the masses of information posted is an injunction to visitors "not to collect any kind of animals or drive a horse with cart". Of the three churches found just south of here – Medelplana, Österplana and Västerplana – the most rewarding interior by far is that at **Västerplana** (May–Sept daily 8am–8pm), with a medieval core. Its an appealing hall church with wide arch-es and beautiful eighteenth-century roof paintings. Its reredos and pulpit, all dark reds and gold, are also worth a look. Directly opposite is a particularly good **antique curio shop**, Kinnekulle Kuriosa (Sun 1–5pm; ☎0510/54 15 06), evocatively housed in an old wooden house. Inside are some real finds, both in the hand-painted original decor and some of the items for sale.

Mariestad and around

Lakeside **MARIESTAD** is smaller, prettier and more welcoming than Lidköping, from where it's just an hour's train ride north. With a splendid medieval quarter and harbour area, Mariestad is a good place for a day's stay, and an excellent base for exploring the surroundings. The compact centre is brought to life by either the self-guided walking **tour** (pick up a map from the tourist office, see below) or the guided tours organized by the tourist office in summer (mid-June to mid-Aug Mon & Thurs 6.30pm; 30kr). What lifts the town beyond mere picture-postcard status is the extraordinary range of building styles crammed into the centre – Gustavian, Carolean, Neoclassical, Swiss-chalet style and Art Nouveau – a living museum of architectural design.

It's also worth taking a look at the late-Gothic **cathedral**, on the edge of the centre, whose construction at the end of the sixteenth century was fuelled by spite. Duke Karl, who named the town after his wife, Maria of Pfalz, was jealous of his brother, King Johan III, and so built the cathedral to resemble and rival the king's Klara kyrka in Stockholm. Karl ensured the new building was endowed with over-the-top Baroque features and some odd niceties – note the stained-glass windows, depicting mint green and yellow wheat sheaves, painted with spiders and other crop insects. The Baroque pulpit is dramatic too, covered in cherubs with silver or black bodies, all dressed in gold wreaths.

Once you've inspected Mariestad's fine architecture, there is little else to do in town – the clutch of seven folk museums in the vicinity aren't up to much. Better prospects are offered at the nearby island of **Torsö**, which now has a bridge connecting it with the mainland and offers good fishing and bathing opportunities (fishing equipment available at the tourist office). To reach Torsö, head up Strandgatan past Snapen, from where the route is signposted; it's a fifteen-minute cycle ride. Perhaps best of all, Mariestad is also an ideal base from which to **cruise** up Lake Vänern to the start of the Göta Canal's main stretch at Sjötorp. There are 21 locks between Sjötorp and Karlsborg (see opposite), with the most scenic section up to Lyrestad, just a few kilometres east of Sjötorp and 20km north of Mariestad on the E20. Canal cruises cost 250kr, no matter where you choose to disembark; the boats return to Sjötorp on the same day (contact Mariestad's tourist office for details). There are no longer lake cruises since EU regulations classified Lake Vänern as a sea, such is its size, and sea-cruising licences are not available.

Practicalities

The **train station** is in a beautiful Art Nouveau building about five minutes' walk from the harbour. Besides providing the usual information, the particularly helpful **tourist office**, in a delightful new building, by the harbour on Hamngatan (June–Aug Mon–Fri 8am–7pm, Sat & Sun 9am–6pm; Sept–May Mon–Fri 8am–4pm; ☎0501/100 01, ⓦwww.turismmariestad.se) also rents out **bikes** for a rather steep 100kr per day.

Opposite is the hugely popular STF **youth hostel** (☎0501/104 48; mid-Aug to mid-June advance reservations necessary; 125kr), with galleried timber outbuildings and an excellent garden café (daily 11am–7pm); it's a great place to stay and close to all the sights. The oldest **hotel** is the 1698 *Bergs Hotell*, in the old town, at Kyrkogatan 18 (☎ & ☎0501/103 24; ❶). The interior is quite basic, with no en-suite rooms, though it's comfortable enough and quiet. Other good-value central hotel options include *Hotel Aqua*, Viktoriagatan 15 (☎0501/195 15, ☎187 80; ❶), which is mundane but cheap and has family rooms, and the far cosier and more appealing *Hotel Vänerport*, Hamngatan 32 (☎0501/771 11, ☎www.vanerport.se; ❹/❸). Rather more luxurious is the *Stadtshotellet*, at Nya Torget 10 (☎0501/138 00, ☎77640, ❹/❸), just five minutes' walk away in the modern centre. The nearest **campsite** is *Ekuddens*, 2km down the river (☎0501/106 37, ☎186 01; 100kr; May–Sept); alternatively you can stay on Torsö at *Torsö Camping* (☎0501/213 02; May–Sept).

In the new town area, Mariestad's trendiest **coffee-house** hangout is *Café Stroget* at Österlånggatan 10 (Mon–Fri 9am–6pm, Sat 9am–2pm), a laid-back place that's popular with young locals. More welcoming, though, is the *Garden Café* at the youth hostel (see above), which serves baguettes for around 30kr, plus ice cream and cakes. The liveliest **bar-restaurants** are *Buffalo* at Österlånggatan 16 and *Hjorten* at Nygatan 21; the latter also has occasional live music. Another popular restaurant is *Björnes Krog* (Mon–Fri 11am–2.30pm, Tues–Thurs 6–11pm, Fri & Sat 6pm–1am; ☎0501 180 50) at Karlsgatan 2, with good lunch specials like ox steak in Provençal sauce or cod with lemon sauce at 62kr. For atmosphere though, there's nothing to beat the lovely *Hamnkrogen Laxhall* in the northwest corner of Torsö island. It's only open in summer (May–Aug Mon–Wed 10am–8pm, Thurs–Sat 10am–10pm) but with superb fish dishes served overlooking the water it's definitely worth a trip. The best pizza place (and almost the only thing open on a Sunday for a bite) is *Candy's Bistro*, Österlånggatan 17A (☎0501/106 20), a simple café serving tasty pizzas (48kr), plus pies, pasta and salad dishes.

One possibility for evening fun is at Björnes Krog (above) where every third Saturday there's an "adults" party (less salacious in reality than it sounds; it's a **nightclub** for over-25s). The only other **club** worth a look in is *Stads* at the Stadshotel (see above), though it's nothing special.

North of Mariestad: Gullspång

Buses head 40km north from Mariestad to **GULLSPÅNG**. Between here and Torved to the south runs 20km of railway track, rebuilt in 1965 in an abortive attempt to run standard trains. In the mid-1980s a craze for railway cycling took hold, and the rusting tracks were cleared for self-propelled trips on pump-action buggies like those in Hollywood westerns. These carry one or two people and can be rented at the tourist office (May–Sept; 40kr for an hour, 400kr per day); the buggies must be returned to the spot where they were rented. The route, which can also be cycled (around 5hr there and back), lies alongside the eminently swimmable Gullspång River. Gullspång is the more convenient end at which to rent a buggy, since there's an STF **youth hostel** there at Järnvägsgatan 4 (open all year). You can book both the buggy rides and the youth hostel through Gullspång's **tourist office** (☎0551/360 00, ☎www.gullspang.se) at Hemgatan 10. They also offer a **package** at the hostel: accommodation, breakfast and a packed lunch for 440kr per person.

Karlsborg and around

Despite the great plans devised for the fortress at **KARLSBORG**, around 70km southeast of Mariestad on the western shores of Lake Vättern, it has survived the years as one of Sweden's greatest follies. By the early nineteenth century, Sweden had lost Finland – after six hundred years of control – and had become jumpy about its own security. In 1818, with the Russian fleet stationed on the Åland

Islands and within easy striking distance of Stockholm, Baltzar Von Platen (see p.179) persuaded parliament to construct an inland fortress at Karlsborg, capable of sustaining an entire town and protecting the royal family and the treasury – the idea being that enemy forces should be lured into the country, then destroyed on Swedish territory. With the town pinched between lakes Vättern and Bottensjön, the Göta Canal – also the brainchild of Von Platen and already under construction – was to provide access, but while Von Platen had the canal finished by 1832, the fortress was so ambitious a project that it was never completed. It was strategically obsolete long before work was finally abandoned in 1909, as the walls were not strong enough to withstand attack from new weaponry innovations. However, parts are still in use today by the army and air force, and uniformed cadets mill around, lending an air of authenticity to your visit.

The complex, which is as large as a small town, can seem austere and forbidding, but you are free to wander through and enter the **museum** of military uniforms (mid-May to mid-June & early Aug to end Aug daily 10am–4pm; mid-June to early Aug daily 10am–6pm; ☎0505/45 18 26; 35kr). The **guided tour** (70kr), with special sound and smoke effects, is a must for children. Apart from the fortress, Karlsborg has one of the most delightful family-run hotels you'll find in Sweden, and a couple of good places to eat.

Practicalities

There is no train service to Karlsborg but there are regular **bus** services from either Lidköping or Mariestad; by road, take the 202 from Mariestad, which brings you to Storgatan when you reach town. Turn left into Strandgatan for the **tourist office** (June–Aug daily 9am–6pm; Sept–May Mon–Fri 9am–3pm; ☎0505/173 50, ©info@karlsborgsfastning). During summer they are in a lovely old building at the entrance to the fortress, and at other times of year in the big yellow house close by. The staff can help reserve **private rooms** from around 150kr per person. The STF **youth hostel** (☎ & ℗0505/446 00; 130kr) is at the fortress entrance too (signposted "*Fästningen*"). Karlsborg's **campsite** is on the banks of Lake Bottensjön (☎0505/449 16, ℗449 12; May–Sept), 2km north along Storgatan. **Bikes** can be rented here for a steep 80kr a day, but they're cheaper from Cykel och Sport on Strandvägen (☎0505/101 80), which has excellent bikes for 70kr per day. One of the real treats of Karlsborg is staying at its most stylish **hotel**, *Kanalhotellet*, at Storgatan 94 (☎0505/121 30, ⓦwww.kanalhotellet.se; ❷), built in 1894 when the present owner's grandparents returned from America after working for President Cleveland at The White House. The dining room, with stately dark panels, oil-paint portraits and glinting chandeliers, overlooks the Göta Canal.

The **restaurant** at the *Kanalhotellet* is very fine too, with classic Swedish dishes for around 200kr a dish – try the speciality, red-belly salmon fresh from Lake Vättern – and a sumptuous breakfast. Another good eating option is *Ida's Brygga* (☎0505/131 11; Mon & Tues 11.30am–11pm, Wed & Thurs 11.30am–midnight, Fri & Sat noon–1am, Sun noon–10pm) just opposite the hotel. With a canal backdrop, it's a romantic spot for dinner, and there's live music in the evenings (50kr entry after 10pm). Next door, *Klangahamns Fiskrokeri* is good for smoked fish. To fill up on a tight budget, a fair choice is *Järnhandel* (Mon–Thurs 4–11pm, Fri & Sat 4pm–3am) on Storgatan, at the junction with Strandgatan. This pub-cum-café, much frequented by locals, plays every ageing rock hit you've ever heard whilst serving up inexpensive *pytt i panna*, chicken sandwiches and fish and chips. Also cheap is *Restaurant San Remo*, on Storgatan 15, a somewhat uninspired pizza restaurant in the disused train station, with pizzas for 45kr and a range of salads.

Forsvik

As far back as the early fourteenth century, the Karlsborg area maintained an important monastic flour mill, 8km northwest at the village of **FORSVIK** (the monastery was founded by Sweden's first female saint, Birgitta). The height differential between lakes Viken and Bottensjön meant that energy could be extracted, first by means of waterwheels and later with turbines, which allowed a sizeable industry to emerge, producing all manner of metal and wood products. During the Reformation, the Crown confiscated Forsvik from the monastery. The creation of the Göta Canal gave the place new life: it once again became a busy industrial centre, with a paper mill operating until the 1940s and a foundry until the Swedish shipyard crises of the 1970s. Today, the area makes for a charming excursion: the mill has been restored to its 1940s condition and converted into an impressive **museum** (June–Aug daily 10am–5pm; 30kr), providing a stimulating picture of Forsvik's industrial past. There's a thorough English booklet about all that's on show and an English-language video for the super-interested. Close by, in the old shipbuilding area, you can observe the work that's currently afoot to build a **steamboat** which, it is hoped, will be ready for use by 2004. The boat will be named *Eric Nordvall II* after the first paddle steamer of that name, which sank in 1856 to the bottom of Lake Vättern, where it has remained ever since.

Bus #420 runs to Forsvik from Karlsborg once a day in summer. Within the clutch of dark red wooden buildings is a well-appointed STF **youth hostel** at Bruksvägen 11 (☎0505/411 37 in summer, ☎411 27 in winter), located in a former workmen's dwelling from the 1860s. A couple of hundred metres away down on the main road is *Forsvik Café* which is *the* place to head for on a summer's evening. As well as sandwiches, cakes and ice cream there are light meals for around 70kr and fuller meals like smoked Vättern perch for 75–175kr.

Tiveden National Park

Located 15km northeast of Karlsborg, **Tiveden National Park** is part of a much larger expanse of forest, lakes and ice-age boulders which takes up this whole region. Follow signs on the Highway E20 or the historic site symbol on Route 49 between Karlsborg and Askersund. There is no public transport to any part of Tiveden. One of southern Sweden's few remaining areas of virgin land, the park has never been inhabited – though charcoal has been produced at the periphery since the seventeenth century. The park, unlike more managed forests, aims to maintain an environment close to that of a primeval forest, with no human intervention, and the old or dead trees throughout Tiveden provide the habitat for a number of rare birds and animals. There are 25km of trails passing though some spectacular scenery, with **organized hikes** tailored for differing abilities (ask at Karlsborg tourist office for details). The Tiveden wilderness is also the site used by the Karlsborg **Survival Training Centre** for its courses (☎505/188 34), each of which usually lasts one to three days. Activities such as baking in a Siberian sauna (complete with birch-twig beatings) on the shores of Lake Vättern, mountain biking and abseiling are also on offer.

Among the easier **trails** to try is the **Stenkälla**, running close by Ödlesjön, a lake. Almost all the forest here originates from after 1835, the date of the last massive fire to devastate the region. One of the best routes is the Stenkälleklack, a short but steep two-hundred-metre trail off the main track. The landscape you see here was shaped hundreds of millions of years ago when the plains cracked and formed valleys, one of which became Lake Vättern.

Just north of the trail, fire marks are still visible on the 250-year-old pines from the 1835 disaster. In order that the bogs here could be crossed in summertime, primitive footbridges were subsequently built; having been trampled down into the peat, their preserved remains can still be seen. **Fishing** is very popular at Tiveden, but comes with a flurry of rules. Licences are available at various places, including Karlsborg's tourist office and Olssons Fiske, back in Mariestad (110kr for 24hr; covers eight lakes in the area); however, you're only allowed to catch three fish. For more information on fishing, contact Hökensås Sportfiske (℗0502/230 00, ℉230 10).

Horse-riding excursions have taken off at Tiveden recently. Tivedens Hästskjuts, based at Uggletorp, just north of Karlsborg guides horseback excursions through the forest (summer 10am–7pm; winter 10am–3pm; book a week in advance on ℗0505/250 44 or 070/512 73 58). The horses are all of a Scandinavian breed known as Nordsvensk. A beginner's excursion costs 175kr, but among the longer trips for more experienced riders are a half-day trip (4hr; 475kr) and a two-day outing offering ten hours' riding and an overnight stay in primitive conditions (1200kr).

Tjolöholm and Äskhult

A couple of sights which make for a most enjoyable day-trip from Gothenburg are located close together just beyond the southernmost suburbs of the city. The splendid manor house on the coast at **Tjolöholm**, 15km south, and the immaculately preserved historic farmstead at **Äskhult**, just on the other side of the E20 from Tjolöholm, are easiest reached by car; public transport, however, only runs to the nearby town of **Kungsbacka**, a residential backwater that's of no particular interest to vistors, unless you time your trip to arrive on the lively market days (first Thurs of every month).

Tjolöholm

The manor house at **TJOLÖHOLM** (pronounced "chewla-home"; mid-June to Aug daily 11am–4pm; Sept Sat & Sun 11am–4pm; Oct Sun 1am–4pm; gardens open all year; 60kr; ⓦwww.tjoloholm.se) was once the dream home of the Scottish merchant and horse-breeder James Dickson. Enormously wealthy, he wanted a unique house that reflected a combination of his British ancestry, contemporary Swedish Romanticism, and the latest comfort innovations of the day. The design of the house was the object of a grand competition in the 1890s, won by the architect Lars Israel Wahlman, who created this stunning Elizabethan-style stately home. Dickson, however, never saw Tjolöholm completed: he died after cutting his finger on a bottle of champagne he was opening, fatally poisoning himself by wrapping the lead cap around the wound.

In 1901, the Dicksons had a village built around the house to provide accommodation for the staff; its little red-and-white wooden cottages, each with just one room and a kitchen, have been immaculately preserved. Walking up the main driveway, you pass the huge stables and indoor riding track, which have been converted into an airy **café** (April to mid-June & mid-Aug to Oct Sat & Sun 11am–5pm; mid-June to mid-Aug Tues–Fri 11am–5pm). It's worth peeking inside the carriage museum next to the stables (same opening times as the house), where among the many stylish carriages and London-built hansom cabs, the most bizarre exhibit is a four-wheeled, horse-drawn electric vacuum cleaner, as large as one of the cabs. Horses gave the carpets a not-so-quick once-over from outside by means of a forty-metre hose, hoisted up through the windows.

The **interior** of the house deserves a good hour or so and there are excellent pamphlets describing the rooms available free at reception. Among the many highlights of the finely detailed interior is the **billiard room**, where the walls are lined with Belgian marble and punctuated by the hot-air vents of the avant-garde central heating system. Sweeping through Blanche Dickson's boudoir and her four fabulous bathrooms with sunken baths and showers that once sprayed from all angles, you're led on to the Charles Rennie Mackintosh-inspired children's nursery, with its simple, white motifs.

The **grounds**, with their ash and oak woods, and the nearby beach, beyond the gardens, are wonderful places to while away a warm summer's afternoon. The transition here from the dramatic rocky cliffs of Bohuslän, to the north, to the open beaches of Halland in the south, made the area a subject for the Varberg group of painters (see p.203).

To get to Tjolöholm, take the **train** from Gothenburg's Central Station to Kungsbacka (20min), from where you catch bus #732 (covered by the train ticket), which goes to within 3km of the estate, from where you'll have to walk. By **car**, turn off the E6 highway just south of Kungsbacka at Fjärås and follow the signs to Åsa for 2km, from where there are signs for Tjolöholm.

Äskhult

Just a few kilometres inland, **Äskhult** is a hamlet of four immaculately preserved farmsteads, which offer a fascinating insight into the lives of Swedish country folk in the eighteenth and early nineteenth centuries. You can get here from Gothenburg by **car** by taking the E6/E20 to Kungsbacka, then Route 135 heading southeast, off which Äskhult is signposted.

At the end of the eighteenth century, **land reforms** meant small patches of cultivated land had to be amalgamated into larger units. The result, all over Sweden, was that villages were split up as people were resettled on larger farms elsewhere. These reforms were brought into force at Äskhult in 1825, but the four local farmers banded together to defy the authorities and kept their land together. By the turn of the century, 15 of the 35 people living here had emigrated to America because of hardships; by the 1930s, there were only six inhabitants. Today, you can wander through the homes (20kr), seeing the primitive wooden bed-chambers and inside the cowshed, where a dead snake was placed, in accordance with local superstition, to protect the animals from snake bites. The pleasant **café**, built into one of the farms, has a plainness about it that's very much in keeping with its surroundings.

Travel details

Trains	Buses
Gothenburg to: Kalmar (Mon–Fri 3 daily, Sat & Sun 2 daily; 4hr 20min); Karlskrona (Mon–Fri 2 daily, Sat & Sun 1 daily; 4hr 40min); Lidköping (6 daily; 45min); Malmö (Mon–Fri 12 daily, Sat 8 daily, Sun 9 daily; 3hr by X2000, 3hr 50min by InterCity); Stockholm (Mon–Fri 13 daily, Sat 9 daily, Sun 12 daily; 3hr 15min by X2000, 4hr 30min by InterCity); Strömstad (Mon–Fri 9 daily, Sat 8 daily, Sun 7 daily; 2hr 40 min); Trollhättan (Mon–Fri 15 daily, Sat 12 daily, Sun 8 daily; 40min); Vänersborg Mon–Fri 10 daily, Sat & Sun 4 daily; 1hr 5min).	**Gothenburg** to: Falun/Gävle (Mon–Thurs & Sat 1 daily, Fri & Sun 3 daily; 10hr 30min); Halmstad (Fri & Sun 3 daily; 2hr); Karlstad (Mon–Thurs & Sat 3 daily; Fri 5 daily, Sun 4 daily; 4hr); Linköping/Norrköping (Mon–Thurs & Sun 3 daily, Fri 4 daily, Sat 1 daily; 4hr 35min); Mariestad (Mon–Fri & Sun 5 daily, Sat 4 daily; 3hr); Oskarshamn (Fri & Sun 2 daily; 5hr 20min); Tanumshede/Strömstad (Mon–Fri 5 daily, Sat & Sun 4 daily; 2hr 30min); Trollhättan (Mon–Thurs & Sun 5 daily, Fri & Sat 2 daily; 1hr 5min);

Varberg/Falkenberg (Fri & Sun 2 daily; 50min/1hr 20min).
Gullspång to: Mariestad (Mon–Thurs & Sun 2 daily, Fri 3 daily; 40min).
Lidköping to: Vånersborg/Trollhättan (Fri & Sun 2 daily; 45min/1hr).
Mariestad to: Gävle (Mon–Fri 1 daily; 7hr 30min); Örebro (Mon–Fri 2 daily, Sat & Sun 1 daily; 1hr 30min); Skövde/Jönköping (Mon–Thurs & Sun 3 daily, Fri 4 daily, Sat 1 daily; 1hr 30min/2hr 10min).

International trains

Oslo–Copenhagen trains involve changing at Gothenburg. Two trains daily.

International ferries

Gothenburg to: Frederikshavn (4–8 daily; 3hr 15min; by catamaran 3–5 daily; 1hr 45min); Harwich (2 weekly; 24hr); Kiel (1 daily; 14hr); Newcastle (1 weekly June to mid-Aug).
Strömstad to: Fredrikstad (mid-June to mid-Aug Mon–Sat 5 daily; 1hr 15min); Halden (mid-June to mid-Aug Mon–Sat 3 daily; 1hr 15min); Sandefjord (mid-June to mid-Aug 2 daily; 2hr 30min).

International buses

Gothenburg to: Oslo (Mon–Fri 5 daily, Sat & Sun 4 daily; 4hr 45min).

2

3

The southwest

CHAPTER 3 Highlights

✱ **Varberg Fortress** Stay in one of the old prison cells in the splendid youth hostel, set in a fortress that dominates the landscape of the west coast. See p.202

✱ **Nimis** Clamber over the extraordinary stairway-and-tower driftwood sculpture that spills dramatically into the sea off the Kullen peninsula. See p.223

✱ **Sofiero Gardens** Best viewed in early summer when the famous rhododendron ravine blazes with colour. See p.228

✱ **Lund cathedral** Beneath the finest Romanesque cathedral in Northern Europe, lies the eerie crypt where Finn the Giant is said to have been turned to stone. See p.233

✱ **Malmö's parks** Escape the bustling energy of Sweden's third city in its peacefully elegant gardens. See p.242

✱ **Sandhammaren** Miles of seamless, fine sands beneath the hot skies of Skäne's southern coast. See p.000

✱ **Gourmet Grön.** The finest vegetarian dishes in Sweden make this gastronomic oasis, in the Blekinge town of Karlshamn, a huge draw. See p.270

The southwest

The southwestern provinces of Halland, Skåne and Blekinge were on the frontiers of the **Swedish–Danish conflicts** for more than three centuries. In the fourteenth to seventeenth centuries, the flatlands and fishing ports south of Gothenburg were constantly traded between the two countries and today, several fortresses still bear witness to the area's status as a buffer in medieval times.

Halland, a finger of land facing Denmark, has a coastline of smooth, sandy beaches and bare, granite outcrops, punctuated by a number of small, distinctive towns. The most charismatic of these is the old bathing resort of **Varberg**, dominated by its tremendous thirteenth-century fortress. Also notable is the small, beautifully intact medieval core of **Falkenberg**; while the regional capital, **Halmstad**, is popular for its extensive beaches and nightlife.

Further south, in the ancient province of **Skåne**, the coastline softens into curving beaches backed by gently undulating fields. This was one of the first parts of the country to be settled, and the scene of some of the bloodiest battles during the medieval conflict with Denmark. Although Skåne was finally ceded to Sweden in the late seventeenth century, the Danish influence died hard; indeed it is still evident today in the thick Skåne accent, often incomprehensible to other Swedes, and in the province's architecture. The latter has also been strongly influenced by Skåne's agricultural economy, the wealth generated by centuries of profitable farming leaving the countryside dotted with **castles**, though the continued income from the land means that most of these are still in private hands, and not open to the public. Skåne has a reputation for mainly flat and uniform countryside, but it doesn't take long here to appreciate the vivid beauty of the landscape: slabs of yellow rape, crimson poppy and lush green fields contrasting with the castles, charming white churches and black windmills.

Skåne is sometimes called "The Basque Province of Sweden" due to the independent spirit of its people. This quality was evident to James Steveni, author of the definitive 1925 guide, *Unknown Sweden*; he wrote, somewhat provocatively, "The people of Skåne are sturdy, very independent and not particularly noted for their love of refinement or high culture. . . they do not believe in outward show. What they prize most is land, property and good food." Steveni was writing, though, before **Båstad** (see p.215) became a showy, glamorous tennis centre. One of the best areas for **walking** and **cycling**, the **Bjäre peninsula**, lies to the west of Båstad and comprises forested hill ranges, spectacular rock formations and dramatic cliffs. To the south of Båstad, both **Helsingborg**, with its laid-back, cosmopolitan atmosphere, and bustling **Malmö**, Sweden's third city, have undergone some

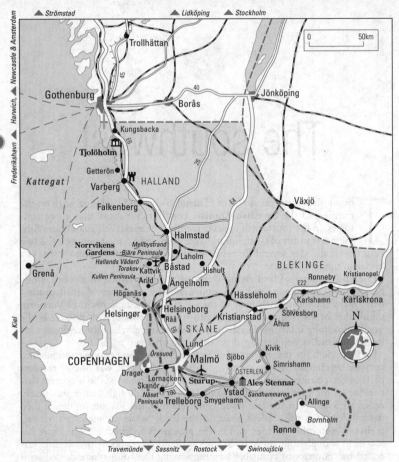

dramatic changes in the last decade. Helsingborg's harbour has been transformed by an explosion of style bars, while Malmö has seen the most significant development of all – the completion of the sixteen-kilometre-long **bridge** linking the city to Copenhagen, and thus Sweden to the rest of Europe. Just north of Malmö, the university town of **Lund**, with its wealth of classic architecture, has a distinctive bohemian atmosphere that's in contrast with Malmö's more down-to-earth heritage.

The southwest corner of Skåne boasts excellent beaches around some minor resorts. Moving east, you encounter the pretty medieval town of **Ystad** along the south coast, and then the splendid countryside of **Österlen**, whose pastoral scenery is studded with Viking monuments, such as the Swedish Stonehenge at **Ales Stennar**. Lined with brilliant white beaches backed by several nature reserves, the area also offers some of Sweden's most enjoyable cycling. As you edge north, the land becomes green and more hilly, the coast dotted with a number of interesting little places, such as **Kivik**, with its apple orchards and Bronze Age cairn, and the ancient and picturesque resort of **Åhus**. At the northeast of the county, **Kristianstad**, built as a flagship town by the Danes, retains its fine, Renaissance layout.

Beyond here to the east, the ledge of land running to the Baltic is **Blekinge** province. Among its several small, not particularly distinguished resorts, **Karlskrona** stands out, a naval base built on a number of islands.

Travel practicalities

South of Gothenburg, the SJ **train** line follows the coast, with frequent trains stopping at all towns as far as Ystad, from where it cuts northeast to Kristianstad. The comfortable, Danish-built Kustpilen Express trains run west–east across the country, linking Malmö, Helsingborg and Lund with Kristianstad and Karlskrona. However, some of the most beautiful and less-frequented areas are not covered by the train network, and the **bus** service is skeletal at best, especially along the south coast. There are also certain transport anomalies to look out for: there are trains but no buses between Malmö and Ystad, whereas there are no trains from Ystad to Kristianstad (to do this route by rail you'll have to take the inland Osterlenaren train from Ystad to Malmö and change). More generally, some train and bus services stop running early in the day. The best places to pick up timetables for the region are Gothenburg and Malmö's train and bus stations and tourist offices.

With no really steep hills, the southwest is wonderful country for **cycling**, and bike rental outlets are numerous; most tourist offices, youth hostels and campsites also rent out bikes. There are several recognized **walking trails**, many of which are referred to in the text.

Varberg

More atmospheric than any other town in Halland, the fashionable little nineteenth-century bathing resort of **VARBERG** boasts surprisingly varied sights – its imposing fortress the most striking, a laid-back atmosphere and plenty of good places to eat. The rocky coastline becomes sandier heading south out of town and there are plenty of opportunities for bathing and windsurfing. Continuing south, **Falkenberg**, has been a centre for fly-fishing for over a century, while **Getterön**, to the north, has an extensive nature reserve that is fascinating for bird-watchers.

Arrival and information

Varberg is a handy entry point to southern Sweden: a year-round **ferry** service comes here from Grenå in Denmark and regular **trains** run down the coast here from **Gothenburg**. From the **train** and **bus stations**, turn right down Vallgatan, and you'll find the town centre off to the left and the fortress to the right. The **tourist office** is at Kyrkogatan, just off Västra Vallgatan (April & May Mon–Fri 9am–5pm, Sat 10am–1pm; June–Aug Mon–Sat 9am–7pm, Sun 3–7pm; Sept–March Mon–Fri 9am–5pm; ☎0340/887 70, @turist@varberg.se), where you can pick up a free map of the town. Varberg itself is easy to get around on foot, but to explore the coast around the town, you can **rent a bike** from Erlan Cykel och Sport, Västra Vallgatan 41 (☎0340/144 55; 70kr a day); or from B.F. Cykelsport at Östralånggatan 47 (☎0340/61 12 55; 85kr a day), both of which are in the centre. Cheaper, and, for those who are camping here, more convenient, is hiring a bike at *Getteröns Camping* or *Apelvikens Camping* (see overleaf), which both charge 50kr per day.

Accommodation

There's a wide variety of really good places to stay in Varberg – some of them representing excellent value. It's worth booking well in advance for the **youth hostel** (℡0340/887 88; 170kr, ❶), housed in the former prison at the fortress; outside the summer season you have to book through the tourist office. Apart from now being spotlessly clean, the place is much as it was: each cell has its own key and original door, complete with spy-hole. Cell 24 on the upper floor has been preserved, without redecoration: push the door open for a chilling glimpse of past conditions. If you do want to stay, ask for Cell 13, the only one with a full-sized (although barred and curtainless) window and a great sea view. Another decent, very central hostel is *Platsamas Vandrarhem* at Villagatan 13 (℡0340/61 16 40; 160kr). A third hostel, *Skeppsgårdens Vandrarhem*, at Krabbesvägen 4 (℡0340 130 35 170kr, ❶), is a couple of streets back from the nudist beaches.

There are a number of **campsites**, the nearest to the centre being the family-oriented *Apelvikens Camping*, 3km south of the fortress along Strandpromenaden (℡0340/141 78, ℗875 38; April–Oct); it adjoins sandy beaches and has a couple of good eating places (see p.205). Close by, *Apelviken Stugby* has neat, clean **cabins** (6-berth cabin 4700kr a week in summer); book at the tourist office. *Getteröns Camping* is near the nature reserve area (see p.206), 5km to the north of the town (℡0340/168 85, ℗104 22; 4-berth cabins 440kr a night); July to early August you can only book for the week at 2300kr. To camp for free, there are plenty of places beyond the nudist beaches (see p.206).

For a B&B, there's **Nils Mårtensgård** (℡ & ℗0340/408 37; ❶), fifteen minutes' drive east, just off the E6. In a comfortable old farmhouse surrounded by woodland, home-made bread is served as part of the excellent breakfasts. **Hotels** in Varberg itself include the following recommendations.

Hotel Bergklinten Västra Vallgatan 25 ℡0340/61 15 45. Close to the station. An old hotel with a spartan wartime feel, but clean and comfortable enough and the cheapest in town. At the time of writing there's a question over its future. ❶

Hotel Fregatten Hamngatan ℡0340/67 70 00, ⓦwww.fregattenhomehotel.se. In a former cold storage warehouse, overlooking the harbour and within a few steps of the fortress. Quite luxurious, boasting a Jacuzzi, sauna, spa and massage. ❺/❹

Hotel Gästis Borgmästaregatan 1 ℡0340/180 50, ⓦwww.hotellgastis.nu. Although you'd never guess it, the hotel building dates from 1786 and is far more appealing inside than out. The en-suite rooms are excellent value, as the price includes an evening meal, afternoon coffee and even cycle hire at just 25kr/day extra. There's a good breakfast buffet plus a sauna, Jacuzzi and gym. ❹/❸

Kust Hotellet Nils Kreugers Vägen 5 ℡0340/62 98 00, ℗62 98 50. For unexpected glamour in an interesting setting, this sumptuous – and costly – hotel is the place. Housed in what was once the sanatorium, at Lilla Apelviken (see p.206), the hotel is full of mock Art Nouveau and Tiffany features and even has its own pool. ❻

Hotel Varberg Norrgatan 16 ℡0340/161 25, ⓦwww.hotellvarberg.nu. A fine choice for its friendly atmosphere, excellent service and good value. Built in 1899, this family-run hotel retains much of its former grandeur and character. The tariff includes a voucher worth 100kr (outside high season) in the restaurant next door, *Knopen*. There's also a great breakfast. ❸

Stadshotell Kungsgatan 24–26 ℡0340/69 01 00, ⓦwww.varbergsstadshotell.com. A traditional place with some Art Nouveau features, right on the main square. It also boasts a good restaurant plus a Jacuzzi. ❺/❹

The Town

All of Varberg's sights are concentrated along or near the seafront, although in summer the main square, Stortorget, throngs with **markets** and pavement cafés. The thirteenth-century moated **fortress**, set on a rocky promontory, is Varberg's most prominent attraction. It was home to the Swedish king Magnus

Eriksson, who signed important peace treaties with Denmark here in 1343. The great bastions were added for protection by Danish king Christian IV in the seventeenth century; ironically, they were completed just in time for him to see the fortress fall, permanently, to Sweden in 1645. The entrance is on its seaward side, either through the great archways towards the central courtyard or by a side route, the uneven stone steps which lead up to a delightful terrace **café** (June–Sept noon–10pm).

Tours (daily 11am–4pm, with hourly tours July to mid-Aug; 40kr) in English will take you into the dungeons and among the impressive cocoa-coloured buildings that make up the inner courtyard. It's the **museum**, though, that deserves most of your attention (mid-June to mid-Aug daily 10am–6pm, 50kr; mid-Aug to mid-June Mon–Fri 10am–4pm, Sat & Sun noon–4pm, 20kr). The most unnerving exhibit is **the Bocksten Man**, a murder victim who was garrotted, drowned, impaled (three stakes were thrust through his body, in the belief this would stop his spirit seeking out his murderers) and thrown into a local bog six hundred years ago – until 1936, when a farmer dug him up while planting crops. His entire garb preserved by the acidity of the bog, the Bocksten Man sports the Western world's most complete medieval costume: a cloak, a hood, shoes and stockings. His most arresting feature is his thick, ringletted red hair, which cascades around his puny-looking skull.

In the neighbouring room, a great deal is made of a small, spotlit brass button that sits on a rotating velvet cushion. The button not only matched those on the uniform of King Karl XII, but exactly fitted the hole in his regal cranium, punctured when he was shot dead while attacking a Norwegian castle in 1718. Convinced that the king had special powers, his assailants believed his life could only be ended by something that belonged to him and so stole a button from his jacket and had it filled with lead. In the same room, there's an oil painting of the rather unattractive king.

The rest of the museum is, for the most part, dispensable, with sections on farming and fishing in Halland from the 1750s onwards and some southern-Swedish peasant wall hangings. A signposted room devoted to the sensitive work of Richard Bergh, Nils Kreuger and Karl Nordström – the so-called **Varberg School** – is, however, worth viewing. These three artists linked up in the last years of the nineteenth century and developed a plein-air National Painting style, reflecting the moods and atmosphere of Halland, and Varberg in particular. Night scenes of the fortress beneath the stars show a strong Van Gogh influence; in other paintings, the misty colours create a melancholy atmosphere.

Overlooking the sea, and painted custard and cream, the 1850 **fortress prison** seems like a soft option next to the looming fortress in whose shadow it lies. The first Swedish prison built after the American practice of having cells for individual inmates, it housed lifers until 1931, when the last one ended his days here. Today you can stay in a private **youth hostel** in the fortress, which has been carefully preserved to retain most of its original features (see opposite).

Back at the main entrance to the fortress, a **bicycle museum** (June–Aug daily 10am–6pm; 50kr or free with ticket for both museum and fortress tour) is largely given over to celebrating the Monark bicycle company. The manufacturers are Sweden's biggest and the founder, Birger Svensson, was born in Varberg. Among the most interesting exhibits is a bizarre, ungainly wooden Draisne bike from 1820.

A couple of fine remnants from Varberg's time as a spa resort are within a minute of the fortress. On the side of the fortress facing the town is the grand Societetshuset, a wedding-dress-like confection of cream-and-green carved

△ The Embrace, Smygehamn

wood, set in its own small park. This was where upper-class ladies took their meals after bathing in the nearby splendid 1903-built **Kallbadhuset** (Cold Bathhouse; mid-June to mid-Aug daily 9am–6pm, Wed till 8pm; 40kr for cold bath and sauna), just to the north of the fortress and overlooking the harbour; there's a pleasant **café** here too. Beautifully renovated to its original splendour, this dainty bathhouse has single-sex nude bathing areas and is topped at each corner by Moorish cupolas. While in the harbour area, take a look inside the busy **Konsthall** (opening hours vary), in a fine old warehouse building, where glass-blowers, silversmiths and several ceramics artists sell their wares.

Eating and drinking

There are plenty of good places to eat in Varberg, mostly along Kungsgatan, which runs north of the main square. Away from the town centre, at Apelviken, there are a couple of very popular **beach eateries** – the laid-back, stylish *Maja's Strand Café*, which has live bands on summer evenings and a full à la carte menu, and *John's Steak House and Bar*, in a rustic wood building on the seafront, serving great meat dishes. A popular place to **drink** is *The Corner Bar & Restaurant*, opposite *Harry's Pub & Restaurant*. Part of the Irish-style pub chain, this one has live music in summer (Wed–Sat), and a happy hour from 5pm till 7pm.

Bagels Coffee House Kungsgatan 28. Cheerful place for a coffee, bagel (45kr) or baked potato (49kr).

Blå Dörren Kafé Corner of Norrgatan and Västra Vallgatan (Mon–Fri 7am–6pm, Sat 7am–4pm, Sun 9am–5pm). The best café in town, with home-made cakes to die for and delicious breakfasts too, all in a friendly setting.

Harry's Pub & Restaurant Kungsgatan 18. Next door to *Ny Fiket*. A large eating place with a rather jumbled identity, its dark interior adorned with chandeliers and statuettes of Liberty and Hiawatha. It has a range of pastas, meat and fish dishes from 85kr and lunch specials at 75kr; service can be less than attentive. There's a wide selection of malt whiskies and beers, and a popular happy hour (4–7pm). Daily noon–midnight, Sat till 2am.

Kärleksparkens Servering Strandpromenaden. A few minutes' walk from the centre, this small café has filled baguettes for 30kr, ice cream and filling lunch specials for 55kr.

Knopen Norrgatan 16. Next door to the *Hotel Varberg* (see p.202). A down-to-earth, cosy place serving good but overpriced steaks and pasta at a steepish 92kr. Really only worth it if you're staying at the hotel and so are entitled to the guests' discount.

Lundquistska Huset Brunnsparken 6 ☎0340/143 90. On the pricey side, the exclusive menu offers Swedish cuisine, such as marinated salmon with a dill/caramel sauce. Mon–Sat 11am–11pm.

Café Mignon Drottninggatan. Opposite Varberg Church. A pleasant, if plain, café serving half baguettes at 30kr as well as salads and panini. Mon–Fri 7.30am–9pm, Sat 7.30am–6pm, Sun 9.30am–7pm.

Ny Fiket Kungsgatan 18. A pleasant café that also serves full meals. Mon–Thurs 8am–9pm, Fri & Sat 8am–1pm.

Sakura Norrgatan 11 ☎0340/101 11. Very popular new addition to the eating scene, serving Japanese, Thai and Chinese food with an excellent value eat-as-much-as-you-want buffet lunch for 63kr. It becomes even more popular in the evening (Mon–Thurs 11am–10pm, Fri to 11pm, Sat noon–11pm, Sun 1–10pm)

Societen In Societets Park ☎0340/67 65 00. Directly behind the fortress. *Dagens Rätt* is 75kr here; for a fine gourmet lunch, it's worth spending a little extra (185kr). The place comes alive in the evenings, with foxtrots on Fridays, and live bands or discos on Saturdays.

Around Varberg

Halland's **coastline** becomes less rocky the further south you go, turning into open beaches at Falkenberg (see overleaf). Although it's still a little rocky around Varberg, there are several excellent spots here for bathing; for the best ones, head south, to the left of the fortress as you face the sea, down Strandpromenaden. In summer, this stretch of the track, built in 1912 as a route from the fortress to the sanatorium 4km beyond, is filled with an assortment of strolling couples, roller skaters and cyclists. After about five minutes, two well-known **nudist beaches** are signposted, with not very private fencing delineating the separate-sex areas, called Goda Hopp ("Good Hope", the men's zone) and Kärringhålan (provocatively, "Pit of Bitches"). A little further along, at **Lilla Apelviken**, is a small sandy beach popular with families. The large grey-and-cream buildings ahead once comprised the Apelviken Hospital, set up at the beginning of the twentieth century as a **sanatorium** for impoverished tuberculosis sufferers; it's now a glamorous hotel (see p.202). Just by the hotel is a specially designed **handicapped bathing beach**, with wheelchair access into the water.

Behind the hotel, **Apelviken cemetery** is a remarkable-looking place carpeted with wild flowers and featuring a chapel like a miniature Parthenon. Created in 1927, the boulder-walled enclosure is the resting place of dozens of children who died of TB in the 1920s and 1930s. The only adult's grave is that of Johan Almer, who created the sanatorium, his huge granite tomb overlooking the rest from one corner of the plot. The north side of Lilla Apelviken is sheltered by a hill, Subbeberget, where you'll find several Bronze Age burial mounds – nothing much to look at. More dramatic is the windy panorama from the secluded **lighthouse**, which looks back towards the fortress across the water. Built in 1934, the lighthouse only takes a few minutes to reach, and is set on a rocky promontory covered with a threadbare carpet of tiny wild orchids and honeysuckle, the waves crashing beneath.

North of Varberg: Getterön

There are regular **buses** in summer from Varberg 2km north to **Getterön**, a fist of land jutting into the sea which, until the 1930s, was an island, where you can bathe amid the secluded coves and the wild flowers that fill the rock crevices in early summer. When the road was built, connecting Getterön to the mainland, two bays were created. The northern bay became a dumping ground for waste from the harbour, making it shallow and providing the appropriate nutritive conditions for it to become a paradise for wetland birds, including gargeney ducks, avocets and greylag geese. There are also falcons and white-tailed eagles, especially in April & May and from August to October. Just before you reach Getterön, there's a nature centre and extensive bird reserve, **Getterön Naturum**, off on the right of the main road (Getterön Nature Centre; July & Aug daily 10am–6pm, Sept–June Fri–Sun 10am–4pm; ☎0340/273 90). Contained in striking thatched houses, the centre is a must for anyone interested in the wildlife – particularly bird-life – of the area. Their biggest project is re-establishing the peregrine falcon as a nesting bird in western Sweden. The staff are enthusiastic and well informed about the site, though you only get the full benefit of their knowledge on the guided tours of the surrounding area (750kr for groups of up to ten).

Falkenberg

It's a twenty-minute train ride south from Varberg to the decidedly likeable medieval town of **FALKENBERG** (falcons were once hunted here, hence the name), with some lively museums and a long beach. It's a well-preserved little town that really comes alive in July and August, when most of the tourists arrive.

Falkenberg has a long-standing reputation as a centre for **fly-fishing**. In the 1820s, Sir Humphrey Davy, the inventor of the miner's safety lamp, visited the town, having heard about its excellent fly-fishing on the River Ätran. A succession of wealthy **English countrymen** came here throughout the nineteenth century, their numbers swelling as Falkenberg's reputation for good fishing spread; one such devotee, London lawyer William Wilkinson, went so far as to write a book about the experience, *Days In Falkenberg* (1894). In it, he described the place where the well-to-do visitors stayed as "an ancient inn with a beautiful garden leading down to the river". This building, one of the few here to have escaped the town fires, now houses *Falkmanska Caféet*, the best café in town (see "Eating and drinking").

These upper-class Englishmen brought considerable wealth with them, and had a tremendous influence on the town. Predictably enough, they made no attempt to adapt to local culture; as a result Falkenbergers had to learn English, and throughout the latter half of the nineteenth century, baby boys here were named Charles instead of the Swedish Karl, while the most popular girls' name was Frances, after Wilkinson's daughter. English influence can be seen even today: near the post office there is a British telephone box, donated by Oswaldtwistle, the English town with which Falkenberg is twinned. The tourist office (see below) will sell you a one-day **licence** that allows you to catch up to three fish (available March–Sept; 80kr).

Arrival, information and accommodation

Regular **buses** and **trains** drop you close to the centre on Holgersgatan, from where it's a couple of hundred metres along to the **tourist office** in Stortorget (mid-June to mid-Aug Mon–Sat 9.30am–6pm, Sun 2–6pm; Sept to mid-June Mon–Fri 9am–5pm; ☎0346/861 00, ⓦwww.falkenbergsturist.se); they'll book **private rooms** from 160kr per person, plus a steep 65kr booking fee. To **rent bikes**, which make trips to the beaches easier, try *Göthes Cykel & Sport* at Storgatan 31 (☎0346/109 26) or *Hertings Cykel*, Plankagårdsvägen 3 (☎0346/100 68). The comfortable and well-equipped STF **youth hostel** (June to mid-Aug; ☎0346/171 11; 150kr) is in the hamlet of **Näset**, 4km south of town, which you can get to on local buses #1 or #2 (no services after 7pm). From the hostel, the southern end of the beach is just a few minutes' walk away, through the neighbouring **campsite** (☎0346/171 07).

The cheapest **hotel** is the plain *Hotel Steria*, a ten-minute walk away from the river at Arvidstorpsvägen 28 (☎0346/155 21, ⓦwww.hotelsteria.se; ❶). In the town centre, the smart *Grand Hotel* overlooks the historic Tullbron bridge (☎0346/144 50, ⓦwww.grandhotelfalkenberg.se; ❺/❹). Its upmarket restaurant offers good but pricey meals, while the bar and disco are popular nighttime haunts for the young. Rather more interesting, and almost next door, the riverside *Hvitan* overlooks a picturesque open courtyard surrounded by low-built houses dating from 1703 (☎0346/820 90, ⓔhwitan@mail.14.calypso.net; ❹). The best-placed hotel for the beach is *Hotel Strandbaden* (☎0346/71 49 00, ⓦwww.strandbaden.elite.se; ❹/❸), 2km from the old town centre (follow Strandvägen all the way to the beach). A plush modern hotel, it lacks any design niceties but does have an excellent lounge with an uninterrupted view of the sea and the rooms are spacious and very well appointed. The cost of a room here includes a fine, varied breakfast and free entry to Klitterbadhuset (see p.208).

The Town and around

Fishing apart, Falkenberg offers several disparate pleasures. The **old town**, to the west of the curving river, comprises a dense network of low, wooden cottages and cobbled lanes. Nestling among them is the fine twelfth-century **St Laurentii kyrka**, its ceiling and interior walls awash with seventeenth- and eighteenth-century paintings. An electronic box by the door lets you choose a taped commentary in a range of languages. It's hard to believe that this gem of a church was – in the early twentieth century – variously a shooting range, a cinema and a gymnasium; indeed its secular usage saved it from demolition after the Neo-Gothic "new" church was built at the end of the nineteenth century. When St Laurentii kyrka was reconsecrated in the 1920s, its sixteenth-century font and silverware were traced to, and recovered from, places all over northern Europe.

The local museum on St Lars Kyrkogatan, with its collections tracing the town's history until 1900, is a pedestrian place that's best bypassed; head straight for the **Falkenberg Museum**, in an old four-storey grain store near the main bridge at Skepparesträtet (June to early Sept Tues–Fri 10am–4pm, Sat & Sun noon–4pm; mid-Sept to May Tues–Fri & Sun noon–4pm; 20kr). In the past, due to a particular interest of the curator, most of the museum has been devoted to the 1950s, but plans are afoot for new approaches from 2003. The fact that Falkenberg had over one hundred dance bands up until the 1970s provides the basis for another of the permanent exhibitions, along with original interiors of a shoe repair shop and stylized café (complete with jukebox) – though labelling in English is minimal.

Falkenberg is full of quirky **sculptures** which make for amusing viewing. You'll find one right outside Falkenberg Museum, a diverting piece called *Wall* – which you may not realize is a sculpture at all. Per Kirkeby, a celebrated Danish artist, built the two brick walls here for a major exhibition in 1997, to close off the wide space below the museum building down to the river. A series of entrances and window openings are designed to let shadows fall at striking angles, and somehow complement the old grain store – though predictably, the more conservative locals loathe the piece. The most fun sculpture, though, is one taking up the whole wall at the corner of Nygatan and Torgatan in the centre: *Drömbanken*, by Walter Bengtsson, is a witty, surrealist explosion of naked women, cats, mutant elks, bare feet and beds.

The town also boasts a rather unusual **Fotomuseum** (late June to Aug Tues–Thurs 1–7pm, Sun 1–5pm; Sept to late June Tues–Thurs 5–7pm, Sun 2–5pm; 40kr; ☏0346/879 28, ✉info@fotomuseet-olympia.com) at Sandgatan 13, the home of Falkenberg's first purpose-built 1907 cinema. It has over one thousand cameras and a remarkable collection of cinematic paraphernalia, including some superb local peasant portraits, taken in 1898. The oldest pictures on show are English and date back to the 1840s. There's also an impressive section on Sweden's well-loved author Selma Lagerlöf at her celebrated home in Mårbacka (see p.420). For a completely different experience, head to the local **Falken Brewery** (July & Aug Mon–Thurs 10am & 1.15pm; 20kr; book tours through the tourist office), where Sweden's most popular beer, Falken, has been brewed since 1896, and is available for sampling at the end of the tour.

Skrea Strand and Klitterbadhuset

Over the river and fifteen minutes' walk south from town, **Skrea Strand** is a fine, four-kilometre stretch of sandy beach. At the northern end, a relaxing diversion is the large bathing and tennis complex of **Klitterbadhuset** (mid-June to mid-Aug Mon–Fri 9am–7pm, Tues & Thurs from 6am, Sat 9am–5pm, Sun 9am–4pm; mid-Aug to mid-June Tues & Thurs 6–9am & noon–8pm, Wed noon–8pm, Fri 9am–noon), which has a fifty-metre pool plus a shallow children's pool nearby, a vast sauna, Jacuzzi and steam rooms, all for 35kr (gym costs 15kr extra). At the southern end of the long beach lie some secluded coves, all the way down past the busy wooden holiday shacks; in early summer the marshy grassland here is full of wild violets and clover. It's a great place for **bird-watching**: ungainly cormorants nest here, while oystercatchers, shell ducks and plover are also thick on the ground.

Eating, drinking and nightlife

The birthplace of Sia Glass – a popular **ice cream** made by Sweden's oldest family firm, established in 1569 – and **Falcon beer**, Falkenberg caters well for the tastebuds. Although the variety of food on offer isn't huge, the town's restaurants and bars are of a standard to make eating and drinking here a pleasure.

Restaurants

The poshest **restaurant** is *Gustav Bratt*, Brogatan 1, near the main square (℡0346/103 31; Mon–Fri 11.30am–2pm & 6pm–midnight, Sat & Sun 3pm–midnight), built as a grain warehouse in 1860; however, its à la carte menu is a disappointingly ordinary selection of fish and pizza dishes; lunch costs around 150kr. There are fine restaurants at two of the town's hotels, the *Grand Hotel* and the *Hvitan*. For good-value meals, head for the friendly *D.D.* on Hotelgatan 3 (June–Aug daily noon–2am; Sept–May Wed–Sat noon–2pm). A smallish restaurant, it serves à la carte pasta dishes and baguettes at very reasonable prices; lunch is 55kr. Fans of salmon really should make the effort to travel 9km south on the old E6 (parallel to the present one) to *Laxbutiken*, in a white building off the highway (℡0345/511 10; summer daily 10am–8pm); their superb dishes have salmon exclusively as the main ingredient. Down at the **beaches**, the *Kattegat Restaurant*, attached to *Strandbaden Hotel* (Mon–Sat 7–11pm) is a gourmet restaurant entered through the hotel. Walk instead around to the beach entrance, and *Strandkrogen Restaurant* (daily noon–11pm) is its casual, budget eaterie with baguettes, baked potatoes and grills for 55–95kr, or try their popular shrimp buffet.

Cafés, bars and nightlife

The best **café** in town is the *Falkmanska Caféet*, Storgatan 42 (Mon–Fri 9am–6pm, Sat 9am–2pm), housed in the oldest (1700) secular building in town, and featuring a stripped wood floor, mellow furnishings and a lovely garden. This place has a welcoming atmosphere and serves huge baguettes (35–45kr) and decadent home-made cakes. For its setting, *Café Rosengården,* (summer daily noon–6pm) with its flowery, shaded outside area at the beginning of Doktorspromenaden (see opposite), just over the old bridge, is hard to beat. For **ice cream**, head to *Slottshagens Glass Café*, at Hamngatan 27, close to Falkenberg Museum, where there's a big range of ices and waffles. (Sun–Fri noon–8pm, Sat 11am–5pm).

Mixing American and British influences, *Harry's Bar* on Rådhustorget (noon till late) is always packed with eaters and drinkers. In the **evening**, a dance floor opens up at *D.D.*, corner of Storgatan and Hotellgatan, for a 20-something crowd. The owner of *Hotel Hvitan* (see above), Bo Persson, runs a popular jazz, blues and folk music **festival** in the first and second weeks of July, setting up stage in the courtyard. One-day tickets to this enjoyable event cost 255kr for the folk festival and 150kr for the jazz, from the tourist office.

Halmstad and around

The principal town in Halland, **HALMSTAD**, was once a grand walled city and an important Danish stronghold. Today, although most of the original buildings have disappeared, Halmstad has a couple of cultural and artistic points of interest, most notably the works, displayed nearby at Mjellby, of the

Halmstad Group, Sweden's first Surrealists. The town also boasts extensive, if rather crowded, **beaches** not far away, and a range of really good places to eat – all in all, a sound choice for a day or two's relaxation.

In 1619, the town's **castle** was used by the Danish king Christian IV to entertain the Swedish king Gustav II Adolf; records show that there were seven solid days of festivities. The bonhomie, however, didn't last much longer, and Christian was soon building great stone-and-earth fortifications around the city, all surrounded by a moat, with access afforded by four stone gateways. However, it was a fire soon after, rather than the Swedes, that all but destroyed the city; the only buildings to survive were the castle and the church. Undeterred, Christian took the opportunity to create a contemporary Renaissance town with a grid of straight streets; today the main street, Storgatan, still contains a number of impressive merchants' houses from that time. After the final defeat of the Danes in 1645, Halmstad lost its military significance, and the walls were torn down. Today, just one of the great gateways, Norre Port, remains; the moat has been filled in and a road, Karl XIs Vägen, runs directly above where the water would have been.

Arrival and information

It takes 25 minutes to get here from Falkenberg by train. From the **train station**, follow Bredgatan to the Nissan river. Within the castle on the opposite river bank, the helpful **tourist office** (Jan–March & Sept–Dec Mon–Fri 9am–5pm; April & May & mid-Aug to end Aug Mon–Fri 9am–6pm, Sat 10am–1pm, June Mon–Fri 9am–6pm, Sat 10am–3pm, Sun 1–3pm; July to mid-Aug Mon–Sat 9am–7pm, Sun 3–7pm; ☏035/13 23 20, ✉info@tourist .halmstad.se) will book **private rooms** from 125kr per person, plus a booking fee (25kr if you visit the office – essential in summer, 50kr by phone).

A good way to get to the beaches or the Mjellby Arts Centre (see p.213) is by a **bike**. Arvid Olsson Cykel, Norra Vägen 11 (Mon–Fri 9.30am–6pm, Sat 9.30am–1pm; ☏035/21 22 51) charges a steep 100kr per day for a five-speed bike, though two days is just 140kr; trailers are 80kr extra. Much cheaper is renting at *Kronocamping* in Tylösand (see p.212; ☏035/305 10; 75kr a day or 285kr a week). No deposit is needed if you're camping there; otherwise there is a 400kr refundable deposit to pay.

Accommodation

The central **youth hostel** is at Skepparegatan 23, 500m to the west of St Nicolai church (☏035/12 05 00; 140kr, ❶; mid-June to mid-Aug); all rooms are en suite. **Camping** is a popular option here, the best site being *Hägons Camping* at Östra Stranden, about 3km from the centre (☏035/12 53 63, ☏12 43 65); there are also **cabins**, each sleeping up to five people (3800kr a week, or 5100kr en suite); the site is next to a nature reserve, to the east of the town centre (see p.212).

The most beautiful **hotel** in town is *Hotel Continental*, Kungsgatan 5 (☏035/17 63 00, ☒www.continental-halmstad.se; ❹/❸), just two minutes' walk from the train station. With a bright, well-preserved interior, this elegant building was built in 1904 in early *Jugendstil* and National Romantic styles. There's a free sauna and solarium and the breakfasts are also very good. Another fine choice is the very comfortable old *Norre Park Hotel*, at Norra Vägen 7 (☏035/21 85 55, ☒www.norrepark.se; ❸/❷), overlooking the beautiful Norre Katt Park; the hotel is reached through the Norre Port arch, north of Storgatan. The price here includes the use of saunas and the fitness room, and an excellent buffet breakfast. Closest to the station is the comfortable and traditional *Grand Hotel*, Stationsgatan 44 (℡035/280 81 00, ⓦwww.grandhotel.nu; ❺/❸), dating from 1905, where there's a sauna, free tea and coffee, and friendly service. The hotel also offers a bar and restaurant (see p.213). The long, low *Hotel Tylösand*, on the Tylösand beach (℡035/305 00, ⓦwww.tylosand.se; ❹), is owned by Per Gessle, better known as the singer/songwriter from the Swedish rock duo Roxette, who hail from the town. Since its renovation, it's become very popular with a young crowd which can make it very noisy at night. There is a big, international restaurant with shows and a casino, plus a pool, sauna and solarium.

The Town

At the centre of the large, lively market square, **Storatorg**, is Carl Milles's *Europa and the Bull*, a fountain with mermen twisted around it, all with Milles's characteristically muscular bodies, ugly faces and oversized nipples. Flanking one side of the square is the grand **St Nikolai kyrka** (daily 8.30am–3.30pm) dating from the fourteenth century, its monumental size bearing witness to the town's former importance. Today, the only signs of its medieval origins are the splodges of bare rock beneath the plain, brick columns. Adjacent to the church, the **Tre Hjärtan** (Three Hearts) *konditori* is a vast, proud building with a cross-beamed ceiling; its name derives from the three hearts that make up the town's emblem, Christian IV having granted the town the right to use it in gratitude for their loyalty to Denmark. It's worth taking your coffee and cake upstairs, where the beams and ceiling are beautifully hand-painted, and photographs of nineteenth-century Halmstad adorn the walls.

Not far from Österbrobron, **Halmstad Castle** is a striking, coral-red affair half hidden by trees, which contains the tourist office (see opposite) and is the private residence of the governor. Moored in front is **Najaden**, a small, fully rigged sailing ship built in 1897, once used for training by the Swedish navy (July & Aug Tues & Thurs 5–7pm, Sat 11am–3pm). With children in tow, a reasonable, though not outstanding, diversion is a trip to the **Tropic Centre**, a few minutes along the river from the tourist office (daily: July 10am–6pm; Aug–June 10am–4pm; adults 60kr), where snakes, monkeys, crocodiles and spiders are on display in a sort of miniature menagerie. A more active time is to be had at the **Sannarpsbadet**, Växjövägen (June–Aug Tues–Fri 10am–5pm, Sat 10am–4pm; Sept–May Mon noon–8pm Tues & Thurs 10am–7pm Wed & Fri 10am–8pm; ℡035/13 96 50; 45kr, family tickets 120kr), a swimming pool complex with a solarium (40kr), slides and Jacuzzis.

Leading north from the square, pedestrianized **Storgatan** – the main thoroughfare for restaurants and nightlife (see p.213) – is a charming street, with some creaking old houses built in the years following the 1619 fire; the great stone arch of **Norre Port** marks the street's end. To the right is the splendid **Norre Katt Park**, a delightful, shady place that slopes down towards the river; the park is dotted with mature beech, copper beech and horse-chestnut trees, with great weeping willows by the water. The town's most serene spot is at the park's centre, where there's a lily pond crossed by a bridge. A popular **café**, housed in an ornate former bandstand, overlooks the spot (June–Aug daily noon–8pm); it serves waffles smothered in jam and cream at 20kr, as well as cakes and ice cream.

The Halmstad Museum and Hallandsgården

At the northernmost edge of the park, by the river, is the fine **Halmstad Museum** (Tues–Sun noon–4pm, Wed till 9pm; 20kr). While the archeological finds and basement collections are unlikely to set many pulses racing, the first-floor displays (rooms 6, 7 & 8) of home interiors from the seventeenth, eighteenth and nineteenth centuries are a lot of fun. There are some exquisitely furnished doll's houses and you can wander through, among others, a room of glorious Gustavian harps and square pianos from the 1780s. The shipping room here avoids the usual nautical maps and bits of old boats, opting for a charismatic collection of ghoulish figureheads from ships wrecked off the Halland coast.

The museum is noted for its tapestries from southern Sweden; the full English commentary amusingly explains the pictorial stories. The top floor is devoted to a fair sampling of the work of the **Halmstad Group** (see opposite). There are also some contemporary sculptures – arresting glass pieces using prismic forms to intriguing effect.

Close by, on so-called Gallows Hill, is a small collection of Halmstad's older houses moved to the site to form a miniature outdoor museum, **Hallandsgården** (early June to mid-Aug 11am–5pm; guided tours 2pm each day and at other times by arrangement on ☎035/21 03 74; free).

Martin Luther Church
One kilometre east of the centre on Långgatan, one of the main roads out of town, stands the gleaming 1970s **Martin Luther Church** (daily 9am–3pm). The first church in Scandinavia to be assembled entirely of steel – it is known by locals as the Tin Factory – this unique creation looks from the outside like a clumsily opened sardine can, with jagged and curled edges, and stained glass. Inside it's just as unusual: all the walls are a rust-orange version of the outer skin, and there are some striking ornaments. The building is famed for its acoustics, and holds concerts (Sun evenings in summer) and a seven-day music festival during the first week of July (☎035/15 19 61 for details).

Out from the centre: Halmstad's beaches and Mini Land
Eight kilometres west of the town centre, Halmstad's most popular **beach** is at **Tylösand** (regular buses run here from town), which in July and August becomes packed with bronzing bodies; by night the same bodies fill the surrounding bars and restaurants. There's a smuggler's cove to wander around at **Tjuvahålan**, signposted directly off the beach, and plenty of excellent spots for bathing, including **Svärjarehålan**, a little further north, where a bathing beach has been adapted for the disabled. To reach less crowded areas, head ten minutes' walk north to **Frösakull** and **Ringenäs**, which is popular for windsurfing.

Between the town and Tylösand is **Mini Land** (late April to Aug Mon–Fri 10am–4pm, Sat & Sun 10am–6pm; late June to mid-Aug daily 10am–7pm; 75kr), a miniature Swedish city complete with historical sites in Lilliputian proportions together with a pleasant **restaurant** (☎035/10 24 38).

The best beach to the east of town is at **Östra Stranden**, where there is also a large, well-equipped campsite. It's reached by crossing the river from Stora Torg and heading along Stationgatan past the train station, then turning southeast for a couple of kilometres down Stålverksgatan. Bus #63 runs here every half-hour from the town centre. Before reaching the beach, you'll see Sweden's biggest **go-karting** tracks, *Gokarthallen* (open all year; ☎035/18 77 00, ⓦwww.gokarthallen.just.nu) hugely popular round here, with special tracks adapted for the disabled. There's a range of prices, but the cheapest is a 'drop in' price of 100kr for eight minutes driving. The long beach – deep, sandy and less crowded than at Tylösand – is excellent for children as the waters are particularly shallow here. Further south is **Hagön**, a secluded **nudist beach** which is principally, though not exclusively, gay. Privacy is afforded by the deep hollows between the dunes; behind it is a nature reserve.

Mjellby Arts Centre

Five kilometres north of the town centre is the **Mjellby Arts Centre** (road signs still use the original "Mjällby"; mid-March to June & mid-Aug to Oct Tues–Sun 1–5pm; July to mid-Aug Tues–Sun 1–6pm; Nov to mid-Dec Sat & Sun 1–5pm; 40kr; ⓦwww.halmstad.se/mjellby.se) containing the largest collection of works by the **Halmstad Group**, a body of six local artists from the 1920s who championed Cubism and Surrealism in Sweden. To get here by car, head out along Karlsrovägen past the tiny airport into the countryside, then take the first road on the left for about 1km; bus #350 from the centre will drop you just after the turning.

The Halmstad Group, comprising brothers Eric and Axel Olson, their cousin Waldemar Lorentzon and three others, worked together as an artists' alliance for fifty years. The group's members had studied in Berlin and Paris and were strongly influenced by Magritte and Dalí, producing work that caused considerable controversy from the Twenties to the Forties. They sometimes worked collectively on a project – an almost unheard-of practice in Swedish art (a good example of one of these group efforts is at the Halmstad City Library, where a fourteen-metre-long painting in six sections hangs above the shelves). If Viveka Bosson, the daughter of Eric Olson, is around (she works here), you may get a free guided tour around Mjellby. There's also an excellent **café** here, *Café Blå*, a cool blue-and-white place serving superb food.

Eating, drinking and nightlife

People congregate in the trendy restaurants, bars and clubs along cobbled, pedestrianized **Storgatan**, many of which have shaded outdoor areas along the street. **Lilla Torget**, just behind Storgatan, also swarms with people on summer evenings. Prices can be steep, but there are also plenty of cheaper cafés and light meal options. **Tylösand** is a night-time spot for the beach crowd, with most of the action concentrated on *Hotel Tylösand* (see p.211). For mouth-watering **picnic** fare, try the deli section of Strömbergs Ost & Delikatessen (Mon–Fri 10am–6pm, Sat 10am–2pm).

Fribergs Konditoria Norrevägen 9. Traditional bakery and coffee house overlooking the park with a relaxed atmosphere. Serves mouthwatering cakes and plates of white-chocolate truffles. A coffee and sandwich is 40kr. Mon–Fri 8am–7pm, Sat & Sun 9am–7pm.

Fridolfs Brogatan 26 ☎035/21 16 66. The food is excellent here and there's a lovely back garden eating area. Several vegetarian choices amongst the substantial, mains of meat, fish, poultry and shellfish. Mon–Sat 6pm–midnight, Sun 5–11pm.

Gastrons Storgatan, corner of Bankgatan ☎035/10 84 80. A locals' favourite. Very popular for pavement-side eating at this grand old building. Fish and meat dishes are dear at 185–215kr, but there's also a big range of pizzas at 65kr, and a lively atmosphere.

Grands Framficka Stationsgatan 44 ☎035/280 81 00. A good solid restaurant, with Swedish and Italian meals housed in the *Grand* hotel.

Lilla Helfwetet Corner Hamngatan and Bastiongatan (Mon–Thurs 11.30am–2pm & 6pm till late, Fri 11.30am–2am, Sat 6pm–2am, Sun 6pm–2am; ☎035/21 04 20). Meaning "Little Hell", this is the most stylish eatery in town serving up chicken, lamb, beef and turbot in this old turbine engine room which overlooks the river, with outside eating at the back.

Nygatan Nygatan 8, off Storatorg. Quite ordinary check-tablecloth café-diner that does a good-value three-course dinner for 129kr. Mon–Sat 9am–midnight, Sun 6pm–midnight.

Pio & Co Storgatan 37 ☎035/21 06 69. A lovely place, where the speciality is steaks served on wooden planks with clouds of mashed potato at 175kr. There's also a massive drinks list. Daily 6pm–1am

Skånska Hembageriet Bankgatan I. Rustic seventeenth-century cake shop and *konditori* just off Storgatan. Mon–Fri 8.15am–6pm, Sat 9am–3pm.

Strömbergs Ost & Delikatessen Storgatan 23. The eating area has a relaxed atmosphere and does great light lunches like pasta with chicken, onions and cream (62kr). July & Aug Mon–Fri 10am–6pm, Sat 10am–2pm. Rest of year delicatessen only.

Tre Hjärtan Storatorg. This beautiful building is more sumptuous than the cakes it serves in its café. There are also light meals like pizzas at 55–65kr and fish and meat courses too.

Ulle's Café Brogatan 7. Café serving snacks and sandwiches. Boasts surreal ceiling paintings and a great little garden at the back. Mon–Fri 9am–6pm, Sat 9.30am–2.30pm.

Verona Laholmsvägen 27. An unexpectedly good restaurant away from the centre, this is a neighbourhood place on the same side of the river as the train station. Superb dishes of steaks, pork, tournedos and great pizzas for around 150kr.

Wayne's Storgatan 42. Part of the laid-back, casual and very likeable chain of coffee houses (Mon–Thurs & Sun 11am–11pm, Fri & Sat to midnight) with huge salads (59kr) pastas and plenty of cakes and pies.

Yoss Storgatan 35 ☏035/18 76 49. This cosy restaurant serves meat, fowl, fish and shellfish main courses, each for 100–200kr, plus several slightly cheaper veggie options. They also do lots of different liqueur coffees for 64kr each.

Bars and discos

For the younger crowd (18–30), summer in Halmstad means the *Monday Club* (Mondag Clubben). This is a huge informal **disco** every Monday night throughout summer. It moves venue frequently, but is currently at *House 17*, Stationsgatan, in an old locomotive shed just beyond the train station. Rather more upmarket are the *Studio 54 nights* every Wednesday, at Lilla Helfwetet (see above, previous page) where Seventies disco music is the order of the day. Other more traditional pubs and clubs are listed below.

Bond Storgatan 34. The discreet facade to this popular night club for the 25–35 age group (summer Wed–Sat 9pm–3am, winter till 2am) belies the glamorous souls within. It's housed, though you'd never believe it from the facade, in Halmstad's former law courts in a seventeenth-century building.

The Bull's Pub Lilla Torg, a step away from Storgatan. Very popular, English-style bar with live music. Sixties sounds on Mon nights. Also serves light lunch specials (Mon–Fri 11.30am–1.30pm; 68kr)

Daltons Storgatan 35. An alternative-music bar offering Swedish music upstairs and dancing on the ground floor, with a bar open to the sky in summer. Entry is by a small doorway two doors down from *Pio & Co* (see previous page).

Harry's Storgatan. On the corner of Klammerdammsgatan. Massively popular pub attesting to the delight taken by some Swedes in all things purporting Britishness. This one has an English phone box and a life-sized Charlie Chaplin dummy. It also does reasonably priced meat, fish and pub meals. Mon–Thurs & Sun 5pm–1am, Fri 5pm–2am, Sat noon–2am.

Gay Halmstad

Halmstad boasts an exceptionally well-designed **gay club** called *Nightlife*, run by RFSL, at Stålverksgatan 2; to get there, head north down Stationgatan from the train station and take the first left, following signs to Östrastranden. Built out of an old factory, the place has a striking dance floor and friendly bar area, though the real eye-opener is in the basement – the main room of which has walls lit up to reveal plaster buttocks on the walls, all modelled from the bodies of club members. Sadly, numbers of regulars have dropped recently, but there's still a disco party here every Saturday night during summer, once a month at other times; you'll have to join RFSL to get in (100kr for three months, which gives you entry to all RFSL venues around Sweden). On Monday and Wednesday there's a welcoming pub night (7–10pm).

Around Halmstad

Around twenty kilometres south of Halmstad, some of the most popular **beaches** along the west coast are to be found at **Mellbystrand**, and the same distance inland from these beaches the backwater hamlet of **Hishult** is well worth seeking out for its art gallery.

Mellbystrand

The beach holiday Mecca of **Mellbystrand** is a twelve-kilometre-long stretch of wide beaches, fringed by dunes and scrubland, behind which lie endless campsites for caravans, tents and cabins. Popular with Swedes, Mellbystrand gets very crowded in summer. **Nude** bathing sections, amongst the most popular in Sweden, are indicated by signs showing a rear view of a family and there are some of the best-known gay beaches in the country to the north of the other beaches.

Mellbystrand is something of a public transport oversight, with no train service and infrequent buses; **taxis** here from the nearby town of Laholm cost 100kr (℡0430/713 10). **Bikes** are a good option for getting around. You can rent a bike in Mellbystrand, at the very cheap Sturesson, Tärnvägen 13 (30kr per day or 100kr per week). In summer, there's an information point at a **café**, *Maxi* (℡0430/278 44) **Camping** is the most popular form of accommodation here, and *Marias Camping* the best campsite (℡0430/285 85), with excellent roomy cabins; you can also pitch tents. There are a couple of **restaurants**, mainly pizza places attached to the campsites. Set in the prettiest wooden lodge trimmed with fancy carving, the *Strand Hotel*, 200m from the beach, is no longer a hotel – it's now a busy restaurant, pizzeria and grill.

Hishult

HISHULT was an old farming village established in the twelfth century, with homes that boasted furnaces in which ore taken from the local swamps was turned into iron. Today the place is very much a backwater, though one set in exquisite forest and lake surroundings. It makes a glorious cycle ride east from Halmstad (40km). One historic sight worth a peek along the way (signposted off the main road) is the ruins of **Sjöboholm**, once the manor of old Hishult County, now reduced to little more than its foundations, jutting out into the lake 3km west of Hishult.

The real reason to seek the village out, though, is **Hishult Gästgivaregård** and **Konsthallen** at Markarydsvägen 10 (gallery; May–Aug Tues–Fri 1–8pm, Sat & Sun 1–5pm; Sept–April Wed–Fri 2.30–6pm, Sat & Sun 1–5pm; ℡0430/403 21 or 400 55, ⌨www.konsthallen.hishult.com); it's well signposted once you reach the village. An old inn had existed here in the middle of Hishult for centuries; it was inherited by its present owner who set about converting part of it into a sensational art gallery. The design is full of inspired ideas, juxtaposing old and new, such as the steel spiral staircase and old stoves which come from old industrial buildings; outside, the gardens are peppered with wacky sculptures. In the grounds, a fine **café**, a good spot for a light lunch, serves almond cream slices and chocolate cake. The inn is a delightful place to **stay**, with nine rooms (❶); dinners can be ordered by arrangement.

Båstad

Back on the west coast, around 30km west of Hishult, lies **BÅSTAD**, the northernmost town in the ancient province of **Skåne**, yet its character is markedly different from other towns along the coast. Cradled by the **Bjäre peninsula** (see p.218), which bulges westwards into the Kattegat (the waters between Sweden and Jutland), Båstad is Sweden's **tennis centre**, where the Swedish Open is played at the beginning of July. The rest of Båstad boasts sixty other tennis courts, five eighteen-hole golf courses and the Drivan Sports

Centre, one of Sweden's foremost sports complexes. The setting is very beautiful, with forested hills on the horizon to the south.

There is a downside, though, which can blunt enthusiasm for the place. Ever since King Gustav V chose to take part in the 1930 tennis championships and Ludvig Nobel (nephew to Alfred of the Nobel Prize) gave financial backing to the tournaments, wealthy retired Stockholmers and social climbers from all over Sweden have flocked here. The result is an ostentatious smugness invading the town for the annual tournaments during the second week of July. The locals themselves, however, are quite down-to-earth, and most view this arrogance as a financial lifeline. Despite all this, Båstad isn't a prohibitively expensive place to stay, and makes a good base from which to explore the peninsula.

Arrival, information and accommodation

There are around twenty **trains** a day here from Halmstad. Båstad's **train station** is a lamentably long walk from the main part of town, a good 25-minute hike east down Köpmansgatan. Båstad's **tourist office**, on the main square (mid-June to mid-Aug Sun–Fri 10am–6pm, Sat 10am–4pm; mid-Aug to mid-June Mon–Sat 10am–4pm; ☎0431/750 45, ⊛www.bastad.com), can supply you with a list of **private rooms** from 150kr per person. The main place to **rent bikes** is Svenn's Cykel, Tennisvägen 31 (Mon–Fri 8am–noon & 1–5pm, Sat 8am–noon; ☎0431/701 26), which charges 80kr per day or 300kr per week. Another good option is at *B&B Malengården* (see below), also charging 80kr per day.

Accommodation in Båstad is plentiful, but to find somewhere to stay during the tennis tournament, you'll need to book months in advance. The cheapest hotels are those nearest the station – and hence furthest from the action. Unlike the rest of Sweden, prices are likely to increase dramatically during the summer due to the tennis tournaments. The **youth hostel** (☎0431/685 00, ⓕ706 19; 160kr, ❶) is next to the Drivan Sports Centre at Korrödsvagen, signposted off Köpmansgatan. It's open all year, but tends to be reserved for groups in winter. **Camping** is not allowed on the dunes – locals can be stuffy if you try; you are better off heading to the Bjäre peninsula.

Falken Hamngatan 22 ☎0431/36 95 94 or 070/641 69 77. This most charming and charismatic bed & breakfast is wonderfully located just above the harbour in delightful gardens. A 1916-built villa, the house has been lovingly maintained and has a welcoming atmosphere. ❷

Buena Vista Tarravägen 5 ☎0431/760 00, ⓕ791 00. With a splendid interior, this vast villa, built out of Cuban stone by a wealthy Cuban émigré, has two grand dining rooms, one overlooking Laholm Bay. To reach it, turn off Köpmansgatan down Pershögsgatan, around 500m east of the church. ❹

Enehall Stationsterrasen 10 ☎ 0431/750 15,
℻ 724 09. A modern hotel just a few metres from
the train station. ❸

Skansen Harbour-side ☎ 0431/55 81 00,
ⓦ www.hotelskansen.se. This beautifully designed
hotel in a century-old cream bathhouse with stylish annexe villas, offers excellent service, a great

health spa and an appealing restaurant, *Sand,*
which is right at the heart of the tennis action.
❹/❺.

Malengården Åhusvägen 41 ☎ & ℻ 0431/36 95
67. A pleasant, traditional wooden house that's
now a B&B; reached by the same turning off
Köpmansgatan as the youth hostel. ❶

The Town

From the train station, it's a half-hour walk eastwards down Köpmansgatan
to the central, old square and tourist office (see opposite). Once you get close
to the centre, you'll see that the street's architecture is unusual for Sweden;
indeed it's somewhat reminiscent of provincial France, with shuttered, low-
rise shops and houses. In the square is the fifteenth-century **St. Maria
Church**, a cool haven on a hot summer's day. The altar painting is unusual,
depicting Jesus on his cross with a couple of skulls and haphazardly strewn
human bones on the ground beneath. For a feel of real old Båstad, take a
stroll down the ancient cottage-flanked Agadhsgatan, off Hamngatat and parallel with the seashore. To reach the **beach**, head down Tennisvägen, off
Köpmansgatan, through a glamourous residential area, until you reach
Strandpromenaden, where you can take a lovely evening stroll as the sun sets
on the calm waters. West of here, the old 1880s bathhouses have all been converted into restaurants and bars which owe much of their popularity to their
proximity to the tennis courts where the famous tournaments are played. Just
a few steps further lies the harbour, thick with boat masts. To get involved in
any **sports activities**, ask at the tourist office for information on booking
tennis courts or renting out sports equipment.

Eating, drinking and nightlife

In Båstad, **eating and drinking** is as much a pastime as tennis, and most of
the waterside restaurants and hotels here have two-course dinner offers, with
menus changing weekly. Although it has a few **nightclubs**, Båstad is much
more geared up for those who prefer to sip wine in restaurants; only teenagers
fill the naff clubs along Köpmansgatan. *Madison's,* next to *Hotel Borgen* on
Köpmansgatan, is grim-looking on the outside but is a fun blackjack joint
inside (June–Aug).

Caffe & Torta Opposite the church. A delightful
café serving newly baked bread (from 6am), gaz-
pacho, focaccia, big salads and lovely coffees and
cake in a fresh, country atmosphere. (Summer
daily 8am–6pm; rest of year shorter hours)

Buena Vista Tarravägen 5. A fine restaurant serving Swedish and European dishes at surprisingly
reasonable prices, or you can pop in just for a coffee. (Summer Wed–Sun noon–5pm)

Pepe's Bodega Up from the harbour, close to the
tennis courts. A very popular place serving pizzas
and pastas. The food is nothing special, but this
being Båstad, along with basic stomach fillers, the
bar will sell you champagne.

Sand A bathhouse attached to *Hotel Skansen*. An
excellent quality à la carte restaurant with wonderful dishes of marinated salmon.

Sveas Skafferi At the harbour. The place to come
to fill up well, cheaply and al fresco. Excellent
smoked mackerel and salmon are served on paper
plates, as are the home-baked pies and chocolate
cake. A plate of fish with potato salad and greens
costs just 60kr.

Våran Next door to *Pepe's*. A pleasant restaurant,
located in a turn-of-the-twentieth-century
bathhouse, offering pricey chicken, meat and fish
dishes.

The Bjäre peninsula

Jutting into the Kattegat directly west of Båstad and deserving of a couple of days' exploration, the **Bjäre peninsula**'s natural beauty has a magical quality to it. Its varied scenery includes wide fertile fields where potatoes and strawberries are grown, splintered red-rock cliff formations, and remote islands ringed by seals, thick with birds and historical ruins.

Travel practicalities

To help you find your way around, it's best to buy a large-scale map of the area from Båstad tourist office (40kr; see p.216). The well-known **Skåneleden walking trail** runs around the entire perimeter; it makes for a great cycle ride, although having a bike with a choice of gears helps, as it can get hilly. **Public transport** around Bjäre is adequate, with **buses** connecting the main towns and villages. Bus #525 leaves Båstad every other hour for **Torekov** (Mon–Fri; 20min; 16kr), running through the centre of the peninsula en route; it stops at the small hamlets of Hov and Karup, on the peninsula's southern coast. For transport to Torekov at weekends, call Båstad taxi (℡0431/696 66) an hour before you want to leave (same charge as the bus; book your return journey on the outward trip). To move on to Ängelholm (see p.221) from Torekov, take bus #523 (6 daily; 50min). **Staying** on the Bjäre peninsula is no problem; there are plenty of spots to pitch a tent for free, several official places to camp and plenty of good hotels in the main towns.

The northern coastline

Heading north out of Båstad along the coast road, it's just a couple of kilometres to **Norrvikens Gardens** (May to mid-Sept daily 10am–6pm; ⓦwww.norrvikenstadgarden.se 60kr), a paradise for horticulturists and lovers of symmetry. With the sea as a backdrop, these fine gardens were designed by Rudolf Abelin at the end of the nineteenth century; he is buried in a magnificent hollow of rhododendrons near the entrance. The best walk is the "King's Ravine", ablaze in late spring and early summer with fiery azaleas and blushing rhododendrons, and leading to a fine Japanese-style garden. At the centre of the grounds there's a villa with a **café–restaurant**. Around July 10, the biggest **classic car show** in Sweden is held in the grounds here (100kr). While at Norrvikens, don't miss the stunning **glassworks** (Mon–Fri 9am–6pm; ℡070 597 9179), just by the carpark. The studio of celebrated British designer Richard Rackham, the glass designs are far more free-spirited and artistic than much of what you can see in the Glass Kingdom (see p.303).

Two to three kilometres further, past the *Norrvikens Camping Site* (for caravans only; ℡0431/691 70, ⓔnorrviken-camp@caravanclub.se; April–Oct), is **KATTVIK**. Once a village busy with stone-grinding mills, it is now largely the domain of wealthy, elderly Stockholmers, who snap up the few houses on the market as soon as they are up for sale. Kattvik achieved its moment of fame when Richard Gere chose a cottage here as a venue for a summer romance, but these days there's little more than the friendly and peaceful *Delfin Bed & Breakfast* (℡070/405 15 49; ❶). With sparklingly clean rooms and serving breakfast with home-baked bruschetta in the garden or on the terrace, it makes an idyllic base for exploring the region.

A kilometre from Kattvik off the Torekov road (follow the sign "*rökt fisk*") is Kai's fish **smokery**, an old farm where fish is smoked in little furnaces fired by sawdust from the nearby clog factory. Here you can have a taste of – and buy – the very best smoked fish in the area; as well as the usual mackerel and salmon, you can sample *horngadda*, a scaly fish with bright green bones, and *sjurygg*, an extraordinarily ugly, seven-crested fish with oily, flavoursome flesh. Just a couple of minutes walk from Kattvik, in the hills behind *Delfin B & B*, is *Westfield Häst Safari* (①& ⑦0431/45 13 53); signposted off the Torekov Route, it's a base for **horse trekking**. The treks are run by an Irishman, John Slattery, and range from a two-hour guided trip (350kr, including lunch), to a two-day trek (1300kr including accommodation) from the forests close by across the valleys to Hovs Hallar (see below).

Heading north along the coast road or the signposted walking trail, the undulating meadows and beamed cottages you'll encounter have a rural, peculiarly English, feel. To continue along the coast after taking the trail from Kattvik, follow the path for **Hovs Hallar nature reserve**, leading off at the T-junction (around a 20min walk). Wandering across to the reserve from the car park, you can clamber down any of several paths towards the sea. The views are breathtaking – screaming gulls circling overhead and waves crashing onto the unique red-stone cliffs, though it's something of a tourist magnet during the summer.

Overlooking the cliffs, *Hovs Hallar Värdhus* is a famed **restaurant** serving fine à la carte meals and lunch specials (daily noon–9pm; ⑦0431/44 83 70, ⑩www.wardshus-hovshallar.com). Unfortunately, it's rested on its laurels recently as custom has been easy to come by, and the standard is not what it has been. There are pretty, four-bed **cabins** just behind the restaurant (June–Aug from 695kr per night for the cabins; Sept–May 455kr). Double rooms are also available between June and August (❶), and there's a **café** here too (10am–10pm; closed outside summer).

Torekov and Hallands Väderö

Leaving Båstad along Route 115 for the sleepy village of **Torekov**, consider stopping for a bite at *Solbackens* waffle bakery and **café** (daily noon–6pm), on Italienskavägen, 2km from town. Nestling amid wild flowers near the start of the peninsula, this place, in a wooden house above a babbling brook, has been dishing up excellent waffles (24kr each) since 1907. Rough-hewn steps lead upwards from the café to countless hidden hillside coves, with tables and chairs and spectacular views.

Torekov

On the peninsula's western coast, **TOREKOV** is just 5km from Hovs Hallar. The village is named after a little girl, later known as St Thora, who, so the story goes, was drowned by her wicked stepmother; the body was washed ashore and given a Christian burial by a blind man, who then miraculously regained his sight. There's precious little to do here, other than have a look at the cut-in-half sailing ship (free), a **museum** with a collection of shipping memorabilia. One odd sight is the daily ritual of elderly men in dressing gowns wandering along the pier – so sought after is the property here, these old boys promenade in bathrobes to set themselves apart from the visitors. Torekov's **tourist office** is at the back of *Café Thora*, close to the harbour (June–Aug daily 10am–6pm; ⑦0431/36 31 80, ⑩www.torekovturism.net). To **stay** in Torekov itself, try the century-old *Hotel Kattegat*, to be found on its cobbled main street (⑦0431/36 30 02; ❺); this fine old building has en-suite rooms with TVs (room no. 9 has the finest view), and a lovely, frescoed dining room. A more rustic, very charming option is found 3km out of Torekov; follow the signposted turning from the main road towards Påarp. This will bring you to *Sjöbyggargården Bed & Breakfast* (☎0431/36 53 86; ❶; mid-June to mid-Aug), in a converted stables dating from the eighteenth century; it oozes country character with hollyhocks outside the front door; advance reservations here are a good idea. For a place to **camp**, there's *Kronocamping* (☎0431/36 45 25, ⓕ36 46 25), 1500m out of Torekov on the Båstad road; it has four-bed, modern cabins with showers and cable TV.

There are three very popular, though rather expensive, **restaurants** in the village. *Hotel Kattegat* has its own restaurant, boasting the revered chef Richard Nilson and international/European food at over 200kr a dish, while just opposite, the vine-roofed *Svenson's* serves fine fish dishes (Tues, Thurs & Sun 6–11pm, Fri & Sat 6pm–1am, open for lunch in summer; ☎0431/36 45 90, ⓦwww.swensons.net). By the harbour, *Hamn Krogan* restaurant (☎0431/36 44 00) looks the cosiest of the three, but its food is the least special. The newest addition is *Café Thora,* (summer daily noon–2am; ☎0431/36 47 48) in between *Hamn Krogan* and *Svenson's*. This laid-back place, with a huge range of cocktails, serves Swedish food in tapas proportions (20–45kr each) and the creative young chefs have established a very friendly, winning atmosphere. You can also buy ciabattas and soups during the day (55–85kr). Alternatively, you can buy a ciabatta bursting with smoked fish (55kr) from the harbour fish shop, *Fiskhuset*. If you're in a car, then it's well worth seeking out the un-touristy *Kvinnaböske Krog* (☎0431/36 21 88) an exceptionally good restaurant on Route 105, near Grevie off Route 115 to Torekov. Superb fresh food with an emphasis on **vegetarian** dishes is served up in an artistically designed place.

Hallands Väderö

Old fishing **boats** regularly leave from Torekov's little harbour for the island nature reserve of **Hallands Väderö** (mid-June to Aug hourly; Sept to mid-June every 2hr; 15min; 70kr return). The last one back leaves at 4.30pm, so it's well worth setting off early (first boats at 9am or 10am at weekends) to give yourself a full day to take in its awesome beauty. You can buy a map (20kr) of Hallands Väderö from Torekov harbour ticket office before you leave.

The island is a scenic mix of trees and bare rocks with isolated fishermen's cottages dotted around its edges, while the skies above are filled with countless birds – gulls, eiders, guillemots, cormorants. One particularly beautiful spot is at its southernmost tip, where weather-smoothed islets stand out amid the tranquil turquoise waters. If you're lucky, you may be able to make out the colony of seals which lives on the furthest rocks; there are organized "**seal safaris**" there (11.30am & 5.30pm; 115kr; ☎0431/36 30 20, ⓦwww.vaderobatarna.se) – ask at the ticket office at Torekov harbour or, outside summer, at Junivägen 13, Halmstad. Also on the south of the island is the English graveyard, surrounded by mossy, dry-stone walls. It holds the remains of English sailors who were killed here in 1809, when the British fleet were stationed on the island in order to bombard Copenhagen during the Napoleonic Wars. Torekov church would not allow them to be buried on its soil as the sailors' faith was, strangely, considered unknown.

There is no camping on the island (heads are counted on the boats' return journeys to check if anyone tries), so if you do want to **stay** overnight, you'll have to rent one of the two idyllic cottages by the northern lighthouse (ask at Torekov tourist office for details).

Ängelholm and around

The best aspects of uneventful **ÄNGELHOLM** are its 7km of popular gold-
en beach and its proximity to two places of interest – Helsingborg (see p.223)
is just thirty minutes south by train, while the **Kullen peninsula** beckons
enticingly to the west. With a good range of accommodation, some agreeable
restaurants and a surprisingly lively nightlife, Ängelhom isn't at all a bad place
to base yourself.

Arrival, information and accommodation

There are regular **trains** here from Båstad (17 daily; 25min), and **buses** from
Båstad (#12) and Torekov (#523). Turn right out of the station and then left
onto Järnvägsgatan, carrying on for 300m past the church to get to the old *rådhus* (town hall), in the main square, containing the **tourist office** (June & Aug
Mon–Fri 9am–6pm, Sat 9am–2pm; July Mon–Fri 9am–7pm, Sat 9am–3pm
Sun 11am–3pm; Sept to May Mon–Fri 9am–5pm; ℡043/821 30, ℮info@
turist.engelholm.se). Central Ängelholm is easy to get around on foot; one useful **bus** route is the #50, which runs from the train station to the square and
on to the harbour. To **rent a bike** – the best way to head out to the Kullen
peninsula (see p.222) – the only option is Harry's Cykel, Södra Kyrkogatan 9
(Mon–Fri 9am–6pm, Sat 9am–1pm; ℡0431/143 25; 100kr per day or 450kr
per week) with seven-speed bikes and excellent service. The shop is a bit tricky
to find; head down Storgatan, then around the back of the building on which
the "Harry's Cykel" sign appears.

For **accommodation**, the tourist office can book hotel rooms with a 30kr
fee, or will provide a list of **private rooms** (from 110kr, with a 30kr fee). There
is an STF **youth hostel** at Magnarp Strand (℡ & ℗0431/45 23 64; 120kr;
bookings necessary Nov–March), 10km north of the train station, and beyond
the beaches detailed below (local buses ply the route). For a friendly **hotel**
that's good value, try *Hotel Lilton* at Järnvägsgatan 29, just a few steps from the
square (℡0431/44 25 50, ℗www.hotel-lilton.se; ❸/❷). There are several
campsites; the most convenient for the beach is *Råbocka Camping*, at the end
of Råbockavägen (℡0431/105 43, ℗832 45). Just opposite is *Klitterbyn*, a large,
leafy holiday village of wooden chalets and apartments (℡0431/586 00, ℗195
72; ❶).

The Town

Ängelholm's efforts to sell itself concentrate not on its beaches but on its mas-
cot, a musical clay cuckoo – unglazed and easily broken toy versions of the bird
are sold everywhere – and **UFOs**. The latter have been big business here since
1946, when a railway worker, Gösta Carlsson, convinced the authorities that he
had encountered tiny people from another world, who travelled in a discuss-
shaped craft. He produced as evidence a piece of stone allegedly harder than
diamond, a strange other-worldly ring, and the supposed imprints made by the
spaceship while landing. Being a UFO guru has made Carlsson a rich man.
And these days Ängelholm hosts international UFO conferences, and the
tourist board, recognizing the potential of the theme, runs tours throughout
the summer to the mysterious site 4km away where the spaceship is meant to
have landed.

The town itself has a small historic core, created when the Danish king
Christian II ("the Good" to the Danes, "the Tyrant" to the Swedes) forced the
people of nearby Luntertun to relocate here in 1518; it's pleasant enough to

wander around but has little to detain you. The least strenuous way to explore the vicinity is a **boat trip** up the river from the harbour (early June to mid-Aug; 4 daily 40min trips, 65kr; or one daily 2hr return trip, 85kr; book on ℡ 0431/203 00). For more freedom of movement, *Skåne Marin*, which runs the tours, also rents out canoes.

Having seen the town, head for the **beaches**, 2km west of the centre. You can take the free bus that runs from the main square in summer (late June to mid-Aug every hour 10am–4pm), or walk (15–20min): from the main square, head down Järnvägsgatan, and turn right onto Havsbadsvägen; this soon turns into Råbockavägen, from where several overground paths lead to the beaches. There are no official demarcations, but in practice, 30-something singles seem to gravitate to the stretch of sand nearest the town; a little further south is the best of the family beaches; to its south is a section for the body beautifuls; while the most southerly beach is nudist (both sexes).

Eating, drinking and nightlife

The best place for **food** is at the harbour, where *Hamn Krogen*, its walls decorated with maritime artefacts, serves the best fish dishes in Ängelholm (April to mid-Aug daily 11am–1am). Their speciality is Toast Skagen – shrimps and red caviar on toast; starters cost from 23kr, main courses from 85kr. The restaurant at *Klitterhus Pensionat* is costly and on the pretentious side (one dish here is "lemon and saffron polenta with black truffle and zucchini yoghurt"). A few metres up the beach, in a whitewashed wartime bunker, *Bunken* restaurant and bar (daily 11am–2am) is much more straightforward, a buzzing, friendly place serving a diverse choice of eats, from barbecue fare to lavish fish and seafood dishes. With local and imported beers, and regular live music, it makes a perfect place to chill out till late in the evening. Back in town, *Nick's*, a bar-restaurant on Stortorget (℡ 0431/129 00), has made a valiant attempt at Mexican-ranch styling; it serves burger-type meals for 80–90kr, and reasonably priced grills, fish and fowl dishes. Nearby, the *Hotel Lilton*, Järnvägsgatan 29, has a great garden **café** (July noon–8pm), tucked away beneath a cluster of beech trees right by the river. While munching waffles and ice-cream here, take a look at the intriguing 1970s design shop Modern Möbel behind the hotel (Tues–Thurs noon–6pm, Sat 10am–3pm).

The most popular **nightclub** is *Bahnhoff Bar*, a cavernous, industrial–looking place (Thurs 7pm–2am, Fri 9pm–3am, Sat 7pm–3am). Occupying old railway buildings just beyond the present train station, it packs out with a crowd of 18- to 30-year-olds. *Kompis*, on Nybrovägen (off Industrigatan, a continuation of Järnvägsgatan), is a loud, relaxed sort of place, catering for a younger crowd.

One of the country's biggest venues for a taste of the peculiarly Swedish obsession with **foxtrots** is *Ekebo*, in the Ängelholm suburb of Munka-Ljungby, around 15km east of town (bus #507 heads there). The place has a live band playing nothing but foxtrots on Saturdays and in July it hosts Sweden's biggest dance festival, attracting a mainly 35-plus clientele – it's quite an eye-opener.

The Kullen peninsula

Jutting out like a stiletto heel, the **Kullen peninsula**, directly west of Ängelholm (though more easily reached by public transport from Helsingborg), is a highlight along the west coast. It is far flatter than the Bjäre peninsula to the north, and so makes for much easier cycling, but still undulates enough to ensure there are some great vistas. The most sensational sight is the sculptural creation of **Nimis**, but this wealthy yet unpretentious triangle of land also boasts **Arild**, one of the prettiest villages you could hope to find.

Arild

There's an undeniable attractiveness to the village of **ARILD**. To get here from Ängelholm (see p.221), take Järnvägsgatan in the opposite direction from the beaches and harbour, initially following directions to Höganäs. At Utvälinge, take the much more scenic northern coastal road leading northwest, which will take you to Arild after a five-minute drive. This waterfront cluster of homes and streets is like a picture postcard come to life – all cottages with fancy ginger-breading and grander houses standing behind. Strolling down Sankt Arilds Väg, parallel to the waterfront, you'll find a simple white chapel, **Arildskapell**, at the end of the street. Inside, the pews take the form of compartments with hand-painted doors.

A good place to **stay** is the *Strand Hotel* on Storavägen 42, just up the hill from the chapel (℡042/34 61 00, ℱ34 61 85; ❸). The sizeable bedrooms have no telephones or TVs and there's a restaurant and bar, although standards seem to have fallen in recent years.

For really good and cheap **food**, wander down to the harbourside *Hamnfiket* (summer daily 10am–6pm) where smoked fish with salads cost 45kr.

Nimis

Continuing northwest along the coast road from Arild, you'll soon reach a right turn signposted for **Himmelstorp**, a fantasically well-preserved eighteenth-century farmstead which you can wander through. Mostly, though, people come here to down ice cream and delicious home-made elderflower juice (*fläderblom*) on their way to or from the stupendous **Nimis**. Arguably Sweden's most sensational – and controversial – **living sculpture** (one that's subject to constant alteration), *Nimis* is the creation of the eccentric sculptor Lars Vilks, Professor of Art at Oslo University. A brilliantly conceived, fantastical structure comprising a tower and corridors, built out of driftwood and the odd item of furniture, the huge design looks as if it ought to collapse at the first breeze, but it effortlessly supports the hundreds of eager visitors who clamber daily over its fascinating bulk. The reason for the controversy is that *Nimis*, as a building of sorts, contravenes the protected status of the surrounding area. Vilks argues, however, that it is art and, being built from driftwood, it enhances rather than detracts from the surroundings – a view accepted by anyone you'll meet hereabouts.

You have to be reasonably fit to get to *Nimis*, as doing so involves a steep clamber down from Himmelstorp into the Kullen ridge, negotiating rough stone steps en route, though plenty of people do it carrying children. Yellow "N"s are painted on trees as you head down to the shore, giving the walk the feel of a treasure hunt.

Helsingborg and around

Long gone are the days when the locals of **HELSINGBORG** joked that the most rewarding sight here was Helsingør, the Danish town whose castle – Hamlet's celebrated Elsinore – is clearly visible, just 4km across the Öresund. Bright and pleasing, Helsingborg has a tremendous sense of buoyancy. With its beautifully developed harbour area, an explosion of stylish bars, great cafés and restaurants among the warren of cobbled streets, plus an excellent **museum**, it is one of the best town-bases Sweden has to offer.

In the past, the links between Helsingborg and Copenhagen were less convivial than they are now. After the Danes fortified the town in the eleventh

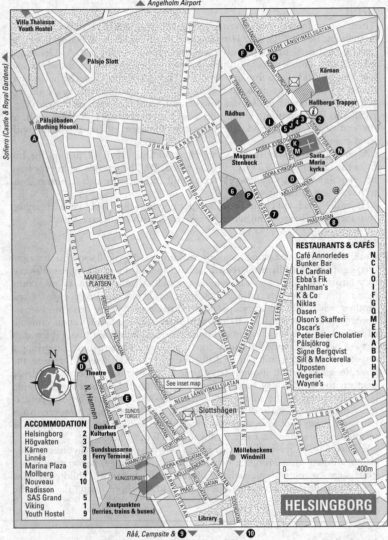

Ångelholm Airport ▲

Sofiero (Castle & Royal Gardens) ◄

RESTAURANTS & CAFÉS

Café Annorledes	N
Bunker Bar	C
Le Cardinal	L
Ebba's Fik	O
Fahlman's	I
K & Co	F
Niklas	G
Oasen	Q
Olson's Skafferi	M
Oscar's	E
Peter Beier Cholatier	K
Pålsjökrog	A
Signe Bergqvist	B
Sill & Mackerella	D
Utposten	H
Vegeriet	P
Wayne's	J

ACCOMMODATION

Helsingborg	2
Högvakten	3
Kärnen	7
Linnéa	8
Marina Plaza	6
Mollberg	4
Nouveau	10
Radisson SAS Grand	5
Viking	1
Youth Hostel	9

See inset map

Slottshagen

Möllebackens Windmill

0   400m

HELSINGBORG

Råå, Campsite & ⑨ ▼   ▼ ⑩

century, the Swedes conquered and lost it again on six violent occasions, finally winning out in 1710 under Magnus Stenbock's leadership. By this time, the Danes had torn down much of the town and on its final recapture, the Swedes contributed to the destruction by razing most of its twelfth-century castle – except for the five-metre-thick walled **keep** (*kärnen*), which still dominates the centre. By the early eighteenth century, war and epidemics had reduced the population to just seven hundred, and only with the onset of industrialization in the 1850s did Helsingborg experience a new prosperity. Shipping and the railways turned the town's fortunes round, as is evident from the formidable late nineteenth-century commercial buildings in the centre and some splendid villas to the north, overlooking the Öresund.

Arrival, information and transport

Unless approaching by car on the E6, chances are you will arrive at the harbourside **Knutpunkten**, the vast, glassy expanses of which incorporate all **ferry** and **train** terminals. On the ground floor, behind the main hall, is the **bus station**, while ticket offices and transport enquiries are in the main hall itself. Below ground level is the **train station**, handling the national SJ trains and the lilac-coloured local Pågatåg services, the latter running south down the coast to Lund and Malmö and north to Ängelholm. There is a Forex **currency exchange** office at ground level (Mon–Fri 9am–7pm, Sat & Sun 9am–4pm) and another on the first floor (daily 7am–9pm). The **Sundsbussarna** passenger-only ferry from Helsingør (see p.226) is just outside at Hamntorget, 100m away.

Outside Kuntpunkten, heading north (left) and then right into Stortorget, the **tourist office** (Sept–April Mon–Fri 9am–6pm, Sat 10am–2pm; May Mon–Fri 9am–6pm, Sat & Sun 10am–2pm; June–Aug Mon–Fri 9am–8pm, Sat & Sun 9am–5pm; ☎042/10 43 50, ⓔturistbyran@stad.helsingborg.se) is at the top of the oblong square, just beneath the steps to kärnen (the keep), on the corner of Södra Storgatan. This is the place to pick up a copy of *Helsingborg This Month*, an events guide with sections in English or the very comprehensive English-language *Helsingborg Guide* (free).

Central Helsingborg is all within easy walking distance of the centre, but for the youth hostel, the gardens of Sofiero and surrounding sights to the north (see p.228), you'll need to catch a **bus**. Tickets bought on board cost 16kr and are valid for two changes within an hour. **Bike rental** is an enjoyable option, as all the best sights are within 5km of town. The tourist office has the monopoly on rental, and charges a very pricey 125kr/day plus a 50kr returnable deposit.

Accommodation

The tourist office will book **private rooms** for upwards of 150kr per person, plus a steep 100kr booking fee; if you're staying three days or more, the booking fee is 200kr. The **youth hostel**, *Villa Thalassa*, is 2.5km north of the town centre at Dag Hammarskjöldsväg (☎042/38 06 60, ⓦwww.villathalassa.com; 180kr, Sept–May 165kr; ❶; June–Aug), next to a peaceful forest. The villa, now the hostel's main building, was built in 1903 by Von Dardel, a courtier to King Gustav Adolf at nearby Sofiero castle. Accommodation is not in the villa itself but in cabins behind, with showers an unwelcome short trek away, but the rooms at least have adjoining toilets. There are also more comfortable holiday cottages (❶) here. Breakfasts (40kr) are served in *Thalassa*'s dining room, with wonderful views over the Öresund. Bus #219 runs north from Knutpunkten to Pålsjöbaden, the old bathhouse (every 30min), from where the hostel is a signposted one-kilometre walk through really beautiful forest. Just five minutes' walk from Knutpunkten, at Järnvägsgatan 39, *Helsingborgs Vandrarhem* (☎042/14 58 50, ⓦwww.hbgturist.com; 175kr, ❶) is a far more central, although less interesting option.

There are plenty of central **hotels**. The most glamorous are around Stortorget, while cheaper establishments are to be found opposite Knutpunkten and along the roads leading away from it. All the following include breakfast in the price.

Helsingborg Stortorget 8–12   ☎02/37 18 00, ⓦwww.hkchotels.se. Lovely hotel with marble stairs, comfortable rooms and a perfect location at the foot of the steps to the castle keep. ❺/❸

Högvakten Stortorget 14 ☎042/12 03 90, ⓦwww.hotelhogvakten.com. A smaller, comfortable hotel in between the *Grand* and *Hotel Helsingborg*. Soft beds and comfy surroundings together with competitive summer rates make this a good choice. **④/③**

Kärnen Järnvägsgatan 17 ☎042/12 08 20, ⓦwww.hotelkarnan.se. Opposite Knutpunkten, this comfortable, recently renovated hotel prides itself on "personal touches", including ominous English-language homilies on each room door (no. 235, for instance, has "He who seeks revenge keeps his wounds open"). There's a small library, cocktail bar and sauna. **⑤/③**

Linnéa Prästgatan 4 ☎042/37 24 00, ⓦwww.hotell-linnea.se. Very cheap, central option, with agreeable rooms as well as apartments for three people at 5000kr per week. **④/③**

Marina Plaza Kungstorget 6 ☎042/19 21 00, ⓦwww.elite.se. Right at the harbourside, next to Knutpunkten. A big, modern and well-equipped hotel, featuring a popular restaurant, *Aqua*; a nightclub, the *Marina*; and the much-frequented *Sailor Pub*. Lively and less austere than other top-class hotels. **⑤/③**

Mollberg Stortorget 18 ☎042/37 37 00,

ⓦwww.elite.se. Every inch a premier hotel, with a grand nineteenth-century facade, elegant rooms and a brasserie. **⑤/③**

Nouveau Gasverksgatan 11 ☎042/18 53 90,ⓕ14 08 85. Despite lacking the grandeur of other Stortorget hotels, it's pretty central and has all the comforts of the top hotels, including a swimming pool and a sauna. Serves exceptionally good breakfasts (also available to nonresidents). Terrible views from the windows, though. **④/③**

Radisson SAS Grand Stortorget 8–12 ☎042/38 04 00, ⓦwww.radissonsas.com. No longer quite as exclusive as it once was since it became part of the Radisson chain, but pleasant nonetheless. Big summer reductions make it much more affordable. **⑤/③**

Viking Fågelsångsgatan 1 ☎042/14 44 20, ⓦwww.hotellviking.se. This is the place to try first. Very appealing, quiet old hotel in a splendid location close to some of the finest buildings in town. Excellent service, cosy atmosphere and really special breakfasts. **⑤/③**

The Town

The most obvious starting point is on the waterfront, by the copper **statue** of Magnus Stenbock on his charger. With your back to the Öresund and Denmark, to your left is the **Rådhus** (town hall), a heavy-handed, Neo-Gothic pile, complete with turrets and conical towers. The extravagance of provincial nineteenth-century prosperity, and the architect's admiration for medieval Italy, make it worth seeing inside (tours mid-June to Aug Mon–Fri at 10am; 40min) – in particular for the many fabulous stained-glass windows, which tell the history of the town. The ones to look out for are those in the entrance hall, depicting Queen Margaretta releasing her rival, Albert of Mecklenburg, in Helsingborg in 1395, and the last window in the city-council chamber, showing John Baptiste Bernadotte arriving at Helsingborg in 1810, having accepted the Swedish crown. When he greeted General Von Essen at the harbour, farce ensued as their elaborate gold jewellery and medals became entangled in the embrace. The original wall and ceiling frescoes were deemed too costly to restore and painted over in 1968, but are currently being uncovered.

Ferries to Helsingør

For a taste of what the locals have traditionally done for fun, buy a **ferry** ticket to **HELSINGØR** at Knutpunkten (ticket office on second floor). Scandlines' ferries run every twenty minutes (40kr return; children 6–11 half price; ☎042/18 60 00), as do Sundbussarna's (☎042/21 60 60); while Tura offer back-and-forth ferry trips (50kr, with a 40kr discount per person on meals). Ask to go on the Swedish boat, *Aurora*, as it has better restaurants and bars than the Danish ones (*Hamlet* and *Tycho Brahe*). The idea is to go back and forth all night; the only reason to get off at Helsingør, apart from having a closer look at **Helsingør Castle** (Hamlet's Elsinore – less thrilling than you may imagine), is to buy cheaper drink, although duty-free can't be bought on the boat. **Car ferries** to Denmark cost 495kr for up to five people.

Crossing over the road towards the Kattegat from the Magnus Stenbock statue, you'll see the **harbour**, divided in two by the new bridge to the pier. To the south of the bridge, at Kungsgatan 11, is the exceptional city museum **Dunkers Kulturhus** (daily 11am–6pm, Tues & Thurs till 10pm; 60kr; Ⓦ www.dunkerskulturhus.com). The white brick building contains a first-rate museum exploring the city's history. The centre is named after Henry Dunker, a local man and pioneer of galoshes – he developed the process for keeping rubber soft in winter and non-sticky in summer and his brand, Tretorn, became a world leader until the factories closed in 1979. When he died in 1962, he left 88 million krona to set up a foundation and this museum is a major recipient. If you're expecting traditional exhibitions, its dramatic special sound-effects and lighting certainly come as a surprise. The history of Helsingborg, with water as the theme, from Ice Age to present day is tremendous fun, though there's no explanation in any language so it's more sensory than educational; the history of the town's social, economic and military history has far more explanation in English though. There are also some **galleries** showing temporary art exhibitions year round. The museum contains a fine **restaurant**, overlooking the Öresund, serving light meals

To the north of the bridge, a chain of stylish contemporary apartment blocks has transformed the area from wasteland into a residential haven with sea views. The ground floor of each block is a bar-cum-café-restaurant, with hip colour schemes and plenty of steel columns and beams. The area is made for strolls on summer evenings, interspersed by sipping wine and serious eating by candlelight (see p.229).

Returning to the statue, you'll find yourself at the bottom of **Stortorget** – the central "square" so elongated that it's more like a boulevard – which slopes upwards to the east, until it meets the steps leading to the remains of the medieval **castle** (June–Aug daily 10am–8pm; Sept–May Mon–Fri & Sun 10am–6pm; 5kr). At the top is the massive castellated bulk of **kärnan** (the keep), surrounded by some fine parkland (daily: April, May & Sept 9am–4pm; June–Aug 10am–7pm; Oct–March 10am–2pm; 15kr). The keep and St Maria kyrka (see below) were the sole survivors of the ravages of war, but the former lost its military significance once Sweden finally won the day. It was due for demolition in the mid-nineteenth century, only surviving because seafarers found it a valuable landmark. What cannon fire failed to achieve, however, neglect and the weather succeeded in bringing about: the keep was a ruin when restoration began in 1894. It looks like a huge brick stood on end and is worth climbing today more for the views than the scant historical exhibitions within.

From the parkland at the keep's base, it's just a few steps to a charming **rose and magnolia garden**, exuding scent and colour all summer. To the side of this, you can wander down a rhododendron-edged path, Hallbergs Trappor, to the **St Maria kyrka** (Mon–Sat 8am–4pm, Sun 9am–6pm), which squats in its own square by a very French-looking avenue of beech trees. Resembling a basilica, and Danish Gothic in style, the church was begun in 1300 and completed a century later. Its rather plain facade belies a striking interior, with a clever contrast between the early seventeenth-century Renaissance-style ornamentation of its pulpit and gilded reredos, and the jewel-like contemporary stained-glass windows.

Walking back to Stortorget, you arrive at **Norra** and **Södra Storgatan** (the streets that meet at the foot of the stairs to the *kärnen*), which comprised Helsingborg's main thoroughfare in medieval times and so are lined with the oldest of the town's merchants' houses. As you head up Norra Storgatan, the 1681 **Henckelska house** is hidden behind a plain stuccoed wall; once you have pushed your way through the trees that have grown over the entrance archway, you'll see a rambling mix of beams and windows, with a fine little topiary garden hidden beyond a passage to the right. The garden was laid out in 1766 for the future wife of King Gustav III, who was to spend one night at the beautiful eighteenth-century **Gamlegård house** opposite.

Take the opening to the left of the old cream brick building, opposite the modern Maria Församling House, to find a real historical gem. After a fairly arduous climb of 92 steps, you'll find a handsome nineteenth-century **windmill**, which you're free to enter using a narrow ramp. Around the windmill are a number of exquisite farm cottages, and inside the low (120cm) doors is a treasure trove of items from eighteenth-century peasant interiors: straw beds, cradles, hand-painted grandmother clocks and the like. A further reward for your climb is the fact that one house, built in 1763 and brought to this site in 1909, serves **waffles**, *Möllebackens Våffelbruk* (May–Aug daily noon–8pm). Established in 1912, they still use the original recipes.

North of the centre: the Royal Gardens of Sofiero

An excursion it would be a shame to miss is to the **Royal Gardens of Sofiero** (April to mid-Sept 10am–6pm; 60kr); take bus #219 from Knutpunkten; or cycle the 4km north along the coast. Built as a summer residence by Oscar II for his wife Sofia in the 1860s, the house is not particularly attractive, as it looks more like an elaborate train station – in fact, its architect was the designer of many of Sweden's stations. The thrill here is in seeing the gardens, given by Oscar to his grandson, Gustav Adolf, on the occasion of the latter's marriage to Crown Princess Margareta in 1905. Margareta created a horticultural paradise, and, as she was a granddaughter of the British queen Victoria, the gardens are strongly influenced by English country-garden design. After Margareta died, aged 38, in 1920, the king's second wife Louise continued her work and the English theme. If you're here in late May or early June, the rhododendron collection really is something special, with a stunning array of ten thousand plants and over five hundred varieties, spreading a blanket of rainbow colours all the way down to the Öresund. In July and August, the rose gardens are the best feature, and in the last week of July entry is free to Sofiero if you bring your own paints, in honour of Princess Margareta's passion for painting.

A couple of kilometres south of Sofiero, near the youth hostel (see p.225), is **Pålsjö Slott**, an immaculate eighteenth-century toy-town palace. While the building has nothing to see inside – it's been converted into offices – you are free to wander behind to its gardens. Walking through a long, narrow avenue of gnarled beech trees, which have become knotted together, and on towards the Öresund, you'll come to a beautiful pathway, Landborgspromenade. Head south along it, back towards town, and you'll pass some large, Art Nouveau villas in fine gardens. At the end of the path (where bus #7 runs into town) stands **Pålsjöbaden**, a classic 1880 bathhouse on stilts (Mon, Wed & Thurs 9am–7.30pm, Tues 6.45am–9pm, Fri 6.45am–7pm, Sat & Sun 8am–5pm; 25kr).

Eating, drinking and nightlife

Some excellent food **shops**, useful for picnic fare, are clustered on the square containing St Maria kyrka (see p.227), notably Maratorgets on the south side of the square, selling fresh fruit, and the adjacent Bengtsons Ost, a specialist cheese shop. The city has a good range of excellent **restaurants**, including a host of stylish **bar-restaurants** along the restored harbourfront. These places can seem samey, though, and it's the older restaurants that continue to provide the variety. During the day, there are some great **cafés** and *konditori*. Helsingborg also has some happening **clubs** for a young crowd.

Cafés

Café Annorledes Södra Storgatan 15. A friendly café with a genteel 1950s atmosphere.

Cyber Space Café Karlsgatan 9. Plenty of screens – and espresso to keep you hyper. There's no minimum charge for Internet access – computer use is charged by the minute, with 30min costing around 25kr. Daily 10am–10pm.

Ebba's Fik Stortorget 20. The most fun café in town: its enthusiastic owners have collected an amazing jumble of 1950s and 1960s furnishings, and the jukebox belts out mambo, bebop and jive. Every detail of the era – from crockery to menu board – is here. The cakes are also very good and you can now buy fish and chips and delicious home-made Swedish beefburgers too. At the back is a bookshop and authentic Fifties bric-a-brac store.

Fahlmans Stortorget 11. This classic bakery/café has been serving elaborate cakes and pastries since 1914 and is *the* place for decadent apple meringue pie – a meal in itself. Also try the coconut and marzipan confections or filling sandwiches.

K & Co Nedre Långwinkelsgatan 9. The best of the laid-back style cafés in town. Very friendly, serving great muffins, cakes and filling ciabattas and panini.

Peter Beier Chocalatier Mariagatan 2. A chocoholics' dream, with an incredible molten chocolate fountain in the window and furnished entirely in shades of, you've guessed it, chocolate, this Danish-owned emporium is a must if you fancy drooling or devouring the stuff over a coffee.

Signe Bergqvist Drottninggatan. Dating from 1889, this *konditori* is the oldest in town, but far less busy than *Fahlmans* (see above) and not quite as good.

Wayne's Stortorget 8. Hip and central, this is part of the growing empire of Wayne's laid-back coffee houses. This place is housed within a grand old building on the main square. The coffee's great, though the cakes can look better than they taste. A relaxed spot and good for young, hip people-watching.

Restaurants

Bunker Bar Near the far end of North Harbour, just 50m from *Sill & Mackerella* (see below). Very crowded, for both lunch and dinner with inevitable concentration on good fish.

Niklas Nedre Långvinkelsgatan 10, opposite Jacob Hansens Hus ☏042/28 00 50. Helsingborg's most exclusive and priciest restaurant is starkly stylish. Truffle-glazed cabbage, local oysters or quail dishes will set you back around 300kr for a main dish. If money's no object at all, feast on the à la carte menu plus a "dessert circus" for a whopping 990kr. The wine list is the best in the city.

Olson's Skafferi Mariagatan 6 ☏042/14 07 80. An absolute must. Despite its Swedish name, this is the very best Italian restaurant in town. Not a pizza in sight: they simply offer wonderfully prepared fish, meat and pasta dishes in a relaxed atmosphere using Italian bases with Swedish overtones. The zabaglione is to drool over.

Oscar's Sundstorget ☏042/11 25 21. At the harbour. The simple decor belies how posh this fish restaurant is. A fine place, longer established but less stylish than Niklas.

Pålsjökrog Attached to the old bathhouse, Drottninggatan 151, Pålsjöbaden, 2km north of the centre ☏042/14 97 30. This fine place is run by an architect, who designed it to feel like a Swedish country eating-house. With traditional, well-presented Swedish food, it's a place for special occasions. Try the melted Toblerone fondue. Main courses 150kr.

Sill & Mackerella End of the North Harbour. This simple-looking place – the one with the white roof – is excellent for fresh fish dishes.

Utposten Stortorget 17 ☏042/28 15 50. Very stylish decor – a pleasing mix of rustic and industrial – at this great, varied Swedish restaurant. Try the delicate and filling seafood-and-fresh-salmon stew at 89kr. Two courses 140kr.

Vegeriet Järnvägsgatan 25 opposite Knutpunkten. ☏042/24 03 03. A good vegetarian café, with simple food that's very good value. There's an elaborate menu, including a wide range of starters, and a small wine list. Hot dishes cost 59–110kr.

Bars and clubs

The glamorous North Harbour **bars** are seen more as places for wine and beer drinking than as restaurants, though they do serve European-influenced food with varying specializations. All located at ground level in the area's upmarket apartment buildings, the bars share a smart, casual clientele of 20- to 40-somethings, in designer-industrial surroundings. At the northern end of the harbour, you'll find *Bunker Bar* and *Sill & Mackerella*, two good-value eating places (see "Restaurants", above).

Jazz Clubben Nedre Långvinkelsgatan 22. Sweden's biggest jazz club and well worth a visit on Wed, Fri and Sat evenings for live jazz, Dixieland, blues, Irish folk and blues jam sessions.

Le Cardinal Södra Kyrkogatan 9. Piano bar and nightclub with a steak-oriented restaurant. The first-floor disco is usually busy, while the second-floor piano bar is quieter, with a roulette table. Cover is 60–70kr and you need to be 25 to get in. Often closed during summer; call ☏042/18 71 71 to check.

Marina Kungstorget 6. At the *Marina Plaza* hotel by the harbour. A very popular nightclub with quite a sophisticated atmosphere; minimum age 24. Thurs–Sat 10pm–3am.

OZ emellan North Harbour. The first bar you encounter as you walk north from Hamn Torget along the harbour. Serves light meals and à la carte meat, fish and vegetarian dishes. Noon–1am.

Piren Hamn Torget. Opposite Sundsbussarna at the harbour, in the old black wooden building that was once the train station. A café by day, it comes alive after dark when it becomes a club with a student-dive atmosphere. Very popular.

Sailor's Inn Kungstorget 6. Part of the *Marina Plaza* hotel at the harbour. A post-dinner, pre-disco drinking spot – extremely popular, too. Mon–Wed 3pm–midnight, Thurs & Fri 3pm–1am, Sat 2pm–1am.

Telegrafen Norra Storgatan 14. A long-term favourite, this cosy bar is full of oddities such as stuffed animals wearing sunglasses. Lively atmosphere; good lunches at 58kr. Daily 11.30am–midnight.

Tivoli Hamn Torget. Lively place occupying the main part of the former train station opposite Knutpunkten, where you'll find lots of concerts and events. There's also a restaurant, *Vinyl Baren*, which is indeed filled with red vinyl bench seats and pop art.

Gay Helsingborg

Gay life in Helsingborg revolves around the RFSL-run **Gay centre** at Pålsgatan 1 (☏042/12 35 32), close to the concert hall, ten minutes' walk north from Knutpunkten. Inside, there's a welcoming **café** (Mon–Fri 10am–5pm) and a **pub** (Fri 10am–2am). A **club**, *Da Klab*, runs regular theme nights throughout the summer (☏042/21 19 11, ⓦ www.daklab.com; 70kr guests, 50kr for members).

Listings

Airport The nearest airport for domestic flights is at Ängelholm, 30km north of town; take the bus from Knutpunkten (1hr before flight departure). For international services, you'll need to go to Copenhagen's Kastrup airport (take the Kustlinjen bus from Knutpunkten; 2hr) or Malmö (see p.238).

Buses The daily bus for Stockholm leaves from Knutpunkten; reservations are essential (☏0625/240 20), but tickets can only be bought on the bus (Mon–Thurs 250kr, Fri–Sun; 355kr). Buses for Gothenburg leave daily (Mon–Thurs 140kr, Fri–Sun; 200kr); tickets must be bought from the bus information section at the train booking office.

Car rental Avis, Garnisonsgatan 2 ☏042/15 70 80; Budget, Gustav Adolfsgatan 47 ☏042/12 50 40; Europcar, Muskötgatan 1 ☏042/17 01 15;

Hertz, Bergavägen 4 ☏042/17 25 40.

Exchange Forex in Knutpunkten (first floor) or Järnvägsgatan 13 (June–Aug 7am–9pm; Sept–May 8am–9pm).

Internet access There's a Net café at Norra Kyrkogatan 17, by St Maria kyrka (Mon–Thurs 11am–9pm, Fri & Sat 11am–6pm, Sun noon–9pm).

Pharmacy Björnen, Drottninggatan 14 (Mon–Fri 9am–6pm, Sat 9am–3pm).

Post office Stortorget 17 (Mon–Fri 9am–6pm, Sat 10am–1pm).

Trains The Pågatåg trains from Knutpunkten require a ticket bought from an automatic machine on the platform; international rail passes are valid. It's 50kr one-way to Lund and 60kr one-way to Malmö.

Lund

"There is a very tangible Lund spirit – those with it have. . . an ironic distance to everything, including themselves and Lund, a barb to deflate pompous self-importance," wrote the Swedish essayist Jan Mårtensson. His compatriot, poet Peter Ortman, for his part once described what he termed "Lund syndrome":

"a mix of paranoia, exhibitionism and megalomania". Whatever it is about the place, there is indeed a special spirit to **LUND** – a sense of tolerance (it's more relaxed than other Swedish cities), and a belief that people should be judged by what they do, not by what they have.

A few kilometres inland and 54km south of Helsingborg, Lund's reputation as a glorious old **university city** is well founded. An ocean of bikes is the first image to greet you at the train station, and like Oxford – with which Lund is usually aptly compared – there is a bohemian, laid-back eccentricity in the air. With its twelfth-century Romanesque **cathedral**, its medieval streets lined with a variety of architectural styles, and its wealth of cafés and restaurants, Lund is an enchanting little city that could well captivate you for a couple of days. It has a wide range of **museums**, a couple of them excellent, a mix of architectural grandeur plus the buzz of student life that lends Lund its distinctive charm. While Lund does lose much of its atmosphere during the summer months some places remain open through June to August.

Arrival and information

Trains arrive at the western edge of the centre. **Buses** use the station south of Mårtenstorget, with many also stopping outside the train station. Flying into Sturup **airport**, located to the east of Malmö, you can catch the hourly Flygbuss into the centre (Mon–Fri 5.30am–7.30pm, Sat 6.30am–5.30pm; 40min; 80kr).

From the train station, the centre is two minutes' walk, and everything of interest is within easy reach, with all the sights no more than ten minutes' away.

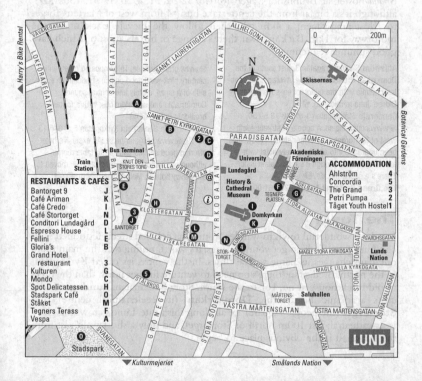

The **tourist office** is at Kyrkogatan 11, opposite the Domkyrkan (May & Sept Mon–Fri 10am–5pm, Sat 10am–2pm; June–Aug Mon–Fri 10am–6pm, Sat & Sun 10am–2pm; Oct–April Mon–Fri 10am–5pm; ☎046/35 50 40, @turist-byran@lund.se); they can provide maps and copies of *I Lund*, a monthly diary of events with museum and exhibition listings (from June to August it's bilingual, with English listings).

You can **rent a bike** at Harry's *Cykelaffar*, Banvaktsgatan 2 (☎046/211 69 46; Mon–Fri 9am–6pm; 90kr a day); for weekend use you'll have to pay to keep the bike until the following Monday, when the shop reopens. The frequent sales of military bikes, most of which take place in Clemenstorget (a couple of minutes' walk northwest of the tourist office), offer excellent value (a typical price is 300kr), particularly if you plan to do a lot of cycling around the region. Large, sturdy and khaki green, these bikes are almost indestructible; you can always sell them back once you're finished with them.

Accommodation

There is a decent range of **accommodation** on offer in Lund – nearly all of it in the centre. The tourist office will book **private rooms** for 175kr per person, plus a 50kr booking fee. You may be surprised at the sight of the town's STF **youth hostel**, *Tåget,* housed in the carriages of a 1940s train at Vävaregatan 22, through the tunnel behind the train station (☎046/14 28 20, ☎32 05 68; 110kr). The novelty soon wears off, however, when you're crammed in three-tier bunks with rope hoists to help pull yourself up; furthermore, the kitchens and showers are pretty basic. An alternative is the *La Strada* hostel, at Brunnshögsvägen (☎046/32 32 51, ☎30 39 31; 130kr, ❶), although it's a bit far from the centre: take bus #4 from west of Martens Torget to Klosterängsvägen, a 4km trip, then follow the bicycle track under the motorway for 1km. Back in town, there's a range of **hotels**, most of which have good summer reductions.

Ahlström Skomakaregatan 3, just south of the Domkyrkan ☎046/211 01 74. Average, very central cheapie with the option of en-suite rooms. Closed June to mid-Aug. ❷

Concordia Stålbrogatan 1 ☎046/13 50 50, @www.concordia.se. A couple of streets southwest of Stortorget, this former student hostel has been upgraded into a very homely hotel with attentive service, though it's rather plain inside. There's a sauna too. ❹/❸

The Grand Bantorget 1 ☎046/280 61 00, @www.grandilund.se. This imposing nineteenth-century pink-sandstone edifice straddles an entire side of a small, stately and central square. Comfortable and unpretentious, with a fantastic breakfast buffet. ❻/❸

Petri Pumpa Sankt Petri Kyrkogatan 7 ☎046/13 55 19, @www.petripumpa.se. An exclusive hotel offering good service and comfortable rooms, although its famous restaurant has now moved to the *Savoy* hotel in Malmö (see p.240). ❺/❸

The Town

Lund is a wonderful town to wander around, its cobbled streets festooned with climbing roses. To help get your bearings, it's worth noting that the main thoroughfare changes its name several times. In the centre, it's called Kyrkogatan; to the north, Bredgatan (there's no need to venture further north than the pretty old brick house at no. 16); to the south, Stora Södergatan. **Lundagård** (the city's academic heart), the **Domkyrkan** (its ecclesiastical centre), and **Stortorget** (the people's square) are all along this route. Lund's crowning glory is its cathedral; just 100m north of Stortorget, and only a short walk east from the station, it is the obvious place to begin.

The Domkyrkan

The magnificent **Domkyrkan** (Mon, Tues & Fri 8am–6pm, Wed & Thurs 8am–7.15pm, Sat 9.30am–5pm, Sun 9.30am–7.30pm; guided tours 3pm, free) is built of storm-cloud charcoal and white stone, giving it an imposing mono-chrome appearance. Before going inside, have a look round the back of the building; on the way there, you'll notice the grotesque animal and bird gargoyles over the side entrances, their features blunted by eight centuries of weathering. At the very back, the most beautiful part of the exterior, the three-storey **apse** above the crypt, is revealed, crowned with an exquisite gallery.

The majestic **interior** is surprisingly unadorned, an elegant mass of watery-grey, ribbed stone arches and stone-flagged flooring. One of the world's finest masterpieces of Romanesque architecture, the cathedral was built in the twelfth century when Lund became the first independent archbishopric in Scandinavia, laying the foundation for a period of wealth and eminence that lasted until the advent of Protestantism. There are several striking features to admire, such as the elaborately carved fourteenth-century choir stalls depicting Old Testament scenes, and the grotesque carvings hidden beneath the seats. The most vividly coloured feature is just to the left of the entrance, an amazing **astronomical clock** dating from the 1440s, which shows hours, days, weeks and the courses of the sun and moon in the zodiac. Each day at noon and 3pm, the clock also reveals its ecclesiastical Punch-and-Judy show, as two knights pop out and clash swords as many times as the clock strikes, followed by little mechanical doors opening to trumpet-blowing heralds and the Three Wise Men trundling slowly to the Virgin Mary.

The dimly lit and dramatic **crypt**, beneath the apse, has been left almost untouched since the twelfth century, and should not be missed. Here, the thick smattering of what look like tombstones is really comprised of memorial slabs, brought down to the crypt from just above; but there is one actual tomb – that of Birger Gunnarsson, Lund's last archbishop. A short man from a poor family, Gunnarsson chose the principal altar-facing position for his tomb, dictating that his stone effigy above it should be tall and regal. Two **pillars** here are gripped by stone figures – one of a man, another of a woman and child. Local legend has it that Finn the Giant built the cathedral for St Lawrence; in return, unless the saint could guess his name, Finn wanted the sun, the moon, or the saint's eyes. Lawrence was just preparing to end his days in blindness when he heard Finn's wife boasting to her baby, "Soon Father Finn will bring some eyes for you to play with." The relieved saint rushed to Finn declaring the name. The livid giant, his wife and child rushed to the crypt to pull down the columns, and were instantly turned to stone. Even without the fable, the column-hugging figures are fascinating to view.

Around the Domkyrkan: museums

Just behind the cathedral, the **History and Cathedral Museum**, on Sandgatan (Tues–Fri 11am–1pm; free), is for the most part rather dull unless you have specialist interests in ecclesiastical history. The statues from Scånian churches, in the medieval exhibition, deserve a look though, mainly because of the way they are arranged – a mass of Jesuses and Marys bunched together in groups. The crowd of Jesuses hanging on crosses have an ominousness worthy of Hitchcock, while in the next room all the Madonnas are paired off with the baby Jesuses.

A few minutes' walk north, on Tegnerplatsen, is the town's best museum, **Kulturen** (May–Sept daily 11am–5pm; Oct–April daily noon–4pm, Thurs till

9pm; 50kr). It's easy to spend the best part of a day just wandering around this privately owned open-air museum, a virtual town of perfectly preserved cottages, farms, merchants' houses, gardens and even churches, brought from seven Swedish regions and encompassing as many centuries. The displays don't have English translations, though you can buy a guidebook in English covering all the exhibits (100kr).

A few streets north from Finngatan, there's another stimulating museum, **Skissernas Museum**, Finngatan 2 (Museum of Sketches; Tues–Sat noon–4pm, Sun 1–5pm; free; 30kr for special exhibitions; ☎046/222 72 83, ⓦwww1.ldc.lu.se/skissernas), which is due to open again after extensive renovation in 2004. Inside is a fascinating collection of preliminary sketches and original maquettes of works of art from around the world. One room is full of work by all the major Swedish artists, while in the international room are sketches by Chagall, Matisse, Léger, Miró and Dufy; the best-known sculptural sketches here are by Picasso and Henry Moore. Outside, the sculptures on display include preliminary versions of pieces found in town squares all over Sweden.

Botanical Gardens

An antidote to museum fatigue, the **Botanical Gardens** are as much a venue for picnicking and chilling out as a botanical experience (mid-May to mid-Sept 6am–9.30pm; mid-Sept to mid-May 6am–8pm, greenhouses noon–3pm). From Finngatan, the gardens are a few minutes' stroll away; head southeast down to the end of the street, then turn left into Pålsjövägen and right into Olshögsvägen. The greenhouses and rock gardens are the best areas to view; the rarest sights here are the Far Eastern paper-mulberry trees and the huge tulip trees – part of the same family as magnolias – with masses of flowers in June.

Eating, drinking and nightlife

There are plenty of charming places to eat and drink in Lund, many of them associated with the university: certain **coffee houses** are institutions with the students, and a number of the better **restaurants** are attached to student bodies or museums. This student connection keeps prices low, especially for beer. During the past few years, a rash of **cafés** have opened up around town, and there's mostly little to choose between them – they invariably serve big mugs of coffee, filled ciabattas and cakes and have a youthful, laid back ambience. One or two perennials still stand out though (see below).

For provisions, the **market** at Mårtenstorget, *Saluhallen*, sells a range of fish, cheeses and meats, including Lund's own tasty speciality sausage, knake. On Sankt Petri Kyrkogata, *Widerbergs Charkuteri* is a long-established food shop, brimming with cooked meats and baguettes for the ultimate picnic, while *Bentsons Ost*, Klostergatan 9, is a must for cheese-lovers (Mon–Fri 9.30am–6pm, Sat 9.30am–2pm).

When it comes to **nightlife**, it's worth knowing that the university is divided into "Nations", or colleges, each named after different geographical areas of Sweden and with its own strong identity. Each nation has its own bar that's active two nights a week, and there are also regular discos. Perhaps unsurprisingly, *Lund Nation*, based in the big red-brick house on Agardhsgatan, is the biggest, with an inexpensive bar. *Småland's Nation* on Kastanjatan, off Mortenstorget (☎046/12 06 80), is the hippest, most left-wing nation. Both are known for supporting music and hosting regular gigs by all the best indie bands. Another lively place on the alternative music scene is the bright lilac-painted **Mejeriet** at the end of Stora Södergatan (daily 9am–5pm), the street running south from the main square. Converted into a music and cultural centre in the 1970s, this former dairy has a **concert hall**, attracting artists as diverse as Iggy Pop and the Bulgarian Women's Choir, as well as an **art-house cinema** (concert information on ☎046/12 38 11, cinema details on ☎046/14 38 13). Its stylish café, whose walls are decorated with 1950s vacuum cleaners, serves wonderful chocolate cake.

Cafés

Café Ariman Kungsgatan 2. Attached to the Nordic Law Department, this classic left-wing coffee house is located in a striking red-brick building. It's frequented by wannabe writers and artists, with goatees, ponytails and blond dreadlocks predominating. Cheap snacks and coffee.

Café Credo Behind the cathedral. This 500-year-old refectory serves coffee and snacks; though the food's nothing special, the setting is very peaceful.

Espresso House Stora Grabrodersgatan 4. Excellent coffee house with big bagels and ciabattas and a lovely easy-going atmosphere, popular with students.

Conditori Lundagård Kyrkogatan 17. *The* classic student *konditori* from the days when this was the only student hangout in which to drink tea and smoke. A delightful institution with excellent caricatures of professors adorning the walls. Justly famous for its apple meringue pie, though sadly closed throughout summer.

Mondo Corner of Sankt Petri Kyrkogatan and Kyrkogatan. In a quaint, beamed house, this newcomer to the café scene serves bagels, cheesecake and brownies. The large baguettes are good value.

Stadspark Café Stadspark at the end of Nygatan. This old wooden pavilion, fronted by a sea of white plastic garden furniture, is busy with families. Big baguettes will fill you up for 35–40kr. Wed nights in summer the park is filled with live music.

Café Stortorget Stortorget. Housed in a National Romantic building that was formerly a bank, this place has walls covered with black-and-white shots of musicians and actors. A large focaccia with a crab-meat, cheese or meat filling costs 56kr.

Restaurants

Bantorget 9 Bantorget 9 ☎046/32 02 00. This very chic restaurant with old, painted ceilings is an established haven for gourmets. The Swedish/International menu is expensive, but bar meals come in under 100kr.

Fellini Banggatan 6, opposite train station ☎046/13 80 20. Stylish and popular Italian restaurant that's all chrome and stripped wood. Two-course meals for 135kr.

Gloria's Sankt Petri Kyrkogatan 9. Serving American food, *Gloria's* is very popular with students and tourists of all ages. Local bands play Friday and Saturday nights. There's a big, lively garden area at the back.

Grand Hotel restaurant Bantorget 1. Part of the *Grand Hotel* (see p.232). Boasting the revered chef Mats Petersson poached from Malmö's *Kocksa Krogen*, this hotel restaurant serves local specialities with international influences. Prices are surprisingly sensible, with mains costing 100–230kr.

Kulturen Just in front of the Kulturen museum. Beneath a giant copper beech and facing ancient rune stones, this busy café, bar and restaurant also attracts people for its cheap beer (28kr). There's a good lunch with a vegetarian option (59kr), although service can be slow.

Spot Delicatessen Klostergatan 14 ☎046/12 43 31. Following on from the success of its sister restaurant in Malmö, this is a wonderful spot for lunch on Italian dishes in the restaurant downstairs, while upstairs delicious Swedish fayre is served. Mon–Sat 11.30am–10pm.

Restaurant Stäket Stora Södergatan 6 ☎046/211 93 67. A step-gabled vaulted house built in 1570 is the setting for this meat-oriented place – seemingly every type of steak can be had for 140–175kr.

Tegners Terass Next to Akademiska Föreningen, the student union. Forget any preconceptions about student cafés being tatty, stale sandwich bars. Lunch for 55kr (49kr with student card) is self-service and you eat as much as you like from a delicious spread.

Bars and clubs

John Bull Pub Bantorget, adjacent to the *Grand Hotel*. Shabby, British-style traditional pub.

Basilika Stora Södergatan 13 ☎046/211 66 60. Hip and firmly established place, just a few steps south of Stortorget. There's a café, and a bar with a huge drinks list (shots at 39kr, cocktails at 53kr), while events (comedy nights, cabaret) and concerts are also staged; there's a minimum age of 20 for these. Closed Sun.

T-Bar Sandgatan 2 ☎046/13 13 33, ⊛www.t-bar.nu. Set in the Tegners Terass building next to the student union, this student nightclub with restaurant seems to change its name annually. With a student card, people aged 18 and over can get in to the club, otherwise it's strictly over-23s only. Thurs 7pm–3am; free entry till midnight, then 20kr.

Vespa Karl II Vägen 1. Chic, well-priced bar with Italian styling in Vespa red; more of a post-grad hangout than the usual student haunts. Also offers good pizzas (62–88kr).

Listings

Buses Information on local and regional buses on ☎020/567 567.

Car rental Avis, Byggmästaregatan 11 ☎046/14 50 30; Budget, Banggatan 13 ☎046/211 34 67; Europcar, Malmövägen Höjebro ☎046/19 79 39; Hertz, Västra Stationstorget 1☎046/30 60 12.

Currency exchange Forex, Bangatan 8 ☎046/32 34 10 (Mon–Fri 8am–7pm, Sat 8am–4pm).

Internet access Studio 9, Lilla Gråbrödersgatan 2 ☎046/70 00 96 (Mon–Fri 10am–midnight, Sat noon–1am, Sun 1–11pm; 10kr/10 mins).

Medical treatment University Hospital,

Getingevägen 4 ☎046/17 10 00.

Police Byggmästaregatan 1 ☎046/16 50 00.

Post Office Banggatan 10, Mon–Fri 8am–6pm, Sat 10am–2pm.

Taxis Taxi Lund ☎046/13 80 00; Royal Cab ☎046/20 20 20.

Travel agent Good deals dramatically cheaper than elsewhere in southern Sweden are found at Caribbean Resor (Golden Sand Tours), Lilla Gråbersgatan 2 (☎046/19 59 90, @caribbeanresor@telia.com)

Malmö

Founded in the late thirteenth century, **MALMÖ** was once Denmark's second most important city, after Copenhagen. The high density of herring in the sea off the Malmö coast – it was said that the fish could be scooped straight out with a trowel – brought ambitious German merchants flocking to the city; the striking fourteenth-century St Petri kyrka in the city centre is heavily influenced by German styles. Eric of Pomerania gave Malmö its most significant medieval boost, when, in the fifteenth century, he built the castle, endowed with its own mint, and gave Malmö its own flag – the gold-and-red griffin of his own family crest. It wasn't until the Swedish king Karl X marched his armies across the frozen Öresund to within striking distance of Copenhagen in 1658 that the Danes were forced into handing back the counties of Skåne, Blekinge and Bohuslän to the Swedes. For Malmö, too far from its own (uninterested) capital, this meant a period of stagnation, cut off from nearby Copenhagen. Not until the full thrust of industrialization, triggered by the tobacco merchant Frans Suell's enlargement of the harbour in 1775 (his jaunty bronze likeness, on Norra Vallgatan opposite the train station, overlooks his handiwork), did Malmö begin its dramatic commercial recovery. In 1840, boats began regular trips to Copenhagen, and Malmö's great Kockums shipyard was opened; limestone quarrying, too, became big business here in the nineteenth century.

During the last few decades of the twentieth century, Malmö was facing commercial crisis after a series of economic miscalculations, which included investing heavily in the shipping industry as it went into decline in the Seventies. But the past few years have witnessed a dramatic renaissance in the city's fortunes, reflected in the upbeat, thoroughly likeable atmosphere pervading the town today. With a very attractive medieval centre, a myriad of cobbled and mainly pedestrianized streets, full of busy restaurants and bars, Malmö has bounced back with style. Since the opening of the **Öresund bridge** linking the town to Copenhagen, the city's fortunes have been further improved, with Danes discovering what this gateway to Sweden has to offer, as opposed to the one-way traffic of Swedes to Denmark in the past.

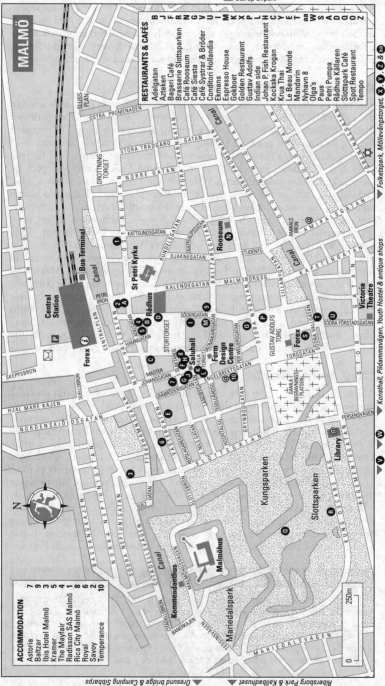

MALMÖ

▲ Sturup airport

► Folketspark, Möllevångstorget ⊗ ⓥ Ⓩ & ⓐⓐ

► Konsthall, Pildammsvägen, Youth Hostel & antique shops

▼ Öresund bridge & Camping Sibbarps

◄ Ribersborg Park & Kallbadhuset

RESTAURANTS & CAFÉS

Adelgatan	B
Azteken	J
Bageri Café	F
Brasserie Slottsparken	R
Café Rooseum	N
Café Siesta	G
Café Systrar & Bröder	V
Conditori Hollandia	I
Ekmans	M
Espresso House	K
Gokboet	X
Golden Restaurant	P
Gustav Adolfs	L
Indian side	H
Johan P. Fish Restaurant	C
Kockska Krogan	Y
Krua Thai	E
Le Beau Monde	T
Mandarin	W
Nyhavn 8	aa
Olga's	S
Paus	A
Petri Pumpa	D
Rådhus Källaren	Q
Slottspark Café	O
Spot Restaurant	Z
Tempo	

ACCOMMODATION

Astoria	7
Baltzar	9
Ibis Hotel Malmö	5
Kramer	4
The Mayfair	1
Radisson SAS Malmö	8
Rica City Malmö	6
Royal	2
Savoy	3
Temperance	10

N

0   250m

Beyond the compact centre, Malmö is endowed with some really superb **parks**, a long and popular **beach** and some interesting cultural diversions south of the centre. **Möllevångstorget**, the culturally diverse neighbourhood to the south, beyond Folketspark, has become the enclave of the well-heeled bohemians. The city's lively **nightlife** is another inducement to stay a while.

Arrival and information

The **train station**, aptly named Central Station, is where SJ national trains and the Danish-built (and very comfortable) Kustpilen trains from Denmark and from Kristianstad, Karlskrona and Linköping arrive and leave. The frequent Pågatåg local trains to and from Helsingborg/Lund and Ystad use platforms 9–13 at the back. It's only a two-minute walk to the main square where you'll find the main **bus terminal**; frequent buses to and from Lund, Kastrup airport (in Denmark), Kristianstad/Kalmar and Ystad all stop here. Buses from Stockholm, Helsingborg and Gothenburg arrive behind Central Station. Flying into Sturup **airport** to the east of Malmö, you can use the hourly Flygbuss to get into the city centre (Mon–Fri 5.30am–7.30pm, Sat 6.30am–5.30pm; 40min; 80kr).

The **tourist office** is inside Central Station (June–Aug Mon–Fri 9am–8pm, Sat & Sun 10am–5pm; Sept–May Mon–Fri 9am–5pm, Sat 10am–2pm; ☎040/34 12 00, ⓦ www.malmo.se/turism). Here, you can pick up a wealth of free information, including an English-language listings brochure, *Malmö This Month*. An excellent weekly guide to the hip and happening is the Swedish-only *Sydsvenskan Dygnet Runt,* available free all over the place; not only does this paper give up-to-the-minute information on films, concerts and sports events, it lists and grades the trendiest places to eat, with categories ranging from "*absolut*" (the best) to "*aldrig*" (meaning "don't touch"). Opposite the tourist office is a Forex **currency exchange** office (daily 8am–9pm).

City transport

Although the city centre is easy to walk around, its central squares and streets all interlinked, you'll need to use the city **bus** service to reach some of the sights and places to stay. Each ride costs 14kr (tickets valid for 1hr); a 200kr magnetic card is also available, which reduces bus fares and can be used by several people at the same time. All tickets are sold on the bus. A useful two-day ticket is the **Öresund Runt** (Round the Öresund; 199kr, under-16s half price), which covers whichever ferry, train and hydrofoil route you choose (or any part of it) to Lund, Helsingborg, Helsingør and across to Copenhagen. You can buy tickets at the tourist office, or by calling ☎0771/77 77 77, ⓦ www.skanetrafiken.skane.se.

When using **taxis**, it's worth stopping several until you find one at a reasonable rate. If you use a minicab (cheaper than using taxis), be on your guard against being cheated on fares, an increasingly common practice used on tourists. To give a rough idea of costs, a trip from Malmö centre to the airport is around 260kr.

The Malmö Card

The very useful **Malmökortet** (Malmö Card; available for 1, 2 or 3 days; 120kr, 150kr or 180kr respectively) entitles you to free museum entry, free parking at public car parks, a guided bus tour of the city and unlimited bus journeys within town. It also gives various other discounts on transport and certain sights around the city, and at cinemas and concerts. With the card, you'll get fifty percent off at Sibbarps and Ribersborgs, an open-air bathhouse and a sauna (see p.244).

There are several **tours** around the city that are worth considering. A ninety-minute guided **sightseeing tour** (late June to early Aug noon; 100kr; half price with Malmö Card, see box) leaves from the tourist office, but it's pricey and conducted in Swedish, English and German, so progress through the streets is necessarily slow. Alternatively you can do your own guided tour on city bus #20; the tourist office will give you a specially designed brochure that details areas of interest en route. The buses also leave from outside the tourist office (several buses an hour; both the bus ride and brochure are free with the Malmö Card; otherwise 12kr). **Canal boat tours** leave daily from the canal opposite the *Savoy* hotel (late June to mid-Aug daily 11am–7pm; rest of year till 4pm; book on ☎040/611 74 88; 1hr; 80kr). Alternatively, **pedal boats** let you tour around the canal network at your own pace. They're moored at Amiralsbron (mid-April to Aug daily 11am–7pm; 90kr per hour, half-price with Malmö Card).

To strike out to the south of the city or further afield, **bike rental** is a good idea. The best place is Fridhems Cykelaffär at Tessinsvägen 13 (Mon–Fri 9am–6pm, Sat 10am–1pm; 65kr/day; ☎040/26 03 35). Head down Citadellvägen past Malmöhus, take first left then right onto Tessinsvägen. Otherwise, try Cykel Kliniken, at the back of the car park directly behind the train station (summer Mon–Fri 10am–6pm, Sat 11am–2pm; rest of year shorter times; ☎040/611 66 66), where new, three-speed unisex bikes are a very steep 120kr a day.

Accommodation

Malmö's **youth hostel**, the STF-run *Vandrarhem*, Backavägen 18 (☎040/822 20, ⓦwww.meravsverige.nu; 175kr; closed mid-Dec to mid-Jan) is 5km south from the city centre, pushed up against the E6 motorway, but new owners have made it a friendly place. To get there, take bus #21A from Centreplan to Vandrarhemmet, cross over the junction past the traffic lights and take the first right; the hostel is signposted to the left. The nearest **campsite**, *Camping Sibbarps*, is at Strandgatan 101 in Limhamn (☎040/15 51 65), not far from the Öresund bridge. Conveniently near the campsite is Sibbarps Saltsjöbad, a fine, open-air bathhouse with a wood-fired sauna (a 10min ride on express bus #82).

There are some really good and surprisingly affordable **hotels** in Malmö: the city is eager to attract tourists, and competition between the hotels can be fierce. Being a commercial city, prices are likely to plummet at the weekend, which for the hotel trade means Friday and Saturday nights; it's worth trying to persuade your hotel to charge you the weekend rate on Sunday night as well. Most hotels also reduce their rates in the summer.

Astoria Gråbrödersgatan 7 ☎040/786 60, ⓦwww.astoria.gs2.com. A few minutes from the train station across the canal, this is a good, plain hotel. ❸

Baltzar Södergatan 20 ☎040/66 57 00, ⓦwww.baltzarhotel.se. Very central (between the two main squares), this is a swanky place done out in swags and flourishes that are more British than Swedish in design. ❺/❸

Ibis Hotel Malmö City Citadellvägen 4 ☎040/664 62 50, ⓦwww.ibishotel.com. Five minutes' walk to the right from the train station, towards Malmöhus, this hotel hides a comfortable and pleasant interior behind the facade of a 1950s apartment tower. Price includes a good breakfast and free parking. ❷

Kramer Stortorget 7 ☎040/693 54 00, ⓦwww.scandic-hotels.com. Beautiful white-stuccoed, turreted hotel from the 1870s, once Malmö's top hotel and still very luxurious. ❻/❹

The Mayfair Adelgatan 4 ☎040/10 16 20, ⓦwww.mayfairtunneln.com. Very central Danish-owned place and one of the finest of Malmö's more intimate hotels. Rooms are well furnished in cherry and Gustavian pastels. Good breakfasts and weekend discounts. ❺/❸

Radisson SAS Malmö Östergatan 10 ☎040/698 40 00, ⓦwww.radissonsas.com. Just beyond the Carolina Church, this hotel's blank and unimposing facade opens into a delightful interior. The stylish rooms are huge, and breakfast is eaten inside one of Malmö's oldest houses, cunningly incorporated into the former apartment building. ⑥/③

Rica City Malmö Stortorget 15 ☎ 040/660 95 50, ⓦ www.rica.se. A grand fin-de-siècle hotel in a fine position on the central square. Recently tastefully renovated. ⑥/②

Royal Norra Vallgatan 94 ☎ 040/664 25 00, ⓦ www.hotellroyal.com. Small, family-run hotel just up from the train station. The price includes breakfast, which is served in the garden in summer. ③

Savoy Norra Vallgatan 62 ☎ 040/664 48 00, ⓦ www.savoy.elite.se. This is where Lenin, Bardot and Dietrich all stayed, with a brass plaque to prove it. Now part of the Best Western chain, it's lost it's edge but the rooms are big, very comfortable and breakfast is in the celebrated (though sometimes overrated) *Petri Pumpa* restaurant. It's right by the canal close to the station.⑥/③

Temperance Engelbrektsgatan 16 ☎ 040/710 20, ⓕ 30 44 06. Pleasant central hotel; price includes sauna, solarium and a big buffet breakfast. ⑥/③

The city centre

Heading south from the heavy-handed nineteenth-century opulence of the train station, with its curly-topped pillars and red-brick ornate arches, the **canal** is immediately in front of you. Dug by Russian prisoners in 1815, it forms a rough rectangle encompassing the **old town** to the south and the moated **castle** to the west. The castle is also surrounded by the first in a series of lovely, connecting **parks**. First off, though, head down Hamngatan to the main square. On the way you'll pass the striking sculpture of a twisted revolver, a monument to nonviolence, standing outside the grand 1890s building that is the former Malmö Exchange.

Stortorget and St Petri kyrka

The laying out of **Stortorget**, the proud main square, necessitated the tearing down of much of Malmö's medieval centre in the mid-sixteenth century. Among the elaborate sixteenth- to nineteenth-century buildings, the 1546 **Rådhus** draws the most attention. It's an impressive pageant of architectural fiddling and crowded with statuary: restoration programmes in the last century robbed the building of its original design, and the finicky exterior is now in Dutch Renaissance style. To add to the pomp, the red-and-gold Scånian flag, of which Malmö is so proud, flaps above the roofs. The interior remains closer to its original form, and there are occasional tours; check with the tourist office for the ever-changing times. The cellars, home to *Rådhus Källaven Restaurant* (see p.246), have been used as a tavern for more than four hundred years. To the south of the town hall, have a look inside **Apoteket Lejonet** (Lion Pharmacy – Swedish pharmacies are always named after creatures of strength): the outside is gargoyled and balconied, the inside a busy mix of inlaid woods, carvings and etched glass. From here, **Södergatan**, Malmö's main pedestrianized shopping street, leads down towards the canal. At the Stortorget end, there's a jaunty troupe of sculptured bronze musicians. On the opposite side of the square, the crumbling, step-gabled red-brick building was once the home of the sixteenth-century mayor and master of the Danish mint, Jörgen Kocks. Danish coins were struck in Malmö on the site of the present Malmöhus castle (see opposite), until irate local Swedes stormed the building and destroyed it in 1534. The cellars of Jörgen's pretty home contain the *Kockska Krogan* restaurant (see p.246), the only entry point for visitors today. In the centre of the square, a statue of Karl X, high on his charger, presides over the city he liberated from centuries of Danish rule.

A block east, on Göran Olsgatan behind the Rådhus, the dark, forbidding exterior of the Gothic **St Petri kyrka** belies a light and airy interior (Mon–Fri 8am–6pm, Sat 9am–6pm, Sun 10am–6pm). The church has its roots in the fourteenth century, and, although Baltic in inspiration, has ended up owing much to German influences, for it was beneath its unusually lofty and elegantly vaulted roof that the German community came to pray – probably for the continuation of the "sea silver", the herrings that brought them to Malmö in the first place. The ecclesiastical vandalism, brought by the Reformation, of whitewashing over medieval roof murals started early at St Petri; almost the whole interior turned white in 1553. Consequently, your eyes are drawn not to the roof but to the pulpit and a four-tiered altarpiece, both of striking workmanship and elaborate embellishment. The only part of the church left with its original artwork was a side chapel, the **Krämare** (merchant's).

Lilla Torg

Despite the size of Stortorget, it still proved too small to suffice as the town's sole main square, so in the sixteenth century **Lilla Torg** was tacked on to its southwest corner, over a patch of marshland. With its half-timbered houses, flowerpots and cobbles, this is where most locals and tourists congregate. During the day, people come to take a leisurely drink in one of the many bars and wander around the summer jewellery stalls. At night, Lilla Torg explodes in a frenzy of activity, the venues all merging into a mass of bodies who converge from all over the city and beyond (see also "Eating and drinking", p.245). Head under the arch on Lilla Torg to get to the **Form Design Centre** (Tues, Wed & Fri 11am–5pm, Thurs 11am–6pm, Sat 10am–4pm, Sun noon–4pm; free). Built into a seventeenth-century grain store, it concentrates on Swedish contemporary design in textiles, ceramics and furniture. It's all well presented, if a little pretentious. The courtyard entrance contains several small trendy boutiques and there's a simple café.

From the end of the nineteenth century until the 1960s, the whole of Lilla Torg was a covered market, and the sole remnant of those days, **Saluhallen**, is diagonally opposite the Design Centre. Mostly made up of specialist fine food shops, *Saluhallen* is a pleasant, cool retreat on a hot afternoon, (see p.245).

Rooseum

A few streets removed from the other sights of the old town, **Rooseum**, on Stora Nygatan (Tues–Sun 11am–5pm, Thurs till 8pm; guided tours Tues–Fri 6.30pm, Sat & Sun 2pm; 30kr, free with a Malmö Card), is well worth a visit if you're interested in contemporary art. This elaborately designed building – a cross between a miniature castle and a shuttered cottage – dates from 1900, and originally housed the Malmö Electricity Company's steam turbines. The main turbine hall has been imaginatively turned into the central gallery, playing host to experimental installations and interesting photographic works. There are regular new exhibitions and an excellent little café for the sweet-toothed (see p.245).

Malmöhus and around

Take any of the streets running west from Stortorget or Lilla Torg and you soon come up against the edge of **Kungsparken**, within striking distance of the fifteenth-century castle of **Malmöhus** (June–Aug daily 10am–4pm, Sept–May noon–4pm; 40kr, free with the Malmö Card). For a more head-on approach, walk west (away from the station) up Citadellsvägen; from here the low castle, with its grassy ramparts and two circular keeps, is straight ahead over the wide moat. It's one of Sweden's least aesthetically pleasing castles, with mean windows and patched-up brickwork, but the inside is worth a peek. There are free guided tours, in English, of Malmöhus (3pm) and the art museum (2pm).

After Sweden's destruction of Denmark's mint here in 1534, the Danish king Christian III built a new fortress two years later. This was only to be of unforeseen benefit to his enemies who, once back in control of Skåne, used it to repel an attacking Danish army in 1677. For a time a prison (its most notable inmate the Earl of Bothwell, Mary Queen of Scots's third husband), the castle declined in importance once back in Swedish hands, and it was used for grain storage until becoming a museum in 1937.

Once in the **museum**, pass swiftly through the natural history section, a taxidermal Noah's Ark holding no surprises; the most rewarding part of the museum is upstairs in the so-called **art museum**, part of the historical exhibition, where an ambitious series of furnished rooms covers most modern styles, from the mid-sixteenth-century Renaissance period through Baroque, Rococo, pastel-pale Gustavian and Neoclassical. A stylish interior from the *Jugendstil* (Art Nouveau) period is also impressive, while other rooms have Functionalist and post-Functionalist interiors, with some wacky colour and texture combinations. It's a fascinating visual feast; unfortunately though, there is no English labelling. Other sections of the historical exhibition include a display of medieval skeletons from Malmö's churchyards, showing the signs of infection with contemporary diseases like leprosy and tuberculosis – less gruesome than you might imagine. It's more interesting to head into the castle itself, with its spartan but authentic interiors.

Just beyond the castle, to the west along Malmöhusvagen, is **Kommendanthuset** (Governor's House; same times as Malmöhus), containing the strange marriage of a military and toy museum. The military section is a fairly lifeless collection of neatly presented rifles and swords. The toy section is more fun, and contains the link between the two museums: a brigade of toy soldiers – of the British army, oddly enough.

A little further west, running off Malmöhusvagen, is a tiny walkway, **Banerkajen**, lined with higgledy-piggledy fishing shacks selling fresh and smoked fish – a rare little area of traditional Malmö that contrasts with the lively pace of the rest of the city.

Malmö is justifiably proud of its beautiful **parks**, a chain of which run southwards from the grounds of Malmöhus. Heading south from the castle, the first of these you encounter is Kungspark, with its graceful trees and classic sculptures, bordering the canal.

South of the centre

Tourists are still rarely encouraged to venture further south of the city than the canal banks that enclose the old town, but those who do are rewarded with the hip multicultural district around **Möllenvågen** (see p.244). The buildings and areas off **Amiralsgatan**, to the southeast, give an interesting insight into Malmö's mix of cultures and its Social Democratic roots (the city has been at the forefront of left-wing politics for the last century, and was central to the creation and development of Sweden's Social Democratic Party). Around **Fersensvägen**, a couple of blocks west of Amiralsgatan, there are some charming enclaves of antique shops, cafés and quirky buildings, and the impressive art exhibition centre, Konsthall.

There's plenty of pleasure to be had from simply strolling around the chain of **parks** that continues south of Kungspark, with free guided tours of the flora and royal history connected with these appealing green swathes also available (ask at the tourist office). Just on the south side of the curving river is Slottspark, with graceful, mature trees and places to picnic; further south is the largest of the parks, Pildammspark, boasting tranquil lakes and a choice restaurant (see p.246).

South towards the Konsthall

Heading south from Malmöhus along Slottsgatan, peer upwards at Regementsgatan 10 as you cross over that street; the building was, until recently, home to Sweden's current prime minister. Now cut across one block east to cobbled Södra Förstadsgatan; at no. 4 is a splendid house designed in 1904, its National Romantic facade covered with flower and animal motifs. A little further along the same road, the **Victoria Theatre** is Sweden's oldest cinema (℡040/23 21 62, ⓦwww.victoria.se; Mon–Fri 11am–6pm), all fine Art Nouveau swirls of dark oak and bevelled glass. Now a place to watch art-house films, it occasionally plays host to theatrical productions.

Back on Fersensvägen, the southward continuation of Slottsgatan, you'll pass the city **theatre** on your right, with its amusing sculpture of tiers of people – the naked supporting the clothed on their shoulders. Arriving at St. Johannesgatan, head for the single-storey glass and concrete building at no. 7: the **Konsthall**, (Art Hall; daily 11am–5pm, Wed till 10pm; free; ⓦwww.konsthall.malmo.se), an enormous white-painted space showing vast contemporary works in regular temporary exhibitions; there's lots of room to stand back and take in the visual feast.

The area between Regementsgatan and the Konsthall is also the best in town for interesting and esoteric **antique** and **curiosity shops** – Kärleksgatan (which runs between Davidshallsgatan and Davidshallstorg) is lined with them. You'll find lovely old silver samovars at Mats Kuriosa, Kärleksgatan 6 (℡040/11 82 23); the more costly Säljer & Köper Kuriosa, on the corner of Davidshallgatan (℡040/97 34 34; Mon & Wed–Fri noon–6pm, Sat 11am–2pm), is one of the biggest antique stores here, selling silverware, glass, furniture and lots more besides.

South to Möllevången

From the canal, head east along Regementsgatan and turn right into Amiralsgatan, where, a few hundred metres down and off to your left along Föreningsgatan, you encounter the restored **Malmö Synagogue**, a splendid copper-domed Moorish building (ask the tourist office to make arrangements to see inside). It serves an Orthodox community, who came mostly from Germany in the latter part of the nineteenth century and during the 1930s. Designed and built in 1894 by the same architect responsible for the neighbouring Betania kyrka, the synagogue is decorated with concentric designs in blue and green glazed brick. The unrenovated interior is rather fine, with its original, German-inspired octagonal wooden ceiling, ark and enormous chandelier of dull brass; there's a separate women's gallery (visitors are permitted access to all parts).

Back on Amiralsgatan, it's a ten-minute walk south to **Folketspark**, Sweden's oldest existing public park was once the prize of the community. Recently restored with an elegant new water feature at the Möllevången exit, Folkespark contains a basic amusement park, and at its centre, a ballroom named the **Moriskan**, an odd, low building with Russian-style golden domes topped with sickles. Both the park and the ballroom are now privately owned, a far cry from the original aims of the park's Social Democratic founders. Severe carved busts of these City Fathers are dotted all over the park. The socialist agitator August Palm made the first of his several historic speeches here in 1881, marking the beginning of a 66-year period of unbroken Social Democratic rule in Sweden.

More interesting than the giant twirling tea-cup fun rides in the park is the multicultural character of the city south from here. Strolling from the park's southern exit down Möllevången to **Möllevångstorget**, you enter an area populated almost entirely by non-Swedes, where Arab, Asian and Balkan émi-gré families predominate. The vast square is a haven of exotic food stores, side by side with shops selling pure junk and more recently established Chinese restaurants and karaoke pubs. On a hot summer afternoon it's easy to forget you're in Sweden at all, the more makeshift and ramshackle atmosphere around the bright fruit and veg stands contrasting with the clean, clinical order of the average Swedish neighbourhood. It's worth taking a close look at the provoca-tive **sculpture** at the square's centre: four naked, bronze men strain under the colossal weight of a huge chunk of rock bearing carved representations of Malmö's smoking chimneys, while two naked women press their hands into the men's backs in support. It's a poignant image, marrying toil in a city found-ed on limestone quarrying with the Social Democratic vision of the working man's struggle.

South of the city: Malmö's beaches to the Öresund bridge

Separated from the city centre by the delightful Ribersborg **park** (bus #20 heads here), Malmö's long stretch of sandy **beach** reaches the several kilome-teres to the old limestone-quarrying area of Limhamn in the southwest. Grand old villas set in glorious gardens overlook the Öresund, and the whole stretch is known as the Golden Coast because of the wealth of its residents. Fringed by dunes and grassland, the beaches here are popular with young families as the water remains shallow for several metres out to sea; throughout the summer months, the area also plays host to groups of teenagers letting their hair down. One bathing area further west (signposted a couple of kilometres from town; bus #20 comes here) is specially adapted for people with disabilities.

A classic Malmö experience at the town end of the beach is the **Ribersborgs kallbadhuset**, a cold-water bathhouse (mid-April to mid-Sept Mon–Fri 8.30am–7pm, Sat & Sun 8.30am–4pm; mid-Sept to mid-April Mon–Fri noon–7pm, Sat & Sun 9am–4pm) and sauna (mid-April to mid-Sept Mon–Fri 11am–7pm, Sat & Sun 9am–4pm; rest of year same as bathhouse); admission is 35kr, half-price with the Malmö Card). Alongside the beaches runs the **Ribersborgs Recreation Promenade**, fringed by dunes and grass-land, where groups of young people hold barbecues and play music (take bus #20 from the train station).

The Öresund bridge

Linking Malmö with Copenhagen in Denmark (and thus Sweden with the rest of con-tinental Europe), the elegant **Öresund bridge** was finally completed in 1999, after a forty-year debate. From Lernacken, a few kilometres south of Malmö, the bridge runs to a four-kilometre-long artificial island off the Danish coast, from where an immersed tunnel carries traffic and trains across to the mainland – a total distance of 16km. The bridge itself has two levels, the upper for a four-lane highway and the lower for two sets of train tracks, and comprises three sections: a central high bridge, spanning 1km, and approach bridges to either side, each over 3km long.

Stockholmers who played down the bridge's importance, fearing it would draw attention to Sweden's west coast, away from the capital, were, it seems, justified. It has fulfilled its promise to make Malmö the ultimate gateway into Sweden, and sig-nificantly raised the city's fortunes.

Eating and drinking

Among Malmö's many **eating places** you'll find some interesting interiors – check out the industrial *Espresso Rooseum* – and much fine food. By day, numerous **cafés** serve good lunches and sumptuous cakes, while at night, there are a couple of top-notch places at which to eat. Most of Malmö's restaurants, brasseries and cafés are concentrated in and around its three central squares, with Lilla Torg attracting the biggest crowds.

For cheaper eats and a very un-Swedish atmosphere, head south of the centre to Möllenvångstorget, the heart of Malmö's immigrant community. More inexpensively still, try *Saluhallen* at the corner of Lilla Torg, an excellent indoor **market** that sells wholefoods; there are also specialist food stores here, like *Krydboden*, which stocks herbal and fruit teas, coffees and crystallized fruits. Cheese fanatics will appreciate the tremendous *Ost huset* at Skomaregatan 10 (Mon–Fri 9am–6pm, Sat 9am–3pm), where the variety is exceptional. There's a good charcuterie, *Spot's Deli*, selling fresh pasta, meats and cakes, next to the Italian restaurant at Stora Nygatan 33.

Cafés

Bageri Café Saluhallen Corner of Lilla Torg. Excellent bagels, baguettes, sweet pies and health food – with some outside eating. Closed Sun.

Conditori Hollandia Södra Förstadsgatan 8. South of Gustav Adolfs Torg, across the canal. Classic, pricey *konditori* with a window full of chocolate fondants. The speciality of the house is strawberry cheesecake.

Café Rooseum Gasverksgatan 22. Inside Rooseum, the contemporary art museum (see p.241). Seating is around the edge of the room, with a giant generator taking up most of the remaining space. Try the superb cheesecakes or the great cookies and filled bagels. Closed Mon.

Café Siesta Corner of Långårdsgatan and Hjorttackegatan. A fun little café specializing in home-made apple cake and offering good daily lunch specials at 60kr.

Café Systrar & Bröder Östra Ronneholmsvägen 26. Superb breads, cakes and sandwiches plus a great-value breakfast buffet for just 45kr are on offer at this hip joint with leatherette bench seats and a Sixties ambience.

Cyber Space Café Engelbrektsgatan 13, a block west of Stortorget. An Internet café where you can surf while sipping coffee or soda and eating baguettes and pastries. Half an hour's Internet use costs 22kr.

Espresso House Skomakaregatan 2. Close to both Stora and Lilla Torg. Part of the excellent chain, this one serves great chocolate cake, muffins and ciabattas, and a delicious Oriental *latte* (30kr) flavoured with cardamom. There's another popular branch at Södra Förstadsgatan 11, just south of the city.

Gustav Adolfs Gustav Adolfs Torg 43. Long established and rather staid, this is still a popular spot, in a grand, white-stuccoed building with seating outside, serving coffee (18kr) and snacks. Open late at weekends.

Nyhavn 8 Möllevångstorget 8. A Danish café-restaurant run by a Danish-Turkish émigré – that could only make sense on this square. Chief among the offerings are *smørrebrod* with all manner of possible toppings for 30–50kr, plus rich Danish meals, all for under 100kr.

Paus Södra Förstensgatan 3. A new entry on the Malmö café scene, this small, intimate place offers generously filled sandwiches and good coffee.

Slottspark Café The park south of the Malmöhus. An appealing spot, overlooking an old black windmill, for home-made carrot or chocolate cake.

Restaurants

Adelgatan Restaurant Adelgatan, next to *Mayfair Hotel*. Part of the *Tunnel* nightclub, this place specializes in flambé dishes, tournedos and seafood.

Azteken Landbygatan 4 ☎040/12 50 45. A mellow restaurant with a lovely outdoor courtyard. Inside is a cosy bar – though service can be brusque – with wooden log walls and a rough-hewn floor.

Le Beau Monde Vastergatan 16. On a quiet street, only a few minutes' walk from the Stortorget action, this attractive choice has a reputation for excellence. The gourmet menu is a wallet strainer at 445kr for a three-course meal, but there are cheaper, à la carte options.

Brasserie Slottsparken Kung Oscarsvägen, running through both Slottspark and Kungspark ☎040/97 11 11. The cheaper of the two parkland eateries, though the setting isn't as attractive as

③

Olga's (see below). Baguettes, open sandwiches and fish or meat dishes for 80–90kr, with outside eating and a friendly, relaxed atmosphere.

Ekmans Södergatan 1. Despite the crisp white cloths and air of chic expense, the prices are reasonable in this appealing eatery in a glorious red sandstone building at the corner of Storgatan. Main dishes of good Swedish food are 125kr.

Golden Restaurant Corner of Södra Parkgatan and Simrishamnsgatan. In the hip neighbourhood of Möllevången, this spartan place serves cheap crepes, pizza and kebabs.

Gokboet Lillatorg 3. With a name that means "cuckoo's nest", this place has a friendly, youthful atmosphere. Mexican food from 48kr, baguettes 38kr, and unusual and delicious cakes.

Indian Side Lilla Torg. Very popular Indian dishes, with house specialities all costing 100–140kr. Within staggering distance of the main bars.

Johan P. Fish Restaurant Saluhallen. With its black-and-white chequer-tiled walls, this place has a good reputation for fairly pricey fish dishes.

Kockska Krogan Corner of Stortorget & Suellgatan ☎040/703 20. Also known as *Arstiderna*, this fine old basement restaurant is within the former home of Malmö's sixteenth-century mayor Jörgen Kock. Pricey but worth the splash for its classic Swedish cuisine and good wines. Daily lunch specials from 75kr.

Krua Thai Möllevångtorget 12 ☎040/12 22 87. In the big square south of the city centre, this informal restaurant serves the best Thai food in town.

Mandarin Södra Vallgatan 3. A young, laid-back crowd and mellow sounds make this a great spot for inexpensive Thai food (dishes 40–75kr) or a beer. The funky atmosphere spills on to outside tables in summer.

Olga's Pildamms Parken ☎040/12 55 26. Superbly set in a wooden lakeside pavilion, this is an expensive place, but a good one, serving Swedish and international cuisine. A vast portrait of the very substantial Olga adorns the wall.

Petri Pumpa Norra Vallgatan 62, at the *Savoy* hotel. This celebrated restaurant – with prices to match – was Lund's culinary pinnacle before moving here. Attempts to win greater custom with endless special offers detract from the former exclusivity of this famous place. Summer special is three courses for 265kr.

Rådhus Källaren Stortorget (Kyrkogatan 6). In the cellars of the gloriously decorated town hall. Main dishes cost 80kr, but there's an excellent daily lunch at 65kr. Outside seating in summer.

Spot Restaurant Stora Nygatan 33 ☎040/12 02 03. A chic Italian daytime restaurant. Light meals based on ciabatta and *panini* breads, with great fillings, are served. Reasonably priced, this is an excellent choice for lunch.

Tempo Norra Skolgatan 30. Near Möllevångstorget, to the south of the city ☎040/12 60 21. A quirky, hip place, whose patrons come to savour the very well-prepared and intriguing food. The menu is short, but inspired and service is friendly but can be absurdly slow.

Nightlife and entertainment

Long gone are the days when the only entertainment in Malmö was watching rich drunks become poor drunks at the blackjack table in the Central Station bar. Nowadays there are some decent **live music** venues and **discos**, most of which are cheaper to get into than their European counterparts. The best place to see live music is *Matssons Musikpub*, Göran Olsgatan 1, behind the Rådhus (☎040/23 27 56; daily 9.30pm–2am), with a variety of Scandinavian R&B and rock bands. Check out *Malmö This Month* for information on what's on here. The cellar bar at *Club Tunnel*, on Adelgatan, boasts a wild dancefloor, and a variety of music on different evenings.

Classical **music** performances take place at the Concert Hall, Föreningsgatan 35 (☎040/34 35 00; two for one with Malmö Card), home of the Malmö Symphony Orchestra, and at Musikhögskolan, Ystadvägen 25 (☎040/19 22 00); check with the tourist office for programme details.

Malmö plays host to two annual **festivals**. The **Folkfesten**, also called Västra Hamnenfest, (ⓦwww.malmo.se) takes place in early June and is devoted to progressive and classic rock. Begun in the early 1970s and now enjoying a renaissance in popularity, this mini-Woodstock is held in Kungsparken (see p.241) and draws a young, tie-dyed and beaded crowd. Much broader in scope is the **Malmö Festival** in August (ⓦwww.malmofestivalen.nu), which mainly takes place in Stortorget. Huge tables are set out with crayfish tails served up for free.

In Gustav Adolfs Torg, other stalls are set up by the immigrant communities, with Pakistani, Somali and Bosnian goodies and dance shows, while at the canal, rowing competitions take place.

Bars

For **drinking**, Lilla Torg is where mainstream Malmöites and tourists head in the evenings. The square buzzes with activity, as the smell of beer wafts between the old, beamed houses, and music and chatter fill the air. With a largely 20- and 30-something crowd, the atmosphere is like that of a summer carnival – orange-jacketed bouncers keep the throng from suffocating. It doesn't make a huge difference which of the six or so bars you go for – expect a wait to get a seat – but roughly speaking, *Mello Yello* is for the 25-plus age group, *Moosehead* for a younger crowd, and *Victors* is even younger and more boisterous. A striking addition to the bar scene is *The Tunnel*, next door to *The Mayfair Hotel*, on Adelgatan (Sun & first Fri of each month; closed in summer) popular with a young, wealthy set. Alternatively, at the *Savoy Hotel*, the *Bishop's Arms* is a cosy but rather staid pub with a heavy-handed insistence on looking British. On Möllenvångstorget, south of the centre in the immigrant quarter, the Danish-style *Nyhavn* at no. 8 is a laid-back place to drink.

Gay Malmö

Though most gay Malmöites head off to Copenhagen for a really good night out, Malmö's **gay nightlife** is livelier than any other Swedish city outside Stockholm. The RFSL-run gay centre is at Monbijougatan 15, to the south of the city centre (head down Amiralsgatan and turn off to the right just before the Folketspark). This is home to *Club Indigo*, at its busiest after midnight (Fri & Sat nights from 10pm). It's a sizeable and friendly place, where all the gay anthems of the past couple of decades are played on disco nights. The first Saturday of the month is women-only and there's a pub night on Wednesdays (9pm–midnight; 80kr, or 40kr for RFSL members). If you're around in the last week of September, try catching the **Regnbågs (Rainbow) Festival** – nine days of nonstop parties, pub nights and a film festival at RFSL and other venues around Malmö (☎040/611 99 62, ⊛www.rfslmalmo.nu). Another place you might want to try on Saturday nights is *Wonk*, Adelgatan 2, next to *The Tunnel* (see above). The nightclub *Etage*, Stortorget 7, is not a gay club, but has a high ratio of gay visitors.

Listings

Airlines British Airways, Sturup airport ☎020/78 11 44; Finnair, Baltzarsgatan 31 ☎020/78 11 00; KLM, Sturup airport ☎020/50 05 30; Lufthansa, Gustav Adolfs Torg 12 ☎040/717 10; SAS, Baltzarsgatan 18 ☎040/35 72 00.
Buses From Centralplan to Lund (#130), Kristianstad/Kalmar (#805) and Ystad (#330).
Car rental Avis, Skeppsbron 13 ☎040/778 30; Budget, Baltzarsgatan 21 ☎040/775 75; Europcar, Mäster Nilsgatan 22 ☎040/38 02 40; Hertz, Jorgenkocksgatan 1B ☎040/749 55.
Doctor On call daily 7am–10pm, ☎040/33 35 00; at other times, ring ☎040/33 10 00.
Exchange Best rates are at Forex; branches are at Norra Vallgatan 60 (daily 7am–9am), Gustav Adolfs

Torg 12 (Mon–Fri 8am–7pm, Sat 9am–3pm), and by the tourist office at Central Station (daily 8am–9pm).
Internet access Cyberspace, Engelbrektsgatan 13a (daily 10am–10pm); Surfer's Paradise, Amiralsgatan 14 (Mon–Fri 10am–midnight, Sat & Sun noon–midnight; ⊛www.surfersparadise.se); Twilight Zone, Stora Nygatan 15 (daily noon–3am); City Library, Regementsgatan 3 (Mon–Thurs 10am–2pm, Fri 10am–6pm, Sat & Sun noon–4pm; ⊛www.msb.malmo.se).
Pharmacy 24hr service at Apoteket Gripen, Bergsgatan 48 ☎040/19 21 13) or Lejonet in Stortorget (Mon–Fri 9am–6pm, Sat 10am–2pm; ☎040/712 35).

Post office Skeppsbron 1 (Mon–Fri 8am–6pm, Sat 9.30am–1pm).
Taxis ☎040/97 97 97 or 040/23 23 23

Train enquiries There's a Pågatåg information office inside the Lokalstationen (Mon–Fri 7am–6pm, Sat 8am–3pm, Sun 9am–3pm).

Southeastern Skåne: from Malmö to Ystad

The people of this province speak a guttural dialect which betrays their Danish origin; a peculiarity so marked that the Swedes playfully say that the Skåne folk "are born with gruel in their throats." They have a great difficulty in managing the letter 'r'. . . They consider themselves as quite a separate nationality – as indeed they really are; for the typical Skåne man is neither a Swede nor a Dane, but distinct from both.

From *Unknown Sweden* (1925) by James Steveni.

Leaving Malmö, the local Pågatåg train and the E6 and E14 highways cut directly east towards Ystad (see p.245). The route bypasses some picturesque, minor resorts such as **Skanör** and **Falsterbo** and the golf-course-studded **Näset Peninsula** with its nature reserves and a couple of the region's best beaches along Sweden's most southwesterly tip; also missed out this way are a remarkable Viking-style settlement at **Foteviken** and an extensive Baltic **amber** workshop at Kämpinge, the latter set in picture-perfect countryside. With time to explore, and particularly with your own transport, this quieter part of the south makes for a few days of delightful exploration.

Twenty-five kilometres south of the city on the old E6 is the village of **VELLINGE**, also reachable on bus #150 from Malmö's Centreplan, or on the cycle paths leading from the city (follow signs first for Tygelsjö and then to Vellinge). Just west of Vellinge (by car or bus #150), you cross an expanse of heathland to which **bird-watchers** flock every autumn. Their goal is to spot nesting plovers and terns, as well as millions of migratory birds fleeing the Arctic for the Stevns peninsula, south of Copenhagen.

Foteviken Viking Museum

From Vellinge, it's 8km southwest to Höllviken, on the way to Skanör and Falsterbo (see p.250). Höllviken itself has nothing to detain you, but signs here point the way to the **Foteviken Viking Museum**, just 500m away (mid-May to Aug daily 11am–4pm; 50kr, 120kr family ticket; ☎040/45 68 40, ⓦwww.foteviken.se). An ancient coastal village and reputedly also a pagan sacrificial site, **Foteviken** was a market town and centre for herring fishing during Viking times. Today, the whole area has been transformed into a working **Viking-style village** comprising houses, workshops, a sacrificial temple and shipyard – a virtually self-sufficient settlement with an astonishing ring of authenticity. The idea was to show the way of life here in the twelfth century, but more than this, the place has become a Mecca for people from all over Europe who want to live as Vikings, together with a not inconsiderable number of characters, sporting wild beards and lots of beads, who firmly believe they *are* Vikings.

The resulting atmosphere is that of a hippy commune in a time warp. Everyone dresses entirely in home-spun garments of loose, coarse linen, coloured with dyes made from local grasses and herbs. The villagers' simply crafted footwear is made from leather which they cure themselves, and if you

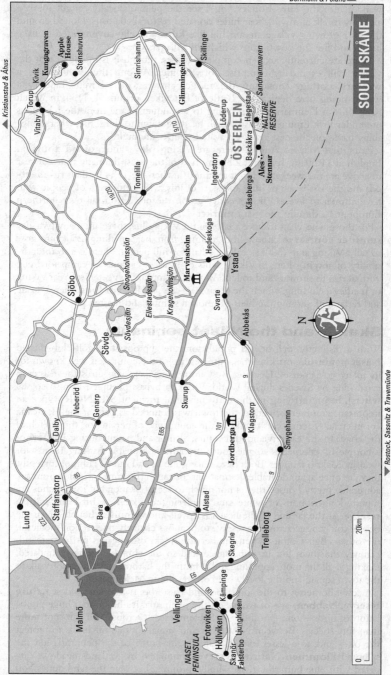

SOUTH SKÅNE

Bornholm & Poland ▲

◀ Kristianstad & Åhus

▼ Rostock, Sassnitz & Travemünde

3

249

20km

0

N

Malmö

Lund

Staffanstorp

Bara

Dalby

Veberöd

Genarp

E22

80

NÄSET
PENINSULA

Vellinge

Höllviken

Foteviken

Skanör
Falsterbo

Ljunghusen

Kämpinge

Skegrie

E6

100

Trelleborg

Alstad

Skurup

E65

Sövde
Sövdesjön

Sjöbo

Snogeholmssjön

Ellestadssjön

Kageholmssjön

13

Marvinsholm

Hedeskoga

Ystad

Svarte

Abbekås

Smygehamn

Klagstorp

Jordberga

9

101

Tomelilla

1570

1570

Ingelstorp

Käseberga

Ales ∴
Stennar

Backåkra

NATURE
RESERVE

Hagestad

Sandhammaren

ÖSTERLEN

Löderup

9/10

Glimmingehus

Skillinge

Simrishamn

Vitaby

Torup

Kivik

Kungagraven

Apple
House

Stenshuvud

wander into the **cure-houses** you'll see the pelts of locally caught mink – along with elk and wild-boar hides donated by local abattoirs. Dotted around the ever-growing village are ant hill-like **kilns** and **clay ovens** used to bake bread, and fire the bowls from which the villagers eat.

There are currently sixteen complete houses, though it is intended that the village will eventually comprise forty homes. Among the highlights is a **weavers' cottage** containing the village's answer to the Bayeux Tapestry: a wall-hanging here depicts the Battle of Foteviken of June 4, 1134, in which King Nils of Denmark is seen trying to reconquer Skåne from the rebellious pretender Erik Emune. It's also worth heading down to the shore, where long-ships, based on the designs of excavated wrecks, are built.

From mid-May to August there are Viking **plays** and **guided tours** in English at 11.30am, 1pm and 2.30pm. Two of the most dramatic times of year to arrive are the weekend closest to June 10, when the 1134 battle is **re-enacted**; and the last week of June and start of July, when hundreds of people who have chosen to live as Vikings converge on the place from all over northern Europe for a shindig and giant **market**.

For those who want to have a taste of the Viking life, there are many two-day **summer courses** to choose from, ranging from bead-making (250kr) to how to sail a Viking ship (500kr); call or email for full details. There is also the possibility of **staying** here in Viking tents or houses (or you can camp for free), with access to showers and toilets. All participants are expected to wear Viking or medieval clothing, which the organizers can provide. For **food**, there's a café and restaurant, serving the likes of smoked salmon and roasted pig.

Skanör and the Näset peninsula

With a distinctly well-heeled population, the appropriately golf-club-shaped **Näset peninsula**, marking the southwest tip of the country, is well known for its many golf courses. Heading west from Foteviken, you cross the Falsterbo canal (dug by Swedes during World War II to bypass occupied Danish coastal waters), before arriving in the early medieval town of **SKANÖR**. Once an important commercial centre, the town was founded as part of the Hanseatic commercial system, exists thanks to the abundance of herring off this stretch of the coast. In the early twentieth century, Skanör and neighbouring **Falsterbo**, a couple of kilometres to the south, became fashionable bathing resorts for wealthy Malmö families. Both have since gone in and out of fashion; currently, they are once again desirable destinations for much the same set. Aside from the admirably pretty houses, there's not much to see in Skanör, but its **beaches** are superb: long ribbons of white sand bordering an extensive **bird** and **nature reserve**. At the far end of the beach is a well-known **nudist beach**. From the beach, you can see across the reserve to Skanör's **church**, one section medieval, the other High Gothic. When the herring stocks disappeared in the sixteenth century, the town lost its importance, and so the church was never updated, making it all the more appealing today. From the harbour, it's a pleasant walk to the town square and the lovely old cottages lining Mellangatan.

A few kilometres to the south, beyond Falsterbo, is Sweden's oldest **nature reserve**, **Nabben**, one of twelve on the peninsula. It's home to a huge population of birds – on a good day in September or October you can spot more than fifty species. Between November and January it's all off-limits to protect the birds and, to a lesser extent, seals. To the north of the peninsula lies the splendid **Flommen Nature Reserve**, dominated by wetland meadows carpeted with blue butterfly iris, sea-holly sprouting between the sand dunes. You can walk southwards, towards the tip of the peninsula, to Sweden's oldest **lighthouse**, Kolabacken, whose beam was created by burning charcoal. At the very tip is **Maklappen Island**, a nature reserve known as a refuge for both grey and harbour seals (closed Feb–Oct).

The Amber Museum

After heavy storms, dull yellow nuggets of rough-textured **Baltic amber**, from submerged prehistoric forest, are regularly washed up on the shores around this part of southwest Sweden, particularly at Skånör beach. Appropriately enough, the hamlet of **Kämpinge**, 5km east of Falsterbo on Route 100 (bus #152 runs here from Höllviken), is home to a remarkable **amber workshop and museum** (June to mid-Aug 9am–7pm; to visit at other times call ☎040/45 08 61 or 45 45 04). Isolated among fields of yellow rape, the museum is signposted off the main road – look for "Bärnstenssnideri 500m". This remarkable centre was set up by one man, the very amiable and knowledgeable Leif Brost, who has dedicated himself to studying all aspects of this fossilized pine-tree resin. The most valuable pieces on show are those with insects trapped inside (known as "inclusions"), most strikingly mating pairs or hapless creatures caught in a web, complete with spider. In the 1990s, Brost's collections drew the attention of the makers of *Jurassic Park* and *The Lost World*, who used some of his specimens in the films. English-language **tours** of the museum, giving you a full run-down on amber and all its uses, are available by prior arrangement.

Practicalities

At Rådhustorget 6, a few metres from Skanör's town hall, *Hotell Gässlingen* is a charming place to **stay**, with weekend discounts outside summer (☎040/47 30 35, ℉47 51 81; ❹); **bikes** are also available to rent (50kr a day). Another pleasant, small hotel is *Spelabacken*, at 58 Mellangarten (☎040/47 53 00, ℉47 32 42; ❹), which boasts a sauna and solarium. There are plenty of places nearby to **camp** for free, but be careful not to pick a protected area for birds: they're marked by signposts.

The town's little harbour boasts a terrific **restaurant**, *Skanör's Fiskroken* (☎040/47 40 50), where you can savour superb fish dishes in a simple, elegant setting. Perhaps the best way to sample the remarkable range of smoked and pickled fish is to have them make up a picnic plate (around 90kr) – in particular, try herring roe marinated in rum, and hot smoked salmon with black bread. At the corner of Dykengatan, near the square, is another quintessential Scånian inn, *Gästgivaregården* (March–Sept Mon & Wed–Fri 5–10pm, Sat 1–11pm, Sun 1–6pm), with its reputation for well-prepared, local produce served in sizeable proportions in a historic setting.

Trelleborg

Heading east around 15km from Kämpinge, you encounter **TRELLEBORG**, which greets traffic with a curtain of low-level industry blocking all views of the sea. Yet behind the graceless factories there's a busy little town; its main attractions are the inspired reconstruction of a recently discovered Viking fortress and a gallery of works by the sculptor Axel Ebbe.

A few minutes' walk from the transport terminals at the harbour, is the **Axel Ebbe Gallery** (Tues–Sun: early June to early Sept 11am–5pm; early Sept to early June 1–4pm; 20kr) in a compact, 1930s Functionalist building that once was the local bank. Ebbe's superb sculptures are powerful nudes in black and white stone, all larger than life. At the turn of the century, Ebbe's gently erotic work was celebrated in Paris, though in Copenhagen, his graceful sprawling female, *Atlas's Daughter*, was regarded as too erotic for public display. Embracing many of the new styles of the era – Art Nouveau, Neoclassical and National Romanticism – his sculptures are elegant, rhythmic and romantic. The exhibition also includes his distinctive, though less interesting, goblin-like figures that provide a lighter touch. A few steps into the **Stadsparken**, opposite, is Trelleborg's main square, dominated by Ebbe's *Sea Monster*, a fountain comprising a serpentine fiend twined around a characteristically sensual mermaid.

Just a few metres from the Stadspark, the main shopping promenade here is **Algatan**, running parallel with the seafront. Walking up the street from the ferry terminal end, you'll soon come to **St Nicolai's kyrka**, which has some bright ceiling paintings, elaborate sepulchral tablets, and chairs from a Franciscan monastery destroyed during the Reformation. A couple of minutes' stroll from here is Trelleborg's most dramatic attraction, the **Trelle Fortress** (open all year; free). Dating from around 980 AD, the original circular fortress was built entirely of earth and wood at the behest of King Harald Blue Tooth; it would have encircled a seventh-century settlement of pit houses and itself been surrounded by a moat. The fortress's heyday was over by the eleventh century, when Vandals had raged along the Skånian coast and the inhabitants had fled inland. By making comparisons with four almost identical forts in Denmark and employing a certain amount of guesswork, archeologists have come up with today's impressive reconstruction, built using split oak logs. Any visitors here seriously interested in Viking matters would be even better off heading west to **Foteviken** (see p.245).

Practicalities

Bus #146 runs every half-hour from Malmö, but there are no trains except the ferry train from Malmö which stops here on trips to Germany. There's a Forex **exchange** at Friisgatan 1, just outside the Rostock ferry terminal (Mon–Fri 7am–7pm, Sat 7am–1pm, Sun 10am–7pm).

The **tourist office** is now at the ferry terminal (mid-June to mid-Aug Mon–Fri 9am–7pm, Sat 9am–6pm, Sun 9am–6pm; mid-Aug to mid-June Mon–Fri 9am–5pm; ☎0410/533 22, ⊛www.trelleborg.se). Staff can supply a good leaflet, *A Couple of Hours in Trelleborg* (free) – its title an accurate reflection of how long most people will stay – and help you book **private rooms** for 130kr plus a 35kr booking fee. For an alternative place to **stay**, *Hotel Prinz* (☎0410/71 32 39, ⊕71 31 44; ❹) is next door and perfectly reasonable. Less appealing but cheaper is *Night Stop* **hostel** close by at Östergatan 59, (☎0410/410 70, ⊛www.hotelnightstop.com; ❶); dismal-looking on the outside, though clean and open all night, it's ideal for late ferry arrivals. Breakfast is 40kr extra. At the other end of the quality spectrum, *Hotel Dannegården*, Standgatan 32 (☎0410/481 80, ⊛www.dannegarden.se; ❺/❽), is a beautiful 1910 villa surrounded by scented bushes, with five double rooms decorated in their original Art Nouveau style; other rooms are available within a much more mundane extension.

The *Hotel Dannegården* is the finest place for a romantic **meal** (Mon–Fri noon–2pm & 6–10pm; closed July), with a good international menu; three courses here will set you back 275kr. On Algatan, there are a couple of reasonable *konditori* **cafés** include *Billings*, with its verandah, and the similar *Palmblads*. The National Romantic water tower, behind the bus station, is a pleasant place for a coffee, and is convenient when you're waiting for a bus.

Smygehamn and Smygehuk

Around a third of the way from Trelleborg to Ystad along coast Route 9 (bus #183 from Malmö stops here hourly Mon–Fri, less often in summer, when schools are on holiday), the hamlet of Smygehamn prides itself on being Sweden's most southerly point. Half a kilometre before you reach this tiny harbour village, neighbouring **SMYGEHUK** is a cluster of pretty, old wooden houses around a quaint **lighthouse**. Built of iron in 1883 and now disused (it's been superseded by an automatic offshore beacon), the lighthouse affords a panoramic sea view, though you'll have to climb its spiral staircase to partake of the privilege.

Walk east through the profuse vegetation along the coast for five minutes, and you'll soon reach **SMYGEHAMN**. Arranged around another minuscule harbour are a few summer-only restaurants, a café and a particularly fragrant smoked-fish shop (daily 10am–6pm), which sells excellent salmon marinated in cognac, and also has bread and cutlery – ideal for a cheap picnic. The only other shop here sells souvenirs and is full of wooden geese, recalling the magic bird in the Swedish children's favourite *The Wonderful Adventures of Nils*, by Selma Lagerlöf (see p.420); in the book, the young hero flew the length and breadth of the country on a magic goose, his travels beginning on the Skånian coast.

The harbour has its origins in a coastal limestone quarry; indeed, lime burning was big business here from Smygehamn's heyday in the mid-nineteenth century until the 1950s. The area is still dotted with lime kilns – odd, igloo-like structures with cupola roofs. There's a lively two-day **folk music festival** here on the weekend after midsummer (free). At the end of July is a **jazz festival**, the cheapest tickets being at 75kr and full-day cards, available from the tourist office, cost 225kr.

Just a hundred metres east of the road sign leaving Smygehamn is a sign for *Spettkaka Bageri*. As its name suggests, this is a bakery specializing in **spettkaka**, concoctions of eggs, sugar and potato starch which taste like done-to-death meringues – the yolks are added to sugar followed by the whites and starch, and the mixture is then dribbled layer on layer on a low heated spit for up to six hours. Despite rarely finding anyone who enjoys eating them, no Swedish celebration is complete without one, and they're synonymous with Skåne. It's a two-kilometre walk from this sign, through rape fields, to the quaint vine-covered farm where Gudrun Olander famously turns out these Skånian specialities. The cheapest way of sampling them here is to buy a twenty-centimetre-long arch of the stuff for 20kr, though the grandest sell for 265kr.

Practicalities

The **tourist office** in Smygehuk is by the harbour (June to mid-Aug daily 10am–6pm; July daily 10am–7pm; ☎ & ℱ0410/240 53, ℰsmygehuktb@ hotmail.com), inside a fine, early nineteenth-century corn warehouse; it's worth a visit if only for the very cheap coffee (10kr including refills). The nearest proper hotels are in Trelleborg, 13km away, but the area around Smygehuk offers a wide variety of other **accommodation** options. The tourist office can book **private rooms** from just 100kr per person. Smygehuk's STF **youth hostel** is housed in what was the lighthouse-keeper's house (☎0410/245 83, ℱ245 09; 100kr; mid-May to mid-Sept), with a spacious kitchen and homely living area packed with books. Just 500m away is *Smygehus Havsbad* (☎0410/243 90, ℳwww.smygehus.se), a former bathhouse that has four-bed cabins for 1350kr, including breakfast; there's a reasonable restaurant, sauna and swimming pool here, too. This place is run by a time-share company, however, and in summer the owners will usually be in residence thus limiting availability.

About 12km east of Smygehuk, and 16km west of Ystad on Route 101, the *Adalen* farm in Skivarp has immaculate self-catering **apartments** (℡0411/307 02) in a converted barn, and is an economical choice at 500kr per night.

The hamlet of Boste, 3km inland (signposted off Route 9), has a **B&B** called *Hedman's* (℡0410/234 73, Ⓦwww.hedmans.nu; ❶), celebrated locally for its gourmet **restaurant** and extensive wine list (daily noon–3pm & 8–10pm; main courses 150–250kr); it has surprisingly cheap and plain rooms.

East to Ystad: Jordberga and Marvinsholm castles

Between Smygehamn and Ystad, the wedge of countryside south of the E65 highway contains a range of attractive **castles**. In southern Skåne, these are rarely castellated fairy-tale confections, more often taking the form of splendid country houses. Not merely pretty, they warrant a visit for the insight they offer into the wealth of this historic region; those described below are particularly rewarding.

From Smygehamn, it's only a few minutes' drive to the spectacular manor house of **Jordberga**: turn off Route 9 at the signpost and head 3km north, first to the village of Klagstorp, then on to another village, Kallstorp. Turn left here at the red-brick church; a single sign on the right points the way into the pretty estate of thatched cottages. To get here by **bus**, get the #184 from Trelleborg, which stops at Klagstorp, just 2km away. A house was first built here in the 1350s, though the present house dates back only to 1906 (the preceding incarnation having been ruined by a fire). Rebuilt in classic Baroque style, the house's very setting makes the foray here worthwhile, with a lake surrounding the house like a moat and formal gardens. In the first week of June, it's well worth checking out the annual **Jordberga Festival** (℡0410/261 09 or 264 25 for information) – a diverse musical celebration attracting well-known Swedish musicians and singers running the gamut from classical to rock.

Driving on past the manor for another 3km brings you to the exceptionally pretty **Marsvinsholm Castle**. Here, amid intricate old outbuildings that practically amount to a village, stands an architectural confection regarded as the finest example of Renaissance splendour in southern Sweden. The present building was constructed for Otto Marsvin, a local aristocrat, and stands on piles in the middle of a lake; though renovated in the 1850s, it retains its original dolphin-shaped door handles (*marsvin* being Danish for "dolphin"). The castle has been in the hands of the Iacobaeus family since 1903, who are happy for visitors to stroll in its grounds beyond the immediate garden. Three hundred metres further is an outsized church, second only in size to Lund Cathedral in the whole of Skåne. It once had the highest spire for miles around, but in the 1850s, the castle's owner decreed that his home must rise higher, and so had lofty towers built to overshadow it.

Every July and August, a wide variety of shows in Danish and Swedish are staged in an open-air **theatre** by the castle (for details ℡0411/600 15). A pleasant restaurant and café is open during performance evenings, which is also when the Pågatåg trains stop at Marvinsholm.

Ystad and around

An hour by Pågatåg train from Malmö, the medieval market town of **YSTAD** is exquisitely well preserved and boasts a prettiness that may come as a surprise

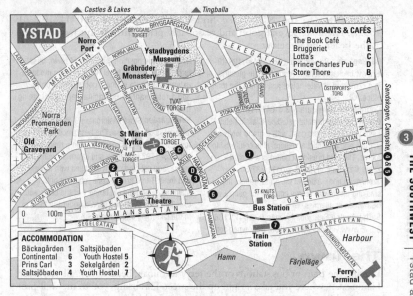

Castles & Lakes ▲   ▲ Tingballa

YSTAD

Norre Port

Ystadbygdens Museum

Gråbröder Monastery

Norra Promenaden Park

Old Graveyard

St Maria Kyrka

STOR-TORGET

Theatre

Bus Station

Train Station

Hamn

Harbour

Färjeläge

Ferry Terminal

N

0   100m

The Book Café	A
Bruggeriet	E
Lotta's	C
Prince Charles Pub	D
Store Thore	B

ACCOMMODATION

Bäckagården	1	Saltsjöbaden	
Continental	6	Youth Hostel	5
Prins Carl	3	Sekelgården	2
Saltsjöbaden	4	Youth Hostel	7

THE SOUTHWEST | Ystad and around

Sandskogen, Campsite, ④ & ⑤

if you've arrived at the train station down by the murky docks. In the historic centre though, you can marvel at the quaint, cobbled lanes, lined with cross-timbered cottages, and the town's chocolate-box central square, oozing rural charm. With the stunningly beautiful coastal region of Österlen stretching northeast from town all the way to Kristianstad (see p.262), and some excellent **walking** in the forests 20km to the north of town, Ystad is a splendid place to base yourself for a day or so.

Arrival and information

From the **train station**, cross over the tracks to the square, St Knuts Torg, where you'll find the **tourist office** (May to mid-June Mon–Fri 9am–7pm, Sat 11am–2pm, Sun 11am–6pm; mid-June to mid-Aug Mon–Fri 9am–7pm, Sat 10am–7pm, Sun 11am–6pm; mid-Aug to April Mon–Fri 9am–5pm; ℡0411/57 76 81, ⓦwww.visitystad.com). Among other things, they can supply copies of a 1753 map of Ystad, that's still a serviceable guide to the old streets. The square is also where buses from Lund, Kristianstad and Simrishamn will drop you off. The **ferry terminal** is 300m southeast of the train station. **Bikes** – a great way to see the surrounding cycle-friendly landscape – can be rented from Roslins Cykelaffär, Jennygatan 11 (℡0411/123 15; 65kr/day or 295kr/week), just east of the bus and train terminals. Alternatively, try Gösta Svenssons Cykel, Kristianstadsvägen 22 (℡0411/55 51 23; 65kr/day) five minutes' walk north of the monastery.

Accommodation

There are two **youth hostels** in Ystad. One is on the beach at Sandskogen, close to the Saltsjöbaden (℡0411/665 66; 135kr; Sept–May group bookings only) – take bus #572 or #304. Much more convenient, and under the same management, is the hostel in the old part of the train station (℡0708/57 79 95;

180kr). Next to the *Saltsjöbaden* hostel is the **campsite** (☎0411/192 70; 155kr). There are several good and reasonably priced **hotels** in town, and one at the beach, listed below.

Bäckagården Bäckagården 36 ☎0411/198 48, ⓦwww.backagarden.nu. A small-scale guesthouse in a converted private-house just behind the tourist office. **②**

Continental Hamngatan 13 ☎0411/137 00, ⓦwww.hotelcontinental-ystad.se. Classic hotel touted as Sweden's oldest, with a grand lobby of marble, and crystal chandeliers, plus comfortable rooms. The cold breakfast buffet is a treat. **④**

Prins Carl Hamngatan 8 ☎0411/737 50, ⓔprinscarl.hotell@brevet.nu. A mid-range, non-smoking place with rooms adapted for people with disabilities or allergies. **②**

Saltsjöbaden Saltsjöbadsvägen 6 ☎0411/136 30, ⓦwww.ystadssaltsjobad.se. Renowned for its beachside position, just east of town, this large, 100-year-old hotel (with endless modern extensions) has a sauna, pool (summer only), and a restaurant in the original saltwater bathing house. **④**

Sekelgården Stora Västergatan 9 ☎0411/739 00, ⓦwww.sekelgarden.se. The best place to stay in town, this small family-run hotel in a merchant's house of 1793 is friendly and informal, with a new sauna, and cobbled courtyard filled with flowers and trees. There are en-suite rooms in both the main house and the old tannery at the back, and excellent breakfasts are served under the trees or in the charming dining room. **③**

The Town

Leaving the train or bus stations or the ferry terminals, head west until you reach Hamngatan, where you take a right up the street. This brings you to the well-proportioned **Stortorget**, a grand old square around which twist picturesque streets. West of the church here is Mattorget, a small square, away from which leads Lilla Västergatan, the main street in the seventeenth and eighteenth centuries; strolling down it today, you'll see the best of the town's Lilliputian cottages.

In Stortorget itself, the thirteenth-century **St Maria kyrka** is a handsome centrepiece (daily 10am–4pm), with additions dating from nearly every century since it was built. In the 1880s, these rich decorative features were removed, as they were thought "unsightly", and only the most interesting ones were put back during a restoration programme forty years later. Inside, the Baroque early seventeenth-century pulpit is worth a look for the fearsome face carved beneath it, while opposite is the somewhat chilling medieval crucifix, placed here on the orders of Karl XII to remind the preacher of Christ's suffering. The figure of Christ wears a mop of actual human hair – sacrificed by a local parishioner in the nineteenth century, in an attempt to make it look realistic. Notice also the green box pews to either side of the entrance, which were reserved for women who had not yet been received back into the church after childbirth.

The Night Bugler of Ystad

Staying in Ystad, you'll soon get acquainted with a tradition that harks back to the seventeenth century: from a room in the church's watchtower, a night watchman sounds a **bugle** every fifteen minutes from 9.15pm to 3am. The haunting sound isn't disturbing, though it's audible wherever you stay in the centre. The sounding through the night was to assure the town that the watchman was still awake (until the mid-nineteenth century, he was liable to be executed if he slept on duty); however, the real purpose of this activity was as a safeguard against the outbreak of **fire**. The idea was that if one of the thatched cottages went up in flames, the bugle would sound repeatedly for all to go and help extinguish the blaze. The melancholic bellowing only ceased during World War II – and then the residents complained they couldn't sleep in the unbroken silence. If you look carefully from Stortorget, you can see just the instrument appear at little openings in the tower walls each time it's played.

Not far from Stortorget, up Lilla or Stora Norregatan, is **Norra Port**, the original northern arched entrance to the town. From here, you can stroll through **Norra Promenaden**, an avenue lined with mature horse-chestnut trees and surrounded by parkland. Here you'll find a white pavilion, built in the 1870s to house a genteel café and a dance hall, with a brass band. Today, the café here, *Café Promenaden* is something of a favourite spot for funeral teas (the small park borders on a graveyard), with many of Ystad's older residents wanting to be remembered at the place where most of them first met and danced with their loved ones.

Another short stroll from Stortorget, past Garvaregränd's art-and craft workshops (one of which, Krukmakaren, is in a fantastically higgledy-piggledy house on the right), then up Klostergatan, brings you to **Ystadbygdens Museum** (Mon–Fri noon–5pm, Sat & Sun noon–4pm; 20kr, under-16s free). Set in the thirteenth-century Gråbröder (Greyfriars) Monastery, the collection is pretty standard local history paraphernalia, but given piquancy by their medieval surroundings. After the monks were driven out during the Reformation, the monastery declined and was used, among other things, as a hospital and a distillery, before becoming a museum in the early twentieth century. The museum has a small **café** serving coffee and cake for just 20kr. Brightly painted low cottages line the streets around here; a brief stroll down the most picturesque of these, **Vädergrand**, off Lilla Östergatan and just one block up from the *Book Café* (see below), makes for a worthwhile foray. Look particularly at no. 4 – the 1727 Gamla Handtwerfargården, a grocery in a time-warp.

Eating, drinking and nightlife

There is a fair selection of places to eat in Ystad, with some atmospheric **cafés** and fine **restaurants**; most of the latter are on or around Stortorget. **Nightlife** is pretty minimal, though things are slowly improving; the only trendy club is *Starshine* at Osterportstorg, east from Stortorget; follow Stora Östergatan (sometimes referred to just as Gågatan). There's a disco and bar here (Thurs minimum age 18, Sat 20) and, just once a month, there's "Stardust", an evening for those over 35. *Laura's* at Stora Östergatan 3 (enter through same door as the *Ronsum* supermarket) has a minimum age of 20; free entrance makes this disco and casino particularly popular. Otherwise, locals tend to take a bus thirty minutes north to the village of **Tingballa**, where there are a couple of dance halls.

Ystad stages its annual **opera festival** through most of July at Ystad Teater at Skansgatan 36, a charming 1890s building and Sweden's best-preserved nineteenth-century theatre, just a few hundred metres from the heart of the old town. You can get information on performances and book tickets at the tourist office.

The Book Café Gäsegrän. Down a tiny, cobbled street off Stora Östergatan, this precariously leaning wooden house has books – all in English – to read while you feast on the home-baked focaccia or sample one of the varieties of coffee. The gardens are delightful too, and retain their layout from 1778.

Bruggeriet Långgatan 20 ☎ 0411/699 99. The rough, beamed interior dominated by two copper beer casks creates a welcoming ambience at this fine restaurant. The well-cooked fish and meat dishes, with one vegetarian option, are usually fairly pricey, and it's a good idea to book a table.

Lotta's Stortorget 11. Justifiably the most popular restaurant in town, packed each evening in summer and serving beautifully presented, scrumptious fish and meat dishes at reasonable prices. Closed Sat & Sun.

Lotta's Källare Stortorget 11. In the cellars below *Lotta's* this cosy bar offers several English beers including the so-called "Manchester United".

Prince Charles Pub Hamngatan 8. Next door to the *Prins Carl Hotel*, this English-style pub and restaurant serves meat and fish dishes in the

evenings, with live music on Fri and Sat nights.
Store Thore Stortorget 1. Located in the cellars of the fourteenth-century Rådhus, and adding a breath of life to Stortorget in summer when tables

are brought into the square itself. At weekends, and out of the high season, the more elegant surroundings inside serve as a fitting backdrop to the less touristy Swedish menu. Meals start at 90kr.

North of Ystad: lakeside hikes and castles

The forested lake region 20km north of Ystad provides plenty of **hiking** possibilities, both along organized trails and in undeveloped tracts where you can camp rough. The trails, some of which have special tracks for wheelchairs, begin just north of the E65. Take any local bus north in the direction of **Sjöbo** (by car take Route 13), and you'll link up with the **Skåneleden** trail, which takes a hundred-kilometre circular route from just outside Ystad. The tourist office (see p.255) can provide route plans as well as details of where to find places to eat and stay en route. You can also head north on foot from Ystad to Hedeskoga and then follow trails that run past a chain of forest-fringed **lakes**: Krageholmsjön, Ellestadssjön, Snogeholmssjön and Sövdesjön (a twenty-kilometre hike).

Taking Route 13 north out of Ystad, the first village you'll see is **Sövestad**, which has nothing to detain you except a good café-bakery, two doors up from the church, serving home-made cake and coffee. The first sizeable lake worth targetting is **Snogeholmsjön**. Though the fifteenth-century castle here was sited on Hagerholmen – the now-overgrown island in the middle of the lake – the present French Baroque house dates from 1870s; it's one of the few castles in this part of Sweden which are run as a commercial proposition, in this case as a hotel (see below). From the outside, it looks like a French chateau in need of a lick of paint, but the inside is a revelation, all antique wardrobes, glittering chandeliers and elegant drawing rooms. The pictures of the current owners, leaning on guns, and the sight of their hunting trophies – boars, ferrets, deer and owls – peering from plinths above every doorway, waver between splendid and grotesque.

Just 3km northwest lies another beautifully sited lake, Sovdesjön, close to the idyllic hamlet of **Sövde**, which boasts some immaculate cottages. The real draw hereabouts, though, is the smallest of Sweden's six remaining traditional apple-presses, **Sövde Musteri**, on Sövdevagen (Fri 9am–5pm, Sat 9am–noon). The affable owner Goran Banke took over this 1890s dairy in 1984, and built a remarkable contraption for pressing apples for the finest juice, cider and scrumpy you'll find anywhere. A bottle of their headily delicious Sovde Glogg, perfumed with cloves, cinnamon, cardamom and ginger, costs just 16kr here.

Just a few minutes' walk away is the enchanting castle, **Sövdeborg Slott**. Only a couple of walls of the original Renaissance manor remain; its fairy-tale medieval facade was in fact the product of renovation in the 1840s. In the 1640s the pile was owned by Otte Thott, whose two wives – Miss Gyllenstierne and Miss Rosenkrantz – each from very wealthy, prominent Danish families, were the inspiration for the characters in *Hamlet*. The grounds are delightful, the castle's moat featuring miniature thatched houses built on stilts; to see the interior, whose highlight is a magnificent ceiling of German baroque gilded oak in the red drawing room, you'll need to make arrangements in advance with Ystad's tourist office (see p.255).

Practicalities

Getting around this region is tricky without a car. **Bus** #341 between Sjöbo and Veberod stops at Sövde (Mon–Fri every 2hr, Sat & Sun 2 daily). For a place to **stay**, there's the **hotel** at Snogeholms Slott, perched at the lake's edge (☎0416/162 00, ⓕ160 18; ❺/❹); it has a fine **restaurant** that takes advantage of the local produce. In Sjöbo, *Sjöbo Gastgiveri* serves excellent meals with daily lunch specials at 55kr. The *gästgivaregård* in Östarp, 3km northwest of Sövde, is in a splendid eighteenth-century setting and has a good à la carte menu and, on Sundays, a smorgasbord special (Tues–Thurs 11.30am–6pm, Fri 11.30am–3pm, Sat & Sun 12.30–6pm).

Österlen and the coast to Åhus

The landscape of the southeastern corner of Skåne, known as **Österlen**, is like a Mondrian painting: horizons of sunburst-yellow fields of rape running to cobalt-blue summer skies, punctuated only by white cottages, fields of blood-red poppies and the odd black windmill. Along with the vivid beauty of its countryside, Österlen has a number of engaging sights, notably picture-perfect villages, plenty of smooth, sandy beaches, and the Viking ruin of **Ales Stennar**. It's not surprising the area has lured writers and artists to settle here more than anywhere else in Sweden. Moving further northeast are the orchards of Sweden's apple-growing region, **Kivik**, with its fragrant Apple House museum and a nearby Bronze Age cairn. At the far northeastern end of this stretch of the coast lies **Åhus**, a fairly low-key resort famous for smoked eels.

Unfortunately, **getting around** this part of the country isn't straightforward without your own transport; the only major road, Route 9 to Kristianstad via Simrishamn, bypasses the most interesting southeastern corner of Österlen. The whole area is poorly served by buses and the only train service is the Pågatåg from Ystad to Simrishamn. If you haven't got a car, the best way to get around is to use a combination of public transport, walking and cycling.

From Ystad to Ales Stenar

There are two ways to get to Ales Stennar from Ystad: either take **bus** #322 (20min) or rent a bike and follow the coastal cycle track for the twenty-kilometre journey. The track runs through an area of pine forest opening onto white sandy beaches, with excellent bathing opportunities. Near Kåseberga is **Ales Stennar**, an awe-inspiring Swedish Stonehenge. Believed to have been a Viking meeting place, it consists of 56 **stones** forming a 67-metre-long boat-shaped edifice, prow and stern denoted by two appreciably larger **monoliths**. The site was hidden for centuries beneath shifting sands, which were cleared in 1958; even now, the bases of the stones are concealed in several metres of sand. It's difficult to imagine how these great stones, not native to the region, might have been transported here. Ales Stennar stands on a windy, flat-topped hill, which most of the tourists snapping away don't bother to climb; once at the top, though (it's a steep, 10min hike), there's a majestic timelessness about the spot that more than rewards the effort.

On the way to the site from the nearby car park, you'll pass a string of single-storey, white cottages, one of which houses the *Café Solståndet* (the owners live here, so opening hours are flexible), where you can have filling baguettes (40kr) or an excellent breakfast. They also do **B&B** (℡ & ℻0411/52 72 73 or 52 72 80, ⓦhttp://travel.to/kaseberga; 150kr, ❶).

The Hagestad Nature Reserve

For a day in really splendid natural surroundings, it's hard to beat the **Hagestad Nature Reserve**, the best of the three reserves around the village of **Backåkra**, a signposted drive 5km east of Kåseberga. Thousands of pines were planted here in the eighteenth and nineteenth centuries to bind the sandy earth, and, together with oaks and birches, they make up a densely forested area; the clumps of gnarled, stunted oaks are particularly distinctive. It's especially beautiful in midsummer when orchids and heathers colour the forest floor; if you're lucky, you may also see elk, badgers and roe deer, while buzzards and golden orioles are often sighted above. The reserve is also the home of the most glorious **beach** in Skåne: walk along any path towards the sea and you'll soon reach a bright white ribbon of sand – marked "Sandhammaren" on signs – backed by steep dunes and lapped by turquoise waters.

In the midst of the nature reserve, uphill on heathland towards Backåkra is an old farmstead (signposted from Backåkra) once owned by **Dag Hammarskjöld**, United Nations secretary-general in the 1950s. His love of the Skånian coast led him to buy the farm and the surrounding sixty acres in order to save it from developers. Killed in a plane crash in 1961, Hammarskjöld willed the farm and its contents to STF, which now runs the house as a **museum** (opening times vary, call ☎0411/260 10 or 261 51; 25kr). It contains amazing pieces of art from all over the world, including an ancient Egyptian painting of the jackal-headed god Anubis, Greek bronzes from 200 BC and contemporary pieces by Barbara Hepworth, Picasso and Matisse.

Practicalities

Backåkra village has a well-equipped STF **youth hostel**, in an old school house with a bus stop right outside (☎0411/260 80; 85kr, ❶; mid-Aug to April; advance booking necessary through Ystad's tourist office). You can **rent bikes** here at 35kr per day and though some of them have seen better days, they're functional and perfect for exploring the nature reserves. At **Löderups Strandbad**, just west of Backåkra, is a beautifully situated **campsite**, with a **café** and **restaurant**.

Simrishamn and Glimmingehus Castle

There's not much to the little fishing town of **SIMRISHAMN** (about 25km north of Backåkra), though its old quarter of tiny cottages and its church, originally built as a fishermen's chapel in the twelfth century, are pretty enough.

One impressive sight, just off Route 9, a few kilometres inland from Simrishamn, is the thirteenth-century **Glimmingehus Castle** (May & mid-Sept to end Sept daily 11am–5pm; June to mid-Sept daily 10am–6pm; ⓦwww.raa.se/glimminge; 45kr). Standing like an upright brick amid the flat landscape and visible for miles around, Glimmingehus lacks any of the aesthetic niceties of most of Sweden's castles, but is remarkably well preserved. One of the few projections on its flat facade is an oriel from which missiles could be dropped, clear evidence of its role as a fortification. In fact, the architect, Adam Van Duran, was drafted in to dream up as many impenetrable features as possible, and his two-metre-thick walls and slits for windows certainly lived up to the brief. The only concession to comfort was an ingenious heating system spreading warmth from the kitchen upwards. Ironically, this was one castle that was never attacked; the only threat to its existence was Karl XI's desire to demolish Glimmingehus, after Skåne had became a Swedish province, in order to prevent Danish guerrillas getting hold of it.

Practicalities

Little Österlenaren **trains** run to Simrishamn from Malmö, stopping at Ystad; from Skillinge, you can get **bus** #575 here. The **tourist office** is by the harbour at Tullhusgatan 2 (☎0414/81 98 00, ⓦwww.turistbyra.simrishamn.se); they can organize **cycling packages**, which include accommodation and cheap bike rental. **Bikes** can be rented at the *Ublivs* supermarket on the harbourfront, where they charge 30kr for the first day and 50kr for subsequent days; for longer periods, it's cheaper to use Österlens Cykel (⑦0414/177 44; 60kr for the first day, thereafter 30kr per day).

Housed in a renovated tavern, *Hotell Kockska Garden*, Storgatan 25, is a comfortable place to **stay** (⑦0414/41 17 55, ⑤41 19 78; ❸). A couple of doors down, *Hotel Turistgarden*, at no. 21, is also pleasant enough (⑦0414/166 22, ⑤137 01; ❸/❷). The town's so-called premier hotel, *Hotel Svea*, Strandvägen 3, by the harbour (⑦0414/41 17 20, ⑤143 41; ❹/❸) is more functional than stylish; its appealing **restaurant** serves a range of Swedish fish and meat dishes, with a couple of vegetarian options. Among other places to eat, one of the best is *Börje Olssons Skafferi*, Storgatan 13 (Mon–Fri 10am–6pm, Sat 10am–2pm), a charcuterie-cum-deli where you can serve yourself from a buffet of pastas, meats and breads for 40kr, or have a filled baguette, also for 40kr. *Hokarn's Café Krog*, on Storgatan (daily 1–6pm), has daily specials for 60kr; next door, the *konditori* and café does good sandwiches and cake (Mon–Fri 6.30am–5.45pm, Sat 6.30am–5pm, Sun 8am–5pm). Equally pleasant is *Mans Byckare*, directly opposite (daily 11.30am–2pm), with lunch specials at 60kr. More elegant evening dining can be had at the candle-lit *Maritim Krog*, on Hamngatan 31, at the harbour, where you can also hear live traditional jazz sounds at their **jazz club** (50kr).

Kivik and around

Not quite halfway along the coast from Simrishamn to Åhus (take Route 9 for about 9km), **KIVIK** is Sweden's **apple-growing region**, the dark forests and hilly green meadows giving way to endless orchards. As you wander through the countryside here, the pungent smell of wild garlic mixes with the fragrance of apple blossom. Kivik village has no obvious centre; the bus stops outside *Kivik Vardhus* hotel (see p.262). The uncommercialized harbour is just a few minutes away down Södergatan, and within a couple of kilometres are a number of worthwhile sights: Sweden's most notable Bronze Age remains, **Kungagraven**; a cider factory with an **Apple House** that has to be seen to be believed; and **Stenshuvud National Park**, which offers fine walks. It all makes for a day's worth of enjoyable sightseeing and meandering. For two days around the middle of July each year, Kivik hosts one of the country's biggest **markets**, an enormous event with stalls and family entertainment centred around the main square.

Kungagraven

Just 500m from the Kivik bus stop lies **Kungagraven** (King's Grave; May–Aug daily 10am–6pm; 10kr), a striking 75-metre-wide Bronze Age cairn, an upturned saucer of rocks that was unearthed by a farmer in 1748. A burial cist at its centre is entered by a banked entrance passage, the design of which makes it look strangely like a hip bar. Once inside, eight floodlit, three-thousand-year-old runic slabs bear pictures of horses, a sleigh and what look like dancing seals. For coffee and cake in a gorgeous setting, try *Café Sågmöllan* (mid-May to mid-Aug), in the old thatched mill-cottage by the stream, next to the ticket kiosk.

Kiviksmusteri and the Apple House

Two kilometres from the grave (follow the signs), **Kiviksmusteri** is a cider factory, with a shop selling apple juices, sauces, ciders, dried apple-rings, and apple or pear wines by the crate. You can't tour the factory; in any case the attraction here is the **Apple House** (April & May 10am–5pm; June–Sept 10am–6pm;

tours 20kr, under-16s free). A non-profit-making venture, the Apple House is aimed at making visitors as obsessed with apples as its dedicated workers. In a new building painted in apple greens and reds is an entire apple museum, each room infused with a different smell. The room devoted to "great apples in history" (Adam and Eve's, Newton's etc) smells of cider, while the room detailing attempts to create an insect-resistant commercial apple smells of apple pie. Other less sane exhibitions concentrate on such topics as "the symphonic soul of apples", while an Internet facility allows addicts to send apple-related messages to one another around the world. You can ask one of the guides here to describe things in English (the displays themselves don't have English labelling).

Stenshuvuds National Park

After the Apple House, **Stenshuvuds National Park**, just 200m away, is the perfect place to come back to reality. The hill which comprises the park is almost 100m high, and the view from the top is superb, particularly over Hanöberg, a village to the east. A self-guided walk (descriptive leaflets are available from boxes at the starting point) will take you to the remnants of an ancient fortress, while wheelchair-accessible paths lead through the beautiful forested hillsides. Close to the car park is a charming café, with good pastries.

Practicalities

The frequent Skåne Express **bus** runs from Simrishamn to Kivik (30min) and from Kristianstad (55min). **Bikes**, a great choice for exploring the local sights and in particular the orchards, can be rented at the harbour kiosk (mid-June to mid-Aug 10am–10pm; 75kr a day). Opposite the bus stop is a **hotel**, *Kivik Vardhus*, in a nineteenth-century vine-covered farmhouse, with pleasant rooms (T0414/700 74, F710 20; ②; May–Aug). For cheaper accommodation, there's the STF **youth hostel** north of the harbour at Tittutvägen (T0414/711 95; 145kr); just five minutes' walk from the bus stop. A good choice for **camping** is 23km north of Kivik along Route 118, and 5km south of Åhus; follow the sign off Route 118 to *Martins Rokeri* and you'll come to the tranquil riverside site, where tents can be pitched for 120kr.

At the *Kivik Vardhus* **restaurant** (daily 11.30am–9pm), the dinnertime speciality is local venison, while lunches cost 65kr. Another good **place to eat** is *Kärnhuset*, at the Apple House (see above). It serves only local produce, with an inevitable emphasis on apple desserts, and exceptionally good fresh-pressed cider. Back near the harbour, *Café Gallile*, on Eliselundsvägen (daily 7.30am–5pm), offers coffee, cakes and Skånian *spettkaka* (see p.253). There's also an excellent harbourside fish **smokery** called Buhres (daily 10am–5pm), where you can sample a dozen varieties of pickled herring and smoked eel before buying.

Kristianstad

Twenty kilometres inland, quiet **KRISTIANSTAD** (for its correct pronunciation, try a gutteral "Krwi-chwan-sta") is eastern Skåne's most substantial historic centre and a convenient gateway to Sweden's southern coast. Dating from 1614, when it was created by Christian IV, Denmark's seventeenth-century "builder-king", during Denmark's 44-year rule here, it's the earliest and most evocative of his Renaissance towns. With beautifully proportioned central squares and broad, gridded streets flanking the wide river, it was a shining example of the king's architectural preoccupations. Christian nurtured plans to make the fortified town one of Denmark's most important, and it wasn't until the mid-nineteenth century that the fortifications were finally levelled, allowing the town to spill beyond the original perimeter. The late-nineteenth century saw the creation of Parisian-style boulevards, pleasant to wander through today, though the too many bland buildings erected during the Sixties and Seventies have left the town with a rather dull appearance.

With its beautiful little **Tivoli Park** containing a fine Art Nouveau theatre, a historic **film museum** and a most elegant **cathedral**, Kristianstad can easily detain you for a relaxed day-long visit.

Arrival and information

The city's sparkling **airport** is 17km south east of the town centre; you can rent a car there from any of the major agencies. Buses from the airport to the centre are timed to leave shortly after flights arrive (20min; 60kr). Local buses from Ystad (1hr 30min, last one Mon–Fri 6.15pm, Sat 3pm), Simrishamn (1hr 30min) and Åhus (30min) all stop outside the central **bus station** on Östra Boulevarden. The fast, ultra-comfortable Kustpilen Express trains stop off here on their Malmö–Karlskrona runs, but there are no trains between the city and Ystad; the **train station**, with left-luggage lockers, is centrally located just opposite the Holy Trinity Church. The **tourist office** is down Nya Boulevarden (mid-June to mid-Aug Mon–Fri 9am–7pm, Sat 9am–3pm, Sun 2–6pm; mid-Aug to mid-June Mon–Fri 10am–5pm, last Sat of each month 11am–3pm; ☎044/12 19 88, ⓦ www.kristianstad.se/turism); to get here, turn right out of the train station and then take the second left. Sadly, this is the only town in Skåne where bikes simply cannot be rented anywhere.

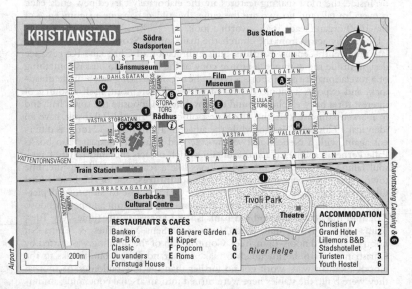

Accommodation

The tourist office can book **private rooms** from 150kr plus a 40kr fee (or you can check the list on the door and arrange things yourself for free). There is a **campsite** at *Charlottsborg Camping*, 2km west of the town centre (☎044/21 07 67; bus #22 or #23; Fri & Sat nights bus #17 to Vä from Busstorget, close to Lilla Torget). There's also a **youth hostel** here (☎044/21 07 67; 110kr) and cottages for two people (❶); campers can use all the hostel facilities including the TV and lounge room.

As Kristianstad isn't a holiday resort, prices at its **hotels**, a selection of which appears below, come down in summer and at weekends.

Hotel Christian IV Västra Boulevarden 15 ☎044/12 63 00, ✉krch.reception@first hotels.se. The most glamorous hotel in town, just south of Stora Torg, located in a rather splendid building that was once home to Sparbank, retaining its original fireplaces and parquet floors; the old bank vaults are now a washroom and a wine cellar. ❻/❸

Grand Hotel Västra Storgatan 15 ☎044/28 48 00, ✉grandkristianstad@choicehotels.se. This modern, modest-looking place offers excellent friendly service and well-equipped en-suite rooms, with supremely comfortable beds. ❺/❸

Lillemors B&B Västra Storgatan 19 ☎044/21 95 25, mobile 070/521 68 00. Built in the 1790s, this cosy hotel has exposed beams, a bright country-style attic dining room and spacious bedrooms. ❷

Stadshotellet Stora Torg ☎044/10 02 55, ⓟ10 25 80. The lobby is all panelled opulence in this old Freemasons' Hall; the rooms, though, have modern decor. ❹/❷

Turisten Västra Storgatan 17 ☎044/12 61 50, ✉info.turisten@swedenhotels.se. A good-value and comfortable option offering a friendly atmosphere, good breakfast and sauna. ❹/❸

The Town

The most obvious starting point for a visit to town is the 1618 **Trefaldighetskyrkan** (Holy Trinity Church; daily 9am–5pm), right opposite the train station. It symbolizes all that was glorious about Christian IV's Renaissance ideas: the grandiose exterior has seven magnificent spiralled gables, and the building's high windows allow light to flood the white interior. Inside, the most striking features are the elaborately carved pew ends: each is over 2m tall, and no two are the same; the gilded Baroque magnificence of the 1630 organ facade is also worth a look.

Diagonally across from the church, the main square, **Stora Torg**, contains the late nineteenth-century **Rådhus**, built in imitation of Christian's Renaissance design. Inside the entrance, a bronze copy of the king's 1643 bust is something of a revelation: Christian sports a goatee beard, one earring and a single dreadlock, and exposes a nipple decorated with a flower motif, itself a source of interest for a baby elephant round the royal neck. Opposite the town hall, and in marked contrast to it, the 1920s post office and the old Riksbank, have an identical 1920s brick design; while the adjacent 1640s Mayor's House is different again, with a Neoclassical yellow-stuccoed facade. The square also boasts Palle Pernevi's splintered *Icarus* fountain, which depicts the unfortunate Greek soul falling from heaven into what looks like a scaffolded building site. The town's streets are peppered with modern **sculptures**; one of the best is Axel Olsson's bronze *Romeo & Julia* at Östra Storgatan 3, close to Storatorg, depicting an accordion player serenading a woman emerging from an open window.

Behind the post office and old bank is the **Länsmuseum** (June–Aug Tues, Thurs & Fri 10am–5pm, Wed 10am–6pm; Sept–May Tues & Thurs–Sat noon–5pm, Wed noon–6pm; free). Construction of the building was started by Christian in 1616; he intended to make it a grand palace, but, thanks to the bloody Skånian wars, work got no further than the low buildings. As soon as they were built, the stables here were turned into an arsenal containing ammunition for the pro-Danish partisans. Today, the museum is home to permanent exhibitions about the Snapphare (from the German *schnappen*, to snatch or steal), as these partisans were called. There's also a new **art gallery** showing good contemporary temporary exhibitions.

Walking back through the town centre, a few minutes east of the Storatorg is the **Film Museum**, ostra Storgatan 53 (June–Aug Tues–Fri 1–4pm, Sun noon–5pm; free), with a bronze model of an early twentieth-century movie camera standing outside its door. This was Sweden's oldest film studio, though little is made of the fact that it closed down within eighteen months of opening in 1909. In order to compete with the other film companies, Svenska Biografteatern, which became the more famous Svensk Filmindustri, had to move to Stockholm in 1911. Inside, the first room is arranged from the set of the 1910 film "*Järnbäraren*" – you can turn handles to see early flickering images and all the original costumes.

Wander down any of the roads to the right and you'll reach **Tivoli Park**, known locally as the "English Park", with avenues of horse-chestnut and copper beech trees. In its centre is a fine Art Nouveau **theatre**, a stylish white building whose designer, Axel Anderberg, also designed the Stockholm Opera (p.79).

If you happen to arrive during the last week of May, expect hotels to be booked full for the five-day **South Swedish Rally**. Billing itself "the third largest car rally in northern Europe", it is much advertised all over town; the tourist office can tell you which are the best vantage points.

Eating, drinking and nightlife

In Kristianstad the prettiest **café** is in *Fornstuga House*, which serves just waffles and coffee in an elaborately carved Hansel-and-Gretel lodge in the middle of Tivoli Park (daily 10am–5pm, stays open later if there are park concerts). A classic and central *konditori* is *Du Vanders*, Hesslegatan 6 (Mon–Fri 8am–7pm, Sat 8am–5pm, Sun 10am–5pm), which has been serving cakes and meringues since 1934.

Banken Stora Torg. In the old Riksbank building. One of the most popular of the town's bars, with around three hundred beers, this place also has a dinner menu, mostly concentrating on meat, with one fish and one vegetarian option. Main courses from 150kr. Mon, Tues & Thurs 4pm–1am, Wed till 2am, Fri till 2am, Sat 5pm–2am.

Bar-B-Ko Tivoligatan 4 ☎044/21 33 55. An inviting, informal place, specializing in grilled Angus beef. Main courses from 100kr. Mon–Thurs 6–11pm, Fri & Sat 6pm–midnight.

Classic Nya Boulevarden 6, just off Storatorg ☎044/21 63 04. The city's only Greek restaurant, with a wide range of main courses from just 75kr. Mon–Sat 4–11pm, Sun 5–11pm.

Kipper Östra Storgatan 9. An atmospheric choice in a building that dates from 1600. The eating area is in the original vaulted cellar, with crispbread hanging from the ceiling to dry. They specialize in steaks and poultry dishes; dinner costs about 250kr, lunches 140kr. Mon 6–10pm, Tues–Thurs 11.45am–1.15pm & 6–10pm, Fri 11.45am–1.15pm & 6pm–2am, Sat 6pm–2am.

Popcorn Västra Storgatan, next to the *Grand Hotel*. A film-themed restaurant with flip-up seats taken from an old cinema. Several fish and meat dishes at 145–165kr and a surprisingly varied wine list.

Roma Östra Storgatan 15. An inexpensive Italian restaurant, worth trying for its generous pizzas at 65kr.

Bars, clubs and entertainment

For loud rock **music**, try *Harry's Bar*, Östra Storgatan (not one of the southern Sweden *Harry's Bar* chain), with a 30-something crowd and a very popular beer garden. German folk music, beers and food are to be had at a little German-owned pub, *Hesslebaren*, opposite the *Du Vanders konditori* at Hesslegatan 9 (Mon–Fri 11am–2pm & every night till late except Mon). The most attractive **drinking venue**, though, has to be *Garvare Gården* on

△ Exterior view of Christian IV's Trefaldighetskyrkan, Kristianstad

Tivoligatan (Mon–Fri 11am–10pm, Sat noon–11pm, Sun noon–9pm), in a lovely old house; there's good food here too from pasta and salads (90kr) to lobster-stuffed steaks at 192kr. On weekdays, your only chance of a late-night drink is at *Kong Christian*, Tivoligatan; this Irish theme bar is open till 1am, or 2am on Fridays and Saturdays, midnight on Sundays.

There's not much choice in the way of **nightclubs**. *Kuppa Bar*, at the train station, caters mainly for teenagers (Wed, Fri & Sat 9.30pm–2am) though on Saturday nights the clientele is a little older. In the basement of the *Grand Hotel* is the glitzy *Grands Nightclub* (Thurs 8pm–2am, Fri & Sat 9pm–1am), for somewhat dated disco sounds and a mid-20s crowd. If you're 30 or older, it's probably best to head to the basement of the *Classic* restaurant (see p.265), which is liveliest on Fridays and Saturdays till 2pm; closed in summer. In summer, the clearest sounds of nightlife emanate from the *Theatre Bar* at Tivoli Theatre in the park where there's a bar and disco.

The town hosts two annual festivals. **Kristianstadsdagarna** is a huge seven-day cultural festival in the second week of July, and the annual **Kristianstad and Åhus Jazz Festival** (Ⓦwww.bluebird.m.se) is spread between the two towns throughout June and October; details of both can be obtained at the tourist office.

Into Blekinge: east to Ronneby

The county of **Blekinge** is something of a poor relation to Skåne in terms of tourism. Tourist offices here put out an endless stream of glossy brochures calling the region "the garden of Sweden", with each of its towns, predictably, the "heart" or "pearl" of that garden. The reality is that there are some good beaches, plentiful fishing, fine walking trails and enough cultural diversions to make Blekinge enjoyable for two or three days. The landscape is much the same as in northeastern Skåne: forests and hills, with grassland fringing the sea. A number of islands and a small archipelago south of Karlskrona make for picturesque destinations on short boat trips. If you only have a day or two in the region, it's best to head to the handsome town of **Karlskrona**, the county capital (see p.272), from where the tiny, fortified hamlet of **Kristianopel** is just 30km away (see p.276).

The Kustpilen Express **train** runs from Malmö and Lund to Karlskrona, and stops at all the towns detailed below. **Public transport** in Blekinge requires some careful scrutiny of timetables so you avoid being stranded in the evenings; at weekends in particular, there are likely to be no regional trains or buses between the towns. The taxi drivers are keenly aware of this fact, charging, for example, 250kr to take you between Ronneby and Karlshamn; hitching is nigh on impossible on this route.

Karlshamn

After **KARLSHAMN** was destroyed by fire in 1763, its wealthy merchants built themselves ever-grander houses, some of which are still standing. The town saw its heyday in the nineteenth century, when it was a centre for the manufacture of such goodies as punch, brandy and tobacco – today, a hideous mess of margarine and ice-cream factories loom above the harbour. In the nineteenth century, this harbour saw a huge number of Swedes leave the country for a new life in America. Karlshamn has some beautiful little streets of pastel-painted houses, a clutch of museums, a couple of summertime festivals that transform the town into a mini-Woodstock, and offshore islands (see overleaf) that offer wooded retreats and the chance of some swimming.

With a smattering of attractive **islands** punctuating the waters to the south of Karlshamn and Ronneby, there are a number of pleasant boat trips to choose from along this stretch of the coast – although at present military restrictions mean that certain islands are off-limits to non-Swedes. Before setting off you need to get a **permit**; if taking a boat from Karlshamn, you apply directly to the boat's captain (permits are free and don't take long to obtain); in Ronneby, ask the tourist office if a permit is needed and how to get one.

One of the most popular island destinations from Karlshamn is **Tjärö**, an hour off the coast (50kr). The island has some great bathing areas among the rocks and is a good place to camp – however, the island comes alive from June onwards with partying Swedes, so finding a secluded spot may be difficult. Alternatively, you can stay at the very popular STF **youth hostel**, with its own restaurant, in an old farm building (☎0454/600 63, ℱ390 63; 160kr, ❶; early May to mid-Sept); it's advisable to book well in advance to stay in summer. A **nature tour** of the island runs all summer and must be pre-booked through the youth hostel.

The only island trip possible from Ronneby is to **Käron**, just 500m off the mainland; take the bus from Ronneby train station to Ekenas, from where an old boat regularly makes the short trip. The island is a beautiful place to wander around during the day, with old wooden houses hiding among the trees. By night, the place is popular with an 18- to 25-year-old crowd. A restaurant-cum-nightclub here, *Restaurant Karön*, serves lunches (Tues–Sun noon–2.30pm) and has dancing four nights a week (Wed–Sat). There are boats back to the mainland after the place closes at night.

From the train station, turn left onto Eric Dahlbergsvägen, and right down Kyrkogatan, which is lined with old, wooden houses painted pale creamy shades. At its junction with Drottninggatan squats Karl Gustav kyrka, an unusually shaped late seventeeth-century church. Walking down Kyrkogatan, you are retracing the steps of nineteenth-century emigrants on their way to "New Sweden" in America; for many this was the last bit of their homeland they would ever see. A grey house, on the left, with flights of external stairs either side of its front door, is the former **Hotel Hoppet** (now offices), which was immortalized by Vilhelm Moberg's *The Emigrants*: the novel's idealistic peasant farmers, Karl Oskar and his wife Kristina, spend their last night in Sweden here. If you carry on to the harbour, you'll see a poignant sculpture of the characters by the Halmstad Group's Axel Olson (a copy of which is at the House of Emigrants in Växjö, see p.299), depicting the husband staring out to sea and an unknown future, his wife glancing wistfully back for a final time.

Traditionally a working people's town, Karlshamn is one of the few areas of the country where there's an active communist party. For a quick taste of this, pop into the **Röde** (red) **bookshop** at Ronnebygatan 42 (Wed–Fri 4–6pm, Sat 10am–1pm, summertime Saturdays only), its walls adorned with simple portraits of the likes of the socialist agitator August Palm, who addressed the masses in Malmö (see p.293), and Anton Nilsson, who was imprisoned for life for blowing up a boat full of strike-breakers during strikes at the beginning of the twentieth century.

The third week of July sees Karlhamn stage its annual **Baltic Festival** (ⓦwww.karlshamn.net) – an impressive, all-consuming town celebration for all ages, with lots of eating, drinking and merriment to the sounds of live music. Karlshamn's annual **rock festival** (ⓦwww.swedenrock.com), a laid-back and pleasingly dated affair, is staged 15km west of town at the small village of **Norje**; extra buses run there for the duration. The crowds, here to see such international acts as Status Quo and Deep Purple, seem to get bigger each year. Tickets cost 880kr for both days.

The museums

The best of the town's **museums** is the amazingly well-preserved eighteenth-century merchant's house, **Skottsbergska Gården**, on Drottninggatan (Tues–Sun noon–5pm; 10kr). Built after the fire that effectively obliterated the town, the place deserves a visit. On the ground floor, the kitchen is of most interest; there's an enormous open fireplace, and all the pots and pans used over the centuries are here too. These were last used to fry up breakfast for Hanna Ljunggren, the final descendant of the original owner; she died in 1941, and her apartments on the ground floor remain as they were at her death. Upstairs there is some splendid Gustavian decoration, although, inexplicably, there don't appear to be any bedrooms; the wardrobes, which still have ancient clothes in them, are all in what seem to be living rooms.

The rest of the museums (June–Aug daily noon–5pm; Sept–May Mon–Fri 1–4pm) are all close together at the junction of Drottninggatan and Vinkelgatan. On the corner, the **Museum of Local History** (Karlshamns Museum; 10kr) is in Smithska House, built in 1765 by Oluf Berg, who was the town's richest man. Inside, there's the usual range of exhibits – old domestic furniture and marine odds and ends. Head instead into the old courtyard, around which are various buildings of more interest (though there's no English translation of the explanatory notes). You can wander up creaking stairs to authentic interiors, including a tobacco-processing works, where there's a collection of tobacco packages and the pervasive smell of the weed. The only other museum likely to fire enthusiasm is the **Punch Museum**, an intriguing place containing all the workings and contents of the Karlshamn Flaggpunsch factory, which once blended the potent mixture of sugar, arrack and brandy (10kr, free with entry to local history museum). You can ask one of the guides to show you around, and even have a serving of the liquor (20kr). The factory was closed down in 1917, when the state monopoly over the trade and distribution of alcohol was begun. A nonalcoholic – and accordingly less celebrated – punch was made here until 1967.

A real treat for **cinema** fans is the little-celebrated Metropol Cinema, Fogdelyckegatan, just off Drottninggatan near the museums. Built in 1923 by celebrated Malmö architect Axel Stenberg, the facade was added in the Sixties, but the inside maintains its hand-painted ceiling, original period lighting and wall paintings. There's a showing a night, usually of mainstream films (Wed–Sun; 65kr).

Practicalities

Karlshamn is a 45-minutes **train** ride from Kristianstad and fifty minutes from Karlskrona. **Ferries** leave for Klapeda in Lithuania every other day (600kr, 1000kr return; ☎0454/190 83, ⓦwww.karlshamn.net, select "kommunikationer"). They dock at Stillerydshamnen, 4km west of town. No buses make this trip, so taxis are necessary (100kr).

A ten-minute walk from the station, or bus #310, the harbourside **tourist office** is on the corner of Ågatan and Ronnebygatan (mid-June to mid-Aug Mon–Fri 9am–7pm, Sat 10am–6pm, Sun noon–6pm; mid-Aug to mid-June Mon–Fri 9am–5pm; ☎0454/812 03, ⓔturistbyran@karlshamn.se). They can book **private rooms** (150kr per person plus 50kr booking fee) and **private cottages** (3000kr per week for two) anywhere in the region. An STF **youth hostel** is next to the train station at Surbrunnsvägen lc (☎0454/140 40, ⓔstfturistkhamn@hotmail.com; 145kr). The nearest **campsite** is at Kollevik, 3km out of town (℡0454/812 10; from 460kr for 4-person cabins; May–Sept). It's nicely positioned by the sea, with beaches and a swimming pool close by but there are no buses. Inland, another campsite is *Långasjönäs*, 10km north of town (℡0454/32 06 91; weekends 370kr for 4-person cabins, minimum bookings for one week; May–Sept); bus #310 gets you to within 3km of the site, from where you'll have to walk.

The cheapest central **hotel** is *Bode Hotel*, at Södra Fogdelyckegatan 28. It's a plain, reasonable sort of place with shared facilities (℡0454/315 00; ❶). For more luxury, there's the harbourfront *First Hotel Carlshamn*, Varvsgatan 1, opposite the tourist office (℡0454/890 00, ℮carlshamn@firsthotels.se; ❺/❷), with a grand atrium hall and a pleasing restaurant.

Karlshamn has an extraordinarily good, principally vegetarian **restaurant**, *Gourmet Grön* at Drottninggatan 61 (Mon–Sat 11.45am–10pm; ℡0454/164 40). Almost justifying a visit to the town in itself, you'll find massive bowls of innovative food elegantly presented in a buffet. Eating as much as you can manage costs a remarkably good-value 75kr during the day, 125–195kr in the evening. *Terrassen Restaurant*, Ronnebygatan 12 (daily 11am–midnight), has a wide range of fish and meat dishes, with outside seating. The most popular **café** is *Christin's* at Drottninggatan 65; though it's nothing special to look at, the location makes it a favourite local meeting place and its *konditori* is rather fine too.

Ronneby

Much of **RONNEBY**, which lies thirty kilometres east of Karlshamn, has been ruined by development: as you arrive here by train, even the summer sun can't disguise the banality of the buildings ahead. There is, however, a tiny **old town**, a few minutes' walk up the hill to the left of the station, testimony to the fact that in the thirteenth century, this was Blekinge's biggest town and a centre for trading with the Hanseatic League. Only when the county became Swedish, four centuries later, did Ronneby fall behind neighbouring Karlskrona. Today, the main attraction is the beautifully preserved collection of spa houses, a couple of kilometres away at **Ronneby Brunnspark** (see opposite); you might also want to consider a trip out to the offshore island of **Käron** (see p.268).

In the town itself, walk uphill to the left of the train station, and turn left again onto the main street, Kungsgatan. There is nothing much of interest until you reach **Helga Korskyrkan** (Church of the Holy Cross). With its whitewashed walls, blocked-in arched windows and red-tiled roof, the church looks like a Greek chapel presiding over the surrounding modern apartment buildings. Dating originally from the twelfth century, this Romanesque church took quite a bashing during the Seven Years' War (1563–70) against the Danes. On the night of what is known as the **Ronneby Blood Bath** in September 1564, all those who had taken refuge in the church were slaughtered – gashes made in the north walls' heavy oak door during the violence can still be seen. The seventeenth-century wood carvings on the pulpit and altar are impressive. If you peer carefully at the south wall through the gloom, you'll see a partly damaged *Dance with Death* wall painting. The most attractive part of town is behind the church. Tiny cobbled alleys on inclines are fringed with perfect wooden cottages peppered with little arts and craft studios. Head down Möllebacksgatan and downhill from Bergslagsgatan into Kyrkogatan for a very pleasant jaunt.

Ronneby Brunnspark

In 1775, the waters here were found to be rich in iron, and Ronneby soon became one of Sweden's principal spa towns. The centre of this activity was **Ronneby Brunnspark**, fifteen minutes' walk from the train station, turning right up the hill and over the river (or take bus #211). Today, the park's houses stand proudly amid blazing rhododendrons and azaleas; one such property is now a fine STF youth hostel (see below). The neighbouring building is the wonderful café-bar **Wiener Café**, with bare floorboards and hand-painted abstract designs on the walls. Built in 1862 as a doctor's home, it was occupied by Danish resistance fighters during World War II. There are pleasant **walks** through the beautifully kept park, past the pond and into the wooded hills behind, picking up part of the **Blekingeleden** walking trail. Also through the trees are some unexpected gardens, including a Japanese Garden. Another of the old spa houses, a gorgeous 1870-built villa, contains **Blekinge Naturum** (June–Aug Tues–Sun 11am–6pm), which can advise on the best walking in the surrounding countryside and also rents out **canoes** (30kr/day, 150kr/week). A full list of **guided walks** in the area is posted outside the front door. The park is also the site of a giant **flea market** every Sunday morning (May–Sept), where genuine Swedish antiques can be picked up amid general tat. **Tours** of the park area run every Sunday from June to August – ask at the tourist office for details.

Practicalities

From Karlshamn, there are frequent **trains** (34min) and **buses** to Ronneby. The **tourist office** is at Västra Torggatan 1, beneath the church (mid-June to end June & Aug Mon–Fri 9am–6pm, Sat 10am–4pm, Sun noon–4pm; July Mon–Fri 9am–7pm, Sat 10am–4pm, Sun noon–4pm; rest of year Mon–Fri 10am–5pm; ☎0457/180 90, ⓦwww.ronneby.se). You can rent **bikes** from Thore's Cykel (Mon–Thurs 8am–6pm, Fri 1–6pm; ☎0457/137 76 or 070/378 95 52), at Gustav Arnoldsgatan, one street back from the train station.

A good place to stay is the STF **youth hostel** in Ronneby Brunnspark (☎ & ℻0457/263 00; 100kr; closed Dec to early Jan); you can bring your wn food and eat alfresco on its balcony. In town, the owners of the hostel also run the inappropriately named *Grand Hotel*, Järnvägsgatan 11 (☎0457/268 80, ℻268 84; ❷), an adequate place in a modern apartment building opposite the train station. Far better, and the place to try first, is the town's best **bed and breakfast** *Villa Vesta*, Nedre Brunnsvägen 25 (☎0457 661 36; ❷), an immaculate, family-run place with en-suite rooms. The new owners have restored this late nineteenth-century house, retaining the original painted ceilings, *Jugendstil* Swedish stove and beautiful conservatory with stained glass, overlooking the river. From the train station, cross the river and head in the direction of Ronneby Brunnspark; it's signed off to the right. Despite being set in the middle of the park, the *SAS Radisson Ronneby Brunn Hotel* (☎0457/750 00, ⓦwww.radissonsas.com; ❺/❹) is little more than a garish chain hotel with with good facilities, including a full-size outdoor pool.

For **eating and drinking** in town, the best café is *Nya Wienerbageriet* on Västra Torgatan, next to the tourist office (not to be confused with *Wiener Café* in the park. An old bakery converted into a bar and **café**, with outside tables (Mon–Thurs 9am–11pm, Fri & Sat 9am–midnight), it serves wholesome lunches, excellent salads, fresh dark breads and coffee and it's where Ronneby's cool folk hang out. At the back is a stylish **bar** (Thurs–Sat 6pm till late) with occasional live music, mostly blues or jazz. Just off Stortorget is the best *konditori*, the *Continental*; this well-stocked bakery has an uncommonly tantalising selection of cakes and is the only place to sit and have a coffee on a Sunday morning. *Wiener Café* in Ronneby Brunnspark has live music and a disco on Thursdays. Fish soup and steaks are on a short, not over-inspired menu at the *Restaurant Karö* in the same attractive old building (Tues 6.30–11pm, Wed–Fri 6pm–midnight, Sat noon–1am, Sun noon–4pm). Another good place for lunch in an airy setting is *Bergslagskrogen*, at the Kulturcentrum close by the church (Mon–Fri 11.30am–2.30pm buffet, Fri 6–11pm, Sat 1–11pm, Sun noon–5pm), serving a range of meat dishes at 100–170kr with some fish and one vegetarian option. For **evening meals**, try the appealing *Garlic House* in a pistachio and strawberry painted old house at Karlskronagatan 29, just up from the train station towards the old town. Mains dishes are offered at 84–159kr and served at comfy, leather seats (℡0457/134 00 Mon–Sat 5.30pm–10.30pm).

Karlskrona and around

Set on the largest link in a chain of breezy islands, **KARLSKRONA**, the capital of Blekinge, is the county's most appealing destination. Founded by Karl XI in 1680, who chose the site as a base for his Baltic fleet because the seas here are ice-free in winter, the town still revolves around its maritime heritage today. Built to accommodate the king's naval parades, Karlskrona's wide avenues and stately squares survive intact, a fact which has earned it a place on UNESCO's World Heritage list, despite the anonymous blocks plonked right between the town's splendid churches. Today, cadets in uniform still career around its streets, many of which are named after Swedish admirals and battleships; the town's biggest museum is, unsurprisingly, dedicated to maritime history (see p.274). Don't despair, though, if you're not a fan of things naval, for Karlskrona has plenty more to offer: a picturesque **old quarter**, around the once-busy fishing port at Fisktorget; and good **swimming** off the nearby island of Dragsö (see below), or, without braving the sea, at the fine pool opposite the train station. If you're around during the first week of August, you'll witness the whole town come alive for a huge **sailing festival** with boats lining the harbour and a party atmosphere with a fair, live music, food stalls and entertainment late into the evening from Friday to Sunday.

Arrival and information

The **train** and **bus stations** are opposite each other, 200m north of Hoglands Park. From either station, the **tourist office**, at Stortorget 2, just behind the Frederikskyrkan (mid-June to mid-Aug Mon–Fri 9am–7pm, Sat & Sun 9am–4pm; Sept–May Mon–Fri 10am–5pm, Sat 10am–1pm; ℡0455/30 34 90, ⓦwww.karlskrona.se/tourism), is an eight-minute stroll away: head south up Landbrogatan, with the park on your left, then proceed along Rådhusgatan to Stortorget. They can book **private rooms** from around 125kr per person and rent out green military **bikes** for 30kr a day (especially useful if you intend to visit Kristianopel; see p.276). A better choice for bikes, however, is the Q8 petrol station, at Järnvägstorget, behind the train station (℡0455/819 93; Mon–Sat 7am–9pm, Sun 9am–6pm), where new multispeed bikes can be rented for 55kr a day.

Accommodation

The STF **youth hostel** at Bredgatan 16 (℡& ⓕ0455/100 20; 115kr; mid-June to mid-Aug) is very central, and has en-suite rooms. A newer STF hostel close by is *Trossö Vandrarhem*, Drottninggatan 39 (same number as Bredgatan hostel), which doesn't have en-suite facilities but does have the advantage of being open all year. You can **camp** out on Dragsö island, around 2.5km away (☎0455/153 54); bus #7 leaves from the bus station to Saltö, the island before Dragsö, from where it's a one-kilometre walk across the bridge.

Aston Landbrogatan 1 ☎0455/194 70, ⓔhotel.aston@trossohotel.se. With the same owners as the *Conrad*, this simple place is of a slightly higher standard. Closed weekends in summer. ❹/❷

Carlskrona Skeppsbrokajen ☎0455/36 15 00, ⓦwww.softwarehotels.se. A pleasant hotel close to the station in a contemporary building right next to the ferry terminal. There's free coffee and tea served throughout the day but it can get very noisy during the sailing festival. ❺/❸

Conrad Västra Köpmangatan 12, ☎0455/36 32 00, ⓔinfor@hotelconrad.se. Plain and basic place up the hill from the station towards Stortorget. ❸/❶

First Hotel Borgmästaregatan 13 ☎0455/270 00, ⓦwww.firsthotels.se. Slightly more relaxed version of its sister hotel (see below), with a friendly ambience and a pleasant informality. There's a 24-hour bistro and free coffee and cake are available from Mondays to Thursdays.

First Hotel Statt Ronnebygatan 37–39 ☎0455/192 50, ⓦwww.firsthotels.se. The Empire-style design rooms in this 1890 building on the main shopping street are aimed at the luxury end of the market. ❺/❹

Siesta Borgmästaregatan 5 ☎0455/801 80, ⓦwwwhotelsiesta.com. Just off Stortorget, this is the plainest of the town's hotels. ❹/❷

The Town

Arriving by train or bus offers an encouraging first glimpse of the island network. The first island you'll pass on the way in is **Hästö**, once home to Karlskrona's wealthiest residents. It's just a few minutes further from Hästö to the centre on the island of **Trossö**, connected to the mainland by the main road, Österleden (the E22). Climb uphill past Hoglands Park, named after an eighteenth-century

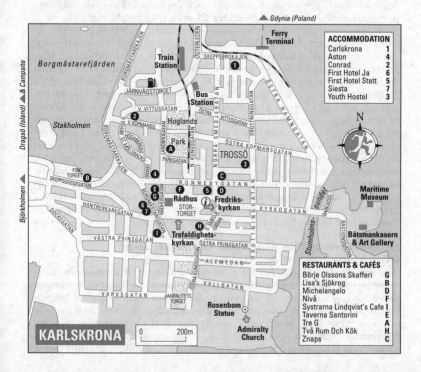

273

battle, to the main square, **Stortorget**, at the highest point and geographical centre of the island. It's a vast and beautiful square, dominated by two complementary **churches**; both were designed by Tessin the Younger and are stuccoed in burnt orange with dove-grey stone colonnades. The more interesting of the churches is the circular, domed **Trefaldighetskyrkan** (Mon–Fri 11am–3pm, Sat 9.30am–2pm; guided tours can be requested here). Built for the town's German merchant community in 1709, its most remarkable feature is its domed ceiling, painted with hundreds of rosettes. The altar is also distinctive with golden angelic faces peering out of a gilded meringue of clouds. In the crypt are the remains of two of Karlskrona's most revered men, Count Hans Wachtmeister, responsible for much of the building of the town in the late seventeenth century; and Johan Törnström, who made most of the fabulous ship figureheads on show at the Maritime Museum (see below). **Fredrikskyrkan**, a few steps away, is an elegant, light-flooded church with towers, but holds fewer surprises inside (Mon–Fri 11am–3pm, Sat 9.30am–2pm).

The Admiralty Church
From Stortorget, head between the churches and walk past the pseudo-medieval castellated waterworks down Södra Kungsgatan. The wide, cobbled street is divided down the centre by the boulder-like stone walls of a tunnel, where a train line (disused) ran from the main station up to the harbour. The leafy square ahead is **Amiralitets Torget**; perched at its centre is the huge, apricot-and-grey-painted wooden bell tower of the Admiralty Church. To see the church itself (signposted "Kungliga Amiralitetskyrkan"), head down Vallgatan on the left of the square, passing the symmetrical austerity of the Marine Officers' School; just before you reach the harbour, the beautifully proportioned, entirely wooden **Admiralty Church** is up on the right. This simple elegant structure, Sweden's biggest wooden church, was built in 1685.

Outside the entrance, take a look at one of the city's best-known landmarks: the wooden statue of **Rosenbom**, around which hangs a sorrowful tale. Mats Rosenbom, one of the first settlers on Trossö island, lived nearby with his family and earned his keep in the shipyard. However, after a fever killed six of his children and left him and his wife too ill to work, he applied for, and was granted, a beggar's licence. One New Year's Eve, while begging at the homes of leading townspeople, he became somewhat drunk from the festive wine on offer and forgot to raise his hat to thank the wealthy German figurehead carver, Fritz Kolbe. When admonished for this, Rosenbom retorted, "If you want thanks for your crumbs to the poor, you can take my hat off yourself!" Enraged, Kolbe struck him between the eyes and sent him away, but the beggar, unable to make it home, froze stiff and died in a snowdrift by the church. Next morning, Kolbe found the beggar frozen to death and, filled with remorse, carved a figure of Rosenbom which stands at the spot where he died. It's designed so that you have to raise his hat yourself to give some money.

Stumholmen: The Maritime Museum and Båtsmanskasern Art Gallery
The best museum Karlskrona has is set on the island of **Stumholmen**, connected to the mainland by road and just five minutes' walk east of Stortorget, down Kyrkogatan. If you prefer, you can take a boat from Fisktorget, but this takes longer. As soon as you cross the bridge onto Stumholmen, there's a large sign indicating all the buildings of interest here. To the left, the prize-winning **Maritime Museum** (June–Aug daily 10am–6pm; Sept–May Tues–Sun 11am–5pm; 50kr; ⓦwww.marinmuseum.se) has a facade like a futuristic Greek

temple. A portrait of Carl XI, who had the navy moved from Stockholm to Karlskrona in 1680, features in the hallway, a pet lion at his feet gazing up at the king's most unappealing, bloated face. Down a spiral staircase from here is a transparent underwater tunnel offering a view of hundreds of fish in the murky depths. The best room, though, contains the **figureheads** designed and made by the royal sculptor to the navy, Johan Törnström. King Gustav III declared that ships of the line should be named after manly virtues, and so have male figureheads, while frigates have female ones. Among the finest is one made for the ship *Försiktigheten* (1784) – a metre-long foot, perfectly proportioned complete with toenails. There's a pleasant, though unambitious, **café** here too, serving light meals for around 55kr.

Just a couple of minutes' walk away is an **art gallery** (Tues–Fri noon–4pm, Wed noon–7pm, Sat & Sun noon–5pm; free), set in the splendid old Seamen's Barracks ("Båtamanskasern"). The building dates from 1842, and was once used to simulate life on the seas during the training of young sailors – the wooden floor is slightly arched to appear like a ship's deck, and the apprentice seamen would have slept here in hammocks, as they did at sea. While the temporary exhibitions downstairs are usually of a good standard, it's well worth heading up to the first floor, where there's a permanent exhibition of the work of the late Erik Langemark. Born in Karlskrona in 1915, he was the best known of those who chronicled the city in art. His paintings of Karlskrona are accompanied here by up-to-date photographs of the places depicted, showing how the city has changed; compare his *Gamla Teatern* (Old Theatre), painted in 1971, with the scene today – only the huge tree now remains.

The harbour and Fisktorget

From the waterside, at the end of Vallgatan, the divide between the picturesque town and the continuing military presence is most apparent: to the left are the old white lighthouse and the archipelago, and the pink- and white-stuccoed county governor's residence; to the right, however, mud-coloured military vessels fill the old quayside, and "Forbidden to Enter" signs abound. For more of a feel of old Karlskrona, wander west past the military hardware towards the **Björkholmen** area. Here, a couple of early eighteenth-century wooden houses survive, homes that the first craftsmen at the then new naval yard built for themselves. All the streets running north–south are named after types of ships, while those from west to east are named after admirals. Nearby **Fisktorget**, once the site of a fish market, is pleasant for a stroll. Nowadays the boats here are mainly pleasure yachts, and there are a couple of pleasant cafés. You'll also find the dull **Blekinge Museum** at the harbourfront (Tues & Thurs–Sun 11am–5pm, Wed till 7pm; 20kr), housed in the 1705 wooden home built for Count Wachtmeister – the pleasant summertime café is more appealing than the exhibits on shipbuilding and the like.

Eating and drinking

Karlskrona is suprisingly poor for good restaurants – most proper eating places are along Ronnebygatan – and, even more strangely given its location, has almost nothing in the way of decent fish places. A couple of the town's **cafés** stand out from the rest.

Börje Olssons Skafferiet Rådhusgatan 9. A really good deli and café combined. Here, you can buy luscious olives, meats, cheeses and exotic pickles for picnics as well as filled baguettes, croissants, great coffees and the best hot chocolate in town. **Café Tre G** Landbrogatan 9, opposite Hoglands

Park. Baked potatoes, cakes and sandwiches served in pleasant surroundings. The city's only café open on a Sunday. **Systrarna Lindkvists Café** Borgmästaregatan 3, across from the tourist office. Coffee is served in fine old gilded china cups, with silver teaspoons and sugar tongs, at this rather genteel establishment.

Ristorante Michelangelo Ronnebygatan 29. The best of the bunch of Italian-style restaurants: slightly pricey but undeniably more elegant than the others in town.

Taverna Santorini Rådhusgatan 11 ☏0455/30 02 02. A Greek restaurant serving a wide choice of dishes including several vegetarian options; dishes cost 30–130kr.

Två Rum Och Kök Södre Smedjegatan 3 ☏0455/104 22. A romantic little place with meat and fowl dishes at a pricey 200kr plus, slightly

cheaper fish dishes, but the draw here is the fondues – meat, fish and vegetarian as well as the popular chocolate.

Nivå Stortorget. A popular steakhouse right on the main square opposite the church.

Lisa's Sjökrog Fisktorget harbour. A floating restaurant with a mix of seafood and meats. Starters are 60–80kr, while mains are mostly around 150kr, and there's a lighter, pub menu.

Znaps Ronnebygatan 30. A laid-back, stylish drinking joint with a varied pasta menu and good burgers served alongside the schnapps and lots of other beverages.

Kristianopel

Arriving by road at the idyllic hamlet of **KRISTIANOPEL**, 30km northeast of Karlskrona (take either the E22 or the coast road to get here), there isn't the slightest hint that this village of just 38 inhabitants was once a strategically positioned fortification with a bloody history. Neither is it obvious – unless you're here during that time – that every July, the place packs out with holiday-makers and acquires an atmosphere of summer revelry that's seldom found elsewhere in Sweden. Only when you've walked past the minute, pristine cottages all the way to the tiny harbour do you see the three kilometres of three-metre-thick **fortification walls** that surround the settlement. The low, squat walls are actually a 1970s reconstruction, built on the foundations of the original fortifications. Erected in 1600 by the Danish king Christian IV to protect against Swedish aggression, the original walls were finally razed by the Swedes after the little town had spent 77 years changing hands with alarming regularity. The only other sight worth a look is the **church**, near the village shop; inside is an eye-catching altar, decorated with vividly drawn trees. The present church replaced a medieval one, whose site, located near the campsite (see opposite), is just a grassy mound today. In 1605, the former church was the scene of great bloodshed: it was burnt to the ground, killing all the women, children and elderly of the village who were huddled inside for what they imagined was protection. They mistakenly believed that the then 16-year-old King Gustav II Adolf would respect it as a place of God.

Though a charming place to visit at any time, Kristianopel is at its very best during summer, when the population jumps to around two thousand. Many of the visitors stay at the tiny hostel and adjacent campsite, tucked inside the low walls and overlooking the sea. Every July, the restaurant here is the focus for a wide range of music and night-time entertainment, ranging from Eurovision Song Contest favourites to folk music. Even if the music doesn't grab you, the bonhomie and the wonderful setting make this a great social event that's well worth dipping into.

Practicalities

Hitching is easier here than in most places in Sweden – which is just as well, as getting to Kristianopel can be tricky by public transport. **Bus** #120 from Karlskrona stops at Kristianopel, but runs only during school terms; throughout the year, you can use the twice-daily bus #500, which runs to Kalmar from Karlskrona along the E22. However, the closest to town you can get on this bus is Fågelmara, 6km from the village; luckily, you can cover the rest of the distance on a bike, which you can take on the bus at no extra cost. Though the signposting on the way can be confusingly ambiguous, **cycling** here from Karlskrona (around 45km) is an enjoyable experience. You don't need to use the relatively busy E22: the prettiest route is to follow minor roads first to Lyckeby, then tracks which lead through cornfields and flowering meadows to Ramdala and the little town of Jämjö. From here, the most appealing way is to cut to the coast (follow signs to Konungshamn), from where Kristianopel is straight up north.

For **accommodation** in the village, there's the **youth hostel** (℡ & ℻0455/36 61 30; 110kr, ❶), with a **campsite** attached (same phone number); at the campsite you can rent a rowing boat (20kr an hour) or – for those who prefer to shoot at wildlife rather than just admire it – go on seabird hunting trips to the local islands (Sept–Jan). The village's one **hotel**, to the left of the main road into the village, is a mellow eighteenth-century farmhouse called *Gästgiferi* (℡ & ℻0455/36 60 30; ❶; April–Sept) set in beautiful gardens.

For provisions, there are a couple of shops on the campsite, and another near the church. You'll find a couple of **restaurants** and one superb café in the village: the *Gästgiferi*, with its charming farmhouse decor, tends to appeal to an older crowd; main courses here start from 95kr. Hans Alerstedt, one of Kristianopel's most enduring and central residents, presides over not only the youth hostel, campsite, and rowing and hunting expeditions, but also the campsite's wooden *Värdshuset Pålsgården* (Fri 6–9pm, Sat noon–9pm, Sun noon–6pm), serving tasty food in cosy surroundings; in July it opens late every night as a pub. Don't leave the village without sampling the lovely home-baked cakes at the *Sött Och Salt* café in the white stone house near the harbour; very good-value lunches are also served here.

Travel details

Express trains

Daily express trains operate throughout the region, in particular Oslo–Copenhagen (via Gothenburg, Varberg, Halmstad and Helsingborg) and Stockholm–Copenhagen (via Helsingborg). Both routes have a branch service through to Malmö. Despite complicated timetabling, the service is frequent and regular north or south between Gothenburg and Helsingborg/Malmö.

Trains

Helsingborg to: Gothenburg (9 daily; 2hr 40min); Lund (13 daily; 40min); Malmö (13 daily; 50min).
Karlskrona to: Emmaboda for connections to Växjö, Stockholm & Kalmar (1–2 hourly; 40min).
Kristianstad to: Karlshamn (hourly; 50min); Karlskrona (hourly; 1hr 45min); Ronneby (hourly; 1hr 20min).
Malmö to: Gothenburg (8–10 daily; 3hr 45min); Karlskrona (hourly; 3hr 15min); Kristianstad (4 daily; 47min); Lund (3 hourly; 13min); Ystad (Mon–Fri hourly, Sat & Sun 5 daily; 50min).

Buses

Ängelholm to: Torekov (5 daily; 45min).
Båstad to: Torekov (5 daily; 30min).
Helsingborg to: Båstad (16 daily; 55min); Halmstad (6 daily; 1hr 50min).
Karlskrona to: Stockholm (Fri & Sun 1 daily; 7hr 30min); Kristianopel (Sat & Sun 2 daily; 25min).
Kristianstad to: Kalmar (1 daily; 3hr); Lund (1 daily; 2hr 30min); Malmö (1 daily; 2hr 45min).
Malmö to: Falkenberg (Fri & Sun 2 daily; 2hr 55min); Gothenburg (Mon–Thurs 1 daily, Fri & Sun 3 daily; 4hr 25min); Halmstad (Fri & Sun 2 daily; 2hr 25min); Helsingborg (Mon–Thurs 1 daily, Fri & Sun 6 daily; 1hr 5min); Jönköping (Mon–Thurs 1 daily, Fri & Sun 3 daily; 4hr 30min); Kalmar (1 daily; 5hr 30min); Kristianstad (1 daily; 2hr); Lund (hourly; 20min); Mellbystrand (Fri & Sun 1 daily; 2hr); Stockholm (Mon–Thurs 1 daily, Fri & Sun 3 daily; 9hr); Trelleborg (hourly; 35min); Varberg (Fri & Sun 2 daily; 3hr 20min).
Ystad to: Kristianstad (Mon–Fri 5–6 daily, Sat & Sun 3 daily; 1hr 55min); Lund (Mon–Fri 3 daily; 1hr 15min); Malmö (3 daily; 1hr); Simrishamn

(Mon–Fri 3 daily, 1 on Sat & Sun; 50min); Smygehamn (Mon–Fri 5 daily, Sat & Sun 3 daily; 30min).

International ferries, hydrofoils and catamarans

Halmstad to: Grenå, Denmark (2 daily; 4hr).
Helsingborg to: Helsingør, Denmark (3 hourly; 25min).

Karlskrona to: Gdynia, Poland (1 daily; 10hr 30min).
Simrishamn to: Allinge (summer only 3–4 daily; 1hr).
Trelleborg to: Rostock, Germany (3 daily; 6hr); Sassnitz (5 daily; 3hr 45min); Travemünde, Germany (2 daily; 7–9hr).
Varberg to: Grenå, Denmark (2 daily; 4hr).
Ystad to: Rønne, Bornholm (3–5 daily; 2hr 30min); Swinoujscie, Poland (2 daily; 7–9hr).

The southeast

CHAPTER 4

Highlights

✱ **Kalmar Castle** Visit the exquisite interior of this sensational, twelfth-century stronghold that has been beautifully remodelled into a Renaissance Palace. See p.284

✱ **Kullzenska Caféet, Kalmar** Tuck in to the scrumptious cakes in the wonderful faded gentility of this eighteenth-century home. See p.287

✱ **House of Emigrants, Växjö** The exhibition of the poignant stories of millions of Swedes forced to emigrate to the United States in the nineteenth century is an essential stop on any visit to Småland. See p.299

✱ **Västänås Slott, Röttle** A bed and breakfast like no other: this grand country house with superb views over Lake Vättern is crammed with antiques. See p.312

✱ **Vadstena** The most atmospheric lakeside town on the eastern shores of Lake Vättern is home to the massive abbey founded by Sweden's first female saint, Birgitta. See p.317

✱ **Norrkoping's textile factories** Described by Carl Milles as Europe's most beautiful industrial landscape, the striking stuccoed buildings reflect in the crashing waters of this lively town. See p.329

✱ **Visby, Gotland** Visit the remarkable walled city of the former Hanseatic League stronghold and party along with the thousands of young Swedes who spill on to this superb Baltic island every Summer. See p.339

The southeast

Although a less obvious target than the coastal cities and resorts of the southwest, Sweden's **southeast** certainly repays a visit. You'll find impressive castles, ancient lakeside sites, and numerous glassworks amid the forests of the so-called "Glass Kingdom", while off the east coast, Sweden's largest Baltic islands offer beautifully preserved medieval towns and fairy-tale landscapes. Train transport, especially between the towns close to the eastern shore of Lake Vättern and Stockholm, is good; speedy, regular services mean that you could see some places on a day-trip from Stockholm.

Småland county in the south encompasses a varied geography and some stridently different towns. **Kalmar** is a very likeable stop; a glorious historic fortress town, it deserves more time than its tag as a jumping-off point for the island of Öland suggests. Inland, great swathes of dense forest are rescued from monotony by the many **glass factories** that continue the county's traditional industry, famous the world over for its design and quality, though today drowning in its own marketing hyperbole. In **Växjö**, the largest town in the south, two superb museums deal with the art of glass-making and the history of Swedish emigration. At the northern edge of the county and perched on the southernmost tip of Lake Vättern, **Jönköping** is known as Sweden's Jerusalem for its remarkable number of Free Churches; it is also a great base for exploring the beautiful eastern shore of Vättern. In the middle of the lake is the island of **Visingsö**, rich in royal history and natural beauty.

The idyllic pastoral landscape of **Östergotland** borders the eastern shores of the lake and reaches as far east as the Baltic. One of its highlights, and popular with domestic tourists, is the small lakeside town of **Vadstena**, its medieval streets dwarfed by austere monastic edifices, a Renaissance palace and an imposing abbey, brought into being by the zealous determination of Sweden's first female saint, Birgitta. The **Göta Canal** wends its way through the northern part of the county to the Baltic, with a number of fine towns lining the route. These include **Linköping**, with its strange open-air museum where people live and work in a re-created nineteenth-century environment. Just to the north, **Norrköping**, a bustling and youthful town, grew up around the textile industry; today it boasts Europe's best collection of preserved red-brick and stuccoed factories.

Outside the fragmented archipelagos of the east and west coasts, Sweden's only two sizeable islands are in the Baltic: Öland and Gotland, adjacent slithers of land with unusually temperate climates for their latitudes. They were domestic tourist havens for years, but now an increasing number of foreigners are discovering their charms – lots of summer sun, delectable beaches and some impressive historic (and prehistoric) sights. **Öland** – the smaller island and

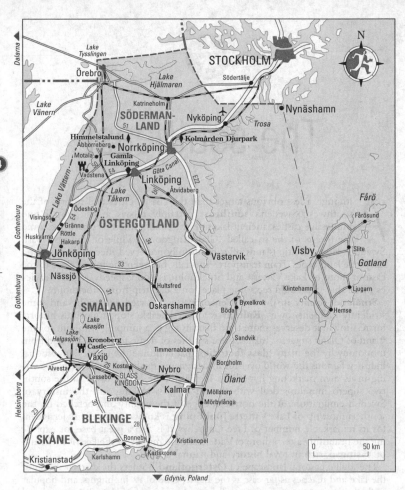

closer to the mainland – has a mix of shady forests and flowering meadows that make it a tranquil spot for a few days' exploration. **Gotland**'s well-known highlight is its Hanseatic medieval capital, **Visby**, a city pervaded by a carnival atmosphere in summer when ferry-loads of young Swedes come to sunbathe and party. The rest of the island, however, is little visited by tourists, and all the more magical for that.

Into Småland: Kalmar

Delightful, breezy **KALMAR**, set on a huddle of islands at the southeastern edge of the county of Småland, has treasures enough to make it one of southern Sweden's most delightful towns. Chief among the town's highlights are the **Länsmuseum**, home to an exhibition on the sunken warship, the *Kronan*, and an exquisite fourteenth-century **castle**, Scandinavia's finest preserved

Renaissance palace. The town is also perfectly sited for reaching the Baltic island of Öland (see p.288), which is just 6km away across the connecting bridge.

Arrival and information

Kalmar's **train station** is at Stationsgatan, at the southern end of the New Town, on the island of Kvarnholmen. The **bus terminal**, used by Öland buses, is a short distance to the west. Within spitting distance of both stations is the **tourist office**, Larmgatan 6, at the junction with Ölandsgatan (early June & late Aug Mon–Fri 9am–7pm, Sat & Sun 10am–4pm; mid-June to mid-Aug Mon–Fri 9am–8pm, Sat & Sun 10am–5pm; May & Sept Mon–Fri 9am–5pm, Sat 10am–1pm; rest of year Mon–Fri 9am–5pm; ⊤0480/153 50, ⓦwww.kalmar.se/turism). They stock an English booklet, with maps, for a **self-guided tour** around the town (30kr), alternatively, in July, English-language **guided city tours** are run from the tourist office at 6pm on Wednesdays (50kr).

Kalmar can be explored easily enough on foot but if you wish to strike out into the surrounding countryside, you can rent a **bike** from Team Sportia, Södravägen 2 (Mon–Fri 10am–6pm, Sat 10am–2pm; 40kr a day).

Accommodation

The tourist office arranges **private rooms**, costing from 200kr per person or 300kr for a double, plus a 50kr booking fee. More popular are the **cottages** which the tourist office rents out by the week (from 3000kr for 4 people). The STF **youth hostel** is at Rappegatan 1c (⊤0480/129 28, ⓕ882 93; 160kr, ❶), on the island of **Ängö**, a pleasant ten-minute walk north of the centre; it's well equipped, with laundry facilities and a shop for basic provisions. *Sjöfartsklubben*, Ölandsgatan 45, which provides accommodation for naval cadets, makes its rooms available to the public from June to August (200kr plus 50kr booking fee; book through the tourist office). The nearest **camping** is on Stensö island (⊤0480/888 03, ⓦwww.camping.se), 3km from the centre, where you can rent cheap cabins (300–400kr for 4 people) and also **canoes**. Local bus #412 heads out this way; check with the tourist office.

There are several really attractive central **hotels** with good summer discounts. The 1906 *Stadshotel*, Stortorget 14 (⊤0480/49 69 00, ⓕ49 69 10; ❻/❹), is in a lovely old building with a stuccoed facade; the price includes an excellent buffet breakfast (available to nonresidents at 55kr). Another fine place, on the lively Larmtorget, is *Frimurarehotellet*, at no. 2 (⊤0480/152 30, ⓦwww.frimurarehotellet.gs2.com; ❹/❸), in a castle-like building owned by the Freemasons. Another very good choice is *Kalmarsund Hotel*, Fiskaregatan 5 (⊤0480 18100, ⓦwww.kalmarsundhotel.se; ❸), which is well positioned with friendly, efficient service and comfortable en-suite rooms. There's a sauna and roof garden too. The prettiest, most regal and also the priciest of Kalmar's hotels is the old *Slottshotellet* at Slottsvägen 7 (⊤0480/882 60, ⓦwww.slottshotellet.se; ❻/❹), which overlooks the castle across the bridge. The authentic interior is extremely tasteful with a charming conservatory area plus a sauna and solarium for use by guests. At the other end of the scale is the perfectly adequate *Hotel Svanen*, next door to the youth hostel and run by the same management (same number as hostel or ⊤0480/255 60; ❷).

The Town

Kalmar is spread across several bridge-connected islands. The seventeenth-century **New Town** sits on the island of Kvarnholmen. The district is surrounded by fragments of ancient fortified walls and the cobbled streets and lively

KALMAR

N

▲ **①**, **②** & Bridge to Öland

Ängöbron (bridge)

FREDRIKSSKANSBRON

Kanalen

Fredriksskans

SÖDRA KANALGATAN

Bus Station

GATAN

LANDS HÖVDINGE GATAN

ÖSTRA VALLGATAN

KVARN-
HOLMEN

STRÖM GATAN

FISKARE-

ÖSTRA SJÖGATAN

PROVIANTGATAN

UNIONSGATAN

Ⓐ

Systra Stömmen

RAVELINSGÅNG

Water tower

Ⓐ Ⓑ

NORRA LÅNG-

VÄSTRA SJÖGATAN

GATAN

Domkyrkan

Ⓐ

Kronan Exhibition
(at Länsmuseum)

SÖDRAVÄGEN

LARM-
GATAN

Ⓒ

STOR-

SÖDRA LÅNGGATAN

GATAN

SÖDRAVÄGEN

Ⓓ

LARM-
TORGET

LILLA
TORGET

Ⓕ

Ⓔ

OLOF PALMSGATAN

Ⓕ

ÖLANDS-

Ⓔ

VÄSTERLÅNGGATAN

Ⓖ

Ⓘ

SÖDRA VALLGATAN

Ⓗ

GAMLA

Ⓖ

STATIONSGATAN

SKEPPSBRONGATAN

SKEPPSBRON

Bus Station
(to Öland)

Train
Station

Gamla
Kyrkogården

City Park

Konstmuseum
(Stadspark)

JÄRNVÄGSGATAN

STAN

Kalmar
Slott

0   200m

Södra Kyrkogården
& Mosaiska Kyrkogården

Kungsgatan

SLOTTSVÄGEN

▼ Stensö Island & Campsite

ACCOMMODATION

Frimurarehotellet	5
Kalmarsund	3
Slottshotellet	6
Stadshotel	4
Svanen	1
Youth hostel	2

RESTAURANTS & CAFÉS

Calmar Hamnkrog	E
Ernesto Salonger	F
Ernesto Steakhouse	I
Krögers	D
Kullzenska Cafeet	C
Ming Palace	B
T&T	A
Taste	G
Trådgårn	6
Znaps Bar och kök	H

squares of its centre are lined with some lovely old buildings. Kalmar was rebuilt after a devastating fire in the 1640s; to the west is the **Gamla Stan** (Old Town), which still retains some winding old streets that are worth a wander. Reaching the **castle** from the centre entails a walk through the appealing **Stadspark**, a few minutes' walk west of the train and bus stations, where every tree has its age on a plaque.

Kalmar Slott

Beautifully set on its own island, just south of Stadspark, is the castle, **Kalmar Slott** (April, May & Sept daily 10am–4pm; June & Aug daily 10am–5pm; July daily 10am–6pm; guided tours in English 11.30am & 2.30pm; 70kr). Its foundations were probably laid in the twelfth century; a century later, it became the best-defended castle in Sweden under King Magnus Ladulås. Today, if the castle doesn't appear to be defending anything in particular, that's because a devastating fire in the 1640s laid waste to the Old Town, after which Kalmar was moved to its present site.

The most significant event to take place within its walls was when the Danish Queen Margareta instigated the **Union of Kalmar** in 1397, which made her ruler over all Scandinavia. With such hatred between the Swedes and Danes, the union didn't stand much chance of long-term success. The castle was subject to eleven **sieges** as the Swedes and the Danes took power in turn; surprisingly, it remained almost unscathed. By the time Gustav Vasa became king of Sweden in 1523, Kalmar Slott was beginning to show signs of wear and tear, and so the king set about rebuilding it, while his sons, who later became Eric XIV and Johan III, took care of decorating the interior. The result, a fine **Renaissance palace**, is still preserved in fantastic detail today.

Unlike many other southern Swedish castles, this one is straight out of a storybook – boasting turrets, ramparts, a moat and drawbridge, and a dungeon. The castle's fully furnished interior – reached by crossing an authentically reconstructed wooden **drawbridge** and through a stone-arched tunnel beneath the grassy ramparts – is great fun to wander through. Among the many highlights is King Johan's bedroom, known as the **Grey Hall**. His bed, which was stolen from Denmark, is decorated with carved faces on the posts, but all their noses have been chopped off – he believed that the nose contained the soul and didn't want the avenging souls of the rightful owners coming to haunt him. The **King's Chamber** (King Eric's bedroom) is the most visually exciting – the wall frieze is a riot of vividly painted animals and shows a wild boar attacking Eric and another man saving him. Eric apparently suffered from paranoia, believing his younger brother Johan wanted to kill him. To this end, he had a secret door, which you can see cut into the extravagantly inlaid wall panels, with escape routes to the roof in event of fraternal attack. As it happened, Eric didn't live that long – Johan is widely believed to have poisoned him with arsenic in 1569.

The adjoining **Golden Room**, with its magnificent ceiling, should have been Johan's bedroom, but sibling hatred meant he didn't sleep here while Eric lived. There are a couple of huge and intriguing portraits: though Gustav Vasa was already of an advanced age when his was painted, he appears young-looking, with unseemly muscular legs. The royal artist had been ordered to seek out the soldier with the best legs and paint those, before attempting a sympathetic portrayal of Vasa's face. The portrait next to his is of Queen Margareta, her ghostly white countenance achieved in real life through the daily application of lead and arsenic. Isolated on another wall is King Eric's portrait, hung much higher up than the others: his family believed that the mental illness from which he supposedly suffered could be caught by looking into his eyes – even images of them.

The tour guides will tell you that the place is rattling with ghosts, but for more tangible evidence of life during the Vasa period, the kitchen fireplace is good enough; it was built to accommodate the simultaneous roasting of three cows. There's a splendidly minimalist **café** just inside the walls dominated by a wonderfully evocative oil painting of a moody chamber interior.

Around Kalmar Slott: Södra Kyrkogården and the Art Museum

A wander through Stadspark with the castle on your left leads you to the tranquil cemetery, **Södra Kyrkogården**. The most poignant section, labelled on city maps as **Mosaiska Kyrkogården**, is hidden away at its extreme southwest corner, where the city's now defunct Jewish community is buried. There is a moving memorial to those who perished in the Nazi Holocaust – surrounded by twenty square granite tablets commemorating Eastern European Jews, all in their teens and 20s, who were brought to Kalmar after surviving the concentration camps. Weak and ill after their ordeal and without sufficient medical backup, most died on Swedish soil during their first few months of liberation. Just to the left of the chapel is another grave of interest, that of Rickard Almskoug. The looming granite tomb is carved with the image of a bent rifle and beneath lie the remains of Sweden's first conscientious objector to be imprisoned for refusing military service. He was imprisoned in Kalmar's damp prison (still very much in evidence as a high security jail), and died there aged 21. The grave is a focal point for sympathizers who leave flowers on the anniversary of Almskoug's death.

On the north side of the cemetery is Kalmar's **Konstmuseum** (daily 11am–5pm, Thurs to 8pm; 40kr, under-15s free; Ⓦ www.kalmarkonstmuseum.nu), where there's an emphasis on Abstract Expressionist work painted by Swedish artists in the 1940s and 1950s. One floor also contains a gallery of nineteenth- and twentieth-century Swedish nude and landscape paintings, include some fine works by Anders Zorn and Carl Larsson. In addition, there are often temporary exhibitions of contemporary art.

Gamla Stan

For a feel of Kalmar's quaint **Gamla Stan** (Old Town), it's best to head into the small warren of cobbled lanes west of the *Slottshotellet*, which overlooks the Stadspark and is only a minute's walk along Slottsvågen from the Södra Kyrkogården. The old wooden cottages, painted egg-yolk yellow and wisteria blue, are at their prettiest on Gamla Kungsgatan and Västerlångatan. These little streets surround the attractive **Old Churchyard**, where the seventeenth- and eighteenth-century gravestones have recently been restored.

The Domkyrkan

The elegantly gridded Renaissance New Town is laid out around the grand **Domkyrkan** in Stortorget (daily 9am–6pm); to get here from the Old Town, head back east along Södravägen across the river, then carry on through Larmtorget and along Storgatan. Designed in 1660 by Nicodemus Tessin the Elder (as was the nearby Rådhus) after a visit to Rome, this vast and airy church in Italian Renassaince-style is today a complete misnomer: Kalmar has no bishop and the church no dome. Inside, the altar, designed by Tessin the Younger, shimmers with gold, as do the *Faith* and *Mercy* sculptures around it. The huge Deposition painting beneath the altar depicts in unusually graphic detail Jesus being taken down from the Cross by men on ladders, his lifeless form winched down with ropes. The pulpit is also worth a look; its roof is a three-tiered confection crowned with a statue of Christ surrounded by gnome-like sleeping soldiers, below which angels brandish instruments of torture, while on the "most inferior" level, a file of women symbolize such qualities as maternal love and erudition.

The Kronan Exhibition

From Stortorget, it's a few minutes' walk south down Östra Sjögatan and then left into Skeppsbrogatan to the **Länsmuseum**, Kalmar's county museum (daily: mid-June to mid-Aug 10am–6pm; mid-Aug to mid-June Tues–Fri 10am–4pm, Sat & Sun 11am–4pm; 50kr). The centrepiece of the museum is the awe-inspiring **Kronan exhibition**, housed in a refurbished steam mill. Built by the seventeenth-century British designer Francis Sheldon, the royal ship *Kronan* was once one of the world's three largest vessels; it had three complete decks and was twice the size of the *Vasa*, which sank off Stockholm in 1628 (see p.87).

The *Kronan* itself went down, fully manned, in 1676, resulting in the loss of 800 of its 842 crew. Its captain, Admiral Creutz, had received a royal order to attack and recapture the Baltic island of Gotland. Pursued by the Danish, Creutz, who had remarkably little naval experience – just one week at sea – was eager to impress his king and engage in combat. To this end, he ignored pleas from his crew and ordered the *Kronan* to turn and face the enemy. A gale caused the ship to heave, and water gushed into her open gun ports, knocking over a lantern, which ignited the entire gunpowder magazine. Within seconds, an explosion ripped the mammoth ship apart.

It wasn't until 1980 that the whereabouts of the ship's remains were detected, 26m down off the coast of Öland, using super-sensitive scanning equipment. A salvage operation began, led by the great-great-great-great-grandson of the ship's captain; the Kronan exhibition displays the resulting finds as part of an imaginative **walk-through reconstruction** of the gun decks and admiral's cabin, complete with the sound of cannon fire and screeching gulls. The ship's **treasure trove** of gold coins is displayed at the end of the exhibition, but it's the incredibly preserved **clothing** – hats, jackets, buckled leather shoes and even silk bows and cuff links – which bring this exceptional show to life. The moments leading up to the disaster have been pieced together brilliantly. The site is still being explored and further finds being made. The most recent, in July 2002, was a complete box of medical equipment which will be added to the exhibition.

Eating, drinking and nightlife

There's a wide range of places **to eat** in Kalmar. The liveliest night-time area is **Larmtorget**, with restaurants, cafés and pubs serving a wide variety of food.

Calmar Hamnkrog Skeppsbrogatan 30 ℡0480/41 10 20. Built right by the water on squat stilts, this swish but pleasantly informal place offers such delights as catfish, duck or lamb with classy sauces for around 200kr.

Ernesto Salonger Lärmtorget 4. Very popular place serving a huge range of very good pizzas and pastas (60–80kr), as well as traditional Italian salads, antipasti and meat dishes (120kr) in quite up-market surroundings. Live music at weekends.

Ernesto Steakhouse Larmgatan 2. All hanging Chianti bottles and no sea view, this Italian-style harbourside restaurant serves substantial and expensive meat and fish meals. The *Dagens Rätt* is good value at 55kr.

Helen & Jörgens Restaurant Olof Palmesgata. Just off Larmtorget ℡0480/288 30. An up-market eatery decorated by frighteningly bad paintings. Menu divided into seafood, Oriental, Swedish, vegetarian and Greek. Mains are 200kr, vegetarian ones a little less.

Krögers Lärmtorget 7. Once the most popular pub/restaurant in town, this place isn't what it was now that live music has stopped. Nonetheless, it's still popular, and serves light Swedish meals such as *kottbullesmörgäs* (meatball sandwiches; 40kr), as well as less Swedish dishes from fish and chips (6kr) to pasta.

Kullzenska Caféet Kaggensgatan 26. Kalmar's best café by far is this charming *konditori* occupying the first floor of an eighteenth-century house. Its eight interconnecting rooms are awash with mahogany furnishings, Indian carpets and crumbling royal portraits – exactly as they were during the lifetime of the twin sisters who lived here for

the best part of a century.

Larmgatan 10 Larmgatan 10. Meat, fish and pasta dishes at this well-placed restaurant which is less up-market than *Taste*, just opposite (see below) but pleasant enough and serves generous portions.

Ming Palace Fiskaregatan 7. The premier Chinese restaurant in town with a beautiful interior to boot. Lunch specials for 50–60kr. To find it, head towards the base of the old castellated water tower.

Peking Restaurant, at the train station ℡0480/105 33. A good spot for Indonesian and Chinese food, and cheaper than *Ming Palace*, though not quite as stylish. Three small dishes cost 62kr.

T & T Unionsgatan 20 ℡0480/235 36. One of Kalmar's hippest eateries, this spot serves unusual (and delicious) pizzas, plus meat and poultry dishes sold by weight. It has a good range of wines and some great desserts.

Taste Lärmgatan 5. Fine restaurant with leather and oak decor, though the menu is short and can be overpriced. Blue mussels followed by lamb, lobster, salmon or ostrich cost around 190kr, though lunch specials are better value at 65kr. The summer bistro menu (99kr) offers four choices of pastas, chicken dishes and salads.

Trädgårn Restaurant at *Slottshotellet* (May–Aug Mon–Fri 5–10pm, Sat & Sun noon–10pm). Swedish specialities with a touch of Provençal in the lovely curved garden pavilion setting of the glamorous old *Slottshotellet* (see above).

Znaps Bar och Kök Corner Södra Vallgatan and Kaggensgatan. A hip joint with a well-designed interior, attracting a youngish crowd. Lots of schnapps and other drinks, and the food isn't bad either – fish soup, salads, wok dishes and pastas – all at reasonable prices.

Öland

Linked to mainland Sweden by a six-kilometre-long bridge, the island of **Öland**, with its unspoilt beaches, mysterious forests, pretty meadows and wooden cottages, has been drawing Swedes in droves for over a century. Now popular with visitors from abroad, too, the island is visited by thousands of people every July and August. Despite this onslaught, which can clog the road from the bridge north to the main town **Borgholm**, this long, splinter-shaped island retains a very likeable old-fashioned-holiday atmosphere. The bathing opportunities here are among the best in Sweden, and the island's attractions include numerous ruined castles, Bronze and Iron Age burial cairns, runic stones and forts, all set amid rich and varied fauna and flora and striking geography. Labyrinthine **walking trails** and **bicycle routes** wend their way past more than four hundred old wooden **windmills**, which give Öland a peculiarly Dutch air. The island is perfect for **camping** and while you can pitch tent anywhere under the rules of *Allemansrätten* (see p.47), there are 25 official campsites. Almost all are open only between April or May and September, and are scattered the length of the island (ⓣ070/948 80 00, ⓦwww.camping-oland.com,)

A royal hunting ground from the mid-sixteenth century until 1801, Öland was ruled with scant regard for its native population. Peasants were forbidden from chopping wood, owning dogs or weapons, or selling their produce on the open market. While protected wild animals did their worst to the farmers' fields, Kalmar's tradesmen exploited the restrictions on the islanders' trade to force them to sell at low prices. Danish attacks on Öland (and a ten-month occupation in 1612) made matters worse, with seven hundred farms being destroyed. A succession of disastrous harvests in the mid-nineteenth century was the last straw, causing a quarter of the population to pack their bags for a new life in America. Last century, mainland Sweden became the new magnet for Öland's young, and, by 1970, the island's inhabitants had declined to just twenty thousand.

The geology of the island varies dramatically due to the crushing movement of ice during the last Ice Age, and the effects of the subsequent melting process, which took place 10,000 years ago. To the south is a massive **limestone** plain known as **Alvaret**; indeed, limestone has been used here for thousands of years to build runic monuments, dry-stone walls and churches. The northern coastline is craggy and irregular, peppered with dramatic-looking **rauker** – stone pillars, weathered by the waves into jagged shapes. Among the island's **flora** are plants that are rare in the region, like the delicate rock rose and the cream-coloured wool-butter flower, both native to Southeast Asia and found in the south of the island. Further north, in the romantically named **Trolls Forest**, you'll find twisted, misshapen pine sand oaks. As regards **fauna**, the south contains a sensational **bird reserve**, where skylarks and lapwings join sea birds, waders and millions of migrating birds in spring and early autumn.

Getting there

The **bus** timetable, available from Kalmar's bus or train station and tourist office, is almost impossible to decipher – Ölanders mostly laugh when you refer to it. Buses #101 and #106 are safe bets, however, and run pretty well every hour from Kalmar bus station to Borgholm (50min; 45kr). These, plus #104, stop at Fårestaden (25 minutes) while buses #103 and #105 head on to

Mörbylånga (55 mins). Even more bizarrely, the bus from Möllstorp to Borgholm initially heads south when you catch it – it will turn a few minutes later to head back north. The evening services are more erratic, but continue in some form until 2am in summer. If you don't want to go to Borgholm, ask at the bus station for the buses that stop at **Färjestaden**, the bus network hub, a couple of kilometres south of Möllstorp.

Heading to Öland **by road,** take the Ängö link road to Svinö (clearly signposted), just outside Kalmar, from where the bridge takes you across onto Öland.

A rule forbidding **cycles** or pedestrians on the bridge has something of a silver lining: there is a free English red bus from Svinö especially for cyclists, with its lower deck stripped to store bikes, which stops outside the island's main tourist office in Möllstorp. (If you're **hitching**, you can try your luck with the free bus, too, citing the bridge's lack of a footpath as the reason to take a free trip.)

Island Practicalities

Öland's main **tourist office** is at **Möllstorp**, next to the end of the bridge (Jan–April & Oct–Dec Mon–Fri 9am–5pm; May, June & late Aug Mon–Fri 9am–6pm, Sat 9am–4pm, Sun 10am–3pm; July to mid-Aug daily 9am–8pm; Sept Mon–Fri 9am–5pm, Sat 10am–3pm; ☏0485/56 06 00, Ⓦwww.olandsturist.se). Here you can pick up a bus **timetable** (but don't expect an explanation) and the *Öland Karten*, a really good map with clear road routes (75kr). In the same building is the nature centre, Naturum, where a model of the island lights up to show all the areas of interest. There's also a good **café** with well-priced meals.

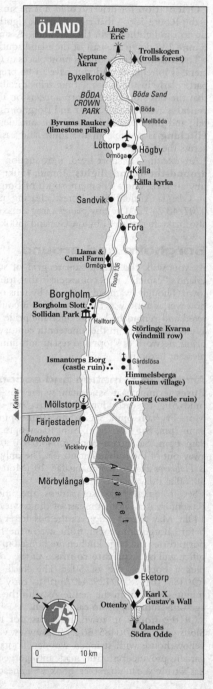

Orientation for drivers could not be simpler. There is only one main road – the Route 136 – that runs from the lighthouse at the island's northernmost tip to the lighthouse in the far south. A smaller (unnumbered) road runs off Route 136 down the east of the island south from Föra.

The **bus** network connects most places in Öland, but the service, though efficient, is infrequent, and you have to be prepared for a lot of waiting around, particularly in the south – time trips carefully to avoid being stranded. Note that the bus stop at Möllstorp appears on the timetable as "tråftpunkt". **Bike rental** is available in Kalmar and Borgholm, at most of the campsites and hostels, and the odd farm with a sign outside; all outlets charge 45–80kr a day. **Hitching** is possible in the south and easiest when you are heading north across the plain.

An exciting, if short-lived, introduction to Öland is to take one of the **around-the-island flights** (15min; 150kr, children 100kr) from one of two tiny airfields, one a kilometre south of Borgholm (℡0485/104 00), the other at Ölanda Airfield, in a forest clearing near Löttorp (℡0485/281 41 or 0707/48 74 72). The tiny planes carry a maximum of three passengers each and also make flights to Visby on Gotland (500kr one-way, 700kr return).

Borgholm and around

As you walk the simple square grid of streets that makes up **Borgholm**, Öland's "capital", it becomes clear that tourism is the lifeblood of this small town. Though swamped each July by tens of thousands of visitors, Borgholm, however, is in no way the tacky resort it could be. Encircled by the flaking, turreted and verandahed villas, once the pride of the town during its first period as a holiday resort in the nineteenth century, most of the centre is a friendly, if bland, network of shops and restaurants lining the roads that lead down to the pleasant harbour.

Arrival, information and accommodation

Buses terminate at Sandgatan, where you'll find Borgholm's **tourist office** (mid-Aug to early June Mon–Fri 9am–3.45pm; early June to late June Mon–Fri 9am–6pm, Sat & Sun 10am–3pm; late June to early Aug Mon–Fri 9am–7pm, Sat 9am–6pm, Sun 10am–6pm; early Aug to mid-Aug Mon–Fri 9am–6pm, Sat 10am–3pm; ℡0485/890 00, ⍟www.olandsturist.se), tucked away out of the hubbub at no. 25. The only place to **rent a bike** in the town is *Hallbergs Hojjar*, Köpmangatan 10 (Mon–Sat 9.30am–6.30pm; ℡0485/109 40; 60kr a day/300kr/week).

Set in quiet, park-like gardens, the fine, stately STF **youth hostel** at Rosenfors is a kilometre east of the town centre (℡0485/107 56, ℻778 78; 140kr; May to mid-Aug); ask the bus driver to stop at the Q8 filling station just before Borgholm proper, from where the hostel is signposted 100m away. Its dormitories and large kitchen are housed in old stone outbuildings. The tourist office will book **private rooms** over the counter only, from 150kr per person, plus a booking fee of 50kr. The local **campsite**, *Kapelludden's Camping* (℡0485/101 78, ℻129 44; April to early Sept), is on a small peninsula five minutes' walk from the centre. As with the rest of the island, there's no shortage of beautiful spots to camp rough.

Of the **hotels** in town, head first for the central yet tranquil *Villa Sol*, Slottsgatan 30 (℡0485/56 25 52, ⍟www.villasol.just.nu; ❶), a charming pale-yellow house with stripped wooden floors and old tiled fireplaces. The lush gardens provide fresh fruit made into gorgeous jams for breakfast and the place has a truly warm character; book well ahead if you're here in July. Also central is *Hotel Borgholm*, Trådgårdsgatan 15 (☎0485/770 60, ℱ12 466; ❸), with smart rooms and pleasant gardens. Straddling one side of the harbour is the vast *Strand Hotel,* Villagatan (☎0485/888 88, ⓦwww.strand.borgholm.se; ❹). Blandly styled like a modern seaside hotel, its massive interior includes a small shopping mall, a disco and nightclub. Guests can use the indoor pool, sauna (free) and solarium (40kr).

Eight kilometres south of Borgholm on Route 136 is one of the few really fine hotels on the island, *Halltorps Gästgiveri* (☎0485/850 00; ❹), based in a beautiful eighteenth-century manor house with striking, modern design features. The breakfasts – included in the price – are superb, and there's an excellent gourmet **restaurant** presided over by celebrated chef Josef Weischel; weekend packages, including meals, are available. Buses #101 or #106 stop outside the hotel every thirty minutes on their way to Borgholm.

The Town

The only real attraction in town is **Borgholms Slotts**, several hundred metres southwest of the centre (May–Aug 10am–6pm; free). A colossal stone fortification with rows of huge arches and corridors open to the skies, it is reached either through a nature reserve, signposted from the town centre, or from the first exit south off Route 136. Built in the twelfth century, the castle was fortified four hundred years later by King Johan III, and given its present shape – with a tower at each corner – in the seventeenth century. Regularly attacked, it eventually fell into disrepair, and when the town was founded in 1816, the castle was already a ruin.

Just a few hundred metres to the south of the castle is the present royal family's summer residence, **Solliden Park**, an Italianate villa built to a design specified by the Swedish queen Victoria (the present king's great-grandmother) in 1903; a huge, austere red-granite bust of her rises out of the trees at the entrance to the car park. Of Austrian stock, Victoria loathed Sweden, and demanded the bust face Italy, the country she most loved. The villa itself is not open to the public, but the formal gardens can be visited (mid-May to late June & mid-Aug & Sept daily 10am–6pm; late June to mid-Aug daily 11am–6pm; gates close at 5pm; 50kr): there's a very ordered Italian Garden, a colourful Dutch Garden and a simple English-style one. Alternatively, you could just head for the delightful **café**, *Kaffetorpet* (same hours as above but open till 7pm), near the car park. Here you can have light lunches, cakes, ice cream and waffles at reasonable prices.

The only other minor diversion in Borgholm is the **Stads Museet** (sometimes still called Forngård; mid-June to Aug Mon–Sat 11am–5pm, daily in July; 20kr), Köpmangatan 23, a museum of Öland life, set in a fine 1840s house boasting a crumbling, though still impressive, glazed porchway. The ground-floor exhibits include bits of ancient skulls, some Viking glass, Bronze Age jewellery and grave finds. Upstairs there are some attractive period rooms, while the outbuildings all contain quaint seventeenth- and eighteenth-century peasant-house interiors; there's a **café** here too. The museum is best seen at the end of your visit to Öland, as the treasures on display are taken from the historical sites you might visit around the island.

To see what the town looked like before the likes of the *Strand Hotel* were built, head along Villagatan, the road to the left of the *Strand* as you face out to sea; the street is lined with classic wooden villas, their porches and eaves all fancy fretwork. You can't drive along the street without authorization, though, as this is the route used by the king and queen to reach their summer home just beyond the reserve.

Just to the north of the town centre is Öland's largest Bronze Age cairn, **Blå Rör**, a huge mound of stones excavated when a coffin was discovered in 1849. People have been turning up artefacts from time to time ever since: in the 1920s, burnt bones, indicating a cremation site, were found, along with bronze swords and tweezers – apparently common items in such tombs. The tourist office promotes it as a major site, but there's not really a lot to see.

Eating, drinking and nightlife

There has traditionally been a pronounced summer-holiday feel to the town's **restaurants** and bars. Pizza places abound around Stortorget and down towards the harbour, cashing in on the summer influx of tourists by charging relatively high prices (65–85kr per pizza). Sadly, the owners of the best eating places have taken to leaving their businesses in the hands of school-leavers during the vital summer weeks, and standards have dropped sharply. The only really good places are the long-standing smart restaurants which are very pricey.

The best pizzas can be eaten at *Pizza Butiken*, at Storgatan 19, with pizzas from 60kr and a vast range of fillings. *Mama Rosa*, right by the harbour at Södra Långgatan 2 (June to mid-Aug daily noon–1am, April & May Wed–Fri 4–11pm, Sat & Sun noon–11pm; ☏0485/129 10), is a smarter pizza parlour than most and has a more varied menu; the three-course dinner is good value at 146kr. On the north side of the harbour, *Skeppet* (☏0485/772 15; May–Sept daily noon–11pm) is a jolly little Italian restaurant, hidden behind 1940s industrial silos. Their special, a pizza piled high with ingredients, is a good choice at 70kr. For the finest Swedish/pan-European food – with prices to match – head for *Backfickan* at *Hotel Borgholm* (daily 6–10.30pm), where main courses here come at a hefty 200kr. For a special atmosphere and wonderful cuisine, it's worth heading south of town to *Halltorps Gästgiveri* (see previous page).

Borgholm's **café** life is limited. The once wonderful **Ebba's Café** on Storgatan has been taken over but next door, at no. 10, however, *Glascafé* is one of the only places that has improved over the past few years. There's now a wide range of home-made ice creams and sorbets and a pleasant eating area in the back garden with a vine-covered verandah. You could check to see if *Villa Harmonie* in the same building upstairs is still in business. It was the best place for **vegetarian** home-cooking, but at the time of writing its future was uncertain. Try also the newer *Hemma Hus*, in a turretted old villa wedged between Västra & Östra Kyrkogatan, facing the church. Its a good spot for pizza, cider, wine or a coffee as well as more ambitious meat, fish and vegetarian choices at around 130kr.

For **drinking**, *Pubben*, Storgatan 18 (daily 3pm–1am), is the first place to try – a cosy pub run by the friendliest of owners, with old radios and crystal sets for decor. As well as lager, stout and bitter, this popular bar specializes in whisky – 46 varieties of malts and blends. *Znaps*, on Södralånggatan at the corner of Hantverkaregatan, is also worth checking out: built originally as a hospital for venereal diseases, and later used as a church, the place features R&B and house music, plus occasional live bands; there's a 40kr cover charge on Friday and Saturday nights. At the harbour, *Robinson Crusoe*, jutting into the water is a fine place for a pint, though the food – including lobster au gratin and fillet steak – is absurdly overpriced. A raucous young crowd invariably swarms into the *Strand Disco* in the *Strand Hotel* every evening, turning it into a sort of Baltic Ibiza throughout the summer nights.

Around Borgholm

Cutting southeastwards from Borgholm (take bus #102), following signs to **Räpplinge**, leads to **Störlinge**, where there's a row of seven windmills by the roadside. At Räpplinge Church, take the road signed Gårdslösa, and after five kilometres the windmills are on the left. There's a very pleasant **café**, *Hus Och Hem*, just opposite (July daily 10am–6pm; rest of year Mon–Fri only; closed Jan & Feb) for a baguette lunch. The shop here stocks the pigments needed to re-create traditional Swedish colours for house painting. A couple of kilometres south, **Gärdslösa** has the island's best-preserved medieval church. The interior is worth a look particularly for its pulpit, completed in 1666, on which stand four fine hourglasses made the same year in Leipzig. The thirteenth-century ceiling paintings were whitewashed over in 1781 but uncovered in 1950. This is where the present king's sister Princess Margaretha married in 1964, and Swedish royalty fanatics have been stealing handfuls of the graveyard gravel on which she walked ever since.

North Öland

The most varied and interesting landscape on the island is to be found towards the north, with no shortage of idyllic villages, dark woods and flowery mead-ows as you head up from Borgholm along the main road, **Route 136**. Though there aren't many proper hotels north of the Borgholm area, **campsites** are marked off the road every couple of kilometres; most of these high-standard sites are close to a beach. Public transport is limited to **buses** heading up Route 136 towards Byxelkrok; the road is safe for **cycling** along too and there are plenty of tracks that lead off the main drag.

Föra to Sandvik

At **Föra**, a village about 20km north of Borgholm, there's a good example of a typical Öland **church**, built in the medieval era (the font is the oldest bit, dating from 1250). It doubled as a fortress, and was capable of accommodating a considerable garrison in times of war. A couple of kilometres north, a sign to **Knisa Mosse** leads to a peaceful nature reserve, centred on a shimmering lake, and to some Bronze Age burial mounds, though there's not much to see at the burial area itself. To see a feat of nineteenth-century engineering, pop in to **SANDVIK**, which is dominated by Scandinavia's largest windmill (ⓦwww.sandvikskvarn.com) built in the 1850s. A Dutch-style construction, with eight floors and ingenious wooden workings, it was a working mill until 1955; today, it's home to a cosy pizza **restaurant**. Sandvik's economy is still based around stone-cutting, one of the few surviving traditional industries on the island. Next door to the stone-cutters, the café and pizza restaurant (daily noon–11pm) has benefited from its neighbour; inside the benches, bar and tables are made of slabs of white marble cut at angles. It's not a bad place for pizza, lasagne and steaks (around 90kr each); there's a range of beers and spir-its too. From the mill, it's just 200m down to the peaceful **harbour**, where the *Hamn Café* does good simple meals, cheap coffee and a wide variety of teas.

Källa and around

Two kilometres outside the village of **KÄLLA** and about 7km north of Sandvik, proud, forlorn **Källa kyrka** sits in splendid isolation (it's not to be confused with the current working church, by the sign for Källa). Surrounded by brightly flowering meadows, this tall, dull-white medieval church, empty since 1888, is bounded by dry-stone walls, its grounds littered with ancient, weathered tombs. Inside, the lofty interior has seen plenty of action: built in 1130 of limestone, to replace an earlier tiny stave church, Källa kyrka was reg-ularly attacked by heathens from over the Baltic Sea. It was modernized in the fourteenth century, when Källa was a relatively important harbour and trading centre, only to be stripped of its furnishings in the nineteenth century; inside, a row of six models of the church at various stages of its history is the only thing left to see.

An authentically Öland culinary experience is the island's speciality, **kroppkakor**; the finest place to try it is undoubtedly *Nini's Kroppskaksbod*, reached by turning left off the main road at Källabygdegård (June–Aug daily 11am–6pm; Sept–May Tues, Wed & Sat 11am–6pm; ☎0485/273 00). These delicacies (each 15kr, or 10kr to take away) are made with boiled and raw potato filled with lightly smoked and boiled pork; their name translating unappetizingly as "body cakes". At *Nini's*, they're made in small batches and served with cream and lingonberries, and a glass of cold milk. They won't become everyone's favourite, but are quite delicious eaten in *Nini's* garden.

One of the most unexpected sights around here is an unsignposted **camel and llama farm**, 14km north of Borgholm at **Ormöga**. Bengt and Christen Erlingsson operate camel rides (☎0485/700 27; from 6pm during the summer; 50kr) in this most unlikely setting, while the llamas are for sale. A sign states reassuringly that although the llamas do spit at each other, they seldom spit at people. Even if you don't feel tempted to make a purchase, they're interesting animals to observe in this pastoral, Baltic island setting.

Högby to Böda Sand

Högby, a few kilometres on, has the only remaining tied church houses on the island, relics of the medieval Högby kyrka nearby; there's not a lot to see though. For a most unusual, though somewhat pricey, dining experience, head for the village of **Löttorp**, off Route 136, and follow the signs east for 4km down country lanes to the *Lammet & Grisen* restaurant, housed in a building like a Spanish hacienda (☎0485/203 50; daily 5.30pm–midnight). The only dishes on the menu are salmon and spit-roasted lamb and pork at over 200kr (hence the restaurant's name), served with baked potatoes, flavoured butters and sauces.

Continuing north and west off Route 136, following signs for Byrums Sandvik and Raukområde, you come to **Byrums Rauker**, a striking sight: solitary limestone pillars formed by the eroding action of the sea, at the edge of a sandy beach. The best **beaches** are along the east coast; starting at Böda Sand, the most popular stretch is a couple of kilometres north at **Lyckesand**, with a nudist beach just to the north, the start of which is marked simply by a large boulder in the sea. Small east coast lanes run from the main road to the beaches, as do the many campsites signposted off Route 136.

The most extensive **campsite** in the north of the island is *Krono Camping* at Böda Sand (☎0485/222 00, ⓦwww.kronocamping-oland.se; mid-May to Sept), 50km north of Borgholm and 2km off Route 136 at the southern end of the beach. It has cabins for rent, costing from 3000kr per week for four people, and a range of facilities including shops, a bakery, and **restaurants**, complete with balladeers for entertainment. Just south of Böda's campsite is an STF **youth hostel**, *Vandrarhem Böda*, at Mellböda (☎0485/220 38, ⓕ221 98; 100kr). A large, well-equipped hostel, it has a cosy kitchen and some single rooms.

North of Böda Sand: the Trolls Forest and Byxelkrok

There are some gorgeous areas of natural beauty in the far north of the island. Some excellent walking is to be had at the island's northeastern tip, within the nature reserve of **Trollskogen** ("Trolls' Forest") with twisted, gnarled trunks of ancient oaks all shrouded in ivy. Around the western edge of the northern coast, the waters lapping against the rocky beaches are of the purest blue. On a tiny island at the very northern tip of Öland stands **Långe Eric lighthouse**, a handsome obelisk built in 1845, and a good target for a walk or cycle ride. **Neptune Åkrar**, 3km south on the western coast, is covered with *blå jungfrun*, lupin-like flowers whose brilliant blue rivals the sea beyond. The name, which was given them by Carl von Linné (see p.124), means "Neptune's Ploughland" – the ridged land formation here looks like ploughed fields.

The only town in this region is **BYXELKROK**, a quiet place with an attractive harbour, where **ferries** from Oskarshamn, on the mainland, dock. You can **rent bikes** here from David Andersson (℡0485/281 09; 40kr a day). The *Solö Värdhus* is a pleasant enough **hotel**, on the town's main road (℡0485/283 70, Ⓔ solo.wardshus@telia.com; ❷). What **nightlife** there is mostly happens here at *Sjöstugan* (April noon–5pm, May noon–8pm, June–Aug noon–2am; ℡0485/ 283 30), a restaurant, pub and disco, right by the shore. The restaurant specializes in salmon (100kr) and flounder (80kr), and also serves pizzas (55–85kr) and a vegetarian dish (70kr). Troubadours sing downstairs every day in June, while Swedish dance bands are their thing in July; there are discos Thursday to Saturday all year round.

South Öland

Dominated by **Stora Alvaret**, the giant limestone plain on which no trees can grow, the south of Öland is sparsely populated, its main town the rather dull **Mörbylånga**. Despite references in the tourist literature to "exposed rock", the landscape here consists of flat meadows which boast, among other unusual plant life, some rare alpine species that have stoically clung to life since the Ice Age. **Buses** run so infrequently here, you'll need to double-check times at Färjestaden (reachable from Borgholm on #101), just south of the bridge, where the few buses south (#101, #103) head to Mörbylånga) start their journey. **Hitching** is feasible – probably because drivers know that without their help, chances are you'll be stranded for long periods of time. Shops and other facilities are sparser than in the north, so if you don't have a car, it's worth stocking up on provisions before you head off. Despite the difficulties, the great advantage of travelling through the south is that the summer crowds thin out here, allowing you to explore peacefully the most untouched parts of the island – and visit Öland's most interesting **fort**, at Eketorp.

Vickleby

The prettiest village south of Borgholm on Route 136 is **VICKLEBY**, a quaint place halfway between Färjestaden to the north and Mörbylånga to the south. It is home to a remarkable art and design school, **Capella Gården**, set up by Carl Malmsten in the early twentieth century. A furniture designer, Malmsten dreamt of creating a school that stimulated mind, body and soul – a sort of educational utopia that was very much against the traditional ethos of teaching supported by the shocked Stockholm society. In 1959, he relocated his art and design school here into a range of picturesque farmhouses at Vickleby; it's still in operation today. Capella Garden isn't for everybody – the atmosphere is more than a little intense – but its courses do attract people from all over the world, who live for a few weeks in a commune environment, brushing up on their textile weaving and pottery, among other skills. The results, including some lovely ceramic and wood pieces, are put on sale during their annual exhibition, held in summer. It's best to call ahead to arrange a visit (℡0485/361 32).

Of all the forts on Öland, the one most worth a visit is in the village of **EKE-TORP** (May to mid-Sept daily 10am–5pm; guided tours in English at 1pm; 50kr, under 14s free). The site, reachable by bus #114 from Mörbylånga, is where three ancient settlements were discovered during a major excavation in the 1970s; these included a marketplace from the fourth century and an agricultural community dating from 1000. Actual physical evidence being thin on the ground, what one sees today is a wonderful achievement in popular archeology: an encircling wall has been constructed on the plain, and pigs, sheep and geese – the same animals that were once reared here (their presence identified by examining food waste in bone fragments found at the site) – wander around. The best of the finds, such as jewellery and weapons, are on show in the adjacent museum, and there's also a workshop where, if you feel inclined, you can have a go at leatherwork or "authentic" ancient cookery.

South of here, a stone wall cuts straight across the island. Called **Karl X Gustav's Wall**, it was built in 1650 to fence off deer and so improve the hunting. A herd of 200 fallow deer, descendents of those introduced by King John III in 1569, still roam about today at **Ottenby**, Öland's largest private estate, in the far south of the island. Built in 1804, this is now a bird-watcher's paradise, boasting a huge nature reserve and the Ottenby **bird station**, which, since 1946, has been Sweden's largest sanctuary for migrating birds – over 300 species have been sighted. There are also two protected observation towers and a bird museum.

Practicalities

The main **tourist office** at Möllstorp (see p.289) will book **private rooms** from 150kr per person per night, with a 25kr booking fee. *Mörby Youth Hostel* (☎0485/493 93, ⓕ406 86 150kr; ❶), 15km south of the bridge to Kalmar, has some hotel-class double rooms with sheets and breakfast provided (❶); bus #105 drops you off outside. Ten kilometres south of the bridge is the *Haga Park* (☎0485/360 30; ❶), offering no-frills B&B in an oldish wooden house. There are four-bed family rooms with a kitchen and bathroom (650kr per night) and the most basic of dormitory accommodation (110kr). There is a **campsite** nearby next to a beach that's popular for windsurfing. For a regular **hotel**, try *Hotel Kajutan* (☎0485/408 10; ❸), a pleasant old place built in 1860; it's at the harbour behind the bus station in Mörbylånga. At Vickleby, a more attractive location, *Hotel Bo Pensionat* (☎0485/360 01; ❸), in a traditional row of village houses, is very popular; it's worth booking ahead in high season. A good, cheap evening **restaurant** can be found at the *Haga Park* hotel, where main dishes go for 75kr.

Further into Småland: Växjö and the Glass Kingdom

Back on the mainland, **Småland county**, thickly forested and studded with lakes, makes up the southeastern wedge of Sweden. Although the scenery is appealing at first, the uniformity of the landscape means it's easy to become blasé about its natural beauty. Småland is often somewhere people travel through rather than to – from Stockholm to the southwest, or from Gothenburg to the Baltic coast. It does, however, have a few vital spots of interest of its own, alongside opportunities for hiking, trekking, fishing and cycling.

Historically, Småland has had it tough. The simple, rustic charm of the pretty painted cottages belies the intense misery endured by generations of local peasants: in the nineteenth century, subsistence farming failed, and the people were starving; consequently a fifth of Sweden's population left the country for America – most of them from Småland. While their plight is vividly retold at the **House of Emigrants** exhibition in **Växjö** (see p.299), a town which makes an excellent base from which to explore the region, the county's main tourist attractions are its myriad **glass factories** hidden in forest clearings. The bulk of these celebrated glassworks lie within the dense birch and pine forests that, together with a thread of lakes, make up the largely unbroken landscape between Kalmar and Växjö. Consequently, the area is dubbed **Glasriket**, or the "Glass Kingdom", with each glassworks signposted clearly from the spidery main roads.

Växjö and around

Founded by Saint Sigfrid in the eleventh century, **VÄXJÖ** (pronounced "vehquer"), deep in the heart of Småland county (120km from Kalmar), is by far the handiest place to base yourself if you are interested in the distinctive **glassware** produced in the region. Though its centre is fairly bland and quiet Växjö, whose name derives from *väg sjö*, or "way to the lake", enjoys some beautifully tranquil lake scenery a few kilometres away. The town itself offers a couple of great **museums**. Once a year, the town comes to life for the **Karl Oskar**

ACCOMMODATION

Elite Växjö Stadshotell	7
Esplanad	4
Royal Corner	6
Teaterpark	5
Tofta Strand Hotel	2
Värend	3
Youth hostel	1

RESTAURANTS & CAFÉS

Askelyckan	**F**	Momento	**M**	Toftastrand Café &	
Broqvists	**G**	Pasta Baren	**K**	Conditori	**B**
Espresso Bar & Café	**H**	P.M. & Friends	**E**	Tomas Skåres Café	**D**
Fiskepiren	**J**	Spisen	**L**	Wibrovski	**I**
Johanssons Lant Café	**A**	Teaterpark	**C**		

Dagens (second week in August) – a long weekend of unbridled revelry in honour of the character Karl-Oskar, created by author Wilhem Moberg, who symbolized the survival struggle of Småland's Swedish peasants in the nineteenth century. In reality, it means Växjö's youth drink themselves silly through the nights while daytime entertainment fills the streets.

Arrival and information

The **train** (hourly from Kalmar; 1hr 45min) and **bus stations** are side by side in the middle of town. Växjö's **tourist office** is in the train station building at Norra Järnvägsgatan (mid-June to mid-Aug Mon–Fri 9.30am–6pm, Sat & Sun 10am–2pm; mid-Aug to mid-June Mon–Fri 9.30am–5pm; ☏0470/414 10, ⊛www.turism.vaxjo.se). **Bikes** – useful for visiting the countryside around Växjö (see p.300) – can be rented from Smålands Cykel, Västra Esplanaden 15 (Mon–Fri 8am–6pm, Sat 10am–2pm, Sun 1–2pm; ☏0470/475 48; 60kr a day). If you're looking for **Internet** access, try *Pax Café*, Willans Park, Storgatan (Tues–Thurs 4–9.30pm, Fri 4pm–1am, Sat 8pm–1am; 30kr/hour), or *Lazergame*, Sandsgårdsgatan 20 (daily 1–9pm; 30kr/hour.)

Accommodation

The helpful tourist office will book **private rooms** around town from 150kr, plus a 50kr booking fee. Växjö's splendid STF **youth hostel** (☏0470/630 70, ☏632 16; 145kr, ❶) at **Evedal**, 5km north of the centre, is among the most civilized and beautifully maintained in the country; even if you normally don't stay in hostels, try this one. Set in parkland by a lake, tranquil Helgasjön, boasting its own beach, this eighteenth-century house was once a society hotel. Today they serve a good breakfast (45kr) and have laundry facilities (40kr). To get there, take Linnégatan north, following signs for Evedal, or take either bus #1C from the Växjö bus terminal to the end of the route (last bus is at 4.15pm, 3.15pm on Sat), or bus #1A; the latter drops you 1500m from the hostel, but has the utility of running daily till 8.15pm. Next to the hostel, and also by the lake, is a **campsite**, *Evedal Camping* (☏0470/630 34, ☏631 22), which has a decent shop for stocking up on food. Tents can be pitched for 130kr; four-person cabins from 500kr, including kitchen and shower.

Växjö has several reasonable central **hotels**, listed below. One good place to stay outside town is the **Tofta Strand Hotel**, Lenhovdavägen 72, in Sandsbro, 5km away (☏0470/652 90, ☏614 02; ❶). Its delightful gardens lead down to Lake Toft, which you can splash about on using the hotel's bizarre motorized raft. There's a wonderful *konditori* too, see p.302. To get to Sandsbro, take Route 23 in the direction of Oskarshamn, or hop on bus #5 from Växjö bus station; the hotel is 400m further on the right from where you leave the bus.

Elite Växjö Stadshotell Kungsgatan 6 ☏0470/134 00, ⊛www.vaxjo.elite.se. The usual executive-class hotchpotch of shiny marble, potted palms and terrible carpets, this hotel serves a generous buffet breakfast. Within the hotel is an English pub, *Bishop's Arms*, and a summertime restaurant, the *Lagerlunden* (Mon–Thurs 6pm–1am, Fri & Sat 6pm–2am). ❹/❷
Esplanad Norra Esplanaden 21A ☏0470/225 80, ☏262 26. A reasonable, central hotel with no frills. ❷/❶
Royal Corner Liedbergsgatan 11 ☏0470/70 10

00, ⊛www.radissonsas.com. Central, comfortable and featureless, this is nonetheless a popular choice for good service. ❹/❷
Teaterpark Västra Esplanaden 10–12 ☏0470/399 00, ⊛www.teaterparken.com. Located in the central Concert Hall building, this ultra-stylish, modern hotel also has some bedrooms designed for disabled guests plus some special allergy-free rooms. ❺/❸
Värend Kungsgatan 27 ☏0470/104 85, ☏ 362 61. Another standard hotel, this one also does good-value triple rooms. ❷

The Town

Växjö boasts two superb museums: the extensive **Smålands Museum**, notable for being home to the **Swedish Glass Museum**; and the **House of Emigrants**, which explores the subject of mass emigration from Sweden in the nineteenth and early twentieth centuries. There's also a romantic **castle ruin** 4km north of town, and a **cathedral** that has been renovated almost as many times as it is centuries old.

Smålands Museum

The enlarged **Smålands Museum**, behind the train station (June–Aug Mon–Fri 10am–5pm, Sat & Sun 11am–5pm; Sept–May Tues–Fri 10am–5pm, Sat & Sun 11am–5pm; 40kr), includes two permanent exhibitions: a history of Småland's manufacturing industries, and the more interesting "500 Years of Swedish Glass". The latter shows sixteenth-century place settings, eighteenth- and nineteenth-century etched glass, and stylish Art-Nouveau-inspired pieces, with subtle floral motifs. "Trees in Fog", designed in the 1950s by Kosta designer Vicke Lindstrand, illustrates just how derivative so much of the twentieth-century work actually is. Most visually appealing among the displays are those of contemporary glass in the museum's extension, though the lighting is poor at times. Look out for the dramatic, innovative work by British-born glass maestro Richard Rackham.

House of Emigrants

Directly in front of the Smålands Museum, and signposted "Utvandrarnas Hus", a plain building is home to the inspired **House of Emigrants** (June–Aug Mon–Fri 9am–6pm, Sat & Sun 11am–4pm; Sept–May daily 9am–4pm; 30kr; ☎0470/201 20, ⓦwww.svenskaemigrantinstitutet.g.se), with its moving "Dream of America" exhibition. The museum presents a picture of the intense hardship faced by the Småland peasant population in the mid-nineteenth century. Due to the agricultural reforms that denied the peasants access to village common land, and a series of bad harvests, more than a million Swedes – a sixth of the population – emigrated to America between 1860 and 1930; most of them came from Småland. By 1910, Chicago had a higher population of Swedes than Gothenburg.

The museum's displays, which include English-language translations and audio narratives, trace the lives of individual emigrants and recount the story of the industry that grew up around emigration fever. Most boats used by the emigrants left from Gothenburg and, until 1915, were British-operated sailings to Hull, from where passengers crossed to Liverpool by train to board the transatlantic ships. Conditions on board were usually dire: the steamer *Hero* left Gothenburg in 1866 with five hundred emigrants, nearly four hundred oxen and nine hundred pigs, calves and sheep sharing the accommodation. Walking through the exhibition, past models of crofters' huts in Småland and a sizeable replica of the deck of an emigrant ship, you are led on to displays on émigré life in America. One man who gets a special mention was known as Lucky Swede; he became America's most successful gold prospector in the Klondike before losing it all to his chorus-girl wife.

There is also a section on **women emigrants**, entitled "Not Just Kristina", a reference to a fictitious character in *The Emigrants*, a trilogy by one of Sweden's most celebrated writers, Wilhelm Möberg. Upon publication, it became the most-read Swedish history book in the country, and was made into a film starring Max von Sydow and Liv Ullman. On display here is Möberg's writing cabin, which was given to the museum after his death in 1973. Möberg would himself have emigrated, only his father sold a farrow of piglets to pay for his son to go to college in Sweden.

One of the saddest tales here is of Mauritz Ådahl, who, like a fifth of those who left, returned to try and live again in his native land. Money pressure forced him to emigrate for a second time in 1912, and due to the English coalminers' strike, which meant his ship could not sail, he took the much-publicized maiden voyage on the *Titanic*. Of the 1500 people killed in the *Titanic* disaster, several hundred were Swedish emigrants who, as third-class ticket holders, had no access to the deck until the lifeboats had all been taken. When his body was discovered twelve days later in the sub-zero waters, his watch had stopped at 2.34am, just as the *Titanic* vanished beneath the waves.

The museum's **Research Centre** (Mon–Fri 9am–4pm; ℡0470/201 20, ⒺInfo@svenskaemigrantinstitutet.g.se) charges remarkably good rates (150kr per half-day, 200kr full day) to help interested parties trace their family roots using passenger lists from ten harbours, microfilmed church records from all Swedish parishes and the archives of Swedish community associations abroad. If you want to use the centre's services during their peak season (May to mid-Aug), it's especially worth booking ahead for an appointment with one of their staff.

The Domkyrkan

In the centre, on Linnégatan, the very distinctive **Domkyrkan**, with its unusual twin green towers and apricot-pink facade (daily 9am–6pm; free; guided tours June–Aug 9am–5pm, book at tourist office), is certainly worth a look. The combined impact of regular restorations, the most recent in 1995, together with a catalogue of disasters, such as sixteenth-century fires and a 1775 lightning strike, have left little of note except an organ. There are, however, some brilliant new glass ornaments by one of the best-known of the contemporary Glass Kingdom designers, Göran Wärff, including a wacky alternative church font. In 2003, a stunning tryptich alterpiece made entirely of glass and designed by one of Sweden's most famous glass designers, Bertil Vallien, will be introduced here. The cathedral is set in **Linné Park**, named after Carl von Linné (see p.124), who was educated at the handsome school next door.

Tegner Cemetery

Just one block west of the train station, and a five-minute walk from the Domkyrkan, the pretty **Tegner Cemetery** is named after the town's most famous nineteenth-century resident, the poet and bishop of Växjö, Esaias Tegner, whose tomb is marked by a very plain white marble tomb along the far wall. Larger and far more lavish is the granite mausoleum built here for the nineteenth-century opera singer Christina Nilsson, who was born in the locality. Her name is embossed in the intricate copper door; a peep through the keyhole reveals her bronze sarcophagus standing proud in the middle.

Out from the centre

Two castles, one a ruin just north of the centre, the other a nineteenth-century affair to the south, make for worthwhile excursions of a couple of hours' duration. Alternatively, you could easily spend a whole day exploring the countryside surrounding Växjö, which is riddled with forest **hiking routes**; the tourist office can supply information and maps. **Cycling** is very popular, though the terrain is by no means flat and the forest lanes are often pretty rough. There are numerous **canoeing** opportunities on the still waters of the lakes, with special designated routes you can row along. Among the many places to rent canoes is Evedals Kanotuthyrning (℡0470/639 93), next to the youth hostel (see p.298); they provide not only equipment but also useful advice on where to go and what activities would suit children.

Kronoberg Castle

The ruin of **Kronoberg Castle** has a beautiful and uncommercialized setting, on a tiny island in a lake, Helgasjön, 5km north of the centre of town. Heading there by car, follow signs for Evedal, and the castle will be signposted off the road; or take bus #1B from Växjö bus station (Mon–Fri hourly, less frequent on Sat). Though the bishops of Växjö had erected a wooden fortress here in the eleventh century, the present stone structure was built by Gustav Vasa in 1540. The grass-roofed **café** *Ryttmästargården*, directly opposite the castle and by the jetty, is worth a visit for its eighteenth-century interior rather than the food. The jetty is used by the old **paddle steamer** *Thor*, which makes regular excursions from here around Helgasjön and up to another lake, Asasjön – a delightful way to see the pretty lakeland scenery (book tours at the café). The options include the so-called "**sluice trip**" along the canal from Helgasjön to Asasjön which enjoys pictureque scenery at a leisured pace, or try a similar trip but with coffee and cake (almost every Wed, 6pm, Sat & Sun at 1pm & 4.30pm except Sun when the Asa Herragård trips are running; 2hr 30min return; 125kr; book at the *Ryttmästargården Café* ☏ 0470/630 00). For a glamorous evening excursion (400kr), take the tour across Lake Asasjön to Asa Herregård (5 times during the summer, leaving at 10am; book through Smålands Museum, ☏ 0470/70 42 00), a country mansion, where you'll be served dinner (included in the price of the trip).

Teleborgs Slott

Just five minutes' drive south of the town centre, the stunning castle of **Teleborgs Slott** is well worth a trip (mid-June to mid-Aug mandatory guided tours; check times and price at tourist office). Standing on a peninsula jutting into Lake Trummen, this 1895 structure is a peculiar and winning concoction, looking like a Renaissance knight's castle in Rhineland but with National Romantic details, such as the beaten copper door handles. A stone staircase of more than fifty steps leads to the main entrance at the side of the castle (there is a lift round the back too). The castle was created as a gift from Count Fredrik Bonde to his new wife Anna Koskull, the idea being to offer her a castle comparable to what he imagined his Småland ancestors called home during the Middle Ages. At the time, the poverty-stricken locals, tinged with jealousy, are reported to have jeered, "what a peasant won't do for the sake of a cow" – a pun on the couple's names (*bonde* meaning "peasant", *ko* meaning "cow").

Eating and drinking

Växjö is a good place to try traditional **Småland cuisine,** which shows the influence of the forests and the poverty associated with the region, and is based around woodland berries, potatoes and game. Among local specialities are **isterband**, a flavoursome, spicy sausage usually served with potatoes and a dill sauce, and **krösamos**, potato pancakes with lingonberry sauce. The classic local dessert is *Smålands Ostkaka*, a rich curd-cheese cake with warm cloudberry sauce. Växjö **restaurants** charge high prices for elk steaks, hare and venison; for cheaper fare, there's a glut of pizza and Chinese restaurants. **Drinking** in Växjö is mostly done in restaurant/bars, as there are few actual pubs in town. This being an inland town, the local population migrates to the coasts in July and part of August, when some of the restaurants shut. The most popular **pub** in town is the *Bishops Arms*, Kungsgatan 6. The Swedes never tire of perceived

English and Irish authenticity, and this is no exception – always full to bursting, it achieves a jolly atmosphere.

Cafés

Askelyckan Storgatan. A mustard-coloured wooden house with a welcoming garden right on the main street. Good for people-watching rather than a gourmet treat.

Broqvists Kronobergsgatan 14, just off Stortorget. Nothing special to look at, but a Växjö institution, nonetheless as, somewhere locals used to come to smoke and gossip. It's now a nonsmoking café.

Espresso Café Bäckgatan. Off Storgatan, and opposite the *Cardinal Hotel*. A cool hangout for younger Växjöites, though the quality of the food – pasta salads, bruschettas and the like, is nothing to write home about. It's still the only stylish place within the bland grid of shopping streets.

Johanssons Lant Café Öhr, about 15km northwest of Växjö. If you've got a car, this is a great trip out to a characterful, nineteenth-century house to which people from all over the countryside flock for a cosy, nostalgia-laden country café with good cakes and sandwiches. One room has a '50s Wurlitzer juke box. Special musical events run throughout summer on Tues evenings (40kr).

Momento Smålands Museum. The best café by far, serving panini and ciabatta, superb Italian pastries (35kr) and decadent desserts, to the background sound of world music. The proprietors also run *PM & Friends*; see opposite.

Tofta Strand Café & Conditori *Tofta Strand Hotel* (see p.298) The daughter of the hotel owner, who runs this café at the back of the premises, specializes in celebration and wedding cakes, and her flair is apparent in the range of delicious fare available. Their speciality is Tofta Torta - white marzipan cake served with cloudberry jam. In summer, you can take the cakes on the hotel's raft onto the lake.

Pastabaren Kungsgatan 3, just twenty metres from the stations. The cheapest place to fill up well in basic surroundings. Vast pasta salads with tuna, cheese and ham or Greek pasta salad are excellent value at 45kr including bread. Also huge baguettes (30kr) and pizza (25kr/slice). Free coffee with food.

Tomas Skåres Kungsgatan 13. A justifiably popular and central *konditori* with coffee-and-cake specials for 22kr. Closed Sun in July.

IKEA

Among Swedish exports, only Volvo and ABBA spring to mind as readily as the furniture store **IKEA**, the letters standing for the name of its founder – **Ingvar Kamprad** – and his birthplace – Elmtaryd, a farm in the hamlet of Agunnaryd. Outside Sweden, the identity of IKEA's originator is played down, and the firm is known for simple, modern design lines and prices that appeal to a mass market. Every item of furniture IKEA produces is assigned a Swedish place name; the styles of certain items are drawn from particular areas of the country, and are given a relevant name.

Founded in 1943 at Älmhult, a small town 20km from Agunnaryd, as a mail-order company, IKEA began producing furniture based on folk designs, which Kamprad had simplified. In the 1950s, Sweden's existing furniture-makers were sufficiently irritated by what they regarded as an upstart that they tried to pressure IKEA's suppliers into boycotting the company. Kamprad responded by importing furniture from abroad.

In his 1976 book, *Testament of a Furniture Dealer*, Kamprad wrote that from the outset, he wanted to promote "constructive fantasies": to change the world's view of design, rather than produce what people already believed they wanted. Having opened in Denmark in 1969, the company began expanding around the world, though it didn't enter the US market until 1985 or the UK until 1987.

Three biographies have been published on Kamprad, one of which (*The History of IKEA*) was authorized. They have revealed Kamprad's Nazi sympathies during World War II which he responds to by blaming his former political leanings on the folly of youth.

Today, if you pass through Älmhult, you can see the original IKEA store, built in 1958; the street on which it stands is called, appropriately enough, Ikeagatan. Ironically, IKEA's headquarters are no longer in Sweden, but in Denmark, and Kamprad himself has chosen to live in London.

Restaurants

Evedal Vardhus Next door to the youth hostel on Lake Helgasjön ☎0470/630 03. The biggest disaster on the Växjö dining scene was when this eighteenth-century lakeside restaurant burnt to the ground in 2001. The owners have worked hard to set it all up again since, serving some of the best food in Växjö with Swedish specialities include roast pike with crayfish, fresh from the local lake. Two courses 260kr; lunches 59kr. July closed Mon.

Fiskepiren Båtmanstorget 1 ☎0470/156 56. In a singularly ugly building on an ugly square, this is nonetheless a very popular and pleasant fish restaurant serving mains for 155–200kr.

PM & Friends Storgatan 24. Popular and stylishly casual, this fine, modern European restaurant is unpretentious and uses fish from the local lakes and organic vegetables from local farms. Lunch specials are 68kr and evening meals won't break the bank either. Cheaper bar menu with light bites at 45–90kr. Closed lunchtime in July.

Spisen Norra Järnvägsgatan 8 ☎0470/123 00. Another gourmet choice – with lunch at 59kr, to give you a taster of the much pricier evening meals. Closed second half of July.

Teaterpark Connected to Hotel Teaterpark in the Concert Hall building. This beautiful restaurant has a well-balanced summertime menu at 150–200kr. Lunch specials are 75kr. Closed July.

Vibrowski Sandgärdsgatan 19 ☎0470/74 04 10. This charming old pink-painted wooden house is where to come for lamb, Wienerschnitzel and pepper steaks at 180kr plus. Inside is simpler than you might expect.

The Glass Kingdom (Glasriket)

Glass-making in Sweden was pioneered by King Gustav Vasa, who'd been impressed by the glass he saw on a trip to Italy in the mid-sixteenth century. He initially set up a **glassworks** in Stockholm; however, it was Småland's forests that could provide the vast amounts of fuel needed to feed the furnaces, and so a glass factory was set up in the county in 1742. Called Kosta, after its founders, Koskull and Stael von Hostein, it is still the largest glassworks in Småland today.

Visiting the glassworks

Of the fifteen glassworks still in operation in Småland, all give captivating **glass-blowing** demonstrations (Mon–Fri 9am–2.30pm, occasionally longer hours; late June to early August, Kosta & Orrefors Sat 10am–4pm & Sun noon–4pm). Several have permanent exhibitions of either contemporary glasswork or pieces from their history, and all have a shop. **Bus** services to the glassworks, or to points within easy walking distance of them, are extremely limited, and without your own transport it is almost impossible to see more than a couple in a day (though this will satisfy most people). While each glassworks has its individual design characteristics, **Kosta Boda** (easiest to reach from Växjö) and **Orrefors** (closer to Kalmar) works have extensive displays and give the best picture of what's available. To get to Orrefors, you first need to get to Nybro; you can do this on Route 25 from Kalmar, or by train from Kalmar or Växjö. Alternatively, you can then drive to the factory on Route 31, or catch bus #138, #139 or #140 from Växjö. Driving from Växjö take Road 25 to Lessebo, then follow signs to Kosta and Orrefors. There are no buses.

Kosta Boda glassworks

The **Kosta Boda** and **Åfors** glassworks are both operated by the same team. While two of Kosta's most celebrated and hyped designers, Bertil Vallien and Ulrica Hydman Vallien, have their studios at Åfors, the bigger glassworks is at Kosta. The **historical exhibition** here (June to mid-Aug Mon–Fri 9am–6pm, Sat 9am–4pm, Sun 11am–4pm) contains some of the most delicate fin-de-siècle glassware, designed by Karl Lindeberg; for contemporary simplicity, Anna Ehrner's bowls and vases are the most elegant. Among the most brilliantly innovative works are those by Göran Wärff – examples of his expressive work

Glass-making and buying in Glasriket

The **glass-making process** can be mesmerizing to watch. The process involves a glass plug being fished out of a shimmering, molten lake (at 1200°C) and then turned and blown into a graphite or steel mould. With wine glasses, a foot is added during the few seconds when the temperature is just right – if the glass is too hot, the would-be stem will slide off or sink right through; if too cold, it won't stick. The piece is then annealed – heated and then slowly cooled – for several hours. It all looks deceptively simple and mistakes are rare, but it nevertheless takes years to become a *servitor* (glass-maker's assistant), working up through the ranks of stem-maker and bowl-gatherer (in the smaller glassworks, all these roles are the responsibility of one person).

The glassware is marketed with a vengeance in Småland – take a look at the often absurd hyberbole in the widely available *Kingdom of Crystal* magazine. If you want to buy glassware, don't feel compelled to snap up the first things you see: the same designs appear at most of the glassworks, testimony to the fact that the biggest factories by far, Kosta Boda and Orrefors, are now under the same umbrella ownership and many of the smaller works have been swallowed up too, even though they retain their own names. Don't expect much in the way of bargains; the more elaborate pieces go for thousands of kronor. Despite all the marketing suggesting the products are innovative and new, there's a lot of emperor's-new-clothes amongst Swedes on the glass design issue. While there's plenty that's interesting to look at, there's a lot of hackneyed, decades-old designs about too. You may find it useful to see the glassware exhibition in Växjö's Smålands Museum first. The historical collections will show how the designs of the mid-twentieth century are simply being reintroduced as new today (see p.299).

can also be found in Växjö's cathedral. Current design trends tend more towards colourful and rather graceless high kitsch; nonetheless, new designer sculptural pieces can go for astoundingly high prices. In the adjacent shop Ulrica Hydman Vallien's commercialized designs go for around 2000kr, although for a single, traditional *akvavit* glass, you're looking at paying something like 115kr.

To get to Kosta from Växjö, take Route 25 to Lessebo, then follow signs to the left. Heading here from Kalmar, you first take Route 25 west to Nybro, turning onto Route 31 northwest, and then left at the Kosta sign. You can do a day-trip here by public transport from Växjö – take bus #218 from Växjö bus station, changing at Lessebo.

Other glassworks

Studio Glass (formerly Strömbergshyttan), near Hovmantorp, is one of the only genuine independents, and one of the best bets for an easy trip from Växjö, with displays of both Kosta and Orrefors merchandise. Nearby **Sandvik** has the best shop for Orrefors glass, as it's part of the Orrefors group. Strömbergshyttan is south down Route 25 from Växjö, or take bus #218 (40min), which runs more frequently here than to Kosta. The simple and distinctive blue-rimmed glassware popular all over Sweden can be seen at **Bergdala**, 6km north of Hovmantorp, although there's no public transport there. A small, traditional factory, it offers a more intimate look at the glass-blowing process.

Heading north on Route 30, the 1905-founded **Lindshammar** works is now Norwegian-owned, and the collection has improved in recent years; the few really good vases cost 3200kr. From Växjö, take Route 23 to Norrhult-Klavreström, then Route 31 north. There is no public transport here.

Johansfors, south of the Boda factory on Route 120, is a small factory set by a river specializing in wine goblets (exhibitions Mon–Fri 9am–6pm, Sat 10am–4pm, Sun noon–4pm; shop daily 9am–6pm). Working here is Astrid Gate, the granddaughter of Simon Gate, who along with Edward Hald, was one of the two design giants at Orrefors in the early twentieth century. They discovered some of the most impressive techniques in glass-blowing still used around the world today. One such skill, used also by Astrid Gate, is **graal** – a method of layering glass then engraving it before blowing it out again to create a subtly curving organic appearance. To get there, take Route 28 from Kosta; there's no bus service here.

Practicalities

There's often local **accommodation** available, particularly at the bigger glassworks; check availability with tourist offices at Kalmar or Växjö. One of the most enjoyable, though costly, eating experiences here – and one that really can claim to be a Småland original – is **hyttsill**, an **evening meal** of smoked sausage, pork and herrings baked in the factory glass furnaces at 300°C. Several of the glassworks – Kosta, Orrefors and Bergdala – cook up *hyttsill*, each on a different night but always at 7pm (240kr; check days with the tourist office). The herring is served with furnace-baked potatoes, Småland curd cake (a rich local cheesecake), coffee and beer. It's fun, but the "wonderful atmosphere" promised in the blurbs rather depends on who turns up. To sample one of these meals, it's important to reserve a place a day or two in advance (Bergdala ☎0478/316 50; Kosta ☎0478/500 00 or 345 00; Orrefors ☎0481/300 65). Most of the glassworks also have simple **cafés** serving coffee, cakes and sandwiches.

Kyrkö Mosse Car Cemetery

For a most bizarre and remarkably un-Swedish sight, head for the **car cemetery** at Ryd, 50km south of Växjö. To reach here take the express bus #240, in direction Ronneby (Mon–Fri 3 daily; 50mins); at the weekends you'll have to change at Tingsryd and take a local bus the 20km west to Ryd. Two kilometres beyond the village, amongst a landscape of dense forest, over a hundred cars were abandoned in the Fifties and early Sixties and promptly forgotten about; nobody knows who left them or where they came from. With moss and trees growing in and through these classic vehicles, the spot is an eerily beautiful melange of greens and browns. Clamber beyond the "cemetery's" main drag, and you'll find older models with split windscreens and running boards lieing half-submerged in the undergrowth, chrome and rusting metal coated by a layer of moss. The subject of much local controversy, the status of the cemetery appears to have been secured recently.

Jönköping

Perched at the southernmost tip of Lake Vättern, northwest of Växjö, along Route 30, one of the oldest medieval trading centres in the country, **JÖNKÖPING** (pronounced "Yun-shurp-ing") won its town charter in 1284. Today, it is famous for being the home of the matchstick, the nineteenth-century manufacture and worldwide distribution of which made the town a wealthy place (see p.307). Despite the town's plum position on the lakeshore, its excess of high-rise offices and bland buildings in the centre detract from what is otherwise a pleasant town. Since the turn of the third millennium, the

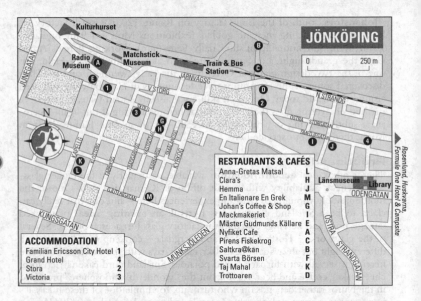

JÖNKÖPING

0   250 m

Kulturhurset

Radio **A**
Museum

Matchstick
Museum

B

Train & Bus
Station

C

JÄRNVAGSG

E

①

V. STORG

D

②

N. STRANDG

N

SKOLG

③

F

ÖSTRA STORGATAN

G

H

SMEDJEGATAN

I

J

④

KAPELLG

KLOSTERG

BARNARPSG

KRISTINAG

SMALANS

KYRKOG

K

L

Rosenlund, Huskvarna,
Formule One Hotel & Campsite

Länsmuseum

Library

ODENGATAN

ÖSTRA STRANDGATAN

G. JUTERGATAN

M

KUNGSGATAN

MUNKSJÖLEDEN

RESTAURANTS & CAFÉS

Anna-Gretas Matsal	L
Clara's	H
Hemma	J
En Italienare En Grek	M
Johan's Coffee & Shop	G
Mackmakeriet	I
Mäster Gudmunds Källare	E
Nyfiket Cafe	A
Pirens Fiskekrog	C
Saltkra@kan	B
Svarta Börsen	F
Taj Mahal	K
Trottoaren	D

ACCOMMODATION

Familian Ericsson City Hotel	1
Grand Hotel	4
Stora	2
Victoria	3

town's pier has been developed into a chain of appealing waterside restaurants and bars, and a dramatic increase in the student population means Jönköping is casting off its image of an provincial town that closes down for the summer. There's an optimistic feel here now, though many Jönköpingers themselves still head for the coast during the summer months, so if you are here between June and August it's still fairly quiet.

At the end of August, the town hosts a five-day **film festival** (ⓦwww .filmfestival.nu). It's not pure art-house, but not mainstream Hollywood either, focusing on films from the rest of Scandinavia, and across Europe.

Arrival and information

At the lake's southern-most edge, the stylish, new **train station** contains the **tourist office**, (mid-June to mid-Aug Mon–Fri 9am–7pm, Sat 10am–3pm, Sun 10am–2pm; mid-Aug to mid-June Mon–Fri 11am–4pm; ☎036/10 50 50, ⓔturist@sfk.jonkoping.se). The bus station is right outside. **Bikes** can be rented from Renbergs Cykel Och Sport at Södra Strandgatan 1 (☎036/16 05 06; 115kr a day or 400kr a week).

Accommodation

The only real budget options in town are the limited number of **private rooms**, at 200–250kr per person, organized by the tourist office. The nearest **youth hostel** is 6km east in Huskvarna (see p.310); to get there, take bus #1 from outside Jönköping's tourist office. Alternatively the *Formula One Hotel* (☎036/30 25 65, ⓦwww.hotelformule.one.com; ❶), 3km from the centre, at Huskvarnavägen 76, next to the Elmia Exhibition Centre at Rosenlund, has very cheap basic rooms for up to three sharing. Several buses head in the right direction, the most frequent being bus #1. There's also a **campsite** at Rosenlund (☎036/12 28 63).

Most of the main **hotels** slash their prices in summer by up to a half. The best choice for style, atmosphere and value for money is the *Hotel Victoria*, F.E.

Elmgrensgatan 5, two blocks south of the tourist office (☎036/71 28 00, ⓦwww.victoriahome.com; ❺/❸). The price includes afternoon tea and an excellent buffet supper in the appealing atrium dining area. The most historical of the hotels is the *Stora*, at Hotellplan (☎036/10 00 00, ⓦwww.elite.se; ❺/❷); built in the 1860s, this imposing place overlooking the lake has rooms decorated in Gustavian-style pastels, and bathrooms that boast that unusual commodity in Sweden – bathtubs. Even if you don't stay in the hotel, ask at reception if you can nip up to the third floor to the old ballroom, the **Spegel Salen** (Hall of Mirrors), where the grand trompe d'oeil ceiling, mirrored arches and massive chandeliers are still in place. For a surprisingly inexpensive but still rather elegant place, try the 1904 *Grand Hotel* at Hovrättstorget, a short distance east of the *Stora* (☎036/71 96 00, ⓦwww.grandhotel-jonkoping.se; ❸/❷). The very comfortable, central *Familjen Ericsson City Hotel*, Västra Storgatan 25 (☎036/71 92 80, ⓕ71 88 48; ❹/❷), is plainer than the other hotels, but is very conveniently positioned just three minutes' walk south from the train station. It's closed in July.

The Town

Jönköping's restored historical core is the most interesting part of town to explore. At its heart, in a quaint cobbled courtyard, is the **Tändsticksmuséet**, Tändsticksgränd 27 (Match Museum; June–Aug Mon–Fri 10am–5pm, Sat & Sun 10am–3pm; Sept–May Tues–Sat 11am–3pm; 30kr), in what was the main building of the town's first match factory (see box). It's not all that thrilling a museum though, being not much more than a collection of matchbox labels and match-making machines. Opposite, at Tandstickgränd 16, is the **Erik E. Karlson Radio Museum** (daily Tues–Fri 10am–5pm, Sat 10am–1pm; June to mid-Aug also Mon 10am–5pm & Sun 11am–3pm; 20kr). Hailing from nearby Huskvarna, Karlson built his first radio receiver aged 16, and later opened Sweden's first radio store. The museum that bears his name contains seemingly every type of radio, from early crystal sets to Walkmans.

The only other museum in town worth bothering with is the **Länsmuseum** on Dag Hammarskjölds Plats 2, on the east side of the canal between lakes Vättern and Munksjön (Tues–Sun 11am–5pm, Wed till 8pm; 40kr, under-18s

---

The rise and fall of the Swedish matchstick

It was in Jönköping, in 1844, that Professor Gustav Pasch invented the **safety match**. Hot on his heels, the Lundström brothers opened the first safety-match factory here the following year; its main building is now the Match Museum (see above). Twenty years after, one Alexander Lagerman designed the world's first machine for churning out matches, transforming the process from a craft into a mechanized industry.

The various Swedish match firms which sprang up over the following decades were amalgamated into the Swedish Match Company in 1917, all under the control of **Ivar Kreugar**, to whom the industry's subsequent downfall is largely attributed. Jönköping's most notorious twentieth-century figure, he lent vast amounts of money he didn't have to countries with large national debts, in exchange for a monopoly on their match sales. For a time one of Sweden's wealthiest men, in 1932, rather than become a bankrupt, he shot himself dead in Paris, an act which signalled the start of his industry's decline; match-making limped on in Sweden until 1971, when it was extinguished by cheaper competition from abroad.

Astrid Lindgren – creator of Pippi Longstocking

Some 90km east of Jönköping on Route 33 is **Vimmerby**, near where one of Sweden's most popular children's authors, **Astrid Lindgren**, was born in 1907. Her most endearing character, **Pippi Longstocking** (in Swedish, Pippi Långstrump), burst upon the world in 1945. Pippi had red hair and long thin legs on which she wore non-matching stockings. Wealthy and energetic, she could do as she pleased, and her adventures have appealed hugely to children everywhere.

The face of Lindgren, who died in 2001, has appeared on a Swedish 6kr stamp; her eighty books have, in total, sold more than 80 million copies worldwide. Yet her writing hasn't simply been about lighthearted adventures: her cleverly conceived tale, *Bröderna Lejonhjärta* ("The Lionheart Brothers"), tries to explain the concept of death to children.

In recent years, she became a Swedish Brigitte Bardot figure, campaigning on animal-rights issues. She was also involved with children's rights: aged 90, she campaigned vigorously against the deportation of an 11-year-old girl from Sweden. Today, Vimmerby is home to Astrid Lindgren World (@www.astridlindgrensworld .com), a theme park where actors take on the roles of her most famous characters. Trains to Vimmerby run from Kalmar, then a free connecting bus (#77) or bus #320 from Växjö leads there.

free). A mishmash of oddities, its exhibits ranging from posters showing Swedish support for Che Guevara through garden chairs throughout the ages to samovars and doll's houses, the place is like a well-stocked junk shop; there's no English labelling, though that won't detract much from the fun. The best part is the well-lit collection of paintings and drawings by **John Bauer**, a locally born artist who enthralled generations of Swedes with his Tolkienesque representations of gnomes and trolls in the *Bland Tomtar och Troll*, a well-known series of Swedish children's books. Upstairs is a constantly changing **art gallery** and the Länsmuseum library (May–Aug Mon–Fri 10am–7pm, Sat 10am–2pm; Sept–April Mon–Thurs 10am–8pm, Fri 10am–7pm, Sat 10am–2pm, Sun 1–5pm), the only place in town with **Internet access** (must be booked before use; free) and worth a stop if you want to peruse the remarkable range of foreign-language **newspapers**.

Back in the centre, a few metres away from the Match Museum, and set in another old match factory, is **Kulturhuset**, on Tändsticksgränd, a trendy arts centre, with an alternative bookshop (Mon–Fri 5–7pm) and a good, cheap café (see opposite). Next door is Bio, a stylish art-house **cinema**. From September to May, there's a bustling early-morning Saturday **market** on the street outside.

Although there's little else to see in the town centre, it is remarkable for the sheer number of **Free Churches** – 23 in the immediate vicinity; consequently, Jönköping has been dubbed "Sweden's Jerusalem". As the traditional Church watches its congregations diminish, people are turning instead to these independent and fundamentalist churches.

Just 3km out of town towards Huskvarna, Rosenlund boasts one of Scandinavia's largest **swimming pool complexes**, *Rosenlundsbadet* at Elmiavågen 4 (leave E4 at Elmia exit; Mon noon–8pm, Tues–Fri 6.30am–8pm, Sat & Sun 10am–5pm; family ticket 150kr), perfect if you have children in tow. There's a range of pools with slides, wave pools, Jacuzzis and massage pools.

Eating, drinking and nightlife

Jönköping's most popular eating and drinking area is the harbour pier, though the rest of town has plenty of good, lively spots too. For a taste of a local food speciality, go for the **Vättern Röding** (Arctic char) from the little fish shop down by the harbour, or at any of the better restaurants. The char is brought here from Vättern, an unusually cold and deep lake which can thereby sustain fish normally found in the Baltic Sea.

The town's trendiest **nightclub** is the stylish *Millennium* (50kr cover charge), in a former match factory by the Match Museum. With a big dance floor and more relaxed bar area, it's packed on Friday and Saturday nights, with a mainly 18- to 23-year-old age group. This is one of the few towns in Sweden where the **gay** community's organisation RFSL is actually growing. They arrange a café night every Thursday (7–10pm) and a party twice-monthly on Saturday nights, but they were moving premises at the time of writing; contact ℡036/71 84 80 for more information.

Be aware that some of the town's establishments close for the summer when many of the residents head for the coast.

Cafés and restaurants

Anna-Gretas Matsal Västra Torget ℡036/71 25 75. The oldest café in town, once serving market traders from daybreak, this pleasant place is now a good-value restaurant with a friendly atmosphere and an eclectic, changing menu.

Saltkråkan Restaurant and Pub End of the pier ℡036/12 53 53. This old boat restaurant appeals to many Swedes, as it's featured in the long-running Swedish children's television programme Saltkråkan. The lower deck has a bar (from 3pm), and the top a restaurant serving fine meat and fish dishes (from 6 pm). This is the best place at the harbour, though it's also the dearest.

Clara's Barnarpsgatan 18. Very relaxed and friendly café on the west side of town close to the university. Terrific salads, pastas (50kr), bagels and lots of coffees, all surrounded by arty photos.

En Italienare En Grek Barnarpsgatan 35B ℡036/30 77 55. Well-priced, tasty Italian and Greek food with good service overlooking the attractive old tram depot in the university district. A fine spot for an evening drink with outside tables in summer.

Johan's Coffee & Shop Barnarpsgatan. With black-and-white marble floors and a pale, lofty interior, this charming place serves superb salads and delicious home-baked pies – both sweet and savoury. Lunch is excellent value at 60kr including coffee. Rather twee pastel furniture and tableware are on sale.

Mackmakeriet Smedjegatan 26. The best café in town housed in a wonderful eighteenth-century building with an original painted ceiling. Lining the walls are sensational photographs by local photographer Andreas Joakimson of a fire which devastated much of the area in 2000; the café was one of the few survivors. Delicious fresh-filled baguettes (44kr) and cakes served in a friendly atmosphere.

Mäster Gudmunds Källar Kappellgatan 2. A

vaulted cellar restaurant serving good, traditional Swedish fare at high prices. Closed Sun in summer.

Nyfiket Café in the Kulturhuset. A friendly, studenty place serving generously filled rolls (25–30kr) and an excellent daily lunch special (40kr).

Pirens Fiskekrog On the pier ℡036/15 00 96. A large selection of fish fresh straight out of Vättern (142–179kr), plus a variety of shellfish and smoked fish for 95–115kr.

Svarta Börsen Kyrkogatan 4 ℡036/71 22 22. The best restaurant in town, in one of the few remaining old buildings on the west side of the centre. Excellent and expensive fish, game and poultry dishes in delicate sauces all beautifully prepared and presented. Booking essential.

Taj Mahal Kapellgatan 15 ℡036/12 82 55. One of the best Indian restaurants in town, specializing in tandoori and grill dishes. Lunch comes at 50kr, including coffee; most à la carte dishes cost 60–130kr.

Trottoaren Restaurant Next to the *Stora Hotell* at Hotellplan. A wacky American-style diner, its decor including a pink Vespa, US number plates and filling-station pumps. In contrast, the tables have crisp linen and silver candlesticks. Full meals from 198kr.

Bars

Balzar's Bar & Brasserie *Hotel Klosterkungen*, Klostergatan 28. A quiet, pleasant place for a meal or a beer, with main courses at 100–150kr or light meals at 65kr. There's occasional live music, a mix of pop and old tunes (Fri & Sat). Happy hours 5–7pm.

Hemma Smedjegatan 36. The town's most popular venue for laid-back live music, with very friendly service and a relaxing terrace garden. There's also decent cooking here with a summer menu of salmon, chicken and veal dishes from 95–200kr, and a wider range of choices during the rest of the year. Lunch specials are 90kr.

Karlsons Salonger Västra Storgatan 9. This buzzing bar attracts a wide age range and is as popular for its tasty meals as for its lively ambience. **Rignes** *Hotel Savoy*, Brunnsgatan 13–15. A candle-lit pub, serving Norwegian beer with blues and rock and roll music, that's often live. There's an inexpensive all-day set menu, mainly offering meat dishes plus a lunch menu (75kr). Mon–Thurs noon till midnight, Fri & Sat noon till 2am (30kr cover charge on Fri & Sat).
Solde Bar next door to the *Trottoaren* restaurant (see above). This bar, part of *Stora Hotell*, is packed all through summer. It offers baguettes, tortillas and salads for 50–75kr each and is a favourite with a young crowd, who come here to make the most of the cider and beer.

Along the shore of Lake Vättern to Vadstena

The eastern shores of **Lake Vättern** offer the most spectacular scenery and delightful historical towns in the region. Jönköping can be used as a base for excursions, but there are plenty of places to eat and stay along the way to Vadstena (see p.315), including some idyllic hotels around the pastoral perfection of **Röttle**, a tiny hamlet 3km south of the splendid little town of **Gränna**. This part of Sweden is perfect for **trekking**, too, with lots of hiking trails to try.

From Jönköping to Gränna

Leaving Jönköping, head out along Östra Storgatan, which soon becomes the E4, towards **HUSKVARNA**, 6km to the east; you can also get there by bus (10min). The little town was named after the 1689 arms factory Husquarna; the company still exists, though today it produces sewing machines and motorbikes. Huskvarna may at first seem very industrial, but there are still some quaint wooden cottages in its old quarter and in the preserved smith's village called **Smedbyn**. Nearby, there's a town museum in the old powder house, **Kruthuset** (May–Aug Sat & Sun 2–5pm; 15kr), and a museum of local industry, **Husqvarna Fabriksmuseum** (April, May & Sept–Nov Sat & Sun 1–4pm; June–Aug Mon–Fri 10am–5pm, Sat & Sun 1–4pm; 20kr), in the company's nineteenth-century musket-barrel factory.

For a place to **stay**, there's Huskvarna's **youth hostel**, at Odengatan 10 (☏036/14 88 70, ℻14 88 40; 130kr), 100m from its bus station. But unless you're particularly interested in the town's history, it's altogether more rewarding to continue north, up either the E4 or the more picturesque Grännavagen (the old E4). **Buses** #120 and #121 make the trip from here to Gränna in around an hour (stopping at Hakarp and Röttle on the way), and there are quicker express buses twice a day, too; there are no trains, though.

A few minutes on from Huskvarna, the crashing waterfalls that used to power the town's industry come into view as Grännavagen winds. A couple of kilometres further is the village of **Hakarp**, whose **church**'s interior is a riot of paintings that were clearly designed to terrify the peasant parishioners (daily 9am–4pm; June–Aug till 6pm). The ceiling bears graphic depictions of hell, with demons stabbing and torturing naked women. Also on the ceiling are interesting paintings of both the present church, built in 1694, and the medieval church that preceded it, together with an interpretation of New Jerusalem, with more naked women climbing from their graves. Note, too, the pew-backs, which are original – despite being painted with leopard-skin spots, which look more like something out of the 1970s than 1770s. Bus #15 runs infrequently from Huskvarna to Hakarp church.

Gränna and around

"Instead of roaring factories with belching chimneys, the visitor to Gränna finds peaceful gardens, fruitful orchards and a soothing quietude in all parts of the town"

Allan Berggren, 'Gränna & Its Surrounds'.

Forty kilometres north of Jönköping, the lakeside town of **GRÄNNA** is associated with the unlikely combination of pears, striped rock candy (see box) and a gung-ho nineteenth-century Swedish balloonist (see overleaf). In late spring, the hills around Gränna are a confetti of pear blossom, Per Brahe (see below) having encouraged the planting of pear orchards hereabouts – the Gränna pear is one of the best-known varieties in the country today. Approaching from the south, the beautiful Gränna Valley sweeps down to your left, with the hills to the right, most notably the crest of Grännaberget, which provides a majestic foil to some superb views over Lake Vättern and its island, Visingsö (see p.313). On a hot summer's day, the trip here from Jönköping has something of the atmosphere of the French Riviera, evoked in particular by the winding roads, red-tiled roofs and the profusion of flowers in the old cottage gardens – not to mention the equal profusion of Porsches and Mercedes cars.

Per Brahe, one of Sweden's first counts (see p.314), built the town in the mid-seventeenth century, using the symmetry, regularity and spaciousness of planning that he had learnt while governor of Finland. The charming main street, **Brahegatan**, was subsequently widened and remodelled, allowing the houses fronting it to have gardens, while the other main roads were designed so Brahe could look straight down them as he stood at the windows of his now-ruined castle, **Brahehus**. The gardens along Brahegatan remain mostly intact, and until the 1920s, there were no additions to the original street layout. Even now, there's very much a village feel to the little town. The best starting point for a great view is to head up behind the market square, containing a statue of Brahe, to *Café Stugan* (see p.313).

Another fine stroll with a fabulous vista over the lake takes you up to *Hembygdsstugan Grännaberget* (May–Aug 10am–9pm), which should not be missed even though there's a climb of 243 steep steps to reach it: from the market square, walk across to the church then south for 200m to the steps in the hillside to your left. Outside seating at the café affords a fabulous vista over the lake. Better still, you can explore inside a range of ancient, grass and thatch-roofed buildings brought from the surrounding areas. The high light is Röttlegärden, a farm brought from Röttle village (sse p.313) in 1919 and exquisitely preserved.

Gränna rock

Gränna has been known for striped rock candy, called **polkagris**, ever since Amalia Eriksson, a penniless widow, began ekeing out a living by producing the red-and-white sugar tubes in the mid-nineteenth century. It's fun to watch it being produced, which you can do at one of the small factories, **Cabbe Polkagrisfabrik**, 3km south of Gränna, just opposite the *Hotel Gyllene Uttern,* or in town at several of the many specialist shops. One of the best is *Grenna Polkagriskokeri*, at Brahegatan 39, where, behind the counter displaying a hundred colours and flavours of the sweet, you can watch as the ingredients (99 percent sugar, a little colouring and a drop of peppermint) are heated to 150°C, melted, poured, twisted, hardened and cut into the sweets.

Gränna Museum, including the S. A. Andree Museum

Within the Grenna Kulturgård on Brahegatan is the fascinating **S.A. Andree museum** (same hours as the tourist office, see below, where you buy your ticket; 40kr), dedicated to Salomon August Andree, the Gränna-born **balloonist** who led a doomed attempt to reach the North Pole by balloon in 1897. Born at Brahegatan 37, Andree was fired by the European obsession of the day to explore and conquer unknown areas; with no real way of directing his balloon, however, his trip was destined for disaster from the start. After a flight lasting only three days, during which time it flew more than 800km in different directions, the balloon made a forced landing on ice just 470km from its departure point. The crew of three attempted to walk to civilization, but the movement of the ice floes meant they made no progress; after six weeks' trekking, they set up camp on a floe drifting rapidly southwards. Sadly, the ice cracked and their shelter collapsed, and with it their hopes. Finally they died from the effects of cold, starvation and trichinosis, caught after they ate the raw meat of a polar bear they had managed to spear. It would be another 33 years before their frozen bodies and their equipment were discovered by a Norwegian sailing ship. They were reburied in Stockholm at a funeral attended by a crowd of forty thousand. The museum exhibition poignantly includes a diary kept by one of the crew and film taken by the team, which makes for pitiful viewing: the men are seen with the polar bear they'd hunted, and other sequences show the three hopelessly pulling their sledges across the ice sheets.

Since 2002, The newly renovated museum has extended its remit to cover exploration of the Polar region including scientific research with exhibitions centring on the Arctic and Antarctic historical expeditions, using Andree as a springboard to a wider picture. There's also a **local history museum**, the most interesting sights being a portrait of a miserable-looking Per Brahe aged 17, his coat of armour, and a model of Västanås Slott before the present count's father removed the top floor in 1928. The stylish first-floor library has free **Internet** access.

Practicalities

Buses will drop you off on the main road, Brahegatan. Bus #121 from Jönköping also stops outside *Hotel Gyllern Ottern*, but it's then a 3km walk to Västenås Slott. The **tourist office** (mid-June to Aug daily 10am–7pm; mid- to end May & Sept–Oct daily 10am–5pm; Nov & Dec daily noon–4pm; ☎0390/410 10, ✆turism@grm.se) is housed in the newly designed Grenna Kulturgård, on Brahegatan, which also contains the museum (see above) and **library** with free Internet access; they can book **private rooms** from 120kr, plus a booking fee of 50kr. Gränna has two **youth hostels**: *Gränna Vandrarhem*, along Brahegatan (book through tourist office; 120kr; mid-June to early Aug), and another hostel right on the beach near where the ferry to Visingsjö puts in (☎0390/107 06; 140kr; May–Sept).

The most sensational place to stay by far is the historic country house **Västenås Slott** (☎0390/107 00; ✆41875; ❸; May–Oct) just south of Röttleby. Built in 1590 by Count Sten Bielke and owned in the seventeenth century by Count Per Brahe, this low grey castle is owned and run by the formidable Rolf Von Otter, a descendent of Bielke, There are no telephones or television in the rooms – hence the very reasonable price – but the sheer majesty of the antique-strewn furnishings and the fabulous lake views from the magnificent first-floor drawing room are worth the stay alone. Breakfast is served in the stunning dining room.

Von Otter's father believed in 1930 that the age of grand car tours had arrived in Sweden, and built Scandinavia's first hotel specifically designed for motor car tourism. The result, close to the main road above Västernås Slott, is *Hotel Gyllene Uttern*, or "Golden Otter" (℡0390/108 00, ⓦwww.gyllerneottern.se; ❺/❹). It looks like a medieval German castle, with stone castellations and a Baronial interior, though compared with the old family home, there is something a bit contrived about the place. The rooms in the annexe are cheaper, but lack the glamour of those in the main building. Other than walking the very pleasant 3km into town from here, you can order a **taxi** from *Gränna Taxi* (℡0390/121 00; 100kr).

There are several excellent **cafés** in Gränna, all of which are on Brahegatan. The best in town is *Café Fiket* (June–Aug daily 8am–7pm; rest of year Mon–Fri 8.30am–6pm), with a quietly 50s themed interior where you can enjoy their speciality, a rich almond pastry tart. Or their excellent Gränna knäckebröd, a crunchy, tasty crispbread made with linseed, sunflower and sesame seeds. *Café Amalia*, just a few steps at no. 47 (June–Aug daily 10am–10pm; Sept–May Mon–Thurs 10am–4pm, Fri & Sat till 10pm), is named after the queen of Gränna rock (see p.311) and specializes in good Swedish home-cooking. They also offer a superb lingonberry ice cream that you can eat on the spacious terrace overlooking the rooftops and lake. A little further up the same road is *Haglunds Konditori,* (Mon–Fri 8.30am–6pm, Sat 8.30am–3pm, Sun 11am–5pm) with a wide selection of delicious cakes and breads.

For something more substantial, *Restaurant Hjorten*, at Brahegatan 42, is a very pleasing **restaurant** and bar (June–Aug daily 11.30am–10pm; rest of year Mon–Fri 11.30am–2.30pm & Sat & Sun all day downstairs only). Their well-prepared fish and meat meals start at 150kr and their pizza and pasta buffet is excellent value – as much as you can eat for 65kr. There's even outside eating in summer on the sunny terrace. *Gränna Golf Krog* (May–Sept 8am–9.30pm; ℡0390/122 22) is the restaurant at Västanå Golf club, itself one of the most celebrated **golf** courses in Sweden located within the grounds of Västanås Slott (see opposite). It's an appealing place with good cakes and coffee during the day and a lovely dinner menu with starters of blue mussel soup or warm smoked Vättern fish at 60–65kr and mains at 145–180kr. Desserts include the locally inspired *polkagris* parfait with Gränna pear sauce (65kr).

Röttle

One of the most idyllic goals for a few hours' wandering, just south of Gränna, is the hamlet of **RÖTTLE**, its name deriving from words meaning "roaring torrent". Industry existed here as early as 1297, when Rytlofors Mill was granted the right to mill flour by the king. The Jerusalem Mill, one of the oldest built here, still stands; it was given by King Magnus to the bishop of Linköping in 1330. The village was once owned by Per Brahe, one of Sweden's most prominent aristocrats, at a time when the professions here included glove-makers, coppersmiths and sword-cleaners. Today, the antiquated wooden cottages that sit snugly amid emerald-green grassland and stands of silver birch are picturesque rather than industrial, and the sound of the water is only a gentle gurgle.

Röttle's tiny harbour is a popular bathing spot during the summer. A couple of minutes' walk from Röttle is **Västanå Nature Reserve**, which runs all the way to the lake and is carpeted with heathers, cowberries and delicate yellow, blue, and white wood anemones in late spring. A splendid **walking trail** to take is the John Bauerleden, which wends its way from Huskvarna northwards for 50km; you can easily pick it up at Röttle (it's signposted).

Visingsö

From Gränna, a twenty-minute **ferry** (June–Aug every 30min; Sept–May hourly; passengers 40kr; car & driver 150kr return) crossing drops you on the island of **Visingsö**, just 14km by 3km wide. In the mid-sixteenth century, Eric XIV decided that Sweden should follow the example of Continental monarchies by bestowing titles and privileges on deserving noblemen. He created the title of Count of Visingsborg, whose lands included the island, and awarded it to Per Brahe the Elder. Brahe's son enjoyed a spate of castle building, and one of his creations was the **Visingsborg Slott**, on the east shore of the island, by the ferry terminal. After Brahe the Younger's death in 1680, the Crown took back much of the estate, including the island; his castle is an empty shell today, its roof having been burned off in 1718 by Russian prisoners celebrating the death of Karl XII, who'd taken them prisoner during his abortive march on Russia.

Visingsö is entirely flat, and so the island is easily covered on foot or by bike; alternatively, if you're not feeling so energetic, hire a *remmalag* or horse and trap. These make trips (50–65kr return) along the quiet lanes to twelfth-century **Kumlaby** church, the oldest relic on the island, with beautifully painted ceiling and walls. The church's truncated tower is the result of astronomy classes organized by Brahe the Younger. The most intriguing aspect of the church is the extremely narrow, pitch-dark stone spiral in the tower (June–Aug 9am–8pm) which gradually opens up as you climb the steep, wooden steps; from the top, you have views right across the island.

The only other sight here is the ruin of **Näs castle**, at the southern tip of the island. This was once a major seat of power in Sweden, though today it's just battlements, revealing little sign of its erstwhile glory. The journey here on the perimeter road is a pleasure, passing through forest and corn fields, and past well-kept old cottages, some with fancy porches and verandahs.

For a spot of summer **swimming**, there's a lagoon at the harbour; the water here is warmer than the much deeper waters of the surrounding Lake Vättern.

Practicalities

Arriving at the dock, you'll find the **tourist office** to your right (mid-May to late June & Aug daily 10am–5pm; late June & July daily 10am–7pm; Sept to mid-May Mon–Fri 8am–2pm; ☎0390/401 93, ⓔvisingsoturist@grm.se); they **rent bikes** at 40kr for three hours, or 60kr for a day. There are plenty of places for **refreshments** on the island. A couple of cafés at the harbour serve lunches, pizzas and coffees, and all around the island are charming wooden houses with signs indicating they're offering home-made cake and cheesecake. There's also a fine smoked-fish shop opposite the dock, selling mackerel, whitefish and salmon smoked with brandy.

Lake Tåkern and around

The E4 runs from Gränna north to **Ödeshög**, crossing into the province of **Östergotland**. From Ödeshog you have a choice of routes: stay on the E4 and you'll be heading east towards Linköping (see p.323); or take Route 50 to continue north to Vadstena. Ten kilometres to the south of Vadstena is **Lake Tåkern**, formed around 7000 BC when the inland ice receded from Östergotland's plains. The lake is surrounded by beautiful open landscapes with excellent walking trails, a sprinkling of medieval churches and the substantial remains of a twelfth-century monastery; also here is one of the country's best bird sanctuaries, on the lake itself. All these sites are probably best visited as daytrips from one of the main towns nearby, such as **Vadstena** and **Motala**, which

Bird-watching on Lake Tåkern

Not impressive in size, Lake Tåkern is one of the best in the country for **bird-watching**, with 260 species to be seen here in the space of a year. There are also several walking trails for a tranquil half-day meander; indeed from April 1 to June 30, you are restricted to trails clearly marked on signs all over the area. There's a **bird-watching tower** close to the car park, where the Tåkern Canal spills out of the lake; in late summer, thousands of wading birds rest on the mud banks in front. Large flocks of geese fill the air in autumn, when up to 45,000 bean geese migrate from Russia and Finland, using Tåkern as their resting point; still later in the year, golden and sea eagles appear, too. There's another tower for bird-watching, with disabled access, at Hor on the lake's eastern shore.

Approaching the lake from the north, take the sign for Strå, 7km off Route 50, for 2km and turn off just past the canal in order to reach the northern visiting area. For the other visiting area, take the E4, turning off at the sign for the tiny village of Kyleberg, then left at Kyleberg. To get to the bird-watching tower to the east, take Route 944 off the E4 and continue for 6km north of Väderstad.

can be reached on **bus** #610 from Ödeshög (Mon–Fri 7 daily, Sat & Sun 2 daily). Also useful is the express bus #840 between Gränna and Vadstena, though it doesn't stop along the way as many times as the #610. There's a handy **youth hostel** at Ödeshög, called *Hernbygdsgården*, at Södra Vägen 63 (☎0144/107 00; 120kr).

Vadstena

With its beautiful lakeside setting, **VADSTENA**, which once served as a royal seat and important monastic centre, is a fine place for a day or two's stay. Sixty kilometres north of Gränna and just 16km southwest of Motala (see p.318), the town's main attraction is its moated **castle**, designed in the sixteenth century by Gustav Vasa as part of his defensive ring protecting the Swedish heartland around Stockholm. The cobbled, twisting streets, lined with cottages covered in climbing roses, also contain an impressive abbey, whose existence is the result of the passionate work of fourteenth-century **Birgitta**, Sweden's first female saint (see box, p.317).

Arrival and information

There are no trains to Vadstena, and the **bus** system has been rendered lamentably poor after drastic cuts to the services. The only way to reach here by public transport from Gränna is to take a local bus to Ödeshög (Mon–Fri 3 daily at 6.45am, 4.10pm & 6.15pm) and then bus #610 from Ödeshög to Vadstena (6 daily; 45 mins). The main **bus stop** is in the centre of town, between the castle and the abbey. By car, it's a straight run along the E4 and Route 50 north from Gränna or southwest on Route 50 from Motala.

The **tourist office** is located in the castle (early May Mon–Fri 11am–3pm; mid-May to end May daily 11am–4pm; June & early Aug daily 10am–6pm; July 10am–7pm; mid- to end Aug daily 10am–5pm; early Sept Mon–Fri 10am–4pm; mid-Sept to April Mon–Fri 11am–2pm; ☎0143/315 70, ℮tourist@vadstena.se) and sells a **combination ticket** (80kr), including a tour of the castle and of the convent area. Vadstena itself is easily walkable, but for striking out into the Östergotland countryside, there's only one place to rent a **bike** – Sport Hörnen at Storgatan, by Rådhustorget (Mon–Fri 9.30am–6pm, Sat 9.30am–2pm; ☎0143/103 62; 100kr/day or 300kr/week).

Accommodation

The tourist office will book **private rooms** from 165kr plus a 40kr fee. Vadstena's STF **youth hostel** at Skänningegatan 20 (☎0143/103 02, ℱ104 04; 145kr) is close to the lake, just up from the abbey. Advance booking is essential outside the mid-June to mid-August period.

Set in converted historic buildings and catering for glamorous tastes, the town's main **hotels** are fairly expensive. The *Vadstena Kloster Hotel* (☎0143/315 30, ℱ136 48; ➎), in the 1369 nunnery next to the abbey, has atmospheric public areas, though the bedrooms are surprisingly dated. It serves breakfasts (open to nonresidents; 55kr) in the old Kings Hall – part of the original Bjällbo Palace (see opposite). Opposite the castle is the rather ungainly *Vadstena Slottshotel,* a former mental hospital (reception is at the *Kloster Hotel,* same telephone number; ➎). The best-value alternative to these pricey hotels is *Pensionat Solgården,* Strågatan 3 (May–Sept; ☎0143/143 50, ⓦhttp://home9.swipnet.se/~-94154/solgarden; ➋), a beautifully maintained villa from 1905 in a quiet, central position.

The Town

While Vadstena boasts numerous ancient sites and buildings, each with an information plate (in English), the two outstanding attractions here are the **castle** and the **abbey**. Vadstena is also made for romantic evening strolls, with wonderful lakeside sunsets and attractive streets of irregularly shaped houses.

Vadstena Slott

Those who've visited the castle at Kalmar will be familiar with the antics of Gustav Vasa and his troubled family, whose saga continues at **Vadstena Slott** (same hours as the tourist office). With four round towers, each with a diameter of 7m, and a grand moat, it was originally built as a fortification to defend against Danish attacks in 1545, but was then prettified to serve as a home to Vasa's mentally ill third son, Magnus. His elder brother, Johan III, was responsible for its lavish decorations, but fire destroyed them all just before their refurbishment was completed, and to save money they simply painted fittings and decor on the walls, including the swagged curtains that can still be seen today.

The castle's last resident was Hedvig Eleanor, the widowed queen of Karl X; after she died in the 1770s the castle was regarded as hopelessly unfashionable, and so no royal would consider living there. At the end of the seventeenth century, the building fell into decay and was used as a grain store; the original hand-painted wooden ceilings were chopped up and turned into grain boxes. As a result, there hasn't been much to see inside, though a recent drive here to buy up period furniture from all over Europe has re-created something of the atmosphere. The place has also been crammed with **portraits** of the Vasa family mainly characterized by some very unhappy and unattractive faces. It's worth joining the regular English-language tours to hear all the Vasa family gossip (late May & mid-Aug to early Sept 2 daily; June to early Aug 3 daily; 50kr) or the atmospheric **night-time tours** of both the castle and through the town (June & Aug Wed & Sat 10pm; July Mon, Wed & Sat 11pm; 95kr) They're in Swedish, but most guides will translate as they go. Price includes a glass of *glögg*, the drink favoured by the Vasa family, in the castle cellars.

Opposite the castle is Vadstena's **glassworks**, Vas Vitreum (glass-blowing Mon 9am–6pm, Tues–Fri 9am–5pm; shop Mon–Fri 10am–6pm, Sat noon–3pm). Founded in 1985, it produces some refreshingly simple designs, along with more traditional pieces. The seconds shop (June to mid-Aug Mon–Fri 10am–6pm, Sat noon–3pm) in one of the two old wooden grain stores outside the castle, has the same items as the factory's shop at forty percent less.

St Birgitta

Birgitta (1303–73) came to the village of Vadstena as a lady-in-waiting to King Magnus Eriksson and his wife, Blanche of Namur, who lived at Bjälbo Palace. Married at thirteen, she gave birth to eight children, and had her first of many visions while living at the palace. Such was the force of her personality, she persuaded her royal employers (to whom she was vaguely related) to give her the palace in order to start a convent and a monastery. To obtain papal approval for the monastery, she set off for Rome in 1349 but the times were against her – the pope was in Avignon, France. She spent the next twelve years in Rome, having more visions, pressing for his return but dying before she could return to Vadstena. She was canonized in 1391, a final vision having already told her this would be the case. Her daughter, Katarina, carried on her work and brought about the building of the monastery and abbey; she too became a saint and her remains lie in the same coffin as her mother's.

The abbey

St Birgitta specified that the **abbey** church (daily: May 9am–5pm; June & Aug 9am–7pm; July 9am–8pm), easily reached by walking towards the lake from the castle, should be "of plain construction, humble and strong". Wide, grey and sombre, the lakeside abbey, consecrated in 1430, certainly fulfils her criteria from the outside; inside it has been embellished with a celebrated collection of medieval artwork. More memorable than the crypt containing the tombs of various royals is the statue of Birgitta, now devoid of the hands "in a state of ecstacy" – as the description puts it. To the right, the poignant "Door of Grace and Honour" was where each Birgittine nun entered the abbey after being professed – the next time they would use the door would be on their funeral days. Birgitta's bones are encased in a red velvet box, decorated with silver and gilt medallions, in a glass case down stone steps in the monks' choir stalls.

The **altarpiece** here is worth a glance, too: another handless Birgitta, looking rather less than ecstatic, is portrayed dictating her revelations to a band of monks, nuns and acolytes, while around her, representations of hell and purgatory depict finely sculpted faces of woe disappearing into the bloody mouth of what looks like a hippopotamus. Other than Birgitta's, a tomb to note inside the abbey is that of Gustav Vasa's mentally retarded son Magnus. His grand, raised tomb is flanked at each corner by obese, glum-faced cherubs; the most impressive feature of the tomb is the remarkably life-like hands raised in prayer on the likeness of Magnus on the top,.

Although now housing the *Vadstena Kloster Hotel* (see opposite), the **monastery** and **nunnery** on either side of the abbey are open for tours. The most interesting part of the nunnery, housed in the thirteenth-century Bjälbo Palace, is the King's Hall with an elegant lofty ceiling. On its conversion to a convent, Birgitta had the ceiling lowered to what she considered a more appropriate level for the nuns – it remains thus today.

The Mental Hospital Museum and Mårten Skinnare's House

Just beyond the gates of the abbey graveyard, the **Mental Hospital Museum** is based in what was Sweden's oldest mental hospital (June & Aug daily 11am–3pm; July daily 11am–noon & 2–4pm, other times call tourist office; 40kr), dating from 1757 and called Stora Dårhuset ("Large Mad House"). The display of terrifying contraptions used to control and "cure" the inmates includes a spinning chair, which difficult patients were tightly strapped to and spun until they vomited; an iron bath, in which patients were tied and then scalded; and a tub, used until 1880, in which patients were held down among electric eels. The most poignant displays on the first floor are the patients' own excellently drawn pictures, depicting the tortures inflicted on them. Also on display are moving photographs of inmates from the nineteenth century (extensive research having first been carried out to ensure that the people shown have no surviving relatives).

Next door, the home of furrier Mårten Skinnare (same times and entrance ticket as Mental Hospital Museum) has been opened to the public as a superb example of a medieval merchant's house. Owned by Mårten, who dealt in both furs and copper, its most intriguing feature is a perfectly intact upstairs privy jutting from its north facade.

Eating and drinking

Vadstena's **eating** places are mostly expensive and not particularly trendy, but some are imbued with considerable historical atmosphere.

Gamla Konditori Storgatan, opposite *Mi Casa* (see below). This busy classic bakery and *konditori* is open every day for traditional cakes and sandwiches in a fine seventeenth-century house.

Kloster Café A few steps from the abbey at the water's edge. An elegant spot for coffee in a former doctor's home. Munch on home-baked cakes outside or in the elegant interior.

Mi Casa Storgatan 9. The nearest Vadstena has to a trendy café, where you can eat quite cheaply. Come here for pies, baguettes, ciabatta and cakes, and a weekday lunch special for 60kr.

På Hörnet Skänningegatan 1. An understated neighbourhood pub that serves great food including marinated mushrooms, various types of herrings and marinated cheese dishes. Well worth seeking out, especially for a fine all-day brunch.

Rådhus Källeren in the cosy cellars of the sixteenth-century courthouse on Rådhustorget. More informal than the other restaurants with main dishes like smoked whitefish, from Vättern, costing 129kr. The place is also a pub where Vadstena locals hang out, particularly on Thurs & Sat evenings.

Sjömagasinet Lilla Hamnarmen. A bar and disco on the far side of the castle relative to the centre that's popular with a young crowd.

Vadstena Kloster Hotel Next to the abbey. Beautifully cooked and presented fish and meat dishes – such as smoked deer at 198kr a course – in the stylish restaurant housed in St Birgitta's old convent. Superb wine cellar too.

Vadstena Valven Storgatan 18. Next door to *Gamla Konditori* (above), this is the smartest restaurant in town with a lunch special (75kr, weekends 85kr) and fine dinners. Their speciality is Vättern char in white wine sauce, but you won't find it on the menu – the fish is only in supply when the waters are warm enough.

Motala

The Göta Canal tumbles into Lake Vättern through a flight of five locks at Motala, 16km north of Vadstena. Designed by the waterway's progenitor, Baltzar Von Platen, this is still a popular spot on the canal, though the particularly engaging **Motor Museum** (see below) is the principal draw here nowadays along with some pleasant canal-side walks. The town centre itself, however, is the dreariest in southern Sweden.

Boats run along the canal to Borensburg, 20km east, leaving Motala at 10.30am (5hr; 200kr return; ☎0141/585 06 or 070/626 0249 for tickets). In June, a fourteen-thousand-strong field takes part in what is claimed to be the world's biggest friendly **cycle race**, around the lake.

The **Motor Museum**, at the harbour edge (June–Aug daily 10am–8pm, May & Sept 10am–6pm, Oct–April 10am–3pm; 40kr), much more entertaining than its name implies. It really a museum of design, and great fun even if you have no particular interest in cars. Each of the unusual, rare and wacky motors – ranging from 1950s American classics to old Jaguars and the occasional Rolls

Royce – is displayed in context, with music of the appropriate era blaring from radio sets.

Practicalities

Trains pull in parallel with the canal about a kilometre from the centre. For the **tourist office** at Folkets Hus (June to mid-Aug daily 10am–7pm; mid-Aug to May Mon–Fri 10am–5pm; ℡0141/22 52 54, ⓦwww.motala.se), turn left along Östermalmsgatan, right along Vadstenavägen and left into Repslagaregatan. This will lead you past the central Storatorget and the **bus station**; the tourist office is on the right, close to the harbour. You can **rent a bike** – the twenty-kilometre ride east to Borensburg is worth considering – from Velosipede at the harbour (℡0141/521 11; 95kr a day); call in advance out of season.

Private rooms can be booked at the tourist office (from 200kr). The STF **youth hostel**, with its own summer café, is at Varamon, right on the beach (June–Aug ℡0141/574 36, rest of year ℡ & ⓕ0141/22 52 85; 100kr) – take bus #301 from Storatorget. There is also a well-equipped **campsite** here, *Z-Parkens Camping* (℡0141/21 11 42), boasting pretty wooden cabins overlooking the lake, which can be booked through the tourist office. Among the better town-centre **hotels**, *Stadshotellet* on Storatorget has big, worn-looking rooms (℡0141/21 64 00, ⓕ21 46 05; ❹/❸). Most of Motala's **restaurants** are nondescript places grouped around Storatorget; they do daily lunches at around 50kr.

North of Vättern: Örebro

Far more appealing than Motala, the lively and youthful town of **ÖREBRO**, 90km north, lies on the shores of the country's fourth largest lake, Hjälmaren. Örebro's development was dictated by its important strategic position: the main route from southwest Sweden to Stockholm, King Eric's Way, ran right through the centre, where a build-up of gravel made the river fordable (Örebro means "gravel bridge"). Nowadays, the E20 links the southwest with the capital – and bypasses the town, but the centre is enjoyable and a good base for a day or so.

Arrival and information

Örebro is just three hours from Stockholm on the main east-west **train** line and straight up Route 50 from Motala by **car**. The **train station** is on Järnvägsgatan, north of the castle; the **bus station**, where the regular buses from Stockholm and Motala stop, is opposite in the recently renovated Resecentrum. From Vadstena, take bus #611 to Motala and change to either bus or train to Örebro. The very helpful and knowledgeable **tourist office** is inside the castle (June–Sept Mon–Fri 9am–7pm, Sat & Sun 10am–5pm; Oct–May Mon–Fri 9am–5pm, Sat & Sun 11am–3pm; ℡019/21 21 21, ⓦwww.orebro.se) sitting four-square on its island. For **Internet** access, head to *Krämaren*, in a shopping arcade at Drottninggatan 29 (Mon–Fri 10am–7pm, Sat 10am–4pm; ℡019/611 49 99). The town centre is easily seen on foot but if you want to get a flavour of the surrounding countryside, it's a good idea to rent a **bike**; you can do this at the kiosk on Hamnplatsen (Mon–Fri 9am–6pm, Sat & Sun 10am–5pm; 50kr a day, tandems 80kr; ℡019/21 19 09), outside *Harry's Bar*.

Accommodation

The tourist office can book **private rooms** from 135kr per person. The STF **youth hostel** at Fanjunkarevägen 5 (☎019/31 02 40, ℗31 02 56; 130kr; ❶) is in a surprisingly pretty nineteenth-century army barracks to the north of town; take bus #31 to Rynninge, getting off one stop before the end of the line. The nearest **campsite** is 2km south of town at Gustavsvik (☎019/19 69 50, ℗19 69 90; late April to late Oct).

Of Örebrö's **hotels**, the best traditional one is the central *Stora Hotellet*, Drottninggatan 1 (☎019/15 69 00, ℗15 69 50; ❺/❸). The oldest hotel in town – built in 1858 – has extremely attractive suites and rooms, especially on the top floor of the annexe. It is supposed to be haunted by the ghost of a young woman and her mother; the girl hanged herself here in the late nineteenth century because her mother forced her into an unrewarding marriage. Örebrö's newest hotel, the well-designed *Radisson SAS Hotel*, Kungsgatan 14 (☎019/670 67 00, Ⓦwww.radissonsas.com; ❺/❸), has remarkable summer discounts on its sumptuous bedrooms and wonderful bathrooms. The *City Hotel*, Kungsgatan 24 (☎019/601 42 00, ℗601 42 09; ❺/❷), and *Hotel Continental*, opposite the train station at Järnvägsgatan 2 (☎019/611 95 60, ℗611 73 10; ❹/❷), are very similar mid-range hotels; while *Hotel Skomakaren*, Järnvägsgatan 20 (☎019/611 90 35, ℗18 94 50; ❹/❷), looks better inside than out. The cheapest hotel in town is the quite adequate *Hotel Linden*, Köpmangatan 5 (☎019/611 78 11, ℗13 34 11; ❶), with a 130kr summer discount.

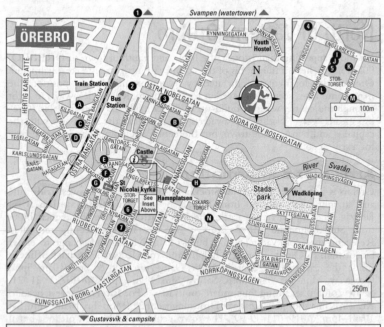

▼ *Gustavsvik & campsite*

ACCOMMODATION				RESTAURANTS & CAFÉS					
City	6	Skomakaren	3	Ågatan 3	F	Drängen	N	Orlando	B
Continental	2	Stora Hotellet	4	Babar	M	Due Amici	D	La Pampa	C
Linden	5	Youth hostel	1	Bishop's Arms	J	Farbror Melkers		Slottskällaren	I
Radisson SAS Örebro	7			Björnstugan	K	Coffee Shop	L	Stallyktan	E
				Den Danske Kroen	A	Harry's Bar	H	Wobbler	G

The Town

The heart of Örebro comes as a pleasant surprise, its much-fortified thirteenth-century **castle** forming a magnificent backdrop to the water-lily-studded **River Svatån**. Aside from the town-centre attractions, **Lake Tysslingen**, a few kilometres west, makes for a good half-day excursion by bike (follow signs for "Garphyttan"). In spring, several thousand whooper swans settle here on their way to Finland and make spectacular viewing from the lakeside observation towers.

You might want to consider taking a **boat trip** around Lake Hjälmaren just west of the town on *M/S Gustav Lagerbjelke* (2hr trips 70kr or day cruises for 275kr including lunch); buy tickets at the tourist office. Also popular are **canal tours** along the attractive stretch of water from Örebro to Kungsör, a village 45km to the east (7hrs 295kr including bus back); tickets can be booked at the tourist office.

Örebro Castle

The town's first defensive fort was built after a band of German merchants settled here in the thirteenth century, attracted by rich iron-mining. It was enlarged in the fourteenth century by King Magnus Eriksson, who lived here; Gustav Vasa's son Karl IX added fortifications and then, following in the footsteps of Vasa's other sons, turned it into a splendid Renaissance castle, raising all the walls to the height of the medieval towers and plastering them in cream-coloured stucco. When the Danes were no longer a threat, the town lost its importance, and **Örebro Castle** fell into disuse and subsequently became a storehouse and a jail. In the old **prison** on the fourth floor, you can see words scratched into the walls by Russian prisoners of war. Another room was used to hold suspected witches and was well furnished by King Karl as a **torture chamber**; at the time, fear of witchcraft was reaching fever pitch, and over four hundred women lost their heads here having survived attempts to drown them in the nearby river. The fairy-tale exterior you see today is the result of renovation in the 1890s. Influenced by contemporary National Romanticism, the architects carefully restored the castle to reflect both Medieval and Renaissance grandeur. The same cannot be said for the interior, where the valiant guides face a real challenge: there's no original furniture left, and many of the rooms are used for conferences. The mandatory **tours** sell the place as a "living castle" to make up for what it lacks (tours June–Aug 5 daily, in English at noon & 2pm; 45kr).

Naturally, it's said to be riddled with ghosts, ranging from that of Magnus Eriksson's wife Blanka, who is said to be in torment for having murdered her son, to Engelbrecht, who had his head lopped off two years after he stormed the castle in 1434 and led a riot on behalf of farmers oppressed by harsh taxes. Among the few features of interest are some fine doors and floors, dating from as recently as the 1920s, the inlays depicting historical events at Örebro, and, in the main state room, a large **family portrait** of Karl XI and his family, their eyes all popping out as a result of using arsenic to whiten their faces.

The Biological Museum

By the castle, in the grand old Karolinska School, is the charmingly dilapidated **Biological Museum** (mid-June to mid-Aug daily 11am–2pm; 20kr). It's interesting for the fact that its musty and fearsome occupants – stuffed polar bears, ostriches, bison and lynx – aren't behind glass, but instead lean over the walkway – a throwback to nineteenth-century museum design. Most unusual is the vast number of badly stuffed sparrows on display; in the late nineteenth century, they were the Swedish equivalent of an apple for the teacher. The gallery floor, up the original spiral staircase, has more stuffed fauna and some gruesome bottles of pickled marine life.

St Nicolai kyrka

Just a few hundred metres south of the castle, **St Nicolai kyrka**, at the top of the very oblong Stortorget, dates from 1260. Extensive restoration in the 1860s robbed it of most of its medieval character, though recent renovations have tried to undo the damage. It was here in 1810 that the relatively unknown figure of Jean Baptiste Bernadotte, Napoleon's marshal, was elected successor to the Swedish throne. The descendants of the new King Karl Johan, who never spoke a word of Swedish, are the current royal family. Engelbrecht was also supposed to be buried here after his execution, but when his coffin was exhumed in the eighteenth century, it was empty, and his bones have never been recovered. Today, the church is home to exhibitions of contemporary art (daily 9am–4pm).

The Art Museum, Stadspark and Wadköping

Following the river eastwards from the castle for about a kilometre leads you to the **Art Museum**, Engelbrektsgatan 3 (daily 11am–5pm, Wed till 9pm; free, except temporary exhibitions), housed in what used to be the Länsmuseum. It has a surprisingly spacious series of galleries, with temporary and permanent collections, though much of what's on show in the latter is mediocre, the best work being a collection of landscapes by the late nineteenth-century local artist Axel Borg.

Örebro's stunning **Stadspark** is one of the most beautiful town parks in the country. Sunbathing locals flock here to picnic surrounded by the park's most exceptional feature – the colour-coded border walks, each section bursting with a rainbow of flowers separated by tone.

A little further up the river, at the far end stands an open-air museum, **Wadköping** (May–Aug 11am–5pm; Sept–April Tues–Sun 11am–4pm; free; shops and exhibitions closed on Mon; for guided tours, ☎019/21 21 21, Ⓦwww.orebro.se/wadkoping). An entire village of centuries-old wooden cottages and shops were brought to the site in the 1950s when urban planning was threatening the historical dwellings with demolition. A local man, Bertil Walden, campaigned to save the better ones, and relocated them here at Wadköping on the banks of the river. The extremely pretty little "high street" is flanked with eighteenth-century low buildings on one side, and on the other with taller houses from after the town fire of 1854. Some of the cottages are now lived in again and there's a very good bakery and **café**. There is also a children's play-barn open all summer.

Eating and drinking and nightlife

Örebro boasts plenty of atmospheric **cafés** and **restaurants** around town, together with some popular **pubs**. In July, expect some of the smaller restaurants to be shut for the holidays. For a superb **café** in beautiful surroundings, head for *Café Stadsträdgården* in the greenhouses at the entrance to Stadspark (daily 11am–5pm); the place isn't to be confused with the newer restaurant next door which is not nearly so appealing. The café's delicious cakes, tasty pies and sandwiches are home-made using organic ingredients, and there's plenty for vegetarians. For a very scenic afternoon tea, head 1500m north of town to the 58-metre-high mushroom-shaped water tower, **Svampen**; buses #11 or #21 head here from Järntorget. There are sweeping views of the surrounding plain and Lake Hjälmaren, and it has a reasonable café inside. The boats which do trips on the lake also play host to popular prawn-eating evenings (220kr, drinks extra; advance bookings on ☏019/18 23 51 for *M/S Linnea*; ☏019/10 71 91, ⓦwww.lagerbjelke.com for *M/S Lagerbjelke*;). Örebro's **gay** community has a pleasant café, *Orlando*, on Slottsgatan 19B, just a minute from the castle (☏019/14 42 32, ⓦwww.rfsl.se/orebro; Tues 7–10pm & Sun 5–9pm).

Cafés and restaurants

Drängen Oskarstorget 9 ☏019/32 32 96. A compact restaurant with intriguing farm-style decor (*drängen* means "farm boy"), this unpretentious place is one of the finer gourmet spots in town serving beautifully prepared dishes. Main courses 150–200kr.

Due Amici Ringgatan 30 ☏019/10 99 96. About ten minutes' walk west from the castle. A wonderful Italian place, romantically and un-Swedishly dark with just candle-light and the dimmest of lighting. Lots of pastas at 119kr, several meat mains (170kr) and fish (190 kr). A lovely, intimate spot.

Farbror Melkers Coffee Shop Stortorget 6. This is where the town's late-night revellers come to fill up on big, fluffy ciabattas (35kr) and coffee after a night out. There's funky apple-green decor and outside seating for daytime snacks.

Harry's Bar on the riverside, a minute's walk east of the castle, in the old red-brick technical museum building. There's a varied menu including the popular shellfish bowl in summer – a sizeable seafood medley for 150kr each.

La Pampa Ringgatan 19. Argentinian steaks and ostrich sold by weight at this heavily meat-oriented restaurant opposite *Due Amici* (above).

Slottskällaren Restaurant & Bar opposite the castle in the *Stora Hotellet* building ☏019/15 69 60. A long-established, popular restaurant, that serves main courses costing upwards of 150kr, plus cheaper, light meals like the classic *pytt i panna* for 59kr.

Wobbler Kyrkogatan 4 ☏019/10 07 40. Classic

Swedish cooking with a modern twist at this oddly named yet elegant spot. Elaborate menu, for example, chilli-baked chicken with strawberry muscat sauce, but tapas choices too. Main dishes from 160kr.

Ågatan 3 Bar & Matsal Ågatan 3, just off Drottninggatan ☏019/10 40 19. Smart little restaurant with a romantic atmosphere and crisp table linen and candles. Interesting fish and meat menu with main courses 120–180kr.

Bars

Babar Kungsgatan 4, directly opposite *Bjornstugan*. The hippest bar-restaurant in town, with a vast oblong bar. They serve European food, with a meat-weighted menu at around 140kr per main course.

Bishop's Arms next door to the *Slottskällaren*. Hugely popular for outdoor drinking; serves British food like fish and chips for 55kr.

Björnstugan Kungsgatan 3. No longer the trendiest bar in town, but still very popular.

Den Danske Kroen Kilsgatan 8. Cosy, relaxed atmosphere in an old, turretted house on the other side of the railway tracks from the rest of town. A Danish bar and restaurant serving homely, filling Danish-inspired dishes at reasonable prices with a lively atmosphere and a mix of age groups.

Stallyktan Södra Strandgatan 3B ☏019/10 33 23. This excellent, rustic pub is a better choice for a quiet drink and dinner than most of the bigger venues. Their freshly cooked chicken, salmon or steak dishes go for 129kr.

East of Vättern: Linköping and around

Sixty kilometres east of Lake Vättern, **LINKÖPING**, in the county of Östergotland, is an appealing 900-year-old town boasting a range of pleasing buildings. The architectural highlights are the remarkable **Domkyrkan**, and a living village a few kilometres to the west, **Gamla Linköping**, caught in a late nineteenth-century time warp. Linköping's best-kept secret, missed by all but a handful of visitors, is a little-known collection of **pictures** by the Osloborn artist Peter Dahl, which reveals more about eighteenth-century Swedish society than any number of preserved dwellings could hope to do. The town has one other hidden treasure: the basement excavations at the often-over-looked twelfth-century **St Lars kyrka**.

Linköping and its sister town Norrköping (see p.329), to the east, have a rela-tionship not dissimilar to that between Lund and Malmö in the west of Sweden. Linköping – like Lund – is essentially a middle-class university town, albeit with relatively recent academic credentials, whereas Norrköping – like Malmö – is staunchly working-class.

Arrival and information

Linköping is easy to walk around, and the Domkyrkan spire is a useful point of reference in the unlikely eventuality that you lose your way. All **trains** and **buses** arrive at and leave from **Resecentrum** (travel centre) in the north of the town centre, at Järnvägsgatan. To get to the **tourist office** it's a fifteen-minute walk from here; cross over to Järnvägsavenyn, turn into Klostergatan and head to its southern end. The tourist office is at no. 68, in the *Ekoxen Hotel* (open 24hr all year; ☎013/20 68 35, ✉turism@linkoping.se). You can rent **bikes** here and pick up a free cycle map with route guides. Other places to rent bikes are *Bertil Anderssons Cykel,* Platensgatan 27 (Mon–Fri 9am-6pm, Sat 10am–2pm, closed Sat in July; ☎013/31 46 46) or *Glyttinge Camping*, Berggårdsvägen (☎013/17 49 28); all charge around 50kr/day. There's free **Internet** access at the splendid new **library** (June–Aug Mon–Fri 10am–7pm; Sept–May Mon–Thurs 10am–8pm, Fri 10am–7pm, Sat & Sun 11am–4pm).

Accommodation

Though the tourist office doesn't book **private rooms**, it provides a free list-ing of the ones on offer, complete with phone numbers. The STF **youth hos-tel**, Klostergatan 52A (☎013/35 90 00, ⊛www.linkopingsvandrarhem.se) is very central and well appointed; every room is en suite and has its own kitch-enette. For a good, modern **campsite**, with four-bed cabins, *Glyttinge Camping* is 3km east of town at Berggårdsvägen (☎013/1759 23, ✉glyttinge@swipnet.se; mid-April to Sept); bus #201 from Resecentrum brings you right to the site.

Some of the hotels listed below close in July others drop their prices dra-matically then.

Du Nord Repslagaregatan 5 ☎013/12 98 95, ⊛www.hotelldunord.se. Just 200m from Resecentrum, this pink detached house is prettier outside than in, though its rooms have en-suite facilities and satellite TV. Closed July. ❸/❷

Frimürarehotellet St Larsgatan 14 ☎013/495 30 00, ✉frimis@scandic-hotels.com. With a grand, National Romantic facade and elegant columns in its dining hall, this hotel is only spoiled by the 1970s interiors. ❻/❸

Park Järnvägsgatan 6 ☎013/12 90 05, ℻10 04 18. Right opposite the train station and dating from the turn of the twentieth century, the *Park* serves a good buffet breakfast. ❸/❶

Quality Ekoxen Klostergatan 68 ☎013/25 26 00, ⊛www.ekoxen.se. Newly renovated large bed-rooms with great beds and big baths, plus a sauna, swimming pool, solarium, and massage and gym facilities (75kr for hotel guests) make this hotel a good place to relax. There's even a 24hr delicatessen and a bistro. ❻/❸

Radisson SAS Stortorget 9 ☎013/12 96 30, ⊛www.radissonsas.com. A plush pile right in the centre of town, this is a glamorous spot, though with a less comprehensive range of amenities than the *Quality Ekoxen* (above). ❻/❸

Östergyllen Hamngatan 2 ☎013/10 20 75, ℻12 59 02. The cheapest and best-value hotel in town, *Östergyllen* includes a good breakfast in the price. The hotel, just 150 metres from the station, also operates packages, with bike or canoe rental, such as three nights in a double room including bike rental and route maps for 890kr per person. Discounts at weekends. ❷

The town and around

The elegant **Domkyrkan**, with its soaring, 107-metre-high spire, is set in a swathe of greenery, Domkyrkoparken, just west of Storatorget (June & July Mon–Sat 9am–7pm, Sun 9am–6pm; Aug–May 9am–6pm, Sun 10am–6pm). It dates from 1232 – though the bulk of the present, sober building was completed in around 1520 – and is built entirely of local hand-carved limestone. Stonemasons from all over Europe worked on the well-proportioned building

Raoul Wallenberg

Descended from a Linköping family, **Raoul Wallenberg** was instrumental in saving 100,000 Hungarian Jews from Nazi murder using unique diplomatic tactics. His great achievement was commemorated with statues all over America and in Budapest, but not until 1999 in Stockholm and 2002 in Linköping. The fate of this man, unsurprisingly honoured as a "Righteous Gentile" at the Holocaust memorial museum, Yad Vashem, in Jerusalem, has never been discovered.

Wallenberg's family have for generations been one of the wealthiest and most influential in Sweden; his father Raoul was an officer in the navy, and his cousins Jacob and Marcus Wallenberg were amongst the country's most prominent bankers and industrialists. Raoul's interest in Jewish life is sometimes attributed to his work at a Dutch bank office in Haifa, then Palestine, where he met Jews who had escaped Hitler's Germany. Another reason may be that one of his great-great-grandfathers was a Jewish immigrant to Sweden in the late eighteenth century.

Wallenberg made numerous business trips to Nazi-occupied France and to Germany itself and, in May 1944, when the first eyewitness reports reached the Western world of what was occuring at Auschwitz, Wallenberg realized the danger for Hungary's 700,000-strong Jewish population (Hungary having allied itself with Germany against the Soviet Union in 1941).

Another diplomat, Per Anger (who died in 2002), negotiated with the Germans that Jewish bearers of protective passes should be treated as Swedish citizens, and thus should be exempt from wearing the yellow Star of David. By 1944, the War Refugee Board in the United States had called a committee with leading Swedish Jews to elect a diplomat to lead a mission to Budapest. Wallenberg was approved, despite having no diplomatic experience, and at the age of 32 he began his rescue operation. By the time he reached Budapest, all but 230,000 of the city's 600,000 Jews had been deported to death camps. Wallenberg was helped both by the Swedish king, Gustav V, who appealed to Hungary's head of state, Miklós Horthy, to stop the deportations – remarkably, Horthy initially complied.

Wallenberg designed protective passes printed in yellow and blue with the coat of arms of the Three Crowns of Sweden in the middle – they actually conveyed no royal authority but were impressive enough to have effect. Wallenberg initially managed to supply 4500 of these passes, and eventually issued more than three times this.

He then built houses in the Pest part of Budapest in which Jews could seek refuge behind the Swedish flag. This saved another 15,000 people. In January 1945, Wallenberg discovered that Adolf Eichmann planned a total massacre in Budapest's largest ghetto. Wallenberg, by threatening retribution after the war was over, managed to have this stopped at the last moment.

On January 17, 1945, Wallenberg was escorted out of Budapest, and was later arrested. He has been missing ever since. In March 1945, Soviet-controlled Hungarian radio announced he had been murdered, although numerous testimonies from Russians imprisoned in various jails indicate that he may have lived through the to the Seventies, and may still be alive, today incarcerated in a Russian mental institution.

and, with a belfry and the west facade added as late as 1885, it incorporates a number of styles from Romanesque to Gothic. Of particular note is the restored south portal, with carved biblical scenes above the Moorish-influenced, geometrically worked doors. The venerable old buildings around the Domkyrkan include the much-rebuilt thirteenth-century **castle** which, like so many others in the south of Sweden, was fortified by Gustav Vasa and beautified by his son Johan III.

Just one block east on St Larsgatan, **St Lars kyrka** (Mon–Thurs 11am–4pm, Fri 11am–3pm, Sat 11am–1pm) is often bypassed as it stands within a few metres of the great Domkyrkan. The church was consecrated by Bishop Kol in 1170 but the present interior has had too many face-lifts to show many signs of its great age. Work undertaken as part of a ground reinforcement plan led to the discovery of twelfth-century engraved stone and wood coffins. Beneath the church, in the half-light of candles, are some complete twelfth-century skeletons lying in new glass coffins, alongside remarkably preserved wood coffins, and the exposed remains of the original church. There are no signs – just ask whomever is selling postcards to unlock the door leading to the basement.

Five minutes' wander down Ågatan in the direction of the Stångån river, the town's most unexpected cultural diversion is in the unlikely setting of the **Labourers' Educational Association** (ABF) at Storgatan 24 (closed July). On the third floor is a collection of 85 wonderful pictures, some shot through with vibrant colour, others fine sepia sketches, depicting the **Epistles of Bellman**. Carl Michael Bellman was an eighteenth-century poet and songwriter who exposed the hypocrisies of contemporary Swedish society; his epistles tell of life in pubs, of prostitutes and of the wild and drunken sexual meanderings of high society, set against fear of the Church and final damnation. The pictures are the work of the Oslo-born artist Peter Dahl, a former head of the Stockholm Art School, who's been adopted by Swedes as one of their own.

It's only a few minutes' walk from here to Raoul Wallenbergplats where, in the summer of 2002, a bronze relief was unveiled in memory of the Swedish war-time hero (see previous page).

Gamla Linköping

Just 3km west of Linköping proper is a real must, **Gamla Linköping**, a living open-air museum (Mon–Fri 10am–5.30pm, Sat & Sun noon–4pm; Ⓦwww.linkoping.se/gamlalinkoping; free). An entire town of houses, shops and businesses has been brought here from the centre of Linköping, along with street lighting, fences, signs and even trees, to re-create the town as an identical copy of its nineteenth-century incarnation; even the street plan is exactly the same. Here you'll find Wallenbergska, the home of financier Andre Oscar Wallenberg great grandfather to Raoul (see box p.325). Fifty people actually live in the village, and there's a massive waiting list for eager new tenants, despite the drawbacks of not being allowed to alter the properties and the fact that tourists trundle through year-round. Craftsmen work at nineteenth-century trades, and most shops are open every day, including a small chocolate factory, gold- and silversmiths, a woodwind workshop and linen shops. An eighteenth-century farmhouse from southern Östergotland is now a very pleasant **café** – *Café Dahlberg* (daily 10am–6pm), owned and occasionally run by a Swedish day time TV celebrity Ragnar Dahlberg, much beloved of middle-aged women across the country. There's also an open-air theatre, with performances throughout the summer. Buses #203 and #205 run there (Sept–May; every 20min) from Resecentrum.

△ Doorway, Norrköping

Canal and lock trips

Linköping is riddled with waterways and offers the chance to see a lot of locks in close proximity. The most obvious one to choose is the **Göta Canal**, which wends its way from Motala through Borensberg to the seven-sluice Carl Johan Lock at Berg, just north of the town, where it meets Lake Roxen. South of the city, the less well-known **Kinda Canal** has a manually operated triple lock at Tannefors, from where you can head south for 35km through a mix of canal and river to Rimforsa. For trips on *M/S Kind* contact ☎070/638 02 30, ⓦwww.kindakanal.se.) There are endless combinations of canal and river trips, from a basic Göta Canal trip for two adults or an adult and two children for 295kr (245kr one-way), to a more glamorous spree to Söderköping (35km east) and back in a 1915 steamer, the *M/S Nya Skärgården* (bookings ☎070/637 17 00). For a less ambitious trip, boats also head down the Kinda Canal/Stångån river to Ringförsa – buses bring you back. There's a pleasant outdoor café at Tannefors, just a kilometre from the town centre. The least expensive canal experience – and probably just as enjoyable as the rest – is cycling along the old towpath at *Hotel Östergyllen* (see p.324).

Eating and drinking

Linköping is a likeable spot to spend an evening. The liveliest and most appealing places to **eat** and **drink** after dark are mostly on **Ågatan** running up to the Domkyrkan. Some of these are open during the daytime, too. The more traditional **café-konditori** around Stortorget serve great cakes and sandwiches: *Lind's*, on the edge of the square, is better than its neighbouring rivals, while *Gyllen* on Lilla Torget is very popular, with outside seating. A friendly **gay** café is the RFSL-run *Joy Café*, Nygatan 58 (Tues 7–10pm; closed July). To get into the RFSL's popular pub (alternate Fri 9pm–1am) and Saturday night discos (10pm–2.30am on alternate weeks to the pub nights), both at the *Joy Café*, you have to be an RFSL member; for information, call the RFSL (☎013/13 20 22; 9am–4pm).

B.K. (Bar & Kök) Ågatan. A cosy, stylish place with a huge cocktail bar and an elegant restaurant, serving unusual and well-presented dishes including a vegetarian option.

Chiccolatta Stortorget, corner of Hantverkaregatan. The best café in town – very popular Italian-run place beneath the *Good Evening Hotel*. The place to come for good, strong coffee, excellent panini, ciabatta and people-watching, particularly the local Italian community.

Harry's Bar & Restaurant Ågatan. A couple of doors down from *B.K.* This ever-popular chain restaurant-bar is always crowded.

Kikkobar Ågatan & Klostergatan corner. Popular but pricey Japanese restaurant. Sushi and chicken dishes are served as well as a smattering of western foods.

Konsert & Kongress Restaurant inside the Concert Hall. With a bright, lofty, modern interior, there's always a choice of three lunches, including a vegetarian option and the biggest salad bar in town, from 55kr.

Metropole Beer Bar and Barbeque St Larsgatan 14, at the *Frimürarehotellet*. Serves good-value

steaks, ribs and baked potatoes in summer only.

People's Café Platengatan 5. Attracts a friendly, young crowd for the wacky LP covers on the walls and Edith Piaf playing in the background. The food's not so good as it was in the past, but still popular.

PM & Co where the Kinda Canal meets the River Stånga ☎013/31 21 00. The trendiest hangout for food and drink, in the only pleasant building in sight at the Kinda Canal guest harbour. Quite costly but well-cooked traditional Swedish fish and meat dishes.

Rivå Ågatan 43 ☎013/14 45 15. New, stylish restaurant serving superb Italian food in a contemporary ambience. The pizzas from a wood-fired oven are very expensive (129kr), but exceptionally good.

Steve's Café Ågatan 30. Next to the Filmstaden cinema. Always crowded with young locals but the service can be rude and the food unexceptional; remains very popular though.

Storan Storatorget 9, at *SAS Radisson Hotel*. The menu boasts such elaborate dishes as "*carpaccio* of ostrich with pears, pistachio and cognac", which comes as a starter for 69kr. Open daily.

Yngves Café Ågatan 38. Linköpings newest and friendliest café, bursting with young people filling up on cheap focaccia, washed down with teas and coffees.

Norrköping and around

It is with good reason that the dynamic, youth-oriented town of **NORRKÖPING** calls itself Sweden's Manchester. Like its British counterpart, Norrköping's wealth came from the textile industry, which was built up in the eighteenth and nineteenth centuries and kept Norrköping booming until the 1950s, when foreign competition began to undermine the town's share of the market; the last big mill here closed its doors in 1992. Such are the parallels between the two towns that the Swedish for corduroy is "Manchester". The town has one of Europe's best-preserved industrial landscapes, with handsome red-brick and stuccoed mills reflecting in the waters of its river, Motala Ström.

Norrköping has one of the highest immigrant populations in Sweden. The first to come were the Jews, who arrived here from Germany and Holland after 1782, when Gustav III granted them the right to settle, hoping they would bring new manufacturing techniques into Sweden. Today's immigrant communities are mostly from Asian and Arabic countries, and in the past few years the most noticeable influx has been from the former Yugoslavia.

Arrival, information and accommodation

The **train** and **bus stations** are opposite each other on Norra Promenaden at the northern end of the centre. From here, walk south down Drottninggatan for five minutes, then head one block across to the right towards the Concert Hall (see p.331). The helpful **tourist office** is housed in an old cotton warehouse opposite the gates of the paper mill, at Dalsgatan 16 (June to mid-Aug daily 10am–7pm, Sat 10am–5pm, Sun 10am–2pm; mid-Aug to May Mon–Fri 10am–6pm, Sat 10am–2pm; ☎011/15 50 00, ⊛www.destination.norrkoping .se). Among other things, they'll be able to explain routes and times for the 1902 **vintage tram**, which circles around on a sightseeing tour during summer. The town's ordinary, yellow **trams** run on two lines all over the town centre, cost a flat 15kr, including any tram changes within the space of an hour. The tourist office also offers **Internet** connection (15mins for 30kr), while the library (Mon–Thurs 8am-8pm, Fri 8am–7pm, Sat 10am–5pm, Sun noon–5pm), just south of the town centre, has free connections too. For night-time use, the only place is the **Internet café** at Prästgatan 48 (Mon–Fri 11am–1am, Sat & Sun 1pm–1am; 25kr/hour.)

Accommodation

There's an STF **youth hostel**, *Turistgården*, at Ingelstadsgatan 31 (☎011/10 11 60, ℻18 68 63; 145kr), just a few hundred metres behind the train station; a much more picturesque hostel can be found at Abborreberg, 5km east of town (see p.333). The closest **campsite** to the rock carvings at Himmelstalund, is *City Camp* on Utställningsvägen (☎011/17 11 90, ℻17 09 87). To get there, either walk west from the centre along the river, or take bus #115 from the bus station, or tram #3, which brings you closer than the bus. The tourist office can arrange **cottages** all over the county. In high season, a secluded cottage – sleeping five – in the countryside 30km away will cost around 1600kr a week

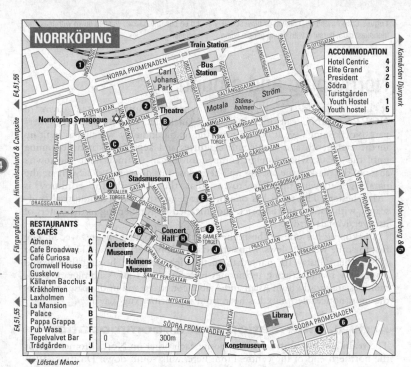

◄ Kolmården Djurpark

◄ Himmelstalund & Campsite

◄ Färgargården

E4,51,55 ◄

E4,51,55 ◄

Alborreberg & ⑤ ►

NORRKÖPING

Train Station

Bus Station

Carl Johans Park

Theatre

Norrköping Synagogue

Motala Ström Strömsholmen

Stadsmuseum

Concert Hall

Arbetets Museum

Holmens Museum

Library

Konstmuseum

0   300m

▼ Löfstad Manor

ACCOMMODATION

Hotel Centric	4
Elite Grand	3
President	2
Södra	6
Turistgården	1
Youth Hostel	1
Youth hostel	5

RESTAURANTS & CAFÉS

Athena	C
Cafe Broadway	A
Café Curiosa	K
Cromwell House	D
Guskelov	I
Källaren Bacchus	J
Kråkholmen	H
Laxholmen	G
La Mansion	L
Palace	B
Pappa Grappa	E
Pub Wasa	F
Tegelvalvet Bar	F
Trädgården	J

including the booking fee, while one more central to Norrköping and sleeping up to eight would cost 3520kr per week.

A cheap, comfortable **hotel**, *Hotel Centric*, Gamla Rådstugugatan 18–20 (☎011/12 90 30, ⒲www.centrichotel.se; ❸/❷), 500m south of the train station, is a decent choice; in the reception is a striking wall fresco by Gothenburg artist Lars Gillies, depicting Norrköping's central areas. More up-market is the classic, turn-of-the-twentieth-century *Elite Grand Hotel*, Tyska Torget 2, bang in the centre (☎011/36 41 00, ⒲www.elite.se; ❺/❸). The *President Hotel*, just as central and next door to the fine theatre at Vattengränd 11 (☎011/12 95 20, ⒲www.president.se; ❺/❸), has secure parking and is very comfortable; there's also a restaurant (see p.333). A calm and pleasant alternative is *Södra Hotellet*, in a sympathetically renovated 1920s house at Södra Promenaden 142 (☎011/25 35 00, ⒲www.sodrahotellet.se; ❹/❷), once a favoured residential street for the textile mill owners.

The Town

Running south from the train station, **Drottninggatan** is a straight north–south central artery, crossing Motala Ström, the small, rushing river that attracted the Dutch industrialist Louis De Geer to the town in the early seventeenth century. He was known as the father of Swedish industry, and his paper mill, which still runs today, became the biggest factory in town. The mill's construction was followed by the creation of many wool, silk and linen factories here. Many of Norrköping's buildings, and the trams, are painted in De Geer's colour of choice – a tortilla-chip yellow – which has become synonymous with the town.

Drottninggatan and around

Just a few steps down from the station, the compact **Carl Johans Park** has 25,000 cacti, formally arranged in thematic patterns, interspersed with brilliantly coloured flowers and palm trees. Glance to the right from here (with the station behind you) down Teatergatan, and you'll see the splendid 1906 city **theatre**, with its Art Nouveau curves and double Ionic columns. Over the river, following the tram lines up cobbled Drottninggatan brings you to a right turn into Repslagaregatan for **Gamla Torget**, overlooked by a charismatic Carl Milles sculpture of Louis De Geer with a bale of cloth slung over his shoulder.

At the southernmost tip of Drottninggatan is Norrköping's **Konstmuseum** (Art Museum; May–Aug Tues–Sun noon–4pm, Wed till 8pm; Sept–April Tues & Thurs 11am–8pm, Wed & Fri–Sun 11am–5pm; 30kr), full of some of the country's best-known modernist works. Founded by a local snuff manufacturer at the turn of the twentieth century, the galleries offer a fine, well-balanced progression from seventeenth-century Baroque through to up-to-the-minute twentieth-century paintings. As you head back north from the art museum, the bunker-like, concrete building to the right is the town **library**; more user-friendly than most, it has a range of newspapers from all over the world and offers free use of the **Internet**.

West of Gamle Torget

Back at Gamla Torget, to the west lies the modern and stylish riverside **Concert Hall**, fronted by trees, providing a lovely setting for the café, *Kråkholmen Louis De Geer* (see overleaf). It's worth stepping inside the Concert Hall for a moment, as its apparent modernity belies the fact that this was once one of De Geer's paper factories. Continuing west from the Concert Hall, go through the impressive, eighteenth-century paper mill gates to the left, across a wooden bridge behind the hall, and you'll pass the new **Norrköping campus** of Linköping University. Next door is the small **Holmens Museum** (Tues & Thurs 9am–12.30pm; free), depicting life in the town's paper mills. It's run on a voluntary basis by retired paper-mill workers; sadly, though, the exhibits aren't labelled in English. The best known of the mills, Holmens, is still functioning just a few metres away.

West along the river on your right is the exceptionally well-presented **Arbetets Museum** (Museum of Work; daily 11am–5pm, Sept–June Tues till 8pm; free), housed in a triangular, yellow-stuccoed factory built in 1917. Known as "The Iron" – though its shape and colour are more reminiscent of a wedge of cheese – the building was described by Carl Milles as Europe's most beautiful factory. The museum has seven floors of exhibitions on living conditions, workers' rights and day-to-day life in the mills. The most poignant, and only permanent exhibit tells the story of Alva Carlsson who worked in the factory all her working life – a fascinating insight into working-class culture and the role of women in the first half of the twentieth century

Next door and over another little bridge is the excellent **Stadsmuseum** (Tues, Wed & Fri 10am–4pm, Thurs 10am–8pm, Sat & Sun 11am–5pm; free), set in an interconnecting (and confusing) network of old industrial properties. The most rewarding of its permanent exhibitions is a street showing various trades from the nineteenth century: there are workshops of a milliner, confectioner, chimney sweep and, in a back yard, a carriage maker. All are cleverly designed and well worth a wander.

The synagogue

Three hundred metres north of the Stadmuseum stands the architectural and cultural gem of Norrköping's **synagogue**, on Bråddgatan (pre-booked tours mandatory; the tourist office can make arrangements). The present synagogue, the city's third, was built in 1858, and has recently been restored; highlights include the enormous central chandelier; the pulpit, finely painted in blues, reds and yellows; and a magnificent ark, with a superb, hand-painted light, representing the "eternal flame" that's kept lit in all synagogues. There are only around thirty synagogue members now living in Östergotland; services are held by rabbis visiting from Stockholm and Malmö, as Norrköping has not had its own rabbi since 1890.

Eating and drinking and nightlife

There is a fair selection of **places to eat** in Norrköping, most of which double as **bars**. It's a town custom to drink at home before heading out, so the centre only starts coming alive from 11pm, particularly from Thursdays to Saturday nights; but from then onwards, it gets very busy.

In the past couple of decades, Norrköping has become a nucleus for music-inspired youth culture. Made fashionable in the 1970s and 1980s by one of Sweden's most famous singer-songwriters, Ulf Lundell, who hails from Norrköping, the town was also home to the country's best-known working-class rock band, Eldkvarn. For a **night club**, the under-25s head to *Otten & Café Bar Hugo* just opposite the station, where they dance to commercial sounds through to the early hours; light food is available too. The town boasts an unusually active **gay** life, run by RFSL, in a blue building down at the harbour at Sjötullsgatan 3. There's a very friendly café (Wed 6–9pm & Sun 3–7pm), and a young peoples' night (under 30s) on Thursdays plus a pub night alternate Friday nights. Even more unusually, lesbians outnumber gay men here.

Athena Kungsgatan 19. Very good Greek restaurant with a wide menu of tasty food a few minutes walk from the Stadsmuseum.

Café Broadway Bråddgatan. Just a few steps east of the synagogue, this simple, slightly dated café is where the celebrated rock group Eldkvarn wrote their classic songs about the Norrköping factories; there's a juke-box (not always working) to hear their hits. Beautifully cool on a hot day, and all the breads are home-baked.

Café Curiosa Hörngatan 6. A super old-fashioned café in the town centre with a little garden, serving home-made cakes, savoury pies and ice cream. Pie and salad costs 42kr. Try the fragrant Kuriosa tea – scented with apricots and vanilla.

Cromwell House Kungsgatan. Dark, faux-English pub full of stained glass and locals. Quite good-value meat dishes cost around 90kr.

Guskelov Dalsgatan 13 ☎011/13 44 00. Next door to the Concert Hall, this Art-Deco-style restaurant serves good Swedish home-cooking at lunch and more Continental dishes in the evening. Becomes a nightclub on Saturday nights when it's the best place to hear non-commercial music.

Källaren Bacchus Gamla Torget 4 ☎011/10 07 40. The cellar restaurant of *Trädgården* (see opposite, serves warm grills and light eats, plus a long list of cocktails, whiskies and beers. The garden is a perfect spot for cold beer and a snack.

Kråkholmen Outside the Concert Hall (enter through the hall, or round the back). The daily lunch menu features steaks and wok dishes and a 55kr buffet served against the backdrop of Motala Ström's crashing waters.

Laxholmen Restaurant sixth floor of the Arbetets Museum. The menu, which changes daily, includes the likes of fish soup, apple pancakes, and baked potato with tuna filling. Warm, filled baguettes for 35kr and a lunch buffet (11.30am–2pm; 65kr) are also available.

La Mansion Södra Promenaden 116. A charming, sedate place for lunch or dinner, in the preserved former home of a mill manager. Dinner menus offering dishes like venison and wild mushrooms or salmon and seafood mousse are 150kr. The two-course lunch is a steep 135kr.

Palace Bråddgatan 13. On the ground floor of a hideous Sixties office block, this nightclub and restaurant is where the tourist office invariably send anyone asking about dinner and evening entertainment. There's a big grill menu – nothing for vegetarians though – and the standard of cooking is mediocre. The nightclub can be something of a middle-aged pick-up joint.

Pappa Grappa Gamla Rådstugugatan 24 ☎011/18 00 14. A terrific Italian restaurant in a dusty 1740s house, serving inventive combinations of fresh ingredients, in a mellow atmosphere. Try raw marinated angler fish, fig cream with amaretto or the fabulous sorbet of peach grappa. The drinks list is also remarkably varied and the celebrated barman game to produce any cocktail you could imagine. Closed Sun.

Pub Wasa Gamla Rådstugugatan 33 ☎011/18 26 25. The upstairs is all done up like a ship's interior (hence the name) with little cannons pointing out of the windows. The cheap food includes *pytt i panna* (58kr), pasta and a bowl of prawns for four people (120kr). The atmosphere is friendly and

there's live music daily from 11pm.

Teater Bar Vattengränd 11. Tiny, French-style restaurant attached to the *President Hotel* that's renowned for its pepper steaks.

Tegelvalvet Bar Gamla Rådstugugatan. In the basement beneath *Pub Wasa*, with live music on Fridays and Saturdays. Closed July.

Trädgården Prästgatan 3 ☎011/10 07 40. The entrance is beneath an iron sign marked "VIP Paraden". This bar and grill is very popular, especially for outdoor eating in summer.

Around Norrköping

Heading out from town there are several places that make for easy and worthwhile excursions from Norrköping. **Himmelstalund** is the closest with a range of particularly well–preserved ancient stone carvings. **Abborreberg** is just outside the city, and boasts some genteel old properties and a charismatic, if basic, youth hostel. The best day-trip targets, however, are the beautiful country house **Löfstad Manor**, with its splendid interior and well-documented history, and **Kolmården Djurpark**, a safari park and zoo which numbers amongst Sweden's biggest attractions.

Himmelstalund

A couple of kilometres west of the centre are the **rock carvings** at **Himmelstalund**. Norrköping's present appearance belies its far more ancient origins; these Bronze-Age carvings show with unusual clarity ships, weapons, animals and men. Some burial mounds at the site, though nothing much to look at, attest to Iron Age and Viking settlements in the area. To get there, take bus #115 from the centre.

Abborreberg

The splendid old wooden villas at **ABBORREBERG**, 5km east of Norrköping, are weathered but charmingly authentic early nineteenth-century summer residences and make a delightful lakeside setting for coffee and cake. Having passed through the affluent suburb of Lindö, Abborreberg looks out onto Lindö Bay from a forested setting. The collection of small, verandahed villas and cottages are all attractive but the drawing room of the main Seaside Villa should be the target of your visit. Although the views from the lovely old windows are fine enough, it's the wallpaper that takes the limelight. Handprinted and brought from Paris in the 1870s, it is one of only four such papers and depicts in gloriously unrealistic detail a panoramic scene called "The Banks of the Bosporus". If you ask at the **café**, they will unlock the larger villa which has a wonderful atmosphere of faded gentility, with fancy woodwork and old furnishings; today it's used for weddings.

Another of the old residences is now an STF **youth hostel** (☎011/31 93 44, ☎31 79 30; 125kr; May–Sept). To reach Abborreberg, take **bus** #111, direction Lindö, from outside the Domino Store on Repslagaregatan, just off Drottninggatan in Norrköping town centre; ask the driver for the nearest stop to *STF Vandrarhem*. After 6pm, take bus #101 from outside the library.

Löfstad Manor

Just 10km southwest of town, **Löfstad Manor** (May Sat & Sun only; June–Aug daily; mandatory tours hourly noon–4pm on the hour, in late Aug, last tour is at 2pm; ℡011/33 50 67; 40kr) is a fine country home dating from the 1650s, though it was rebuilt a hundred years on after a fire left it a shell. Bus #481 runs from Norrköping bus terminal to Löfstad (ask for Löfstad Slott). Getting back to town on the infrequent buses can be a problem, especially on weekend afternoons, so it's best to check the return times with the bus driver.

The same family owned Löfstad until 1926, when Emily Piper, who died unmarried, bequeathed the whole estate to the Museum of Östergotland. The house contains a splendid collection of Baroque and Rococo furniture and pictures, though presented in a rather more stiff and formal way than the billing "as she left it" implies. The areas with the most authentic, lived-in feel are the kitchen and servants' quarters; a bathroom in the latter became Emily Piper's, with her ancient bathrobe still hanging from the door. In the scullery there's an elaborate candle-making gadget and a machine for twisting metal into bed springs (the house was meant to be as self-sufficient as possible). During the summer, the house plays host to a **cultural programme** ranging from classical and jazz concerts to Swedish poetry recitations.

There's a pleasant **restaurant** in one wing of the house, *Löfstad Värdhus* (daily 11am–10pm), which serves traditional Swedish food; their *Dagens Rätt* costs 65kr. For a less formal and very enjoyable cold lunch, a **café** in the stables does delicious smoked beef with mounds of potato salad for 55kr (daily 11am–5pm).

Kolmården Djurpark

One of Sweden's biggest attractions, **Kolmården Djurpark**, (⊛www.kolmarden .com) lies 28km northeast of Norrköping. A combined zoo, safari park and dolphinarium, it's understandably popular with children, for whom there's a special section. If your views on zoos are negative, it's just about possible to be convinced that this one is different. There are no cages; instead sunken enclosures, rock barriers and moats prevent the animals from feasting on their captors. There's certainly no shortage of things to do either: try the cable-car ride over the safari park, tropical house, working farm or dolphin shows.

If you're interested in just one or two specific attractions in the park, it might be as well to confirm those are open before you visit (call ℡011/24 90 00); the safari park only opens when the weather is calm and the temperature above -10C. Generally, though, most things are open daily (May–Sept 10am until around 4–6pm); the dolphinarium has between one and four shows a day for most of the year. The entrance price varies according to what you want to see, but a combined ticket for everything runs from 195kr to 235kr, depending on the season. You can **camp** at *Kolmården Camping* (℡011/39 82 50, ℻39 70 81).

Nyköping and around

Heading northeast from Norrköping, after 30km or so you enter the county of **Södermanland** – known as Sörmland. Its capital, the very small historic town of **NYKÖPING**, has seen a lively past. Its underrated charms include an excellent museum, in and around the ruins of its thirteenth-century **castle**, and a harbour – a regular target for the Stockholm yachting set – that bustles with life in summer.

Arrival and information

The **train station** and, 500m to the south, the **bus station** are ten minutes' walk west of the winding Nyköping river. Conveniently, all the sights lie between the stations and the river, or by the river itself. The harbour is at the other end of town from the stations, but the distance is easily walkable in around fifteen minutes. The central and enthusiastic **tourist office** is in the

Rådhus, the only hideous building on the otherwise graceful Storatorget (June to mid-Aug Mon–Fri 8am–6pm, Sat & Sun 10am–5pm; mid-Aug to May Mon–Fri 8am–5pm; ☎0155/24 82 00, ⓔturism@nykoping.se). Bikes are also available to rent here (40kr a day or 200kr a week).

Accommodation

The delightful **youth hostel** is set in the castle grounds, at Brunnsgatan 2 (☎0155/21 18 10; 150kr, ❶), in an eighteenth-century former hospital and overlooking the King's Tower. You can get here from the train station by heading south down Järnvägsgatan, then cutting east along Västra Kvarngatan; Brunnsgatan is the third right off this street. There's a **campsite**, *Strandstuvikens*, 6km south on the Baltic coast (☎0155/978 10; mid-May to mid-Sept).

The most stylish and well-positioned **hotel** is the excellent-value *Kompaniet* on Folkungavägen, near the harbour (☎0155/28 80 20, ⓦwww.choicehotels .se; ❻/❸); the price includes breakfast, afternoon tea and a buffet dinner. The cheap and basic *Hotel Wiktoria,* Fruängsgatan 21 (☎0155/21 75 80, ⓕ21 44 47; ❸/❷), is close to the town's picturesque theatre and quite adequate. Out of town, off the E4, the more upmarket *Blommenhof Hotel*, Blommenhovsvägen, has private saunas, a heated pool and a stylish restaurant (☎0155/20 20 60, ⓦwww.blommenhof.se; ❻/❸).

The Town

Opposite the tourist office stands the vast **St Nicolai Kyrka**, with its white, vaulted ceiling. The building dates from the 1260s, although most of what you see is the result of sixteenth-century refurbishment. The pillars here are adorned with dozens of beautiful, heavily moulded silver candle sconces. It's the pulpit, though, that's the highlight of the church; crafted in Norrköping, it was modelled on the one in the Storkyrkan in Stockholm. Outside, standing proudly on a nearby rocky outcrop, is the red 1692 bell tower, the only wooden building not destroyed in 1719 when the town's worst fire struck.

The castle

From the tourist office, it's just a couple of minutes' wander south, down Slottsgatan with the river to your left, to Kungsgatan. Here you'll see the museum complex and beyond it, the King's Tower. A late twelfth-century defensive tower, built to protect the trading port at the estuary of the Nyköping river, it was subsequently converted into a **fortress** by King Magnus Ladulås. It was here in 1317 that the infamous **Nyköping Banquet** took place: one of Magnus's three sons, Birger, invited his brothers Erik and Valdemar to celebrate Christmas at Nyköping and provided a grand banquet. Once the meal was complete, and the visiting brothers had retired to bed, Birger had them thrown in the castle's dungeon, threw the key into the river and left them to starve to death. In the nineteenth century, a key was caught by a boy fishing in the river; whether the rusting item he found, now on display in the museum, really is the one last touched by Birger, no one knows.

In the sixteenth century, Gustav Vasa fortified the castle with gun towers; his son Karl, who became duke of Södermanland, converted the place into one of Sweden's grandest Renaissance palaces. A fire here in the 1660s reduced all lesser buildings to ash and gutted the castle. With no money forthcoming from the national coffers, it was never rebuilt; only the King's Tower was saved from demolition and became used as a granary. Today, the riverside tower and the adjoining early eighteenth-century house built for the county governor form a **museum complex** (July daily noon–4pm; Aug–June closed Mon; 20kr).

Wandering through the original gatehouse beneath Karl's heraldic shield, you reach the extensively restored **King's Tower**. On the first floor, a stylish job has been done of rebuilding the graceful archways that lead into the Guard Room. The museum is fairly uninspiring with the best exhibition being a display of medieval shoes and boots, and the small leaflet available at reception doesn't help explain things much either.

It's far more rewarding to head instead to the old **Governor's Residence** which has exquisite collections. Downstairs is the original kitchen, with shiny copper pots and utensils, and a souvenir shop, selling expensive medieval-style clothes for both sexes. Climb the stairs, lined with menacing portraits, to gain access to an exceptional run of magnificently decorated rooms from each stylistic period in Sweden. Among the many highlights are the red-silk bed in the Baroque room, a copper steam bath in a nineteenth-century bedroom, and best of all, the *Jugendstil* room – about the finest example you'll see in the country. Amid the stylish finery are some splendid early twentieth-century portraits by twin brothers, Bernard and Emil Österman, who were famous for their passionate and sensual style.

Eating and drinking

Most of the **eating** and **drinking** options are, unsurprisingly, at the harbour, but for the best daytime **café** by far, head for *Café Hellmans* on Västra Trädgårdgatan 24 (Mon–Fri 7.30am–6pm, Sat 9am–4pm, Sun 10am–4pm), just off Storatorget; head down Västra Storgatan from the square, then turn left). In a converted grain warehouse with a summer courtyard, it attracts a young, relaxed crowd and serves great sandwiches, fruit flans, the gooiest chocolate cake and large mugs of good coffee; there's also a great breakfast (40kr).

For a bright and fun **restaurant** and **bar** scene head for the old wooden storage buildings along the harbourside. The first warehouse you'll see when you arrive is a fine **fish smokery** (Rökeriet) with outside eating and a lunch menu of smoked salmon, mackerel, and gravadlax for 75kr. It's a popular place to drink as the evening progresses. Beyond this, the next handsome eighteenth-century grain store is home to *Hamnmagasinet,* where there are plenty of simple dishes for 65–100kr, as well as some more substantial dishes and a wide wine and drinks list. The food is lighter and the atmosphere quieter next door at *Café Krogen*. After a couple of big red wooden storehouses is the popular and more economical *Café Aktersnurran*, with tables outside. The most laid-back place is *Lotsen* (daily 11am–2pm), in a picturesque wooden house serving ice cream and snacks at lower prices. On cooler summer nights, the stylishly nautical, candle-lit interior is a pleasant place to drink and listen to regular live music.

Gotland

Tales of good times on **Gotland** are rife. Wherever you are in Sweden, one mention of this ancient Baltic island will elicit a typical Swedish sigh, followed by an anecdote about what a great place it is. You'll hear that the short summer season is an exciting time to visit; that the place is hot, fun and lively. These claims are largely true: the island has a distinctly youthful feel, with young, mobile Stockholmers deserting the capital in summer for a boisterous time on its beaches. The flower-power era still makes its presence felt with a smattering of elderly VW camper vans lurching off the ferries, but shiny Saabs outnumber

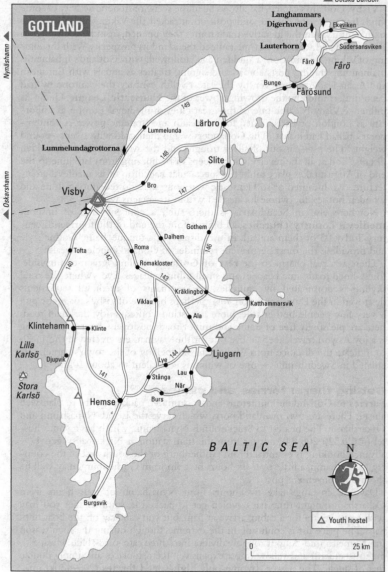

GOTLAND

Gotska Sandön

Langhammars
Digerhuvud

Ekeviken

Lauterhorn

Sudersansviken

Fårö

Fårö

Bunge

Fårösund

149

Lärbro

Lummelunda

Lummelundagrottorna

Slite

Bro

147

148

Visby

Gothem

Dalhem

146

Roma

Tofta

Romakloster

142

140

143

Viklau

Kräklingbo

Katthammarsvik

Ala

Klintehamn

Klinte

Lilla
Karlsö

Djupvik

Lye

144

Ljugarn

Stora
Karlsö

141

Stånga

Lau

När

Hemse

Burs

BALTIC SEA

N

△ Youth hostel

0   25 km

Burgsvik

them fifty to one. During summer, the bars, restaurants and campsites are packed, the streets swarm with revellers, and the sands are awash with bodies. It's not everyone's cup of tea: to avoid the hectic summer altogether, come in late May or September when, depending on your level of bravado, you might still manage to swim in the waters around the island. To experience the setting at its most frenetic, come in August during **Medieval Week** (see p.345), when people put a huge effort into dressing the part.

Visby, Gotland's capital, has always been the scene of frenetic activity of some kind. Its temperate climate and position attracted the Vikings as early as the sixth century, and the lucrative trade routes they opened, from here through to Byzantium and western Asia, guaranteed the island its prosperity. With the ending of Viking domination, a "golden age" followed, with Gotland's inhabitants maintaining trading posts abroad and signing treaties as equals with European and Asian leaders. However, by the late twelfth century their autonomy had been undermined by the growing power of the **Hanseatic League**. Under its influence, Visby became one of the great cities of medieval Europe, as important as London or Paris, famed for its wealth and strategic power. A contemporary ballad had it that "The Gotlanders weigh their gold with twenty-pound weights. The pigs eat out of silver troughs and the women spin with golden distaffs." Today, all the revelry which keeps Visby buzzing from late June to the end of August takes place amid the spectacular backdrop of its medieval architecture; two hundred or so Hanseatic warehouses are dotted among stone and wooden houses, the whole lot nestled within its ancient walls.

Nowhere else in Scandinavia is there such a concentration of unspoilt **medieval country churches**, all built before the end of the fourteenth century. Today 93 of them are still in use, displaying a unique Baltic Gothic style and providing the most permanent reminder of Gotland's ancient wealth.

There is a real charm to the **rest of Gotland** – rolling green countryside, forest-lined roads, fine beaches and small fishing villages. Everywhere the rural skyline is dominated by churches, the remnants of medieval settlements destroyed in the Danish invasion. Yet – perhaps because of Visby's magnetic pull – very few people bother to explore the island; consequently, the main roads here are pleasingly free of traffic and minor roads positively deserted – cycling is a joy. As you travel, keep an eye out for the waymarkers erected in the 1780s to indicate the distance from Wisby (the old spelling of the town's name), calculated in Swedish miles – one of which is equivalent to about 10km.

Getting there: ferries and planes

Ferries to Gotland are numerous and, in summer, packed, so try to plan well ahead. There are two mainland ports which serve the island: Nynäshamn and Oskarshamn. The nearest to Stockholm is Nynäshamn, which has a youth hostel (☏09/520 208 34), not far from the train station at Nickstbadsvägen 17 – advance booking is essential. From Gothenburg or the southwest of the country, Oskarshamn, a little over six hours by train from Gothenburg, may well be the more convenient port.

Daytime crossings take five hours from Nynäshamn or four hours from Oskarshamn; night-time trips, which get so packed in summer that you may wish to pay extra for a cabin, arrive at 5am, but you can stay on the boat until 8am. The price list is confusing in the extreme, though during the high season (mid-June to mid-Aug) it roughly divides into three categories: blue (cheapest), green (standard) and yellow (most expensive). Return prices are simply double that of single. The newer, daytime-only **high-speed ferries** (205–430kr one-way, depending on season), make the same crossing in just three hours. The supplement for carrying a bike across starts at 35kr. Destination Gotland run a range of ferries to the island (reservations on ☏0498/20 10 20 in Visby, ☏08/20 10 20 in Stockholm, ✆www.destinationgotland.se); as phone lines are notoriously busy it may be quicker to book online. Another option is to try Gotland City (☏08/406 15 00, ✆www.gotlandcity.se), at Kungsgatan 57, in Stockholm, which can provide plenty of information and sells advance tickets at prices roughly equivalent to Destination Gotland.

Cycling around Gotland

- Gotland is flat but even so, cycling can get tiring, and so it's worth renting a bike with gears.
- **Luggage** can usually be left at the bike rental office, although paying a few kronor more gets you baskets or bicycle trolleys to take your gear with you as you cycle.
- Most bike rental outlets offer **bike insurance** (around 25kr a day). The built-in rear wheel lock should be enough to deter most joyriders, but if you're not satisfied with that level of security, buy an extra chain and padlock. Be warned, though, that if your machine goes walkabout when insured, you'll still be liable for the first 200kr of a claim.
- Most rental places are down by the ferry terminals, and it's fairly standard practice – ask about this – for them to let you keep the bike overnight to ride down to the harbour the next morning. In the unlikely event you have to return your bike the same day you rented it, you may well be left with a long hike from your hostel the next morning if you want to catch an early ferry.
- You can take bikes on the island's buses for a flat fee of 20kr.
- A cycle route circumnavigates almost the entire island, signposted out of Visby. You can pick up a free route map from the tourist office.

Two airlines **fly** to Gotland: Skyways (☎0498/75 00 00, ⓦwww.skyways.se) has services to Visby from Arlanda airport, Stockholm (Mon–Fri 10 daily, Sat 5 daily, Sun 7 daily; 40min) and from Norrköping airport (Mon–Fri 3 daily; 30min); and Gotlands Flyg (☎0498/22 22 22, ⓦwww.gotlandsflyg.se) has services from Bromma, Stockholm's domestic airport (Mon–Thurs 2–3 daily, Fri 4 daily, Sat 1 daily, Sun 2 daily). Cheapest standard ticket prices for both airlines are around 500kr, though if you're under 26, the price is closer to a very competitive 300kr.

Transport on Gotland

For **getting around** the island, it's hard to resist the temptation to **rent a bike**, given the flat terrain and empty roads. Most ferry arrivals at Visby are plagued by people hustling bikes outside the terminal; there are also outlets in town where you can rent bikes too (see p.342). Handy for striking out into the countryside beyond Visby (a real joy that's little visited by most of the young summer crowd), bikes can also easily be rented at various towns to the south of Visby, less so further north. As for Gotland's **buses**, services are pretty sparse; outside Visby, buses tend to run only twice daily – morning and evening. **Hitching**, however, is an accepted means of transport; unless you have a specific destination, the general attractiveness of the countryside, especially in the south, means it's often just as well to go wherever the driver is heading.

Visby

VISBY is much older than its medieval trappings suggest: its name comes from *vi*, "the sacred place", and *by*, "the settlement", a derivation that reflects its status as a Stone Age sacrificial site. After the Gotlanders had founded their trading houses in the eleventh and twelfth centuries, the Hansa or Hanseatic League was created, comprising a group of towns that formed a federation to assert their interests and protect their seaborne commerce. Visby became the place where all lines of Baltic trade met. Following the foundation of Lübeck in the 1150s, German merchants began to expand into the eastern Baltic area

VISBY

ACCOMMODATION

Alleskolan	1
Donnersplats	6
Fångelset	10
Sjumastam	8
Gute	4
Hamn	2
Jernvägshotell	5
Solhem	9
Strand	3
Villa Borgen	7
Wisby	

RESTAURANTS & CAFÉS

Bakfickan	C
Björkstugan	L
Café Boheme	A
Burmeister	K
Clematis Medeltidskrogen	I
Friheten	H
Gula Huset	J
Gutekällaren	E
Munk Källeren	F
Skafferiet	B
Vinäger	G
Vinäger Café Bar	D

4, Ferry Terminal & Gotlandsresor (Room Booking Service) ▲   ▲ Fångelset Sjömastarn

① ◄
Valdemar's Cross ◄
Bus Terminal & Östercentrum ◄

Söderport

SÖDERTORG
SÖDRA MURGATAN
ADELSGATAN
VÄRDKLOCKEGATAN
HÄSTGATAN
WALLERSPLATS
BREDGATAN
VISBORGSGATAN
SLOTTSBACKEN
SKEPPARGATAN
SLOTTSTERRASSEN
FÄRJELEDEN
SKEPPSBRON

Skansporten
Visborgs Slott
Österport
MÄSTGATAN
BREMERGRAND
SCHWEITZERGRAND
SLOTTS-BACKEN
KILGRAND
STRANDGATAN
KORSGATAN
HAMNPLAN
CRAMERGATAN
STRANDVÄGEN

Art Museum
Gotlands Fornsal Museum
MELLANGATAN
HÄSTGATAN
DONNERS PLATS
HAMNGATAN
PACKHUS PLAN

Almedalen

St Karin
SÖDRA KYRKOGATAN
S:T KATARINEG
LILLA TORGRAND
ST HANSGATAN
ST MELLANGATAN
STORA TORGET
NYGATAN
TRAPPGATAN
STRANDGATAN
SPECKSGRÄND
Kruttornet

Domkyrkan Sankta Maria
KYRK-BERGET
Helge And (ruins)
ST DROTTENSGATAN

Botanical Gardens
SILVERHÄTTAN
STUDENTALLEN
TRANHUSGATAN

St Nikolai (ruins)
SMEDJEGATAN
ST NIKOLASGATAN
ODALGATAN
NORRA KYRKOGATAN
NORDERKLINT
NYGATAN
NORRA MURGATAN
PACKARBACKEN
Norderport

N

0   250m

in order to gain access to the coveted Russian market. A trading agreement between Gotlanders and the League in 1161 gave the islanders the right to trade freely throughout the whole Saxon area, while Germans were able to settle in Visby, which became the principal centre of the Hanseatic League. As Visby metamorphosed from Gotlandic village to international city, it was the Germans who led the way in form and architecture, building warehouses up to six storeys high with hoists facing the street, still apparent today.

In 1350 the **Black Death** swept through Gotland, creating ghost towns of whole parishes and leaving more than eight thousand people dead. Eleven years later, during the power struggle between Denmark and Sweden, the Danish king, Valdemar III, took Gotland by force and advanced on Visby. The burghers and traders of the city, well aware of the wealth here, shut the gates and sat through the slaughter which was taking place outside, only surrendering when it was over. Hostilities and piracy were the hallmarks of the following two centuries. In 1525, an army from Lübeck stormed the much-weakened Visby, torching the northern parts of the town. With the arrival of the Reformation and the weakness of the local economy, the churches could no longer be maintained, and Visby's era of greatness clanged to a close.

Undoubtedly the finest approach to **Visby** today is by ship, seeing the old trading centre as it should be seen – from the sea. If you sail on one of the busy summer night-time crossings, it's good to get out on deck for the early sunrise. By 5am the sun is above the city, silhouetting the towers of the cathedral and the turrets in the magnificent old wall.

Visby is a city made for wandering around and lingering over coffees and slices of cake. Whether climbing the **ramparts** of the surrounding walls, or meandering up and down the warren of cobbled, sloping streets, there's plenty to tease the eye. If you feel like something more educational, head for the fine **Fornsal Museum** which covers pretty well all there is to know about Gotland, and Visby in particular, with a rather good art gallery close by.

Arrival, information and orientation

Visby **airport** is 3km from town, a five-minute ride by **taxi** into the centre (not more than 105kr). All the **ferries** serving Visby dock at the same terminal, just outside the city walls; for the centre, turn left out of the terminal and keep walking for five minutes.

The main **tourist office** is within the city walls at Hamngatan 4, conveniently en route between the ferries and the old city (Oct–April Mon–Fri 8am–noon & 12.30–4pm; May to mid-June & mid- to end Aug Mon–Fri 8am–5pm, Sat & Sun 10am–4pm; Sept Mon–Fri 8am–5pm, Sat & Sun 11am–2pm; mid-June to mid-Aug Mon–Fri 8am–7pm, Sat & Sun 8am–6pm; ☎0498/20 17 00, ⓦwww.gotland.com). Here you can buy the excellent *Turistkarta Gotland* (25kr), a map marking and describing all the points of interest on the island, or take one of the free Visby guides – though you'll need to fork out 35kr for the best guide, entitled *Visby On Your Own*. There's also a selection of **tours** available, one of which, the walking tour of the town (May–Aug 2–3 times a week; 85kr), is worth considering especially if time is short.

Visby's main square, **Storatorget**, is signposted from most places. The town is best **walked** around; despite its warren-like appearance, it's a simple matter to get the hang of the narrow, crisscrossing cobbled streets. Modern Visby has spread beyond the limits defined by its old city walls, and today the new town gently sprawls from beyond **Österport** (East Gate), a few minutes' walk up the hill from Storatorget. Here, in **Östercentrum**, is the **bus terminal**, used by the buses serving all over the island; the tourist office has free timetables.

Bikes can be rented just outside the ferry terminal (three-gear bikes 60kr a day, bikes with up to seven gears 70kr a day; tandems 110kr a day). Rental is also possible at several outlets on Korsgatan. To secure a tandem, it's best to arrive early as they are popular. There are no **Internet** cafés in Visby, but the library by Almedalen (Mon–Fri 9am–7pm, Sat noon–4pm) provides 30 minutes for free, and they'll usually oblige if you ask for longer.

Accommodation

Finding **accommodation** in Visby should seldom be a problem; the abandoned-looking souls wrapped in sleeping bags in the parks are only there through alcoholic excess the night before, not homelessness. There are plenty of hotels (though few are particularly cheap), several campsites with cabins, and three good youth hostels. Both the Gotlandsresor office at Färjeleden 3 (Gotland reservations; ℡0498/20 12 60, ⓦwww.gotlandsresor.se) and the tourist office can help with **private rooms** (from 285kr per person, 425kr for doubles), as well as **cottages** both in and outside Visby. More information is available at the Gotlands Turist Service at Österport (Mon–Fri 9am–6pm; ℡0498/20 33 00, ℗20 33 90), which has access to accommodation information as the tourist office.

Of Visby's several **youth hostels**, all of which have double rooms (❶) as well as regular dorms, the two most central are the *Visby Jernvägshotell*, Adelsgatan 9 (℡0498/27 17 07 or 21 98 19) and the more interesting and well-placed *Fångelset Sjumastam* (℡0498/20 60 50 or 070/426 57 60), situated in a former prison building near the harbour just opposite the ferry terminal. There's a café and sauna here, and it's lively in the evenings. The town's only STF hostel, *Alleskolan*, Fältgatan (℡0498/26 98 42, ⓦwww.meravsverige.nu; June to early Aug) has a café, washing machines, nonsmoking rooms and rooms equipped for people with disabilities. It's twenty minutes' walk south from the harbour; go through Söderport (the South Gate) and down Peder Hardingsvägen onto Artillerigatan, and the hostel is off on the right.

Chiefly, though, Gotland is a place for **camping**. After the success of Ulf Lundell's Seventies youth-culture novel *Jack*, which extolled the simple pleasure of getting wasted on a beach, Gotland became the place to go for wild summer parties: at many campsites, the most exercise you'll get is cycling to and from the Systembolaget. The closest campsite, *Nordenstrands* (℡0498/21 21 57, ⓦwww.norderstrandscamping.se; late April to mid–Sept), is 1km outside the city walls – follow the cycle path that runs through the Botanical Gardens along the seafront.

Donnersplats Donnersplats 6 ℡0498/21 49 45, ⓦwww.donnersplatshotell.nu. A popular, central hotel also offering two- and three-bed apartments for 950kr, and suites for six people for 1800kr. Booking essential in July and Aug. ❸

Gute Mellangatan 29 ℡0498/20 22 60, ⓦwww.hotellgute.se. Very central and reasonably comfortable; reductions may be possible if you appear at the last minute. ❹/❸

Hamn Färjeleden 3 ℡0498/20 12 50, ⓦwww.gotlandsresor.se/boende/hh.asp?flik=boende. Opposite the harbour, and convenient for early-morning ferries back to the mainland. All rooms have TV, shower and toilet; breakfast (included) is served from 5am. Open May–Sept. ❸

Solhem Solhemsgatan 3 ℡0498/27 90 90, ⓦwww.strandhotel.net/solhem. Just outside the

city walls at Skansporten, this large, comfortable hotel has recently been renovated. It has a basement sauna and is quieter than the more central hotels. ❺/❸

Strand Strandgatan 34 ℡0498/25 28 00, ⓦwww.strandhotel.net. A rather glamorous place in the heart of town, with a sauna, steam bath, indoor pool and a stylish atmosphere. ❻/❺

Villa Borgen Adelsgatan 11 ℡0498/27 99 00, ⓦwww.guteinfo.com/villaborgen. Attractive family hotel in the middle of the action, yet with lovely, peaceful gardens. En-suite rooms, sauna and solarium. ❹

Wisby Strandgatan 6 ℡0498/25 75 00, ⓦwww.wisbyhotell.se. Splendid, central hotel in a building dating back to the Middle Ages. Fine breakfasts (open to nonresidents for 65kr). ❺/❻

The Town

The old **Hanseatic harbour** at Almedalen is now a public park and none of the town's attractions are much more than a few minutes' walk from here. Pretty **Packhusplan**, the oldest square in the city, is bisected by curving Strandgatan, which runs southwards to the fragmentary ruins of **Visborg Castle**, overlooking the harbour. Built in the fifteenth century by Erik of Pomerania, the castle was blown up by the Danes in the seventeenth century. In the opposite direction, Strandgatan runs northwest towards the sea and the lush **Botanical Gardens**, just beyond which is the **Jungfrutornet** (Maiden's Tower), where a local goldsmith's daughter was walled up alive – reputedly for betraying the city to the Danes. Today, you can climb the tower for the fine view.

Strolling around the twisting streets and atmospheric walls is not something that palls quickly, but if you need a focus, aim for **Norra Murgatan**, above the cathedral, once one of Visby's poorest areas. At the end nearest Norderport is the best view of the walls and city rooftops, and there's a rare opportunity to climb up onto the ramparts. The dark, atmospheric tower on Strandgatan, **Kruttornet** (June–Aug daily 10am–6pm), affords more grand views; while the roof of the **Helge And** church ruin (May–Sept daily 10am–6pm), which has been reinforced to allow access to the second floor, provides another central vantage point. Or head for the water's edge, where **Studentallén** is a popular late-evening haunt and the sunsets are magnificent – brilliant fiery reds, glinting mirrored waters and bobbing sailing boats in the distance.

Strandgatan itself is the best place to view the impressive **merchants' houses** looming over the narrow streets, with storerooms above the living quarters and cellars below; most notable among these properties is the clearly signposted **Burmeisterska house**, which is attractive and in good condition. One of the most picturesque buildings on the street is the old pharmacy nearby, **Gamla Apoteket**, a lofty old place with gloriously higgledy-piggledy windows.

Gotlands Fornsal Museum

At Strandgatan 14 is the fine **Gotlands Fornsal Museum** (early May & early Sept, daily noon–4pm; mid-May to Aug daily 10am–5pm; rest of year Tues–Sun noon–4pm; 60kr). Housed in a mid-eighteenth-century distillery, it comprises five storeys of exhibition halls covering eight thousand years of history, plus a good café and bookstore. Among the most impressive of the exhibitions is the **Hall of Picture Stones** in Room 1. Dating mostly from the fifth to seventh centuries, these large, keyhole-shaped stones are richly ornamented. The earlier ones are covered in runic inscriptions and are more intriguing, with vivid depictions of people, animals, ships and houses. The **Hall of Prehistoric Graves** is also fascinating, with skeletons dating back six thousand years displayed in glass cases. The occupant of one was killed by a flint arrowhead lodged in his hip (the site of the wound is indicated by red arrows); another case contains the body of a 20-year-old woman from 2500 BC, alongside whom are the decorative pins she once used to fix her hair. Rooms 9 to 13 trace the history of **medieval Visby**; in room 9, you can see an actual trading booth, the sort of place where the burghers of Visby and foreign merchants would have dealt in commodities – furs, lime, wax, honey and tar – brought from all over northern Europe.

The years **1500 to 1900** are cleverly represented in a series of **tableaux**, starting with one on Eric of Pomerania, the first resident of Visborg Castle, and leading through the years of Danish rule to the Peace of Brömsebro, when Gotland was ceded to Sweden. Take a look at the eighteenth-century farmhouse interior – the oddest bit is the "unrest" – a sort of dream-catcher cube made of pigs' bristle and wax swinging above the kitchen table apparently to denote where the man of the house sits. In the same section is a wax model of Anna Margareta Donner, a member of the Visby-based **Donner** family who ran one of Sweden's largest trading houses of the time. The Donner name can still be seen all over the centre of the city, notably the square close to where the tourist office stands.

Gotland's Art Museum

A couple of streets up on St Hansgatan, Gotland's **Art Museum** at no. 21 (early May & early Sept daily noon–4pm; mid-May to Aug daily 10am–5pm; rest of year Tues–Sun noon–4pm; 40kr, outside July & Aug 20kr) has some innovative temporary exhibitions of contemporary painting and sculpture, and installations which tease the eye. Though for the most part much less exciting, the permanent work on the top floor is given over to twentieth-century Gotlandic art, and among the few notable classics is Axel Lindman's 1917 oil of Visby from the beach, showing brilliant dabs of sun before a storm. The eye is also drawn to a stunning picture by William Blair Bruce of his wife, the sculptress Carolina. The painting from 1891 shows her working on a sculpture, and the lifelike qualities of the style are remarkable.

The town wall and Valdemar's Cross

The oldest of the towers in Visby's town wall is the **Gunpowder Tower**, built in the eleventh century to protect the old harbour. The **wall** itself, a three-kilometre circuit enclosing the entire settlement, was built around the end of the thirteenth century for a rather different purpose: it was actually aimed at isolating the city's foreign traders from the locals.

Valdemar's Cross, a few hundred metres east of Söderport (South Gate), marks the mass grave, excavated in the twentieth century, of two thousand people, more than half of them women, children and invalids; they were slaughtered when the Danish king Valdemar attacked the town in 1361. Erected by the survivors of the carnage, it reads: "In 1361 on the third day after St James, the Goths fell into the hands of the Danes. Here they lie. Pray for them."

A section of the wall near Söderport was broken down to allow Valdemar to ride through as conqueror. **Valdemar's Breach** is recognizable by its thirteen crenellations representing, so the story goes, the thirteen knights who rode through with the Danish king. Valdemar soon left, in possession of booty and trade agreements, and Visby continued to prosper while the countryside around it stagnated, its people and wealth destroyed.

Visby's churches

At the height of its power, Visby maintained more **churches** than any other town in Sweden – sixteen in all, most of which are dramatic ruins today. However, one, the **Domkyrkan Sankta Maria** (Cathedral of St Mary; Mon–Fri & Sun 8am–9pm, Sat 8am–6.30pm), is still in use. Constructed between 1190 and 1225, it was built for visiting Germans, becoming the German Parish Church when they settled in the city. In 1300, a large Gothic chapel was built to the south, the eastern tower was elevated, and the nave was raised to create storage space; this was where the burghers kept their money, papers and records. It's been heavily restored, and about the only original fixture left is the thirteenth-century sandstone font inside. Most striking are its **towers**, a square one at the western front end and two slimmer eastern ones, standing sentry over the surrounding buildings. Originally each had spires, but following an eighteenth-century fire, they were crowned with fancy Baroque cupolas, giving them the appearance of inverted ice-cream cones. Inside, have a look beneath the pulpit, decorated with a fringe of unusually ugly angels' faces.

Seventeenth- and eighteenth-century builders and decorators found the smaller churches in the city to be an excellent source of free limestone, tiles and fittings – which accounts for the fact that most are ruins today. Considering the number of tourists clambering about them, it's surprising that the smaller church ruins manage to retain a proud yet abandoned look. Best of what's left is the great **St Nicolai** ruin, just down the road from the Domkyrkan. Destroyed in 1525, its part-Gothic, part-Romanesque shell hosts a week-long **chamber music festival**, starting at the end of July; tickets range from 150kr to 300kr and are available from the tourist office. One of the loveliest ruins to view at night is **St Karins** (St Catherine's; mid June to mid-Aug daily 10am–6pm; 10kr) on Storatorget; its Gothic interior is one of the finest here, having belonged to one of Visby's first Franciscan monasteries, founded in 1233. This church was built in 1250; at night its glorious arches, lit creamy yellow, frame the blue-black sky.

The tourist office gives away a reasonably informative English-language **guide**, *The Key to all of Gotland's Churches*, which lists the key features of all 92 churches on the island in alphabetical order. These are also found near the entrance of most of the churches themselves.

Eating, drinking and nightlife

Adelsgatan is lined with cafés and snack bars. At lunchtime, the eateries at Wallersplats, the square at Adelsgatan's northern end, and Hästgatan, the street leading off the square to the southwest, are particularly busy; Strandgatan is the focus of Visby dining in the evening while Hästgatan also boasts a number of evening options. For good, cheap food all day, try *Saluhallen,* the **market** opposite the old harbour. Here you can buy freshly baked bread, fish and fruit, and eat at tables overlooking the water. For inexpensive fare at night, the lively **Donnersplats** has lots of stalls selling takeaway food during summer.

Youthful **nightlife** is mainly down at the harbour. The unmarked *Anton's Pub*, within the glamorous new *Hamnplan 5* at the northern end, is filled with old rock hits and folk music, both live and on record. A couple of good bars are housed on boats: *Graceland* is popular with a 35-plus crowd and *Priscilla Bar* pours out Elvis hits (noon–2am). Many of Visby's discos and clubs open in the late afternoon (around 4pm onwards) for people to have cheap beer, postbeach. One place to try within the city walls is *Effe's*, Adelsgatan 2 (T0498/21 51 11), built into one of the defence towers just inside the city walls at Södra Port. There are plenty of live bands playing here, usually with a low cover (20kr) and a good-value bar menu including meat and fish dishes at just 70kr.

Medieval Week

During the second week of August, Visby becomes the backdrop for a boisterous re-enactment of the conquest of the island by the Danes in 1361. **Medieval Week** (Wwwww.medeltidsveckan.com) sees music in the streets, medieval food on sale in the restaurants – they hadn't yet been brought to Europe) and on the Sunday a procession re-enacting Valdemar's triumphant entry through Söderport to Storatorget. Here, people in the role of burghers are stripped of their wealth, and then the procession moves on to the Maiden's Tower. Locals and visitors alike really get into the spirit of this festival, with a good fifty percent of everyone all dressed up and on the streets. There are weekly **tournaments** throughout July and early Aug.

Gotlanders enjoy a unique licence from the state to brew their own **beer** and the recipe differs from household to household. Though it's never for sale, summer parties are awash with the stuff – be warned that it's extremely strong and murky.

Daytime cafés

Björkstugan Speksgränd. In a fabulous, lush garden on Visby's prettiest central cobbled street, this little café serves tasty pies and coffee. Open till 10pm.

Gula Huset Tranhusgatan 2. Close to the Botanical Gardens and a favourite amongst locals: cosy and serving delightful home-baked port-wine cake and concoctions of almonds, chocolate and fruit in an unspoiled garden setting outside a vine-covered cottage.

Skafferiet Adelsgatan. A lovely eighteenth-century house turned into an appealing, characterful café boasting a lush garden at the back. Baked potatoes, great cakes and vast, generously filled baguettes which suffice for a full meal.

Vinäger Café Hästgatan 3. Great place for giant muffins, terrific cakes and pies and a relaxed, mellow atmosphere, all in an anachronistically modern pharmacy building dating from 1896 (note that there's no sign outside). Its bakery, directly opposite, has fresh loaves from 6am, and the café opens till 9pm.

Restaurants and bars

Bakfickan Corner of St Katarinegatan and Storatorget. A quiet, relaxed little restaurant with a tiled interior that specializes in seafood – around 200kr a dish but for some of the best food in town. Also good for a drink.

Burmeister Strandgatan 9. Busy place serving a full à la carte menu with starters around 80kr,

pasta 90kr and main courses at 160kr. Expect long queues.

Café Boheme Hästgatan 9. This mellow but lively candle-lit place is a really good bet, serving inexpensive salads, sandwiches and pizzas and lots of cakes, including a rather good *kladdkaka* (gooey chocolate pie).

Clematis Medeltidskrogen Strandgatan 20. Set in the vaulted cellars of a thirteenth-century house, this is Visby's most atmospheric and evocative restaurant by far. Lit with candles, mead is served in flagons and food in rough ceramic bowls and on wooden platters. Try the pear cake with lavender cream.

Friheten Donnersplats 6. A lively pub attached to the *Wisby Hotel*. Loud, live bands reverberate on Fri & Sat evenings.

Gutekällaren Lilla Torggränd. Fronting onto Storatorget, this is less frenetic than the other nearby restaurants, cleverly designed with striking primary-colour paintings to complement the vivid harlequin chairs. Excellent food, but quite costly, with mains from 140kr.

Munk Källeren Lilla Torggränd, opposite *Gutekällaren*. Massively fashionable, and subsequently crowded. There's an extensive à la carte menu, with good soups, meat and fish dishes and simpler, burger-type dishes.

Vinäger Hästgatan 3. Just opposite its sister-café, with a garden and comfortable low seating, this is a great place for pasta dishes or simply a drink. Summer only.

Listings

Banks and exchange Östercentrum has the largest concentration of branches for changing money; the tourist office also has fairly good rates and charges no fee.
Car rental Avis, Donnersplats 2 ☎0498/21 98 10, ☎21 84 20; Hertz, at the airport ☎0498/24 85 50.
Ferries Buy tickets down at the terminal buildings

or at the travel agency on Södertorg.
Market Souvenirs in Storatorget. Open Mon–Fri all year, and Sat also in summer.
Post office In the grocery store Hemköp, outside Österport.
Systembolaget In Storatorget and at Östervägen 3.

Central Gotland: Roma, Romakloster and around

Heading first onto Route 148, then straight down Route 143 southeast of Visby leads after 15km to **ROMA**; bus #11 from Visby's bus station runs six times a day. Nothing to do with Rome, this small settlement gleans its name from "room" or "open space", as this was the original location of ancient Gotland's courthouse. The place looks something of a ghost town as its century-old sugar-beet factory, to the right of the main road as you approach from Visby, has recently closed, and the early twentieth-century cottages fronting Route 143 are also deserted (they can't be demolished, though, as they're protected for their rarity value). The church here, dating from 1215, is large and pretty; the three-aisled nave gives it a surprisingly Romanesque appearance, and because of this the church is known as the False Basilica.

Just 1km further down the road, the Cistercian cloister ruins, **Romakloster**, are the real draw of the area; follow the sign left down a long avenue of beech trees. The crumbling Roma monastery, dating from 1164, lacks both apse and tower, being Romanesque in design; it would once have comprised a church with three wings built around a rectangular cloister. What is left is sturdy stuff – big arches of grey stone blocks so regular they could be breeze block. The multitude of spotlights set in the ground here make it very dramatic as a backdrop for night-time **theatre**, with Shakespeare being performed here every summer, though they detract from the site's timeless character by day. The ruin is not the isolated site one might expect, as it's behind the cream-stucco **manor house** built in the 1730s for the county governor. Part of the monastery was in fact destroyed by the Danish crown during the Reformation of the early sixteenth century, and it was further ruined when the governor used materials from it in the building of the house.

Temporary art exhibitions are held within (20kr), and there's a **café** serving delicious sweet pies and sandwiches (July to mid-Aug daily 10am–9pm; May, June & mid- to end Aug daily 10am–6pm; Sept Sat & Sun 10am-6pm).

Practicalities

For cheap and basic **accommodation**, the very amiable guide Peter Doolk provides rooms in his manor-house home at the hamlet of Viklau, five kilometres south of Roma (☎0498/512 12; 100kr). This very affable and knowledgeable Gotlander will also take you round the island by arrangement – a good choice if time is limited. *Konstnärsgården* (☎0498/550 55) is a complex of art galleries at Ala, south of Roma, just off Route 143; the main reason to come here, though, is to **eat** at the appealing and popular **restaurant** (summer daily noon–9pm) round the back, serving filling meals including excellent fish and meat dishes for 55–85kr. There's also a **café**, offering the usual baguettes and cakes.

The south of Gotland: Hemse to Ljugarn

The so-called "capital" of the south, **HEMSE**, around 50km from Visby (buses come here along Route 142), is little more than a main street. There's a good local café and bakery, *Bageri & Conditori Johansson* on Storgatan and you can rent **bikes** from Ondrell's, Ronevägen, which is the cheapest place in town (☎0498/48 03 33; 40kr per for the first day, 20kr on each subsequent day after or 160kr per week).

Taking Route 144 east from Hemse, signposted for Burs, you'll find the countryside is a glorious mix of meadows, ancient farms and dark, mysterious forest. One of the most charming villages just a couple of kilometres further on, **BURS** has a gorgeous thirteenth-century saddle church, so-called because of its low nave and high tower and chancel. There's a fabulously decorated ceiling, medieval stained-glass windows and ornately painted pews. For a really friendly, locals' **café**, the nearby *Burs Café* (June–Aug daily noon–10pm; Sept–May Tues–Sun 4–9pm) serves cheap, filling meals like beef stroganoff, or hamburgers made with Gotland beef for just 30kr.

Heading east from Burs, following signs to the pretty, tranquil hamlet of När, you encounter a paradise of wild, flowering meadows and medieval farm holdings, with ancient windows and carved wooden portals untouched by the centuries. **När** itself is notable for its church, set in an immaculate churchyard. The tower originally served as a fortification in the thirteenth century; more arresting are the bizarre portraits painted on the pew-ends right the way up the leftside of the church. All depict women with demented expressions and bare, oddly placed breasts. A couple of kilometres north and just beyond the village of **LAU**, *Garde* **youth hostel** (℡0498/49 11 81, ℻49 11 81; pre-book outside summer) provides accommodation in a cluster of buildings situated right by the local football pitch. There's a food shop (daily 9am–7pm) around the corner from the hostel reception.

Ljugarn

For beaches, and the nearest thing Gotland has to a resort, the lively and charming town of **LJUGARN** makes a good base. You can get here from Roma by heading straight down Route 143 for around thirty kilometres; from Lau, just head north for about 8km following the signs for Ljugarn. Ljugarn, though full of restaurants and obviously aimed at tourists, no longer has a tourist office. It's famous for its *rauker* – tall limestone pillars rising up from the sea.

From the main street, it's only 100m to the popular beaches from here. A delightful cycle or stroll down Strandvägen follows the coastline through woods and clearings carpeted in *blåeld,* the electric-blue flowers for which the area is known. The *rauker* along the route stand like ancient hunched men, their feet lapped by the waves.

Ljugarn has a range of eating places and accommodation to suit most tastes. Rooms ("*Rums*") are advertised in appealing-looking cottages all over the little town, and Ljugarn's STF **youth hostel** (℡0498/49 31 84; 105kr; May–Aug), on Strandridaregården, has two- to six-bed rooms. Just off this street and 150 metres from the sea is Gotland's oldest **B&B**, *Badpensionatet* (℡0498/49 32 05 or 070 339 79 30; ❷); it opened its doors in 1921. All the rooms are en suite and a fine outdoor swimming pool has recently been added and there's also a restaurant (July to early Aug daily noon–10pm; May, June & late Aug Tues–Fri 6–8pm; rest of year Sat & Sun only). Cheap but perfectly functional rooms are available at *Storvägen 91*, (℡0498/49 34 16; ❶); **bike rental** here costs 35kr per day.

For a splendid **café**, *Café Espegards* on Storvägen is a must (daily 9am–8pm) serving some of the best cakes around – try their almond and blueberry tart. Their famously good breads, in particular *Ljugarslimpa*, a dark, slightly chewy loaf, have been made here and shipped to the mainland since the 1930s. The place is very popular, so expect a queue in summer. Further down Storvägen, on the corner of Claudelinsvägen, is *Kräkan*, the best fish **restaurant** in town (daily 5pm–1am), with main courses at 130–240kr. A lovely, relaxed place, it also has plenty of meat options and a decent wine list. A few steps further down the street is *Bruna Dörren* (Mon–Thurs & Sun noon–midnight, Fri & Sat noon–1am), a pizza place in a pleasant old stuccoed house (pizzas 60kr, other light meals 35–65kr). *Strandcafé,* located on the beach itself (daily 10am–10pm) isn't anything special for food nowadays, but it's beautifully placed for a drink right on the beach.

The north of Gotland: from Visby to Slite

Thirteen kilometres north of Visby on Route 149, or by bus from Österport (June to early Aug daily at 2pm) are the **Lummelundagrotta** (daily: May to late June & mid- to late Aug 9am–4pm; late June to mid-Aug 9am–6pm; late

Aug to mid-Sept 10am–2pm; 45kr; ⓦwww.lummelundagrottan.se), limestone caves, stalagmites and stalactites that are disappointingly dull and damp despite being marketed as Gotland's most visited tourist attraction. The cave adventures here are of interest if you enjoy clambering around in the damp, and are not recommended if you suffer from claustrophobia (minimum age 15).

There's a more interesting natural phenomenon 10km to the north, where you'll see the highest of Gotland's coastal *rauker* (see opposite). The remnants of reefs formed over four hundred million years ago, the fact that the stacks are now well above the tide line is proof that sea levels were once much higher. This particular stack, 11.5m high and known as **Jungfruklint**, is said to look like the Virgin and Child – something you'll need a fair bit of imagination to discern.

Instead of taking the coastal road from Visby, you could head inland around 10km towards the village of **BRO**, which has one of the island's most beautiful churches. Several different stages of construction are evident from the Romanesque and Gothic windows in its tower. The most unusual aspect is the south wall, with its flat-relief picture stones, carved mostly with animals, that were incorporated from a previous church that once stood on the site. On the whole, though, it's better to press on further into the eminently picturesque north, where many of the secluded cottages are summer-holiday homes for urban Swedes.

At the village of **BUNGE**, it's worth visiting the bright fourteenth-century fortified church, and the open-air museum of seventeenth- to nineteenth-century buildings (mid-May to mid-Aug daily 10am–6pm; 30kr). **SLITE**, around 8km south of Lärbro, is the island's only really ugly place – the day-trip buses pass right by its cement factories, quarries and monumentally dull architecture. Beyond, though, Slite has a sandy beach and good swimming; its **campsite** (ⓣ22 08 30, ⓦwww.guteinfo.com; May to mid Sept), right on the beach, is a reasonable place to stay.

The islands around Gotland

The two islands of **Stora Karlsö** and **Lilla Karlsö**, lying over 6km off the southwest coast, have been declared nature reserves: both have **bird sanctuaries** where razorbills, guillemots, falcons and eider duck breed relatively undisturbed. On Lilla Karlso you'll also see the unique horned Gute sheep. It's possible to reach Stora Karlsö from Klintehamn some 30km south of Visby on Route 140; tickets are available from the harbour office for sailings (May to mid-Sept 10am, returning 3.30pm; late May to early Aug, 10am & 11.30am, returning 5pm; 200kr return; ⓣ0498/24 05 00, ⓦwww.storakarlso.com). There are also daily **tours** from Visby (May–Sept; 250kr per person). Lilla Karlsö is reached from Djupvik (120kr return; tickets from the harbour office or book on ⓣ0498/48 52 48), 7km south of Klintehamn (no buses). You can stay in hostel-style accommodation, near the pier (ⓣ0498/24 11 39; 100kr).

The only **accommodation** on Stora Karlsö is at the STF **youth hostel**, which puts guests up in tiny fishermen's huts sleeping up to four people (ⓣ0498/24 05 00, ⓕ24 52 60; 200–280kr per night for a hut); as picturesque as it sounds, it's also extremely basic, with no showers. There are restaurant facilities for breakfast and dinner. Any other kind of camping is not allowed on the islands.

Fårö

Most of **Fårö** island is flat limestone heath, with shallow lakes and stunted pines much in evidence. In winter (and sometimes in summer, too) the wind whips over the Baltic, justifying the existence of the local windmills – and of the sheep shelters, with their steeply pitched reed roofs, modelled on traditional Fårö houses.

Ingmar Bergman

Since the mid-1960s, Sweden's best-known film director and screenwriter, **Ingmar Bergman**, has lived for much of the time on Fårö. He was born in Uppsala in 1918, the son of a Lutheran pastor. The combination of his harsh upbringing, his interest in the religious art of old churches, and the works of August Strindberg inspired Bergman constantly to consider the spiritual and psychological conflicts of life in his films. The results – he made forty feature films between 1946 and 1983 – are certainly dark, and for many, deeply distressing and/or depressing. He made his first breakthrough at the Cannes Film Festival in 1944, winning the Grand Prix for his film *Hets* (*Persecution*), based on his school life. Among his best-known movies are the *The Seventh Seal,* starring Max von Sydow, and *Wild Strawberries.* The two most prevalent themes in his films were marriage and the motives for marital infidelity, and the divide between sanity and madness. One of his finest films, *Fanny and Alexander* (1983), portrays bourgeois life in Scandinavia at the turn of the twentieth century; it's actually based on the lives of his own maternal grandparents and was to be the last major film he made.

Bergman married five times (divorcing all but the last of his wives, who died in 1995). He had eight children, one of whom – Lin – was born out of marriage to the actress Liv Ullman.

The best place to head for is the five-kilometre arc of white sand at **Sudersandsviken**, or alternatively, for more swimming, try **Ekeviken**, on the other side of the isthmus. The rest of the coastline is rocky, spectacularly so at **Lauterhorn** and, particularly, **Langhammars**, where limestone stacks (see p.348) are grouped together on the beach. At Lauterhorn you can follow the signs for Digerhuvud, a long line of stacks leading to the tiny fishing hamlet of **Helgumannen**, which is no more than a dozen shacks on the beach, now used as holiday homes. There are fine **diving** opportunities here. Continuing along the same rough track brings you to a junction; right runs back to the township of Fårö; left, a two-kilometre dead-end road leads to Langhammars.

You can get to Fårö by taking a bus from Visby to the town of **Fårösund** and making the ferry crossing from there (daily every 15min; 30min; free). There's a down-at-heel but surprisingly good **café** in town, *Fårösund Grill*, which serves excellent sandwiches (25kr), an almond tart (10kr), and good, cheap coffee. Just opposite is Bungehallen, a very well-stocked supermarket (daily till 10pm). You can **camp** at Fårösund or take a chalet at Fårosunds Stugor, Strandgatan 80 (from 950kr a week; mid-April to Sept; ☎0498/22 16 94, ⓦ www.guteinfo.com/stugor).

Travel details

Trains

Hallsberg to: Gothenburg (hourly; 2hr 40min); Stockholm (hourly; 1hr 30min).

Jönköping to: Falköping for Stockholm and Gothenburg (hourly; 45min); Nässjo, for Stockholm and Malmö (hourly; 35min).

Kalmar to: Emmaboda (16 daily; 35min); Gothenburg (5 daily; 4hr 15min); Malmö (8 daily; 3hr 40min); Stockholm (5 daily; 6hr 30min); Växjo (10 daily; 1hr 45min).

Motala to: Hallsberg, for Örebro, Stockholm and Gothenburg (6 daily; 45min); Mjölby, for Malmö and Stockholm (2 daily; 1hr 15min).

Norrköping to: Linköping (1–2 hourly; 25min); Malmö (11 daily; 3hr 15min); Nyköping (5 daily; 40min); Stockholm (hourly; 1hr 40min).

Oskarshamn to: Gothenburg (3 daily; 5hr 30min); Nässjo (3 daily; 2hr 25min); Jönköping (3 daily; 3hr 20min).

Växjö to: Gothenburg (8 daily; 3hr 20min); Kalmar (6 daily; 1hr 40min); Karlskrona (2 daily; 1hr

30min); Copenhagen (8–10 daily; 3hr).
Örebro to: Gävle (6 daily; 3–4hr); Hallsberg, for Stockholm and Gothenburg (1–2 hourly; 20min); Motala (6 daily; 1hr 30min); Stockholm (7 daily; 3hr 10min).

Buses

Jönköping to: Gothenburg (Mon–Fri 2–3 daily; 2hr 15min); Gränna (up to 3 daily; 30min); Växjö (Mon–Fri 2 daily, Sat & Sun 1 daily; 1hr 55min).
Kalmar to: Gothenburg (1 daily; 6hr); Lund/Malmö (1 daily; 5hr 30min/5hr 45min); Oskarshamn/Västervik/Stockholm (3 daily; 1hr 25min/2hr 35min/6hr 50min).
Motala to: Norrköping/Stockholm (Fri & Sun 2 daily; 1hr 35min/3hr 25min).
Norrköping to: Linköping/Jönköping/Gothenburg (6 daily; 30min/2hr 40min/4hr 55min); Kalmar (5 daily; 4hr 15min); Stockholm (5 daily; 2hr 10min).

Växjö to: Jönköping/Linköping/Norrköping/ Stockholm/Uppsala (Fri & Sun 1 daily; 1hr 20min/3hr 30min/4hr/6hr 30min/7hr 30min).

Ferries

Nynäshamn to: Visby (mid-June to mid-Aug 3 daily; 5hr day, 6hr night; rest of year night sailings only; 5–6hr).
Oskarshamn to: Visby (mid-June to mid-Aug 1 daily plus 1 night sailing; rest of year night sailings only; 4hr day, 6hr night).

Fast ferries

Nynäshamn to: Visby (June–Aug 5 daily; 3hr; rest of year 1 daily; 3hr).
Oskarshamn to: Visby (June–Aug 5 daily; 2hr 30min).

5

The Bothnian coast: Gävle to Haparanda

CHAPTER 5

Highlights

✳ **A boat trip on the Ångerman river, Härnösand** Sail to peaceful Sollefteå along one of Sweden's most graceful rivers. See p.372

✳ **Högbonden, High Coast** A night in the former light-house on this unspoilt island complete with shoreside sauna is unbeatable. See p.379

✳ **Elk farm, Bjurholm** Come face to face with the elusive King of the Forest at this fascinating farm outside Umeå. See p.391.

✳ **Pite Havsbad, Piteå** Northern Sweden's premier beach resort is renowned for long hours of sunshine and warm waters. See p.397

✳ **Gammelstad, Luleå** Four hundred and fifty knarled wooden cottages make up Sweden's most extensive parish village offering an insight into the country's reli-gious past. See p.403

✳ **Luleå archipelago** Take a boat trip to one of the dozens of pine-clad islands at the very top of the Gulf of Bothnia. See p.403

The Bothnian coast:
Gävle to Haparanda

Sweden's east coast forms one edge of the **Gulf of Bothnia** (Bottenhavet), a corridor of land that is quite unlike the rest of the north of the country; the forest, so apparent in other parts of the north, has been felled here to make room for settlements. Although the entire coastline is dotted with towns and villages that reveal a faded history – some, like **Gävle** and **Hudiksvall**, still have their share of old wooden houses, though sadly much was lost during the Russian incursions of the eighteenth century – it is cities like **Sundsvall**, **Umeå** and **Luleå** that are more typical of the region – modern, bright and airy metropolises that rank as some of northern Sweden's liveliest and most likeable destinations.

Throughout the north you'll find traces of the religious fervour that swept the north in centuries past; **Skellefteå**, **Piteå** and particularly **Luleå** (included on the UNESCO World Heritage List) all boast excellently preserved **kyrk-städer** or parish villages, clusters of old wooden cottages dating from the early eighteenth century, where villagers from outlying districts would spend the night after making the lengthy journey to church in the nearest town. Working your way up the coast, perhaps on the long train ride to Swedish Lapland, it's worth breaking your trip at one or two of these places.

The highlight of the Bothnian coast is undoubtedly the stretch known as the **Höga Kusten**, or the High Coast (see p.376), between Härnösand and Örn-sköldsvik – for peace and quiet, this is easily the most idyllic part of the Swedish east coast. Its indented coastline is best seen from the sea, with shimmering fjords that reach deep inland, tall cliffs and a string of pine-clad islands that make it possible to island-hop up this section of coast. There's also good **hiking** to be had here in the **Skuleskogen National Park** (see p.383). The weather along this stretch of coast may not be as reliable as further south, but you're guaranteed clean beaches (which you'll often have to yourself), crystal clear waters and some of the finest countryside for walking.

Getting around

Unlike southern Sweden, travel anywhere in the north of the country requires careful planning. Many **trains**, including the Tågkompaniet departures to Swedish Lapland, only operate once-daily and **bus** services to destinations off

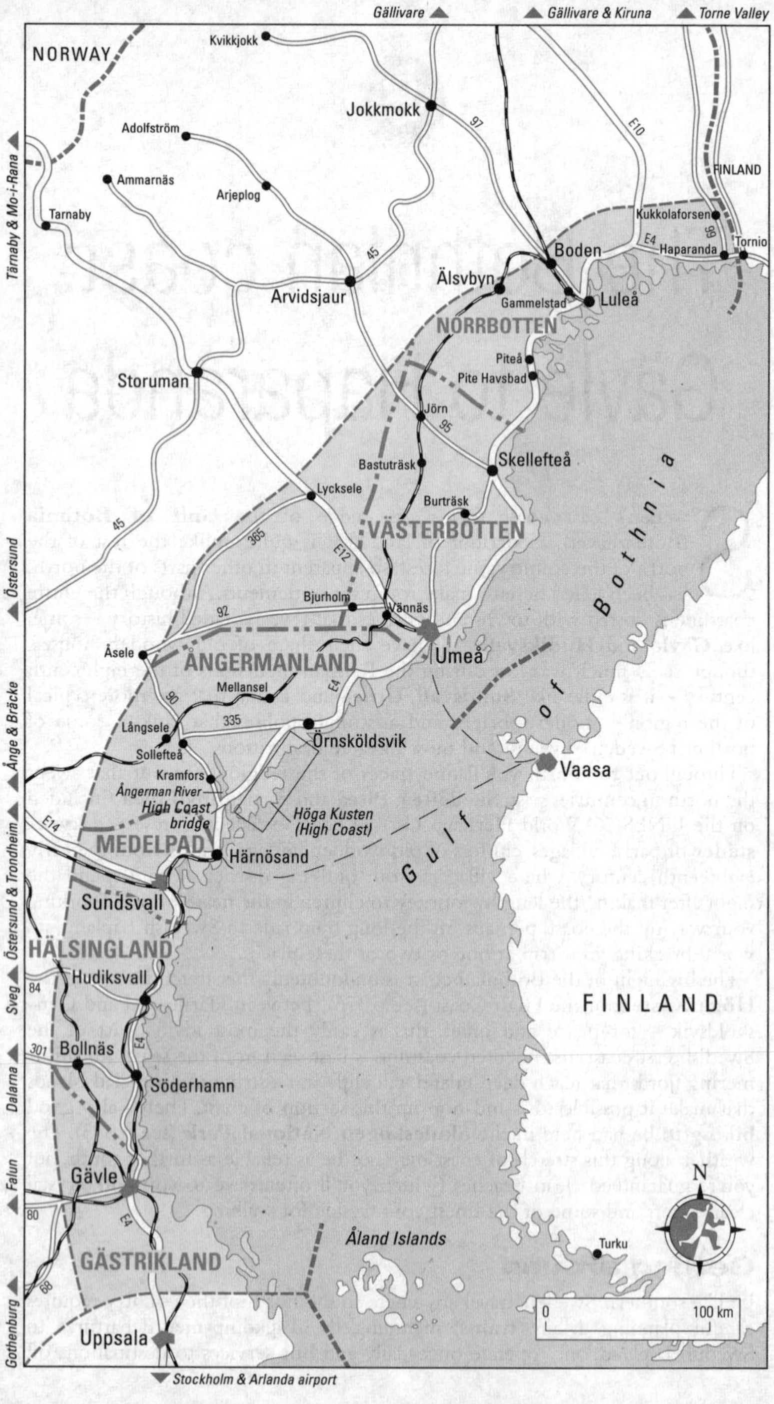

Gällivare
Gällivare & Kiruna
Torne Valley
NORWAY
Kvikkjokk
Jokkmokk
97
E10
Adolfström
Ammarnäs
Arjeplog
FINLAND
Kukkolaforsen
Tarnaby
99
Tornio
E4
Haparanda
Boden
45
Älvsbyn
Arvidsjaur
Gammelstad
Luleå
NORRBOTTEN
Piteå
Pite Havsbad
Storuman
Jörn
95
Bastuträsk
Skellefteå
Lycksele
Burträsk
45
365
VÄSTERBOTTEN
E12
Bjurholm
Vännäs
92
Umeå
Åsele
ÅNGERMANLAND
Mellansel
E4
90
335
Långsele
Örnsköldsvik
Sollefteå
Kramfors
Vaasa
Ångerman River
High Coast bridge
Höga Kusten (High Coast)
E14
MEDELPAD
Härnösand
Gulf of Bothnia
Sundsvall
HÄLSINGLAND
Hudiksvall
84
FINLAND
E4
301
Bollnäs
Söderhamn
Gävle
N
80
E4
Åland Islands
Turku
GÄSTRIKLAND
68
0
100 km
Uppsala
Stockholm & Arlanda airport
Tärnaby & Mo-i-Rana
Östersund
Ånge & Bräcke
Östersund & Trondheim
Sveg
Dalarna
Falun
Gothenburg

the beaten track can be skeletal – particularly between mid-June and mid-August when, arguably, the need for transport is greatest. Before setting off, make sure you check all travel details thoroughly – two good places to start are the SJ and Tågkompaniet websites, ⓦ www.sj.se and ⓦ www.tagkompaniet.com. Also worth a look is ⓦ www.dintur.se which provides details of bus services in and around the High Coast.

Buses and trains

The **train** route north from Uppsala hugs the **coast** from Gävle until Härnösand, where SJ services terminate. From here, **buses** head northwest to inland Långsele to meet Tågkompaniet trains running on the main line to Swedish Lapland and on to the Norwegian port of Narvik; the branch line from Härnösand to Långsele has recently been closed.

To head north along the High Coast from Härnösand, you'll need to catch one of the Norrlandskusten buses via Örnsköldsvik to either Umeå or Luleå, where you can connect back onto the train. Things look set to improve in the near future since work is now well under way on a new rail line, the 190km-long Botniabanan, which will finally close the gap between Härnösand, Örnsköldsvik and Umeå when it opens in 2008. This new route will allow daytime rail journeys between these places for the first time; at present all services north run overnight.

If you're planning to head **inland** from the Bothnian coast (or vice versa), it's worth noting that there's also a handy train and bus connection between Sundsvall and Östersund (see p.446). From Luleå you can travel by overnight Tågkompaniet train to Östersund by changing at Bräcke, or Sundsvall by changing at Ånge (see p.372). There are also several bus services running inland from Örnsköldsvik, Umeå and Skellefteå, which can whisk you up into the mountains of central Sweden should you wish to head inland from further up the Bothnian coast.

Ferries

Along the High Coast, island-hopping between Härnösand and Örnsköldsvik – via Högbonden, Ulvön and Trysunda (see p.376) – is a wonderful way to make your way north and to take in one of northern Sweden's most beautiful regions at the same time. **Ferry** tickets here are good value; see p.378 for details. Once again, though, you'll need to carefully check departure times to make sure you're not left stranded either on the islands or the mainland – the general pattern of services is given in the text.

Gävle and around

It's only one and a half hours north by train from Stockholm to **GÄVLE** (pronounced "Yev-luh", and confusingly similar to a much-used Swedish swearword), capital of the county of Gästrikland. Gävle is also the southernmost city of **Norrland**, the region – comprising almost two-thirds of Sweden – which represents wilderness territory in the minds of most Swedes. To all intents and purposes, Norrland, Sweden's main reservoir of natural resources with vast forests and large ore deposits, means everything north of Uppsala; crossing into here from Svealand (which together with Götaland makes up the southern third of the country) is – as far as the Swedish psyche is concerned – like leaving civilization behind.

Gävle's town charter was granted as long ago as 1446, a fact that's at variance with the modernity of the centre's large squares, broad avenues and proud monumental buildings. The city was almost completely rebuilt after a devastating fire in 1869, and its docks and warehouses reflect the heady success of its late nineteenth-century industry, when Gävle was the export centre for locally produced iron and timber. Today, the city is more famous as the home of **Gevalia coffee** ("Gevalia" being the old Latinized name for the town), which you'll no doubt taste during your time in Sweden and certainly smell in the air in Gävle.

If you're heading north for Höga Kusten only, Gävle makes a good stop, as its charming old town is a good spot for a stroll and it's also one of the few towns in Norrland to boast a couple of decent beaches. If you're travelling all the way into Swedish Lapland, you'd do better to break your journey further north than Gävle, in Sundsvall (see p.367) or Umeå (see p.386), say.

Arrival and information

The city centre is concentrated in the grid of streets spreading southwest from the **train station** on Stora Esplanadgatan. You'll find left-luggage lockers (15kr) on the main platform. The **bus station** is linked to the train station by

RESTAURANTS & CAFÉS
Bali Garden	E
Brända Bocken	H
Café Artist	G
Church Street Saloon	K
Heartbreak	J
Janssons	A
Kungshallen	C
O'Leary's	L
Österns Pärla	F
Skeppet	B
Tennstoppet	D
Wayne's Coffee	I

ACCOMMODATION
Aveny	7
Boulogne	4
Engeltoffa Youth Hostel	5
Nya Järnvägshotellet	2
Scandic Grand Central	1
Winn	3
Youth hostel	6

the subway that goes under the train tracks. A new **resecenturm**, or travel centre, is scheduled to open in 2003 on the site of the current bus and train stations from where all buses and trains will leave. A two-minute walk from the train station is the **tourist office** at Drottninggatan 37 (June–Aug Mon–Fri 9am–6pm, Sat 9am–2pm, Sun 11am–4pm; Sept–May Mon–Fri 9am–5pm; ⊤026/14 74 30, ⓦwww.gavle.se). They will book private **apartments** from 400kr per person per night. If you need **Internet** access, head for the library (Mon–Thurs 10am–8pm, Fri 10am–6pm, Sat & Sun 10am–3pm; free), near the corner of Södra Strandgatan and Rådmansbron.

Accommodation

Gävle has two **youth hostels**, one of which is superbly located in the old quarter at Södra Rådmansgatan 1 (⊤026/62 17 45, ⓕ026/61 59 90). The other is on the coast at Bönavägen 118 in **Engeltofta**, 6km northeast of the city (⊤026/961 60, ⓕ960 55; June–Aug); to get there, take the frequent bus #5 from Rådhuset. Gävle's **campsite**, which has cabins for rent, (⊤026/980 28) is by the amusement park, off Östnäsvägen, out at Furuvik (see p.362), a bus ride away on either #821 or #838, which leave roughly every half-hour. It's much better to make use of **Allemansrätt** and camp rough somewhere on the outskirts of town.

Aveny Södra Kungsgatan 31 ⊤026/61 55 90, ⓦwww.aveny.nu. A small and comfortable family-run hotel south of the river, offering a small breakfast buffet. ❸/❷

Boulogne Byggmästargatan 1 ⊤026/12 63 52, ⓦwww.hotellboulogne.com. Cosy, basic hotel, with breakfast brought to your room on a tray. Close to Boulognerskogen park. ❷

Nya Järnvägshotellet Centralplan 3 ⊤026/12 09 90, ⓕ10 62 42. The cheapest hotel in Gävle; fine, though rooms aren't en suite, and it's located on a busy corner opposite the train station. ❷/❶

Scandic Grand Central Nygatan 45 ⊤026/495 84 00, ⓦwww.scandic-hotels.com. One of the smartest hotels in town, with old-fashioned en-suite rooms yet an inescapable chain-hotel feel. ❻/❸

Winn Norra Slottsgatan 9 ⊤026/64 70 00, ⓦwww.softwarehotels.se/winngavle. Another smart hotel, with its own pool, sauna and sunbeds. Rooms are tasteful, if characterless, with neutral decor and wooden floors. ❺/❸

The town

Although Gävle is one of the bigger towns in Norrland, you can comfortably see everything in a day. Your first point of call should be **Gamla Gefle**, the old town district, where you'll also find the town's two museums, **Joe Hill-Gården** and **Länsmuséet Gävleborg**. Nearby, the **Heliga Trefaldighets kyrka** is a riot of seventeenth-century woodcarving and makes a pleasant stop en route to Gävle's city park, **Boulognerskogen**, a vast expanse of forested parkland ideal for a picnic or a leisurely stroll.

Gamla Gefle

It's only a ten-minute walk from the train station, across the Gavleån river, to the district of **Gamla Gefle**, which escaped much of the fire damage and today passes itself off as the authentic old town. Unfortunately, although it's the most interesting part of the city, it doesn't amount to much. The few remaining narrow cobbled streets – notably Övre Bergsgatan, Bergsgränd and Nedre Bergsgränd – boast pastel-coloured wooden cottages, window boxes overflowing with flowers in summer and old black lanterns. It's all very attractive and quaint; the jumbled lanes now house the odd craft shop and a café or two.

For a glimpse of social conditions a century ago, visit the **Joe Hill-Gården** at Nedre Bergsgatan 28 (June–Aug daily 11am–3pm; free; other times by arrangement on ☏026/61 34 25), the birthplace of one Johan Emanuel Hägglund in 1879. He emigrated to the United States in 1902, changed his name to Joe Hill, and became a working-class hero – his songs and speeches became rallying cries to comrades in the International Workers of the World, a Utah-based syndicalist organization, which runs the museum today. Its collection of standard memorabilia – pictures and belongings – is given piquancy by the inclusion of the telegram announcing his execution in 1915 – he was framed for murder in Salt Lake City – and his last will and testament.

On the northern edge of Gamla Gefle on the riverside, is an unusually thoughtful county museum, **Länsmuséet Gävleborg**, at Södra Strandgatan 20 (Tues–Sun noon–4pm, Wed until 9pm; 30kr; ⓦwww.lansmuseetgavleborg.se). It has extensive displays of artwork by most of the great Swedish artists from the seventeenth century to the present day, including Nils Kreuger and Carl Larsson, which attract visitors from across the country. Also on display is the work of a local artist, Johan-Erik Olsson (popularly known as "Lim-Johan"), whose vivid imagination and naive technique produced some strange childlike paintings.

Gävle Slottet and the Church of the Holy Trinity

Follow the river west from the museum to the double bridges of Rådmansbron and Kungsbron and you'll come to **Gävle Slott**, the seventeenth-century residence of the county governor, which lost its ramparts and towers years ago and now lurks behind a row of trees like some minor country house. It's not possible to get inside for a poke around, although you can ask the tourist office to arrange a visit to the **Fängelsemuséet** (Prison Museum), on the premises. Housed in what was the county's first prison, dating from the seventeenth century, the museum gives some idea of how jails were back then.

From Gävle Slott, a short walk west following the river leads to a wooden bridge, across which is Kaplansgatan and the **Heliga Trefaldighets kyrka**, the Church of the Holy Trinity, a seventeenth-century masterpiece of **wood-carved** decoration: check out the pulpit, towering altarpiece and screen – each the superb work of the German craftsman, Ewardt Friis.

Central Gävle and Boulognerskogen park

The modern city lies north of the river, its broad streets and avenues designed to prevent fires from spreading. A slice through the middle of the centre is comprised of parks, tree-lined spaces and fountains, running north from the spire-like **Rådhus** to the beautiful nineteenth-century theatre designed by Axel Nyström. All the main banks, shops and stores are in the grid of streets on either side of Norra Kungsgatan and Norra Rådmansgatan; the new **resecentrum** is about 700m to the east. From the train station, look across the tracks and you'll see the beginnings of an industrial area. Home to three parallel streets of old dock-side **warehouses**, off Norra Skeppsbron just by the river, it's a reminder of the days when ships unloaded coffee and spices in the centre of Gävle. To get to the warehouses, use the subway to head under the railway tracks, and walk east to the riverside. Today, with company names emblazoned on the red, wooden fronts of the empty buildings, the area feels more like a Hollywood movie set than a Swedish town. Continue to the far eastern end of the warehouses and the heady smell of roasting coffee with become ever stronger: Gevalia has its production centre here right next to the harbour at Nyhamn, north off Norra Skeppsbron.

Especially on a rainy day, you may find yourself contemplating the Sveriges Järnvägsmuseum, **Swedish Railways' museum**, at Rälsgatan 1 (June–Aug

daily 10am–4pm; Sept–May Tues–Sun 10am–4pm; 40kr; ☯http://message.sj.se/
museum); from the station cross Islandsbron bridge, then head south along
Fältskärsleden which later becomes Upplandsgatan, turn right onto Österbå-
gen, right again into Växelgatan and finally left into Rälsgatan; it's less than half
an hour's walk. In what used to be Gävle's engine shed, it's a train enthusiast's
paradise, stuffed to the gills with nearly fifty locomotives – sixteen of which are
over one hundred years old – and other paraphernalia. The highlight is the
hunting coach dating from 1859, one of the world's oldest railway carriages; it
once belonged to King Carl XV. One of the 1950s carriages houses the museum's own **café**.

Boulognerskogen park and swimming complex

West of the city centre and a twenty-minute stroll down picturesque
Kungsbäcksvägen, a narrow street lined with brightly painted wooden houses
beginning at Heliga Trefaldighets kyrka, you'll come to the rambling nineteenth-century park, **Boulognerskogen**. It's a good place for a picnic and a
spot of sunbathing or a visit to the music pavilions, open-air **café** or the sculpture, by Carl Milles, of five angels playing musical instruments.

Beyond the sculptures, on the southern edge of the park, Västra Ringvägen
slices south through the well-tended streets of suburban Gävle to an altogether more enticing proposition, the Fjärran Höjder **swimming complex** on
Lantmäterigatan. Downstairs is an impressively large – and often deserted –
pool and Jacuzzi plus an outdoor pool, whilst upstairs is a health suite with a
couple of saunas.

Eating, drinking and nightlife

The roomy Stortorget, just west of the central esplanade formed by
Drottinggatan and Nygatan, has an open-air **market** that's worth visiting for
its fruit and veg (Mon–Sat 9am–4pm). There's a fair choice of **eating places**
in Gävle, with the best options in the central grid of streets around Stortorget
and up and down the streets running from Rådhus to the theatre. Nearly all
cafés and restaurants double as **bars**. For dancing, **Heartbreak** and **O'Leary's**
are fun and always very busy.

Bali Garden Nygatan 37. Good Indonesian food,
with meat dishes from 85kr, served in this centrally
located restaurant that's handy for the train station.

Café Artist Norra Slottsgatan 9. A trendy hangout
offering fish and meat dishes for around 150kr, plus
smaller, cheaper dishes such as *pytt i panna*. In the
evenings, the café mutates into a piano bar and is a
relaxed place for a beer or two on cosy sofas.

Church Street Saloon Kyrkogatan 11. Tries too
hard to be an old-fashioned American saloon diner.
There may be Wild West grills on the plates and
dancing on the tables, but you can't forget you're
still in Gävle. Meaty mains from around 100kr.

Brända Bocken Stortorget. Young and fashionable, with outdoor seating in summer. Beef and
pork mains, hamburgers and salmon, each for
around 80kr. Lunch for 65kr. Also a popular place
for a drink.

Heartbreak Norra Strandgatan 15. A pub, bistro-
style bar and nightclub, that attracts a 35-plus
crowd.

Janssons Norra Rådmansgatan 20. Without a
doubt, the trendiest eatery in town, with rough
brick walls and tiled floors, specializing in Swedish
home-cooking, everything from herring to apple
pie. Reckon on 120kr for mains.

Kungshallen Norra Kungsgatan 17. Serves mammoth pizzas for 40–56kr; lunch portions, often
lasagne, are excellent value at 50kr. Cheap beer
available, too.

O'Leary's Södra Kungsgatan 31. A 20-minute
walk from the centre, this incredibly busy bar
caters for a 20- to 30-something crowd – *the*
place to do your boozing and boogieing. Closed
Mon.

Skeppet *Scandic Grand Central Hotel*, Nygatan
45. Fine fish and seafood dishes served amid maritime decor: main courses start from 150kr.

Tennstoppet Nygatan 38. Cheap and cheerful grill
restaurant close to the station, with chicken fajitas
for 90kr, pork fillet 95kr and *Janssons frestelse* for
79kr.

Österns Pärla Ruddammsgatan 23. Fairly standard Chinese restaurant, serving the usual favourites for 80–90kr each; lunch is 52kr.
Wayne's Coffee Drottninggatan 16. As always with this chain café, excellent coffees and cakes make this the best and busiest café in Gävle, centrally located in the main square.

Listings

Banks FöreningsSparbanken and Handelsbanken are both on Nygatan, west of Norra Kungsgatan; Nordea, Norra Kungsgatan 3–5.
Bus information Local buses operated by XTrafik (☎020/91 01 09); long-distance buses to Bollnäs (direct trains to Swedish Lapland and Östersund), Uppsala and Stockholm operated by Swebus (☎0200/21 82 18).
Car rental Europcar Södra Kungsgatan 62 ☎020/78 11 80; Hertz Kryddstegen 19 ☎026/51 18 19; Statoil Krickvägen 4 ☎020/25 25 25.
Cinemas Filmstaden, Drottninggatan 9–11; Sandrew, Norra Slottsgatan 3; Royal, Norra Slottsgatan 3B.
Pharmacy Drottninggatan 12 ☎020/66 77 66 (Mon–Fri 9am–6pm, Sat 9.30am–3pm, Sun 11am–3pm).
Police Södra Centralgatan 1 ☎026/65 50 00.
Systembolaget at Södra Kungsgatan 7 near Gävle Slottet; also at Nygatan 13 (both Mon–Wed 10am–6pm, Thurs & Fri 10am–7pm, Sat 10am–2pm).
Taxi Gävle Taxi ☎026/12 90 00; Taxi Stor och Liten ☎026/10 70 00.
Travel agent Ticket, Drottninggatan 27. Mon–Fri 9am–6pm, Sat 10am–1pm.

Around Gävle

If the sun's shining, you'll find locals catching the rays at the nearby sandy beach of **Rullsand**, which stretches for about 3km northeast of town. The beaches at **Engeltofta** or **Engesberga**, a few kilometres further on are the easiest to reach without your own transport; catch bus #5 from the Rådhus. From Engesberga, the bus continues to **Bönan**, where an old lighthouse marks a good spot for swimming. Other enjoyable beaches are on the island of **Limön**, connected by a summer ferry, **MS Drottning Silvia** (ⓦwww.swed.net/drottning-silvia), from Norra Skeppsbron, reached by heading east along the banks of the Gavleån river from behind the Resecentrum (3 daily; 40mins; 30kr), with one departure making a stop in Engeltofta on the way.

In the other direction from town is the **Furuvik amusement park** (daily: mid-May to mid-June & mid-Aug to early Sept noon–4pm; mid-June to mid-Aug noon–6pm; day-pass for 130kr; ⓦwww.furuvik.se); buses #821 and #838 leave for here roughly every half-hour from Gävle's bus station; the place boasts a zoo, fairground, parks and playgrounds.

Söderhamn and Hudiksvall

On the first leg of the coastal journey further into Norrland, train services, are reasonably frequent. Along this stretch of coast, **Söderhamn** and **Hudiksvall** both make for a leisurely stop en route to the bigger towns and tourist centres further north. Hudiksvall's wood-panelled architecture and convenience for visiting the natural beauty of the Hornslandet peninsula gives it the edge over sleepy Söderhamn; a few hours at most is all you'll need to get to grips with either place. Out of the main tourist season, it's best to avoid spending Sundays in either town, when you'll probably be the only person in the streets.

Söderhamn

It's easy to see that **SÖDERHAMN**, founded in 1620, was once much more important than it is today. The seventeenth-century **Ulrika Eleonora kyrka** (daily 8am–4pm), named after Karl XI's wife and designed by Nicodemus Tessin the Younger, towers over the Rådhus hinting at the wealth which once accrued to the city, primarily from fishing. Relics from an earlier church that stood on the same spot are kept in **Söderhamns Stadsmuseum** (mid-June to mid-Aug Tues–Sun noon–5pm; free), halfway up Oxtorgsgatan from Rådhustorget, the main square. The museum is housed in what was once a rifle-manufacturing workshop, a reminder of Söderhamn's seventeenth-century role as supplier of the weapons that helped Sweden dominate northern Europe; the permanent exhibitions upstairs canter through the town's history.

A number of devastating fires took their toll on the town; the largest, on July 22, 1876, destroyed virtually everything in its path. As a result, the modern town is built on a grid pattern, with space for central parks and green spaces. The best of which, **Källparken**, barely a five-minute walk from Rådhustorget – cross Smäckbron and go under the railway bridge – explodes into colour every summer with 9000 flowers crowded into a series of well-kept beds and borders. The familiar Swedish mix of pedestrianized shopping streets and parkland gives the town a likeable air, one that's inviting enough to while away some time at a pavement café. However, the wide open spaces in the centre of town don't give a true impression of the surrounding area, as a climb up the 125 steps of the white, 23-metre-tall **Oskarsborg tower** (mid-June to mid-Aug daily 10am–8pm; free) will demonstrate; there's a path to it signposted from down by the train tracks, off Södra Hamngatan. Over the years the tower, which opened in 1895, has become known across Sweden as the symbol of Söderhamn – locals are only too ready to tell you that the town's singing group, short of somewhere to practice their vocal skills, collected money for its construction. From the top, the surrounding forests that hem the town in stretch away as far as the eye can see. If you want to a take a **walk** out into the countryside, head down Kyrkogatan, from under the railway bridge south of Rådhustorget, and continue up the hill onto the footpath; turn left into Krongatan and on towards the hospital past the helipad, then head right along any one of a series of paths into the forest.

Practicalities

Söderhamn's **resecentrum** ("Travel Centre") on Söderhamnsporten not only houses both the **train** and **bus stations** but also the town's **tourist office** (mid-June to mid-Aug Mon–Fri 9am–5pm, Sat & Sun 10am–3pm; rest of year Mon–Fri 9am–5pm; ☎0270/753 53, ⊛www.turism.soderhamn.se). From here it's a fifteen-minute walk east along Brädgårdsgatan, past the **First Hotel Statt**, into the main square, Rådhustorget. In town, the best of the **accommodation** options is the central and swanky **First Hotel Statt**, Oxtorgsgatan 17 (☎0270/735 70, ⊛www.firsthotels.com; ❺/❸). Close by, in the main square, **Centralhotellet** (☎0270/700 00, ℗0270/160 60; ❸/❷) is a cheaper alternative whose rooms, though all en-suite, are on the small side and cursed with floral curtains in the worst possible taste. The wonderfully situated **youth hostel** is at **Mohed**, 13km west of town, in a deep pine forest (☎0270/42 52 33, ⊛www.camping.se/plats/X06; June–Aug). Right by a lake, the hostel occupies an old sanatorium, built here so that patients could benefit from Mohed's famous clean air; swimming, boat rental, fishing, horse-riding and mini-golf are all available in the vicinity. There's a year-round **campsite** here, too. To get to Mohed from Söderhamn, take the hourly buses #63 or #100 (the latter continues to **Bollnäs**, about thirty minutes' ride west from Mohed, which is handy for catching direct buses north to Swedish Lapland and Östersund).

Eating and **drinking** establishments in Söderhamn have come on in leaps and bounds in recent years, and there are now a fair number vying for your custom, though they're nothing spectacular. For **daytime** coffee, cakes, sandwiches, salads and pies, try **Mackeriet** on the main pedestrian street, Köpmangatan; it's open daily. Most restaurants are to be found along the same thoroughfare: at the Rådhus end of the street, **Mousquet** has pizzas for around 50kr, pasta 60kr and fish dishes for 100–120kr. The Chinese restaurant, **Mandarin Palace**, in Köpmantorget, has various rice dishes for 72kr; they also offer chicken and beef mains for 83kr and 87kr respectively. However, the best restaurant, the intimate **Tassili**, at Kungsgatan 23, opposite the police station, serves an excellent pork cutlet in chanterelle sauce with fried potatoes for just 110kr; pizzas are from 60kr, pasta dishes 85kr. Up-market food is also served at the **Restaurang Stadshotellet**, inside the **First Hotel Statt** on Oxtorgsgatan. **Drinking** is best done at **O'Leary's** at Oxtorgsgatan 14 or at **Blue Heaven** on Kungsgatan. Free **Internet access** can be found at the library on Köpmangatan in the town centre.

Hudiksvall and around

Granted town status in 1582 by King Johan III and accordingly the second oldest town in Norrland, **HUDIKSVALL** has seen its fair share of excitement over the years. Though the original settlement was built around what had been the bay of Lillfjärden, at the mouth of the Hornån river, the harbour began to silt up, and so it was decided in the early 1640s to move the town to its current location: the old bay is now a lake, connected to the sea by a small canal. The town has suffered no less than ten **fires**, the worst occurring in 1721 when Russian forces swept down the entire length of the Bothnian coast, burning and looting as they went. Then an important commercial and shipping centre, the town bore the brunt of the onslaught; only its **church** (June–Aug Mon–Fri 10am–4pm, Sat 11am–3pm; rest of year Mon–Thurs 11am–3pm), still pockmarked with cannonball holes today, remained standing. Although St Jakob's white stone exterior topped with a green onion dome is elegant enough, it's the interior that really impresses; unusually ornate for Swedish Orthodox, nineteenth-century renovators opted for brown marble hand-painted wall decoration, delicately lit by ornate candle-bearing chandeliers. The incongruous cannonball by the steps to the pulpit is a replica of the original fired by the Russians at the church. A further blaze, east of Rådhustorget, in 1792 led to a rethink of the town's layout, following which the street plan which exists today was conceived.

The oldest part of the rebuilt town – the most interesting part of the city – is split into two main sections. Turn right out of the train station and cross the narrow canal, Strömmingssundet ("Herring Sound"), and you'll soon see the small old **harbour** on the right; this area is known as **Möljen**. Here the wharfside is flanked by a line of red, wooden fishermen's cottages and storehouses, all leaning into the water; it's a popular place for locals to while away a couple of hours in the summer sunshine, dangling their feet into the water. The back of the warehouses hides a run of handicraft studios and the tourist office (see opposite). More impressive and much larger than Möljen, **Fiskarstan** (Fishermen's Town), beyond **First Hotel Statt** down Storgatan, contains neat examples of the so-called "Imperial" wood-panel architecture of the late eighteenth and nineteenth centuries. It was in these tightly knit blocks of streets, lined with beautiful wooden houses and fenced-in plots of land, that the fishermen used to live during the winter. Take a peek inside some of the little courtyards – all window boxes, summer flowers and cobblestones.

The history of these buildings is put into context in the excellent **Hälsinglands Museum** at Storgatan 31 (late June to mid-Aug Mon & Fri

9am–4pm, Wed & Thurs 9am–7pm, Sat 11am–3pm; rest of year Mon & Thurs noon–4pm, Wed 9am–7pm, Sat 11am–3pm; 20kr; ⓦwww.halsinglandsmuseum .se), which traces the development of Hudiksvall as a harbour town since its foundation. The museum's real showstoppers, however, are the ornately decorated **Malsta rune stone**, from around 1000, ornately engraved with the letter-less Helsinge runic script – ask at the museum reception for a translation of the inscription – and the quite breathtaking collection of **medieval church art** kept in a dimly lit room, just to the right of the reception desk. From altar screens to intricately carved wooden figures of Sweden's saints, this astounding array of outstanding craftsmanship is sure to impress; the centrepiece is the sixteenth century figure of the Madonna by renowned local artist, Haaken Gulleson from the village of Enånger in Hälsingland. Whilst here, be sure also to see the paintings by **John Sten** on the ground floor: born near Hudiksvall in 1879, he moved to Paris at the age of thirty, where he was greatly influenced by Gauguin. Tragically, Sten died of dysentery at the age of 42 in Bali; like many artists of his day, he travelled extensively in Southeast Asia collecting impressions and designs and became one of the first to work with Cubism, from which his work extends towards a more decorative fanciful style.

Undoubtedly the best time to visit Hudiksvall is during the second week of July, when the town hosts the **Musik vid Dellen**, a multifarious cultural festival, including folk music and other traditional events (for more information, contact the tourist office), held in churches and farms in the surrounding countryside.

Practicalities

The **train** and **bus stations** are opposite each other on Stationsgatan. It takes two minutes to walk from either, along Stationsgatan, to the town centre around Möljen. Close by, behind the old warehouses in what once was the town's bus station terminal off Hamngatan, is the **tourist office** (mid-June to mid-Aug Mon–Fri 9am–7pm, Sat & Sun 10am–5pm; mid-Aug to mid-June Mon–Fri 9am–4pm; ☎0650/191 00, ⓦwww.hudiksvall.se). For **Internet** access, head for the library inside Folkets Hus, opposite the **First Hotel Statt** on Storgatan, or the Hälsinglands Museum.

The **youth hostel** (☎0650/132 60, ⓦwww.malnbadenscamping.com) is out at the Malnbaden **campsite**, 3km from town. Bus #5 runs there hourly in summer (10am–6pm); at other times you'll have get there by taxi (100kr one-way; there's a rank at the train station). Situated on the bay, the hostel overlooks a large sandy beach and jogging tracks on the opposite side of the road; there are also cottages for rent, which can be booked through the tourist office. For **hotel** accommodation, there's **Hotell Temperance** (☎0650/311 07, ⓦwww.home .swipnet.se/~w-77808; ❸/❷) a cheapish place at Håstagatan 16, near the train station, which also has utilitarian rooms. The swishest hotel in town is the 1878 **First Hotel Statt**, at Storgatan 36 (☎0650/150 60, ⓦwww.firsthotels.com; ❺/❸). It was here that the barons of the timber industry did their best to live up to the town's nickname of "Glada Hudik" ("Happy Hudiksvall"), a phrase coined in the first half of the nineteenth century, when the people here became known for their lively social life and generous hospitality.

Today, Hudiksvall continues this tradition with a few decent eating and drinking places, though none will form the highlight of a trip to Sweden. For **snacks** and cakes, try **Dackås Konditori** at Storgatan 34, a Hudiksvall institution that's been here since the 1950s – with decor to match. A popular **restaurant** is **Bruns** at Brunnsgatan 2, where main dishes consisting of tasty Swedish home-cooking cost around 85kr. Alternatively, try the Chinese restaurant, **Ming**, at Bankgränd 1 near the station, which has dishes for around 80kr. In summer, though, the best place to eat is the open-air terrace at **Gretas Krog,** Västra Tvärgatan, right behind the tourist office beside the railway line; lunch here is 59kr, meat and fish mains around 180kr. The poshest place in town is **StadtNöje**, the restaurant attached to **First Hotel Statt** on Storgatan; the reindeer stew here is superb at 118kr, as is their salmon wrapped in bacon with tagliatelle at 135kr; you'll need to dress smartly, though, if you want to blend in. The one and only **bar** is the **Pub Tre Bockar** at Bankgränd, opposite the fishermen's warehouses at Möljen, with occasional evening jazz. For those empty evenings, you'll find the **cinema** at Drottninggatan 1 and the **swimming pool** at Norra Kyrkogatan 9B.

The Hornslandet Peninsula

For a day-trip, head southeast out to the beautiful and unspoilt **Hornslandet peninsula**, renowned for its quaint fishing villages of red wooden cottages and sandy **beaches**. This egg-shaped chunk of land is the geological result of continuous land rise since the last Ice Age; as recently as the Viking era, the Arnösund sound which once separated Hornslandet from the mainland was easily navigable and remained an important channel for seafarers until the tenth century. Today, though, the sound has silted up and the peninsula is effectively an extension of the Bothnian coast. This whole area is rich in flora and fauna, as well as being ideal for swimming, fishing and walking; there are two villages to head for in particular: Hölick and Kuggörarna.

Located at the southern tip of the peninsula, **Hölick**, the larger of the two villages, traces its history back to the sixteenth century when a small fishing community became established here. Although there are no sights to speak of, the main purpose for coming here is to enjoy the plentiful peace and tranquillity on the very edge of the Gulf of Bothnia; indeed, a set of wooden steps lead up from the pilot boat station (**lotsstation**) in the centre of the village onto the rocks from where there are unsurpassed **views** out over the sea. A 7km circular **walking path** (allow around 2hr) will take you through the surrounding nature reserve to some of the peninsula's finest **beaches**: from the village the path leads southeast out to the Hornslandsudden promontory – there are sandy streches of coast all the way to the furthest point of the promontory – from where the path cuts inland, heading over a series of low hills, back towards Hölick.

If you want to stay here, **accommodation** is restricted to the **Natura Camping Hölick** campsite (℡0650/56 50 32, ℻0650/56 51 00; June–Aug), which also has around fifteen **cabins** (❶) for rent; look out for the signs where the road into the village ends. Hölick also boasts one **restaurant**, **Sjöboa**, whose fish buffet for 120kr is truly superb.

Tiny **Kuggörarna**, actually located on a small island, is joined to the rest of the peninsula by a narrow bridge across the dividing sound. Once again, it's for solitude and great sea vistas that most visitors come here, although the hamlet does have a couple of things worth seeking out: the eighteenth-century **chapel** up on the hill above the houses is worth a quick look (you'll find the key hanging by the door) and, just to the north of the cluster of houses, is a well-preserved stone **labyrinth**, a collection of winding walkways delineated by large stones on the ground, used in centuries past by superstitious fishermen to ensure a good catch. There's neither accommodation nor eateries here.

Getting to the Hornslandet peninsula by public transport is only possible in summer: take bus #37 (mid-June to mid-Aug, 2 daily) which runs from the bus station via Hölick (40min) to Kuggörarna (1hr), otherwise, with your own transport, route 778 leads to Kuggörarna from Hällby, just north of Hudiksvall.

Sundsvall and around

The capital of the tiny province of Medelpad, **SUNDSVALL**, is often referred to as "Stone City", for the simple reason that most of its buildings are made of stone – a fact that distinguishes it immediately from other coastal towns here. Once home to a rapidly expanding timber industry, the whole city burned to the ground the day after Midsummer in June 1888. A spark from the wood-burning steamboat **Selånger** (promptly dubbed "The Arsonist") set fire to a nearby brewery, and the rest, as they say, is history – so much so that the remark "that hasn't happened since the town burned down" is now an established Sundsvall saying. Nine thousand people lost their homes in the resulting blaze. The work of rebuilding the city began at once, and within ten years a new centre had been constructed, entirely of **stone**. The result is a living document of turn-of-the-twentieth-century urban architecture, designed and crafted by

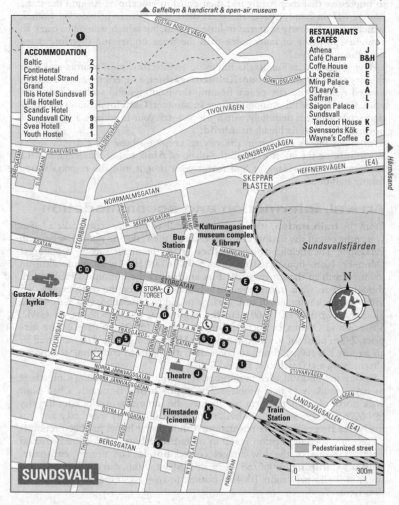

▲ Gaffelbyn & handicraft & open-air museum

ACCOMMODATION

Baltic	2
Continental	7
First Hotel Strand	4
Grand	3
Ibis Hotel Sundsvall	5
Lilla Hotellet	6
Scandic Hotel Sundsvall City	9
Svea Hotell	8
Youth Hostel	1

RESTAURANTS & CAFÉS

Athena	J
Café Charm	B&H
Coffe House	D
La Spezia	E
Ming Palace	G
O'Leary's	A
Saffran	L
Saigon Palace	I
Sundsvall Tandoori House	K
Svenssons Kök	F
Wayne's Coffee	C

Gustav Adolfs kyrka

Bus Station

Kulturmagasinet museum complex & library

Sundsvallsfjärden

STORA-TORGET

N

Theatre

Filmstaden (cinema)

Train Station

Pedestrianized street

SUNDSVALL

0   300m

► Härnösand

architects who were involved in rebuilding Stockholm's residential areas at the same time. Wide streets and esplanades that would serve as firebreaks in the event of another fire formed the backbone of their work. These thoroughfares are home to 573 residential buildings, all of which went up in four years; the centrepiece is the house that dominates the main square, Storatorget.

The reconstruction, however, was achieved at a price: the workers who had laboured on the city's refurbishment became the victims of their own success. They were shifted from their old homes in the centre and moved out south to a run-down suburb – the glaring contrast between the wealth of the new centre and the poverty of the surrounding districts was only too obvious. When **Nils Holgersson**, a character created by the children's author Selma Lagerlöf (see p.420), looked down from the back of his flying goose (see the picture on 20kr notes), he remarked: "There was something funny about it when you saw it from above, because in the middle there was a group of high stone houses, so impressive that they hardly had their equal in Stockholm. Around the stone houses was an empty space, and then there was a circle of wooden houses, which were pleasantly scattered in little gardens, but which seemed to carry an awareness of being of lesser value than the stone houses and therefore dared not come too close."

Having gawped at Sundsvall's imposing architecture, most visitors make for the city's other main attraction: **Kulturmagasinet**, a superb museum complex located right in the city centre housing the paintings and sculptures of local artist, Carl Frisendahl, amongst others. In summer, **Gaffelbyn**, Sundsvall's outdoor craft village is definitely worth a look – try your hand here at baking the northern Swedish flatbread, **tunnbröd**.

Although there's enough in the city to keep you busy for a day or so, it's worth making the effort to reach the island of **Alnö**, east of Sundsvall, and the traditional fishing village of Spikarna, for an insight into the region's strong fishing traditions.

Arrival, information and accommodation

From the **train station**, it's a five-minute walk to the city centre; take a left as you come out of the station, cross the car park then take the underpass beneath Parkgatan. The helpful **tourist office** is in the main square, Storatorget (Mon–Fri 10am–6pm, Sat 10am–2pm; ☎060/61 04 50, ⦁www.sundsvallturism .com). North of the square is the **bus station**, at the bottom of Esplanaden, though if you want information or advance tickets for the daily express bus south to Stockholm, north to Umeå, or inland to Östersund, visit Y-Bussen at Sjögatan 7 (☎060/17 19 60). For the express bus to Gothenburg via Gävle, Västerås and Örebro, contact Perssons Bussar on (☎026/66 01 60). The **airport**, 24km north of town on the way to Härnösand, is linked to Sundsvall by an airport bus (60kr), timed to coincide with flights to and from Stockholm; alternatively, a taxi will cost around 330kr.

Rooms in Sundsvall, even in summer, are plentiful, and so finding somewhere to stay is unlikely to be a problem. The **youth hostel** is roughly a half-hour walk north of town at Norra Stadsberget, the mountain overlooking the city (☎060/61 21 19, ⦁www.sundsvall.norraberget.se); to get there, take any bus for Norra Berget from the bus station. Although the hostel has been renovated recently, accommodation is still in minuscule cabins and you are better off opting for one of the low-budget central **hotels**. The nearest **campsite**, **Fläsians Camping** (☎060/55 44 75; mid-May to Aug), also has four-bed cabins (200–400kr per cabin). It's 4km outside town – ask at the tourist office for directions.

Baltic Sjögatan 5 ☎ 060/14 04 40, 🖥 www
.baltichotell.com. Centrally located, near the
Kulturmagasinet and the harbour, with perfectly
adequate rooms. ④/③

Continental Rådhusgatan 13 ☎ 060/15 00 60,
📠 15 75 90. A fairly cheap centrally located hotel
offering en-suite rooms with cable TV, and a sun
terrace. ③/②

First Hotel Strand Strandgatan 10 ☎ 060/64 19
50, 🖥 www.firsthotels.com. The smartest hotel in
town, with two hundred rooms, an indoor pool and
a superb breakfast buffet. ⑥/④

Grand Nybrogatan 13 ☎ 060/64 65 60,
🖥 www.grandhotelsundsvall.se. The basement
sauna and jacuzzi suite are excellent; the rooms,
however, are on the small side, with rather worn
furnishings. ④/②

Ibis Hotel Sundsvall Trädgårdsgatan 31–33

☎ 060/64 17 50, 🖥 www.ibishotel.com. All rooms
are en suite and some even have baths. Worth trying, especially if the cheaper hotels are full; breakfast is an extra 50kr. ②/①

Lilla Hotellet Rådhusgatan 15 ☎ 060/61 35 87,
🖥 www.home.swipnet.se/lilla-hotellet. One of the
most reasonably priced hotels in town with just
eight rooms, all of which are en suite and have
cable TV. ②

Scandic Hotel Sundsvall City Esplanaden 29
☎ 060/785 6200, 🖥 www.scandic-hotels.com. This
chain hotel boasts saunas, sunbeds, eight cinemas
and a golf simulator, with prices to match the opulence. ⑥/③

Svea Hotell Rådhusgatan 11 ☎ 060/61 16 05. The
ten rooms at this, the cheapest hotel in Sundsvall,
soon fill up in summer. Doubles every day in summer and Fri and Sat all year for just 395kr. ②/①

The City

As you walk in from the train station, the sheer scale of the rebuilding here
after the 1888 fire is clear to see. **Esplanaden**, the wide central avenue, cuts the
grid of streets in two; towards its northern end it's crossed by **Storgatan**, the
widest road in town. **Storatorget**, the central square, is a delightfully roomy
shopping and commercial centre, home to the city hall, various impromptu
exhibitions and displays, as well as a fresh fruit and veg market (May to early
Sept Mon–Sat from 8am). The limestone and brick buildings are four- and
five-storey palatial structures. As you stroll the streets, you can't help but be
amazed by the tremendous amount of open space that surrounds you, even in
the heart of the city; Sundsvall is unique among Swedish cities in this respect,
yet it's the most densely populated metropolis in northern Sweden.

Several of the buildings in the centre are worth a second look, not least the sturdy Kulturmagasinet museum, housed within two blocks of late nineteenth-century warehouses, spanned by a glass roof, on Hamngatan, down by the harbour. The
buildings stood empty for twenty years before a decision was taken to turn them
into what's now the **Kulturmagasinet** (Mon–Thurs 10am–7pm, Fri 10am–6pm,
Sat & Sun 11am–4pm; June–Aug 20kr, Sept–May free), comprising museum,
library and café. The museum is actually built over an old street, Magasinsgatan,
once boasting train tracks running between the warehouses to carry coffee and
rice to export. Deserving of a quick look, the museum does its best to depict the
history of Sundsvall and the province of Medelpad. Upstairs, the art exhibition
warrants a few minutes of your time: the works of twentieth-century Swedish
artists are on show here, in particular, those of the local artist and sculptor Carl
Frisendahl (1886–1948) whose early style is heavily influenced by Rodin. At the
age of twenty, Frisendahl studied in Paris where he met his wife, Marie Barbaud.
Forsaking his native Sweden for a studio in Montparnasse, he began painting in
the 1920s; his works, which often depict animals and mythological figures in combat, clearly show inspiration from Delacroix and Orthon Friesz.

Continue west along the main pedestrian street, Storgatan, and at the far end
you'll come across a soaring red-brick structure, **Gustav Adolfs** kyrka
(Mon–Thurs 10am–7pm, Fri 10am–6pm, Sat & Sun 11am–4pm; June–Aug 20kr,
Sept–May free) which marks the western end of the new town. The church's interior looks like a large Lego set, its pillars, vaults and window frames all constructed from smooth bricks, making a pleasing picture of order for the eye.

Norra Berget and Gaffelbyn

Beyond the city's design, the most attractive diversion is the tiring three-kilometre climb to the heights of **Gaffelbyn** on **Norra Berget**, the hill that overlooks the city to the north; walk up Storgatan, cross over the main bridge and follow the sign to the youth hostel. If you'd prefer to spare your legs, any bus for Norra Berget will take you there. The view on a clear day is fantastic, giving a fresh perspective on the city's planned structure and the restrictive nature of its location, hemmed in on three sides by hills and the sea. From here you can see straight across to Södra Berget, the southern hill, with its winter ski slopes. The best views can be had from the top of the **viewing tower** which has stood on this spot since 1897. Originally made entirely from wood, the tower fell victim over the years to the Swedish winter. By the 1930s it was in such poor condition that during one particularly severe autumn storm, the entire tower blew down; the present concrete replacement, 22m high, dates from 1954. The nearby **Norra Bergets Hantverksmuseum** (June–Aug Mon–Fri 9am–4pm, Sat & Sun 11am–4pm; Sept–May Mon–Fri 9am–4pm; free) is an open-air handicrafts museum with the usual selection of twee wooden huts and assorted activities, though you can try your hand at baking some **tunnbröd**, the thin bread that's typical of northern Sweden. The idea is to roll out your dough extra thin, brush off as much flour as you can, slip the bread into the oven on a big, wooden pizza-type paddle, and count slowly to five.

Eating, drinking and entertainment

Restaurants have mushroomed in Sundsvall over the last couple of years, and there's a good choice of places to eat and cuisines to choose from, including unusual options such as Vietnamese, Spanish and Indian – something you may want to make the most of if you're heading further north, as culinary options up there are limited. There are a handful of inexpensive pizza places and restaurants on Storgatan, most offering daily lunches. **Bars** in the city generally have a good atmosphere, and there are several places serving cheap beer. **Nightclubs** are a bit thin on the ground; the best one to head for is **Primero** at the **First Hotel Strand**, Strandgatan 10, where over-23s gather to shake their stuff to the latest sounds or **Casino** on Hamnplan, at the eastern end of Storgatan.

Cafés

Café Charm Storgatan 34 and Köpmangatan 34. A good choice for coffee and cake, with free refills and naughty-but-nice cream concoctions.

Coffee House Storgatan 31, opposite *O'Leary's*. Small and agreeable modern café with Swedish coffee, tea, sandwiches and newspapers.

Wayne's Coffee Storgatan 33. Located in new premises at the western end of the main drag, this is *the* coffee house in Sundsvall, with dozens of varieties of coffee and excellent sandwiches and cakes.

Restaurants

Athena Köpmangatan 7. Run by a Moroccan football star who ended up in Sundsvall. This place has all your Greek favourites, from tzatziki to souvlaka, as well as good pizzas. Main courses from 100kr.

Ming Palace Esplanaden 10. The best Chinese restaurant in Sundsvall with a range of dishes from 80kr to eat in, or take away

La Spezia Sjögatan 6. Serves decent bargain-basement pizzas 35kr; also has a takeaway service.

Saffran Rådhusgatan 7. A Spanish restaurant whose fare includes a reasonable selection of tapas, all at moderate prices.

Saigon Palace Trädgårdsgatan 5. Vietnamese and Chinese restaurant with some good-value dishes – try the chicken in peanut sauce for 78kr; the buffet lunch costs 65kr.

Sundsvall Tandoori House Södra Järnvägsgatan 9. One of Sweden's best Indian restaurants serving up first-class meals in a basement restaurant just 10min on foot from the centre. Reckon on 145kr for main courses.

Svenssons Kök Torggatan 8. Always busy at lunchtime, thanks to its central location in the main square. Has a *Dagens Rätt* that changes daily.

5

Bars

Dublin Nybrogatan 16. This Irish pub has a broad selection of beers, including Cafferys and Kilkennys, plus Irish food, music – and darts.
Harry's Storgatan 33. Another in the chain of popular American-style bars sweeping Sweden. This one's a pub, restaurant and nightclub all rolled into one.
JOP's Trädgårdsgatan 35. A popular place for a mid-evening tipple with an extensive choice of foreign beers; darts is also available.
Mercat Cross Esplanaden 29. Part of the Filmstaden complex, at the southern end of Esplanaden, this Scottish theme pub serves just about every variety of whisky you can think of.
O'Bar Bankgatan 11. A good, lively bar; try the excellent, pricey cocktails (100kr and up). The staff are happy to make up any concoction you throw at them.
O'Leary's Storgatan 40. A sports-oriented pub with a good choice of beer, and pub food with a Tex-Mex flavour. Big screens show the latest football and ice hockey matches.

Listings

Airlines SAS and Skyways ☎060/608 80 10.
Banks Handelsbanken, Storgatan 23; Nordea, Kyrkogatan 15; SEB, Storgatan 19.
Buses ☎020/51 15 13.
Car rental Hertz, Bultgatan 1 ☎060/66 90 80; Europcar, Trafikgatan 42 ☎060/12 33 10.
Cinema Filmstaden, at the southern end of Esplanaden.
Hospital Lasarettsvägen 19 ☎060/18 10 00.
Pharmacy Storgatan 18 ☎060/18 11 17 (Mon–Fri 10am–6pm, Sat 10am–3pm).
Police Storgatan 37 ☎060/18 00 00.

Post office Köpmangatan 19 ☎060/19 60 00 (Mon–Fri 8.30am–6pm, Sat 10am–1pm).
Systembolaget Torggatan 1 Stora Torget ☎060/61 36 69 (Mon–Wed 10am–6pm, Thurs 10am–7pm, Fri 9.30am–6pm; Sat 10am–2pm).
Taxi Taxi Sundsvall ☎060/19 90 00; Taxi Centralen ☎060/15 00 00.
Train station Parkgatan ☎0771/75 75 75.
Travel agent Ticket, on the corner of Rådhusgatan and Esplanaden (Mon–Fri 9am–6pm, Sat 10am–2pm).

Around Sundsvall: Alnö

The island of **Alnö** is within easy striking distance of Sundsvall and makes for a good day-trip. Alnö's empty roads and tranquil scenery are particularly popular with cyclists (ask at Sundsvall tourist office for **bike** rental information), who come to navigate the narrow country lanes that wind their way past pine forests, sandy coves and the odd farmstead. The main place to head for here is the tiny, pretty fishing village of **SPIKARNA** in the southeast corner of the island. Its red, wooden fishermen's cottages, snuggled round a tiny bay for protection from the wind and snow that sweeps in from the Gulf of Bothnia, are evidence of a long fishing tradition, still going strong today: you'll see nets laid out to dry on frames all around the village. To get into what passes for the village centre, cross the wooden bridge from the spot where the bus drops you, and continue along the footpath for just a couple of minutes. In summer, you can buy smoked whitefish from small huts by the side of the path, while to the right there's a cluster of rocks that are good for sunbathing. Once a week in summer there are jazz evenings, held by the side of the fishermen's cottages – a wonderful way to enjoy the light nights.

To **get to Alnö**, take the frequent bus #1 from Sundsvall's bus station over the arched Alnöbron bridge. The bus will stop at the main village, Vi, from where you can get to Spikarna on the bus for Södra Alnö. In summer a special bus, Badbussen, runs directly to Spikarna from Sundsvall's bus station – ask at Sundsvall's tourist office for departure times; in winter, the water in the channel below freezes, allowing people with their own snow scooters to nip across. For a **place to stay** in Spikarna, the tourist office back in Sundsvall has **cottages** for rent, which get snapped up very quickly (1500–3500kr a week); alternatively, you could always camp rough.

Regular **direct trains** run west from Sundsvall to Östersund, for connections inland; and south to Stockholm via Hudiksvall, Söderhamn, Gävle, Uppsala and Arlanda airport. There are also very limited services north to Härnösand. To continue further north to Swedish Lapland, you'll have to time your departure carefully, since there's just one daily bus leaving Sundsvall at 10pm for Långsele, where there's a connection for the night train to Kiruna (arrival 9.48am), via Boden, Luleå and Gällivare.

To get to the **High Coast** or any of the **coastal towns** between Sundsvall and Luleå, it's a much better idea to travel by **bus**. **Norrlandskusten** services, bound for Luleå, begin their trek north at Sundsvall's bus station four times daily, with stops en route including Härnösand, Örnsköldsvik and Umeå. For more on getting to the High Coast, see p.378.

⑤

Härnösand and Sollefteå

Full of architectural delights, including a number of old wooden cottages dating from the 1730s, the town of **Härnösand** is definitely worth a stop on the way north. An hour's train or bus trip along the coast from Sundsvall, Härnösand marks the beginning of the stunningly beautiful county of **Ångermanland** – one of the few areas in Sweden where the countryside resembles that of neighbouring Norway. The coastline here, between Härnösand and Örnsköldsvik, is known as **Höga Kusten** (the High Coast, see p.976), with craggy shorelines, long fjords that reach far inland and low mountains – this is the most scenic coastal stretch in northern Sweden. Alternatively, you can go inland to **Sollefteå** and on to **Långsele** (see p.375) to connect up with the main line north to Swedish **Lapland**.

Härnösand and around

A pleasant little place at the mouth of the Ångerman river, **HÄRNÖSAND** was founded in 1585 by King Johan III. In 1647, the town was selected as the capital of the second most northerly diocese in Sweden and, accordingly, the new bishop decreed that the old stone church, which already stood in the town, be enlarged into a cathedral. The town has since had more than its fair share of disasters: in 1710, flames tore through the town after drunken churchgoers accidentally set fire to a boathouse; just four years after, Härnösand fell victim to a second great fire, started by a group of school students. Newly rebuilt, the town was razed by a third blaze in 1721, during the Great Northern War, when invading Russian forces burnt every house to the ground – bar one (see p.374).

Striking **architecture** awaits at every turn in Härnösand, notably around the harmonious main square, **Stora Torget** and winding **Östanbäcksgatan** with it's eighteenth-century wooden houses painted in gentle pastel shades. A short walk from the town centre, the extensive open-air museum at **Murberget** showcases vernacular architecture from around the country. If you tire of buildings head out of town to the peninsula and some of the county's best **beaches**.

Arrival, information and accommodation

The closest **airport**, with regular flights from Stockholm, is 34km south of Härnösand; you can get to the centre by airport bus (110kr) and taxi (around 525kr). Trains from Sundsvall and Stockholm at the **train station** on Järnvägsgatan, from where the **tourist office** is a couple of minutes' walk down the road at no. 2 (June–Aug Mon–Fri 9am–6pm, Sat & Sun 10am–2pm; Sept–May Mon–Fri 9am–4.30pm; ☏0611/881 40, ◍www.turism.harnosand .se), inside the building marked "Spiran". It has free maps, bus times and accommodation details for the town and further afield in Ångermanland, in particular, up the High Coast; there's also free **Internet** access here, as well as in the library, Sambibloteket, at Trädgårdsgatan 17. The **bus station** is east along Nybrogatan from the small roundabout in front of the train station.

The cheapest place to stay in town is the **youth hostel**, a fifteen-minute walk from the centre of town up Nybrogatan and then left (☏0611/104 46; mid-June to early Aug); it's located in a student village, **Statens Skola För Vuxna**, at Volontären 14. Staying here gets you a flat to yourself, complete with kitchen and bathroom for 120kr. The **campsite**, **Sälstens Camping** (☏0611/181 50), has a small selection of four-bed cabins for 300kr per person per night. It's around 2km northeast of the town centre, next to a string of pebble beaches; to get there, take Storgatan off Nybrogatan and follow the road as it swings eastwards along the coast. Of the town's three **hotels**, **Hotell Royal**, close to the train station at Strandgatan 12 (☏0611/204 55, ℻0611/267 90; ❸/❷) is the cheapest, while **Hotell City** at Storgatan 28 (☏0611/277 00, ◍www.kaju-tan.com; ❸/❷) is only marginally more expensive when discounted, though there's little to choose between the modern uninspired decor of both places. Much bigger and a lot plusher than either is the **First Hotel Härnösand**, at Skeppsbron 9, (☏0611/55 44 40, ◍www.firsthotels.com; ❻/❸).

The Town

For a small, provincial place, Härnösand reeks of grandeur and self-importance, each of its proud civic buildings a marker of the confidence the town exudes. The main square, **Stora Torget**, was once declared by local worthies as the most beautiful in Sweden and it's easy to see why – the western edge of the square is proudly given over to the governor's residence built in Neoclassical style using local brick by the court architect, Olof Tempelman. It rubs shoulders with the Neo-Renaissance former provincial government building on the southwestern edge. From the square take a stroll up Västra Kyrkogatan to the heights of the Neoclassical **Domkyrkan** (daily 10am–4pm), the smallest cathedral in the country. Dating from the 1840s, it incorporates elements from earlier churches on the site; the Baroque altar is from the eighteenth century, as are the VIP boxes in the nave.

From the Domkyrkan, turn right and follow the road round and back down the hill until you come to the narrow old street of **Östanbäcksgatan**, with its pretty painted wooden houses from the 1730s. This is one of the oldest parts of town, Östanbäcken, where the houses were among the first to be built after the Russian incursions. For a further taste of the town's architectural splendour, take a walk up the hilly main street, **Nybrogatan**: the Neoclassical pastel orange **Rådhuset** here, complete with white semicircular portico, originally served as a school and home to the diocesan governors; while further up the hill, at the corner of Brunnshusgatan, the headquarters of the county adminis-tration is particularly beautiful, housed in a Neo-Baroque and Art Nouveau building with a yellow ochre facade. From the top of Nybrogatan, there are good **views** back over the town and the water.

Murberget and the beaches

Whilst in town it's worth retracing your steps back down Nybrogatan to the train station, from where Stationsgatan (turning into Varvsallén) turns right, passing through the docks and past the terminal for the **ferry** to Vaasa in Finland on its way to the impressive **open-air museum** at **Murberget**

(June–Aug daily 11am–5pm; free), the second biggest in Sweden after Skansen (see p.86). It's a thirty-minute walk up here from the town centre, or, alternatively bus #2 runs hourly from Nybrogatan in front of the Rådhuset.

The first building to take up its location here was a bell tower, which was moved from the village of Ullånger on the High Coast to its current position in 1913. There are around eighty other buildings, most notably traditional Ångermanland farmhouses and the old Murberget church, once a popular venue for local weddings. Look out for the Rysstugan, the one and only wooden building to escape the devastating fire caused by the Russians in 1721. The nineteenth-century **Spjute Inn** here is still home to a restaurant, and also contains a skittle alley dating from 1910, where you can have a game. In the nearby **Länsmuseum** (County Museum; daily 11am–5pm; ⓦwww.ylm.se; free), there are worthy exhibitions showing how people settled the area two thousand years ago, as well as very dull displays of wheels, silver goblets and accordions from more modern times. Those with an interest in weaponry are in luck, though: the museum has a collection of weapons used by huntsmen, peasants and the military from the seventeenth, eighteenth and nineteenth centuries.

If the weather's good it's definitely worth heading in the opposite direction, east across the Härnön peninsula to **Smitingen**, barely 5km out of Härnösand, to some of the best **sandy beaches** in the whole of Norrland; undoubtedly the best way to get here is to **hire a boat** (80kr per half-day, 120kr for a whole day) and sail around the peninsula; book at the tourist office from where the boats are a 200m walk at Nattviken (the small bay behind the tourist office). It's also possible to take **bus** #14 from the bus station (4 daily; 15min), located on Nybrogatan opposite **McDonald's** just before the bridge across to the town. There are also **pebble beaches** near the Sälsten campsite, within walking distance of the town centre.

Eating, drinking and nightlife

The most popular **restaurant**, also a pub, is **Kajutan**, on the pedestrianized Storgatan, which links Stora Torget and Nybrogatan. It has special eat-as-much-as-you-can lunch deals for 89kr; otherwise reckon on 90kr for pasta, 145kr for something more meaty; a beer here costs around 48kr. A good place to **drink** and grab a bite to eat is **Highlander** at Nybrogatan 5, a Scottish theme pub (Tues–Sat from 6pm) with a surprisingly good-value menu – fried chicken with mozzarella and tortilla bread is just 98kr. To splash out, **Restaurang Apothequet**, Nybrogatan 3, is the place: its two-course set meals cost around 200kr. The restaurant is in an old pharmacy, which dates from 1909; on the ground floor there's also a bar, where locals ask for a glass of "medicine" at what was the pharmacist's counter. Other decent non-Swedish places to eat include **New China Restaurant**, in the centre of town at Storgatan 34, with Chinese (from 84kr) and Indonesian (from 120kr) dishes; the Greek **Mykonos**, at Storgatan 20, with moussaka for 95kr and garlic lamb steak with potatoes for 145kr; and **Östanbäckens Pizzeria**, Östanbäcksgatan 1, where pizzas cost around the 70kr mark. Härnösand has now finally joined the growing ranks of Swedish provincial towns to sport an **O'Leary's** – it's at Skeppsbron 9 – and is currently the most popular place to imbibe.

For a cup of coffee or good lunchtime dishes, head for the **Rutiga Dukan Café** at Västra Kyrkogatan 1, near the cathedral; here lunch goes for 65kr, and good home-baked pastries and apple pie are also on the menu. In summer, a refreshing place to sit with a coffee or a beer is **Café Skeppet & Restaurang**, a small wooden house which has a terrace overlooking the water; it's on Skeppsbron, by the bridge over to the train station. For **nightlife**, try the disco at **Kajutan** at Storgatan 28, though don't expect too much. The Saga **cinema**, at the junction of Storgatan and Nybrogatan, is your best bet for films.

Since all trains now terminate in Härnösand, your journey onwards from here must be either by bus, or more interestingly, by boat. A daily bus leaves the bus station at 10.45pm for **Långsele** where you can connect on to the night train **north** to Swedish Lapland. A much more picturesque way of heading for Långsele is to take a **boat** trip; departing from Skeppsbron, the *M/S Ådalen III* sails up the Ångerman river as far as **Sollefteå** (late June to mid-Aug; single trip 120kr; for information call ✆0612/505 41 or visit ⌨www.hogakustenturist.se), from where there are buses the short distance to Långsele. To head **west** or **south** from Härnösand, there are a handful of trains and frequent buses to Sundsvall, for connections inland; there's currently one through service from Härnösand to Stockholm. You can also fly to Stockholm from the Midlanda airport, 34km south of town, reachable by airport bus (110kr) and taxi (525kr).

To reach the beauty of the **High Coast** there are two options: one is to take the daily 8am Norrlandskusten express bus bound for Luleå; it passes through the tiny village of Docksta, from where a ferry sails for the island of Ulvön (see p.380). The bus also skirts round the Skuleskogen National Park with its excellent **hiking** opportunities. Much more enjoyable, though, is island-hopping up the coast (see p.378). All Norrlandskusten services leave from the bus station and operate daily via the High Coast to the coastal towns of Örnsköldsvik, Umeå, Skellefteå, Piteå and Luleå.

Sollefteå

Eighty kilometres northwest of Härnösand, **SOLLEFTEÅ** is an appealingly peaceful little town, beautifully located on the banks of the Ångerman river, which was once the main transport artery of the region, carrying logs from the great inland forests down to the sawmills on the coast. Although the practice ceased in the early 1960s, the river is still the focal point of the town and the location for the hydroelectric plant, right in the heart of the town. Arriving by road, you'll probably cross the river via the bridge on Kungsgatan, the main road north, affording good views of the Ångerman and the powerful **monument** of three log drivers, perched high on a stone pillar rising from the waters.

Today though, Swedes know Sollefteå for two things: the hometown of one of their most famous, and infamous, politicians, Mona Sahlin, a former deputy prime minister, who resigned amid a scandal linking use of her government credit card to the private purchase of nappies and chocolates for her young children; but, also, as the home of one of the country's best beers, Zeunerts. Indeed, the main thing to do whilst in town is visit the **brewery** (tours: mid-June to mid-Aug Tue 1pm & Fri 10am; 30kr) at the junction of Storgatan, Sollefteå's main street, and Bellevuevägen, a ten minute walk from the centre. Offering an insight into the different stages of the brewing process, the tours last roughly 1hr 15min and end with that very un-Swedish event – a free tasting.

From the brewery it's another ten minutes west along Storgatan, then left for a further five minutes or so on Route 90 to the junction with Kyrkvägen, to the elegant **Sollefteå kyrka** (June–Aug daily 7am–4.30pm; Sept–May daily 8am–dusk), on a small hill to the south of the town overlooking the river. This eighteenth-century church encompasses bits of the original medieval building within its shell; inside you'll find an eighteenth-century Rococo pulpit and a carved altarpiece. The separate wedding-cake bell tower is a later addition.

On the pedestrianized main street, the **tourist office**, at Storgatan 49 (June to mid-Aug Mon–Fri 9.30am–7pm, Sat & Sun 10am–2pm; mid-Aug to May Mon–Fri 9.30am–6pm, Sat 10am-1pm; ℡0620/68 29 00, Ⓦwww.solleftea.se/turism), has useful information on local hiking trails and the whole province of Ångermanland. You can get to the tourist office from the **bus station** (there are no longer any trains to Sollefteå) by following Kungsgatan downhill to its junction with Storgatan. **Buses** run every 1–2 hours between Sollefteå and Långsele, providing connections to and from Swedish Lapland. Arriving by **boat** from Härnösand, take Djupövägen (across the car park in front of the jetty) until it meets Storgatan and turn right; this will take you to the main square opposite the tourist office. The **airport** (℡0612/71 81 10, Ⓦwww.ksf.nu), shared with neighbouring industrial Kramfors and served by daily Skyways flights from Stockholm, is 30km southeast of the town, from where there are taxis into the centre (300kr) but no buses. **Internet** access is available (free) at the library at Storgatan 59.

The **youth hostel** (℡0620/158 17, Ⓦwww.hotellbjorklunden.com) shares its management with the adjacent **hotel**, the **Björklunden** (same contact details; ❷). To get to either, turn right out of the bus station and follow Storgatan east beyond the Zeunerts brewery, over the train tracks and the Bruksån river, turning left at the T-junction into Övergårdsvägen and finally right into Tegelvägen; it's about a two-kilometre walk. The tourist office itself has a few rooms and cabins for rent – ask there for the latest details and prices. Back in town, the cheapest place to stay is **Hotell Appelberg**, at Storgatan 51, which represents excellent value for money with its traditional-style rooms (℡0620/121 30, ℱ0620/121 58; ❷/❶). More up-market accommodation is nearby at **City Hotell**, Storgatan 47, with en-suite rooms and cable TV in every room (℡0620/167 00, ℱ0620/167 03; ❶). The town's **campsite** is the beautifully situated **Sollefteå Camping** (℡0620/68 25 42 or 68 25 43), right on the river and by far the most enjoyable place to stay; there are water slides and outdoor heated swimming pools on site. It has twelve four-bed **cabins**, with kitchen, for rent at around 300kr per cabin, though in July they cost 375kr. To get there, head down Kungsgatan, cross the river and head right.

Eating opportunities in Sollefteå are severely limited; for good pizza at reasonable prices, try **City 93** at Torggatan 4, opposite the tourist office, or for Chinese food there's **June Hine** at Storgatan 52 which has the usual run of meaty dishes for 85–95kr; at lunchtime there's **Dagens Rätt** for 60kr. The **pub** and restaurant, **Old House,** at the corner of Storgatan and Kungsgatan, is worth checking out for its agreeable atmosphere; while you're here, remember to try the local beer, Zeunerts.

Höga Kusten – the High Coast

Designated a UNESCO World Heritage Site in late 2000, **HÖGA KUSTEN** (Ⓦwww.visitmidsweden.com & Ⓦwww.highcoast.net), or the High Coast, is the highlight of any trip up the Bothnian Coast. This stretch of striking coastline between Härnösand and Örnsköldsvik is elementally beautiful: rolling mountains and verdant valleys plunge precipitously into the Gulf of Bothnia, and the rugged shoreline of sheer cliffs and craggy outcrops, gives way to gently undulating pebble coves. The dramatic landscape is the result of the rapid isostatic uplift that has occurred since the last Ice Age; as the ice melted, the land, no longer weighed down by ice up to three kilo-

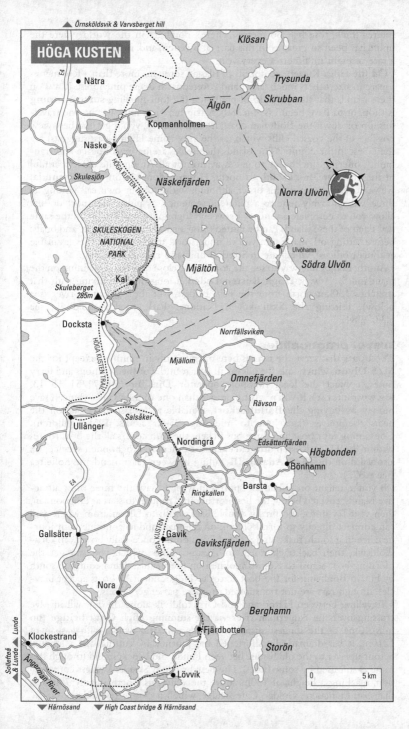

metres thick, rose by 286 metres. There's nowhere in the world where the uplift has been so great as in this part of Sweden, and, in fact, is still rising at a rate of eight millimetres every year.

Off the Höga Kusten are dozens of islands, some no more than a few metres square in size, others much larger and covered with dense pine forest. It was on these islands that the tradition of preparing the foul-smelling **surströmming** is thought to have begun (see p.380). A trip here is a must for anyone travelling up or down the Bothnian coast; from out at sea, you'll get the best view possible of the coastal cliffs which (as the very name High Coast suggests) are the tallest in the country. The islands themselves are havens of peace and tranquility, offering the chance to get away from it all. Among the most beautiful in the chain are, from south to north, **Högbonden**, **Ulvön** and **Trysunda**; we've covered them in this order, although without your own car, visiting all three will probably require a different sequence, as public transport doesn't allow you to complete a journey between Högbonden and Ulvön on the same day. Each of these islands can be visited using a combination of buses and boats; before setting off, make sure you've understood the boat timetables (available at tourist offices), which are in Swedish only and can be confusing.

Another enjoyable way to see the coastline at close quarters, remaining on the mainland, is to walk **Höga Kusten Leden**, a long-distance hiking path that stretches 130km north from the new bridge over the Ångerman river (see below), skirting the Skuleskogen National Park, to Örnsköldsvik; see p.383–384.

Travel practicalities

The **boats** that serve the islands here operate only in summer, except for the **M/S Ulvön**, which sails for Ulvön all year round. For the latest bus and ferry times, contact the local transport operator, Din Tur (☎0771/51 15 13, ⓦwww.dintur.se). If you're visiting more than one of the islands, you can save money by buying the **Båtluffarkort**, available at tourist offices or on the boats themselves (late June to mid-Aug; 250kr adults, 125kr children). Containing four boat and three bus tickets, the card covers all the boat routes within the Höga Kusten area except the Bönhamn–Högbonden service; it's also valid on the **M/S Ådalen III**, sailing between Härnösand and Sollefteå (see p.375).

If you're reliant on public transport and want to visit the three most attractive islands, covered below, the best northbound route is to start at Högbonden, then visit Trysunda, and finally double back south to Ulvön, from where you can connect directly to Örnsköldsvik on the mainland to continue your journey; heading south, make straight for Ulvön on the once-daily boat from Örnsköldsvik, then backtrack north to Trysunda, after which you can get the morning boat across to Köpmanholmen on the mainland and continue south by bus to Bönhamn for the boat across to Högbonden. All boats accept bicycles, though cars are not transported on these passenger vessels.

Travelling between Härnösand and Örnsköldsvik along the E4 will involve crossing over the Ångerman river via the stunning High Coast **bridge** (no tolls). One of the longest suspension bridges in the world, with a span of 1210m, it has dramatically shortened the journey by cutting out a lengthy detour upriver to the old bridge between Lunde and Klockestrand (though this route is still used by some buses). The new bridge is Sweden's tallest construction, reaching a height of 180m above the water; its length is only 70m less than San Francisco's Golden Gate Bridge, which it closely resembles.

Högbonden

After a mere ten-minute boat ride from Bönhamn on the mainland, the steep sides of the tiny island of **Högbonden** rise up in front of you. Though the island can feel a little overcrowded in peak season, as dozens of people come over on day-trips, at its best, the place is a wonderfully deserted, peaceful haven. There are no shops – so bring any provisions you'll need with you – and no hotels on the island; in fact the only building here is a former lighthouse, now converted into a **youth hostel** (see below). It's situated on a rocky plateau at the island's highest point, where the pine and spruce trees, so prominent else-where on the island, have been unable to get a foothold; Högbonden's flora also includes rowan, sallow, aspen and birch trees, as well as various mosses that compete for space with wild bilberries.

You'll only get to know the special charm of Högbonden if you stay a cou-ple of nights and take time to explore: a narrow gorge runs north–south across the island, and there are also forested hillsides and a shoreline where eider ducks glide by with their young. The **views** out across the Gulf of Bothnia are stunning; on a sunny day you could easily imagine you're in the middle of the Mediterranean. At any time, you can head for the traditional **wood-burning sauna** down by the sea, two minutes' walk from the jetty (it's signposted "**bastu**" off the island's one and only path); you'll need to book your slot with the youth hostel staff, who keep the sauna's key. The logs, which fuel the fire, are piled behind the sauna; if it's been raining, you'll need to pick out some of the driest ones from underneath. If no one's used the sauna for several hours, you may need to restart the fire: matches will start it off, and putting some newspaper in the burner will help get it going. Afterwards, you can take a quick skinny-dip in the cool waters of the Gulf of Bothnia. The sunsets, seen from the boardwalk in front of the sauna, are truly idyllic.

Practicalities

Sailing from the mainland village of **Bönhamn**, the **M/F Högbonden** makes the ten-minute trip out to Högbonden (mid-June to mid-Aug daily 10am, noon, 3pm & 6pm; 70kr return). To get to Bönhamn by car, turn off the E4 at Gallsäter onto the minor road leading there via Nordingrå. The ferry doesn't take cars, so you'll need to leave your vehicle in Bönhamn. To get to Bönhamn on public transport **from Härnösand**, take the 11am Norrlandskusten bus to Ullånger (45min), where you change for a connection at 12.20pm to Nordingrå; once there, catch the once-daily connecting bus at 12.45pm to Bönhamn (mid-June to mid-Aug weekdays only). To head straight for Högbonden **from Stockholm**, take the 6.25am train to Sundsvall, where you can change for the direct Norrlandskusten bus to Ullånger, then follow the route described above. Heading for Högbonden **from Trysunda**, take the 9.15am boat to Köpmanholmen, and from there the 10am bus to Örnsköldsvik, departing there for Ullånger at 11.45pm; at 12.20pm take the bus from Ullånger to Nordingrå, where you change again for the 12.45pm bus to Bönhamn.

Högbonden's **youth hostel** is in the former lighthouse (☎0613/230 05, ⊛www.hogbonden.se; May–Oct; advance bookings necessary at other times of the year), reached by several sets of steep wooden steps from the path that begins at the jetty. Inside the building there is a kitchen, two bathrooms and two decent sized dorms (with creaking floorboards) though if the hostel is full, you may find that the separate-sex rule which normally applies is waived to accommodate as many guests as possible. To add to the novelty of sleeping in a converted lighthouse, the building's clifftop vantage point affords sweeping sea views from the kitchen and the dorms. If you fancy a dip in the sea before breakfast, head through the forest and down to the shoreline. A word of warning though: from July to mid-Aug the island can be busy with daytrippers so if you're looking for peace and tranquillity it's probably wise to avoid the peak Swedish holiday season.

Ulvön

ULVÖN (⊛www.ulvon.com), 20km northeast of Högbonden and 12km southwest of Trysunda, is really two islands, Norra and Södra Ulvön, their combined area making it the largest in the High Coast archipelago. The southern island is uninhabited, separated from its northern neighbour by a narrow channel, Ulvösund, which provides a well-protected harbour. During the seventeenth and eighteenth centuries, Ulvön became home to the High Coast's biggest fishing community, as fishermen from Gävle came here to exploit the rich fishing grounds off the island; in subsequent centuries, though, many islanders moved to the mainland, especially after World War II, when the industry started to decline. Today, there are only around fifty permanent residents.

Ulvön is famous for its production of **surströmming**, fermented Baltic herring (see box); two of the firms involved, Söderbergs Fisk and Ruben Madsén, are based in the main village of Ulvöhamn (see opposite) and it's possible to buy the locally produced stuff in the island's shops.

Travel practicalities

To reach Ulvön **from Härnösand**, take the 9am bus to the village of **Docksta**. There's an **STF hostel** here, 3km south of the village (☎0613/130 64, ⊛www.dockstavandrarhem.nu; mandatory advance bookings Sept to late May), though you probably won't need to use it; the bus will drop you by the Docksta jetty, from where the **M/S Kusttrafik** leaves at 10.15am (June–Aug daily; ☎0613/105 50, ⊛www.hkship.se; 95kr one-way), arriving in **Ulvöhamn**, on Ulvön, at 11.30am, heading back to the mainland at 3pm.

Surströmming

Mention the word **surströmming** to most Swedes and they'll turn up their noses in disgust. It's best translated as "fermented Baltic herring" – though to the non-connoisseur, the description "rotten" would seem more appropriate. The tradition of eating the foul-smelling stuff began on Ulvön sometime during the sixteenth century when salt was very expensive; as a result just a little was used in preserving the fish, a decision which inadvertently allowed it to ferment.

The number of **salthouses** producing the herring has dwindled from several hundred early in the twentieth century to around twenty to thirty manufacturers now. Today, *surströmming* is made in flat tins containing a weak salt solution. Over the course of the four- to ten-week fermentation process, the tins blow up into the shape of a soccer ball under the pressure of the odious gases produced inside. Restaurants refuse to open the tins on the premises because of the lingering stink that's exuded, not unlike an open sewer; the unpleasant job has to be done outside in the fresh air.

The **season** for eating *surströmming* begins on the third Thursday in August, ending around two to three weeks later, when supplies run out. The fish can accompanied with the yellow, almond-shaped variety of northern Swedish potatoes and washed down with beer or *akvavit*; alternatively it's put into a sandwich, perhaps with onion or tomato, all rolled up in a piece of *tunnbröd*, the thin unleavened bread traditional in this part of the country.

Ulvön is easily reached all year round **from Trysunda**, via Köpmanholmen, on the **M/F Ulvön** (☎0660/29 90 21, ✆www.ornskoldsvik.se/oviksbuss/mfulvon/turlista; 2hr 30min; 40kr one-way). Sailings are roughly twice daily on weekdays, at 9.15am and 6.20pm, and once daily at weekends. Better and faster is the once-daily direct service on the **M/F Otilia II**, which takes an hour to reach Ulvön from Trysunda; it departs **from Örnsköldsvik** for Sandviken and Ulvöhamn, via Bockviken on Trysunda (late June to early Aug daily; 2hr 30min; ☎0660/22 34 31; 70kr one-way). The boat leaves Örnsköldsvik at 9.30am, returning from Ulvöhamn at 3pm.

Ulvöhamn

All boats to the island dock at the main village, **ULVÖHAMN**, a picturesque one-street affair with red and white cottages and tiny boathouses on stilts snuggling up eave to eave. Walking along the waterfront, you'll pass the pretty fishermen's chapel, dating from 1622 and now the oldest wooden building in Ångermanland (June–Aug daily 1.45–2.15pm); inside, its walls are covered with flamboyant eighteenth-century murals. The church was established by Gävle fishermen who began summer fishing forays up the Baltic coast in the sixteenth century. Its detached bell tower was once used to signal that it was time to assemble for the daily fishing trip. To get to the **beaches**, follow the sign marked "Strandpromenaden" from the village shop (see below); it's about ten minutes by bike past small sandy coves to the harbour entrance and a promontory of red rocks, Rödharen, beyond which lie several pebbly stretches. The unusual red rock here is a granite known by its Finnish name, **rappakivi**.

The **tourist office** is in a tiny wooden hut (mid-June to mid-Aug daily 11am–3.30pm; ☎0660/23 40 93), a short distance from the quay where the **M/S Kusttrafik** from Docksta puts in. You can **rent bikes** here (30kr for 4hr) and pick up information about the **Ulvön Regatta**, an annual gathering for ostentatious yachting types that takes place in July. The island's only **hotel**, **Ulvö Skärgårdshotell**, is just to the right of the quay as you come off the boat (☎0660/22 40 09, ✆22 40 78; ❸; June–Aug); it has cosy, modern rooms with good views of the sea. At the other end of the road from the hotel is the jetty where the **M/S Otilia II** puts in; the village **shop** is here too. To get to the non-STF **youth hostel**, about 2km from the harbour, take the road, just beyond the chapel midway between the jetties, that leads uphill to the right (☎0660/22 41 90; late May to mid-Aug). Pine **cabins** with cooking facilities can be rented (☎0660/22 40 14 or ☎22 41 57; early June to mid-Aug 650kr for one night, 2490kr per week; Sept–May 450kr for one night, 1990kr per week); there are four four-bed cabins at Fiskeläget, just by the village shop, with fantastic views out over the harbour and the bay; and ten four-bed cabins at Fäbodvallen, a ten-minute walk up the hill behind the harbour. Residents at the latter can use the **hälsohus**, a small health spa, containing a sauna, Jacuzzi and solarium.

For **eating**, there's the **Almagränd** restaurant, with its limited menu, near the tourist office; and the excellent restaurant at **Ulvö Skärgårdshotell**, with main courses from 100kr; or, for light snacks, **Café Måsen** (11am–3pm only). If you are self-catering, the village shop, at the southern end of Ulvöhamn's main street, has a decent array of provisions. There's a pleasant **pub** below the hotel that buzzes in summer. Out of season, you'll have no choice but to self-cater since all eateries close down for the winter.

Sandviken

To get to the island's second village, **SANDVIKEN**, take the road to the youth hostel and continue out of town, past Ulvön's cemetery on a tiny island in the middle of a lake. About 5km further from the hostel, over a few hills, lies Sandviken, a fishing village for over three hundred years, now restored to its seventeenth-century prime, its unpainted wooden cabins standing in a row. You can also get here on **M/S Otilia II**, which puts in at Sandviken fifteen minutes after sailing from Ulvöhamn for Örnsköldsvik; the same boat, heading from Örnsköldsvik, can take you back to Ulvöhamn. With its long, peaceful beach, Sandviken is certainly the place to come if you want to get away from it all.

For a place to **stay**, there are fourteen small cottages (300kr a night, 1800kr a week) and eight boathouses (300kr a night, 2050kr a week) on the beach which function as a sort of tiny holiday resort for about six weeks from the end of June – both the cottages and the boathouses sleep four. There are toilets, showers and a wood-burning sauna in the service building plus a small kiosk that sells limited provisions, including smoked fish, and rents out **cycles**. To book accommodation here, call ☎0660/752 23 or 22 40 33.

Trysunda

The charming fishing village of **TRYSUNDA**, on the tiny island of the same name, is the best preserved in Ångermanland, hemmed in around a narrow U-shaped harbour, with forty or so red-and-white houses right on the waterfront. The village's wooden chapel, which is usually unlocked, is one of the oldest on the Bothnian coast, dating from around 1655. Like the church on neighbouring Ulvön, the interior is decorated with colourful murals.

Trysunda is crisscrossed with walking paths, leading through the forests of dwarf pine that cover the island – many of which have become gnarled and twisted under the force of the wind. The island's gently sloping rocks make it ideal for bathing, and you'll find plenty of secluded spots where you can do so. There's a **sandy beach** at **Björnviken**, a bay on the eastern part of the island, and some smooth rocks on the north coast, just to the east of **Bockviken**, where **M/S Otilia** from Örnsköldsvik puts in. An easily walked path from the village will take you to both beaches and round the entire island in an hour or two. To continue east from Björnviken, don't be tempted to strike off round the headland, as the rocks there are impassable; instead, stay on the path, which cuts inland, and follow the signs for Storviken.

As you approach or leave the island, you might be lucky enough to catch a glimpse of elk on the neighbouring island, the volcanic and uninhabited **Skrubban**. Although the island has been a nature reserve since 1940, every year some hunting is allowed to control the animal population and prevent unnecessary suffering from starvation, a practice followed elsewhere in Sweden too.

Practicalities

The **M/S Otilia II** sails here **from Ulvön** and **Örnsköldsvik** (summer 1 daily; 60kr). Heading here from **Högbonden**, you'll need to get to **Köpmanholmen**, from where you can catch the twice-daily ferry to Trysunda; regular buses connect Örnsköldsvik and Köpmanholmen. From Högbonden, take the 1.45pm bus from Bönhamn to Nordingrå (Mon–Fri), where you change for the bus to Gallsäter at 2.35pm. There's a connection at 4pm north from Gallsäter to Bjästa where you change again to catch the bus to Köpmanholmen at 4.55pm, from where the ferry leaves for Trysunda at 5.40pm (30kr; 50min). The journey isn't as complicated as it may sound; in fact every bus on your route will know you're coming because each driver is informed by radio of connecting passengers.

For **accommodation** on Trysunda, seven simple **rooms** (℡0660/430 29 or ℡430 38; ❶; June–Sept) are available in the service building of the small marina at the harbour entrance; three rooms have four beds (360kr per room per night, 2160kr per week), another three have three beds (290kr per night, 1740kr per week), and the remaining room sleeps two (200kr per night, 1200kr per week). There's a kitchen and a sauna in the same building. There are also two **cabins** for rent: one, with a kitchen and hot and cold water, is located close to the village shop by the marina and sleeps six (400kr per night, 2400kr per week); the other, which has no electricity or running water, stands by itself in one of the island's bays and also sleeps six in one room (200kr per night, 1200kr per week). Both the rooms and the cabins can be booked at the village shop (Mon–Sat 9am–8pm, Sun 10am–6pm; ℡0660/430 11 or 430 38), where you can also buy the bare necessities, including fresh and smoked fish, and the dreaded **surströmming**. Ask at the shop for their free map of the island.

The High Coast Trail and Skuleskogen National Park

It's possible to walk the entire length of the High Coast along **Höga Kusten Leden**, or High Coast Trail, which stretches 130km from the High Coast bridge at the mouth of the Ångerman river to **Varvsberget**, the hill overlooking the centre of Örnsköldsvik. The trail is divided into thirteen stages, which vary in difficulty and length (all are between 7km and 15km long); see overleaf for details. There's accommodation at each break between stages, mostly in the form of cabins. The buses between Härnösand and Örnsköldsvik stop very close to several stages along the way: Lappudden, Ullånger, Skoved, Skule Naturum (for Skuleberget) and Köpmanholmen. For more **information** on the trail, contact the tourist offices in Härnösand or Örnsköldsvik (see p.372 and p.385), both of which sell the excellent **Small Map Book for the High Coast**, which includes not only good maps of the region but also detailed descriptions of the trail (60kr). For more general guidance on the do's and don'ts of hiking in Sweden, see p.487.

Skuleskogen National Park

The High Coast Trail takes in the eastern edge of the magnificent, 26-square-kilometre **Skuleskogen National Park**, noted for its dense evergreen forests, coastal panoramas and deep ravines. Its main sight is the gorge known as Slåtterdalsskrevan, located at the eastern edge close to the coast; though only 200m long and 7m wide, it's 40m deep.

The park is home to a rich mix of **flora and fauna**, including many varieties of bird. Woodpeckers thrive here, alongside the grey-headed, black, three-toed, lesser spotted, greater spotted and even the rare whitebacked woodpecker. All four of Sweden's forest game birds, namely the capercaillie, hazelhen, black grouse and willow grouse, are also found here, along with other birds such as the wren, coal tit and crested tit. Among the numerous forest animals in the park are elk, roe deer, lynx, fox, gopher, stoat, pine marten, mink, mountain hare and red squirrel. Spruce is the dominant tree here; some of the large, mature specimens have regenerated naturally after logging ended one hundred years ago. Half of the park consists of bare stone outcrops, home only to a few gnarled and stunted pines – some of these trees are over five hundred years old. You'll also see the slow-growing long beard lichen (**Usnea longissima**), which is entirely dependent on old spruce trees, on whose branches it's found.

Stages in the High Coast Trail

Below, we list the thirteen sections of the High Coast Trail, with accommodation details for each. Most parts of the trail can be easily covered by anyone of average health, but where we've described a section as "demanding", you'll need to be pretty fit in order to complete it. Further details of each stage are given in the booklet *Walking Guide to The High Coast Path* (40kr), available in both English and Swedish at tourist offices.

High Coast Bridge–Sör–Lövvik (9.3km; demanding). Cabins with kitchen at Sjöbodviken. **Lövvik–Fjärdbotten** (9.6km; moderate). Four wooden cabins at Fjärdbotten by the promontory at Häggnäset.
Fjärdbotten–Gavik (12.8km; demanding). Cabin Nipstugan Lidnipan for a maximum of five or six people.
Gavik–Lappudden (11.5km; easy). Six cabins available in Lappudden on the edge of the Vågfjärden.
Lappudden–Ullånger (15km; demanding). *Hotell Erikslund* (℡0613/104 75).
Ullånger–Skoved (10.5km; average). Cabins on the beach at Lake Mäjasjön; no cooking facilities.
Skoved–Skule Naturum (6.8km; easy). Youth hostel in Docksta at Dockstavägen 47 (Sept to mid-May advance bookings only; ℡0613/130 64, ℻403 91; 100kr; open all year), complete with sauna.
Skule Naturum–Käl (9.2km; moderate). Cabins at Bergsbodarna, 5km north of Skuleberget mountain; a path leads there from Skule Naturum.
Käl–Näske (8.5km; demanding). Passes through wilderness. Simple hut by Lake Tärnettvattnet in Skuleskogen National Park.
Näske–Köpmanholmen (7km; easy). Youth hostel in Köpmanholmen by the ferry quay (℡0660/22 34 96; 100kr; May–Sept; rest of year book in advance on ℡0660/22 37 64).
Köpmanholmen–Sandlågan (12.3km; demanding). One cabin at Bodviken in the Balesudden nature reserve.
Sandlågan–Svedjeholmen (12km; moderate). Restored farm storehouse at Småtjärnarna.
Svedjeholmen–Varvsberget (5.5km; easy). Accommodation in Örnsköldsvik (see opposite).

Leading inland through the park are a number of well-marked paths off the High Coast trail that take you past some wonderful, if very steep, countryside. You can also go **mountain climbing** in Skuleskogen; trails up **Skuleberget** (285m), near Docksta, afford stunning views from the top, and anyone in normal shape can make it safely to the summit; for the less-energetically minded a **cable car** (mid-June to mid-Aug daily 9am–6pm; 50kr) also makes the ascent. Skule Naturum nature centre (see below) at the foot of the mountain rents out equipment for serious climbing and offers sound advice from experts.

Örnsköldsvik

Just beyond the northern edge of the High Coast, and about 110km north of Härnösand, lies the port of **ÖRNSKÖLDSVIK** (usually shortened to Ö-vik). A busy, modern place stacked behind a superbly sheltered deep-water harbour, Örnsköldsvik began life as a market town in 1842 (when it was known as Köping), becoming a city in 1894. The town's present name comes from that of the eighteenth-century county governor, Per Abraham Örnsköld; the ending "-**vik**" simply means "bay". Try not to get stuck in Örnsköldsvik, since a night spent here can be a pretty depressing experience: bars and restaurants are thin on the ground, and the streets are virtually empty after 8pm. Much better is to head 100km north to buzzing Umeå, or south to the beautiful High Coast or the architectural delights of Härnösand.

Things will, however, undoubtedly improve once the new **Botniabanan** railway, linking the town to Härnösand and Umeå, opens in 2008. Building work is continuing apace across town and the new railway station will be constructed at the foot of the Varvsberget hill.

Arrival, information and accommodation

The **bus station** is on Strandgatan, right in the centre and **boats** to and from Trysunda and Ulvön dock at the Arken quay, in front of the bus station. For the time being, the nearest **train station** is about 30km to the northwest in **Mellansel**, on the main line from Stockholm to Swedish Lapland; to get into town, get a Tågtaxi (train-taxi), which you need to book in advance by calling ☎0660/104 00. A ten-minute walk from the bus station is the **tourist office** at Nygatan 18 (mid-June to mid-Aug Mon–Fri 9am–7pm, Sat 10am–3pm, Sun 10am–3pm; mid-Aug to mid-June Mon–Fri 10am–5pm; ☎0660/881 00, ⓦwww.ornskoldsvik.se), where you can get free town maps, bus and boat schedules and accommodation information for both the city and the Höga Kusten islands. It's a ten-minute walk to the tourist office from the bus station: head up the steps by the side of the terminal building, following the sign marked "Turistbyrå"; then cross Lasarettsgatan into Fabriksgatan, which you head down until the junction with Nygatan, where you turn right. There's free **Internet** access at the library on the corner of Lasarettsgatan and Torggatan.

Among the most central of Örnsköldsvik's **hotels** is **Strand City Hotell**, a cheap and cheerful hostel-like establishment at Nygatan 2 (☎0660/106 10, ⓕ21 13 05; ❸/❷). The swanky exterior of the **First Hotel Statt** (☎0660/881 00, ⓦwww.firsthotels.com; ❺/❸), down the road at no. 2, is a sign of what's waiting inside in the expensive chain-hotel rooms. The **youth hostel** is in Överhörnäs, 7km to the southwest (☎ & ⓕ0660/702 44); to get there, take the local bus for Köpmanholmen from the bus station, and tell the driver where you're going.

The town

A tour of the town will occupy you for no more than a couple of hours: Örnsköldsvik holds little of appeal. The city's only saving grace is its **museum** at Läroverksgatan 1 (Tues–Sun noon–4pm; 20kr), five minutes from the tourist office. You can ignore its predictable collections of prehistoric finds, nineteenth-century furniture and town history, and ask instead to be let into the adjacent workshop, which conceals a sparkling documentation of the work of **Bror Marklund**, a twentieth-century artist who was born in 1907 in the nearby town of Husum. Most of his art was commissioned for public spaces and goes unnoticed by passers-by; for example, his **Thalia** – a sculpture of the goddess of the theatre – rests outside Malmö's City Theatre, and his figures adorn the facade of the Historical Museum in Stockholm. On his death in 1977, he left his plaster models and sketches to the local municipality; inside the workshop, look for the plaster casts used to make one of his best-known works – the wonderful jesters which now decorate the hospital in Sundsvall. An English-language commmentary played through loudspeakers, detailing all the work on display, is available by pressing a button just inside the entrance.

The liveliest part of town is the **harbourside**, a pleasant place to eat or drink, or stroll past the old warehouses. For further relaxation or some exercise, you might want to visit the indoor **swimming complex**, Paradisbadet (June to early Aug Mon–Fri 10am–7pm, Sat & Sun 10am–5pm; rest of year Mon–Thurs 10am–8pm, Fri 10am–9.30pm, Sat & Sun 10am–5.30pm; ☎0660/885 90, ⊛www.paradisbadet.nu), off Centralesplanaden behind the bus station, boasting Sweden's longest water slide at 100 metres, a 25-metre indoor pool, Jacuzzis, a sauna, and a heated outdoor pool.

Eating, drinking and entertainment

The best **café** in Ö-vik is undoubtedly **Café Brittas II,** in the pedestrianized Storgatan, with a homely feel and home-made cakes and bread. For snacks, check out **Brittas Delikatesser** at Skolgatan 4, serving sandwiches and pies.

There are a number of pizza **restaurants** in the city centre: the best are **Il Padrino** on Läroverksgatan, a dark and dingy little place just off Stora Torget, with pizzas for around 70kr, pasta at 85kr and steaks from 170kr, and the much larger **Restaurangen Mamma Mia**, with outdoor seating on Storgatan and a yard where people play boules in summertime – pizzas here are around 65kr, pasta dishes 85kr. For more stylish eating and drinking, head for the lively harbourside, where restaurants with outdoor tables offer good views out over the water of Örnsköldsviksfjärden. **Church Street Saloon**, an American Western theme restaurant, feels very much out of place but is worth a stop if you feel like large portions of something-and-chips, for around 160kr. Among the handful of **drinking** holes, the best are the brasserie-style place, **Harry's**, next to the harbour, which also does tasty bar meals, and **O'Leary's** at Storgatan 24, an Irish-style sports pub with the same Tex-Mex style menu to others in the chain. Having exhausted the town's few attractions seek out the **cinema** at Köpmangatan 3 which generally screens the latest releases a few weeks after Stockholm.

Umeå and around

UMEÅ is the biggest city in the north of Sweden, with a current population of 105,000 people which means that an astonishing one in ten of the residents of Norrland (see p.357) live here. Demographically speaking, it's probably Sweden's youngest city, a notion borne out by taking a stroll round the airy modern centre: you'll form the impression that anyone who's not in a pushchair is pushing one, and that the cafés and city parks are full of teenagers. Indeed one in five people are in their twenties, figures that are partly due to the presence of Norrland University. Its youthfulness may well be responsible for the fact that Umeå is the only town or city in northern Sweden where there's an air of dynamism: new restaurants and bars are opening all the time, there's a thriving cultural scene, and by 2008, the **Botniabanan** high-speed rail link to Stockholm should be completed, making it possible to reach the capital in just five and a half hours.

With its fast-flowing river – a feature few other Swedish coastal cities enjoy – and wide, stylish boulevards, Umeå is an appealing metropolis. It would be no bad idea to spend a couple of days here, sampling some of its bars and restaurants – the variety of which you won't find anywhere else in Norrland.

Arrival and information

Trains from Stockholm, Gothenburg and Swedish Lapland arrive at the **train station**, at the northern end of the city centre on Järnvägsallén. Opposite is the

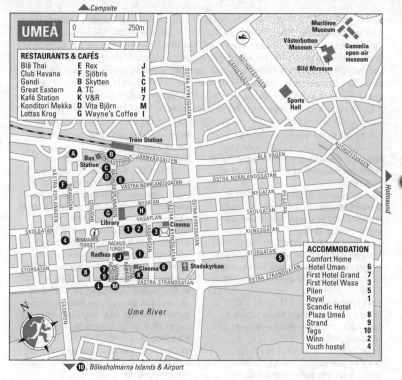

UMEÅ   0   250m

RESTAURANTS & CAFÉS

Blå Thai	E	Rex	J
Club Havana	F	Sjöbris	L
Gandi	B	Skytten	C
Great Eastern	A	TC	H
Kafé Station	K	V&R	7
Konditori Mekka	D	Vita Björn	M
Lottas Krog	G	Wayne's Coffee	I

ACCOMMODATION

Comfort Home Hotel Uman	6
First Hotel Grand	7
First Hotel Wasa	3
Pilen	5
Royal	1
Scandic Hotel Plaza Umeå	8
Strand	9
Tegs	10
Winn	2
Youth hostel	4

long-distance **bus station** used by services from Dorotea, Vilhelmina and Östersund, and by the Norrlandskusten buses. The city centre is a ten-minute walk south from here. Six kilometres from the city is Umeå's busy **airport**, with direct flights to and from Stockholm, Kiruna, Luleå and Östersund; it's linked with the centre by airport buses (30kr) and taxis (110kr). RG Line and Botnialink ferries from Vaasa in Finland dock at Holmsund, 20km from Umeå, from where connecting buses run inland to Umeå.

The city centre is easy to get around on foot, and many of its streets are pedestrianized, including the main east–west drag, Kungsgatan. A good first stop is the **tourist office** in Renmarkstorget (May to mid-June & mid-Aug to late Sept Mon–Fri 10am–6pm, Sat 10am–2pm; mid-June to mid-Aug Mon–Fri 8am–7pm, Sat 10am–5pm, Sun 11am–5pm; Oct–April Mon–Fri 10am–5pm; ☎090/16 16 16, ⓦwww.umea.se), a concrete square whose ugliness is at odds with its romantic name, meaning "reindeer-country square". The helpful staff here dish out assorted literature, including a free multilingual newspaper, **Umeåguiden**, with detailed listings of local events. From the train and bus stations, it's a ten-minute walk down the main north–south thoroughfare, Rådhusesplanaden, to the square.

Accommodation

The tourist office will book **private rooms** from 170kr per night (booking fee 25kr). Umeå boasts one of the best STF establishments in the bright and airy **youth hostel**, centrally located at Västra Esplanaden 10, just 450m from the stations (☎090/77 16 50, ⊛www.vandrarhemmet.se). The nearest **campsite** is **Umeå Camping Stugby** (☎090/70 26 00, ℗090/70 26 10), 5km from town on the shore of a lake beside the E4 at **Nydala**. Open all year, it has **cabins** for four to six people (685kr a night per cabin), individual double rooms in other cabins (❶) and **trätält** (tiny two-bed huts; ❶); washing machines are also available. To get there, take buses #67 or #69, get off at Nydala and walk for around five minutes towards Nydalabadet, which is signposted.

Umeå has a good selection of central **hotels**, the like of which you won't experience anywhere north of here; in short, splash out and treat yourself.

Comfort Home Hotel Uman Storgatan 52 ☎090/12 72 20, ℗090/12 74 20. Home from home, with evening coffee and newspapers for all guests. Not recommended if you want to be left alone. ❺/❸

First Hotel Grand Storgatan 46 ☎090/77 88 70, ⊛www.firsthotels.com. A relatively chic, newly renovated hotel, right in the heart of town overlooking the river. ❺/❸

First Hotel Wasa Vasagatan 12 ☎090/77 85 40, ⊛www.firsthotels.com. A comfortable hotel with modern rooms, in a lively central location, though its rooms have that tired chain-hotel feel to them. ❺/❸

Pilen Pilgatan 5 ☎090/14 14 60, ℗13 42 58. One of the smaller, cheaper hotels, with clean, basic rooms, and weekend and summer discounted rates of 500kr. ❷

Royal Skolgatan 64 ☎090/10 07 30, ⊛www.royalhotelumea.com. A good, centrally located hotel, with modern rooms, a sauna,

Jacuzzi and solarium. Summer discounts make this one a real steal. ❺/❸

Scandic Hotel Plaza Umeå Storgatan 40 ☎090/205 6300, ⊛www.scandic-hotels.com. For a treat, head for this very smart place which is popular with business travellers. There are superb views from the fourteenth-floor sauna suite which is worth a stay in itself. ❻/❹

Strand Västra Strandgatan 11 ☎090/70 40 00, ℗090/70 40 90. A perfectly adequate budget-class hotel, though make sure you get a room overlooking the river to make it worth it. ❹/❷

Tegs Verkstadsgatan 5 ☎090/12 27 00, ℗13 49 90. The cheapest hotel in town but south of the river (less than 30mins on foot from the centre) and some way from the action. Discounted rooms are just 460kr, but correspondingly dingy. ❷/❶

Winn Skolgatan 64 ☎090/71 11 00, ℗090/71 11 50. Close to the bus station, and good for nearby restaurants and bars, although the traffic noise can be obtrusive. ❺/❸

The City

The sound of the **rapids** along the Ume river gives the city its name: **uma** means "roar". Umeå is sometimes also referred to as the "City of Birch Trees", after the trees that were planted along every street after a devastating fire in 1888. Most of the city was burnt to the ground in the blaze, and two-thirds of the town's three thousand inhabitants lost their homes. In the rebuilding which soon began apace, two wide esplanades, one of which is Rådhusesplanaden, were constructed to act as fire breaks and help prevent such a disaster happening again. A decree was then handed down stating that the birch was the most suitable tree to add life to the town's newly reconstructed streets; even today, the city council places ads for free trees in the local papers and provides free birch saplings every spring to anyone who wants them.

Most visitors to Umeå make an immediate beeline for the city's excellent museum complex, **Gammlia**, home to a terrific collection of exhibitions on everything from photojournalism to skiing. In summer, the open-air section even has people dressed in period costume going about their daily tasks much as their predecessors did several centuries ago. When the weather's fine, you'll also find people relaxing on the **Bölesholmarna** islands in the river. Whilst in Umeå don't miss the opportunity, though, to take a trip to the **elk farm** in nearby Bjurholm where you can come face to face with these elusive creatures.

The Gammlia museum area

The highlight of Umeå is undoubtedly its terrific museum complex, **Gammlia**, which merits a good half-day's exploration. It's a twenty-minute walk from the train or bus stations: head east along Järnvägsallén and turn left into Östra Kyrkogatan, crossing under the railway tracks. After the bridge, turn right into Hemvägen, which after its junction with Rothoffsvägen becomes Gammliavägen, leading to the museum.

Gammlia grew out of the **Friluftsmuseum** (mid-June to mid-Aug daily 10am–5pm; ⓦwww.vasterbottensmuseum.se; free), an open-air cluster of twenty regional buildings, the oldest of which is the seventeenth-century gatehouse you pass on the way in. The grounds are home to the customary farmyard animals – cows, pigs, geese and the like – and the guides dressed in period costume are very willing to tell you about life in their mock town. It all helps to create a rural ambience including a windmill, church, two threshing floors and a smokehouse for pork. At the bakery, there are demonstrations of how to make the thin unleavened bread, **tunnbröd**, that used to be baked in people's homes. You can also take a ride through the grounds in a horse-drawn carriage, an experience that's bound to entertain kids.

The indoor **Västerbottens Museum** (mid-June to mid-Aug daily 10am–5pm; rest of year Tues–Fri 10am–4pm, Sat noon–4pm, Sun noon–5pm; 20kr; ⓦwww.vasterbottensmuseum.se) houses Gammlia's main collection: three exhibitions that canter through the county's past, from prehistoric times (the section on this period contains the oldest ski in the world, over five thousand years old) to the Industrial Revolution. It's all good stuff, well laid out and complemented by an array of videos and recordings; a useful English guidebook is available at reception.

Housed in the same building as Västerbotten Museum but run by Umeå university is the **Bildmuséet** (mid-June to mid-Aug noon–5pm; rest of year Tues noon–8pm, Wed–Sat noon–4pm, Sun noon–5pm; free; ⓦwww.umu.se/bildmuseet), which houses interesting displays of contemporary Swedish and international art, photojournalism and visual design.

Back outside, you can resume your exploration of provincial history in the separate **Fiske och Sjöfartsmuseum** (Fishing and Maritime Museum; late June to late Aug daily noon–5pm; late Aug to late June Tues–Sat noon–4pm, Sun noon–5pm; free), which tries its best to be a regional maritime museum: a tug and several fishing boats are squeezed into the small hall.

Bölesholmarna and Norrfors

On the southern side of the river, following the **cycle path**, Umeleden, west from the centre leads you to **Bölesholmarna**, two islands in the river that are an ideal spot for picnics and barbecues. One island even contains a small lake where you can have a quick dip. It takes about twenty minutes to get here on foot from the centre; both the cycle path and the route to the islands are detailed on a free map available from the tourist office. By bike (see "Listings" for rental details), you can carry on further west along the cycle path to the rapids of **Norrfors**, with its five-thousand-year-old rock carvings in the former riverbed; it takes about an hour to get here from the centre.

Winter activities

Visiting Umeå in winter can be a wonderful experience. What gives the city the edge over many smaller places further north, is not only easy access by both plane and train, but also the chance to experience the northern winter right on the city limits by day and Umeå's extensive range of bars and restaurants by night.

During the coldest winter months the Ume river freezes over providing a ready opportunity to take **snow-scooter safaris** upriver. The easiest way to arrange this is to book through the **Scandic Hotel** who charge 800kr per person (minimum five people) for a three-hour trip, which ends with a dip in a wooden hot pot (an additional 200kr) right on the riverbank. Another wintertime attraction here is the **northern lights**; January and February are both good months for observing this phenomenon – most spectacularly from a snowmobile.

Eating, drinking and entertainment

Eating and **drinking** opportunities are varied and generally of a high standard in Umeå, partly because of the size of the city and partly due to the large student population. Most restaurants and cafés are centred around the main pedestrianized Kungsgatan or Rådhusesplanaden. For fresh fruit and vegetables try the daily market in the main square, Rådhustorget, outside the old Town Hall.

Cafés

Konditori Mekka Rådhusesplanaden 15, close to the train station. Serves delicious pastries and cakes, and free coffee refills.

Kafé Station Östra Rådhusgatan 2L, next to the Filmstaden cinema. Rough brick walls, wooden floors and great coffee.

Rex Rådhustorget. Located in the old town hall. More a restaurant than a café though it's a stylish place to sip coffee, with outdoor seating in summer.

Vita Björn in a boat moored off Västra Strandgatan, near the old Town Hall. Sit on deck and enjoy a view over the river.

Wayne's Coffee Storgatan 50. Another branch of the highly successful chain sweeping Sweden. This one's stylish, elegant and, above all, has a fantastic range of excellent coffee.

Restaurants

Blå Thai Corner of Rådhusesplanaden and Västra Norrlandsgatan. Genuinely tasty Thai food in the basement of the pretentious street-level bar of the same name. Look out for the eat-until-you-drop buffet deal for just 99kr.

Club Havana Västra Norrlandsgatan 5. The upstairs restaurant specializes in tasty Italian and Cuban buffets on weekdays for around 99kr. It's hard to find better value for money – though you will have to pay around 15kr to check in your coat.

Gandi Järnvägstorget. Despite the dingy basement location in a building opposite the railway station, this place has excellent Indian food with good-value dishes for around 140kr-although the

restaurant is rather down at heel.

Great Eastern Magasinsgatan 17. The best Chinese restaurant in Norrland. Very busy at lunch (60kr); evening chicken and beef dishes from 86kr as well as a Mongolian barbecue for 159kr.

Lottas Krog Nygatan 22. Pub-restaurant that's a good place for lunch at 73kr, though in the evening there's a much more extensive menu, featuring fish and chips for 99kr and salmon pasta for 112kr – both excellent. Also has some sixty different beers, and darts.

Rex Bar och Grill Rådhustorget. Probably the most popular – and stylish – place to eat in Umeå. Avoid the fussy à la carte menu offering northern Swedish specialities at sky-high prices and choose instead from the bar meals priced from 85kr.

Sjöbris Boat moored off Västra Strandgatan at Kajplats 10. An excellent fish restaurant on board an old white fishing boat. Fresh fish dishes from 100–160kr. Open all year.

Skytten Järnvägstorget. Near the train station. Two restaurants in one, an up-market place with fine cooking, including good fish dishes, and a brasserie with simpler fare including a burger and a beer for 95kr.

TC Vasaplan. A bar-restaurant with grill specialities and light dishes that's a firm Umeå favourite for its good-value Swedish home-cooking – reindeer for 105kr, salmon burger 99kr and mushroom soup 74kr. There's outdoor seating in summer.

V&R *Scandic Hotel Plaza Umeå*, Storgatan 40. Very smart and chi-chi restaurant specializing in traditional Swedish dishes given an international flavour. Mains around 200kr.

Bars and nightlife

Umeå buzzes at night, with plenty of stylish and friendly **bars** to choose from, most of them British-style pubs or brasseries. Much of the **nightlife** revolves around the students, and Umeå is liveliest when they're in town; there are usually discos in the union building, Universum, on term-time weekends (best reached from the centre by taxi as it's a bit far to walk). Strictly, you need to be a student to get in, but you may be let in if you're accompanied by one of the students. For non-student **clubs**, head for the **Scandic Hotel Plaza Umeå** on Storgatan where there's late-night music and dancing on Friday and Saturday; in winter **Sportpuben Dragonen**, Västra Norlandsgatan 5, is also popular – note there's a lower age limit of 23 on Saturday nights only.

Blå Rådhusesplanaden 14. Although meals are on offer, people flock here to pose. This place has the distinction of being the trendiest place to imbibe in town. Lined with blue mosaic tiles, glass and chrome, and people with attitude. Be prepared to check in your coat though for around 15–20kr.
Droskan Storgatan 60. The place to hear catch live bands – blues is particularly popular here. In summer the whole bar spills out into the garden.
Lottas Nygatan 22. If people are drinking anywhere it's here. Another of the British-style pubs the Swedes love so much, with heavy wooden panelling and carpets. Always a good choice for either a pre- or post-dinner drink.

Mucky Duck Vasaplan. Around forty types of beer in this smoky British-style pub; attracts an older crowd.
Rex Rådhustorget. Attracting a trendy 20-something crowd, this all-round establishment – café, pub and restaurant rolled into one – is definitely worth a visit.
Skytten Rådhusesplanaden 17. One of the most popular bars to be seen and to do the seeing in – always packed.
Sportpuben Dragonen Västra Norrlandsgatan 5. A popular pub with large video screens showing various sports. Also has dancing on Friday and Saturday nights.

Listings

Airlines Malmö Aviation, ☏020/44 00 10; SAS, at the airport ☏090/728 30 10. For other airlines and general information, call SAS on ☏090/728 30 10.
Banks FöreningsSparbanken, Rådhustorget; Handelsbanken, Storgatan 48; Nordea, Rådhusesplanaden 3; SEB, Kungsgatan 52.
Beaches Nydala, at Umeå's campsite; Bettnesand, 20km south of town; Bölesholmarna, 15min walk west from the centre along the south bank of the river. There's a nudist beach at Dragonudden, 10km south of Umeå, on Stocksjö lake – ask the tourist office for precise directions.
Bike rental Reckon on 150kr a day any of these places: Bike, Storgatan 38 ☏090/14 28 00 (Mon–Fri 11am–6pm, Sat 10am–2pm); Cykel & Mopedhandlar'n, Kungsgatan 101 ☏090/14 01 70 (Mon–Fri 9.30am–5.30pm, Sat 10am–1pm).
Buses Long-distance bus station, Järnvägstorget 2 ☏020/91 00 19, ✆www.lanstrafikeniac.se. City buses at Vasaplan ☏090/16 22 50.

Cinemas Filmstaden, Östra Rådhusgatan 2D; Royal, Skolgatan 68.
Ferry tickets Contact the tourist office in Renmarkstorget.
Pharmacy Renmarkstorget 6 ☏090/77 05 41 (Mon–Fri 9.30am–6pm, Sat 9.30am–2pm).
Police Ridvägen 10 ☏090/15 20 00.
Post office Vasaplan ☏090/15 07 00 (Mon–Fri 8am–6pm, Sat 10am–2pm).
Swimming pools Indoor swimming at Umeå *simhall*, Rothoffsvägen 12 ☏090/16 16 40.
Systembolaget Kungsgatan 50A and Vasagatan 11 (both Mon–Wed & Fri 10am–6pm, Thurs 10am–7pm, Sat 10am–2pm).
Taxi City Taxi ☏090/14 14 14; Taxi Direkt ☏090/13 20 00; Umeå Taxi ☏090/77 00 00.
Train station Järnvägsallén 7 ☏020/44 41 11.
Travel agent Ticket, Kungsgatan 58 (Mon–Fri 10am–6pm, Sat 10am–4pm); Kilroy Travels, Kungsgatan (Mon–Fri 10am–6pm).

Around Umeå

Umeå is ideally placed for a jaunt to the Älgens hus **elk farm** (early June to mid-Aug Tue–Sun noon–6pm; rest of year by advance booking on ☏0932/500 00; 80kr; ✆www.swedishadventure.com/elk.house) at Västernyliden 23 in **Bjurholm**, a small village 65km west. Driving around Sweden you may well have caught the briefest glimpse of the king of the forest, Europe's largest land animal, as tall as a horse but with antlers. The farm, though, provides an excellent opportunity to come face to face with these cumbersome looking beasts and to learn all about their behaviour from the knowledgeable staff, who also make cheese from elk milk – a rare and inordinately expensive delicacy. Although the

Scandic Hotel Plaza Umeå can arrange minibus or car hire to visit the elk farm, it's also possible to reach Bjurholm by bus (daily: every 1–2hr) from Umeå. Incidentally, elk love bananas, so you may wish to pack a few for your visit.

Holmön island

The Gulf of Bothnia is at its narrowest between **Holmön**, part of an island group 30km northeast of Umeå, and the Finnish island of Björkö. Consequently, the sea route between the two islands was for centuries used to transport goods, people, soldiers and mail. Sweden and Finland were one country until 1809, and there are still strong links between the respective island communities here; every summer, the **postrodden** (literally "mail row") is held, when a number of boats row and sail their way between Holmön and Björkö just as the mail boats used to do (the starting point alternates between Sweden and Finland from one year to the next). It's worth making the effort to get there for the event, which is usually held in early July; more details can be obtained from Umeå's tourist office (see p.387). Other summer events worth checking out are the **Sea Jazz Festival**, in the middle of August, and **Holmöns Visfestival**, a **song contest** held in late July, when people get up to sing traditional ditties at drinking parties.

To get to **Holmön**, take the bus from Umeå to the tiny port of **Norrfjärden** (1 daily from Vasagatan; 50min), the departure point for the free **ferry** to the islands (June–Aug 3 daily, Sun 2 daily; 40min; Sept–May Mon–Sat 2 daily, Sun 1 daily; more information on ☏070/346 48 19). The island's **tourist office** (June–Aug daily 9am–5.30pm; ☏090/552 20), which provides **maps** of the island and **rents bikes**, is a few metres from the jetty where the boat puts in. **Cycling** is a wonderful way to see the small farmsteads, flower meadows and pine forests that fill the landscape; conveniently, this part of Sweden is arguably the sunniest in the country, as has been borne out by 150 years' worth of records from the weather station here. On a bike, you'll also easily be able to find your own secluded little nook where you can swim, though for proper facilities, head to Holmö Havsbad. For a place to **stay**, there's **Holmögården**, not far from the tourist office (☏090/550 70; ❶), a charming, though simple, bed-and-breakfast-style establishment.

Skellefteå

There used to be a religious fervour about the town **SKELLEFTEÅ**, 140km northeast of Umeå. In 1324, an edict in the name of King Magnus Eriksson invited "all those who believed in Jesus Christ or wanted to turn to him" to settle between the Skellefte and Ume rivers. Many heeded the call, and parishes mushroomed on the banks of the Skellefte river. By the end of the eighteenth century, a devout township was centred around the town's monumental church, which stood out in stark contrast to the surrounding plains and wide river. Nowadays, though, more material occupations, including computer and electronics industries, and the mining of gold and silver, support the town. If you're heading north for Swedish Lapland, Skellefteå can make an appealing stop on the way. There are enough attractions to keep you busy for a day or so, namely its superb parish village, **Bonnstan**, an engaging collection of battered log cottages gathered together around the proud Neoclassical **church** housing one of Norrland's proudest exhibits – the **medieval carving** of the Virgin of Skellefteå. Nearby, the rickety **Lejonströmsbron** is Sweden's

△ Bonnstan Row

oldest wooden bridge, offering elevated views of the Skellefte river. Skellefteå is also well placed for jaunts into the Swedish inland with good bus connections to Arvidsjaur and Arjeplog.

Arrival, information and accommodation

The small centre is based around a modern paved square flanked by the streets Kanalgatan and Nygatan; at the top of the square is the **bus station** and, at the bottom, the **tourist office** (end–June to early Aug Mon–Fri 9am–6pm, Sat 10am–4pm, Sun 10am–3pm; rest of year Mon–Fri 9am–5pm, Sat 10am–4pm; ☏0910/73 60 20, ⓦwww.skelleftea.se), at Trädgårdsgatan 7. The **airport** is 18km southeast of town, from where buses (50kr) and taxis (400kr) will bring you into the centre. The library at Kanalgatan 73 has plenty of **Internet** terminals for free use.

The **youth hostel** – at Brännavägen 25 (☏0910/72 57 00, ⓦwww .stiftsgardenskelleftea.com), a rustic red two-storey building by the banks of the Skellefte river, half an hour's walk from the centre – is well worth seeking out. Head west along Nygatan (which later becomes Brännavägen) until the junction with Kyrkvägen, where the hostel is on the corner. There are four central **hotels**; the cheapest is **Hotell Viktoria** at Trädgårdsgatan 8 (☏0910/174 70, ⓦwww .hotelocafevictoria.com; ❸/❷), a family-run establishment on the top floor of one of the buildings on the south side of the main square. Virtually next door at Torget 2, **Rica Hotel Skellefteå** (☏0910/73 25 00, ⓦwww.rica.cityhotels.se; ❹/❸) has perfectly adequate rooms and is the centre of Skellefteå's nightlife (see p.396). The smartest hotel is **Scandic Hotel** (☏0910/75 24 00, ⓦwww.scandic-hotels.com; ❻/❸) at Kanalgatan 75, next to the library, replete with plush rooms and a gym, sauna and swimming pool in the basement; its discounted rooms are definitely worth the money. For **campers**, **Skellefteå Campingplats** is about 1500m north of the centre on Mossgatan, just off the E4 (☏0910/188 55, ⓦwww.skelleftea.se/ skellefteacamping); you can rent four-bed **cabins** here for 275kr per night per cabin. Popular with dozens of holidaying Norwegians, who, quite inexplicably, drive hundreds of kilometres down the E95 to visit Skellefteå, the site also has a heated outdoor swimming pool, wave machine and Jacuzzi.

The Town

There's little to see in the town centre; you should concentrate on nearby **Bonnstan**, comprising Skellefteå's **church** and **kyrkstad** (parish village). The only museum in town that deserves a visit is the **Anna Nordlander Museum**, one of just three in the world dedicated to women artists, at Kanalgatan 73; it's due to move to new premises on the corner of Storgatan and Viktoriagatan; ask at the tourist office for the latest details. Born in 1843, Anna Nordlander made plain that art was her first love, showing a remarkable talent for painting in her childhood; she went on to become one of the few successful women artists of her time. The museum is exclusively devoted to her work, mostly landscapes and portraits.

A fifteen-minute walk west from the centre along Nygatan brings you to the **Nordanå Kulturcentrum**, a large and baffling assortment of old wooden buildings that's home to a theatre, an old-world grocer's store (labelled "Lanthandel" – the Swedish word for a country grocer's) and a dire **museum** (Mon & Fri–Sun noon–4pm, Tues–Thurs 9am–5pm; ⓦwww.museet.skelleftea.se; 20kr), containing three floors of mind-numbing exhibitions on everything from the region's first settlers to swords. Tucked away to the side of the grocer's store is a pleasant restaurant, **Nordanå Gårdens Värdshus**, with outdoor seating in summer.

Sweden's parish villages

After the break with the Catholic Church in 1527, the Swedish clergy were determined to teach their parishoners the Lutheran fundamentals, with the result that, by 1681, church services had become compulsory. There was one problem with this requirement, though – the population in the north was spread over considerable distances, making weekly attendance impossible. The clergy and the parishes agreed a compromise: it was decreed that those living within 10km of the church should attend every Sunday; those between 10km and 20km away, every fortnight; and those 20–30km away, every three weeks. The scheme worked, and within a decade, **parish villages** (**kyrkstäder**) had appeared throughout the region to provide the travelling faithful with somewhere to spend the night after a day of praying and listening to powerful sermons.

Of the 71 parish villages Sweden originally had, only eighteen are left today, predominantly in the provinces of **Västerbotten** and **Norrbotten**. Each *kyrkstad* consists of rows of simple wooden houses grouped tightly around the church. The biggest and most impressive, at **Gammelstad** near Luleå (see p.403), is included on the UNESCO World Heritage List; another good example, aside from the one in Skellefteå, is at **Öjebyn**, near Piteå (see overleaf). Today, they are no longer used in the traditional way, though people still live in the old houses, especially in summer, and sometimes even rent them out to tourists.

The church and Bonnstan parish village

Skellefteå's church and **parish village** known as **Bonnstan** are within easy striking distance of the centre: walk west along Nygatan and keep going for about fifteen minutes. An evocative sight, the **kyrkstad** (see box, above) here comprises five long rows of weather-beaten log houses, with battered wooden shutters. The houses are protected by law: any renovations, including the installation of electricity, are forbidden. You can take a peek inside, but bear in mind that these are privately owned summer houses today. Next to these cottages is the **kyrka** (daily 10am–4pm), a proud white Neoclassical church which so enthused Leopold von Buch, a traveller who visited here in the nineteenth century, that he was moved to describe it as "the largest and most beautiful building in the entire north of Sweden, rising like a Palmyra's temple out of the desert". Its domed roof is supported by four mighty pillars along each of the walls; inside, there's an outstanding series of medieval sculptures. Look out too for the 800-year-old **Virgin of Skellefteå**, a walnut **woodcarving** immediately behind the altar on the right – it's one of the few remaining Romanesque images of the Virgin in the world. Nearby, on the Skellefte river, is a pretty place to sit and while away an hour or two: the islet of **Kyrkholmen**, reached by a small wooden bridge. It's home to an outdoor **café** that's handy for a cup of coffee and simple sandwiches (mid-June to mid-Aug).

From the church you have two walking routes back to the centre: either take Strandpromenaden along the river's edge, interrupted by barbecue sites and grassy stretches; or cross **Lejonströmsbron**, the longest wooden bridge in Sweden, beneath the hill where the church stands. Dating from 1737, the bridge was the scene of mass slaughter when Russian and Swedish forces clashed there during the war that started in 1741. Once on the south side of the river, you can stroll back to Parksbron, past the occasional boat and silent fisherman.

Eating and drinking

For all its contemporary go-ahead industry, modern Skellefteå is quiet and retiring; its restaurants and bars though come as a pleasant surprise – they are among the best in Norrland.

For **cafés**, try the fussy **Carl Viktor** at Nygatan 40, or, much better, the popular **Lilla Mari** at Köpmangatan 13, set in an old-fashioned wooden cottage in a small courtyard off the main drag. The **M/S Norway restaurant** opposite the **Scandic Hotel** offers gorgeous Nordic specialities such as fillets of ptarmigan or reindeer from 270kr. Among the usual cluster of pizzerias, the best and most popular is **Monaco**, Nygatan 31, which also does takeaways. An excellent choice for Greek food, though, is the **Kriti Stekhus** at Kanalgatan 51, with steaks from 79kr, moussaka at 95kr and lamb cutlets for 160kr. In the main square, **Tatong** has the best Chinese food in town – though that's not exactly saying much.

Drinking is best done at **O'Leary's** at Kanalgatan 31 or at the traditional-English-style **Old Williams Pub** in the main square – though it's also worth checking out the **Mr Greek Bar & Pub**, at Kanalgatan 51, in the same building as the **Kriti** steakhouse, which has beers for 39kr. On long summer evenings people also gravitate towards **UnderBar**, in the main square, for a drink or three.

Moving on from Skellefteå

The easiest way to continue **north** from Skellefteå is by one of the frequent **Norrlandskusten buses** which stop in Piteå, before terminating in Luleå. The nearest **train station** is at Jörn, which is on the main line; you can get there by bus (7 Mon–Fri, 2 Sat & Sun; 1hr). For Swedish Lapland, take the 7.25am bus to Jörn (Mon–Fri only) to connect with the northbound train to Boden and Luleå; change at Boden for Gällivare, Kiruna and beyond. To travel **south** by train, take the 5.20pm bus (Mon–Fri only) to Jörn, where you can connect onto the night train south to both Stockholm and Gothenburg. Skellefteå is also connected by **air** to Stockholm; for airport information call ☎0910/68 32 10.

Piteå and around

Located in the province of Norrbotten at the head of the Gulf of Bothnia, and, unexpectedly, northern Sweden's main beach resort, the small town of **PITEÅ** has a history that goes back to the beginning of the fourteenth century, when the village was founded at **Öjebyn**, site of one of northern Sweden's oldest **parish villages** (see previous page). At the time Piteå was granted its town charter, in 1621, it was still situated 5km west of its current location, but a fire in 1666 destroyed much of the town, and it was decided to up sticks and move it to the coast. Although the Russians burnt the new town to the ground in 1721 during the Great Northern War, the layout of the town's streets still dates from that time.

Piteå today consists mostly of nineteenth-century houses, at their most elegant along the main pedestrian drag, **Storgatan**, and the main square, **Rådhustorget**, at the street's southern end. Built in Venetian style and one of only two in the country (the other is Stora Torget in Uppsala) to boast closed corners – access is from the middle of each of the four sides rather than the corners – the square is lined with well-kept wooden buildings painted in pastel shades of yellow, green and grey and overlooked, from its northern end, by the mighty **Rådhus**, from 1830. This is one of Sweden's best preserved examples of timber architecture, inspired by the Classicist style commonly found in towns on the Finnish side of the northern Gulf of Bothnia. Inside, the **Piteå Museum** (Mon–Fri 8am–4pm, early June to late Aug Sat 11am–2pm; free) does its best to recount the district's cultural history with a couple of rambling displays, but the most interesting exhibit is the model of what Piteå used to look like until the early twentieth century – complete with street after street of traditional wooden houses, sadly now long gone.

Indeed, the rest of Piteå is a mish-mash of characterless concrete buildings, pedestrianized shopping streets and anodyne little squares; however, before moving on, have a look inside **Piteå kyrka** off Sundsgatan. Dating from 1686 and consequently one of the oldest wooden churches in Norrland, the invading Russians forces spared the building in 1721, when they razed the rest of Piteå to the ground, because they had their headquarters here. Notwithstanding its dramatic past, the church's main attractions are the Baroque altar, which was bought in 1700 from Maria kyrka in Södermalm in Stockholm, which portrays the suffering of Christ, and the ornate pulpit carved by local craftsman, Nils Fluur – though neither will hold your attention for longer than five minutes. Instead it's a much better idea to head off in search of Piteå's other main draws: Öjebyn parish village and the beach resort of Pite Havsbad.

Pite Havsbad

The superb sandy **beaches** and swimming complex at **Pite Havsbad**, 10km to the southeast, come as a pleasant surprise so far north. In fact, Havsbadet, as it's known locally, is one of the most popular summer resorts in Sweden, renowned for its long hours of summer sunshine, relatively warm water temperatures and long sweeping strands of golden sand that are well looked after, friendly and a great place to unwind after the long journey up from the south. There's even an official **nudist beach**, quite a rarity in northern Sweden, given that you can sunbathe nude more or less anywhere you choose away from the crowds. The best way to find it is to follow the side of the main building of the swimming complex down to the sea, turn left along the beach and look out for a large rock, with the words "Naturist Bad" painted on, approximately where the caravan park ends, or look for another sign on the red toilet block around here; the beach runs as far as the wooden post marked "Här slutar naturistbad".

Back at the **swimming complex**, you'll find open-air pools with water slides, and the indoor Tropikbadet (☎0911/327 33; June–Aug daily 10am–9pm; rest of year Mon–Fri 3pm–8pm, Sat & Sun 10am–6pm; 135kr); with fun pool, Jacuzzis, saunas, steam room and yet more water slides.

For **accommodation** here try the on-site **Hotell Pite Havsbad** (☎0911/327 00, ☎0911/327 99; ❹/❸) with its modern rooms, or next door, right on the beach, there are four-bed **cabins** (same contact details; 790kr per night, 4000kr per week) though you'll need to book at least three weeks ahead to be sure of getting one.

You can get here easily from Piteå bus station on **bus** #1 (they'll display the destination "Havsbadet"; hourly until 8pm; 14kr).

Öjebyn parish village

Centred around a fifteenth-century medieval stone church on Kyrkovägen, the **parish village** at **Öjebyn** is one party in an ongoing debate as to whether it's the oldest in Sweden, a title also claimed for the parish village at nearby Gammelstad outside Luleå. Although smaller than its more famous neighbour, the parish village contains equally impressive clusters of knarled wooden cottages perched on piles of stones to protect them from the cold and damp. Today, although they're privately owned, most have been kept in their original state and still have no electricity. Inside the church there are two things you shouldn't miss: the carved pulpit, dating from 1706, by local carpenter, Nils Fluur, who was greatly praised for his highly individual Baroque style and also produced the pulpits for the churches in Gammelstad and Piteå; and the altar, in Swedish Baroque, made by court sculptor, Caspar Schröder, and brought from Stockholm at the start of the eighteenth century. To get to Öjebyn from Piteå, it's a twenty-minute hop on **bus** #1 (20min) from the bus station. Öjebyn is also the location of one of Piteå's best **restaurants**, serving up the traditional **pitepalt** – see Practicalities.

Practicalities

Piteå's **bus station** is located at the western end of the town's two main parallel streets, Storgatan and Prästgårdsgatan. Inside, the **tourist office**, at Sundsgatan 42 (June–Aug Mon–Sat 9am–8pm, Sun noon–8pm; Sept–May Mon–Fri 8am–5pm; ☏0911/933 90, ⓦwww.pitea.se), can fix up **private rooms** for around 300kr per person per night (there are also a couple available for just 150kr). The **youth hostel** is located in the old hospital, on the southern edge of the town centre at Storgatan 3 (☏ & ⓕ0911/158 80): from the bus station, simply walk the length of Storgatan, passing through Rådhustorget until the T-junction with Trädgårdsgatan, where the hostel is then in front of you. Of the town's two **hotels**, the Art Nouveau **Stadshotellet** from 1906, at Olof Palmes Gata 1, is not to be missed (☏0911/197 00, ⓦwww.piteastadshotell .com; ❺/❹). Built on the instigation of the local doctor who was keen that Piteå should have a grand hotel to mark the arrival of the railway, its smart rooms have an old-world atmosphere, with grand furnishings complemented by a modern Jacuzzi and sauna suite in the basement. Even if you don't stay here, it's worth poking your head around the door of this Piteå fixture to see the sweeping main staircase that leads up to the breakfast room. Cheaper, and correspondingly less charming, is **Skoogs City Hotell** at Uddmansgatan 5, off the main square (☏0911/10 000, ⓦwww.skoogs.net/cityhotell; ❹/❸). The **campsite** at Pite Havsbad, one of the largest in the country, has a variety of four-bed cabins, which can be rented for 690–1390kr per night (☏0911/327 00, ⓕ327 99). There's also a modern hotel here, **Hotell Pite Havsbad** (same contact details as campsite; ❺/❹).

Whilst in Piteå it's worth trying to sample the local delicacy, **pitepalt**, akin to large dumplings and eaten with butter; they're made from potato and flour rolled up into balls, stuffed with meat, then boiled. In **Öjebyn**, the **restaurant** just east of the parish village at Gammelstadsvägen 1, **Paltzerian**, is the place of choice to sample them – their menu is truly enormous though most plates go for around 65kr. In the middle of July, there's a good chance they'll be served up along Storgatan in Piteå – for no reason in particular. Otherwise eating out in Piteå is rather uninspiring as the range of restaurants in town is pretty limited; the best bet is the Chinese restaurant **Pentryt** at Sundsgatan 29, with lunch deals for around 60kr; in the evenings it has Chinese dishes and pizzas for around 120kr – on Fridays, though, it only serves food until 10pm, when, bizarrely, it turns into a bar and disco. Another reasonable choice is **Pigalle**, across the road at Sundsgatan 36, renowned for its big portions; a meat-based main dish will cost around 160, lunch is 59kr. The best pizzeria is **Blå Ängeln** at Källbogatan 2, with pizzas and pastas from 50kr.

Drinking dens include the **Cockney Pub**, serving expensive beer downstairs at the **Stadshotellet**; and **Karls Källa**, where beer costs slightly less, at Sundsgatan 35. There's also the English-style **Olivers Inn** at Storgatan 41, which attracts a slighter older crowd.

Moving on from Piteå

Taking the **Norrlandskusten bus** to Luleå is the easiest way to continue your journey north. You can also use buses to connect with the **trains** to and from Stockholm and Gothenburg. To head north by train, take the Norrlandskusten service to Luleå and change there; to head south, take the 4.30pm bus (not Sat) from Piteå to Älvsbyn (55min), which connects with the sleeper to Gothenburg and Stockholm.

Luleå and around

When **LULEÅ**, twenty-five minutes down the train line from Boden and 55km from Piteå up the E4, was founded in 1621, it had at its centre a parish village (see p.395) and medieval church. Numerous trading ships would load and unload their goods at its tiny harbour, reflecting the importance of trade with Stockholm even in those days. The harbour soon proved too small, thanks to the growth in business, and so, by royal command, the settlement was moved to its present site in 1649; only the church and parish village, today part of Luleå's **Gammelstad** (Old Town), remained **in situ**. Up until the end of the eighteenth century, Luleå was still little more than a handful of houses and storage huts; indeed Linnaeus, Sweden's famous botanist, who passed through here

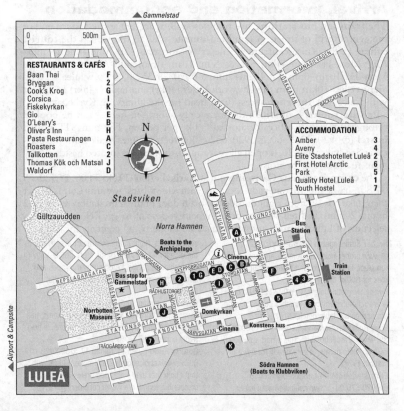

RESTAURANTS & CAFÉS

Baan Thai	F
Bryggan	2
Cook's Krog	G
Corsica	I
Fiskekyrkan	K
Gio	E
O'Leary's	B
Oliver's Inn	H
Pasta Restaurangen	A
Roasters	C
Tallkotten	2
Thomas Kök och Matsal	J
Waldorf	D

ACCOMMODATION

Amber	3
Aveny	4
Elite Stadshotellet Luleå	2
First Hotel Arctic	6
Park	5
Quality Hotel Luleå	1
Youth Hostel	7

LULEÅ

in 1732 on his journey to Swedish Lapland, described Luleå as a village. Though the town had started to become something of a shipbuilding centre in the nineteenth century, it wasn't until the construction in 1888 of the Malmbanan, the railway built to transport iron-ore from the Gulf of Bothnia for wintertime export at the ice-free Norwegian port of Narvik, that Luleå's fortunes really started to flourish. Luleå was at one end of the line, and its port was vital for lucrative iron exports (the main ironfields were – and are – around Kiruna and Malmberget).

Although shipping is still important today, in recent years Luleå has become the hi-tech centre of the north, specializing in metallurgy; it also has an important **university**. The town's wide streets and lively, friendly atmosphere make Luleå immediately likeable, and if you're heading north for the wilds of the Torne valley, Gällivare and Kiruna, or to the sparsely populated regions of Swedish Lapland, Luleå represents your last chance to enjoy a decent range of restaurants and bars before entering the forest and wilderness that spreads north and west from here. Be mindful of the weather, though: Luleå is built on a peninsula which takes the full brunt of the northerly winds. If you're here in summer (see below for times), taking a boat out into the **archipelago** makes a wonderful day-trip – departures are daily and there's a whole array of islands in the Gulf of Bothnia to choose from: beaches, walking trails and plenty of peace and solitude are the main draws.

Arrival, information and accommodation

The **train** and **bus stations**, five minutes' walk apart, are at the eastern end of the central grid of streets. A good ten-minute walk to the west is the **tourist office**, in the Kulturcentrum Ebeneser at Storgatan 43B (mid-June to mid-Aug Mon–Fri 9am–7pm, Sat & Sun 10am–4pm; mid-Aug to mid-June Mon–Fri 10am–6pm, Sat 10am–2pm; ☏0920/29 35 00, ⓦwww.lulea.se). The **airport** lies 10km from the city, with buses (40kr) and taxis (145kr) linking it with Luleå. For **Internet** access (free) head for the library on Kyrkogatan.

Private rooms – of which there are only about ten here – can be booked through the tourist office for around 300kr per person. The non-STF **youth hostel** (☏0920/22 26 60, ⒻO920/652 67), fifteen minutes' walk from the centre at Sandviksgatan 26, is open all year round, though it is located beside a busy main road and can be noisy.

The **campsite**, **Arcus Camping** out at **Karlsvik** (☏0920/43 54 00, Ⓕ0920/25 04 80), has a superb waterside location with views back towards Luleå. To get there, take bus #6 from right outside the main door of the train station (every 1–2 hours; 20min), and tell the bus driver where you want to go. Below we give a selection of Luleå's **hotels**, most of which are modern and centrally located.

Amber Stationsgatan 67 ☏0920/102 00, ⓦwww.amber-hotell.nu. A small and cosy family-run place in an old wooden building. Summer doubles for 600kr. ❹/❷.

Aveny Hermelinsgatan 10 ☏0920/22 18 20, ⓦwww.hotellaveny.com. Another compact, modern and comfortable hotel. ❹/❷

First Hotel Arctic Sandviksgatan 80 ☏0920/109 80, ⓦwww.arctichotel.se. This smart little hotel, with en-suite rooms, is very handy for the train station. ❺/❸

Elite Stadshotellet Luleå Storgatan 15 ☏0920/670 00, ⓦwww.elite.se/hotell/lulea/

stadshotellet. Right in the centre of town, this is the oldest and smartest of the city's hotels, with old-fashioned rooms, kitted out with drapes and large armchairs, and a huge breakfast buffet. ❺/❸

Park Kungsgatan 10 ☏0920/21 11 49, ⓦwww.parkhotell.se. Without en-suite rooms, this basic place, the cheapest of Luleå's hotels, is perfectly acceptable. ❸/❷

Quality Hotel Luleå Storgatan 17 ☏0920/20 10 00, ⓦwww.choicehotels.se. A modern hotel with that chain feel to it – a bit too dreary, though its discounted rooms are worth considering. ❻/❷

The City

Just to the south of **Storgatan**, the main street, lies Luleå's main square, **Rådhustorget**, with the **Domkyrkan** (Mon–Fri 10am–3pm; free) in the corner. The medieval incarnation of the cathedral disappeared centuries ago and the present one, built in 1893 on the same spot as its predecessor, is a modern barrage of copper chandeliers hanging like Christmas decorations. Unusually for northern Sweden, it's built of brick, in late-Gothic style to the design of the architect Adolf Emil Melander. The interior was completely renewed in 1938 when the original wooden walls and fittings were removed, revealing the brickwork underneath which was then painted white. Southeast of the Domkyrkan, **Konstens Hus** (Tues, Thurs & Fri 11am–6pm, Wed 11am–8pm, Sat & Sun noon–4pm; free) at Smedjegatan 2 is worth a look, with interesting displays of work from modern Swedish artists and sculptors; to get there, head east from the Domkyrkan until you reach Smedjegatan, when you turn right and walk about 200m south.

Back at the main square, walk 300m west along Köpmangatan, and you'll come to the **Norrbottens Museum** at Storgatan 2 (Mon–Fri 10am–4pm, Sat & Sun noon–4pm; closed Mon in winter; free; ⓦ www.norrbottensmuseum.se). Although most of the collection is a rather dull resumé of county history, the museum's worth a look mainly for the informative displays and exhibitions on **Sámi** life and culture that predominate northwest of Luleå (see p.472). Don't leave without seeing the superb short **film** (in Swedish with English subtitles) about a young **Sámi** woman from Skåne who travels to Jokkmokk to find her roots; the difficulties she faces as an outsider reveal a side to the **Sámi** rarely seen by foreigners. The museum also has a pleasant **café**.

When the weather's good, it's worth heading to the oddly named **Gültzauudden**, a wooden promontory that has a great **beach**; it was named after the German shipbuilder, Christian Gültzau, who helped to make Luleå a shipbuilding centre. It's easily reachable on foot from the centre: head north from the cathedral along Rådstugatan, which later changes its name to Norra Strandgatan and veers northwest past the Norrbotten theatre to the junction with Fagerlindsvägen. Turn right and follow the road down to the beach. On warm days, it can seem like Luleå's population have all come down to the beach.

Eating, drinking and nightlife

While the city often has a busy feel in summer, from a **cultural** standpoint Luleå is most busy when the university is in session. The best bet for music recitals and theatre productions all year round is the Kulturcentrum Ebeneser at Storgatan 43B, in the same building as the tourist office, who also sell tickets; there's a good café on the ground floor. There are two **cinemas** in town: Filmstaden at Timmermansgatan 19 (☎0920/27 02 00) and Sandrews at Nygatan 1 (☎0920/21 10 15).

Drinking is generally done at the main restaurants listed, although a couple of British-style **pubs** have become inordinately popular. You can go **clubbing** at the raucous **Cleo Nightclub**, Storgatan 17; **Bryggeriet** on Västra Varvsgatan, popular with 20- to 25-year olds and known for its house and soul music; and, during the summer months, the very loud **Terrazzen**, inside the **Elite Stadshotellet Luleå**, on Skeppsbrogatan. The most lively and interesting **places to eat** are all found along Storgatan.

Baan Thai Corner of Storgatan and Kungsgatan. Authentic and extensive Thai menu with meat dishes at 89kr. Vegetarian and noodle dishes are 79kr; a strong beer is just 38kr. Don't miss it.

Bryggan *Elite Stadshotellet*, Storgatan 15. Offering great views out over the northern harbour, and international fare, with main courses at around 150kr.

Cook's Krog *Quality Hotel*, Storgatan 17. Intimate and cosy, this is the best place in Luleå for steak cooked over a charcoal grill, for around 200kr.

Corsica Nygatan 14. The dark and dingy interior notwithstanding, this place offers a welcome change from Swedish fare, serving some traditional Corsican dishes for 100–150kr as well as lots of steak and pizzas. Lunch here is 59kr.

Fiskekyrkan in Södra Hamnen. Walk down Nygatan, cross Sandviksgatan, and you'll see the seafront orange warehouse building housing this place. One of the cheaper restaurants in town, with pasta and other simple dishes for around 120kr, it's also a popular drinking hole in the evenings.

Gio Storgatan 27. Wear your sharpest clothes, darkest shades and sip a chilled foreign beer before going clubbing. Predictably voguish – yet surprisingly good value – menu featuring modern Swedish food for around 120kr.

O'Leary's Skomakargatan 22. Definitely *the* place to watch, from its adjoining terrace, the summer sun set over the northern harbour. Has Tex-Mex-style food for around 120kr, with a good choice of beer too.

Oliver's Inn Storgatan 11. Serving pub food and a good selection of beer, this bar is known for its 1970s and 1980s music, which attracts a large crowd at weekends.

Pasta Restaurangen In a side street at Magasinsgatan 5. Serves hefty pizzas from around 70kr and pasta dishes for 80kr; takeaway service is available.

Roasters Storgatan 43, next to the tourist office. The best café in Luleå with magnificient espressos, cappucinos and lattes. Also has a good selection of sandwiches, light snacks, quiches and salads.

Tallkotten Inside the *Elite Stadshotellet* at Storgatan 15. A smart business person's restaurant, serving high-quality, high-price dishes. Expense-account stuff.

Thomas Kök och Matsal Köpmangatan 16, near the Domkyrkan. Serving delicious French cuisine-style dishes including wild boar with forest mushroom sauce from around 200kr,

Waldorf Storgatan 33. Inside the Wasa City shopping centre. Renowned for its pizzas, this restaurant also serves decent Chinese and Japanese food. Pizzas from 60kr upwards, more substantial dishes over 120kr.

Listings

Airport ☎0920/58 70 08.
Banks Handelsbanken, Storgatan, between the *Elite Stadshotellet* and tourist office; Nordea, Köpmangatan, near the pharmacy.
Buses City bus information on ☎020/99 00 00 or at ⊛www.llt.lulea.se; long-distance bus information is on ☎020/47 00 47 and at ⊛www.ltnbd.se.
Car rental Avis, Banvägen 6 ☎0920/183 50; Budget, Stationsgatan 26 ☎0920/881 88; Hertz, Gammelstadsvägen 23 ☎0920/873 44; Statoil,

Stationsgatan 30 ☎0920/186 22.
Hospital Luleå Lasarett, Repslagaregatan 2–6 ☎0920/714 00.
Pharmacy Köpmangatan 36c (Mon–Fri 9am–6pm, Sat 9am–2pm, Sun 1–4pm).
Police Skeppsbrogatan 37 ☎0920/29 50 00.
Post office Storgatan 53 ☎020/23 22 21 (Mon–Fri 8am–6pm, Sat 10am–2pm).
Swimming pool Pontusbadet, Bastugatan 6–8 ☎0920/29 32 72, with a decent sauna suite, too.

Moving on from Luleå

From Luleå, **trains** run northwest along the Malmbanan to Boden, Gällivare, Kiruna, Abisko, Riksgränsen and ultimately Narvik in Norway. Services along this route can be subject to lengthy delays, particularly in winter, so plan your journey with flexibility in mind. **Buses** complement the train service in this part of Sweden; particularly useful routes from Luleå are bus #21 (for Älvsbyn and Arvidsjaur); bus #44 (for Jokkmokk and Gällivare); bus #10 (for Gällivare and Kiruna); buses #11 and #300 (for Haparanda); and buses #53 and #54 (for Pajala).

Three **night trains** run **south** from Luleå; the first leaves at 4.26pm for Stockholm, followed by a train for Gothenburg at 5.11pm and finally one to Stockholm at 9pm. The first Stockholm service operates via Boden, Umeå, Gävle, Uppsala and Arlanda airport – but, importantly, not Bräcke. By taking the later Stockholm train at 9pm, which does stop in Bräcke, you can reach Östersund (change in Bräcke at 5.51am) and Sundsvall (change in Ånge at 6.15am). There are four daily **Norrlandskusten buses** from Luleå to Sundsvall via the towns along the Bothnian coast.

Systembolaget Storgatan 25 (Mon–Wed
10am–6pm, Thurs & Fri 10am–7pm, Sat
10am–2pm).
Taxi Taxi Luleå ℡ 0920/100 00; 6:ans Taxi
℡ 0920/666 66.

Trains Prästgatan. For train times call ℡ 020/44
41 11.
Travel agent Ticket, Storgatan 27 (Mon–Fri
9am–6pm, Sat 10am–1pm).

Gammelstad

One of the most significant places of historical interest north of Uppsala,
GAMMELSTAD (Ⓦ www.lulea.se/gammelstad), the original settlement of
Luleå and 11km northwest of the present city, is included on UNESCO's
World Heritage List. The **church** here (daily 9am–6pm; free) was completed at
the end of the fifteenth century; originally intended to be a cathedral, it's one
of the largest churches in Norrland, and among the most impressive in the
whole of Sweden. The building was worked on by artists from far and wide.
On the outside are decorative brick and plaster gables and there's an opening
above the south door through which boiling oil was poured over unwelcome
visitors. The high altar, made in Antwerp, is adorned with finely carved biblical scenes; the decorated choir stalls and ornate triptych are other medieval
originals. Have a close look at the sumptuous 1712 pulpit, too, a splendid
example of Baroque extravagance, its details trimmed with gilt cherubs and red
and gold bunches of grapes, made by local craftsman Nils Fluur, who also produced the pulpits for the churches in Öjebyn and Piteå.

When Luleå moved to the coast, a handful of the more religious among the
townsfolk stayed behind to tend the church, and the attached **parish village**,
the largest in Sweden, remained in use. It comprises over four hundred **cottages**, which can only be occupied by people born in Gammelstad (even people from Luleå must marry a local to gain the right to live here). Down the hill
from the cottages is **Friluftsmuséet Hägnan** (June to mid-Aug daily
11am–5pm; free; Ⓦ www.lulea.se/hagnan) an open-air heritage park, whose
main exhibits are two old farmstead buildings from the eighteenth century.
During summer, it plays host to displays of rural skills, such as sheep-rearing,
making traditional wooden roof slates and baking of northern Sweden's
unleavened bread, **tunnbröd**.

Practicalities

Gammelstad, 10km northwest of the modern city centre, is readily reached by
bus from Luleå: buses #9 and #32 run twice-hourly leaving from
Hermelinsparken at the western end of Skeppsbrogatan. The **tourist office** is
right by the old church (mid-June to mid-Aug daily 9am–6pm; mid-Aug to
mid-June Mon–Fri 11am–4pm; ℡ 0920/29 35 81, Ⓔ worldheritage.gammelstad@
lulea.se) and the staff organize guided walks around the village and have
brochures telling you all about the historical significance of the place. For a
place to **eat**, there's **Margaretas Wärdshus,** in a beautiful old wooden house
at Lulevägen 2, close to the old church; among the fine fare it serves up are
Norrbotten delicacies like reindeer and Arctic char for around 120kr.

The Luleå archipelago

Luleå's **archipelago** (Ⓦ www.lulea.se/skargard) is the only one in the world
surrounded by brackish water (the Atlantic Ocean off the Norwegian port of
Narvik contains ten times more salt than this part of the Gulf of Bothnia).
Made up of over 1700 islands and skerries, most of which are uninhabited and
unexploited, it's well worth a visit; the islands are renowned for rich bird-life
and a profusion of wild berries: lingonberries, blueberries and raspberries are

5

THE BOTHNIAN COAST | Luleå and around

very common, with arctic raspberries, cloudberries, wild strawberries and sea buckthorns also found in large numbers. The **islands** mentioned below are among the most **popular** destinations in the archipelago; being served by once-daily passenger boats from Luleå, they're also the most easily accessible. With a few notable exceptions, the islands are relatively small – no more than a couple of square kilometres in size – and are therefore ideal for short **walks**. Few are inhabited year-round and, hence, there are barely any facilities – you should take all provisions with you and shouldn't count on being able to buy anything once you leave the boat. Although it's perfectly feasible to take a tent and camp on the islands, other **accommodation** is severely limited (we have listed where cabins exist) and most visitors to the islands are day-trippers.

The wildest and most beautiful of all the islands is **Brändöskär**. Located far out in the Gulf of Bothnia, the island can often by very windy; its best features are some terrific upland scenery and smooth rocks along the coast, ideal for sunbathing.

People have lived and worked on **Hindersön**, one of the bigger islands here, since the sixteenth century. Then, fishing, farming and catching seals were the main occupations; today, this is the only island north of Arholma in the Stockholm archipelago which is still farmed.

Kluntarna has a little of everything – small fishing villages, dense pine forest and thousands of seabirds – and is a good choice, especially if you've only time to visit one island. You can rent a simple **cottage** here (book at Luleå's tourist office; 300kr), and there's a sauna for your use as well.

South of Luleå in the outer archipelago is **Rödkallen**. Site of an important lighthouse, this tiny island offers fantastic sea and sky views; parts of it have been declared a nature reserve.

Klubbviken, a bay on the island of **Sandön**, is the place to come for good sandy beaches, and has the added advantage of regular boat connections to Luleå. Walking paths crisscross the island, taking in some terrific pine moorland scenery. **Cabins** on Klubbviken can be booked at the tourist office; reckon on 550kr for four people per night.

Småskär is characterized by virgin forest, flat cliff tops and countless small lakes. The island traces its history back to the seventeenth century, when it was a base for Luleå's fishermen. Its small chapel, dating from 1720, was the first to be built in the archipelago. There's a small **cottage** available for rent here (300kr per night) – book through the tourist office in Luleå.

Travel practicalities

Four or five **boats** serve the various islands in the archipelago from mid-June to mid-August, with a reduced service running from early to mid-June and from mid-Aug to mid-Sept. From Luleå's northern harbour, **M/S Favourite** and **M/S Ronja** go to **Brändöskär, Hindersön, Rödkallen, Altappen, Junkön, Småskär** and **Kluntarna**. You're most likely to find yourself on board these two boats since they serve more islands than the others; information on routes and times can be obtained from Luleå's tourist office. The **M/S Laponia** sails, also from the northern harbour, to **Kluntarna, Småskär, Altappen** and **Brändöskär** (details of sailings on ☏0920/120 84 or ☏070/530 33 44, ⊛www.laponia.net). From the southern harbour, day-trips out to the sandy beaches of **Klubbviken** on the island of **Sandön** are made by the **M/S Stella Marina** (details of sailings on ☏0920/22 38 90 or ☏070/565 0761). During the first two weeks of June and from mid-Aug to mid-Sept the small boat **M/S Gajecha** sails once daily on Fridays and Sundays to Klubbviken, Junkön, Kluntarna, Småskär, Brändöskär and Hindersön, making it possible to spend a weekend out in the archipelago.

Boden

Roughly halfway along the coast of Norrbotten, at the narrowest bridging point along the Lule river, **BODEN** is a major transport junction for the entire north of the country; from here, trains run northwest to Gällivare and Kiruna and eventually on to Narvik in Norway, and south to Stockholm, Gothenburg and Arlanda Airport. From the station, you simply walk west for ten minutes along Kungsgatan to get to the town centre. Although first impressions of Boden are of a drab northern town, things get considerably better around the **Överluleå kyrka** (late June to early Aug daily 10am–7pm; rest of year Mon–Fri 9am–3pm) and its **parish village**, which were founded in 1826. It's roughly a twenty-minute walk here from the station, turning right into Strandplan once you've crossed the Kungsbron bridge on Kungsgatan. Pleasant enough in itself, the church's appeal benefits considerably from its location, perched on a hillock, surrounded by whispering birch trees and overlooking the water. The surrounding cottages of the parish village once spread down the hill to the lake, Bodträsket, lining narrow little alleyways. Today, the cottages that remain are rented out as superior **hostel accommodation** during the summer (see overleaf).

Boden happens to have the distinction of being Sweden's largest military town: everywhere you look, you'll see young men in camouflage gear strutting purposefully (if somewhat ridiculously) up and down the streets. If you're interested in military attire through the ages, head for the **Garnisonsmuseum** (June–Aug daily 11am–4pm; free; ⓦwww.boden.mil.se), housing the largest collection of uniforms north of Stockholm. It's at the southwestern edge of town; bus #1 (direction Sävast; 14kr) comes here from the train station.

Two places in Boden will almost certainly appeal to kids. Located in the town centre, roughly midway between the two military establishments, is Boden's fantastic **swimming complex**, Nord Poolen (mid-June to mid-Aug daily 9am–6pm; mid-Aug to mid-June Mon–Fri 8am–9pm; 60kr; ⓣ0921/624 00, ⓦwww.nordpoolen.com), at Garnisonsgatan 1. It boasts indoor and outdoor pools (all edged with tropical palms), two water slides, Jacuzzis and saunas. The complex is a ten-minute walk south on Lulevägen from the Kungsbron bridge on Kungsgatan. For a taste of the Wild West, head out to **Western Farm** (June–Aug Tues–Sun 11am–6pm; 75kr; ⓦwww .western-farm.com), a theme park 3km from town at Buddbyvägen 6 in the village of **Buddbyn** (reached by bus #8 from the train station; 14kr). There's a re-creation of an American frontier town (the year is supposedly 1879) complete with re-enactions of cowboys and Indians showdowns, all unfolding on the edge of the Arctic Circle.

Practicalities

The **train station**, on Stationsgatan, is at the eastern edge of town; buses leave from in front of the station). The **tourist office** is in the town centre at Kungsgatan 40 (June–Aug Mon–Fri 9am–7pm, Sat 9am–4pm, Sun noon–4pm; Sept–May Mon–Fri 10am–5.30pm, Sat 10am–1pm; ⓣ0921/624 10, ⓦwww.turistbyran.com). There's **Internet** access immediately across the road at the town library, located inside Folkets Hus at Kungsgatan 51. Boden's **youth hostel** is 100m from the train station at Fabriksgatan 6 (ⓣ0921/133 35 & ⓣ070/681 33 35). One of the most convenient **hotels** for the station is the cheap and cheerful **Hotell Standard**, at Stationsgatan 5 (ⓣ0921/160 55, ⓕ175 58; 495kr per person); it's the first thing you'll see when coming out of the station building. For more comfort and style, there's **Hotell Bodensia**, in the centre of town at Kungsgatan 47 (☏0921/177 10, ⓦwww.bodensia.se; ❹/❸). The **campsite** (☏0921/624 07, ⓦwww.boden.se/camping) is a few minutes' walk from the church following the path along the lakeside to Björknäs. It has six-bed cabins for 750kr per night, and four-bed cottages for 550kr per night; **canoes** (40kr an hour, 160kr a day) and **bikes** can also be rented here (50kr a day), and there's a heated outdoor pool too. You might want to consider staying in one of Boden's **parish cottages** (to rent one, call ☏0921/198 70; ❶ or ❷ depending on size), though it's worth noting that these usually get booked up months in advance, particularly for July.

Of the very few **restaurants** in town, the best of the bunch is the excellent and unexpectedly chic **Pär och Mickes Kök** at Kungsgatan 20 (at the station end of the street), where fine food is served up every evening; a three-course affair is only 195kr. Opposite is another restaurant, the unpretentious **Panelen**, in an old wooden building; orders are taken at the counter, with meat dishes here starting at 80kr. For pizza, head for **Restaurang Romeo** on Drottninggatan in the pedestrianized centre, with pizzas from 62kr and meat dishes starting at 100kr. Your best bet for a good lunch is **Café Ollé** at Drottninggatan 4 (opposite **Restaurang Romeo**), where the **Dagens Rätt** goes for 59kr; this place is also good for open sandwiches. Chinese dishes can be had for about 100kr each at **Ming Palace** in the square on Drottninggatan; lunch here is 63kr.

For a **drink**, the best spots are **Olivers Inn** just before Kungsbron bridge on Kungsgatan, and the oddly named **Puben med stort P** (its name means "Pub with a capital P") at Kungsgatan 23. Alternatively, you can buy drink at the local Systembolaget at Drottninggatan 8 (Mon–Wed & Fri 10am–6pm, Thurs 10am–7pm, Sat 10am–2pm).

Haparanda and around

Right by the Finnish border, at the very northern end of the Gulf of Bothnia, **HAPARANDA** is hard to like. The signpost near the bus station reinforces the fact that the town is a very long way from anywhere: Stockholm, 1100km away; the North Cape in Norway, 800km away; and Timbuktu – 8386km distant. The train station, eerily empty today after the branch line to Boden and Tornio in Finland became another victim of SJ closures in 1992, only serves to reinforce the town's backwater status. A grand-looking building, it was the result of Haparanda's aspirations to be a major trading centre after World War I. The hoped-for takeoff never happened, and walking up and down the streets around the main square, Torget, is a pretty depressing experience.

The key to Haparanda's grimness is the neighbouring Finnish town of Tornio. Finland was part of Sweden from 1105 until 1809, with Tornio an important trading centre, serving markets across northern Scandinavia. Things began to unravel when Russia attacked and occupied Finland in 1807; the Treaty of Hamina followed, forcing Sweden to cede Finland to Russia in 1809 – thereby losing Tornio. It was decided that Tornio had to be replaced, and so in 1821, the trading centre of Haparanda was founded – on the Swedish side of the new border, which ran along the Torne river. However, the new town was never more than a minor upstart compared to its neighbour across the water – until recently. With both Sweden and Finland now members of the European Union, Haparanda and **Tornio** have declared themselves a **Eurocity**

– one city made up of two towns from different countries. A regional council, the Provincia Bothiensis (a neutral name – neither Swedish nor Finnish) has been set up to foster cooperation between the towns. The inhabitants of Haparanda and Tornio are bilingual and use both the euro and the Swedish krona; roughly half of the children in Haparanda have either a Finnish mother or father. Services are also shared between the two: everything from central heating to post delivery is centrally coordinated. If a fire breaks out in Tornio, for example, Swedish fire crews from Haparanda will cross the border to help put out the flames.

There are only two real sights in town. The **train station**, built in 1918, dominates the suburban streets of southern Haparanda. Constructed from red brick and reached by a flight of steps leading up from the small square in front, complete with stone tower and lantern on Järnvägsgatan, it once provided Sweden's only rail link to Finland. From the platforms, you'll be able to discern two widths of track – Finnish trains run on the wider, Russian, gauge. The empty sidings, overgrown with weeds and bushes, backed by the towering station building, with its vast roof of black tiles and chimneys, give the place a strangely forlorn air. The only other place worthy of some attention is the peculiar copper-coloured **Haparanda kyrka** on Östra Kyrkogatan, a monstrous modern construction that looks like a cross between an aircraft hangar and an apartment building. When the church was finished in 1963, its design caused a public outcry: it even won the prize for being the ugliest church in Sweden.

Practicalities

Arriving from Luleå **buses** will drop you at the **bus station** at the northern end of Haparanda's main street, Stationsgatan, which runs parallel to the Torne river (the buildings you can see here across the river are in Finland). From here it's a five-minute walk south along Storgatan to the main square, Torget, where it's possible to get limited tourist information from the reception of the **Stadshotel** between June and August. The main **tourist office** (Finnish time: June to mid-Aug Mon–Fri 9am–7pm, Sat & Sun 11am–7pm; rest of year Mon–Fri 9am–5pm; ☎0922/120 10, ⊛www.haparanda.se), is actually in Finland in the Green Line Welcome Center and also has information about Tornio and the rest of Finland; there are two telephones in the office, one for calls from Sweden, the other with enquiries from Finland; staff switch effortlessly from one language to another depending on which phone is ringing. To get here from the bus station head towards the "Finland" signs on the nearby bridge – there are no border formalities, and so you can simply walk over the bridge to Finland and wander back whenever you like. It's worth remembering that **Finnish time** is one hour ahead of Swedish time and that Haparanda and Tornio have different names in Swedish (Haparanda and Torneå) and Finnish (Haaparanta and Tornio).

The cheapest beds in town are at Haparanda's STF **youth hostel**, a smart riverside place at Strandgatan 26 (☎0922/611 71, ⊛www.haparandavandrarhem .com), affording good views across to Finland. Another inexpensive place is the cheap and cheerful pension, **Resandehem**, in the centre of town at Storgatan 65B (☎0922/120 68; ❶). **Haparanda Stadshotel** is the only **hotel** in town, at Torget 7 (☎0922/614 90, ℻102 23; ❺/❸); an elegant and sumptious place dating from 1900, full of wooden flooring and opulent chandeliers, some rooms even have their own sauna.

Two **bus** routes head north on the Swedish side of the border through the beautiful Torne valley: #54 runs to Pajala (Mon–Fri 2 daily; 140kr), whereas #53 makes the six-hour journey via Pajala and Vittangi to Kiruna (Mon–Thurs & Sun 1 daily, 2 buses on Fri; 240kr). Connections can be made in Vittangi for bus #50 to Karesuando. To head west take bus #11 or #300 to Luleå (Mon–Fri 12 daily, Sat & Sun 5 daily). Finnish-operated buses connect Haparanda with Tornio and Kemi every hour; times are posted up at the bus station in Haparanda. In addition, there are direct buses from Haparanda to Rovaniemi (Mon–Fri 2 daily, Sat & Sun 1 daily; 3hr) and from Haparanda to Oulu (Uleåborg in Swedish; 2 daily; 2hr 30min).

As far as eating, drinking and nightlife go, you're better off in Tornio in every respect. Friday nights there are wild, the streets full of people trying to negotiate the return leg over the bridge; meanwhile, Haparanda sleeps undisturbed. It used to be the case that Tornio was much cheaper than Haparanda, but prices are now roughly the same, although drinking is still a little less expensive in Finland. For **eating** without trekking over to Finland, there are several options: the lunches at the plastic-looking **Prix Restaurant** at Norra Esplanaden 8 are fine, though not particularly inspiring (50kr). The youth hostel has its own restaurant that does a **Dagens Rätt** (55kr); however, your best bet is **Hasans Pizzeria** at Storgatan 88, close to Torget, which has lunch for 50kr. As well as a range of Chinese and Thai dishes (80–100kr), the local Chinese restaurant, **Leilani** at Köpmangatan 15, also does pizzas. **Nya Konditoriet** on Storgatan is good for coffee and cakes; for open sandwiches and baguettes try **Café Rosa**, in the Gallerian shopping centre on Storgatan. For **drinking** in Haparanda, head for the **Ponderosa** pub at Storgatan 82 or alternatively, try the **Gulasch Baronen** pub, attached to the **Stadshotel**, which serves slightly more expensive beers.

Around Haparanda

Having travelled so far to reach Haparanda, the northernmost point on the Swedish east coast, it seems churlish to leave without making at least one for-ray into the surrounding area. Other than popping over the Finnish border into Tornio, there are a couple of other diversions worth exploring, notably a day-trip to one of several nearby **islands** or, inland, to the impressive rapids at **Kukkolaforsen** at the start of the Torne Valley.

Twenty-four kilometres to the southwest and attached to the mainland by a slender road-bridge, you'll find the sandy island of **Seskarö** (www.seskaro.nu), a favourite refuge for windsurfers and swimmers. There's a **campsite** here (0922/201 50, 0922/202 44), with cabins for 4–6 people available (490kr), as well as cycle and boat rental. To get to the island, take **bus** #322 from the bus station in Haparanda (Mon–Fri 4 daily; 32kr).

South of Seskarö is the start of the Haparanda **archipelago**, which extends into the Baltic's northernmost arm; the two main islands, **Seskar-Furö** and the larger **Sandskär**, were declared a national park in 1995 and contain impor-tant fauna and flora, including the razorbill and little tern, as well as the lesser butterfly orchid. A boat leaves for Sandskär from the quay on Strandgatan, 400m south of the youth hostel (July Wed & Thurs only; boat information on 0922/133 95, www.bosmina.bd.se).

Fifteen kilometres north of Haparanda, reached on buses #53 and #54 to Pajala, the impressive rapids at **Kukkolaforsen** (www.kukkolaforsen.se) are best visited during the **Sikfesten** ("Whitefish Festival"), held on the last weekend in July. The **whitefish**, a local delicacy grilled on large open fires, are caught in nets at the end of long poles, fishermen dredging the fast, white water and scooping the fish out onto the bank. The festival celebrates a sort of fisherman's harvest, centuries old, although it's now largely an excuse to get drunk at the beer tent, with evening gigs and dancing the order of the day. It costs 100kr to get in on the Saturday, 60kr on the Sunday; if you're staying in the adjacent **campsite** (T0922/310 00, F0922/310 30), which has four-berth cabins for 420kr per night or larger cottages at 660kr per night, you should be able to sneak in for free. Also worth checking out is the local **Fiskemuseum** (mid-June to mid-Aug daily 10am–6pm; free), which gives accounts of local fishing activities; there's also a freshwater aquarium, a working nineteenth-century mill and enormous salmon.

The Swedish Sauna Academy has rated the **sauna** at Kukkolaforsen the country's finest; after you've sweated to your heart's content here, you can breathe the crisp air on the verandah, heavy with the scent of pine, look across the rapids and wave to Finland on the other side of the river. To get out onto the water, **river rafting** down the rapids can be arranged through the tourist office in Haparanda or at the campsite at Kukkolaforsen – 200kr rents the gear, pays for a short trip downriver, and gets you a certificate at the end.

Travel details

Trains

Boden to: Gällivare (3 daily; 2hr); Gävle (2 daily; 11hr); Gothenburg (1 daily; 16hr); Kiruna (3 daily; 3hr); Luleå (6 daily; 25min); Stockholm (2 daily; 13hr); Uppsala (2 daily; 12hr).

Gävle to: Boden (2 daily; 11hr); Falun (8 daily; 1hr); Gällivare (2 daily; 13hr 30min); Härnösand (1 daily; 3hr); Hudiksvall (8 daily; 1hr 15min); Kiruna (2 daily; 15hr); Luleå (2 daily; 12hr); Östersund (4 daily; 4hr); Stockholm (hourly; 1hr 30min); Sundsvall (8 daily; 2hr); Umeå (1 daily; 9hr); Uppsala (hourly; 45min).

Härnösand to: Gävle (1 daily; 3hr); Hudiksvall (1 daily; 2hr); Stockholm (1 daily; 4hr 30min); Sundsvall (1 daily; 1hr).

Hudiksvall to: Gävle (8 daily; 1hr 15min); Härnösand (1 daily; 2hr); Stockholm (8 daily; 2hr 30min); Sundsvall (8 daily; 45min); Söderhamn (13 daily; 25min); Uppsala (8 daily; 2hr).

Luleå to: Boden (5 daily; 25min); Gällivare (3 daily; 2hr 30min); Gävle (2 daily; 12hr); Gothenburg (1 daily; 16hr 45min); Kiruna (3 daily; 3hr 30min); Stockholm (2 daily; 14hr); Umeå (2 daily; 4hr 15min); Uppsala (2 daily; 13hr).

Sundsvall to: Gävle (8 daily; 2hr); Härnösand (1 daily; 1hr); Hudiksvall (8 daily; 45min); Östersund (5 daily; 2hr 20min); Stockholm (8 daily; 3hr 30min).

Söderhamn to: Gävle (8 daily; 50min); Hudiksval (13 daily; 25min); Härnösand (1 daily; 2hr 30min); Stockholm (8 daily; 2hr); Sundsvall (8 daily; 1hr

15min); Uppsala (8 daily; 1hr 30min).

Umeå to: Gävle (1 daily; 9hr); Gothenburg (1 daily; 13hr 30min); Luleå (2 daily; 4hr 15min); Stockholm (1 daily; 11hr 15min); Uppsala (1 daily; 10hr 30min).

Buses

The reliable **Norrlandskusten** buses run four times daily between Sundsvall and Luleå, generally connecting with trains to and from Sundsvall. Tickets should be bought from the bus driver when boarding. The buses have toilets on board. From Sundsvall, the buses call at Härnösand (45min); Gallsäter (1hr 35min); Ullånger (1hr 45min); Docksta (1hr 50min); Örnsköldsvik (2hr 30min); Umeå (4hr); Skellefteå (6hr 15min); Piteå (7hr 30min) and Luleå (8hr 30min).

Other bus services run from the coast into central northern Sweden, often linking up with the Inlandsbanan. Key routes are:

Boden to: Luleå (Mon–Fri every 30mins, Sat & Sun 9 daily; 50min).

Haparanda to: Luleå (Mon–Fri 12 daily, Sat & Sun 5 daily; 2hr 30min); Pajala (Mon–Fri 2–3 daily, Sun 1 daily; 3hr 30min).

Hudiksvall to: Sveg (Mon–Fri 2 daily, Sat & Sun 1 daily; 3hr).

Luleå to: Arvidsjaur (Mon–Fri 2 daily, Sat & Sun 1 daily; 3hr); Boden (Mon–Fri 43 daily, Sat & Sun 9 daily; 50min); Gällivare (Mon–Thurs 2 daily, Fri & Sun 3 daily, Sat 1 daily; 3hr 15min); Haparanda

(Mon–Fri 12 daily, Sat & Sun 5 daily); Jokkmokk (Mon–Fri 3 daily, Sat 1 daily, Sun 2 daily; 2hr 45min); Kiruna (Mon–Thurs 2 daily, Fri & Sun 3 daily, Sat 1 daily; 5hr); Pajala (Mon–Fri & Sun 2 daily, Sat 1 daily; 3hr 30min).

Piteå to: Arvidsjaur (Mon–Fri & Sun 1 daily; 2hr).

Skellefteå to: Arjeplog (3hr 15min), Arvidsjaur (2hr), Jäckvik (4hr) and Vuoggatjålme (5hr), Mon–Fri & Sun 1 bus.

Sollefteå to: Örnsköldsvik (Mon–Fri 2 daily, Sat & Sun 1 daily; 1hr 45min); Östersund (Mon–Fri 3 daily, Sat & Sun 1 daily; 3hr).

Umeå to Dorotea (2 daily; 3hr); Vilhelmina (Mon–Fri 3 daily, Sat & Sun 2 daily; 3hr 30min); Storuman and Tärnaby/Hemavan (Mon–Thurs & Sat 3 daily, 4 buses on Fri, 1 bus on Sun; 3hr 40min to Storuman, 6hr to Tärnaby/Hemavan.

Örnsköldsvik to: Dorotea (Mon–Sat 2 daily, Sun 1 daily; 5hr); Sollefteå (Mon–Fri 2 daily, Sat & Sun 1 daily; 1hr 50min); and Östersund (Mon–Fri 2 daily, Sat & Sun 1 daily; 4hr 30min).

International trains

Boden to: Narvik, Norway (1 daily; 6hr).
Luleå to: Narvik, Norway (1 daily; 6hr 30min).

International buses

Haparanda to: Oulu, Finland (2 daily; 2hr 30min); Rovaniemi, Finland (Mon–Fri 2 daily; 3hr).
Skellefteå to: Bodø, Norway (Mon–Fri & Sun 1 daily; 9hr); Fauske, Norway (Mon–Fri & Sun 1 daily; 7hr 30min).
Umeå to: Mo-i-Rana, Norway (1 daily; 8hr).

International ferries

Härnösand to: Vaasa, Finland (3–4 weekly; 10hr)
Umeå to: Vaasa, Finland (1 daily; 4hr).

Central Sweden

CHAPTER 6

Highlights

* **Riding the Inlandsbanan** A chance to see Sweden's vast forests and fast-flowing rivers close up – but without leaving the comfort of your train seat. See p.424.

* **Island beaches, Kristinehamn** A chain of islands in Lake Vänern offer the perfect opportunity to chill out and work on your all-over tan. See p.421.

* **Hiking in the Härjedalen mountains** Get back to nature and experience the wild side of central Sweden in this remote mountainous province. See p.438.

* **Rafting on the Klarälven river, Karlstad** Build your own raft and glide down one of Värmland's most enchanting rivers. See p.420.

* **Monster spotting, Östersund** Go hunting for Sweden's version of the Loch Ness monster in this appealing lakeside town. See p.429.

* **Orsa Grönklitt bear park, Dalarna** Europe's largest bear park offers a unique chance to see these shy animals at close quarters. See p.434.

Central Sweden

n many ways, the long wedge of land that comprises **central Sweden** – from the shores of **Lake Vänern** up to the border with the province of Lappland – encompasses all that is most typical of the country. This vast area of land is really one great forest, broken only by the odd village or town. Rural and underpopulated, it epitomizes the image most people have of Sweden: lakes, log cabins, pine forests and wide, open skies. Until just one or two generations ago, Swedes across the country lived in this sort of setting, taking their cue from the people of these central lands and forest, who were the first to rise against the Danes in the sixteenth century.

At the extreme southwest of the region, the province of **Värmland**, with its shimmering lakeside capital, **Karlstad**, is best known for sweeping forests, fertile farmland and lazy rivers, once used to float timber into Lake Vänern and now the best means of seeing this most peaceful part of central Sweden, through one of the trips downstream on ready-built pontoon rafts. Just to the northeast, **Dalarna** province, centred around **Lake Siljan**, is an intensely picturesque – and touristy – region, its inhabitants maintaining a cultural heritage (echoed in contemporary handicrafts and traditions) that goes back to the Middle Ages. You won't need to brave the crowds of visitors for too long, as even a quick tour around one or two of the more accessible places here gives an impression of the whole: red cottages with white door and window frames, sweeping green countryside, water that's bluer than blue and a riot of summer festivals. Dalarna is *the* place to spend midsummer, particularly **Midsummer's Eve**, when the whole region erupts in a frenzy of celebration.

The privately owned **Inlandsbanan**, the great Inland Railway, cuts right through central Sweden and links many of the towns and villages covered in this chapter. Running from **Mora** in Dalarna to **Gällivare**, above the Arctic Circle, it ranks with the best of European train journeys, covering an enthralling 1067km in two days; the second half of the journey, north of Östersund (where you have to change trains), is covered in the Swedish Lapland chapter, see p.457. Buses connect the rail line with the mountain villages that lie alongside the Norwegian border, where the surrounding Swedish *fjäll*, or fells, offer some spectacular and compelling hiking, notably around **Ljungdalen** and **Tänndalen** in the remote province of **Härjedalen**. Marking the halfway point of the line, **Östersund**, the only town of any size along it, is situated by the side of Storsjön, the great lake that's reputed to be home to the country's own Loch Ness monster, Storsjöodjuret. From here trains head in all directions: west into Norway through Sweden's premier **ski** resort, **Åre**, south to Dalarna and Stockholm, east to Sundsvall on the Bothnian coast and north into the wild terrain of Swedish Lapland.

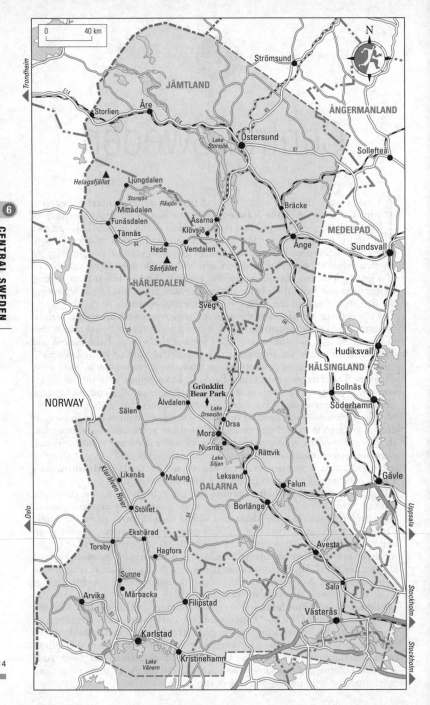

The northern shore of Lake Vänern

Connected to Stockholm by fast and frequent trains, the northern shore of **Lake Vänern** and the adjoining province of **Värmland** (@www.varmland.org) is the easiest region of central Sweden to travel, with direct trains from the capital passing south of Lake Mälaren bound for here, via Katrineholm and Hallsberg. The latter, a major transport hub for this part of the country, is where you change to get to Värmland from Swedish Lapland, Östersund, Dalarna and Västerås. Once you've arrived in the vicinity of the lake, the places to seek out are the enjoyable provincial capital **Karlstad** and the shy and retiring **Kristinehamn** (see p.421), both at the lakeside. If you're looking for nature rather than culture, you'll find it in plentiful supply along the banks of the Klarälven river where rafting is one of the province's most popular outdoor activities.

Karlstad and around

"Wherever I look I see fire – fire in the houses, fire in the air, fire everywhere. The whole world is burning. There is thundering, crackling, shouting, hissing and howling."

The recollections of Karlstad's most famous son, the poet Gustaf Fröding, on the Great Fire of 1865.

Sitting elegantly on Lake Vänern, **KARLSTAD**, capital of the province of Värmland, is named after King Karl IX, who granted the place its town charter in 1584. Since then, the town has been beset by several disaster; devastating **fires** ripped through the centre in 1616 and 1729, but it was in 1865, when fire broke out in a bakery on the corner of Östra Torggatan and Drottninggatan, that Karlstad suffered its worst calamity: virtually the entire town, including the Cathedral, burned to the ground – giving rise to the local saying "the bishop swore and doused the flames whilst the governor wept and prayed". Of 241 buildings that made up the town then, only seven survived the flames. Sweden had not experienced such a catastrophe in living memory, and a national emergency fund was immediately set up to help pay for reconstruction. Building began apace, with an emphasis on wide streets and large open squares to act as firebreaks and so prevent another tragedy. The result is an elegant and thoroughly likeable town, full of life, which makes an altogether more agreeable base from which to tour the surrounding country and lakeside than nearby Kristinehamn.

Karlstad is served by international **trains** between Stockholm and Oslo (it's roughly halfway between the two), as well as the more frequent X2000 service from Stockholm. Direct train services also run along the western side of the lake from Gothenburg. Heading here from southeastern Sweden, Västerås and towns in Norrland, you'll need to change in Hallsberg. From Dalarna it's quickest to get here by **bus**, with a handy Swebus Express service, the #800 (2 daily; 3hr 30min; 160kr), making the trip from Falun and Borlänge to Karlstad (and on to Gothenburg); leaving from Mora, Rättvik or Leksand, you can change onto this bus in Borlänge. Karlstad is also linked by **air** with Stockholm (SAS) and Copenhagen (Skyways).

Arrival and information

The modern centre of Karlstad is built upon the island of **Tingvalla**. The **bus station** is located at the western end of Drottninggatan; close by is the **train station** on Hamngatan. Karlstad's **airport**, 18km from the centre, is served by buses (75kr) and taxis (200kr). At the opposite end of the town centre from the stations is the **tourist office**, located in the Carlstad Conference Centre on Tage Erlandergatan 10 (June–Aug Mon–Fri 9am–7pm, Sat 10am–6pm, Sun 11am–4pm; Sept–May Mon–Fri 9am–5pm; ℡054/22 21 40, ⓦwww.karlstad .se). It's a good place to pick up general information and make bookings for river rafting trips on the Klarälven river (see p.420); they also have timetables for buses throughout Värmland, which can help you plan a trip elsewhere in the province.

Accommodation

Karlstad's **youth hostel** is located 3km from the centre in Ulleberg (℡054/56 68 40, ℱ054/56 60 42), in a rambling old house; it's reached on buses #11 or #32 in the direction of Bellevue. The nearest **campsites** are a nine-kilometre drive west out of the town along the E18: *Skutbergets camping* is open all year (℡054/53 51 39, ⓦwww.camping.se), whereas *Bomstad Badens camping* next door (℡054/53 50 68), beautifully situated on the lakeshore, is only open from June to August. The daily Badbussen, bus #18 (mid-June to mid-Aug hourly 10.30am–5.30pm; 25min) runs from Stora Torget via Drottninggatan to the beaches at Bomstad; ask at the tourist office for information on getting to the campsites by public transport at other times of the year. To claim the **summer discount** offered by all Karlstad's hotels – 550kr for a double room – you must book at least one day in advance.

Carlton Järnvägsgatan 8 ℡054/21 55 40, ℱ18 95 20. One of the cheaper hotels in Karlstad, with simple unadorned rooms, located in the pedestrianized centre. ❷

Drott Järnvägsgatan 1 ℡054/10 10 10, ⓦwww.drotthotel.se. Just 50m from the train station. Built in 1980, this is a smart, elegant hotel, next to a busy main road, though the double-glazing is effective against the noise. ❺/❸

Elite Stadshotellet Kungsgatan 22 ℡054/21 52 20, ⓦwww.elite.se. Beautifully located next to the river, with well-appointed rooms and good views, this is the best hotel in town. However, rooms in the wings of this cavernous place are rather dowdy and not worth the money; ask for one closer to the central staircase. ❺/❸

First Hotel Plaza Västra Torggatan 2 ℡054/10 02 00, ⓦwww.plaza-karlstad.nu. Large, modern, plush hotel, with a fantastic sauna offering panoramic views over the city. ❻/❸

Freden Fredsgatan 1A ℡054/21 65 82, ⓦwww.fredenhotel.com. Cheap and cheerful place, close to the bus and train stations. ❷/❶

Ibis Hotel Karlstad City Västra Torggatan 20 ℡054/17 28 30, ⓦwww.ibishotel.com. Good-value hotel in the centre of town, boasting a large breakfast buffet and free evening parking for guests. ❷

Solsta Drottninggatan 13 ℡054/15 68 45, ⓦwww.solstahotell.se. A good, central option with cable TV in all rooms and some adapted for the disabled. ❸/❷

The Town

It's best to start your wanderings around town in the large and airy market square, Stora Torget. The Neoclassical **Rådhuset**, on the square's western side, was the object of much local admiration upon its completion in 1867, just two years after the great fire; local worthies were particularly pleased with the two stone Värmland eagles that adorn the building's roof, no doubt hoping the birds would help ward off another devastating blaze.

In front of the town hall, the rather austere **Peace Monument** commemorates the peaceful dissolution of the union between Sweden and Norway in 1905, which was negotiated in the town. Unveiled fifty years later, it portrays an angry woman madly waving a broken sword whilst planting her right foot firmly atop a soldier's severed head; "feuds feed folk hatred, peace promotes people's understanding" reads the inscription. Across Östra Torggatan, the nearby **Domkyrkan** was consecrated in 1730, although only its arches and walls survived the flames of 1865. Its most interesting features

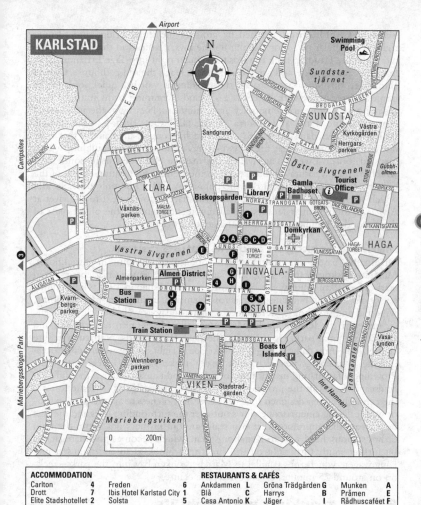

ACCOMMODATION

Carlton	4	Freden	6
Drott	7	Ibis Hotel Karlstad City	1
Elite Stadshotellet	2	Solsta	5
First Hotel Plaza	8	Youth hostel	3

RESTAURANTS & CAFÉS

Ankdammen	L	Gröna Trädgården	G	Munken	A
Blå	C	Harrys	B	Pråmen	E
Casa Antonio	K	Jäger	I	Rådhuscaféet	F
Glada Ankan	D	Kebab House	H	Tom Yam	J

are the altar, made from Gotland limestone with a cross of Orrefors crystal, and the font, also of crystal. The site where the Cathedral stands, Lagberget on Kungsgatan, was only selected after previous churches located by the river on the island of Tingvalla (now the modern centre of Karlstad) were destroyed by various fires.

Continuing east along Kungsgatan and over the narrow Pråmkanalen into Hagatorget square, the road swings left and changes its name to Nygatan ahead of the longest arched **stone bridge** in Sweden, Östra Bron. Completed in 1811, this massive construction is made up of twelve arches and spans 168m across the eastern branch of the Klarälven river. It's claimed the bridge's builder, Anders Jacobsson, threw himself off the bridge and drowned, afraid the achievement of his life would collapse; his name is engraved on a memorial stone tablet in the centre of the bridge. On sunny days, the nearby wooded island of **Gubbholmen**, reached by crossing the stone bridge and turning right, is a popular place for soaking up the rays; if you head there, take a picnic with you. Heading back towards town, turn right into Tage Errlandergatan from the stone bridge, and carry on until you reach the old bathhouse, **Gamla Badhuset**, on Norra Strandgatan; the building is worth a quick look for its impressive red stonework. Used as a spa and swimming baths until 1978, it today houses occasional temporary art exhibitions. Nearby, at the junction of Norra Strandgatan and Västra Torggatan, the Bishop's Residence, **Biskopsgården**, dates from 1781 and, as such, is one of the handful that were not destroyed in the great fire. A two-storey yellow wooden building with a mansard roof, it owes its survival to the massive elm trees on its south side, which formed a natural firebreak, and to the sterling firefighting efforts of the bishop of the time, alluded to in the phrase on p.415. The only other houses which survived are located in the Almen district of town, next to the river at Älvgatan; though their facades are all nineteenth century, the oldest parts of these wooden buildings date from the century before.

Mariebergsskogen and the nature centre
Originally based on the Skansen open-air museum in Stockholm, **Mariebergsskogen** (June–Aug daily 7am–10pm; free; ⓦwww.mariebergsskogen .karlstad.se), 2km southwest of the centre, was established in 1920 when a number of old wooden buildings from across Värmland, including a smoking house, windmill and storehouse, were relocated here. Today, as well the original open-air museum, the **leisure park** (May–Aug daily 11am–6pm) has a funfair and children's animal park. However, it's the new **Värmlands Naturum** nature centre (May–Aug daily 10am–6pm; 40kr), built right on the water's edge overlooking Mariebergsviken bay, that really makes a trip here worthwhile. Providing a fascinating insight into local flora and fauna as well as the different landscapes found in the province – anything from marshland to dense forest – the centre has been designed to accentuate the closeness to nature: glass exterior walls offering cinemascope views out over the surrounding trees and the lake help create the impression that you really are out in the wilds. From the train or bus stations, head west to Klaraborgsgatan, which becomes Jungmansgatan a bit further south; turn right off this street into Hööksgatan and then left into Långövagen, which runs parallel to Mariebergsviken bay, into the park – reckon on around 25 minutes on foot from the centre.

Eating, drinking and nightlife
Eating and **drinking** in Karlstad are a joy. There's a good selection of **restaurants**, specializing in everything from Thai and Spanish to vegetarian dishes. **Bars** are thick on the ground too for a Swedish town; the *Bishops Arms* and the *Woolpack Inn* are especially popular and packed out most nights, particularly at weekends.

Cafés and restaurants
Ankdammen Magasin 1, Tynäsgatan, in the Inner Harbour. Open-air restaurant with a large wooden jetty that catches the afternoon sun. A nice place for coffee and a snack. Open June to mid-Aug only.
Blå Kungsgatan 14. Currently the most pretentious and chi-chi of Karlstad's restaurants, attracting upwardly mobile young Swedes who come here to be seen through the semi-frosted windows. Top-

notch Swedish cooking at around 200kr per dish.
Casa Antonio Drottninggatan 7. Good Spanish restaurant with tapas from 35kr and paella for two at 260kr. The *Dagens Rätt* here is 60kr
Glada Ankan Kungsgatan 12. A lively first-floor restaurant with a balcony overlooking the main square, this place serves mostly Swedish dishes from around 130kr. Nice place for coffee.
Gröna Trädgården Västra Torggatan 9. With a

small balcony overlooking the pedestrianized street below, this first-floor vegetarian restaurant has a large salad buffet, and serves home-made bread with all meals. Open lunchtimes only; reckon 60–80kr.

Harrys Kungsgatan 16. An American-style bar, café and restaurant in the main square, with open-air seating in summer. Main courses, including burgers, from 75kr. The evening bar is pretty popular.

Jäger Västra Torggatan 8. Main courses of salmon, chicken and pork from 95kr at this trendy restaurant that really buzzes in the evening, when it's open till 2am.

Kebab House Västra Torggatan 7. Small but pleasant pizza and kebab place with outdoor seating in summer taking up a large chunk of the pedestrian street in front. Pizzas from 60kr.

Munken Västra Torggatan 17. Just off the main square. A cosy little restaurant, with stained-glass windows and a vaulted roof. Imaginative menu with fine food from 175kr.

Pråmen Älvgatan 4. A restaurant and café on a boat moored close to the main square, with good views over the river and the centre. Serving uncomplicated Swedish home-cooking, it's also a great place for a cup of coffee out on deck.

Rådhuscaféet Tingvallagatan 8. Elegant café in the town hall, entered from the left side of the building. In summer there's outdoor seating making this the premier spot for people-watching in the main square.

Tom Yam Fredsgatan 3B. A very small and friendly Thai restaurant with just a handful of tables, making it a good idea to arrive early to avoid disappointment. Excellent Thai food such as chicken in coconut milk with lime leaves and lemongrass for 93kr. Closed lunchtimes.

Bars and clubs

Bishops Arms Kungsgatan 22. Classic British-style pub enjoying a great location overlooking the river, with outdoor seating in summer and a wide range of beers.

Glada Ankan Kungsgatan 12. With seats out in the main square, this place is known for its wide choice of beers and lively evening atmosphere.

Harrys Kungsgatan 16. Good-sized American-style bar, with a wooden interior and plenty of people eager to practise their English.

Jäger bakgården Västra Torggatan 8. Behind the Jäger restaurant and actually accessed from Drottninggatan. A wooden beer terrace and dance-floor make this a great place to spend a summer evening.

Plaza Nattklubb Västra Torggatan 2. Inside the *First Hotel Plaza*. Definitely *the* in place for anyone over 23, with late night dancing – and much drinking. Fri & Sat evenings only.

Woolpack Inn Järnvägsgatan 1. Just across the road from the train station. Very popular, this is one of a few pubs in town doing their best to create traditional-British-style drinking establishments.

Listings

Airport SAS and Skyways on ☏054/55 60 00.
Banks FöreningsSparbanken, Kungsgatan 10; Handelsbanken, Tingvallagatan 17; Nordea, Tingvallagatan 11-13; S-E Banken, Drottninggatan 24.
Beaches Sundstatjärnet, at the swimming pool on Drottning Kristinas väg; Mariebergsviken, by the shore at Mariebergsskogen and also on the opposite side of the the bay (bus #20 or #31 head here); Bomstad, at the campsite southwest of Karlstad (#18).
Buses Information on buses in Värmland on ☏020/22 55 80 or at ☻www.kollplatsen.com.
Car rental Avis, Hamngatan 24 ☏054/15 26 60; Europcar, Hagalundsvägen 29 ☏054/18 23 20.
Cinemas Filmstaden, Drottninggatan 33A ☏054/770 40 00; Sandrews, Östra Torggatan 9

☏054/18 47 00.
Internet At the library on Västra Torggatan; free.
Police Drottninggatan 4 ☏054/14 50 00.
Swimming pool Sundsta Bad-och Idrottshus, Drottning Kristinas väg, reached by crossing Tingvallbron from Tingvall ☏054/29 68 71. (Mon 2pm–8pm, Tues–Fri 6.30am–8pm, Sat 8.30am–5pm, Sun 8.30am–1pm; 30kr)
Systembolaget Drottninggatan 26 (Mon–Wed 10am–6pm, Thurs & Fri 10am–7pm, Sat 10am–2pm).
Taxis Taxi Kurir ☏054/15 02 00.
Trains For information call ☏054/14 33 50 or ☏0771/75 75 75.
Travel agent Ticket, opposite the cinema on Drottninggatan (Mon–Fri 9am–6pm, Sat 10am–1pm).

Around Karlstad

Karlstad's importance as an inland port is in no small measure due to the sheer scale of **Lake Vänern**. The city makes an ideal base from which to explore the northern reaches of the lake and see some of the twenty-two thousand islands and skerries off Karlstad, which comprise the largest freshwater **archipelago** in Europe. You can do both by taking a ride on the charming old steamer *M/S Vestvåg*, built in 1885 (T054/21 99 43, Wwww.tillsjoss.se), which sails from Karlstad's Inre Hamnen (July to mid-Aug 3–4 weekly; 80kr one-way) out into the archipelago. Incidentally, the fresh smell of roasting coffee that fills the air down by the harbour comes from the nearby Löfbergs Lilla factory producing one of Sweden's most popular blends. Karlstad's also a good place from which to sail down one of the longest waterways in Scandinavia, the **Klarälven river**. An interesting day-trip from Karlstad is a visit to the house, at nearby Mårbacka, where the Nobel-prize-winning author **Selma Lagerlöf** once lived and wrote many of her books.

Rafting on the Klarälven river

The 500km-long **Klarälven river** begins over the border in Norway near Lake Femunden, entering Sweden at Långflon in the north of Värmland for slightly over half of its course. The Klarälven was one of the last Swedish rivers where timber was floated downstream to sawmills; the practice only ceased in 1991 here. Two companies, Sverigeflotten (T0564/402 27, Wwww.sverigeflotten .se) and Vildmark i Värmland (T0560/140 40, Wwww.vildmark.se), now operate **trips** along the river on sixteen-square-metre **timber rafts**, each of which takes two people. A three-day trip with either company costs around 2000kr. Travelling with Vildmark i Värmland, you must even build the raft yourself, supervised by one of their staff, using the three-metre-long logs and the rope provided; no other materials are allowed. Once you're under way, you'll find the water flows at around 2km per hour, which gives you time to swim, fish and study the countryside and animals along the river (beavers and elk are plentiful, and there are also wolverine, wolf, lynx, marten and bears out in the forest). At night, you sleep in a tent either on the raft, which is moored, or on the riverbank. Both companies begin their trips at Branäsberget near Ransby, though you need to assemble on day one at **Gunnerud** near **Ekshärad** for trips with Vildmark i Värmland; to **get there**, take bus #304 from Karlstad bus station and tell the driver you're going to the rafts (Mon–Fri 3 daily, Sat 1 daily, Sun 2 daily; 2hr 15min). Sverigeflotten's trips start at **Ransby** (also #304; 3hr) and end 90km south of here at *Byns Camping*, near Ekshärad; with Vildmark i Värmland, you'll end up a little further downriver back at Gunnerud. You can get back to Karlstad from both places on bus #304.

Mårbacka: the home of Selma Lagerlöf

About forty kilometres north of Karlstad by bus is **Mårbacka**, the house where the author, **Selma Lagerlöf**, was born and died. The first woman winner of the Nobel Prize for Literature, in 1909, Lagerlöf is arguably Sweden's best-known author of her generation, familiar to every Swede. Her fantastical prose was seen as a revolt against the social realism of late nineteenth-century writing. Commissioned to write a geography book for Swedish children, Lagerlöf came up with *The Wonderful Adventures of Nils*, a saga of myth and legend, infused with affection for the Swedish countryside; the book became compulsory reading at every school in the country. Lagerlöf never married; she had a long-term relationship with another woman, though the fact wasn't generally acknowledged until their love letters were published some fifty years after Lagerlöf's death. The first woman to gain membership of the Swedish Literary Academy, her hatted face now appears on 20kr notes, which Swedes affectionately refer to as "Selmas".

The house, complete with portico supporting a wonderfully long balcony, was completely rebuilt after Lagerlöf won the Nobel Prize. Upstairs is her

study, much as she left it, along with a panelled library and an extensive collection of her work. Mårbacka is not easy to reach but with some careful advance planning it's possible to get there and back by public transport between mid-June and mid-August on Monday, Wednesday and Thursday; from Karlstad take bus #302 to **Sunne** (1hr 10min), from where you can connect onto bus #345 (usually this service is operated by a taxi, charging bus fares; 15min). There's just the one connection, which allows you to spend a couple of hours at Mårbacka before returning, via the same route.

Kristinehamn and around

The pretty harbour town **KRISTINEHAMN**, on the northeastern fringes of Lake Vänern 36km east of Karlstad, has been a significant trading centre since the fourteenth century, and soon also became the point of export for iron ore from Sweden's upland mining area, Bergslagen, a role that was further strengthened with the arrival of the railway in the middle of the nineteenth century. A quick walk around the prosperous town soon confirms its strategic importance to Swedish industry: rail and lake transport have made Kristinehamn the compact industrial and maritime centre that it is today. Apart from the handful of old wooden houses nestled together around central Trädgårdsgatan, and the town hall from 1798, Kristinehamn's main attraction is its pleasant setting directly on the lakeside. Once you've taken in the town's most famous piece of artwork (see below), there's precious little else to do here other than use it as a convenient base from which to see the **Nobel museum** in nearby Karlskoga (see p.422).

The **Inlandsbanan** (see p.424) once began in town and, strictly speaking, it's still possible to begin a trip on the railway here (services resumed in 2000) but trains (late June to early Aug daily 1pm) only operate as far as Persberg, a mere ninety-minutes north of Kristinehamn, before everybody piles off for the connecting bus to Mora, over three hours away – the track between Persberg and Mora has been dismantled. It is, therefore, much better to spare yourself a very dull bus journey through a string of uneventful small towns and start your journey 300km to the north in Mora (see p.432), from where trains run uninterrupted to Gällivare.

The Picasso sculpture and the beaches

Having got a flavour of the place, it's much better to make for the lakeside, where the towering 15-metre-high **sculpture**, of which the folk of Kristinehamn are justifiably proud, stands guard where the river that runs through town enters the lake. A sandblasted concrete pillar, the striking piece is one of the *Les Dames des Mougins* series, based on Picasso's wife, Jaqueline, and was realized and decorated by the Swedish artist Carl Nesjar. He was working from a photograph, provided by Picasso, of a model of the sculpture; seeing as Picasso never even set foot in Sweden, the tag "Picasso sculpture" – as the work is generally referred to – is a little unfair to Nesjar. The statue is 6km from the centre: heading there from the train station, take Karlstadsvägen west until its junction with Västra Ringvägen; turn left into this road and carry on until the right-hand turning, Presterudsvägen just over the Varnan river; the sculpture is signposted from here.

Looking out at the lake from the sculpture, the large island immediately offshore is **Vålön**, the favourite summer destination for locals looking to catch a few rays. This tooth-shaped island, covered in spruce, pine and deciduous forest, is blessed with two long sandy **beaches** as well as a separate **nudist beach**, all close to where the boat from the the the mainland docks at Sandvikarna. Between mid-June and mid-August eight daily services (roughly hourly 10am–6pm; 20kr return) leave for the ten-minute crossing over to the island from the *Restaurant Sjöjungfrun* at Rönneberg (see below), about 20min on foot north of the sculpture. What Vålön has in abundance is unspoilt nature and superb views out over Vänern; walking and cycling paths crisscross the island leading to a small bridge at the southern point of the island which provides access to the adjoining neighbouring islet of Kalvön, equally unspoilt but with only rocky beaches, and via a second bridge to the nature reserve of larger Sibberön island; all three places are ideal for **camping** in the wilds.

Practicalities

The **train station** is only a short distance from the large main square, Södra Torget, reached by turning left out of the station and walking straight ahead along Tullportsgatan for about five minutes, past the library at no. 13 where there's free **Internet** access, and over the small Varnan river. The **tourist office** is at the western edge of the square, at Västerlånggatan 22 (late June to mid-Aug Mon–Fri 10am–7pm, Sat 11am–4pm, Sun 1pm–46pm; rest of year Mon–Fri 8.30am–4pm; ☏0550/881 87 and 881 83, ⊚www.kristinehamn.se) and has free **bike rental**; you can also book **private rooms** here (from 120kr).

The **youth hostel** (☏0550/147 71, ℗0550/123 94; May–Aug) and **campsite** (same number as hostel) are on the same site in the village of Kvarndammen, 5km east of town. You can drive there by taking the E18 east in the direction of Örebro; alternatively, take bus #1 from the train station. The campsite **rents bikes** at 55kr a day. The biggest **hotel** in Kristinehamn is *Stadshotellet*, on Kungsgatan 27 (☏0550/150 30, ⊚www.stadshotelletkristinehamn .se; ❹/❷), in a lovely turn-of-the-nineteenth-century building with modern rooms and a restaurant. A cheaper alternative is *Hotel Fröding*, at Kungsgatan 44 (☏0550/151 80, ⊚www.hotellfroding.com; ❸/❷). The cheapest hotel in town, though, is *Park* (☏0550/150 60, ⊚www.parkhotell-kristinehamn; ❸/❷) at Floragatan 2, off Kungsgatan between the library and the train station, where en-suite rooms are small and cramped. At all hotels, you'll need to book one day before arrival to claim their summer rate – 685kr at the two former hotels, 575kr at the latter – and ask for their *Värmlandsrum* discount.

For **food**, *Restaurant Sjöjungfrun*, at Vålösundsvägen 117 (June–Aug), has top-quality fish and meat dishes; it's on the way to the Picasso statue and is a wonderful place to watch the sun set over Lake Vänern with outdoor seating in summer. A good cheap choice for lunch (65kr) in town is *China Garden*, at Kungsgatan 21, where the usual range of dishes starts at 92kr. *Maxim*, a busy Italian restaurant at the corner of Kungsgatan and Södra Staketgatan, has *Dagens Rätt* for 66kr, plus beef and pork dishes in the evenings costing around 95kr. The most popular central place for a **drink**, *Bulls 'n Bricks*, is at Tegelslagaregatan 17.

Around Kristinehamn: the Alfred Nobel Museum

A half-hour bus ride east of Kristinehamn, **Karlskoga** is an ugly industrial town that's home to the Swedish armaments manufacturer, Bofors. Yet it has one saving grace: the **Alfred Nobel Museum** (June to mid-Aug daily 10.30am–4pm; Sept–May advance booking required on ☏0586/834 94; 60kr; ⊚www.nobel.se), situated in the Karlskoga house and laboratory, Björkborn Herrgård, that Nobel once owned (see box opposite). There are four sections to the museum, including

Alfred Nobel and the Nobel prizes

Born in Stockholm in 1833, **Alfred Nobel** is known across the globe as the inventor of **dynamite**, the explosive which played such a central role in the industrial development of the world. Yet by his death in 1896, Nobel held the patent for not only dynamite but 354 other inventions, ranging from safety fuses to smokeless gunpowder. The immense fortune he amassed during his life, roughly thirty million kronor at the time (equivalent to 1.5 billion kronor today), came mostly from his industrial activities in Sweden and other European countries.

Nobel stipulated in his will that the income from his estate be divided annually into five equal parts and distributed "in the form of prizes to those who during the preceding year have conferred the greatest benefit on mankind". Upon his death, his wealth was used to establish the **Nobel Foundation**, which still administers the award of these prizes today. In selecting the five fields for his **prizes** – physics, chemistry, physiology or medicine, literature and peace – Nobel emphasized that "no consideration shall be given to the nationality of the candidates . . . the most worthy shall receive the prize, whether he is a Scandinavian or not".

All the prizes, except the one for peace, are presented to the recipients by the Swedish king at a **ceremony** held in Stockholm Concert Hall on December 10, the anniversary of Nobel's death in Italy in 1896; the peace prize presentation takes place on the same day at Oslo City Hall. Nobel gave no explanation why he selected Norway as a venue, although it wasn't a separate country during his lifetime, as the union between Sweden and Norway was only dissolved in 1905.

one that contains his original **laboratory equipment**, and another that's an experimental workshop for children. If you're keen to really get to grips with Nobel and understand more about his legacy, the museum is definitely the place to come. However, the exhibitions tend towards worthiness and the whole place, including the attitude of the staff, is somewhat stuffy.

There are frequent direct buses from Kristinehamn to Karlskoga (roughly hourly; 40min); alternatively, take the train to Degerfors (10 daily; 20min) and then the frequent buses from there to Karlskoga (25min). It's not possible to get to the museum by public transport; from Karlskoga's train and bus stations, which are together, it's a forty-minute walk. You begin by heading east along Järnvägsgatan, continuing from the road's end onto the footpath which leads into Centralplan square. From here, continue east along Kungsvägen to the main square, Torget, from where you head north along a road called, at various stages along the route, Stadshusgatan, Bergmansgatan or Björkbornsvägen. The last of these becomes a cycle path, which you follow under the busy Norrleden and then right, over the canal, where the road picks up again and leads to the museum.

Dalarna

A sizeable province, **DALARNA** takes in not only the area around **Lake Siljan** (see p.429) but also the ski resorts of **Sälen** (see p.436) and **Idre** (see p.437), close to the Norwegian border. Dalarna holds a special misty-eyed place in the Swedish psyche and should certainly be seen, although not to the exclusion of places further north. Verdant pastures, gentle rolling meadows sweet with the smell of summer flowers, and tiny rural villages make up most of the county, backed by the land to the northwest of Lake Siljan, which rises slowly to meet the chain of mountains that forms the border with Norway. One small lakeside town can look pretty much like another, so if time is short, restrict yourself to visiting just one or two: **Leksand** (see p.429) and **Mora** (see p.432) are the best options; the latter is also the starting point for Sweden's most beautiful train journey, along the **Inlandsbanan** to the Arctic Circle.

If you're staying in the area for a few days or more and tire of the lakeside area's predominantly folksy character and tourist crowds, the nearby industrial towns of **Borlänge** (see opposite) and **Falun** (see p.426) can provide light relief. North of Mora, the county becomes more mountainous and less populous, the only place of note here being **Orsa**, with its fascinating **bear park** (see p.434). There's no need to worry about **accommodation** in the province: there are numerous hotels, hostels and campsites around.

Travel practicalities

SJ and locally operated **trains** (all accepting rail passes) call at Borlänge – where you can get a connection to Falun – and at all the towns around Lake Siljan, terminating in Mora; north of here, the privately operated **Inlandsbanan**, the great Inland Railway that links Dalarna with Swedish Lapland, takes over (see box below). With special guides on board the trains to provide commentaries and information about places along the route, it's certainly a fascinating way to reach the far north of the country, though the Inlandsbanan today is a mere shadow of its former self. Spiralling costs and low passenger numbers forced SJ to sell the line, and the last state-run trains trundled down the single-line track in the autumn of 1992. Trains on the southern section between Mora and Kristinehamn had ceased running several years earlier, and part of the track there has been dismantled. The railway was then sold to the fifteen municipalities that the route passes through, and a private company, Inlandståget AB, was launched to keep the line going.

The Inlandsbanan – Practical details

The Inland Railway is now only operated as a tourist venture in summer, generally from late June to early August. **Timetables** are only approximate, and the train will stop whenever the driver feels like it – perhaps for a spot of wild-strawberry picking or to watch a beaver damming a stream. Generally there are daily trains north from Mora at around 6.35am, but this can change slightly from year to year. Done in one go, the whole journey (Mora–Gällivare, 1067km) lasts two days, with an overnight stop in Östersund. Take it at a more relaxed pace, with a couple of stops along the route (you can break your journey as many times as you like on one ticket), and you'll get much more out of it. More details of Inlandsbanan services are given in the text and in "Travel Details", p.455.

All trips cost 0.75kr per kilometre, with tickets bought on the train; Mora–Östersund, for example, costs 240kr and takes around seven hours. Under-26 InterRail pass holders travel for free, whereas Over-26 InterRail pass holders and those with ScanRail passes don't get a discount on individual journeys but do get 25 percent off the price of an **Inland Railway Card** (normal price 950kr), which gives unlimited travel on the entire stretch of the railway for fourteen days. Seat reservations are best made at least 24 hours in advance and cost 50kr per seat. Two children under 16 can travel free if accompanied by an adult; otherwise they pay half price. Bicycles can be carried on board at a cost of 50kr per day. For **train times**, ring ☏020/53 53 53 or check out ⦿www.inlandsbanan.se.

Paradoxically, in summer, when Dalarna is inundated with visitors, its **bus** system is down to a skeleton service; buses to some places, like Idre and Sälen, are reduced to one bus a day then. It's worth picking up a timetable from the tourist office and organizing your route before you go, otherwise you could find yourself facing a very long wait for your next connection. Mora is one of the main interchanges in Dalarna's bus network; the only way to get to Sälen or Idre by public transport is by bus from Mora, and if you want to visit both, you'll be forced to retrace your steps back to Mora to get from one village to the other, adding about five hours to your journey. A good way to get about locally, especially around Lake Siljan, is to rent a **bike** from one of the tourist offices.

Borlänge

Boring **BORLÄNGE**, the biggest and dullest town in Dalarna, developed into a centre for the steel and papermill industries, which still dominate the town today. It's a workaday place where, sadly, the concepts of service-mindedness and urban sophistication have yet to make their mark. To be frank, there is no reason whatsoever to come here other than to change trains or catch the handy twice daily Swebus express to Karlstad and Gothenburg. If, however, you are caught between connections, the place does have a few saving graces, most of which lie in the centre. The **Jussi Björling Muséet**, at Borganäsvägen 25 (mid-May to mid-Sept Mon–Fri 11am–6pm, Sat 10am–2pm, Sun noon–5pm; mid-Sept to mid-May Tues–Fri noon–5pm; 40kr; ⓦwww.borlange.se/kommun/jussi), not far from the tourist office, commemorates the life and career of the world-renowned tenor, Borlänge's most famous son; in its listening rooms, you can have Jussi sing for you at the flick of a button. It's a toss-up as to which of the town's other two museums is the more interesting: the **Geologiska Muséet**, at Floragatan 6, has mind-numbing displays of rocks, minerals and fossils (Mon–Fri 11am–5pm, May–Sept also Sat 11am–2pm; 20kr), whereas at **Framtidsmuséet**, Jussi Björlingsvägen 25 (Museum of the Future; Mon 1–5pm, Tues–Fri 10am–5pm, Sat & Sun noon–5pm; 50kr), the best section is the planetarium.

You could well pass up the museums in favour of a stroll along the river. A pleasant trail starts at the open-air **Gammelgården** craft village (mid-June to mid-Aug Tue–Sun 11am–5pm; 20kr), with its small collection of old wooden houses on Stenhålsgatan. From here, head away from the main road bridge to the left and follow the riverside path as far as the impressive power station built across the river; you can get across to the opposite bank here and retrace your steps. All in all, it's a passable walk of around an hour or so, with plenty of places to stop for a picnic. To get to Gammelgården itself, take the footbridge over the main road, Siljansvägen, which begins just beyond Svea Torget, and follow it till you get to Kontorsvägen.

Practicalities

Direct trains run daily to Borlänge from Stockholm. The Swebus Express #800 bus service comes here twice daily from Gothenburg and Karlstad, with a stop at Filipstad for the connecting #401 from Kristinehamn. Borlänge's **bus** and **train stations** are centrally located at Ovanbrogatan, from where it's a five-minute walk following the "Turistbyrå" signs to the **tourist office** at Sveavägen 1 (mid-June to mid-Aug daily 9am–7pm; mid-Aug to mid-June Mon–Fri 10am–6pm; ☎0243/665 66, ⓦwww.borlange.se).

One **accommodation** option within easy walking distance of the centre is the **youth hostel** at Kornstigen 23A (℡0243/22 76 15, ⓦwww.borlange.se/kommun/vandrarhem). The town's several central, very similar **hotels** cater mainly to business people offering modern, well-decorated rooms. There's little to choose between the four hotels in the centre of town. At Stationsgatan 21–23, *Scandic Hotel Borlänge* has the largest and most modern rooms (℡0243/79 90 00, ⓦwww.scandic-hotels.com; ❻/❸). The *Quality Hotel Galaxen*, at Jussi Björlings väg 25, is more dated, looking a bit 1980s (℡0243/21 61 00, ⓦwww.galaxen.to; ❻/❸), although it's bright, en-suite rooms are quite adequate. The second-best place, after the *Scandic*, is *First Hotel Brage* at Stationsgatan 1 (℡0243/21 76 60, ⓦwww.firsthotels.com; ❻/❸). *Hotel Gustaf Wasa*, at Tunagatan 1, is distinguished by having actual bathtubs (℡0243/21 74 00, ⓦwww.gustafwasa.se; ❻/❸). The **campsite**, *Mellsta Camping* (℡0243/23 82 55, ⓦwww.camping.se/plats/w15), is beautifully located by the river at **Mellstavägen**, a bit of a trek from the centre; take bus #58 there.

When it comes to **restaurants**, Borlänge specializes in pizzerias; the best is the tasty *La Cantina* at Tunagatan 9. For Greek specialities, head to *Akropolis* at Vattugatan 2 or there's Mexican and Cajun delights at around 100–130kr at *Broken Dreams* inside *Hotel Gustaf Wasa*. The very best food, though, is served up in the smart *Stationsgatan 1*, the restaurant inside *First Hotel Brage* – their fish dishes are legendary. The most popular **pubs** in town – though they're nothing exceptional – are the *Flying Scotsman*, in the same building as the Framtidsmuséet on Jussi Björlings väg, and the *Golden Bear* at Målaregatan 12.

Falun and around

Twenty-four kilometres northeast of Borlänge, **FALUN** is essentially an industrial town – a pleasant one at that – known for copper mining, which began in the eleventh century; today, the mines, which closed as recently as 1992, can be visited on hour-long guided tours (see opposite). Falun is also known for a much more sobering event: in 1994, the town witnessed Sweden's worst case of mass murder, when a young soldier, inflamed with jealousy after seeing his girlfriend with another man, ran amok and shot dead seven local people; there's a simple stone monument to the event, bearing an inscription to "young people killed by meaningless violence", at the junction of Parkgatan and Vasagatan between the hospital and train station.

Arrival, information and accommodation

Falun is easily reached by train from Börlange, or by direct bus services from Stockholm. The **train** and **bus stations** are to the east of the centre; if you walk through the bus station, then take the underpass below the main road and head towards the shops in the distance, you'll soon come to Falun's **tourist office**, at Trotzgatan 10–12, opposite the *First Hotel Grand* (mid-June to mid-Aug Mon–Fri 9am–7pm, Sat 9am–6pm, Sun 11am–5pm; mid-Aug to mid-June Mon–Fri 9am–6pm, Sat 10am–2pm; ℡023/830 50, ⓦwww.visitfalun.se). There's **Internet** access, as usual, at the library, Kristinegatan 15.

The nearest **youth hostel** (℡023/105 60, ⓦwww.stfvandrarhem.falun.just.nu) is at Hälsinggårdsvägen 7. 3km away in the Haraldsbo part of town (bus #701 or #712 from the centre). Housed in a couple of long, low-rise modern buildings, the hostel is close to Runnsjö lake which is an ideal spot for a swim. Up at Lugnet hill is Falun's best **hotel**, *Scandic Hotel Falun*, at Svärdsjögatan 51

(☎023/669 22 00, ⓦwww.scandic-hotels.com; ❺/❸), which has fantastic views over the town, as well as ultramodern rooms and a basement pool and sauna complex. The swankiest hotel in town is the central *First Hotel Grand* at Trotzgatan 9–11 (☎023/79 48 80, ⓦwww.firsthotels.com; ❺/❸), whose rooms are sumptuous to say the least. For a more homely feel, try *Hotell Winn* at Bergskolegränd 7, near the train station (☎023/70 17 00, ⓦwww.softwarehotels .se/winnfalun; ❺/❷).The nearest **campsite** (☎023/835 63) is up at Lugnet by the National Ski Stadium.

The Town and around

Falun grew in importance during the seventeenth and eighteenth centuries, when its **copper mines** produced two-thirds of the world's copper ore. Commensurate with its status then as the second largest town in Sweden, Falun acquired grand buildings and an air of prosperity. The few old, wooden houses that survive in the town (in 1761, two fires wiped out virtually all of central Falun) are worth seeking out to gain an idea of the cramped conditions mine workers had to live in; you'll find these buildings in the districts of **Elsborg** (southwest of the centre), Gamla Herrgården and Östanfors (both north of the centre).

By far the most interesting attraction in Falun is its **mines** (ⓦwww .kopparberget.com), reached from the centre along Gruvgatan – head along this street right to the far end, about a kilometre away. Mandatory **guided tours** (May–Sept daily 10am–5pm; rest of year Mon–Fri only; 80kr; English commentary available), lasting around an hour, are organized on the site, beginning with an elevator ride 55m down to a network of old mine roads and drifts. The temperature down below is only around 6–7°C, so make sure you bring warm clothing; try also to wear old shoes, as your footwear is likely to come out tinged red.

The site has a worthy **museum** (same hours as above; admission includes the museum), recounting the history of Falun's copper production. Conditions below ground in the mines were appalling, said by the botanist Carl von Linné to be as dreadful as hell itself. One of the most dangerous aspects of eighteenth-century copper mining was the presence everywhere in the mines of **vitriol** gases, which are strong preservatives. It's recorded that the body of a young man known as *Fet Mats* (Fat Mats) was found in the mines in 1719; though he'd died 49 years previously in an accident, his corpse was so well preserved when discovered that his erstwhile fiancée, by then an old woman, recognized him immediately. Be sure not to miss peering into the **Great Pit** (Stora Stöten), just nearby, which is 100m deep and 300–400m wide. It suddenly appeared on Midsummer Day in 1687, when the entire pit caved in – the result of extensive mining and the unsystematic driving of galleries and shafts.

Back in the centre, the riverside **Dalarnas Museum** at Stigaregatan 2–4 makes for a worthwhile visit (Mon–Fri 10am–5pm, Sat & Sun noon–5pm; ⓦwww.dalarnasmuseum.se; 40kr). Containing sections on the province's folk art, dresses and music, it includes among its exhibits a reconstruction on the ground floor of the dark, heavily wood-panelled study where the author Selma Lagerlöf worked when she moved to Falun in 1897; a copy of her most famous work *Nils Holgerssons underbara resa genom Sverige* (The wonderful Adventures of Nils) still lies open on her desk (for more on Lagerlöf, see p.420).

In fine weather, it's well worth getting out of the centre and heading up Svärdsjögatan to **Lugnet** (a 25min walk), the hill overlooking the town, where you'll find Sweden's **National Ski Stadium** (*Riksskidstadion*).You can take a lift (mid-May to mid-Aug daily 10am–6pm; 20kr) 90m up to the top of the ski jump for great views of the town and the surroundings. Close to the ski arena is an outdoor **swimming pool** and a **nature reserve**, where you can sit undisturbed in a carpet of blue harebells in July.

If you want to take a dip, you should head out north from the centre along Slaggatan for the **beach** at **Kålgårdsudden**, near the area of wooden houses at Östanfors – a ten- to fifteen-minute walk from the centre of town; alternatively there's also a pleasant bathing area at **Uddnäs**, which can be reached from the centre by bus #20.

Eating, drinking and nightlife

The variety and quality of the places to **eat** and **drink** in Falun, all of them in or around the main square, Stora Torget, far outstrip the selection in the other towns around Lake Siljan. One of the most popular is the trendy bistro *Banken*, at Åsgatan 41, which, as the name suggests, is housed in what used to be a bank. The excellent Swedish home cooking here isn't cheap though – meat dishes weigh in at around 170kr. Next door is the gourmet *Två rum och kök*, a restaurant whose cosy feel is like eating in a friend's dining room – top-notch mains are from 200kr, the usual array of meat and fish, though served in exquisite French-style sauces; seafood ragout with aioli is delicious at 235kr. Another busy spot is *Rådhuskällaren*, under the Rådhus in Stora Torget, in what looks to be a wine cellar; here you can indulge in delicious, if somewhat pricey, food – roast duck breast in an orange and leek sauce with potato florets, for example, is 200kr. Good Greek fare can be had at the *Akropolis* restaurant, opposite Dalarnas Museum, at Hälsingtorget 1.

One of *the* places to be seen, as far as Falun's young and trendy are concerned, is the *Bakfickan* **bar**, next door to *Rådhuskällaren* which also serves light bar snacks. Other drinking establishments include enjoyable *Harry's* at Trotzgatan 9–11 (the entrance is round the corner in pedestrianized Åsgatan), another in the chain of American-style bars with rough brick walls and wooden panels sweeping Sweden; the excellent *Pub Engelbrekt*, Stigaregatan 1, with its old wooden benches; and the British-style *King's Arms* at Falugatan 3.

Without doubt the best time to be here is during the annual four-day **International Folk Music Festival** (generally July 10–13; ⓦwww.falufolk .com), when the streets come alive to the sound of panpipes, bagpipes and every other type of pipes. The tourist office can provide details of the festival programme and how to get tickets.

Around Falun: Sundborn

The delightful **Carl Larssongården** (May–Sept daily 10am–5pm; 70kr), once the home of the artist **Carl Larsson**, lies in the nearby village of **SUNDBORN**, 13km from Falun; to get there, take bus #64 from Falun's train station (Mon–Fri 5 daily). One of Sweden's most visited tourist attractions, the cottage was at first the summer dwelling of Carl and his wife Karin, later becoming their permanent home. The artist's own murals and portraits of his children form part of the decor, as do the embroidery and tapestries of his wife. At the start of the twentieth century, when the Larssons had done the place up, the house represented an entirely new decorative style for Sweden, its bright, warm interior quite unlike the dark and sober colours used until that time. Other paintings by Carl Larsson are displayed in the village church as the artist is buried outside in the churchyard.

Around Lake Siljan

Things have changed since Baedeker, writing in 1889, observed that "Lake Siljan owes much of its interest to the inhabitants of its banks, who have preserved many of their primitive characteristics. In their idea of cleanliness they are somewhat behind the age." Today it's not the people who draw your attention but the setting. **Lake Siljan** (Ⓦ www.siljan.se), created millions of years ago when a meteorite crashed into the earth, is what many people come to Sweden for, its gently rolling surroundings, traditions and local handicrafts weaving a subtle spell on the visitor. There's a lush feel to much of the region, the charm of the forest heightened by its proximity to the lake, all of which adds a pleasing dimension to the low-profile towns and villages that interrupt the rural scenery. Only **Mora** (see p.432) stands out as being bigger and busier, with the hustle and bustle of holidaymakers and countless caravans crowding the place in summer.

Leksand

Perhaps the most traditional of the Dalarna villages, **LEKSAND**, 43km northwest of Borlänge, is certainly worth making the effort to reach at midsummer, when it stages festivals recalling age-old dances performed around the **maypole** (Sweden's maypoles are erected in June – in May the trees here are still bare and the ground can be covered with snow). The celebrations culminate in the **church boat races**, a waterborne procession of sleek wooden longboats, which the locals once rowed to church on Sundays. Starting on Midsummer's Day in nearby **Siljansnäs** – take bus #84 from Leksand (Mon–Fri only) – and continuing for ten days at different locations around the lake, the races hit Leksand on the first Saturday in July and Rättvik on the first Tuesday after Midsummer's Day. Leksand's tourist office will have details of the arrangements for each summer's races.

Another event you should try to catch is **Musik vid Siljan** (Ⓣ 0248/102 90, Ⓦ www.musikvidsiljan.se), nine days of musical performances in lakeside churches and at various locations out in the surrounding forest. The range of music covered is pretty wide, including chamber music, jazz, traditional folk songs, and dance-band music. It all takes place during the first week of July, with proceedings starting in the early morning and carrying on until late evening every day.

There's little else to do in Leksand other than take it easy for a while. A relaxing stroll along the riverside brings you to **Leksands kyrka** (daily 9.30am–3pm), one of Sweden's biggest village churches; it's existed in its present form since 1715, although the oldest parts of the building date back to the thirteenth century. The church enjoys one of the most stunning locations of any in the land, its peaceful churchyard lined with whispering spruce trees and looking out over the lake to the distant shore. Next door is the region's best open-air **Hembygdsgård** homestead museum (free) – about a dozen old timber buildings grouped around the maypole ranging from simple square huts used to store hay during the long winter months to a magnificent *parstuga* which forms the centrepiece of the collection. Built in 1793, this two-storey dwelling, constructed of thick circular logs, is notable because buildings of the period were rarely more than one storey in height since timber was expensive. From directly behind the musuem a narrow track leads down to the lake where there's a reconstruction of a church boat house used to house the *kyrkbåtar* boats for which Dalarna is known throughout Sweden.

Whilst in Leksand, it's worth taking one of the **cruises** on Lake Siljan on the lovely old steamship *M/S GustafWasa* (timetables vary; check sailing times with the tourist office or ☎010/252 32 92, ⊛www.wasanet.nu), which leaves from the quay near the homestead museum; take the track down to the reconstructed boathouse (see above) and turn left following the lakeside to the bridge and the quay. The excursions include a round trip to Mora and back (120kr), or a two-hour lunch cruise round a bit of the lake (80kr including lunch).

Practicalities

There are frequent **trains** between Mora and Borlänge in both directions, all of which stop at Leksand. The **tourist office** is in the station building (mid-June to mid-Aug Mon–Fri 9am–7pm, Sat & Sun 10am–5pm; mid-Aug to mid-June Mon–Fri 10am–5pm, Sat 10am–1pm; ☎0247/79 61 30). The centre of town is a five-minute walk up Villagatan, the street opposite the station.

Leksand's cosy **youth hostel**, one of the oldest in Sweden, is around 2.5km from the train station, over the river at Parkgården (☎0247/152 50, ℻0247/101 86); bus #58 will take you there. The **campsite**, *Leksands Camping* at Orsandbaden, is a twenty-minute walk from the tourist office along Tällbergsvägen (☎0247/803 13 or 803 12, ⊛www.leksand.se/camping_stugby). Four-bed **cabins** in the vicinity of Leksand are available (450–500kr a night); you can book them at the tourist office, which is also where to head in the afternoon for any last-minute **hotel** deals. Comfortable rooms in log cabins are to be found at *Hotell Moskogen*, Insjövägen 50 (☎0247/146 00, ⊛www.moskogen.com; ❸). But by far the best place to stay in Leksand is *Hotell Korstäppen* at Hjortnäsvägen 33 (☎0247/123 10, ⊛www.korstappan.se; ❹), a wonderful hotel tastefully decked out in traditional Dalarna colours. Its sitting and dining rooms look out over the lake, whose lapping waters can be reached by a path behind the hotel.

A good place to **eat** is *Siljans Konditori & Bageri*, in the main square; their summer terrace is a wonderful place from which to watch the world go by while sipping a cup of coffee. They serve up sandwiches with fantastic homemade bread, and salads and pies; make this place your first choice for lunch (they're not open in the evenings). Alternatively, try *Bosporen* in the tiny pedestrianized centre of town; the village's main restaurant, it serves pizzas from 60kr as well as meat and fish dishes from 93kr. Chinese food can be had at *Lucky House*, in the main square, with the usual array of dishes from 98kr. Down at the station, *Håkans Bodega* serves up lunch and dinner and is a good place for a **drink** when evening comes; there's outdoor seating here in summer. Alternatively, try the bar and disco in the *Bosporen* or the pub attached to the *Lucky House*.

Tällberg

If you believe the tourist blurb, then **TÄLLBERG**, all lakeside log cabins amid rolling hills, *is* Dalarna. Situated on a promontory in the lake halfway between Leksand and Rättvik, this folksy hillside village, whose wooden cottages are draped with flowers in summer, first became famous in 1850, when the Danish writer Hans Christian Andersen paid it a visit; on his return to Copenhagen, he wrote that everyone should experience Tällberg's peace and tranquillity, and marvel at its wonderful lake views. Ever since, hordes of tourists have flooded into the tiny village to see what all the fuss was about – prepare yourself for the crowds that unfortunately take the shine off what is otherwise quite a pretty little place. Tällberg today is also a prime destination for wealthy middle-aged Swedes, who come to enjoy the good life for a few days, savour the delicious food dished up by the village's seven hotels, and admire the fantastic views out over Lake Siljan. To escape the crowds, walk down the steep hill of Sjögattu, past the campsite, to the calm lapping water of the lake and a small sandy beach; keep going through the trees to find quieter spots for nude bathing.

Tällberg is on the main **train** line round Lake Siljan; the **station** is a ten- to fifteen-minute walk from the village. There's no tourist office here. For **accommodation**, avoid the expensive hotels and walk down Sjögattu to *Siljansgården* (℡0247/500 40, ⊛www.siljansgarden.com; ❷), a wonderful old wooden farm building with a cobbled courtyard and a fountain. Its rooms are comparable to those in youth hostels; prices fluctuate, but reckon on around 200kr per night – one of the best deals in Dalarna. Alternatively, head for the **campsite** (℡0247/503 01), a little further along from *Siljansgården* – head down to the lakeshore and turn left.

Rättvik

On the eastern bulge of the lake, **RÄTTVIK**, 8km from Tällberg, has one claim to fame: the longest **lake pier** in the world, at 628 metres in length, which you'll glimpse through the train window on arriving at the station. The railway reached the town in 1890, a period of great development in Rättvik, when a large tourist hotel was built to accommodate visitors and, six years later, a pier was constructed to provide easy access to the town's swanky new open-air bathing house on an artificial island just offshore. Over the years the pier became known as the symbol of Rättvik across the country and, indeed, many local people got engaged here. Sadly though, the Swedish winter took its toll on the original structure and in 1989 it was decreed that a new pier, identical to the old one, should be built to re-establish Rättvik's claim to a place in the record books. Whilst in town take a stroll to the end of the pier (it's a fifteen-minute walk) for superb views of the lake and its sweeping shore-line – and also to get an idea of the scale of the achievement; each of the two and a half thousand or so planks used bears the name of its sponsor, who paid 500kr for the privilege.

Other than the pier, though, and the town's tiny shopping street, there's little else to see in Rättvik. It's a better idea to get out of the village and head up to the **viewing point** at **Vidablick** – it's about an hour's walk and quite a climb, but the view is worth the effort. From the top, you'll be able to survey the surrounding forest-covered hillsides, with the occasional small farm interrupting the greenery, and get a view of virtually all of Lake Siljan, even all the way to Mora. There's a small **café** and a shop at Vidablick. To get to the viewing point, walk along one of the marked **trails** through the forests above Rättvik. The most appealing route is the well-signposted walk that begins at Bockgatan: head down the road towards *Hotell Lerdalshöjden* (see below), then follow the signs for Tolvåsstugan by walking right along Märgatan and then right again up Werkmästargatan – take another right into the forest at the sign for Fäbodarstigen. Right here there are a couple of information boards showing the different onward trails. The quickest way back to Rättvik from Vidablick is to take the steep road down the hill (there are a couple of them, so ask the staff in the shop to point out the right one), go left at the end onto Wallenkampfvägen and then right along Mårsåkervägen towards Lerdal again, all the time coming down the hill. As you head back along this route, you'll see some of the most beautifully located homes in Dalarna – all log cabins, gardens and views out over the lake.

Practicalities

Rättvik's **train station** contains the **tourist office** (mid-June to mid-Aug Mon–Fri 9am–7pm, Sat & Sun 10am–5pm; mid-Aug to mid-June Mon–Fri 10am–5pm, Sat 10am–1pm; ☎0248/79 72 10). The most central place to stay in Rättvik is the **youth hostel** at the aptly named Centralgatan (☎0248/105 66, ℻0248/561 13), its buildings constructed using large pine logs, in the old Dalarna style. To get there, take either Järnvägsgatan and Vasagatan (which run either side of the square outside the station) northeast to their junction with Centralgatan, where you turn right and walk another 200m. There's not much variety when it comes to **hotels**; the closest to the centre is *Hotell Lerdalshöjden*, on Bockgatan (☎0248/511 50, ⓦwww.greenhotel.se; ❸), with good views of the lake, though the rooms are pretty average. The only other hotel worth considering is *Hotell Vidablick* (☎0248/302 50, ⓦwww.hantverksbyn.se; ❸), with pine cabins that have been converted into comfortable rustic apartments; it's about 3km out of Rättvik and can be reached by heading south from the station along Faluvägen. There are two **campsites** in town: one is across the road from the youth hostel, close to Rättviksparken (☎0248/561 10); the other, *Siljansbadet* (☎0248/516 91), has its own swimming pool – it's 200m from the station, right on the lakeside behind the train lines.

Rättvik has a dearth of good places to **eat and drink**; indeed, things are so bad that the local youth take off to Leksand and Mora of an evening in search of a decent pub or restaurant. The best of the bunch is the cosy *Restaurant Anna*, at Vasagatan 3, with a *Dagens Rätt* and evening meals that include local dishes – reindeer noisette in juniper sauce is 170kr, salmon fillet just 98kr. The main alternative is *Krögar'n*, on the pedestrianized shopping street, Storgatan, serving burgers and meat dishes at good prices. For cheap pizzas (around 45kr), head for *Bella Pizza* at Ågatan 11; good home-made bread, cakes, sandwiches and pies can be had at *Fricks Konditori*, in the main square.

Mora and around

At the northwestern corner of the lake, 37km from Rättvik, **MORA** is the best place to head for, handy for onward trains on the Inlandsbanan (see p.424) and for moving on to the ski resorts of Idre (see p.437) and Sälen (see p.436). The town's main draw is its excellent **Zorn Museum** at Vasagatan 36 (mid-May to mid-Sept Mon–Sat 9am–5pm, Sun 11am–5pm; mid-Sept to mid-May Mon–Sat noon–5pm, Sun 1–5pm; 35kr; ⓦwww.zorn.se), showcasing the work of Sweden's best-known painter, **Anders Zorn** (1860–1920). Most successful as a portrait painter (he even went to the United States to paint American presidents Cleveland, Theodore Roosevelt and Taft), Zorn came to live in Mora in 1896. At the museum, look out for his self-portrait and the especially pleasing *Midnatt* (Midnight) from 1891, which depicts a woman rowing on Lake Siljan, her hands blue from the cold night air. You might also want to wander across the museum lawn and take in his home, **Zorngården** (mid-May to mid-Sept Mon–Sat 10am–4pm, Sun 11am–4pm; mid-Sept to mid-May Mon–Sat noon–3pm, Sun 1–4pm; 45kr), where he lived with his wife, Emma, during the early 1900s. What really makes this place unusual is the cavernous ten-metre-high hall with its steeply V-shaped roof, entirely constructed from wood and decked out in traditional Dalarna designs and patterns, where the couple lived out their roles as darlings of local society.

The other museum in town worth considering is the **Vasaloppsmuséet** (mid-June to mid-Aug daily 10am–5pm; mid-Aug to mid-June Mon–Fri 10am–5pm; 30kr; ⓦwww.vasaloppet.se), telling the history of the ski race,

Vasaloppet (see p.436); it's east of the Zorn Museum, on the other side of Vasagatan. The longest cross-country ski race in the world, the competition was the idea of a local newspaper editor who organized the first event in 1922; it was won by a 22-year-old from Västerbotten who took seven and a half hours to complete the course; today professionals take barely four hours to cover the 90km which is always held on the first Sunday in March. Although the race enjoys royal patronage (the current Swedish king has skied it), it does have a somewhat chequered past since women were forbidden from taking part until 1981 – something the museum makes no reference to and which the embarrassed staff are unable to explain. Whilst here, make sure you watch the half-hour **film** (with English subtitles) about the race – the impressive aerial shots really help to portray the massive scale of the competition.

Practicalities

For the centre of town you should leave the **train** at Mora Strand station (which consists of little more than a platform), one stop after the main Mora Station on trains coming from the south; the Inlandsbanan begins at Mora Strand before calling at Mora Station. The bus station is at Moragatan, close to Mora Strand, just off the main Strandgatan. The **tourist office**, at Stationsvägen 3, actually in Mora Station (mid-June to mid-Aug Mon–Fri 9am–7pm, Sat & Sun 10am–5pm; mid-Aug to mid-June Mon–Fri 10am–5pm, Sat 10am–1pm; ☎0250/56 76 00), has all the usual literature, including a map of the Vasaloppsleden hiking route, which you can follow north from Mora to Sälen (see p.436).

By the finishing line for the Vasaloppet is the STF **youth hostel**, at the corner of Fredsgatan and Prostgatan, 100m off Vasagatan (☎0250/381 96, ⓦwww.maalkullann.se). From Mora station, turn left and keep walking for about five minutes along Vasagatan; from Mora Strand station, turn right and head northeast on Strandgatan, turning left at the junction with Fredsgatan. The biggest and best **hotel** is the *First Hotel Mora*, opposite Mora Strand station at Strandgatan 12 (☎0250/59 26 50, ⓦwww.firsthotelmora.com; ❺/❸), with modern and old-fashioned rooms, as well as free Internet access for guests. *Hotel St Mikael*, at Fridhemsgatan 15 (☎0250/150 70, ⓦwww.trehotell .nu; ❺/❷), is a sweet little place with tasteful rooms; it's five minutes' walk from Mora Strand (turn left out of the station into Strandgatan, then take the first right). Close to the main station, *Hotell Kung Gösta* (☎0250/150 70, ⓦwww.trehotell.nu; ❹/❷), is handy for those early-morning departures on the Inlandsbanan; the hotel annexe functions as an **independent hostel** *Kristineberg* (contact details same as the hotel) where there are both double rooms (❶) and dorms sleeping up to ten. Travelling with children, your best bet is *Mora Park Hotell*, at Parkvägen 1 (☎0250/276 00, ⓦwww.moraparken.se; ❷), which has a playground nearby; it's a ten-minute walk from the centre along Hantverkaregatan, which begins near the bus station. Nearby is the **campsite**, *Mora Camping* (contact details same as *Mora Park Hotel*), with a good beach as well as a lake for swimming.

In summer, coffee and cakes can be enjoyed outside at two **cafés**, *Helmers Konditori* and *Mora Kaffestugan*, which are virtually next door to each other on the main shopping street, Kyrkogatan. For more substantial **eating**, all the hotels serve up a decent *Dagens Rätt*, with little to choose between them. Among the town's **restaurants**, the tiny *Pizzeria Prima* in Fridhemplan, off Fridhemsgatan, and *Pizzeria Torino* at Älvgatan 73 serve up virtually any pizza you can imagine at reasonable prices; for bland Chinese *Dagens Rätt* or evening meals (set menu and a beer 149kr), try *China House*, at the corner of Hamngatan and Moragatan near the church. The most popular place to eat is *Wasastugan*, a huge log building at Tingnäsvägen, between the main train station and the Vasaloppsmuséet, where you can have reasonably priced lunch (60kr), though in the evenings it becomes a pub which attracts a young crowd, especially to its disco evenings. The town's most popular **drinking** place, though, is the trendy *Jérnet* at Strandgatan 6, but if you're looking for something more traditional, *Lilla Krogen*, Moragatan 1, has darts and billiards as well as good beer.

Around Mora: Nusnäs

Whilst in Mora you might want to consider a visit to **Nusnäs**, just east of town on the lakeside, where you'll find the **workshop** of the Olsson brothers known as *Nils Olsson Hemslöjd* (mid-June to mid-Aug Mon–Fri 8am–6pm, Sat & Sun 9am–5pm; mid-Aug to mid-June Mon–Fri 8am–5pm, Sat 10am–2pm; free; ⓦwww.nohemslojd.se), creators of Sweden's much-loved **Dala horses** (see box below). Skilled craftsmen carve the horses out of wood from the pine forests around Lake Siljan and then hand-paint and varnish them. You can get to Nusnäs from Mora on bus #108 (Mon–Fri 4 daily; 20min).

Orsa and the bear park

A dull little place barely 20km from Mora, sitting aside Lake Orsasjön, a northerly adjunct of Lake Siljan, **ORSA**'s draw is its location – right in the heart of Sweden's bear country – and its fascinating bear park. It's reckoned that there are a good few hundred **brown bears** roaming the dense forests around town, though few sightings are made in the wild, except by the hunters who cull the steadily increasing numbers. The nearby **Orsa Grönklitt björnpark** (mid-May to mid-June & mid-Aug to mid-Sept daily 10am–3pm; mid-Sept to mid-Oct Sat & Sun only; mid-June to mid-Aug daily 10am–6pm; 75kr; ⓦwww.orsa-gronklitt.se) is the biggest **bear park** in Europe. The bears here aren't tamed or caged, but wander around the nine hundred square kilometres of the forested park at will, hunting and living as they would in the wild. It's the human visitors who are confined, having to clamber up viewing towers and along covered walkways.

The bears are fascinating to watch: their behaviour is amusing, and they're gentle and vegetarian for the most part (though occasionally they're fed the odd dead reindeer or elk that's been killed on the roads). Until recently, the king of the park was the enormous male bear called Micke, who weighed in

The Dala Horse

No matter where you travel in Sweden, you'll come across small wooden figurines known as **Dala horses** (*dalahästar*). Their bright red colour, stumpy legs and garish floral decorations are, for many foreigners, high kitsch and rather ugly; the Swedes, however, adore bright colours (the redder the better) and so love the little horses – it's virtually an unwritten rule that every household in the country should have a couple on display. Two brothers from the town of **Nusnäs**, **Nils** and **Jannes Olsson**, began carving the horses in the family baking shed in 1928, when they were just teenagers. Though they were simply interested in selling their work to help their cash-strapped parents make ends meet, somehow the wooden horses started catching on – Swedes are at a loss to explain why – and soon were appearing across the country as a symbol of rural life.

at a staggering 450 kilos; quite the celebrity after his teeth were fixed live on Swedish TV, he's now stuffed and on display for all to admire. Trying hard not to be upstaged by the bears are two lynx and a couple of wolves – although you'll be lucky to see them; in fact, it's a good idea to bring along a pair of binoculars to help you pick out any rustlings in the undergrowth.

The bear park is located 16km from Orsa, and can be reached by taking the bus #118 (Mon–Fri 2 daily, Sun 1 daily) from either Mora or Orsa bus stations. From late autumn to early spring the park closes, when the bears hibernate in specially constructed lairs, monitored by closed-circuit television cameras.

Practicalities

Given that all Inlandsbanan trains arrive in Orsa at ridiculous times (7am & 9.30pm), you're unlikely to use the train to visit the bear park; however, the **train station** is right in the centre of town on Järnvägsgatan, opposite the **bus station**. Nearby, at Dalagatan 1, the **tourist office** (mid-June to mid-Aug Mon–Fri 9am–7pm, Sat & Sun 10am–5pm; mid-Aug to mid-June Mon–Fri 10am–5pm, Sat 10am–1pm; ☎0250/55 25 50), can help with local accommodation. Right in the centre near the station on Järnvägsgatan is the *Orsa* **hotel** (☎0250/409 40, ⓦwww.stab.se/fi/orsdahotell; ❷), a decent enough place with modern rooms, though it's a much better bet to head for the beautifully located **youth hostel** by the side of Orsasjön lake, at Gillevägen 3, just 1km west of the centre (☎0250/421 70; ⓕ0250/423 65). However, should you want to stay up at the bear park there's also a second, well-equipped hostel at Grönklitt (☎0250/462 00, ⓦwww.orsa-gronklitt.se), easily reached on the #118 bus. You might want to be careful what you eat in the *Värdshuset Björnidet* restaurant next door – if it looks like pink roast beef, it's likely to be bear meat (sometimes an excess number of bears in the park means that one or two have to be killed – and end up being served up here).

Northwestern Dalarna

The area to the northwest of Mora offers travellers approaching from the south a first taste of what northern Sweden is really all about. The villages in this remote part of Dalarna lie few and far between, separated by great swathes of coniferous forest which thrive on the poor sandy soils of the hills and mountains which predominate here. On its way to the Norwegian border, **Route 70**, the main artery through this part of the province, slowly climbs up the eastern side of the Österdalälven river valley. After the tiny village of Åsen, the road leaves the river behind and strikes further inland towards the mountains which mark the border between Sweden and Norway. Buses to Särna, Idre and Grövelsjön follow this route, whereas services to Sälen only travel as far as Älvdalen before heading west towards Route 297.

It is predominantly to ski (in winter) or to hike (in summer) that most visitors come to this part of Dalarna. Indeed, **Sälen** and **Idrefjäll** are two of Sweden's most popular **ski resorts** and, in season, the slopes and cross-country trails here are busy with Swedes from further south where snowfall is less certain. In summer, though, **Grövelsjön** makes a better destination than its sleepy neighbours, thanks to some superb hiking trails through the surrounding mountains which begin right on the doorstep of the Fell Station (see below).

Sälen

Considered as one entity, **SÄLEN** and the surrounding resorts of Lindvallen, Högfjället, Tandådalen, Hundfjället, Rörbäcksnäs and Stöten constitute the biggest **ski centre** in the Nordic area, with over a hundred pistes and guaranteed snow from November to May. It isn't unreasonable to lump all these places together, as each of the minor resorts, despite having its own ski slope, is dependent on Sälen for shops (not least its Systembolaget) and services. Novice skiers can take advantage of Sälen's special lifts, nursery slopes and qualified tuition; there are also plenty of intermediate runs through the densely forested hillsides and, for advanced skiers, twenty testing runs as well as an off-piste area. To get the best value for money, it's really worth buying a package rather than trying to book individual nights at local hotels; prices are high and in season they're packed to capacity. During the **summer**, Sälen specializes in assorted **outdoor activities** – fishing, canoeing and beaver safaris are all available, and the hills, lakes and rivers around the town will keep you busy for several days. There's also some fantastic hiking to be had in the immediate vicinity (see box below).

Bus #95 heads from Mora to Sälen (mid-June to mid-Aug 1 daily; mid-Aug to mid-June 2–3 daily; 2hr). Heading here from Borlänge, take the train to **Malung**, from where bus #157 takes just an hour to reach Sälen. The bus calls at each resort in turn, terminating at Stöten. Annoyingly, to get to **Idre** by public transport (see opposite), you'll need to backtrack to Älvdalen or Mora and set out from there as there's no transport to Idre from Sälen. By car it's much more straightforward; take Route 297 north from Sälen to Särna, from where you head northwest on Route 70 to Idre.

Sälen's **tourist office** is on the straggly main street that runs through the village (late April to late June & mid-Aug to Dec Mon–Fri 9am–6pm; late June to mid-Aug & Dec to late April Mon–Fri 9am–6pm, Sat & Sun 10am–4pm; ☎0280/202 50, ⓦwww.salen.se). **Accommodation** is best at the wonderfully situated *Högfjällshotellet*, at Högfjället (3–4 buses daily from Sälen; ☎0280/870 00, ⓦwww.salen-hotell.se; ❻/❸), just in the tree line; it has a restaurant and a

---

Hikes around Sälen

The **Vasaloppsleden** from Sälen to **Mora** (90km) is the route taken by skiers on the first Sunday in March during the annual **Vasaloppet race**. The event commemorates King Gustav Vasa's return to Mora after he escaped from the Danes on skis; two men from Mora caught up with him and persuaded him to come back to their town, where they gave him refuge. The path starts just outside Sälen, in **Berga**, and first runs uphill to Smågan, then downhill all the way to Mora via Mångsbodarna, Risberg, Evertsberg, Oxberg, Hökberg and Eldris. For **accommodation**, there are eight **cabins** along the route, each equipped with a stove and unmade beds; it's also possible to stay in a number of the hamlets on the way too – look out for *rum* or *logi* signs. A detailed map of the route is available from the tourist offices in Sälen and Mora.

Another hike to consider is the little-known **southern Kungsleden** (for the main Kungsleden, see pp.495–500). It starts at the *Högfjällshotellet* on **Högfjället**, one of the slopes near Sälen, and leads to **Drevdagen**, a thirty-minute drive west of Idre off Route 70 (bus #128 runs once daily Mon–Fri between Idre and Drevdagen), where it continues to Grövelsjön and all the way north to **Storlien**. With the notable exception of the Grövelsjön to Tänndalen stretch (see p.442), although it's an easy path to walk, it doesn't pass through particularly beautiful scenery, and so is best suited to serious walkers who are not averse to covering large distances and camping as there is no accommodation on the Högfjället–Drevdagen stretch.

bar with fantastic panoramic views. There's also a superb sauna suite in the basement, and a swimming pool with whirlpool and jet streams. To be out in the wilds, head for the **youth hostel** at Gräsheden, near Stöten (℡0280/820 40, ℡0280/820 45); buses from Sälen to Stöten will drop you close by. Meals can be ordered in advance and there's also a kitchen, laundry room and sauna.

Idre and Idrefjäll

The three daily buses (#170) from Mora follow the densely forested valley of the Österdalälven on their three-hour journey to **IDRE** – one of Sweden's main **ski resorts** and home to its southernmost community of reindeer-herding *Sámi*. However, if you're expecting wooden huts and reindeer herders dressed in traditional dress, you'll be disappointed – the remaining six herding families live in conventional houses in the area around Idre and dress like everyone else.

The continental climate here – Idre is located at one of the wider points of the Scandinavian peninsula, and thus isn't prone to the warming influence of the Atlantic – means that the summers are relatively dry; consequently Idre, like its fellow ski resort, Sälen (see above), offers plenty of seasonal **outdoor activities**. Its tourist office can help arrange fishing trips, horse riding, mountain biking, tennis, climbing and golf. There are some good sandy beaches along the western shore of **Idresjön**, a lake that's a kilometre east of town; to go canoeing, you can rent a boat through the tourist office. Advice about local hiking routes is available at the tourist office. By far the best hiking hereabouts is to be had around **Grövelsjön**, 3km northwest of Idre and reachable by bus from Idre (Mon–Fri 3 daily; Sun 1 daily). The area is renowned throughout Sweden for its stark, beautiful mountain scenery and is well worth making the extra effort to reach; see overleaf.

Continuing up the mountain (three daily buses; 20min), you'll come to the ski slopes at **IDREFJÄLL**, one of the most reliable places for snow in the entire country, with particularly cold winters. Although not quite on the scale of Sälen, Idre's ski resort manages to be Sweden's third largest and one of the most important in the Nordic area, with 32 lifts and thirty slopes. In winter the place is buzzing – not only with skiers but also with reindeer, who wander down the main street at will hoping to be able to lick the salt off the roads for minerals. Unfortunately for them, though, Route 70 is not salted north of Mora, which means you should be especially careful if you're driving here in winter.

Practicalities

Idre is a tiny one-street affair; if you come in summer, it's where you should stay, rather than up at Idrefjäll. The main street, where the bus drops you, is where you'll find everything of any significance here, including a supermarket and bank. The **tourist office** is near the entrance to the village when approaching from Mora (mid-June to mid-Aug daily 10am–7pm; mid-Aug to mid-June Mon–Fri 9am–5pm; ℡0253/200 00, ⓦwww.idreturism.se) in the Idre Kulturhus on Byvägen. For **accommodation** in the village itself, try the small and comfortable *Hotell Idregården* on the main road just as you come in from Mora (℡0253/205 10, ℡0253/204 78; ❸). When it comes to **eating and drinking**, there's precious little choice: you can either go to the *Idregården*'s restaurant for traditional Swedish home cooking, or *Restaurant Älgen*, right at the other end of town, which does pizzas and pasta dishes for around 100kr.

Idrefjäll consists of one **hotel**, *Idre Fjäll* (℡0253/410 00, ⓦwww.idrefjall.se; ❻/❸), and the surrounding ski slopes and lifts. The place also boasts snowboard areas, indoor swimming pools, saunas, five hotel restaurants and a sports hall. All other facilities, such as banks, are down in the town. Room prices are fiendishly complicated and vary almost week to week through the season, depending on when Stockholmers take their holiday (don't just turn up here in winter and expect to find a room – you won't). You can get a much better rate if you book a package for a week or so; contact the tourist office down in the village for details.

Around Idre: the Njupeskär waterfall

From Idre, it's well worth a trip to **Särna**, 30km away, to see the impressive **Njupeskär waterfall**, Sweden's highest, with a drop of 125m. In winter it's particularly popular with **ice climbers**, as the waterfall freezes completely. An easy, circular **walking route** is clearly signposted from the car park to the waterfall and back, making for a good, two-hour hike. There's no public transport from Idre; by **car**, take the main road to Särna, then turn right following signs for Mörkret and later for Njupeskärsvattenfall.

Grövelsjön

Surrounded by nature reserves and national parks, **GRÖVELSJÖN**, 45km northwest of Idre and reachable by bus #170 from Mora via Idre (Mon–Fri 3 daily, Sun 1 daily; 4hr), is where the road ends and the mountains and wilderness really start. The area is renowned throughout Sweden for its stark, beautiful mountain scenery; in summer, the pasture around here is home to hundreds of grazing reindeer. Virtually the only building here is the STF **fell station**, with a variety of rooms and prices depending on the season (℡0253/59 68 80, Ⓦwww.stfgrovelsjon.com; ❶; closed May to mid-June & Oct–Jan except Christmas & New Year); it boasts a restaurant, kitchen, sauna, massage room and solarium. The fell station makes an ideal base for **hikes** (summer only) out into the surroundings, with a variety of routes available, some lasting a day, others several days.

Among the established **day-hikes** is the clearly marked route (16km round trip) from the fell station up to Storvätteshågnen (1183m), with fantastic views over the surrounding peaks and across the border into Norway. Another worthwhile hike starts with a short walk from the fell station to Sjöstugan on Lake Grövelsjön (roughly 1500m away), from where you take the morning boat to the northern (Norwegian) end of the lake. You can now return along the lake shore to the fell station (9km) by way of the Linné path, following in the footsteps of the famous botanist who walked this route in 1734. It's possible to do the whole route in the opposite direction, heading out along the Linné path in the morning and returning by boat in the late afternoon; ask at the fell station for details of boat departure times. A third option is to strike out along the path leading northwest from Sjöstugan, heading for the Norwegian border and Salsfjellet (1281m) on the other side of it (16km round trip). There's no need to take your passport with you as the border is all but invisible; people wander back and forth across it quite freely.

Härjedalen

From Mora and Orsa, the Inlandsbanan trundles through the northern reaches of Dalarna before crossing the provincial border into **HÄRJEDALEN**, a sparsely populated fell region containing some of the best scenery anywhere in Sweden, stretching north and west to the Norwegian border. Indeed, the region belonged to Norway until 1645, and the influence of the Norwegian language is still evident today in the local dialect. Härjedalen got its name from the unfortunate Härjulf Hornbreaker, a servant to the Norwegian king, who mistakenly killed two of the king's men and was banished from the court. He fled to Uppsala, where he sought protection from King Amund, but after falling in love with Amund's cousin, Helga, and arousing the king's fury, he was forced to make another hasty exit. It was then he came across a desolate valley in which he settled and which he named after himself: Härjulf's dale, or Härjedalen as it's known today.

From the comfort of the Inlandsbanan, you'll be treated to a succession of breathtaking vistas of vast forested hill and mountainsides (Härjedalen boasts more than thirty mountains of above 1000m) – these are some of the emptiest tracts of land in the whole country, also home to the country's largest population of bears. Although the sleepy provincial capital, **Sveg**, holds little of appeal, it's from here that **buses** head northwest to the remote mountain villages of **Funäsdalen** and **Tänndalen**, both with easy access to excellent and little-frequented **hiking trails** through austere terrain that is also home to a handful of shaggy musk oxen that have wandered over the border from Norway. Nearby, across the lonely **Flatruet plateau**, with its ancient rock paintings, tiny **Ljungdalen** is the starting point for treks to Sweden's southernmost glacier, **Helags**, on the icy slopes of Helagsfjället (1797m).

Sveg and around

A good three hours north of Mora by the Inlandsbanan, **SVEG** is the first place of any significance after Lake Siljan. With a tiny population of just four thousand, the town is by far and away the biggest in Härjedalen – though that's not saying much. Even on a Friday night in the height of summer you'll be hard pushed to find anyone in the streets. Though there's not an awful lot to do here, Sveg's a pretty enough place: the wide streets are lined with grand old wooden houses, and the beautiful and very graceful Ljusnan river runs through the centre of town. Although there's very little to see in Sveg, there are a couple of diversions worthy of attention, the first of which is ideally located for arrivals by both train and bus. On permanent display inside the train station building on Järnvägsgatan (which is also used as the bus station) is an **exhibition** (daily; free) of the life and times of the Inlandsbanan, in old photos and maps. Unfortunately the text and captions are only in Swedish but it's pretty evident that without the railway Sveg probably wouldn't be here at all. The town's lifeblood since 1909, when the line to Orsa was opened by King Gustaf V and Queen Viktoria, the line not only brings visitors to the region during the short summer months, but also provides a means of transporting timber and peat pellets (see below) to southern Sweden.

From the station, your next port of call should be **Svegs kyrka**, the parish church on Vallarvägen; head right out of the station on Järnvägsgatan and walk to the T-junction with Fjällvägen, then turn left into this road which later becomes Vallarvägen. A church has stood on this spot since the latter part of the eleventh century when Sveg was also the site of an ancient Viking *ting*, or parliament. In 1273 a border treaty between Sweden and Norway was hammered out here, when the church was part of the bishopric of Trondheim. Sadly, though, the glory days are long gone and the present building only dates from 1847 and contains few of the fittings which once made its predecessors so grand; it's predominantly the woven textiles inside that catch the eye today. Given the paucity of other sights in Sveg, the church is worth a quick look, but if the weather's fine, a stroll along the river is certainly more appealing.

At the western end of Fjällvägen, a pleasant **walk** of around 20–30min (total) takes you across the road and train bridge on Brogatan to the riverbank, ideal for a picnic and a bit of skinny-dipping. Once over the bridge, just beyond the point where the railway line veers left and leaves the road, head right over a little stream into the forest, all the time walking back towards the river's edge. Hidden from the road by the trees is a wonderful sweet-smelling open flower meadow, but don't forget your mosquito repellent – the countryside around Sveg is made up of vast tracts of uninhabited marshland and countless small lakes, ideal breeding grounds for the insect. However, Sveg also has the surrounding swamps to thank for its livelihood; Härjedalen's biggest factory, on the outskirts of town, turns the peat into heating pellets which are then transported down the Inlandsbanan to Uppsala.

Practicalities

The **train** and **bus stations** are on Järnvägsgatan. The **tourist office** at Kyrkogränd 1 (mid-June to mid-Aug Mon–Fri 9am–4pm; rest of year Mon–Fri 1pm–5pm; ℡0680/107 75, ⓦwww.haerjedalen.se) has leaflets about local hiking routes, useful for their maps even if you don't understand Swedish.

For a place to **stay**, try the ramshackle and very welcoming **youth hostel** (℡0680/103 38; bookings mandatory Oct–May), a ten- to fifteen-minute walk from the station at Vallarvägen 11, near the main square. Next door, in the same building, is *Hotell Härjedalen* (same contact details; ❷), with rather shabby rooms. More up-market and just the other side of Torget, at the corner of Fjällvägen and Dalagatan, is the smart *Hotell Mysoxen* (℡0680/170 00, ℻0680/100 62; ❸/❷). The campsite (℡0680/130 25) is by the riverside, a stone's throw from the tourist office.

Most of the town's **eating places** seem pretty deserted. One that isn't is the *Knuten* pizzeria, in the main square, serving standard pizzas for around 60kr. For bargain-basement meals, try the greasy spoon *Inlandskrogen*, next to the train and bus stations, which offers fry-ups and burgers for around 70–80kr; the fare may not be excellent and the place rather smoky but there's a sporting chance you'll find people in there. Finer food can be had at the restaurant in the *Hotell Mysoxen*.

Tännäs and Funäsdalen

Although Sveg may be shy and retiring and void of major attractions, what it does have is some blockbuster scenery right on its doorstep. It's worth leaving the Inlandsbanan at Sveg to travel into the far reaches of Härjedalen to explore one of Sweden's least visited and most rewarding landscapes, where compelling views of the uninhabited vastness of seemingly unending forest unfold at every turn. From Sveg, **bus** #633 winds its way (Mon–Fri 2 daily) northwest towards the tiny village of Lofsdalen, where you change buses to continue to the remote outpost of **TÄNNÄS**, at the junction of Routes 311 and 84, remarkable for its **parish village**, consisting of a handful of knarled wooden cottages clinging to the south-facing valley side where, quite unbelievably for such a high altitude and latitude location, corn was once grown. Should you want to stay here, the well-equipped **youth hostel** (℡0684/240 67, ⓦwww.tannasgarden .nu) lies just to the west of the main road junction and is open all year though advance booking is required in May and November.

From here the bus heads a further 15km west to reach the pretty mountain resort of **FUNÄSDALEN** which is surrounded by kilometres of superb hiking trails. Curling gracefully around the eastern shore of Funäsdalssjön lake, this appealing little village, barely 30km from the Norwegian border, enjoys some fantastic views of the surrounding mountains. It's best seen from the top of the sheer Funäsdalsberget mountain (977m), which bears down over the village and is reached by **chairlift** – you can get to the base station by walking ten minutes along the road signed to Ljungdalen at the eastern end of the village. The main thing to do in the village is visit **Härjedalens Fjällmuseum** (same times as tourist office; 60kr), at Rörosvägen 30, which has a short slide show about the province as well as informative explanations of how the mountain farmers of these parts managed to survive in such a remote location; the transhumance practice of moving animals to higher ground during summer to fatten them on the fresh lush pasture is given particular prominence. The adjacent outdoor **Fornminnesparken** homestead museum, the oldest in Sweden, established in 1894 by a local trader, contains the usual collection of old timber buildings, plus a former customs house from the early nineteenth century used to regulate cross-border trade with Norway.

Practicalities

The best place for advice on the dozens of local **hiking trails** is the **tourist office**, at Rörosvägen 30 (☎0684/164 10, ⓦwww.funasdalsfjall.se), which also has useful information about **canoe hire**. The top place to **stay** in the village is *Hotell Funäsdalen* (☎50684/214 30, ⓦwww.hotell-funasdalen.se; ❷), the huge red building with the green roof down by the lakeside, which has comfortable modern rooms with unsurpassed views out over the lake. Alternatively, five **cabins** are available at *Norrbyns Stugby* (☎0684/212 05, ⓦwww.norrbyns-stugby.nu; ❶), by the chairlift, with terrific views out over Anåfjället mountain. The delightfully named *Veras Krog*, opposite the tourist office on the main road, is the best place to **eat**, not only for its delicious fish (Arctic char is 175kr), pasta dishes (140kr) or grilled meats (145kr), but also its wonderful views of the lake.

Tänndalen

From Funäsdalen, Route 84, covered by **bus** #623 (Mon–Fri 2–3 daily; 15min), climbs steeply uphill bound for dramatic **TÄNNDALEN**, an altogether better destination if you want to get out and do some proper hiking rather than just take in the mountain scenery. Considerably smaller than its easterly neighbour, consisting of barely a dozen or so houses strung out along the main road which crosses this highland plateau, the village boasts Sweden's highest **hotel** and **youth hostel**, *Skarvruet* (☎0684/221 11, ⓕ0684/223 11) at 830m above sea level, run by an engaging couple who fled their native Skåne to enjoy the peace and tranquillity of the north. The hotel is made up of one main building with double rooms (❶), a sauna and restaurant, as well as a number of smaller cabins (❶) which function as the youth hostel – all with breathtaking views of Rödfjället mountain (1243m). In winter, Tänndalen is not only surrounded by 300km of prepared cross-country ski tracks (there's another 450km of marked expedition trails up on the surrounding mountains), the most extensive anywhere in the world, but also a variety of downhill slopes; **ski hire** is available in the village from *Tänndalens Skiduthyrning* (☎0684/222 25) – ask at the hotel for directions. In summer, though, it's the extensive **hiking** routes which attract people here. One of the better routes is outlined in the

From Tänndalen there are two main hiking routes, both along the **southern Kungsleden**. Heading **south**, the stretch to **Grövelsjön** in Dalarna (see p.438) makes an excellent hike, taking three to four days to complete (76km) and begins with an ascent of Rödfjället. For much of the time the route passes through sparse pine forest relatively untouched by modern forestry; an eight-kilometre stretch also runs alongside Lake Rogen, known for its rich birdlife and unusual moraine formations. Between Tänndalen and the lake, you might be lucky enough to see the only herd of **musk oxen** in Sweden. They spend the winter in the mountain area between Storvålen and Brattriet before nipping over the border into Norway's Femundsmarka national park (close to the western edge of Lake Rogen) for the summer months. It's wise to keep your distance should you come across them, as musk oxen can be ferocious creatures; also bear in mind they're one of the few animals which can run faster uphill than downhill! The route then crosses the provincial border from Härjedalen into Dalarna to the east of Slagufjället, skirts round Töfsingdalens National Park and finally goes over the reindeer-grazing slopes of Långfjället. This hike takes in three STF **cabins** (all closed May, June & late Sept to early March), with about 20 beds each and selling provisions, at: Skedbro (21km from Tänndalen), Rogen (17km from Skedbro) and Storrödtjärn (16km from Rogen and 22km to Grövelsjön).

Heading **north**, the trail leads to **Storlien** (see p.454), first heading to the ski slopes of Ramundberget (20km from Tänndalen), then climbing steeply towards Helagsfjället and Sweden's southernmost **glacier**; at an altitude of 1796m, it's disappointingly small, only a couple of square kilometres in size. From Helags it's possible to either descend 18km to **Ljungdalen** and pick up bus #613 to Åsarna and Östersund (see p.446) or continue north towards Storlien via the fell stations at **Sylarna** and **Blåhammaren** and the youth hostel at **Storvallen** outside Storlien (see p.454), a magnificent 50km stretch across central Sweden's most enchanting mountain range.

There are several places for overnight **accommodation**: Fältjägaren cabin (late Feb to early May & late June to late Sept), 15km from Ramundberget; Helags cabin at the foot of the glacier (late Feb to early May & late June to late Sept), 12km from Fältjägaren; Sylarna fell station (March to early May & late June to late Sept; ☏0647/750 10, ⊛www.stfsylarna.com), 19km from Helags; Blåhammaren fell station at 1086m (March to early May & late June to late Sept; ☏0647/701 20, ⊛www.stf-blahammaren.stfturist.se), 19km from Sylarna and 12km from Storvallen youth hostel (see p.454) just outside Storlien, from where there are trains to Östersund.

box above. **Buses** from Tänndalen leave for Funäsdalen, where there are direct connections to Östersund via Klövsjö and Åsarna (see p.444) or, with a change in Lofsdalen, back to Sveg. There are no buses, however, over the border into Norway or to Ljungdalen.

The Flatruet plateau and Ljungdalen

From Funäsdalen, an unnumbered road, actually the highest in the country, sets out for the bumpy ascent to the hamlet of Mittådalen and beyond to the **Flatruet plateau** (975m), a bare stretch of desolate, rocky land, punctuated only by electricity poles and herds of grazing reindeer. The plateau is renowned for its 4000-year-old Stone Age **rock paintings** (*hällmålningar* in Swedish) at the foot of the Ruändan mountain at the eastern edge of this extensive upland area; get here by turning right in Mittådalen for another hamlet, Messlingen, where you should leave your vehicle. East of the settlement, a track off to the left leads towards Byggevallen and Ruvallen, from the latter a footpath then leads to the paintings; from the road it's a walk of around 5–6km. Fashioned from a mix of iron ochre and animal fat and etched into slabs of rock, the twenty or so figures show, in remarkable clarity, elk, reindeer and even bears.

Once over the plateau, the road descends steeply towards the charming village of **Ljungdalen**, hemmed in on three sides by high mountains, occupying an area of flat grassland near the head of the Ljungan river. Though the fifty or so wooden houses are pleasant enough, it's as a base from which to reach the Helags glacier that Ljungdalen really comes into its own. From the ICA supermarket in the centre of the village, take the road signed for "Helags/Kläppen" which leads to a car park after 6km, from where the hiking trails starts. Before the car park, though, the road passes a small settlement, Kläppen, where you should take Kläppenvägen uphill, following the signs. Once at the car park it's 12km to the STF mountain cabin at Helags. For details of the route towards Storlien see the box opposite.

Practicalities

The **tourist office** (℡0687/200 79, ⊛www.ljungdalen.com) occupies a small shed in the centre of the village. They have good advice about hiking to Helags and about onward travel possibilities; there's no bus over the plateau to Funäsdalen though it is possible to hike there; see box opposite for details.

Ljungdalen is an excellent place to rest up for a few days and the *Dunsjögården* **youth hostel** (℡0687/202 85, ℻0687/203 64) also has a swimming pool and sauna nearby, for relaxing those aching muscles after hiking. Whilst you can cook here, the best **eating** alternative in the village is *Restaurant Ljungan*, down by the phone box, which serves good Swedish cooking dishes for around 140kr.

From Ljungdalen to Åsarna

From Ljungdalen, one of the most beautiful journeys anywhere in northern Sweden unfolds. Although the 110km trip to Åsarna certainly requires stamina – the road is in a truly appalling condition, unsurfaced all the way to the border with Jämtland and with some alarmingly large ruts and potholes – it offers a real taste of wild Sweden. Threading its way around serpentine bends and across narrow isthmuses between the extensive areas of swampland and spruce forest that characterize this forgotten corner of the country, this switchback road cuts through some of the most spectacular mountain and lakeside landscapes you'll witness in the north.

Curiously for such a remote route, it is served by **bus**; #613 runs to Åsarna (Mon–Fri 2 daily, Sat & Sun 1 daily; 2hr) providing a rare insight, for anyone without their own transport, into life in backwoods Sweden – as the bus trundles through the tiny villages, you'll notice how the lumberjack culture is alive and well in these parts.

Indeed, the stretch of road between the Härjedalen/Jämtland border and the village of **Börtnan** (1hr 15min from Ljungdalen) runs through one of the region's most important forestry areas; mountains of timber line the roadside awaiting transport to the nearest railhead.

Jämtland

Stretching from just north of Sveg to the border with Lappland, a distance of around 250km, the sizeable province of **JÄMTLAND** is centred round one of Sweden's greatest lakes, Storsjön, and its associated watercourses. Altogether more pastoral than its wilder and more mountainous neighbour to the south,

Härjedalen, it was the plentiful supply of fish from the lake coupled with successful cultivation of the rich lands around its shores that enabled the region's first settlers to eke out an existence so far north – Stockholm, for example, is 600km to the south. Although the province can trace its history back to the early Iron Age, Jämtland has only been Swedish since 1645, before which it was part of Norway. The people here have a strong sense of regional identity and, in recent years, have even called (albeit rather half-heartedly) for independence from Sweden. Spend any length of time here and you'll soon encounter the tremendous pride the locals have in their villages, forests and lakes – on the ground Jämtland may represent one tenth of Sweden's total area, but the free-minded straight-talking mentality of the local people is known well beyond the provincial borders.

Approaching from the south, it's the cross-country skiing centre of **Åsarna** and the pretty village of **Klövsjö** that you'll reach first, though an altogether more upbeat destination is **Östersund** situated on Storsjön lake, whose murky waters reputedly hide Sweden's own version of the Loch Ness monster. West of the provincial capital, **Åre** is Sweden's most popular ski destination for foreign tourists whilst nearby **Storlien** has some great summer hiking right on its doorstep.

Åsarna and around

From Sveg, the Inlandsbanan veers eastwards in order to get around the vast area of marshland north and east of the town. The train line finally swings west at Överhogdal, where the Viking Age tapestries now on display in Östersund were discovered (see p.446), before crossing the provincial border into Jämtland and continuing north to **Åsarna**, a lowkey cross-country skiing centre in winter. From here, **buses** run southwest to **Klövsjö**, one of northern Sweden's prettiest villages, all log cabins and rolling meadows, before crossing back into Härjedalen, where, close to the provincial border, **Vemdalen** is deservedly known for its ornate eighteenth-century Rococo wooden church.

Åsarna

Blink and you'll miss **Åsarna**, a tiny one-street affair, 109km north of Sveg, that serves as a diminutive service centre for the southern part of Jämtland. Other than the railway station, a filling station and a hotel, all lined up along the nameless main road, there's nothing to recommend an overnight stay here. Even the all-year **Skicenter**, at the southern end of the town (to the left of the railway station as you exit) holds little of appeal. Established by four of the region's many skiing champions – Tomas Wassberg, Torgny Mogren, Jan Ottosson and Hans Persson – the centre organizes cross-country skiing in winter and provides advice on hiking in summer. If, however, you're waiting for a bus to nearby Klövsjö, the real reason for breaking your journey at Åsarna, you may want to check out its **ski museum** (daily: June–Aug 9am–8pm; Sept–May 9am–7pm; 20kr), which has worthy displays of the Åsarna ski club's Olympic and World Championship medals and equipment, as well as photographs of famous Swedish skiers and a couple of video exhibits.

For a stroll or an afternoon picnic in summer, wander past the campsite cabins, behind the ski centre, down to the river, turn right, and follow the age-old Kärleksstigen – Lover's Lane – along the water's edge; you can cross the river over an old stone bridge, further upstream by the rapids, and return on the opposite bank along a minor road. The smooth, low rocks by the bridge make an ideal spot at which to fish or catch a few rays of sunshine.

Åsarna's **tourist office** is housed in the Skicenter complex (daily: June–Aug 8am–8pm; Sept–May 8am–7pm; ☎0687/301 93, ⓦwww.asarnaskicenter.se) where you'll also find a post office and a branch of *Sparbanken*. While it's virtually impossible to **stay** in Åsarna in winter without an advance booking, in summer you can just turn up and find a room. The Skicenter's **youth hostel** (☎ & ⓕ0687/302 30) and **campsite** (same contact details as youth hostel); are down by the river's edge, with a small bathing pool and a sauna. Three non-STF four-berth **cabins** are available to rent here from 500kr per day via the tourist office. The *Åsarna Hotell* (☎0687/300 04; ❷), opposite the train station, has smarter rooms than the hostel's, and a restaurant and bar. The Skicenter **restaurant** is hard to beat for cheap meals (closes around 8pm), with breakfast for 40kr, *Dagens Rätt* and evening meals for 65kr. When the Inlandsbanan is running, a northbound **train** for Östersund generally leaves around midday, while the southbound service to Sveg and Mora doesn't go until around 5pm.

Klövsjö and Vemdalen

Åsarna is well placed for a quick jaunt out to charming **KLÖVSJÖ** (3–4 daily buses from Åsarna; 20min). The village has gained the reputation as Sweden's most beautiful village, with some justification: the distant lake and the forested hills that enclose Klövsjö give it a special, other-worldly feeling. In and around the village itself, the flower meadows, streams, wooden barns and the smell of freshly mown hay drying on frames in the afternoon sun cast a wonderful spell on all who pass through.

The ten farms here work the land in much the same way as in medieval times: ancient grazing rights, still in force, mean that horses and cows are free to roam through the village. Once you've taken a look at **Tomtangården** (July to mid-Aug daily; free), a preserved seventeenth-century farm estate, there's not much else to do except breathe the biting, clean air and admire the beauty. Unfortunately there's nowhere to stay in the village, but the **tourist office** on the main road (Mon–Fri noon–3.30pm; ☎0682/41 36 60) has cabins to rent in the vicinity (around 500kr a day). Bus #164 from Åsarna continues to **Funäsdalen** (where you can change for **Tänndalen** and hike along the southern Kungsleden to Grövelsjön, see p.442), passing within fifteen minutes' walk of *Katarina Wärdshus* (tell the driver if you wish to go here), a guesthouse which has **cabins** for rent (☎0682/41 31 00, ⓦwww.klovsjofjall.se; ❶); they're popular in winter with the skiers who make the most of the thirteen ski slopes nearby.

The road from Klövsjö to Funäsdalen is especially worth travelling. Once beyond the turn for *Katarina Wärdshus*, the route crosses the provincial border back into Härjedalen and follows the ancient track used by the region's merchant farmers through the Vemdalsskalet pass. Bound for **VEMDALEN** the road descends sharply offering clear views of another of Härjedalen's mighty peaks: the impressive sugarloaf-shaped **Sånfjället** mountain (1278m) to the southwest. Back in the 1900s the forest and fell terrain around the mountain was declared a national park in an attempt to maintain its delicate ecosystem, and, it would seem with great success, since the park is now a favourite habitat for Härjedalen's bear population. Once through the pass and down into Vemdalen, you'll find a stunning octagonal **wooden church** right by the roadside in the centre of the village. Built in Rococo-style in 1763, eight years after its separate onion-domed bell tower, the church supports a deep two-stage roof and a central onion turret. Inside, the work of a couple of local craftsmen is proudly displayed: the pulpit with its bowing cherrywood panels was made in Ljungdalen, whilst the altar was carved by a local carpenter from Klövsjö. From

Vemdalen **bus** #164 continues to Tännäs and Funäsdalen; in the opposite direction it runs back to Åsarna and Klövsjö, continuing on to Östersund (Mon–Fri 3 daily, Sat 2 daily, Sun 1 daily).

Östersund

Having reached **ÖSTERSUND**, just 78km north of Åsarna, which sits gracefully on the eastern shore of the mighty **Storsjön** (Great Lake), it's worth stopping at what is the only large town along the Inlandsbanan until Gällivare inside the Arctic Circle. King Gustav III gave Östersund its charter two hundred years ago with one thing in mind: to put an end to the lucrative trade the region's merchant farmers carried out with neighbouring Norway. Travelling through the Vemdalsskalet pass (see above) they bartered and sold their goods in Trondheim before returning back over the mountains to the Storsjön region. Although rival markets in Östersund gradually stemmed the trade, it took another century for the town's growth to really begin, heralded by the arrival of the railway from Sundsvall in 1879.

Today, the town is a major **transport hub**: the E14 runs through town on its way to the Norwegian border; the Inlandsbanan stops here (the town is 2hr north of Åsarna by this line); and other trains run west to Åre and Storlien (with connections in Storlien to Trondheim in Norway), east to Sundsvall (a very beautiful run which hugs lakeshore and riverbank the entire way) and south to both Stockholm and Gothenburg, through some of Sweden's most stunning primeval forest. Coming from Swedish Lapland, train connections can be made for Östersund in nearby Bräcke.

Most visitors head straight for Östersund's top attraction, **Jamtli**, home to the beautiful **Överhogdal Viking tapestries**. The adjoining **open-air museum** expertly – and enjoyably – brings to life Östersund from years past. However, it's for its lake **monster**, the Storsjöodjuret, that Östersund is perhaps best known. Reached by bridge from the town, the nearby island of **Frösön** is worth checking out for the oldest rune stone in Sweden and its elaborate wooden church.

Arrival and information

From the **train station**, on Strandgatan, it's a five-minute walk north to the town centre; the **bus station**, on Gustav IIIs Torg, is more central. The town's **airport** is on Frösön, an island 11km from town, from where buses (50kr) and taxis (250kr) run to the centre. A couple of blocks north of the bus station is the **tourist office** at Rådhusgatan 44 (June Mon–Fri 9am–7pm, Sat & Sun 9am–3pm; late June to early Aug Mon–Sat 9am–9pm, Sun 9am–7pm; Aug Mon–Fri 9am–5pm, Sat & Sun 9am–3pm; rest of year Mon–Fri 9am–5pm; ☎063/14 40 01, ⓦ www.turist.ostersund.se), opposite the minaret-topped Rådhus. Here you can obtain the **Östersundskortet** (valid June to mid-Aug; 120kr), a nine-day pass giving free bus rides, museum entry and fifty percent discounts on bus and boat sightseeing trips in and around the town.

Accommodation

For a place to **stay**, the modern and central STF **youth hostel** is at Södra Gröngatan 32, a few minutes' walk south from the tourist office (☎063/341

30, Ⓕ063/13 91 00; late-June to early Aug). Another option, accessed from the platform at the train station, is the cosy *Rallaren* hostel, Bangårdsgatan 6 (℡063/13 22 32) with beds in rooms sleeping 2–6. More atmospheric, though, is a night spent inside *Jamtli*, a wonderful STF hostel set in the old buildings at the museum (℡063/12 20 60, Ⓦwww.jamtli.com); you should be guaranteed free entry to the museum if you smile politely. Campers can stay either at *Östersunds Camping* (℡063/14 46 15, Ⓦwww.camping.se/plats/z11), a couple of kilometres south from Rådhusgatan and handy for the fantastic indoor swimming complex, Storsjöbadet; or over on Frösön at *Frösö Camping* (℡063/432 54; mid-June to mid–Aug), reached by bus #3 or #4 from the centre. Unlike many other places in central northern Sweden, Östersund has good quality **hotels** at reasonable prices; you won't find their like north of here until Gällivare.

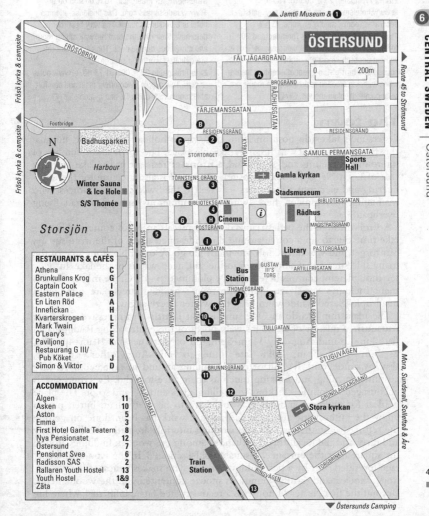

ÖSTERSUND

▲ Jamtli Museum & ❶

◄ Fröső kyrka & campsite

► Route 45 to Strömsund

► Mora, Sundsvall, Sollefteå & Åre

0 — 200m

FRÖSÖBRON

FÄLTJÄGARGRÄND

BROGRÄND

RÅDHUSGATAN

FÄRJEMANSGATAN

Footbridge

Badhusparken

N

Harbour

RESIDENSGRÄND

RESIDENSGRÄND

STORTORGET

KYRGATAN

SAMUEL PERMANSGATA

Sports Hall

Winter Sauna & Ice Hole

S/S Thomée

Storsjön

TÖRNSTENS GRÄND

Gamla kyrkan

BIBLIOTEKSGATAN

Stadsmuseum

BIBLIOTEKSGATAN

Cinema

Rådhus

MAGISTRATSGRÄND

POSTGRÄND

HAMNGATAN

Library

PASTORGRÄND

SJÖTORGET

STRANDGATAN

RESTAURANTS & CAFÉS

Athena	C
Brunkullans Krog	G
Captain Cook	I
Eastern Palace	B
En Liten Röd	A
Innefickan	H
Kvarterskrogen	L
Mark Twain	F
O'Leary's	E
Paviljong	K
Restaurang G III/ Pub Köket	J
Simon & Viktor	D

Bus Station

GUSTAV III'S TORG

ARTILLERIGATAN

THOMÉEGRÄND

KÖPMANGATAN

STORGATAN

PRÄSTGATAN

KYRGATAN

SÖDRA GRÖNGATAN

TULLGATAN

RÅDHUSGATAN

STUGUVÄGEN

Cinema

BRUNNSGRÄND

GRUNDLAGGARGRÄND

GRÄNSGATAN

Stora kyrkan

N HAMNVÄGEN

BANGÅRDSGATAN

RINGVÄGEN

TORGBRINKEN

ACCOMMODATION

Älgen	11
Asken	10
Aston	5
Emma	3
First Hotel Gamla Teatern	8
Nya Pensionatet	12
Östersund	7
Pensionat Svea	6
Radisson SAS	2
Rallaren Youth Hostel	13
Youth Hostel	1&9
Zäta	4

Train Station

▼ Östersunds Camping

Älgen Storgatan 61 ☎063/51 75 25, ⓦwww.hotelalgen.se. Handy for the train station, this is yet another of the town's small central hotels, with plain and comfortable en-suite rooms. There are also thirteen smaller hostel-style shared rooms for 180kr per person. ❹/❷

Asken Storgatan 53 ☎063/51 74 50. Only has eight rooms (all en suite and rather plain and simple), one of which is for the use of people with allergies. ❸/❷

Aston Köpmangatan 40 ☎063/51 08 51. Entrance in Postgränd. This small hotel is the cheapest in town, with plain rooms, some of which are en suite. ❸/❷

Emma Prästgatan 26 ☎063/51 78 40, ⓦwww.hotelemma.com. Nineteen tiny, garishly decorated rooms, mostly en suite. ❹/❷

First Hotel Gamla Teatern Thoméegränd 20 ☎063/51 16 00, ⓦwww.gamlateatern.se. This is without doubt the most atmospheric hotel in town, housed in a turn-of-the-twentieth-century theatre with sweeping wooden staircases; the rooms are disappointingly plain though. ❺/❸.

Nya Pensionat Prästgatan 65 ☎063/51 24 98. Near the train station, this tastefully decorated house – dating from around 1900 – has just six rooms, all with washbasins, but the bathrooms are shared. ❷/❶

Östersund Kyrkgatan 70 ☎063/57 57 00, ⓦwww.scandic-hotels.com. A massive modern hotel with 126 rooms; high on quality – with carpeted rooms and leather chairs – but low on charm. ❺/❸

Pensionat Svea Storgatan 49 ☎063/51 29 01. Seven tweely decorated rooms, with shared bathroom. Discounted rates are available for long-term stays. ❷

Radisson SAS Prästgatan 16 ☎063/55 60 00, ⓦwww.radissonsas.com. This business-oriented hotel is Östersund's finest. The very best rooms here have their own marbled hallway, sitting room and sumptious double beds. The discounted rates are definitely worth the splurge. ❺/❸

Zäta Prästgatan 32 ☎063/51 78 60, ⓦwww.hotel-z.com. This simple place offers plain and comfortable rooms with cable TV, and a sauna. ❹/❷

The town

Östersund's **lakeside** position lends it a seaside-holiday atmosphere, unusual this far inland, and it's an instantly likeable place. The town has a number of interesting museums and, so it's said, a **monster** resident in the lake, rivalling that of Loch Ness (see box opposite). Östersund is also a centre for the engineering and electronics industries – as well as the Swedish armed forces, who maintain two regiments here (witness the numerous military aircraft flying overhead).

A stroll through the pedestrianized centre reveals an air of contented calm – take time out to sip a coffee around the wide-open space of the main square, Stortorget, and watch Swedish provincial life go by, or amble along one of the many side streets that slope down to the still, deep waters of the lake. In winter, though, temperatures here regularly plummet to -15°C; the modern apartment buildings you'll see lining the town's gridded streets are fitted with quadruple-glazed windows to keep the winter freeze at bay.

The main thing to do in Östersund is visit **Jamtli**, an impressive **open-air museum**, a quarter of an hour's walk north of the centre along Rådhusgatan (late June to mid-Aug daily 11am–5pm; rest of year Tues–Fri 10am–4pm, Sat & Sun 11am–5pm; 90kr late June to mid-Aug, otherwise 60kr; ⓦwww.jamtli.com). It's full of people milling around in nineteenth-century costume, farming and milking much as their ancestors did. Everyone else is encouraged to join in – baking, tree felling, grass cutting, and so on. The place is ideal for children, and adults would have to be pretty hard-bitten not to enjoy the enthusiastic atmosphere. Intensive work has been done on getting the settings right: the restored and working interiors are authentically gloomy and dirty, and the local store, Lanthandel, among the wooden buildings around the square near the entrance, is suitably old-fashioned. In the woodman's cottage (presided over by a bearded lumberjack, who makes pancakes for the visitors), shoeless and scruffy youngsters snooze contentedly in the wooden cots. Beyond the first cluster of houses is a reconstructed farm, Lillhärdal, where life

Storsjöodjuret – the "Great Lake Monster"

The people of Östersund are in no doubt: **Storsjöodjuret** is out there, in their lake. Eyewitness accounts – there are hundreds of people who claim to have seen it – speak of a creature, with a head like a dog, long pointed ears and bulging eyes, that sweeps gracefully through the water, sometimes making a hissing or clucking sound, often several hundred metres away from the shore; every summer come new reports of sightings. Although several explanations have been given that dispel the myth – a floating tree trunk, a row of swimming elk, the wake from a passing boat, a series of rising water bubbles – the monster's existence is taken so seriously that a protection order has now been slapped on it, using the provisions of paragraph fourteen of Sweden's Nature Conservation Act. For most people, though, the monster will be at its most tangible not in the lake, but on the Web (@www.storsjoodjuret.jamtland.se).

In 1894, the hunt for this sinister presence began in earnest, when King Oscar II founded a special organization to try to catch it. Norwegian whalers were hired to do so, but the rather unorthodox methods they chose proved unsuccessful: a dead pig gripped in a metal clasp was dangled into the water as bait; and large, specially man-ufactured pincers were on hand to grip the creature and pull it ashore. Their tackle is on display at Jamti, together with photographs claimed to be of the creature.

If you fancy a bit of monster spotting, consider taking a **steamboat cruise** on the lake on board *S/S Thomée*, a creaking 1875 wooden steamship. Routes and timeta-bles vary, but in general the boat does a two-hour trip (75kr) round the lake leaving from the harbour in town. Also available are three-hour trips out to the island of **Andersön**, with its nature reserve and virgin forests (85kr); five-hour trips to **Verkön**, where there's a nineteenth-century castle (95kr); as well as one-hour trips across the water towards **Sandviken** and back (65kr); for more information, contact the tourist office. Also, ask about special **monster spotting tours** with onboard guides – there are generally two in July and one in early August – during which the boat heads out for places on the lake where previous sightings have been recorded.

goes on pretty much as it did in 1785 when the land was ploughed using hors-es and crops were sown and harvested by hand – even the roaming cattle and the crop varieties are accurate to the period.

The indoor **museum** on the same site is the place to get to grips with Öster-sund's **monster**. Ask to see the fascinating film (with English subtitles) about the creature which contains a series of telling interviews with local people who claim to have seen the creature; one very Swedish thing leaps out at you – hav-ing witnessed something unusual out on the lake, many people took several months, even years, to talk about their experience for fear of ridicule. Having seen the film, head downstairs for a further display of monster-catching gear devised by lakeside worthies in the nineteenth century, alongside what's claimed to be a pickled embryo of a similar monster found in 1895; this quite grotesque thing is kept in a small glass jar on a shelf next to the foot of the stairs. However, the museum's prize exhibits are the awe-inspring Viking **Överhogdal tapestries**, crowded with brightly coloured pictures of horses, reindeer, elk and dogs, and different types of dwellings. Dating from the ninth and tenth centuries, most of the tapestries were discovered by accident in an outhouse in 1910. One piece was rescued after being used as a doll's blanket – rumour has it the child had to be pacified with a 2kr reward to hand it over.

There's nothing much else to see back in the town centre, apart from the **Stadsmuseum** on Rådhusgatan (Mon–Fri 10am–4pm, Sat & Sun 1–4pm; 30kr), housing a crowded two hundred years of town history in a building the size of a shoebox. The **harbour**, where a fleet of tiny boats bobs about on the

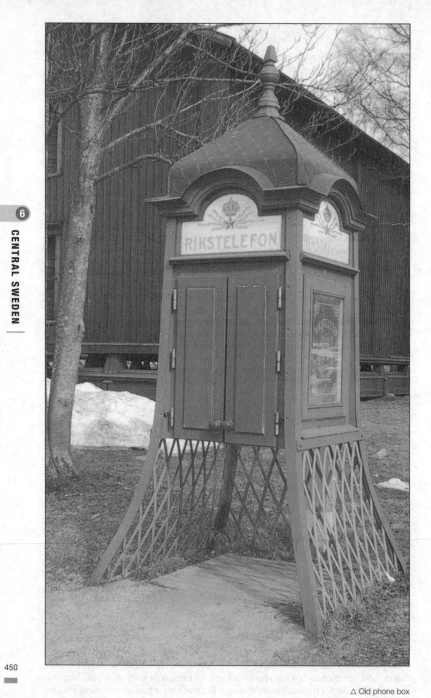

△ Old phone box

clean water, is a better bet for a place to head. Immediately to the north of the harbour is the tiny **Badhusparken**, an extremely popular sunbathing spot in summer; in winter it's the place for a quick dip in the invigorating waters of Lake Storsjön – a hole in the ice is kept open here for this purpose (mid-Jan to late March). Once you're out of the water, though, head straight for the nearby mobile **sauna** or you'll be covered in frost faster than you can say "Storsjöodjuret".

Frösön

Take the footbridge across the lake from Badhusparken, or the road bridge a little further north, and you'll come to the island of **Frösön**. People have lived here since prehistoric times; the island's name comes from the original Viking settlement here, which was associated with the pagan god of fertility, Frö. There's plenty of good walking on Frösön, as well as a couple of historical sights. Just over the bridges, in front of the red-brick offices, look for the eleventh-century **rune stone** telling of Östmadur (East Man), son of Gudfast, the first Christian missionary to the area. From here, you can clamber up the nearby hill of Öneberget to the fourth-century settlement of **Mjälleborgen**, where a pleasant walking trail of around 1hr leads through the area.

Five kilometres west of the bridges along the island's main road, and up the main hill, is the beautiful **Frösö kyrka** (bus #3 from the centre comes here), an eleventh-century church with a detached bell tower. In 1984, archeologists digging under the altar came across a bit of old birch stump surrounded by animal bones – bears, pigs, deer and squirrels – evidence of the cult of ancient gods, who were known as the *æsir*. Today, the church is one of the most popular in Sweden for weddings – to tie the knot here at midsummer, you have to book years in advance.

From Frösön, there are fantastic **views** across the lake back to Östersund, which appears to tumble down the hill towards the water. In **winter**, when the trees hang heavy under the weight of snow and ice, and the town's streetlights cast a soft glow into the dark sky, the view across the frozen lake to the streets buried deep under a fresh snowfall is one of the most romantic and beautiful in Sweden.

Eating, drinking and nightlife

Gastronomically, there's more **choice** in Östersund than for a long way north, with good Swedish, Thai and even Australian food. Most of the city's eating places, many of which double as bars, are to the south of Stortorget. For **breakfast** (and convenient for the several trains that leave early in the morning), the train station café is good value and always busy. **Coffee and cakes** can be had at *Törners Konditori*, at Storgatan 24, or better, *Wedemarks Konditori* at Prästgatan 27, where you can have sandwiches made to order. **Nightlife** can be found at *G III* in *Hotell Östersund*, the most popular **club** in town, which attracts a 20-something crowd.

Athena Stortorget 3. Tucked away in one corner of Stortorget, this pompously decorated pizza restaurant serves tasty, authentic pizzas from 55kr, as well as steaks for around 185kr.

Brunkullans Krog Postgränd 5. Östersund's premier eating place, this old-fashioned, home-from-home restaurant, with polished lanterns and a heavy wooden interior, offers traditional Swedish dishes as well as more international fish and meat options for around 170kr. In summer a cheaper menu can be enjoyed at tables in the garden at the rear.

Captain Cook Hamngatan 9. This moderately priced place has a selection of delicious Australian-style surf-and-turf delights that really draws in the crowds – try the Ayers Rock mixed grill for 154kr, which includes ostrich and kangaroo. It's also one of the most popular places for a drink, and offers an extensive beer and whisky selection.

Eastern Palace Storgatan 15. The town's best Chinese restaurant, with the usual dishes for 95–135kr. They also have a Mongolian barbecue at 99kr.

En Liten Röd Brogränd 19. A cosy neighbourhood restaurant with a good choice of meat dishes from 159kr; their chocolate fondue for 129kr is the stuff dreams are made of (must be booked one day in advance).

Innefickan Postgränd 11. A small basement place serving up some of the tastiest Italian meals in Östersund. Meat dishes add to the usual array of pasta specials for 120–200kr.

Kvarterskrogen Storgatan 54. A linen tablecloth place, with high prices to match, serving lamb, entrecôte, beef and Arctic char as well as northern Swedish delicacies from 170kr.

O'Leary's Storgatan 28. A popular Irish-style pub, offering a large selection of beer and a Tex-Mex-inspired menu – burgers are 99kr, fajitas 168kr.

Mark Twain Biblioteksgatan 5. A noisy American-style bar and restaurant with up-market dishes such as grilled turbot with blue mussels for 192kr, as well as a cheaper bar menu featuring the likes of fish soup (72kr) and wok-fried chicken and vegetables (69kr).

Paviljong Prästgatan 50B. This is the best Indonesian/Thai restaurant in central Sweden – make the most of it. Excellent chicken with garlic, chilli and Thai basil. Dishes around 119kr; lunch for 60kr.

Restaurang G III/Pub Köket Both inside the Hotel Östersund, Kyrkgatan 70. A standard, fairly expensive à la carte restaurant, but right beside one of the town's popular drinking holes, *Pub Köket*.

Simon & Viktor Prästgatan 19. An English-style pub with up-market pub food, featuring fish and chips for 75kr.

Listings

Airlines SAS, at the airport ☎063/635 10 06.
Banks FöreningsSparbanken, Handelsbanken and Sparbanken are all on Prästgatan.
Bike rental Cykelogen ☎063/12 20 80 at Kyrkogatan 45 has mountain bikes from about 100kr per day.
Buses Information on all buses on ☎020/61 62 63, or visit ⊛www.lanstrafiken-z.se.
Car rental Avis Bangårdsgatan 9 ☎063/10 12 50; Europcar, Hofvallsgränd 1 ☎063/57 47 50; Hertz, Kyrkgatan 32 ☎063/57 50 30.
Cinemas Filmstaden 1–6, Biblioteksgatan 14; Filmstaden 7–8, corner of Tullgatan and Prästgatan.
Doctor Health Centre Z-gränd ☎063/14 20 00

(Mon–Fri 8am–5pm).
Left luggage Lockers at the train station for 15kr.
Pharmacy Prästgatan 51 (Mon–Wed & Fri 9am–6pm, Thurs 10am–7pm, Sat 9am–4pm, Sun 11am–4pm).
Police Köpmangatan 24, ☎063/15 25 00.
Systembolaget Prästgatan 18 (Mon–Wed & Fri 10am–6pm); Kyrkgatan 82 (Mon–Wed & Fri 10am–6pm, Thurs 10am–7pm, Sat 10am–2pm)
Taxi Taxi Östersund ☎063/51 72 00.
Trains Information from the station on Strandgatan. SJ trains also on ☎0771/75 75 75; Inlandsbanan on ☎020/53 53 53.
Travel agents Ticket, Kyrkgatan 45 (Mon–Fri 9am–6pm, Sat 10am–1pm).

Moving on from Östersund

Direct **trains** from Östersund include services **south** to Gävle, Arlanda airport, Uppsala, Stockholm and Gothenburg, **east** to Sundsvall, and **west** to Åre and Storlien and on to Trondheim in Norway. By changing in Bräcke it's possible to travel by night train to Boden, Luleå and Swedish **Lapland**. For the **Bothnian Coast**, take the train to Sundsvall, then change to the Norrlandskusten bus services up the coast. **Inlandsbanan** services (late June to early Aug) operate north to Gällivare and south to Mora. The **Inlandsexpressen bus** (#45) covers the same route as the Inlandsbanan and operates year round. Other key bus services include the #40 to Sollefteå and Örnsköldsvik and the #164 to Tännas and Funäsdalen via Åsarna and Klövsjö. There's also a daily direct express bus to Stockholm with Y-Bussen.

West to Åre and Storlien

Heading west from Östersund, the **E14** and the **train** line follow the course trudged by medieval pilgrims on their way to Nidaros (now Trondheim in Norway) over the border, a twisting route that threads its way through sharp-edged mountains rising high above a bevy of fast-flowing streams and deep, cold lakes. Time and again, the eastern Vikings assembled their armies beside the holy Storsjön lake to begin the long march west, most famously in 1030 when King Olaf of Norway collected his mercenaries for the campaign that led to his death at the Battle of Stiklestad. Today, although the scenery is splendid, the only real attractions en route are the winter skiing and summer walking centres of **Åre** and **Storlien**.

Åre

The alpine village of **Åre** is Sweden's most prestigious ski resort, with 42 lifts, 100 ski slopes and guaranteed snow between December and May; it can be reached from Östersund either by **train** (2–3 daily; 1hr 45min) or on the late-afternoon **bus** (#155, 1hr 30min). During the skiing season, rooms here are like gold dust and prices sky high: book accommodation for this period well in advance through the tourist office or, better yet, take a package trip. Equipment isn't that expensive to rent (details of where to do so can be obtained at the tourist office): downhill and cross-country gear costs from 180kr per day.

In summer, the village is a quiet, likeable haven for ramblers, sandwiched as it is between the Åresjön lake and a range of craggy hills that's overshadowed by Sweden's seventh highest peak, the mighty **Åreskutan** mountain (1420m). A network of tracks crisscrosses the hills; the tourist office has endless information about **hiking routes** in the nearby mountains and further afield – ask them for the excellent *Hiking in Årefjällen* booklet, which will tell you all you need to know, with detailed mountain maps. A popular route is the **Jämttriangle** from Sylarna via Blåhammaren to Storulvån, which takes in fantastic wilderness scenery close to the Norwegian border and involves two overnight stays in STF fell stations.

A cable car, the **Kabinbanan** (100kr return), whisks you from just behind Storlien's main square to the viewing platform and *Stormköket* restaurant, some way up Åreskutan. The ride takes just seven minutes, and it'll take you a further thirty minutes to clamber to the summit. Take sensible shoes with you and warm clothes, as the low temperatures are intensified by the wind, and it can be decidedly nippy even in summer. From the top the view is stunning – on a clear day you can see over to the border with Norway and a good way back to Östersund. There's a tiny wooden **café** at the summit, serving coffee and extortionately priced sandwiches. Even the shortest route back down to Åre (2hr) requires stamina; other, longer, paths lead more circuitously back down to the village. One word of warning: there are phenomenal numbers of **mosquitoes** and other insects up here in July and August, so make sure you are protected by repellent. The mountains around Åre are also as good a place as any to go **mountain biking**; the tourist office can help sort out a bike for you.

Back in the centre, Åre's **kyrka** (use the key hanging on a hook outside the door to get in), just above the campsite, is a marvellous thirteenth-century stone building: inside, the simple blue decoration and the smell of burning candles create a peaceful ambience.

Practicalities

The **tourist office** is in the main square (mid-June to Aug & early Dec to April daily 9am–6pm; May to mid-June & Sept to early Dec Mon–Fri 9am–5pm, Sat & Sun 10am–3pm; ☎0647/177 20), 100m up the steps opposite the train station building. **Accommodation** in the village, of which there's plenty, is packed in winter; in summer, however, most places are either closed or only take groups, but it's worth asking the tourist office about fixing up a **private room** (from around 150kr per person), almost all of which will have a kitchen, shower and TV. The cheapest place to stay is the unofficial **youth hostel**, known as *Parkvillan*, in the park below the square (☎0647/177 33; ❶) though in summer they only accept groups. Alternatively there's the **campsite** (☎0647/136 00; closed Sept–Nov), five minutes' walk from the station. The nearest STF hostel is Brattlandsgården in **Brattland**, 8km to the east (☎0647/301 38, ⓦwww.host.bip.net/brattlandsgarden; booking mandatory Sept to mid-June). It's a 4km hike from the train station at Undersåker, a stop on the train line from Östersund to Åre; you can also get to the hostel on the weekday buses (#157) from Åre.

Åre's not up to much in terms of **food**, but there are several cheap options around the square: try the pie or sandwich lunches served at *Café Bubblan*, or the pizzas and more substantial dishes at *Werséns*. At the bottom of the cable car, *Bykrogen* serves lunches at 60kr and reasonably priced main meals, but note the early closing time of 7pm. More palatable and very good value fare can be sampled at *Villa Tottebo*, opposite by the train station, which cooks up local meat and fish for around 150–200kr. Two winter-only restaurants are the upmarket *Bakfickan* at Åregården, and the American-style bar and grill *Broken* in the main square.

Storlien

Just six kilometres from the Norwegian border, **STORLIEN** is an excellent place to stop if you're into hiking, surrounded as it is by rugged, scenic terrain. The **southern Kungsleden** starts here and winds its way south via Sweden's southernmost glacier on the slopes of Helagsfjället, continuing on to Tänndalen and Grövelsjön, terminating on the hills above Sälen. Storlien is also prime berry-picking territory (the rare cloudberry grows here); mushrooms can also be found in great numbers hereabouts, in particular the delicious chanterelle.

There are infrequent **trains** here from Åre (2–3 daily; 1hr). The **tourist office** is inside the train station at Vintergatan 1 (Mon–Fri 9.30am–2.30pm; ☎0647/705 70, ⒻC0647/703 51). Aside from this, Storlien is little more than a couple of hotels and a supermarket amid open countryside. The **youth hostel** is a 4km walk across the tracks to the E14 and then left down the main road to Storvallen (☎0647/700 50, ⓦwww.scout.se/km/storvallen). There's also a youth hostel in **Ånn**, halfway between Åre and Storlien (☎ & ⒻC0647/710 70); which is served by all Östersund–Storlien trains. Finding **hotel** accommodation in summer isn't easy as many places close; **apartments** though can be rented at *Fjäl-lyor* (☎0647/701 70; ❶), just to the right of the station. In winter, *Storliens Högfjällshotell,* a luxury affair (☎0647/701 70, ⓦwww.storlienfjallen.se; ❷; closed summer) ten minutes away up in the chain of mountains that border Norway, has nearly two hundred well-appointed hotel rooms and its own swimming pool.

Eating and **drinking** opportunities in Storlien are very limited. The best bet is *Le Ski* restaurant, nightclub and bar at the station, which has cheapish eats for lunch and dinner; otherwise, coffee, pizzas and burgers are available at

Sylvias Kanonbar in the main square in front of the station.

Moving on from Storlien, two trains leave Storlien daily for Trondheim. In the opposite direction, there are through overnight SJ trains to Stockholm and Gothenburg via Östersund.

Travel details

Trains

Borlänge to: Falun (hourly; 20min); Mora (every 2hrs; 1hr 20min); Stockholm (hourly; 2hr 30min).
Falun to: Gävle (4 daily; 1hr); Stockholm (10 daily; 2hr 40min); Uppsala (10 daily; 2hr 20min).
Karlstad to: Kristinehamn (hourly; 25min); Stockholm (5 daily; 2hr 40min).
Mora to: Leksand (5 daily; 40min); Rättvik (5 daily; 20min); Stockholm (6 daily; 4hr); Tällberg (5 daily; 30min); Uppsala (8 daily; 3hr 40min).
Östersund to: Åre (2–3 daily; 1hr 45min); Gothenburg (1 daily; 11hr); Stockholm (6 daily; 6hr); Storlien (2–3 daily; 3hr); Sundsvall (6 daily; 2hr 15min); Uppsala (6 daily; 5hr 40min).

The Inlandsbanan

Timetables change slightly from year to year, but the following is a rough idea of Inlandsbanan services and times. The Inlandsbanan runs in two sections from late June to early August: from Kristinehamn (Mon–Fri at 1pm) to Persberg with an onward bus connection at 2.40pm to Mora; southbound a bus leaves Mora (Mon–Fri at 11.10am) for Persberg with a train connection at 2.40pm, arriving in Kristinehamn at 4pm; and from Mora to Gällivare via Östersund daily. Northbound trains leave Mora daily at 6.35am calling at Orsa and Sveg and many other wayside halts en route for Östersund. From Östersund, trains leave daily for Gällivare at 7.05am. From Östersund a train leaves at 3pm daily for Mora.

International trains

Karlstad to: Oslo (3 daily; 2hr).
Östersund to: Trondheim (2 daily; 4hr).
Storlien to: Trondheim (2 daily; 1hr 40min).

Buses

The Inlandsexpressen (#45) runs north from Mora to Östersund via Orsa, Sveg and Åsarna. It operates daily all year, leaving Mora at 8am and 2pm for Östersund. Heading south, two buses leave Östersund for Mora at 6.45am and 12.25pm.
Funäsdalen to: Östersund (3 daily; 3hr 30min).
Mora to: Orsa (hourly; 25min).
Åsarna to: Klövsjö (2–3 daily; 15min); Östersund (3 daily; 1hr 20min).
Östersund to: Umeå (3 daily; 6hr).

Swedish Lapland

* **Wilderness Way, Strömsund** Witness the austere beauty of northern Sweden on this remote switchback road that leads into Lappland. **See p.462.**

* **Lapland delicacies, Klippen** The hotel restaurant in this isolated village is *the* place to taste delicious local cuisine: reindeer, elk and bear are all on the menu. **See p.469.**

* **Lappstaden, Arvidsjaur** The square timber huts and cabins at this *Sámi* parish village offer an insight into the life of Sweden's indigenous people. **See p.474.**

* **Kungsleden trail, Jäkkvik** Walk one of the quietest and most beautiful sections of the north's premier hiking trail through the Pieljekaise national park. **See p.477.**

* **The Arctic Circle, Jokkmokk** Crossing the magic line is a real sense of achievement and undoubtedly the best place to see the Midnight Sun. **See p.478.**

* **Icehotel, Jukkasjärvi** Spend a night in a thermal sleeping bag in one of the most famous hotels in the world at a chilly –5C. **See p.492.**

Swedish Lapland

Swedish **Lapland**, the heartland of the indigenous **Sámi** people, is Europe's last wilderness, characterized by seemingly endless forests of pine and spruce, thundering rivers that drain the snow-covered fells, and peaceful lakeside villages high amongst the hills. The irresistible allure of this vast and sparsely populated region is undoubtedly the opportunity to experience raw nature at first hand. This unsullied corner of the country is a very long way away for many Swedes; in terms of distance for example, Gothenburg is closer to Venice than it is to Kiruna. The reputation of the local people for speaking their mind, or, alternatively not speaking at all, has confirmed the region's image within Sweden: remote, austere yet still rather fascinating.

One constant reminder of how far north you've come is the omnipresent **reindeer** that are still fundamental to the livelihood of many families here, but the enduring *Sámi* culture, which once defined much of this land, is now under threat. Centuries of mistrust between the *Sámi* and the Swedish population have led to today's often tense standoff; *Sámi* accusing Swede of stealing his land, Swede accusing *Sámi* of scrounging off the state. Back in 1986, the Chernobyl nuclear accident led to a fundamental change in *Sámi* living patterns: the fallout affected grazing lands, and even today the lichen (the reindeer's favourite food) in certain parts of the north is unfit for consumption, a fact which the *Sámi*, perhaps understandably, are keen to play down. The escalating problems posed by tourism – principally the erosion of grazing land under the pounding feet of hikers – have also made the *Sámi's* traditional existence increasingly uncertain.

The best way to discover more about Sámi culture is to drive the 320km-long Wilderness Way from **Strömsund**, a notable canoeing centre, over the barren Stekenjokk plateau to isolated **Fatmomakke**, a parish village of dozens of traditional wooden *kåtor* or huts beside the steely waters of Kultsjön lake. The road terminates at **Vilhelmina**, whose tiny parish village makes an interesting diversion on the way north. **Storuman** and neighbouring **Sorsele**, have handy train and bus connections that are useful access points for a small handful of charming mountain villages close to the Norwegian border where hiking is the main draw (see below). More accessible **Arvidsjaur**, reached by the Inlandsbanan, also offers a worthwhile insight into indigenous culture at its *lappstad*, a diverting collection of religious dwellings and storehuts. However, it's nearby **Jokkmokk**, just north of the **Arctic Circle**, that is the real centre of *Sámi* life – not least during its Winter Market when thousands of people brave the winter chill to buy and sell everything from reindeer hides to Wellington boots. Moving further north, the iron-ore mining centres of **Gällivare** (where the Inlandsbanan ends) and **Kiruna** share a rugged charm, though it's undoubtedly the world-famous **Icehotel** in nearby **Jukkasjärvi** that is the real winter draw. Beyond, the rugged **national parks** offer a chance to hike and commune with nature like nowhere else: the **Kungsleden trail** runs for 500km from **Hemavan**, northwest of Storuman, through some of the most gorgeous stretches anywhere in the Swedish mountains to the tiny village of **Abisko** – oddly, yet reassuringly, the driest place in all of Sweden.

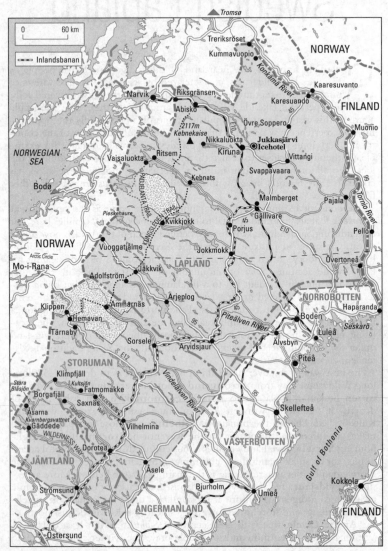

Whilst Lapland's strong cultural identify is evident in every town and village across the north, it's a much trickier task to try to pin down the region geographically. The word **Lapland** means different things to different people. Mention it to a Swede (the Swedish spelling is **Lappland**) and they'll immediately think of the northern Swedish province of the same name which begins just south of Dorotea, runs up to the Norwegian and Finnish borders in the north, and stretches east towards (but doesn't include) the Bothnian Coast. For the original inhabitants of the north, the *Sámi*, the area they call **Sápmi** (the indigenous name for Lapland) extends from Norway through Sweden and Finland to the Russian Kola peninsula, an area where they've traditionally lived a semi-nomadic life, following their reindeer from valley bottom to fell top. Most foreigners have but a hazy idea of where Lapland is; for the sake of this guide, we've assumed Swedish Lapland (the English spelling) to be located within the borders of the administrative province of Lappland but have included all of Route 342 – The Wilderness Way – beginning in Strömsund (see overleaf), which crosses into Lappland, as well as the Torne Valley, which also lies partly within the province.

Getting around Swedish Lapland

Covering a whopping 110,000 square kilometres – an area only fractionally smaller than the whole of England – getting from one place to another in Lapland is inevitably going to take up a lot of time. During the short summer months, the **Inlandsbanan** provides the easiest and most enjoyable form of transport. Slowly snaking its way across the northern hinterland, the train often has to stop so that elk and reindeer – and occasionally bears – can be cleared from the tracks. Otherwise, it'll come to a halt – when no station's in sight – for a spot of berry picking, or for the guard to point out a beaver damming a nearby stream; the train also stops at least once by a lake for everyone to take a quick dip, usually at Varjisträsk (1hr 30min north of Arvidsjaur). At the **Arctic Circle** it stops again, so that everyone can jump off and take some photos. The train terminates in Gällivare, 100km north of the Arctic Circle, where there are mainline train connections linking most of the major centres and attractions. Route 45 – the **Inlandsvägen** – is the best road north through Swedish Lapland; from Östersund, it sticks close to the train line on its way to Gällivare. It's easy to drive and well surfaced for the most part, although watch out for reindeer with a death wish – once they spot a car hurtling towards them they seem to do their utmost to throw themselves in front of it. You could drive from Östersund to Gällivare in a day if you left very early and put your foot down, but you are better off taking it in stages. The **Inlandsexpressen**, the daily bus service that runs from Östersund to Gällivare, follows Route 45; it's not as much fun as the train, but is faster and very comfortable (see p.505).

Strömsund and routes north

At seven o'clock every morning between late June and early August, the Inlandsbanan sets out from Östersund (see p.446) on its fifteen-hour journey to Gällivare, north of the Arctic Circle. Shortly outside the town, the train crosses the Indalsälven river, one of Sweden's greatest natural sources of power, the first sure sign that civilization is slowly being left behind and only the wilds of nature lie ahead. Indeed, it's a good two hours before the train makes the first stop of any significance: the small waterside town of **Strömsund**, which is the starting point for Route 342, the **Wilderness Way**, a circular road looping out towards the Norwegian border. The route passes through stunning scenery more than worthy of its name, rejoining the main Inlandsvägen in Vilhelmina, which, in turn, is directly linked to Strömsund via the appealing little town of **Dorotea**.

The town and around

Built on a narrow isthmus of land between Russfjärden lake and the extensive network of **waterways** that stretches northwest of here known as **Ströms Vattudal**, STRÖMSUND is a shy and retiring sort of place. It consists of no more than a couple of parallel streets sporting the odd shop or two the town, however, is a centre for **canoeing** along the surrounding rivers and lakes. The tourist office (see below) can rent out canoes and also provide information (walking routes, details of places to stay and maps) on the road known as the **Wilderness Way** (see below), which starts here and leads through some wonderful scenery.

The town's other claim to fame is its proximity to the impressive **Stone Age rock paintings** (*hällmålningar* in Swedish), at **Brattfors**, around 45km southeast of Strömsund; bus #421 runs here via Ulriksfors (Mon, Wed & Fri 1 daily) on its way to Backe. Once at Brattfors, you can reach the site on foot using the map provided by the Strömsund tourist office. The paintings, created by hunter-gatherers around 2500 BC, were a plea to their gods for plentiful hunting.

Practicalities

Although there's no actual train station in Strömsund, you can get off at nearby Ulriksfors and either walk the 3km or so into town or take connecting **bus** #420 (Mon, Wed & Fri only). The town's **tourist office**, in the Kommunhuset, at Storgatan 6 (late June to early Aug daily 9am–4pm; mid-Aug to late June Mon–Fri 8am–4pm; ☎0670/164 00, ⓦwww.stromsund.se), can fix you up with canoes (25kr an hour, 125kr a day). The Inlandsexpressen **bus** #45 stops in the town itself. For a **place to stay**, there's a simple **youth hostel** (☎ & ⒻFax0670/300 88), 5km south of the town in Tullingsås, which can be reached by the Inlandsexpressen bus or bus #142 (Mon–Fri 5 daily, Sat 1 daily, Sun 2 daily), which runs between Östersund and Strömsund. The **campsite** is just on the outskirts of town – about 1km out – on the way to Östersund (☎0670/164 10). Good **hotel** accommodation is available at *Hotell Vattudalen* at Ramselevägen 6 (☎0670/61 10 00, Ⓕ0670/133 70; ❸/❷). **Eating** opportunities in this pint-sized town are few but the best option is *Pizzeria Granen* at Storgatan 7, opposite the tourist office, which serves the usual array of pizzas as well as a few steak dishes.

The Wilderness Way

From Strömsund, **Route 342**, the Wilderness Way, strikes out northwest towards the mountains at Gäddede, before hugging the Norwegian border and crossing the barren treeless Stekenjokk plateau. It then swings inland again, joining Route 45 at Vilhelmina. The route ranks as one of the most beautiful and dramatic in Sweden, passing through great swathes of **virgin forest**, tiny forgotten villages and true wilderness where the forces of nature have been left undisturbed. There are also plenty of **lakes** along the way ideal for nude bathing – you can choose whichever one you want to make your own; there'll be nobody else there. One of the most beautiful stretches of rocky beach is just south of the tiny village of Alanäs on the beautiful Flåsjön lake, before you get to Gäddede.

The #425 **bus** runs from **Strömsund** to **Gäddede**. On weekdays there are two daily services, one in the afternoon and another in the evening; on Saturdays and Sundays there's one service daily, in the morning and evening respectively. Travelling on a weekday, you can stock up with picnic delights in Strömsund, catch the earlier of the two buses, get off wherever you like (just tell the driver to stop), and spend the afternoon and early evening walking or chilling out by the side of a lake. You can then catch the evening bus on to Gäddede; alternatively on Monday to Friday the afternoon bus connects in Gäddede with the #472 to Storviken, beside the pretty Stor-Blåsjön lake (see below), arriving at 6.45pm. Unfortunately from here there's no connection over the Stekenjokk plateau to **Klimpfjäll**, from where bus #420 runs down to Saxnäs and Vilhelmina (Mon–Fri 3 daily, Sat 2 daily, Sun 1 daily); on weekdays the last bus from Klimpfjäll goes at 3.30pm. It may be best to **hitch** between the two places – there are a lot of German and Dutch campervans on this stretch of the road who may be able to help out with a lift over the plateau. Another option would be to **hike** towards Ankarede (see p.464) and Raukasjön lake before heading north across the Norra Borgafjällen mountains for Slipsiken lake and onto Klimpfjäll – a distance of approximately 40km, best covered over two days, breaking the hike at the small cluster of cottages on the eastern shore of Raukasjön.

It's also the part of Sweden with the densest population of **bears**. If you're driving, stop wherever you can, turn off the engine and listen to the deep silence broken only by the calls of the birds and the whisper of the forest.

If you have your own transport, you should turn left at **Bågede** and follow the minor, very rocky road along the southern shore of **Fågelsjön lake** to reach **Hällsingsåfallet**, an impressive **waterfall**. Sweden's answer to Niagara Falls, it has an 800-metre-long canyon, into which the falls plummet, that's getting longer every year due to continuing erosion.

The only town along the route is **Gäddede**, whose name means "the spot where the northern pike can no longer go upstream". The name may be cute but the place certainly isn't; give it a miss and instead turn off the main road and follow the road signed "Riksgränsen" (National Border) for a few kilometres to the long and empty sandy beach of **Murusjöen lake**, right on the border with Norway (the beach is in Sweden, the water in Norway). You'll be hard pushed to find a more idyllic spot: the silence is total, the deep blue water still and calm, and the mountains in the distance dark and brooding.

Heading back towards Gäddede, take the left turn for **BJÖRKVATTNET**, a tiny village reached by a twenty-kilometre road with not even one building along its entire length. On the edge of the village is the **youth hostel** (℡0672/230 24; mid-Feb to mid-Nov). Complete with a sauna, the hostel has information on some good local **hiking** trails and a local bus that runs to Gäddede, where there's a **tourist office** (℡0672/105 00, ✉gaddede.turistbyra@ stromsund.se; June–Aug) at Storgatan 40 that can help out with **hiking** maps and advice about getting from Storviken to Klimpfjäll (see box above) and a **campsite** (℡0672/100 35) on the lake shore. From Björkvattnet, it's possible to rejoin the Wilderness Way by nipping briefly over the border into Norway, driving along the northern shore of **Kvarnbergsvattnet lake** and taking a poorly surfaced minor road through dense forest to Jormlien and on to Åsarna (a different village to the one covered on p.444).

Stor-Blåsjön, a lake to the north of Gäddede, is surrounded by blue mountains; the village of Stora Blåsjon is where the road starts to climb above the tree line to cross the desolate, boulder-strewn **Stekenjokk plateau** into the province of Lappland. Just outside Stora Blåsjön, look out for the minor road leading to **Ankarede**, an age-old meeting place for the local *Sámi*; even today families from Sweden and Norway get together here at midsummer and again in the autumn. Its old wooden **church** dates from 1896 and is located by the lake, between the two rivers. In addition there are around twenty *Sámi* circular wooden huts – *kåtor* – close by. The Stekenjokk plateau is the temporary summer home of several *Sámi* families, who tend their reindeer on the surrounding slopes, including those of the magnificent peak of **Sipmeke** (1424m) to the west of the road.

After dropping into the minuscule village of **Klimpfjäll** (the stretch of road over the plateau between Leipikvattnet lake and Klimpfjäll is open mid-June to mid-Oct only), the Way continues east. Taking the first turn to the left, after about 12km and then following the signs, you'll reach **Fatmomakke**, a fascinating **Sámi parish village** made up of eighty *kåtor*, gathered neatly around the church, and twenty log cabins lined up by the side of Kultsjön lake. The first church on the site was built in 1790, but the *Sámi* met together here long before that for special religious celebrations including marriages, christenings and funerals, travelling vast distances on skis, horseback or by boat to reach here. The huts are made out of birch wood, with a hole in the roof to let the smoke out, and birch twigs on the floor to sit on. Everything inside is orderly, the fireplace in the middle, the cooking area at the back; there's a strict code of behaviour as well – you must first wait in the entrance before being invited to enter. Look out for the *visningskåta* (signposted), the "show hut" near the church, and have a peek inside.

SAXNÄS, about 20km to the east, has a **youth hostel** at Kultsjögården on the main road (☏0940/700 44, ⓦwww.kultsjogarden.se), next door to a luxury **hotel** complex, *Saxnäsgården* (☏0940/377 00, ⓦwww.saxnas.se; ❹; simpler rooms in the annexe ❷; both prices include breakfast). On Friday and Saturday nights the hotel offers a weekend price of 1295kr for a double room and full board for two people. The hotel also has lakeside **cabins** for rent, each sleeping up to ten people, with open fireplaces and a sauna (❸ for 1–4 people, ❹ for 5–10 people). The place also doubles up as a **health complex** (☏0940/310 80 or 710 68, ⓦwww.slit.net/flygtjanst): surrounded by water and situated at the foot of the Marsfjällen mountains, it is quite literally an oasis in the surrounding wilderness and a wonderful place to pamper yourself for a day. This alcohol-free spot boasts a divine 34°C swimming pool, herbal health baths, massage facilities, saunas, a fitness centre and sports hall. It also **rents** out mountain **bikes**, **canoes**, **fishing tackle** and **motor boats**. In summer the hotel runs a boat service to the Fatmomakke *Sámi* village as well as a **seaplane** up into the mountains for **hiking**. In winter, **dog-sledge** trips can be arranged by the hotel, which also has **snow scooters** for hire.

Opposite the hotel's front door, the Marsfjällen Naturum **nature centre** (no fixed hours; if it's closed ask at the hotel for the key) is worth a quick look; try to ignore the cheesey mobile of stuffed snow grouse revolving from the ceiling and look instead for the impressively large dropping of one of the bears resident in the nearby Marsfjällen nature reserve. Between mid-October and mid-April, whilst in their lair, bears neither eat nor defecate, hence the size (the length of a child's arm) of this first movement which was collected close to the exit of the bear's lair – the surrounding tracks, each measuring a whopping 30cm in length and 22cm in width, give an idea of the mighty size of this male bear.

North to Dorotea

Avoiding the Wilderness Way detour, it's possible to head directly north both along the Inlandsbanan and the Inlandsvägen from Strömsund to tiny **DOROTEA**, 71km north, a journey of around an hour. A textbook example of a linear village, houses and shops strung out in a long line either side of the main road, Dorotea has a few attractions which merit a stop on the long journey north. Firstly, it has the biggest bear population in Sweden; **bears** regularly wander into town during the night to rummage through rubbish bins for scraps of food. If you decide to stay here and fail to spot the creatures, it's also possible to take a 4–5hr **bear-spotting tour** (550kr; arrange through the tourist office, see below) out into the surrounding forests where there's an even better chance of a sighting. At the top of the village, the **Jakt och Fiskemuseum** in the same building as the tourist office (same hours; see below; 40kr), at Storgatan 46, is a taxidermist's dream: inside there's a varied collection of stuffed local wildlife, everything from a bear to a wolverine, as well as a tired exhibition of glass boxes containing a motley collection butterflies, grasshoppers and beetles. More interesting, however, is the adjacent aquarium where there are live specimens of bream, perch, pike, trout and Arctic char, found in vast numbers in the surrounding lakes.

Whilst in Dorotea, make sure to see the powerful Björn Martinius group **sculpture** of the Last Supper. Housed in a small chapel in the church graveyard on a low hill just off the main road, the life-size wooden figures sit around three long trestle tables – the very size of the sculpture, filling an entire room, the striking bright colours used to paint the figures, as well as the intense expressions, creates a sense of life and motion that's enough to send a shiver down the spine of the most ardent agnostic.

Practicalities

The **tourist office** (mid-June to mid-Aug Mon–Fri 9am–8pm, Sat & Sun 11am–6pm; rest of the year Mon–Fri 9am–5pm; ☎0942/140 63, ⓦwww.dorotea.se) is located at the top of the village, at Storgatan 46, a ten-minute walk along the main road from the train station. As well as booking bear-spotting tours, they also have good advice on local **hiking routes** and **fishing trips**. The only **hotel** in the village is the swanky *Hotell Dorotea* (☎0942 47780, ⓦwww.hotelldorotea.se; ❹/❸) at Bergsvägen 2. However, a much more agreeable option is *Björnens Camping* (☎0942/102 38, ⓦwww.camping.se/plats/AC01) beautifully sited beside the Bergvattenån river. As well as four-bed **cabins** (❶), there are also a number of simple hostel-style rooms (❶) with access to showers and a sauna in the nearby service building. A popular café for locals to swap gossip in is *Görans Konditori*, at Parkvägen 2, which serves set lunch for 55kr, as well as a number of open sandwiches and cakes. More substantial meaty **meals**, including pizzas and a daily *Dagens Rätt*, are available at *Ankis Bar* at Storgatan 37, opposite the bank. For **Internet** access, head to the library on Storgatan opposite *Görans Konditori*.

Around Dorotea: Borgafjäll

The 106km journey northwest from Dorotea to **Borgafjäll** offers a superb taste of wild northern Swedish landscapes. Passing a handful of remote village communities high on the hills of southern Lappland, the road winds its way around steely grey lakes and over barren outcrops of rocky land before climbing steeply towards the southern extent of the Norra Borgafjällen mountains; **bus** #436 operates here from Dorotea (Mon–Fri 2 daily, Sun 1 daily). The main reason to come is to experience the unspoilt and exhilarating terrain along the 20km **hike** (allow 5–6hr) over to Saxnäs on the Wilderness Way. From *Hotell Borgafjäll* (☎0942/421 00, ⓦwww.borgafjallen.com; ❹; end Sept to end April), the path climbs steeply up towards the highest peak of the Norra Borgafjällen mountain chain, Jengegietje (1477m), before skirting the mountain on its eastern edge – this is the highest stretch of the trail at 1160m. From here, it's a graceful and gradual descent down towards the Satsån river (bridged), a section which offers unsurpassed views of the low dusky hills and extensive swamps of the Gitsfjället nature reserve to the east. Once across the Satsån, the trail climbs once again towards the Satsfjället mountain (1105m) from where a minor road leads down the valley side into Saxnäs.

In addition to the hotel (see above), Borgafjäll also boasts a year-round **campsite**, *Polarbyn* (☏0942/420 42), at the entrance to the village when approaching from Dorotea, with twelve four-berth cabins (❶) and a sauna. The simple **restaurant**, *Idet*, on site, is a good place to taste local game dishes, including reindeer stew. Borgafjäll also has a general **food store** which doubles up as the village filling station and pharmacy.

Vilhelmina

The Inlandsvägen and the Wilderness Way meet up again in the pretty little town of **VILHELMINA**, 54km north of Dorotea. Once an important forestry centre, today the timber business has moved away and the main source of employment is a telephone booking centre for Swedish Railways and the package tour company, Fritidsresor. The town, a quiet little place with just one main street, is named after the wife of King Gustav IV Adolf, Fredrika Dorotea Vilhelmina (as is its southerly neighbour Dorotea). The principal attraction is the **parish village**, nestling between Storgatan and Ljusminnesgatan, whose thirty-odd wooden cottages date back to 1792, when the first church was consecrated. It's since been restored, and the cottages can be rented out via the tourist office (from 150kr per night). The **museum** here, at Storgatan 7 (daily June–Aug 10.30am–4pm; 10kr), contains a mind-numbingly dull display of local history from prehistoric times to the present day; give it a miss and instead have a look inside the couple of *Sámi* **handicraft stores** nearby, a little further down Storgatan.

Practicalities

The **tourist office** is on the main Volgsjövägen (mid-June to mid-Aug Mon–Fri 8am–8pm, Sat & Sun noon–6pm; mid-Aug to mid-June Mon–Fri 9.30am–5pm; ☏0940/152 70, ⓦwww.vilhelmina.se), a five-minute walk up Postgatan from the **train station**, which also serves as the **bus** arrival and departure point. The airport, with handy flights to and from Stockholm, is just 12km away, from where a taxi into Vilhelmina will cost around 138kr. There are two **hotels** in town: the showy *Hotell Wilhelmina*, at Volgsjövägen 16 (☏0940/554 20, ⓦwww.hotell.vilhelmina.com; ❹/❸), and the simpler and friendlier *Lilla Hotellet*, at Granvägen 1 (☏0940/150 59, ⓦwww.lillahotellet .vilhelmina.com; ❸/❷). The **campsite**, *Rasten Saiva Camping* (☏0940/107 60), has two- to six-berth cabins for rent (250–525kr depending on size) and a great sandy **beach**; to get there, walk down Volgsjövägen from the centre and take a left turn after about ten minutes. **Eating** and **drinking** doesn't exactly throw up a multitude of options: try the à la carte restaurant at *Hotell Wilhelmina* for traditional northern Swedish dishes and a *Dagens Rätt* for 65kr, or the plain *Pizzeria Lascité*, Volgsjövägen 27, for cheap pizzas. In the evenings, locals gravitate towards *Krogen Besk*, opposite the *Lilla Hotellet*, for a **drink** or two.

Storuman, Tärnaby and around

The one defining factor that unites the small settlement of **Storuman** with its northwesterly neighbours, **Tärnaby** and Hemavan, is the **Blå Vägen** (Blue Way) or E12, as it is less poetically known, running through all three villages. This major artery, one of northern Sweden's better roads, is so named because it follows the course of the great Ume river that flows down from the mountains of southern Lappland to Umeå on the Bothnian Coast. Water is omnipresent hereabouts, not only in Storuman, a dreary little town which sits on the banks of the eponymously named lake best used as an access point to the mountains, but also all the way up to Tärnaby, a small-time skiing centre, and **Hemavan**, the start of Sweden's longest and best hiking trail, the Kungsleden, leading 500km north to Abisko.

Storuman

In 1741, the first settler arrived in what was to become **STORUMAN**, 68km north of Vilhelmina. His first neighbours didn't appear until forty years later and even by World War I, Storuman, then called Luspen (the Swedish name for a river which emerges from a lake) numbered barely forty inhabitants working just eight farms. Things changed, though, with the arrival of the railway in the 1920s; today Storuman is an important centre for the generation of hydroelectric power. That said, there's not much to the town: the centre consists of one tiny street that supports a couple of shops and banks. You can head off into the mountains west of here for some good **hiking** and **fishing**; ask at the tourist office for maps and information. If you find yourself at a loose end whilst waiting for buses or trains, one diversion is the worthwhile short walk signed "Utsikten" from the main square which leads up to a wooden **viewing platform** from where there are fantastic views out over the surrounding lakes and forest towards the mountains which mark the border with Norway; it's around a 2km uphill walk to the platform from the town centre.

Practicalities

An hour by the Inlandsbanan from Vilhelmina, Storuman is a **transport hub** for this part of southern Lappland. From here, **buses** run northwest up the E12, skirting the Tärnafjällen mountains to Tärnaby and Hemavan, before wriggling through to Mo-i-Rana in Norway; in the opposite direction, the road leads down to Umeå via Lycksele, from where there are bus connections to Vindeln and Vännäs on the main coastal train line. A direct bus, **Lapplandspilen**, links Storuman with Stockholm. Skyways also operate twice-daily flights to Stockholm and Arvidsjaur.

The **tourist office** is on Järnvägsgatan, 50m to the right of the **train station** (late June to mid-Aug Mon–Fri 9am–8pm, Sat & Sun 10am–5pm; rest of the year Mon–Fri 9am–5pm; ☎0951/333 70, ⊛www.storuman.se), and can supply a handy map of town and a few brochures; **buses** (3–4 daily from Vilhelmina; 1hr) stop outside the station. While you're here, check out the wonderful old **railway hotel**, diagonally opposite the tourist office, which now houses the library; built in association with the Inlandsbanan, the wide-planked wooden exterior hides an ornate interior, complete with wrought-iron chandeliers, that's well worth a peek.

The **youth hostel** is just 200m from the station (☎0951/333 80), and is attached to the luxurious **hotel**, *Hotell Toppen* (☎0951/777 00, ⊛www .hotelltoppen.com; ❹/❷), with pine and birchwood rooms; to get here, walk up the hill from the station to BlåVägen 238. In the middle of the local **camp-site**, by the lakeside at Vallnäsvägen (℡0951/106 96), is a church built in the style of a *kåta*, a traditional *Sámi* hut. The **restaurant** at *Hotell Toppen* should be your first choice for **food**, with a 65kr lunch buffet; alternatively, the basic *Blå Stjärnan* behind the Konsum supermarket in the main square serves cheap *Dagens Rätt* and pizzas. *Restaurant Storuman*, opposite the station, has Chinese food, pizzas and lunch for much the same prices. For good Greek food, it's a twenty-minute walk to *Grill 79*: take the E12 road towards Tärnaby and head underneath the railway bridge towards the Statoil filling station.

Tärnaby and around

Buses (Mon–Fri 5 daily, Sat 3 daily, Sun 1 daily) make the two-hour drive northwest from Storuman to the tiny mountain village of **TÄRNABY**, the birthplace of Sweden's greatest skier, Ingemar Stenmark. A double Olympic gold medallist, he occasionally spiced up his training with a spot of tightrope walking and monocycling. It's a pretty place: yellow flower-decked meadows run to the edge of the mountain forests, the trees felled to leave great empty swathes that accommodate World Cup ski slopes. At the eastern edge of the village as you approach from Storuman, the **Samegården** (end June to mid-Aug daily 9am–5pm; 20kr) in the hamlet of Tärnafors is a pleasant introduction to *Sámi* history, culture and customs. Among other things, the museum recalls a practice in older times when, after a kill in a bear hunt, the gall bladder was cut open and the fluid drunk by the hunters. A popular **walk** here leads across the nearby mountain, **Laxfjället**, with its fantastic views down over the village – it can be reached by chair lift from either of the two hotels listed below.

The **tourist office**, on the one main road (mid-June to mid-Aug daily 9am–8pm; mid-Aug to mid-June Mon–Fri 8.30am–5pm; ℡0954/104 50, ⊛www.tarnaby.se) can supply advice about local **fishing**, which is reputed to be excellent, and information on **hiking trails** in the surrounding mountains. When it's sunny, head for the beach at **Lake Laisan**, where the water is often warm enough to swim; to get there, take the footpath that branches off right from Sandviksvägen past the **campsite** (℡0954/100 09, ⊛www.campa-it.se/tarnaby) which also has dorm beds for 100kr per person. There are several inexpensive places **to stay** – try the decent *Tärnaby Fjällhotell*, Östra Strandvägen 16 (℡0954/301 50, ℻106 27; Dec–April; ❶), which also has four-bed apartments for 445kr per day; or the *Tärnaby Skilodge* (℡0954/104 25, ⊛www.tarnabyskilodge.com; Dec–April; ❷) on Skyttevägen, which also rents out two- to six-berth cabins for 545kr per day during the summer. For something to **eat** the best bet is the *Tärnaby Wärdshus*, opposite the tourist office at Västra Strandvägen 2B, where decent pizzas and some good Swedish home-cooking is served up; there's also a tolerable **bar** here.

Around Tärnaby: Hemavan and Klippen

Buses (Mon–Sat 4 daily, Sun 2 daily) continue from Tärnaby on to **HEMA-VAN**, 18km northwest, which marks the beginning and the end of the five-hundred-kilometre **Kungsleden** trail (for more information on the trail and hiking in general, see p.487). The village is also reachable from Stockholm on direct Skyways flights (℡0951/305 30, ⊛www.hemavansflygplats.nu; journey time 1hr 45min). This tiny nondescript village, straddling the main road, is totally devoid of attractions. It is pure and simply a service centre which provides accommodation and eating opportunities to hikers starting and ending the trail here. The village can be busy during the peak summer season (mid-June to mid-

Aug) and it is therefore wise to book a bed in advance to be sure of somewhere to stay.

There's a **youth hostel**, *FBU-Gården* (☎0954/300 02, ⊛www.fbu.to), on the main road; it's always busy with hikers, so it's essential to book ahead here. On site there's also a swimming pool, sauna, steam room, Jacuzzi and even a climbing wall.

Although there's a greasy spoon, *Sibylla Grill*, in Hemavan, when it comes to **eating** you're much better catered for in neighbouring **KLIPPEN**, just 6km away, and reached by **bus** (Mon–Sat 3 daily, Sun 2 daily). This tiny village sheltering beneath the bulk of Artekenvalle mountain (1188m) is an unlikely location for one of Sweden's top restaurants. Housed in the gay-friendly *Hotell Sånninggården* (☎0954/330 00, ⊛www.sanninggarden.com; ❶), the kitchen is renowned across the north of the country for culinary excellence. In fact, it's worth making a special journey here just to eat in the award-winning **restaurant**, as the northern Swedish delicacies they serve up here – everything from fillet of bear with red berries, mushroom and blueberry sauce (398kr) to elk stew with rowanberry gelé (110kr) – really are some of the best you'll find. Run by two Swedes and an Englishman, everything on the menu is locally produced – even the duck is likely to have come from the lakes around Tärnaby. Make sure you try the various local akvavits – the angelica is particularly good. In addition to the extensive à la carte menu there's an all-day lunch buffet for 99kr or simpler dishes such as meatballs for 65kr and spaghetti bolognaise at 60kr. Although the cuisine here is world-class, the accommodation, unfortunately, is not – rooms, although adequate, are cramped and share facilities. *Sånninggården* is the last stop for the Lapplandspilen bus to and from Stockholm as well as a destination on the Umeå to Mo-i-Rana service.

Sorsele and around

The next major stop on the Inlandsbanan north of Storuman (also served by three daily buses from Storuman; 1hr 20min) is **SORSELE**, 76km away – a pint-sized, dreary town on the **Vindelälven** (Vindel river). The town became a *cause célèbre* among conservationists in Sweden when activists forced the government to abandon its plans to build a hydroelectric power station, which would have regulated the river's flow. Consequently, the river remains in its natural state today – seething with rapids – and is one of only four in the country that hasn't been tampered with in some way or other. During the last week in July, the river makes its presence felt with the **Vindelälvsloppet**, a long-distance race that sees hundreds of competitors cover, in stages, over 350km from nearby Ammarnäs (see p.470) down to Vännäsby, near Umeå. It's quite a spectacle, but needless to say accommodation at this time is booked up months in advance. The other big event here is the **Vindelälvsdraget**, a dog-sleigh race held over the same course in the third week of March.

Sorsele is an ideal base for **fly-fishing**: the Vindelälven and the other local river, Laisälven, are teeming with grayling and brown trout, and there are a number of local lakes stocked with char. Ask at the tourist offices for details.

The town's only other attraction is the Inland Railway **museum,** in the same building as the tourist office (same opening times as the tourist office; 20kr), detailing the life and times of the Inlandsbanan; the labelling here is in Swedish only, though there is an English-language fact sheet available which will help make sense of the evocative black and white photographs of German troops travelling up and down the line during the Second World War; during the height of the conflict, 12,000 German soldiers and significant amounts of war material were moved every week between Narvik and Trondheim in occupied Norway, travelling via Gällivare and Östersund along the Inlandsbanan in supposedly neutral Sweden.

Practicalities

The **tourist office** (end June to Aug Mon–Fri 9am–6pm, Sat & Sun 11am–4pm; end Aug to end June Mon–Fri 8.30am–11.30am; ☎0952/140 90, ⊛www.sorsele.se) at the **train station** on Stationsgatan has information about local activities such as fishing and **canoe hire** (330kr per day); **buses** stop outside. **Internet** access is available at the village library at Storgatan 11. For **accommodation**, there are **cabins** at the riverside **campsite** (☎0952/101 24; 285–550kr), as well as a small **youth hostel** at Torggatan 1–2 (☎0952/100 48; ❶; 140kr in a cabin; mid-June to end-Aug), just 500m from the station. The only **hotel** in town is *Hotell Gästis*, a plain and rather drab affair at Hotellgatan 2 (☎0952/100 10, ⊛www.hotellgastis.se; ❸/❷). **Eating** choices in Sorsele are scant too, although what food is on offer is cheap, with few dishes costing more than 60kr. At lunchtime, head for the hotel, which has simple fare, or *Grillhörnan*, near the station, with its burgers and pizzas; there's a more palatable *Sibylla Grill* in the same building. As with many of the villages in this part of Sweden, there are no **bars** here, but expensive beer can be found at all the restaurants. The **Systembolaget** is over the river from the train station on the main shopping street.

Around Sorsele: Ammarnäs

The tiny mountain village of **AMMARNÄS**, with a population of just two hundred and fifty, lies ninety minutes' bus ride northwest of Sorsele, the road finally reaching this remote corner of Sweden in 1939. Set in a wide river valley by the side of the **Gautsträsk lake** and at the foot of the towering **Ammarfjället mountains**, the village offers peace and tranquillity of the first order. This is **reindeer** country (one-third of the villagers here are reindeer herders), and for hundreds of years the local *Sámi* are known to have migrated with their animals from the coast to the surrounding fells for summer pasture.

Hikes around Ammarnäs

There's some excellent **hiking** to be had around Ammarnäs, not least along the Kungsleden (see p.500), which passes through the village. For the less adventurous, **Mount Kaissats** (984m) is ideal for a day spent in the mountains; to get there, take the road at the western end of the village that leads to the lake of **Stora Tjulträsk**, from where a marked trail for Kaissats (not particularly difficult) leads off to the right (2hr). Even less strenuous is taking a **chair lift** from the village and up **Näsberget**, from where trails lead back down into Ammarnäs. Another hiking possibility is along the road up to the village of **Kraipe**; this small turning, to your left before you reach Ammarnäs on Route 363, is one of the steepest in Sweden. From Kraipe you can easily reach the surrounding summits, and if you take the route in September you may well encounter the marking and slaughtering of reindeer at Kraipe corrals. From any of these bare mountain tops, the spectacular views look out over some of the last remaining wilderness in Europe – mountains and dense forest as far as the eye can see.

The first settlement began here in 1821 when two *Sámi* brothers, Måns and Abraham Sjulsson, were granted permission to set up home at Övre Gautsträsk. When they failed to keep the terms of their agreement, a new tenant, Nils Johansson, took over. He eked out an existence by cultivating the land and is responsible for *Potatisbacken* or Potato Hill, adjacent to the church at the eastern end of the village at the junction of Kyrkvägen and Nolsivägen (get here by following Nolsivägen from opposite the *Ammarnäsgården Hotel*, signed "Norra Ammarnäs"), where the northern Swedish potato (a sweet, yellow variety), is grown – unusual for a location so far north. With the founding of a postal station in 1895, the village changed its name from Gautsträsk (a *Sámi* word meaning "bowl" – an accurate description of its valley-bottom location) to Ammarnäs – the foreland between the Tjulån and Vindelälven rivers. A stone plinth now stands in Nils Johansson's memory across from the church on Strandvägen.

The **Sámi parish village**, near the potato hill on Nolsivägen, was built in 1850, moving to its present site in 1911. The dozen or so square wooden huts, which are perched on horizontal logs to help keep them dry, are still used today. Three times a year *Sámi* families gather here, much as they have done for centuries, to celebrate important **festivals**: the *Sámi* festival (Sunday before midsummer), Vårböndagshelgen (spring intercession day, on the first Sunday in July) and Höstböndagshelgen (autumn intercession day, on the last Sunday in September).

The nearby **Samegården** on Strandvägen has a simple display of *Sámi* history and traditions (mid-June to mid-Aug Mon–Fri 9am–2pm). At **Vinkas Sameviste**, at the edge of town, however, you can obtain a much better insight into local culture; this is the place to come face to face with **reindeer**, try your hand at a spot of lassoing and learn about the traditional methods of building a wooden *kåta*.

Adjoining the tourist office on Tjulträskvägen is the **Naturum Vindelfjällen** (mid-June to mid-Aug Mon–Fri 9am–5pm, Sat & Sun 1–5pm), which has information about the local geology, flora and fauna, and an unflattering selection of stuffed animals, including a bear, lynx and wolverine. It also shows a 1940s film of bears in the woods along the Vindelälven – just ask them to put it on. Look out also for their model of the surrounding peaks, which will give you an idea of just how isolated Ammarnäs is, locked in on three sides by mountains.

Practicalities

Buses take an hour to reach here from Sorsele (Mon–Thurs 2 daily, Fri & Sat 3 daily, Sun 1 daily), and will drop you along the main road, Tjulträskvägen, where you'll find the **tourist office** (mid-June to mid-Aug Mon–Fri 9am–6pm, Sat & Sun 1–6pm; ☎0952/600 00, ⓦwww.ammarnas.com). They have plenty of maps and brochures on the surrounding countryside and useful information on hiking, and can also help with the renting of **Icelandic ponies**, **dog sledges** and **snowmobiles** in winter.

Virtually opposite the tourist office is the **youth hostel** (☎0952/600 45, ⓦwww.ammarnasturism.com; 140kr; advance booking required Oct–May); it's in an annexe to *Jonsstugan*, a small and simple pension (☎0952/600 45, ⓕ602 51; ❶). The only **hotel** is the busy and popular *Hotell Ammarnäsgården* (☎0952/600 03, ⓕ602 43; ❸), on the main road, which has rather simple en-suite rooms aimed at hikers walking the Kungsleden; its decent sauna and pool complex in the basement makes up for the lack of creature comforts in the rooms. For **eating** and **drinking**, your only option is the hotel's bar and restaurant; it's much cheaper to bring some beer with you from the nearest Systembolaget, 90km away in Sorsele.

Among the oldest people in Europe, the **Sámi** – better known, erroneously, to many as "Lapps" – are probably descended from the original, prehistoric inhabitants of much of Scandinavia and northern Russia. Today, there are around 58,000 *Sámi*, stretched across the whole of the northernmost regions of Norway, Sweden, Finland and Russia; traces of their nomadic culture have even been discovered as far south as Poland. Rather than Lapland, the *Sámi* name for their lands is *Sápmi*. In Sweden itself, they number around 17,000 (the population is declining, however), their domain extending over half the country, stretching up from the northern parts of Dalarna.

The *Sámi* **language** is a rich one, strongly influenced by their harmonious natural existence. There are no words for certain alien concepts (like "war"), but there are ninety different terms to express variations in snow conditions. One of the Finno-Ugric group of languages, which also contains Finnish and Hungarian, the *Sámi* language is divided into three dialects: Southern (spoken in southern parts of the *Sámi* region) and Central and Eastern (both spoken only in Russia). In Sweden you'll come across two words for *Sámi*: the politically correct *Sámi* (as used by the *Sámi* themselves), and, more commonly, the Swedish corruption *Same* (plural *Samer*). Opposite is a brief glossary of some of the *Sámi* words, many related to snow and reindeer, that you may come across while travelling in northern Sweden.

Reindeer, of which there are estimated to be 238,000 in Sweden, have been at the centre of *Sámi* life and culture for thousands of years, with generations of families following the seasonal movements of the animals. Accordingly, the *Sámi* year is divided into eight separate seasons, ranging from early spring, when they traditionally bring the reindeer cows up to the calving areas in the hills, through to winter, when they return to the forests and the pastures.

The *Sámi* were dealt a grievous blow by the **Chernobyl** nuclear disaster of 1986, which contaminated not only the lichen that their reindeer feed on in winter, but also the game, fish, berries and fungi that supplement their own diet. Contamination of reindeer meat meant the collapse of exports of the product to southern Scandinavia, Germany, America and the Far East; promises of government compensation came

---

Travelling on from Ammarnäs is quite tricky – all connections are via Sorsele. The best way to reach Stockholm is to take a bus to Sorsele, change for a connection to Östersund and change again for the train to Stockholm. On Saturdays, there's a direct afternoon bus from Ammarnäs to Vännäs, which connects with the Stockholm night train (more information on ☎020/91 00 19 or at ⓦwww.lanstrafikeniac.se).

Arvidsjaur and around

An hour and a quarter north of Sorsele by Inlandsbanan, **ARVIDSJAUR** was for centuries where the region's **Sámi** gathered to trade and debate. Their presence was of interest to Protestant missionaries, who established the first church here in 1606. The success of this Swedish settlement was secured when silver was discovered in the nearby mountains, and the town flourished as a staging point and supply depot. While these developments unfolded, the *Sámi* continued to assemble on market days and during religious festivals. At the end of the eighteenth century, they built their own parish village of simple wooden huts. Today, out of a total population of five thousand, there are still twenty *Sámi*

late in the day and failed to address the fact that this disaster wasn't just on an economic level for the *Sámi*, their traditional culture being inseparably tied to reindeer herding. However, perhaps as a consequence of Chernobyl, there has been an expansion in other areas of *Sámi* culture. Traditional **arts and crafts** have become popular and are widely available in craft shops, and *Sámi* **music** (characterized by the rhythmic sounds of **joik**, a form of throat singing) is being given a hearing by fans of world music. On balance, it would appear that the *Sámi* are largely managing to retain their culture and identity in modern Sweden.

A glossary of Sámi words

aahka	grandmother, old woman	*lopme*	storm
aajja	grandfather, old man	*lopme-aajma*	snow storm
aaltoe	reindeer cow	*lopmedahke*	surface of the snow in autumn
aehhtjie	father	*lopme-moekie*	snow shower
båtsuoj	reindeer	*miesie*	reindeer calf
daelvie	winter	*nejpie*	knife
geejmas	black reindeer	*ruvveske*	water on the surface of the ice in spring
giedtie	reindeer pasture		
gierehtse	sledge drawn by reindeer	*sarva*	reindeer bull
giesie	summer	*saevrie*	loose, heavy snow that you can't walk on
gijre	spring		
gåetie	house, hut, tent	*sahpah*	powdery wet snow that doesn't stick
jiengedahke	autumn frost		
klomhpedahke	sticky snow surface	*sieble*	slush
klöösehke	grey and white reindeer	*soehpenje*	lasso
		tjakje	autumn
kåta	tent	*tjidtjie*	mother
lijjesjidh	to snow lightly on bare (snowless) ground	*vielle*	brother
		åabpa	sister

families in Arvisdjaur who make their living from reindeer husbandry, and the town is a good place to get a real hands-on experience of *Sámi* life.

Arvidsjaur is not one of Sweden's more attractive towns – its streets of drab houses strung out either side of the main drag lined with a dozen or so shops make a pretty depressing impression on any first-time visitor. However, although the modern town is decidedly unappealing, it hides one of northern Sweden's top attractions in the traditional *Sámi* village of **Lappstaden**.

Arrival, information and accommodation

The **train station** is on Järnvägsgatan. Five minutes' walk away, up Lundavägen, is the **tourist office** (mid-June to mid-Aug daily 8.30am–6.30pm; mid-Aug to mid-June Mon–Fri 9am–5pm; ℡0960/175 00, ⓦwww.arvidsjaurturism.se) at Östra Skolgatan 18C, just off Storgatan. The **bus station** is at Gökstigen from where you simply walk west along Gökstigen, across Stationsgatan, to reach Östra Skolgatan to get to the tourist office. Flights from Storuman and Stockholm's Arlanda airport land at the modern **airport** terminal, 15km from town, which has been designed to resemble a *Sámi* wooden *kåta*; you can get from here to the centre by bus (45kr) or taxi (112kr). For **Internet** access, the library is in Medborgarhuset at Storgatan 12.

By far the best place to **stay** in Arvidsjaur, is *Rallaren* (℡070/682 32 84; ❶; late June–Aug), a wonderful old wooden house which ranks as one of the best deals in northern Sweden. With just eight beds and a kitchen, it's been tastefully restored by a local artist, and now boasts stripped floorboards, painted walls and dried flowers. There's also a cosy private **youth hostel**, *Lappugglan*, conveniently situated at Västra Skolgatan 9 (℡0960/124 13; ❶). The tourist office will fix you up with a **private room** for around 130kr, plus a booking fee of 20kr, or the **campsite**, *Camp Gielas* (℡0960/556 00), has **cabins** for 520kr with TV, shower and running water. It sits beside one of the town's dozen or so lakes, Tvättjärn, with its bathing beaches; there's a sports hall here, too, as well as a gym, sauna, tennis courts and mini-golf. The site is a ten-minute walk from the tourist office (head south down Lundavägen, left along Strandvägen and left again into Järnvägsgatan). There's just one **hotel** in town: *Laponia Hotel*, at Storgatan 45 (℡0960/555 00, ⓦwww.laponia-gielas.se; ❹/❸), with comfortable, modern en-suite rooms and a swimming pool. Between October and April much of the accommodation will be full of test drivers from Europe's leading car companies, who come to the area to experience driving on the frozen lakes – book well in advance to secure a room during this period, especially in March.

Lappstaden

A good way to find out more about the *Sámi* culture (which manifests itself more and more as you travel north from here) is to visit **Lappstaden** (free; daily tours in July at 6pm, 25kr), reached by walking west along Storgatan and turning right into Lappstadsgatan. Although you probably won't meet any *Sámi* here, you will at least be able to see how they used to live in traditional huts or *kåtor*. About eighty of these huts in the eighteenth-century *Sámi* **parish village** have survived, and are clumped unceremoniously next to a yellow, modern apartment building. The design of these square wooden buildings supporting a pyramid-shaped roof is typical of the Forest *Sámi* who lived in the surrounding forests, constructing their homes of indigenous timber. Local Sámi schoolteacher, Karin Stenberg, made it her life's work to preserve Lappstaden and, indeed, the huts are still used today during the last weekend in August as a venue for a special **festival**, Storstämningshelgen.

Steam trains and trolley trekking

From early July to early August, an incredibly popular **steam train**, pulling vintage coaches from the 1930s, runs from Arvidsjaur along sections of the Inlandsbanan. The trips head west to **Slagnäs** on Fridays and north to **Moskosel** on Saturdays (140kr for either trip, under-16s free); en route to Slagnäs the train stops at Storavan beach for swimming and a sausage barbecue. Alternatively, you can strike out through the surrounding countryside under your own steam on a **rail-inspection trolley** (a bike with train wheels; *dressin* in Swedish), which can be booked through the tourist office (90kr for up to 5hr, 160kr for 24hr). Each trolley can carry two people, with camping gear provided. Thus equipped, you can cycle along the disused rail line from Arvidsjaur 75km southeast to **Jörn** – a stopping-off point for trains on the main coastal route – though there's an extra 250kr fee if you leave the trolley in Jörn.

Eating and drinking

For **snacks**, coffee, fresh pastries and bread, try *Kaffestugan* at Storgatan 21, which also has cheap lunches, sandwiches (often filled with reindeer meat) and salads;

there's outdoor seating here in summer. Arvidsjaur also has a small selection of **restaurants**: you can sit down to Italian food at *Athena*, Storgatan 10, with averagely priced lunches, pizzas, meat and fish dishes; next door at Storgatan 8, *Cazba*, serves up pizzas for the same price but has less atmosphere; but for finer food and higher prices, head for the restaurant at the *Laponia Hotel*, where the delicious à la carte meals include local reindeer and other Lapland delicacies. The **bar** here is the place to be seen of an evening, particularly on Friday nights when there's also a disco; be prepared though to shell out at least 55kr for a beer.

Around Arvidsjaur: Båtsuoj Forest Sámi Center

Seventy kilometres to the west of Arvidsjaur, in the village of **GASA**, the **Båtsuoj Forest Sámi Center** (June–Aug daily noon–9pm; at other times book ahead ☎0960/65 10 26, ✆same-id@algonet.se) is a good place to get to grips with the everyday life of the *Sámi*. Here, you'll not only come face to face with **reindeer** (*båtsuoj* in *Sámi*) but also meet real reindeer herders, who'll teach you about their religion and way of life, including the way to milk a reindeer and the tricks of baking their traditional bread; frozen reindeer meat is also available for purchase.

A half-day visit to Båtsuoj costs 390kr and includes dinner (of reindeer cooked over an open fire); a full day costs 590kr and adds an overnight stay in a *kåta* (tent); for children under twelve both trips are half price. From late June to early July you can go on **branding** trips here, which generally take place in the evenings (375kr). The centre also arranges **cloudberry-picking** expeditions with pack-bearing reindeer (Aug to mid-Sept; 600kr); these rare berries grow in the most inaccessible of northern Sweden's marshlands – hence the hefty price. To get here from Arvidsjaur, head west on Route 45 until the village of Slagnäs, from where you take the unnumbered minor road 19km north towards Arjeplog. Although you can reach Slagnäs by the Inlandsbanan, there's no public transport on to Gasa from there.

Arjeplog and around

Stretching northwest of Arvidsjaur out towards the Norwegian border, the municipality of **ARJEPLOG**, roughly the size of Belgium, supports a population of just three and a half thousand – half of whom live in the eponymous lakeside town, 85km from Arvidsjaur. It's one of the most beautiful parts of Sweden, with nearly nine thousand lakes and vast expanses of mountains and virgin forests. Here the air is clear and crisp, the rivers clean and deep and the winters mighty cold – in 1989 a temperature of -52°C was recorded. January and February, in particular, are bitter, dark and silent months. However, it's during winter that Arjeplog is at its busiest: hundreds of test drivers from Korea, Australia, Germany, Britain, Italy, America and France descend on the town to put cars through their paces in the freezing conditions, with brakes and road-holding being given a thorough examination on the frozen lakes. In summer, Arjeplog is a likeable little place away from the main inland road and rail routes, where **hiking**, **canoeing** and **fishing** are all popular activities, each offering the chance of blissful isolation, be it by the side of a secluded mountain tarn or in a clearing deep in the pine forest. In late July you can go **cloudberry picking** in the surrounding marshland, and in the autumn, you can hunt for lingonberries, blueberries and wild mushrooms.

Arjeplog town itself is a tiny unassuming sort of place, barely one main street leading to what passes as a main square, but is really only a car park between the tourist office and the **Silvermuséet** (mid-June to mid-Aug daily 9am–6pm; mid-Aug to mid-June Mon–Fri 10am–4pm, Sat 10am–2pm; 40kr), the only sight in town. Housed in a yellow wooden building opposite the tourist office and founded by the Lapland doctor Einar Wallquist, it's home to fascinating collections of *Sámi* silver, including several ornate silver collars that were handed down from mother to daughter; if a mother had several daughters she would divide her chain amongst them. Whilst in the museum, make sure to visit the newly constructed cinema in the basement where you can see a **slide slow** about the surrounding countryside and nature and how people in this remote part of Sweden learnt to adapt to the harsh climate. If you're around in the first week of July, the **Lapplands festspel** (Ⓦwww.arjeplog.se/festspel/index.html) is an orgy of chamber music, fiddles, folk music and dancing.

Practicalities

There are daily **buses** here from Arvidsjaur (Mon–Fri 4 daily, Sat & Sun 2 daily; 1hr 10min). The **tourist office** is in the main square (mid-June to mid-Aug Mon–Fri 9am–7pm, Sat 10am–5pm, Sun noon–5pm; mid-Aug to mid-June Mon–Fri 9am–4pm; Ⓣ0961/142 70, Ⓦwww.arjeploglappland.se) and can help with local hiking trails, fishing (90kr will rent equipment for a day) and **bike rental** (50kr a day). The best-value **accommodation** is the central and palatial **youth hostel** on Silvervägen (Ⓣ0961/612 10, Ⓕ0961/101 50; May to late Nov), where every room sleeps a maximum of four and has en-suite facilities. The hostel is part of *Hotel Lyktan* (Ⓣ0961/612 10, Ⓕ101 50; ❸/❷), which offers comfortable modern rooms of the highest standard. At *Arjeplog Hotel* (Ⓣ0961/107 70, Ⓦwww.arjeploghotel.com; ❸/❷), 1500m up Öberget hill from the centre (a 30min walk), the accommodation is dowdy but comfortable, and the views over the village and surrounding lake are fantastic. Ten minutes' walk along Silvervägen, the lakeside **campsite**, *Kraja* (Ⓣ0961/315 00, Ⓦwww.kraja.se) has simple **cabins** for 220–775kr a day, the price depending on the size and the facilities included; there's also an outdoor swimming pool which is open to non residents (free). To get away from it all in your own private **cabin in the wilds**, speak to the tourist office: it has dozens for rent in **Jäkkvik** or **Adolfström** (both on the Kungsleden); for complete isolation head for stunning **Vuoggatjálme**, tucked right up in the mountains close to the Norwegian border, see opposite. Bear in mind that in winter, accommodation hereabouts is often booked months in advance by the major car manufacturers.

Eating and **drinking** in the centre of Arjeplog isn't a joy – more agreeable surroundings can be found at the campsite and the *Arjeplog Hotel*. There are two cut-price options: the basic *Mathörnan*, on Drottninggatan, which serves up moderately priced reindeer, Arctic char and traditional Swedish home-cooking amid hideously tacky decor; the other is the cavernous *Pizzeria Verona*, next door, with an equally dingy 1970s interior, offering salads and pizzas at similar prices. For gourmet food head for *Kraja Wärdshus* at the campsite, where you can tuck into fillet of elk or saddle of reindeer; there's also a pub and disco here on Fridays. Fine food, including Arctic char and salmon, is also served in the light and airy restaurant at the *Arjeplog Hotel*, complete with open fire. For a **coffee** in summer try the kiosk next to the tourist office, which has outdoor seating; or better *GKs Fiske och Café* on Storgatan, which serves up sandwiches, coffee and cakes. The *Mathörnan's* downstairs **bar**, *Källarn*, attracts the town's hardened drinkers who seem prepared to pay 45kr for a beer.

The Kungsleden in one day: Jäkkvik–Adolfström

From the shop in **Jäkkvik**, walk back along the main road to the sign for Kungsleden car parking. The trail begins at the car park, climbing first through mountain birch forest, before emerging on bare upland terrain dominated by **Mount Pieljekaise** (1138m), which is said to look like a large ear (hence its name, which means just that in *Sámi*). From here, the views over the surrounding mountains are truly spectacular. The trail winds round the mountain and descends below the tree line into virgin birch woodland, carpeted with stately flowers like the northern wolfsbane, alpine sow-thistle and angelica. Pieljekaise National Park is also home to elk, bear, Arctic fox, wolverine, golden eagle and the gyrfalcon. It's a moderate 27km hike from Jäkkvik to Adolfström (all downhill after climbing out of Jäkkvik; allow 6–7 hours). Cabin **accommodation** can be rented in Adolfström at *Adolfströms Handelsbod och Stugor* (☎0961/230 41, ℻0961/230 44; from 230kr) and *Johanssons Fjällstugor* (☎0961/230 40, ℻0961/230 23; from 230kr); there's an old-world village shop at the former. Buses usually only leave once daily, at 10.20am, from the post box on Monday, Wednesday & Friday for **Laisvall** (change here for Arjeplog), so time your hike carefully and check the bus information on ☎020/47 00 47 before setting out.

Around Arjeplog: Jäkkvik and Vuoggatjålme

From Arjeplog, the **Silver Road** (Route 95) strikes out for the craggy chain of mountains which marks the border with Norway. The **views** on this stretch of the road are stunning – unlike in so many other parts of Lapland, the forest here is set back from the road, rising and falling over the surrounding hills, giving an awe-inspiring sense of the scale of the uninhabited territory you're passing through. The **Silverexpressen** bus #200, running between Skellefteå and Bodø in Norway, via Arvidsjaur and Arjeplog, is the only public transport on this section of the road (daily except Sat). Thirty minutes northwest of Arjeplog, the bus reaches the minuscule settlement of **JÄKKVIK**, little more than a cluster of houses dependent on the tiny shop and petrol station which doubles as the bus station. From here, one of the least walked sections of the Kungsleden trail (see box, above) heads across to **Adolfström**, a tiny village on Lake Gautosjön, 27km away, where the summer air is sweet with the smell of freshly scythed hay. The route makes an ideal day's hike through the beauty of the **Pieljekaise national park** just south of the Arctic Circle, containing the least disturbed flora and fauna in the entire Swedish mountains. There are **cabins** in Jäkkvik at the *Stugby* (☎0961/211 20, ℻0961/210 62; from 350kr) or simple hostel rooms and a **campsite** at *Kyrkans Fjällgård* (☎0961/210 39; ❶).

Vuoggatjålme

To get away from it all, **VUOGGATJÅLME** (*Sámi* for "fish hook channel"), 45km from Jäkkvik, is the place to come. The Silverexpressen **bus** stops here on its way between Norway and Skellefteå; jump off at the petrol station, and walk around 2km following the sign for the village. Only two families live here, one of which comprises Björn and Monica Helamb who manage the **cabin accommodation** (☎0961/107 15, ℻0961/613 57), while the other, Björn's sister and her husband, run the petrol station and small food store across the main road. The cabins couldn't be better situated, with a view of Vuoggatjålmejaure lake from one window, the majestic snowcapped Tjidtjak mountain from the other. From mid-June to end August they cost 550kr or 635kr per night depending on size (the ones on the lakeshore have open fireplaces); in winter both types of cottage go for around 300kr per night. Bear in mind, though, if you're here out of season, that Vuoggatjålme proudly boasts one of the coldest temperatures ever recorded in Sweden (-53°C, in 1966), although the minimum here is generally -40°C.

The surrounding area offers superb **hiking** and a chance to enjoy nature. Björn operates a **helicopter service** (1600kr per person) which can take you right up into the mountains, allowing you to establish a base from which to strike out, thus avoiding the hassle of getting up there with heavy packs. An excellent trip takes you by helicopter up to the **Pieskehaure cabins**, stunningly located in the Arjeplogsfjällen mountains, from where you can hike across to Kvikkjokk (64km, see p.500) and the Kungsleden in around three days. There's also good hiking closer to the cottages; ask Björn for advice. Before you leave, look carefully at the forest beside the main house – the eyes you might be lucky enough to see are likely to be those of elk, as there are dozens of them around the cottages.

Jokkmokk and around

During his journey in Lapland, the botanist Carl von Linné said, "If not for the mosquitoes, this would be earth's paradise". His comments were made after journeying along the river valley of the Lilla Luleälven during the short

The Arctic Circle and the midnight sun

Just 7km south of Jokkmokk, the Inlandsbanan finally crosses the **Arctic Circle**, the imaginary line drawn around the earth at roughly 66°N, which links the northernmost points along which the sun can be seen on the shortest day of the year. Crossing into the Arctic is occasion enough for a bout of whistle-blowing by the train, as it pulls up to allow everyone to take photos. However, the painted white rocks that curve away over the hilly ground here, a crude delineation of the Circle, are completely inaccurate. Due to the earth's uneven orbit, the line is creeping northwards at a rate of about 14–15m every year; the real Arctic Circle is now around a kilometre further north than this line. It won't be for another ten to twenty thousand years that the northward movement will stop – by which time the Circle will have reached 68°N – and then start moving slowly south again.

Thanks to the refraction of sunlight in the atmosphere, the **midnight sun** can also be seen south of the Arctic Circle – Arvidsjaur marks the southernmost point in Sweden where this happens – for a few days each year. The further north you travel, the longer the period when the phenomenon is visible, and conversely the longer the polar winter. True midnight sun occurs when the entire sun is above the horizon at midnight. The following is a list of the main towns and the dates when the midnight sun can be seen; remember, though, that even outside these periods, there is still 24-hour daylight in the north of Sweden in summer, since only part of the sun ever dips below the horizon.

Arvidsjaur and Haparanda	June 20 /21
Arjeplog	June 12 /13 to July 28 /29
Jokkmokk and Övertorneå	June 8 /9 to July 2 /3
Gällivare	June 4 /5 to July 6 /7
Kiruna	May 28 /29 to July 11 /12
Karesuando	May 26 /27 to July 15 /16
Treriksröset	May 22 /23 to July 17 /18

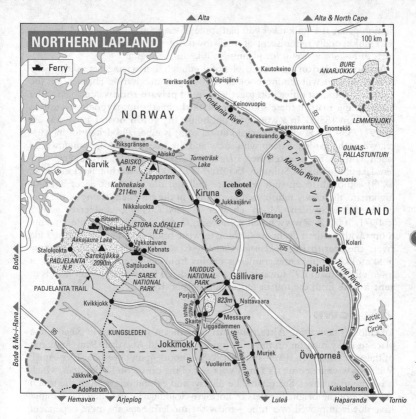

summer weeks, when the mosquitoes are at their most active. Along this valley is the town of **JOKKMOKK**, its name deriving from one particular bend (*mokk* in *Sámi*) in the river (*jokk*). The densely forested municipality through which the river runs is the size of Wales and has a tiny population of 6500.

The town is a welcome oasis, although not an immediately appealing one. At one time winter quarters for the *Sámi*, by the beginning of the seventeenth century the site had a market (see p.481) and church, which heralded the start of a permanent settlement. Today, as well as being a well-known handicraft centre, the town functions as the capital of the *Sámi* and is home to Samernas Folkhögskola, the only further education college in Sweden using the *Sámi* language, teaching handicraft making, reindeer husbandry and ecology.

Arrival, information and accommodation

It's a four-hour journey here on the Inlandsbanan from Arvidsjaur, 161km away, or just over two hours on the Inlandsexpressen **bus**. If you're arriving here for the Winter Market (when the Inlandsbanan isn't running), take the Connex **train** to Murjek (between Boden and Gällivare), from where bus #94 runs west to Jokkmokk (2 daily; 1hr). Jokkmokk's **tourist office** is at Stortorget 4 (mid-June to mid-Aug daily 9am–7pm; mid-Aug to mid-June Mon–Fri 8.30am–4pm; during the winter market 8am–6pm; ☎0971/121 40, ⓦwww.turism.jokkmokk.se), five minutes' stroll from the train station along

Stationsgatan; the walk takes you past some of the prettiest houses and shops in Jokkmokk, oddly reminiscent of small-town America. The tourist office has all sorts of literature, useful for planning a hike in the region.

Accommodation in town is plentiful enough, but staying here during the Winter Market will require booking a good year in advance. That said, in the autumn the tourist office puts together a list of **private rooms** available for the forthcoming market; these should be booked directly, not through the tourist office (from 155kr). In a wonderful old house, the **youth hostel** at Åsgatan 20 (☎0971/559 77; ⓦwww.jokkmokkhostel.com) is especially delightful in winter, when the garden is deep with snow and the trees outside the windows are laden with ice. For a **hotel**, there's *Hotell Jokkmokk*, in an attractive and convenient lakeside setting at Solgatan 45 (☎0971/777 00, ⓦwww.hoteljokkmokk.se; ⑤/③); although its en-suite rooms are dull and the restaurant decor a 1970s nightmare, the newly refurbished sauna suite in the basement is one of the best in northern Sweden. Much cheaper is *Hotell Gästis*, at Herrevägen 1 (☎0971/100 12, ⓦwww.hotell-gastis.com; ④/③), though its simple en-suite rooms with modern decor are nothing to write home about either. By the Lule river, the **campsite**, *Jokkmokk-Camping-Center* (☎0971/123 70; ⓦwww.jokkmokkcampingcenter.com), has **cabins** from 550kr; it's 3km southeast of town off the main E97 towards Luleå and Boden. The best way to get here is to **rent a bike** from the tourist office for 60kr per day.

The Town

Jokkmokk's fascinating **Ájtte museum** (*ájtte* means storage hut in *Sámi*) is the place to really mug up on the *Sámi* (mid-June to mid-Aug daily 9am–6pm; rest of the year Mon–Fri 10am–4pm, Sat & Sun noon–4pm, closed Sat Oct–April; 50kr; ⓦwww.ajtte.com); it's a brief walk east of the centre on Kyrkogatan, which is off the main street, Storgatan. The displays and exhibitions recount the tough existence of the original settlers of northern Scandinavia, and show how things have slowly improved over time – today the modern *Sámi* are more dependent on snow scooters and helicopters to herd their reindeer than on the age-old methods employed by their ancestors. The museum also has imaginative temporary exhibitions on *Sámi* culture and local flora and fauna; its staff can arrange day-trips into the surrounding marshes for a spot of mushroom picking.

Close to the museum on Lappstavägen, the **Alpine Garden** (late June to early Aug Mon–Fri 10am–4pm, Sat & Sun 10am–3pm; other times by arrangement on ☎0971/101 00; 25kr) is home to moor-king, mountain avens, glacier crowfoot and other vegetation that's found on the fells around Jokkmokk. Also worth a quick look is **Naturfoto** (daily 9am–5pm July to early Aug), in Klockartorget square, near the corner of Klockarvägen and Storgatan; it's an exhibition of work by the local wilderness photographer, Edvin Nilsson – a good place to pick up a few postcards or posters.

Have a look, too, at the **Lapp kyrka** (daily 8am–4pm, early June to early Aug to 6pm), off Stortorget, a recent copy of the 1753 church on the same site (the original burnt down in 1972). The octagonal design, curiously shaped tower and colours inside the church represent *Sámi* styles; outside, notice the space in between the coarsely hewn timbers which was used to store coffins during winter, waiting for the thaw in May when the *Sámi* could go out and dig graves again (temperatures in this part of Sweden regularly plunge to -30°C and below).

During the summer, Talvatissjön, the lake behind *Hotel Jokkmokk*, is the preferred spot for catching Arctic char and rainbow trout. To **fish** here you'll need a **permit** (*fiskekort*), available from the tourist office. There's a barbecue on the lakeside behind the hotel, should you catch anything. It's also possible to go **canoeing** on the unspoilt surrounding lakes and rivers. For more information and bookings, contact Jokkmokkguiderna (☎0971/122 20, ⓦwww .jokkmokkguiderna.com; 450kr for a day tour) who're based in the village of Skabram, 3km west of Jokkmokk. They'll collect you from Jokkmokk once you've made a firm booking.

The Winter Market

Known simply in Swedish as *Jokkmokks marknad*, the town's 400-year-old **Great Winter Market** (ⓦwww.jokkmokksmarknad.com) traces its origins back to 1602, when King Karl IX decreed that a series of market sites should be set up in the north to help extend Swedish territory and increase taxes to fund his many wars. A chapel, a parsonage and a row of market sheds were built here, and the rest is history. Today the market is held on the first Thursday to Sunday of each February, when thirty thousand people force their way into town – ten times the normal population. It's the best (and coldest) time of year to be here; with lots of drunken stallholders trying to flog reindeer hides and other unwanted knick-knacks to even more drunken passers-by, there's a Wild West feeling in the air at this time. Held on the frozen Talvatissjön lake behind *Hotell Jokkmokk* (see below), the **reindeer races** run during the market can be a real spectacle, as man and beast battle it out on a specially marked-out ice track. The reindeer, however, often have other ideas and every now and then veer off with great alacrity into the crowd, sending spectators fleeing for cover. A smaller and less traditional autumn fair around August 25 is an easier, but poorer, option.

Eating and drinking

Jokkmokk has a limited number of **eating** and drinking possibilities. At the cheap and cheerful *Restaurang Kowloon*, on Berggatan, lunch is 62kr and Chinese meals start at 90kr at other times. The *Restaurang Opera*, Storgatan 36, offers pizzas from 60kr, Greek salad also for 60kr, simple fry-ups including *pytt i panna* for 70kr and reindeer for 80kr, though its clientele is often predominantly male and heavily drunk; it also has the usual range of meat and fish à la carte dishes. For Swedish home-cooking or burgers, head for *Smedjan* on Föreningsgatan, the cheapest place in town, where lunch deals go for 45kr. It's better to avoid the overpriced restaurant at *Hotell Jokkmokk* and savour the traditional *Sámi* dishes at the Ájtte museum's restaurant instead – the cloudberry and ice cream is simply divine. Perfectly decent meals, including pizza and pasta, are also served up at the restaurant out at the campsite. For pastries and a cup of coffee, try *City Konditoriet* at Storgatan 28, which also serves up good sandwiches.

Your first choice for **drinking** should be *Restaurang Opera* (beer costs just 40kr); failing that try *Restaurang Kowloon*, and of an evening the bar inside *Hotell Jokkmokk* – if you've drunk your way round Jokkmokk this far you won't mind the late-night drunken company but mind the prices, such as a totally outrageous 55kr for a *storstark*.

Around Jokkmokk: Vuollerim

Forty-five kilometres southeast of Jokkmokk on the E97 to Boden and Luleå lies the tiny village of **VUOLLERIM**, site of a 6000-year-old **Stone Age winter settlement**. Archeological digs here have uncovered well-preserved remains of houses, storage pits, tool and weapon shards, rubbish dumps and drainage works. A small and excellent **museum** on the edge of the village at Murjeksvägen 31 (Nov to early May Mon–Fri 11am–3pm; early May to June

Recommended for novice hikers, **Muddus National Park** (ⓦwww.fjallen.nu/parker/muddus.htm) is a five-hundred-square-kilometre pine-forested and marshland park between Jokkmokk and Gällivare, hemmed in by the Inlandsbanan on one side and the train line from Boden to Gällivare on the other. Muddus is home to bears, lynx, martens, weasels, hares, elk and (in summer) also reindeer; among birds, the whooper swan is one of the most common sights. The terrain here is gently undulating, consisting of bog and forest, though there are clefts and gorges in the southern stretches. The park's western edges are skirted by Route 45; the easiest approach is to leave the highway at **Liggadammen** (there are also buses here from Gällivare) and then follow the small road to **Skaite**, where an easy hiking **trail** begins; two suggested routes are Skaite–Muddusfallet–Måskoskårså–Skaite (24km) or Skaite–Muddueluobbal–Manson–Skaite (44km). There are cabins along the trail (April–Sept; rest of the year keys can be obtained from Jokkmokk and Gällivare tourist offices), with a campsite at Muddus Falls. Distances between the various stages are as follows: Liggadammen to Skaite 13km; Skaite to Muddus Falls 7km; Muddus Falls to Muddusluobbal 9km; Muddusluobbal to Manson 5km; Sarkavare to Muddus Falls 14km; Solaure to Manson 7km. There are no outlets for buying food or provisions en route.

& mid-Aug to Sept Mon–Fri 10am–4pm; July to mid-Aug Mon–Fri 10am–5pm; 50kr; ⓦwww.vuollerim6000.se) covers the development of the various sites and finds, with a slide show that takes you on a journey through time, depicting how the inhabitants probably lived. The whole thing really comes alive when you see the digs themselves, with archeologists providing a guided tour in English (without it, the whole thing would be nothing more than a mudbath to the untrained eye). To **get here** from Jokkmokk, you can take the #44 Boden–Luleå bus, and get off at the Statoil filling station, from where it's a one-kilometre walk up the road towards the village; or better, the #94 to Murjek, which goes via Vuollerim and right to the museum.

Porjus

Forty-three kilometres north of Jokkmokk, Route 45 and the Inlandsbanan pass through pretty **PORJUS**, blighted only by the ugly hydroelectric power station constructed in the 1910s. Situated on the fast-flowing Stora Luleälven river, the town was an obvious choice at which to site the power plant – usefully for Swedish State Railways, who required power for the electrification of the new line between Luleå and the Norwegian border. But the spot proved to be a disaster logistically: the nearest train station was then 50km away at Gällivare, and there was no road to Porjus. For the first year until the inland rail stretch was complete, men carried loads of up to seventy kilos on their backs along planked paths all the way from Gällivare here. The **heritage park** at **Porjus Kraftbyggarland** (mid-June to mid-Aug daily 9am–6pm; free), by the station, documents the power plant's history; another part of the park, **Porjus EXPO**, tells of the men who made the power plant a reality.

Gällivare and around

Following a brief halt at the Mosquito Museum in Avvakajjo (see p.486), the Inlandsbanan reaches its last stop, **GÄLLIVARE**, two hours up the line from Jokkmokk and over 600km north of Strömsund. Although the town is not immediately appealing, it is one of the few population centres in this part of northern Sweden and it's a good idea to spend a day or two here enjoying the relative civilization before striking out in the wilds beyond – Gällivare is a good starting point for walking in the national parks, which fill most of the north-western corner of the country (see pp.487–489). The town is also one of the most important areas for iron ore in Europe – if you have any interest in see-ing a working mine, don't wait until Kiruna's tame "tourist tour" (see p.491); instead take a trip down the more evocative mines here.

Arrival and information

The **train station** is on Lasarettsgatan, about five minutes' walk from the tourist office. Gällivare's **airport**, 10km from the town, is served by direct flights with *Skyways* from Stockholm taking just 2hr, compared to 20hr by train; you can get into town by taxi (150kr). The very accommodating **tourist office**, at Storgatan 16 (late June to late Aug Mon–Fri 9am–8pm, Sat & Sun 10am–5pm; rest of the year Mon–Fri 9am–4pm; ☎0970/166 60, ⓦwww.gallivare.se), has good free maps and hiking information; upstairs in the same building is a simple **museum** deal-ing with *Sámi* history and forestry. Gällivare is an easy place to walk around, with nearly everything you could want located east of the train line, except the youth

RESTAURANTS & CAFÉS

Björnfällan	F
Kilkenny Inn	3
New Delhi	B
Restaurang Peking	C
Strandcaféet	E
Tre Kronor	A
Vassara Pub	5
Åhults	D

ACCOMMODATION

Dundret	7
Gällivare Värdshus	2
Grand	3
Hotell Dundret	4
Kilkenny Inn	3
Malm Hotel	1
Quality Hotel Gällivare	5
Youth hostel	6

▲ *Malmberget (5 km), Kåkstan,* **❶** & **Ⓐ**

Vassara träsk

Bus Station

Library

Train Station

Kyrka

Lappkyrkan

Vassara älv

Campsite

▲ *Jokkmokk Campsite & Muddus National Park*

▶ *Kiruna & Airport*

N

0   250m

INLANDSVÄGEN 45

PORJUSVÄGEN

GÄLLIVARE

SWEDISH LAPLAND | Gällivare and around

7

483

▼ **❼** *(1 km),* **Ⓕ** *, Sámi Camp at Repisvare & Dundret Hill* hostel, which is west of the tracks. The main sight in town, the **Lappkyrkan**, is barely five minutes on foot from the centre. Outside the town in Malmberget, the mines are easily reached on a tourist office bus.

Accommodation

Advance bookings for places to **stay** in Gällivare are a good idea from mid-June to mid-August, when the town receives trainloads of backpackers – thanks to its strategic location at the junction of two major rail routes. The tourist office can fix you up with a **private room** for around 150kr per person, plus a booking fee of 25kr. The **youth hostel** (℡0970/143 80; ℻0970/165 86; open all year but bookings required Sept–May), behind the train station (cross the tracks by the metal bridge), offers a good sauna and accommodation in small cabins. It's a wonderful place to stay in winter when the Vassara träsk lake is frozen and snow scooters whizz up and down its length under the eerie northern lights, which are clearly visible in Gällivare. The premier place to stay, however, is 5km north in the reconstructed shantytown up at Malmberget, **Kåkstan** (reached by bus #1; ℡0970/183 96 or book through the tourist office; 90kr; four-bed hut 360kr), where the iron miners once lived. You can rent one of the simple four-berth wooden huts here (toilets and showers are located across the unpaved road) and pretend you're back in 1888, when iron ore was first loaded onto trains at the beginning of the great iron-ore boom. The town's **campsite** is close to the centre, at Malmbergsvägen 2 (mid-May to mid-Sept; ℡0970/100 10), by the river and off Porjusvägen (Route 45 to Jokkmokk). Gällivare is also one of the few places in northern Lapland to offer a good range of affordable **hotel** accommodation, a selection of which appears below.

Dundret ℡0970/145 60, ✆www.dundret.se. At the top of the Dundret mountain and not to be confused with *Hotell Dundret* in the town centre. With unparalleled views out over the town, you'll need your own transport or be prepared to walk: take Route 45 south out of town for about 2km and take the signed turning left up to Dundret; the hotel is just 1km from the main road. ❺/❹

Hotell Dundret Per Högströmsgatan 1 ℡0970/550 40. A small pension, with just eight comfortable rooms and shared facilities. ❸/❷

Grand Per Högströmsgatan 9 ℡0970/164 20, ✆www.grand-hotel.nu. The second-best hotel in town, with decent rooms; it's handily situated for the *Kilkenny Inn*, which shares the same building. ❸/❷

Gällivare Värdshus Klockljungsvägen 2 ℡0970/162 00, ✆www.home.swipnet.se/vardshuset.index.html. A cheap, central German-run place close to the swimming pool with small hostel-style rooms which make it a good place to meet other backpackers. ❸/❷

Malm Hotel Torget 18, in Malmberget ℡0970/244 50. The rooms here are basic and not en suite, but reasonable enough. ❶

Quality Hotel Gällivare Lasarettsgatan 1 ℡0970/550 20, ✆www.nexhotel.se. The best of the bunch in the town centre, with smart, tastefully decorated rooms and a good restaurant (see opposite); sit in the sauna and enjoy views of the station and the main street below. ❹/❸

The town and the mines

Though an industrial town, Gällivare is quite a pleasant place to fetch up after so long on the road; it's certainly a far cry from the small inland villages that predominate along the Inlandsbanan. If you've come here from the Bothnian Coast, the town's steely grey mesh of modern streets will, on the surface at least, appear familiar. Located just north of the 67th parallel, Gällivare has a pretty severe climate: as you stroll around the open centre of town, have a look at the double-glazed windows here, all heavily insulated to protect against the biting Arctic cold.

What makes Gällivare immediately different from other towns is its large *Sámi* population – this is, after all, the heart of Lapland. The site the town occupies was once that of a *Sámi* village, and one theory has it that the name Gällivare comes from the *Sámi* for "a crack or gorge (*djelli*) in the mountain (*vare*)". The *Sámi* church, **Lappkyrkan** (mid-June to late Aug 10am–3pm), down by the river near the train station, is a mid-eighteenth-century construction; it's known as the *Ettöreskyrkan* ("1 öre" church) after the sum Swedes were asked to contribute to the subscription drive that paid for its construction.

Though there's precious little else to see or do in the town centre, there are some magnificent views to be had from the top of **Dundret** hill, one of the two peaks dominating Gällivare; the walk up here is around 3–4km on a well-signposted path – ask at the tourist office for the best starting point. The hill is also a favourite destination for **midnight sun** spotters; special buses run from the train station to the end of the winding road up the hill (mid-June to mid-July daily at 11pm, returning 1am); tickets, available from the tourist office, cost 200kr return and include the ubiquitous Swedish waffle covered with cloud-berries and cream.

The mines at Malmberget

Tucked away at **Malmberget**, the other hill that overlooks the town, the modern mines and works are distant, dark blots down which the tourist office ferries relays of tourists in summer. There are two separate tours, both running from June to August: one of the underground **iron-ore mine** (Mon–Fri 1.30pm; 200kr), the other to the open-cast **copper mine** known as Aitik (Mon–Fri 1.30pm; 200kr), the largest of its kind in Europe (and also Sweden's biggest gold mine – the metal is recovered from the slag produced during the extraction of the copper). The ear-splitting noise produced from the mammoth-sized trucks (they're five times the height of a human being) in the iron-ore mine can be quite disconcerting in the confined darkness.

Eating, drinking and entertainment

If you're arriving from one of the tiny villages on the Inlandsbanan, the wealth of **eating** possibilities in Gällivare will make you quite dizzy; if you're coming from Luleå, grit your teeth and bear it. As for **drinking**, the place to be seen is the *Kilkenny Inn* inside the *Grand Hotel*, at Per Högströmsgatan 9, which often has special deals on beer; there's also a **nightclub** here on Friday and Saturday (entrance 50–60kr) which has occasional live music, although their choice of artistes can leave a lot to be desired. *Vassara Pub* in the *Quality Hotel Gällivare* is also a popular drinking hole.

Björnfällan at *Dundret* hotel out of town. Good northern-Swedish food in this friendly restaurant but at a price – nothing here is under 200kr.

Kilkenny Inn Per Högströmsgatan 9. With decent pub food, including burgers, and an Irish-style atmosphere, this is a good place to meet other travellers and locals.

New Delhi Storgatan 19. Indian food has finally made it north of the Arctic Circle in this newly opened restaurant in the centre of town. Unfortunately though, meals are rather bland and lacking in gusto; however, this place does make a welcome change from the omnipresent pizzerias. Reckon on around 120kr for a main dish.

Restaurang Peking Storgatan 21 B. Reasonable Chinese food and pizzas from 60kr. A good place for lunch – 65kr.

Strandcaféet Malmbergsvägen 2 at the campsite. Beautifully located café right by the graceful Vassara river. Open until 10pm, but shut outside summer.

Tre Kronor Kaptensvägen 4 in Malmberget. Very popular with locals, no doubt because they serve pizzas that are so big they're just about falling off the plates.

Vassara Pub Lasarettsgatan 1, in the *Quality Hotel Gällivare*. Although a little pretentious and expensive, this bar-restaurant does a range of good lunches and serves excellent local delicacies such as Arctic char and reindeer.

Åhults Bageri & Café Lasarettsgatan 19. A Gällivare institution that's great for coffee and cakes.

Listings

Airport Information on ☎0970/780 00.
Banks FöreningsSparbanken, Storgatan 5; Handelsbanken, Storgatan 12; SEB, Storgatan 21.
Buses For long-distance bus information call ☎020/47 00 47.
Camping equipment Falkens Sport, Lasarettsgatan 256; Fjällsport, Järnvägsgatan in Malmberget.
Car rental Avis, Lasarettsgatan 1 at the *Quality Hotel Gällivare* ☎0970/160 30; Statoil, Malmberget ☎0970/229 00.
Doctor Treatment available at the hospital at Källgatan 14 ☎0970/190 00.
Internet Stacken youth centre, Storgatan (Mon–Thurs 3pm–9pm, Fri 3pm–11pm, Sat

6pm–11pm); library Hantverkargatan.
Left luggage At the railway station (15kr).
Pharmacy Storgatan 15 (Mon–Fri 9am–6pm, Sat 10am–1pm).
Police Lasarettsgatan 20 ☎0970/770 00.
Post office Hantverkaregatan 15.
Swimming pool Hellebergs väg, near the post office, with an excellent sauna suite.
Systembolaget Västra Kyrkallén 10 (Mon–Wed & Fri 10am–6pm, Thurs 10am–7pm, Sat 10am–2pm).
Taxi Gällivare Taxi ☎0970/10 000.
Trains For information call Connex ☎0771/260 000.

Around Gällivare

To dip into *Sámi* culture – meet (and taste) reindeer, and see how the *Sámi* make their handicrafts and throw lassoes – you can visit a **Sámi camp** at **Repisvare**, 2.5km from the town centre (book on ☎0970/140 80). A one hour visit there costs 350kr including transport to and from Gällivare; in theory they only take group bookings but you might be able to persuade them otherwise. You'll return smelling of wood smoke after sitting around an open fire inside a traditional *kåta*, so it may be wise not to wear your best gear on the trip.

The **Sjaunja Myggmuseum** (Mosquito Museum; free), the only one of its kind in the world, is within easy swatting distance of Gällivare at nearby Avvakajjo – a wayside halt on the Inlandsbanan. If you haven't yet been bitten by a **mosquito** (unlikely), the chances are you will be here; the museum (actually a three-walled wooden shed open at the rear) is full of live specimens buzzing around at leisure waiting for their next free lunch. Just how important the insects are for the Lapland countryside – they're responsible for pollinating the cloud-berry bushes out in the surrounding marshes – is demonstrated by the exhibitions. The only public transport to the museum is the Inlandsbanan: you simply dash in and out again (and use your mosquito repellent) while the train waits in the station. The best way to **get there** from Gällivare is to take the 5.10pm bus to either Porjus or, better, to Jokkmokk (there's less time to wait for the train here) and then ride the Inlandsbanan back north to the museum. Alternatively, though you have to be keen: take the 6.45am southbound Inlandsbanan, which stops for ten minutes at the museum, then get back on the train and disembark at Porjus, from where you can travel back to Gällivare on the 9am bus.

Moving on from Gällivare

From Gällivare, **trains** run south daily at 6.45am from late June to early August to Östersund on the Inlandsbanan; northwest to Kiruna and on to Narvik in Norway; and southeast to Boden, Luleå and then all points south. **Buses** run west to the **Laponia World Heritage Area** of Stora Sjöfallet National Park and Ritsem (see p.488), east to Pajala (see p.501) and northeast to Svappavaara, where connections can be made to Karesuando (see p.503); and from there via Finland to Treriksröset (see p.503) – the northernmost point in Sweden, where the country meets Norway and Finland. Especially handy when the Inlandsbanan isn't running are the year-round **Inlandsexpressen** buses, which run south via Jokkmokk and Arvidsjaur to Östersund.

Swedish Lapland's national parks

It's not a good idea to go **hiking in the national parks** of northern Sweden on a whim. Even for experienced walkers, the going can be tough and uncomfortable in parts, downright treacherous in others. **Mosquitoes** are a real problem: it's difficult to describe the utter misery of being covered in a blanket of insects, your eyes, ears and nose full of the creatures (for more on practicalities and safety guidelines see the box below). Yet the beautiful landscape here is one of the last wilderness areas left in Europe – it's one vast expanse of forest and mountains, where roads and human habitation are the exception rather than the norm. **Reindeer** are a common sight, as the parks are their breeding grounds and summer pasture, and **Sámi** settlements are dotted throughout the region – notably at **Ritsem** and **Vaisaluokta**.

The five **national parks** (@ www.fjallen.nu) here range in difficulty from moderately challenging to a positive assault course. Four of these lie about 120km northwest of Gällivare in the tract of Swedish wilderness edging Norway (the only national park not in this zone is the easy Muddus National

Hiking: some practical information

The best time to go **hiking** in the Swedish mountains is from late June to September: during May and early June the ground is still very wet and boggy as a result of the rapid snow melt. Once the snow has gone, wild flowers burst into bloom, making the most of the short summer months. The weather is very changeable – one moment it can be hot and sunny, the next it can be cold and rainy – and snow showers are not uncommon in summer.

It's always wise to keep to the **designated trails**, which, for summer hikes, are worn paths marked here and there by stone cairns or ribbons on trees and poles (a red "X" on a pole marks a winter snow-scooter trail). Many routes cross large streams – bridges or rowing boats are provided. **Rest shelters** are always open but aren't intended for overnight stays only for shelter from bad weather; head instead for **mountain cabins** (*fjällstugor*) or **STF fell stations** (*fjällstationer*), which appear at intervals of roughly 15–20km. Only the fell stations can be booked in advance and offer bed and breakfast accommodation; at cabins you'll need your own sheets or sleeping bags. There are telephones in cabins and some rest shelters. Safety advice and some guidelines on how to reduce damage to the land are posted at the park entrances and on huts and cabins; these are worth reading and remembering. A few tips:

- Get decent **maps**, boots and proper advice before setting out.
- Bring several bottles of **mosquito repellent**.
- Take a good **sleeping bag**, and for longer treks a **tent**, as parts of some trails don't have overnight cabins.
- **Other essentials** for a day-hike pack include rain gear, scarf, gloves, cap, matches, a compass and a knife.
- When **fording streams** never wade in water above your knees; wade across where the stream is shallow and wide. Go one at a time and wear training shoes if possible. Unbuckle the hip belt and chest strap on your pack.
- Watch out for **snow bridges** across streams – take great care not to fall into the water, which is likely to be deep and cold.
- Never go on a **glacier** without a knowledgeable guide – concealed crevasses can be fatal.

For additional detailed information, advice and encouragement for all the routes and parks covered here, contact **Svenska Turistföreningen** (Swedish Touring Club; Box 25, 101 20, Stockholm; @ www.meravsverige.nu) or speak to any of the tourist offices in Ammarnäs, Arjeplog, Jokkmokk, Gällivare, Kiruna or Tärnaby.

"It is one of the last and unquestionably largest and best preserved examples of an area of transhumance, involving summer grazing by large reindeer herds", said the UNESCO World Heritage Committee when they established **Laponia** as a **heritage area** in 1996. Covering a vast area of 9400 square kilometres, including the Padjelanta, Sarek and Stora Sjöfallet **national parks**, Laponia is the home and workplace of Forest and Mountain **Sámi** families from seven different villages, who still tend their reindeer here much as their ancestors did in prehistoric times. The Forest *Sámi* move with their herds within the forests and the Mountain *Sámi* follow their animals from the lichen-rich forests, where they spend the winter, up to the tree line by the time spring comes, then on into the mountains for summer; in August they start making their way down. Come September, many animals will be slaughtered either at the **corrals** in Ruokto, on the road between Porjus and Kebnats, or at highland corrals between Ritsem and Sitasjaure.

Park, covered on p.482). The low fells, large lakes and moors of **Padjelanta** (see below), **Stora Sjöfallet** (see below) and **Abisko** (see p.496) parks act as the eyebrows to the sheer face of the mountainous and inhospitable **Sarek** park (ⓦwww.fjallen.nu/parker/sarek.htm). Classed as "extremely difficult", Sarek (not covered in this book) has no tourist facilities, trails, cabins or bridges; the rivers are dangerous and the weather rotten – in short, you need good mountaineering experience to tackle it. For up-to-the-minute **information** on walking in the parks, contact the fell station at Saltoluokta ☎0973/410 10; or Kvikkjokk youth hostel ☎0971/210 22.

For coverage of the Kungsleden hiking trail see pp.495–500.

Padjelanta and Stora Sjöfallet national parks

Padjelanta (ⓦwww.fjallen.nu/parker/padje.htm) is the largest of Sweden's national parks; its name comes from *Sámi* and means "the higher country", an apt description for this plateau that lies almost exclusively above the tree line. The **Padjelanta trail** (150km) runs from **Vaisaluokta** through the **Laponia World Heritage Area** (see box above) south to **Kvikkjokk**, and is suited to inexperienced walkers – allow at least a week to finish it. You can get to Vaisaluokta by taking a **bus** from Gällivare to Ritsem (which will take you through the beautiful **Stora Sjöfallet** national park (ⓦwww.fjallen.nu/parker/ storasjo.htm) with its luxuriant forests and sweeping vistas, from where a boat takes you across Akkajaure lake to Vaisaluokta (details from the Ritsem mountain cabin; see below). To get to Kvikkjokk, hop on a bus in Jokkmokk; times can be obtained from Länstrafiken Norrbotten on ☎020/47 00 47, or from any tourist office in the area. There's also a helicopter service, operated by Lapplandsflyg, between Kvikkjokk, Staloluokta and Ritsem (late June to early Sept daily; 1260kr per person over whole route, 700kr over part of route; ☎0971/210 40, ⓦwww.lapplandsflyg.se).

For **accommodation**, there's an STF mountain cabin at Ritsem (☎0973/420 30, ☎0970/420 50; late Feb to mid-May & late June to late Sept) and a **youth hostel** at the end of the trail, in Kvikkjokk (☎0971/210 22, ⓦwww.jokkmokkhostel .com; mid-Feb to late April & mid-June to mid-Sept). **Cabins** can be found elsewhere along the route; distances between points where they're located are as follows: Ritsem to Vaisaluokta (by boat) 16km; Vaisaluokta to Kutjaure 18km; Kutjaure to Låddejokk 19km; Låddejokk to Arasluokta 12km; Arasluokta to Staloluokta 10km; Staloluokta to Tuottar 18km; Tuottar to Tarraluoppal 11km;

SWEDISH LAPLAND | Swedish Lapland's national parks

7

Tarraluoppal to Såmmarlappa 15km; Såmmarlappa to Tarrekaise 13km; Tarrekaise to Njunjes 7km; Njunjes to Kvikkjokk 17km. The wardens at the cabins or fell stations can tell you the locations of the nearest **food** stores.

Kiruna and around

One hundred and twenty-three kilometres northwest of Gällivare **KIRUNA** (the town's name comes from the *Sámi* word "Giron", meaning "ptarmigan") was the hub of the battle for the control of the iron-ore supply during World War II; ore was transported north from here by train to the great harbour at Narvik over the border in Norway. Much German firepower was expended in an attempt to interrupt the supply to the Allies and wrest control for the Axis. In the process, Narvik suffered grievously, whilst Kiruna – benefiting from supposed Swedish neutrality – made a packet selling to both sides. Today the train ride to Kiruna, 200km north of the Arctic Circle, rattles through sidings, slag heaps and ore works, a bitter contrast to the surrounding wilderness.

Partly due to its proximity to the world-famous **Icehotel** in the nearby village of **Jukkasjärvi**, and partly because it's the most northerly town in Sweden, Kiruna has become *the* destination in Swedish Lapland, the place that everyone wants to visit. However, don't come here expecting monumental architectural delights, tree-lined avenues and big-city sophistication – it has none of that.

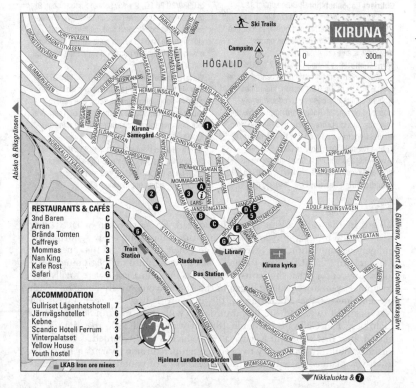

What it does have is a strangely likeable down-to-earth feel, influenced by its total dependence on iron ore mining. Although there are a few sights in town, it's more attractive as a base to visit this corner of northern Lappland, with rail connections northwest to the start of the Kungsleden trail (see p.495) and Riksgränsen as well as bus connections into the Torne Valley (see p.500).

Arrival, information and accommodation

The **train** station is at Bangårdsvägen, from where it's a brisk ten-minute walk up the steep hill, Konduktörsgatan, to the **tourist office** in Folkets Hus, in the central square off Mommagatan (mid-June to Aug Mon–Fri 8.30am–8pm, Sat & Sun 8.30am–6pm; Sept to mid-June Mon–Fri 9am–5pm, Sat 10am–4pm; ☎0980/188 80, ⓦwww.lappland.se). The **bus station**, where regular daily buses from Gällivare stop, is at the corner of Biblioteksgatan and Hjalmar Lundbohmsvägen; turn off the latter street and into Lars Janssonsgatan to get to the main square. Served by flights from Stockholm and Umeå, the **airport**, 10km away, is linked to town by summer bus (40kr) and taxi (170kr) all year round.

For a place to **stay**, the **youth hostel** is 900m from the train station at Bergmästaregatan 7 (☎0980/171 95, ⓕ0980/841 42). Boasting its own sauna, it fills quickly in summer, as does the *Ripan* **campsite** (☎0980/630 00, ⓦwww.ripan.se), with four-berth cabins (❸) and an open-air swimming pool; it's on Campingvägen in the Högalid area of town, a twenty-minute walk north of the centre. Though the town has only a limited range of **hotels**, some of which are listed below, reservations are generally not required.

Gullriset Lägenhetshotell Bromsgatan 12 ☎0980/109 37, ⓦwww.fabmf.se. Cheap and cheerful boasting apartments for one to four people, costing 350–660kr depending on size. Breakfast is an extra 45kr.

Järnvägshotellet Bangårdsvägen 7 ☎0980/844 44, ⓦwww.jarnvagshotellet.com. Located on the main platform of the train station, this rambling old timber building has been restored and newly reopened as a hotel. Rooms are comfortable and spacious, though plainly decorated – noise from the passing iron ore trains can be a problem. ❷

Kebne Konduktörsgatan 7 ☎0980/681 80, ⓦwww.hotellkebne.com. Good-quality rooms with wooden floors make this a sound choice. ❹/❷

Scandic Hotell Ferrum Lars Jansongatan 17 ☎0980/39 86 00, ⓦwww.scandic-hotels.com. By far the most expensive place in town, has characterless chain hotel rooms and indifferent staff, although the palatial sauna suite on the top floor is a wonderful place to relax and watch the midnight sun. ❻/❸

Vinterpalatset Järnvägsgatan 18 ☎0980/677 70, ⓦwww.kiruna.se/~vinterp. A listed building with wooden floors, large double beds, and superb sauna and jacuzzi suite on the top floor. There are four cheaper, more basic rooms in the annexe. ❺/❸

Yellow House Hantverkaregatan 25 ☎0980/137 50, ⓦwww.yellowhouse.nu. Budget hotel with dorm beds (130kr) and shared rooms for 2–4 people. Breakfast not included. ❶

The Town

When, in the early 1600s, Swedish pioneers first arrived in what is now Kiruna, they found the *Sámi* already in place here. Completely ignoring the indigenous population, the Swedes opened their first mine in 1647, nearby at Masugnsbyn ("Blast Furnace Village"), but it wasn't until the beginning of the following century that the **iron-ore** deposits in Kiruna itself were finally discovered. Exploratory drilling began in the 1880s, which nicely coincided with the building of the **Malmbanan**, the iron-ore railway between Luleå and Narvik in Norway, and the first train laden with iron ore trundled out from Malmberget in Gällivare in March 1888. It wasn't until 1900 that the settlers braved their first winter in Kiruna, a year which is now regarded as the town's birthday. Built on a hill to try to keep the temperature up (warm air rises), the town was planned to withstand the coldest snaps of winter – even the streets are curved as protection against the biting polar wind. Sadly, though, much of the wooden architecture, gloriously painted in reds, greens and yellows, of Kiruna's early days was ripped down to make way for today's unprepossessing concrete structures; the town even won an award in the 1960s for its out-with-the-old-in-with-the-new policy.

Not surprisingly, most sights in town are firmly wedded to iron in one way or another. The tower of the **Stadshus** is a strident metal pillar, designed by Bror Marklund (see p.385) and harbouring an intricate latticework, clock face and 23 sundry bells that chime raucously at noon, 1pm and 6pm; incomprehensibly, the Stadshus won an award in 1964 for being the most beautiful Swedish public building. Inside, there's a tolerable art collection and, in summer, occasional displays of *Sámi* handicrafts.

The **mines**, ugly brooding reminders of Kiruna's prosperity, still dominate the town, much more depressingly so than in Gällivare (see p.482); despite its new central buildings and open parks, Kiruna retains a grubby industrial feel. The tourist office arranges **guided tours** around the mines (July to mid-Aug 3 daily; late June & mid- to late Aug 2 daily; 140kr; minimum age 6), on which visitors are bussed to a "tourist mine", a closed-off section of the rabbit warren of tunnels comprising a working mine. Inside you'll see facilities such as petrol stations and a workers' canteen; and mining paraphernalia, including trains for transporting ore and equipment, and mills for crushing the ore-bearing rock. Oddly enough, the mine provides a perfect habitat for *shiitake* mushrooms, which are grown here at a depth of 540m and can be sampled during the tour.

Back in town, **Kiruna kyrka**, on Kyrkogatan (daily 11am–4.45pm; July till 10pm), causes a few raised eyebrows when people see it for the first time: built in the style of a *Sámi* hut, it's an origami-like creation of oak beams and rafters, the size of a small aircraft hangar. LKAB, the iron-ore company (and the town's main employer) which paid for its construction, was also responsible for the **Hjalmar Lundbohmsgården** at Ingenjörsgatan 1 (June–Aug daily 10am–5pm; Sept–May Mon–Fri 10am–4pm; 30kr), fifteen minutes' walk away (take Gruvvägen south, turn left at Hjalmar Lundbohmsvägen, then right into Ingenjörsgatan). The displays in this country house once used by the managing director of the company, who was the town's "founder", consist mostly of turn-of-the-twentieth-century photographs featuring the man himself and assorted *Sámi* in their winter gear. Try to visit the house, in order to get a perspective on the town's history, before going down the mine; you'll be all the more aware afterwards how, without the mine, Kiruna would be a one-reindeer town instead of the thriving place it is today – quite a feat when you consider its location on the map (don't be surprised to see snow on the slag heaps in the middle of June).

For the most rewarding exhibition of *Sámi* culture in town, head for the handicraft centre, **Kiruna Samegård**, at Brytaregatan 14 (mid-June to Sept daily 10am–6pm; Oct to mid-June Mon–Fri 10am–4pm; 20kr). The handicrafts you'll see here may well be familiar by now; what probably won't be is its small but impressive display of *Sámi* art featuring scenes from everyday life in the north. It also has a souvenir shop, where you can pick up a piece of antler bone or reindeer skin.

Eating, drinking and nightlife

Eating and **drinking** in Kiruna is not a joy. Restaurants and bars are few and far between, and in summer you may even find several closed: frustratingly, the staff take their holidays just when the town is full of tourists. That said, Kiruna is a good place to try some traditional *Sámi* delicacies such as reindeer.

Brända Tomten inside the Gallerian shopping centre at the corner of Mangigatan and Föreningsgatan. Decent coffee, cakes and sandwiches but a bit soulless.

Caffreys Bergmästaregatan 7. *The* place in Kiruna for pizza and pasta – both around 90kr – although the surrounds are rather dark and dingy. The adjoining bar, which is much more light and airy, is one of the most popular – and pleasanter – places for an evening drink.

Kafe Rost Torget, inside Folkets Hus. This open-plan first floor café serves up decent sandwiches and cakes and has good views out over the main square.

Mommas inside the *Scandic Hotel Ferrum* in the main square. An American-style place with a dreary interior, serving up burgers and the like.

Nan King Mangigatan 26. This friendly little restaurant is the most northerly Chinese restaurant in Sweden, serving – besides the expected fare – pizza and spaghetti. Main dishes from 100kr. Lunch here is 60kr. Closed Mon.

Restaurang Arran Föreningsgatan 9. A grotty drinking den offering the cheapest beer in town. Go in with a friend and be prepared to be stared at.

Safari Geologgatan 4. The best choice in town for tea and coffee, with outdoor seating in summer and a wonderful continental feel.

3nd Baren Föreningsgatan 11. A great old wooden building with coarsely hewn floorboards, attracting a trendy crowd during the evenings, this is undoubtedly the best restaurant in town. Mains include reindeer for 99kr, salmon 133kr and lasagne 69kr. There's outdoor seating under the trees at the rear in summer.

Listings

Airport Information on ☎0980/28 48 10.

Banks Nordea, in the main square opposite the tourist office.

Buses For long-distance bus information call ☎020/47 00 47.

Car rental Avis, at the railway station and the airport ☎0980/130 80; Budget, Industrivägen 18 ☎0980/831 65; Europcar, Forvägen 33 ☎0980/807 59.

Cinema There are weekly films inside Folkets Hus in the main square ☎0980/157 00.

Internet Ask at Kafe Rost, Torget, inside Folkets Hus (Mon–Fri 10am–5pm, Sat 10am–4pm). Staff here will give you access to the nearby computer room.

Left luggage At the railway station (20kr).

Medical treatment At the hospital ☎0980/730 00.

Pharmacy Inside the Gallerian shopping centre on Föreningsgatan (Mon–Fri 9.30am–6pm, Sat 10am–1pm).

Police Lars Janssonsgatan ☎0980/744 00.

Post office Meschplan ☎0980/100 55 (Mon–Fri 9.30am–6pm, Sat 10am–1pm).

Swimming pool Simhallsbadet at Bergmästaregatan 10.

Systembolaget Geologgatan.

Taxi Taxi Kiruna ☎0980/120 20.

Trains For information call Connex on ☎0771/260 000..

Travel agent Kiruna Affärs och Privatresebyrå, Arent Grapegatan 27 ☎0980/831 80.

Jukkasjärvi and the Icehotel

An obvious destination for any tourist travelling around Kiruna in winter is the tiny village of **JUKKASJÄRVI** (known locally simply as "Jukkas"), 17km east of Kiruna, the location for Swedish Lapland's blockbuster attraction, 200km north of the Arctic Circle: the **Icehotel**. What's effectively the world's largest igloo, the Icehotel is built every year by the side of the Torneälven river in late October, from when it stands proudly until temperatures rise definitively above zero in May, and it finally melts away back into the river.

Jukkasjärvi village

Although the Icehotel totally dominates tiny **Jukkasjärvi**, from its position at the entrance to the village, it's worth taking a stroll down the main (and only) road, Marknadsvägen, past the handful of simple dwellings owned by locals who're not all in favour of the changes the Icehotel has brought to their village. A much more traditional sight awaits at the end of the dead-end road: an old wooden *Sámi* **church** (June–Aug daily 8am–10pm; restricted hours in winter), parts of which date from 1608, making it the oldest surviving church in Lapland. Check out the richly decorated altarpiece by Uppsala artist, Bror Hjorth, depicting the revivalist preacher, **Lars Levi Laestadius** (see p.502), alongside the woman who inspired him to rid Lapland of alcohol, Maria of Åsele. The triptych was given to the church in 1958 by the mining company, LKAB, who were then celebrating their 350th anniversary. Under the floor are the mummified remains of villagers who died here in the eighteenth century (not on display). The sandy ground and frost are thought to have been responsible for keeping the bodies, including that of a woman dressed in a white wedding dress and high-heel shoes, so remarkably well preserved. The organ above the door is made from reindeer horn and birch wood; the artwork in the centre of the organ, suspended over the pipes, symbolizes the sun rising over the Lapporten, the two mountain tops near Abisko which have come to represent the gateway to Lapland. Across the road from the church, the wooden houses of the tedious Hembygdsgården **homestead museum** (daily 11am–4pm; 20kr) contain the usual suspects: a stuffed reindeer, an old sleigh, a rickety spinning wheel and other equally dull how-we-used-to-live paraphernalia.

The Icehotel

The brains behind the **Icehotel** belong to Yngve Bergqvist, a southern Swede who moved to Lapland thirty odd years ago. In 1989 he built an igloo – barely sixty square metres in size – as an art gallery to showcase local *Sámi* crafts and design. Won over by visitors who asked to sleep in the igloo, the concept was born. Today, covering a colossal 4000 square metres, the *Icehotel* (℡0980/668 00, ⊛www.icehotel.com; ❻) is constructed of thirty thousand cubic metres of snow and three thousand tonnes of ice (cut from the Torne river); its exact shape and design changes from year to year though there's always an exhibition hall, a cinema, and a chapel where couples can marry. From the entrance hall there's usually one main walkway filled with ice **sculptures**, from which smaller corridors lead off to the fifty or so bedrooms (all with electric lights and beds made out of blocks of compact snow covered with reindeer hides) which make up the bulk of the hotel.

Overnight guests are required to leave their valuables and most of their clothes in lockers in a heated cabin on the edge of the hotel, from where there's access to toilet facilities (also heated). When it's time to go to bed, you make a run for it from here to your room (wearing as little as possible; see below) and dive into your sleeping bag as quickly as you can – the temperature inside the hotel is –5C, outside it's generally around –20 or –30C. Guests are provided with specially made, tried-and-tested, **sleeping bags** of a type used by the Swedish army, who have used the hotel for Arctic survival training; the bags are supposed to keep you warm in temperatures down to -35°C. However, as they enclose your entire body and head (bar a small area for your eyes and nose) they are rather claustrophobic. You should take off all the clothes you're still wearing and sleep naked to prevent sweating; stuff your clothes into the bottom of the sleeping bag to keep them warm and place your shoes on the bed with you to stop them freezing. Don't expect to sleep – you won't – it's simply too cold and uncomfortable. In the morning, you can refresh yourself with a sauna and have a hearty breakfast at the *Wärdshus* restaurant across the road, though you'll soon notice from people's faces that nobody else has slept a wink either.

Whilst there is no doubt that this is one of the most unusual places in the world to spend a night, and simply seeing the Icehotel is an experience in itself, it's worth noting that, sadly, the whole operation has become money-driven of late; prices have more than doubled in recent years as demand for rooms has surged, and even **day visitors** now have to pay an entrance fee (100kr). The separate-sex shower blocks (a good ten-minute walk from some rooms) are not up to scratch; the handful of shabby cubicles are of youth hostel standard; and you'll be forced to queue to shower and share the facilities with at least fifty other people. Due to a local dispute with the inhabitants of the village, the only place to socialize before retiring is the *Icebar* (sponsored by Absolut Vodka), certainly an amazing piece of ice construction with its domed ceiling, though a drink here (there's only vodka available) costs a stinging 85kr, with a refill coming in at 60kr; there is no other bar or communal area anywhere on site, or indeed nearby, leaving you at a loose end once the sun has gone down early afternoon.

Practicalities

The Icehotel is open from mid-December each year until it thaws, though the dubious pleasure of spending a night in subzero temperatures doesn't come cheap; we've given the high-season price first (it runs from late Dec to early April), whilst the second price in brackets is the low-season rate, applicable for just a month or so. The **double rooms** cost a pricey 2490kr (1960kr), while a more stylish **decorated suite**, adorned with ice carvings and ornaments, is a totally outrageous 3490kr (2960kr). There are also six-person en-suite **cabins** for rent on the site, all with kitchens (Dec–April ❻; four-bed cabins also available). Hotel rooms and cabins can be booked through Jukkas AB, on the main road at Marknadsvägen 63 (☎0980/668 00, ⓦwww.icehotel.com); you should book in advance, especially in the peak season from Christmas until mid-March.

Organized **activities** – also inordinately expensive – include a 90min dog-sledging trip through the neighbouring forests with a short stop for coffee and cake (975kr per person), an accompanied daytime drive on snow scooters down the Torne river and into the wintry forests (995kr; 4hr), or a night-time spin to see the northern lights (995kr; 3hr 30min). In **summer** there's organized river rafting (550kr per person; 6 hrs), fishing and hiking – details can be obtained from Jukkas AB. In the Icehotel's all-year Art Center, you can also see the massive blocks of ice (3500 tonnes in total) cut from the river in March and stored ready for the next Icehotel, and, should you wish to escape the summer mosquitoes, it's even possible to spend a night inside specially constructed igloos in the Art Center – once again the hotel staff on site have details.

You can **eat** all meals across the road at *Jukkasjärvi Wärdshus* in winter (only open lunchtimes in summer); for **provisions**, there's a small supermarket in the village.

To get here from Kiruna, take bus #006 (Mon–Fri 1 daily; 20min). Undoubtedly the best way to arrive, though, is by **dog sledge** from Kiruna airport; for a hefty 4350kr (price includes up to four people) you can be met at your plane and pulled all the way to your room.

Nikkaluokta and Kebnekaise

Nikkaluokta, 66km west of Kiruna and reached on the twice-daily bus, is the starting point for treks towards and up Sweden's highest mountain, **Kebnekaise** (2114m). From the village, a 19km trail leads to the **fell station** at Kebnekaise (☎0980/550 00, ⓦwww.stfkebnekaise.com; ❶; early March to early May & mid-June to mid-Sept) at the foot of the mountain. There's also a **helicopter** connection here; see p.496. The mountain was first conquered in 1883 by a Frenchman, Charles Robot; today it can be reached in 8–9 hours by anyone in decent physical condition. Two paths lead to the peak: the eastern route goes over Björling glacier, includes some climbing and is only recommended for experts; the western route is much longer and is the one most people opt for.

The Kungsleden

The **Kungsleden** (literally "King's Trail") is the most famous and popular hiking route in Sweden. A well-signposted, five-hundred-kilometre path from **Abisko** (see p.496) in the north to **Hemavan**, near Tärnaby (see p.468), it takes in Sweden's highest mountain, **Kebnekaise** (2114m), en route. If you're

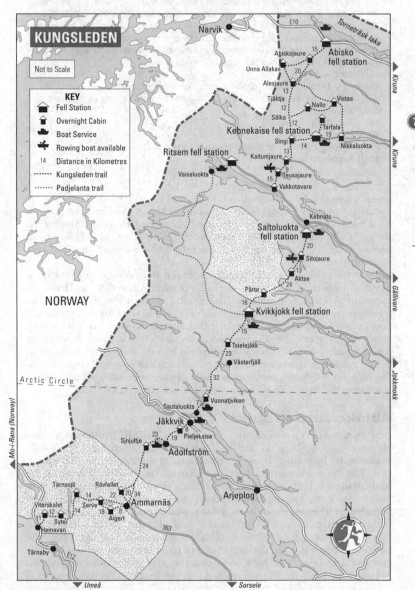

You can get to **Abisko** pretty easily by **train**; it's just before the Norwegian border on the Kiruna–Narvik run. The **Inlandsbanan** will get you to Jokkmokk, from where you can get a bus to Kvikkjokk, another point on the trail. A **helicopter** service, run by Norrlandsflyg, operates between Nikkaluokta and Kebnekaise (late June to mid-Sept; 390kr per person; information on ☎0970/140 65 or ☎0971/210 68).

There are also several useful **bus** routes that you can take to link up with the trail, listed below; most of these services are run by Länstrafiken Norrbotten (☎020/47 00 47) and Länstrafiken Västerbotten (☎020/91 00 19). The buses operate a *bussgods* service, which allows you to send your pack ahead to your destination or alternatively back to your starting point, sparing you the effort of lugging your stuff around; ask about this service at bus stations or on the bus.

#31: Hemavan to Umeå
#92: Kiruna to Nikkaluokta (19km from Kebnekaise fell station)
#93: Gällivare to Ritsem (passes through Vakkotavare and Kebnats for the boat to Saltoluokta)
#94: Jokkmokk to Kvikkjokk
#200: Arjeplog to Jäkkvik
#303: Arjeplog to Laisval (change there for Adolfström)
#341: Ammarnäs to Sorsele

looking for splendid isolation, this isn't the trail for you; it's the busiest in the country, though it's really only the section from Abisko to Kebnekaise that sees most hikers (one of the least busy sections is between Jäkkvik and Adolfström, see p.477). Although most people start the trail at Abisko, it's equally feasible to begin further south – see the box above for possible starting points and how to get to them.

There are **cabins** along the entire route, and from Abisko to Saltoluokta, north of the Arctic Circle, and in the south between Ammarnäs and Hemavan, there are also STF **fell stations**. The ground is easy to walk, with bridges where it's necessary to ford streams; marshy ground has had wooden planks laid down to ease the going, and there are either boat services or rowing boats with which to get across several large lakes. The route, which passes through the national parks (see p.487), is traditionally split into the five segments described below. For the distances between the places mentioned on each segment, see the map on p.495; the best map to have of the entire area is Lantmäteriet Kartförlagets *Norra Norrland* (scale 1:400,000), available in Gällivare.

Abisko and around

Leaving Kiruna, it's a further 98km northwest to **ABISKO**. Although accessible since 1984 by both rail and road, once the E10 from Luleå was finally extended, it's by **train** that most people arrive at the start of the Kungsleden trail. The train route from Luleå, via Kiruna, to Narvik, known as the **Malmbanan**, is Europe's northernmost line, and would never have been built had it not been for the rich deposits of iron ore around Gällivare and Malmberget. The idea to construct the line, which connects the Bothnian coast with the Atlantic coast (170km), passing through some of the remotest and most inhospitable parts of Europe, was talked about on and off throughout the nineteenth century, when the only means of transporting the ore was by reindeer and sleigh. Finally, in 1884, an English company was awarded the contract to build it; by 1888, the line had reached Gällivare from the Bothnian coast and the company was bankrupt. Ten years passed before the state took over the project; in July 1902, the navvies – who'd been subject to temperatures of below -30°C in incredibly harsh conditions – finally shovelled their way through deep snow at Riksgränsen to cross the Norwegian border. A year later the line was officially opened by King Oscar II.

Arriving by train from Kiruna, the first stop, Abisko Ö (short for Östra meaning east) is the location of the tiny village of Abisko, nothing more than a couple of streets of houses of little interest to visitors. Instead stay on the train for another five minutes and alight at the next stop, **Abisko Turiststation**, the name of the eponymous STF establishment (☎0980/402 00, ⊛www.stfabisko .com; ❶) and the only **accommodation** option (booking ahead is wise), superbly located beside the vast Torneträsk lake. There are 300 beds here in both private rooms (from 170kr per person) and two-berth cabins (Jan–May ❷, otherwise ❹), a great basement sauna suite, restaurant and bar (with views over the lake). There's also a food store which hires out hiking equipment. The friendly staff have expert knowledge of the Kungsleden and surrounding area and more than compensate for the lack of a dedicated tourist office.

Even if you don't intend to walk the Kungsleden (see below), there are a couple of attractions right on the doorstep. Departing from directly opposite the *Turiststation*, you can take a **cable car** (*linbanan*; 85kr return) 500m up Nuolja mountain (1169m) for fantastic views of the surrounding wilderness: the spectacular U-shaped mountain tops of **Lapporten** (used as landmarks by the *Sámi* for guiding their reindeer between their summer and winter grazing land), the seventy-kilometre-long Torneträsk lake, and the vast wooded expanses of **Abisko National Park** (⊛www.fjallen.nu/parker/abisko.htm). The mountain is a popular place from which to observe the midnight sun. From the café at the end of the cable car, an easy walking path (7km; allow 2–3hr) leads downhill to nearby **Björkliden**, 9km away by road, comprising nothing more than a few houses gathered around the railway station. From here, the **Navvy Road** (Rallarvägen) leads to Rombaksbotn, near Narvik, in Norway; the road was built alongside the Malmbanan, then under construction, in order to transport materials needed for the line. Today it provides a walking or mountain-biking route between Abisko and Narvik – though it can be fairly narrow and rough going in parts.

Riksgränsen

From Abisko and Björkliden, the train line and the E10 continue on to **RIKSGRÄNSEN**, 34km from Abisko, a self-contained mountain ski and spa resort 400km north of the Arctic Circle in the shadow of the Norwegian border. The proud claim of Riksgränsen is that plentiful precipitation means there's never any need for artificial snow; you can ski and snowboard until Midsummer. Although the minuscule settlement consists of barely a couple of houses supplemented by a top-notch **hotel**, *Hotell Riksgränsen* (☎0980/400 80, ⊛www.riksgransen.nu; ❻/❹) opposite the train station, it's the chance to explore the only high Alpine area in Sweden with 60 peaks over 1350m that brings trainloads of people here, predominantly during the winter season (mid-Feb to late June). The hotel certainly buzzes in season – it's one of the Swedes' favourite ski destinations, despite its isolated location – advance booking is therefore essential. The hotel also has 3–6-bed self-catering **apartments** (1230–2055kr per night), which, although adequate, are a little cramped; in summer (late June to late Sept) individual **bunks** in the apartments are let as simple youth hostel-style accommodation (150kr per person per bunk). In addition to the ski trails here, the hotel also boasts a well-appointed **spa cen-**

△ Ski action, Lapland

tre complete with five massage rooms, gym, Jacuzzi and outside hot tubs from where there are breathtaking views over the Vassijaure lake; this is certainly one of the best places in the whole of Sweden to completely chill out. During the summer months, there's some great **fishing** and **hiking** to be had in these parts; the hotel can supply detailed information as well as rent **mountain bikes** to cycle along the Rallarvägen (see p.497) or **canoes** for use on the lake here (both cost 250kr a day). Bear in mind, though, that Riksgränsen is one of the wettest places in the entire country in summer (unlike neighbouring Abisko which is in a rain shadow).

While you're in Riksgränsen, be sure to check out the fantastic **landscape and wildlife photographs** of local photographer, Sven Hörnell, who lived up here for fifty years (mid-June to mid-Sept daily 9am–6pm; 60kr; ⓦwww.sven -hornell.se). He made it his life's work to record the changing seasons in the Sarek national park and the Lofoten archipelago over the hills in Norway, with much of his output consisting of aerial photos taken while flying his own pro-peller plane across the wilds of Lapland. His photographs, together with an hour-long slide show (3pm) of his work can be seen in the exhibition hall next to the railway station, Riksgränsvägen 10, marked "Sven Hörnell".

Abisko to Kebnekaise – 6 days, 105km

From its starting point at Abisko Turiststation, the Kungsleden winds through the elongated Abisko National Park which contains some of the most lush and dense vegetation of the trail, including beech forest lining the valley bottom. From the Alesjaure cabins, perched on a mountain ridge 35km from the start, you'll get a fantastic view over the open countryside below; there's a sauna here, too. The highest point on this segment is the Tjäktja pass (1105m), 50km from the start, from where there are also wonderful views. There are **cabins** en route at Abiskojaure, Alesjaure, Tjäktja (before the pass), Sälka and Singi.

At the end of this section of cabins lies **Kebnekaise fell station** (14km from Singi; early March to early May & mid-June to mid-Sept; ☏0980/550 00, ⓦwww.stfkebnekaise.com; ❶; advance booking necessary), from where it's possible to leave the main trail and head to Nikkaluokta, 19km away (served by buses to Kiruna). **Provisions** are available at Abisko, Alesjaure, Sälka and Kebnekaise.

Kebnekaise to Saltoluokta – 3 days, 51km

One of the quietest sections of the trail, this segment takes in beech forest, open fells and deep valleys. First of all you backtrack 14km to **Singi**, before heading south again with an unobstructed view of the hills and glaciers of Sarek National Park. You then paddle across the river at **Teusajaure** and climb over a plateau, from where you drop steeply through more beech forest to **Vakkotavare**. Here a bus runs to the quay at Kebnats, and then a short boat trip brings you to **Saltoluokta fell station**, an STF fell station at Saltoluokta (☏0973/410 10, ⓦwww.stfsaltoluokta.com; ❶; March to early April & mid-June to mid-Sept) and the start of the next section. There are **cabins** en route at Singi, Kaitumjaure, Teusajaure and Vakkotavare.

Provisions are available at all the cabins apart from Singi.

Saltoluokta to Kvikkjokk – 4 days, 73km

This segment involves crossing two lakes and also passes through a bare land-scape edged by pine and beech forests. A long uphill climb of around five to six hours leads first to **Sitojaure** on a bare high fell. The shallow lake here, which you have to cross, is choppy in the strong wind; take the boat service operated by the cabin caretaker. You then cross the wetlands on the other side of the lake, making use of the wooden planks laid down here, to **Aktse**, where there's a vast field of yellow buttercups in summer. Row across **Laitaure lake** for Kvikkjokk; as you approach you'll see pine forest. There are **cabins** en route at Sitojaure, Aktse, and Pårte; at **Kvikkjokk** there's a **youth hostel** (☎0971/210 22, ⓦwww.jokkmokkhostel.com; mid-Feb to late April & mid-June to mid-Sept). **Provisions** are available at Saltoluokta, Aktse and Kvikkjokk.

Kvikkjokk to Ammarnäs – 8 days, 166km

Not recommended for novices, this is one of the most difficult stretches of the trail (distances between cabins can be long and there are four lakes to cross); it is, however, also one of the quietest. From **Kvikkjokk** you take the boat over Saggat lake and walk to the first cabin at **Tsielejåkk**. It's 55km to the next cabin at **Vuonatjviken**.

You then take the boat across Riebnesjaure and walk to Hornavan for another boat across to the village of **Jäkkvik**; there are cabins available here (see p.477). It's a short hike of 8km to the next cabin, then on to the village of **Adolfström**, where once again there is accommodation (see p.477). Then you get another boat over Iraft lake and on to the cabins at **Sjnjultje**. From here there's a choice of routes: 34km direct to Ammarnäs, or 24km to Rävfallet and then another 20km into Ammarnäs. **Accommodation** en route is at Tsielejåkk, Vuonatjviken, Jäkkvik village, Pieljekaise, Adolfström village, Sjnjultje, Rävfallet and Ammarnäs. **Provisions** are available in Jäkkvik and Adolfström.

Ammarnäs to Hemavan – 4 days, 78km

This is the easiest part of the trail: on it you'll pass over low fells and heather-covered moors and through beech forests and wetlands, the horizon lined with impressive fell peaks. The only steep climb is eight kilometres long between **Ammarnäs** and **Aigert**, where there's an imposing waterfall and a traditional steam sauna in the cabin. On the way to the **Syter** cabin, 48km from Aigert, you'll pass a network of bridges, which cross the various lakes in what is called the **Tärnasjö archipelago**. There are no fell stations on this stretch of the trail; cabins en route are at Aigert, Serve, Tärnasjö, Syter, Viterskalet and Hemavan. **Provisions** are available at all the cabins apart from Hemavan (see also p.468).

The Torne Valley

Along the border with Finland, the lush, gentle slopes of the **TORNE VALLEY** (Tornedalen in Swedish) are among the most welcoming sights in northern Sweden. Stretching over 500km from the mouth of the Gulf of Bothnia to Sweden's remote northern tip, the three rivers, Torne, Muonio and Könkämä, mark out the long border between Sweden and Finland. The valley is home to Swedes, Finns and *Sámi*, who all speak an archaic **dialect** of Finnish known, in Swedish at least, as *tornedalsfinska* (Torne Valley Finnish, now an official minority language), though Swedish is understood by most people here and is the language of choice for the younger generation. Refreshingly different from the coast and from the heavily wooded inland regions of the country, the area is dotted with small villages, often no more than a couple of wooden cottages near a river, bordered by flower meadows that run down to the water's edge. To either side of Route 400, the main road along the valley, lie open fields providing much-needed grazing land for the farmers' livestock.

Arriving from the west, you can enter the valley by **bus** at its midway point, **Pajala**; take the #46 here from **Gällivare** (Mon–Fri 3 daily, Sat & Sun 1 daily; 2hr 30min), or the #53 from **Kiruna** (Mon–Thurs & Sun 1 daily, Fri 2 daily; 3hr). From the north, bus #50 runs from Karesuando to Vittangi (Mon–Fri & Sun 1 daily), where you change onto the #53 for Pajala. From the **Bothnian coast**, buses run daily from Haparanda (see p.407) up the valley as far as **Pajala**. The main **bus** routes through the Torne Valley (there are no trains here) are the #53 and #54 between Pajala and Haparanda (Mon–Thurs 3 daily, Fri 4 daily, Sun 1 daily; 3hr).

Pajala

Over time we understood that Pajala didn't actually belong to Sweden… we'd made it by chance. A northerly appendage, desolate swampland where a few people just happened to live, who only partly managed to be Swedish…no roe deer, hedgehogs or nightingales. Just interminable amounts of mosquitoes, Torne Valley Finnish swearwords and Communists.

Popular Music, Mikael Niemi, on growing up in Pajala during the 1960s and 1970s.

The valley's main village is pretty **PAJALA**, a place that has earned itself a reputation and a half throughout Sweden. The predominance of heavy labouring jobs in the north of Sweden has produced a gender imbalance here – around three men to every woman (a fact which also explains the ridiculously macho behaviour that seems to prevail in these parts). So, to celebrate the village's four-hundredth anniversary in 1987, the local council placed advertisements in the national papers inviting women from the south of the country up to Lapland to take part in the birthday festivities. Journalists outside Sweden soon heard of the ads, and articles about the unusual invitation began to appear in newspapers across Europe. Before long, busloads of women from all over the continent were heading for the village. The anniversary festivities proved to be a drunken, debauched bash that tiny Pajala won't forget in a long time, but they did help to redress the gender problem: dozens of East European women lost their hearts to gruff Swedish lumberjacks, and began new lives north of the Arctic Circle. It remains to be seen whether these women will adapt to a lifetime of winters spent in darkness, in temperatures of -25°C – to date, though, thirty women have stayed the course.

Taking place in the last week in September, the **Römpäviiko** ("romp week"; (Ⓦ www.pajala.se/welcome/culture/festivals.shtml#Romp%20) cultural festival, featuring live music and street stalls selling food and handicrafts, is undoubtedly the liveliest time to be in the village. However, the second weekend after Midsummer is another time to visit the village, when up to forty thousand people flood into town for the Pajala **market**, one of the biggest in Norrland selling everything from chorizos to reindeer antlers; it's an excellent opportunity to pick up a few *Sámi* handicrafts. A smaller market is also held during the last weekend in February during the **Norrkskensfestivalen**. As the Swedish name suggests, this festival provides a good chance to see the northern lights, most enjoyably from aboard a **snow scooter tour** (400kr for an accompanied one-hour tour; 850kr per day), which can be booked at the tourist office.

At any other time, Pajala is a great place to rest up in for a day or so – take a walk along the riverside, or head off in search of the great grey **owl** (*strix nebulosa*) that sweeps through the nearby forests. The huge wooden **model** of the bird in the bus station will give you an idea of its appearance: lichen grey, with long, slender tail feathers and a white crescent between its black and yellow eyes. Close by, on Torggatan, is the largest **sundial** in the world, a circular affair with a diameter of 38m which tells the real solar time – always 18–25min different to that of a regular watch or clock.

While you're in Pajala, make an effort to visit the **grave** of the revivalist preacher, Lars Levi Laestadius (see box below), who came to Pajala in 1849. Although he strived throughout his life to rid Lapland of alcohol abuse, he was rarely popular hereabouts since many workers were paid for their toils in hard liquor. He died in Pajala in 1861, and his grave is located in the middle section of the old graveyard next to Pajala kyrka on Kyrkallén. Close by, on Prästgårdsallén, **Laestadiuspörtet** (mid-June to mid-Aug daily 10am–6pm; 40kr) is the simple unassuming house he once lived in; the entrance fee includes a guided tour and coffee.

Practicalities

The **bus station**, right in the centre of town, contains the **tourist office** (May–Aug Mon–Fri 9am–5pm; mid-June to mid-Aug also Sat & Sun 9am–5pm; Sept–April Mon–Fri 9am–5pm; ℡0978/100 15, ⍟www.pajalaturism.bd.se). For **accommodation**, the *Bykrogen Hotell*, close by at Soukolovägen 2 (℡0978/712 00, ⍟www.bykrogen.se; ❹/❸) has cosy little rooms; *Hotell Smedjan*, Fridhemsvägen 1 (℡0978/108 15, ⍟www.fa-hotell-rest.se/se/index.html; ❹/❷), has similar en-suite rooms. The best place to stay, however, is right at the other end of the village at *Pajala Camping* (℡0978/741 80; May–Sept), with its stunning views over the lazy Torne river; there are simple two-bed **cabins** here with cold water and a hotplate only (nos. 1–16 285kr per night) or fully equipped larger four-berth ones with a kitchen (nos. 17 & 18 for 485kr per night). During any of the festivals accommodation is in short supply and it's necessary to book well ahead. For **eating** and **drinking**, head for the *Bykrogen Hotell* at lunchtime for the cheapest meals – *Dagens Rätt* goes for 66kr, traditional northern Swedish delicacies start at 120kr. For pizzas, head for the *Tre Kronor* pizzeria in the centre of town on Tornedalsvägen and reckon on around 60kr.

Laestadius and the demon drink

No other man has made a greater impression on northern Scandinavia than **Lars Levi Laestadius**, the Swedish revivalist preacher who dedicated his life to saving people in three different countries from the perils of **alcoholism**. Born in Jäkkvik in 1800 and educated in Kvikkjokk, the young Laestadius soon developed a close relationship with the indigenous *Sámi*, many of whom had turned to drink to escape the harsh reality of their daily lives. It was while the priest was working in Karesuando (1826–49) that he met **Maria of Åsele**, the *Sámi* woman who inspired him to steer people towards a life of total purity. Following Laestadius's death in Pajala in 1861, the movement continued under the leadership of Juhani Raattamaa before splitting into two opposing branches: a conservative western group in Sweden and Norway, and a more liberal eastern one in Finland. Today tens of thousands of teetotal Swedes, Finns, Norwegians and *Sámi* across the Arctic area of Scandinavia still follow Laestadius's teachings; they're not allowed to have flowers or curtains in their homes, nor are they permitted to wear a tie, listen to the radio or watch TV. Drinking, of course, is totally out of the question.

Karesuando and around

Sweden's northernmost village, **KARESUANDO**, 180km north of Pajala, is a surprisingly likeable little place that you can reach from Pajala by bus by changing in nearby Vittangi. This is as good a spot as any to take stock of just where you've reached: the North Cape is barely 500km away, you're as far north as Canada's Baffin Island and the northern tip of Alaska, and the tree line slices through the edge of the village. **Winters** up here can be particularly severe; the first snow falls at the end of September or early October and stays on the ground until late May, when the Muonioälven, the river which curls around the village, also finally melts. Just a few centimetres beneath the surface, the ground is in the grip of **permafrost** all year round. Summer here is short and sweet – except that the region becomes a mosquito paradise then.

Karesuando is right in the midst of *Sámi* heartland; reindeer husbandry, particularly in the nearby villages of Övre and Nedre Soppero, as well as in Idivuoma, where many herders live, is of primary importance to the local economy. Nevertheless unemployment remains stubbornly high.

The only sight to speak of in Karesuando is beyond the tourist office: the wooden cabin here was once the rectory of **Lars Levi Laestadius**, the village's most famous son (see box opposite). Complete with simple wooden pews, it was used as a meeting place while Laestadius was rector in Karesuando; the cabin is now a simple **museum** of his life and works. Also worth a quick look, along the road to the campsite, is the village **museum** (Mon–Fri 10am–noon & 1pm–3.30pm; 20kr), known as *Vita Huset*, containing a few atmospheric black and white photographs from 1944 when Karesuando was inundated by Finns fleeing the approaching German forces – with their cattle. Look, in particular, for the picture of Olga Raattamaa, known locally as Empress Olga, who once lived in nearby Kummavuopio, and single-handedly

Treriksröset

Heading north for **Treriksröset** – the **three-nation marker post** where Sweden, Norway and Finland all meet – walk over the bridge to Karesuvando in Finland, from where a daily bus leaves at 2pm (remember Finland is an hour ahead of Sweden) for **Kilpisjärvi** (journey time 2hr). From June to mid-Sept a second daily bus leaves at 4.30pm for Tromsø in Norway travelling via Kilpisjärvi. From here, there are two ways to get to Treriksröset. One of these is a hike of 11km down a track which passes through an area of dwarf woodland before running around a small lake to reach Sweden's northernmost point, marked by a yellow bell-shaped piece of concrete, suspended in a lake and surrounded by wooden walkways; don't forget your camera and mosquito repellent. The path then continues (14km) towards the **northernmost peak** in Sweden, **Pältsan** (1445m); the going here is rocky in parts. The STF **cabins** at the foot of the mountain, two of Sweden's most northerly buildings, boast thirty beds and a sauna (late March to early May & early July to mid-Sept). There's an easy hike (40km) from the Pältsa cabins back to **Keinovuopio** (see p.504), then across the river to the main E8 road in Finland, where you can catch the bus back towards Karesuando (daily; late morning).

Alternatively, you can reach Treriksröset from Kilpisjärvi by getting a **boat ride** across the lake on board *M/S Malla*, which shortens the hike to just 3km. The boat requires at least four passengers if it's to sail (July to mid-Aug 9am, 1pm & 5pm Swedish time; 20min; 80kr return); for boat information ask at the tourist office in Karesuando or call the Finnish number ℡00358/16 53 77 83 or the boat directly on ℡00358/49 394 173.

saved the lives of dozens of Finns by rowing them across the Könkämä river to safety in neutral Sweden. Beyond the museum, further along the same road, is the **Sámiid Viessu**, a **photography** and **handicraft exhibition** (July to mid-Aug daily 10am–7pm), which has some atmospheric black and white shots of *Sámi* gatherings from generations past; there's also a small **café** serving up coffee and cakes.

With your own transport, it's well worth the short drive south along Route 400 for fantastic **views** over the surrounding tundra: about 5–10 minutes after leaving the village, take the right turn marked "Kaarevaara" and continue past a small lake, whereupon the road begins to climb up past a TV mast and eventually ends in a small car park. On a clear day you can see for miles across the Swedish and Finnish tundra from up here. The vast tract of land you'll see stretching away to the northwest contains **Treriksröset**, the point where Sweden, Finland and Norway meet (see box, above).

Practicalities

National **borders** in northern Scandinavia carry little significance: people cross them without as much as batting an eyelid as they go about their everyday duties. Since Finland is just a stone's throw away across the river, business in Karesuando is done in both Swedish kronor and euro.

The **tourist office** (mid-June to mid-Aug daily 8am–8pm; rest of the year Mon–Fri 8am–3pm; ☏0981/202 05, ⓦwww.karesuando.com) is in the customs house on the bridge across to Finland. There are various **accommodation** options including *Karesuando Camping* (☏0981/201 39; June to mid-Sept), a 2km walk past the church, heading out of the village along the main road towards Pajala. A number of four-berth **cabins** are available at the campsite; those with a simple kitchen go for 375kr, those without are a little smaller and cost 275kr; there's a separate toilet and shower block. On the same road, though 5min before the campsite, the **youth hostel** (☏0981/200 00, ☏0981/203 70; mid-May to mid-Sept) enjoys a fantastic waterside location and is the best place to stay in the village. Immediately opposite, the dowdy *Hotell Karesuando* (☏0981/203 30, ⓦwww.hotellkaresuando.com; ②) is useful only as a last resort. To get away from it all, there are **cabins** in the wilds at **Keinovuopio**, a tiny settlement that's home to just fifteen people, right on the Könkämä river in the far northwestern corner of Sweden; these can be booked through the tourist office for 250kr per day. To reach Keinovuopio, cross the river to **Karesuvanto** in Finland, and then take a Finnish bus towards **Kilpisjärvi**, from where there's a footbridge back over the river to Swedish Keinovuopio.

There's just one **eating** place in Karesuando, a greasy-spoon grill-restaurant at the opposite end of the village to all accommodation options, between the Statoil and OK filling stations, run by the same people who look after the youth hostel. Both these stations have limited supplies of food for sale, but a better option for **provisions** is the ICA shop opposite Statoil.

Travel details

Trains	
The Inlandsbanan runs from Mora to Gällivare via Östersund from late June to early Aug. Northbound trains leave Östersund daily for Gällivare at 7.05am calling at Ulriksfors (for Strömsund), Dorotea, Vilhelmina, Storuman, Sorsele, Arvidsjaur, the Arctic Circle, Jokkmokk and Gällivare.	Southbound trains leave Gällivare daily at 6.45am for stations to Östersund. For details of the Mora-Östersund stretch, see Travel Details p.455 (Central Sweden). Abisko to: Boden (2 daily; 4hr 20min); Gällivare (2 daily; 2hr 30min); Kiruna (3 daily; 1hr 20min); Narvik (3 daily; 1hr min); Riksgränsen (3 daily; 40min); Stockholm (1 daily; 18hr).

Gällivare to: Boden (3 daily; 2hr); Gävle (2 daily; 14hr); Gothenburg (1 daily; 19hr 30min); Kiruna (3 daily; 1hr); Luleå (3 daily; 2hr 20min); Stockholm (2 daily; 16hr 30min); Umeå (1 daily; 7hr); Uppsala (2 daily; 15hr 30min).

Kiruna to: Boden (3 daily; 3hr); Gothenburg (1 daily; 20hr 30min); Luleå (3 daily; 3hr 20min); Narvik (3 daily; 3hr); Stockholm (2 daily; 17hr 30min); Uppsala (2 daily; 16hr 30min).

Riksgränsen to: Abisko (3 daily; 40min); Boden (2 daily; 5hr); Gällivare (2 daily; 3hr); Kiruna (3 daily; 2hr); Narvik (3 daily; 1hr); Stockholm (1 daily; 19hr).

Buses

The **Inlandsexpressen** (#45) runs north from Östersund to Strömsund, Dorotea, Vilhelmina, Storuman, Sorsele, Arvidsjaur, Jokkmokk and Porjus. It operates daily all year round, leaving Mora at 8am and 2pm for Östersund, and leaving from Östersund at 7am for Gällivare, at 1.40pm for Arvidsjaur and at 4.55pm for Storuman.

Southbound, a bus leaves Gällivare at 9.30am for Östersund, from Arvidsjaur at 8.35am for Öster-sund and from Storuman at 7.10am for Östersund. The **Lapplandspilen** express runs overnight from Stockholm to Hemavan via Arlanda airport, Uppsala, Gävle, Söderhamn, Hudiksvall, Sundsvall, Härnösand, Sollefteå, Vilhelmina, Storuman and Tärnaby. Northbound services leave Stockholm on Wed and Fri, southbound services return from Hemavan on Thurs and Sun. For information call ☎0951/779 50 or check
ⓦwww.lapplandspilen.se.

Arjeplog to: Arvidsjaur (4 daily; 1hr 15min).

Arvidsjaur to: Arjeplog (4 daily; 1hr).

Gällivare to: Jokkmokk (5 daily; 1hr 30min); Kiruna (4 daily; 2hr); Pajala (3 daily; 2hr 20min); Ritsem (3 daily; 3hr 30min).

Jokkmokk to: Gällivare (5 daily; 1hr 30min); Kvikkjokk (2 daily; 1hr 50min)

Kiruna to: Gällivare (3 daily; 2hr); Karesuando (2 daily; 3hr); Pajala (2 daily; 3hr 15min); Nikkaluokta (3 daily; 1hr 10min).

Kvikkjokk to: Jokkmokk (2 daily; 1hr 50min).

Sorsele to: Ammarnäs (3 daily; 1hr 30min).

Storuman to: Tärnaby (4 daily; 2hr); Hemavan (3 daily; 2hr 20min).

7

SWEDISH LAPLAND | Travel details

Contexts

Contexts

History

Sweden has one of Europe's longest documented histories, but for all the upheavals of the Viking times and the warring of the Middle Ages, the country has, in modern times, seemed to delight in taking a historical back seat. For one brief period, when Prime Minister Olof Palme was shot dead in 1986, Sweden was thrust into the limelight. Since then, however, the country has regained some of its equilibrium, though political infighting and domestic disharmony can often threaten the one thing that the Swedes have always been proud of and that other countries aspire to: the politics of consensus, the potential passing of which is arguably of far greater importance than even the assassination of their prime minister.

Early Civilizations

It was not until around 6000 BC that the **first settlers** roamed north and east into Sweden, living as nomadic reindeer hunters and herders. By 3000 BC people had settled in the south of the country and were established as farmers; from 2000 BC there are indications of a development in burial practices, with **dolmens** and **passage graves** found throughout the southern Swedish provinces. Traces also remain of the **Boat Axe People**, named after their characteristic tool/weapon, shaped like a boat. The earliest horse riders in Scandinavia, they quickly held sway over the whole of southern Sweden.

During the **Bronze Age** (1500–500 BC) the Boat Axe People traded furs and amber for southern European copper and tin. Large finds of finished ornaments and weapons show a comparatively rich culture. This was emphasized by elaborate burial rites, the dead laid in single graves under mounds of earth and stone.

The deterioration of the Scandinavian climate in the last millennium before Christ coincided with the advance across Europe of the Celts, which halted the flourishing trade of the Swedish settlers. With the new millennium, Sweden made its first mark upon the Classical world. In the *Historia Naturalis*, Pliny the Elder (23–79 AD) mentioned the "island of Scatinavia" far to the north. Tacitus was more specific: in 98 AD he mentioned a powerful people who were strong in men, weapons and ships, the *Suinoes* – a reference to the **Svear**, who were to form the nucleus of an emergent Swedish kingdom by the sixth century.

The Svear settled in the rich land around Lake Mälaren and became rulers of most of the territory comprising modern Sweden, except the south. They gave Sweden its modern name: *Sverige* in Swedish or *Svear rik*, the kingdom of the Svear. More importantly, their first dynastic leaders had a taste for expansion, trading with Gotland and holding suzerainty over the Åland Islands.

The Viking period

The Vikings – raiders and warriors who dominated the political and economic life of Europe and beyond from the ninth to the eleventh centuries – came from all parts of southern Scandinavia. But there is evidence that the **Swedish**

Vikings were among the first to leave home, the impetus being rapid population growth, domestic unrest and a desire for new lands. Sweden being located on the eastern part of the Scandinavian peninsula, the raiders turned their attention largely eastwards, in the knowledge that the Svear had already reached the Baltic. By the ninth century, the trade routes were well established, with Swedes reaching the Black and Caspian seas and making valuable trading contact with the **Byzantine Empire**. Although more commercially inclined than their Danish and Norwegian counterparts, Swedish Vikings were quick to use force if profits were slow to materialize. From 860 onwards Greek and Muslim records relate a series of raids across the Black Sea against Byzantium, and across the Caspian into northeast Iran.

The Vikings were settlers as well as traders and exploiters, and their long-term influence was marked. Embattled Slavs to the east gave them the name **Rus**, and their creeping colonization gave one area in which the Vikings settled its modern name, Russia. Russian names today – Oleg, Igor, Vladimir – can be derived from the Swedish – Helgi, Ingvar, Valdemar.

Domestically, **paganism** was at its height; dynastic leaders would claim descent from Freyr, "God of the World". It was a bloody time: nine **human sacrifices** were offered at the celebrations held every nine years at Uppsala. Adam of Bremen recorded that the great shrine there was adjoined by a sacred grove where "every tree is believed divine because of the death and putrefaction of the victims hanging there".

Viking **law** was based on the *Thing*, an assembly of free men to which the king's power was subject. Each largely autonomous province had its own assembly and its own leaders: where several provinces united, the approval of each *Thing* was needed for any choice of leader. For centuries in Sweden, each newly elected king had to make a formal tour to receive the homage of each province.

The arrival of Christianity and the Early Middle Ages

Christianity was slow to take root in Sweden. Whereas Denmark and Norway had accepted the faith by the turn of the eleventh century, the Swedes remained largely heathen. Missionaries met with limited success: no Swedish king was converted until 1008, when **Olof Skötonung** was baptized. He was the first known king of both Swedes and Goths (that is, ruler of the two major provinces of Västergötland and Östergötland), and his successors were all Christians. Nevertheless, paganism retained a grip on Swedish affairs, and as late as the 1080s the Svear banished the then king, Inge, when he refused to take part in the pagan celebrations at Uppsala. By the end of the eleventh century, though, the temple at Uppsala had gone and a Christian church was built on its site. In the 1130s, Sigtuna – original centre of the Swedish Christian faith was replaced by Uppsala as the main episcopal seat, and in 1164 Stephen, an English monk, was made the first archbishop.

The whole of the early Middle Ages in Sweden was characterized by a succession of struggles for control of a growing central power. Principally two families, the Sverkers and the Eriks, waged battle against each other throughout the twelfth century. **King Erik** was the first Sverker king to make his mark: in 1157 he led a crusade to heathen Finland, but was killed in 1160 at Uppsala by a Danish pretender to his throne. Within 100 years he was to be recognized as patron saint of Sweden, and his remains interred in the new Uppsala Cathedral.

Erik was succeeded by his son **Knut**, whose stable reign lasted until 1196, a period marked by commercial treaties and strengthened defences. Following his death, virtual civil war weakened royal power. As a result, the king's chief ministers, or **Jarls**, assumed much of the executive responsibility for running the country, so much so that when Erik Eriksson (last of the Eriks) was deposed in 1229, his administrator **Birger Jarl** assumed power. With papal support for his crusading policies he confirmed the Swedish grip on the south-west of Finland. His son, Valdemar, succeeded him but proved a weak ruler, and didn't survive the family feuding after Birger Jarl's death.

In 1275, Valdemar's brother, **Magnus Ladulås**, assumed power. He earned his nickname "Ladulås", or "Barn-lock", from his having prevented the nobility from claiming maintenance at the expense of the peasantry, who travelled from estate to estate. Magnus's reign represented a peak of Swedish royal might not to be repeated for 300 years. While he was king, his enemies dissipated; he forbade the nobility to meet without his consent, and began to issue his own authoritative decrees. He also began to reap the benefits of conversion: the clergy became an educated class upon whom the monarch could rely for diplomatic and administrative duties. By the thirteenth century, there were ambitious Swedish clerics in Paris and Bologna, and the first stone churches were appearing in Sweden, the most monumental of which is the early Gothic **cathedral** built at Uppsala.

Meanwhile, the nobility had come to constitute a military class, exempt from taxation on the understanding that they would defend the crown. In the country the standard of living was still low, although an increasing population stimulated new cultivation. The forests of Norrland were pushed back, more southern heathland turned into pasture, and crop rotation introduced. Noticeable, too, was the increasing **German influence** within Sweden as the Hansa traders spread. Their first merchants settled in Visby and, by the mid-thirteenth century, in Stockholm.

The fourteenth century – towards unity

Magnus died in 1290, power shifting to a cabal of magnates led by **Torgil Knutsson**. As marshal of Sweden, he pursued an energetic foreign policy, conquering western Karelia to gain control of the Gulf of Finland, and building the fortress at Viborg, only lost with the collapse of the Swedish Empire in the eighteenth century.

Magnus's son Birger came of age in 1302 and soon quarrelled with his brothers Erik and Valdemar, who had Torgil Knutsson executed. They then rounded on Birger, who was forced to divide up Sweden among the three of them. An unhappy arrangement, it lasted until 1317 when Birger had his brothers arrested and starved to death in prison – an act that prompted a shocked nobility to rise against Birger and force his exile to Denmark. The Swedish nobles restored the principle of elective monarchy by calling on the three-year-old **Magnus** (son of a Swedish duke, and already declared Norwegian king) to take the Swedish crown. During his minority, a treaty was concluded in 1323 with Novgorod in Russia to define the frontiers in eastern and northern Finland. This left virtually the whole of the Scandinavian peninsula (except the Danish provinces in the south) under one ruler.

Yet Sweden was still anything but prosperous. The **Black Death** reached the country in 1350, wiping out whole parishes and killing perhaps a third of the population. Subsequent labour shortages and troubled estates meant that the nobility found it difficult to maintain their positions. German merchants had driven the Swedes from their most lucrative trade routes: even the copper and iron-ore **mining** that began around this time in Bergslagen and Dalarna relied on German capital.

Magnus soon ran into trouble and was threatened further by the accession of Valdemar Atterdag to the Danish throne in 1340. Squabbles concerning sovereignty over the Danish provinces of Skåne and Blekinge led to Danish incursions into Sweden; in 1361, Valdemar landed on Gotland and sacked **Visby**. The Gotlanders were massacred outside the city walls, refused refuge by the Hansa merchants.

Magnus was forced to negotiate and his son **Håkon** – now king of Norway – was married to Valdemar's daughter Margaret. When Magnus was later deposed, power fell into the hands of the magnates who shared out the country. Chief of the ruling nobles was the Steward **Bo Jonsson Grip**, who controlled virtually all Finland and central and southeast Sweden. Yet on his death, the nobility turned to Håkon's wife **Margaret**, already regent in Norway (for her son Olof) and in Denmark since the death of her father, Valdemar. The nobles were anxious for union across Scandinavia, to safeguard those who owned frontier estates and strengthen the crown against any further German influence. In 1388 she was proclaimed "First Lady" of Sweden and, in return, confirmed all the privileges of the Swedish nobility. Called upon to choose a male king, Margaret nominated her nephew, **Erik of Pomerania**, who was duly elected king of Sweden in 1396. As he had already been elected to the Danish and Norwegian thrones, Scandinavian unity seemed assured.

The Kalmar Union

Erik was crowned king of Denmark, Norway and Sweden in 1397 at a ceremony in **Kalmar**. Nominally, the three kingdoms were now in union but, despite Erik's kingship, real power remained in the hands of Margaret until her death in 1412.

Erik was at war with the Hanseatic League throughout his reign. He was vilified in popular Swedish history as an evil and grasping ruler, and the taxes he raised went on a war that was never fought on Swedish soil. He spent his time instead in Denmark, directing operations, leaving his queen Philippa (sister to Henry V of England) behind. Erik was deposed in 1439 and the nobility turned to **Christopher of Bavaria**, whose early death in 1448 led to the first major breach in the union.

No one candidate could fill the three kingships satisfactorily, and separate elections in Denmark and Sweden signalled a renewal of the infighting that had plagued the previous century. Within Sweden, unionists and nationalists skirmished, the powerful unionist **Oxenstierna** family opposing the claims of the nationalist **Sture** family, until 1470 when **Sten Sture** (the Elder) became "Guardian of the Realm". His victory over the unionists at the **Battle of Brunkeberg** (1471) – in the centre of what's now modern Stockholm – was complete, gaining symbolic artistic expression in the **statue of St George and the Dragon** that still adorns the Great Church in Stockholm.

Sten Sture's primacy fostered a new cultural atmosphere. The first **university** in Scandinavia was founded in Uppsala in 1477, with Sweden's first printing press appearing six years later. Artistically, German and Dutch influences were great, traits seen in the decorative art of the great Swedish medieval churches. Only remote **Dalarna** kept alive a native folk art tradition.

Belief in the union still existed though, particularly outside Sweden, and successive kings had to fend off almost constant attacks and blockades emanating from Denmark. With the accession of **Christian II** to the Danish throne in 1513, the unionist movement found a leader capable of turning the tide. Under the guise of a crusade to free Sweden's imprisoned archbishop Gustav Trolle, Christian attacked Sweden and killed Sture. After Christian's coronation, Trolle urged the prosecution of his Swedish adversaries (who had been gathered together under the pretext of an amnesty) and they were found guilty of heresy. Eighty-two nobles and burghers of Stockholm were executed, their bodies burned in what became known as the **Stockholm Blood Bath**. A vicious persecution of Sture's followers throughout Sweden ensued, a move that led to widespread reaction and, ultimately, the downfall of the union.

Gustav Vasa and his sons

Opposition to Christian II was vague and disorganized until the appearance of the young **Gustav Vasa**. Initially unable to stir the locals of the Dalecarlia region into open revolt, he was on his way to Norway, and exile, when he was chased on skis and recalled, the people having had a change of heart. The chase is celebrated still in the **Vasaloppet** race, run each year by thousands of Swedish skiers.

Gustav Vasa's army grew rapidly. In 1521 he was elected regent, and subsequently, with the capture of Stockholm in 1523, king. Christian had been deposed in Denmark and the new Danish king, Frederick I, recognized Sweden's de facto withdrawal from the union. Short of cash, Gustav found it prudent to support the movement for religious reform propagated by Swedish Lutherans. More of a political than a religious **Reformation**, the result was a handover of Church lands to the Crown and the subordination of Church to state. It's a relationship that is still largely in force today, the clergy being civil servants paid by the state.

In 1541 the first edition of the Bible in the vernacular appeared. Suppressing revolt at home, Gustav Vasa strengthened his hand with a centralization of trade and government. On his death in 1560, Sweden was united, prosperous and independent.

Gustav Vasa's heir, his eldest son **Erik**, faced a difficult time, not least because the Vasa lands and wealth had been divided among him and his brothers Johan, Magnus and Karl (an uncharacteristically imprudent action of Gustav before his death). The Danes, too, pressed hard, reasserting their claim to the Swedish throne in the inconclusive **Northern Seven Years' War**, which began in 1563. Erik was deposed in 1569 by his brother who became **Johan III**, his first act being to end the war by the **Peace of Stettin** treaty. At home, Johan ruled more or less with the goodwill of the nobility, but matters were upset by his Catholic sympathies: he introduced Catholic liturgy and the Catholic-influenced *Red Book*. On Johan's death in 1592, his son and heir, Sigismund (who was Catholic king of Poland) agreed to rule Sweden in accordance with Lutheran practice, but failed to do so. When Sigismund returned to Poland the way was clear for Duke Karl (Johan's brother) to assume the regency, a role he filled until declared King **Karl IX** in 1603.

Karl, the last of Vasa's sons, had ambitions eastwards but was routed by the Poles and staved off by the Russians. He suffered a stroke in 1610 and died the year after. His heir was the seventeen-year-old Gustav II, better known as **Gustav II Adolf**.

The rule of Vasa and his sons made Sweden a nation, culturally as well as politically. The courts were filled with and influenced by men of learning; art and sculpture flourished. The **Renaissance** style appeared for the first time in Sweden, with royal castles remodelled – Kalmar being a fine example. Economically, Sweden remained mostly self-sufficient, its few imports being luxuries like cloth, wine and spices. With around eight thousand inhabitants, Stockholm was its most important city, although **Gothenburg** was founded in 1607 to promote trade to the west.

C

Gustav II Adolf and the rise of the Swedish Empire

Sweden became a European power during the reign of **Gustav II Adolf**. Though still in his youth he was considered able enough to rule, and proved so by concluding peace treaties with Denmark (1613) and Russia (1617), the latter pact isolating Russia from the Baltic and allowing the Swedes control of the eastern trade routes into Europe.

In 1618, the **Thirty Years' War** broke out. It was vital for Gustav that Germany should not become Catholic, given the Polish king's continuing pretensions to the Swedish crown and the possible threat it could pose to Sweden's growing influence in the Baltic. In 1629, the Altmark treaty with a defeated Poland gave Gustav control of Livonia and four Prussian seaports, and the income this generated financed his entry into the war in 1630 on the Protestant side. After several convincing victories, Gustav pushed on through Germany, delaying an assault upon undefended Vienna. The decision cost him his life: Gustav was killed at the **Battle of Lützen** in 1632, his body stripped and battered by the enemy's soldiers. The war dragged on until the **Peace of Westphalia** in 1648.

With Gustav away at war for much of his reign, Sweden ran smoothly under the guidance of his friend and chancellor, **Axel Oxenstierna**. Together they founded a new Supreme Court in Stockholm (and did the same for Finland and the conquered Baltic provinces); reorganized the national assembly into four Estates of nobility, clergy, burghers and peasantry (1626); extended the university at Uppsala (and founded one at Åbo – modern Turku in Finland); and fostered the mining and other industries that provided much of the country's wealth. Gustav had many other accomplishments, too: he spoke five languages and designed a new light cannon, which assisted in his routs of the enemy.

The Caroleans

The Swedish empire reached its territorial peak under the **Caroleans**. Yet the reign of the last of them was to see Sweden crumble.

Following Gustav II Adolf's death and the later abdication of his daughter Christina, **Karl X** succeeded to the throne. War against Poland (1655) led to some early successes and, with Denmark espousing the Polish cause, gave Karl the opportunity to march into Jutland (1657). From there his armies marched across the frozen sea to threaten Copenhagen; the subsequent **Treaty of Roskilde** (1658) broke Denmark and gave the Swedish empire its widest territorial extent.

However, the long regency of his son and heir, **Karl XI**, did little to safeguard Sweden's vulnerable position, so extensive were its borders. On assuming power in 1672, Karl was almost immediately dragged into war: beaten by a smaller Prussian army at Brandenberg in 1675, Sweden was suddenly faced with war against both the Danes and Dutch. Karl rallied, though, to drive out the Danish invaders, and the war ended in 1679 with the reconquest of Skåne and the restoration of most of Sweden's German provinces.

In 1682, Karl XI became **absolute monarch** and was given full control over legislation and *reduktion* – the resumption of estates previously alienated by the Crown to the nobility. The armed forces were reorganized too: by 1700, the Swedish army had 25,000 soldiers and twelve regiments of cavalry; the naval fleet had expanded to 38 ships and a new base had been built at **Karlskrona** (which was nearer to the likely trouble spots than Stockholm).

Culturally, Sweden began to benefit from the innovations of Gustav II Adolf. *Gymnasia* (grammar schools) continued to expand, and a second university was established at **Lund** in 1668. A national **literature** emerged, helped by the efforts of **George Stiernhielm**, father of modern Swedish poetry. **Olof Rudbeck** (1630–1702) was a Nordic polymath whose scientific reputation lasted longer than his attempt to identify the ancient Goth settlement at Uppsala as Atlantis. Architecturally, this was the age of **Tessin**, both father and son. Tessin the Elder was responsible for the glorious palace at **Drottningholm**, work on which began in 1662, as well as the cathedral at **Kalmar**. His son, Tessin the Younger, succeeded him as royal architect and was to create the new royal palace at Stockholm.

In 1697, the fifteen-year-old **Karl XII** succeeded to the throne; under him, the empire collapsed. Faced with a defensive alliance of Saxony, Denmark and Russia, there was little the king could have done to avoid eventual defeat. However, he remains a revered figure for his valiant (often suicidal) efforts to take on the rest of Europe. Initial victories against Peter the Great and Saxony led him to march on Russia, where he was defeated and the bulk of his army destroyed. Escaping to Turkey, where he remained as guest and then prisoner for four years, Karl watched the empire disintegrate. With Poland reconquered by Augustus of Saxony, and Finland by Peter the Great, he returned to Sweden only to have England declare war on him.

Eventually, splits in the enemy alliance led Swedish diplomats to attempt peace talks with Russia. Karl, though, was keen to exploit these differences in a more direct fashion. Wanting to strike at Denmark, but lacking a fleet, he besieged Fredrikshald in Norway (then united with Denmark) in 1718 – and was killed by a sniper's bullet. In the power vacuum thus created, Russia became the leading Baltic force, receiving Livonia, Estonia, Ingria and most of Karelia from Sweden.

The Age of Freedom

The eighteenth century saw absolutism discredited in Sweden. A new constitution vested power in the Estates, who reduced the new king **Frederick I**'s role to that of nominal head of state. The chancellor wielded the real power, and under **Arvid Horn** the country found a period of stability. His party, nicknamed the "Caps", was opposed by the hawkish "Hats". The latter forced war with Russia in 1741, a disaster in which Sweden lost all of Finland and had its whole east coast burned and bombed. Most of Finland was returned with the agreement that **Adolphus Frederick** (a relation of the crown prince of Russia) would be elected to the Swedish throne on Frederick I's death. This duly occurred in 1751.

During his reign, Adolphus repeatedly tried to reassert royal power, but found that the constitution was only strengthened against him. The Estates' power was such that when Adolphus refused to sign any bills, they simply utilized a stamp bearing his name. The resurrected "Hats" forced entry into the **Seven Years' War** in 1757 on the French side, another disastrous venture, as the Prussians were able to repel every Swedish attack.

The aristocratic parties were in a state of constant flux. Although elections of sorts were held to provide delegates for the *Riksdag* (parliament), foreign sympathies, bribery and bickering were hardly conducive to democratic administration. Cabals continued to rule Sweden, the economy was stagnant, and reform delayed. It was, however, an age of **intellectual and scientific advance**, surprising in a country that had lost much of its cultural impetus. **Carl von Linné**, the botanist whose classification of plants is still used, was professor at Uppsala from 1741 to 1778; **Anders Celsius** initiated the use of the centigrade temperature scale; **Carl Scheele** discovered chlorine. A royal decree of 1748 organized Europe's first full-scale **census**, a five-yearly event by 1775. Other fields flourished, too. The mystical works of **Emmanuel Swedenborg**, the philosopher who died in 1772, encouraged new theological sects; and the period encompassed the life of **Carl Michael Bellman** (1740–95), the celebrated Swedish poet (see also p.325) whose work did much to identify and foster a popular nationalism.

With the accession of **Gustav III** in 1771, the Crown began to regain the ascendancy. A new constitution was forced upon a divided *Riksdag* and proved a watershed between earlier absolutism and the later aristocratic squabbles. A popular king, Gustav founded hospitals, granted freedom of worship and removed many of the state controls over the economy. His determination to conduct a successful foreign policy led to further conflict with Russia (1788–90) in which, to everyone's surprise, he managed to more than hold his own. But with the French Revolution polarizing opposition throughout Europe, the Swedish nobility began to entertain thoughts of conspiracy against a king whose growing powers they now saw as those of a tyrant. In 1792, at a masked ball in Stockholm Opera House, the king was shot by an assassin hired by the disaffected aristocracy. Gustav died two weeks later and was succeeded by his son **Gustav IV**, with the country being led by a regency during his minority.

The wars waged by revolutionary France were at first studiously avoided in Sweden but, pulled into the conflict by the British, Gustav IV entered the **Napoleonic Wars** in 1805. However, Napoleon's victory at Austerlitz two years later broke the coalition and Sweden found itself isolated. Attacked by Russia the following year, Gustav was later arrested and deposed, and his uncle was elected king.

A constitution of 1809 established a liberal monarchy in Sweden, responsible to the elected *Riksdag*. Under this constitution **Karl XIII** was a mere caretaker, his heir a Danish prince who would bring Norway back to Sweden – some compensation for finally losing Finland and the Åland Islands to Russia (1809) after 500 years of Swedish rule. On the prince's sudden death, however, Marshal Bernadotte (one of Napoleon's generals) was invited to become heir. Taking the name of **Karl Johan**, he took his chance in 1812 and joined Britain and Russia to fight Napoleon. Following Napoleon's first defeat at the Battle of Leipzig in 1813, Sweden compelled Denmark (France's ally) to exchange Norway for Swedish Pomerania.

By 1814 Sweden and Norway had formed an uneasy union. Norway retained its own government and certain autonomous measures. Sweden decided foreign policy, appointed a viceroy and retained a suspensive (but not absolute) veto over the Norwegian parliament's legislation.

The nineteenth century

Union under Karl Johan, or **Karl XIV** as he became in 1818, could have been disastrous. He spoke no Swedish and just a few years previously had never visited either kingdom. However, under Karl and his successor **Oscar I**, prosperity ensued. The **Göta Canal** (1832) helped commercially, and liberal measures by both monarchs helped politically. In 1845 daughters were given an equal right of inheritance. A Poor Law was introduced in 1847, restrictive craft guilds reformed, and an Education Act passed.

The 1848 revolutions throughout Europe cooled Oscar's reforming ardour, and his attention turned to reviving **Scandinavianism**. It was still a hope, in certain quarters, that closer cooperation between Denmark and Sweden–Norway could lead to some sort of revived Kalmar Union. Expectations were raised with the **Crimean War** of 1854: Russia as a future threat could be neutralized. But peace was declared too quickly (at least for Sweden) and there was still no real guarantee that Sweden would be sufficiently protected from Russia in the future. With Oscar's death, talk of political union faded.

His son **Karl XV** presided over a reform of the *Riksdag* that put an end to the Swedish system of personal monarchy. The Four Estates were replaced by a representative two-house parliament along European lines. This, together with the end of political Scandinavianism (following the Prussian attack on Denmark in 1864 in which Sweden stood by), marked Sweden's entry into modern Europe.

Industrialization was slow to take root in Sweden. No real industrial revolution occurred, and development – mechanization, introduction of railways, etc – was piecemeal. One result was widespread **emigration** amongst the rural poor, who had been hard hit by famine in 1867 and 1868. Between 1860 and 1910 over one million people left for America (in 1860 the Swedish population was only four million). Given huge farms to settle, the emigrants headed for land similar to that they had left behind – to the Midwest, Kansas and Nebraska.

At home, Swedish **trade unionism** emerged to campaign for better conditions. Dealt with severely, the unions formed a confederation (1898) but largely failed to make headway. Even peaceful picketing carried a two-year prison sentence. Hand in hand with the fight for workers' rights went the **temperance movement**. The level of alcohol consumption was alarming and various abstinence programmes attempted to educate the drinkers and, if necessary, eradicate the stills. Some towns made the selling of spirits a municipal monopoly – not a big step from the state monopoly that exists today.

With the accession of **Oscar II** in 1872, Sweden continued on an even, if uneventful, keel. Keeping out of further European conflict (the Austro–Prussian War, Franco–Prussian War and various Balkan crises), the country's only worry was growing dissatisfaction in Norway with the union. Demanding a separate consular service, and objecting to the Swedish king's veto on constitutional matters, the Norwegians brought things to a head, and in 1905 declared the union invalid. The Karlstad Convention confirmed the break and Norway became independent for the first time since 1380.

The late nineteenth century was a happier time for Swedish culture. **August Strindberg** enjoyed great critical success and artists like **Anders Zorn** and **Prince Eugene** made their mark abroad. The historian **Artur Hazelius** founded the Nordic and Skansen museums in Stockholm; and the chemist, industrialist and dynamite inventor **Alfred Nobel** left his fortune to finance the Nobel Prizes. It's an instructive tale: Nobel hoped that the knowledge of his invention would help eradicate war, optimistically believing that humankind would never dare unleash the destructive forces of dynamite.

The two World Wars

Sweden declared strict neutrality on the outbreak of **World War I**, influenced by much sympathy within the country for Germany, stemming from the longstanding cultural, trade and linguistic links. It was a policy agreed with the other Scandinavian monarchs, but a difficult one to pursue. Faced with British demands to enforce a blockade of Germany and with the blacklisting and eventual seizure of Swedish goods at sea, the economy suffered grievously; rationing and inflation mushroomed. The **Russian Revolution** in 1917 brought further problems to Sweden. The Finns immediately declared independence, waging civil war against the Bolsheviks, and Swedish volunteers enlisted in the White Army. But a conflict of interest arose when the Swedish-speaking Åland Islands wanted a return to Swedish rule rather than stay under the victorious Finns. The League of Nations overturned this claim, granting the islands to Finland.

After the war, a Liberal–Socialist coalition remained in power until 1920, when **Branting** became the first socialist prime minister. By the time of his death in 1924, franchise had been extended to all men and women over 23, and the state-controlled alcohol system (Systembolaget) set up. Following the Depression of the late 1920s and early 1930s, conditions began to improve after a Social Democratic government took office for the fourth time in 1932. A **welfare state** was rapidly established, offering unemployment benefit, higher old-age pensions, family allowances and paid holidays. The **Saltsjöbaden Agreement** of 1938 drew up a contract between trade unions and employers to help eliminate strikes and lockouts. With war again looming, all parties agreed that Sweden should remain neutral in any struggle, and so the country's rearmament was negligible, despite Hitler's apparent intentions.

World War II was slow to affect Sweden. Unlike in 1914, there was little sympathy in the country for Germany, but Sweden again declared neutrality. The Russian invasion of Finland in 1939 brought Sweden into the picture, with the Swedes providing weapons, volunteers and refuge for the Finns. Regular Swedish troops were refused though, the Swedes fearing intervention from either the Germans (then Russia's ally) or the Allies. Economically, the country remained sound – less dependent on imports than in World War I and with no serious shortages. The position became stickier in 1940 when the Nazis marched into Denmark and Norway, isolating Sweden. Concessions were made – German troop transit allowed, iron ore exports continued – until 1943–44, when Allied pressure had become more convincing than the failing German war machine.

Sweden became the recipient of countless refugees from the rest of Scandinavia and the Baltic. Instrumental in this process was **Raoul Wallenberg**, who rescued Hungarian Jews from the SS and persuaded the Swedish government to give him diplomatic status in 1944. Anything up to 35,000 Jews in Hungary were sheltered in "neutral houses" (flying the Swedish flag), and fed and clothed by Wallenberg. But when Soviet troops liberated Budapest in 1945, Wallenberg was arrested as a suspected spy and disappeared; he was later reported to have died in prison in Moscow in 1947. However, unconfirmed accounts had him alive in a Soviet prison as late as 1975; in 1989 some of his surviving relatives flew to Moscow in an unsuccessful attempt to discover the truth about his fate.

The end of the war was to engender a serious crisis of conscience in the country. Though physically unscathed, Sweden was now vulnerable to **Cold War** politics. The Finns had agreed to let Soviet troops march unhindered through Finland, and in 1949 this led neighbouring Sweden to refuse to follow the other Scandinavian countries into **NATO**. The country did, however, much to Conservative disquiet, return into Stalin's hands most of the Baltic and German refugees who had fought against Russia during the war – their fate is not difficult to guess.

Postwar politics

The wartime coalition quickly gave way to a purely Social Democratic government committed to welfare provision and increased defence expenditure – now nonparticipation in military alliances did not mean a throwing-down of weapons.

Tax increases and a trade slump lost the Social Democrats seats in the 1948 general election, and by 1951 they needed to enter into a coalition with the Agrarian (later the Centre) Party to survive. This coalition lasted until 1957, when disputes over the form of a proposed extension to the pension system brought it down. An inconclusive referendum and the withdrawal of the Centre Party from government forced an election. Although the Centre gained seats and the Conservatives replaced the Liberals as the main opposition party, the Social Democrats retained a (slim) majority.

Sweden regained much of its international moral respect (lost directly after World War II) through the election of **Dag Hammarskjöld** as secretary-general of the United Nations in 1953. His strong leadership greatly enhanced the prestige (and effectiveness) of the organization, which under his guidance participated in the solution of the 1956 Suez crisis and the 1958 Lebanon–Jordan affair. He was killed in an air crash in 1961, towards the end of his second five-year term.

Domestic reform continued unabated throughout the 1950s and 1960s. It was during these years that the country laid the foundations of its much-vaunted social security system, although at the time it didn't always bear close scrutiny. A **National Health Service** gave free hospital treatment, but only allowed for small refunds on doctor's fees and the costs of medicines and dental treatment – hardly as far-reaching as the British system introduced immediately after the war.

The Social Democrats stayed in power until 1976, when a **non-Social-Democrat coalition** (Centre–Liberal–Moderate) finally unseated them. In the 44 years since 1932, the socialists had been an integral part of government in Sweden, their role tempered only during periods of war and coalition. It was a remarkable record, made more so by the fact that modern politics in Sweden has never been about ideology so much as detail. Socialists and non-socialists alike share a broad consensus on foreign policy and defence matters, even on the need for the social welfare system. The argument in Sweden has instead been about economics, a manifestation of which is the issue of **nuclear power**. A second non-Socialist coalition, formed in 1979, presided over a referendum on nuclear power (1980); the pro-nuclear lobby secured victory, with the result being an immediate expansion of nuclear power generation.

Olof Palme

The Social Democrats regained power in 1982, subsequently devaluing the krona, introducing a freeze on prices and cutting back on public expenditure. They lost their majority in 1985, having to rely on Communist support to get their bills through. Presiding over the party since 1969, and prime minister for nearly as long, was **Olof Palme**. He was assassinated in February 1986, and his death threw Sweden into modern European politics like no other event. Proud of their open society (Palme had been returning home unguarded from the cinema), Swedes were shocked by the gunning down of a respected politician, diplomat and pacifist. The country's social system was placed in the spotlight, and shock turned to anger and then ridicule as the months passed without his killer being caught. Police bungling was criticized and despite the theories – Kurdish extremists, right-wing terror groups – no one was charged with the murder.

Then the police came up with **Christer Pettersson**, who – despite having no apparent motive – was identified by Palme's wife as the man who had fired the shot that night. Despite pleading his innocence, claiming he was elsewhere at the time of the murder, Pettersson was convicted of Palme's murder and jailed. There was great disquiet about the verdict, however, both at home and abroad. Pettersson was eventually acquitted on appeal; it was believed that Palme's wife couldn't possibly be sure that the man who fired the shot was Pettersson, given that she had only seen the murderer once, on the dark night in question, and then only very briefly. The police appear to believe they had the right man all along, but in recent years some convincing evidence of the involvement of the South African secret services has come to light (Palme having been an outspoken critic of apartheid).

Carlsson and Bildt

Ingvar Carlsson was elected prime minister after Palme's murder, a position confirmed by the **1988 General Election** when the Social Democrats – for the first time in years – scored more seats than the three non-socialist parties combined. However, Carlsson's was a minority government, the Social Democrats requiring the support of the Communists to command an overall majority – support that had usually been forthcoming but, after the arrival of the **Green Party** into parliament in 1988, could no longer be taken for granted. The Greens and Communists jockeyed for position as protectors of the Swedish environment, and any Social Democrat measure seen to be anti-environment cost them Communist support. Perhaps more worryingly for the government, a series of **scandals** swept the country, leading to open speculation about a marked decline in public morality. The Swedish **Bofors** arms company was discovered to be involved in illegal sales to the Middle East, and early in 1990 the Indian police charged the company with paying kickbacks to politicians to secure arms contracts. In addition, there was insider dealing at the stock exchange, and the country's ombudsman resigned over charges of personal corruption.

The real problem for the Social Democrats, though, was the economy. With a background of rising inflation and slow economic growth, the government announced an **austerity package** in January 1990. This included a two-year ban on strike action, and a wage, price and rent freeze – strong measures which astounded most Swedes, used to living in a liberal, consensus-style society. The Greens and Communists would have none of it and the Social Democrat government resigned a month later. Although the Social Democrats were soon back in charge of a minority government, having agreed to drop the most draconian measures of their programme, the problems didn't go away.

The **General Election of 1991** merely confirmed that the consensus model had finally broken down. A four-party centre-right coalition came to power, led by **Carl Bildt**, which promised tax cuts and economic regeneration, but the recession sweeping western Europe did not pass Sweden by. Unemployment hit a postwar record and in autumn 1992 – as the British pound and Italian *lira* collapsed on the international money markets – the krona came under severe pressure. Savage austerity measures did little to help: VAT on food was increased, statutory holiday allowances were cut, welfare budgets slashed, and – after a period of intense currency speculation – short-term marginal interest rates raised to a staggering 500 percent. In a final attempt to steady nerves, Prime Minister Bildt and Carlsson, leader of the Social Democratic opposition, made the astonishing announcement that they would ignore party lines and work together for the good of Sweden – and then proceeded with drastic **public expenditure cuts**.

The fat was trimmed off the welfare state – benefits were cut, health care was opened up to private competition and education was given a painful shake-up. But it was too little too late. Sweden was gripped by its worst **recession** since the 1930s and unemployment had reached record levels of fourteen percent – the days of a jobless rate of one or two percent were well and truly gone. Poor economic growth coupled with generous welfare benefits, runaway speculation by Swedish firms on foreign real estate and the world recession all contributed to Sweden's economic woes. With the budget deficit growing faster than that of any other Western industrialized country, Sweden also decided it was time to tighten up its asylum laws – in a controversial step it introduced visas for Bosnians, to try to stem the flood of refugees from the Bosnian war.

The return of the Social Democrats

A feeling of nostalgia for the good old days of Social Democracy swept through the country in September of 1994, and Carl Bildt's minority Conservative government was booted out. Swedes voted in massive numbers to return the country's biggest party to power, headed by **Ingvar Carlsson**. He formed a government of whom half the ministers were women. Two ministers subsequently decided they no longer wanted to work in Stockholm – the minister for culture upped sticks and moved her office out to Lake Vänern to be with her family, while the minister for employment thought he could be closer to the people by working from home in Piteå, up in the far north. Social Democracy, with all its quirks and foibles, was back.

During 1994, negotiations on Sweden's planned **membership of the European Union** were completed and the issue was put to a referendum, which succeeded in splitting Swedish public opinion right down the middle. The *Ja till EU* lobby argued that little Sweden would have a bigger voice in Europe and would be able to influence pan-European decisions if it joined. *Nej till EU* warned that Sweden would be forced to lower its standards to those of other EU countries, unemployment would rise, drug trafficking would increase, and democracy would be watered down; they also argued that the additive-free Swedish food market would be swamped with cheap additive-packed Eurosausages. But in November of that year, the Swedes followed the Austrians and the Finns in voting for membership from 1 January 1995 – by the narrowest of margins, just five percent.

In 1995, Sweden allowed **gay couples** effectively to marry, adopting a law on registered partnerships similar to that already in force in neighbouring Denmark and Norway. Same-sex couples won virtually the same rights as straight couples, the exceptions being that gay couples aren't allowed to adopt children, lesbians can't apply for artificial insemination, and gay partnership ceremonies can't be carried out in a church.

The Swedish authorities also faced the seemingly impossible task of stopping the smuggling of refugees into the country by organized gangs based, in particular, in Iraq, Afghanistan and Pakistan. However, the influx of illegal refugees was overshadowed by the problem of how to get the massive **state debt** under control. The krona fell to new lows as money-market fears grew that the minority government wouldn't be able to persuade parliament to approve cuts in state spending. However, the cuts were duly introduced – the welfare state was trimmed back further and new taxes were announced to try to rein in the spiralling debt. Unemployment benefit was cut to 75 percent of previous earnings, benefits for sick leave were reduced, and lower state pension payments also came into force; a new tax was also slapped on newspapers. To try to keep public support on his side, Finance Minister **Göran Persson** reduced the tax on food from a staggering 21 percent to just 12 percent.

Just when everything appeared under control, Carlsson announced his resignation – he was retiring to spend more time with his family, a very Swedish way of bowing out. He was replaced by the bossy Persson, known to friends and enemies alike as HSB – short for *han som bestämmer,* he who decides. Following elections in September 1998, marked by a drift to the far left and the traditional right, Persson clung on to power by the skin of his teeth, remaining prime minister of a coalition government but with a much-reduced majority. As the new millennium approached, the Swedish government concentrated its efforts on turning the economy round and experts argue this quiet period was necessary to muster strength to face the challenges to come.

Sweden today

Sweden's export-led **economy** has rendered the country extremely susceptible to changes in world finances. Since the turn of the millennium as globalization has gathered momentum, Sweden has faced a number of difficult choices which would have been unthinkable during the heady days of Social Democracy. During the past couple of years, privatizations, mergers and general cost-cutting measures – most visibly the virtual disappearance from the Swedish high street of the post office and the much-lamented fragmentation of the national rail network – have brought Sweden more into line with countries that went through equally painful economic change decades ago. Some economists argue it is this enforced shaking up of the business environment from outside, rather than any direct government measures, that is responsible for Sweden's improved economic fortunes since 1998 – today Swedish markets are once again flourishing.

As Sweden prepares for a heated debate on whether or not to adopt the **euro,** it is this refound growth and prosperity that will be at the centre of discussion. Things look set to come to a head during 2003 when a public referendum on the question is expected. Debate currently rages over whether it is in Sweden's financial interest to join and opinion polls consistently show public opinion divided on the issue. At stake, naturally, is not only Sweden's blossoming economy but also the amount of influence the Swedes can bring to bear on events inside the European Union, should the country opt to stay outside the single currency. The prime minister, Göran Persson, is strongly pro-euro and following his resounding general election success in September 2002, which saw his Social Democratic party increase its share of the vote, it's likely he will throw his weight behind the campaign for the single currency – the betting is that Swedes will vote "yes" to the euro.

The other issue set to become a focus for debate is the planned decommissioning of the country's four **nuclear power** stations, whose dozen reactors produce half of Sweden's energy. Following the Three Mile Island incident in 1979, Swedes voted in a referendum to close all nuclear plants by 2010, but already the government is trying to wriggle out of this commitment, in view of the vast cost of making up the energy shortfall.

Swedish architecture

The all-encompassing Swedish preoccupation with design and the importance attached to the way buildings interact with their wider environment have provided Sweden with a remarkable wealth of buildings, both domestic and commercial, during the past century. Despite this, planning for a perceived shortage of affordable housing has also meant that almost every town of any size is blighted with a plethora of postwar, faceless apartment blocks which can look more Soviet than Scandinavian. To really get the most out of Sweden's hugely rich architectural history, it's invariably worth seeking out the historic heart of a settlement – from small country towns to larger commercial cities.

There are rich pickings of **Romanesque** and **Gothic** buildings, particularly ecclesiastical and royal ones, and the number of **Renaissance** and **Baroque** buildings is quite remarkable. But Sweden's architectural heritage is not always so grand; the more vernacular constructions – from rural cottages to fisherman's homes – provide a fascinating insight into how Swedes have lived and worked for centuries.

Prehistoric buildings

Discussion of **prehistoric** building in Sweden is mostly a matter of conjecture, for the only structures to have survived from before 1100 are ruined or fragmentary. The most impressive structures of **Bronze Age** Sweden are the numerous grassy burial barrows and the coastal burial sites (particularly apparent on the island of Gotland) that feature huge boulders cut into the shapes of a prow and stern. One of the best known of the latter type is at **Ales Stennar** on the South Skåne coast – a Swedish Stonehenge set above windy cliffs.

More substantial are the **Iron Age** dwellings from the **Celtic** period (c. 500 BC to 800 AD). The best example of a fortification from this era is at **Ismantorp** on the Baltic island of Öland. Dating from the fifth century AD, this remarkable site has limestone walls up to fifteen feet high and some eighty foundations arranged into quarters, with streets radiating like spokes of a wheel.

From the remnants of pre-Christian-era houses a number of dwelling types can be identified. The open-hearth hall, for example, was a square house with an opening in the roof ridge by which light entered and smoke exited. The two-storey gallery house had an open upper loft reached via an exterior stair, while the post larder was a house on stilts allowing for ventilation and protection from vermin.

Romanesque to Gothic

The Christianization of Sweden is dated from 1008, the year St Sigfrid is said to have baptized King Olof. In the eleventh and twelfth centuries the Church and the monastic orders were the driving force behind the most significant building projects, with the most splendid example of Romanesque architecture being **Lund Cathedral**. Consecrated in 1145, when Lund was the largest town in Scandinavia and the archiepiscopal see, this monumental building was designed as a basilica with twin western towers, and boasts some tremendously rich carvings in the apsidal choir and vast crypt. The chief centre of Romanesque church building, however, was the royal town of **Sigtuna** to the northwest of Stockholm. Apart from boasting Sweden's oldest street, Sigtuna has the ruins of three eleventh-century churches – one of which, St Peter's, features the country's oldest groin vault.

Round arches, a distinctive feature of Romanesque architecture, flourished wherever limestone and sandstone were found – principally in regions of southern and central Sweden, such as Västergötland, Östergötland and Närke as well as Skåne. An easy supply of both types of stone was to be found on the Baltic island of Gotland, from where numerous baptismal fonts and richly carved sandstone decorations were exported to the mainland both to the west (Sweden proper) and the east (Swedish-controlled Finland).

Of the great monastic ruins from this period, the finest is **Alvastra Monastery** (1143), just south of Vadstena near the eastern shores of Lake Vättern. A portion of the huge barrel-vaults can still be seen, though much of the graceful structure was carted off by Vasa to build his castle at Vadstena.

Gothic architecture emerged in the thirteenth century, one of the finest early examples being the **Maria Church** in Sigtuna (1237), which with its red-brick step gables is markedly unlike the austere grey-stone churches of a century earlier. The cathedral at **Strängnäs**, due east of Stockholm, is another superb piece of Gothic brick architecture, while in Sweden's third city of Malmö, the German-inspired **St Peter's Church** survives as a fine example of brick Gothic, a style often known as the Hanseatic Style. The cathedral at Uppsala (the largest in Scandinavia) is another intriguing specimen, designed by Parisian builders as a limestone structure to a French High Gothic plan, but eventually built in brick in a simpler, **Baltic Gothic** form. A good example of late Gothic is **Vadstena Convent Church**; begun in 1384, this austere limestone and brick hall was built exactly as decreed by St Birgitta, the founder of the church, and is flanked by her monastery and nunnery. However, the most rewarding place to explore Sweden's Gothic architecture is **Gotland** – the countryside is peppered with almost one hundred richly sculpted medieval churches, while the island's capital, the magnificently preserved Hanseatic seat of **Visby**, is replete with excellent domestic as well as ecclesiastical Gothic.

Few examples of the castles and fortifications of this period exist today. One of the best examples, **Varberg's Fortress** in Halland, just south of Gothenburg, was built by the Danes, while the best Swedish-built medieval fortifications are in Finland, a Swedish province until the early nineteenth century. One stark and beautifully unmolested example of a fortification in Danish-controlled Skåne is the castle of Glimmingehus; dating from around 1500, it was built by Adam van Duren, who also supervised the completion of the cathedral of Lund.

Renaissance and Baroque architecture

Gustav Vasa (1523–60) could not have had a more pronounced effect on Swedish architecture. In 1527, with his reformation of the Church, Catholic properties were confiscated, and in many instances the fabric of monasteries and churches was used to build and convert castles into resplendent palaces. Wonderful examples of such Renaissance palaces are **Kalmar Castle**, in the south of Småland, and **Vadstena's Castle** – though, unlike Kalmar, the latter's interior has been stripped of its original furnishings. Another magnificent Vasa palace, a glorious ruin since a nineteenth-century fire, is **Borgholm Castle** on the Baltic island of Öland.

While few churches built in this period enjoyed much prominence, one of outstanding elegance is the **Trefaldighetskyrkan** (Trinity Church) in Kristianstad, Danish king Christian IV's model Renaissance city in Skåne. With its tall windows, slender granite pillars and square bays, it is the epitome of sophistication and simplicity.

By the time Gustav II Adolf (Gustavus Adolphus) ascended the throne in 1611, a greater opulence was becoming prevalent in domestic architecture. This tendency became even more marked in the **Baroque** area, which in Sweden commenced with the reign of Queen Kristina, art-loving and extravagant daughter of Gustav II Adolf. The first wave of Baroque was largely introduced by the German Nicodemus Tessin the Elder, who had spent much time in Italy.

The most glorious of palatial buildings from this era is **Drottningholm** outside Stockholm, a masterpiece created by Tessin for the Dowager Queen Hedvig Eleonora. Tessin's other great creation was **Kalmar Cathedral**, the finest church of the era and a truly beautiful vision of Italian Baroque. Nicodemus Tessin the Younger followed his father as court architect and continued his style. He designed the new **Royal Palace at Stockholm** following the city's great fire of 1697 and the two contrasting **Karlskrona** churches: the domed rotunda of the Trefaldighetskyrkan (Trinity Church) and the barrel-vaulted basilica of the Fredrikskyrkan (Fredrik's Church). Karlskrona, like **Gothenburg**, is a fine example of regulated town planning, a discipline that came into being during this era.

The Eighteenth Century

In the eighteenth century **Rococo** emerged as the style favoured by the increasingly affluent Swedish middle class, who looked to France for their models. This lightening of architectural style paved the way for the Neoclassical elegance which would follow with the reign of Gustav III, who was greatly impressed by the architecture of classical antiquity. Good examples of this clear Neoclassical mode are the **Inventariekammaren** (Inventory Chambers) at Karlskrona, and the **King's Pavilion at Haga**, designed for Gustav III by Olof Temelman, complete with Pompeiian interiors by the painter Louis Masreliez.

Another, and quite distinct aspect of late eighteenth-century taste, was the fascination with **chinoiserie**, due in large measure to the power and influence of the Gothenburg-based Swedish East India Company, founded in 1731. The culmination of this trend was the **Kina Slott** (Chinese Pavilion) at Drottningholm, a tiny Palladian villa built in 1763 and now beautifully restored.

The Nineteenth Century

Two vast projects dominated the Swedish architectural scene at the beginning of the nineteenth century: the remarkable **Göta Canal**, a 190-kilometre waterway linking the great lakes of Vänern and Vättern, Gothenburg and the Baltic; and the **Karlsborg Fortress** on the western shores of Vättern, designed to be an inland retreat for the royal family and the gold stocks, but abandoned ninety years later in 1909.

By the mid-nineteenth century, a new style was emerging, based on Neoclassicism but flavoured by the French-born king's taste. This **Empire Style** (sometimes referred to as the Karl Johan Style) is most closely associated with the architect **Fredrik Blom** of Karlskrona, whose most famous building is the elegant pleasure palace **Rosendal** on Djurgården, Stockholm.

During the reign of Oskar I (1844–59), while the buildings of Britain's manufacturing centres provided models for Sweden's industrial towns, the styles of the past couple of centuries began to reappear, particularly Renaissance and Gothic. One of the most glamorous examples of late nineteenth-century neo-Gothic splendour is **Helsingborg Town Hall**, built around 1890 as a riot of fairy-tale red-brick detail. The names which crop up most often in this era include Fredrik Scholander, who designed the elaborate **Stockholm Synagogue** in 1861, and Helgo Zetterwall, whose churches of the 1870s and 1880s bear a resemblance to neo-Gothic buildings in Britain and Germany.

The Twentieth Century to the present

Some of the most gorgeous buildings in Sweden's cities are the result of a movement which germinated in the final, resurgent years of the nineteenth century – **National Romanticism**, a movement that set out to simplify architecture and use local materials to create a distinctive Swedish style. The finest example of this new style, which was much influenced by the Arts and Crafts movement in Britain, is **Stockholm City Hall**, built in 1923 from plain brick, dressed stone and rustic timber. Another luscious example is Lars Israel Wahlmann's **Tjolöholm Castle**, just south of Gothenburg – a city in which some of the finest apartment buildings are those produced in the associated Art Nouveau style, known in Sweden as **Jugendstil**. One beautifully renovated building in full *Jugendstil* form is the theatre in Tivoli Park in **Kristianstad**, a town otherwise known for its Renaissance buildings. Stockholm's 1910-built *Hotel Esplanade* is a fine example, though the cities of Gothenburg, Malmö and Lund amongst others are rich in the heritage. The small town of Hjö on the western shores of Lake Vättern has a fine clutch of *Jugendstil* houses.

In the second quarter of the century a new movement – **Functionalism** – burst onto the scene, making great use of "industrial" materials such as stainless steel and concrete. The leading architect of his generation was **Gunnar Asplund**, famed for Stockholm City Library (mid-1920s) and his contribution to many other buildings – his interior of the law courts in **Gothenburg's Rådhus** is a Mecca for architecture students and enthusiasts today. Asplund was also responsible for the famed **Woodland Cemetery** in Stockholm, a magnificent project that also involved another designer, **Sigmund Lewerentz**.

The creation of the welfare state went hand in hand with the ascendancy of a functionalist approach to architecture which rejected many of the individualistic features of traditional Swedish design. By the 1960s, the faceless International Style had gained dominance in Sweden, as town planning gave way to insensitive clearance of old houses and their replacement with bland high-rises.

The late 1980s and early 1990s saw restoration becoming the order of the day with areas that had been left to decay – such as the old working-class neighbourhood of **Haga** in Gothenburg – gently gentrified and preserved. More recently the emphasis has shifted towards environmentally sympathetic architecture. Intrinsically Nordic in their tone these new buildings are often low-level structures constructed from locally sourced wood with vast areas of glass capitalizing on natural light. A wonderful example of this sympathy with Sweden's natural habitat is on the Bohuslän coast where the **Nordic Water-Colour Museum** (Akvarellmuseet) explores the interplay between a sizeable constructed space and the surrounding wild landscape. A little further south, in Gothenburg, the natural science museum, **Universeum** is a splendidly organic building – all rough-hewn wood, glass and concrete reflecting in the pools of water outside. One of the highest profile projects of the last decade is the **Modern Museum** and **Museum of Architecture** (Moderna Museet and Arkitekturmuseet) on the island of Skepsholm, in Stockholm Harbour. Designed by the Spaniard **Rafael Moneo**, the building eloquently complements the diverse structures of the city's waterfront without trying to overshadow them.

Geography and wildlife

Sweden is known above all else for its forests and lakes, yet the sheer diversity of its terrain is less familiar. While there are indeed a vast number of lakes, the largest – Vättern and Vänern – home to a wide variety of fish, and swaths of forest blanket vast tracts of the country, the southern shores are fringed with sandy beaches and the east and west coasts are a myriad of rocky islands forming archipelagos. The Baltic islands of Gotland and Öland provide an entirely different habitat to anywhere on mainland Sweden, with limestone plateaux, dramatic sea-stacks and a variety of flora found nowhere else in Scandinavia.

Reindeer are the most celebrated animals associated with Sweden, and are a common sight – especially in the centre and north of the country – though the rarest mammals, such as brown bears and wolverines, are found only in the very far north.

Geography

The appearance of Sweden's terrain owes most to the last **Ice Age**, which chafed the landscape for 80,000 years before finally melting away 9000 years ago. Grinding ice masses polished the mountains to their present form, a process particularly evident in scooped-out U-shaped mountain valleys such as **Lapporten** (The Lapp Gateway) near Abisko, in the extreme north of the country. Subsequent to the thaw, the land-mass rose, so that former coastlines are now many kilometres inland, manifested by the form of huge plains of rubble, while the plains of Sweden were created by the deposition of vast quantities of silt by the meltwater.

The northwest of the country is dominated by **mountains**, which rise well above the timber line. Deciduous trees are most prevalent, except in the most southerly regions, where coniferous forest predominates. Sweden also boasts some of Europe's most impressive **archipelagos**, such as the dramatically rugged Bohuslän coast on the west, and Stockholm's own archipelago of 24,000 islands, many covered in meadows and forest, on the east.

Allemansrätten

The relationship between the Swedish people and their environment is characterized by an intense reverence – as one might expect of the country that produced the world-renowned botanist Carl von Linné, whose system of plant classification is still used today. Many Swedes regard regular communion with the lakes and forests as an absolute necessity, and their respect for the natural world is encapsulated by the **Allemansrätten** or **Right of Common Access**. An unwritten right, it permits anyone to walk anywhere and spend a night anywhere, as long as this does not infringe the privacy of home-owners or impinge upon land where crops are grown. The only other exceptions are nature reserves and protected wildlife zones at sensitive times of the year, such as bird sanctuaries, which are entirely closed to visitors during breeding season.

The general rules of the Allemansrätten, which appear in English-language leaflets all over the country, forbid such actions as tree felling, the removal of twigs or bark from living trees, the lighting of fires in dry terrain or on bare rock, and off-road driving (unless there is lying snow). Fishing is allowed along the shores of the country's five largest lakes; in all other bodies of water, a permit to fish is required.

The country is also known for its **lakes**, which number more than 100,000. These support rich aquatic life, mostly salmon and salmon trout, although the coastlines are where most of the country's fishing takes place.

The North

Sweden's mountainous north is home to many of the country's national parks. The mountains here are part of the **Caledonian range**, the remains of which are also to be found further south in Europe, notably in Scotland and Ireland. Formed around 400 million years ago, the range is at its highest at **Kebnekaise** and **Sarek**, both above 2000m, in the extreme northwest of Sweden. Ancient spruce, pine and birch forest extends continuously along most of the 1000-kilometre range, providing an unspoilt habitat for birds such as the golden eagle. The tree line here lies at around 800m above sea level; higher up are great expanses of bare rockface and heathland, the latter often covered in wild orchids. In addition to eagles, the bird life in these raw mountain areas includes snow bunting, golden plovers and snowy owls, while the woodlands support willow grouse and bluethroat, among other species.

Central Sweden

The most extensive of Sweden's plains is in the **central Swedish lowlands**, a broad belt spanning from the Bohuslän coast in the west to Uppland and Södermanland in the east. Divided by steep ridges of rock, this former seabed was transformed by volcanic eruptions that created rocky plateaux such as Ålleberg and **Kinnekulle** (Flowering Mountain) to the west of Lidköping. The latter is Sweden's most varied natural site, comprising deciduous and ever-green woodland, meadows and pastures, and treeless limestone flats. Particularly notable among the flora here are cowslips, lady's-slipper orchids, wild cherry trees and, in early summer, the unusual and intensely fragrant bear-garlic.

Stretching some 160km north from Gothenburg up to the Norwegian border, the rough and windswept **Bohuslän coast** possesses a considerable **archipelago** of around three thousand islands. Most of these are devoid of trees – any which existed were cut down to make into boats and houses during the great fishing era of the eighteenth century. This low coastal landscape is peppered with deeply indented bays and fjords, interspersed with islands and peninsulas. To the north of the region, the waves have weathered the pink and reddish granite, and the resulting large, smooth stone slabs with their distinctive cracks are characteristic of the province. Inland from this stretch of coast are steep hills and plateaux which are separated from one another by deep valleys, the inland continuations of the fjords. Long, narrow lakes have developed here, the Bullaren lakes being the largest. Until around a thousand years ago, these comprised a journeyable waterway from Norway to the Gota river.

One of the region's most splendid areas of virgin forest is **Tiveden National Park**, around 50km northeast of Karlsborg and just to the northwest of **Lake Vättern**, one of the two enormous lakes in this part of Sweden. The other, **Lake Vänern**, is home to nesting seabirds such as the turnstone, water pipit and Caspian tern. Fishing being a major sport in Sweden, Vänern and Vättern attract thousands each year who wish to try their luck. Around 1300 tonnes of fish are taken from Vänern alone each year, with commercial fisheries accounting for around eighty percent of the catch. The lake's waters were once the most productive for salmon in Sweden, but the construction of hydroelectric dams ruined the spawning grounds, and by the 1970s salmon was almost extinct here. In an effort to complement natural reproduction, salmon and brown trout have been raised in hatcheries and released into the lake with considerable success, though stocks are still not high.

The plains of central Sweden are dotted with lakes, and many wetland and migratory birds shelter here. **Kvismaren**, near Örebro, is an area of reed marsh and open waters where geese and ducks live in their thousands. **Lake Tysslingen**, just to the west of Örebro, is also well worth heading for, especially during March and April, when as many as 2500 whooper swans gather here. Just east of Vättern is **Lake Tåkern**, one of northern Europe's finest bird habitats. Like Kvismaren, it was largely drained in the nineteenth century and has an average depth of just a metre. Some 250 species of bird spend time here, particularly huge flocks of geese in autumn.

Sweden's most famous lowland lake is **Hornborgasjön**, southeast of Lidköping, which boasts 120 species of wetland birds. Every April, thousands of cranes briefly settle in the potato fields just to the south of the lake on their migration to the northern marshes.

The South

The southernmost third of Sweden, the country's most highly populated and industrialized region, is a mixture of highlands (in the north), forests, lakes and cultivated plains. In southeastern Sweden, the forests of **Småland** have kept the furnaces of the province's glass factories alight since the seventeenth century. In the south, where the highlands give way to a gently undulating landscape, the combination of pastures and fields of rape and poppy makes for some glorious summertime scenery in **Skåne**. Though this province has a reputation for being monotonous and agricultural (true of much of its southwest), it also boasts tracts of conifers, a dramatic coastline and lush forests of beech, best seen in the first weeks of May. The province also boasts dramatic natural rock formations at **Hovs Hallar**, a stunning castellation of red rock sea-stacks on the northern coast of the Bjäre peninsula.

To the east of Skåne, the **Stenshuvud National Park** has rocky coastal hills surrounded by woods of hornbeam and alder and moorlands full of juniper. Animals untypical of Sweden live here, such as tree frogs, sand lizards and dormice.

Öland and Gotland

Sweden's two largest islands, **Gotland** and **Öland**, lying in the Baltic Sea to the east of the mainland, have excited botanists and geologists for centuries. When Carl von Linné first arrived in Öland in the mid-eighteenth century, he noted that the terrain was "of an entirely different countenance" from the rest of the country, and indeed the island's limestone plateaux – known as *alvar* – are unique in Sweden. In southern Öland, **Stora Alvaret** (Great Limestone Plain) is a thin-soiled heathland with vividly colourful flora in spring and summer – Öland rockrose, red kidney vetch and blue globe daisy are among the unusual flowers which grow here. Bird-life is also rich and varied on Öland. The **Öland goose**, one of the oldest domesticated breeds in the country, originated here from interbreeding with wild geese. **Ottenby**, on the island's southern point, is Öland's largest nature reserve, supporting golden oriole as well as fallow deer, which have lived here since the time when the entire island was a royal hunting ground.

Gotland is the more dramatic of the two great islands, thanks to its tall sea-stacks, the remains of old coral reefs which loom like craggy ghosts along the island's shoreline. Like Öland, Gotland sustains rich floral life, including at least 35 species of orchid. This is also the home of the **Gotland sheep**, an ancient (and now rare) breed characterized by a dark, shaggy coat and powerful, bow-shaped horns. Nearby, off Gotland's western shores, is **Stora Karlsö**, an island breeding ground for guillemot and razorbill.

Fauna

Stretching over two thousand kilometres from the northern temperate zone into the Arctic Circle, Sweden is unsurprisingly home to a considerable diversity of flora and **fauna**. To see endangered species from Sweden in conditions approaching those in the wild, it's worth visiting **Nordens Ark**, near Lysekil on the Bohuslän coast. A not-for-profit breeding park, it is home to wolves, wolverines and lynxes, as well as to lesser pandas and snow leopards from the Himalayas.

Sweden's attitude to wild animals is in marked contrast to that of, say, Britain, in that Swedes deeply concerned with animal rights will often also be in support of **hunting**, regarding the practice as working hand in hand with nature conservation. Elk, bear, deer, fox and grouse are all hunted during specified seasons.

Mammals

The animal with the highest profile in Sweden is the **reindeer**: "reindeer crossing" signs are common all over the country, as is serious damage to vehicles involved in collisions with them. Throughout the year, reindeer are to be seen not just on mountainsides but also in the wooded valleys and lowlands throughout the country, except for Gotland and in the far north.

The most common deer in the country is the **roe deer**, one of the smaller breeds; it numbers around a million in Sweden. Roe deer are much more likely to be seen in the south and centre of the country than the north. One of the best places to see it, as well as **red deer** and (in particular) **elk** (a close relation of the American moose) is the plateau of Halleberg, just south of Vanersborg in Västergötland. Used as a royal hunting ground for elk since the 1870s, Halleberg has around 140 of these creatures in winter and 200 in summer. The elk, which is the largest species of deer in the world, can be over 2m tall and weigh up to five hundred kilograms. The best times to see elk and deer are dawn and dusk, when they emerge to seek food in cleared areas. Also seen in this area are Swedish **woodland hare**, **badgers** and even **lynx** – the only member of the cat family living in the wild in Sweden. It lives off roe deer and hare, and is characterized by its triangular tufted ears. Although it's a rare practice today, some provinces still organize small-scale hunting of the creature.

Sweden's **wolves** have been hunted almost to extinction. A rare few – believed to be fewer than forty – still live in the north, and can on rare occasions be heard howling in groups. Thanks to intensive efforts at conservation, the wolf population is slowly beginning to recover. Also found in the north are **Arctic foxes**, which have adapted to the conditions of extreme cold; they live only in the mountain regions above the tree line. Although the animals were common in Sweden at the beginning of the twentieth century, excessive hunting for their fur has reduced numbers dramatically. Ironically, the recent minor decline in the **fur trade**, due in part to animal rights activism, has posed a danger to Arctic foxes. A recent project aimed at conserving the Arctic fox in Sweden and Finland has found that where red foxes (also hunted for their fur) are left uncontrolled, they dominate over Arctic foxes, even preying on juvenile Arctic foxes.

Far closer to extinction than the Arctic fox are **wolverines**, placed under protection in 1969; there are now under one hundred individuals left in Sweden, entirely found in the north and mountain regions. One of their difficulties is that they depend on offal left by other predators, mainly wolves. The near demise of the wolf has clearly put considerable pressure on wolverines and recently they have been known to damage the tame reindeer herds owned by the *Sámi* people.

The Swedish **brown bear** may grow to 2.3 metres in length and weigh around 350 kilograms. Though rarely seen, they still live in the northernmost reaches of Sweden; it is estimated that there are around seven hundred of them in the wild.

Birds

While Sweden is not particularly noted for its avian wildlife, the variety of **native birds** is considerable and as a staging post for great numbers of **migratory birds** there is some spectacular viewing as they make their way between the far north and hotter climes.

Unsurprisingly, the country's coastlines are thick with seagulls, ducks and herons, while swans make beautiful additions to inland lakes and coastal inlets. Kingfishers and dippers can be found around the country's rivers and streams. The mountain regions of Sweden are home to capercaillie, mountain grouse, black grouse and a range of owls. Two varieties of **eagle** are seen throughout the country, though their numbers are small, while hawks and buzzards make an occasional appearance. Many of these birds are threatened with extinction, and so the hunting of all birds of prey is forbidden.

Among the finest bird areas in the country is **Getterön Nature Reserve**, just a few kilometres north of Varberg on the west coast of Halland. The area is seen as hugely valuable for bird-life, due to its large mosaic of wetlands in an otherwise exploited region. The mix of open water and dramatic clumps of reeds and rushes here make an ideal home for **nesting birds**. Among the rare birds which nest at Getterön are the black-tailed godwit and the southern dunlin; also found here are lapwings, redshanks, skylarks and yellow wagtail. The number of birds peaks in April and May (though spring migration begins as early as February) and from August to October. April is the time to see the most ducks; in May, flocks of dunlins and other waders gather in the bay. The last waders head northwards in June, while female curlews and spotted redshanks meet them heading south. This latter southbound migration goes on through July and August. In autumn, Canada geese and greylag geese arrive. During the winter months it's possible to see white-tailed eagles; peregrine falcons are seen all year. During the wintertime some of the best bird-viewing can be found at Lake Åsnen in south Småland, where up to ten thousand goosanders and the rare white-tailed eagles have made a spectacular sight.

Fish and reptiles

Fish play an important role in Swedish life, with fishing a national sport and almost every restaurant boasting about its local, fresh fish. Pike perch, roach, bream and carp are the most common types in all but northern Swedish lakes, which are home to salmon trout and char. Lake Vättern, being particularly cold for its latitude, is also rich in Arctic char. The country's rivers are filled with trout, salmon and salmon trout. Off the coasts can be found shoals of herring, mackerel, Baltic herring, spiny dogfish and some sharks. **Shellfish** also appear on thousands of tables throughout the land, with crab, lobster, crayfish and oyster all harvested from offshore waters.

The only poisonous **snake** found in Sweden is the **viper**, its bite only comparable to the sting of a wasp. **Grass snakes** tend to live near the water's edge; in Sweden, neither grass snakes nor vipers reach more than 1m in length. **Frogs** and **toads** are very common, particularly in southern and central Sweden.

Books

English-language **books** on Sweden are remarkably scant. Although Swedish publishing houses are producing quality titles – particularly fiction – that are translated into most European languages, remarkably few find their way into English. The books listed below are the pick of a meagre crop; those that are currently out of print (o/p) shouldn't be too difficult to track down; Internet auctions and secondhand bookstores can offer rich pickings on older titles. The UK publisher is given first in each listing, followed by the publisher in the US, unless the title is available in one country only, in which case we've specified which country.

Travel and general

★ **James William Barnes Steveni** *Unknown Sweden* (Hurst & Blackett, o/p). A fascinating account of journeys through Sweden in the early years of the twentieth century. With its excellent illustrations, this book is a superb social record.

Mary Wollstonecraft *A Short Residence in Sweden, Norway and Denmark* (Penguin). A searching account of Wollstonecraft's three-month solo journey through southern Scandinavia in 1795.

History and politics

Sheri Berman *The Social Democrat Movement* (Harvard University Press). A comparison between the Swedish and German social democratic systems between the First and Second World Wars. Whilst Sweden placed itself at the forefront of the drive for democratization after the Great Depression, Germany lacked direction and opted for Hitler.

H.R. Ellis Davidson *The Gods and Myths of Northern Europe* (Penguin). A Who's Who of Norse mythology, including some useful profiles of the more obscure gods. Displaces the classical deities and their world as the most relevant mythological framework for northern and western European culture.

Eric Elstob *Sweden: A Traveller's History* (Boydell & Brewer). An introduction to Swedish history from the year dot to the twentieth centu-

ry, with useful chapters on art, architecture and cultural life.

Bridget Morris *St. Birgitta of Sweden* (Boydell & Brewer). A comprehensive and intelligently researched book offering a rounded perspective of Sweden's first female saint and her extraordinary life. Accessible and educational without being over academic in approach.

Lee Miles *Sweden and European Integration* (Ashgate Publishing Limited). A political history of Sweden comparing the period 1950–66 with the accession to the European Union in 1995.

Michael Roberts *The Early Vasas: A History of Sweden 1523–1611* (Cambridge University Press, o/p). A clear account of the period. Complements the same author's *Gustavus Adolphus and the Rise of Sweden* and *The Age of Liberty:*

Sweden 1719-1772 (Cambridge University Press), which, more briefly and enthusiastically, covers the period from 1612 to Gustav's death in 1632.

Jan-Öjvind Swahn *Maypole, Crayfish and Lucia – Swedish Holidays and Traditions* (The Swedish Institute). This little edition is superbly written and informative about how and why Swedish tradi-

tions have evolved. In contrast to the pictures, the prose is historically accurate and both entertaining and frank about what makes Sweden tick.

Franklin Daniel Scott *Sweden, The Nation's History* (Southern Illinois University Press). A good all-round account of Sweden's history from a poor, backward warrior nation to the prosperous modern one of today

Art, architecture and design

★ **Henrik O. Andersson and Fredric Bedoire** *Swedish Architecture 1640–1970* (Swedish Museum of Architecture). With superb colour plates, this is the definitive survey of the subject, with parallel English/Swedish text.

Katrin Cargill *Creating the Look: Swedish Style* (Frances Lincoln; Pantheon Books). A great book to help you create cheerful Swedish peasant interiors. Includes lots of evocative photographs by Christopher Drake and a long list of stockists of the materials you'll need. A practical guide, the book includes some background information to place the designs in context.

Görel Cavalli-Björkman and Bo Lindwall *The World of Carl Larsson* (Simon & Schuster, US). A charming and brilliantly illustrated volume, charting the life and work of one of Sweden's most admired painters.

Barbro Klein and Mats Widbom *Swedish Folk Art* (Abrams). A lavishly illustrated and richly documented history of its subject, relating ancient crafts to modern-day design ideas.

Mereth Lindgren, Louise Lyberg, Birgitta Sandström and Anna Greta Wahlberg *A History of Swedish Art* (Coronet, US). A fine overview of Swedish painting, sculpture and, to a lesser extent, architec-

ture, from the Stone Age to the present. Clear text and good, mostly monochrome, illustrations.

★ **Nils-Olof Olsson Skåne** *Through The Artist's Eye* (Fårgtrappan AAA) A cleverly balanced, illustrated book encompassing from prehistoric to the present day in its coverage of the country's southernmost province. Steering clear of the usual demarcations in art history, this very likeable hardback shows how much contemporary art work can help with our understanding of history.

Lars Sjöberg and Ursula Sjöberg *The Swedish Room* (Frances Lincoln; Pantheon Books). An exceptionally well-documented journey through developments in the design of Swedish homes, covering the period from 1640 through to the nineteenth century (stopping short of National Romanticism, Art Nouveau and Functionalism). The book sets design patterns in their historical and political context, and includes beautiful photographs by Ingalill Snitt. There's also a section on achieving classic Swedish decor effects, and a good list of suppliers of decorative materials, though without exception all are in America.

★ **Håkan Sandbring & Martin Borg** *Skåne – Wide Horizons* (Salix Förlag, Lund). A glorious visual study of Skåne – the ultimate coffee-table tome for anyone who loves the sort of beauty at which Sweden excels. From country scenes to urban visions and all the quirks of Swedish life in between, these brilliantly hued photographs will keep you absorbed for hours.

Literature

Hugh Beach *A Year in Lapland* (University of Washington Press). As a young man Hugh Beach went to live with the *Sámi* reindeer herders of Jokkmokk. In later life he returns to the Arctic Circle to charter the fascinating changes that have occurred to northern Sweden and its traditionally nomadic inhabitants.

Frans G Bengtsson *The Long Ships: A Saga of the Viking Age* (HarperCollins). A real gem of historical fiction bringing the Viking world vividly alive with solid background on arcane Norse traditions such as "trollcraft", "gold-luck" and "the Ale-death". A marvellously pacy adventure story that is literally laugh-out-loud funny.

Marikka Cobbold *Frozen Music* (Orion). Cobbold – who is herself Swedish, though lives in England – paints a very true-to-life picture of Swedish mannerisms and way of life. This novel about the relationship between a Swedish architect and an Englishwoman is set on a very well-drawn Swedish island.

Stig Dagerman *A Burnt Child* (Quartet, UK). One of the author's best works, this intense, short narrative concerns the reactions of a Stockholm family to the death of the mother. A prolific young writer, Dagerman had written short stories, travel sketches, four novels and four plays by the time he was 26; he committed suicide in 1954 at the age of 31.

Kerstin Ekman *Blackwater* (Vintage; St Martin's Press). A tightly written thriller by one of Sweden's most highly rated novelists.

Set in the forests of northern Sweden, the plot concerns a woman whose lover is murdered; years later, she sees her daughter wrapped up in the arms of the person she suspects of the killing.

Kerstin Ekman *Under the snow* (Vintage). In a remote Lapland village, a police constable investigates the death of a teacher following a drunken brawl. The dark deeds of winter finally come to light under the relentless summer sun. This is an excellent book to get to grips with the mentality of northern Swedes.

Robert Fulton *Preparations for Flight* (Forest Books, UK). Eight Swedish short stories from the last 25 years, including two rare prose outings by the poet Niklas Rådström.

Lars Gustafsson *The Death of a Beekeeper* (New Directions Press). Keenly observed novel structured around the journal of a dying schoolteacher-turned-beekeeper.

Pers Christian Jersild *A Living Soul* (Norvik Press; Dufour). The work of one of Sweden's best novelists, this is a social satire based around the "experiences" of an artificially produced, bodyless human brain floating in liquid. Entertaining, provocative reading.

Selma Lagerlöf *The Wonderful Adventures of Nils* (Floris, Edinburgh; Dover, New York). Lagerlöf is Sweden's best-loved children's writer, and it's an indication of her standing in her native land that she's featured on the 20kr banknote. The tales of Nils Holgren, a little boy who flies all over the country on the back of a magic goose, are continued in *The Further Adventures of Nils* (Tomten, US).

Sara Lidman *Naboth's Stone* (Norvik Press; Dufour). A novel set in 1880s Västerbotten, in Sweden's far north, charting the lives of settlers and farmers as the industrial age – and the railway – approaches.

Ivar Lo-Johansson & Rochelle Wright *Peddling My Wares* (Boydell & Brewer). An intriguing exploration of life for a young, self-educated Swede. This autobiographical tale is written by the last surviving member of the "Thirties Generation" and the narrative ranges from funny to very sad and is as popular today in Sweden as when the book first appeared in 1953.

Torgney Lindgren *Merab's Beauty* (HarperCollins). Short stories capturing the distinctive flavour of family life in northern Sweden.

★ **Vilhelm Moberg,** *The Emigrants* (Minnesota Historical Society, US). From one of Sweden's greatest twentieth-century writers, this is one of four novels based on the lives of characters Karl Oskar and Christina Nilsson as they struggle their way from Småland to Minnesota. It's a highly poignant story dealing with the emigration of Swedes to the US in the second half of the nineteenth century.

★ **Michael Niemi** *Popular Music* (Flamingo). The enchanting tale of two boys, Matti and Niila, growing up in Pajala in northern Sweden during the Sixties and Seventies. Dreaming of an unknown world beyond the horizons of the Torne Valley, they use their fantasy to help take them there. Winner of the *August Prize* for Sweden's best novel 2000 and recently translated into English.

Leo Perutz *The Swedish Cavalier* (Harvill; Arcade). Two men meet in a farmer's barn in 1701 – one is a thief, the other an army officer on the run. An adventure story with a moral purpose.

Agneta Pleijel *The Dog Star* (Peter Owen, UK). By one of Sweden's leading writers, *The Dog Star* is the powerful tale of a young girl's approach to puberty. Pleijel's finest novel yet, full of fantasy and emotion.

Clive Sinclair *Augustus Rex* (Andre Deutsch, UK). August Strindberg dies in 1912 – and is then brought back to life by the Devil in 1960s Stockholm. Bawdy, imaginative and very funny treatment of Strindberg's well-documented neuroses.

August Strindberg *Plays: One* (including *The Father, Miss Julie* and *The Ghost Sonata*); *Plays: Two* (*The Dance of Death, A Dream Play* and *The Stronger*) (both Methuen). The major plays by the country's most provocative and influential playwright, scrutinizing and analysing the roles of the sexes both in and out of marriage. Only a fraction of Strindberg's sixty plays, twelve historical dramas, five novels, numerous short stories, autobiographical volumes and poetry has been translated into English.

Bent Söderberg *The Mysterious Barricades* (Peter Owen; Dufour). In which a leading Swedish novelist writes of the Mediterranean during the wars – a part of the world in which he's lived for many years.

Hjalmar Söderberg *Short Stories* (Norvik Press; Dufour). Twenty-six short stories from the stylish pen of Söderberg (1869–1941). Brief, ironic and eminently suited to dipping into.

Biography

Peter Cowie *Ingmar Bergman* (Andre Deutsch; Scribner; both o/p). A fine critical biography of the great director; a well-written, sympathetic account of Bergman's life and career. Bergman's major screenplays are published by Marion Boyars.

Michael Meyer *Strindberg* (Oxford University Press). The best and most approachable biography of the tormented genius of Swedish literature.

Andrew Oldham, Tony Calder and Colin Irwin, *Abba* (Pan; Music Book Services). The last word on the band, here described as the "greatest composers of the twentieth century".

Alan Palmer *Bernadotte* (John Murray, o/p). A lively and comprehensive biography of Napoleon's marshal, who later became King Karl XIV Johan of Sweden.

Language

Language

Swedish

For most foreigners Swedish is nothing more than an obscure, if somewhat exotic, language spoken by a few million people on the fringe of Europe, and whose most famous speaker is the Swedish chef from TV's *The Muppet Show*. Many travellers take their flirtation with the odd hurdy-gurdy sounds of the language no further than that, since there is no need whatsoever to speak Swedish to enjoy a visit to Sweden. Recent surveys have shown that 95 per-cent of Swedes speak English to some degree. However, Swedish deserves clos-er inspection, and if you master even a couple of phrases you'll meet with nothing but words of encouragement.

Despite what you might think, Swedish is one of the easiest languages for English-speakers to pick up; its grammar has developed along similar lines to that of English and therefore has no case system to speak of (unlike German). Many everyday words are common to both English and Swedish, having been brought over to Britain by the Vikings, and anyone with a knowledge of north-ern English or lowland Scottish dialects will already be familiar with a good number of Swedish words and phrases. Your biggest problem is likely to be per-fecting the "tones", different rising and falling accents which Swedish uses (the hurdy-gurdy sounds you're no doubt already familiar with).

Swedish is a Germanic language and, as such, related to English in much the same way as French is related to Italian. However its closest cousins are fellow members of the North Germanic group of tongues: Danish, Faroese, Icelandic, Norwegian. Within that subgroup, Swedish is most closely linked to Danish and Norwegian, and the languages are mutually intelligible to quite an extent. A knowledge of Swedish will therefore open up the rest of Scandinavia to you; in fact Swedish is the second official language of Finland. Unlike Danish though, Swedish spelling closely resembles pronunciation, which means you stand a sporting chance of being able to read words and make yourself under-stood.

Basics

Swedish **nouns** can have one of two **genders**: common or neuter. The good news is that three out of four nouns have the common gender. The **indefinite article** precedes the noun, and is *en* for common nouns, and *ett* for neuter nouns. The **definite** article, as in all the other Scandinavian languages, is suf-fixed to the noun, for example, *en katt*, a cat, but *katten,* the cat; *ett hus*, a house, but *huset,* the house. The same principle applies in the plural: *katter*, cats, but *kat-terna*, the cats; *hus*, houses, but *husen*, the houses. The plural definite article suf-fix is therefore -*na* for common nouns and -*en* for neuter nouns (and confus-ingly identical with the definite article suffix for common nouns).

Forming **plurals** is possibly the most complicated feature of Swedish. Regular plurals take one of the following endings: -*or*, -*ar*, -*er*, -*r*, -*n*, or no end-ing at all. Issues like the gender of a word, whether its final letter is a vowel or consonant, and stress can all affect which plural ending is used. You should learn each noun with its plural, but to be honest, the chances are you'll forget the plural ending and get it wrong. Swedes have no apparent difficulty in forming plurals and can't understand why you find it so hard. Show them the plurals section in any grammar and savour their reaction.

Adjectives cause few problems. They generally precede the noun they qualify and agree in gender and number with it; *en ung flicka*, a young girl (ie no ending on the adjective); *ett stort hus*, a big house; *fina böcker*, fine books. The -*a* ending is also used after the definite article, irrespective of number, *det stora huset*, the big house, *de fina böckerna*, the fine books; and also after a possessive, once again irrespective of number, *min stora trädgård*, my big garden, or *stadens vackra gator*, the town's beautiful streets.

Verbs are something of a mixed blessing. There is only one form for all persons, singular and plural, in all tenses, which means there are no irksome endings to remember: *jag är* – I am, *du är* – you (singular) are, *ni är* – you (plural) are, *han/vi är* – we are, *de är* – they are. All verbs take the auxiliary *att ha* (to have) in the perfect and pluperfect tenses (eg *jag har gått* – I have gone, *jag har talat* – I have spoken; *jag hade gått* – I had gone, *jag hade talat* – I had spoken). The price for this simplicity is unfortunately four different conjugations which are distinguished by the way they form their past tense. Verbs are always found as the second idea in any Swedish sentence, as in German, which can often lead to the inversion of verb and subject. However, there are no "verb scarers" in Swedish which are responsible for the suicidal pile-up of verbs which often occurs at the end of German sentences.

How to say "you" in many Germanic languages poses considerable problems – not so in Swedish. In the 1960s a wave of liberalism and equality swept through the language and the honorific form, *ni* (the equivalent of *Sie* in German), was dropped in favour of the more informal *du*. However, the change in the language has left many elderly people behind, and you'll often still hear them using *ni* to people they don't know very well. In modern Swedish *ni* is really only used to express the plural of you (the equivalent of both *ihr* and plural *Sie* in German).

Pronunciation

Rest assured – you're never going to sound Swedish, for not only can **pronunciation** be difficult, but the sing-song **melody** of the language is beyond the reach of most outsiders. Swedish uses two quite different **tones** on words of two or more syllables – one rises throughout the entire word, while the other falls in the middle before peaking at the end of the word. It's this second down-then-up accent which gives Swedish its distinctive melody. Unfortunately identical words can have two different meanings depending on which tone is used. For example, *fem ton* with a rising accent throughout each word means "five tons", whereas *femton* where the accent dips during the *fem-* and rises throughout the *-ton* means "fifteen". A mistake in tones can often have hilarious consequences! Equally, *komma* with a rising tone throughout means "comma", whereas *komma* with a falling tone followed by a rising tone is the verb "to come". In short, try your best, but don't worry if you get it wrong. Swedes are used to foreigners saying one word but meaning another and will generally understand what you're trying to say.

Vowels can be either long (when followed by one consonant or at the end of a word) or short (when followed by two consonants). Unfamiliar or unusually spelt vowels are as follows:

ej as in mate
y as in ewe
å when short, as in hot; when long, sort of as in raw

ä as in get
ö as in fur

Consonants are pronounced approximately as in English except:
g before e, i, y, ä or ö as in yet; before a, o, u, å as in gate; sometimes silent

j, dj, gj, lj as in yet
k before e, i, y, ä or ö approximately as in shut and
similar to German ch in "ich", otherwise hard
qu as in kv
rs as in shut (also when one word ends in r and
the next begins with s, for example för stor, pronounced "fur shtoor")
s as in so (never as English z)

sj, skj, stj approximately as in shut (different from
soft k sound and more like a sh-sound made
through the teeth but with rounded lips – this
sound takes much practice; see below)
tj approximately as in shut and with same value
as a soft k
z as in so (never as in zoo)

The soft sound produced by **sj, skj** and **stj** is known as the **sj-sound** and is a peculiarity of Swedish. Unfortunately it appears widely and its pronunciation varies with dialect and individual speakers. To confuse matters further there are two variants, a back sj-sound formed by raising the back of the tongue and a front sj-sound formed by raising the middle or front of the tongue. Gain instant respect by mastering this Swedish tongue twister: *sjuttiosju sjuksköterskor skötte sju sjösjuka sjömän på skeppet till Shangai*, meaning seventy-seven nurses nursed seven seasick sailors on the ship to Shanghai.

Books

Swedes are always keen to practise their English, so if you're intent on learning Swedish, perseverance is the name of the game. The excellent *Colloquial Swedish* by Philip Holmes and Gunilla Serin (published by Routledge) is the best **textbook** around and should be your starting point. It will guide you through everything from pronunciation to the latest slang. Make sure you buy the companion cassette so you get a chance to hear the spoken language.

Of the handful of **grammars** available, by far the most useful is the six-hundred-page *Swedish: A Comprehensive Grammar* by Philip Holmes and Ian Hinchliffe (Routledge) which is head and shoulders above anything else on the market. An abridged version, *Essentials of Swedish Grammar* (Routledge), is handy as a first step on the road to learning the language.

Until just a couple of years ago, it was virtually impossible to buy an English–Swedish **dictionary** outside Sweden; now most bookshops will supply the *Collins Gem Swedish Dictionary*, perfect for checking basic words whilst travelling around. It's also available in Sweden under the title *Norstedts engelska fickordbok* but costs twice as much. Incidentally, the Swedish word for dictionary, *ordbok* – meaning "wordbook" – is a good example of how Swedish builds new words from existing ones.

Of the **phrasebooks**, the most useful is *Swedish Phrase Book and Dictionary* (Berlitz); alternatively, you can use the forty-page Swedish section in the *Scandinavian Phrase Book and Dictionary* (also Berlitz).

Useful words and phrases

Basic phrases

yes; no	ja; nej	women; men	kvinnor; män
hello	hej/tjänare	toilet	toalett
good morning	god morgon	bank; change	bank; växel
good afternoon	god middag	post office	posten
good night	god natt	stamp(s)	frimärke(n)
today/tomorrow	idag/imorgon	where are you from?	varifrån kommer
please	tack/var så god		du?
here you are/		I'm English	jag är engelsman/
you're welcome	var så god		engelska
thank you (very much)	tack (så mycket)	Scottish	skotte
where?; when?	var; när/ hur dags	Welsh	walesare
what?; why?	vad; varför	Irish	irländare
how (much)?	hur (mycket)	American	amerikan
I don't know	jag vet inte	Canadian	kanadensare
do you know? (a fact)	vet du...?	Australian	australier
could you...?	skulle du kunna...?	a New Zealander	nyzeeländare
sorry; excuse me	förlåt; ursäkta	what's your name?	vad heter du?
here; there	här; där	what's this called in	vad heter det här
near; far	nära; avlägsen	Swedish?	på svenska?
this; that	det här; det där	do you speak English?	talar du engelska?
now; later	nu; senare	I don't understand	jag förstår inte
more; less	mera; mindre	you're speaking too fast	du talar för snabbt
big; little	stor; liten	how much is it?	hur mycket kostar
open; closed	öppet; stängt		det?

Getting around

how do I get to...?	hur kommer jag till...?	Gothenburg?	Göteborg?
		what time does it leave?	hur dags går det?
left; right	till vänster/ till höger	what time does it arrive in...?	hur dags är det framme i...?
straight ahead	rakt fram	which is the road to...?	vilken är vägen
where is the bus station?	var ligger busstationen?		till...?
		where are you going?	vart går du?
the bus stop for...	busshållplatsen till...	I'm going to...	jag går till...
		that's great, thanks a lot	jättebra, tack så mycket
railway station	järnvägsstationen		
where does the bus to .... leave from?	varifrån går bussen till...?	stop here please	stanna här, tack
		ticket to	biljett till
is this the train for	åker detta tåg till	return ticket	tur och retur

Accommodation

where's the youth hostel?	var ligger vandrarhemmet?	can I see it?	får jag se det?
		how much is it a night?	hur mycket kostar det per natt?
is there a hotel round here?	finns det något hotell i närheten?	I'll take it	jag tar det
		it's too expensive,	det är för mycket, jag
I'd like a single/	jag skulle vilja ha ett	I don't want it now	tar det inte
		can I/we leave the bags here until...?	kan jag/vi få lämna väskorna här till...?
double room	enkelrum/ dubbelrum		

have you got anything cheaper?	**har du något billigare?**	with a shower can I/we camp here?	**med dusch får jag/vi tälta här?**

Days and months

Sunday	**söndag**	April	**april**
Monday	**måndag**	May	**maj**
Tuesday	**tisdag**	June	**juni**
Wednesday	**onsdag**	July	**juli**
Thursday	**torsdag**	August	**augusti**
Friday	**fredag**	September	**september**
Saturday	**lördag**	October	**oktober**
January	**januari**	November	**november**
February	**februari**	December	**december**
March	**mars**	Days and months are never capitalized.	

The time

what time is it?	**vad är klockan?**	one forty	**tjugo i två**
it's....	**den/hon är...**	one forty-five	**kvart i två**
at what time...?	**hur dags...?**	one fifty-five	**fem i två**
at...	**klockan...**	two o'clock	**klockan två**
midnight	**midnatt**	noon	**klockan tolv**
one in the morning	**klockan ett på natten**	in the morning	**på morgonen**
		in the afternoon	**på eftermiddagen**
ten past one	**tio över ett**	in the evening	**på kvällen**
one fifteen	**kvart över ett**	in ten minutes	**om tio minuter**
one twenty-five	**fem i halv två**	ten minutes ago	**för tio minuter sedan**
one thirty	**halv två**		
one thirty-five	**fem över halv två**		

Numbers

1	**ett**	19	**nitton**
2	**två**	20	**tjugo**
3	**tre**	21	**tjugoett**
4	**fyra**	22	**tjugotvå**
5	**fem**	30	**trettio**
6	**sex**	40	**fyrtio**
7	**sjö**	50	**femtio**
8	**åtta**	60	**sextio**
9	**nio**	70	**sjuttio**
10	**tio**	80	**åttio**
11	**elva**	90	**nittio**
12	**tolv**	100	**hundra**
13	**tretton**	101	**hundraett**
14	**fjorton**	200	**två hundra**
15	**femton**	500	**fem hundra**
16	**sexton**	1000	**tusen**
17	**sjutton**	10,000	**tio tusen**
18	**arton**		

Swedish sayings

Just two generations ago Sweden was a predominantly rural country which had yet to experience the Industrial Revolution. As a result the language is still full of **phrases and expressions** which refer to the Swedish countryside. When something goes wrong, you'll often hear *det gick åt skogen*, literally "it went to the forest", the implication being that the uncivilized world began at the forest edge; hence also *dra åt skogen!*, "be off to the forest", which is a polite way of telling someone to leave you alone. Animals also feature in Swedish phrases: *gå som katten kring het gröt* is cats walking around hot porridge, as opposed to the hot tin roofs familiar to their English cousins. Equally, every good Swede is told *sälj inte skinnet förrän björnen är skjuten*, "don't sell the skin before the bear is shot". Swedes don't talk of the devil but instead of the trolls (the Swedish word for "devils", *djävlar*, is one of the worst swear-words in the language). When they're in a crowd, Swedes are never packed like sardines but *packade som sillar* – like herrings. If a Swede is singularly unimpressed about something, it's definitely *ingenting att hänga i julgran*, literally "nothing to hang in the Christmas tree".

Food and drink terms

Basics and snacks

Bröd	Bread	Pommes	Fries
Bulle	Bun	Ris	Rice
Glass	Ice cream	Salt	Salt
Grädde	Cream	Senap	Mustard
Gräddfil	Sour cream	Småkakor	Biscuits
Gröt	Porridge	Smör	Butter
Kaka	Cake	Smörgås	Sandwich
Keks	Biscuits	Socker	Sugar
Knäcke-bröd	Crispbread	Sylt	Jam
Olja	Oil	Tårta	Cake
Omelett	Omelette	Vinäger	Vinegar
Ost	Cheese	Våffla	Waffle
Pastej	Paté	Ägg	Egg
Peppar	Pepper	Ättika	Vinegar for pickling

Meat (kött)

Biff	Beef	Lammkött	Lamb
Fläsk	Pork	Lever	Liver
Kalvkött	Veal	Oxstek	Roast beef
Korv	Sausage	Renstek	Roast reindeer
Kotlett	Cutlet/chop	Rådjursstek	Roast venison
Köttbullar	Meatballs	Skinka	Ham
Kyckling	Chicken	Älg	Elk

Fish (fisk)

Ansjovis	Anchovies	Räkor	Shrimps/prawns
Blåmusslor	Mussels	Rödspätta	Plaice
Fiskbullar	Fishballs	Sardiner	Sardines
Forell	Trout	Sik	Whitefish
Hummer	Lobster	Sill	Herring
Kaviar	Caviar	Sjötunga	Sole
Krabba	Crab	Strömming	Baltic herring
Kräftor	Freshwater crayfish	Torsk	Cod
Lax	Salmon	Ål	Eel
Makrill	Mackerel		

Vegetables (grönsaker)

Blomkål	Cauliflower	Sallad	Lettuce; salad
Brysselkål	Brussels sprouts	Spenat	Spinach
Bönor	Beans	Svamp	Mushrooms
Gurka	Cucumber	Tomater	Tomatoes
Lök	Onion	Vitkål	White cabbage
Morötter	Carrots	Vitlök	Garlic
Potatis	Potatoes	Ärtor	Peas
Rödkål	Red cabbage		

Fruit (frukt)

Ananas	Pineapple	Jordgubbar	Strawberries
Apelsin	Orange	Lingon	Lingonberry; red
Aprikos	Apricot		whortleberry
Banan	Banana	Persika	Peach
Citron	Lemon	Päron	Pear
Hallon	Raspberry	Vindruvor	Grapes
Hjortron	Cloudberry	Äpple	Apple

Culinary terms

Blodig	Rare	Lagom	Medium
Filé	Fillet	Pocherad	Poached
Friterad	Deep fried	Rökt	Smoked
Genomstekt	Well done	Stekt	Fried
Gravad	Cured	Ungstekt	Roasted/ baked
Grillat/halstrat	Grilled	Varm	Hot
Kall	Cold	Ångkokt	Steamed
Kokt	Boiled		

Drinks

Apelsinjuice	Orange juice	Rödvin	Red wine
Chocklad	Hot chocolate	Saft	Juice
Citron	Lemon	Starköl	Strong beer
Fruktjuice	Fruit juice	Storstark	Large strong beer
Grädde	Cream	Te	Tea
Kaffe	Coffee	Vatten	Water
Lättöl	Light beer	Vin	Wine
Mellanöl	Medium-strong beer	Vitt vin	White wine
Mineral-vatten	Mineral water	Öl	Beer
Mjölk	Milk	Skål	Cheers!

Swedish specialities

Bruna bönor	Baked, vinegared brown beans, usually served with fried pork	Getost	Goat's cheese
		Glögg	Mulled wine usually fortified with spirits to keep out the cold, and drunk at Christmas
Filmjölk	Soured milk		
Fisksoppa	Fish soup usually including several sorts of fish, prawns and dill	Gravad lax	Salmon marinated in dill, sugar and

	seasoning; served with mustard sauce and lemon
Hjortron	A wild, orange-coloured berry, served with fresh cream and/or ice cream. Also made into jam
Janssons frestelse	A potato and anchovy bake with cream
Kryddost	Hard cheese spiced with seeds, sometimes caraway seeds or cloves
Köttbullar	Meatballs served with a brown creamy sauce and lingonberries
Kräftor	Crayfish, often served with **kryddost**, and eaten in August
Lingon	Lingonberry (sometimes known as red whortleberries), a red berry made into a kind of jam and served with meat dishes as well as on pancakes and in puddings eaten at Christmas
Långfil	A special type of soured milk from northern Sweden
Lövbiff	Sliced, fried beef with onions
Matjessill	Sweet-pickled herring
Mesost	Brown, sweet whey cheese; a breakfast favourite
Ostkaka	Curd cake made from fresh curds and eggs baked in the oven served with jam or berries
Pepparkakor	Thin, spiced gingerbread biscuits popular at Christmas
Plättar	Thin pancakes often served with pea soup
Potatissallad	Potato salad often flavoured with dill or chives
Pytt i panna	Cubes of meat and fried potatoes with a fried egg and beetroot
Semla	Sweet bun with almond paste and whipped cream; associated with Lent
Sillbricka	Various cured and marinated herring dishes; often appears as a first course in restaurants at lunchtime
Sjömansbiff	Sailor's beef casserole, thin slices of beef baked in the oven with potatoes and onion topped with parsley
Smultron	Wild strawberries, known for their concentrated taste
Strömming	Baltic herring
Surströmming	Baltic herring fermented for months until it's rotten and the tin it's in buckles – very smelly and eaten in very, very small quantities. Not for the faint-hearted!
Ärtsoppa	Yellow pea soup with pork spiced with thyme and marjoram; a winter dish traditionally eaten on Thursdays
Ål	Eel, smoked and served with creamed potatoes or scrambled eggs (**Äggröra**)

Glossary

bad swimming (pool)
bastu sauna
berg mountain
biljett ticket
bio cinema
björn bear
bokhandel bookshop
bro bridge
brygga jetty/pier
båt boat/ferry
cyckelstig cycle path
Dagens Rätt dish of the day
dal valley
domkyrka cathedral
drottning queen
ej inträde no entrance
extrapris special offer
färja ferry
färjeläge ferry terminal/berth
gamla old
gamla stan old town
gata (g.) street
gränd alley
hamn harbour
hembygdsgård homestead museum
hiss lift
järnvägsstation railway station
kapell chapel
klockan (kl.) o'clock
kung king
kyrka church
liggvagn couchette car
lilla little
muséet museum
pressbyrå newsagent
rabatt discount

rea sale
ren reindeer
restaurangsvagn train buffet
restaurang restaurant
riksdagshus parliament building
rådhuset town hall
rökning förbjuden no smoking
simhallen swimming pools
sjö lake
skog forest
storstark strong beer
slott palace/castle
smörgåsbord spread of different dishes
sovvagn sleeping car
spår track
stadshus city hall
stora big
strand beach
stuga cottage
systembolaget alcohol store
stängt closed
torg square/market place
tunnelbana underground (metro)
turistbyrå tourist office
tältplats campsite
tåg train
universitet university
vandrarhem youth hostel
väg (v.) road
vrakpris bargain
ångbåt steamboat
älg elk
ångbad steamroom
öppet open
öppettider opening hours

Index

+ small print

Index

Map entries are in colour

Note that the order used below is for the Swedish alphabet which is the English with å, ä, ö on the end in that order.

INDEX

I

INDEX

Twenty Years of Rough Guides

In the summer of 1981, Mark Ellingham, Rough Guides' founder, knocked out the first guide on a typewriter, with a group of friends. Mark had been travelling in Greece after university, and couldn't find a guidebook that really answered his needs. There were heavyweight cultural guides on the one hand – good on museums and classical sites but not on beaches and tavernas – and on the other hand student manuals that were so caught up with how to save money that they lost sight of the country's significance beyond its role as a place for a cool vacation. None of the guides began to address Greece as a country, with its natural and human environment, its politics and its contemporary life.

Having no urgent reason to return home, Mark decided to write his own guide. It was a guide to Greece that tried to combine some erudition and insight with a thoroughly practical approach to travellers' needs. Scrupulously researched listings of places to stay, eat and drink were matched by careful attention to detail on everything from Homer to Greek music, from classical sites to national parks and from nude beaches to monasteries. Back in London, Mark and his friends got their Rough Guide accepted by a farsighted commissioning editor at the publisher Routledge and it came out in 1982.

The Rough Guide to Greece was a student scheme that became a publishing phenomenon. The immediate success of the book – shortlisted for the Thomas Cook award – spawned a series that rapidly covered dozens of countries. The Rough Guides found a ready market among backpackers and budget travellers, but soon acquired a much broader readership that included older and less impecunious visitors. Readers relished the guides' wit and inquisitiveness as much as the enthusiastic, critical approach that acknowledges everyone wants value for money – but not at any price.

Rough Guides soon began supplementing the "rougher" information – the hostel and low-budget listings – with the kind of detail that independent-minded travellers on any budget might expect. These days, the guides – distributed worldwide by the Penguin group – include recommendations spanning the range from shoestring to luxury, and cover more than 200 destinations around the globe. Our growing team of authors, many of whom come to Rough Guides initially as outstandingly good letter-writers telling us about their travels, are spread all over the world, particularly in Europe, the USA and Australia. As well as the travel guides, Rough Guides publishes a series of dictionary phrasebooks covering two dozen major languages, an acclaimed series of music guides running the gamut from Classical to World Music, a series of music CDs in association with World Music Network, and a range of reference books on topics as diverse as the Internet, Pregnancy and Unexplained Phenomena. Visit **www.roughguides.com** to see what's cooking.

Rough Guide credits

Text editor: Lucy Ratcliffe
Series editor: Mark Ellingham
Editorial: Martin Dunford, Jonathan Buckley,
Kate Berens, Ann-Marie Shaw, Helena Smith,
Olivia Swift, Ruth Blackmore, Geoff Howard,
Claire Saunders, Gavin Thomas, Alexander
Mark Rogers, Polly Thomas, Joe Staines,
Duncan Clark, Peter Buckley, Lucy Ratcliffe,
Clifton Wilkinson, Alison Murchie, Matthew
Teller, Andrew Dickson, Fran Sandham,
Sally Schafer (UK); Andrew Rosenberg,
Yuki Takagaki, Richard Koss, Hunter Slaton
(US)
Cover art direction: Louise Boulton
Picture research: Sharon Martins,
Mark Thomas

Production: Link Hall, Helen Prior,
Julia Bovis, Katie Pringle, Rachel Holmes,
Andy Turner, Dan May
Cartography: Maxine Repath, Ed Wright,
Katie Lloyd-Jones
Online: Kelly Martinez, Anja Mutic-Blessing,
Jennifer Gold, Audra Epstein,
Suzanne Welles, Cree Lawson (US)
Finance: John Fisher, Gary Singh,
Edward Downey, Mark Hall, Tim Bill
Marketing & Publicity: Richard Trillo,
Niki Smith, David Wearn, Chloë Roberts,
Demelza Dallow, Claire Southern (UK);
David Wechsler, Megan Kennedy (US)
Administration: Julie Sanderson,
Karoline Densley

Publishing information

This third edition published June 2003 by
Rough Guides Ltd,
80 Strand, London WC2R 0RL.
345 Hudson St, 4th Floor,
New York, NY 10014, USA.
Distributed by the Penguin Group
Penguin Books Ltd,
80 Strand, London WC2R 0RL
Penguin Putnam, Inc.
375 Hudson Street, NY 10014, USA
Penguin Books Australia Ltd,
487 Maroondah Highway, PO Box 257,
Ringwood, Victoria 3134, Australia
Penguin Books Canada Ltd,
10 Alcorn Avenue, Toronto, Ontario,
Canada M4V 1E4
Penguin Books (NZ) Ltd,
182–190 Wairau Road, Auckland 10,
New Zealand
Typeset in Bembo and Helvetica to an
original design by Henry Iles.

The publishers and authors have done their
best to ensure the accuracy and currency of
all the information in **The Rough Guide to
Sweden**; however, they can accept no
responsibility for any loss, injury, or
inconvenience sustained by any traveller as a
result of information or advice contained in
the guide.

Help us update

We've gone to a lot of effort to ensure that
the third edition of **The Rough Guide to
Sweden** is accurate and up to date.
However, things change – places get
"discovered", opening hours are notoriously
fickle, restaurants and rooms raise prices or
lower standards. If you feel we've got it
wrong or left something out, we'd like to
know, and if you can remember the address,
the price, the time, the phone number, so
much the better.

We'll credit all contributions, and send a
copy of the next edition (or any other Rough
Guide if you prefer) for the best letters.
Everyone who writes to us and isn't already a
subscriber will receive a copy of our full-
colour thrice-yearly newsletter. Please mark
letters: **"Rough Guide Sweden Update"** and
send to: Rough Guides, 80 Strand, London
WC2R 0RL, or Rough Guides, 4th Floor, 345
Hudson St, New York, NY 10014. Or send an
email to **mail@roughguides.com**

Have your questions answered and tell
others about your trip at
www.roughguides.atinfopop.com

Acknowledgements

James would like to extend grateful thanks to Emelie Klein at the Swedish Travel and Tourism Council in London for helping with such an extensive visit to Sweden; best wishes too to Ann-Charlotte now in Gothenburg. In Sweden thanks also to the following: Robert Lundgren, top busman in Kiruna; Mina Dahl in Riksgränsen; archipelago expert Linda in Luleå; Anders Granberg in Piteå for expert knowledge on paths; Annica in Umeå; the wonderfully helpful Olle Lidgren at Mitt Sverige Turism; the Tre Små Rum boys and Sylvie Kjellin in Stockholm; Jan Svensson, the Scanrail man at SJ; Europcar in Borlänge for some quite breathtaking customer service; cheery Gunnar Bäckström (and Claude the postman) in Leksand; Sara Wänseth in Östersund; Linda, Bjarne and especially Duncan for such fantastic hospitality and angelica schnaps in Klippen; Monika Juhlin and her lunch in Arjeplog and Kerstin in Pajala for Populärmusik från Vittula and her printer for an angry letter from the Cape. Also, as ever,

a big thanks to Per and Gerd in Stockholm for a warm welcome after the north but most of all, to Lance whose support, patience and words of encouragement from Montclus made this update possible.

Neil: I would like to thank Kalle & Janis Sundin of Kalmar, Ingvar Grimberg and Stigake Berkin in Gothenburg for their much appreciated friendship. I am also very grateful for all the enthusiasm and help shown by Lena Larsson at Gothenburg & Co, Stefanie Feldmann in Lund, a special thanks to Lena Birgersson at Skane Tourist Board, to Torgney Andersson at Destination Gotland, to Cecilia Theisen in Visby, Kerstin Hallberg at Kronoberg and Sylva Schaefer at Örebro.

The editor would like to thank Link Hall for layout, PC Graphics for cartography, David Price for proofreading, Veneta Bullen for picture research and Karoline Densley for indexing.

Readers' letters

Thanks to all the readers who took the trouble to write in with their comments and suggestions (and apologies to anyone whose name we've misspelt or omitted):

Felix Corley, Bart Hansen, Clemens Kurek, Joanna Leapman, Iain Molyneux, Brendan Mcglyn, Glyn Richards and Gareth Wright.

Photo credits

Cover credits

Main front picture Medle © FPG
Small front top picture Bronze Age rock carvings, Tanumshede © Robert Harding
Small front lower picture Detail from City Hall, Stockholm © Robert Harding
Back top picture Lapland © Robert Harding
Back lower picture Kalmar Slott © Robert Harding

Introduction

Scania, Rape Field & Red house © Art Directors/Trip/Viesti Collection
View of Archipelago, Stockholm © Impact Photos/Petteri Kokkonen
Sami man & reindeer © Swedish Tourist Board
Sunlight through forest walk © Neil Roland
Medieval carvings, Ystad © Neil Roland
Kalmar Palace © Neil Roland
Mural painting in Stockholm subway © Corbis/Bob Krist

Child with crown of flowers & flag © Corbis/Staffan Widstrand
Haga street scene © Neil Roland
Huskies and sleigh through snow © Harjedalen/James Proctor
Jugendstil architecture; Bath house © Neil Roland
Red Windmill, Oland Storlimga © Neil Roland
A rune stone © Impact Photos/June Read
Colourful doorway, Fiskebackskil © Neil Roland
Northern Lights: Northen Lights, Sweden © Corbis/Torleif Svensson

Things not to miss

Herrings © Anthony Blake Library
Living sculpture of Nimis © Neil Roland
Ship at Vasa Museum © Impact Photos/Ray Roberts
Midnight Sun © Naturbild
Street scene, Gamla Stan © Art Directors/Trip/T Bognar

Swimmers at Fjordholman © Naturbild/Kate Karrberg

Wooden cottage Store & Kator © James Proctor

Ice Hotel © Axiom/Ian Cook

Nude Sauna Bathing Saami style © Corbis/Staffan Widstrand

Arches of the ruins at St. Katarin's © Neil Roland

Snowmobiling in winter © Harjedalen/James Proctor

Café at Marina, Fjallbacka Harbour © Corbis/Macduff Everton

Artic Circle signs at lake area © Naturbild/Eddie Granlun

Hogbonden lighthouse at night © Naturbild/Sven Halling

Glass blowers making a vase © Corbis/Macduff Everton

Altar piece at Vadstena Church © Corbis/Patrick Ward

Jokkmokks market scene © Naturbild/Kate Karrberg

Dunes © Corbis/Dennis Marsico

Hip Hip Hooray by Peter Koyer, Furstenburg Gallery, Gothenburg Art Museum © Neil Roland

Gammelstad street scene © Powerstock/AGE

Hikers arrive at boat area © Naturbild/Stefan Rosengren

Skins drying in the sun at Foteviken © Neil Roland

View across to island of Marstrand © Art Directors/Trip/C Rennie

Interior of Lund Cathedral © Corbis/Hubert Stadler

Buildings at the Gamla industrial area © Naturbild/Bengt Hedberg

Buildings at the Gamla industrial area ©

Naturbild/Bengt Hedberg

Car corpses © Neil Roland

Exterior of Dunkers Museum © Naturbild/Dickclevestam

St Mana Church street scene © Neil Roland

Fjaderholmarnas Xmas Smorgasbord © Corbis/Bo Zaunders

Inlandsbanan Railway steams through © Arvidsjaur Turism/James Proctor

Black and whites

Vista of Gamla Stan & Riddarholmen © Art Directors/Trip/T. BognarVista (p.58)

Stockholm harbour © Impact Photos/Ray Roberts (p.76)

Wooden house along the river, Västeras © Naturbild/Hasse Schrode (p.119)

View over Gothenburg Office & Utkiket Ship © Powerstock/AGE Fotostock (p.130)

Poseidon sculpture, Gothenburg © Powerstock/AGE Fotostock (p.148)

Varberg's Kallbadhuset © Naturbild/Christer Fredriksson (p.198)

Axel Ebbe's "The Embrace", Smygehamn © Neil Roland (p.204)

Exterior view of Christian IV's Trefaldighetskyrkan, Kristianstad © Neil Roland (p.266)

Street scene, Kalmar © Neil Roland (p.280)

Doorway, Norrköping © Neil Roland (p.327)

River view at Hudiksvall © James Proctor (p.354)

Bonnstan Row © James Proctor (p.393)

View of Lake © Swedish Tourist Board (p.412)

Old phone box © James Proctor (p.450)

Snowy scene and mountains © Naturbild/Kenneth Bengstsson (p.458)

Ski action, Lapland © Swedish Tourist Board (p.498)

Rough Guides publishes new books every month

TRAVEL • MUSIC • REFERENCE • PHRASEBOOKS •

The ideas expressed in this code were developed by and for independent travellers.

Learn About The Country You're Visiting

Start enjoying your travels before you leave by tapping into as many sources of information as you can.

The Cost Of Your Holiday

Think about where your money goes - be fair and realistic about how cheaply you travel. Try and put money into local peoples' hands; drink local beer or fruit juice rather than imported brands and stay in locally owned accommodation. Haggle with humour and not aggressively. Pay what something is worth to you and remember how wealthy you are compared to local people.

Embrace The Local Culture

Open your mind to new cultures and traditions - it will transform your experience. Think carefully about what's appropriate in terms of your clothes and the way you behave. You'll earn respect and be more readily welcomed by local people. Respect local laws and attitudes towards drugs and alcohol that vary in different countries and communities. Think about the impact you could have on them.

Exploring The World – The Travellers' Code

Being sensitive to these ideas means getting more out of your travels - and giving more back to the people you meet and the places you visit.

Minimise Your Environmental Impact

Think about what happens to your rubbish - take biodegradable products and a water filter bottle. Be sensitive to limited resources like water, fuel and electricity. Help preserve local wildlife and habitats by respecting local rules and regulations, such as sticking to footpaths and not standing on coral.

Don't Rely On Guidebooks

Use your guidebook as a starting point, not the only source of information. Talk to local people, then discover your own adventure!

Be Discreet With Photography

Don't treat people as part of the landscape, they may not want their picture taken. Ask first and respect their wishes.

We work with people the world over to promote tourism that benefits their communities, but we can only carry on our work with the support of people like you. For membership details or to find out how to make your travels work for local people and the environment, visit our website.

www.tourismconcern.org.uk

TourismConcern
Campaigning for Ethical and Fairly Traded Tourism

hot hotels,
cool prices!
...in stockholm
with up to 50% off standard rates in quality hotels.
We offer a superb range of quality hotels, from 2 star to deluxe in over 85 European cities and coastal resorts.
Booking is extremely easy with no booking fee and offered through both our call centre and on our website.
3* from £35
4* from £36
*prices are per person per night based on 2 people sharing a twin/double room with breakfast & taxes included.
book now on:
020 8731 7000
www.hotelconnect.co.uk
hotelconnect
the hotel specialist